CLASSIC REPRINTS

Genealogies, Local Histories, and More

Library-quality reprints
available from
NEW ENGLAND HISTORIC
GENEALOGICAL SOCIETY

ISBN-13: 978-0-88082-250-3
Library of Congress Control Number: 2010942860

Cover design by Carolyn Sheppard Oakley
Printed by Yurchak Printing, Landisville, Pennsylvania

NEW ENGLAND HISTORIC GENEALOGICAL SOCIETY®
99–101 Newbury Street
Boston, Massachusetts 02116-3007
www.AmericanAncestors.org

TABLE OF CONTENTS

table of contents continues on next page . . .

Books listed in this catalog are printed and bound to order. You will be charged for the special order books at the time you place the order. Books take **4–8 weeks** to bind. Please allow sufficient time for shipping in your delivery estimates. Standard delivery takes 1–8 business days and economy shipping takes 10–15 business days within the United States. Please call for international shipping rates and policies. Books may be returned for credit. Unless the book is damaged or defective, the return will incur a **15% reshelving fee** and credit will not be given for shipping charges.

Questions? Call toll-free at **1-888-296-3447** or email *thebookstore@nehgs.org*.

Local Histories continued . . .

SECTION THREE: Miscellaneous

✂ –

Ordering from NEHGS

To order, visit our online store at *www.AmericanAncestors.org,* call us toll-free at 1-888-296-3447, or mail or fax the order form below.

All of the books listed in the *Classic Reprints* catalog are softcover editions. For hardcover, please add $12 per book on the appropriate line on the order form below. If you are ordering a multi-volume set and would like them in hardcover, add $12 per volume (e.g., for a three-volume set in hardcover, please add $12 x 3 volumes = $36). If you do not add the $12 per book, you will receive softcover books. Once your order has been placed with our bindery, you will receive a confirmation via USPS mail. Books take 4–8 weeks to be produced before being shipped. Questions? Send email to *thebookstore@nehgs.org* or call 1-888-296-3447.

✂ —

Ship to:

Name_____

Address _____

City, State, ZIP_____

Daytime phone no._____

Email address _____

NEHGS member no. _____

Bill to *(if different)*:

Name_____

Address _____

City, State, ZIP_____

Daytime phone no._____

Email address _____

NEHGS member no. _____

Item no.	Description	Price
	membership *Enroll me as a member* *$75 individual; $90 family*	

Shipping options:

Standard/UPS Ground (2–8 days):
$9.50 for the first book and $3 for each additional book.

Economy /USPS Book Rate (10–15 business days):
$6 for the first book and $3 for each additional book.

Expedited or international shipping: call 617-226-1212 or email *thebookstore@nehgs.org.*

subtotal $_____

hardcover option *($12 each book—see above)* $_____

6.25% sales tax *(only if Mass. resident)* $_____

shipping *(see above)* $_____

TOTAL $_____

Payment Information

___ check enclosed, payable to NEHGS *(please do not staple to order form)*   ☐VISA   ☐MasterCard   ☐Discover   ☐American Express

Account no. _____Exp._____

Signature _____

Please mail to: NEHGS Bookstore, 99–101 Newbury St., Boston, MA 02116
or fax: 617-536-7307   •   or call: 1-888-296-3447, toll-free, M–F, 9 a.m.–5 p.m. (Eastern time)

How to Use This Book

The 12,000-plus classic reprints listed in this book are divided into several categories: genealogies and family histories; local histories; and miscellaneous.

Genealogies and family histories (which also include biographies) are alphabetized by surname. Please be sure to peruse the entire list for any surnames that might be allied with your family, as some books cover more than one family. For ease of presentation, we have chosen to list books by the first family given in the title.

Local histories are divided into Canada, Europe, and the United States. General U.S. entries are followed by regional entries and then by state-by-state listings. Within states, general statewide publications are listed first, followed by specific localities, alphabetized by locality. Be sure to scan through the entire list for a state, as some publications apply to more than one locality, and we have listed each under only the first locality mentioned in the title. For example, you'll find a history of Essex and Norfolk Counties, Massachusetts, alphabetized under Essex.

The "Miscellaneous" section comprises books about wars, emigrant groups, heraldry, *Mayflower* descendancy, and other topics that are not necessarily tied to specific locations or families. We have chosen to list some state-specific books about wars under the relevant war in the Miscellaneous section. You will find, for example, *Records of California Men in the War of the Rebellion* under both the Civil War and under California—general. Books about specific battles, or about specific cities' involvement in a war, will be found only in the statewide listings, however.

Please note that all titles are available as paperback and hardcover editions. **All prices listed are for the paperback version**. As noted elsewhere, please add $12 to the price of the book for a hardcover version, and specify hardcover when you place your order. You can find more information on the order form on page v.

GENEALOGIES
&
FAMILY
HISTORIES

A

AAKER: The Aaker Saga: A Family History. By A.A. Rowberg. 1951. 206p.
P4-S00105 — $33.50.

ABBE: ABBEY Genealogy; In Memory of John Abbe & His Desc. By C. Abbe & J.G. Nichols. 1916. 525p.
P4-S00111 — $82.00.

ABBEY: Memorial of Capt. Thomas Abbey; Anc & Desc. of the Abbey Family: Pioneers of CT, West. Reserve in OH & the Great West, 2nd ed. By A. Freeman. 1917. 175p.
P4-S00117 — $26.50.

ABBOT: A Genealogical Register of the Desc. of George Abbot of Andover, George of Rowley, Thomas of Andover, Arthur of Ipswich, Robert of Branford, CT & George of Norwalk, CT. By A. & E. Abbot. 1847. 217p.
P4-S00123 — $32.50.

ABBOTT: Desc of George Abbott of Rowley, MA & George Abbott, Jr. of Andover. By Lemuel A. Abbott. 1906. 2 vols, lxxx + 1157p.
P4-S00129 — $156.00.

ABBOTT: A Pioneer Family of the West. A.A. Abbott. 1926. 81 + 8p.
P4-S00130 — $13.50.

ABEEL: & Allied Families. By Henry Whittemore. 1899. 24p.
P4-S00134 — $10.00.

ABELL: Anc. & Desc of Jonathan Abell, Who Came from CT & Settled in Schenectady Co, NY about 1812. By H.A. Abell. 1933. 61p.
P4-S00138 — $12.00.

ABELL: Fam in America: Robert Abell of Rehobeth, MA, his English Anc. & Immigr.; Abell Fams. in England. By H.A. & L.P. Abell. 1940. 339p.
P4-S00135 — $51.00.

ABENAKIS: Historie Des Abenakis. [text in French] L.J.A. Maurault. 1866. 631 + 18p.
P4-S00139 — $97.00.

ABERCROMBIE: The Abercrombies of Baltimore: Gen & Bio Sketch of the Family of David Abercrombie Who Settled in Baltimore, MD, in 1848. By R.T. Abercrombie. 1940. 35p.
P4-S00141 — $10.00.

ABERNATHY: ALEXANDER, the Forneys, the Sims. By Mabel B. McClure. 1934. 48p.
P4-S00142 — $10.00.

ACHENBACH: Family Memorial of John Phillip Achenbach & Desc in the US. By Mrs Sarah J. Houtz. 1890? 39p.
P4-S00143 — $10.00.

ACHESON: History of the Acheson Family on the Paternal Side. By A.W. Acheson. 1878. 60p.
P4-S00144 — $12.00.

ACHILLES: Family from NH, 1776-1961: Henry the Hessian Soldier & His Desc, with Mention of the Family in Europe & its other American Branches. By Walter B. Smith II. 1962. xi + 416 + 41p.
P4-S00153 — $70.00.

ACIE: Some Gen Notes on Early American families [incl. Acie, Atwood, Batchelder, Barnard, Barnes, et al]. By Mrs. F.W. Culver. 1925. 175p., typescript.
P4-S00159 — $25.00.

ACKER: Brief Hist of the Acker-Halbert Family, Composed of Bio Sketches & Descent Diagrams. By E.D. Acker. 1928. 179p.
P4-S00165 — $26.00.

ACKERMAN: Family; Comprising the Desc of George Ackerman, Mennonite, of Lower Milford Twp, Bucks Co. & Some Desc of Stephen Ackerman, Lutheran, of Haycock Twp, Bucks Co., PA. By Clair A. Vliet. 1950. 258 + 43p.
P4-S00171 — $45.00.

ACKERMAN: Genealogy of the Ackerman Family. By Kathlyne K. Viele. 1922. vi + 296p.,typescript.
P4-S00177 — $45.00.

ACKLEY: Ancestry of Lorenzo Ackley & his Wife Emma Arabella Bosworth. By N. Grier Parke II. 1960. xii + 325 + 48p.
P4-S00183 — $58.00.

ADAIR: History & Genealogy. By J.B. Adair. 1924. 330 + 78p.
P4-S00189 — $61.00.

ADAMS: The Genealogy of the Descendants of Several Ancient Puritans, By the Names of Adams, Bullard, Holbrook, Rockwood, Sanger, Wood, Grout, Goulding & Twitchell. Rev. Abner Morse. 1857. 362p.
P4-S00220 — $54.00.

ADAMS: Family Records: Gen & Bio Hist of all Branches of the Adams family, incl Addams, Adam, Adamson, McAdams & Corresponding Names in Other Languages (Volume I). By James T. Adams. 1929. 106p.
P4-S00216 — $19.50.

ADAMS: Hist of Adams Family of N. Staffordshire; with Numerous Pedigree Charts & Notes on Allied Fams. By Percy W.L. Adams. 1914. 417 + 63p.
P4-S00249 — $72.00.

ADAMS: Gen. & Hist. of Part of the Newbury Adams Fam., Formerly of Devonshire, Eng., Desc. of Robert Adams & Wife Eleanor. By S. Adams. 1895. 61p.
P4-S00219 — $12.50.

ADAMS: John Adams & His Descendants, with Notes & Incidents. By Gardner Adams. 1874. 139p.
P4-S00267 — $22.00.

ADAMS: History of the Adams & Evarts Families. By J.M. Adams. 1894. 87p.
P4-S00243 — $16.50.

ADAMS: History of the Adams Family. By H. Whittemore. 1893. 84p.
P4-S00255 — $17.00.

ADAMS: Family records of the Adams, Mills & Humason families. By Franklin Burwell Mills. 1921. 135p.
P4-S00210 — $13.50.

ADAMS: Desc of James & William Adams of Londonderry, Now Derry, NH. By A.N. Adams. 1894. 87p.
P4-S00204 — $15.00.

ADAMS: Jeremy Adams of Hartford, CT & Some Desc. 1905. 6p.
P4-S00206 — $10.00.

ADAMS: Jeremy Adams of Cambridge, MA, & Hartford, CT & his Desc. By A. Adams. 1955. 45p.
P4-S00207 — $10.00.

ADAMS: Genealogy: Hist of Robert Adams of Newbury, MA & his Desc, 1635-1900. By A. Adams. 1900. vi + 564 + 58p.
P4-S00192 — $94.00.

ADAMS: Henry Adams of Somerset, Eng. & Braintree, MA, Eng. anc. & some desc. By J.G. Bartlett. 1927. 185p.
P4-S00237 — $25.00.

ADAMS: Gen. Hist. of Henry Adams of Braintree MA & His Desc.; Also John of Cambridge. By A. Adams. 1898. 1246p.
P4-S00231 — $155.00.

ADAMS: Genealogy of the Adams Family of Kingston, MA. By G. Adams. 1861. 64p.
P4-S00225 — $12.50.

ADAMS: The Rev. Amos Adams (1728-75) of Roxbury, MA & His American Ancestors. By R. Lawrence. 1912. 17p.
P4-S00208 — $10.00.

ADAMS: Ancestry & Desc. of Elias Adams, the Pioneer, 600-1930. By F.D. Adams. 1930. 274p.
P4-S00198 — $41.00.

ADAMS: History of the Thomas Adams & Thomas Hastings Families of Amherst, MA. By H. Adams. 1880. 66p.
P4-S00248 — $12.50.

ADDINGTON: History of Addington family in US & England, Vol. I. By H. M. Addington. 1931. 101p.
P4-S00273 — $20.00.

ADDINGTON: History of Addington family in US & England, Vol. II, including a multitude of related families. By Hugh M. Addington. 1960. 59p.
P4-S00276 — $12.00.

ADDIS: Family history: Edward Addis of Preble, OH, 1843, his wife, Alice Reynols, & their descendants. By Wanda L. DeMooy. 1999. 97p.
P4-S00285 — $18.00.

ADGER: LAW Ancestral notebook. By John Adger Law. 1936. 159p.
P4-S00291 — $26.00.

ADSIT: Descendants of John Adsit of Lyme, CT. By Norman W. Adsit. 1950? 226p., typescript.
P4-S00297 — $34.00.

AGEE: A record of the Agee family. By P.M. Agee. 1937. 330p.
P4-S00303 — $52.50.

AGNEW: Hereditary Sheriffs of Galloway, their forebears & friends, their courts & customs of their times . . . By Sir Andrew Agnew. 1893. 2 vols., 507 + 501p.
P4-S00309 — $153.00.

AGNEW: The book of the Agnews; James Agnew of PA, His Race, Ancestry & Descendants. By Mary Virginia Agnew, et al. 1926. xx + 587p.
P4-S00321 — $89.50.

AINSWORTH: Gen. of the Ainsworth families in America. By F. J. Parker. 1894. 212p.
P4-S00327 — $32.00.

AKERS: Our Kinsfolk (descendants of Wm. Akers of NJ, ca. 1698). By W.R. Akers. 1957. 114p.
P4-S00339 — $19.50.

AKERS: Family of Franklin Co., VA, Combined with the Boone, Cannaday, Hickman & Pridgen families. By A.E. Akers. 1953. 159 + 20p.
P4-S00333 — $27.00.

ALBEE: Family records. By R.S. Albee. 1920 221p.
P4-S00342 — $30.00.

ALBRIGHT: Some records of the Albright family, with additional findings. By Claribel Albright. 1941, 1950. 135 + 16p.
P4-S00348 — $23.00.

ALDEN: Memorial of the desc. of the Hon. John Alden, incl suppl. to 1869. By E. Alden. 1867. 184p.
P4-S00369 — $22.50.

ALDEN: The desc. of Daniel Alden, 6th in desc. from John Alden, the Pilgrim. By F. Alden. 1923. 113p.
P4-S00381 — $17.00.

ALDEN: The anc. & desc. of Isaac Alden & Irene Smith, his wife, 1599-1903. By H. C. Fielding. 1903. 144p.
P4-S00375 — $21.50.

ALDEN: Gen. (repr. NEHGR). By C.L. Alden. 1898-1900. 25p.
P4-S00377 — $10.00.

ALDEN: John Alden of Ashfield, MA & Chautauqua Co., NY: his Alden ancestors & his descendants. By Frank W. Alden. 1909. 84p.
P4-S00366 — $17.00.

ALDEN: Misc. Alden data (repr. NEHGR). 9p.
P4-S00378 — $10.00.

ALDEN: Gen. of fourteen fams. of the early settlers of New England, of the names of Alden, Adams, Arnold, Bass, Billings, Capen et al. By E. Thayer. 1835. 180p.
P4-S00360 — $28.00.

ALDEN: Eliab Alden of Middleborough, MA & Cairo, NY: his Alden ancestors & his descendants. By Charles Henry Alden. 1905. 55p.
P4-S00379 — $11.00.

ALDEN: Descendants of Polly & Ebenezer Alden, who were 6th in descent from John Alden, the Pilgrim. By E. Alden & H. Shaw. 1903. 100p.
P4-S00354 — $19.50.

ALDEN: The story of a Pilgrim family from the Mayflower to the Present Time (1899), with autobiography, recollections, letters, incidents & genealogy. By Rev. John Alden 1889. 441p.
P4-S00387 — $68.00.

ALDERMAN: The Aldermans in America. By William A. Parker. 1957. xv + 714p.
P4-S00393 — $109.00.

ALDIS: Family in America, 1640-1800. By Fred. H. Whitin. 1905. 28p.
P4-S00396 — $10.00.

ALDRICH: "Hi, Cousin": the Mason J. Aldrich fam. hist. By M.M. Aldrich. 1967. 125p.
P4-S00399 — $21.00.

ALDWORTH: ELBRIDGE Fam., 1590-1811. By E. Salisbury. 1885. 40p.
P4-S00404 — $10.00.

ALEXANDER: AUSTIN — ARNOLD. Alexander Family of Scotland, Ireland & America; Austin Family of Wales & America; Arnold Family of England & America. By Frances A. Arnold. 1896. 25p.
P4-S00412 — $10.00.

ALEXANDER: Family Bios of the Families of Alexander, Wilkinson, Sparr & Guthrie, with Sketches & Memorials. By Wm. G. Alexander. 1892. 180p.
P4-S00411 — $29.00.

ALEXANDER: Family records. By W.M. Clemens. 1914. 20p.
P4-S00413 — $10.00.

ALEXANDER: The Alexanders of ME. By D. Alexander. 1908. 129p.
P4-S00438 — $19.00.

ALEXANDER: Notes on the Alexander fam. of SC & GA & connections. By H.A. Alexander. 1954. 142p.
P4-S00417 — $23.00.

ALEXANDER: Earlier gen. of the Alexander fam. of VA. By S. M. Culbertson. 1934. 46p.
P4-S00414 — $10.00.

ALEXANDER: Records of a Family of the House of Alexander, 1640-1909. By Francis A. Butterworth. 1909. 89p.
P4-S00415 — $17.50.

ALEXANDER: Record of the descendants of John Alexander of Lanarkshire, Scotland, & his wife Margaret Glasson, who emigrated from Co. Armagh, Ireland By J.E. Alexander. 1878. 220p.
P4-S00423 — $36.00.

ALEXANDER: Descent of the Scottish Alexanders; gen. sketch, with discussions of some hist. matters. By F.A. Sondley. 1912. 73p.
P4-S00405 — $15.00.

ALEXANDER: Sketch of Alexander Alexander, who emigrated from Co. Down, Ireland, in the year 1770 & settled in Cumberland Co., PA. By Walter S. Alexander. 1898. 79p.
P4-S00435 — $16.00.

ALGER: The Thomas Alger family, Jabez Alger line, 1645-1994, of Taunton, MA. By Eleanor M. Crouch. 1994. 165p.
P4-S00450 — $19.50.

ALGER: Gen. hist. of fam. of Thomas Alger of Taunton & Bridgewater. By A. M. Alger. 1876. 60p.
P4-S00441 — $12.00.

ALLAN: Mem. of Col. John Allan, an officer of the Rev., with a gen. By G. H. Allan. 1867. 32p.
P4-S00452 — $10.00.

ALLEN: Memorial, 1st series; Desc. of Edward Allen of Nantucket, MA, 1690-1905. By O.P. Allen. 1905. 123p.
P4-S00480 — $21.50.

ALLEN: Family history. By J.M. Seaver. 86p.
P4-S00462 — $17.50.

ALLEN: Brief history of the Allen family in America. By John H. Allen. 1915. 28p.
P4-S00463 — $10.00.

ALLEN: Jesse Allen of Wysox, PA, 1784, patriot of the American Revolution, & some of his descendants. By Edw. C. Hoagland. 1952. 47p., typescript.
P4-S00464 — $10.00.

ALLEN: Charles Allen of Portsmouth, NH, 1657, & some desc. By F.W. Allen. 1902. 7p.
P4-S00465 — $10.00.

ALLEN: Genealogy of the Allen family [of Prudence Isl., RI]. By Dan'l Gould Allen. 1898. 154p.
P4-S00531 — $24.00.

ALLEN: History & genealogy. By Geo. W. Allen. 1937. 120p.
P4-S00474 — $19.00.

ALLEN: Phinehas Allen's desc. of Lincoln, MA, 1745 & gen. of the desc. of Benj. Allen of Ashby, MA, 1777. By G. Allen. 1898. 27p.
P4-S00466 — $10.00.

ALLEN: Genealogy of the Allen family from 1568-1882. By Wm. Allen, revised By Joshua Allen. 1882. 36p.
P4-S00467 — $10.00.

ALLEN: Fam. of Salisbury, Gloucester & Manchester, MA (Ex. from Essex Antiquarian). 28p.
P4-S00469 — $10.00.

ALLEN: Lewis Allen of Watertown Farms (Weston), MA, 1665 & his descendants, including the Walpole & Lancaster Allens. By Allen H. Bent. 1900. 35p.
P4-S00470 — $10.00.

ALLEN: Fourteen Generations, Desc. & Anc. of Diarca Allen, Lebanon, NH. Allene Beaumont Duty. 1973. 257p.
P4-S00471 — $39.00.

ALLEN: Family: descendants of Ralph Allen (b. 1540, England) through his son George of Weymouth, England & MA. By Art Reierson. 1998. 213 + 32p.
P4-S00472 — $37.00.

ALLEN: Some Prudendce Island Allens. By Devere Allen. n.d. 338p., typescript.
P4-S00501 — $53.00.

ALLEN: George Allen, Ralph Allen: one line of their descendants in NJ, with some fragments of history. By David A. Thompson. 1901. 66p.
P4-S00537 — $13.00.

ALLEN: Our Childrens Ancestry: Whitaker, Cantey, Gaines, Harvie, Cosby, Leonard, Moran & Allen Families. Sarah C.W. Allen. 1935. 513 + 74p.
P4-S00473 — $88.00.

ALLEN: Brief hist. of Lewis Allen of Fisher's Island & New London, CT & his desc., from 1699-1954. By M.A. Phinney. 1954. 207 + 30p.
P4-S00475 — $36.00.

ALLEN: A brief history of the family of Nathan Allen & Mary Putnam, his wife, late of Ft Plain, Montgomey Co., NY & of the families of Rev. Aaron Putnam By A.L. Allen. 1895. 132p.
P4-S00476 — $25.00.

ALLEN: Memorial, 2nd ser.; Desc. of Samuel Allen of Windsor, CT, 1640-1907. By O.P. Allen. 1907. 303p.
P4-S00483 — $39.50.

ALLEN: Family of Manchester, MA to 1888. By J. Price. 1888. 47p.
P4-S00477 — $10.00.

ALLEN: Anc & Desc Andrew Lee Allen & Clarinda Knapp Allen. By Gerald R. Fuller. 1952. 445p.
P4-S00489 — $67.50.

ALLEN: Gen. sketches of the Allen fam. of Medfield; with an account of the golden wedding of Ellis & Lucy Allen, also of Gershom & Abigail (Allen) Adams. By J. Allen. 1869. 88p.
P4-S00510 — $15.00.

ALLEN: Some early settlers, being a history of Allen, Littler, Metcalfe, Shouse[& other] families. By Mary C. McCabe. 1921. 68p.
P4-S00555 — $13.50.

ALLEN: History & genealogical record of the Allens-Begleys-Mays of KY: Descendants of John Allen from 175- to the present time[1953], rev. By Jackson A. Begley. 1953. 147p.
P4-S00543 — $21.00.

ALLEN: Gen. history of the Allen family & some of their connections. By F. M. Stoddard. 1891. 136p.
P4-S00504 — $23.00.

ALLEN: Gen. & hist. of the Allen fam. of Dedham & Medfield, MA, 1637-1898. By F. Hutchinson. 1896. 80p.
P4-S00519 — $16.00.

ALLEN: Family, from "Family Sketches." By J.R. Wood. 1870. 13p.
P4-S00478 — $10.00.

ALLEN: The Allens, from William (1602-79) of Manchester, England, & Salem & Manchester, MA in the direct line through Nathaniel of Beverly, MA. By Raymond F. Allen. 1958. 121p.
P4-S00561 — $19.50.

ALLEN: Memorial of Joseph & Lucy Clark Allen (Northborough, MA]. By E. W. Allen. 1891. 246p.
P4-S00549 — $37.00.

ALLEN: Walter Allen of Newbury, MA, 1640, & some descendants. By A.H. Bent. 1896. 66p.
P4-S00567 — $13.00.

ALLEN: Genealogy of the Allen & Witter family & their desc. By A. W. Allen. 1872. 251p.
P4-S00525 — $37.50.

ALLEN: Genealogy of Samuel Allen of Windsor, CT & some of his desc. By W. S. Allen. 1876. 76p.
P4-S00519 — $15.00.

ALLEN: Genealogical statement by Capt. C.T. Allen [desc. of William if Lunenburg Co., VA]. 1895. 48p.
P4-S00479 — $10.00.

ALLERTON: Hist. of the Allerton fam. in the US, 1585-1885, & desc. of Isaac Allerton. By Allerton & Currier. 1900. 149p.
P4-S00573 — $27.50.

ALLERTON: Allertons of New England & VA (Repr. NEHGR). By I.J. Greenwood. 1890. 7p.
P4-S00574 — $10.00.

ALLERTON: Mem, of Isaac Allerton, (repr. NEHGR). By H.W. Cushman. 1854. 6p.
P4-S00575 — $10.00.

ALLING: Genealogical sketches of Roger Alling of New Haven CT, 1639; Gilbert Allen of Morristown NJ, 1736; & Thomas Bancroft of Dedham, MA. By J.K. Allen & Edwin Salter. 1883. 33p.
P4-S00577 — $10.00.

ALLING: Historical & genealogical record of the Alling-Allens of New Haven, CT, the descendants of Roger Alling, 1st, & John Alling, Sr., from 1639. By G.P. Allen. 1899. 317p.
P4-S00576 — $47.50.

ALLIS: Genealogy. By Chas. Allis. 1893. 32p.
P4-S00583 — $10.00.

ALLIS: Genealogy of William Allis of Hatfield, MA & desc, 1630-1919. By Horatio D. Allis. 1919. 237 + 44p.
P4-S00582 — $42.00.

ALLISON: History of the Allison family, that Branch Belonging to PA, A.D. 1750-1912. By J. L. Allison. 1912. 115p.
P4-S00591 — $22.50.

ALLISON: NJ — NY Familes: Allison, Davenport, Shawger (Shauger), Wendel (Wandle). By John P. Rogers. 1954. 108p.
P4-S00597 — $17.50.

ALLISON: History of the Alison-Allison family in Europe & America, 1135-1893. By L. Morrison. 1893. 328p.
P4-S00585 — $41.00.

ALLYN: Ancestry & descendants of Nancy Allyn (Foote) Webb, Rev. Edw. Webb & Jos.Wilkins Cooch, By Mary Evarts (Webb) Cooch. 1919. 157p.
P4-S00603 — $24.00.

ALLYN: Matthew Allyn of Cambridge, MA. By C. C. Baldwin. 1882. 20p.
P4-S00605 — $10.00.

ALLYN: Sketch of Matthew Allyn of Cambridge, MA. By J. Allyn. 1884. 37p.
P4-S00606 — $10.00.

ALMEY: Ancestry of Wiliam Almey of Lynn & Sandwich, MA & Portsmouth, RI (ex Essex Inst. Hist. Coll.). By G.A. Moriarty. 1913. 5p.
P4-S00613 — $10.00.

ALRICKS: Jacob Alrocks & his nephew Peter Alricks. By Edw. A. Price. 1898. 60p.
P4-S00606 — $12.00.

ALSTON: Alstons of NC & SC, Comp. from English, Colonial & family records, with personal reminiscences & notes of some allied fams. By J.A. Groves. 1901. 367p.
P4-S00615 — $58.50.

ALT: Valentin Alt, his children & his grandchildren. By Nellie W. Reeser. 1949. 122p., typescript.
P4-S00621 — $21.00.

ALTIZER: Emera Altizer & his desc, with sketches of connected families. Ruby A. Roberts & Rosa A. Bray. 1937. 263p.
P4-S00627 — $39.00.

ALVORD: Descendants of Alexander Alvord of Windsor, CT & Northampton, MA. By S. M. Alvord. 1908. 823 + 30p.
P4-S00633 — $128.00.

AMBLER: The Amblers in America: historical sketch, early families & their descendants directory. 1937. 35p. typescript.
P4-S00634 — $10.00.

AMBLER: Descendants of Jaquelin Ambler. By Geo. D. Fisher. 1890. 23p.
P4-S00635 — $10.00.

AMBROSE: Ambrose fam. records. By W. M. Clemens. 1925. 7p.
P4-S00636 — $10.00.

AMES: The Ames Family of Easton, MA. Winthrop Ames. 1938. x + 248p.
P4-S00637 — $39.00.

AMES: Charles Gordon Ames: a spiritual autobiography, with an epilogue by Alice Ames Winter. 1913. 229p.
P4-S00639 — $35.00.

AMES: The Ames Family of Bruton, Somerset, England. Faber K. Ames. 1969. 291p.
P4-S00638 — $44.00.

AMES: Gen. mem. of desc. of Samuel Ames of Canterbury, NH. By J. Kimball. 1890. 55p.
P4-S00640 — $11.00.

AMES: Ames & Eames fam. of Woburn, MA & Jefferson, ME. By F. M. Ames. 1913. 30p.
P4-S00641 — $10.00.

AMES: Some gen. notes (Ames & others). By P. Ames. 1900. 32p.
P4-S00642 — $10.00.

AMHERST: Jeffery Amherst: a Biography. By Lawrence Shaw Mayo. 1916. 344p.
P4-S00643 — $45.00.

AMIDON: A record of the descendants of Roger Amadowne of Rehoboth, MA. By Frank E. Best. 1904. 165p.
P4-S00639 — $26.00.

AMORY: The descendants of Hugh Amory, 1605-1805. By G. Meredith. 1901. 385p.
P4-S00645 — $58.50.

AMOS: "Our ancestry" [Amos, Beverly, Goodale, Graham, Keeney, Miller, Walton]. By Hazel Crane Amos. 1955. 202p.
P4-S00651 — $32.00.

AMSDEN: Some descendants of Isaac Amsden of Cambridge, MA. By Murray M. Brown. 1934. 116p., typescript. P4-S00657 — $18.00.

ANCKETELL: A short history, with notes & references, of the ancient & honourable family of Ancketill or Ancetell. By "One of its Members." 1901 60p. P4-S00660 — $12.00.

ANDERSEN: Desc. of Andrew Andersen. Lawrence T. Fadner. 2005. 168p. P4-S00668 — $25.00.

ANDERSON: KROGH Genealogy: anc. lines & desc. By L.W. Hansen. 1956. 323p. P4-S00669 — $51.50.

ANDERSON: DENNY; William Anderson & Rebecca Denny & their descendants, 1706-1914. By Mary Anderson Leonard. 1914. 287 + 98p. P4-S00717 — $58.00.

ANDERSON: PERRINE — BARBOUR — SMITH, Howell-Clark, Porter & Savery families, with a genealogical & biographical records of some who were pioneers in America. By Henriette E.S. Smith. 1902. 186 + 42p. P4-S00705 — $34.00.

ANDERSON: OVERTON genealogy. A continuation of "Anderson Fam. Records" (1936) & "Early Desc. of Wm. Overton & Elizabeth Waters of VA." By W.P. Anderson. 1945. 376p. P4-S00723 — $59.50.

ANDERSON: CHEVALIER Families of VA, 1678-1847. By E.E. Salisbury. 1885. 28p. P4-S00670 — $10.00.

ANDERSON: Notes of family history, the Anderson, Schofield, Pennypacker, Yocum, Crawford, Sutton, Lanes, etc., families. By Isaac C. Sutton. 1948. 210p. P4-S00699 — $32.00.

ANDERSON: Genealogy, in part, of the Anderson-Owen-Beall families. By G.J. Anderson. 1909. 159p. P4-S00687 — $24.00.

ANDERSON: Family history, containing a brief account of the families of Anderson, Davies, Wersler. By Julius A. Lloyd. 1880 80p. P4-S00681 — $15.50.

ANDERSON: Family records, By W.P. Anderson. 1936. 174p. P4-S00671 — $25.00.

ANDERSON: Andersons of Goldmine, Hanover County, VA. By E. L. Anderson. 36p. P4-S00672 — $10.00.

ANDERSON: Monograph of the Anderson, Clark, Marshall & McArthur connection. By T. Anderson. 1908. 32p. P4-S00673 — $10.00.

ANDERSON: The Andersons from the Great Fork of the Patuxent. By Cora A. DuLaney. 1948. 223p. P4-S00711 — $34.00.

ANDERSON: Genealogical history of the Leroy Anderson & Idell Anderson families. By Larry A. Anderson. 1998. 2 vols. In 1. 165 + 289p. P4-S00693 — $59.00.

ANDREW: History of the Andrew family, from various sources. By Adelia Elmer. 1889. 79p. P4-S00729 — $16.00.

ANDREW: Thomas Andrew, immigrant. A gen. of the posterity of Thomas Andrew, one of the early settlers of New England. By L.C. Andrew. 1971. 166p. P4-S00735 — $26.50.

ANDREWS: HAYWARD Genealogies. By Elizabeth H. Andrews. 1950. 115p. P4-S00753 — $18.50.

ANDREWS: A few family notes, genealogical & otherwise. By Avery D. Andrews. 1942. 48p. P4-S00742 — $10.00.

ANDREWS: Wm. Andrews of Hartford, CT & his desc. in the direct line to Asa Andrews of Hartland, CT & Hartford, OH. By F. Andrews. 1938. 69p. P4-S00789 — $14.00.

ANDREWS: "Postmarked Hudson": Letters of Sarah Andrews to her brother James A. Andrews, 1864-5, with gen. of the Andrews fam. Ed. by W. Miller. 1955. 76p. P4-S00741 — $15.00.

ANDREWS: Anc. of Henry L. & John C. Andrews, Woburn, MA. By H.L. & J.C. Andrews. 1914. 2nd ed. 19p. P4-S00743 — $10.00.

ANDREWS: Samuel George Andrews & Family. J.S. Andrews 1919. 49p. P4-S00748 — $10.00.

ANDREWS: Genealocical history of John and Mary Andrews, who settled in Farmington, CT, 1640, desc. to 1872. By A. Andrews. 1872. 652p. P4-S00777 — $82.00.

ANDREWS: Genealogy & alliances By Clara B. Wyker. 1917. 126p. P4-S00759 — $19.00.

ANDREWS: Genealogical biography of Charles T. & Mary E. Clark Andrews. By C.Y. Andrews. 1917. 63p. P4-S00771 — $13.00.

ANDREWS: Ancestors & descendants of Laban Andrews, Revolutionary patriot, & his wife, Pridence Stanley Andrews. By Adele Andrews. 1943. 136p., typescript. P4-S00747 — $21.00.

ANDREWS: John Andrews of Ipswich, MA & Norwich, CT & some desc. By H.A. Goodell. 1916. 28p. P4-S00755 — $10.00.

ANDREWS: Memorial, genealogy of the Andrews of Taunton & Stoughton, MA, Desc. of John & Hannah Andrews of Boston, 1656-1886. By G. Andrews. 1887. 86p. P4-S00765 — $14.50.

ANDREWS: Lt. John Andrews of Chebacco, MA, 1637-1708. By H.F. Andrews. 1909. 17p. P4-S00756 — $10.00.

ANDRUS: A few facts about the Andrus family, its relatives & ancestors (some descendants of Wm. of Wallingford, CT). By L.R. Andrus. 1932. 58p. P4-S00792 — $12.00.

ANDRUS: Supplement to "A Few Facts About the Andrus Family" By L.R. Andrus. 1933. 329p. P4-S00801 — $49.00.

ANGEL: Genealogy of Charles Angel, Sr., Pioneer of Frederick Co., MD. By Walter W. Gruber, Sr. 1948. 152p. P4-S00807 — $29.00.

ANGELL: Genealogy of desc. of Thomas Angell, who settled in Providence, 1636. By A.F. Angell. 1872. 210p. P4-S00813 — $37.50.

ANGELL: Looking backward four score years, 1845-1925 (author's reminiscences of life & family in Centerdale, RI, with some genealogy). By Frank C. Angell. 1925. 178p.
P4-S00819 — $25.00.

ANKENY: Sketch of the life & some descendants of Dewald Ankeny: b. Germany, 1728; came to America, 1746, & settled in Lancaster Co. By C. Shultz. 1948. 112 + 82p.
P4-S00825 — $28.00.

ANNIN: Centennial celebration of the Annin fam. at the old Stone House in Somerset Co., NJ. 1866. 17p.
P4-S00830 — $10.00.

ANNIS: Genealogy of David Annis of Hopkinton & Bath, NH, his ancestors & descendants. 1909. 73p.
P4-S00831 — $14.00.

ANSLEY: "Our Ansley Family:" record of the lives & times of the early members of the Ansley house in America, with ancestral tables Harold A. Davidson. 1933. 97p., typescript..
P4-S00837 — $18.00.

ANTHON: Ancestry of Charles Anthon, professor of classics at Columbia Univ. By A.A.G. Anthon. 1901. 48p.
P4-S00842 — $10.00.

ANTHON: Genealogy. By S. Fish. 1930. xl + 214p.
P4-S00843 — $39.50.

ANTHONY: Genealogy of the Anthony family, 1495-1904. By C.L. Anthony. 1904. 379p.
P4-S00846 — $49.00.

ANTHONY: Michael Anthony & Anne Sheild-Lambing: their ancestors & desc. By A.A. Lambing. 1896. 42p.
P4-S00847 — $10.00.

ANTILL: Edward Antill, a NY merchant of the 17th century, & his descendants, particularly Edward Antill 2nd of Piscataway, NJ; Lt-Col. Edward Antill 3rd of Quebec and Montreal By Wm. Nelson. 1899. 34p.
P4-S00851 — $10.00.

ANTISELL: Gen. of the desc. of Lawrence & Mary Antisell of Norwich & Willington, CT; Incl. some records of Christopher Antisell of Sraduff, Birr, (King's Co.) Ire. By M. Wyman. 1908. 335 + 40p.
P4-S00852 — $56.00.

ANTRIM: Records of the Antrim family of America. By H. S. Antrim. 1899. 232p.
P4-S00858 — $35.00.

APGAR: Desc. of Herbert Apgar & John Peter Apgar. Dorothy E. Apgar. 2005. v + 517 + 165p.
P4-S00860 — $103.00.

APPELTON: Fam. of Ipswich, MA. 17p.
P4-S00866 — $10.00.

APPLER: Family history. By Charles Ross Appler. 1976. 280p.
P4-S00864 — $44.00.

APPLETON: Monumental memorials of the Appleton family. By J. A. Appleton. 1867. 30p.
P4-S00867 — $10.00.

APPLETON: Family genealogy. By W.S. Appleton. 1874. 54p.
P4-S00868 — $10.00.

APSLEY: BATHURST Families. By A.B. Bathurst. 1903 (England). 136p.
P4-S00870 — $22.00.

ARAM: Family. By Alice Aram. (n.d. — ca. 1940?) 25p.
P4-S00878 — $10.00.

ARBOGAST: Descendants of Michael Arbogast (ca. 1734-1812) Volumes 1-5. Charles J. Eades. 1995-1996 5 vols; 3432p.
P4-S00880 — $350.00.

ARCHER: SYLVESTER families: a history written in 1870. By Dr Robert Archer. 1937. 29p.
P4-S00885 — $10.00.

ARCHER: Genealogical history of the Archer family, from the time of the settlement of James Archer 1st to the 5th generation By M.B. Archer. 1919. 100 + 70p. Index.
P4-S00882 — $25.00.

ARCHER: George Archer I, or the Umberland Archers of Henrico Co., VA & his descendants. By Wassell Randolph. 1966. 83p.
P4-S00888 — $17.00.

ARDERY: Descendants of James Ardery of Franklin Co., PA, Incl. allied families Read, Elder, McNutt, McGriffin & Others. By E. C. Floyd. 1984. 112p.
P4-S00894 — $14.00.

AREY: Richard Arey of Martha's Vineyard & some of his desc. By R.V. Chamberlin. 1932-1933 51p.
P4-S00894 — $10.00.

ARMISTEAD: Family, 1635-1910. By V.A. Garber. 1910. 319p.
P4-S00900 — $49.50.

ARMISTEAD: Family of VA. By W.S. Appleton. 1899. 23p.
P4-S00901 — $10.00.

ARMS: A gen. record of the Arms fam. in this country, embracing all the known desc. of William 1st. By E. W. Arms. 1877. 57p.
P4-S00902 — $11.00.

ARMSTRONG: Fam. of Windham, NH. By L. Morrison. 19p.
P4-S00904 — $10.00.

ARMSTRONG: Life of a woman pioneer, as illustrated in the life of Elsie Strawn Armstrong, 1789-1871. By James Elder Armstrong. 1931. 124p.
P4-S00921 — $18.00.

ARMSTRONG: Chronicles of the Armstrongs. By J.L. Armstrong. 1902. iv + 407 + 11p.
P4-S00903 — $63.00.

ARMSTRONG: History of the Armstrong family, 980-1939, & genealogy of David Armstrong & Sarah Harris Armstrong, 1746-1939. By T.E. Armstrong & J.H. Moyer. 1939. 272p.
P4-S00915 — $43.00.

ARMSTRONG: Genealogical record of the descendants of Nathan Armstrong, early settler of Warren Co., NJ,with sketches of family history. By Wm. Clinton Armstrong. 1895. 201p.
P4-S00909 — $31.00.

ARNDT: The story of the Arndts: The Life, Antecedents & Descendants of Bernhard Arndt, who emigr. to PA in 1731. By J.S. Arndt. 1922. 428 + 54p.
P4-S00927 — $72.00.

ARNOLD: LUCKEY Family ties: authorized hist. & gen., complete. By L.W. Arnold & E.Z. Luckey. 1931. 168p.
P4-S00933 — $25.00.

ARNOLD: Descendants of Wm. Arnold of Hingham, MA, With Cooke, Harris & Mowry families. By E. Richardson. 1876. 69p.
P4-S00957 — $14.00.

ARNOLD: The Arnold Family. By W.H. Arnold. 1935. iv + 210p.
P4-S00945 — $33.50.

ARNOLD: Family record: 323 years in America, a record of some of the descendants of Wm. Arnold & his son Benedict Arnold of RI & his grandson. By Ethan L. Arnold. 1958. 101p.
P4-S00939 — $18.00.

ARNOLD: Redway & Earle families. Descendants of Edward Arnold, b. perhaps in 1730-40; Comfort Redway, b. 1760; William Earle, b. about 1760 By Willis Arnold Boughton. 1948. 102 + 17p.
P4-S00963 — $19.00.

ARNOLD: Genealogy of the family of Arnold in Europe & America, with brief notes. By John Ward Dean, Henry T. Drowne & Edwin Hubbard. 1879. 16p.
P4-S00940 — $10.00.

ARNOLD: Family, as entered upon the records of the towns of Braintree, 1640-1853. comp. By Sam'l A. Bates. 1902. 48p.
P4-S00941 — $10.00.

ARNOLD: Lawrence Arnold (1650-1692) of Perquimans County, NC, with some of his descendants. Sidney C. Arnold, Jr. 2004. 443p.
P4-S00938 — $66.50.

ARNOLD: Memorial; Wm. Arnold of Providence & Pawtuxet, 1587-1675, & gen. of his desc. E. Arnold. 1935. 311p.
P4-S00951 — $49.50.

ARNOT: John Arnot of Scotland & Albany NY & desc. 1914. 12p.
P4-S00965 — $10.00.

ASHBY: BADGER Ancestry. By Robert L. Ashby. 1955. v + 445p.
P4-S00969 — $67.50.

ASHBY: TURNER records; Ashby of Fauquier Co., VA. 1952. 18p.
P4-S00970 — $10.00.

ASHBY: Ancestry: something of the origin of the name & family; family pedigree; story of Nathaniel & Susan Hammond Ashby; autobiogr. of Benj. Ashby. By Robert L. Ashby. 1941. 38p.
P4-S00971 — $10.00.

ASHBY: Family history of William Hardy Ashby & Nancy Maria Badger Ashby. By Robert L. Ashby. 1944. 226p.
P4-S00975 — $34.00.

ASHFORD: Some of the Ancestors & Descendants of James & George Ashford, Jr, of Fairfield Co., SC. By Charlie R. Ashford, Sr. 1956. iv + 123p., typescript.
P4-S00981 — $25.00.

ASHLEY: Family history. By Mary K.A. Casper & Mabel E. Ashley. 1943. 153 + 8p., typescript.
P4-S00987 — $25.00.

ASHLEY: Genealogy. History of the desc. of Robert Ashley of Springfield, MA. By F.B. Trowbridge. 1896. 483p.
P4-S00990 — $60.00.

ASHMEAD: Fam. of PA; Desc. of John Ashmead. 5p.
P4-S00991 — $10.00.

ASPINWALL: The Aspinwall & Aspinall Families of Lancashire, 1189-1923. By Henry O. Aspinall. 1923 viii + 394p.
P4-S00993 — $62.00.

ASPINWALL: The Aspinwall Genealogy. By Algernon A. Aspinwall. 1901. 262p.
P4-S00999 — $41.00.

ATHEY: Genealogy of the Athey family in America, 1642-1932. By Dr C.E. Athey. 1932. 95p.
P4-S01005 — $17.50.

ATKINS: Joseph Atkins: The Story of a Family. By F.H. Atkins. 1891. 158 + 60p.
P4-S01011 — $40.00.

ATKINS: A New England Family. Helen A. Claflin 1956. 154p.
P4-S01012 — $24.00.

ATKINSON: The Atkinsons of N.J. from the record of Friends Meetings a& from the offices of record in the state. By John N. Atkinson. 1890. 40p.
P4-S01019 — $10.00.

ATKINSON: Families of Bucks Co., PA, Pts. I & II. By Oliver Hough. 116p.
P4-S01017 — $21.00.

ATKINSON: Families of Atkinson of Roxby & Dearman of Braithwaite. By Harold W. Atkinson. 1933 516p.
P4-S01023 — $77.00.

ATLEE: Genealogical record of Atlee family of Lancaster Co., PA. By E. A. Barber. 1884. 130p.
P4-S01029 — $22.00.

ATTERBURY: Descendants of Job Atterbury. By L. Effingham de Forest. 1933. 157p.
P4-S01035 — $23.00.

ATWATER: Atwater History & Genealogy; Vol. I. By F. Atwater. 1901. vii + 492 + 8p.
P4-S01041 — $76.50.

ATWATER: Atwater History & Genealogy; Vol. II. By F. Atwater. 1907. 304 + 44p.
P4-S01047 — $48.00.

ATWATER: Atwater History & Genealogy; Vol. III. F. Atwater. 1918. 289p.
P4-S01053 — $45.00.

ATWATER: Atwater History & Geneealogy; Vol. IV. F. Atwater. 1927. 364p.
P4-S01059 — $56.00.

ATWATER: Atwater History & Genealogy; Volume V, The Great Adventure, 1456-1956. By Charles H. Attwater. 1956. vi + 316p.
P4-S01065 — $48.00.

ATWATER: Gen. register of the desc. in the male line of David Atwater, of New Haven, CT to the 6th generation. By E. E. Atwater. 1873. 64p.
P4-S01068 — $12.50.

ATWELL: Gen. of the Atwell fam. of New London, CT, By C.B. Atwell. 1896. 11p.
P4-S01067 — $10.00.

ATWOOD: Philip Atwood, 1619/20-1700, of Malden & Bradford, & descendants of early generations. By E.F. Atwood. 1931. 48p.
P4-S01075 — $10.00.

ATWOOD: Family, dating from 1741. By Arvilla Atwood. 1916. 52p.
P4-S01076 — $11.00.

ATWOOD: Ye Atte Wode Annals, 1-4. By E. Atwood. 1928. 90p.
P4-S01074 — $16.50.

AUCHINCLOSS: John & Elizabeth Auchincloss; their ancestors & descendants. By J.R. Auchincloss & C.A. Fowler. 1957. 67p.
P4-S01080 — $13.50.

AUCHMUTY: Family of Scotland & America. By Annette Townsend. 1932. xxxviii + 215 + 76p.
P4-S01086 — $50.00.

AUDENRIED: The Audenried Genealogy with the Allied Families of Musche, Wills, Wallace & Fulton. Col. Joseph Crain Audenried 1933. 132p.
P4-S01085 — $23.00.

AUGUR: Family history & genealogy of the desc. of Robert Augur of New Haven colony. By E. P. Augur. 1904. 260p.
P4-S01092 — $39.00.

AULL: MARTIN Genealogy. By W.F. Aull. 1920. 190p.
P4-S01098 — $28.50.

AUSTIN: Descendants of Richard Austin of Charlestown, MA, 1638. By E.A. Moore & W.A. Day. 1951 (?) 608p.
P4-S01104 — $89.50.

AUSTIN: Anc. of Jeremiah Austin of Charlestown, RI. By J.O. Austin. 26p.
P4-S01105 — $10.00.

AUSTIN: Genealogy of the descendants of Robert Austin of Kingstown, RI. By E.A. Moore. 1951. 738p.
P4-S01110 — $109.00.

AUSTIN: History of Rev. Wm. Austin & his wife Elizabeth with the names & addresses of their living descendants [1940], volumes I & II. By Marshie & Florence Austin. 1940-1953 40 + 64p.
P4-S01116 — $17.00.

AUTRY: Fam. & desc. of Capt. John Autry. By M.B. Autry. 1964. 209p.
P4-S01128 — $31.00.

AUTRY: Descendants of Cornelius Autry, immigrant, of Edgecombe Co., NC; Neil Culbreth of Sampson Co., NC & allied families. By V. Mayo Bundy & Robert Autry Brooks. 1996. 1247p.
P4-S01122 — $125.00.

AVERELL: AVERILL — AVERY Family: A Record of the Desc of William & Abigail Averell of Ipswich, MA. By C.A. Avery. 1906, 1914. 2 vols., 1094 + 10p.
P4-S01134 — $165.00.

AVERY: FAIRCHILD — PARK Families of MA, CT & RI. By S.P. Avery. 1919. 169p.
P4-S01158 — $25.00.

AVERY: Warren, Little, Lothrop, Park, Dix, Whitman, Fairchild, Platt, Wheeler, Lane & Avery ped. of Sam'l Putnam Avery. By S. Avery. 1925. 292p.
P4-S01179 — $44.00.

AVERY: Capt. John Avery, Pres. Judge at the Whorekill in Dela. Bay & his desc. By E.J. Sellers. 1908. 55p.
P4-S01180 — $11.00.

AVERY: The Groton Avery clan. By E.M. & C.H. Avery. 1912. 2 vols., xi + 785 + 736p.
P4-S01140 — $200.00.

AVERY: Notes & Queries. A quarterly magazine devoted to the hist. of the Groton Averys, # 1-18. ed. by E.M. Avery. 1898-1902. 246p.
P4-S01170 — $37.00.

AVERY: Genealogical record of the Dedham branch of the Avery family in America. By Carter & Holmes. 1893. 366 + 17p.
P4-S01164 — $58.00.

AVERY: The Averys of Groton, Ct., gen. & biogr. By H.D. Sweet. 1894. 698p.
P4-S01173 — $88.00.

AXFORD: The Axfords of Oxford, NJ: a genealogy beginning in 1725. By Wm. C. Armstrong. 1931. 78p.
P4-S01185 — $16.00.

AXTELL: Genealogy. By Carson A. Axtell. 1945. 380p + 11 charts.
P4-S01191 — $62.00.

AXTELL: Record: desc. of Henry Axtell, of Morris Co., NJ. By E.S. Axtell. 1886. 68p.
P4-S01197 — $14.00.

AYARS: Robt. Ayars & his descendants. By Frank D. Andrews. 1918. 98p.
P4-S01203 — $18.00.

AYDELOTT: History of the Aydelott family in the US. By George C. Aydelott. 1931. 101p.
P4-S01215 — $18.00.

AYLSWORTH: Arthur Aylsworth & his descendants in America. By H.E. Aylsworth; ed. J.N. Arnold. 1887. 632p.
P4-S01221 — $95.00.

AYRES: Genealogy of the Ayres fam. of Fairfield Co., CT. By J. N. States. 1916. 127p.
P4-S01233 — $22.50.

AYRES: Record of desc. of Capt. John Ayres of Brookfield, MA. By W. H. Whitmore. 1870. 55p.
P4-S01204 — $11.00.

B

BABBITT: The Babbitt Family history, 1643-1900, By W.B. Browne. 1912. 761 + 136p.
P4-S01236 — $135.00.
BABCOCK: Babcock Genealogy. Comp by S. Babcock. 1903. xxx + 640 + 130p.
P4-S01245 — $120.00.

BABCOCK: & Allied families. By L.E. de Forest. 1928. 137p.
P4-S01242 — $23.50.

BABCOCK: Genealogical Record of Nathaniel Babcock, Simeon Main, Isaac Miner & Ezekiel Main. Comp by C.H. Brown. 1909. 362 + 66p.
P4-S01251 — $64.00.

BABCOCK: Isaiah Babcock, Sr., & desc. By A.E. Babcock. 1903. 119p.
P4-S01257 — $19.50.

BABSON: & Allied families in America. By Robt. B. Alling. 1930. 77p.
P4-S01263 — $14.50.

BABSON: Genealogy, 1637-1930. By Geo. W. Chamberlain. 1934. 104p.
P4-S01269 — $19.00.

BABSON: Fam. of Gloucester, MA, [Ex Essex Antiq]. 8p.
P4-S01264 — $10.00.

BACK: WALLIS Fams: gen. notes. By H. Back. 1911. 12p.
P4-S01270 — $10.00.

BACKENSTOSS: Backenstoss Family Association of America. comp. by the Family. 1949. 188 + 40p.
P4-S01275 — $34.00.

BACKHOUSE: Descendants of John Backhouse, Yeoman, of Moss Side Near Yealand Redman, Lancashire. Comp by Joseph Foster. 1894 222 + 90p.
P4-S01281 — $47.00.

BACKUS: Families of early New England. By Reno W. Backus. 1966. iv + 199p.
P4-S01287 — $32.50.

BACKUS: Genealogical mem. of the Backus family, with private journal of James Backus bearing on 1st settlement of OH at Marietta. By W. Backus. 1889. 392p.
P4-S01293 — $60.00.

BACON: Genealogy. Michael Bacon of Dedham, 1640 & His desc. By T.W. Baldwin. 1915. 422p.
P4-S01317 — $44.00.

BACON: "Bacon's adventure," with Bacon & Wood genealogies. By Herbert M. Bacon. 1948. 197p.
P4-S01299 — $29.50.

BACON: Bacon & Allied families: A Family Directory. Comp by Committee. 1958 iv + 370p.
P4-S01305 — $56.00.

BACON: Genealogy of Asa Bacon, native of Wrentham, MA, Also a condensed report of his English ancestry. By Erdix N. Bacon. 1915. 32p.
P4-S01306 — $10.00.

BACON: Family genealogy. By Arthur L. Taylor & Cassius F. Bacon. 1922. 132p.
P4-S01311 — $21.00.

BADCOCK: Family of MA. By W. Appleton. 1881. 11p.
P4-S01325 — $10.00.

BADGER: Giles Badger & his desc. By J. C. Badger. 1909. 64p.
P4-S01320 — $12.50.

BAER: Genealogy of Johannes Baer, 1749-1910. By D.M. & R.B. Bare. 1910. 288p.
P4-S01335 — $44.00.

BAER: Genealogy of Henry Baer of Leacock, PA (Baer-Bear-Bare). By Willis N. Baer. 1955. xvi + 290p.
P4-S01329 — $45.00.

BAILEY: The Baileys of Baileytown, a genealogy of the So. Jersey Bailys with especial reference to the descendants of Edw. Bailey, Sr, of Cumberland Co By Norman W. Bailey. 1945. 152p.
P4-S01392 — $24.00.

BAILEY: Ancestry of Jos. Trowbridge Bailey of Philadelphia, & Catherine Goddard Weaver of Newport, RI. By Jos. Trowbridge Bailey. 1892. 54p.
P4-S01342 — $11.00.

BAILEY: History & genealogy of the family of Baillie of Dunain, Duchfour & Lamington, with a short sketch of McIntosh, Bulloch & other families. By Joseph Gaston Baillie Bulloch. 1898. 111p.
P4-S01380 — $18.00.

BAILEY: History & genealogy of the family of Bailie of North of Ireland . . . including the parish[es] of Duneane, Ireland & Dunain, Scotland. By Geo. A. Bailie. 1902. 96p.
P4-S01374 — $18.00.

BAILEY: Bailey Genealogy: James, John & Thomas & Their Descendants, in three parts, 1899. vi + 479p.
P4-S01350 — $61.00.

BAILEY: Genealogy of the descendants of Richard Bailey. By Alfred Poor. 1858. 91p.
P4-S01368 — $18.00.

BAILEY: Baillies of Inverness, Scotland, & some of their descendants in the US. By J.G.B. Bulloch. 1923. 86p.
P4-S01356 — $17.00.

BAILEY: Accts. of 2nd, 3rd & 12th Annual Gatherings of the Bailey-Bayley Fam. Assoc. 1894-1908. 123p.
P4-S01341 — $18.75

BAILEY: Family: history & genealogy of descendants of Richard Bailey of Rowley, MA, Who came to MI by Way of ME, NH, VT & NY. By Jeanne Bailey Ransom. 1991. xxiv + 478p.
P4-S01347 — $75.00.

BAILEY: Rec. of the Bailey fam., desc. of Wm. Bailey of Newport, RI, chiefly the line of his son Hugh, E. Greenwich, RI. By H. Hopkins. 1895. 207p.
P4-S01386 — $31.00.

BAILEY: Genealogical record of the descendants of James Bailey — Levi Bailey, in Westchester & Putnam Cos., NY. By Geo. A. Taft, et al. 1948. 139p.
P4-S01362 — $23.00.

BAILLEULS: Bailleuls of Flanders & Bayleys of Willow Hall. By F. Bayley. 1881. xxxvii + 272 + 24p.
P4-S02088 — $50.00.

BAILY: Genealogy of the Baily family of Bromham, Wiltshire, England, & more particulary of the descendants of Joel Baily. By Gilbert Cope. 1912. ix + 672 + 84p.
P4-S01398 — $115.00.

BAINBRIDGE: Ancestry of Wm. Seaman Bainbridge. By Louis E. de Forest. 1950. 164p.
P4-S01404 — $25.00.

BAIRD: BEARD Families: Genealogical, Biographical & Historical. By F.B. Catchings. 1918. 230 + 12p.
P4-S01410 — $36.00.

BAIRD: Family centennial, with a sketch of the life of Francis Baird, the pioneer, who settled in Warwick, NY, in 1765, & a genealogical list of some of his descendants. 1912. 45p.
P4-S01411 — $10.00.

BAKER: Genealogy of the fam. of Deacon Smith Baker of Litchfield, ME, 1874. By S. Baker. 1874. 18p.
P4-S01414 — $10.00.

BAKER: Descendants of William Baker, Jr. Silas Kenneth Baker, Jr. 2006. xvi + 502p.
P4-S01415 — $78.00.

BAKER: Genealogy & collateral branches. By Amenzo W. Baker. 1910. 226p.
P4-S01425 — $34.00.

BAKER: Anc. of Priscilla Baker, wife of Isaac Appleton of Ipswich. By W. S. Appleton. 1870. 143p.
P4-S01413 — $21.50.

BAKER: Gen. of the desc. of Edward Baker of Lynn, MA, 1630. By N.M. Baker. 1867. 99p.
P4-S01443 — $13.00.

BAKER: Henry Baker & some of his descendants. By Miles White, Jr. 1901. 32p.
P4-S01426 — $10.00.

BAKER: Short notes on the Baker fam. By C. Baker. 1896. 12p.
P4-S01428 — $10.00.

BAKER: Genealogical record of Rev. Nicholas Baker (1610-78) & his descendants. By Fred A. Baker. 1917. 147p.
P4-S01431 — $25.00.

BAKER: Genealogy of Eber & Lydia Smith Baker of Marion, OH & their descendants to Oct. 1909. By Elwood T. Baker. 1909. 87p.
P4-S01437 — $16.50.

BAKER: Family gen: desc. of John Nicholas Baker, 1701-63 (native of Germany; came to US in 1754) with some connecting lines. By R.H. Baker. 1955. 233p.
P4-S01419 — $38.50.

BALCH: WHITE. Bio. Sketches of Rev. James Balch, William White & Their Descendants, including Genealogical Records of their families Rev. A.F. White, LL.D. 1890. 176p.
P4-S01442 — $26.50.

BALCH: Balch Genealogica. By T.W. Balch. 1907. x + 410 + 34p.
P4-S01449 — $68.00.

BALCH: Leaflets. Vol. I, # 1-12. By E. Putnam. 1897. 75p.
P4-S01455 — $15.00.

BALCH: Genealogy of the Balch family in America. By G.B. Balch. 1897. xxxii + 553 + 62p.
P4-S01458 — $97.00.

BALCOM: Gen. of the Balkcom (Balcom) fam. of Attleboro, MA. By D. Jillson. 16p.
P4-S01463 — $10.00.

BALCOMBE: First book of the Balcombe family. By F.W. Balcomb. 1942. 95p.
P4-S01464 — $17.00.

BALDWIN: Investigations concerning the fam. of Baldwin of Ashton, Clinton, Bucks (Eng.). By J.L. Chester. 1884. 28p.
P4-S01477 — $10.00.

BALDWIN: John Baldwin of Stonington, CT. By J.D. Baldwin. 1873. 6p.
P4-S01478 — $10.00.

BALDWIN: Genealogy, 1500-1881. By C.C. Baldwin. 1881. 974p.
P4-S01476 — $146.00.

BALDWIN: Genealogy; Supplement to "Baldwin (1881)." By C. C. Baldwin. 1889. 398p.
P4-S01470 — $55.00.

BALDWIN: Brief genealogy of the Baldwins. By N.A. Baldwin. 1891. 70p.
P4-S01482 — $14.00.

BALDWIN: Genealogy notes. By Karl F. Baldwin. 1928. 31p.
P4-S01481 — $10.00.

BALDWIN: Descendants of Dea. Aaron Baldwin of N. Branford, CT, 1724-1800, with brief account of his ancestors. By Geo. E. Baldwin. 1907. 102p.
P4-S01488 — $17.00.

BALL: Family records; genealogical mem. of some Ball families of Gr. Britain, Ireland & America. By W.B. Wright. 1908. lxxii + 199 + 62p.
P4-S01512 — $50.00.

BALL: Descendants of John Ball, Watertown, MA, 1630-1635, By F.D. Warren & G.H. Ball. 1932. 161p.
P4-S01506 — $26.00.

BALL: Gen. of the fam. of Peter & Josiah Ball. By J. Ball. 1894. 8p.
P4-S01496 — $10.00.

BALL: Genealogy of the Ball & Weston families. By J.E.B. Jewett. 1867. 40p.
P4-S01498 — $10.00.

BALL: Conquering the frontiers, a biography & history of one branch of the Ball family. By R.H. Ball. 1956. 102p.
P4-S01500 — $18.50.

BALL: Col. William Ball of VA; The great-grandfather of Washington. By E.L.W. Heck. 1928 (London). 47p.
P4-S01501 — $10.00.

BALL: Recollections of the Ball family of SC & the Comingtee Plantation. By Anne Simons Deas. 1909. 190p.
P4-S01503 — $28.00.

BALL: Hist. of the Ball fam. Gen. of the New Haven branch; Allen Ball & some of his desc., 1638-1864. By L.A. Bradley. 1916. 59p.
P4-S01515 — $12.00.

BALLARD: William Ballard, a genealogical record of his descendants in Monroe Co., WV. By Margaret B. Ballard. 1957. 410p.
P4-S01545 — $62.00.

BALLARD: Genealogy: descendants of Israel Ballard (1748-1810) & Alice Fuller, his wife (1751-1796). By M.G. Dodge. 1942. 375p.
P4-S01536 — $58.00.

BALLARD: Gen. Wm. Ballard (1603-1639) of Lynn, MA & Wm. Ballard (1617-1689) of Andover, MA & their desc. By Farlow & Pope. 1911. 203p.
P4-S01539 — $30.00.

BALLARD: From the "Edward Pleasants Valentine Papers" abstr. of rec. in the local & general archives of VA. Comp. by Valentine Museum. 67p.
P4-S01530 — $13.50.

BALLARD: & Allied families. By Louis E. DeForest. 1924. 64p.
P4-S01524 — $13.00.

BALLARD: History, 1635-1935. By Newton A. Ballard. 1935. 35p.
P4-S01526 — $10.00.

BALLORD: Some of the descendants of Zaccheus Ballord, a private in the Revolutionary War; also in the last French & Indian War. By Esek S. Ballord. 1907. 74p.
P4-S01551 — $15.00.

BALLOU: An elaborate history & genealogy of the Ballous in America. By A. Ballou. 1888. xiv + 1323 + 54p.
P4-S01563 — $209.00.

BALLOU: The Ballous in America: An Addendum to the Original "Hist & Gen of the Ballous in America." Ballou Family Assn. 1937. vii + 210p., typescript.
P4-S01557 — $33.00.

BALLOU: The Ballous in America: An Addendum to the original "Hist & Gen of the Ballous in America." By Myrtle M. Jillson. 1942. 353p., typescript.
P4-S01569 — $53.00.

BALTZLY: BALSLEY-POLSLEY Family, with other variations of the name; also, a sketch of Maj. Wm. Haymond. By Katherine A.P. Bryan. 1939. xx + 373 + 28p.
P4-S01575 — $63.00.

BANCKER: Partial hist. & gen. record of the Bancker or Banker families of America, in particular the desc. of Laurens Mattyse Banker. Howard J. Banker. 1909. 458 + 12p.
P4-S01586 — $70.00.

BANCROFT: Charles Bancroft of Montreal: his ancestors Thomas of England & Reading, MA; John of Lynnfield, MA; his father James of Boston By George Abbott-Smith & James Bancroft. 1943. 126p.
P4-S01581 — $21.00.

BANGS: Family in America hist. & gen.; the desc. of Edw. Bangs of Plymouth & Eastham. By D. Dudley. 1896. 360p.
P4-S01584 — $46.50.

BANKS: Genealogical record of the Banks family of Elbert Co., GA, coll. By **E.A. Banks (2nd ed.)** Comp. & ed. by G.B. Young & S.B. Franklin. 1934. 215 + 16p.
P4-S01596 — $35.00.

BANKS: Descendants of Frances "Frankie" Banks from 1802-2004, Buncombe County, NC. Marshall L. Styles. 2004. 2 vols., 577 + 894p.
P4-S01597 — $162.00.

BANKS: Banks & Allied. J.L. Banks. 1938. 145p.
P4-S01598 — $24.00.

BANNING: Gen. & biogr. records of the Banning & allied fam. from the Amer. Hist. Soc. 1924. 161p.
P4-S01602 — $24.00.

BANTA: A Frisian family, the Banta gen. desc. of Epke Jacobse who came from Friesland, Netherlands to New Amsterdam, February 1659. By T. M. Banta. 1893. 427p.
P4-S01608 — $67.00.

BANTA: Pioneers, & records of the wives & allied families. By Elsa M. Banta. 1983. 303p.
P4-S01614 — $45.00.

BARBER: Genealogy of the Barber-Eno family of Homer, NY. By Geo. R. Howe. 1893. 40p.
P4-S01628 — $10.00.

BARBER: Genealogy of the Barber fam: desc. of Robt. Barber, Lancaster Co., PA. By E. Barber. 1890. 166p.
P4-S01638 — $25.00.

BARBER: Genealogy of desc. of Lyman Barber of Newark Valley, NY. By L. B. Barber. 1944. 60p.
P4-S01629 — $12.00.

BARBER: The Barbers of Daviess Co, IN, Including Collateral & Allied Lines of Baldwin, Boyd, Gilley, Horrall, McKnight, Myers, Ratton & Stone. John C. Clement. 2001. vii + 234p.
P4-S01636 — $36.00.

BARBER: Genealogy; Pt. 1. Desc. of Thomas Barber of Windsor, CT, 1614-1909. Pt 2; Desc. of John Barber of Worcester, MA, 1714-1909. By J.B. White & L.M. Wilson. 1909. 826p.
P4-S01626 — $103.00.

BARBER: Record of anc. & desc. of Edward Barber of Hopkinton, RI & Wife Phebe Tillinghast, By D.W. Matteson. 1892. 80p.
P4-S01644 — $16.00.

BARBOUR: Family history & genealogy of the Dryden Barbour family, Traer IA. By C.R. Green. 1911. 20p.
P4-S01646 — $10.00.

BARCLAY: Our branch of Barclays. By Cornelia Barclay Barclay. 1915. 78p.
P4-S01656 — $15.50.

BARCLAY: Barclays of NY: Who they are & who they are not, & other Barclays. By R.B. Moffat. 1904. 481p.
P4-S01650 — $75.00.

BARCROFT: Family record; Account of the family in England & desc. of Ambrose Barcroft, the emigrant of Solebury, PA. By E.T. Runk. 1910. 334p.
P4-S01662 — $53.00.

BARD: Fam.; hist. & gen. of the Bards of "Carroll's Delight" & gen. of the Bard kinship. By G. Seilhamer. 1908. 515p.
P4-S01668 — $79.50.

BARDWELL: BORDWELL Descendants, book II. By Robert Bardwell Descendants Amer. Ancestry Assoc. 2000. 637 + 14p.
P4-S01674 — $98.00.

BARGER: Journal; Bargers & Allied kindred. By A. L. Barger. 1924. 144p.
P4-S01686 — $29.00.

BARGER: Journal: . . . the genealogy & history of the Bargers & allied kindred. 1939. 588p.
P4-S01680 — $89.50.

BARKER: Family. By E. F. Barker. 1927. 553p.
P4-S01698 — $78.50.

BARKER: (Repr. Newport Hist. Mag.) By J. Austin. 1880. 13p.
P4-S01694 — $10.00.

BARKER: Fam. of Plymouth Col. & Co. By B. Newhall. 1900 102p.
P4-S01692 — $19.00.

BARKER: Genealogy, giving the names & descendants of several ancestors who settled in the US previous to the Declaration of Independence By James C. Parshall. 1897. 36p.
P4-S01699 — $10.00.

BARKER: Story with genealogy of some of the descendants of Nathan Barker of Sandisfield, MA. By Wm. G. Lord, et al. 1931. 101p.
P4-S01704 — $19.50.

BARKSDALE: Genealogy of part of the Barksdale family of America. By Sarah Donelson Hubert. 1895. 46p.
P4-S01711 — $10.00.

BARKSDALE: Family history & genealogy (with collateral lines). By Capt. J.A. Barksdale. 1940. xxii + 634p.
P4-S01710 — $98.00.

BARLOW: Family genealogy, comprising the anc. & desc. of Jonathan Barlow & Plain Rogers, of Delaware Co., NY. By G. Barlow. 1891. 508p.
P4-S01716 — $76.00.

BARNARD: MILLER & Allied families. By Kenneth D. Miller. 1952-1954. 278p.
P4-S01715 — $42.00.

BARNARD: Robert Barnard of Andover, MA & His desc. By R. M. Barnard. 1899. 40p.
P4-S01714 — $10.00.

BARNES: BAILEY Genealogy. By Walter D. Barnes. 1939. 100p.
P4-S01728 — $19.00.

BARNES: Fam. of Easthampton, L.I. By R. Wynkoop. 1906. 25p.
P4-S01723 — $10.00.

BARNES: Gen., incl. a coll. of anc., gen., & fam. records & bio. sketches of Barnes people. By G.N. Barnes. 1903. 226p.
P4-S01746 — $34.00.

BARNES: Thomas Barnes (c.1615-1689/90) of Hartford & Farmington, CT. By F.R. Barnes. 1943. 89p.
P4-S01758 — $17.00.

BARNES: Ten generations of the Barnes family in Bristol, CT. By F.F. Barnes. 1946. 280 + 90p.
P4-S01752 — $62.00.

BARNES: Ancestry of Fanny Barnes & her husband Thomas Knight: family relationships in CT, MA & L. Isl., 1620-1820. By Brian J.L. Berry. 1989. 106p.
P4-S01722 — $19.50.

BARNES: Family year book, Vols. I-III. By Trescott C. Barnes. 1907-10. 64 + 44 + 49p.
P4-S01740 — $25.00.

BARNES: Family in WV; Being a brief account of this branch of the family in WV. By Rev. I.A. Barnes. 1920. 126p.
P4-S01734 — $21.00.

BARNEY: Barney (1634) — Hosmer (1635) [family records]. By W.F. Adams. 1912. 133p.
P4-S01764 — $21.00.

BARNEY: Many interesting facts connected with the life of Commodore Joshua Barney, hero of US Navy, 1776-1812 By W.F. Adams. 1912. 228p.
P4-S01770 — $36.00.

BARNHAM: Life of Alice Barnham, (1592-1650) Wife of Sir Francis Bacon. A. Chambers Bunten. 1928. 79 + 3p.
P4-S01772 — $12.00.

BARNHART: The desc of John & Mariah (Hiveley) Barnhart: a gen of the anc & desc of John Barnhart & Mariah Hively of Eastern OH, By James K. Raywalt. 1990. 109p.
P4-S01788 — $19.00.

BARNUM: Barnum Genealogy: 650 Years of Family History, Vols 1 & 2. P.W. Barnum. 2006. 2 vols., 1387p.
P4-S01777 — $208.00.

BARNUM: Gen Chart of the Barnum Family, 1517-1904; 2nd Ed. Barnum Family, 1350-1907. Noah G. Barnum. 1904, 1907 22 + 33p.
P4-S01778 — $10.00.

BARNUM: Gen Rec of the Barnum Family; Conspectus of the Male Desc of Thomas Barnum, 1625-1695. E.L. Barnum & F. Barnum. 1912. 127p.
P4-S01779 — $19.00.

BARR: Hist. of the Barr fam., beginning with gr-grandfather Robt Barr & Mary Wills: their desc. down to the latest child. By W.B. Barr. 1901. 216p.
P4-S01788 — $32.00.

BARRET: Volume III, families of VA: Barret. By Geo. W. Chappelear. 1934. 208p.
P4-S01794 — $31.00.

BARRETT: Barrett Genealogy. Frederick Berrett Emery. 1957. 119 + 10p.
P4-S01801 — $20.00.

BARRETT: Descendants of Reuben Barrett 1755-2000. Janet Barrett Walker. 2000. 572p.
P4-S01802 — $86.00.

BARRETT: Genealogy of some of the descendants of Thomas Barrett, Sr., of Braintree, MA, 1635. By Wm. Barrett. 1888. 295p.
P4-S01800 — $46.00.

BARRETT: Some descendants of Wm. Barrett of Cambridge, 1656, who married four times: Sarah Champney, Mary Barnard, Mary Sparhawk, Margaret Bartlett. By Geo. C. Martin. 1912. 24p.
P4-S01803 — $10.00.

BARRETT: Leaves from family trees [biographical & genealogical sketches of Barrett & related families]. 1989. 249p.
P4-S01806 — $39.00.

BARRETT: Thomas Barrett of Braintree, Wm. Barrett of Cambridge & early desc. By J.H. Barrett. 1888. 8p.
P4-S01804 — $10.00.

BARROLL: in Gt. Britain & America, 1554-1910. By Hope H. Barroll. 1910. 124p.
P4-S01812 — $18.00.

BARROW: A few early families in America. By Grace Barrow Johnson. 1941. 262p.
P4-S01818 — $39.50.

BARRY: BARRYMORE, Records of the Barrys of County Cork, from the Earliest to the Present Time, with Pedigrees. By E. Barry. 1902. 214p.
P4-S01824 — $35.00.

BARRY: William & Esther Barry & their descendants: a mem'l record. By Esther S. Barry. 1909. 84p.
P4-S01836 — $16.00.

BARRY: Family records, Vol. I: Capt. Charles Barry & his desc. By L.H. Parker. 1951. 148p.
P4-S01830 — $25.00.

BARTH: Descendants of Nicholas Barth of Strasbourg. By Jay Norwalk. 1998. 120p.
P4-S01842 — $19.50.

BARTHOLOMEW: Collection of family records from Bartholomew, Botsford & Winston lines of genealogy. By Sarah A.W. Pond. 1899. 60p.
P4-S01845 — $12.00.

BARTHOLOMEW: Record of the Bartholomew Family: Historical, Genealogcal & Biographical. By G.W. Bartholomew, Jr. 1885. xviii + 752p.
P4-S01851 — $94.00.

BARTLETT: Fam. of Newbury, MA. 19p.
P4-S01858 — $10.00.

BARTLETT: A genealogy of the descendants of Joseph Bartlett of Newton, MA for seven generations. By Aldis E. Hibner. 1934. 291 + 78p.
P4-S01857 — $57.00.

BARTLETT: Fams. of Guildford, CT (Repr. NEHGR). By R.D. Smyth. 1902. 8p.
P4-S01859 — $10.00.

BARTLETT: Forefathers & descendants of Willard & Genevieve Wilson Bartlett, & allied families Moulton — McGehee — Endress. By G.W. Bartlett. 1952. 270p.
P4-S01881 — $42.00.

BARTLETT: Aaron Bartlett of Brookfield, MA, With some of his descendants. By Nellie A. Bartlett. 1931. 90+ 17p., typescript.
P4-S01863 — $17.00.

BARTLETT: Desc. of Samuel Colcord Bartlett & Eleanor Pettengill, his wife, of Salisbury, NH to Jan. 1, 1909. By E.J. Bartlett. 1930. 11p.
P4-S01860 — $10.00.

BARTLETT: Ancestry & descendants of Sam'l Bartlett & Lucy Jenkins. By Edith B. Sumner. 1951. 169p.
P4-S01869 — $25.50.

BARTLETT: Gen. & biogr. sketches of the Bartlett fam. in England & America. By L. Bartlett. 1876. 114p.
P4-S01887 — $19.50.

BARTLETT: Anc., Gen., Biogr., Hist: Acct. of the Amer. progenitures of the Bartlett fam. with special ref. to the desc. of John Bartlett of Weymouth & Cumberland. By T.E. Bartlett. 1892. 112p.
P4-S01875 — $19.00.

BARTON: Biography of Revolutionary heroes: containing the life of Gen. Wm. Barton & also of Capt. Stephen Olney, By Mrs Williams. 1839. 312p.
P4-S01893 — $42.00.

BARTON: Lt. William Barton of Morris Co., NJ & his desc. By W.E. Barton. 1900. 148p.
P4-S01899 — $22.00.

BARTON: Genealogy of the Barton Family of the Town of Marshall, Oneida Co., NY. Edward S. Barton. 1920. 40p.
P4-S01900 — $10.00.

BARTON: Roger Barton's kinsmen: general record of the Barton family & a detailed list of Roger Barton's descendants. By Margaret A.B. McLean. 1940. 115p.
P4-S01905 — $19.50.

BARTON: The Barton's Quest for Liberty. One Family's Sojourn Through RI & VA During the Nation's Formative Years. Peyton F. Carter, III. 2003. 62p.
P4-S01901 — $18.00.

BARTON: Descendants to the Tenth Generation of Jedediah Barton (1707 — after 1798) of Oxford and Ward, Worcester County, MA. Joan A. Hunter. 2004. 183 + 31p.
P4-S01902 — $32.50.

BARTOW: Genealogy; parts 1 & 2, with suppl. By E. Bartow. 1878-79. 318p.
P4-S01917 — $49.50.

BARTOW: Genealogy, containing every one of the name of Bartow, descended from Dr Thomas Bartow. By Evelyn Bartow. 1875. 60p.
P4-S01915 — $12.00.

BARWICK: Family of the US: Concise history of Barwicks from the time of their coming to this country in . . . 1652 & 1664 up to [1907], the lost links. By Sam'l O. Barwick. 1907. 78p.
P4-S01923 — $16.00.

BASCOM: Gen. record of Thos. Bascom & his desc. By E.D. Harris. 1870. 79p.
P4-S01929 — $16.00.

BASKERVILLE: Genealogy of the Baskerville Family & Some Allied Families, Including English Descent, from 1266 a.d. By Patrick H. Baskervill. 1912. xiv + 214 + 82p.
P4-S01935 — $47.00.

BASKIN: BASKINS Family, SC & PA. By Raymond Martin Bell. 1963. 85p., typescript.
P4-S01941 — $16.00.

BASKIN: BASKIN Family, PA, VA & SC. By Raymond M. Bell. 1957. 104p., typescript.
P4-S01947 — $16.50.

BASS: Descendants of Dea. Samuel & Ann Bass. By Charissa T. Bass & Emma L. Walton. 1940. 223p.
P4-S01959 — $34.00.

BASS: Family history: Esau Bass (Revolutionary Soldier), his brother Jonathan Bass, & their decendants. By Ivan E. Bass. 1955. xiv + 449 + 8p.
P4-S01953 — $71.00.

BASS: Jeriah Bass & his descendants: leaves from memory's scrapbook & facts from authentic sources. By L.E. Bass. 1940. 195p.
P4-S01965 — $29.50.

BASS: Anc. of Moses Belcher Bass, 1735-1817; also the anc. of his two wives Elizabeth Wimble & Margaret Sprague. By S. A. Smith. 1896. 14p.
P4-S01954 — $10.00.

BASSETT: One Bassett family in America with all connections in America & Many in Great Britain & France. By B.B. Bassette. 1926. 867p.
P4-S01974 — $115.00.

BASSETT: Edward M. & Annie Preston Bassett. By B. Preston. 1930. 359p.
P4-S01971 — $49.00.

BASYE: Family in the US. By O. Basye. 1950. 987p.
P4-S01980 — $135.00.

BATCHELDER: BATCHELLER; desc. of Rev. Stephen Bachilar of Eng., leading non-conformist who settled the town of New Hampton, NH, & Joseph, Henry, Joshua and John By F.C. Pierce. 1898. 623p.
P4-S01992 — $93.50.

BATCHELDER: Anc. & desc. of Deacon David Batchelder of Hampton Falls, NH. By M. J. Greene. 1902. 80p.
P4-S01986 — $16.00.

BATCHELOR: A Batchelor's Delight: The Adventures of a Family Historian. Anne Batchelor. 1990. vi + 78p.
P4-S01995 — $16.00.

BATES: FLETCHER Gen. register. By T.C. Bates. 1892. 60p.
P4-S02015 — $12.50.

BATES: BEARS & Bunker Bill. By E. Deacon. 1911. 90p.
P4-S02016 — $18.00.

BATES: Brief history & genealogy of Joseph Harrison Bates. By Madison C. Bates. 1915. 52p.
P4-S02000 — $10.00.

BATES: Ancestral lines for eight generations of Capt. Lemuel Bates, 1729-1820, with some records of his descendants. By Albert C. Bates. 1943. 68p.
P4-S01998 — $14.00.

BATES: Bulletin (misc. Bates material). By the Bates Fam. Assoc. 1908. 8p.
P4-S02001 — $10.00.

BATES: Gen. of the desc. of Edward Bates of Weymouth, MA. By S.A. Bates, ed. By F. Bates. 1900. 145p.
P4-S02025 — $24.00.

BATES: of VA & MO. By O. Bates. 1914. 160p.
P4-S02010 — $24.00.

BATES: The Bates Bulletin: Series I-VI. Bates Assn. 1907-1934. 630p.
P4-S02019 — $95.00.

BATT: The English anc. of the fam. of Batt & Biley (Repr. NEHGR). By J. H. Lea. 1897. 26p.
P4-S02027 — $10.00.

BATTELLE: Battelle gen. record. By L. Battelle. 1889. 21p.
P4-S02028 — $10.00.

BATTEY: Samson Battey of Rhode Island, the immigrant ancestor & his descendants. H.V. Battey. 1932. 400p.
P4-S02031 — $61.00.

BATTLE: Book: Genealogy of the Battle family in America. By Herbert Battle & Lois Yelverton. 1930. xv + 768p.
P4-S02037 — $99.50.

BATZ: BAATZ Family in America, which branch descended from the ancient dukes of Gascony, France. By Claude C. Hamel. 1951. 61p., typescript.
P4-S02040 — $12.00.

BAUERSACHS: Family history & chronology. By Dr U.S.G. Baowersox. 1941. 168p.
P4-S02049 — $25.00.

BAXTER: Memorial of the Baxter family. By J. Baxter. 1879. 114p.
P4-S02058 — $19.00.

BAXTER: Family: Desc. of George & Thomas Baxter of Westchester Co., NY as well as some WV & SC lines. By F. Baxter. 1913. 157p.
P4-S02055 — $25.00.

BAXTER: Some MD Baxters & their desc., includng fams. with surnames Anderson, Baker, Bonner, Brown, Butler, et al. A.S. Humphreys. 1948. 139p.
P4-S02064 — $22.50.

BAYARD: History & genealogy of the families of Bayard, Houstoun of GA & the descent of the Bolton family from Assheton, Byron & Hulton of Hulton Park. By Jos. G.B. Bulloch. 1919. 76p.
P4-S02070 — $14.00.

BAYARD: Col. John Bayard (1738-1807) & the Bayard family of America. By Jas. G. Wilson. 1885. 24p.
P4-S02071 — $10.00.

BAYLES: Families of Long Island & NJ & their descendants; also ancestors of James Bayles & Julia Halsey Day. By H.G. Bayles & F.P. Bayles. 1944. viii + 270p.
P4-S02076 — $42.00.

BAYLES: Supplement to "Bayles (1944)." 1946. 274p.
P4-S02082 — $42.00.

BAYLES: Ancestors of the Bayles family in the US, 1617-1900. By Eliza M.B. St John. 1900. 41p.
P4-S02077 — $10.00.

BAYLIES: Reminiscences of the Baylies & Richmond families. By "M.R.A." 1875. 28p.
P4-S02095 — $10.00.

BAYLIS: Family of VA, With supplements on the Chunn, Fawcett, Hawkins & Turner families & Baylis family in England. By W.B. Blum & Wm. Blum, Sr. 1958. xiii + 669p.
P4-S02094 — $102.00.

BAYLOR: History of the Baylors: collection of records & important family data. By O.W. Baylor & Henry B. Baylor. 1914. 48p.
P4-S02097 — $12.00.

BAYNE: Historical Genealogy of the Family of Bayne of Nedderdale; Showing also how Bayeux became Baynes. By J. Lucas. 1896. xxiv + 635p.
P4-S02106 — $99.00.

BEACH: Descendants of Thomas Beach of Milford, CT. By M. E. Beach. 1912. 51p.
P4-S02126 — $10.00.

BEACH: Beach in America, containing general information regarding the brother Richard, John & Thomas Beach By Elmer T. Beach. 1923. 149p.
P4-S02118 — $24.00.

BEACH: Rev. John Beach & descendants, with historical & biographical sketches, & ancestors & desc. of John Sanford of Redding, CT. By Beach & Gibbons. 1898. 397p.
P4-S02130 — $61.00.

BEACH: Ancestry & Posterity of Obil Beach. 1936. 456p.
P4-S02112 — $69.00.

BEACH: Genealogy of the Beach family of CT, with portions of the genealogies of the allied families By Charles C. McClaughry. 1905. 248p.
P4-S02124 — $38.50.

BEACH: The John Beach & John Wade Families. Anna C. Smith Pabst. 1960. 228 + 30p.
P4-S02127 — $39.00.

BEACHY: Family record of Samuel J. Beachy & Elizabeth Yoder & their descendants. By Lucy Eash. 1959. 201p.
P4-S02142 — $33.00.

BEAL: Joseph Beal & his wife Elizabeth (Cleghorn) Beal of Perinton, Monroe Co., NY & Rollin, Lenawee Co., MI. 1910. 114p., typescript.
P4-S02148 — $19.00.

BEAL: John Beal of Hingham & one line of his desc. N. B. Shurtleff. 1865. 8p.
P4-S02143 — $10.00.

BEAL: John Beal of Hingham & one line of his descendants. By Granville Beal. 1901. 42p.
P4-S02144 — $10.00.

BEAL: John Beal the centenarian & descendants: fourteen generations, 1588-1956; also other Beal families from England. By Bertha B.B. Aldridge. 1956. 263p.
P4-S02145 — $39.50.

BEALE: The Genealogy of the Beale Family, 1399-1956. By Frances Beal S. Hodges. 1956. 391p.
P4-S02154 — $61.00.

BEALES: Beales of Chester Co., PA. By Mary B. Hitchens. 1957. 57p.
P4-S02155 — $11.00.

BEALL: Ancestry & descendants of Gustavus Beall & Thos. Heugh Beall. By Josiah Shinn. 1911. 28p.
P4-S02159 — $10.00.

BEALS: Chronology of the Beals family of NC, desc. from John Beals of Chester Co., PA. n.a. 1912. 114p.
P4-S02166 — $19.00.

BEAMAN: CLARK Genealogy: history of the desc. of Gamaliel Beaman & Sarah Clark of Dorchester & Lancaster, MA, By E.B. Wooden. 1909. 219p.
P4-S02172 — $35.00.

BEAN: Joshua Bean of Exeter, Brentwood & Gilmanton, NH & some of his desc. By J. H. Drummond. 1903. 116p.
P4-S02178 — $20.50.

BEAN: Autobiography of George Washington Bean & His Family Records. G.W. Bean. 1945. 377p.
P4-S02177 — $56.00.

BEAR: Gen of the Bear Family & Biographical Record of the Descendants of Jacob Bear, 1747-1906. By W. S. Bear. 1906. 216 + 116p.
P4-S02184 — $50.00.

BEARD: Family history & genealogy. By Ruth Lindenberger. 1939. 130p.
P4-S02190 — $21.00.

BEARD: Gen. of desc. of widow Martha Beard of Milford, CT. By R. Beard. 1915. 99p.
P4-S02196 — $19.50.

BEARD: History of Adam Beard & his descendants. By Irene Beard. 1952. 93p.
P4-S02202 — $18.50.

BEARDEN: Preserving the Past: Vol. I. Roots Stems & Branches of our Familly Bearden/Burden & Winn. Bertha Irene Keller. 1998. 521 + 88p.
P4-S02204 — $86.00.

BEARDSLEY: Genealogical history of Beardsley-lee family in Amer., 1635-1902. By I.H. Beardsley. 1902. 453p.
P4-S02208 — $69.50.

BEARDSLEY: William Beardsley of Stratford, CT desc. By H. F. Johnston. 108p.
P4-S02214 — $20.00.

BEARE: Capt. Henry Martin Bear (1760-1828), life, ancestry & descendants. By Sam'l Seabury. 1938. 275p.
P4-S02183 — $41.50.

BEARSE: Gen. of the Bearse fam. in America 1618-1871. By J. B. Newcomb. 1871. 16p.
P4-S02213 — $10.00.

BEATH: The Beath-Pelham families. By M.R.B. Potter. 1870. 13p.
P4-S02212 — $10.00.

BEATH: Fam. of Scotland & America. By K.G. Stone. 1898. 20p.
P4-S02211 — $10.00.

BEATTY: ASFORDBY, the ancestry of John Beatty & Susanna Asfordby, with some of their descendants. By S.R. Turk. 1909. 183p.
P4-S02220 — $29.50.

BEATTY: Record of the family of Charles Beatty, who emigrated from Ireland to America in 1729. By Charles C. Beatty. 1873. 120p.
P4-S02215 — $19.50.

BEATTY: Gen. record of the fam. of Beatty, Egle, Muller, Murray, Outh & Thomas. By W.H. Egle. 1886. 129p.
P4-S02260 — $21.00.

BEAVERS: History of Sol. Joseph Beavers (NJ Militia) (1728-1816) of Hunterdon Co., NJ, his family. By Harold Alfred Sonn. 1948. 173p., typescript.
P4-S02232 — $25.00.

BEBOUT: Family, in Flanders & North America. By Alexander C. Flick. 1943. 80p.
P4-S02238 — $16.00.

BECHTEL: Karl Bechtel of Hanau, Germany & some of his desc. By J. W. Hook. 1936. 30p.
P4-S02239 — $10.00.

BECK: History of the Beck fam. together with a gen. record of the Alleynes & the Chases from whom they are desc. By C. R. Conover. 1907. 259p.
P4-S02244 — $39.00.

BECKER: Biographical history of the Becker family & their early settlement in America. By Leah B. Becker. 1901. 136p.
P4-S02250 — $21.00.

BECKER: The Adam Becker family, with Kessler & Dierker connections, from the Rhineland, Germany, to St. Louis, MO. By Gerry B. Meier. 2000. 177p.
P4-S02256 — $27.00.

BECKHAM: Family in VA. By J.M. Beckham. 1910. 98p.
P4-S02262 — $19.00.

BECKLEY: The Descendants of Richard Becley of Wethersfield, CT. C.B. Sheppard. 1948. xi + 406p.
P4-S02268 — $61.50.

BECKSTEAD: Desc John Beckstead, b. abt. 1738, Saxony, Germany, d. 1808, Schoharie Co., NY. By Lee Allen Beckstead. 1963. 901p.
P4-S02274 — $129.00.

BECKWITH: Additional Beckwith notes, including Avery, Ely, Gilbert, Holmes, Lee, Smith, Southerland, Wightman & Williams families. By F.W. Beckwith. 1956. 49p.
P4-S02281 — $10.00.

BECKWITH: "The Beckwiths." By P. Beckwith. 1891. 384p.
P4-S02280 — $51.50.

BECKWITH: Notes, Nos. 1-6; Marvin Beckwith & his wife Abigail Clark; their colonial ancestors & desc., with some notes on allied fams. 1899-1907. 378p.
P4-S02286 — $57.00.

BEDELL: Desc. of John Bedell of Passaic Valley, NJ. By E. Bedell. 1885. 29p.
P4-S02287 — $10.00.

BEDON: Family of SC. 4p.
P4-S02288 — $10.00.

BEEBE: Lucius Beebe of Wakefield & Sylenda Morris, his wife: forebears & desc. By L. Wilder. 1930. 255p.
P4-S02310 — $38.00.

BEEBE: Genealogy of the family of Beebe, from the earliest known immigrant, John Beebe of Broughton, Eng., 1650, Vol. I. comp. & ed. by Clifford Beebe. 1991. 217p.
P4-S02298 — $31.00.

BEEBE: Genealogy of the family of Beebe, The Second Emigration, Vol. II. By J.B. Fisher & C. Beebe. 1993. 282p.
P4-S02304 — $42.50.

BEEBE: Monograph of desc. of Beebe family. By Clarence Beebe. 1904. 127p.
P4-S02316 — $25.00.

BEEBE: Add. misc. Beebe data. By F.S. Whelan. 1949. 11p.
P4-S02306 — $10.00.

BEEBE: Some anc. & desc. of Alex Beebe of New London, By A. B. Seger. 1951-1958 20p.
P4-S02305 — $10.00.

BEECHER: Ancestors of Henry Ward Beecher & his wife Eunice White Bullard. By J.C. Frost. 1927. 126p.
P4-S02322 — $19.50.

BEEKMAN: Distinguished families in America, descended from Wilhelmus Beekman & Jan Thomasse Van Dyke. By Wm. B. Aitken. 1912. 266p.
P4-S02328 — $42.00.

BEEM: Daniel Beem & his descendants, embracing some facts relating to the early history of Spencer & Owen Co., IN. By David Beem. 1917. 102p.
P4-S02334 — $17.00.

BEEM: History of the Michael Beem family. By Nelson Beem. 1936. 96p.
P4-S02340 — $18.00.

BEERY: Family history. By Wm. Beery & Judith B. Garber. 1957. 783p.
P4-S02346 — $105.00.

BEERY: Hist of the desc of Nicholas Beery, b. 1707, emigrated from Switzerland to PA in 1727. By Jos. H. Wengler. 1911. 496p.
P4-S02358 — $74.50.

BEERY: Hist. of the desc. of Abraham Beery, b. in 1718, emigr. to Penn. in 1736, & comp. gen. fam. register. By J.H. Wenger. 1905. 328p.
P4-S02352 — $51.50.

BEESON: Genealogy. By Jasper L. Beeson. 1925. 144p.
P4-S02364 — $25.00.

BEESON: Family: direct line of descendants from Edward Beeson, who came from England in 1682, down to 1898. By B.A. Beeson. 1898 12p.
P4-S02365 — $10.00.

BEGGS: Book of Beggs; gen. study of the Beggs fam. in Amer. By R. & C. Beggs. 1928. 135p.
P4-S02370 — $27.00.

BEHARRELL: Family history. By N.C. Messenger with V.B. Chapman. 1974. 130p.
P4-S02376 — $24.00.

BEIDLER: Genealogical record of the desc. of Jacob Beidler of Lower Milford Twp., Bucks Co., PA. By A.J. Fretz. 1903. 565p.
P4-S02382 — $84.50.

BEIGHLEY: 1737-1934: Acorns from Colonial Oaks, Vol. I. By Wm. B Rodenbaugh. 1934. 86p.
P4-S02388 — $17.00.

BELCHER: Record of the desc. of Andrew Belcher (Repr. NEHGR). By W. H. Whitmore. 1873. 8p.
P4-S02395 — $10.00.

BELCHER: Family in England & America, comprehending a period of 765 years with part. reference to desc. of Adam Belcher of Southfields, Orange Co., NY. By W. & J. Belcher. 1941. 481p.
P4-S02394 — $75.00.

BELDEN: Some of the anc. & desc. of Royal Denison & Olive Cadwell Belden. By J.P. Belden. 1898. 248p.
P4-S02400 — $37.00.

BELKNAP: Family of Newburgh & vicinity. By Wm. E. Warren. 1889. 78p.
P4-S02406 — $15.50.

BELKNAP: English anc. of Abraham Belknap, who settled in Lynn, MA, 1635. By H.W. Belknap. 1914. 20p.
P4-S02407 — $10.00.

BELL: Genealogy of the Bell family, a record of the descendants of Lancelot. By family committee. 1907. 112p.
P4-S02418 — $18.00.

BELL: Bells in the Revolution. By W. M. Clemens. 1916. 16p.
P4-S02413 — $10.00.

BELL: Family in America. By W. Clemens. 1913. 45p.
P4-S02414 — $10.00.

BELL: Family records. By J. Montgomery Seaver. 1929. 36p.
P4-S02415 — $10.00.

BELL: Family of Mifflin Co., PA: Ancestors & descendants of John Henderson Bell of Decatur Twp., By Raymond M. Bell. 1941. 77p., typescript.
P4-S02412 — $15.00.

BELL: John Bell of Barree Twp, PA, his anc. & desc. By R. M. Bell. 1937. 4p.
P4-S02416 — $10.00.

BELL: Colonial Families of the US, Descended from the Immigrants Who Arrived Before 1700; Bell, Beal, Bale, Beale, Beall. By M.M. Beall. 1929. 296p.
P4-S02417 — $46.00.

BELL: John Bell of Londonderry, NH & his Scottish anc. By L. Bell. 1920. 19p.
P4-S24019 — $10.00.

BELL: Genealogy of the Bell family of Hagerstown, MD, with supplement. n.a. 1894. 40 + 19p.
P4-S02420 — $11.50.

BELLEVILLE: Jean Belleville the Huguenot, his descendants. By Paul Belville Taylor. 1973. 610p.
P4-S02430 — $89.00.

BELLINGER: History & genealogy of the families of Bellinger & DeVeaux, & other families. By Jos. G. Bulloch. 1895. 109p.
P4-S02436 — $18.00.

BELLOWS: Genealogy; or, John Bellows the boy emigrant of 1635 & His desc. By T. B. Peck. 1898. 673p.
P4-S02442 — $83.50.

BELLOWS: Parentage of Ezra Bellows of MA & VT. By T. B. Peck. 1902. 9p.
P4-S02443 — $10.00.

BELSER: Fam. of SC. By W.G. Belser, et al. 1941. 67p.
P4-S02448 — $13.50.

BELVILLE: Fam. of VA, GA & FL & several allied families, north & south. By A.B.V. Tedcastle. 1917. 212p.
P4-S02449 — $34.00.

BEMIS: Family in ME. By C. N. Sinnett. 1922. 6p.
P4-S02452 — $10.00.

BEMIS: Hist. & gen.; an acct. of the desc. of Jos. Bemis of Watertown, MA. By T. Draper. 1900. 295p.
P4-S02451 — $37.50.

BENDER: Descendants of Dan'l Bender. By C.W. Bender, with D.B. Swartzendruber. 1948. 192p.
P4-S02457 — $28.50.

BENEDICT: Story of the Benedicts: genealogy of the Benedict fam. for the descendants of Ira & Seely Benedict of the 7th gen. in America. By Lyle Benedict. 1939 31p.
P4-S02461 — $10.00.

BENEDICT: Genealogy of the Benedicts in America. By H.M. Benedict. 1870. 494p.
P4-S02460 — $60.00.

BENJAMIN: Gen. of the Benjamin fam. in US, 1632-1898. By E. B. Baker. 1898. 88p.
P4-S02466 — $17.50.

BENJAMIN: Genealogy of the family of Lt. Sam'l Benjamin & Tabitha Livermore, his wife, early settlers of Livermore, ME, with a record of their descent from John Benjamin & John Livermore By Mary Louise Benjamin. 1900. 92p.
P4-S02472 — $18.00.

BENNET: Fam. of Ipswich, MA. By J.M. Bradbury. 1875. 8p.
P4-S02473 — $10.00.

BENNETT: BENTLY — BEERS Families of NY. By S.B. Bennett. 1899. 50p.
P4-S02479 — $10.00.

BENNETT: Bennett & allied families. Addenda to Bullard & allied families. By E. J. Bullard. 1931. 43p.
P4-S02480 — $10.00.

BENNETT: Origin & hist. of the name Bennett, with biogr. of the most noted persons of the name. 1905. 112p.
P4-S02496 — $19.50.

BENNETT: Family history: Wm. Bennett & Grace Davis (m. 1789); their ancestry & their descendants. By Mary E.B. Durand & Edw. Dana Durand. 1941. 220p.
P4-S02484 — $34.00.

BENNETT: Family, 1628-1910. By E.B. Bennett. 1910. 50p.
P4-S02483 — $10.00.

BENNETT: Book: family history, Tunis, Fowler, Myers, Nichols, Wiley, Shields, et al. By John A. Shields. 1956. 112p., typescript.
P4-S02478 — $18.00.

BENNETT: Fam. of Sussex Co., DE, 1680-1860, with branches into the Warren, Shockley & other fams. By J.B. Hill. 1970. 71p.
P4-S02490 — $14.00.

BENNION: Family of UT, Vol. I. By Harden Bennion. 1931. 241p.
P4-S02502 — $36.50.

BENSCHOTER: Desc. of Byron Benschoter (1845-1933). By Rachel Saul Tefft. 1999. 133p.
P4-S02508 — $21.00.

BENSON: A pioneer family. By E. L. Benson. 1919. 11p.
P4-S02531 — $10.00.

BENSON: Jacob Benson, pioneer & his desc. in Dover & Amenia, NY. By A. T. Benson. 1915. 130p.
P4-S02526 — $26.00.

BENSON: Genealogy of the Benson, Latimer, Reed, Durham & associated families. By Mary B. Maxwell. 1931. 57p.
P4-S02527 — $11.00.

BENSON: Family records. By F. H. Benson. 1920. 207p.
P4-S02520 — $31.00.

BENSON: Family of Newport, RI, with an appendix concerning the Bensons in America of English desc. By W.P. Garrison. 1872. 65p.
P4-S02514 — $13.00.

BENSON: Narrative history of the family of Caleb Ellis Benson & Alice Anzanette Hatch, 1603-1924. By Harold E. Benson. 1957. 103p.
P4-S02532 — $16.50.

BENT: "Who begot thee?" — some genealogical & historical notes made in an effort to trace the American progenitors of one individual living in America in 1903. By Gilbert O. Bent. 1903. 78p.
P4-S02538 — $15.50.

BENT: Family in America, being mainly a gen. of the desc. of John Bent, who settled in Sudbury, MA in 1638. By A. H. Bent. 1900. 313p.
P4-S02541 — $49.50.

BENT: Supplement to The Bent Family in America: Descendants of Orlando Brown (1837-1919) & Mary Ann Luther (1840-1901). By Elva Spiker. 1992. 21p.
P4-S02539 — $10.00.

BENTLEY: One branch of the Bentley family of RI. By Emilie Sarter. 1953. 121p., typescript.
P4-S02550 — $19.00.

BENTLEY: Bentley gleanings, by J.H. Lobdell; fam. of John Witherstine. By W. Witherstine. 1905. 128p.
P4-S02545 — $21.00.

BENTLEY: The Diary of William Bentley, D.D, Pastor of East Church, Salem, MA. W. Bentley. 1784-1792 4 vols., 536 + 548 + 663 + 783p.
P4-S02546 — $275.00.

BENTLEY: Fam.; gen. record of OH Bentleys. By G.R. Brinkerhoff. 1897. 20p.
P4-S02547 — $10.00.

BENTON: Samuel Blade Benton, his anc. & desc., 1620-1901. By J. H. Benton, Jr., 1901. 366p.
P4-S02574 — $58.00.

BENTON: Edward Benton of Guildford, CT & his desc. (Repr. NEHGR). By R. D. Smyth. 6p.
P4-S02573 — $10.00.

BENTON: David Benton, Jr. & Saral Bingham, their ancestors & descendants & other ancestral lines. By John H. Benton. 1906. 88p.
P4-S02568 — $17.00.

BENTON: David Benton & Nancy Pitts, their ancestors & descendants, 1620-1920. By Edith E. Davenport. 1921. 101p.
P4-S02562 — $17.50.

BENTON: Caleb Benton & Sarah Bishop, their ancestors & descendants. By Chas. E. Benton. 1906. 92p.
P4-S02556 — $18.00.

BENTON: Extr. from Gen. Notes of NY & New Eng. Fams. By S. V. Talcott. 1883. 12p.
P4-S02572 — $10.00.

BENTON: Andrew Benton of Milford & Hartford, CT & his desc. (Repr. NEHGR). By J.H. Benton. 1906. 14p.
P4-S02571 — $10.00.

BERGEN: Family; or, the desc. of Hans Hansen Bergen of New York & Brooklyn, with notes on other Long Island families. By T.G. Bergen. 1876. 658p.
P4-S02580 — $83.50.

BERGER: Desc. of Philip D. Berger (1814-80). By Rachel Saul Tefft. 1999. 262p.
P4-S02586 — $35.00.

BERGEY: Genealogy; record of the desc. of John Ulrich Bergey & his wife Mary. By D. Bergey. 1925. 1166p.
P4-S02592 — $168.00.

BERKELEY: The Berkeleys of Barn Elms. F.B. Young. 1954. 123p.
P4-S02598 — $21.00.

BERRY: The Berry Family of Lawrence County, KY. David V. Agricola, MD. 1985. xiii + 70p.
P4-S02600 — $13.00.

BERTOLET: Genealogical hist. of the Bertolet fam.; descendants of Jean Bertolet. By D.H. Bertolet. 1914. 260p.
P4-S02604 — $41.00.

BEST: Hist. of Peter & Mary Best & fam. By N. Best 1897. 15p.
P4-S02608 — $10.00.

BETTS: Thomas Betts & desc. By C.W. & F. Betts. 1888. 136p.
P4-S02613 — $24.50.

BETTS: Family history, 1634-1958. By W. Robbins. 1959. 122p.
P4-S02610 — $22.00.

BEUSSE: Sketches of the Beusse & Evans families, & items of interest. By HJ.H. Beusse. 1923. 119p.
P4-S02619 — $18.00.

BEVERIDGE: Family, 'Yarmouth (N.B.) Genealogies' No. 109. By George S. Brown. 1909. 6p.
P4-S02622 — $10.00.

BEVIER: Family; History of the desc. of the desc. of Louis Bevier, who came from France & settled in New Paltz, NY. By K. Bevier. 1916. 291p.
P4-S02625 — $41.00.

BEWLEY: & Related families. By Donald D. Parker. 1946. 135p., typescript.
P4-S02637 — $21.00.

BIARD: Family [of Scotland & TX]. By Maud Biard Smith. 1928. 79p.
P4-S02649 — $15.50.

BIARD: Family. By Maud Biard Smith. 1929. 100p.
P4-S02643 — $19.00.

BIBB: Family in America, 1640-1940. By C.W. Bibb. 1941. 149p.
P4-S02655 — $24.00.

BIBIGHAUS: Descendants of John Bibighaus of Bedminster, Bucks Co., PA. 1888. 44p.
P4-S02658 — $10.00.

BICKNELL: History & genealogy of the Bicknell family & some collateral lines, of Normandy, Great Britain & America. By T. W. Bicknell. 1913. 620p.
P4-S02661 — $93.00.

BICKNELL: A memoir of a respectable & respected fam., esp. of Joshua Bicknell, With tombstones inscrp. in Sarrington, RI, By T. Bicknell. 1880. 48p.
P4-S02662 — $10.00.

BIDDLE: A sketch of Owen Biddle, to which is added a short acct. of the Parke fam., with a list of his desc. By H.D. Biddle. Rev. & enl. ed. 1927. 111p.
P4-S02673 — $21.00.

BIDDLE: A sketch of Owen Biddle, to which is added a short account of the Parke fam., together with a list of his desc. By H. D. Biddle. 1892. 87p.
P4-S02667 — $17.50.

BIDWELL: Gen. to the 7th gen. of Bidwell fam. in America. By E. M. Bidwell. 1884. 123p.
P4-S02679 — $25.00.

BIDWELL: Some Bidwell occupations; read at Bidwell fam. mtg. at Buffalo, NY, 1914. By F. Bidwell. 1917. 8p.
P4-S02680 — $10.00.

BIEBER: History & genealogy of the Bieber, Beaver, Biever, Beeber family [desc. of George Bieber of Germany & PA]. By I.M. Beaver. 1939. 984p.
P4-S02685 — $129.50.

BIERBAUER: House of Bierbauer, two hundred years of family history, 1742-1942. By James C. Bierbower & Chas. W. Beerbower. 1942. 188p.
P4-S02691 — $25.00.

BIERCE: Ancestors in the US of Byron Bierce & his wife Mary Ida Cottrell, of Cortland Co., NY. By T.H. Bierce & L. Cottrell. 1962. 289p.
P4-S02697 — $44.00.

BIGELOW: Genealogy of the Bigelow family of Amer., from the marr. in 1642 of John Bigelow & Mary Warren to the year 1890. By G.B. Howe. 1890. 517p.
P4-S02712 — $65.00.

BIGELOW: Ancestors of Chas. Dana Bigelow & his wife Eunice Ann Howe. By Josephine C. Frost. 1926. 172p.
P4-S02703 — $26.00.

BIGELOW: Background. By Ashley Bigelow. 1933. 107p.
P4-S02709 — $18.00.

BIGNOLD: Five generations of the Bignold fam., 1761-1947, & their connection with Norwich Union [Insurance]. By Sir Robert Bignold. 1948. 320p.
P4-S02718 — $49.50.

BILL: History of the Bill family. By L. Bill. 1867. 368p.
P4-S02721 — $47.50.

BILLINGS: Gen. of some desc. of William Billing(s) of Stonington, CT. By F. Billings. 49p.
P4-S02724 — $10.00.

BILLINGS: Family of CT. By C. Spencer-Mounsey. 1927. 23p.
P4-S02725 — $10.00.

BINFORD: Family Genealogy. By Mary L. Bruner. 1925? 375p.
P4-S02727 — $57.00.

BINFORD: Genealogy supplement. By M.L. Bruner. 1934. 126p.
P4-S02733 — $19.50.

BINGHAM: Genealogy of the Bingham family in the US, especially of CT. By T.A. Bingham. 1898. 288p.
P4-S02760 — $37.50.

BINGHAM: Family in the US, especially of CT, including notes on the Binghams of Phila. & of Irish desc: medieval records; arm. bearings, etc., Three-volume set By T.A. Bingham. 927-1930 3 vols., 473 + 434 + 447p.
P4-S02739 — $190.00./set

BINGHAM: Family in the US, especially of CT . . . , Vol. I. 473p.
P4-S02739A — $69.00.

BINGHAM: Family in the US, especially of CT . . . , Vol. II. 434p.
P4-S02739B — $69.00.

BINGHAM: Family in the US, especially of CT . . . , Vol. III. 447p.
P4-S02739C — $69.00.

BINNEY: Gen. of the Binney fam. in the US. By C.J.F. Binney. 1886. 278p.
P4-S02766 — $36.50.

BIRD: Descendants of Andrew Bird of Colonial Long Island, NY, 2nd ed. By Prof. E.O. Bennett. 1999. 329p.
P4-S02778 — $49.50.

BIRD: Genealogy of the Bird family of Hartford. By I. Bird 1855. 24p.
P4-S02773 — $10.00.

BIRD: Family history. By Booth, Maycock & Poulson. 1961. 171p.
P4-S02772 — $26.50.

BIRD: Genealogy [descendants of Col. Abraham Bird of VA]. By William B. Wylie. 1903. 13p.
P4-S02773 — $10.00.

BISBEE: Genealogy of the Bisbee family, descendants of Thomas Besbeech (Bisbee) of Scituate, Duxbury & Sudbury, MA. By Frank J. Bisbee. 1956. 558p.
P4-S02784 — $82.50.

BISBEE: Fam. records of some of the desc. of Thomas Besbedge (Bisbee) of Scituate, MA, 1634. By W.B. Lapham. 1876. 48p.
P4-S02785 — $10.00.

BISHOP: Bishop families in ME. By C. N. Sinnett. 1922. 13p.
P4-S02797 — $10.00.

BISHOP: Record of desc. of John Bishop , one of the founders of Guilford, CT, in 1639. By W.W. Cone & G.A. Root. 1951. 277p.
P4-S02814 — $42.50.

BISHOP: Family history of John Bishop of Whitburn, Scotland; Robt. Hamilton Bishop of Oxford, OH; Ebenezer Bishop of McDonough Co., IL, By Stanley R. Scott & Robt. H. Montgomery. 1951. 148p.
P4-S02808 — $23.50.

BISHOP: Families in Amer., Book III: Richard of Salem. I.E. Bishop. 1966. 80p.
P4-S02790 — $16.00.

BISHOP: Families of America, Book VIII: Edward Bishop of Salem. By I.E. Bishop. 1967. 115p.
P4-S02796 — $21.00.

BISHOP: Family history of John Bishop of Whitburn, Scotland; Robt. Hamilton Bishop of Oxford, OH; Ebenezer Bishop of McDonough Co., IL. By Stanley R. Scott & Robt. H. Montgomery. 1951. 148p.
P4-S02808 — $23.50.

BISPHAM: Memorial concerning the family of Bispham in Great Britain & the US. By W. Bispham. 1890. 348p.
P4-S02820 — $57.00.

BISSELL: General Daniel Bissell: his ancestors & descendants & the Hoyt, Strong & other families with which they intermarried. By Edith N. Jessop. 1927. 146p.
P4-S02826 — $22.50.

BITTINGER: BEDINGER families: descendants of Adam Budinger. By Lucy F. Bittinger. 1904. 63p.
P4-S02832 — $13.00.

BITTNER: Gen. record & hist. of the Bittner-Werley fams: desc. of MIchael Bittner & Sebastian Werley (1753-1930). By J.W. Bittner. 1930. 239p.
P4-S02838 — $28.00.

BIXBY: Genealogy of descendants of Joseph Bixby, 1621-1701, of Ipswich & Boxford, MA, who spell the name Bixsby, Bigsby, Byxbee, etc By W.G. Bixby. Pts. I-III 1914. 707p.
P4-S02844 — $99.00.

BLACK: Record of the posterity of Joseph Smith Black & Nancy Cynthia Allred Black. By Alta A. Dayton. 1956. 117p.
P4-S02856 — $19.00.

BLACK: Family marriages. By W.M. Clemens. 1916. 32p.
P4-S02851 — $10.00.

BLACK: Historical record of the posterity of Wm. Black, who settled in this country in the year 1775; also a sketch of 23 English families By Cyrus Black. 1885. 209p.
P4-S02850 — $32.00.

BLACKBURN: Genealogy, with notes on the Washington family through intermarriage, containing certain hist. facts on VA lore & Mt. Vernon. By Vinnetta W. Ranke, 1939. 158p.
P4-S02862 — $26.00.

BLACKHALL: The Blackhalls of that Ilk & Barra: hereditary coroners & foresters of the Barloch. By A. Morison. 1905. 180p.
P4-S02868 — $28.00.

BLACKMAN: & allied families. By A. L. Holman. 1928. 258p.
P4-S02874 — $39.00.

BLACKMAN: The Blackmans, Darrows, Booses, Joneses et al. By H.B. Plumb. 1894. 22p.
P4-S02785 — $10.00.

BLACKSHEAR: Blacksheariana genealogy, history, anecdotes. By Perry L. Blackshear, Sr. 1954. 476p.
P4-S02880 — $72.00.

BLACKSTONE: Desc. of Wm. Blackstone. By L. Sargent. 1857. 42p.
P4-S02883 — $10.00.

BLACKSTONE: Lineage & History of William Blackstone, First Settler of Boston & of His Descendants. John Wilford Blackstone. 1907. v +292p.
P4-S02884 — $44.00.

BLACKWELL: Genealogy: Ancestors, descendants & connections of Moore Carter & Sarah Alexander (Foote) Blackwell (Book I, Genealogy only). By E.M. Blackwell. 1948. 126p.
P4-S02886 — $23.00.

BLAINE: Family: James Blaine, emigrant, & his children, Ephraim. Alexander, Wm., Eleanor. By John Ewing Blaine. 1920. 109p.
P4-S02892 — $18.00.

BLAIR: MOFFETT Families: history & genealogy between the years 1600 & 1935. By Eva Pogue Kirkman. 1935. 192p.
P4-S02898 — $28.50.

BLAIR: Family of New England. By E.W. Leavitt. 1900. 197p.
P4-S02901 — $34.50.

BLAIR: History of the Blair, Banister & Braxton families, before & after the Revolution, with a brief sketch of their descendants. By F. Horner. 1898. 257p.
P4-S02913 — $37.00.

BLAIR: Blairs of Richmond, VA: descendants of Rev. John Durburrow Blair & Mary Winston Blair. By Rolfe E. Glover, Jr. 1933. 177p.
P4-S02907 — $27.50.

BLAKE: The anc. & allied fam. of Nathan Blake, 3rd, & Susan (Torrey) Blake of East Corinth, VT. By A. T. B. Fenno-Gendrot. 1916. 212p.
P4-S02949 — $32.00.

BLAKE: Family. A gen. hist. of William Blake of Dorchester & his desc. By S. Blake. 1857. 140p.
P4-S02925 — $21.00.

BLAKE: Ancestry of Edward Wales Blake & Clarissa Matilda Glidden, with 90 allied families. By Edith B. Sumner. 1948. 322p.
P4-S02919 — $49.50.

BLAKE: Gen. desc. of Amos Blake of Waterbury, CT. 7p.
P4-S02920 — $10.00.

BLAKE: Descendants of Jasper Blake, emigrant from England to Hampton NH, ca. 1643, 1649-1979. By Carlton E. Blake. 1980. 553p.
P4-S02931 — $79.50.

BLAKE: Increase Blake of Boston, his anc. & desc.; Wm. of Dorchester & his five children. By F. Blake. 1898. 147p.
P4-S02937 — $24.00.

BLAKE: Record of the Blakes of Somersetshire, especially in the line of Wm. Blake of Dorchester, MA, the emigrant to New England By Horatio G. SomerBy. 1881. 64p.
P4-S02943 — $13.00.

BLAKENEY: SABIN. Anc. of Benj. Ferris Blakeney & his wife Stella Peronne Sabin. By J.C. Frost. 1926. 309p.
P4-S02955 — $48.00.

BLAKENEY: Blakeneys in America, with reference to English-Irish families. By J.O. Blakeney. 1928. 103p.
P4-S02961 — $19.50.

BLAKESLEY: Samuel Blakesley of New Haven, CT & his desc. (Repr. NEHGR). By J. Shepard. 1902. 15p.
P4-S02968 — $10.00.

BLAKESLEY: Family, 1630-1957. By F.B. Hopkins & P.D. Flint. 1958. 75p.
P4-S02967 — $15.00.

BLAKEY: Genealogy of the Blakey family & descendants, with George, Whitsitt, Haden, Anthony, Stockton, Gibson By L.A. Kress. 1942. 96p.
P4-S02973 — $19.00.

BLANCHARD: Memorial, being a brief account of our ancestors . . . through various branches back to colonial times. By Arthur W. Blanchard. 1935. 190p.
P4-S02979 — $28.00.

BLANCHARDS: of RI. By Adelaide B. Crandall. 1942. 263p.
P4-S02985 — $40.00.

BLATCHFORD: Memorial II: A gen. rec. of the fam. of Rev. Samuel Blatchford, D.D., with some mention of allied fams. By E.W. Blatchford. 1912. 123p.
P4-S02991 — $21.00.

BLAUVELT: Family genealogy: a comprehensive compilation of the descendants of Gerrit Hendricksen (Blauvelt) (1620-1687) By Louis L. Baluvelt. 1957. 1064p.
P4-S02997 — $149.50.

BLETHEN: Gen. of the Blethen fam. By A. Blethen. 1911. 108p.
P4-S03003 — $19.50.

BLICKENSDERFER: History of the Blickensderfer family in America. By Jacob Blickensderfer. (1900?) 56p.
P4-S03005 — $11.00.

BLISH: Family genealogy, 1637-1905. By J.K. Blish. 1905. 10 + 366p.
P4-S03022 — $47.50.

BLISH: Supplement to Bliss Genealogy (1905). By Matthew R. Blish. 1957. 154p.
P4-S03021 — $24.00.

BLISS: HOLMES Descendants: genealogical data, biogr. sketches of the desc. of Ephraim Bliss of Savoy, MA & Israel Holmes of Waterbury, CT. By E.B. & A.B. Dayton. 1961. 184p.
P4-S03027 — $28.00.

BLISS: Genealogy of the Bliss family in America, from about 1550-1880 By J. H. Bliss. 1881. 811p.
P4-S03039 — $99.00.

BLISS: Book: romantic history of the Bliss family from the time of its beginning in England to its advent into America By C.A. Hoppin. 1913. 184p.
P4-S03033 — $29.50.

BLIVEN: Five families of Charlestown, RI: Bliven, Crandall, Macomber, Money & Taylor, with appendix. By Earl P. Crandall. 1993. 165 + 120p.
P4-S03045 — $29.00.

BLODGET: Hon. Sam'l Blodget, pioneer of progress in the Merrimack Valley. By Geo. Waldo Browne. 1907. 56p.
P4-S03049 — $11.00.

BLODGETT: Seth Blodgett of Brooksville, ME, 1747-1817, his ancestors & descendants. By Grace Limeburner. 1933. 88p.
P4-S03057 — $17.50.

BLODGETT: Asahel Blodgett of Hudson & Dorchester, NH, his Amer. anc. & desc. By I.D. Blodgett. 1906. 144p.
P4-S03051 — $23.00.

BLOOD: Desc. of Richard Blood of Bellingham & Charlton, MA. By C. W. Barlow. 1952. 37p.
P4-S03066 — $10.00.

BLOOD: Genealogy of the Noal D. Blood & Elanda F. D'Onofrio Family. Bernard S. Sadowski, PhD. 2003. 389p.
P4-S03064 — $50.00.

BLOOD: The story of the Bloods, incl an acct. of the early gen. of the fam. In Amer. in geneal. lines from Robt. Blood of Concord & Richard Blood of Groton By R.D. Harris. 1960. 201p.
P4-S03069 — $32.50.

BLOOD: Gen record of the descendants of Richard Blood — Baptist Hicks & allied families, 1470-1933. By Grace Cabot Toler. 1933. 101p.
P4-S03063 — $18.50.

BLOOD: English ancestry & miscellanea: Blood-Hicks & allied families, 1150-1939, supplement to 1933 edition. By Grace C.B. Toler. 1939. 32p.
P4-S03065 — $10.00.

BLOSS: Genealogy. By J. O. Bloss. 1887. 19p.
P4-S03072 — $10.00.

BLOUNT: BLUNT Fam. records. By J.H. Wheeler. 1884. 10p.
P4-S03073 — $10.00.

BLUE: A Viking Odyssey to the New World: from Ancient Sweden to AL, via Norway, Normandy, England, Scotland, VA, NC & GA. By James J. Blue. 1992. 183p.
P4-S03075 — $25.00.

BLUNT: Family; Desc. of William Blunt of Andover, MA (in Goodhue fam.) By E. G. Fuess. 1930. 10p.
P4-S03078 — $10.00.

BOARDMAN: Genealogy, 1525-1895. By C. Goldthwaite. 1895. 791p.
P4-S03084 — $99.50.

BOARDMAN: Family in Topsfield, MA (Repr. Topsfield Hist. Coll.) By H. R. Towne. 1902. 29p.
P4-S03082 — $10.00.

BOARMAN: The Boarmans [of England & MD]. By C.F. Thomas. 1934. 89p.
P4-S03090 — $18.00.

BOARDMAN: Ancestry of William Francis Joseph Boardman, Hartford, CT, By W. F. J. Boardman. 1906. 419p.
P4-S03081 — $66.00.

BOAZ: Thomas Boaz family in America, with related families. By Hiram A. Boaz. 1949. 286p.
P4-S03096 — $43.50.

BOCKEE: BOUCQUET Family, 1641-1897. By Martha B. Flint. 1897. 168p.
P4-S03102 — $26.00.

BODDIE: & Allied families. By John T. Boddie & John B. Boddie. 1918. 250p.
P4-S03108 — $38.00.

BODURTHA: Record of the Bodurtha family, 1645-1896. By H. Maria Bodurtha. 1896. 116p.
P4-S03114 — $18.00.

BOEKEL: Family Association of America, with supplement. 1942-1943. 66 + 39p.
P4-S03120 — $19.00.

BOGARDUS: Genealogical history of the ancestors & descendants of Gen. Robert Bogardus. By M. Gray. 1927. 281p.
P4-S03126 — $45.00.

BOGART: Family: Tunis Gysbert Bogaert & his desc. By J.A. Bogart. 1959. 280p.
P4-S03132 — $44.00.

BOGART: Some notes on the history of the Bogart family in Canada, with genealogical record of Lewis Lazier Bogart & Elizabeth Cronk Bogart. By Marshall C. Bogart. 1918. 71p.
P4-S03138 — $14.00.

BOGERT: Five Bogert families: descendants of Evert, Jan Laurencz, Cornelis, Guysbert & Harmense Myndertse Bogert. By Herbert S. Ackerman. n.d. 488 + 40p., typescript.
P4-S03144 — $78.00.

BOGERT: More Bogert families: descendants of Cornelise Jansen, Gysbert Uyten, & Henry Bogert, with other Bogert families. By Herbert S. Ackerman. n.d. 374 + 56p., typescript.
P4-S03150 — $66.00.

BOGGS: Genealogical record of the Boggs family; the descendants of Ezekial Boggs. By W.E. Boggs. 1916. 100p.
P4-S03156 — $18.00.

BOGLE: Family records [descendants of Jos. Bogle, pioneer to PA & TN]. By Leila Mason Eldridge. 1937. 49p.
P4-S03158 — $10.00.

BOGMAN: Genealogy of the Bogman family, 1767-1890. By Emily W. Leavitt. 1890. 36p.
P4-S03160 — $10.00.

BOGUE: Genealogy: descendants of John Bogue of East Haddam, CT & his wife Rebecca Walkley; also the NC Bogues By Flora Bogue Deming. 1944. 322p.
P4-S03168 — $49.50.

BOGUE: & Allied families. By V.T. Bogue. 1947. 439 + 49p.
P4-S03162 — $75.50.

BOHLANDER: Family & early hist. of DuPage Co., IL. By W.F. Bohlander. 1937. 72p.
P4-S03174 — $14.00.

BOHRER: BORAH — BORER Genealogy. By Camden Borah Meyer. 1965. 519p.
P4-S03180 — $79.50.

BOIT: Chronicles of the Boit family & their descendants, & other allied families. By R.A. Boit. 1915. 260p.
P4-S03186 — $39.00.

BOLICH: Family in America, with genealogies. By Mary M. Bolich. 1939. 142p.
P4-S03192 — $23.00.

BOLLES: Gen. of the Bolles fam. in Amer. By J. Bolles. 1865. 71p.
P4-S03204 — $14.00.

BOLTON: The Boltons of old & New England, with a gen. of the desc. of William Bolton of Reading, MA, 1720. By C. K. Bolton. 1889. 98p.
P4-S03228 — $19.50.

BOLTON: Family records of Peter Bolton, son of Peter of Pocklington, England. By T.L. Bolton. 1923. 28p.
P4-S03211 — $10.00.

BOLTON: Genealogical & biographical account of the family of Bolton in England & America, deduced from an early period & Continued to the present time By Robert Bolton. 1862. 223p.
P4-S03222 — $35.00.

BOLTON: Family of Bolton in England & America, 1100-1894; a study in genealogy. By H.C. & R.P. Bolton. 1895. 540p. + charts
P4-S03216 — $89.00.

BOLTON: Family in Ireland with their Eng. & Amer. kindred. By C.K. Bolton. 1937. 109p.
P4-S03210 — $18.50.

BOMBERGER: Chronicles. By Henry H. Bomberger. 1935. 22p.
P4-S03230 — $10.00.

BOND: Autobiogr. reminiscences of Rev. Alvan Bond, D.D., 1793-1882; anc. & desc., ped. charts of Alvan Bond & Sarah Richardson, his wife; By H.R. Bond. 1896. 214p.
P4-S03234 — $32.00.

BOND: Family record or genealogies of Robert Bond; also the descendants of Jacob Price. By Mrs D. Price. 1872. 36p.
P4-S03241 — $10.00.

BOND: Genealogy: history of the desc of Joseph Bond, b. 1704 in Wiltshire, England, d. 175- in NC, By Sam'l B. Garrett. 1913. 208p.
P4-S03240 — $31.00.

BONHAM: Bonham, 1631-1908. By Emmet L. Smith. 1911. 40p.
P4-S03242 — $10.00.

BONNEY: Family. By Chas. L. Bonney. 1893. 178p.
P4-S03243 — $26.50.

BONNIFIELD: Family, Descendants of Gregory Bonnifield of MD. By Charles J. Maxwell. 1918. 72p.
P4-S03249 — $14.50.

BONNIFIELD: Descendants of Gregory Bonnifield (1726-94). By C.J. Maxwell. 1949. 183p., typescript.
P4-S03255 — $26.00.

BONTECOU: The ancestry of Daniel Bontecou of Springfield, MA: a record of forty successive generations, extending through thirteen centuries. By John E. Morris. 2nd ed. 1887. 271p.
P4-S03267 — $41.00.

BONTECOU: Anc. of Daniel Bontecou of Springfield, MA. J. E. Morris. 1887. 29p.
P4-S03262 — $10.00.

BONTECOU: Genealogy: A records of the descendants of Pierre Bontecou, Huguenot refugee from France, in the lines of his sons. By John E. Morris. 1885. 271p.
P4-S03261 — $43.00.

BONYTHON: Fam. of ME. By C.E. Banks. 1884. 7p.
P4-S03270 — $10.00.

BOODEY: Annals of the Boodeys in New England, with lessons from John Eliot. By R. B. Caverly. 1880. 297p.
P4-S03273 — $46.50.

BOOKER: History of the Booker family in ME. By C.N. Sinnett. 1922. 31p.
P4-S03274 — $10.00.

BOONE: Boone, Mayfield, Short & Tate fam. hist., (VA) By R. N. Mayfield. 1902. 6p.
P4-S03277 — $10.00.

BOONE: Family; Genealogical history of desc. of George & Mary Boone, who came to America in 1717. By H. Spraker. 1922. 707p.
P4-S03276 — $91.00.

BOORSE: Family. By Harry Emerson Boorse. 1953. 298p.
P4-S03282 — $45.00.

BOOTH: Genealogy. By A. Booth. 1903. 12p.
P4-S03289 — $10.00.

BOOTH: Genealogy. By H. S. Booth. 1908. 18p.
P4-S03290 — $10.00.

BOOTH: Genealogy, including allied families representing the American ancestry in the Booth line of the compiler. By Henry Slader Booth. 1923. 116p.
P4-S03288 — $19.00.

BOOTH: One branch of Booth fam., showing connections with 100 Mass. Bay Col. By C.E. Booth. 1910. 237p.
P4-S03291 — $31.00.

BOOTH: Genealogy of the Booth fam. in England & US. By W. S. Booth. 1892. 25p.
P4-S03292 — $10.00.

BOOTH: The Cranbrook (Kent, England) Booth family of America. comp. By the Cranbrook Foundation. 1955. 68p. + charts
P4-S03303 — $16.00.

BOOTHE: Genealogy [desc. of Daniel of NC]. By Ross Boothe, Jr. 1958. 31p.
P4-S03305 — $10.00.

BOOZER: Our heritage: history of Smyrna Church (Newberry Co., SC) & of the Boozers of Smyrna. By Mildred W. Goodlett. 1963. x + 272p.
P4-S03309 — $42.50.

BORDEN: Richard Borden of Portsmouth, RI & desc. ed. by H. F. Johnston. 56p.
P4-S03313 — $11.00.

BORDEN: History & gen. record of the desc. of Richard & Joan Borden, who settled in Portsmouth, RI, May 1638. By H. B. Weld. 1899. 348p.
P4-S03312 — $45.00.

BORDWELL: Ancestry of Lavern Bordwell, 420 a.d.-1928 a.d., with every traceable line in America, all colonials & some earlier royal ancestors. By Lavern Bordwell. 1928. 70p.
P4-S03318 — $14.00.

BORLAND: Family. By Constance Borland. 1911. 40p.
P4-S03320 — $10.00.

BORLASE: Descent, name & arms of Borlase of Borlase, in the Co. of Cornwall. By W. Borlase. 1888. 207p.
P4-S03324 — $36.00.

BORNEMAN: History of Borneman fam. in America since first settlers, 1721-1878. By J. H. Borneman. 1881. 114p.
P4-S0330 — $22.50.

BORROR: Jonas Borror family history. By Charles E. Borror. 1999. 393p.
P4-S03336 — $59.50.

BORROR: The Desc of Jacob Borror II & Magdaline Strader Borror. ed. By Dick Shover, 2003. 879p.
P4-S03337 — $90.00.

BORTHWICK: Family: history & genealogy of the family of Borthwick, chiefly in Scotland & America, By H.M. Borthwick, with additional information By Wm. S. Borthwick. 1903, 1936. 148p.
P4-S03342 — $22.50.

BORTON: History of the Borton & Mason families in Europe & America. By Freeman C. Mason. 1908. 304p.
P4-S03354 — $46.50.

BORTON: Desc. of John of Eng., who settled in Burlington Co., NJ [Ex. from Haines Gen]. 1902. 5p.
P4-S03355 — $10.00.

BOSBYSHELL: Descendants of Christian & Elizabeth (Oliver) Bosbyshell, 1782-1910. By Oliver C. Bosbyshell. 1910. 61p.
P4-S03357 — $12.00.

BOSS: An inquiry concerning the Boss family & the name Boss, corresponding between Wm. Graham Boss (Edinburgh, Scotland) & Henry Rush Boss. 1902. 187p.
P4-S03366 — $28.00.

BOSTWICK: Genealogical register of the name of Bostwick 1668-1850. By E. Bostwick. 1851. 50p.
P4-S03370 — $10.00.

BOSTWICK: Genealogy of the Bostwick family in America; Desc. of Arthur Bostwick of Stratford, CT. By H.A. Bostwick. 1901. 1172p.
P4-S03369 — $146.50.

BOSWORTH: Genealogy: history of the descendants of Edward Bosworth who arrived in America in 1634. By M.B. Clarke. 1926. 122p.
P4-S03385 — $23.00.

BOSWORTH: Hist. of the desc. of Edward Bosworth, who arrived in Amer. in 1634, with appendix containing other lines of Amer. Bosworths. By M.B. Clarke. 1926-1931 Pts. 1-4, 551p.
P4-S03375 — $81.50.

BOSWORTH: Hist. of the desc. of Edward Bosworth, who arrived in America in 1634. By M.B. Clarke. 1936-1940 Pts. 5 & 6, 464p.
P4-S03384 — $69.50.

BOTSFORD: Family origins. By O. Botsford. 1937. 20p.
P4-S03397 — $10.00.

BOTSFORD: Family genealogy, the line of Jospeh, youngest son of Elnathan, grandson of Henry: ten generations, 1639-1939. By the Botsford Family Assoc. 1939. 200p.
P4-S03402 — $30.00.

BOTSFORD: An American family: Botsford-Marble ancestral lines. By D.L. Jacobus. 1933. 267p.
P4-S03396 — $39.50.

BOTTUM: LONGBOTTOM Family album: an historical & biographical genealogy of the descendants of Daniel (— 1732) & Elizabeth (Lamb) Longbottom of Norwich. By R.D. Oliver. 1970. 341p.
P4-S03408 — $52.00.

BOUCHER: Family (Bowsher, Bauscher, Bausher, Bousher), comprising a gen. of branches of Strawn, Harpster, Tedrow, Cryfer et al; desc. of Daniel Boucher By F.A. Burkhardt. 1917. 402p.
P4-S03414 — $62.00.

BOUDINOT: Family records for six generations, 1685-1868. E.L.S. 1883. 73p.
P4-S03420 — $14.50.

BOURGO: BOURGAULT — BRUNET & Other Allied Lines. Jeffrey D. Fraser — Bourgo. 2003. 301p.
P4-S03422 — $46.00.

BOURN: Sketch of the desc. of Jared Bourn, who settled in Boston about 1630. By Augustus O. Bourn. 1875. 32p.
P4-S03423 — $10.00.

BOUTON: BOUGHTON family, descendants of John Bouton of France, who landed at Boston, 1635 & settled at Norwalk, CT. By J. Boughton. 1890. 684p.
P4-S03426 — $90.00.

BOUTON: BOUGHTON; An informative INDEX to the names of persons & their essential genealogical data, as given in "Bouton-Boughton Family" (above). By Willis A. Boughton. 1958. 200p.
P4-S03432 — $30.00.

BOUTON: BOUGHTON — FARNAM Families. By Willis A. Boughton. 1949. 214p.
P4-S03438 — $34.00.

BOVEE: Descendants of Matthew Bovee. Lawrence T. Fadner. 2005. xii + 1215p.
P4-S03440 — $160.00.

BOWDEN: Hist. & biogr. sketch of Bowden, Bodine, Beaudoin, Boden, Bowdoin fam. 32p.
P4-S03441 — $10.00.

BOWDEN: Michael Bowden & some desc. By W. Bowden. 1960. 54p.
P4-S03442 — $11.00.

BOWDITCH: Fam. of Salem, MA; a gen. sketch. 1936. 50p.
P4-S03443 — $10.00.

BOWDOIN: Some account of the Bowdoin fam., with a notice of the Erving fam. T. Prime. 1900. 3rd. ed. 18p.
P4-S03445 — $10.00.

BOWDOIN: Some account of the Bowdoin fam., with notes on the fam. of Pordage, Lynde, Newgate, Erving. By T. Prime. 1894. 2nd. ed. 52p.
P4-S03446 — $10.00.

BOWEN: Descendants of John Bowen. By Fanny C. Bowen. 1941. 182p.
P4-S03444 — $24.00.

BOWEN: Family of Griffith Bowen, Welsh Puritan imgr., Boston, 1638-9, esp. the branch of Silas Bowen, born in Woodstock, CT, 1722. By D. Bowen. 1893. 278p.
P4-S03450 — $44.00.

BOWEN: Mem. of the Bowen family. By E.C. Bowen. 1884. 102p.
P4-S03459 — $19.50.

BOWEN: Lineage of the Bowens of Woodstock, CT. By E. A. Bowen. 1897. 251p.
P4-S03453 — $32.50.

BOWIE: The Bowies & Their Kindred of Scotland & the Colonies. Robert M. & Richard S. Bowie. 1997. 351 + 36p.
P4-S03470 — $58.00.

BOWIE: The Bowies & their kindred: a gen. & biogr. hist. By W.W. Bowie. 1899. 523p.
P4-S03471 — $78.50.

BOWIE: George Bowie of Stilinshire, Scot., & Boston & Truro, MA: his ancestry & descendants, By Leola Bowie Ellis. 1962. 110p.
P4-S03465 — $18.50.

BOWLBY: Families in England & America. By Raymond E. Bowlby. 1985-1991 5 pts in 1, 534p.
P4-S03477 — $79.50.

BOWLER: Record of the desc. of Charles Bowler, England--1740--America, who settled in Newport, RI. By N. Bowler & C. Malone. 1905. 298p.
P4-S03483 — $44.50.

BOWLES: Thomas Bowles line of Hanover Co., VA; Leroy Samuel line of Marion Co., MO; Warren Moore line of Marion Co.; J.W. Friley line of Saline Co., MO. By Inez M. Bowles. 1947. 87p.
P4-S03495 — $16.00.

BOWLES: History & related families: historical note of the Bowles family, 1066 to & Including the 20th century in the US & Great Britain By Mary Ann Bowles. 1960. 244p., typescript.
P4-S03489 — $37.00.

BOWMAN: Elder Jacob Bowman family record. By Floyd R. & Kathryn Garst Mason. 2000. 476p.
P4-S03507 — $61.50.

BOWMAN: Genealogy, fragmentary annals of a branch of the Bowman family, to which is appended data relating to other Bowmans & Spencers. By Chas. W. Bowman. 1912. 108p.
P4-S03501 — $19.00.

BOWMAN: History of the Bowman family. By H,M Smiley, R.M. McConnell & S.O. Manchester. 1909. 213p.
P4-S03519 — $33.50.

BOWMAN: The Bowmans: history of Hans Dieterick Bauman & his descendants. By Augusta D. Thomas. 1934. 466p.
P4-S03537 — $71.50.

BOWMAN: Jesse Bowman, Sr, lineage. By Alfred S. Bowman. 1931. 99p.
P4-S03525 — $18.00.

BOWMAN: Genealogy of a Bowman family. By Byron W. Bowman. 1956. 203p., typescript.
P4-S03513 — $31.00.

BOWMAN: The Bowmans, pioneering fam. in VA, KY & the NW territory. By J.W. Wayland. 1943. 185p.
P4-S03531 — $29.50.

BOWMAN: John Bowman & Elizabeth Ikenberry Family Record of Pennsylvania & Franklin Cos., VA. Floyd R. Mason. 2003. 426p.
P4-S03532 — $64.00.

BOWNE: William Bowne of Yorkshire, England & his descendants. By M.K. Reading. 1903. 47p.
P4-S03540 — $10.00.

BOWSER: Family history. By A.B. Bowser. 1922. 309p.
P4-S03543 — $46.00.

BOYCE: The journey of Boyce family. By Cynthia J. Crumb. 2001. 373p.
P4-S03549 — $54.00.

BOYD: PATTERSON Ancestry. By H.M. Pitman & K.P.B. Hunt. 1967. 6 + 191p.
P4-S03555 — $29.00.

BOYD: Family, including allied families of Bell, Bracken, Culler, Cunningham, Finley, et al . . . with special reference to Mercelia Louise Boyd. By Scott Lee Boyd. 1935. 330p.
P4-S03561 — $49.50.

BOYD: History of the Boyd family & descendants, with an historical chapter of the "ancient family of Boyds" in Scotland & a complete record of their descendants By Wm. P. Boyd. 1884. 318p.
P4-S03567 — $46.50.

BOYD: History of the Boyd family & desc., with hist. sketches of the fam. In Scotland & Ireland, with records of their desc. By W. P. Boyd. 1912. 521p.
P4-S03573 — $81.50.

BOYDEN: Here & there in the family tree. By A. Boyden. 1949. 294p.
P4-S03579 — $46.00.

BOYDEN: Thomas Boyden & descendants. By W. Boyden, etc. 1901. 267p.
P4-S03582 — $39.50.

BOYDSTUN: BOYDSTON Family. By Gladys Boydston Domonoske. 3rd ed., 1979. 386p., typescript.
P4-S03588 — $58.00.

BOYDSTUN: Family. By G.C. Weaver. 1927. 147p.
P4-S03594 — $24.00.

BOYER: The Boyers: descendants Abraham Beyer, Sr, of Silesia, Germany, & Montgomery Co., PA. By Art Reierson. 1998. 190p.
P4-S03606 — $28.00.

BOYER: The House of Boyer. By Edith B. Suggs. 1963. 111p.
P4-S03612 — $19.50.

BOYER: American Boyers. By Charles C. Boyer; 1940. 663p.
P4-S03600 — $99.50.

BOYKIN: Family. By R. Arthur. 1964. 34p.
P4-S03620 — $10.00.

BOYLE: Genealogy, John Boyle of VA & KY; notes on lines of descent with some collateral references. By John Boyle. 1909. 174p.
P4-S03618 — $27.50.

BOYNTON: Reprint of Betham's Hist., Gen. & Baronets of the Boynton Fam. in Eng. By J. Boynton. 1884. 40p.
P4-S03630 — $10.00.

BOYNTON: A genealogy of the desc. of Wm. & John Boynton. By J.F. & C.H. Boynton. 1897. 386p.
P4-S03621 — $45.00.

BOYNTON: Ancestry & descendants of Jonathan & Sally Martin Boynton, late of Baltimore, VT; also ancestry & descendants of Caleb & Lakin Willard Leland, By Oscar H. Leland. 1907. 93p.
P4-S03633 — $16.50.

BOYNTON: Amer. Boynton directory, with the address of all known Boyntons, Boyingtons & Byingtons in the US & Brit. dominions. By J. Boynton. 1884. 147p.
P4-S03627 — $22.00.

BOZARTH: Historical & genealogical record of the Bozarth family, from landing in America to 1918. By Charles A. Bozarth. 1919. 96p.
P4-S03936 — $17.00.

BRAASCH: Pioneer history of the Braasch family, 1803-1956. By Mrs H Wagner. 1956. 89p.
P4-S03645 — $17.50.

BRACE: Lineage. By J.S. Brace. 1927. 224p.
P4-S03651 — $40.00.

BRACKEN: Wm. Bracken of New Castle Co., DE & his descendants. By H.M. Bracken. 1901. 79p.
P4-S03657 — $16.00.

BRACKENBURY: of Lincolnshire, Vol. I: Wills, etc. 1954. 68 + 15p.
P4-S03663 — $16.00.

BRACKETT: Descendants of Anthony Brackett of Portsmouth & Capt. Richard Brackett of Braintree. By H.I. Brackett. 1907. 624p.
P4-S03666 — $80.00.

BRACKETT: Desc. of Anthony Brackett of Portsmouth, NH. By A. L. Brackett. 1897. 8p.
P4-S03667 — $10.00.

BRACKETT: Eight hundred years of the history of the name of Brackett, the Keepers of the Hounds. By Wm. Brackett. 1999. 240p.
P4-S03672 — $36.00.

BRADBURY: Memorial; Records of some of the desc. of Thomas Bradbury of Agamenticus (York) in 1634 & of Salisbury, MA in 1638 By W.B. Lapham. 1890. 320p.
P4-S03678 — $41.00.

BRADFORD: The James Frank Bradford Family. Marteal Wells. 1999. 178p.
P4-S03685 — $27.00.

BRADFORD: Governor William Bradford & his son Major William Bradford. By J. Shepard. 1900. 103p.
P4-S03690 — $18.50.

BRADFORD: Genealogy. By G. Fessenden. 1850. 26p.
P4-S03686 — $10.00.

BRADFORD: Anc. of the Bradfords of Austerfield, Co. York. (Repr. NEHGR). By W. B. Browne. 1929. 38p.
P4-S03987 — $10.00.

BRADFORD: The Bradfords of Charles City County, VA & Some of Their Descendants, 1653-1993. David Thomas Bradford. 1994. xvii + 243p.
P4-S03688 — $45.00.

BRADFORD: Family, 1660-1906. By Henry Darrach. 1906. 25p.
P4-S03689 — $10.00.

BRADFORD: One branch of the Bradford fam.; desc. of Capt. Gamaliel Bradford. By H.S. Bradford. 1898. 27p.
P4-S03691 — $10.00.

BRADFORD: Our New England ancestors & their descendants, 1620-1900, historical, genealogical, biographical [Gov. Bradford} By Henry Whittemore. 1900. 84p.
P4-S03696 — $16.50.

BRADFORD: Extr. from The Hist. of Bridgewater. 7p.
P4-S03692 — $10.00.

BRADFORD: Record of the descendants of James Bradford. By James W. Bradford. 1900. 24p.
P4-S03693 — $10.00.

BRADFORD: One branch of the descendants of Gov. Wm. Bradford. 1895. 29p.
P4-S03694 — $10.00.

BRADFORD: Descendants of Gov. Wm. Bradford through the first seven generations. By R.G. Hall. 1951. 645p.
P4-S03684 — $96.50.

BRADHURST: My forefathers: Bradhurst, Broadhurst, de Bradehurst. By A.M. Bradhurst. 1910 364p.
P4-S03702 — $56.00.

BRADLEE: Hist. of the Bradlee fam., with particular reference to the desc. of Nathan Bradley of Dorchester, MA. By S.B. Doggett. 1878. 45p.
P4-S03706 — $10.00.

BRADLEY: Ancestors & desc. of Morris A. Bradley. By Mrs G. Rideout. 1948. 176p.
P4-S03708 — $28.00.

BRADLEY: Bradleys of New Haven & Guildford, CT (Repr. NEHGR). By R. D. Smyth. 1903. 8p.
P4-S03709 — $10.00.

BRADLEY: Gen. Fam. of Aaron & Sarah Bradley of Guilford, CT. By A. P. Lloyd. 1879. 46p.
P4-S03710 — $10.00.

BRADLEY: Desc. of Isaac Bradley of CT, 1650-1898; with a brief hist. of the Bradley families in New England. By L.A. Bradley. 1917. 171p.
P4-S03720 — $25.50.

BRADLEY: A Tribute of Affection to the Memory of Hon. William C. Bradley. S.B. Willard. 1869. 112p.
P4-S03713 — $17.00.

BRADLEY: of Essex County, MA: early records, 1643-1746. By E.B. Peters. 1915. 8 + 213p.
P4-S03714 — $35.00.

BRADLEY: Brief sketches of a few American Bradleys, with reference to their English progenitors. By John C. Bradley. 1889. 46p.
P4-S03712 — $10.00.

BRADLEY: Notes respecting the Bradley fam. of Fairfield, with notices of coll. anc. on the female side, By J.P. Bradley, ed. By C. Bradley. 1894. 69p.
P4-S03723 — $12.50.

BRADT: A Norwegian family in colonial America. By Peter Christoph. 1994. 250p.
P4-S03732 — $32.50.

BRADT: Descendants of Albert & Arent Andriessen Bradt. By Cynthia Brott Biasca. 1990. 776p.
P4-S03732 — $89.50.

BRADT: Supplement to Descendants of Albert & Arent Andriessen Bradt. By Cynthia Brott Biasca. 1993. 190p.
P4-S03744 — $27.00.

BRADT: Second supplement to Descendants of Albert & Arent Andriessen Bradt, including Van Dersee. By Laurene Matthews Grimes. 2002. 252p.
P4-S03745 — $37.50.

BRADY: James Cox Brady & his ancestry. By L. Effingham DeForest & Anne L. DeForest. 1933. 520p.
P4-S03750 — $78.50.

BRAINERD: Genealogy of the Brainerd-Brainard family history, 1649-1908; descendants of Daniel, the emigrant ancestor. By L.A. Brainard. 3 Vols. 1908. 1908
P4-S03762 — $230.00.

BRAINERD: Genealogy of the Brainerd fam. in the US; with sketches of individuals. By D. Field. 1857. 303p.
P4-S03774 — $48.50.

BRAINERD: Ancestry of Thomas Chalmers Brainerd. comp. & ed. by D.L. Jacobus. 1948. 351p.
P4-S03768 — $54.00.

BRALEY: Genealogy: the desc. of Roger Braley, 1696-1913. By G.L. Randall. 1913. 393p.
P4-S03780 — $61.00.

BRANCH: Branchiana, being partial account of the Branch family in VA. By James Branch Cabell. 1907. 177p.
P4-S03786 — $28.00.

BRANCH: History of the descendants of Peter Branch, 1638-1914. By A.E.B. Paulson. 1914. 63p.
P4-S03789 — $12.50.

BRANCH: Family of New England: line of Wm. Farrand Branch. By Wm. F. Branch & Roger E. Branch. 1935. 43p.
P4-S03787 — $9.00.

BRANCH: History of the leading Branch families in American, 1633-1904. By A.E.B. Paulson. 1904. 50p.
P4-S03788 — $10.00.

BRAND: Family of Monongalia Co., VA (now WV). By Franklin M. Brand. 1922. 426p.
P4-S03798 — $64.00.

BRANN: Desc. of Nicholas Brann of Westmoreland Co., VA. By M.W. Brann. 1942. 18p.
P4-S03808 — $10.00.

BRANNER: Casper Branner of VA & desc. By J. Branner. 1913. 477p.
P4-S03810 — $74.50.

BRANT: Genealogy, Somerset Co., PA. By Alvin A. Cober. 1932. 135p.
P4-S03816 — $33.00.

BRASFIELD: BRASSFIELD Genealogies. By Annabelle C. and Edward N. McAllister. 1959. 720p.
P4-S03822 — $109.00.

BRASHEAR: BRESHEAR Family, 1449-1929. Henry S. Brashear. 1929. 170p.
P4-S03828 — $26.00.

BRASSINGTON: Family to England & America. By Jane Brassington Burns. 1999. 174p.
P4-S03834 — $26.50.

BRATTLE: Account of some of the descendants of Capt. Thomas Brattle. By E.D. Harris. 1867. 90p.
P4-S03840 — $18.00.

BRAY: Seven generations of Brays, of MA, ME, WI & MN. By W.M. Bray. 1956. 43p.
P4-S038439 — $10.00.

BRAYNE: Who was Richard Brayne? A look at the father-in-law of VA's greatest colonial governor Alexander Spotswood & his descendants. By Peyton F. Carter, III. 2002. 86p.
P4-S03841 — $16.00.

BREAKENRIDGE: Genealogy of the descendants of James Breakenridge, who emigrated from Ireland, July, 1727. By Cornelia A. gould. 1887. 65p.
P4-S03846 — $13.00.

BRECK: Fam. of Sherborn & Gardner, MA. By A. Bent. 1902. 16p.
P4-S03850 — $10.00.

BRECK: Gen. of the Breck fam., desc. from Edward of Dorchester & his brothers in Amer. By S. Breck. 1889. 281p.
P4-S03849 — $40.00.

BREED: Record of the descendants of Allen Bread, who came to America from England in 1630. By J. Howard Breed. 1892. 224p.
P4-S03855 — $35.00.

BREESE: Family of England & America, 1709-1875. By E. E. Salisbury. 1885. 61p.
P4-S03858 — $12.00.

BREESE: Personal reminisc., with gen. sketch of Amer. branch of the Breese fam. J. Montgomery. 1884. 73p.
P4-S03867 — $15.00.

BRENEMAN: History of the descendants of Abraham Breneham, born in Lancaster Co., PA, 1744, & settled near Edom, Rockingham Co., VA. By Charles D. Breneman. 1939. 566p.
P4-S03873 — $85.00.

BRENNEMAN: History. By Albert H. Gerberich. 1938. 1217p.
P4-S03879 — $159.50.

BRENNER: JAMES Genealogy. By A.L. Brenner & B.A.B. Fleming. 1949. 304p.
P4-S03885 — $47.50.

BRENT: Descendants of Col. Giles Brent, Capt. George Brent & Robert Brent, immigrants to MD & VA. By C.H. Brent. 1946. 195p.
P4-S03891 — $31.00.

BRENT: Descendants of Hugh Brent, immigrant to Isle of Wight Co., VA, 1642, & some allied families By Chester H. Brent. 1936. 274p.
P4-S03897 — $41.50.

BRENTLINGER: Genealogy & biography of the Brentlinger family. By Ellsworth Brentlinger, et al. 1927. 168p.
P4-S03903 — $25.00.

BRETT: Genealogy. By L.B. Goodenow. 1915. 545p.
P4-S03909 — $84.00.

BRETZ: Gen. of Ludwig Bretz fam. 1750-1890. By E. Parthemore. 1890. 149p.
P4-S03915 — $30.00.

BREWER: The long Brewer line: Colonial family genealogy, with ancestors, descendants & connecting families, research & general information By Ben R. Brewer. 1993. 395p.
P4-S03933 — $59.50.

BREWER: Hist. of the Brewer fam. of NC, TN, IN & IL. 1936. 75p.
P4-S03921 — $15.00.

BREWER: House of Brewer. By Edw. D. Brewer. 1947. 159p.
P4-S03927 — $24.50.

BREWER: Genealogy. By Harriet A. Robinson. 1903. 49p.
P4-S03930 — $10.00.

BREWSTER: Genealogy, 1566-1907; desc. of Wm. Brewster of the Mayflower. By E. Jones 1908. 2 vols., 1493p.
P4-S03936 — $187.50.

BREWSTER: Early genealogy of the Brewster family. By L. Greenlaw. (Repr. NEHGR) 1899. 20p.
P4-S03937 — $10.00.

BRIDGE: An account of the desc. of John Bridge, Cambridge, 1632. By W. F. Bridge. 1884. 122p.
P4-S03939 — $19.50.

BRIDGE: Family of NJ, OH & WI. By Annie M.H. Karrer & Ferne M.D. Bridge. 1956. 39p., typescript.
P4-S03940 — $10.00.

BRIDGE: Genealogy of the John Bridge fam. in Amer., 1632-1924, rev. ed. By W.D. Bridge. 1924. 547p.
P4-S03945 — $81.50.

BRIDGES: Genealogy of Samuel Willard Bridges (1874-1943) & Caroline Britton Bridges (1873-1958). By R.E. Thomas. 1960. 129p.
P4-S03951 — $19.50.

BRIDGMAN: Family; descendants of James Bridgman, 1636-1894. By B.N. & J.C. Bridgman. 1894. 168p.
P4-S03957 — $27.50.

BRIGGS: We & our kinfolk: Ephraim & Rebeka Waterman Briggs, their desc. & anc. ed by M.B. Briggs. 1887. 150p.
P4-S03972 — $22.50.

BRIGGS: Genealogical tree: Colonial ancestry of the family of John Greene Briggs, son of Job Briggs & Patience Greene, & Isabell Gibbs de Groff By Harry T. Briggs & John G. Briggs. 1940. 498p.
P4-S03969 — $75.00.

BRIGGS: Genealogy with allied White lines, incl. Anc. & Desc. of Ichabod White Briggs, 1609-1953. 116p.
P4-S03963 — $21.00.

BRIGHAM: The hist. of the Brigham fam., a record of several thousand desc. of Thomas Brigham the emigrant, 1603-1653. By W.I.T. Brigham. 1907. 636p.
P4-S03987 — $80.00.

BRIGHAM: History of the Brigham family, Vol. II, with English origins of Thomas Brigham, the emigrant, 1603-35. By E.E. Brigham. 1927. 300p.
P4-S03984 — $45.00.

BRIGHAM: The Genealogy of the Descendants of Several Ancient Puritans, By the Names of Brigham, Hapgood, Pettee, Hewins & Frary. Rev. Abner Morse. 1859. 180p.
P4-S03985 — $27.00.

BRIGHAM: Gen. register of several ancient Puritans; Vol. II., the Brigham fam. By A. Morse. 1859. 96p.
P4-S03978 — $20.00.

BRIGHT: Historical sketch of the Bright family of Berks Co., PA. By Albert G. Green. 1900. 29p.
P4-S03994 — $10.00.

BRIGHT: The Brights of Suffolk, England, & desc. of Henry Bright, Jr., who came to New England in 1630, & settled in Watertown, MA. By J.B. Bright. 1858. 365p.
P4-S04005 — $57.50.

BRIGHT: KY Brights & their kin, including the Crabb, Drane, Ford, Hopkins & King families. By Grace H. Ford. 1929. 198p.
P4-S03999 — $30.00.

BRIGHT: Descendants of Henry Bright, Sr (b. 1760) of Lincoln Co., KY, By Harry W. Mills. 1941. 71p., typescript.
P4-S03993 — $14.00.

BRILLHART: Pictorial history of the Brillharts of Amer. By J.A. Brillhart. 1926. 268p.
P4-S04011 — $42.00.

BRINGHURST: History of the Bringhurst family with notes on the Clarkson, de Peyster & Boude families. By J.G. Leach. 1901. 152p.
P4-S04017 — $24.00.

BRINKERHOFF: Family of Joris Dircksen Brinckerhoff, 1638 (with 1994 every-name index by Jerri Burket). By T. Van Wyck Brinkerhoff. 1887. 188p.
P4-S04023 — $29.50.

BRINKMAN: Desc. of Otto Henrich Wilhelm Brinkman. By I. H. De Long. 1925. 55p.
P4-S04024 — $10.00.

BRISTOL: Richarde & Henry Bristow or Bristok, or Guilford & New Haven, CT & their descendants. By D.L. Jacobus. 9p.
P4-S04030 — $10.00.

BRISTOL: Family of Henry Bristol. By D. Jacobus. 1905. 7p.
P4-S04031 — $10.00.

BRISTOL: Genealogy. By W.E. Bristol. 1967. 561p.
P4-S04029 — $86.00.

BRITT: Family in ME. By C.N. Sinnett. 1923. 7p.
P4-S04033 — $10.00.

BRITTAIN: BRITTEN Family of NY, VA & PA. Purcel, Brand & Mathews. 12p.
P4-S04034 — $10.00.

BRITTON: Ancestors of Dan'l Freeman Britton of Westmoreland NH & Ganaoque, Ont., 1808-1887: Part I, ancestry of Daniel Britton; Part II, ancestry of Sally Wood By Eva L. Moffat. 1953. 135 + 81p., typescript.
P4-S04035 — $33.00.

BRITTON: Genealogy Britton. By E.E. Britton. 1901. 50p.
P4-S04036 — $10.00.

BROADDUS: History of the Broaddus family from the time of the settlement of the progenitor of the family in the US down to the year 1888. By Andrew Broaddus. 1888. 208p.
P4-S04041 — $31.50.

BROCAS: Family of Brocas of Beaurepaire & Roche Court, hereditary masters of the royal buckhounds, with some account of the English rule in Aquitaine. Montagu Burrows. 1886. 496p.
P4-S04044 — $75.00.

BROCKBANK: Historical & Genealogical record of Isaac Brockbank, Sr. By the Brockbank Org. 1959. 335p.
P4-S04050 — $51.00.

BROCKETT: The desc. of John Brockett of New Haven Colony. By E.J. Brockett, et al. 1905. 266p.
P4-S04056 — $40.00.

BROCKMAN: Record of the Brockman & Drake-Brockman family. By D.H. Drake-Brockman. 1936. 158p.
P4-S04068 — $25.00.

BROCKMAN: Scrapbook: Bell, Bledsoe, Brockman, Burrus, Dickson, James, Pedan, et al. By W.E. Brockman. 1952. 442p.
P4-S04062 — $67.50.

BROCKWAY: Genealogy of a branch of the descendants of Wolston Brockway, who settled in Lyme, CT about 1660. By Asahel N. Brockway. 1888. 34p.
P4-S04072 — $10.00.

BROCKWAY: Family, desc. of Wolston Brockway. D. W. Patterson. 1890. 167p.
P4-S04071 — $23.50.

BROCKWAY: Gen. of branch of desc. of Wolston Brockway, who settled in Lyme, CT, 1660. B. Brockway. 1887. 22p.
P4-S04073 — $10.00.

BROMFIELD: The Bromfields. By D.D. Slade. 1872. 19p.
P4-S04075 — $10.00.

BROMLEY: Genealogy, being a rec. of the desc. of Luke Warwick, RI & Stonington, CT. V. Bromley. 1911. 452p.
P4-S04077 — $69.50.

BROMWELL: Genealogy, including descendants of Wm. Bromwell & Beulah Hall with data relating to others of the Bromwell name in America By Henrietta E. Bromwell. 1910. 244 + 77p., typescript.
P4-S04083 — $47.50.

BRONSDON: BOX Fams Pt.1: Robt. Bronsdon, merchant, & his desc; Pt. 2: John Box, ropemaker, & his desc. By Marsh & Parker. 332p.
P4-S04089 — $53.00.

BRONSON: Lineage, 1636-1917, ancestors & descendants of Capt. Wm. Bronson of the Revolutionary War, & other ancestral lines. By Harriet B. Sibley. 1917. 62p.
P4-S04092 — $12.50.

BRONSON: Anc. & Desc. of Leman Bronson, 1640-1963. S.B. Boden. 1963. vi + 264p.
P4-S04100 — $42.00.

BROOKE: Fam. of Whitchurch, Hampshire, Eng.; acct. of Acting-Gov. Robert Brooke MD & Col. Ninian Beall of MD & desc. By T.W. Balch. 1899. 69p.
P4-S04098 — $12.50.

BROOKFIELD: Twelve generations in American lineage of W.L. Brookfield, H.M. Brookfield & S.L. Brookfield. By H.M. Brookfield. 1937. 310p.
P4-S04113 — $49.00.

For hardcover versions, see the order form on page v. To order, call 1-888-296-3447.

BROOKFIELD: The Brookfields of
NJ, CT & N.S. By H.M. Brookfield. 159p.
P4-S04107 — $22.00.

BROOKS: Timothy Brooks of MA &
his desc. By R. P. Brooks. 1927. 40p.
P4-S04120 — $10.00.

BROOKS: Anc. of Jonas Hapgood
Brooks. 1897. 6p.
P4-S04121 — $10.00.

BROOKS: William Brooks of Spring-
field, MA & some desc. By J.N. Eno.
(Repr. NEHGR) 1918. 7p.
P4-S04122 — $10.00.

BROOKS: & Kindred Families. By I.B.
Kellam. 1950. 392p.
P4-S04119 — $59.50.

BROOKS: My Ancestors & Their
Descendants [the Brooks, Brown,
Faulkner & Gillenwater families). By
Wm. L. Brown. 1937. 222p.
P4-S04125 — $34.00.

BROSIUS: Genealogy of Henry &
Mary Brosius & their Descendants;
Also some Sort Accounts of other
Families Bearing the Brosius Name.
By Lewis W. Brosius. 1928. 472p.
P4-S04131 — $63.00.

BROUGHTON: Family of
Marchwiel, Contribution to the
History of the Parish of Marchwiel. By
Alfred N. Palmer. 1900 45p.
P4-S04232 — $10.00.

BROWN: COMLY Families Gene-
alogy. By Jas. C. Brown. 1912. 123 + 62p.
P4-S04161 — $27.50.

BROWN: James Brown of Middleton,
CT. By E. Hill. 1911. 13p.
P4-S04138 — $10.00.

BROWN: Desc. of Ipswich, Newbury,
Salisbury & Salem. (Ex. Essex
Antiquarian). 47p.
P4-S04139 — $10.00.

BROWN: Report to the Brown Assn,
US. By C. Smith. 1868. 126p.
P4-S04227 — $22.00.

BROWN: Genealogy of the Brown
Family of Prince William Co., VA &
Allied Families. J.E. Brown. 1930. 874p.
P4-S04203 — $117.50.

BROWN: Rev. Daniel Brown of
Culpeper Co., VA & Allied Families
Webster, Finnell, McCain, Pemberton.
By Col. Woolsey Finnell, Sr. 1954. 72p.
P4-S04233 — $15.00.

BROWN: Ancestors of Florence Julia
Brown & Some of Their Descendants.
By W.L. and M.T.H. Brown. 1940. 341p.
P4-S04155 — $52.00.

BROWN: Ancestors & Descendants
of Robert Brown of Madison Co., NY,
1768-1850. By Leon R. Brown. 1934.
57p., typescript.
P4-S04141 — $11.50.

BROWN: Handbook of Our
Extended Family: An Account of
Some of the American & European
Ancestors of James M. Brown &
Cherly (Gustafson) Brown By James M.
Brown. 1992. 523p.
P4-S04209 — $79.50.

BROWN: The NJ Browns & Allied
Families. 1931. 110p.
P4-S04239 — $21.50.

BROWN: Ten Irish Families: Gene-
alogical Essays on the Families of
Brown, Davison, Ferguson, Lavery,
Maguire, McCarty, McNally. Andrew
Clandermond & Dr. Terence MacCarthy
2002. 136p.
P4-S04142 — $22.00.

BROWN: Desc. of James Brown,
1716-1922. J.J. Brown (n.d.) 264p.
P4-S04144 — $40.00.

BROWN: Memorials of the Browns of
Fordell, Finmount & Vicarsgrange. By
Robert R. Stodart. 1887. 240p.
P4-S04221 — $42.00.

BROWN: Genealogy of Rasselas
Wilcox Brown & Mary Potter
Brownell Brown, their Desc. &
Ancestral Lines. By Isaac Brownell
Brown. 1922. 139p.
P4-S04197 — $21.00.

BROWN: Genealogy; Desc. of
Thomas, John & Eleazor Brown, sons
of Thomas & Mary (Newhall) Brown
of Lynn, MA, 1629-1915. By C.H.
Brown. 1907. 2 vols., 618 + 611p.
P4-S04134 — $152.00.

BROWN: Alexander Brown & his
descendants, 1764-1916 [b. Cairnlirn,
Co. Antrim, emigr. to MD]. By Mary E.
Brown. 1917. 158 + 14p.
P4-S04149 — $24.00.

BROWN: Genealogical Record of the
Descendants of Brown, Runyan,
Peters, Needham & Ackerman
Families, Together with Historical &
Biographical sketches By David E.
Peters. 1925. 138p.
P4-S04185 — $21.50.

BROWN: Family History, Tracing the
Clark Brown Line. By Ella B. Spooner.
1929. 231p.
P4-S04179 — $34.50.

BROWN: History of the Michael
Brown Family of Rowan Co., NC,
Tracing its Line of Posterity from
Michael Brown to the Present [1921]
Generation. By Rev. Richard L. Brown.
1921. 190p.
P4-S04215 — $28.00.

BROWN: Genealogy of John Brown
of Ipswich, MA. T.F. Waters. 1909. 29p.
P4-S04145 — $10.00.

BROWN: & Allied Families. By Mabel
F. Moore. 1939. 82p., typescript.
P4-S04173 — $16.00.

BROWN: Genealogical Record of the
Descendants of Brown, Runyan,
Peters, Needham & Ackerman fam-
ilies, with hist. & biogr. sketches. By
D.E. Peters. n.d. 137p.
P4-S04191 — $21.00.

BROWN: Ancestors & Kinfolk, Being
a Genealogical & Historical Record of
[the author's] Immediate & Related
Families, from Colonial days to the
Present [1940]. Thos. S. Brown. 1940. 99p.
P4-S04167 — $19.00.

BROWNE: The Brownes of
Bechworth Castle. John Pym Yeatman.
1903. xxiii + 238p.
P4-S04243 — $39.50.

BROWNE: John Browne of
Rehoboth, MA, Benjamin William
Brown. 1912. 12p., typescript.
P4-S04244 — $10.00.

BROWNE: John Browne, Gentleman,
of Plymouth, Assistant, Commissioner
Magistrate, Pioneer in New England
Colonial Life & One Branch of Descen-
dants. By Geo. T. Brown. 1919. 55p.
P4-S04241 — $11.50.

BROWNE: John Browne, Gentleman
of Wannamoisett. Benjamin William
Brown. 1951. 170p., typescript.
P4-S04245 — $25.50.

BROWNE: Chad Browne Memorial, Consisting of Gen. Memoirs of a Portion of the Desc. of Chad & Elizabeth Browne, 1638-1888. By A.I. Bulkley. 1888. 173p.
P4-S04242 — $23.50.

BROWNELL: Gen Rec of the Desc of Thomas Brownell. G.G. Brownell. 1910. 366p.
P4-S04249 — $55.00.

BROWNELL: Genealogy, 1619-1930. By Lowell L. Rogers. 1931. 173p.
P4-S04248 — $26.00.

BROWNELL: Gen. Record of Desc. of John Brownell, 1773-1903. By S. Brownell. 1903. 53p.
P4-S04250 — $11.00.

BROWNING: Genealogy of the Brownings in America from 1621-1908. By Edw. F. Browning. 1908. 982p.
P4-S04254 — $139.50.

BRUBACHER: Genealogy in America. By J.N. Brubacher. 1884 244p.
P4-S04260 — $50.00.

BRUBAKER: Genealogical Information Regarding the Families of Brubaker, Bomberger & Fogelsanger. By Elizabeth S. Claude J. Rahns. 1952. 105p.
P4-S04272 — $16.00.

BRUBAKER: Genealogy. By Henry S. Brubaker. 1912. 344p.
P4-S04266 — $52.00.

BRUCE: Book of Bruce: Anc. & desc. of King Robert of Scotland. By L.H. Weeks. 1907. 352p.
P4-S04281 — $45.00.

BRUCE: "In love, Carrie:" Letters of Carrie Augusta Bruce of Newfane, VT. 2000. 71p.
P4-S04279 — $15.00.

BRUCE: Family, 1788-1992, Desc. of John & Clarissa Bruce. By Bill Denny & Howard C. Bruce. 1992. 95p.
P4-S04287 — $17.00.

BRUCE: William Thatcher Bruce, Jr., of Newfane & Brattleboro, VT & Walpole, MA; his Ancestors & Some of his Descendants. By Claudia E.S. Cridland. 2000. 415p.
P4-S04299 — $62.50.

BRUCE: Family Rec. of the Bruces & the Cumyns, with an Hist. Intro. & Appendix. By M.E.C. Bruce. 1870 692p.
P4-S04293 — $99.00.

BRUMBACH: Genealogy of the Brumbach Family, Incl. Those Using Variations of the Original Name & Many other Connected Fams. By G.M. Brumbaugh. 1915. 850p.
P4-S04305 — $115.00.

BRUMFIELD: Descendants of Thomas Brumfield of Berks Co., PA; Genealogy & Family History, 1720-1960. By Ray C. Brumfield, 1962. 493p.
P4-S04311 — $76.00.

BRUNER: Genealogy of the Bruner family, 1728-1967. By Anita Fisher. 1967. 296p.
P4-S04317 — $37.50.

BRUSH: PHILLIPS; Concise Genealogy of Isaac Elbert Crush & Delia Williams Phillips, His Wife & of Their Descendants. 1932. 51p.
P4-S04324 — $10.00.

BRUSH: BOWERS Genealogy. By Maria A. Brush. 1904. 118p.
P4-S04323 — $18.00.

BRUSH: Crean Brush, Loyalist & his Descendants. Jane N. Smith. 1938. 30p.
P4-S04325 — $10.00.

BRYANT: Stephen Bryant of Plymouth Colony & His Desc. By J. A. Boutelle. 1870. 4p.
P4-S04330 — $10.00.

BRYANT: Family History, Ancestry & Desc of David Bryant (1756) of Springfield, NJ, Washington Co., & Wolf Lake, Noble Co., IN. By C.V. Braiden. 1913. 270p.
P4-S04329 — $42.50.

BRYANT: Fam. of Stoneham. By W.F. Bucknam. 3p.
P4-S04331 — $10.00.

BUCHANAN: COPELAND — RIBBLE Genealogy. By Ida R. Duckworth. 1929. 130p.
P4-S04347 — $21.00.

BUCHANAN: Book, The Life of Alexander Buchanan. By A. W. P. Buchanan. 1911. 501p.
P4-S04359 — $78.00.

BUCHANAN: Ancestry. By M.G. Buchanan. 1962. 93p.
P4-S04353 — $18.00.

BUCHANAN: First Gathering of the Buchanan Clan, Trotters creek, Miami Co., OH, with gen. notes, 10/1/1892. 55p.
P4-S04348 — $10.00.

BUCHANAN: Family records. By W. M. Clemens. 1914. 15p.
P4-S04349 — $10.00.

BUCK: Genealogy of the Samuel Buck Family of Portland, CT, to the Year 1894. By Horace B. Buck. 1894. 54p.
P4-S04366 — $11.00.

BUCK: Johannes Buck, 1747-1790; Christian & Catherine Buck & their Descendants, 1754-1958. By Fisher, Ulrey & Hetrick. 1958. xii + 138p.
P4-S04377 — $25.00.

BUCK: History & Genealogy Supplment or Appendix, 2nd edition, as a sequel to the first edition of 1917. By Samuel Buck. 1924. 147p.
P4-S04371 — $24.00.

BUCK: Account of the Buck Family of Bucks Co., PA & of the Bucksville Centnnial Celebration. 1893. 141p.
P4-S04365 — $22.00.

BUCK: History of a Part of the Family & Near Connections. By Buck & Washburn. 1906. 20p.
P4-S04367 — $10.00.

BUCK: Origin, history & genealogy of the Buck family, including a brief narrative of the earliest emigration to & Settlement of, its branches in America By Cornelius B. Harvey. 1889. 273p.
P4-S04383 — $42.00.

BUCKINGHAM: Family: Descendants of Thomas Buckingham of Milford, CT. By F.W. Chapman. 1872. 384p.
P4-S04398 — $49.50.

BUCKINGHAM: Family, Book II. By Robert J. Buckingham. 1999. 179p.
P4-S04395 — $27.50.

BUCKINGHAM: The Anc. of Ebenezer Buckingham, Born in 1748, & of his Desc. By J. Buckingham. 1892. 256p.
P4-S04404 — $38.50.

BUCKINGHAM: Colonial Ancestors. By Geo. T. Buckingham. 1920. 163p.
P4-S04389 — $25.00.

BUCKNER: The Buckners of VA & the Allied Families of Strother & Ashby. 1907. 303 + 26p.
P4-S04410 — $61.50.

BUDD: Family, First Reunion 8/14/1878, with Brief Hist. of the Fam., 1632-1881. E. G. Budd. 1881. 68p.
P4-S04416 — $13.50.

BUELL: History of the Buell Family in England, from Remotest times . . . in America, from Town, Parish, Church & Fam. Records By A. Welles. 1881. xix + 384p.
P4-S04428 — $61.50.

BUELL: A Memory of the Buell Centennial Reunion, With a Genealogical Table of the Descendants of Capt. Timothy Buell. 1899. 87p.
P4-S04422 — $16.50.

BUFFALOE: Descendants of Buffaloe. Sidney Carey Arnold, Jr. 2001. 114p.
P4-S04430 — $19.00.

BUFFUM: Partial List of Buffums Interred in the Old Buffum Cemetery of E. Douglas, MA. M.E. Buffum. 3p.
P4-S04433 — $10.00.

BUFORD: Genealogy of the Buford Family in America, With Records of a Number of Allied Families. By Marcus B. Buford. 1903. 409p.
P4-S04440 — $62.00.

BUFORD: History & Genealogy of the Buford Family in America, With Records of a Number of Allied Families. By Marcus B. Buford. 1903, 1924. 512p.
P4-S04446 — $77.00.

BUHRER: Ancestry & History of the Buhrer Families. By Jas. D. Buhrer. 1916. 51p.
P4-S04447 — $10.00.

BUKER: James Buker of Bowdoin, ME & Desc. By C.N. Sinnett. 1923. 31p.
P4-S04448 — $10.00.

BULKELEY: Desc. of Rev. Peter Bulkeley, Who Settled at Concord, MA in 1636. F.W. Chapman. 1875. 289p.
P4-S04452 — $43.50.

BULKELEY: Rev. Peter Bulkeley; an acct. of His Career, His Anc. & Anc. of His Two Wives & His Relatives in Eng. & New Eng. By D.L. Jacobus. 1933. 1073p.
P4-S04458 — $139.00.

BULL: Record of the Desc. of John & Elizabeth Bull, Early Settlers in PA. By J. H. Bull. 1919. 387p.
P4-S04482 — $60.00.

BULL: John Bull of Perkiomen, Early Philadelphia Co., now Montgomery Co., PA & His Desc, 1674-1930. By Comm. James H. Bull. 1930. 436 + 63p.
P4-S04464 — $75.00.

BULL: Misc. Notes, Pedigrees, Etc., Relating to Persons of the Surname of Bull. By Joseph C. Bull. 1911 128p.
P4-S04470 — $19.00.

BULL: The Bulls of Parkeomink, Montgomery Co., PA & their Descendants. ByJames H. Bull. 1907. 70p.
P4-S04488 — $14.00.

BULL: Miscellaneous Notes, Pedigrees, etc., Relating to Persons of the Surname of Bull. James H. Bull. 1918. 105p.
P4-S04476 — $18.50.

BULL: The family of Stephen Bull of Kinghurst Hall, Co. Warwick, England & Ashley Hall, SC, 1600-1960. By H.D. Bull. 1961. 161p.
P4-S04494 — $25.00.

BULLARD: & Allied Fams.; Amer. Anc. of George Newton Bullard & Mary Bullard. By E. Bullard. 1930. 337p.
P4-S04500 — $53.50.

BULLARD: Other Bullards, a Genealogy Supplementary to "Bullard & Allied Families," E.J. Bullard. 1928. 86p.
P4-S04506 — $16.00.

BULLARD: Gen. Sketch of Dr. Artemas Bullard of Sutton, MA & his desc. By W. S. Barton. 1878. 22p.
P4-S04501 — $10.00.

BULLEN: Anc. & Desc. of Phillip of Jersey, Eng. & Charlestown, MA. By M. L. & W. L. Holman. 1930. 170p.
P4-S04512 — $25.00.

BULLEN: Samuel Bullen & Some of His Descendants. By Philipps Train. 1941. 64p.
P4-S04518 — $13.00.

BULLOCH: Hist. & Gen. of the Fams. of Bulloch, Stobo & Irvine of Cults, By J.G.B. Bulloch. 1911. 102p.
P4-S04521 — $16.50.

BUNKER: Family; Branches Early Identified with Charlestown & Nantucket, MA; DE & MD. By C.W.O. Bunker. 1931. 797p.
P4-S04527 — $115.00.

BUNKER: Origins of the Bunker Fam. & Bunker Hill, with other Bunker Material. By C. W. O. Bunker. 1942. 7p.
P4-S04534 — $10.00.

BUNKER: Genealogy; The Charlestown & Nantucket, MA Branches & Some Unconnected Groups. By E.C. Moran, Jr. 1965. 302p.
P4-S04545 — $46.50.

BUNKER: Genealogy. Ancestry & Descendants of Benjamin 3 (James 2, James 1) Bunker, Vol II. By E.C. Moran, Jr. 1942. 232p.
P4-S04551 — $37.50.

BUNKER: Genealogy, by Edward C. Moran, Jr., Vol. III, Dover branch. rev. By R.B. Christiansen, H.L. Bunker, & W. Bunker. 1982. 389p.
P4-S04533 — $59.50.

BUNKER: Genealogy; Descendants of James Bunker of Dover, NH. By E.C. Moran, Jr. 1961. 405p.
P4-S04539 — $61.50.

BUNN: History of the Bunn Family of America. By James A. Ellis. 1928. 466p.
P4-S04557 — $71.50.

BUNTING: Family; Our People & Our Selves. By A.M. Bunting. 1909. 245p.
P4-S04563 — $39.50.

BURBANK: John Burbank of Suffield, CT & Some Desc. (Repr. NEHGR). By L.M. Dewey. 1907. 6p.
P4-S04670 — $10.00.

BURBANK: Genealogy of the Burbank Family & the Family of Bran, Wellcome, Sedgley & Welch. By G. Sedgley. 1928. 586p.
P4-S04569 — $87.00.

BURBANK: Contribution to the Gen. of the Burbank & Burbanck Fam. in the US. By G.T. Ridlon. 1880. 24p.
P4-S04671 — $10.00.

BURBEEN: Acct. of John Burbeen, Who Settled at Woburn, MA about 1660 & Such of his desc. as have borne the surname of Burbeen. By J. Walker. 1892. 52p.
P4-S04673 — $10.00.

BURCH: Book, Comprising a General Study of the Burch Ancestry in America & a Specific Record of the Desc of Jonathan Burch. By Edwin W. Burch. 1925. 285p.
P4-S04575 — $44.00.

BURCHAM: & Allied Families, Boxley, Cole, Gaylor, Messer, Pillow, Rogers & Shelton. By Charleta J. Sisk Dunn. 2000. 2 vols, 1521p.
P4-S04581 — $189.00.

BURCHETT: A Family History: Burchetts in America. By Anthony Crury Burchett. 2003. 1018.
P4-S04585 — $129.00.

BURDICK: Descendants of Robert Burdick of RI. By Nellie W. Johnson. 1937. 1398p.
P4-S04587 — $159.00.

BURFORD: Genealogy, Showing the Ancestors & Descendants of Miles Washington Burford & Nancy Jane Burford. By Wesley B. Burford. 1914. 132p.
P4-S04599 — $21.00.

BURGESS: Memorial of the Fam. of Thomas & Dorothy Burgess Who Were Settled at Sandwich, Plymouth Col., 1637. By E. Burgess. 1865. 212p.
P4-S04611 — $26.50.

BURGESS: Colonists of New Eng. & Nova Scotia: Burgess & Heckman Fams. By K.F. Burgess. 1956. 134p.
P4-S04605 — $24.00.

BURGNER: Hist. & Gen. of the Burgner Fam. in the US, as Desc from Peter Burgner, a Swiss emigr. of 1734. By J. Burgner. 1890. 171p.
P4-S04617 — $23.00.

BURGWIN: John Burgwin, Carolinian, John Jones, Virginian: their Ancestors & Descendants. By Walter B. Jones. 1913. 119p.
P4-S04623 — $18.00.

BURHANS: Descendants from the First Ancestor in Amer., Jacob Burhans, 1660, & his son, Jan Burhans, 1663. By S. Burhans, Jr. 1894. 799 + 11p.
P4-S04629 — $114.00.

BURKE: ALVORD Memorial; A Gen. Acct. of the Desc. of Richard Burke of Sudbury, MA. By J. Boutelle. 1864. 239p.
P4-S04635 — $35.50.

BURKET: Desc. of Jehu Burket. By Burkett, Raber & Burkett. 1940. 10p.
P4-S04637 — $10.00.

BURLEIGH: Gen. of the Burley or Burleigh Fam. of America. By C. Burleigh. 1880. 200p.
P4-S04641 — $27.50.

BURLINGAME: Family, Descendants of Thomas Burlingame of Kent, England & RI. By Art Reierson. 1998. 347p.
P4-S04647 — $54.50.

BURNAP: BURNETT Genealogy. By Henry Wyckoff Belknap. 1925. 351p.
P4-S04653 — $55.50.

BURNETT: Genealogy, Supplementing the Burnap-Burnett Genealogy (1925). Edgar A. Burnett. 1941. 148p.
P4-S04665 — $23.00.

BURNETT: The Family of Burnett of Leys, with Collateral Branches. comp. by G. Burnett. 1901 xxii + 367p.
P4-S04671 — $61.00.

BURNETT: Family with Coll. Branches. By C. Burnett. 1950. 316p.
P4-S04659 — $48.00.

BURNHAM: Genealogical Records of Thomas Burnham, the Emigr., Who was Among the Early Settlers at Hartford, CT & his Desc. By R.H. Burnham. 1884. 292p.
P4-S04680 — $38.50.

BURNHAM: Family; or Gen. Records of the Desc. of the Four Emigr. of the Name Who were Among the early Settlers in America. By R.H. Burnham. 1869. 546p.
P4-S04674 — $84.00.

BURNHAM: Report of the Board of Trustees of the Burnham Assn. of America, incl. The report of Edward Payson. 1873. 16p.
P4-S04675 — $10.00.

BURNLEY: Our Burnley Ancestors & Allied Families. By Emma Dicken. 1946. 262p.
P4-S04686 — $41.00.

BURNS: Family History. By J. Montgomery Seaver. 32p.
P4-S04688 — $10.00.

BURR: A General History of the Burr Family, 1193-1891. By C.B. Todd. 1891. 2nd ed. 572p.
P4-S04700 — $78.50.

BURR: Bures of Suffolk, Eng. & Burr of Mass. Bay Colony, New Eng. By C. R. Burr. 1926. 131p.
P4-S04695 — $19.50.

BURR: General History of the Burr Family, with a Gen. Record from 1193-1902. By Charles B. Todd. 4th ed. 1902. 600p.
P4-S04701 — $76.00.

BURRAGE: Memorial. A Gen. Hist. of the Desc. of John Burrage, who Settled in Charlestown, MA in 1637. By A. A. Burrage. 1877. 265p.
P4-S04707 — $39.50.

BURRILL: Fam. of Lynn During the Colonial & Provincial Periods, with Some Desc.; a Paper Read Before the Lynn Hist. Society. By E.M. Burrill. 1907. 54p.
P4-S04714 — $10.00.

BURRILL: Family of John & Mary Burrill, 1767-1931. C.W. Burrill. 1931. 92p.
P4-S04713 — $18.00.

BURRITT: One Line of the Burritt Family [of Wales & CT], with addendum. By Mary L. Foster. 1898. 46 + 8p.
P4-S04720 — $11.00.

BURRITT: Family in America: Descendants of William Burritt of Stratford, CT, 1635-1940. By Lewis L. Burritt. 1940. 321p.
P4-S04719 — $49.00.

BURRITT: Family of Blackleach Burritt, Jr, Pioneer & One of the First Settlers of Uniondale, Susquehanna Co., PA. By Alice Burritt. 1911. 68p.
P4-S04725 — $14.00.

BURROUGHS: Family of Burroughs, Burrows, Burris (in Brockman Scrapbook). By W. E. Brockman. 1952. 27p.
P4-S04727 — $10.00.

BURT: Genealogical Records of Henry & Eulalia Burt, the Emigrants, Who Early Settled at Springfield, MA & Their Desc. Through Nine Generations Roderick H. Burnham. 1892. 347p.
P4-S04731 — $47.00.

BURT: Early Days in New England. Life & Times of Henry Burt of Springfield & Some of His Desc. By H. M. Burt & S. W. Burt. 1893. 620p.
P4-S04728 — $78.50.

BURTON: Chronicles of Colonial VA; Particularly Relating to the Burtons of the Valley of the James & Appomatox By Francis B. Harrison. 1933. 449p.
P4-S04743 — $67.50.

BURTON: Descendants of Josiah Burton of Manchester, VT. By W. L. Holman. 1926. 310p.
P4-S04737 — $49.00.

BURWELL: Record of the Burwell Family, Copied in Part from the Manuscript by the Rev. Robt. Burwell, rev. ed. By Geo. H. Burwell. 1908. 43p.
P4-S04746 — $10.00.

BUSBY: Hist. Sketch of Nicholas Busby the Emigrant. By A. C. Kingsbury. 1924. 26p.
P4-S04747 — $10.00.

BUSH: Desc. of John Bush & Jane Osterhoudt of Kingston, Ulster Co., NY, 1791-1914. By B. Bush. 1914. 63p.
P4-S04752 — $12.50.

BUSH: Genealogy. By Ann S. Bush. 1967. 130p., typescript.
P4-S04749 — $21.00.

BUSHMAN: The Bushman Family, Orig. of PA & The Rocky Mtn. States. N.I. Butt. 1956. 262 + 4p.
P4-S04750 — $40.00.

BUSHNELL: Ancestry of Daniel Bushnell. J. Gardner Bartlett. 1918. 55p.
P4-S04814 — $11.50.

BUSHNELL: Bushnells of CT (Repr. NEHGR). 1898-1899 20p.
P4-S04754 — $10.00.

BUSHNELL: Family Genealogy: Anc. & Posterity of Francis Bushnell (1580-1646) of Hursham, England, & Guilford, CT. By G. E. Bushnell. 1945. 276p.
P4-S04761 — $41.50.

BUTLER: COX — HALE Connections: Thirteen Generations. By Genevieve C. Kennedy. 1978. 96 p.
P4-S04773 — $15.00.

BUTLER: Book of the Family & Lineal Desc. of Medad Butler. By W. A. Butler. 1887. 61p.
P4-S04764 — $12.50.

BUTLER: Family. By Albert W. Rook. 1901. 111p.
P4-S04791 — $18.50.

BUTLER: Family in America. By W. Butler et al. 1909. 306p.
P4-S04779 — $48.50.

BUTLER: Genealogy; Dedication of the Monument to Deacon John Butler, Pelham, NH, 1886. 1887. 36p.
P4-S04774 — $10.00.

BUTLER: Tales of Our Kinsfolk Past & Present: The Story of Our Butler Anc for Ten Generations, 1602-1919. By H.L. Butler. 1919. 552p.
P4-S04809 — $84.50.

BUTLER: Family of Rev. John Butler [b. 1789 in Nottingham NH]. By Chas. B. Fillebrown. 1908. 44p.
P4-S04775 — $10.00.

BUTLER: Butleriana, Genealogica et Biographica, or Genealogical Notes Concerning Mary Butler & Her Descendants. By J.D. Butler. 1888. 162p.
P4-S04797 — $25.00.

BUTLER: Butlers & Kinsfolk: Butlers of New England & Nova Scotia, & Rel Fams of Other Names, incl. Durkees. By E.E. Butler. 1944. 362p.
P4-S04803 — $56.00.

BUTLER: Family of Northwestern NJ: Their Ancestors & Descendants & Related Families By John W. Butler. 1996. 157p.
P4-S04785 — $22.00.

BUTLER: Thomas Butler & His Desc., 1674-1886, By G.H. Butler. 1886. 199p.
P4-S04815 — $26.50.

BUTTERS: Gen Reg of the Butters Family, Desc. of William Butter of Woburn, MA, 1665, & Others in America. By G. Butters. 1896. 476p.
P4-S04821 — $74.00.

BUTTOLPH: BUTTOLPH Family; [ex History of Wethersfield, CT]. 1904. 9p.
P4-S04822 — $10.00.

BUTTON: Outline of Earliest Desc. of Matthias Button, Who Settled at Salem, MA in 1628. A. Button. 1889. 16p.
P4-S04823 — $10.00.

BUTTON: Same, 2nd ed. Supplement. 1903. 18p.
P4-S04825 — $10.00.

BUTTS: John Butts: His Ancestry & Some Descendants. By A. Butts. 1898. 153p.
P4-S04824 — $24.50.

BYE: History of the Bye Family & Some Allied Fams. A.E. Bye. 1956. 450p.
P4-S04830 — $69.00.

BYERLY: The Byerlys of Carolina. By W.G.Byerly. 1960. 69p.
P4-S04836 — $14.00.

BYRAM: Abby Byram & Her Father, Their Anc. & Desc. By J. M. McElroy. 1898. 65p.
P4-S04842 — $13.00.

BYRD: Hist & Gen of the Byrd Family, From the Early Part of 1700 a.d. When They First Settled at Muddy Creel, Accomack Co., VA. By Colwell P. Byrd. 1908. 126p.
P4-S04848 — $21.00.

C

CABELL: The Cabells & Their Kin. By A. Brown. 1939. 708p.
P4-S04860 — $99.00.

CABOT: History & Genealogy of the Cabot Family. By L. Vernon Briggs. 1927. 2 vols. in 1, 885p.
P4-S04866 — $135.00.

CADENHEAD: Family of Cadenhead. By Geo. M. Cadenhead. 1887. 57p.
P4-S04869 — $12.00.

CADLE: List of 115 Colonial Anc. of Cornelius Cadle of Muscatine, IA. By C. F. Cadle. 12p.
P4-S04870 — $10.00.

CADMUS: COLE Genealogy. By Bell S. Cadmus. 1933. 165p., typescript.
P4-S04878 — $26.00.

CADY: Descendants of Nicholas Cady of Watertown, MA. By O. P. Allen. 1910. 546p.
P4-S04881 — $69.50.

CADY: Supplement to above. 1911. 33p.
P4-S04882 — $10.00.

CADY: Some Notes on Nicholas Cady of Watertown & Desc. ed. by H. F. Johnston. 4p.
P4-S04883 — $10.00.

CAHOON: History of the Cahoon Family. By I. M. Cahoon. 47p.
P4-S04890 — $10.00.

CAITHNESS: The Caithness Family History. By J. Henderson. 1884. 341p.
P4-S04893 — $53.00.

CALDWELL: Records. John & Sarah (Dillingham) Caldwell, Ipswich, MA. By A. Caldwell. 1873. 82p.
P4-S04899 — $16.00.

CALDWELL: John Caldwell & Sarah Dillingham Caldwell, Ipswich, MA. By A. Caldwell & S. Kimball. 1904. 318p.
P4-S04905 — $49.50.

CALDWELL: William Coaldwell, Caldwell or Coldwell By C. T. Caldwell. 1910. 82p.
P4-S04917 — $16.50.

CALDWELL: The Caldwells & Collateral Branches in France, Scotland, Ireland & America. By Annie C. Escott. 1931. 90p.
P4-S04911 — $18.00.

CALEF: Robert Calef of Boston & Roxbury & Some of His Desc. By W. W. Lunt. 1928. 68p.
P4-S04923 — $14.00.

CALHOUN: Family of SC. By A. Salley. 42p.
P4-S04930 — $10.00.

CALHOUN: The Story of the Calhouns of Judea, CT. By M.B. Calhoun. 1956. 57p.
P4-S04926 — $12.00.

CALKINS: Family in America. By Kenneth W. Calkins. 2000. 517p.
P4-S04942 — $75.00.

CALKINS: Memorial Military Roster. By W.M. Calkins. 1903. 204p.
P4-S04935 — $31.00.

CALKINS: Genealogy of the Calkins Family [Descendants of Hugh Calkins of MA & CT], Parts I & II. By Mrs T Sharps. 1949? 580 + 490p., typescript.
P4-S04941 — $139.00.

CALL: The Calls of Norfold & Suffolk. By Chas. S. Romanes. 1920 103p.
P4-S04947 — $16.50.

CALL: Genealogy of the Call Family in the US. By S. Call. 1908. 56p.
P4-S04948 — $11.00.

CALLAWAY: Clan [of VA, GA, TN]. By Bessie C. Hoffmeyer. 1948. 100p.
P4-S04953 — $19.50.

CALTHORPE: Notes on the Calthorpe & Calthrop in the Counties of Norfolk & Lincolnshire & Elsewhere. By C.W. Carr-Calthrop. 1933, 3rd ed. 129 + 22p.
P4-S04959 — $24.00.

CALVERT: My Calvert Ancestry & Extended Family, Holmes, Gleason, Naughton, Rogers, Hayden, Shawm. By Louise Naughton Shaw. 1996. 277p.
P4-S04971 — $42.00.

CALVERT: Descendants of VA Calverts. By E.F. O'Gorman. 1947. 763p.
P4-S04965 — $99.00.

CALVIN: Families: Origin & Hist. of the American Calvins with a Partial Gen. By C.W. Calvin. 1945. 405p.
P4-S04977 — $62.00.

CALVIN: Our Huguenot Anc. & Their Emigration. By C.W. Calvin. 1955. 7p.
P4-S04977 — $10.00.

CAME: Genealogy of the Came Family. By Susan C. Conant. 1909. 60p.
P4-S04980 — $12.00.

CAMP: Ancestry & Descendants of Frederick Tracy Camp & His Wife Marion Fee. By John F. Camp., Jr. & N. Grier Parke II. 1961. 171p.
P4-S04989 — $25.00.

CAMPBELL: The Campbell Family Magazine; Volume I, No 1-4; Volume II, No 1. 1916-1917 80 + 22p.
P4-S04996 — $15.00.

CAMPBELL: Robert Campbell & Desc. By H. Douglas. 1878. 6p.
P4-S04997 — $10.00.

CAMPBELL: The Campbells of Drumaboden on the River Lyennon, New Rathmelton, Co. Donegal, North of Ireland. By John F. Campbell. 1925. 147p.
P4-S05025 — $24.00.

CAMPBELL: Clan in VA. By L.L. Campbell. 1954. 154p.
P4-S04995 — $27.00.

CAMPBELL: Genealogy of the Campbell, Noble, Gorton, Shelton, Gilmour & Byrd Families. By M.C. Whitaker. 1927. 230p.
P4-S05007 — $36.50.

CAMPBELL: Historical Sketches of the Campbell, Pilcher & Kindred Families. By M.C Pilcher. 1911. 444p.
P4-S05013 — $68.50.

CAMPBELL.: House of Argyll & the Collateral Branches of the Clan Campbell. 1871. 239p.
P4-S05019 — $37.00.

CANBY: William Canby of Brandywine, DE: His Descendants, 4th to 7th Generations in America. 1883. 59p.
P4-S05028 — $12.00.

CANDEE: Genealogy, with Notices of Allied Families. By C. Baldwin. 1882. 240p.
P4-S05037 — $32.00.

CANFIELD: Our Canfield Ancestors & Some Related Families. By Clifford R. Canfield. 1956. 131p., typescript.
P4-S05049 — $21.00.

CANFIELD: A History Thomas & Matthew Canfield with a Gen. of Their Desc. in NJ. By F.A. Canfield. 1897. 228p.
P4-S05043 — $34.00.

CANNON: Andrew Cannon & His Desc., 1651-1912. By C. S. Williams. 1912. 54p.
P4-S05055 — $17.50.

CANNON: Descendants of Samuel (Carnahan) Cannon of Ulster, Ireland, & Blandford, MA. By Almon Brown Cannon. 1932. 168p., typescript.
P4-S05061 — $26.50.

CANTEY: Six Generations of the Cantey Family of SC. By Jos. S. Ames. 1910. 56p.
P4-S05064 — $11.00.

CANTINE: Family: Descendants of Moses Cantine. By Alice C. Huntington. 1957. 82p. typescript.
P4-S05067 — $16.00.

CANTINE: Preliminary Statement of the Cantine Genealogy, or the Desc in America of the Huguenot Refugee Moses Cantine, By Matthew C. Julien. 1903. 14p.
P4-S05068 — $10.00.

CANTRELL: CANTRELL— POTTER — MAGNESS Ancestry of Alvin Edw. Potter, Sr. By E.R. Whitley. 1938. 100p.
P4-S05073 — $19.00.

CANTRELL: Family: A Biographical Album & History of the Desc. of Zebulon Cantrell. By C.G. Cantrell. 1898. 156p.
P4-S05079 — $25.00.

CANTRILL: CANTRELL Genealogy: Record of the Desc. of Richard Cantrill of Philadelphia. By S.C. Christie. 1908. 271p.
P4-S05085 — $35.00.

CAPEN: Family; Descendants of Bernard Capen of Dorchester, MA. By C. Hayden, rev. By J. Tuttle. 1929. 312p.
P4-S05091 — $49.00.

CAPERS: Pedigree of the Capers Family. By Francis L. Capers. 1908. 28p.
P4-S05094 — $10.00.

CAPEWELL: First Annual Genealogical & Heraldic Report on the Capewell & Capwell Families. By Clarence L. Capewell. 1906. 66p.
P4-S05097 — $13.00.

CAPEWELL: Second Annual Genealogical & Heraldic Report on the Capewell & Capwell Families. By Clarence L. Capewell. 1907. 80p.
P4-S05103 — $16.00.

CAPRON: Genealogy of the Desc. of Banfield Capron (with 1999 every-name index by Martin Irons) By F. A. Holden. 1859. 263p.
P4-S05109 — $39.00.

CAREY: The Careys of KS & Some of their Ancestors. Albert D. Bill. 1950. 81p.
P4-S05115 — $15.00.

CARHART: Descendants of Thomas Carhart. By M. Dusenbury. 1880. 142p.
P4-S05121 — $25.00.

CARLOCK: History of the Carlock Family & Adventures of Pioneer Americans. By Marion P. Carlock. 1929. 654p.
P4-S05127 — $97.50.

CARLSON: The Family of Ekeremma Sweden. n.d. 250p.
P4-S05128 — $38.00.

CARNEGIE: The Carnegies, Earls of Southesk, Vols. I-II. Wm. Fraser. 1867. 2 vols., cx + 240 + 360p.
P4-S05129 — $90.00.

CARNEY: Gen. of the Carney Family, Desc of Mark Carney & Suzann Gow of Pownalboro, ME. By S.H. Carney, Jr. 1904. 227p.
P4-S05130 — $29.50.

CARNEY: Descendants of John Carney, Stafford Co., VA. D.E. Page. 2002. xii + 167p.
P4-S05131 — $27.00.

CARPENTER: WIER Family of Upper SC & Other Ancestors. By H.B. McCoy. 1959. 326p.
P4-S05136 — $51.00.

CARPENTER: Genealogy & Historical Record of the Carpenter Family. By J. Usher. 1883. 70p.
P4-S05142 — $14.00.

CARPENTER: Genealogical History of the Rehoboth Branch of the Carpenter Family in America. By A. Carpenter. 1898. 921p.
P4-S05145 — $112.00.

CARPENTER: Samuel Carpenter & His Desc. By E. & L. H. Carpenter. 1912. 320p.
P4-S05151 — $49.50.

CARPENTER: History & Genealogy of the Carpenter Family in America from the Settlement at Providence, RI. By D.H. Carpenter. 1901. 375p.
P4-S05148 — $55.25

CARR: Family Records, Embracing the Record of the First Family who Settled in America. E.C. Carr. 1894. 540p.
P4-S05166 — $68.00.

CARR: House of Carr: A Historical Sketch of the Carr Family. By W. L. Watson. 1926. 58p.
P4-S05169 — $12.00.

CARR: Genealogy of Joseph Carr of Jamestown, RI. Mary E. Burt. 1902. 36p.
P4-S05164 — $10.00.

CARR: Sketches of the Lives of Many of the Descendants of Robert & Caleb Carr. By Arthur A. Carr. 1947. 598p.
P4-S05157 — $89.50.

CARR: Family of Duplin Co., NC. By James O. Carr. 1929. 65p.
P4-S05163 — $13.00.

CARRELL: Descendants of James Carrell & Sarah Dungan his Wife. By E. P. Carrell. 1928. 708p.
P4-S05178 — $99.00.

CARRIER: History of the Carrier Family (New England). By C.C. McLean, Jr. n.d. 9p., typescript.
P4-S05180 — $10.00.

CARRINGTON: Brief Historical Sketch of the Name & Family. By Mary E. Tilley. 1943. 88p.
P4-S05184 — $18.00.

CARROLL: History of the William Carroll Family of Alleghany Co., NY. By K. Stevenson. 1929. 100p.
P4-S05190 — $19.00.

CARRUTH: Family: Brief Background & Genealogical Data of Twenty Branches in America. By Harold B. Carruth. 1952. 273p.
P4-S05196 — $42.50.

CARRUTH: Genealogy of a Branch of the Carruth Family, or the Desc. of James Carruth of Phillipston, By A. J. Carruth. 1926. 67p.
P4-S05199 — $12.50.

CARSON: McCORMICK Family Memorials. By Thos. C. McCormick. 1954. 158p., typescript.
P4-S05208 — $26.00.

CARTER: FISHER & Allied Families: Genealogical Study with Biographical Notes. By Thomas H. Bateman. 1950. 241p.
P4-S05238 — $36.50.

CARTER: Gen. of the Desc. of Thomas Carter of MA & CT. By H.W. Carter. 1909. 341p.
P4-S0524 — $54.00.

CARTER: Descendants of Samuel & Thomas, Sons of Rev. Sam'l Carter, 1640-1886. By C. & S. Carter. 1886. 272p.
P4-S05226 — $41.00.

CARTER: The Carters of Amelia County, VA: 350 Years of American History. Peyton F. Carter III. 2003. 253p.
P4-S05214 — $38.00.

CARTER: The Carter Tree, Tabulated & Indexed. By R.R. Carter & R.I. Randolph. 1951. 241p.
P4-S05262 — $38.00.

CARTER: Family of Thomas Carter of Salisbury, MA. By Horace C. Hovey. 1914. 84p., typescript.
P4-S05232 — $16.00.

CARTER: Descendants of Capt. Thomas Carter of "Barford," Lancaster Co, VA With Allied Families. By J. Miller. 1912. 430p.
P4-S05220 — $67.50.

CARTER: Bi-Centenary Mem. of Jeremiah Carter Who Came to the Prov. of PA in 1682. By T.M. Potts. 1883. 304p.
P4-S05214 — $49.00.

CARTER: Descendants of Samuel Carter of Deerfield, MA & Norwalk, CT. By Sam'l Carter. 1885. 27p.
P4-S05216 — $10.00.

CARTER: Family of NC: Descendants of Robert Carter of Bertie Co. By Carolyn A. Foster. 1914. 40p.
P4-S05217 — $10.00.

CARTER: Giles Carter of VA: A Genealogical Memoir. By Gen. Wm. G.H. Carter. 1901. 134p.
P4-S05250 — $19.50.

CARTER: History of the Isaac P. Carter Family & Their Descendants. By Howard Carter. 1905. 134p.
P4-S05256 — $21.00.

CARTER: The Carters of Blenheim: Gen of Edward & Sarah Champe Carter of "Blenheim" Albemarle Co., VA. By George S. Wallace. 1955. 139p.
P4-S05268 — $22.50.

CARTWRIGHT: Edward Cartwright of Nantucket, MA, Some of his Descendants & Their Allied Families. By Stanley L. Mack. 1937? 38p., typescript.
P4-S05269 — $10.00.

CARVER: DANNER, History of Christian Carver & Frederick Danner & Their Descendants. By J.D. Danner & Rose Carver Danner. 1931. 47p.
P4-S05275 — $10.00.

CARVER: John Carver, First Governor of the Colony of New Plymouth (Repr. NEHGR). 6p.
P4-S05276 — $10.00.

CARVER: Jonathan Carver of Kent, CT & Kinston, PA. By R.M. & H.C. Search. n.d. 7p.
P4-S05277 — $10.00.

CARVER: Genealogy of William Carver from Hertfordshire, England, in 1682. By Elias Carver. 1903. 146p.
P4-S05280 — $22.50.

CARVER: Family of New England: Robert Carver of Marshfield & His Desc. By C.N. Carver. 1935. 204p.
P4-S05274 — $31.00.

CARVER: Robert Carver of Marshfield, MA & Some Desc. By W. Jones. 1934. 49p.
P4-S05278 — $10.00.

CARY: COOPER Marriages & deaths, Otsego Co., NY. 2p.
P4-S05299 — $10.00.

CARY: ESTES Genealogy. By May F. Webb & Patrick M. Estes. 1939. 242p.
P4-S05292 — $37.00.

CARY: Memorial. S.F. Cary. 1874. 306p.
P4-S05307 — $45.00.

CARY: Family in England. By H. G. Cary. 1906. 105p.
P4-S05304 — $16.00.

CARY: Family in America, by H.G. Cary; Appendix, Jonathan Cary ye third. By I. H. Cary. 1907. 120p.
P4-S05298 — $17.00.

CARY: John Cary, Plymouth Pilgrim. By S. Cary. 1911. 274p.
P4-S05313 — $41.00.

CARY: The VA Carys; Essay in Genealogy. By F. Harrison. 1919. 29 + 194p + charts.
P4-S05319 — $42.00.

CARY: John Cary, 1755-1823. Rev. S.C. Cary. 1908. 48p.
P4-S05300 — $10.00.

CARY: Eleazer Cary Family, With Affiliated Lines. By May A.C. Smith. 1908. 55p.
P4-S05301 — $11.00.

CARYL: Family in England & America, By Arthur S. Caryl. 1937. 320p.
P4-S05325 — $49.00.

CASE: John Case of CT. A. P. Case. 24p.
P4-S05338 — $10.00.

CASE: Jonathan Case of Ontario Co., NY. By C. Case. 1915. 104p.
P4-S05337 — $20.00.

CASE: Desc. of Stephen Case of Marlboro NY, Including Allied Families. By Lynn M. Case. 1971. 82p.
P4-S05331 — $17.00.

CASEY: Early Family of Casey in RI. By T. Casey. 1893. 45p.
P4-S05342 — $10.00.

CASS: Ada Ball Cass, Desc. of John Cass, 1620-1675. E. M. Cass. 1945. 8p.
P4-S05344 — $10.00.

CASS: Ancestry of Ada Ball Cass. By Earle M. Cass. 1945. 93p., typescript.
P4-S05343 — $17.00.

CASSEL: Gen Hist of the Cassel family in America, desc of Julius Kassel or Yelles Cassel of Germany. By D.K. Cassel. 1896. 465p.
P4-S05349 — $71.50.

CASTLE: Gen. Notes on the Ancestry & Desc. of Lester Delos Castle & Lucy Angelia (Taylor) Castle By Chas. W. Coltrin. 1923. 125p.
P4-S05355 — $21.00.

CASTLE: History of the Castle Family, from 1635-1900, With 1903 appendix, 1997 addendum & index. By Wm. W. Ingraham, addendum & index By Roger P. Kohin. 1900. 210p.
P4-S05361 — $33.50.

CASTOR: Family, Holmesburg Branch. By R.A. Martin. 1909. 11p.
P4-S05368 — $10.00.

CASTOR: Family of PA & the Castor Family of NY. By George C. Martin, Henry A.J. Castor, et al. 1910. 119 + 42p.
P4-S05367 — $26.00.

CATCHINGS: HOLLIDAY Families & Various Related Families in VA, GA, MS & Other Southern States. T.C. Catchings & Mrs M.C. Torrey. 1921. 190p.
P4-S05373 — $28.00.

CATE: CATES Family of New England. By Cates & Sanborn. 1904. 52p.
P4-S05375 — $10.00.

CATHER: The Jasper Cather Family of Frederick Co., VA. By Flavius J. Cather. 1902. 42p., typescript.
P4-S05376 — $10.00.

CATLETT: Family, extr. "Zimmerman & Allied Fams." 14p.
P4-S05378 — $10.00.

CATT: WILLETT Families of Sussex, England & British Columbia, Canada, 1595-1993. By Glenna Willett Metchette. 1993. 132p.
P4-S05379 — $21.00.

CAUDEBEC: in America: Descendants of Jacques Caudebec, 1700-1920. By Wm. L. Cuddeback. 1919. 276p.
P4-S05385 — $41.50.

CAUTHORN: Record of the Cauthorn Family. By R.C. Phillips. 1909. 59p.
P4-S05388 — $12.00.

CAVENDISH: An Account of the Cavendish, Candish or Candage Family. By R. G. A. Candage. 1889. 9p.
P4-S05390 — $10.00.

CAVERLY: Family Genealogy, 1116-1880. By R.B. Caverly. 1880. 201p.
P4-S05397 — $33.00.

CAVERNO: Record of the Caverno Family. By A. Caverno. 1874. 36p.
P4-S05400 — $10.00.

CAWOOD: Who is this Fellow Cawood. A History of the Cawood Family from Johannes de Cawood [John Cawood]. Richard Lawrence Cawood. 1962. 133p.
P4-S05402 — $22.50.

CESSNA: House of Cessna. By H. Cessna. 1903. 120p.
P4-S05403 — $25.00.

CESSNA: House of Cessna, 2nd series. By H. Cessna. 1935. 199p.
P4-S05409 — $31.00.

CHACE: Gen. Record of Chace & Hathaway Family, 1630-1900. By C. V. Case. 1900. 42p.
P4-S05411 — $10.00.

CHADBOURNE: CHADBOURN Genealogy. By W.M. Emery. 1904. 66p.
P4-S05415 — $13.00.

CHADWICK: Notes on Descendants of John & Joan Chadwick & Related Families. By A.D. Kilham. 1966. 120p.
P4-S05421 — $19.50.

CHAFEE: LeBOSQUET Fams: Informal Gen. of Olivia K. Chaffee, Husband Maurice LeBosquet & Their Children. O.K. LeBosquet. 1955. 228p.
P4-S05427 — $23.00.

CHAFFEE: Genealogy; Desc. of Thomas Chaffee of Hingham, Hull, Rehoboth & Swansea, MA. By W.H. Chaffee. 1909. 663p.
P4-S05430 — $83.00.

CHAFFEE: The Berkshire, VT Chaffees & Their Desc. By A.J. Elliot. 1911. 356p.
P4-S05436 — $57.50.

CHAFFIN: History of Robert Chaffin & His Desc. & Other Chaffins in America, By W.L. Chaffin. 1912. 337p.
P4-S05442 — $54.00.

CHALK: The Chalk Family of England & America. Minna Chalk Scott Hyman 1942. xxii + 156p.
P4-S05444 — $27.00.

CHAMBERLAIN: A Genealogical Record of the Desc of Benjamin Chamberlain, of Sussex Co, NJ. A.J. Fretz. 1907. iv + 104 + 70p.
P4-S05449 — $27.00.

CHAMBERLAIN: One Branch of the Desc. of Thomas Chamberlain of Woburn G. W. Chamberlain. 1897. 16p.
P4-S05450 — $10.00.

CHAMBERLAIN: Annual Report of the Chamberlain Assoc. of America; Desc of William Chamberlin of Woburn & Billerica, MA. 1911. 159p.
P4-S05454 — $26.00.

CHAMBERLAIN: The Chamberlain Association of America. Chamberlain Family Association. 1898-1905. 568p.
P4-S05451 — $85.50.

CHAMBERLAIN: Annual Report of the Chamberlain Assoc. of America 1908. 90p.
P4-S05448 — $18.00.

CHAMBERLAINE: Genealogical Notes of the Chamberlaine family of MD (Eastern Shore). By John B. Kerr. 1880. 99p.
P4-S05460 — $18.00.

CHAMBERS: Evolution of the Chambers, Bowlus & Remsburg Families. By Charley D. Bowlus. 1901. 108p.
P4-S05472 — $17.00.

CHAMBERS: History: Trails of the Centuries. By Wm. D. Chambers. 1925. 198p.
P4-S05466 — $31.00.

CHAMBLIN: James Chamblin of SC & His Children. 1914. 16p.
P4-S05473 — $10.00.

CHAMNESS: Family in America: Hist & Gen of the American Desc of John & Ann Chamness of London, England. By Zimri Hanson. 1922. 123p.
P4-S05478 — $19.00.

CHAMPION: Genealogy; History of the Descendants of Henry Champion of Saybrook & Lyme, CT. By F. Trowbridge. 1891. 575p.
P4-S05484 — $71.50.

CHANCELLOR: Family Data. By G. Chancellor. 8p.
P4-S05491 — $10.00.

CHANCELLOR: Chancellor Family. By J. C. Chancellor. 1963. 69p.
P4-S05490 — $13.50.

CHANDLER: PARSONS; Edmond Chaundeler, Geoffrey Parsons & Allied Families. By Mary Chandler Lowell. 1911. 112p.
P4-S05496 — $17.50.

CHANDLER: Anc. of Lydia Mehitable Chandler. By F. W. Goding. 1904. 11p.
P4-S05400 — $10.00.

CHANDLER: Of Oare Co., Wilts., Eng; Report of Researches Regarding Anc. of John & George Chandler who Sailed to PA in 1686. By Chandler & Glenn. 1913. 23p.
P4-S05401 — $10.00.

CHANDLER: Sketch of the Chandler Family in Worcester, MA. By E.O.P. Sturgis. 1903. 37p.
P4-S05402 — $10.00.

CHANDLER: Family, Geanealogy of a Branch. By A.M. Pickford. 1903. 31p.
P4-S05403 — $10.00.

CHANDLER: Partial Genealogy of the Chandler Family. n.d. 14p.
P4-S05404 — $10.00.

CHANDLER: Record of the Desc of George & Jane Chandler Who Emigrated to PA from Wiltshire, England. 1937. 762p.
P4-S05511 — $105.00.

CHANDLER: Family, Desc of William & Annis Chandler Who Settled in Roxbury, MA, 1637. By G. Chandler. 1883. 1323p.
P4-S05499 — $157.00.

CHANDLER: John Chandler Family of Green & Taylore Cos., KY. By Walter R. Sanders. 1947. 57p., typescript.
P4-S05506 — $11.50.

CHANDLER: Descendants of Roger Chandler of Concord, MA, 1658. By C.H. Chandler. 1949. 152p.
P4-S05505 — $24.50.

CHAPIN: Book of Gen. Data, with Brief Bio. Sketches of the Desc. of Dea. Samuel Chapin, Volume I. By G.W. Chapin. 1924. 1320p.
P4-S05517 — $153.00.

CHAPIN: Book, Eight to Twelfth Generation, Volume II. By G.W. Chapin. 1924. 1417p.
P4-S05523 — $155.00.

CHAPIN: Genealogy, Containing Desc. of Dea. Samuel Chapin, Who Settled in Springfield, MA, 1642. By O. Chapin. 1862. 376p.
P4-S05535 — $58.50.

CHAPIN: Proceedings at the Meeting of the Chapin Family in Springfield, MA, Sept. 17, 1862. 1862. 97p.
P4-S05541 — $18.50.

CHAPIN: Chapins Who Served in the French & Indian Wars 1754-1764; Rev. War 1775-1783; War of 1812-1815 & Others. By G.W. Chapin. 1895. 47p.
P4-S05536 — $10.00.

CHAPIN: From the Connecticut Valley of MA to NE, 1638-1996: Hist & Gen of the family of Maxine Chapin. By Rev. Leopold H. Hoppe. 2002. 308p.
P4-S05529 — $45.00.

CHAPLIN: Elder Asa Chaplin, Revolutionary Soldier 1739/40-1807, Mittie Myers Chaplin 1956. 258p.
P4-S05546 — $39.00.

CHAPLIN: John Chaplin (1758-1837) of Rowley, MA & Bridgton, ME, his Anc. & Desc. M. & L. Ellis. 1949. 139p.
P4-S05547 — $21.00.

CHAPMAN: Family, or the Desc. of Robert Chapman, One of the First Settlers of Saybrook, CT. By F.W. Chapman. 1854. 414p.
P4-S05556 — $52.00.

CHAPMAN: Family; From Hunter Family of VA. By Sidney M. Culbertson. 1934. 25p.
P4-S05554 — $10.00.

CHAPMAN: A History of Chapman & Alexander Families. Sigismunda Mary Frances Chapman 1946. 305p.
P4-S05557 — $46.00.

CHAPMAN: Northern Neck Families: Ancestors of Susan Frances Chapman, Alexander, Chapman & Pearson Plus Connecting Lines. Brian J.L. Berry. 125p.
P4-S05568 — $21.00.

CHAPMAN: Descendants of Ralph Chapman. Charles B. Gerard. 1876. 86p.
P4-S05562 — $16.50.

CHAPMAN: A Gen; Edward Chapman of Ipswich, MA, 1642-1678 & His Desc. By J. Chapman. 1893. 147p.
P4-S05553 — $22.00.

CHAPMAN: Edward Chapman of Ipswich, MA in 1644 & Some Desc. By Chapman & Lapham. 1878. 36p.
P4-S05555 — $10.00.

CHAPMANS: The Chapmans of Old Saybrook, CT; A Family Chronicle. By Edw. M. Chapman. 1942. 74p.
P4-S05574 — $15.00.

CHAPPELEAR: Family of VA & Connecting Lines. By G.W. Chappelear. 1932. 122p.
P4-S05580 — $23.00.

CHAPPELL: DICKIE & Other Kindred Families of VA, 1635-1900. By P.E. Chappell. Rev. ed. 1900. 384p.
P4-S05592 — $59.00.

CHAPPELL: Records of the Chappells in England & the Chappells in VA, TN, AL & Other States. By Mrs J.M. Guttery. n.d. 61p., typescript.
P4-S05583 — $12.00.

CHASE: A Gen. Memoir of the Chase Family of Chesham, Bucks in Eng. & of Hampton & Newbury in New Eng. By G. B. Chase. 1869. 19p.
P4-S05599 — $10.00.

CHASE: Family Records. By J. Montgomery Seaver. 84p.
P4-S05598 — $17.00.

CHASE: Records of the Desc. of Rev. Nathaniel Chase of Buckfield, ME. By W. B. Lapham. 1878. 18p.
P4-S05600 — $10.00.

CHASE: Gen. of the Portion of the Desc. of William Chase, Who Came to America in 1630. 1886. 31p.
P4-S05601 — $10.00.

CHASE: Gen. of the Anc. & Desc. of Joseph Chase. 1874. 86p.
P4-S05604 — $17.00.

CHASE: Reminiscenses of the Fam. of Moody Chase of Shirley, MA. By W. M. Chase. 1888. 32p.
P4-S05602 — $10.00.

CHASE: Gen. of Champion Spalding Chase & Mary Sophronia Butterfield By C. S. Chase. 1894. 19p.
P4-S05605 — $10.00.

CHASE: Seven Generations of the Descendants of Aquila & Thomas Chase. By J. C. Chase & G. W. Chamberlain. 1928. 624p.
P4-S05610 — $93.50.

CHATFIELD: The Chatfield fam. of Derby, CT (Repr. NEHGR). By D. L. Jacobus. 1924. 8p.
P4-S05614 — $10.00.

CHATFIELD: Family of Naugatuck Valley, CT. By W. Sharpe. 1896. 32p.
P4-S05613 — $10.00.

CHAUNCY: Memorial of the Chaunceys, Incl. President Chauncey, His Anc. & Desc. By W. C. Fowler. 1858. 377p.
P4-S05616 — $58.50.

CHEEVER: Family. By J. T. Hassam. 1896. 54p.
P4-S05618 — $10.00.

CHEEVER: Bartholomew & Richard Cheever & Some of Their Desc. (Repr. NEHGR). J. Hassam. 1882. 11p.
P4-S05617 — $10.00.

CHEEVER: Ezekiel Cheever & Some of His Desc., Part Second. (Repr. NEHGR). By J. T. Hassam. 1884. 26p.
P4-S05620 — $10.00.

CHEEVER: Ezekiel Cheever; add. notes. By J. Hassam. 1887. 6p.
P4-S05621 — $10.00.

CHEEVER: Ezekiel Cheever & Some of His Desc. John T. Hassam. 1879. iv + 64p.
P4-S05622 — $10.00.

CHENEY: John Cheney of Plaistow, NH, Orange Co., VT & Monroe Co., NY & his Desc. E. Gundry. 1959. 55p.
P4-S05624 — $11.00.

CHENEY: Genealogy [Descendants of Wm. of Roxbury & John of Newbury]. Charles H. Pope. 1897. 582p.
P4-S05619 — $75.00.

CHENOWETH: History of the Chenoweth Family, Beginning 449 a.d., By C.C. Hiatt. 1925. 240p.
P4-S05625 — $37.50.

CHENOWETH: Gen. & Chart of the Chenoweth & Cromwell Family of MD & VA. A. C. Chenoweth. 1894. 35p.
P4-S05626 — $10.00.

CHERRY: Ancestry of My Three Children, Lewis W. Cherry, George Denison Cherry, Carolyn Vandegrift Cherry McDonnell. By Lina Vandegrift (Denison) Cherry. 1945. 704p., typescript.
P4-S05631 — $109.00.

CHESEBROUGH: Genealogy of the Descendants of William Chesebrough of Boston, Rehoboth, MA. By A.C. Wildey. 1903. 688p.
P4-S05634 — $86.00.

CHESEBROUGH: Biogr. Sketch of Wm. Chesebrough, First Settler of Stonington, CT. By A. Chesebrough. 1893. 25p.
P4-S05635 — $10.00.

CHESTER: Extr. Gen. & Hist. of Watertown, MA. 8p.
P4-S05637 — $10.00.

CHESTER: Desc. of Leonard Chester of Wethersfield, CT. E. Strong. 1868. 8p.
P4-S05638 — $10.00.

CHESTER: Gen. Notes of the Fam. of Chester, (Eng. & CT) By R.E.C. Waters. 1886. 31p.
P4-S05639 — $10.00.

CHESTER: The Desc. of Christopher Chester, 1796-1896. By A.H. Chester. 1896. 11p.
P4-S05636 — $10.00.

CHESTER: Extr. from Hist. of Wethersfield, CT. 1904. 15p.
P4-S05641 — $10.00.

CHESTON: The NJ Chestons. By F.C Cheston. 1901. 45p.
P4-S05642 — $10.00.

CHETWODE: Family of England, with the Line of Desc to Grace Chetwode, Wife of Peter Bulkeley of Concord, MA. By Frank B. Smith. 1910. 65 + 76p. + charts
P4-S05640 — $24.00.

CHICKERING: ALLEYNE Family of Dedham. By W. Cheney. 1927. 25p.
P4-S05644 — $10.00.

CHILD: Genealogy of the Child, Childs, & Childe Family, in the US & the Canadas By E. Child. 1881. 856p.
P4-S05643 — $105.00.

CHIPMAN: Family: Genealogy of the Chipmans in America, 1631-1920. By Bert Lee Chipman. 1920. 321p.
P4-S05649 — $49.00.

CHIPMAN: Chipmans of America. By A. L. Chipman. 1904. 232p.
P4-S05655 — $34.50.

CHIPMAN: The Chipman lineage, particularly as in Essex Co., MA. By R.M. Chipman. 1872. 59p.
P4-S05658 — $12.00.

CHIPMAN: Family in ME, A Genealogy. By A.L. Chipman. 1897. 44p.
P4-S05650 — $10.00.

CHIPP: Family, in Eng. & Amer., with gen. Tree By C.H. Burnett. 1933. 182p.
P4-S05667 — $29.50.

CHISOLM: Gen; being a record of the name from 1254, with sketches of allied fam. By W. Chisolm. 1914. 101p.
P4-S05673 — $19.50.

CHISOLM: Our Chisolm Clan in America & Connecting Families. E. Doris Chisolm-Cooper. 2000. 331 + 41p.
P4-S05672 — $58.00.

CHITTENDEN: A History of Chittenden-Field Lane, Madison, CT, 1896-1996. David Willis. 1996. 112p.
P4-S05677 — $19.00.

CHITTENDEN: Family; William Chittenden of Guilford, CT & his desc. By A. Talcott. 1882. 263p.
P4-S05676 — $39.00.

CHOATE: Choates in America, 1643-1896: John Choate & his descendants, Chebacco, Ipswich, MA. By E. Jameson. 1896. 474p.
P4-S05679 — $58.00.

CHOUTEAU: Creoles of St. Louis. By P. Beckwith. 1893. 174p.
P4-S05691 — $26.00.

CHOUTEAU: Family: genealogy of descendants of collateral branches, with addendum. By Beatrice C. Turner. 1934. 143 + 5p.
P4-S05685 — $23.00.

CHRISTIAN: Genealogy. By Alfred R. Christian. n.d. 132p., typescript.
P4-S05697 — $19.00.

CHRISTLIEB: Family. By Benj. F. Christlieb. 1895. 52p.
P4-S05700 — $11.00.

CHRISTOPHERS: Genealogy; Jeffrey & Christopher Christophers of New London, CT & their descendants. By J.R. Totten. 1921. 178p.
P4-S05703 — $28.00.

CHURCH: Desc. of Capt. Samuel Church of Churchville. By E. A. Emens. 1920. 80p.
P4-S05709 — $14.00.

CHURCH: Descendants of Richard Church of Plymouth, MA. By J. A. Church. 1913. 354p.
P4-S05715 — $45.00.

CHURCH: Simeon Church of Chester, CT, 1708-1792, & his descendants, By Charles W. Church. 1914. 241p.
P4-S05727 — $38.00.

CHURCH: The hist. of the Church fam. Chase, French & Wade. 1887. 144p.
P4-S05733 — $21.00.

CHURCH: Genealogy & history of the Church family in America, descended from Richard Church of Hartford CT & So Hadley MA By Alice M. Church. 1948. 261 + 90p. typescript.
P4-S05721 — $52.50.

CHURCHILL: Facts concerning the anc. & desc. of Asaph Churchill of Milton. By G.A. Churchill. 1887. 18p.
P4-S05737 — $10.00.

CHURCHILL: Family in America. By G.A. & N.W. Churchill. 1904. 722p.
P4-S05736 — $89.50.

CHURCHILL: Genealogy & biography of the CT branch of the Churchill family in America. By Sam'l J. Churchill. 1901. 109p.
P4-S05742 — $17.00.

CHUTE: Genealogy & history of the Chute family in America By W.E. Chute. 1894. 493p.
P4-S05751 — $63.00.

CHUTE: Family in American in the 20th century. By George M. Chute, Jr. 1967, 123 + 20p.
P4-S05748 — $22.50.

CILLEY: The Cilley Family Roots in New England. A Continuation of Volume I with additions & Corrections. Annie M. Cilley. 2004. xiii + 786p.
P4-S05753 — $118.00.

CILLEY: Fam.; desc. of Robert Seely. By J.P. Cilley. 1878. 47p.
P4-S05754 — $10.00.

CLAFLIN: Genealogy of the Claflin family, being a record of Robt. Mackclothlan, of Wenham, MA & his desc. By C.H. Wight. 1903. 473p.
P4-S05757 — $60.00.

CLAGGETT: Genealogical narrative: history of the Claggett-Irvine clans. By Edith K. Chambers. 1940. 150p.
P4-S05763 — $24.00.

CLAGHORN: The barony of Cleghorne, A.D. 1203, Lanarkshore, Scotland, to the family of Claghorn, A.D. 1912, US. By W.C. Claghorn. 1912. 132p.
P4-S05769 — $24.00.

CLAIBORNE: Pedigree; a gen. table of the desc. of Secretary Wm. Claiborne of the junior branch of the US. By G.M. Claiborne. 1900. 51p.
P4-S05777 — $10.00.

CLAP: Lemuel Clap family chart, 1630-1902-1961. By F.L. Weis. 1961. 59p.
P4-S05772 — $12.00.

CLAPP: Mem. Record of the Clapp family. By E. Clapp. 1876. 536p.
P4-S05784 — $79.00.

CLAPP: Fifty ancestors of Henry Lincoln Clapp, who came to New England, from 1620-1650, parts I & II. Henry Lincoln Clapp. 1902, 1907. 68 + 72p.
P4-S05781 — $25.00.

CLARK: DIXON Family, the ancestry & desc. of James Clark & his wife Jane (Dixon) Clark of Fairton, Cumberland Co., NJ. H. Stanley Craig. n.d. 127 + 14p. P4-S05808 — $22.00.

CLARK: Loyalist Clarks, Badgleys & allied fam. By E. Watson. 1954. 338p. P4-S05874 — $54.00.

CLARK: Genealogies of the Clark, Parks, Brockman & Dean families in three parts. Henry W. Clark. 1905. 371p. P4-S05844 — $56.50.

CLARK: American ancestors of Oratio Dyer Clark & his wife Laura Ann King . . . By John E. Salisbury, enl. By Geo. C. Martin. 1917. 170p. P4-S05796 — $27.00.

CLARK: Ancestry of General Emmons Clark of New York City. 1891. 32p. P4-S05791 — $10.00.

CLARK: Family genealogy in the US, 1541-1907. By Dr A.W. Clark 1907. 149p. P4-S05826 — $25.00.

CLARK: Misc. Clark data (Repr. NEHGR), 6p. P4-S05827 — $10.00.

CLARK: Ancestors of my children & other related children . . . By Wm. C. Clark. 1906. 215p. P4-S05802 — $33.00.

CLARK: Jacob Clark of Abbeville, SC & some of his descendants By Eva T. Clark. 1926. 121p. P4-S05862 — $18.50.

CLARK: Genealogy: some desc. of Daniel Clark of Windsor, CT, 1639-1913. By E. L. Walton. 1913. 278p. P4-S05826 — $42.00.

CLARK: History of the descendants of Cephas Clark, b. Medfield, MA, 1745. By C.W. Clark. 1926. 102p. P4-S05856 — $19.00.

CLARK: Records of the desc. of Hugh Clark of Watertown, MA. By J. Clark. 1866. 261p. P4-S05880 — $39.00.

CLARK: of Elizabethtown in NJ. By Elmer S. Clark. 1942. 223p., typescript. P4-S05832 — $34.50.

CLARK: Deacon George Clark(e), & some of his desc. G.C. Bryant. 1949. 258p. P4-S05838 — $41.00.

CLARK: James Clark, [Robert] Mansfield, Christopher Clark & allied families. By Virginia E.H. McNaught. 1934. 245p., typescript. P4-S05868 — $37.00.

CLARK: A record of the desc. of John Clark of Farmington, CT. By J. Gay. 1882. 94p. P4-S05790 — $18.50.

CLARK: Ebenezer Clark family history. By Audria Clark. 1959? 38p., typescript. P4-S05728 — $10.00.

CLARK: Family. By Ella A. Eustis. 1957. 31p., typescript. P4-S05729 — $10.00.

CLARK: History & genealogy of one branch of the Clark family & its connections By George Washington Clark. 1898. 74p. P4-S05850 — $15.00.

CLARKE: KELLOGG; Some New England families. By Mrs J.A. King. 1922. 207p. P4-S05904 — $31.00.

CLARKE: CLARK Gen.; rec. of the desc. of Thomas Clarke (1623-1697) of Plymouth. 1884. 192p. P4-S05898 — $23.50.

CLARKE: History of Patrick Clarke & Catherin Wade Clarke, their ancestors & descendants. Wm. P. Clarke. 1946. 138p. P4-S05934 — $22.00.

CLARKE: Voyage of Geo. Clarke, Esq., to America, with intro & notes. By E.B. O'Callaghan. 1867. 126p. P4-S05946 — $19.50.

CLARKE: Records of some of the desc. of Thomas Clarke of Plymouth, 1623-1697. By S. C. Clarke. 1869. 43p. P4-S05899 — $10.00.

CLARKE: Clarke's kindred gen. A gen. hist. of certain desc. of Joseph Clarke, Dorchester By A.P. Clarke. 1896. 185p. P4-S05913 — $26.50.

CLARKE: Richard Clarke of Rowley, MA & his desc. in the line of Timothy Clark of Rockingham, VT, 1638-1904. By T.B. Peck. 1905. 93p. P4-S05940 — $18.00.

CLARKE: Anc. of Jeremy Clarke of RI & Dungan gen. By A. R. Justice. 1922. 538p. P4-S05892 — $80.50.

CLARKE: Descendants of Nathaniel Clarke & his wife Elizabeth Somerby of Newbury, MA. By G. K. Clarke. 1902. 468p. P4-S05916 — $55.00.

CLARKE: Ancestry & writings of Rev. Dorus Clarke [of MA]. By Dorus Clarke. 1876. 25p. P4-S05908 — $10.00.

CLARKE: Genealogy of the descendants of Nathaniel Clarke of Newbury By Geo. K. Clarke. 1885. 216p. P4-S05928 — $33.00.

CLARKE: Families of RI. By George A. Morrison, Jr 1902. 337p. P4-S05907 — $43.50.

CLARKE: Genealogy of the descendants of Nathaniel Clarke of Newbury, MA. By Geo. K. Clarke. 1883. 121p. P4-S05922 — $19.00.

CLARKE: Ancestors & descs of Rev. Henry Clarke & his wife Catherine Pendleton, of Madison Co., NY. By Cyrus C. Nan Deventer. 1902. 128p. P4-S05886 — $19.00.

CLARKSON: Memorial of Matthew Clarkson of Phila., 1735-1800, by J. Hall; & of his brother Gerardus, 1737-1790. By S. Clarkson. 1890. 259p. P4-S05952 — $39.00.

CLARY: Desc. of Selected Fams. of Clary, Ruggles, Hooe, Livermore, Murdoch, Fahlen, Murphy, Poikela, Ross, Sibilsky, Sincook. Lawrence T. Fadner. 2005. 201p. P4-S05955 — $30.00.

CLASON: CLAWSON — CLASSON — Classon, Closson, Clauson; Stephen Clason of Stamford, CT. By W. B. Lapham. 1892. 160p. P4-S05958 — $24.00.

CLAUNCH: "Aaron's Ancestry:" Claunch, Littleon & connecting lines. By Brian J.L. Berry. 2000. 190p. P4-S05964 — $27.00.

CLAWSON: "Princess Eleanor," being the genealogy (paternal & maternal) of Mary Eleanor Clawson Knaus. By Francis A. Knaus. 1991. 1109p. P4-S05970 — $129.50.

CLAY: Family of Clay of New Castle, DE & Phildelphia, PA. By Cecil Clay. 1895. 51p.
P4-S05977 — $10.00.

CLAY: Gen. & hist. of the Clay fam. By H. H. Clay. 1916. 159p.
P4-S05976 — $24.00.

CLAYPOOLE: The Claypoole Family in America, volumes I-V. Evelyn Claypoole Bracken 1986. 5 vols in 1, 1158p.
P4-S05979 — $162.00.

CLEEK: Early Western Augusta pioneers, including the families of Cleek, Gwin, Lightner & Warwick, & related families. By Geo. W. Cleek. 1957. 492p.
P4-S05982 — $74.00.

CLEMENS: Clemens fam. chronology, births, marriages, deaths. By W. M. Clemens. 1914. 63p.
P4-S05985 — $12.50.

CLEMENTS: — SPALDING, Origins of Clements-Spalding & allied families of MD & KY, with appendix. By J.W.S. Clements. 1928, 1929. 87 + 11p.
P4-S06000 — $18.00.

CLEMENTS: Ancestors & descendants of Robert Clements of Leicestershire & Warwickshire, Eng., first settler of Haverhill, MA. By P. W. Clement. 1927. 2 vols., 1092p.
P4-S05994 — $163.50.

CLEMENTS: Fam. of Dover, NH, By J. Scales. 1923. 18p.
P4-S05995 — $10.00.

CLEMENTS: Robert Clements of Haverhill, MA & some of his desc. By A.W. Greely. 1911. 18p.
P4-S05996 — $10.00.

CLENDINEN: MYERS — MILLS Families, & various related families in the South. By Baird, Catchings & Torrey. 1923. 181p.
P4-S06006 — $28.00.

CLEVELAND: The Clevelands of Leicestershire, Eng. (Repr. NEHGR). By H. G. Cleveland. 1885. 7p.
P4-S06019 — $10.00.

CLEVELAND: Acct. of the lin. of Gen. Moses Cleaveland of Canterbury, CT. By H. Cleveland. 1885. 14p.
P4-S06020 — $10.00.

CLEVELAND: Gen. of Benj. Cleveland, gr-grandson of Moses Cleveland of Woburn, MA, Native of Canterbury, Windham Co., CT. By H. Cleveland. 1879. 260p.
P4-S06036 — $28.00.

CLEVELAND: Genealogy of the Cleveland-Cleaveland families, Three-volume set By E.J. & H.G. Cleveland. 1899. 3 vols; 2900p.
P4-S06012 — $357.00./set

CLEVELAND: Genealogy of the Cleveland-Cleaveland families, Vol. I By E.J. & H.G. Cleveland. 1899.
P4-S06012A — $125.00.

CLEVELAND: Genealogy of the Cleveland-Cleaveland families, Vol. II By E.J. & H.G. Cleveland. 1899.
P4-S06012B — $125.00.

CLEVELAND: Genealogy of the Cleveland-Cleaveland families, Vol. III By E.J. & H.G. Cleveland. 1899.
P4-S06012C — $125.00.

CLEWELL: History of the Clewell family in the US, 1737-1907. By Lewis B. Clewell & L.P. Clewell. 1907. 391p.
P4-S06042 — $59.50.

CLIFT: PENLAND Family [descendants of Wm. Clift & Mary Penland of Oakdale, TN]. By Essie G. Gaston. 1949. 116p., typescript.
P4-S06048 — $18.00.

CLINE: KLINE Family history. By Floyd R. & Kathryn Garst Mason. 1997. 484p.
P4-S06054 — $62.00.

CLINTON: Fam. of CT. By E.J. Clinton. 1915. 40p.
P4-S06057 — $10.00.

CLOPPER: An American family: eight generations in New Amsterdam, NY, PA, MD, OH & TX. By Edw. N. Clopper. 1950. 624p.
P4-S06060 — $92.50.

CLOPTON: Ancestry of Wm. Clopton of York Co., VA. By Lucy L. Erwin. 1939. 333p.
P4-S06066 — $52.00.

CLOUGH: Genealogy & desc. of John Clough of Salisbury, MA, Volume I. Ed. by E.C. Speare. Pub. By the John Clough Soc. 1952. 511p.
P4-S06072 — $75.00.

CLOUGH: Genealogy & desc. of John Clough of Salisbury, MA, Volume II. 1966. 286p.
P4-S06078 — $43.50.

CLOYD: Genealogy of the Cloyd, Basye & Tapp families in America By A.D. Cloyd. 1912. 297p.
P4-S06084 — $46.50.

CLUVER: Cluverii Chronica: history of the ancient Clawen, the medieval Cluvers, de Clauen, de Claven, de Cluwen, de Kluuen . . . By Herman C. Kluever. 1958. 317p.
P4-S06090 — $47.50.

CLYMER: SOUDER Search. By Winifred L. Holman. 1937. 87p., typescript.
P4-S06096 — $16.50.

COALE: Coale fam. of MD. By I. Coale, Jr. 1933. 8p.
P4-S06099 — $10.00.

COAN: Descs of Capt. Elisha Coan & his wife Mary Atkins Coan of Truro, MA; Castine, ME & Exeter, ME. By Myrtie Fisher Seaverns. 1932. 26p., typescript.
P4-S06100 — $10.00.

COAN: Lineage, with supplement. By W.L. Holman. 1960. 122 + 20p., typescript.
P4-S06102 — $21.50.

COATES: Genealogy of Moses & Susanna Coates, who settled in PA in 1717, & their descendants. By T. Coates. 1906. 319p.
P4-S06108 — $44.00.

COATES: Family Memorials & Recollections; or, Aunt Mary's Patchwork. Mary Coates. 1885. 171 + 34p.
P4-S06107 — $32.00.

COATES: Thomas Coates, Eng. to PA, 1683, & the Coates fam. in Phila. City Dir., 1785-1901. 43p.
P4-S06106 — $10.00.

COBB: History of the Cobb family, pt. 1-4. By P. Cobb. 1907-1923. 278p.
P4-S06111 — $38.50.

COBLEIGH: Genealogy of the Cobleigh family & desc. from the first John Cobleigh & his wife Mary (Bosworth) Cobleigh at Swansea, MA. By Arthur M. Cobleigh. 1960. 757 + 124p., typescript.
P4-S06117 — $105.00.

COCHRAN: Chronicles of the Cochrans. By Ida C. Haughton. 1915, 1925. 147 + 186p.
P4-S06123 — $49.50.

COCHRAN: History & Genealogy of the Cochran Family of Kirkcudbright & NY. comp. by James H. Callender. 1932. 291 + 72p.
P4-S060134 — $56.00.

COCHRANE: The Cochranes of Renfrewshire, Scotland; The anc. of Alexander Cochrane of Billerica & Malden, MA, By W.K. Watkins. 1904. 53p.
P4-S06128 — $11.00.

COCKBURN: The house of Cockburn of that ilk & the cadets thereof. By T. H. Cockburn-Hood. 1888. 394p.
P4-S06129 — $61.00.

COCKRELL: Desc. of Lyttleton Cockrell, Jr, 1802-1877. By Elizabeth S. Stevenson. 1922. 26p.
P4-S06130 — $10.00.

CODDINGTON: Records: descendants of Isaac, Reuben & Uzziah Coddington of Woodbridge, NJ. By Rev. Herbert G. Coddington. 1920. 42p.
P4-S06136 — $10.00.

CODDINGTON: Wm. Coddington in RI Colonial affairs: an historical inquiry. By Henry E. Turner. 1878. 69p.
P4-S06135 — $14.00.

CODDINTON: Records #2, descendants of Wm. & Benj. Coddington of MD. By Rev. Herbert G. Coddington. 1930. 45p.
P4-S06139 — $10.00.

CODMAN: The Codmans of Charlestown & Boston, 1637-1929. By C.C. Wolcott. 1930. 89p.
P4-S06141 — $17.50.

CODY: Family in Amer., 1698: desc. of Philip & Martha of MA, biogr. & gen. comp. By the Cody Fam. Assoc. 1954. 257p.
P4-S06153 — $41.00.

CODY: Family handbook-directory: descendants of Philip & Martha at Beverly, MA, 1698. 1941. 224p.
P4-S06147 — $34.00.

COE: WARD Mem'l, & immigr. ancestors. By L.E. Coe. 1897. 136p.
P4-S06159 — $21.50.

COE: Descendants of Matthew Coe. By Henry F. Coe. 1894. 47p.
P4-S06160 — $10.00.

COE: Robert Coe, Puritan, his anc. & desc., 1340-1910, with notices of other Coe families. J. G. Bartlett. 1911. 664p.
P4-S06162 — $85.00.

COE: Record of the Coe family. By D.B. Coe. 1856. 18p.
P4-S06161 — $10.00.

COFFEY: Thomas Coffey & desc. By L. H. Coffey. 1931. 102p.
P4-S06168 — $19.50.

COFFIN: Life of Tristram Coffyn of Nantucket, MA. A. Coffin. 1881. 64p.
P4-S06189 — $12.50.

COFFIN: "Trustum" & his grand-children [Tristram Coffin of Nantucket]. By "One of Them." 1881. 261p.
P4-S06174 — $39.50.

COFFIN: Gatherings toward a gen. of the Coffin family. W. Appleton. 1896. 53p.
P4-S06175 — $10.00.

COFFIN: Family. 1962. 579p.
P4-S06180 — $59.50.

COFFIN: Early wills illus. the anc. of Harriot Coffin, with gen. & biogr. notes. By W. Appleton 1893. 89p.
P4-S06186 — $18.00.

COFFIN: Armorial bearings & origin of the name (Repr. NEHGR). By J.C.J. Brown. 1881. 8p.
P4-S06176 — $10.00.

COFFIN: Genealogy of the early generations of the Coffin fam. in New England, (repr. NEHGR). By S.J. Macy. 1870. 17p.
P4-S06177 — $10.00.

COFFINBERRY: Genealogy of the Coffinberry family, desc. of George Lewis Coffinberry, & his wife Elizabeth (Little) Coffinberry. comp. By B.B. Scott. 1927. 64p.
P4-S06198 — $13.00.

COGGESHALLS: in Amer.; gen. of the desc. of John Coggeshall of Newport. 1930. 395p.
P4-S06204 — $62.50.

COGHILL: Family of Coghill, continued: supplement to & continuation of "The Family of Coghill (1879)." By Wm. H. Coghill. 1956. 292p.
P4-S06210 — $45.00.

COGSWELL: The Cogswells in America. By E. O. Jameson. 1884. 707p.
P4-S06213 — $85.00.

COGSWELL: A sermon delivered at the funeral of Dr. William Cogswell of Atkinson, NH, 1831, (with Cogswell gen. appendix) By J. Kelly. 16p.
P4-S06214 — $10.00.

COIT: Family: or, the desc. of John Coit, at Salem, MA, in 1638, at Gloucester in 1644, & at New London, CT in 1650. F. W. Chapman. 1874. 341p.
P4-S06219 — $54.00.

COLBURN: Desc. of Isaac Colburn, Jr. of W. Dedham, MA. E. J. Cox. 28p.
P4-S06223 — $10.00.

COLBURN: Genealogy of the desc. of Edward Colburn, come from Eng., 1635. By G.A. Gordon & S.R. Coburn. 1913. 474p.
P4-S06222 — $60.00.

COLBY: History of the Colby family, with genealogical tables. By J.W. Colby 1895. 119p.
P4-S06234 — $22.00.

COLBY: A gen. of the desc. of Abraham Colby & Elizabeth Blaisdell, his wife, who settled in Bow in 1768. By one of them (H. Colby). 1895. 152p.
P4-S06228 — $22.50.

COLBY: Family (of Colby College), something of its hist. in Europe & America, 1931. 24p.
P4-S06229 — $10.00.

COLCORD: Desc. of Edward Colcord of NH. By D.B. Colcord. 1908. 166p.
P4-S06240 — $24.00.

COLE: Ancestry & descendants of Edward Smith Cole of Upper Montclair, NJ, & Little Compton, RI. Benj. F. Wilbour. 1941-1945 200p., typescript.
P4-S06246 — $31.00.

COLE: Genealogy of the family of Cole of the Co. of Devon. By Jas. E. Cole. 1867 66p.
P4-S06267 — $13.00.

COLE: Isaac Kool (Cool or Cole) & Catherine Serven. D. Cole. 1876. 269p.
P4-S06273 — $40.00.

COLE: Descendants of James Cole of Plymouth, 1633 & More. By E. B. Cole. 1908. 449p.
P4-S06261 — $55.00.

For hardcover versions, see the order form on page v. To order, call 1-888-296-3447.

COLE: The early genealogy of the Cole family in America (including Coles & Cowles). F.T. Cole. 1887. 340p. P4-S06276 — $44.50.

COLE: Family of Stark, NH Desc. of Solomon Cole of Beverly, MA, with 1935 supplement. By H.W. Hardon. 1932. 90 + 71p. P4-S06252 — $23.00.

COLEMAN: Extr. from "Gen. Notes of Barnstable Families." 7p. P4-S06283 — $10.00.

COLEMAN: Robert Coleman family from VA to TX, 1652-1965. By J. P. Coleman. 1965. 451p. P4-S06294 — $69.50.

COLEMAN: Descendants of Thomas Coleman, in line of the oldest son. By E. Stearns, ed. By L. Coleman. 1867. 24p. P4-S06284 — $10.00.

COLEMAN: Genealogy of William Coleman of Gloucester. By J.C. Coleman. 1906. 240p. P4-S06282 — $40.00.

COLEMAN: Memoirs of Louis Harrison Coleman, with genealogical notes. Christopher B. Coleman. 1920. 62p. P4-S06285 — $12.50.

COLEMAN: Family: descendants of Thos. Coleman of Nantucket, in line of the oldest son, ten generations, 1602-1898. By Silas B. Coleman. 1898. 36p. P4-S06286 — $10.00.

COLER: Family history & genealogy. By S.J. Williams. 1900. 195p. P4-S06300 — $29.50.

COLES: Family of VA, its numerous connections, from emigration to America to 1915. W.B. Coles. 1931. 885p. P4-S06306 — $125.00.

COLEY: Family of Prudden & Coley of CT (in Goodwin Gen.) By Starr & Goodwin. 1915. 8p. P4-206309 — $10.00.

COLGATE: Robert Colgate, the Immigrant: a Genealogy of the NY Colgates & some associated lines. By T. Abbe & H.A. Howson. 1941. 464p. P4-S06318 — $72.00.

COLHOUN: Family of PA; From Hunter Family of VA. By Sidney M. Culbertson. 1934. 7p. P4-S06320 — $10.00.

COLLAMER: Gen. of the desc. of Anthony Collamer of Scituate, MA. By C. Hatch. 1915. 198p. P4-S06324 — $30.00.

COLLIN: Desc. of John Collin formerly a resident of Milford, CT. By J.F. Collin. 1872. 124p. P4-S06330 — $17.50.

COLLINS: Reminisc. of Isaac & Rachel Budd Collins By J. Collins etc. 1893. 164p. P4-S06351 — $24.50.

COLLINS: Address by Dr. S.C. Beane at the Collins fam. gathering 1892. ed. By L.W. Collins. 1898. 34p. P4-S06340 — $10.00.

COLLINS: Our folks & your folks: a volume of family history & biographical sketches, including the Collins, Hardison, Merrill, Teague & Oak families, & extending over a period of two centuries. By Florence C. Porter & Clara W. Gries. 1919. 246p. P4-S06345 — $38.00.

COLLINS: The Collins Family: Desc of William Collins & Esther Morris, 1760-1897. W.H. Collins. 1897. 188p. P4-S06339 — $28.00.

COLLINS: Henry Collins of Lynn & some of his desc., in Southborough, MA & Fitzwilliam, NH. By A. Collins & C. Pope. 1916. 21p. P4-S06346 — $10.00.

COLLINS: Ancestors & desc. of James Harrah Collins & Jane Hill Collins, of Batavia IA, Monte Vista CO, & Del Norte CO. By Roy E. Collins. 1954. 82p., typescript. P4-S06336 — $16.00.

COLLINS: Edw. & John Collins & their desc. (Repr. NEHGR) By R. D. Smyth. 1907. 8p. P4-S06347 — $10.00.

COLT: Genealogical memoirs of the families of Colt & Coutts. By Charles Rogers. 1879 59p. P4-S06354 — $12.00.

COLTER: Family records of the Colters & Culbertsons, with biographical sketches. By James F. Colter. 1889. 141p. P4-S06363 — $22.00.

COLTON: 1644-1911; A gen. records of the desc. of Quartermaster George Colton. By G.W. Colton. 1912. 598p. P4-S06369 — $89.00.

COLTRANE: Descendants of David Coltrane & James Frazier of NC, By Robert H. Frazier. 1961. 121p. P4-S06375 — $19.50.

COLVER: CULVER Gen., desc. of Edward Colver of Boston, Dedham & Roxbury, MA. & New London & Mystic, CT By F. L. Colver. 1910. 271p. P4-S06381 — $40.50.

COLWELL: Robert Colwell of Providence & his descendants. By Ruth S.D. Eddy. 1936. 66p., typescript. P4-S06387 — $13.00.

COMEY: COMEE Fam. in Amer. Desc. of David Comey of Concord, MA With notes on the Maltman fam. By A. H. Bent. 1896. 50p. P4-S06390 — $10.00.

COMINS: Family: desc. of John Comins of Woburn, MA. By W.B. O'Connor. 1915. 30p. P4-S06391 — $10.00.

COMLY: Family in America; descendants of Henry & Joan Comly who came to America in 1682 from Beaminster, Somerset, Eng. By G.N. Comly. 1939. 1148p. P4-S06393 — $170.00.

COMLY: Supplement to Comly Family in America, Being additions and Corrections to the volume published in 1939. George Norwood Comly 1952. 145p. P4-S06399 — $24.00.

COMPTON: Family & direct ancestors of Herman Everett Compton, 0006-1996. By Nancy L. Baron Compton. 1996. 504p. P4-S06405 — $74.50.

COMSTOCK: Genealogy: descendants of William Comstock of New London, CT, who died after 1662, ten generations. By Cyrus B. Comstock. 1907. 314p. P4-S06411 — $47.50.

COMSTOCK: History & gen. of the Comstock fam. in America. By J.A. Comstock. 1949. 715p. P4-S06417 — $99.50.

COMSTOCK: Anc. of Richard Wilmot Comstock. By H.M. Pitman. 1964. 452p. P4-S06423 — $69.50.

CONANT: Genealogy. By F.O. Conant. 1914 44p. P4-S06427 — $10.00.

CONANT: History & genealogy of the Conant family in Eng. & Amer., 1520-1887. By F.O. Conant. 1887. 654p. P4-S06426 — $94.00.

CONANT: Roger Conant, a founder of MA. Clifford K. Shipton. 1944. 171p. P4-S06432 — $25.00.

CONARD: Descendants of John Conard of Loudoun Co., VA. By Amy M. Bowen 1939. 91p., typescript. P4-S06438 — $18.00.

CONDIT: Genealogical rec. of the Condit fam., desc. of John Cunditt, a native of Gt. Brit. who settled in Newark, NJ By J.H. & E. Condit. 1916. Rev.ed. 470p. P4-S06444 — $69.50.

CONE: Some account of the Cone family in America, principally the descendants of Daniel Cone By W.W. Cone. 1903. 546p. P4-S06450 — $84.00.

CONEY: Ancestors & descendants of John Coney of Boston, England & Boston, MA. Mary L. Holman. 1928. 319p. P4-S06456 — $47.00.

CONGDON: Great Grandma was a Congdon: some lines of descent of John Congdon of Wales. By Earl P. Crandall. 1995. 462p. P4-S06468 — $69.50.

CONGDON: One hundred thirty-eight gen. from Adam By G. E. Congdon. 1910. 55p. P4-S06463 — $11.00.

CONGDON: Congdon chronicle, #1-18. By G.E. Congdon. 1921-1934. 240p. P4-S06462 — $36.00.

CONGER: The Conger family in America: desc. of John Belconger, 1640, & his six sons. By Helen Maxine C. Leonard. 1972. 844p. P4-S06480 — $99.50.

CONGER: Record of births, marr. & deaths of the desc. of John Conger of Woodbridge, NJ. By C.G.B. Conger. 1903. 165p. P4-S06474 — $25.50.

CONKLING: Salem, MA & the Conkling fam. F. J. Conkling. 1894. 11p. P4-S06481 — $10.00.

CONNET: Hist. & gen. of author's branch of the Connet fam. By A. Connet. 1905. 53p. P4-S06482 — $10.00.

CONNIN: Brief study in genealogy: Connin, Conny, Cony, Coney, Cony. By Jos. H. Williams. 1885. 39p. P4-S06483 — $10.00.

CONRAD: Clan; Family of John Stephen Conrad, Sr, & allied lines. By F.W. Coffman. 1939. 355p. P4-S06486 — $52.50.

CONVERSE: Some anc. & desc. of Sam'l Converse, Jr., Maj. James Convers, Hon. Heman Allen, Capt. Jonathan Bixby, Sr. By C. Converse. 1905. 2 vols., 989p. P4-S06504 — $132.00.

CONVERSE: Fam. records of Deacons James W. Converse & Elias S. Converse By W. G. Hill. 1887. 246p. P4-S06498 — $37.00.

CONVERSE: Fam. hist. in the line of Jos. Converse of Bedford, MA, 1739-1828. By J. J. Putnum. 1897. 97p. P4-S06492 — $15.00.

COOK: Family history. By J. Montgomery Seaver. 32p. P4-S06511 — $10.00.

COOKE: The Cooke anc. By Van Dycke & Cooke. 1960. 162p. P4-S06534 — $27.50.

COOKE: Family of Elizha Cooke. By Florence ooke Newberry. 1934. 202p. P4-S06528 — $32.00.

COOKE: Desc. of Mordecai Cooke of "Mordecai's Mount" & Thomas Booth of Ware Neck, Gloucester Co., VA, By Dr & Mrs W.C. Stubbs. 1923. 286 + 35p. P4-S06522 — $49.50.

COOKE: Book: Cooke ancestry. By J.N. VanDyke. 1960. 114 + 28p. P4-S06516 — $23.00.

COOKE: Cooke Family: Descendants & Relatives of Francis of the Mayflower, 1577-1820. (n.d.) 295p. P4-S06517 — $44.00.

COOLBAUGH: Family in American, from their earliest appearance at New Amsterdam, 1686-1938 By Edw. Coolbaugh Hoagland. 1938. 71p. P4-S06540 — $15.00.

COOLBAUGH: Rec. of desc. of Wm. Coolbaugh, 1765-1918. 40p. P4-S06547 — $10.00.

COOLBAUGH: Twigs from family trees, or 162 early American & Foreign lineages of first settlers in this country Edw. Coolbaugh Hoagland. 1940. 192p. P4-S06552 — $29.00.

COOLBAUGH: More twigs from family trees (Coolbaugh & allied families). By Edward C. Hoagland. 1954-1956 101p. P4-S06546 — $17.50.

COOLEY: Genealogy: desc. of Ensign Benj. Cooley, early settler of Springfield & Longmeadow, MA. By M.E. Cooley. 1941. 1199p. P4-S06558 — $149.00.

COOLEY: Descendants of Dr Asahel & Sally Wilbur Cooley (suppl. to "Cooley Gen."). A.S. Cooley. 1952. 153p. P4-S06564 — $23.00.

COOLIDGE: Genealogy of some desc. of John Coolidge of Watertown, 1630. 1892. 32p. P4-S06571 — $10.00.

COOLIDGE: One branch of the Coolidge family, 1427-1963. By F.C. Crawford. 1964. 91p. P4-S06576 — $17.50.

COOLIDGE: Descendants of John & Mary Coolidge of Watertown, MA, 1630. By E.D. Coolidge. 1930. 418p. P4-S06570 — $58.00.

COOMBS: The story of Anthony Coombs & his desc. By W. C. Coombs. 1913. 226p. P4-S06582 — $38.00.

COON: The Koon-Coons fams. of Eastern NY: hist. of the desc. of Matthaies Kuntz & Samuel Kuhn By W.S. Coons. 1937. 502p. P4-S06588 — $78.50.

COOPER: Thomas Cooper of Boston & his desc. By F. Tuckerman. 1890. 13p. P4-S06595 — $10.00.

COOPER: Family of Buckingham-shire, England, & Long Island. By Art Reierson. 1998. 187p. P4-S06600 — $27.00.

COOPER: History & gen., 1681-1931. By M. Cooper 1931. 116p. P4-S06594 — $22.50.

COOPER: Desc. of Peter Cooper of Rowley, MA (repr. MHGR) By A.K. Cooper. 1885. 11p.
P4-S06596 — $10.00.

COPE: Records of the family of Cope. By Emma E. Cope. 1901 31p.
P4-S06607 — $10.00.

COPE: Memoirs of the Copes of Wiltshire. J.C Biddle-Cope. 1882? 100p.
P4-S06606 — $19.00.

COPE: Record of the Cope family, as established in America by Oliver Cope By Gilbert Cope. 1861. 251p.
P4-S06612 — $38.00.

COPELAND: Family: A Copeland genealogy. W.T. Copeland. 1937. 821p.
P4-S06618 — $114.50.

COPINGER: History of the Copingers or Coppingers of the County of Cork, Ireland & the Counties of Suffolk & Kent, England. Walter Arthur Copinger. 1884. vi + 428p.
P4-S06620 — $66.00.

COPLEY: Thomas Copley of Suffield, CT & his desc. (Repr. NEHGR) By L. M. Dewey. 1910. 5p.
P4-S06621 — $10.00.

COPP: Family of NH. By Frank M. Ferrin. 1940. 173p., typescript.
P4-S06624 — $28.00.

COPPAGE: COPPEDGE Family bulletin, Vol. I. 1950. 55p.
P4-S06631 — $11.00.

COPPAGE: COPPEDGE Family, 1542-1955. By Monahan & Coppage. 1955. 126p.
P4-S06630 — $25.00.

COQUILLETTE: History of James Coquillette & Celestia Wayne Burnside Qoquitte & Their ancestors & descendants. Emma E. Flint 1891. 46p.
P4-S06635 — $10.00.

CORBETT: Gen. of the Corbett fam., By E. Corbett. 1917. 85p.
P4-S06636 — $17.50.

CORBETT: Fam. in Eng. & Amer. By H.R. Corbett. 8p.
P4-S06637 — $10.00.

CORBIN: The Corbins of Virginia: gen. record of the descs of Henry Corbin, who settled in VA in 1654. By Return Jonathan Meigs. 1940. 49p., typescript.
P4-S06643 — $11.00.

CORBIN: History & genealogy of the descendants of Clement Corbin of Muddy River (Brookline), MA & Woodstock, CT. H. Lawson. 1905. 378p.
P4-S06642 — $58.50.

CORBOULD: Genealogy [in England]. G.C.B. Poulter. 1935. 165p.
P4-S06648 — $25.00.

CORDELL: Records: a VA family. By Allan S. Humphreys. 1940. 103p.
P4-S06654 — $19.00.

CORDER: Wm. Corder of Barbour Co., WV. By H.B. Grant. 1934. 14p.
P4-S06655 — $10.00.

COREY: Fam. of Southampton & Southold, L.I., NY, 1644-1779. By L.D. Akerly. 1900. 12p.
P4-S06656 — $10.00.

CORLETT: Family in America. By Elsie C. Hamilton. 1952. 128p.
P4-S06660 — $19.00.

CORLEY: Genealogy of Corleys beginning with Caniel Corley of Bedford Co., VA. By DeWitt C. Corley. 1927. 222p.
P4-S06666 — $34.00.

CORLISS: Genealogical record of the Corliss fam. of Amer. By A. W. Corliss (& others). 1875. 343p.
P4-S06672 — $54.00.

CORN: Our family tree [Corn family with related families of Barker, Perry, Leonard, Cole, Taylor, Glenn & Lewallen,] By Si & Shirley Corn. 1959. 449p., typescript.
P4-S06678 — $67.00.

CORNELIUS: History of the Cornelius family in America: Historical, genealogical & biographical. By C.S. & S.F. Cornelius. 1926. 292p.
P4-S06684 — $46.00.

CORNELIUS: Volume 2, containing supplemental information & additions & corrections to 1929, with historical & biographical sketches. By Chas. S. Cornelius. 1929. 116p.
P4-S06690 — $19.00.

CORNELL: Family: descendants of George Cornell (b.1550, Essex, England) in England & NY. By Art Reierson. 1998. 339p.
P4-S06696 — $51.00.

CORNELL: Genealogy of the Cornell family, being an acct. of the desc. of Thomas Cornell of Portsmouth, RI. By J. Cornell. 1902. 468p.
P4-S06699 — $59.50.

CORNEWALL: The House of Cornewall [family in England]. By C. Reade. 1908 316p.
P4-S06705 — $47.50.

CORNING: Samuel Corning of Beverly, MA & his Nova Scotia desc. By G. S. Brown. 1897. 15p.
P4-S06706 — $10.00.

CORNISH: Cornish gen. By C. N. Sinnett. 1922. 26p.
P4-S06709 — $10.00.

CORNISH: History & genealogy of the Cornish family in America. By J. E. Cornish. 1907. 353p.
P4-S06708 — $45.00.

CORNMAN: CORMAN — KORMAN Genealogical record of descendants of Ludwig Kornman, Sr., in America. By Chas. A. Cornman. 1916. 168p.
P4-S0614 — $26.00.

CORNWALL: Wm. Cornwall & his desc. By E. Cornwall. 1901. 185p.
P4-S06717 — $28.00.

CORNWALL: Family of Wm. Cornwall. By E.E. Cornwall. 1895. 6p.
P4-S06718 — $10.00.

CORRY: History of the Corry family of Castlecoole. By the Earl of Belmore. 1891. 296 + 13p.
P4-S06723 — $46.50.

CORSER: Genealogy of the Corser family in America By Samuel B.G. Corser & Elwood S. Corser. 1902. 336p.
P4-S06729 — $52.00.

CORSON: The Corson Family: A Hist of the Desc of Benjamin Corson. H.Corson. 1906? 192 + 62p.
P4-S06742 — $38.00.

CORSON: Three hundred years with the Corson fams. in America By O. Corson. 1939 2 vols., 303 + 336p.
P4-S06735 — $97.00.

CORWIN: William Corwin family [descendants of Wm. Corwin of NJ & PA]. By Art Reierson. 1998. 86p.
P4-S06759 — $17.00.

CORWIN: Genealogy (Curwin, Curwen, Corwine) in the US. By E.T. Corwin. 1872. 318p.
P4-S06753 — $47.50.

CORY: James Cory & Susan Mulford [ancestry]. 1922. 72p.
P4-S06777 — $14.00.

CORY: Lineal anc. of Rhoda Axtell Cory, mother of Capt. James Cory: gen., hist., & biogr., pts. 1 & 2. By C.H. Cory, Jr. 1937. 300p.
P4-S06783 — $44.00.

CORY: Lineal anc. of Susan Kitchell Mulford, mother of Susan Mulford Cory: gen., hist. & biogr., pts. 1 & 2. By C.H. Cory, Jr. 1937. 295p.
P4-S06789 — $43.50.

CORY: Family genealogy, with brief records of many branches of the Cory family in America. By Harry H. Cory. 1941. 117p.
P4-S06771 — $19.00.

CORY: Ancestral lines of Thomas Judd Cory, Clarence Richard Cory & John Harry Cory . . . By H.T. Cory 1943. 270p., typescript.
P4-06765 — $42.00.

CORY: Lineal anc. of Susan Mulford Cory, wife of Capt. James Cory: gen., hist., & biogr., pts. 1 & 2. By C.H. Cory, Jr. 1937. 437p.
P4-S06795 — $64.00.

CORY: Some chronicles of the Cory family relating to Eliakim & Sarah Sayre & their descendants By Harriett C. Dickinson. 1914. 113 + 21p.
P4-S06801 — $19.00.

COSSIT: Family: genealogical history of Rene Cossitt, a Frenchman who settled in Granby, CT, a.d. 1717 & His descendants. By P.S. Cossitt & F.H. White. 1925. 220p.
P4-S06807 — $35.00.

COTTON: Fam. of Portsmouth, NH. By F. E. Cotton. 26p.
P4-S06814 — $10.00.

COTTON: Eng. anc. of Rev. John Cotton of Boston. By H. G. Somerby. 1868. 12p.
P4-S06815 — $10.00.

COTTON: A short biogr. of Rev. John Cotton of Boston & gen. of his Cotton desc. By L. Cooley. 1945. 125p.
P4-S06816 — $24.00.

COUCH: Ancestors & desc. of Joseph Couch & Deborah Adams. By J.J.W. Howes. (1946?) 22p.
P4-S06818 — $10.00.

COUENHOVEN: The Couenhovens & kinsfolk: some descendants of Wolphert Gerritse vanKouenboven & Neehtje Janse By Lincoln C. Cocheu. 1947. 93p., typescript.
P4-S06819 — $18.00.

COULTRAP: CRAMBLIT; Data concerning the Coultrap-Cramblit lineage, including Eichors, Randals, Simms & their descendants By M.W. Coultrap. 1938. 133p.
P4-S06825 — $21.50.

COUNTER: Genealogy of the Counter family, primarily of Chas. Counter, son of George & Alice Caunter. Wm. Charles Counter. 1955. 94p.
P4-S06831 — $18.50.

COUNTRYMAN: Genealogy. By Alvin Countryman. 1925. 364p.
P4-S06837 — $55.00.

COUNTRYMAN: Genealogy, 1925-1963; Suppl. to earlier book. 1963 32p.
P4-S06838 — $10.00.

COURSEN: Coursens from 1612-1917, with the Staten Island branch. By P. G. Ullman. 1917. 88p.
P4-S06843 — $18.00.

COURTICE: Family tree. By Cyril C. Jeffrey. 1952. 82p., typescript.
P4-S06849 — $16.00.

COURTNEY: Courtney fam. of E. TN (Extr. from Gen. of Some E. TN Fam.) 1945. 20p.
P4-S06850 — $10.00.

COURTRIGHT: KORTRIGHT Family, descendants of Bastian Van Kortryk, a native of Belgium who emigrated to Holland about 1615. By John H. Abbott. 1922. 147p.
P4-S06861 — $23.50.

COURTRIGHT: History of the Van Kortryks or Courtrights, also families Staudt, Vattier, Moore. By Dudley V. Courtright. 1924. 105p.
P4-S06867 — $17.50.

COURTRIGHT: Ancestors & descendants of Rheuben Courtright. By Pardon & Harriett Head. 1915. 79p.
P4-S06855 — $15.50.

COURTWRIGHT: A family name. By Morris Courtwright, Jr. 1985-1998 34p.
P4-S06856 — $10.00.

COVERT: Covert anc. By Jones & Horton. 1906. 20p.
P4-S06868 — $10.00.

COVERT: Bassett's notes on Covert. By L.A. Bryan. 1957. 32p.
P4-S06869 — $10.00.

COVINGTON: The Covingtons: being a collection of family info. By W.S. Covington. 1942. 201.
P4-S06879 — $32.00.

COVINGTON: Cousins, a genealogy of the Covingtons & some related families. By Eurie C. White. 1956. 151p., typescript.
P4-S06873 — $24.00.

COWAN: History of the Cowan family, with list of descendants of Dr James Jones Cowan & Sarah Ann Cook Cowan. By Dr Zachary S. Cowan & Martha W. Cowans. 1959? 71p., typescript.
P4-S06885 — $14.50.

COWAN: Chronological genealogy of James Cowan, Sr., & his descendants. By Julia E. Sellers. 1911-1919. 44p.
P4-S06886 — $10.00.

COWAN: Henry Cowan family of VA. Frank B. Lamb. 1950 (?) 43p., typescript
P4-S06887 — $10.00.

COWDEN: GILLILAND; Illustrated hist. & biogr. sketch of the desc. of William Cowden, (with charts). By R. Cowden. 1915. 179p.
P4-S06897 — $27.50.

COWDEN: Southern Cowdens. By John B. Cowden. 1933. 112p.
P4-S06903 — $19.00.

COWDEN: Ancestry & kin of the Cowden & Welch families. By Rev. James M. Welch. 1904. 203p.
P4-S06891 — $32.00.

COWDREY: COWDERY – COWDRAY Gen.; Wm. Cowdery of Lynn, MA, 1630 & his desc., By M.B.A. Mehling. 1911. 451p.
P4-S06909 — $69.50.

COWIE: North American descendants of Wm. Cowie. By George E. Sands. 1946. 145p.
P4-S06915 — $23.00.

COWING: Genealogy of the Cowing family. Janet McKay Cowing. 1923. 11p.
P4-S06917 — $10.00.

COWLES: Genealogy of the Cowles families in America. By C.D. Cowles. 1929. 2 vols., 1510p.
P4-S06921 — $198.00.

COX: TAYLOR Families. By Nora Hawkins. 1963? 80p., typescript.
P4-S06933 — $15.50.

COX: Families of Holderness, with partial gen. of the Cox, Randall, Nutter & Pickering fams. By L.S. Cox. 1939. 235p.
P4-S06939 — $37.00.

COX: Additions & corrections for "The Cox families of Holderness." 1949, 1957 58 + 90p.
P4-S06927 — $21.00.

COX: History & genealogy of the Cock-Cocks-Cox family, descended from James & Sarah Cock of Oysterbay, Long Isl. By Geo. W. Cocks, with John Cox, Jr. 1914. 2nd ed. 415p.
P4-S06969 — $62.50.

COX: Genealogy; Some materials towards a history of the early Cox families of New England. By John H. Cox. 1899. 143p.
P4-S06951 — $25.00.

COX: Family of Delaware River. 7p.
P4-S06934 — $10.00.

COX: Descendants of Solomon Cox of Cole Creek, VA. W.E. Cox. 1955. 89p.
P4-S06963 — $17.50.

COX: Family in America: history & genealogy of the older branches of the family By H.M. Cox. 1912. 325 + 11p.
P4-S06945 — $51.00.

COX: Ancestors & Descendants of Jehu Cox. W.D. Stout. 1957. 394p.
P4-S06935 — $59.00.

COX: Joseph Cox, ancestors & descendants. By Stanley M. Cox. 1955. 144p., typescript.
P4-S06975 — $24.00.

COX: Descendants of John Cox. By C.S. Williams. 1909. 89p.
P4-S06957 — $17.50.

COXE: & Connected families. By Douglas Merritt. 1915. 49p.
P4-S06976 — $10.00.

COXE: Family. By F.W. Leach & A. duBin. 1938. 60p.
P4-S06978 — $12.00.

CRAFTS: Nabby Crafts & her family. By Tenah Porter. 1908. 47p.
P4-S06988 — $10.00.

CRAFTS: Family; A gen. & biogr. hist. of the desc. of Griffin & Alice Craft of Roxbury, MA, 1630-1890. By J.M. & W.F. Crafts. 1893. 807p.
P4-S06987 — $99.00.

CRAGIN: Gen. of the Cragin fam. By C. H. Cragin. 1860. 42p.
P4-S06989 — $10.00.

CRAIG: Samuel Craig, Sr., Pioneer to Western PA & His Desc. By Jane M. Craig. 1915. 143p.
P4-S06993 — $23.00.

CRAIG: Fam. of PA, 1708-1895. By W.M. Clemens. 1921. 12p.
P4-S06994 — $10.00.

CRAIG: The Craigs of Goulbourn & N. Gower. James B. Craig. 1929. 220p.
P4-S06999 — $33.50.

CRALL: Anc. of Leander Howard Crall, monographs on the Crell, Haff, Beatty & others. F. Allaben. 1908. 426p.
P4-S07005 — $66.50.

CRAMPTON: Fam. of Guildford, CT. By H. Johnston. 1949. 8p.
P4-S07007 — $10.00.

CRANDALL: Elder John Crandall of RI & his desc. J.C. Crandall. 1949. 797p.
P4-S07011 — $109.00.

CRANDALL: Gen. of Elder John Crandall & his desc. By A. P. Crandall. 1888. 62p.
P4-S07014 — $12.50.

CRANDALL: A New England Childhood. Dorothy Crandall Bliss. 1997. 63 + 30p.
P4-S07013 — $17.50.

CRANDALL: One Crandall Family, 1651-1996. Alice Crandall Park. 1996. vii + 166p.
P4-S07015 — $26.00.

CRANDALL: Supplement to One Crandall Family, 1651-1996 Alice Crandall Park. 1999. 83p
P4-S07012 — $17.00.

CRANE: A branch of the Crane family tree. By Elinor Lexington et al. 1923. 21p.
P4-S07024 — $10.00.

CRANE: Family history. By Sarah S. Crane. 1911. 67p.
P4-S07023 — $13.50.

CRANE: Henry Crane of Milton, MA, 1654, & some of his desc. By E. W. Leavitt. 1893. 29p.
P4-S07025 — $10.00.

CRANE: Green is the Valley, Blue are the Hills; or The Search for My Irish and PA Dutch Roots. Thomas J. Crane. 1986. 241 + 80p
P4-S07026 — $42.00.

CRANE: Genealogy of the Crane family, descendants of Henry Crane of Wethersfield & Guilford, CT, By E. Crane. 1900. 2 vols., 839p.
P4-S07029 — $115.00.

CRANMER: Gen. memoir of the kindred families of Thomas Cranmer, archbishop of Canterbury, & Thomas Wood, Bishop of Lichfield. By Robert E.C. Waters. 1877. 162p.
P4-S07035 — $24.50.

CRAPO: Certain comeoverers. By H. H. Crapo. 1912. 2 vols., 1044p.
P4-S07041 — $139.00.

CRARY: Peter Crary of Groton, CT & his desc., (Repr. NEHGR) By L. M. Dewey. 1907. 9p.
P4-S07042 — $10.00.

CRAUN: Family in America, & its connections with other families. By Victor S. Craun. 1950. 354p.
P4-S07047 — $55.00.

CRAWFORD: "Laurus Crawfurdiana": Memorials of that branch of the Crawford family, with decendants of John Crawford of VA. By Robert Leighton Crawford. 1883. 185p.
P4-S07053 — $28.50.

CRAWFORD: The William Crawford Memorial. John Crawford and Jennings Crawford. 1904. 298p.
P4-S07054 — $45.00.

CRAWFORD: Early ancestors of the Crawfords in America By Fred E. Crawford. 1940. 81p.
P4-S07065 — $16.00.

CRAWFORD: Histories of the families of James & Martha Crawford & of John & Isabella Whitesides. By Amelia C. Ferguson & Margaret C. Pearson. 1939. 65p.
P4-S07071 — $13.00.

CRAWFORD: Partial record of the descendants of James Crawford & his wife Huldah Thompson Crawford, of Brunswick ME. By Chauncey E. Crawford. 1947. 315p., typescript.
P4-S07077 — $46.00.

CRAWFORD: Family records. By W.M. Clemens. 1914. 30p.
P4-S07055 — $10.00.

CRAWFORD: Genealogy. By Lucinda F. Stephens. 1936. 203p.
P4-S07059 — $32.00.

CRAWFORD: The Crawfords of Adams Co., OH. By H. Marjorie Crawford. 1943. 110p.
P4-S07083 — $18.50.

CRENSHAW: Fam. record. (in Valentine Papers). 70p.
P4-S07089 — $14.00.

CRESAP: The story of Thos. Cresap, a MD pioneer. By Lawrence C. Writh. 1928. 44p.
P4-S07096 — $10.00.

CRESAP: History of the Cresaps. By J. & B. Cresap. 1937. 506p.
P4-S07095 — $76.50.

CRESSEY: Gen. of the Cressey fam., desc. of Mighill Cressey (Mighel Cresse) of Salem & Ipswich, MA (Repr. NEHGR) G. Blodgette. 1877. 13p.
P4-S07102 — $10.00.

CRESSEY: Story of your ancestors: Cressey, 286 years in America. By Ernest W. Cressy. 1935. 155p.
P4-S07101 — $24.00.

CREW: Genealogy, 1397-1966. By L. Frank Bedell. 1969. 59 + 22p.
P4-S07107 — $17.00.

CREWS: My kinsfolk: story & geneal. of the Crews, Sampson, Wilber & Waddel families. By Laura E. Crews. 1941. 169p.
P4-S07113 — $24.50.

CRISPE: History of the Crispe family . . . in the Old World & the New World. By B.J. Cigrand. 1901. 409p.
P4-S07119 — $61.50.

CRISPELL: Descendants of Anthony Crispell, 1660-1950, PA branch. By E. Cobleigh. 1950. 102p.
P4-S07125 — $19.50.

CRISPIN: The Crispins of Kingston-on-Hull. M. Jackson Crispin. 1928. 20p.
P4-S07132 — $10.00.

CRISPIN: Biographical & historical sketch of Capt. Wm. Crispin of the British Navy By Rev. Wm. F. Crispin. 1901. 144p.
P4-S07131 — $24.00.

CROCKER: Nathaniel Crocker, 1758-1855, his descendants & ancestors By Henry G. Crocker. 1923. 76p.
P4-S07143 — $15.00.

CROCKER: Genealogy [descendants of Wm. Crocker of Barnstable MA, 1612-1692]. By J.R. Crocker, et al. 1962? 246 + 75p.
P4-S07137 — $49.00.

CROCKETT: Family & connecting lines [Vol. V, "Notable Southern Fams."]. By French & Armstrong. 1928. 611p.
P4-S07149 — $91.00.

CROCKETT: Fam. of New Eng., 1632-1943. By O. Crockett. 1943. 41p.
P4-S07150 — $10.00.

CROFT: Genealogy of the Croft family [of SC]. Robert Wilson. 1901 46p.
P4-S07151 — $10.00.

CROMWELL: The House of Cromwell. A gen. hist. of the fam. & desc. of the Protector (incl. Amer. desc.). By J. Waylen; rev. By J. G. Cromwell. 1897. 298p.
P4-S07155 — $48.00.

CRONE: History of the Crone, Pence, Switzer, Weaver, Heatwole, Stout, Steel & Fissell families By F.L. Crone. 1916. 50p.
P4-S07156 — $10.00.

CROOK: An American family, 1698-1955: documented genealogy By Chas. Henry Leavitt. 1956. 254p.
P4-S07161 — $34.00.

CROOM: Family. By Doris C. Outlaw. 1955-1957 332p., typescript.
P4-S07167 — $51.00.

CROSBY: A Crosby fam. Josiah Crosby, Sarah Fitch, & their desc. By N. Crosby. 1877. 143p.
P4-S07173 — $23.00.

CROSBY: Simon Crosby, the emigrant; his Eng. anc. & some of his Amer. desc. E.D. Crosby. 1914. 183p.
P4-S07194 — $26.50.

CROSBY: Family line, chiefly concerning Benj. Lewis Crosby, 1797-1893, of Halcott Ctr., Greene Co., NY. Emerson C. Kelly. 1957. 75p., typescript.
P4-S07185 — $15.00.

CROSBY: Crosby anc., Robert, Jonah & Joel Crosby of ME. By M. A. Crosby. 1939. 70p.
P4-S07176 — $12.50.

CROSBY: Crosbys of Henry Co., IL, 1851-1936. Eva M.C. Kellogg. 1951. 230p.
P4-S07191 — $35.00.

CROSLAND: Family of Edward & Ann Snead Crosland, 1740-1957. By Lulu C. Ricaud. 1958. 546p.
P4-S07200 — $83.00.

CROSS: HOWELL — GLOVER — Stoddert & Related Families. comp. by Kate A. C. Vandervelde 1959. 125p.
P4-S07207 — $19.00.

CROSS: Memoir of the Cross family. By Alfred E. Goodman. n.d. 168p.
P4-S07206 — $25.00.

CROSS: Wm. Cross of Botetourt Co., VA & his descendants, 1733-1932. By J.N. Cross & M.C. Cole. 1932. 258p.
P4-S07218 — $39.50.

CROSS: My children's ancestors; N.E. ancestors of Roselle Theodore Cross & his wife, Emma Asenath (Bridgman) Cross. By R. T. Cross. 1913. 212p.
P4-S07212 — $31.50.

CROUCH: Family of Stafford, CT & some other descendant of Wm. Crouch of Charlestown, MA, 1654. By Grace O. Chapman. 1943. 36p., typescript.
P4-S07225 — $10.00.

CROUCH: The Crouches, 1627-1998. By Eleanor Crouch with Marilyn Labbe. 2003 232 +36p.
P4-S07224 — $40.00.

CROWE: John Crowe & his desc. By L. Crowell. 1903. 109p.
P4-S07227 — $19.00.

CROWEL: History, or "Footprints in the sands of time." H. Crowel. 1899. 55p.
P4-S07228 — $11.00.

CROWELL: Hist & Gen of the Crowell & Allied Fams. K.W. Buchanan. 1938. 73 + 30p.
P4-S07229 — $16.00.

CRUMB: Genealogy: desc. of Daniel Crumb of Westerly, RI. By C.C. Fisk. 1956. 310p.
P4-S07233 — $47.00.

CUBBERLEY: Genealogy of the Cubberley family. By Bertha C. Righter & Sharon Cubberley. 1968. 380 + 29p., index, typescript.
P4-S07239 — $59.00.

CUDAHY: Patrick Cudahy: His Life. Patrick Cudahy. 1912. 290 + 18p.
P4-S07241 — $46.00.

CULBERTSON: Genealogy of the Culbertson-Culberson family who came to Amer. Before the year 1800 By L. Culbertson. 1923. Rev. ed. 477p.
P4-S07251 — $74.50.

CULBERTSON: Family of PA & OH; From Hunter Family of VA. By Sidney M. Culbertson. 1934. 12p.
P4-S07246 — $10.00.

CULBERTSON: John Culbertson, Ransom Thacker, John Cummings & related families. By A.B. Culbertson. 1962? 28p., typescript.
P4-S07247 — $10.00.

CULLISON: Descendants from MD Westward: Baltimore County roots. By Norma L. Cullison Myers. 2000. 717p.
P4-S07257 — $105.00.

CULLISON: Descendants from MD Westward, St. Mary's County Roots; Also Some VA Families. Volume II. By J.R. Cullison, J. Painter, M.E. Miller & N.L.C. Myers. 2001. 334 + 61p.
P4-S07257 — $59.50.

CULPEPER: Proprietors of the Northern Neck: chapters of Culpeper genealogy. Fairfax Harrison. 1926. 178p.
P4-S07263 — $25.00.

CULVER: BUELL; Genealogy of Reuben Culver & Oliver Buell Culver By Reuben D. Culver. 1921-1924. 51p.
P4-S07270 — $10.00.

CULVER: LODER Genealogy. By F. G. Lewis. 1940. 13p.
P4-S07271 — $10.00.

CULVER: The ancestry of Donald Colburn Culver & Related familiies Acie (Agee), Atwood, Bachelder, etc. 1933. 90p., typescript.
P4-S07275 — $18.00.

CULVER: Genealogical notes on the family of Fred Wm. Culver (Culver, Backus, Baldwin, Caulkins, Close, etc.), By Mrs F.W. Culver. 1925. 71p., typescript.
P4-S07269 — $14.00.

CUMMINGS: Our Cummings Family: A Chronicle of Some Plain New England People, Books 1-3. L.B. Cummings. 1953. 392p; typescript
P4-S07279 — $59.00.

CUMMINGS: Isaac Cummings of Topsfield, MA & some of his desc. By M. Clark & others. 1899. 39p.
P4-S07280 — $10.00.

CUMMINGS: Memorial; gen. hist. of the desc. of Isaac Cummings, an early settler of Topsfield, MA. By G. Mooar. 1903. 535p.
P4-S07278 — $67.50.

CUMMINGS: Isaac Cummings, 1601-1677, of Ipswich in 1638, & some of his desc. By A.O. Cummins. 1904. 661p.
P4-S07284 — $99.00.

CUNNABELL: Genealogical memoir of the Cunnabell, Conable or Connable fam. 1650-1886. By Connable & Newcomb. 1886. 187p.
P4-S07290 — $34.50.

CUNNABELL: Pictorial genealogy of the Cunnabell, Connable, Conable family, 1886-1935 (Vol. II of 1886 book, above). By Ralph Connable. 1935. 190p.
P4-S07296 — $29.50.

CUNNINGHAM: Andrew Cunningham of Boston & some desc. (Repr. NEHGR) H. Cunningham. 1901. 16p.
P4-S07297 — $10.00.

CUPIT: History of the Cupit family. By John T. Cupit. 1954. 204p.
P4-S07302 — $32.00.

CUPPLES: Family, a record & family memorial. By Jos. E. Cupples. 1887. 69p.
P4-S07308 — $14.00.

CURD: Family in America: genealogy of some of the descendants of Edw. Curd of Henrico Co., VA. By F.D. Fuller & T.H.S. Cird. 1938. 152p.
P4-S07320 — $24.00.

CURD: & allied families. By Wm. B. Curd & Lucy P.R. Truog. 1927. 96p.
P4-S07314 — $18.00.

CURRENT: Genealogy of the Current & Hobson families, in two parts. By Annie E. Current. 1906. 350p.
P4-S07326 — $53.50.

CURRIER: Hist. sketch delivered at a Currier reunion, Toledo, OH, 1910. By E.M. Currier. 1913. 19p.
P4-S07333 — $10.00.

CURRIER: Genealogical history of the Currier family. By Richard S. Currier. 1935. 341p.
P4-S07332 — $52.00.

CURRIER: Genealogy of Richard Currier of Salisbury & Amesbury, MA & many of his desc. By J. McN. Currier. 1910. 271p.
P4-S07338 — $41.00.

CURTIS: Rec. of some of the desc. of Wm. Curtis, Roxbury 1632. By S. C. Clarke. 1899. 29p.
P4-S07351 — $10.00.

CURTIS: Family: a record of some of the descendants of Deodatus Curtis of Braintree, MA. By Laura G.C. Preston. 1945. 166p.
P4-S07350 — $25.00.

CURTIS: The fam. of Henry Curtis of Sudbury, MA (Repr. NEHGR) By H. E. Woods. 1907. 10p.
P4-S07345 — $10.00.

CURTIS: Ancestry & descendants of Wm. Curtis of Marcellus, NY; also some allied families By Lorissa E. Steele. 1912. 110p.
P4-S07344 — $17.50.

CURTISS: Genealogy of the Curtiss family; record of the desc. of widow Elizabeth Curtiss, who settled in Stratford, CT. By F. Curtiss. 1903. 283p.
P4-S07356 — $42.00.

CURTISS: Genealogy of the Curtiss-Curtis family of Stratford, CT; a suppl. to the 1903 ed. comp. by H.D. Curtis. 1953. 585p.
P4-S07362 — $87.00.

CURWEN: History of the ancient house of Curwen, of Workington in Cumberland & its various branches By J.F. Curwen. 1928. 363p.
P4-S07368 — $57.50.

CURZON: Family of NY & Baltimore, & their English descent. By J. Hall Pleasants. 1919 75p.
P4-S07374 — $15.00.

For hardcover versions, see the order form on page v. To order, call 1-888-296-3447.

CUSHING: & Allied families. By Elizabeth G. Fuess. 1931. 469p., typescript.
P4-S07380 — $71.50.

CUSHING: Sketches from the history of the Cushing family, which relate to Laban & Nancy Whitney Cushing By Effie A.W. Rideout. 1928. 63p.
P4-S07395 — $12.50.

CUSHING: Genealog of the Cushing family; anc. & desc. of Matthew Cushing who came to Amer. in 1638. By J. S. Cushing. 1905. 668p.
P4-S07392 — $84.00.

CUSHING: Gen. of the Cushing fam. By L. Cushing. 1877. 117p.
P4-S07386 — $23.50.

CUSHMAN: A hist. & biogr. gen.; the desc. of Robert Cushman, Puritan, 1617-1855. H.W. Cushman. 1855. 666p.
P4-S07401 — $84.00.

CUSHMAN: Genealogy & general hist., incl. the desc. of the Fayette Co., PA & Monongalia Co., VA, families, By A.W. Burt. 1942. 432p.
P4-S07407 — $67.00.

CUSHMAN: A grandson of Elder Thomas Cushman & his desc. (Repr. NEHGR) By J. T. Cushman. 1918. 8p.
P4-S07400 — $10.00.

CUSHMAN: The proceedings at the Cushman celebration at Plymouth, MA, 1855 By N. B. Shurtleff & H. W. Cushman. 1855. 84p.
P4-S07413 — $17.00.

CUSTER: The Custer fam. By M. Custer. 1912. 27p.
P4-S07420 — $10.00.

CUSTER: Genealogies. By Milo Custer. 1944. 91 + 23 + 34p.
P4-S07419 — $23.00.

CUTHBERT: The Cuthberts, barons of Castle Hill, & their desc. in SC & GA. By J. Bulloch. 1908. 100p.
P4-S07425 — $19.00.

CUTLER: A gen. record of several fam. bearing the name of Cutler in the US. By A. Morse. 1867. 80p.
P4-S07431 — $16.00.

CUTLER: Memorial & genealogical history. By N.S. Cutler. 1889. 665p.
P4-S07437 — $99.50.

CUTLER: History of the Holliston branch of the Cutler family, parts 1 & 2. By Henry Cutler. 1897. 59 + 36 + 41p.
P4-S07443 — $22.00.

CUTTER: History of the Cutter family of New England. By Benj. Cutter, rev. By Wm. R. Cutter. 1871, 1875. 363p.
P4-S07449 — $52.00.

CUTTING: Kin. T.A. Cutting. 1939. 224p.
P4-S07455 — $34.00.

CUTTS: Genealogy of the Cutts fam. in Amer. By C. Howard 1892. 658p.
P4-S07461 — $98.00.

CUYLER: Earliest Cuylers in Holland & America & some of their descendants. By Maud C. Nicoll. 1912. 69p.
P4-S07467 — $14.00.

D

DABNEY: Sketch of the Dabneys of VA, with some of their family records. By Wm. H. Dabney. 1888. 107p.
P4-S07473 — $18.00.

DAGUE: The history & genealogy of the Dague family. By Carrie M. Dague. 1938. 253p.
P4-S07479 — $39.00.

DAILEY: Fam.; biogr. hist. & gen. of desc. of Ebenezer Dailey of Columbia Co., NY. By E. Fox. 1939. 186p.
P4-S07485 — $30.00.

DAKIN: Descendants of Thomas Dakin of Concord, MA. By A.H. Dakin. 1948. 716p.
P4-S07491 — $99.00.

DAKIN: Descendants of Thos. Dakin of Concord, MA & Rev. Simon Dakin of North East, NY, 1624-1920. By A. Dakin, Jr & Emily L. Reed. 1920. 79p.
P4-S07497 — $16.00.

DALEY: The Journey of Mary Ann Eliza Daly, Wife of Amos Switzer of Limerick, Ireland & Some of Her Descendants. Claudia E. Cridland. 2003. 87p.
P4-S07498 — $16.50.

DALLAS: History of the family of Dallas & their connections & desc. from the 12th cent. J. Dallas. 1921. 611p.
P4-S07503 — $89.00.

DALLENBACH: The Dallenback family in America, 1710-1935. By A. Dillenbeck & K. Dallenbach. 1935. 439p.
P4-S07509 — $67.50.

DALLETT: Genealogy of the Dallett family. Francis J. Dallett, Jr. 1946. 112p.
P4-S07515 — $17.50.

DALRYMPLE: The name of Dalrymple, with gen. of one branch in the US. By W. H. Dalrymple. 1878. 68p.
P4-S07521 — $14.00.

DAME: Gen. of the Dame fam. for 10 gen. in Amer. E. & M. Estes. 1890. 16p.
P4-S07521X — $10.00.

DAMON: Genealogy of six generations of descendants of John Damon of Scituate, MA. By D. Bradford Damon. 1935. 112 + 26p., typescript.
P4-S07539 — $21.00.

DAMON: Damon memorial. By B. M. Damon. 1897. 60p.
P4-S07530 — $12.00.

DAMON: Genealogy of the descendants of Simeon Damon. By Flora A. Teel. 1922. 77p.
P4-S07545 — $15.00.

DAMON: The Damon Family of Reading, MA. Richard A. Damon, Jr. 1999. 733p.
P4-S07540 — $109.00.

DAMON: Family, listing some of the Ohio descendants of Amos Damon of Chesterfield, MA. By Richard Van Deusen. n.d. 158p.
P4-S07527 — $24.00.

DANA: Family in America. By E.E. Dana. 1956. 685p.
P4-S07551 — $99.00.

DANA: The Dana Saga: three centuries of the Dana family in Cambridge. By Henry W.L. Dana. 1941. 61p.
P4-S07560 — $12.00.

DANA: Memoranda of some of the desc. of Richard Dana of Cambridge. By J. Dana. 1865. 64p.
P4-S07554 — $12.50.

DANCE: Family in VA, By Leslie Lyle Campbell. 1951. 134p.
P4-S07569 — $22.50.

DANFORTH: Genealogy; Nicholas Danforth of Framingham, Eng. & Cambridge, MA & Wm. of Newbury, MA. By J. May. 1902. 492p.
P4-S07572 — $62.00.

DANIELS: Family: a gen history of the descendants of William Daniels of Dorchester & Milton, MA, 1630-1951, Vol I. By J.H. Daniels, Jr. 1952. 264p.
P4-S07584 — $41.50.

DANIELS: Family, Vol. II, 1630-1957. 1957. 484p.
P4-S07578 — $73.00.

DANIELS: Note on a Franklin [MA] branch of the Daniell or Daniels family. By Geo. F. Daniels. 1897. 62p.
P4-S07587 — $12.00.

DANN: Descendants of Abraham Dann, married 1760. By Rachel Saul Tefft. 1997. 66p.
P4-S07596 — $13.00.

DARBY: Gen.; George Darby (1726-1788) of Montgomery Co., MD. By R.C. Darby. 172p.
P4-S07602 — $29.00.

DARE: Genealogy of the Dare family. By Clara Dare Ettinger. 1901. 123p.
P4-S07614 — $19.00.

DARE: Family History. By W.H. & N.L. Montgomery. 1939. 340p.
P4-S07608 — $54.00.

DARLING: Benjamin Darling of Casco Bay, ME & desc. By C. N. Sinnett. 1923. 14p.
P4-S07615 — $10.00.

DARLING: Fam. in Amer: Early settlers prior to 1800. By W.M. Clemens. 1913. 31p.
P4-S07616 — $10.00.

DARLINGTON: Gen of the Darlington family: record of the descendants of Abraham Darlington of Chester Co., PA. G. Cope. 1900. 693p.
P4-S07620 — $87.00.

DARLINGTON: Gathering of Clan Darlington, with desc. of Abraham Darlington, et al. 1853. 52p.
P4-S07621 — $10.00.

DARNALL: DARNELL Family, incl. Darneal, Darnielle, Darnold, Durnell, et al, with allied fams. By Dr. H.C. Smith. 421p.
P4-S07626 — $66.00.

DART: Gen. of the Dart fam. in Amer. By T. L. Bolton. 1927. 235p.
P4-S07638 — $35.00.

DART: Family in America. By Suessa L.D. Boice. 1954. 119p., typescript.
P4-S07632 — $18.00.

DARY: Lewis Dary of Norton, MA & some of his desc. G. A. Dary. 1903. 25p.
P4-S07639 — $10.00.

DASHIELL: Family records, Volume I (some descendants of James Dashiell of MD). By Benj. J. Dashiell. 1928. 256p.
P4-S07644 — $39.00.

DASHIELL: Family records, Vol. II (some descendants of Thos. Dashiell of MD). By Benj. J. Dashiell. 1929. 330p.
P4-S07650 — $51.00.

DASHIELL: Family records, Volume III [some descendants of George Dashiell of Quantico]. By Benj. J. Dashiell. 1932. 214p.
P4-S07656 — $34.00.

DASHWOOD: The Oxfordshire Dashwoods. James Townsend. 1922. 52 + 20p.
P4-S07663 — $12.00.

DAVENPORT: James & Elizabeth Davenport of TN: their desc, & Some speculation regarding their ascendants. By James H. Davenport. 1995. 327p.
P4-S07680 — $49.50.

DAVENPORT: Ancestry & descs of John & Jane Anne (Lounsbery) Davenport, of Ulster Co., NY & Meadsville, PA. By Eleanor B.D. Grant. 1960. 35p., typescript.
P4-S07681 — $10.00.

DAVENPORT: Genealogy of the Davenport family & connections. By Henry B. Davenport, Jr. 1947. 99p.
P4-S07668 — $18.50.

DAVENPORT: History & genealogy of the Davenport family in Eng. & Amer., 1086-1850. By A.B. Davenport. 1851. 398p.
P4-S07674 — $55.00.

DAVENPORT: Suppl. to the 1851 Davenport gen., continued to 1876. By A. B.Davenport. 1876. 437p.
P4-S07686 — $68.00.

DAVES: Sketch of the mil. career of Capt. John Daves of the NC continental line of the army of the Rev. By G. Daves. 1892. 16p.
P4-S07687 — $10.00.

DAVIDSON: The Davidsons/ Davisons of Ulster, A Genealogical Guide. J.A.B N. Davison, Count of Clandermond. 2002. 195p.
P4-S07693 — $30.00.

DAVIDSON: Genealogy. By Elizabeth D. Harbaugh. 1948. 482p.
P4-S07692 — $74.50.

DAVIES: Memoir, a genealogical & biogr. monograph on the family & descendants of John Davies of Litchfield, CT. By H.E. Davies. 1895. 138p.
P4-S07698 — $19.50.

DAVIS: WOODRUFF Families of Western KY. Virginia Couchot. 1992. 74p.
P4-S07716 — $15.00.

DAVIS: ADAMS Genealogy. By Bell Shank Cadmus. 1931. 82 + 38p.
P4-S07710 — $19.50.

DAVIS:- KINDER - NOBLE: Reunions & family trees. 1926. 223p.
P4-S07746 — $33.50.

DAVIS: Gen. of Jefferson Davis; address delivered Oct. 9, 1908, before Lee Camp # 1, Conf. Vets, Richmond, VA. By W.H. Whitsitt. 1908. 16p.
P4-S07705 — $10.00.

DAVIS: Our pioneer ancestors, Volume I: genealogy of the Davis family, Middlesex Co., VA & Montgomery Co., KY. By Ruth H. DeVerter. 1957. 275p., typescript.
P4-S07788 — $42.00.

DAVIS: Family: history of the descendants of William Davis & his wife Mary Means. By T.K. Davis. 1912. 248p.
P4-S07740 — $39.00.

DAVIS: Family of early Roxbury & Boston. By S. F. Rockwell. 1932. 326p.
P4-S07734 — $49.00.

DAVIS: History of the descendants of John Davis, native of England, who died in Easthampton, L.I., in 1705. By A. Davis. 1888. 199p.
P4-S07776 — $30.00.

DAVIS: Samuel Davis of Oxford, MA & Joseph Davis of Dudley, MA & their descendants. G. Davis. 1884. 618p.
P4-S07794 — $77.00.

DAVIS: Dolor Davis, a sketch of his life, with record of his earlier desc. By H. Davis. 1881. 46p.
P4-S07706 — $10.00.

DAVIS: A brief genealogical history of the Davis family & allied lines. By T.C. & W.C. Davis. 1934. 40p.
P4-S07707 — $10.00.

DAVIS: Family history, special emphasis on ancestors of Philip C. Davis, Geo. G. Davis, Jos. G. Davis, James C. Davis & John Edw. Davis. By Geo. W. Davis. 1955. 122p., typescript.
P4-S07728 — $21.00.

DAVIS: Records (Deaths, Marr., Bible), Washington Co., OH — Early Gateway to the West. By H.C. Biedel. 1952. 43p.
P4-S07708 — $10.00.

DAVIS: Fam. of NJ & Upstate NY. By H. Johnston. 10p.
P4-S07709 — $10.00.

DAVIS: Genealogies of the Davis & Goss families, in two parts. By H.W. Clark. 1905. 122 + 141p.
P4-S07752 — $59.50.

DAVIS: Genealogy of the Davis family: Wm. Davis of London, England, 1764-1809, & his descendants. By Mildred F.D. Barr. 1957. 71p., typescript.
P4-S07764 — $14.00.

DAVIS: Three generations of Northboro Davises, 1781-1894. By John D. Estabrook. 1908. 84p.
P4-S07800 — $17.00.

DAVIS: Genealogy of the Clinton H. Davis family; short sketch of the Lost Creek 7th Day Baptist Church. By W.M. Davis. 1935. 100p.
P4-S07758 — $19.00.

DAVIS: Ancestry & posterity of Joseph Davis (1773-1865) of Norway, NY, & his wilfe Elizabeth Hallock Davis. By Wm. Church Davis. 1927. 172p.
P4-S07704 — $27.00.

DAVIS: One line of desc. from Dolor Davis & Richard Everett. By W. S. Crosby. 1911. 59p.
P4-S07788 — $12.50.

DAVIS: Fam. of Haverhill & Dover, MA (Extr. from The Old Fam. of Sal., Part Nine & Ten). 40p.
P4-S07711 — $10.00.

DAVIS: John Davis of Chebacco (Ipswich) & some of his desc. By E. A. Davis. 1934. 24p.
P4-S07712 — $10.00.

DAVIS: Family (Davies and David) in Wales & America: Genealogy of Morgan David of PA. By Harry A. Davis. 1927. 445p.
P4-S07722 — $67.00.

DAVIS: Gen. of the desc. of Col. John Davis of Oxford, CT, with partial gen. of his anc. By G.T. Davis. 1910. 338p.
P4-S07770 — $53.50.

DAVIS: Genealogy of the descendants of Charity Davis of Oxford CT. By G.T. Davis. 1883. 4p.
P4-S07713 — $10.00.

DAVISON: Gen. record of the Davison, Davidson, Davisson fam. of New. Eng. By H.R. Coles. 1899. 143p.
P4-S07812 — $24.00.

DAVISON: Family. By A. A. Davison. 1905. 78p.
P4-S07806 — $16.00.

DAVISON: The Davisons of Knockboy, Broughshane, Co. Antrim. By Alexander Davison. 1995. 115p.
P4-S07811 — $18.50.

DAVOL: Ancestors of Frank Herbert Davol & his wife Phebe Downing Willits, showing Mayflower descent. By Josephine C. Frost. 1925. 222p.
P4-S07818 — $33.50.

DAWES: GATES ancestral lines: a mem'l vol. containing the Amer. ancestry of Rufus R. Dawes, Vol. I: Dawes & allied families. By M.W. Ferris. 1943. 758p.
P4-S07824 — $105.00.

DAWES: Wm. Dawes & his ride with Paul Revere, & Dawes genealogy. By Henry W. Holland. 1878. 128p.
P4-S07830 — $21.00.

DAWS: Some descendants of Frank Daws of Co. Sussex, England, with information on assoc. Kiplinger family. By Steve Roth. 1992. 89p.
P4-S07836 — $17.50.

DAWSON: A record of the desc. of Robert Dawson, of East Haven, CT, incl. Barnes, Bates & 31 other fam. By C. C. Davidson. 1874. 119p.
P4-S07848 — $21.00.

DAWSON: A coll. of fam. records with biogr. sketches & other mem. of those bearing the name Dawson. By C. C. Dawson. 1874. 572p.
P4-S07842 — $87.00.

DAWSON:- GRAHAM & allied families, By Gid Graham. 1938. 144p.
P4-S07854 — $23.00.

DAY: The desc. of Anthony Day of Gloucester, MA, 1645. By J. A. Day. 1902. 11p.
P4-S07858 — $10.00.

DAY: Gen; A record of the desc. of Jacob Day & an incomplete record of Anthony Day. By the Gen. Comm. of the Day Assoc. 1916. 210p.
P4-S07863 — $35.50.

DAY: Some chronicles of the Day fam. By E. Putnam. 1893. 159p.
P4-S07869 — $25.50.

DAY: A gen. reg. of the desc. in male line of Robt. Day of Hartford, CT, who died in 1648. 1848. 2nd ed. 129p.
P4-S07857 — $22.00.

DAYTON: Record of a family descent from Ralph Dayton & Alice Goldhatch Tritton By Edson C. Dayton. 1931 96p.
P4-S07881 — $18.00.

DAYTON: Genealogical story: Dayton & Tomlinson. By L.D. Fessenden. 1902. 230p.
P4-S07875 — $34.50.

DEACON: Descendants of the Deacon fam. of Elstowe & London, & sketches of allied families. E. Deacon. 1898. 420p.
P4-S07887 — $66.00.

DEAN: Gen. of Dean fam., desc. of Ezra Dean of Plainfield, CT & Cranston, RI. By A. Dean. 1903. 158p.
P4-S07896 — $25.00.

DEAN: Life, experiences & incidents of Rev. Gardner Dean, with gen. of the Gardner, Dean & Hinds families. By Rev. G. Dean, genealogy By Ebenezer W. Peirce. 1883. 307p.
P4-S07914 — $46.00.

DEAN: A gen. of the desc. of James Dean, one of the first settlers of Oakham, MA. G. M. Dean. 1889. 29p.
P4-S07894 — $10.00.

DEAN: Gen. of Isaac Dean of Grafton, NH, 4th in desc. from John of Taunton. ed. by J. Drummond. 1902. 35p.
P4-S07895 — $10.00.

DEAN: Descendants of John Dean, 1650-1727, of Dedham MA. By Marion D. Cooper. 1957. 217p. typescript.
P4-S07893 — $33.00.

DEAN: Hist. of William Dean fam. of Cornwall, CT & Canfield, OH. By B. S. & J. E. Dean. 1903. 69p.
P4-S07902 — $14.00.

DEANE: Desc. of Thomas Deane of MA & NH. By J.W. Dean. 1883. 12p. P4-S07915 — $10.00.

DEANE: Brief mem. of John & Walter Deane, two of the first settlers of Taunton, MA & the early gen. of their desc. By W.R. & J.W. Dean(e). 1849. 16p. P4-S07916 — $10.00.

DEARBORN: The Dearborns of Hampton, NH; Desc. of Godfrey Dearborn of Exeter & Hampton (Repr. from his Hist. of Hampton, NH) By J. Dow. 1893. 16p. P4-S07919 — $10.00.

DeARMOND: Families of America & Related families (d'Armand, D'Armond, DeArman, Dearmont, etc.). By Roscoe C. d'Armand. 1954. 699p. P4-S07920 — $99.00.

DEAVOR: Brief history of the Deavor family in America. By Rev. Wm. T.S. Deavor. 1896. 100p. P4-S07926 — $19.00.

DeBEAUFORT: Family of DeBeaufort in France, Holland, Germany & England. By Wm. Morris Beaufort. 1886. 163p. P4-S07932 — $24.50.

DeBLOIS: Family ("Old Boston Fams." #1). A.W.H. Eaton. 1913. 15p. P4-S07933 — $10.00.

DeBRAOSE: Family of DeBraose, 1066-1326. Dudley G.C. Elwes. 1883. 57p. P4-S07934 — $11.00.

DeCAMP: Record of the desc. of Ezekial & Mary Baker DeCamp of Butler Co., OH. J.M. DeCamp. 1896. 177p. P4-S07944 — $24.00.

DeCAMP: Gen., Laurent DeCamp of New Utrecht, NY, 1664 & his desc. By G. A. Morrison. 1900. 77p. P4-S07938 — $16.00.

DeCARPENTIER: Allied ancestry of Maria de Carpentier, wife of Jean Paul Jaquet of New Netherland. By E.J. Sellers. 1928. 236p. P4-S07950 — $37.50.

DeCARPENTIER: Gen. of the DeCarpentier fam. of Holland. By E.J. Sellers. 1909. 59p. P4-S07953 — $12.00.

DECKARD: Gen. of the Deckard fam. showing also those desc. from Decker, Deckert, Decher, Dechert, Decherd, etc. By P. E. Deckard. 1932. 893p. P4-S07962 — $133.00.

DeCOU: Gen. of the De Cou fam., showing the desc. from Leoren des Cou. By S.E. & J.A. de Cou. 1910. 219p. P4-S07968 — $37.00.

DEERING: Genealogical notes on some of the descendants of George Dearing from Co. Devon, & John Whipple, from Co. Essex, England By Charles Deering. 1914. 464p. P4-S07980 — $61.50.

DeFOREST: The de Forests of Avesnes (& of New Netherland). A Huguenot thread in Amer. colonial hist., 1494-1900, By J. W. De Forest. 1900. 307p. P4-S07986 — $49.00.

DeGRAFFENRIED: The family of Christopher DeGraffenried IV, in Switzerland & America & allied families By Irene B. Spence. 1968. 143p. P4-S08004 — $25.00.

DeGRAFFENRIED: History of the DeGraffenried family, from 1191-1925. By T.P. DeGraffenried. 1925. 282p. P4-S07998 — $44.50.

DeGRAFFENRIED: Family Scrapbook, 1191-1956. By Thomas P. de Graffenried. 1956. 270p. P4-S07992 — $44.00.

DeHAVEN: Hist. of the DeHaven fam. By H. D. Ross. 1929. 4th ed., 43p. P4-S08005 — $10.00.

DeHAVEN: Hist. of the DeHaven Fam., 3rd ed. By H. Ross. 1914. 33p. P4-S08006 — $10.00.

DEISCH: TEUSCH Family (1560-1985). By Frank J. Deisch. 1985. 644p. P4-S08010 — $94.50.

DeJARNETT: Allied families in America (1699-1954). By Earl C. & May M. Frost. 1954. 338p. P4-S08016 — $52.00.

DeJONGH: & Allied families: genealogy & history in Europe & America. By Dirk P. de Young. 1934. 111p. P4-S08022 — $18.50.

DELAMATER: Desc. of Claude Le Maitre who came from France & settled at New Netherlands, now NY, in 1652. By L. De La Mater. 1882. 229p. P4-S08028 — $34.00.

DeLANCEY: The DeLanceys: romance of a great family, with notes on allied families By D.W. Story. 1931. 180p. P4-S08034 — $27.50.

DELAND: Family in America; a biogr. gen. By F. Leete. 1943. 414p. P4-S08040 — $66.00.

DELANO: Genealogy, hist. & alliances of the Amer. house of Delano, 1621-1899 By J.A. Deland & M.D. de Lannoy. 1899. 561p. P4-S08043 — $71.00.

DeLONG: Pioneer Palatine pilgrims [PA]. By Irwin H. Delong. 1928. 36p. P4-S08050 — $10.00.

DeLONG: Jacob Jansen Van Etten, otherwise known as Jacob Jansen DeLange. By I. H. DeLong. 1922. 5p. P4-S08051 — $10.00.

DeLONG: Early occurences of the fam. name DeLong in Europe & Amer. By I. H. DeLong. 1924. 17p. P4-S08052 — $10.00.

DeLONG: The DeLongs of NY & Brooklyn: a Huguenot family portrait. By Thomas A. DeLong. 1972. 203p. P4-S08049 — $29.50.

DeLOTBINIERE: the De Lotbinieres. A bit of Canadian romance & hist. By I.J. Greenwood. 1896. 8p. P4-S08054 — $10.00.

DeMARANVILLE: Genealogy, descendants of Louis DeMaranville. By G. L. Randall. 1921. 152p. P4-S08055 — $28.00.

DEMAREST: David des Marest of the French Patent on the Hackensack & his desc. W. & M. Demarest. 1938. 576p. P4-S08061 — $89.00.

DEMING: Genealogy of desc. of John Deming of Wethersfield, CT, with hist. notes. By J. Deming. 1904. 702p. P4-S08064 — $87.00.

DENHAM: Denham fam. of ME. By C. N. Sinnett. 1922. 8p. P4-S08069 — $10.00.

DENIO: Genealogy of Aaron Denio of Deerfield, MA, 1704-1925. By F.B. & H.W. Denio. 1926. 345p. P4-S08070 — $53.00.

DENISON: Denison mem., Ipswich, MA, 1882. By A. Caldwell. 1871. 52p. P4-S08077 — $10.00.

DENISON: Record of the descendants of Samuel Denison, late of Floyd, Oneida Co., NY By Geo. B. Denison. 1884. 72p.
P4-S08088 — $14.50.

DENISON: Genealogy: record of the ancestors & descendants of James Post Denison By E. Glenn Denison & Harry E. Bolton. 1939. 130p.
P4-S08076 — $22.00.

DENISON: Record of the desc. of Capt. Geo. Denison, of Stonington, CT. By Baldwin & Clift. 1881. 424p.
P4-S08082 — $54.50.

DENMAN: Denman fam. hist. from earliest records to the present time. By H. N. Harris. 1913. 88p.
P4-S08094 — $18.00.

DENNISON: Family of N. Yarmouth & Freeport, ME, Abner Dennison & desc., by G.M. Rogers; David Dennison & desc. By A.L. Dennison. 1906. 148p.
P4-S08100 — $24.00.

DENNISON: Gen. of the Dennison fam. from George Dennison, 1725. 1880. 15p.
P4-S08101 — $10.00.

DENNISTON: Record of the descendants of Ezekial Denniston, son of Chas. Denniston By Gerda D. DeForest. 1912. 112p.
P4-S08106 — $18.00.

DENNY: Family in England & America: desc. of John Denny of Combs, Suffolk, England, 1439. By C.C. Denny. 1886. 267p.
P4-S08118 — $40.00.

DENNY: Genealogy. By Margaret C.D. Dixon & Elizabeth C.D. Vann. 1944. 565p.
P4-S08136 — $86.50.

DENNY: Genealogy, second book: descendants of Wm. Denny of Chester Co., PA & allied families Elizabeth C.D. Vann & Margaret C.D. Dixon. 1947. 404p.
P4-S08124 — $62.00.

DENNY: Genealogy, third book: descendants of David Denny, Sr, of PA & the Shenandoah Valley of VA. By Margaret C.D. Dixon & Elizabeth C.D. Vann. 1951. 489p.
P4-S08130 — $75.00.

DENNY: Family history; The Hugh & Susan Denny family of Jefferson Co., NY, 1850. Bill Denny. 1995. 300p.
P4-S08112 — $45.00.

DEPPEN: Counting kindred of Christian Deppen & History of Christian Ruchty & Other collateral lines. E.E. & M.L. Deppen. 1940. 625p.
P4-S08142 — $92.50.

DePRIEST: Hist. of the Wm. Allen DePriest fam. of WV & PA, & Depriest gen. 1790-1965. P. DePriest. 5p.
P4-S08153 — $10.00.

DERBY: Genealogy: record of desc. of John Darby of Marblehead (10 gen.) By W.D. Derby. 22p.
P4-S08155 — $10.00.

DERBY: Genealogy, being a record of the desc. of Thomas Derby of Stow, MA. V.A. Derby Bromley. 1905. 141p.
P4-S08154 — $23.00.

DERBY: Life & times of Richard Derby, Merchant of Salem, 1712-1783. By James Duncan Phillips. 1929. 116p.
P4-S08160 — $18.50.

DeREIMER: Family, a.d. 1640-1903. By Rev. W.E. DeRiemer. 1905. 47p.
P4-S08161 — $10.00.

DeRHAM: "Smaller New York" & Fam. reminiscences: De Rham, Schmidt, Bache, Barclay, Paul Richard. By "O.E.S." 1899. 78p.
P4-S08166 — $16.00.

DeRIEUX: Our French ancestors & how the came to VA. By Edwin R. Lancester. 1917. 31p.
P4-S08165 — $10.00.

DERTHICK: Genealogy & history of the Derthicks & related Derricks: eight centuries of the Derthicks & related Derricks in America & England. By J.T. Spencer & R. A. Goodpasture. 1986. 585p.
P4-S08172 — $84.50.

DETREVILLE: Fam. of SC, extr. Habersham gen. 1901. 16p.
P4-S08174 — $10.00.

DeTURK: History & genealogy of the DeTurk-DeTurck family, descendants of Isaac DeTurk & Maria DeHarcourt, with supplement. By Eugene P. DeTurk. 1934. 368 + 15p.
P4-S08178 — $57.50.

DeVEAUX: Genealogy of the DeVeaux family. By T. F. Devoe. 1885. 302p.
P4-S08184 — $48.00.

DEVENDORF: Family. By O.W. Bell. 1932. 111p.
P4-S08190 — $19.50.

DEVENISH: Historical & genealogical records of the Devenish families of England & Ireland. By R.J. Devenish & C.H. McLaughlin. 1948. 409p.
P4-S08196 — $62.50.

DEVEREAUX: Genealogy of the family of Devereaux of the line of Jonathan Deveraux, born in Wethersfield, CT, with some additions. By C. A. Herrick & C. F. Haight. 1929. 266p.
P4-S08202 — $41.00.

DEVEREUX: Genealogy of Reuben Devereus of the 58th generation of the Devereux family. By A.D. & D.C. Reed. 1930? 149p., typescript.
P4-S08214 — $22.00.

DEVEREUX: Genealogy of Arthur Forrester Devereux & his family. By A.D. & D.C. Reed. 1930? 146p., typescript.
P4-S08208 — $21.00.

DEW: Genealogy of some descendants of Thomas Dew, colonial VA Pioneer immigrant By Ernestine D. White. 1937. 349p.
P4-S08220 — $52.50.

DEWEY: Descendants of William Dewey. Thomas P. Dewey. 1998. 116p.
P4-S08226 — $19.50.

DEWEY: Life of Adm. Geo. Dewey, by A.M. Dewey. Dewey family history. By L.M. Dewey, et al. 1898. 1120p.
P4-S08232 — $139.00.

DEWING: Desc. of Andrew Dewing of Dedham, MA, with notes on some Eng. fam. of the name. By B. Dewing. 1904. 173p.
P4-S08238 — $25.00.

DeWITT: Fam. of Ulster Co., NY. By T.G. Evans. 1886. 18p.
P4-S08239 — $10.00.

DeWOLF: Charles D'Wolf of Guadalupe, his anc. & desc.; a complete gen. of the "R.I. D'Wolf's" By C.B. Perry. 1902. 325p.
P4-S08244 — $49.00.

DEXTER: Genealogy of the Dexter family in Amer., desc. of Thomas Dexter & Other allied fam. By W.A. Warden & R.L. Dexter. 1905. 353p.
P4-S08252 — $56.00.

DEXTER: Gen.; being a record of the fam. desc. from Rev. Gregory Dexter, with notes & biogr. sketches. By S.C. Newman. 1859. 108p.
P4-S08256 — $19.50.

DEXTER: Genealogy, 1642-1904, history of the desc. of Richard Dexter of Malden, MA, By O.P. Dexter. 1904. 279p.
P4-S08250 — $41.50.

DEXTER: Life of Lord Timothy Dexter; with Sketches of the Eccentric Characters that Composed his Associates, Including his own Writings, "Dexter's Pickle for the Knowing Ones" et al. Samuel L. Knapp. 1858. 157.
P4-S08251 — $25.00.

DEYO: DEYOE Family. By K.E. Hasbrouck & R.P. Heidgerd. 1958. 272p., typescript.
P4-S08268 — $42.50.

DIAL: DYALL Genealogy. By E. Dunklin. 1912. 7p.
P4-S08275 — $10.00.

DIAL: Martin Dial & Related families, with their ancestors, descendants & connections. Harris 1951. 251p.
P4-S08274 — $39.00.

DIBBLE: Dibble fam. of CT. By V. Lamb. 1949. 124p.
P4-S08280 — $25.00.

DICKERMAN: Genealogy; desc. of Thomas Dickerman, an early settler of Dorchester, MA, with suppl. By E.D. & G.S. Dickerman. 1897 & 1922. 705p.
P4-S08286 — $98.00.

DICKERSON: Daniel Dickerson 1740-1826, & desc. of NJ (in Genung Gen.) By M. & L. Nichols. 1906. 14p.
P4-S08287 — $10.00.

DICKEY: Genealogical history of the Dickey family. R.S. Currier. 1935. 340p.
P4-S08292 — $54.00.

DICKEY: Genealogy of the Dickey family. By J. Dickey. 1898. 322p.
P4-S08298 — $49.50.

DICKINSON: Descendants of Nathaniel Dickinson. By Addie M. Dickinson & the Dickinson Assoc. 1955. 387p., typescript.
P4-S08304 — $58.00.

DICKINSON: To the descendants of Thomas Dickinson, son of Nathaniel & Anna Gull Dickinson By F. Dickinson. 1897. 144p.
P4-S08307 — $22.00.

DICKSON: Genealogy of the Dickson family & its immediate collateral branches. 1908. 189p.
P4-S08313 — $29.00.

DICKSON: Some of the descendants of William Dickson & Elizabeth Campbell of Cherry Valley, NY. By Tracy C. Dickson. 1937. 367p.
P4-S08319 — $57.00.

DICKSON: The Border or Riding clans followed by a hist. of the clan Dickson & a brief acct. of the fam. of the author. By B.H. Dixon. 1889. 223p.
P4-S08314 — $29.50.

DIEHL: Addenda to Diehl genealogy, 1915 [above]. By E.H. Diehl. 1930. 227p.
P4-S08331 — $33.50.

DIEHL: Families of America: history, genealogy, reminiscences, etc. By E.H. Diehl. 1915. 227p.
P4-S08337 — $34.00.

DIEHL: Account of the family reunion of the descs of Sam'l Diehl of Friend's Grove, Bedford Co., PA. 1891. 60p.
P4-S08322 — $12.00.

DIETER: John Dieter of Northampton Co., PA & his descendants. By E.E.D. Gundry. 1972. 699p.
P4-S08343 — $105.00.

DIKE: Genealogy of the Dike & Torrance families, from 1623 and 1701. By Nellie K.T. Burkhart. 1959. 54p., typescript.
P4-S08344 — $11.00.

DILKS: Communication to John Hyland Dilks & Wm. Alburger Dilks concerning the Dilks, Durfor, Alburger & related families. By W.H. Dilks, Jr. 1962. 85p.
P4-S08349 — $17.00.

DILL: Mathew Dill genealogy: study of the Dill family of Dillsburg, York Co., PA, 1698-1935, parts I & II. By Rosalie J. Dill. 1934-5. 79 + 98p.
P4-S08361 — $27.50.

DILL: Mathew Dill genealogy, a study of the Dill family of Dillsburg, York Co., PA, 1698-1935, part III. By Rosalie J. Dill. 1935. 67p.
P4-S08355 — $14.00.

DILLE: Family. Three hundred years in Amer. By G.E., J.K. & E.K. Dille. 1965. 138p.
P4-S08367 — $21.00.

DILLER: Family [of PA]. By J.L. Ringwalt. 1877. 56p.
P4-S08374 — $11.00.

DILLER: Desc. of Christian Theuller (Diller) (1757-1807). By Rachel S. tefft. 1998. 218p.
P4-S08375 — $35.00.

DILLINGHAM: Genealogy of the Dillingham family of New England. By Winthrop Alexander. 1943. 311p., typescript.
P4-S08379 — $46.00.

DILLON: Ancestors. By Dr Charles R. Dillon. 1959. 209p., typescript.
P4-S08397 — $32.00.

DILLON: Ancestors of Arthur Orison Dillon & his poems. By Authur O. Dillon. 1927. 111p.
P4-S08385 — $18.50.

DILLON: Ancestral record of the Dillon, Hodgson, Risher & Leonard families. By Isaiah Dillon. 1909. 183p.
P4-S08391 — $26.00.

DIMOND: Gen. of the Dimond-Dimon fam. of Fairfield, CT. By E. Dimond. 1891. 179p.
P4-S08403 — $28.50.

DINGS: Family in America: genealogy, memoirs & comments. By M. Dings. 1927. 182p.
P4-S08409 — $25.00.

DINKINS: Dinkins & Springs fam., By J. Dinkins. 1908. 24p.
P4-S08410 — $10.00.

DINSMOOR: Hist. & gen. of the Dinsmoor-Dinsmore fam. of Scotland, Ireland & Amer. L.M. Morrison. 1891. 48p.
P4-S08416 — $10.00.

DINSMORE: Genealogy from about 1620-1925. By M.H. Savage. 1927. 141p.
P4-S08415 — $24.00.

DINWIDDIE: Family records, with especial attention to the line of William Walthall Dinwiddie, 1804-1882. By E.D. Holladay. 1957. 191p.
P4-S08421 — $29.50.

DINWIDDIE: Genealogical records of the Dinwiddie clan of Northwestern IN. By T.H. Ball. 1902. 120p.
P4-S08421 — $21.00.

DINWIDDIE: of Lake Co., VA fam. records. By T. Ball 8p.
P4-S08422 — $10.00.

DISTLER: Ohio River Valley families [Distler, Morris, MacDonald, Hobbs, Koehler, Vogl, Goessl, Garreis, Allison, Douglas, Stephenson, Rennard, Keith, Jones, Rand, Pate, Hopkins] By Allen David Distler. 1995. 358p.
P4-S08433 — $55.00.

DIX: Life of Dorothea Lynde Dix. By Francis Tiffany. 1891. 392p.
P4-S08439 — $35.00.

DIXON: NORTHUP Families; Genealogy for descendants of John S. Dixon, Stephen Northup, Nicholas Northup By Frank Dixon. 1952. 73p.
P4-S08445 — $15.00.

DIXON: History of Charles Dixon, one of the early English settlers of Sackville, N.B. J.D. Dixon. 1891. 204p.
P4-S08451 — $30.50.

DIXON: Dixons of Dixon's Ford, with "the Soldier's Tale," a story of the people of Derry [PA] in 1776. By Wm. Darby. 1878. 21p.
P4-S08446 — $10.00.

DIXON: Kith & kin, genealogical data of Dixon & collateral lines. By W. M. Dixon. 1922. 83p.
P4-S08457 — $16.50.

DOAK: Family. B. E. Hanes. 1931. 100p.
P4-S08469 — $19.50.

DOAK: The Doak Family [from Notable Southern Families].
J.S. French. 1933. 98p.
P4-S08470 — $15.00.

DOANE: Family: I. Deacon John Doane, of Plymouth; II. Dr. John Done, of MD & their descendants By A. Doane. 1902. 554p.
P4-S08475 — $70.00.

DOBBIN: John Dobbin of Connagher descendants. Wm. J. Foster. 1936. 98p.
P4-S08481 — $18.00.

DODD: Gen. of the male desc. of Daniel Dod, of Branford, CT & native of Eng., 1646-1863. By B. Dodd & J. Burnet. 1864. 221p.
P4-S08493 — $33.00.

DODD: Genealogy & history of the Daniel Dodd fam. in Amer., 1646-1940. By A. Dodd & J.F. Folsom. 1940. 442p.
P4-S08487 — $68.50.

DODD: Anc. & desc. of Lewis Dodd & Elizabeth (Baldwin) Dodd. By B. Dodd. 19p.
P4-S08488 — $10.00.

DODDS: Gen. & hist. of fams. of Francis Dodds & Margaret Craig Dodds of Spartanburg, SC & of the Dodds fams. of Baltimore, IN & IL By L. Colby. 1929. 177p.
P4-S08499 — $29.50.

DODGE: Tristram Dodge & his desc. in America By R. Dodge. 1886. 248p.
P4-S08520 — $37.00.

DODGE: Genealogy of the Dodge family of Essex Co., MA, 1629-1894. By J. T. Dodge. 1894. 456p.
P4-S08511 — $65.00.

DODGE: Gen. of the Dodge fam. of Essex Co., MA, Second Part, 1629-1898. By J.T. Dodge. 1898. 218p.
P4-S08516 — $30.00.

DODGE: Family [of Block Isl, RI]. By Louis L. Dodge & Wm. Carrol Hill. 1947. 40p., typescript.
P4-S08515 — $10.00.

DODGE: Anc. of Nathan Dane Dodge & his wife, Sarah Shepard Dodge, with notes. M. Parson. 1896. 76p.
P4-S08517 — $15.00.

DODGE: Desc. of Tristram Dodge. By T.R. Woodward. 1904. 241p.
P4-S08508 — $32.00.

DODGE: Gen. hist. of one branch of the Dodge fam. T. H. Dodge. 1880. 20p.
P4-S08506 — $10.00.

DODGE: Early records of the Dodge fam. in Amer. R. R. Dodge. 1879. 12p.
P4-S08507 — $10.00.

DODGE: Report, full, authentic, & complete, of all the addresses & proceedings of the memorable first reunion of the Dodge fam. in Amer. By R. Dodge. 1879. 53p.
P4-S08521 — $10.00.

DODGE: The Dodge lands at Cow Neck; an appendix. By R. D. Dodge. 1896. 32p.
P4-S08522 — $10.00.

DODGE: The Dodge fam. of Essex Co., MA, first three gen. (Repr. NEHGR). By J. Dodge. 1892. 11p.
P4-S08523 — $10.00.

DODSON: DOTSON, Lucas, Pyles, Rochester & allied families, By S.E. Lucas, Jr. 1959. 239p.
P4-S08526 — $37.50.

DOE: Descendants of Nicholas Doe. By E. Doe. 1918. 375p.
P4-S08532 — $49.00.

DOGGETT: History of the Doggett-Daggett family. S. B. Doggett. 1894. 696p.
P4-S08535 — $86.50.

DOLBEARE: A few facts relating to the origin & hist. of John Dolbeare of Boston & some of his desc. By A.D. Osborne. 1893. 32p.
P4-S08537 — $10.00.

DOLMAN: Compendium, a.d. 1340-1940. By Paul H. Dolman, 1940. 139p.
P4-S08541 — $22.00.

DOMMERICH: Our col. & continental anc; Anc. of Mr. & Mrs. Louis Wm. Dommerich. I. de Forest. 1930. 328p.
P4S08547 — $49.25

DONALD: Fam. with notes on rel. fam. By D. Gordon. 1906. 79p.
P4-S08553 — $16.00.

DONALDSON: Genealogical rec. of one branch of the Donaldson family in Amer. By M. McKitrick. 1916. 332p.
P4-S08559 — $54.00.

DONIPHAN: Ancestral lines of the Doniphan, Frazee & Hamilton families. Frances F. Hamilton. 1928. 700p.
P4-S08565 — $99.50.

DONNELL: Family: history & genealogy of the descendants of Thos. Donnell of Scotland. By Camilla & Emma A. Donnell. 1912. 174p.
P4-S08571 — $26.50.

DONNELL: The Donnells & their Macdonald ancestors: history & gen., 157-1927, a.d. E. & J. Donnell. 1928. 251p.
P4-S08577 — $41.00.

DOOLITTLE: Abraham Doolittle & some of his desc. O. P. Allen. 1893. 38p.
P4-S08584 — $10.00.

DOOLITTLE: Family in America, Pts. I-VII, 1901-1908. By W.F. Doolittle. 1908. 730p.
P4-S08589 — $92.00.

DOOLITTLE: Family in America, Part VIII. By L.S. Brown & M.R. Doolittle. 1967. 619p.
P4-S08583 — $87.50.

DOOLITTLE: Index to "The Doolittle Family in America." compiled By Victoria Reed. 1988. 247p.
P4-S08595 — $30.00.

DOPP: Dopp fam. in America. By C. N. Sinnett. 1922. 18p.
P4-S08602 — $10.00.

DOPP: "We're from Iowa?" Revisited: a family hist tracing Doop, Marr, Sandvig & Omundson ancestors. By Roy Dopp. 1993. 370p.
P4-S08601 — $56.00.

DOREMUS: Genealogy of the Doremus family in America, descendants of Cornelis Doremus By Wm. Nelson. 1897. 232p.
P4-S08607 — $36.00.

DORLAND: Records of the Dorland fam. in Amer., incl. principal branches Dorland, Dorlon-an, Durland, Darling By J. Cremer. 1898. 320p.
P4-S08613 — $49.50.

DORLANDT: Jan Gerretse Dorlandt & His American Descendants. Enid Dickinson Collins. 1946. 259p.; typescript.
P4S08614 — $39.00.

DORMAN: Some descendants of Jabez Dorman of Arundel (1678-1765): ten generations of Dormans in ME. By Franklin A. Dorman. 1992. 112p.
P4-S08619 — $16.50.

DORR: Records of Lineage in the Dorr, Dalton, Odin, Walter & other allied New England families. By Dalton Dorr. 1898. 144 + 20p.
P4-S08625 — $26.00.

DORRANCE: Fam. in the US. By A.A. Dorrance. 1901. 24p.
P4-S08626 — $10.00.

DORRANCE: Dorrance inscr. Old Sterling Twp. burying ground, Oneco, CT. By E.F. Welch. 1909. 24p.
P4-S08627 — $10.00.

DORSEY: Family; Descendants of Edward Darcy-Dorsey of VA & MD for five generations, & allied families. By Maxwell J. & Jean M. Dorsey, & Nannie B. Nimmo. 1947. 270p.
P4-S08631 — $42.00.

DOSTER: Genealogy. By Mrs Ben Hill. 1945. 286p.
P4-S08643 — $44.50.

DOTTERER: Family. By Henry S. Dotterer. 1903. 164p.
P4-S08643 — $25.00.

DOTY: DOTEN Family in America; Descendants of Edw. Doty, an emigrant by the Mayflower, 1620. By E.A. Doty. 1897. 2 vols., 1035p.
P4-S08655 — $145.00.

DOTY: Continuing the line of Doty-Lawrence family, as found in "Doty-Doten family," by Ethan Allen Doty. Ethel V. Lawrence. 1940. 78p., typescript.
P4-S08649 — $16.00.

DOTY: Family history & genealogy. By E. E. VanSant. 1935. 104p.
P4-S08661 — $20.00.

DOUDE: DOWD: Descendants of Henry Doude who came from England in 1639. W. W. Dowd. 1885. 342p.
P4-S08667 — $44.00.

DOUGHERTY: Family history of James Dougherty & lineage of descent, By Wm. C. Dougherty. 1930. 50p.
P4-S08668 — $10.00.

DOUGHTY: Records of the Doughty fam. in ME. By C. N. Sinnett. 1923. 23p.
P4-S08669 — $10.00.

DOUGLAS: History of the House of Douglas, from the earliest times to the legislative union of England & Scotland. By Sir H. Maxwell. 2 vols. in 1. 1902 324+318p.
P4-S08688 — $99.50.

DOUGLAS: My father's family, Douglas-Haden-Churchill-Blakey-George-Perkins-Oglesby -Attkisson & allied families. By Edith A. Rudder. 1947. 119p.
P4-S08700 — $18.50.

DOUGLAS: Coll. of family records, with biogr. sketches & other mem. of various various families & individuals of the name Douglas. By C. Douglas. 1879. 563p.
P4-S08670 — $71.00.

DOUGLAS: Genealogy of the families of Douglas of Mulderg & Robertson of Kindeace with their descendants. 1895. 84p.
P4-S08682 — $16.00.

DOUGLAS: Lineage of Amelia S. (Douglas) Howard-Smith, with the added gen. of her son Douglas Sparks Howard-Smith By Frances Houston Irwin. 1943. 81p.
P4-S08694 — $16.00.

DOUGLAS: Genealogy: descs of John Douglas of Middleborough, MA, the first of this branch in America. By J. Lufkin Douglas. 1890. 226p.
P4-S08676 — $34.00.

DOUGLASS: Life & ancestry of Francis Douglass, bookseller & author, of Aberdeen & Paisley, Scotland. By Walter K. Watkins. 1903. 37p.
P4-S08701 — $10.00.

DOUKHOBOR: Their History in Russia, Their Migration to Canada. Joseph Elkinton. 1903. 336p.
P4-S08703 — $37.50.

DOW: The Book of Dow: genealogical memoirs of the descendants of Henry Dow, Thomas Dow & Others of the name By Robert P. Dow. 1929. 1013p.
P4-S08706 — $139.00.

DOWLER: Story of the Dowler-Hartshorne Fisher-Lybarger families. By Donald F. Lybarger. 1938. 63p.
P4-S08712 — $13.50.

DOWLING: A Dowling Family of the South. R.A. Dowling. 1959. 245p.
P4-S08714 — $37.00.

DOWNER: The Downers of America. By D. R. Downer. 1900. 244p.
P4-S08718 — $36.50.

DOWNES: Researches into the gen. history of families bearing the name of Downes. Leonard Downes. 1891 69 + 34p.
P4-S08724 — $19.50.

DOWNEY: McDONALD Families of Kentucky: ancestors of Donald G. Downey, with revised McDonald genealogy. By D.G. Downey. 1993, 1997. 89 + 24p.
P4-S08730 — $19.50.

DOWNEY: History of the Protestant Downeys of the Cos. of Sligo, Leitrim, Fermanagh & Donegal & their desc. By C.C. Downey. 1931. 173p.
P4-S08736 — $27.00.

DOWS: DOWSE Family in America:descendants of Lawrence Dows, including the Masterman, Newman, Morse families. By A.M Dows. 1890. 348p.
P4-S08742 — $51.00.

DOWSE: Lawrence Dowse of Legbourne, Eng.; his ancestors, desc., & connections in Eng., MA & Ireland. By W.B.H. Dowse. 1926. 359p.
P4-S08748 — $56.50.

DOYLE: Fam. of Harpswell, ME. By C.N. Sinnett. 1922. 8p.
P4-S08750 — $10.00.

DRAKE: Gen. & biogr. acct. of the fam. of Drake in America. By S. G. Drake. 1845. 51p.
P4-S08755 — $10.00.

DRAKE: Family in Eng. & Amer. 1360-1895, & the desc. of Thomas Drake of Weymouth, MA, 1635-1691. By L. S. Drake. 1896. 347p.
P4-S08757 — $42.00.

DRAKE: Descendants of John Drake of Windsor, CT. F.B. Gay. 1933. 380p.
P4-S08754 — $59.00.

DRAKE: The family of Nelson Drake back to 1630: NY & MI pioneers, with genealogy supplement. By F.N. Drake. 1963. 146p.
P4-S08769 — $22.50.

DRAKE: Gen, in the line of Samuel Drake of Lower Smithfield Twp, Northampton (now Monroe) Co., PA. By Lillian D. Avery. 1926. 130p.
P4-S08763 — $21.00.

DRAPER: Drapers in America, being a history & genealogy of those of that name & connection. By T. Draper. 1892. 324p.
P4-S08772 — $45.00.

DRAPER: Account of the silver wedding of Mr. & Mrs. F. P. Draper at Westford, NY, 1871, Incl. the Draper & Preston fam. 1871. 32p.
P4-S08779 — $10.00.

DRAPER: The Mormon Drapers. By Delbert M. Draper. 1958. 377p.
P4-S08778 — $55.00.

DRAYTONS: of SC & Philadelphia. By Emily H.D. Taylor. 1921. 120p.
P4-S08784 — $19.00.

DRESSER: Family in America. By C. & W. Dresser. 1925. 14p.
P4-S08785 — $10.00.

DRESSER: John Dresser of Rowley, MA & some of his desc. By F. S. Kinsey. 12p.
P4-S08787 — $10.00.

DRESSER: Wentworth Dresser & desc., By C. Sinnett. 1914. 6p.
P4-S08786 — $10.00.

DRINKARD: The Drinkards in the US; their history & genealogy. By Charles A. Drinkard. n.d. 161p.
P4-S08790 — $25.00.

DRINKER: Family in America. By H.D. Biddle. 1893. 30p.
P4-S08791 — $10.00.

DRINKWATER: Fam. of Drinkwater of Cheshire, Lancashire, etc. in Eng. By Drinkwater & Fletcher 1920. 112p.
P4-S08796 — $19.50.

DRINKWATER: Anc. & desc. of Micajah Drinkwater of Northford, ME, 1620-1825. By J.S. Fernald. 29p.
P4-S08797 — $10.00.

DRIVER: Family; gen. memoir of the desc. of Robert & Phebe Driver of Lynn, MA; with appendix containing 23 allied fam. H.R. Cooke. 1889. 556p.
P4-S08802 — $85.00.

DROWNE: Partial list of the descendants of Leonard & Elizabeth (Abbott) Crowne of Sturgeon's Creek, ME & Boston, MA, 1646-1941. By Henry R. Drowne with Theodore D. Mitchell. 1942. 141p., typescript.
P4-S08808 — $23.00.

DRUMMOND: Descendants of Alexander Drummond of Georgetown ME, including Campbell, Chamberlain, Crane, Morse. By Josiah H. Drummond. 1942. 171p.
P4-S08814 — $25.00.

DRUSE: Genealogy [descendants of Stepehn Druse of RI & NY]. By Geo. McKenzie Roberts. 1931. 204p., typescript.
P4-S08820 — $32.00.

DRYER: Ancestry of Rufus K. Dryer, with notes on William Dryer of Rehobeth & some of his desc. By J.F. Dryer. 1942. 280p.
P4-S08826 — $43.50.

DuBOIS: Documents & genealogical chart of the family of Benj. DuBois. By Anson DuBois & James G. DuBois. 1878. 104p.
P4-S08832 — $17.00.

DUDLEY: History of the Dudley family. By D. Dudley. 1894. 2 vols., 1253p.
P4-S08847 — $158.00.

DUDLEY: Supplement to 1894 "Hist. of Dudley Fam." 1898. 96p.
P4-S08859 — $18.00.

DUDLEY: Gen. & fam. records. By D. Dudley. 1848. 150p.
P4-S08838 — $24.50.

DUDLEY: History of the Dudley fam., with gen. tables, pedigrees, etc., Number V. By D. Dudley. 1891. 100p.
P4-S08853 — $18.50.

DUDLEY: Number VII. 1891. 100p.
P4-S08844 — $18.00.

DUDLEY: Life & Work of Thomas Dudley, Second Governor of MA. A. Jones 1899. 485 + 38p.
P4-S08839 — $75.00.

DUDLEY: Yearbook of Gov. Thomas Dudley Fam. Assoc. 1930-1939 364p.
P4-S08871 — $55.00.

DUDLEY: The Sutton-Dudleys of Eng. & the Dudleys of MA in New Eng., from the Norman Conquest to the present time. G. Adlard. 1862. 186p.
P4-S08865 — $27.50.

DUFFIELD: Family: sketch of Wm. Duffield of Venango Co., PA & his descendants. John T. Duffield. 1905. 74p.
P4-S08877 — $15.00.

DUFOUR: The Dufour saga: story of 8 Dufours who came from Switzerland & founded Vevay, Switzerland Co., IN. By J.L. Knox. 1942. 167p.
P4-S08883 — $29.00.

DUKE: SYMES Family. By Jane Morris. 1940. 263p.
P4-S08889 — $41.00.

DUKE: Henry Duke, Councilor, & his descendants & connections, comprising partial records of many allied families. Walter Garland Duke. 1949. 452p.
P4-S08898 — $69.50.

DUKE: Genealogy of the Duke-Shepard-Van Metre family, from civil, military, church recs. & documents. By S.G. Smyth. 1902. 454p.
P4-S08892 — $58.00.

DUKEHART: My heritage: collection of authenticated bio.l sketches of the author's ancestors By Morton McI. Dukehart. 1947. 160p., typescript.
P4-S08904 — $25.00.

DULANEY: Something about the Dulaney (Dulany) family & sketch of the southern Cobb family. By Benj. Lewis Dulaney. 1921. 94p.
P4-S08910 — $18.00.

DUMARESQ: Sketch of family of Dumaresq, with added reminiscences of James Dumaresq. 1863. 23p.
P4-S08911 — $10.00.

DUNAWAY: The Dunaways of VA. By A.E. Clendening. 1959. 156p. P4-S08922 — $25.00.

DUNCAN: GIBSON Family. By H. W. Duncan. 1905. 44p. P4-S08923 — $10.00.

DUNCAN: The North East Duncans, their kith & Kin, 1769-1932, By Wm. M. Duncan. 1932. 126p. P4-S08934 — $22.00.

DUNCAN: Descendants of William Duncan the Elder. N.R. Roy. 1959. 267p. P4-S08922 — $42.50.

DUNCAN: The story of Thomas Duncan & his six sons. By K.D. Smith. 1928. 174p. P4-S08940 — $29.00.

DUNCAN: Family register of Lewis Duncan & Harriet Kinnaird, his wife, with numerous bio. sketches. By R.S. Duncan. 1905. 88p. P4-S08928 — $17.00.

DUNCKLEE: Sketch of the Duncklee family & a history of the descendants of David Duncklee of Amherst NH. By A,M.L. Duncklee. 1908. 260p. P4-S08946 — $39.50.

DUNDAS: HESSELIUS. By Francis Dundas. 1938. 122p. P4-S08952 — $19.00.

DUNDORE: Genealogical record of the Dundore family in America By Nathan Dundore. 1881. 58p. P4-S08953 — $11.00.

DUNHAM: Jacob Dunham of Lebanon, CT & Mayfield, NY, his anc. & desc. By S. D. Moore. 1933. 51p. P4-S08960 — $10.00.

DUNHAM: Ancestors & desc. of Richard Dunham of PA & his wife Laura Allen. By J. Crary. 1916. 102p. P4-S08958 — $20.00.

DUNHAM: Genealogy of Dea. John Dunham of Plymouth, MA, 1589-1669, & his descendants. By I.W. Dunham. 1907. 384p. P4-S08967 — $49.50.

DUNHAM: Suppl. English & Amer. branches of the Dunham family. By I. Dunham. 1907. 52p. P4-S08959 — $11.00.

DUNHAM: Genealogy, & related families Billings, Powell, Hice, Gray, Root, Andrus. By Chester Forrester Dunham. 1956. 160p., typescript. P4-S08964 — $24.50.

DUNLAP: The House of Dunlap. By Rev. James A. M. Hanna. 1956. 412p. P4-S08973 — $62.00.

DUNLEVY: Genealogical history of the Dunlevy family (Don Levi, Dunlavey, etc.). G.D. Kelley. 1901. 373p. P4-S08979 — $59.50.

DUNLOP: House of Dunlop. By Freda Dunlop White. 1951. 257p. P4-S08985 — $39.50.

DUNNELL: Genealogy of the Dunnell-Dwinell fam. of New Eng. By H. G. Dunnel. 1862. 84p. P4-S08991 — $17.00.

DUNNING: Ebenezer Dunning (1761-1838) of Norfield Parish, Fairfield, CT; Stillwater, Champlain & Milton, NY; Benninton, VT. By Alice D. Haskell. 1940. 54p. typescript. P4-S08992 — $11.00.

DUNNING: Genealogical notes on the Dunning fam. in America. By M. B. Dunning. 1915. 30p. P4-S08993 — $10.00.

DUNSTER: Henry Dunster & his descendants. By S. Dunster. 1876. 343p. P4-S08997 — $44.00.

DUNWOODY: Genealogy of the Dunwoody & Hood fams. & coll. branches; their hist. & biogr. By G. Cope. 1899. 172p. P4-S09003 — $26.00.

DuPONT: Early generations of the DuPont & allied families. By H.A. DuPont. 1923. 2 vols., 802p. P4-S09009 — $119.50.

DUPUY: A gen. hist. of the Dupuy fam. By C.M. Dupuy, with add. By H. Dupuy. 1910. 175p. P4-S09015 — $30.00.

DUPUY: The Huguenot Bartholomew Dupuy & his desc. By B.H. Dupuy. 1908. 455p. P4-S09018 — $58.00.

DURAND: WHALLEY, Barnes & Yale fam. By F. Hewitt. 1912. 115p. P4-S09036 — $22.00.

DURAND: Family: descendants of Dr John Durand, a Huguenot, born 1664, La Rochelle, France. By Samuel R. Durand. 1965. 278p. P4-S09024 — $55.00.

DURAND: Genealogy of the Durand family: record of the desc. of Francis Jos. Durand. Celia C. Durand. 1925. 136p. P4-S09030 — $21.00.

DURELL: Family: descendants of Peter of Newton, MA & Moses of Gloucester, MA. By Harold C. Durrell. 1925, 1928. 23 + 25p. P4-S09038 — $10.00.

DURFEE: Descendants of Thomas Durfee of Portsmouth, RI, vol I. By W.F. Reed. 1902. 593p. P4-S09042 — $89.00.

DURFEE: Desc of Thomas Durfee of Portsmouth, RI, Vol II. W.F. Reed. 1905. 668p. P4-S09048 — $97.00.

DURHAM: The name & family of Durham. By Wm. Clark Durham. n.d. 99p., typescript. P4-S09054 — $18.00.

DURLING: My Mother & Her Ancestors: The Durlings & Pardees of Wadsworth, OH. John H. Fullerton. 2002. 90p. P4-S09059 — $18.00.

DURRELL: Genealogy: descendants of Phillip. By H.C. Durrell. 1918. 204p., typescript. P4-S09060 — $31.00.

DURYEA: TURNER Lines, By Rhea Duryea Johnson. 1959. 102p. P4-S09066 — $17.50.

DUSEN: GAYDEN Family record. By Wm. L. Duren. 1959. 74p., typescript. P4-S09072 — $14.50.

DUSENBURY: Dusenbury fam. By B. A. Dusenbury. 1932. 69p. P4-S09078 — $14.00.

DUSENBURY: Family [of Holland & NY: some descendants of Willamd, Henry & Moses]. n.d. 51p. typescript. P4-S09079 — $10.00.

DUSTON: DUSTIN Fam. gen., 3rd & 4th gen. 1948. 48p. P4-S09085 — $10.00.

DUSTON: DUSTIN Family genealogy. Kilgore & Curtis. 1937-1960. 247p.
P4-S09084 — $39.00.

DUTCHER: Family: our Colonial ancestors & their descendants, historical, genealogical, biographical. By Henry Whittemore. 1902. 76p.
P4-S09090 — $15.00.

DUTTON: Memorials of the Duttons of Dutton in Cheshire, with notes repecting the Sherborne branch of the family. n.a. 1901 296p.
P4-S09102 — $47.50.

DUTTON: Gen. of the Dutton fam. of PA with a hist. of the fam. In Eng., & appendix containing a short acct. of the Duttons of CT. G. Cope. 1871. 112p.
P4-S09096 — $17.00.

DUVAL: Genealogy & history of a branch of the Duval family: Peter (Pierre) Duval (I) & his descendants. By Prescott C. Crafts. 1951. 94 + 6p., typescript.
P4-S09114 — $18.00.

DuVAL: DuVals of KY from VA, 1794-1935, descendants & allied families. By Margaret G. Buchanan. 1935. 265p.
P4-S09108 — $41.00.

DUYCKINCK: & allied fams: record of the desc. of Evert Duyckinck who settled in New Amsterdam, now NY in 1638. Duyckinck & Cornell. 1908. 256p.
P4-S09120 — $41.00.

DWIGHT: History of the desc. of John Dwight of Dedham, MA. By B. W. Dwight. 1874. 2 vols., 1173p.
P4-S09126 — $154.50.

DYAR: Preliminary gen. of Dyar fam. By H. G. Dyar. 1903. 32p.
P4-S09127 — $10.00.

DYER: FINN; Descendants of James Dyer & Jane Finn of Jackson Co., TN. By Richard E. Preator, Jr. 1998. 240p.
P4-S09144 — $36.00.

DYER: Some records of the Dyer fam. By C. Joy-Dyer 1884. 130p.
P4-S09156 — $19.50.

DYER: Settlement. Ft. Seybert, WV massacre, with gen. notes. By M. Talbot. 1937. 64p.
P4-S09147 — $12.00.

DYER: "Tar Heel Born:" A Dyer family from Lincoln County, NC. By Jerry L. Dyer. 1999. 484p.
P4-S09132 — $72.00.

DYER: Descendants of John Dyer & Mary "Polly" Youngblood of Jackson Co., TN. By Richard Preator. 1998. 80p.
P4-S09138 — $16.00.

E

EAGER: Family. By Grace Olive Chapman. 1942. 91p., typescript.
P4-S09162 — $18.00.

EAGER: History of the Eager family, from the coming of the first immigrant, William Eager, in 1630-1952. By S.E. Trotter. 1952. 251p.
P4-S09168 — $43.00.

EAKLEY: Family of Ontario & MI: Vincent Egle & his descendants. By Barbara Brown Eakley. 1996. 157p.
P4-S09174 — $24.50.

EAMES: AMES Genealogy: descendants of Robert of Woburn & Thomas of Framingham, MA, 1634-1931. By Wilmot S. Ames. 1931. 251p.
P4-S09180 — $38.00.

EAMES: Robert Eames (Ames), 1640-1693, of Andover & Boxford, MA. By Wilmot S. Ames. 1943. 400p.
P4-S09186 — $61.50.

EAMES: Robert Eames of Woburn, MA & some of his desc. By A.G. Loring. 1908. 17p.
P4-S09181 — $10.00.

EAMES: Gen. of one branch of the Thomas Eames fam., who came from Eng. About 1630 & first settled at Dedham, MA in 1640. By M. Eames. 1887. 34p.
P4-S09182 — $10.00.

EANES: Descendants of Edward Eanes of Henrico & Chesterfield Counties in VA. By Richard H. Eanes, et al. 1940. 172 + 63p., typescript.
P4-S09192 — $35.00.

EARLE: Descendants of the Earle & Morris families of NY & NJ. n.d. 70p., typescript.
P4-S09204 — $13.50.

EARLE: Amos S. Earle branch of the Ralph Earle family in America. By Amos E. Voorhies. 1940. 111p.
P4-S09198 — $18.50.

EARLE: Family; Ralph Earle & desc. By P. Earle. 1888. 516p.
P4-S09207 — $65.50.

EARLE: History & genealogy of the Earles of Secaucus, with an acct. of other English & Amer. branches. By I.N. Earle. 1924. 828p.
P4-S09213 — $115.00.

EARLY: The family of Early which settled upon the eastern shore of VA, By R. H. Early. 1920. 343p.
P4-S09219 — $54.50.

EARLY: Hist. of the Early fam. in Amer. By S.S. Early. 1896. 53p.
P4-S09220 — $10.50.

EARNEST: Genealogy: Indian Eve & her descendants, an Indian story of Bedford Co. By Emma A.M. Replogle. 1911. 128p.
P4-S09225 — $21.00.

EASTBURN: Family: Gen. & Hist. Record of the Descendants of John Eastburn, who came to America in 1684 By Hettie A. Walton & Eastburn Reeder. 1903 206p.
P4-S09231 — $31.00.

EASTBURN: Memoirs of the Rev. Joseph Eastburn, stated preacher in the Mariner's Church, Phildelphia By Ashbel Green. 1828. 208p.
P4-S09237 — $32.00.

EASTERDAY: History of the Easterday family. By L.F.M Easterday. 1908. 32p.
P4-S09238 — $10.00.

EASTMAN: Hist. & Gen. of the Eastman family of America, cont. biogr. sketches & genealogy of both males & females. By G. S. Rix. 1901. 1000p.
P4-S09252 — $139.00.

EASTMAN: Hist & gen of Dea. Jos. Eastman of Hadley, MA, grandson of Roger Eastman of Salisbury, MA. By Guy S. Rix. 1908. 263p.
P4-S09249 — $39.50.

EASTMAN: The puritan ancestors in America of Georgia Ann Eastman (Mrs Wm Morris Bennett) By R.W. Bennett. 1929. 132p.
P4-S09258 — $21.00.

EASTMAN: "That Man Eastman" volumes I & II [bio. sketches & continuation of 1908 Eastman genealogy]. By Charles J. Eastman. 1952, 1954. 128 + 260p.
P4-S09243 — $58.00.

EASTMAN: Genealogy of the Eastman family for the first four gen. By Rev. L. R. Eastman. 1867. 11p.
P4-S09248 — $10.00.

EASTON: Descendants of Joseph Easton, Hartford, CT, 1636-1899. By Wm. S. Easton. 1899. 257p.
P4-S09264 — $38.50.

EATON: FOX — NEWCOMB — SEWARD Ancestry of Geo. Blunt Wendell & Edw. Eaton Wendell. By Davis G. Maraspin. 1939. 106p., typescript.
P4-S09288 — $17.50.

EATON: Fam. assoc. report of the 6th annual reunion at Boston, 1890. 1891. 35p.
P4-S09271 — $10.00.

EATON: Family of Nova Scotia, 1760-1929. By A. Eaton. 1929. 253p.
P4-S09282 — $38.00.

EATON: Ancestry & descendants of Syvanus Eaton, Jacob Swetland & Christopher Reynolds. By Jane A.E. Wight. 1900. 69p.
P4-S09270 — $14.00.

EATON: History, gen. & biogr., of the Eaton family. By N.Z.R. Molyneux. 1911. 782p.
P4-S09297 — $99.00.

EATON: Family of Dedham & the Powder House Rock. By John Eaton Alden. 1900. 67p.
P4-S09276 — $13.50.

EATON: Report of the 6th annual reunion of the Eaton Family Assoc., Boston, Aug. 19th, 1890. 1891. 35p.
P4-S09289 — $10.00.

EATON: Grange & notes of Andrews, Kimball & Eaton family. By Christie L. Eaton. 1890. 88p.
P4-S09294 — $17.00.

EBAUGH: John Jacob Ebaugh: The First "Ebaugh" in America; Origin of His Provincial Name. John Lynn Ebaugh. 1941. 100 + 6p.
P4-S09298 — $20.00.

EBERHART: Hist. of the Eberharts in Germany & the US, from 1265-1890, with an autobiogr. of the author. By Rev. U. Eberhart. 1891. 263p.
P4-S09303 — $39.50.

EBERLY: Biographic mem'l of John Eberly & genealogical family register of the Eberly family. By Levi E. Martin. 1896. 78p.
P4-S09309 — $15.50.

EBERSOL: Families in America, 1727-1937, including Ebersole, Ebersol, Eversole, Eversull. By Charles E. Ebersol. 1937. 281p.
P4-S09315 — $44.00.

EBY: The Aby family of Peoria Co., IL, the Eaby family of Lancaster Co., PA. By Mavina S. Aby & Franklin S. Aby. 1924. 101p.
P4-S09321 — $17.00.

EBY: Swiss Eby family, pioneer millwrights & millers of Lancaster Co. PA (family bulletin #2). By Franklin S. Aby. 1924. 55p.
P4-S09322 — $11.00.

EBY: Bio Hist of the Eby Family. E.E. Eby. 1889. 144p.
P4-S09323 — $22.00.

ECCLES: Geo. Eccles of Sherbrooke, P.Q. & Plymouth, NH, also the Eccles fam. of Ind. 4p.
P4-S09331 — $10.00.

ECK: Zacharias Eck fam. record. By L.E. Cooper. 1959. 126p.
P4-S09333 — $19.50.

ECKARDT: History of an Eckhar(d)t family, whose three sons (John, Henry, George) came to America before 1850 By Chas. M. Reinuehl & Geo. B. Eckhart. 1952. 78p., typescript.
P4-S09339 — $15.50.

ECKEL: Family of MD, PA, TN, NC & DE. By Milton Rubicam. 1955. 70p.
P4-S09345 — $14.00.

ECKERT: Record: story of Georg Bernhardt Eckert & his descendants, 1793-1957, By Estrella H. Orrison. 1957. 124p.
P4-S09351 — $19.50.

ECKLER: ACKLER — ACKLEY Family. By A. Ross Eckler. 1970. 446p.
P4-S09357 — $67.00.

ECKLER: Family of the Mohawk Valley; five generations of the descendants of Hendrick & Margaret (Young) Eckler of Canajoharie & Warren, NY. By A.R. Eckler. 1949. 75p.
P4-S09363 — $15.00.

EDDY: Gen. memoir of Rev. William Eddye, vicar of the Parish of Cranbrook, England. Robert Henry Eddy. 1881. 265p.
P4-S09381 — $41.00.

EDDY: Family in America, 1940 suppl. By R.S. Eddy. 1940. 180p.
P4-S09375 — $28.00.

EDDY: Ancestors & desc. of Zachariah Eddy of Warren, PA. By B.B. Horton. 1930. 332p.
P4-S09369 — $51.00.

EDDY: Mem. of Col. Jonathan Eddy of Eddington, ME. J. Porter. 1877. 73p.
P4-S09387 — $14.00.

EDDY: Ancestry of Mary Baker Eddy. By Wm. M. Clemens. 1924. 44p.
P4-S09370 — $10.00.

EDGAR: An account of the sirname Edgar, & particularly of the family of Wedderlie in Berwickshire. By J.H. Lawrence-Archer. 1873. 171p. + charts.
P4-S09393 — $27.00.

EDGAR: Letters & genealogy of the Edgar family. By C.G. Edgar. 1930. 82p.
P4-S09405 — $16.00.

EDGAR: Gen. collections concerning the Scottish House of Edgar, with a memoir of James Edgar. 1873 103p.
P4-S09399 — $17.00.

EDGERLY: Rec. of the Edgerly fam., desc. of Thomas Edgerly of Durham, NH, 1630. By E. Edgerly. 43p.
P4-S09412 — $10.00.

EDGERLY: & Allied families. By Edwin L. Edgerly. 1959? 269 + 68p., typescript.
P4-S09411 — $52.00.

EDGERTON: Edgerton gen. 1762-1927. By J. Edgerton. 1927. 29p.
P4-S09143 — $10.00.

EDMONSTONE: Extr. from "Zimmerman & allied fams." 19p.
P4-S09144 — $10.00.

EDNEY: My North Carolina heritage, Volume VI: Descs of Robt. Edney & Anna A. Wrensher of NC & TN. By Marshall L. Stiles. 1997. 537p.
P4-S09417 — $79.50.

EDSON: Family history & genealogy: descendants of Samuel Edson of Salem & Bridgewater, MA, Vol. I: English origin of the family 1969. 1535p.
P4-S09423 — $150.00.

EDSON: Family history & genealogy, Volume III. comp. By the Edson Family Assoc. 2003. 572p.
P4-S09424 — $86.50.

EDSON: Gen. acct. of the Edsons of Bridgewater. By T. Edson. 1864. 62p. P4-S09438 — $12.00.

EDSON: Nathan Edson & his desc. By G. T. Edson. 1926. 48p. P4-S09425 — $10.00.

EDSON: Several anc. lines of Josiah Edson & his wife, Sarah Pinney. With a full gen. hist. of their desc. By H.H. Wells & H.W. Van Dyke. 1901. 98p. P4-S09453 — $19.00.

EDSON: Genealogy of the Edsons. By J. B. Edson. 1903. 184p. P4-S09447 — $30.00.

EDWARDS: Family of Barren Co., KY, history & traditions. By Cyrus Edwards. 1924. 88p. P4-S09465 — $17.00.

EDWARDS: A condensed gen. of one branch of the Edwards fam. of Concord & Acton, MA & of allied fam. By J.H. Edwards. 1907. 28p. P4-S09460 — $10.00.

EDWARDS: Family in the Chenango country. By Mary E. Twitchell & Richard H. Edwards. 1947. 97p., typescript. P4-S09459 — $19.00.

EDWARDS: Richard Edwards & his wife Catherine Pond May; their anc., lives & desc. M. Edwards. 1931. 209p. P4-S09477 — $31.50.

EDWARDS: Timothy & Rhoda Ogden Edwards of Stockbridge, MA & desc. By W. Edwards. 1903. 172p. P4-S09483 — $26.00.

EDWARDS: Our Patronymics, Edwards, Parsons, Cleveland & allied fam. By E.E. Gifford. 1886. 28p. P4-S09466 — $10.00.

EDWARDS: Genealogical record of the desc. of John Edwards, 168?-1915. By L.N. Edwards. 1916. 395p. P4-S09471 — $61.00.

EELS: Fam. of Dorchester, MA in the line of Nathaniel Eels of Middletown, CT, 1633-1821, with notes on the Lenthall fam. By F. Star. 1903. 224p. P4-S09489 — $33.50.

EGE: History & genealogy of the Ege family in the US, 1738-1911. By Thompson P. Ege. 1911. 281p. P4-S09495 — $54.00.

EGLER: Descendants of Peter Egler, By Janet Egler. 1997. 423p. P4-S09501 — $62.50.

EHLE: "Dominie" John Jacob Ehle & his descendants. Boyd Ehle. 1930. 55p. P4-S09502 — $11.00.

EICHELBERGER: Hist. sketch of Philip Frederick Eichelberger, who came from Ittlinger, Germany, in 1728, & of his descendants By A.W. Eichelberger. 1901. 160 + 79p. P4-S09507 — $38.00.

EICHENBERG: History & genealogy of Peter Eichenberg family in the US. By Chas. S. Ikenberry & W.L. Eikenberry. 1955. 511p. P4-S09513 — $78.00.

EISENBERG: JONES Family record: Eisenberg branchm a record of Lawrence Eisenberg & his descendants. The Historical Comm. 1923. 120p. P4-S09519 — $21.00.

EISENHART: Ancestry of the John Franklin Eisenhart family, with supplement. By W.W. Eisenhart. 1951. 150 + 7p. P4-S09525 — $24.00.

EISENHOWER: Lineage & reference, 1691-1957: complete set of the series of bulletins on Eisenhower, Eisenhauer, Isenhour, Icenhower, etc. By Fannie B. Taylor-Richardson. 1956-1957 914p., typescript. P4-S09531 — $129.00.

ELA: Gen. of the Ela fam., desc. of Israel Ela of Haverhill, MA. By D. H. Ela. 1896. 44p. P4-S09532 — $10.00.

ELAM: Family, with special reference to Josiah Elam & his descendants. By Harvey W. Elam. 1933. 200p. P4-S09537 — $31.00.

ELDER: Gen. of David Elder & Margery Stewart. T. A. Elder. 1905. 52p. P4-S09439 — $10.00.

ELDERKIN: Genealogy of the Elderkin family, with intermarriages By Dyer W. Elderkin. 1888. 245p. P4-S09543 — $38.00.

ELDERKIN: John Elderkin, a founder of CT & some of his desc. By J. Elderkin. 1896. 19p. P4-S09544 — $10.00.

ELDRED: Family, particularly the descs of Wm. Eldred of Yarmouth & more particularly the Eldreds of Greene Co., IL. By Orville W. Eldred. 1940. 51p. P4-S09545 — $10.50.

ELDREDGE: STORY & allied familes, gen. & biogr. 1943. 130p. P4-S09555 — $23.00.

ELDREDGE: Ancestors of Edw. Irvin Eldredge & his wife Helen Louise Dutcher. Josephine C. Frost. 1929. 129p. P4-S09549 — $21.50.

ELDREDGE: Gen., (Repr. NEHGR). y Z. Eldredge. 1897. 9p. P4-S09550 — $10.00.

ELIOT: A sketch of the Eliot family. By W.G. Eliot. 1887. 177p. P4-S09561 — $25.00.

ELIOT: Family of Wm. Greenleaf Eliot & Abby Adams Eliot of St. Lous, MO, 3rd ed., 1811-1943. 1943. 157p. P4-S09567 — $24.00.

ELIOT: Genealogy of the Eliot family. By Wm. H. Eliot; rev. By W.S. Porter. 1854. 184p. P4-S09576 — $29.50.

ELIOT: Genealogy of the descendants of John Eliot, "Apostle to the Indians," 1598-1905. By W. H. Emerson. 1905. 356p. P4-S09570 — $53.50.

ELKINTON: The anc. & desc. of George Elkinton of Burlington Co., NJ. By A. Adams. 1945. 48p. P4-S09581 — $10.00.

ELLER: George Michael Eller & his desc. in America, incl. info. on related fams. By J.W. Hook. 1957. 485p. P4-S09582 — $75.00.

ELLIOT: The John Elliot fam. of Boscawen, NH. By H. A. Kimball. 1918. 132p. P4-S09588 — $19.50.

ELLIS: Gen. data regarding the descendants of John Ellis of Sandwich, MA. By Mary W. Bates. 1935. 118p. typescript. P4-S09618 — $19.00.

ELLIS: Family. K. S. Foos. 1900. 128p. P4-S09612 — $19.00.

ELLIS: History of the Ellis family, & desc. of William Ellis of Bideford, P.E.I. By P. Ellis. 1950. 368p. P4-S09630 — $58.50.

ELLIS: Bio. sketches of Richard Ellis, first settler of Ashfield, MA & his desc. By E. Ellis. 1888. 483p.
P4-S09594 — $61.50.

ELLIS: A few desc. of Richard Ellis, 1621-1694, of Dedham, MA. By H.D. Ellis. 1985. 19p.
P4-S09613 — $10.00.

ELLIS: Millwood, a family tree; Partial history of the descendants of John Ellis of Rehoboth, MA. By Frances O. Ellis. 1909. 109p.
P4-S09636 — $18.00.

ELLIS: History & genealogy of the John Ellis family, 1797-1935. By Milo H. Miller. 1936. 33 + 165p.
P4-S09624 — $29.50.

ELLIS: Gen. of Ellis fam. 1632-1920, & Coburn fam. 1618-1911, By H.W. & A.S. Ellis. 1920. 12p.
P4-S09625 — $10.00.

ELLIS: Early New England People: some acct. of Ellis, Pemberton, Willard, Prescott, Titcomb, Sewall, Longfellow & allied families. By S.E. Titcomb. 1882. 293p.
P4-S09600 — $45.00.

ELLISON: James Ellison memorial 1778-1820, with Ellison gen. By M. H. Curran. 1903. 19p.
P4-S09637 — $10.00.

ELLITHORPE: Facts about the Ellithorpe family: Thomas Ellithorpe 1601-1654, Abigail Sumner — 1680. By H.F. Ellithorpe. 1974. 2 vols. in 1, 147 + 185p.
P4-S09642 — $45.00.

ELLITHORPE: Ellithorpes of Killingly (Thompson Parish) & Stafford, CT. By Grace. O. Chapman. 1944. 47p., typescript.
P4-S09643 — $10.00.

ELLSWORTH: Our Ellsworth Ancestors. By G.E., M.S. & J.O. Ellsworth. 257p.
P4-S09648 — $38.50.

ELLSWORTH: Desc. of Selected Fams: Ellsworth & Morse. Lawrence T. Fadner. 2005. 146p.
P4-S09649 — $22.00.

ELLYSON: Dr Robert & Elizabeth Ellyson, their ancestors & descendants. L. Frank Bedell. 1969. 283 + 42p.
P4-S09654 — $37.00.

ELMER: ELMORE Gen. By W. W. Johnson. 1899. 96p.
P4-S09660 — $20.00.

ELMER: Genealogy of the Elmer & More families. By L.Q.C. Elmer, rev. By Brookes More. 1930. 91p.
P4-S09666 — $18.00.

ELMORE: Fam. memorials, hist. & gen. of Elmore fam. By T. J. Elmore. 1880. 40p.
P4-S09667 — $10.00.

ELSTON: Family in America. By J.S. Elston. 1942. 632p.
P4-S09672 — $94.50.

ELTING: Family. By Wm. & Ruth Heidgard. 1955. 68p.
P4-S09678 — $13.50.

ELWELL: Fam. in America; a gen. of Robert Elwell of MA. By J.T. Elwell, rev. By C.H. Pope. 1899. 30p.
P4-S09679 — $10.00.

ELY: Ancestry; lineage of Richard Ely of Plymouth, Eng., who came to Boston about 1655 & settled at Lyme, CT in 1660. M.S. Beach, et al. 1902. 639p.
P4-S09684 — $80.00.

ELY: Hist. narrative of the Ely, Revell & Stacye fam., of Trenton & Burlington, West Jersey, 1678-1683 By R.P. Ely et al. 1910. 445p.
P4-S09690 — $56.50.

ELY: Rec. of the descendants of Nathaniel Ely, the Emigrant, who settled first in Newtown, now Cambridge, MA. By Heman Ely. 1885. 515p.
P4-S09699 — $77.50.

ELY: Hist. of the Ely reunion held at Lyme, CT, July 10th, 1878. By M.E.D. Stuart. 1879. 158p.
P4-S09696 — $23.50.

EMERSON: The Ipswich Emersons, 1636-1900. A gen. of the desc. of Thomas Emerson, with some acct. of his Eng. anc. B.K. Emerson. 1900. 544p.
P4-S09726 — $68.00.

EMERSON: The Haverhill Emersons. By C. H. Pope. 1913. Part 1, 106p.
P4-S09720 — $15.00.

EMERSON: The Haverhill Emersons. By C. H. Pope. 1916. Part 2. 248p.
P4-S09723 — $37.00.

EMERSON: The English Emersons: gen. history of the fam. from earliest times to the end of the 17th cent., incl. modern pedigrees. By P.H. Emerson. 1898. 320p.
P4-S09711 — $41.00.

EMERSON: The Emerson, alias Emberson family of Cos. Herts & Essex, etc., with "further notes" & "penultimate notes," By P.H. Emerson. 1919, 1925 (England) 47 + 35 + 21p.
P4-S09705 — $17.00.

EMERY: Genealogical records of desc. of John & Anthony Emery of Newbury, MA, 1690-1890. By R. Emery. 1890. 621p.
P4-S09729 — $93.00.

EMERY: Four gen. of the desc. of John Emery, Sr., of Newbury, MA & Anthony Emery of Kittery, ME. By R. Emery (& others). 1889. 22p.
P4-S09730 — $10.00.

EMERY: D'Amerie-Emery-Amory. By J.W. Thornton. 1869. 6p.
P4-S09731 — $10.00.

EMISON: Supplement: partial genealogies of Emison families of KY & VA. By James W. Emison, Jr. 1962. 399p.
P4-S09741 — $59.50.

EMISON: Families, revised: origin & history of the KY Emisons. By James W. Emison, Jr. 1954. 360p.
P4-S09735 — $55.00.

EMMERTON: Materials toward a gen. of the Emmerton fam. By J. A. Emmerton. 1881. 248p.
P4-S09753 — $37.00.

EMMONS: Family genealogy; Thomas Emmons of Newport, RI, with desc. from 1639-1905. By E.N. Emmons. 1905. 287p.
P4-S09753 — $43.00.

ENDECOTT: Some descendants of John Endecott, Governor, Mass. Bay Colony. By Mabel McF. McCloskey. 1943. 286p.
P4-S09759 — $42.50.

ENGLAR: Genealogy of the Englar family, the descendants of Philip Englar, 1736-1817 V.E. Barnes. 1929. 79p.
P4-S09765 — $16.00.

ENGLE: History & family records of Dauphin & Lancaster Cos., PA; the numerous lineal descendants of Ulrich Engel, 1754-1927. By Morris M. Engle. 1927. 161p.
P4-S09777 — $24.00.

ENGLE: Fam. Desc. of Robt. of Cambridgeshire, Eng. who settled in Evesham, NJ. By G. Haines. 1902. 5p.
P4-S09778 — $10.00.

ENGLE: Melchor Engle family history & genealogy, 1730-1940, By Winfield S.H. Engle. 1940. 500p.
P4-S09783 — $75.00.

ENO: Family, NY branch. By H.L. Eno. 1920. 35p.
P4-S09784 — $10.00.

ENOCH: Partial gen. of desc. of Henry Enoch of PA. By A. Gibbens. 1894. 12p.
P4-S09785 — $10.00.

ENSIGN: Record of the descendants of James Ensign, the Puritan, 1634-1939. By M.E. Ensign, et al. 1939. 340p.
P4-S09789 — $53.00.

EPLER: History & genealogy of the Epler, Oldwiler, Huckleberry, Carr & Ewing families.
E.E. Knudson. 1913. 137p.
P4-S09795 — $24.50.

EPPERSON: The story of David Epperson & his family of Albemarle Co., VA, with supplementary notes on the Epperson family in America. By Edna E. Brinkman. 1933. 304p.
P4-S09801 — $46.50.

EPPLEY: Hist. & gen. of the descendants of Jacob (Eppli, Aeply, Ebli) Eppley, the pioneer Eppley of America 1936. 200p.
P4-S09807 — $30.00.

ERSKINE: Fam. of Bristol, ME. By F.E. Woodward. 1920. 31p.
P4-S09808 — $10.00.

ERWIN: Erwin fam. record. By F. Brandt. 1895. 8p.
P4-S09809 — $10.00.

ESCHBACH: Gen. annals of Anthony & Barbara Eshbach, with brief records of their children & descendants. By Edmund R. Eschbach. 1902. 55p.
P4-S09810 — $11.00.

ESH: Genealogy of the descendants of Christopher Esh. By Benj. L. Blank. 1949. 201p.
P4-S09813 — $32.00.

ESPY: History & genealogy of the Espy family in America. By Florence M. Espy. 1905. 126p.
P4-S09819 — $21.00.

ESSELTINE: Ancestry and descendants of Conrad Esseltine (Esselstyne, Asselstine), some allied families with 1946 addendum By Inez Fowler Johnson. 1943. 69 + 11p.
P4-S09825 — $16.00.

ESSLINGER: Two hundred years of the Esslinger family. By W.F. Esslinger. (n.d.) 116p.
P4-S09831 — $19.50.

ESTABROOK: Gen. of the Estabrook family, incl. the Esterbrook & Easterbrooks in the US. By W. B. Estabrook. 1891. 359p.
P4-S09834 — $46.00.

ESTABROOKS: Gen. of the Anglo-Dutch Estabrooks family of the St John River, New Brunswick, revised ed. By Florence C. Estabrooks. 1935, rev. 1958. 211p.
P4-S09840 — $32.00.

ESTEP: Estep: Thomas, Sr. (c.1709-c.1772) of Frederick County, MD & His Descendants. Margaret E. Vidal. 1994. x + 798p.
P4-S09841 — $120.00.

ESTES: Genealogy, 1097-1893. By C. Estes. 1894. 417p.
P4-S09843 — $53.00.

ESTILL: Family history. By "One of the Family." 1903. 144p.
P4-S09849 — $22.50.

ESTY: Isaac Esty of Topsfield & some of his desc. (Repr. Essex Inst. Hist. Coll.) By G. E. Bangs. 1900. 12p.
P4-S09850 — $10.00.

ETHEREDGE: Our Etheredge fam. circles from 1753-1953. By H. Etheredge. 1953 (?). 72p.
P4-S09855 — $14.50.

EUSTIS: Genealogy of the Eustis family. By H.L. Eustis. 1878. 27p.
P4-S09856 — $10.00.

EVANS: JACKSON. The Jones & Evans fam. of Portage & Mahoning Cos., OH & the Jackson & Somers fam. of Portsmouth, NH & Buffalo, NY. By O.O. & A.J. Evans. 1954. 74p.
P4-S09897 — $15.00.

EVANS: WHITTING, Davis [of PA]. 1922. 163p.
P4-S09891 — $24.50.

EVANS: Genealogy of the Evans, Nivin & allied families. By Septimus E. Nivin. 1930. 270p.
P4-S09879 — $42.00.

EVANS: Descendants of David Evans of Charlestown, MA, By S.A. Evans. 1893. 107p.
P4-S09867 — $17.00.

EVANS: History of Nathaniel Evans of Cat Fish Creek [DE]. By James D. Evans. 1905. 104p.
P4-S09885 — $17.50.

EVANS: Ancestry & descendants of Thomas Stickney Evans & Sarah Ann Fifield of Fryeburg, ME. By Walter L. Sheppard. 1940. 214p.
P4-S09861 — $33.50.

EVANS: Family. S. Evans. 1895. 21p.
P4-S09862 — $10.00.

EVANS: Genealogy of the Evans family, the VA Biddles & other related families. By Esther M. Leithold. 1940? 68 + 10p., typescript.
P4-S09873 — $15.00.

EVARTS: John Evarts of Guilford, CT & his desc. (Repr. NEHGR) By R. D. Smyth. 1907. 7p.
P4-S09898 — $10.00.

EVERENDEN: Descendants of Walter Everenden, Powdermaker in MA, 1684. By L.E. Wagstaff. 1966. 110p.
P4-S09909 — $19.00.

EVEREST: Descendants of Andrew Everest of York, ME. By W.L. Holman. 1955. 488p.
P4-S09915 — $74.00.

EVERETT: Early 17th century immigrant British ancestors of Jean Gilman Everett Bonafide, Malcolm Gould Everett, Peter Stowell Everett . . . By Harold H. Everett. 1997. 255p.
P4-S09924 — $39.00.

EVERETT: Descendants of Richard Everett of Dedham, MA. By E. F. Everett. 1902. 389p.
P4-S09918 — $61.50.

EVERTON: KNOWLES Book: life story of Walter Marion Everton & his wife Laura Knowels Everton By Walter M. Everton. 1942. 132p., typescript.
P4-S09930 — $21.00.

EWBANK: John & Ann Ewbank family [immigr. from England in 1807, to IN, 1811]. Richard L. Ewbank & Louis B. Ewbank. 1948? 104p.
P4-S09936 — $18.00.

EWING: Alexander Ewing (1676/7-1738) & descendants, Ireland to America in 1727. By James R. McMichael. 1999. 647p.
P4-S09942 — $95.00.

EWING: Clan Ewing of Scotland: early history & contribution to America. By Elbert W.R. Ewing. 1922. 382p.
P4-S09954 — $57.00.

EWING: Ewing in Early America. Margaret Ewing Fife. 2002. 472p.
P4-S09943 — $71.00.

EWING: Rec. of the fam. of Thomas Ewing, who emigr. from Ireland to Amer. In 1718. R.P. DuBois. 1858. 38p.
P4-S09944 — $10.00.

EWING: Sketches of the fam. of Thomas, William & James Ewing & their desc. By J. L. Ewing. 1910. 123p.
P4-S09960 — $25.00.

EWING: Genealogy, with cognate branches. P.K. & M.E. Ewing. 1919. 244p.
P4-S09954 — $36.50.

EYERMAN: The anc. of Marguerite Eyerman: (Oster, Schaeffer, Roessel, Schneider, Black, etc.). By J. Eyerman. 1898. 48p.
P4-S09962 — $10.00.

EYERMAN: The anc. of Marguerite & John Eyerman. By J. Eyerman. Suppl. to 1898 ed. 1899. 35p.
P4-S09961 — $10.00.

EYESTONE: Genealogy of Eyestone & Related Families. J. Bruce Eyestone 1948. 186p.
P4-S09963 — $24.00.

EYRE: Genealogy, tracing the ancestors & descendants of Isaac & Eleanor Cooper Eyre. By Barclay Eyre. 1921. 16p.
P4-S09964 — $10.00.

F

FABENS: Some of the descendants of Jonathan Fabens of Marblehead. By G. A. Perkins. 1881. 26p.
P4-S09965 — $10.00.

FAHNESTOCK: Genealogy; Anc. & desc. of Johann Diedrich Fahnestock. By H.M. Pitman. 1945. 442p.
P4-S09966 — $67.50.

FAHNESTOCK: Fam. mem. of the Fahnestocks in the US. By A.K. & W.F. Fahnestock. 1879. 69p.
P4-S09972 — $14.00.

FAIN: Notable Southern families: Fain of TN, descendants of Nicholas Fain. By Augusta Bradford. 1930. 31p.
P4-S09973 — $10.00.

FAIRBANK: Ye Fayerbanke historical [biography & genealogy], Vol. I, Nos. 1-3. 1903-1904 54 + 34p
P4-S09978 — $17.00.

FAIRBANK: Antecedents & Descendants of Nathaniel Kellogg Fairbank. Dorr Bradley Carpenter. 2005. iv + 268p.
P4-S09979 — $41.00.

FAIRBANKS: Family, rev. ed. By Thaddeus Fairbanks. 1892. 55 + 17p.
P4-S09984 — $14.50.

FAIRBANKS: Genealogy of the Fairbanks fam. in America, 1633-1897. By L. S. Fairbanks. 1897. 967p.
P4-S09987 — $121.00.

FAIRCHILD: Revised ed. of the name & family of Fairchild. By T.M. Fairchild with S.E.F. Filter. 1944. 278p.
P4-S09999 — $44.00.

FAIRFAX: The Fairfaxes of Eng. & Amer. in the 17th & 18th cent. By E.D. Neill. 1868. 234p.
P4-S10005 — $34.50.

FAIRFIELD: Desc. of John Fairfield of Wenham, Vol. I: First five generations, with an appendix on Fairfield Fams. in Eng. W.C. Fairfield. 1953. 82p.
P4-S10011 — $16.50.

FAIRMAN: Desc. of John Fairman of Enfield, CT, 1638-1898. By O. P. Allen. 1898. 38p.
P4-S10012 — $10.00.

FALES: Family of Bristol, RI; anc. of Haliburton Fales of NY, By DeCoursey Fales. 1919. 332p.
P4-S10017 — $53.00.

FALES: Fales Family: The First Ten Generations in America. J. T. Fales. 2005. xviii + 475p.
P4-S010018 — $74.00.

FANCHER: Family. By W. H. Fancher. 1947. 144p.
P4-S10023 — $24.00.

FANNING: History of the Fanning family; gen. record to 1900 of the desc. of Edmund Fanning, who settled in CT in 1655. By W.F. Brooks. 1905. 2 vols., 872p.
P4-S10029 — $131.00.

FARABEE: Genealogy of the Farabess in America. By Louis T. Farabee. 1918. 345p.
P4-S10035 — $52.00.

FARGO: Record of the Fargo family. By John J. Giblin. 1907. 35p.
P4-S10036 — $10.00.

FARIS: Eight generations of the VA branch of the Faris family in the US. By Nellie L. Flack. 1917? 117p.
P4-S10041 — $17.00.

FARLEY: Twelve generations of Farleys. By J. Farley, Jr. 1943. 260p.
P4-S10047 — $39.00.

FARMAR: Hist. of Thos. & Anne (Billopp) Farmer & some of their desc. By C. F. Billopp. 1907. 137p.
P4-S10053 — $23.50.

FARMER: Farmer fam. of E. TN (Extr. from Gen. of some E. TN Fam.) 1945. 24p.
P4-S10060 — $10.00.

FARMER: Descendants of Thomas Farmer, who came to VA in 1616. By Ellery Farmer. 1956. 88p.
P4-S10059 — $18.00.

FARMER: Genealogy of the Farmer, Cox & Hopkins families of Fayette Co., IL. By Mrs F.C. Harrington. 1942. 113p.
P4-S10065 — $17.00.

FARNHAM: John Farnham (Farnum, Varnum) of Dorchester & desc. By H.F. Johnston. 1959. 18p.
P4-S10078 — $10.00.

FARNHAM: Genealogy of the Farnham family. By J.M.W. Farnham. 1886. 92p.
P4-S10079 — $18.50.

FARNHAM: Ralph Farnham of Andover, MA & his desc. By H.F. Johnston. 1950. 74p.
P4-S10083 — $15.00.

FARNHAM: Genealogy of the Farnham family, 1603-1926. By Levi L. Farnham. 1926. 107p.
P4-S10077 — $17.00.

FARNSWORTH.L: Memorial. Record of Matthias Farnsworth & his descendants in America. By M.F. Farnsworth. 1897. 514p.
P4-S10086 — $65.00.

FARNUM: "Know thyself": a genealogy. By Leora E. Belknap. 1948. 105p., typescript.
P4-S10092 — $16.50.

FARR: Descendants of Thomas Farr of Harpswell, ME & ninety allied families. By E.B. Sumner. 1959. 390p.
P4-S10098 — $59.50.

FARRAR: Some American Farrars. By Calvin L. Farrar. 1948. 214p.
P4-S10104 — $32.00.

FARREN: FERRIN, Capt. Jonathan Farren of Amesbury, MA & some desc. By Ferrin & Brennan. 1941. 222p.
P4-S10110 — $37.00.

FARRINGTON: Mem.; a sketch of the anc. & desc. of Dea. John Farrington of Wrentham, MA & ME. By Farrington Reunion Comm., 1880. 23p.
P4-S10111 — $10.00.

FARWELL: Ancestral memorial; Henry Farwell of Concord & Chelmsford, MA. By D.P. & F.K. Holton. 1879. 258p.
P4-S10116 — $43.00.

FARWELL: Fam. A hist. of Henry Farwell & his wife Olive (Welby) Farwell of Boston, Eng., & Concord & Chelmsford, MA, 1605-1927 By Farwell, Abbott & Wilson. 1929. 2 vols. 941p.
P4-S10122 — $139.00.

FAUBION: The Faubions. By Sarag F. Pangle. 1922. 82p.
P4-S10128 — $16.00.

FAUCONNIER: Pierre Fauconnier & his descendants, with some acct. of allied Valleaux. By A.E. Helffenstein. 1911. 266p.
P4-S10134 — $42.00.

FAULKNER: My anc. & their desc., the Faulkner fam. By W. L. Brown. 38p.
P4-S10135 — $10.00.

FAVILL: Favill fam. S. Favill. 1899. 44p.
P4-S10136 — $10.00.

FAXON: History of the Faxon family, containing a gen. of the desc. of Thomas Faxon of Braintree, MA & allied fam. By G.L. Faxon. 1880. 377p.
P4-S10140 — $48.50.

FAY: One branch of the Fay family tree: ancestors & descendants of William & Elizabeth Fay of Westboro MA & Marietta, OH. By G. Johnson. 1913. 130p.
P4-S10152 — $25.00.

FAY: Genealogy, John Fay of Marlborough & his desc. By O.P. Fay. 1898. 420p.
P4-S10150 — $54.00.

FAY: Index to 1898 FAY genealogy. 119p., typescript.
P4-S010144 — $17.00.

FEARN: Desc. of John Fearn & Mary Lee of VA, mar. 1687, By McAllister & Tandy. 1906. 9p.
P4-S10155 — $10.00.

FEATHERSTONE: Featherstones & Halls; gleanings from old fam. letters & mss. By M. Irwin. 1890. 99p.
P4-S10158 — $18.00.

FEETER: History of Wm. Feeter, a soldier in the War of American independence, & his father Lucas Vetter . . . John B. Koetteritz. 1901. 125p.
P4-S10164 — $18.00.

FELCH: Memorial history of Felch family in America & Wales. By W. F. Felch. 1881. 98p.
P4-S10167 — $16.50.

FELL: Genealogy of the Fell fam. in America desc. from Joseph Fell who settled Bucks. Co., PA, 1705. By S.M. Fell. 1891. 515p.
P4-S10173 — $65.50.

FELLOWS: FALLOWES — FELLOW & like names: Fellows ancestry in New England & Old England, with data on English origins. By Louis D. Scisco. 1926. 113p.
P4-S10179 — $18.00.

FELLOWS: Family of Shelburne. By Robt. F. Wood. 1957. 159 + 9p.
P4-S10185 — $25.00.

FELLOWS: Genealogy of William Fellows of Ipswich, MA. By T.F. Waters. 1909. 16p.
P4-S10180 — $10.00.

FELLOWS: Joseph & Philena (Elton) Fellows: their ancestors & descendants. By M.M. Morris. 1940. 404p.
P4-S10197 — $61.00.

FELLOWS: Gen. of the Fellows-Craig & allied fam. from 1619-1919. By F. H. Craig. 1919. 151p.
P4-S10191 — $22.50.

FELT: Genealogy, a record of the desc. of George Felt of Casco Bay. By J.E. Morris. 1893. 568p.
P4-S10209 — $87.00.

FELT: A register of the anc. of Dorr E. Felt & Agnes McNulty Felt. By A. L. Holman. 1921. 267p.
P4-S10203 — $40.00.

FELTON: Brief acct. of the desc. of Nathaniel & Mary Felton of Salem, MA. By C. Felton. 1877. 19p.
P4-S10216 — $10.00.

FELTON: Family: desc. of Lt. Nathaniel Felton, who came to Salem, MA in 1633, (extension of 1886 & 1935 books). By N.F. Koster. 1963. 251p.
P4-S10221 — $38.50.

FELTON: A gen. hist. of the Felton fam., desc. of Lt. Nathaniel Felton who came to Salem, MA, 1633. By C. Felton. 1886. 260p.
P4-S10215 — $39.00.

FELTON: Gen. hist. of the Felton family: anc. & desc. of Lt. Nathaniel Felton who came to Salem, MA from Gt. Yarmouth, Eng., in 1633 By W.R. Felton. 1935. 467p.
P4-S10227 — $72.00.

FELTUS: Family book containing a biographical sketch of the Rev. Henry James Feltus & Descendants. By Geo. H. Feltus. 1917. 61p.
P4-S10239 — $12.00.

FENTON: Family history of Jeremiah Fenton (1764-1841), of Adams Co., OH & his descendants. By Wm. B. Brown. 1910. 206p.
P4-S10239 — $31.50.

FENTON: The Fenton fam. of America & Great Britain. By T. A. Atkins. 1912. 154p.
P4-S10245 — $23.00.

FENTON: Gen. of Fenton fam., desc. of Robert Fenton of Windham, CT. By W. L. Weaver. 1867. 34p.
P4-S10240 — $10.00.

FENWICK: Allied ancestry; Ancestry of Thomas Fenwick of Sussex Co., DE. By Edwin J. Sellers. 1916. 101p.
P4-S10251 — $19.00.

FERGUSON: Family in Scotland & America. By M.L. Ferguson. 1905. 142p.
P4-S10257 — $25.50.

FERGUSON: Susanna Cornell Ferguson & her descendants. By Edw. Cornell. 1937. 78p.
P4-S10275 — $16.00.

FERGUSON: Records of the Clan & name of Fergusson, Ferguson & Fergus. ed. by J. & R.M. Fergusson. 1895 xxx + 618p.
P4-S10269 — $94.00.

FERGUSON: Gen. of desc. of John Ferguson of Scotland & US. By A.B. Ferguson. 1911. 112p.
P4-S10263 — $22.50.

FERRIER: Thos. Ferrier & some desc. By E.E. Lane. 1906. 56p.
P4-S10276 — $11.00.

FERRIS: Ancestry. By Louise Austin. 1934. 85p., typescript.
P4-S10281 — $16.00.

FERRIS: Genealogy of the Ferris family: descendants of Zachariah Ferris. By Harriet Scofield. 1954. 72 + 14p., typescript.
P4-S10287 — $16.00.

FERRIS: Part. gen. of the Ferris fam. By C. Crowell. 1899. 60p.
P4-S10290 — $12.00.

FERRY: The Ferry's of Staffordville, CT & their New England ancestry. By G.O. Chapman. 1942. 47p.
P4-S10288 — $10.00.

FIELD: Genealogy, being the record of all of the Field fam. in America whose anc. were in this country prior to 1700, By F.C. Pierce. 1901. 2 vols., 1196p.
P4-S10299 — $159.00.

FIELD: Gen. of the Fields of Providence, RI. By H. A. Brownell. 1878. 65p.
P4-S10311 — $13.00.

FIELD: Fields of Sowerby near Halifax, Eng. & Flushing, NY. By O. Field. 1895. 138p.
P4-S10305 — $21.00.

FIELD: Record of the fam. of Rev. David D. Field, D.D., of Stockbridge, MA. By H.M. Field. 1880. 147p.
P4-S10317 — $22.00.

FILLMORE: So soon forgotten; Three thousand Fillmores: the descendants of John, the Mariner, & his wife, Abigail (Tilton) Fillmore. By Charles L. Fillmore. 1984. 715p.
P4-S10329 — $85.00.

FILLMORE: Memorials of the family of Fynmore, with notes on the origin of Fynmore, Finnimore, Phillimore, Fillmore, etc. By Wm. P.W. Phillimore. 1886. 77p.
P4-S10323 — $15.00.

FILLMORE: Mem. of Capt. John Fillmore. By A. Woodward. 1857. 13p.
P4-S10324 — $10.00.

FILLOW: PHILO — PHILEO Gen: a rec. of the desc. of John Fillow, Huguenot refugee from France. By D.H. Van Hoosear. 1888. 274p.
P4-S10335 — $43.50.

FINCH: Family Association bulletins. 1945-1956 138p., typescript.
P4-S10341 — $23.00.

FINGON: Memoirs of Clan Fingon, with famly tree. By Donald D. MacKinnon. 1909. 246p.
P4-S10347 — $39.00.

FINLEY: The Clan Finley, Vol. I. By Herald F. Stout. 1956. 176p.
P4-S10353 — $25.00.

FINLEY: The Clan Finley, Vol. II. 1957. 217p.
P4-S10359 — $33.00.

FINNEY: PHINNEY Families in America: descendants of John Finney of Plymouth & Barnstable, MA & Bristol, RI. By Howard Finney, Sr. 1957. 298p.
P4-S10365 — $45.00.

FINNEY: Bristol branch of the Finney fam. By F. Clark. 1906. 13p.
P4-S10364 — $10.00.

FISCHER: Jacob Fischer, the immigr. Early settler in the Perkioman Val. By Dotterer & Strassburger. 1927. 39p.
P4-S10370 — $10.00.

FISH: Ancestors of Hamilton Fish & Julia Ursin Niemcewicz Kean, his wife. Stuyvesant Fish. 1929. 177 + 40p.
P4-S10371 — $33.00.

FISH: Family in England & America: gen. & bio. records & sketches. By Lester W. Fish. 1948. 530p.
P4-S10377 — $79.50.

FISH: Genealogy of the Fish & Van Wagenen-Van Wagner families. By Dr F.E. Weeks. 1938. 50p., typescript.
P4-S10372 — $10.00.

FISH: The gen. & desc. of Luke Fish, Sr., in chronological order from 1760-1904. By D. Fish. 1904. 80p.
P4-S10383 — $16.00.

FISHBACK: Family in America: Desc. of John Fishback, the emigr., with historical sketch of his family By W.M. Kemper. 1914. 356p.
P4-S10389 — $56.50.

FISHER: STOMBAUGH families & allied lineages of MD & PA, 1715-1949. By Florence H. Petersen. 1950. 409p.
P4-S10395 — $62.00.

FISHER: One dozen pre-Revolutionary War families of eastern NC & some of their descendants [incl. Fisher, Paquinet, Pelletier, etc.) By P.W. Fisher. 1958. 629p.
P4-S10422 — $69.50.

FISHER: Gen. of Joseph Fisher & his desc., & of the allied fam. of Farley, Farlee, Feherman, Pitner, Reeder, & Shipman. By C. W. Fisher. 1890. 243p.
P4-S10410 — $36.50.

FISHER: & Allied families [some descendants of Thos. Fisher of England & Dedham, MA] n.d. 66p., typescript.
P4-S10398 — $12.50.

FISHER: Genealogical record of the desc. of Joshua, Anthony & Cornelius Fisher, of Dedham, MA, 1636-40. By P.A. Fisher. 1898. 474p.
P4-S10404 — $60.00.

FISHER: Life of George Fisher (1795-1873) & the hist. of the Fisher fam. in MS. By Parmenter, Fisher & Mallette. 1959. 299p.
P4-S10416 — $47.00.

FISKE: FISK Family; descendants of Symond Fiske, Lord of the Manor, Studhaugh, Suffolk Co., Eng. By F.C. Pierce. 1896. 660p.
P4-S10425 — $82.00.

FISKE: Family; Hist. of the fam. (anc. & desc.) of Wm. Fiske, Sen., of Amherst, NH, with brief notices of other branches. A.A. Fiske. 1867. 216p.
P4-S10431 — $32.50.

FISKE: Genealogy of a Fiske family, 16 generations, 1399-1867. By A. Poor. 1867. 20p.
P4-S10426 — $10.00.

FITCH: History of the Fitch family, 1400-1930. R. C. Fitch. 1930. 2 vols., 557p.
P4-S10443 — $89.00.

FITCH: Genealogy of the Fitch family in North America. J.G. Fitch. 1886. 116p.
P4-S10437 — $17.50.

FITCH: Genealogy; Rec of six gen. of the desc. of Dea. Zachary Fitch of Reading, MA (Repr. NEHGR) By E. S. Stearns. 1902. 23p.
P4-S10438 — $10.00.

FITE: The biographical & genealogical records of the Fite families in the US, By E.M.S. Fite. 1907. 175p.
P4-S10449 — $28.00.

FITTS: FITZ; Genealogy of the Fitts or Fitz family in America. By James H. Fitts. 1897. 170p.
P4-S10455 — $27.50.

FITTS: Gen. of the Fitts of Fitz fam. in Amer. By J.H. Fitts. 1869. 91p.
P4-S10461 — $18.00.

FITZ RANDOLPH: Edward Fitz Randolph Branch Lines. Allied Families & English & Norman Ancestry, A Family Genealogy, 860-1976. Oris H. F. Randolph 1976, 1980 x + 841p.
P4-S10468 — $115.00.

FITZ RANDOLPH: Traditions: a story of a thousand years. By L.V.F. Randolph. 1907. 134p.
P4-S10467 — $24.00.

FITZRANDOLPH: Family, from "Family Sketches." J.R. Wood. 1870. 49p.
P4-S10469 — $10.00.

FIX: Family; Digging up our German roots: adventures in genealogy. By Ed Fix. 2000. 438p.
P4-S10473 — $67.50.

FLAGG: Genealogical notes on the founding of New Eng.; my ancestors' part in that undertaking. By E. Flagg. 1926. 440p.
P4-S10497 — $39.00.

FLAGG: Descendants of Eleazer Flagg & his wife Huldah Chandler of Grafton, MA. By Chas. Alcott Flagg. 1903. 228p.
P4-S10479 — $32.50.

FLAGG: Fam. records of the desc. of Gershom Flagg of Lancaster, MA. By N.G. Flagg & L.C.S. Flagg. 1907. 173p.
P4-S10491 — $26.00.

FLAGG: Descendants of Josiah Flagg of Berkeley Co. WV, with sketches of Flagg, Keyes, Foss, Shiveley, Hughes, Slemons & Campbell. comp. by C.A. Flagg. 1920. 93p.
P4-S10485 — $18.00.

FLANDERS: Descendants of Stephen Flanders of Salisbury, MA, 1646 By Ellery K. Taylor. 1932. 117p.
P4-S10503 — $19.00.

FLANDERS: Family from Europe to Amer: being a hist. of the Flanders fam. In Amer. & its probable origin in Europe. By E.F. Dunbar. 1935. 1032p.
P4-S10509 — $139.00.

FLANDERS: Family. By W. Prescott. 1873. 8p.
P4-S10504 — $10.00.

FLEEK: George Fleek & his desc: hist. of the Fleeks & Maloneys of NW PA, with add. notes on the hist. of Little Cooley, PA. By G. Southworth. 1958. 120p.
P4-S10515 — $21.00.

FLEMING: Family & allied lines: Baird, Blair, Butler, Cook, Childs, Clark, Cole, Crane, et al. By P.V. Lawson. 1903. 304p.
P4-S10521 — $46.50.

FLEMING: History of the Fleming family. By H. Teetor. 9p.
P4-S10522 — $10.00.

FLEMING: William Fleming family, a genealogy, with a brief account of some other Flemings of DE. By Franklin M. Brand. 1941. 652p.
P4-S10527 — $98.00.

FLEMING: Family records. By J.M. Seaver. 1929. 40p.
P4-S10526 — $10.00.

FLETCHER: Genealogy; an acct. of the desc. of Robert Fletcher of Concord, MA. E.H. Fletcher. 1871. 279p.
P4-S10536 — $36.50.

FLETCHER: The Fletchers of Auchallader. 1916. 17p.
P4-S10537 — $10.00.

FLETCHER: Gen. in part of the Fletcher-Crowder-Tucker fam. By G. J. Anderson. 1909. 92p.
P4-S10542 — $15.00.

FLETCHER: Lineage. By Winifred L. Holman. 1928. 58p., typescript.
P4-S10541 — $11.50.

FLETCHER: The Desc of Robert Fletcher of Concord, MA. Edward H. Fletcher. 1881. 563 + 85p.
P4-S10540 — $97.00.

FLETCHER: Case: account of the descent & relationships of the late Christopher Fletcher of Netherwasdale, yeoman, & of his will. By Rev. C. Moor. 1910 86p.
P4-S10533 — $16.50.

FLEWELLEN: "Family skeleton:" history & genealogy of the Flewellen, Fontaine, Copeland, Treutland, McCormick, Allan & Stuart. By Henrietta McC. Hill. 1958. 186p.
P4-S10548 — $27.50.

FLICKINGER: Family history. By R.E. Flickinger. 1927. 820p.
P4-S10554 — $109.00.

FLINT: Thomas Flint & Wm. Flint of Salem, MA & their desc. By A.M. Smith. 1931. 232p.
P4-S10569 — $30.00.

FLINT: Family: Robert Flint (the Pioneer) & his descendants: history & genealogy of the Flint family By C. Ellis Flint. 1932. 119p.
P4-S10566 — $21.00.

FLINT: A gen. reg. of the desc. in a direct line of Thomas Flint to Capt. Benj. Flint, & the desc. of Cheney Flint. By N. & R. Flint. 1915. 20p.
P4-S10565 — $10.00.

FLINT: Genealogical register of the desc. of Thomas Flint, of Salem, By J. Flint & J. H. Stone. 1860. 150p.
P4-S10560 — $21.50.

FLINT: A Supplement to the Gen. Register of the Descendants of Thomas Flint of Salem. Carrie E. Crowell 1939. 71p. P4-S10561 — $14.00.

FLINT: Genealogy of Ephraim Flint of Baldwin, ME. By Edw. F. Brown. 1882. 29p. P4-S10564 — $10.00.

FLORA: Genealogy & history of descendants of Jacob Flora, Sr., of Franklin Co., VA. By Joel C. Flora. 1951. 375p. P4-S10575 — $57.00.

FLORY: Genealogy of the Flory-Dinkey family, with direct ancestors incl. Boyd, Wallace, Carnahan, Cobb, etc. By G.F. Dinkey. 1946. 98p. P4-S10581 — $19.00.

FLOWER: FLOWERS Family. n.d. 66p., typescript. P4-S10584 — $12.50.

FLOYD: JONES; Thomas Jones, Ft. Neck, Queens Co. Long Island, 1695, & his descendants By T. Floyd-Jones. 1906. 183 + 11p. P4-S10599 — $29.50.

FLOYD: Biogr. gen. of the VA-KY Floyd fam. By N. J. Floyd. 1912. 113p. P4-S10593 — $20.00.

FLOYD: Family of Rumney Marsh. By C.H. Floyd. 1909. 15p. P4-S10594 — $10.00.

FLYNN: Descs of Charles Flynn & Margaret Faherty, Co. Longford, Ireland, & Crawford Co., WI, 1850-1998. By Genevieve C. Kennedy. 1998. 240p. P4-S10605 — $36.00.

FOGG: Fam. of Amer. Reunions of the Fogg fam. (1st to 6th) 1902-06. By Fogg & Willis. 1907. 141p. P4-S10617 — $24.00.

FOGG: Gen. of the Fogg fam. desc. of Samuel Fogge. By H. Fogg. 1903. 49p. P4-S10612 — $10.00.

FOLGER: Highlights of the Folger family, with a brief genealogy. By Harriet M. Grover. 1939. 73p., typescript. P4-S10623 — $14.50.

FOLKINS: Family: some descendants of Joseph Folkins & Anna Lydekker to the 7th generation. By Wm. H. Folkins, with John R. Elliott. 2nd ed., 1994. 551p. P4-S10624 — $75.00.

FOLLETT: DEWEY, Fassett-Safford anc. of Capt. Martin Dewey Follett (1765-1831) & his wife, Persis Fassett (1767-1849). By H. P. Ward. 1896. 249p. P4-S10626 — $37.00.

FOLLIN: Genealogical history of the Follin family in America. By Gabriel Edmonston. 1911. 142p. P4-S10632 — $22.50.

FOLLIN: Follin Family Tree Update. Donna D. Anderson Follin. 2005. vi + 419p. P4-S10633 — $64.00.

FOLLMER: History of the Follmer family. By Chas. C. Follmer. 1899. 128p. P4-S10638 — $19.00.

FOLSOM: Genealogy of the Folsom family: John Folsom & his desc. 1615-1882. By J. Chapman. 1882. 297p. P4-S10647 — $39.00.

FOLSOM: Genealogy of the Folsom family, 1638-1938. Revised & ext. ed. Including English records. By E. Folsom. 1938. 2 vols., 1135p. P4-S10644 — $159.00.

FONES: Family: [NY & New England] descendants of William Fones of Saxby, England. By Art Reierson. 1998. 250p. P4-S10653 — $38.00.

FONTAINE: Gen. presenting data of the Fontaine, Maury, Dupuy, Trabue, Marye, Chastain, Cooke & other families By R.A. Brock. 1886. 132p. P4-S10659 — $22.00.

FONTAINEE: Memoirs of a Huguenot Family: Translated & Compiled from the Original Autobiography of the Rev. James Fontainee, & other Family Manuscripts. Ann Maury. 1872. 512p. P5-FR0002 — $57.00.

FOOTE: BINGHAM; Some New England families. Mrs J.A. King. 1922. 206p. P4-S10665 — $30.00.

FOOTE: Family, or the desc. of Nathaniel Foote, one of the first settlers of Wethersfield, CT. By Nathaniel Goodwin. 1849. 360p. P4-S10677 — $52.00.

FOOTE: Family, compr. the gen. & hist. of Nathaniel Foote, of Wethersfield, CT & his desc., vol I. By A.W. Foote. 1907. 607p. P4-S10671 — $89.00.

FOOTE: Family, vol II, 2nd ed. 1932. 723p. P4-S10683 — $99.00.

FORBES: FORBUSH Gen.; the desc. of Daniel Forbush, who came from Scotland about 1655 & settled in Marlborough, MA in 1675. By F.C. Pierce. 1892. 199p. P4-S10701 — $30.00.

FORBES: Ancestry of Wm. Forbes of Barre , MA & Montreal, Que., 1778-1833. Eva L. Moffatt. 1953. 103p., typescript. P4-S10695 — $18.50.

FORBES: Ancestors & descendants of Ephraim Forbes & Amy Fitch. By Clarence W. Vogel. 1957. 170p.; typescript P4-S10689 — $22.00.

FORBES: The House of Forbes. ed. By A. & H. Tayler. 1937. 494p. P4-S10707 — $76.50.

FORD: Family history: Richard Ford (Foord) of VA, his wife Elizabeth, & their descendants. By Wanda L. DeMooy. 2000. 196p. P4-S10713 — $29.00.

FORD: Family history. By J.M. Seaver. 33p. P4-S10714 — $10.00.

FORD: The Fords, 1854-1954 [descendants of John Ford & Rebecca Chandler]. 1954. 250p., typescript. P4-S10731 — $38.00.

FORD: The valley of the shadow; a gen. study of the anc. & desc. of Capt. Paul Ford of Lyman, ME, 1577-1952. By P. G. Ford. 1953. 59p. P4-S10715 — $11.50.

FORD: Genealogy of the Ford family. By James Ford. 1890. 291p. P4-S10725 — $45.00.

FORD: Gen; an acct. of some of the Fords: early settlers in New Eng., particularly the desc. of Martin-Mathew Ford of Bradford, MA By E.R. Ford. 1916. 249p. P4-S10719 — $37.00.

FOREMAN: FARMAN — FOMAN Gen. Desc. of Wm. Foreman, who came from London, Eng., in 1675 & settled near Annapolis, MD. By E. Farman. 1911. 232p. P4-S10737 — $34.50.

FORESMAN: Genealogy, [with] Brown, Morris, Barney. By Laverna Foresman. 1946. 163p.
P4-S10743 — $23.50.

FORMAN: Gen. Desc. of Robt. Forman of Kent Co. MD, Robt. Forman of L.I., NY & the Forman fam. of Monmouth Co. NJ. By A.S. Dendridge. 1903. 151p.
P4-S10749 — $23.00.

FORNEY: Forney's five family records of genealogy of Benners, Blappers, Ettlemans, Forneys & Studys, with historical sketches. By Chas. W. Forney. 1931. 371p.
P4-S10755 — $57.00.

FORNEY: Sketches of the Forney family. By H.O.F. 1911. 129p.
P4-S10767 — $19.50.

FORNEY: Sketches & genealogy of the Forney family from Lancaster Co., PA, in part. John K. Forney. 1926. 115p.
P4-S10761 — $18.00.

FORRER: Christian Forrer the clockmaker & his descendants. By Frank Bruen. 1939. 249p.
P4-S10773 — $39.00.

FORREST: History of the antecedents & descendants of Wm. & Dorothy Worthen Forrest of Canterbury Borough, NH. By Lucy Rogers Cross. 1897. 146p.
P4-S10779 — $23.00.

FORRESTER: Simon Forrester of Salem & his descendants. By Henry W. Belknap. 1935. 48p.
P4-S10780 — $10.00.

FORSTER: The pedigree & desc. of Jacob Forster, Sen., of Charlestown, MA. By E. J. Forster. 1870. 25p.
P4-S10781 — $10.00.

FORSYTH: A gen. Record; Forsyth of Nydie. By F. de Fronsac. (F. G. Forsyth) 1888. 29p.
P4-S10786 — $10.00.

FORSYTH: Memorial of the fam. of Forsyth de Fronsac. By F.G.F. de Fronsac. 1903. 104p.
P4-S10791 — $18.50.

FORSYTH: History of the Forsyth family. By Jennie F. Jeffries. 1920. 340p.
P4-S10785 — $52.00.

FORT: A family called Fort: the Descendants of Elias Fort of VA. By Homer T. Fort, Jr. & Drucilla Stovall Jones. 1970. vi + 757 + 19p.
P4-S10799 — $117.00.

FOSDICK: Annals of the Fosdick family. By R. Fosdick. 1953. 189p.
P4-S10803 — $28.50.

FOSDICK: Family, Oyster Bay branch 1583-1891, record of anc. & desc. of Samuel Fosdick of Oyster Bay. By L. L. Fosdick. 1891. 137p.
P4-S10809 — $26.50.

FOSTER: Grandchildren of Col. Jos. Foster of Ipswich & Gloucester, MA, 1730-1804. By J. Foster. 1885. 32p.
P4-S10816 — $10.00.

FOSTER: Family record of the Foster, Penny & Squires families, from their settling on Long Island to the present time [1895]. Alonzo Foster. 1895. 85p.
P4-S10839 — $17.00.

FOSTER: Fostors of Charlestown, MA (Repr. NEHGR). By Forster & Appleton. 1871. 5p.
P4-S10817 — $10.00.

FOSTER: Christopher Foster family history, Book One (Parts 1 & 2): hist. of the desc. of Christopher Foster & Frances Stevens By Helen Foster Shaw. 1953. 169 + 110 + 61p., typescript.
P4-S10821 — $52.50.

FOSTER: Christopher Foster family history, Book Two (Parts 3 & 4). By Helen Foster Shaw. 1953. 108 + 106p., typescript.
P4-S10827 — $33.50.

FOSTER: Christopher Foster family history, 1603-1953, supplement. Helen F. Snow. 1953. 125+38p; typescript.
P4-S10815 — $22.00.

FOSTER: Family, CA Pioneers, 1849. By Lucy F. Sexton. 1925. 285p.
P4-S10845 — $43.50.

FOSTER: Record: account of Thos. Foster of Billerica, MA & some of his descendants Frank M. Hawes. 1889. 139p.
P4-S10854 — $23.00.

FOSTER: Genealogy. A record of the posterity of Reginald Foster, early inhabitant of Ipswich & all other American Fosters. F. C. Pierce. 1899. 1081p.
P4-S10848 — $135.00.

FOSTER: Pedigree of Jesse W. Foster G.E. Foster. 1897. 503p.
P4-S10866 — $76.00.

FOSTER: of Dowsby & Moulton, Co. Lincoln. By Everard Green. 1875 6p.
P4-S10849 — $10.00.

FOSTER: Family; One line of the desc. of William Foster, son of Reginald Foster of Ipswich, MA, By P. Derby. 1872. 35p.
P4-S10850 — $10.00.

FOSTER: Col. Joseph Foster (1730-1804), his children & grandchildren, with supplemental records, 1887-1947. By J. Foster & E.A. Foster. 1947. 416p.
P4-S10833 — $62.00.

FOULKE: Allied families: . . . some of the descendants of Andreas Volck-Foulke & Mathias Lupfer. By Sunshine F. Chambers. 1952. 188p.
P4-S10872 — $29.00.

FOUSE: Genealogy of the desc. of Theobald Fouse (Fauss), incl. many other connected families. By G. M. Brumbaugh & J. G. Fouse. 1914. 302p.
P4-S10878 — $48.00.

FOWLE: Immigrant anc. of the various Fowle fam. of Amer. & hist. Facts pertaining to them & their desc. By E. P. Pierce. 1912. 22p.
P4-S10879 — $10.00.

FOWLER: Wives of the Fowlers, in one line from Wm. the magistrate. By W. C. Fowler. 24p.
P4-S10918 — $10.00.

FOWLER: William Fowler, the magistrate, & one line of his desc. By W. C. Fowler. 41p.
P4-S10891 — $10.00.

FOWLER: House of Fowler: history of the Fowler families of the South By Grover P. Fowler. 1940. 754p.
P4-S10908 — $109.00.

FOWLER: Genealogy of the Fowlers in England & America. By Wharton Dickinson. 1904. 65p.
P4-S10896 — $13.00.

FOWLER: Annals of the Fowler family, with branches in VA, NC, SC, TN, KY, AL, MS, CA & TX. By G.D.F. Arthur. 1901. 327p.
P4-S10884 — $51.00.

FOWLER: Gen. mem. of desc. of Ambrose & Wm. Fowler. 1857. 27p.
P4-S10903 — $10.00.

FOWLER: Desc. of Philip & Mary Fowler of Ipswich, MA, 1590-1882. By M. Stickney. 1883. 269p.
P4-S10890 — $40.00.

FOWLER: History of the Fowlers [descendants of Henry Fowler & William Fowler]. By Christine C. Fowler. 1950. 938p.
P4-S10902 — $129.50.

FOWLER: John Fowler of Guilford, CT & his desc. (Repr. NEHGR) By R. D. Smyth. 1899. 7p.
P4-S10905 — $10.00.

FOWLER: Our predecessors & their descendants. Robt. L. Fowler. 1888. 78p.
P4-S10920 — $16.00.

FOX: Genealogy, including the Metherd, Benner & Leiter descendants By D.G. Fox. 1924. 172p.
P4-S10938 — $27.50.

FOX: Hist. of that pt. of the Fox fam. desc. from Thomas Fox of Cambridge, MA. By N. Fox. 1899. 240p.
P4-S10944 — $36.00.

FOX: Fox family marriages. By W. M. Clemens. 1916. 44p.
P4-S10939 — $10.00.

FOX: Some Fox trails in old VA: John Fox of King Wm. Co., ancestors, descendants, near kin. By Ellen M. Cocke. 1939. 165p.
P4-S10950 — $25.00.

FOX: The desc. of Thos. Fox of Concord, MA, through his sixth son Isaac, of Medford, MA & New London, CT. By G.H. Fox. 1931. 54p.
P4-S10949 — $10.00.

FOX: Daniel Fox of E. Haddam, CT & some desc. 1890. 29p.
P4-S10948 — $10.00.

FOX: Biographical & historical accounts of the Fox, Ellicott & Evans families & the different families connected with them. By Chas. W. Evans. 1882. 289p.
P4-S10926 — $44.50.

FOX: Cousins by the dozens (includes allied lines Aldridge, Ballard, Berryman, Brookshire, Conkwright, Fish, etc.) By Nellie Fox Adams & Bertha Fox Walton. 1976. 408p.
P4-S10932 — $59.50.

FRACHE: Out of the House of Frache: Christopher & Peter & their associated American families. By Genevieve C. Kennedy. 1980. 311p.
P4-S10956 — $47.50.

FRAME: Some ancestors of the Rev. John Selby Frame & his wife Clara Winchester Dana. By Julia L.F. Bunce. 1948. 396p.
P4-S10962 — $64.50.

FRAMPTON: Family, with especial reference to Wm. Frampton, register general, Prov. of PA, 1686, & his desc. By J.S. Wrightnour. 1916? 208p.
P4-S10968 — $35.00.

FRANCIS: Descendants of Joseph Francis of MD & VA. By L.M. Dickson. 1949. 165 + 15 + 31p.
P4-S10974 — $32.00.

FRANCIS: Descendants of Robt Francis of Wethersfield CT; gen. records of various branches of the Francis fam. of CT origin. By C.E. Francis. 1906. 226p.
P4-S10980 — $29.50.

FRANCIS: Extr. from Hist. of Wethersfield, CT. 1904. 15p.
P4-S10975 — $10.00.

FRANK: Hist. of the Matthew Frank fam. By H. Nelson. 1921. 24p.
P4-S10981 — $10.00.

FRANKLIN: Descendants of James Isaiah Franklin (b. 1825, St Helena Parish LA). By Chaplain Dan Franklin. 1992. 257p.
P4-S10986 — $41.50.

FRANKLIN: Historical sketches of Roswell Franklin & family, By Robert Hubbard. 1839. 103p.
P4-S10992 — $19.00.

FRASER: History of the Frasers of Lovat, with gen. of the principal fams. of the name; By A. Mackenzie. (Publ. in Scotland) 1896. 761p.
P4-S11010 — $105.00.

FRASER: Some Fraser pedigrees [of Inverness-shire, Scotland]. By D. Warrand. 1934 8 + 177p.
P4-S11016 — $29.50.

FRASER: Descendants of Simon Fraser of Laggan, Inverness-shire, Scotland, & allied families in Scotland, Canada & US. By M.I.F. Brewster. 1956. 219p.
P4-S11004 — $34.00.

FRAY: History & genealogy of John Fray (Johannes Frey) of Culpeper Co., VA: his descendants & their related families. Florence V.F. Lewis. 1958. 207p.
P4-S11022 — $37.00.

FREED: Partial history of the Freed family & connecting families. By Jacob A. Freed. 1923. 113p.
P4-S11034 — $18.00.

FREED: History of the Freed family. By Isaac G. Freed. 1919. 130p.
P4-S11028 — $21.00.

FREEMAN: Genealogy, Pt. I: Mem. of Edmund of Sandwich & his desc.; II: Samuel of Watertown & his desc. & III: F. Freeman. 1875. 2nd ed. 457p.
P4-S11043 — $58.00.

FREEMAN: Family: genealogical & historical record of 160 years, extending from the 18th to the 20th. By Mosees D.A. Steen. 1900. 77p.
P4-S11040 — $15.50.

FREEMAN: The Freemans: Eastham branch of the Sandwich fam. (Repr. NEHGR). By J. Paine. 1866. 8p.
P4-S11044 — $10.00.

FREESE: Families, 1749-1800. By John W. Freese. 1906. 78p.
P4-S11049 — $15.50.

FREESE: Freese gen. By C. N. Sinnett. 1929. 68p.
P4-S11055 — $14.00.

FREMONT: La famille Fremont. By Pierre-Georges Roy. 1902. 71p.
P4-S11061 — $14.00.

FRENCH: Genealogy of the Billerica, MA, French family, 1599-1914. By H. Martin Kellogg (1884), Bonibel F. Hodgkins (1915). 1958. 129p., typescript.
P4-S11121 — $21.00.

FRENCH: An American ancestry. Anna Richmond Warner French. 1894. 186p.
P4-S11109 — $28.00.

FRENCH: Ancestors & descendants of Samuel French the Joiner, of Stratford, CT with biographies, illustrations, maps & charts. By Mansfield J. French. 1940. 369 + 50p
P4-S11091 — $63.50.

FRENCH: Gen of the Desc. of Thomas French, Who Settled in Berlinton (Burlington) West NJ, vol I. By H.B. French. 1909. 501p.
P4-S11073 — $76.00.

FRENCH: Gen. of the desc. of Thomas French, vol II. 1913. 743p.
P4-S11079 — $105.00.

FRENCH: County records of the surnames Francus, Franceis, French in Eng., A.D. 1100-1350. By A.D.W. French. 1896. 602p.
P4-S11097 — $76.50.

FRENCH: John French of Braintree, MA, notes on the Frenches in connection with France, Eng., Ireland, Scotland, & the US. By A.D.W. French. 1885. 15p.
P4-S11080 — $10.00.

FRENCH: Genealogical history of the French & allied families. By M.Q. Beyer. 1912. 373p.
P4-S11115 — $58.50.

FRENCH: Family, 1555-1995: genealogy of Thomas French & Susan Riddlesdale (Boston, 1629) By Eleanor M. Crouch. 1995. 170p.
P4-S11103 — $29.50.

FRENCH: Family, anc. & desc. of Capt. John French of Stoughton, MA. By S. French. 1870. 12p.
P4-S11081 — $10.00.

FRENCH: Amer. anc. of Charles E. French & his wife Anna Richmond Warner. By A.R.W. French. 1894. 187p.
P4-S11085 — $25.00.

FRENCH: Gen. of the French family of Hartland, CT. 1927. 28p.
P4-S11082 — $10.00.

FRENCH: Notes on the surnames of Francus, Franceis, French, etc., in Scotland, with an acct. of the Frenches of Thorndykes. A.D.W. French. 1893. 109p.
P4-S11127 — $19.00.

FRETZ: Genealogical record of the descendants of Abraham Fretz of Bedminster, Bucks Co., PA. By A.J. Fretz. 1911. 42p.
P4-S11135 — $10.00.

FRETZ: Brief history of John & Christian Fretz & complete genealogical register to the fourth generation By A.J. Fretz. 1904. 125p.
P4-S11133 — $22.00.

FRETZ: Brief history of John & Christian Fretz, & a complete gen. family reg. By A. J. Fretz. 1890. 609p.
P4-S11139 — $83.00.

FREY: Ancestry & posterity of Gottfried Frey, 1605-1914. By Sam'l C. Frey. 1914, 1926 388p.
P4-S11145 — $59.00.

FREY: Notes on the Twigs of the Tree of Heinrich (Henry) Frey 1663-2003. Paul Eugene Frye. 2003. xvi + 492p.
P4-S11146 — $76.00.

FRISBIE: Edw. Frisbie of Branford, CR & his desc. (Repr. NEHGR) By R.D. Smyth. 1904. 6p.
P4-S11152 — $10.00.

FRISBEE: FRISBIE Edward Frisbye of Branford, CT & his desc., with appendix of brief lin. of Fiskes, Haskells, Mabvies, Parkes, By E. Frisbee. 1926. 778p.
P4-S11151 — $109.00.

FROST: Genealogy. By A.A. Doane. 1910. 8p.
P4-S11164 — $10.00.

FROST: Fam. in Eng. & Amer., with special ref. to Edmund Frost & some desc. By T. & E. Frost. 1909. 177p.
P4-S11154 — $22.50.

FROST: Genealogy in five families. By N.S. Frost. 1926. 410p.
P4-S11160 — $64.00.

FROST: The Nicholas Frost fam., incl. suppl. By J.E. Frost. 1943. 170p.
P4-S11169 — $25.50.

FROST: Genealogy; desc. of Wm. Frost of Oyster Bay, NY, showing conn. with the Winthrop, Underhill, Feke, Brown & Wickes fams. By J. Frost. 1912. 458p.
P4-S11163 — $57.00.

FROTHINGHAM: Genealogy. By Wyman & Frothingham. 1916. 170p.
P4-S11175 — $25.50.

FRY: The Saxon orig. of the Fry fam. By G. S. Fry. 1928. 27p.
P4-S11182 — $10.00.

FRY: Memoir of Col. Joshua Fry of VA with gen. of his desc. & allied lines. By F. Slaughter. 113p.
P4-S11181 — $23.50.

FRYE: Frye gen; Adrian of Kittery, Maine: John of Andover, MA, Joshua of VA, Thomas of RI, NY. By E.F. Barker. 1920. 194p.
P4-S11187 — $29.00.

FUESS: & Allied families. By Elizabeth G. Fuess. 1929. 341p., typescript.
P4-S11193 — $52.50.

FULHAM: Genealogy, with index of names. By Volney S. Fulham. 1909. 291p.
P4-S11199 — $44.00.

FULLER: Genealogy of some descendants of Edward Fuller of the Mayflower. By W.H. Fuller. 1908. 306p.
P4-S11235 — $40.00.

FULLER: A brief sketch of Thomas Fuller & his desc., with hist. notes. By J. F. Fuller. 1896. 47p.
P4-S11206 — $10.00.

FULLER: Desc. of Ens. Thomas Fuller of Dedham. F. Fuller. 1894. 24p.
P4-S11207 — $10.00.

FULLER: Bible records. comp. by J. P. Fuller. 1915. 4p.
P4-S11208 — $10.00.

FULLER: Genealogy of some descendants of Thomas Fuller of Woburn, with suppl. to Vols. I, II, III. By W.H. Fuller. 1919. 271p.
P4-S11241 — $42.50.

FULLER: Alden-Fuller record. A record of the desc. of Lemuel Fuller, Sr. By M. Percy Black. 1896. 76p.
P4-S11205 — $15.00.

FULLER: Benjamin Fuller & some of his desc., 1765-1958. By R.E. Banta. 1958. 143p.
P4-S11211 — $22.50.

FULLER: Genealogy; record of Joseph Fuller, desc. of Thomas Fuller of Woburn & Middleton, MA. By E. Abercrombie. 1897. 101p.
P4-S11223 — $18.50.

FULLER: Genealogy of the Fuller family, desc. from Robert Fuller of Salem & Rehoboth, MA. By N. Fuller. 1898. 50p.
P4-S11209 — $10.00.

FULLER: Genealogy of some descendants of Dr. Samuel Fuller of the Mayflower. W.H. Fuller. 1910. 263p.
P4-S11232 — $34.00.

FULLER: Gen. of some desc. of Capt. Matthew Fuller, John of Newton, John of Lynn, etc, With supplement to vol. I & II By W. H. Fuller. 1914. 325p.
P4-S11229 — $49.00.

FULLER: Early New England Fullers & Eng. desc. (Repr. NEHGR). By F.H. Fuller. 1901. 12p.
P4-S11210 — $10.00.

FULLER: Historical notices of Thomas Fuller of Middleton, MA & his descendants. By Fuller & Dean. 1859. 17p.
P4-S11212 — $10.00.

FULTON: HAYDEN — WARNER Anc. in Amer. C. E. Leonard. 1923. 629p.
P4-S11247 — $94.50.

FULTON: Gen. of the Fulton fam., being desc. of John Fulton, born in Scotland 1713. Settled in Nottingham, Chester Co., PA, 1762 By H. R. Fulton. 1900. 238p.
P4-S11259 — $35.50.

FULTON: Family of Westmoreland Co., PA, 1712-1772-1940: account of the descendants of Abraham Fulton & Margaret Guthry By Ernest S. Craighead. 1940. 216p., typescript.
P4-S11253 — $33.50.

FULTZ: A North American family [Fultz, Walsh, Lawrence, et al. By Neil R. Walsh, Jr. 2002. 157p.
P4-S11260 — $25.00.

FUNK: Brief hist. of Bishop Henry Funck & other Funk pioneers By A.J. Fretz. 1899. 874p.
P4-S11265 — $121.00.

FUNSTEN: MEADE Ancestors & descendants of Col David Funsten & his wife Susan Everard Meade, By Howard S.F. Randolph. 1926. 93p.
P4-S11271 — $18.00.

FURRY: History of Johannes Furry (or Forrer) & his descendants to the end of the 8th generation. By Henry S. Furry. 1911. 68p.
P4-S11277 — $13.50.

FUSON: VA-OH Fusons, a genealogical history of the VA-OH branch of the Fuson family in America. By Sylvia S.F. Ferguson. 1939. 224p.
P4-S11289 — $34.00.

FUSON: History of the Fuson family, Volume II (Vol. I pub. 1932). By Henry H. Fuson. 1938. 220p.
P4-S11283 — $25.00.

FUTCH: NC Palatine-Germans (Futch family). Evelyn Futch Smith. n.d. 115p.
P4-S11295 — $17.00.

G

GABLE: History of the Gable family. 1902. 80p.
P4-S11301 — $15.50.

GAFFNEY: Descendants of Michael Gafney (1750-1838) of Gloucester, MA. By Mary H. Sibbalds. 1998. 344p.
P4-S11307 — $51.00.

GAGE: SHEPARD: A family record including information on the principal related families, 2nd ed. By Clyde V.T. Gage. 1961? 142p., typescript.
P4-S11313 — $22.00.

GAGE: Rec. of Pierce Gage & his desc. By G. Gage. 1894. 62p.
P4-S11322 — $12.50.

GAGE: The New Eng. anc. of Lyman J. Gage (Repr. NEHGR) By A.E. Gage. 1899. 8p.
P4-S11314 — $10.00.

GAGE: Family: John Gage of Ipswich & Thomas of Yarmouth; William of Freetown; Robert of Weston; William of Canada; etc. Rev. W. Gage. 1922. 65p.
P4-S11319 — $13.00.

GAINES: Henry Gaines of Lynn, MA & some of his desc. (Repr. NEHGR). By H. W. Brainard. 17p.
P4-S11320 — $10.00.

GALE: Gen. of the desc. of David Gale of Sutton, MA. By L.A.E. Gale. 1909. 57p.
P4-S11329 — $11.50.

GALE: Fam. records in Eng. & US & the Tottingham fam. of New Eng., sone accts. of the Bogardus, Waldon & Young fam. of NY. By G. Gale. 1866. 254p.
P4-S11328 — $33.00.

GALE: Records of Gale fam. of Salem. By C. Townes. 1937. 3p.
P4-S11330 — $10.00.

GALL: WILLIAMS Genealogy. By Olive G. Newcomer. 1953. 108p., typescript.
P4-S11340 — $16.00.

GALLATIN: NICHOLSON; Ancestry of Albert Gallatin, & Hannah Nicholson with a list of their descendants to the 2nd & 3rd generation By Wm. P. Bacon. 1916? 57p.
P4-S11341 — $11.00.

GALLEY: History of the Galley family, with local & old-time sketches in the Yough region. By H. Galley & J.O. Arnold. 1908. 271p.
P4-S11346 — $53.00.

GALLOWAY: Genealogy of the descendants of George Galloway & Rebekah Junkin, 1700-1925, in the US. By George W. Kendall & Wm. A. Galloway. 1926. 61p.
P4-S11349 — $12.00.

GALLUP: Genealogical history of the Gallup family in the US, with biogr. sketches. By J.D. Gallup. 1893. 329p.
P4-S11358 — $55.00.

GALPIN: Family in America. By Wm. F. Galpin. 1955. 289p.
P4-S11364 — $44.50.

GALT: Families: notes on their origin & their history with genealogical lists. By Howard S. Galt. 1938. 163p.
P4-S11370 — $26.00.

GAMAGE: Desc. of John Gamage of Ipswich, MA. A.L.G. Morton. 1906. 83p.
P4-S11376 — $16.00.

GAMBLE: The Mount Desert Widow: Genealogy of the Maine Gamble family By G. & J.P. Cilley. 1896. 196p.
P4-S11382 — $30.00.

GARBER: MILLER; The John H. Garber & Barbara Miller family of PA, MD, VA. By Floyd R. & Kathryn G. Mason. 1998. 1560p.
P4-S11400 — $155.50.

GARBER: MILLER, Elder Samuel Garber & Elizabeth Miller of Augusta Co., VA. By Floyd R. & Kathryn Garst Mason. 2000. 161p.
P4-S11394 — $25.00.

GARBER: Niclous Garber family record. By Floyd R. & Kathryn G. Mason. 1997. 310p.
P4-S11388 — $46.50.

GARDINER: The Gardiners of Narragansett, a gen. of the desc. of Geo. Gardiner, colonist, 1638. By C. E. Robinson. 1919. 320p.
P4-S11418 — $49.50.

GARDINER: 1599-1890; Lion Gardiner & his desc. By C.C. Gardiner. 1890. 195p.
P4-S11412 — $29.00.

GARDINER: Chronicle of everyday people, being . . . the American ancestry of George Schuyler Gardiner & his wife Cathering Larison Marshall By Catherine M. Gardiner. 1929. 268p.
P4-S11406 — $41.00.

GARDINERS: of Gardiner's Island. By John Lion Gardiner. 1927. 345p.
P4-S11424 — $52.00.

GARDNER: Desc. of Richard Gardner of Woburn, MA, By W.W. Greenough. 1858. 14p.
P4-S11428 — $10.00.

GARDNER: Ancestry of Daniel Gardner V and Mary (Hodges) Gardner of Champaign, IL, with other Gardner & Hodges records & notes By D. Hodges Gardner. 1915. 56p.
P4-S11429 — $11.00.

GARDNER: Hist & gen.; desc. of Thomas Gardner (Extr. from Headley gen.) By A.J. Fretz. 1905. 49p.
P4-S11430 — $10.00.

GARDNER: Mem'l: biogr. & gen. rec. of the desc. of Thom. Gardner, Planter. of Cape Ann, 1624; Salem, 1626-74. By F.A. Gardner. 1933. 295p.
P4-S11433 — $44.00.

GARDNER: History & genealogy. By L.M. & C.M. Gardner. 1907. 407p.
P4-S11427 — $52.50.

GARDNER: Thomas Gardner, Cape Ann 1623-1626, Salem 1626-1674, & some of his desc. By F.A. Gardner. 1907. 347p.
P4-S11436 — $49.50.

GARESHE: DeBAUDY — Des CHAPELLES Families: history & genealogy. By Dorothy G. Holland. 1963. 299p.
P4-S11442 — $45.00.

GARLAND: The desc. of Peter Garland, mariner, of Charlestown, MA, 1637 By J. Garland. 1897. 219p.
P4-S11445 — $28.00.

GARLING: Genealogy of the Garling family. By Abraham Crider. 1910. 183p.
P4-S11451 — $16.00.

GARNER: KEENE Families of Northern Neck, VA. By Ruth Ritchie & Sudie Rucker Wood. 1952. 240p.
P4-S11457 — $37.00.

GARNETT: Genealogy & story of the family of Robert Kirtley Garnett. By H.E. Hobble & C.H. Garnett. 1955. 124p.
P4-S11463 — $23.00.

GARR: Genealogy of the descendants of John Gar, & his son Andreas Gaar, who emigrated from Bavaria to America in 1732. By J.W. & J.C. Garr. 1894. 608p.
P4-S11475 — $89.50.

GARRARD: Governor Garrard of KY, his descendants & relatives. By Anna R. des Cognets. 1898. 134p.
P4-S11481 — $19.50.

GARRETT: Hist. of Welcome Garrett & his desc. By S.B. Garrett. 1909. 141p.
P4-S11487 — $24.50.

GARRETT: The Genealogy in part of Stephen & William Garrett of Buckingham, VA. Rev. Clyde B. Garrett & Mary E. Gaither. n.d. 58p.
P4-S11488 — $10.00.

GARRISON: Descendants of Caleb Garrison & His wife, Sarah Fleming. By J.G. Ross & Q. Garrison. 1966. 305p.
P4-S11493 — $47.00.

GARST: Our Garst family in America. By W.T. Garst. 1950. 363p.
P4-S11499 — $55.00.

GARST: Our Garst Family in America — Revised. Floyd & Kathryn Mason, et al. 2004. 790p.
P4-S11501 — $110.00.

GARST: Elder Jeremiah H. Garst & his descendants. Floyn R. Kathryn G. Mason. 2000. 27p.
P4-S11500 — $10.00.

GARY: The desc. of Authur Gary of Roxbury, MA, with an acct. of the posterity of Stephen Gary of Charlestown, MA. By L. Brainerd. 1918. 235p.
P4-S11505 — $35.00.

GASKILL: Descendants of Edward Gascoigne (Gaskill). By Rachel Saul Tefft. 1997. 79p.
P4-S11511 — $16.00.

GASTON: Fam. in the US. By H.F. Johnston. 1948. 10p.
P4-S11512 — $10.00.

GATES: Our American anc. By F.T. Gates. 1928. 289p.
P4-S11523 — $33.00.

GATES: Silas Gates of Stow, MA & the desc. of his son Paul Gates of Ashby. By J. & S. Gates. 1907. 147p.
P4-S11529 — $22.00.

GATES: Ancestry & descendants of William Gates of Frankfort NY; Appendix I, descendants of Alfred Gates of Franklin LA; Appendix II, ancestry of Mary Ann Deuel. By Frederick Gates. 1921. 32p.
P4-S11518 — $10.00.

GATES: Stephen Gates of Hingham & Lancaster, MA & his desc. By C.O. Gates. 1898. 370p.
P4-S11535 — $47.50.

GATES: Dawes — Gates ancestral lines: a mem'l vol. containing the American anc. of Rufus R. Dawes, Vol. II: Gates & allied families. By M.W. Ferris. 1931. 918p.
P4-S11517 — $117.50.

GAUER: GOWER Family. By Irene M. Gower. 1939. 68p.
P4-S11541 — $14.00.

GAY: John Gay of Dedham, MA & some of his desc. F.L. Gay. 1879. 16p.
P4-S11542 — $10.00.

GAYER: Memoirs of the Family of Gayer. A.E. Gayer. 1870. 47+11p.
P4-S11543 — $10.00.

GAZZAM: DeBLEEN: History of the Gazzam family, together with a bio. sketch of the American branch of the family of DeBleen. By A. DeB. MacKenzie. 1894. 72p.
P4-S11547 — $15.00.

GEARHART: Fam. in Amer., By E.B. Gearhart. 1962. 24p.
P4-S11548 — $10.00.

GEDNEY: CLARKE Fam. of Salem, MA. By H. Waters. 1880. 52p.
P4-S11549 — $10.00.

GEE: Family of Union Co, SC. By W. Gee. 1935. 29p.
P4-S11554 — $10.00.

GEE: Family: desc. of Charles Gee (d. 1709) & Hannah G. (d. 1928) of VA, with a chapter on the English background. W.J. Fletcher. 1937. 157p.
P4-S11553 — $29.00.

GEER: Genealogy of Aaron Geer of Pitcairn & his descendants. 1956. 24p.
P4-S11560 — $10.00.

GEER: Genealogy of the Geer family in Amer. from 1635-1914. By W. Geer & F.E. Youngs. 1914. 256p.
P4-S11565 — $38.00.

GEER: Genealogy: hist record of George & Thomas Geer & their descs in the US, from 1623-1923. By Walter Geer. 1923. 447p.
P4-S11559 — $68.00.

GEHLING: The Proven Ancestry of Charles Gehling & John B. Leist of Manitowoc Co, WI & Baden, Germany. S. C. Gehling. 2006. 291 + 14p.
P4-S11566 — $47.00.

GEIB: John Geib & his children. By A. Gildersleeve. 1945. 23p.
P4-S11567 — $10.00.

GEIGER: The Geigers of SC. Compiled By Percy L. Geiger. 1950 191p.
P4-S11571 — $29.50.

GEIL: Hist. of the Desc. of J. Conrad Geil & His Son Jacob Geil, Emigrated from Wurttemberg, Germany to America in 1754. Joseph H. Wengler. 1914. 275p.
P4-S11572 — $41.00.

GEIST: Relation: two hundred years in America [desc. of Christopher Geist]. By A.F. Geist. 1940. 925p.
P4-S11577 — $129.50.

GENDRON: Fa famille de Nicolas Gendron: dictionnaire genealogique. par P.S. Gendron. 1929 570p., in French
P4-S11583 — $85.00.

GENTRY: Family in America; 1676-1909 incl. notes on the Claibourne, Harris, Sharp & twelve other fams. By R. Gentry. 1909. 406p.
P4-S11589 — $52.50.

GEORGIA: Gen. record & history of the Georgia family in America, descendants of Wm. & Sarah (Cable) Georgia, Elijah Burr (1st) & Keziah (Stewart) Georgia. By Elmore L. Brooks. 1921. 314p.
P4-S11595 — $46.50.

GERBERICH: History of the Gerberich Family in America, 1613-1925. A.H. Gerberich 1925. 288 + 22p.
P4-S11596 — $46.50.

GERNHARDT: Heinrich Gernhardt & his desc. J.M.M. Gernerd. 1904. 315p
P4-S11601 — $49.50.

GEROULD: Gen. of the family of Gamaliel Gerould, son of Dr. Jacques Jerauld, of the Province of Languedoc, France. By S.L. Gerould. 1885. 85p.
P4-S11607 — $17.00.

GEROULD: Supplements 1 & 2 to above. 1890. 15 + 17p.
P4-S11608 — $10.00.

GETCHELL: Stephen Getchell Bible records. 8p.
P4-S11609 — $10.00.

GETCHELL: Fam. of Samuel Getchell of Salisbury, MA. By E. & F. Getchell. 1909. 10p.
P4-S11610 — $10.00.

GETTY: Gen. notes of the Getty & Lytle families of Salem, NY. By Horace R. Currier. 1902. 87p.
P4-S11613 — $16.50.

GIBBLE: History & gen. of Henry Gibble family in the US. By Gibble, Longenecker & Gibble. 1961 315p.
P4-S11619 — $47.50.

GIBBS: Family of RI & some related families. By Geo. Gibbs. 1933. 193p.
P4-S11631 — $29.00.

GIBBS: A golden legacy to the Gibbs in America. By M. B. Gibbs. 1893. 77p.
P4-S11625 — $15.50.

GIBBS: Fam. notices. collected by W. Gibbs. 1845. 8p.
P4-S11626 — $10.00.

GIBSON: John Gibson of Cambridge, MA & his desc., 1634-1899. By M.C.C. Wilson. 1900. 547p.
P4-S11634 — $69.50.

GIDDINGS: Family; or, the desc. of George Giddings who came from St. Albans, Eng. to Ipswich, MA in 1635. By M. S. Giddings. 1882. 227p.
P4-S11637 — $34.00.

GIDEON: A Southern Gideon family. By Marteal Wells. 1999. 318p.
P4-S11643 — $46.00.

GIFFEN: Gen. family history of desc. of Robt. Giffen & Mary Bane Giffen, settlers at Big Spring, PA, 1777 By J.W. Giffin. 1927. 174p.
P4-S11649 — $25.00.

GIFFIN: Pioneers in America prior tp 1742, following the descent of Andrew Giffin I, from Eastern PA. 1933. 222p.
P4-S11655 — $34.50.

GIFFORD: Genealogy, 1626-1896; desc. of Wm. Gifford of Sandwich, MA, 1650, with 1932 index, By H.E. Gifford. 1896, 1932. 101 + 61p.
P4-S11661 — $22.50.

GIFT: History of the Gift, Kern & Royer families. By Aaron K. Gift. 1909. 179p.
P4-S11667 — $28.00.

GILBERT: BARBER Families [descendants of Orrin Gilbert & Mary Barber, m. 1807, of CT & OH] By Harlow Gilbert, et al. 1903. 129p.
P4-S11673 — $21.00.

GILBERT: Family. (Repr. NEHGR). 1850. 21p.
P4-S11674 — $10.00.

GILBERT: Family, descendants of Thomas Gilbert, 1582(?)-1659, of Mt Wollaston (Braintree), Windsor & Wethersfield. By Brainard, Gilbert & Torrey. 1953. 508p.
P4-S11679 — $76.50.

GILBERT: Gilberts of New England: Pt. I, descendants of John Gilbert of Dorchester; Pt. II, descendants of Matthew of New Haven, Humphrey of Ipswich & Wm. of Boston. Geo. & Geoffrey Gilbert (Pt. I) & H.W. Brainard & C.A. Torrey (Pt.II) 1959. 484p.
P4-S11685 — $75.00.

GILBERT: The Gilberts of Clare & Colchester. By G. Andrews Moriarty. 1924. 19p.
P4-S11675 — $10.00.

GILBERT: Ancestors of Moses Haskell Gilbert of VT & Montreal, 1790-1843. Part I, father, Solomon Gilbert; Part II, mother, Thankful Haskell. By G. Gilbert & E.L. Moffat. 1954. 144p.
P4-S11691 — $22.00.

GILDART: GELDART Families. By C.R. Gildart. 1962. 78p.
P4-S11697 — $15.50.

GILDERSLEEVE: Pioneers. By W.H. Gildersleeve. 1941. 337p.
P4-S11703 — $54.00.

GILES: Memorial; Gen. mem'l of the fam. bearing the names Giles, Gould, Holmes & others. J.A. Vinton. 1864. 608p.
P4-S11709 — $81.00.

GILFILLAN: Sketches, our lands & people, Gilfillan fam. By J. B. Gilfillan. 1918. 25p.
P4-S11710 — $10.00.

GILKEY: The Gilkeys: history of the early American Gilkeys & their descendants. By Geo. L. Gilkey. 1950. 362 + 60p; typescript.
P4-S11715 — $64.00.

GILL: Notes hist. sur l'origine de la fam. Gill de Saint-Francois du Lac & St Thomas de Pierreville; hist. de ma propre fam. By C. Gill. 1887. 96p.
P4-S11727 — $15.00.

GILL: Abstracts from records in Southern states & genealogical notes. By Eva T. Clark. 1939. 196p.
P4-S11721 — $29.50.

GILL: Notes additionnelles a l' hist. de la fam. Gill. By C. Gill. 1889. 30p.
P4-S11722 — $10.00.

GILLET: Desc. of Jonathan Gillet of Dorchester, MA & Windsor, CT (Repr. NEHGR) By S.C. Gillette, ed. By H.C. Alvord. 1893. 11p.
P4-S11728 — $10.00.

GILLINGHAM: Family: descendants of Yeamans Gillingham. By Harrold E. Gillingham. 1901. 117p.
P4-S11733 — $18.50.

GILLMAN: Searches into the history of the Gillman or Gilman family, incl. various branches in Eng., Ire., Amer. & Belgium. A.W. Gillman. 1895. 360p.
P4-S11739 — $57.00.

GILLSON: Genealogy of the Gillson/ Jillson family. By D. Jillson. 1876. 266p.
P4-S11745 — $40.00.

GILMAN: The story of the Gilmans & a Gilman gen. of the descendants of Edward Gilman of Hingham, England, 1550-1950. By Constance L.G. Ames. 1950. 190p.
P4-S11754 — $27.00.

GILMAN: Genealogy of Gilman family in Eng. & Amer. By A. Gilman. 1864. 24p.
P4-S11749 — $10.00.

GILMAN: Gen. & bio. record of that branch of the family of Gilman, descended from the Hon. John Gilman of Exeter NH By Arthur Gilman. 1863. 51p.
P4-S11750 — $10.00.

GILMAN: Family traced in the line of Hon. John Gilman of Exeter, NH, & an acct. of many other Gilmans in Eng. & Amer. By A. Gilman. 1869. 337p.
P4-S11748 — $52.50.

GILMER: The Gilmers in America. By J. G. Speed. 1897. 208p.
P4-S11760 — $31.00.

GILMOR: William Gilmor-Sarah Hanna, 1778; Arthur Scott, Jr-Ann Hamilton, 1788. E. Gilmor. 1932. 238p.
P4-S11766 — $36.00.

GILMORE: Robert & James Gilmore who settled in Southern NH & their descendants By Frank S. Osgood. 1926. 201p., typescript.
P4-S11772 — $31.00.

GILMORE: Anc.; desc. of John Gilmore of MA, down to Pascal P. Gilmore, et al. P. P. Gilmore. 1928. 25p.
P4-S11773 — $10.00.

GILPIN: Gen. of the fam. of Gideon Gilpin, grandson of Jos. Gilpin of Dorchester, Co. of Oxford, Eng., Settled in Chester Co., PA. By J.E. Gilpin. 1897. 23p.
P4-S11779 — $10.00.

GILPIN: Family, from Richard de Gylpyn in 1206 . . . to Joseph Gilpin, emigrant to America By George G. Perkins. 1927. 130p.
P4-S11778 — $25.00.

GINGERICH: Descendants of Johannes Gingerich & Catherine Schlabaugh. Mr. & Mrs. David Gerig. n.d. 259p.
P4-S11783 — $39.00.

GIRTY: History of the Girtys, a concise account of the Girty brothers - Thomas, Simon, James & George & Their half-brother John Turner, By Consul Willshire Butterfield. 1905. 425p.
P4-S11784 — $42.50.

GIST: Family. C. T. Cockey. 1885. 12p.
P4-S11791 — $10.00.

GIST: Family of SC & its MD anc. By W. Gee. 1934. 101p.
P4-S11790 — $20.00.

GIVEN: David Given & desc. By C. N. Sinnett. 1923. 30p.
P4-S11791 — $10.00.

GLADDING: Book; hist. record & gen. chart of the Gladding fam. & accts. of reunions of 1890 & 1900 at Bristol RI, their anc. home. By H. Gladding. 1901. 189p.
P4-S11796 — $28.00.

GLADNEY: [Update of "Gladneys in America"]. By the Gladney Family Association. 2003. 1248p.
P4-S11795 — $135.00.

GLASS: Henry Glass & desc. By C. N. Sinnett. 1922. 4p.
P4-S11797 — $10.00.

GLASSELL: Virginia genealogies: gen. of the Glassel family of Scotland & VA, also of the families of Ball, Brown, Conway, Daniel, etc. By H.E. Hayden. 1891. 777p.
P4-S11808 — $49.50.

GLATTFELDER: Record of Casper Glattfelder of Glattfelden, Canton Zurich, Switzerland, immigrant, 1743, & of his descendants By Noah M Glatfelder. 1901. 124p.
P4-S11814 — $21.00.

GLAZIER: Family, mainly of Willington & Stafford, Tolland Co., CT. By Grace O. Chapman. 1943. 54p., typescript.
P4-S11815 — $11.00.

GLEASON: Genealogy of the desc. of Thomas Gleason of Watertown, MA, 1607-1909. By L. Wilson. 1909. 672p.
P4-S11817 — $84.00.

GLEN: History of the Glen fam. of SC & GA. By J.G.B. Bulloch. 1923. 134p.
P4-S11823 — $22.00.

GLENN: Fam. of Armstrong Co., PA. By M. Williamson. 1941. 15p.
P4-S11824 — $10.00.

GLICK: Genealogy of the Glick family. By George H. Glick, et al. 1918. 134p.
P4-S11829 — $21.50.

GLIDDEN: Descendants of Charles Glidden of Portsmouth & Exeter, NH. By G.W. Chamberlain. 1925. 420p.
P4-S11835 — $65.00.

GLOVER: Memorial & genealogy: an acct. of John Glover of Dorchester & descendants By A. Glover. 1867. 612p.
P4-S11838 — $76.00.

GLOVER: Genealogy of the Glover Clans. By C. M. Glover. 1938. 50p.
P4-S11839 — $10.00.

GLOYD: Family tree of Daniel Gloyd, Sr., Prince George's Co., MD. By Cleo G. Wilkens. 1949. 45p., typescript.
P4-S11840 — $10.00.

GNAGEY: Complete history of Christian Gnaegi & a complete family register of his lineal descendants By Elias Gnagey. 1897. 198p.
P4-S11844 — $29.50.

GODDARD: Giles Goddard & his descendants. By Kingston G. Hadley. 1942? 89p. typescript.
P4-S11856 — $16.50.

GODDARD: Genealogy of the desc. of Edward Goddard. By W.A. Goddard. 1833. 95p.
P4-S11850 — $19.00.

GODING: Gen. of the Goding fam. By F.W. Goding. 1906. 176p.
P4-S11862 — $24.50.

GOLDSMITH: Joseph Goldsmith, 1796-1876, & his descendants. Comp. by Goldsmith Reunion Committee. 1955 95p.
P4-S11868 — $18.00.

GOLDTHWAIT: Gen. Notes: New Eng. anc. of the children of William Johnson Goldthwait & Mary Lydia Pitman-Goldthwait of Marblehead, MA. By H. Tutt. 39p.
P4-S11872 — $10.00.

GOLDTHWAITE: Desc. of Thomas Goldthwaite of Salem, MA, with some acct. of the Goldthwaite fam. in Eng. By C. Goldthwaite. 1899. 418p.
P4-S11871 — $56.00.

GOOCH: History of a surname, with some account of the line of John Gooch on New England, with appendix. By Frank A. Gooch. 1926-1927 160 + 16p.
P4-S11877 — $26.00.

GOOD: The Adam Good family history. Christiana B. Latsha. 1914. 150p.
P4-S11883 — $23.50.

GOODALE: Gen: notes on the lives of Edw. & Sarah Temple Goodale, pioneer settlers of Shrewsbury, MA, 1738-1786 By Leon A. Goodale. 1948. 86p., typescript.
P4-S11889 — $16.00.

GOODE: Virginia cousins. A study of the anc. & posterity of John Goode of Whitby, VA. By G. Goode. 1887. 526p.
P4-S11895 — $82.00.

GOODELL: Goodell mem. tablets. By I. Goodell. 1892. 38p.
P4-S11896 — $10.00.

GOODHUE: History & genealogy of the Goodhue fam. in Eng. & Amer. to the year 1890, By Rev. J. E. Goodhue. 1891. 398p.
P4-S11898 — $62.50.

GOODHUE: Family of Ipswich, 1636-1833. By W. Goodhue. 16p.
P4-S11899 — $10.00.

GOODLOCK: & Allied families. By Katie R. Mills. 1951. 250p.
P4-S11904 — $38.00.

GOODMAN: The Goodmans of Bolton, NY, their ancestry & descendants. Edith W.G. West. 1930. 100p.
P4-S11922 — $19.50.

GOODMAN: History of the George & Catherine Goodman family, 1730-1942. By Esther Mae Warner. 1942. 107p.
P4-S11916 — $19.00.

GOODMAN: From Ledde to Champion Twp: family history of the Goodmans & Klingemeiers of Ledde, 1690-2000. David F. Sprunk. 2001. 875p.
P4-S11910 — $89.50.

GOODNOW: Desc. of Edmund Goodnow in the line of Daniel Goodnow of Roxbury, MA & Sullivan, NH. By J.L. Seward. 1904. 11p.
P4-S11923 — $10.00.

GOODRICH: Family memorial, part I, containing the english history of the fam as collected by Hiram P. Goodrich. comp. By Edwin Hubbard. 1883-1884 109p.
P4-S11931 — $17.50.

GOODRICH: Mayflower ancestry of Elizabeth Ely Goodrich & her descendants. By Inglis Stuart. 1932. 136p.
P4-S11943 — $21.00.

GOODRICH: Family tree: American ancestors of my children. By Merton T. Goodrich. 1932. 192p., typescript.
P4-S11937 — $29.50.

GOODRICH: Family in America. Gen. of the desc. of John & William Goodrich of Wethersfield, CT, Richard of Guilford, CT & William of Watertown, MA. By L. W. Case. 1889. 423p.
P4-S11925 — $53.50.

GOODRICKE: Abstracts of Goodricke will, Lincolnshire, Cambridge & Yorkshire. 1891 35p.
P4-S11944 — $10.00.

GOODRIDGE: Mem; Desc. & anc. of Moses Goodridge of Marblehead, MA, Oct. 9, 1764, & died at Constantine, MI, Aug 23, 1838. S. Perley. 1884. 87p.
P4-S11955 — $17.00.

GOODRIDGE: Genealogy. The desc. of William Goodridge who came to Watertown, MA from Bury St. Edmunds, Eng. in 1636. By E. A. Goodridge. 1918. 313p.
P4-S11949 — $49.50.

GOODSELL: Family of CT. By Percy Hamilton Goodsell, Jr. 1986. 190 + 45p.
P4-S11961 — $36.00.

GOODSPEED: Hist of the Goodspeed family, being a genealogical & Narrative record extending from 1380-1906. By Weston A. Goodspeed. 1907. 561p.
P4-S11967 — $86.00.

GOODWIN: The Goodwins of Delaware Gap, PA & Tompkins Co., NY. By J.S. Goodwin. 1898. 10p.
P4-S11974 — $10.00.

GOODWIN: Family. Various ancestral lines of James Goodwin & Lucy Morgan Goodwin of Hartford, CT, vol I. By F.F. Starr. 1915. 317p.
P4-S11973 — $49.50.

GOODWIN: Family. Various ancestral lines of James Goodwin & Lucy Morgan Goodwin of Hartford, CT, vol II. 1915. 481p.
P4-S11979 — $75.00.

GOODWIN: The Goodwins of E. Anglia. By A. Jessop. 1889. 37p.
P4-S12025 — $10.00.

GOODWIN: The Goodwins with Hartford, CT; desc. of Wm. & Ozias Goodwin. Goodwin & Starr. 1891. 809p.
P4-S12027 — $99.00.

GOODWIN: The Goodwins of Kittery, York Co., ME. By J. S. Goodwin. 1898. 125p.
P4-S12024 — $19.00.

GOODWIN: English Goodwin fam. papers, being material coll. in the search for the anc. of William & Ozias Goodwin, Hartford, CT. Vols. I & II. 1921. 1196p.
P4-S11997 — $144.50.

GOODWIN: English Goodwin fam. papers. V. III, Index 1921. 349p.
P4-S11991 — $54.50.

GOODWIN: Family in America. By J. Goodwin. 1897. 200p.
P4-S12015 — $31.50.

GOODWIN: Family in America, Supplement. 1899. 169p.
P4-S12021 — $27.50.

GOODYEAR: Genealogy of the Goodyear family. G. Kirkman. 1899. 250p.
P4-S12033 — $37.50.

GOOGINS: Family in America. By Charlotte H. Googins. 1914. 68p.
P4-S12039 — $13.50.

GOOKIN: Gookin fam. of Eng. & Amer., 1400-1831. By E.E. Salisbury. 1885. 84p.
P4-S12045 — $17.00.

GOOKIN: Historical & genealogical sketch of the Gookin family of England, Ireland, America. By R.N. Gookin. 1952. 191p.
P4-S12051 — $31.00.

GOOLD: Genealogy of the Twitchell Goold families. By Mrs W.J. Slayton. 1957. 76p.
P4-S12057 — $15.00.

GORBY: Family origin, history & genealogy; desc. of Samuel & Mary (May) Gorby. By A. Gorby. 1936. 304p.
P4-S12063 — $47.00.

GORDON: Gordons in VA, with notes on Gordons of Scotland & Ireland. Armistead C. Gordon. 1918. 188p.
P4-S12075 — $28.00.

GORDON: Our Gordon family, a genealogical & biographical records. By Spencer Gordon. 1941. 50p.
P4-S12070 — $11.00.

GORDON: Gordons of Spotsylvania Co., VA, with notes on the Gordons of Scotland. By Frances B.S. Hodges. 1934. 35p., typescript.
P4-S12071 — $10.00.

GORDON: Family of ME & NH. By Blanche G. Cobb. 1946? 57p., typescript.
P4-S12072 — $11.50.

GORDON: The Gordons of Nethermuir. John M. Bulloch. 1915. 52p.
P4-S12073 — $10.50.

GORDON: Genealogy of the related families of Gordon & Cameron of Caledonia, NY, & John MacKinnon of Tyree, Scotland. By Chas. H. Gordon. 1933. 28p.
P4-S12074 — $10.00.

GORDON: Family records. By J.M. Seaver. 52p.
P4-S12076 — $10.00.

GORDON: The Gordons of Pitlurg & the desc. of Thomas Gordon, who came to America in 1684 & settled in Perth Amboy, NJ. By Franklin S. Gordon. 1941. 127p., typescript.
P4-S12081 — $21.00.

GORDON: The Gordons in Forfarshire, with the lairds of Ashludie, Dnavourd, Trview, Threave & Charleton. By John M. Bulloch. 1909. 31p.
P4-S12077 — $10.00.

GORDON: The House of Gordon, 3-volume set. 1903. 3 vols.
P4-S12087 — $250.00./set

GORDON: MACY Allied families: Gordon-Macy & Hiddleston-Curtis et al, M.G. Carman & J.G. Flack. 1967. 293p.
P4-S12069 — $45.00.

GORE: Brief gen. of the Gore fam. By W. Whitmore. 1875. 7p.
P4-S12092 — $10.00.

GORHAM: Family: ancestors & descendants of Ephraim Gorham (1753-1830), Rev. Soldiers of Canterbury, CT & Elbridge, NY. By Gerald J. Parsons & Louis Wm. Hagen. 1955. 93p.
P4-S12099 — $18.50.

GORHAM: New Eng. Gorhams: misc. notes from NEHGR. 1896-1915. 40p.
P4-S12094 — $10.00.

GORHAM: Family of NC. By Webb & Colburn. 17p.
P4-S12095 — $10.00.

GORHAM: Capt. John Gorham, a genealogy. Alfred A. Knapp. 1961. 90p.
P4-S12093 — $18.00.

GORSUCH: Lost in a Wilderness: Lines of the Gorsuch Families of Huntingdon & Blair Cos., PA. Todd A. Johnson. 2005. xv + 429p.
P4-S12100 — $67.00.

GORTON: Samuell Gorton: a forgotten founder of our liberties; first settler of Warwick RI. By Lewis G. Janes. 1896. 141p.
P4-S12111 — $17.50.

GORTON: The life & times of Samuel Gorton: the founders of the col. of Providence & RI, with a gen. of Samuel Gorton's desc. By A. Gorton. 1907. 966p.
P4-S12114 — $121.50.

GOSNEY: Family records, 1740-1940, & related families. By Georgia G. Wisda. 1940. 325p.
P4-S12120 — $49.50.

GOSNOLD: Gosnold & Bacon, the anc. of Bartholomew Gosnold. A collection. By J. H. Lea. 1904. 36p.
P4-S12121 — $10.00.

GOSS: Family of Philip Goss of Lancaster, MA & Winchester, NH (Extr. Lawrence-Goss-Pomroy Gen.) By J. Lawrence. 1881. 37p.
P4-S12122 — $10.00.

GOSS: Goss fam., an hist. romance, (Incl. 9th reunion) By W. H. Boomer. 1886. 27p.
P4-S12123 — $10.00.

GOSSETT: The family of Gossett. By Evangeline G. Newcomer. 1954. 188p.
P4-S12126 — $27.50.

GOTT: The family of Robert & Lydia (Nichols) Gott. By Steve Roth & Beverly Franks. 1992. 575 + 95p.
P4-S12132 — $89.50.

GOTT: Daniel Gott, Mt. Desert pioneer, his anc. & desc. By W.O. Sawtelle. 28p.
P4-S12133 — $10.00.

GOTTSHALL: Gen. hist. of Gottshall fam., desc. of Jacob Gottshall. By N.B. Grubb. 1924. 112p.
P4-S12138 — $22.50.

GOULD: Desc. of Richard Gould of Chatham, MA, 1788-1871. By Ames & Sawyer. 1902. 31p.
P4-S12142 — $10.00.

GOULD: Family of Zaccheus Gould of Topsfield. By B.A. Gould. 1895. 360p.
P4-S12141 — $45.50.

GOULDS: of RI. By R.G. Mitchell. 1875. 99p.
P4-S12147 — $18.00.

GOURLEY: Gen. of Samuel Gourley & his desc., 1784-1909. By C. T. Heydecker. 1909. 32p.
P4-S12148 — $10.00.

GOVE: Book: history & genealogy of the American family of Gove & notes of European Goves, By W.H. Gove. 1922. 692p.
P4-S12153 — $99.00.

GOVE: The Gove & McDaniel Family, Revised. Barbara Evelyn Gove. 2003. 248p.
P4-S12154 — $37.50.

GOWDY: Family hist. comprising the surnames of Gade, Gaudie, Gawdy, Gowdy, Gaudern, etc. By M.H. Gowdy. 2 v. in 1, 1919. xx + 628p.
P4-S12156 — $89.50.

GOYETTE: Histoire genealogique et livre de famille des Goyette, 1659-1959, or The Goyette's family book and genealogy By Armand Goyette. 1959 487 + 75p.
P4-S12165 — $82.00.

GRABER: Peter Graber family record, 1839-1948. By Jacob M. & Anna G. Goering. 1948. 444p.
P4-S12171 — $68.00.

GRADY: Some Grady & Newcomb Families. Annie Self Arnold 2004. 109p.
P4-S12178 — $16.50.

GRADY: John Grady (1710-87) of Dobbs & Duplin, with some of his descendants. By Benj. Grady with Louis C. Hendry. 1930. 93p.
P4-S12177 — $18.00.

GRAFF: History of the Graff family of Westmoreland Co. (PA). By Paul Graff. 1891. 103p.
P4-S12183 — $19.00.

GRAFTON: Family of Salem. By H.W. Belknap. 1928. 103p.
P4-S12189 — $19.50.

GRAHAM: GRIMES Genealogy, with cognate branches, 1756-1926. By Frances G. Sitherwood. 1926. 175p.
P4-S12195 — $26.00.

GRAHAM: Condition of the Border at the Union: Destruction of the Graham Clan. John Graham. 1907. 202 + 34p.
P4-S12196 — $36.00.

GRAHAM: History of the Graham family [of VA]. David Graham. 1899. 119p.
P4-S12201 — $21.00.

GRAHAM: The Rev. John Graham of Woodbury, CT & his desc. By H.G. Carpenter. 1942. 550p.
P4-S12207 — $84.50.

GRANBERRY: Family & allied families, incl. the anc. of Helen Woodward Granberry. By Waterman & Jacobus. 1945. 383p.
P4-S12213 — $61.00.

GRANGER: Launcelot Granger of Newbury, MA & Suffield, CT, A genealogical history. By J.N. Granger. 1893. 587p.
P4-S12216 — $78.00.

GRANNIS: Descendants of Edward Grannis, who was in New Haven, CT, as early as 1649 & died there Dec. 10, 1719. By F. A. Strong. 1927. 288p.
P4-S12222 — $43.00.

GRANNIS: Genealogical history of the Grannis family in America from 1630-1901. Sidney S. Grannis. 1901. 55p.
P4-S12223 — $11.00.

GRANT: Family; Gen. history of the desc. of Matthew Grant of Windsor, CT, 1601-1898. A.H. Grant. 1898. 602p.
P4-S12240 — $89.00.

GRANT: Family magazine, suppl. to the Grant Family History. ed. By A.H. Grant. 1901. 228p.
P4-S12234 — $34.00.

GRANT: Ancestry of General Grant & their Comtemporaries. By Edw. C. Marshall. 1869. 186p.
P4-S12228 — $27.00.

GRANT: Report of the 1st reunion of the Grant Family Assoc. at Windsor & Hartford, CT on Oct. 27, 1899. 1899. 58p.
P4-S12243 — $12.00.

GRANT: American ancestry of US Grant. By H.E. Robinson. 1885. 17p.
P4-S12229 — $10.00.

GRANT: The Edward Grant Family & Related Families. Verne Grant. 1997. 186p.
P4-S12242 — $38.00.

GRANT: Supplement to the Edward Grant Family & Related Families in MA, RI, PA & CA. Verne Grant. 2003. 24p.
P4-S12241 — $10.00.

GRANTS: & Their Relatives. By John P. Grant. 1926. 121p.
P4-S12252 — $21.00.

GRANVILLE: The history of the Granville family, traved back to Rollo, first Duke of Normandy, with pedigrees, etc. By R. Granville. 1895 489p.
P4-S12258 — $74.50.

GRAVES: Family of ME. By C. Sinnett. 1922. 32p.
P4-S12265 — $10.00.

GRAVES: Notes on the anc. & connections of "Rear Admiral" Thomas Graves of Charlestown, MA (Repr. Essex Inst. Hist. Coll.) By E. Putnam. 1895. 17p.
P4-S12266 — $10.00.

GRAVES: Genealogy of the Graves family in America, Volume I By J.C. Graves. 1896. 546p.
P4-S12264 — $82.00.

GRAY: William Gray of Lynn, MA & some desc. (Repr. Essex Inst. Hist. Coll.) By E. Gray. 1916. 35p.
P4-S12298 — $10.00.

GRAY: Family & allied lines. Bowman, Lindsay, Millis, Disk, Peebles, Wiley, Shannon, Lamar, McGee, By Jo White Linn. 1976. Reprinted by permission. 607p.
P4-S12282 — $75.00.

GRAY: Genealogy, being a gen. record & history of the desc. of John Gray of Beverly, MA. M.D. Raymond. 1887. 316p.
P4-S12285 — $45.00.

GRAY: Family record of Edw. Gray & his wife Mary Paddock, & their descendants. By Alonson Gray. 1889. 195p.
P4-S12270 — $29.50.

GRAY: Gen. records & notes on the Gray family of NH & ME, particularly descendants of James & Tamson Gray of NH. Casimir P. Stevens. 1916. 195p.
P4-S12276 — $29.00.

GRAY: Hon. George Gray 4th of Philadelphia, his ancestors & descendants. By Mary Stanley Field Liddell. 1940. 226p.
P4-S12291 — $34.00.

GRAY: Joshua Gray of Yarmouth, MA & his desc. By J. E. Thacher. 1914. 136p.
P4-S12297 — $20.00.

GRAY: William Gray of Salem, merchant: a biographical sketch. By Edw. Gray. 1914. 124p.
P4-S12303 — $17.00.

GREELY: Genealogy of the Greely-Greeley family. G.H. Greeley. 1905. 915p.
P4-S12309 — $114.50.

GREEN: An acct. of Percival & Ellen Green & some of their desc. By S. A. Green. 1876. 67p.
P4-S12315 — $13.50.

GREEN: 1712-1901: Gen. of the family of Wm. Green of Long Island, referring especially to the desc. of his son Ambrose Green. By Sarah E. Frazier & W.C. Green. 1901. 47p.
P4-S12316 — $10.00.

GREEN: Genealogy of the family of Timothy & Eunice Ellsworth Green. By J.M. Greene. 1904. 227p.
P4-S12321 — $34.50.

GREENE: GREEN Family of Plymouth Colony. R.H. Greene. 1909. 145p.
P4-S12348 — $22.50.

GREENE: Family of RI, with hist. rec. of Eng. anc., 1534-1902. By L.B. Clarke. 1903 2 vols. In 1, 892p.
P4-S12375 — $119.00.

GREENE: Family of Plymouth col. (Repr. NEHGR) R.H. Greene. 1903. 5p.
P4-S12331 — $10.00.

GREENE: Ancestors of Forrest Greene in England & America: Greene of Boughton & Greene's Norton, Greene of Gillingham & new England. n.d. 48p., manuscript.
P4-S12332 — $10.00.

GREENE: Family in Eng. & Amer., with pedigree charts. 1901. 168p.
P4-S12366 — $30.00.

GREENE: Genealogical sketch of the desc. of Robert Greene of Wales, MA. By R. Greene. 1885. 64p.
P4-S12333 — $12.50.

GREENE: Genealogical sketch of the desc. of Thomas Green of Malden, MA. By S. Green. 1858. 80p.
P4-S12342 — $16.00.

GREENE: Family & its branches from 861-1904, by Lora S. la Mance, together with poems, descriptions of the text. By A.A. Stowe. 1904. 305p.
P4-S12354 — $49.00.

GREENE: Desc of Edward (2) Greene, eldest son of John (1) Greene of Quidnessett (Kingstown), RI, rev ed. By Ella Greene. 1986, 1997. 118p.
P4-S12327 — $18.00.

GREENE: Family history: an account of the ancestors & descs of Nathan & Job Greene, St. Albans, VT By Walter & Ella Greene 1981. Rev. 1997. 198p.
P4-S12360 — $29.50.

GREENE: Supplement to a Greene family history, with added sections on some branches of the RI Greenes By Walter & Ella Greene. 1969, 1998. 229p.
P4-S12390 — $34.00.

GREENE: History of Levi Greene of RI, MA, NY, MI & His descendants. By M.S. Green. 1944. 413p.
P4-S12384 — $62.00.

GREENE: Desc. of Joseph Greene of Westerly, RI; also, other branches of the Greenes of RI & in America By F.L. Greene. 1894. 500p.
P4-S12330 — $65.00.

GREENE: Greenes of Warwick in colonial hist. By H. Turner. 1877. 68p.
P4-S12378 — $13.50.

GREENLAW: Family of Deer Isle, ME. By C. Greenlaw. 1955. 5p. + 21 charts
P4-S12391 — $10.00.

GREENLEAF: Genealogy of the Greenleaf family. By J.E. Greenleaf. 1896. 564p.
P4-S12399 — $86.50.

GREENLEAF: The anc. of Jane Maria Greenleaf, wife of Wm. F. Boardman, Hartford. By W. Boardman. 1906. 133p.
P4-S12408 — $20.00.

GREENLEAF: Genealogy of the Greenleaf family. J. Greenleaf. 1854. 116p.
P4-S12399 — $16.00.

GREENLEE: Genealogy of the Greenlee families in America, Scotland, Ireland & England. By R.S. & R.L. Greenlee. 1908. 744p.
P4-S12420 — $105.00.

GREENLEE: Descendants of Edward Greenlee of WV. By W.C. Greenlee. 1956. 436p.
P4-S12414 — $66.00.

GREENOUGH: Notes on the anc. of Ebenezer Greenough, 1783-1847, & his wife, Abigail Israel, 1791-1868, & a list of their desc. By F. Platt. 1895. 38p.
P4-S12421 — $10.00.

GREENWOOD: Family of Norwich, Eng. in Amer. By H.M. Pitman & M.M. Greenwood. 1934. 396p.
P4-S12426 — $61.00.

GREENWOOD: Chronological history of the Greenwood family [of OH]. By Erastus Alderman. 1879. 19p.
P4-S12427 — $10.00.

GREENWOOD: Anc. & desc. of Thomas of Newton, MA; Nathaniel & Samuel of Boston, John of VA & many later arrivals in Amer. By F. Greenwood. 1914. 548p.
P4-S12432 — $84.50.

GREER: & related families Sanders, Sims, Glenn, Christmas, Smith, Ferris & Carver of the Carolinas & VA. By Brent H. Holcomb. 1987 (reprinted by permission). 109p.
P4-S12438 — $18.50.

GREGG: Desc. of Wm. Gregg, the Friend immigrant to DE, 1682 By Hazel May M. Kendall. 1944. 274p.
P4-S12444 — $52.00.

GREGORY: Ancestors & descendants of Henry Gregory. G. Gregory. 1938. 492p.
P4-S12450 — $76.00.

GRENVILLE: Pedigree of the family of Grenville, with the descent of High R.C. Birley & Bevil L. Birley fro Sir Bevil Grenville. Ernest Axon. 1893. 24p.
P4-S12451 — $10.00.

GRESHAM: Biogr. & hist. sketches of Gresham of Amer. & overseas. By A. Strange. 1913. 53p.
P4-S12452 — $10.00.

GRIFFIN: Samuel Griffin of New Castle County on Delaware, Planter, & his descendants to the 7th generation. By Thos. H. Streets. 1905. 235p.
P4-S12462 — $36.00.

GRIFFIN: Ancestors & descendants of Richard Griffin of Smithville, Ont: a pioneer family. Justus A. Griffin. 1924. 168p.
P4-S12456 — $25.00.

GRIFFING: Stephen Griffing [of NY], his anc. & desc. By E.W. West. 1911. 234p.
P4-S12474 — $37.00.

GRIFFING: Genealogy of the desc. of Jasper Griffing. C.J. Stone. 1881. 194p.
P4-S12468 — $30.00.

GRIFFITH: Genealogy of the Griffith family: the descendants of William & Sarah MacCubbin Griffith. By R.R. Griffith. 1892. 323p.
P4-S12480 — $49.50.

GRIFFITH: Genealogy of the Griffith family (from "Early History of Fluvanna NY"). By Mary Griffith. 1926? 126p.
P4-S12481 — $18.00.

GRIFFITTS: Gen. Tables of Griffitts Family. F.P. Griffitts. 1887. 88p.
P4-S12482 — $14.00.

GRIGG: Five generations of Mormonism: Grigg family gen embracing the ancestry, life & desc of Dr Anderson Irvin Grigg. Cleo G. Johnson. 1956. 345p.
P4-S12486 — $52.00.

GRIGGS: Gen. of the Griggs fam. By W. S. Griggs. 1926. 116p.
P4-S12498 — $22.50.

GRIGSBY: Gen. of Grigsby fam. By W. H. Grigsby. 1878. 8p.
P4-S12493 — $10.00.

GRIMES: Family from MD to OH. By Rachel Saul Tefft. 1996. 69p.
P4-S12498 — $14.00.

GRIMES: Family. By E. B. Grimes. 1946. 70p.
P4-S12504 — $14.00.

GRIMMETT: Genealogy of the Grimmett family, concerning the lineage of Mrs Paul Brown (Eloise Renfro). By Mrs P. Brown. 1985. 64p., handwritten.
P4-S12510 — $13.00.

GRISWOLD: Family research in England. Charles C. Griswold. 1932. 12p.
P4-S12517 — $10.00.

GRISWOLD: Family of Eng. & Amer: Edward of Windsor, Matthew of Lyme, Michael of Wethersfield (CT). By G.E. Griswold. 1943. 391p.
P4-S12522 — $61.00.

GRISWOLD: Records of the Griswold, Crane, Paddock, Howes, Smith & Russell families. By Anna R. Vance. 1889 57p.
P4-S12531 — $12.00.

GRISWOLD: Family. By E.E. Salisbury. 1884. 82p.
P4-S12528 — $16.50.

GRISWOLD: Ancestors & descendants of Edward Griswold of NY. By Arthur M. Buell. 1930. 82p.
P4-S12516 — $16.50.

GROOME: Family & connections: a pedigree, with biographical sketches. By Harry C. Groome. 1907. 113p.
P4-S12540 — $19.00.

GROUT: From "Genealogy of Several Ancient Puritans," By Rev. Abner Morse. 1857. 61p.
P4-S12555 — $12.00.

GROUT: "A Family Affair" concerning certain desc. of Capt. John Grout, who came from Eng. to New Eng. early in the 17th cent. By H.S.B. Osgood. 1949-1952. 116p.
P4-S12546 — $19.50.

GROUT: Capt. John Grout of Watertown & Sudbury, MA, & some of his desc. By E.E. Jones. 1922. 124p.
P4-S12552 — $18.50.

GROVE: Family of Halesowen. By James Davenport. 1912. 84p.
P4-S12564 — $16.00.

GROVER: Ancestry & genealogy of Thomas Grover - b. 1807, Whitehall, NY, d. 1886 Farmington, Ut. - Utah Pioneer, 1847, By Joel P. Grover. 1959. 359p.
P4-S12570 — $54.00.

GROVES: A hist. & gen. of the Groves fam. in Amer., desc. of Nicholas La Groves of Beverly, MA. By W.T. Groves. 1915. 56p.
P4-S12565 — $11.00.

GROW: John Grow of Ipswich. John Groo (Grow) of Oxford. By G.W. Davis. 1913. 274p.
P4-S12576 — $41.00.

GROWDON: Family, from "Fam. Sketches." By J. Wood. 1870. 37p.
P4-S12577 — $10.00.

GUELPH: Gen. Hist. of the House of Guelph, or royal family of Great Britain Andrew Halliday, M.D. 1821 472 + 29p.
P4-S12582 — $75.00.

GUERIN: One Guerin Family's Dutch Connection, 1600-2000. Denise Guerin Rice. 2002. 186p.
P4-S12585 — $31.00.

GUERIN: Transcriptions of Original & Photocopied Documents. Denise Guerin Rice. 1996. 152p.
P4-S12586 — $23.00.

GUERIN: Guerin Family & Allied Lines. Denise Guerin Rice. 1989. 209p.
P4-S12583 — $31.50.

GUERIN: Guerins in America. D. Rice. 2003. 642p.
P4-S12584 — $96.00.

GUIGNARD: Genealogie des Guignard. par Guignard de Buttelville. 1892. In French, 259p.
P4-S12588 — $39.00.

GUILD: Genealogy & history of the Guild, Guile & Gile family. By C. Burleigh. 1887. 381p.
P4-S12594 — $49.00.

GUILD: Genealogy of the descendants of John Guild, Dedham, MA. By C. Guild. 1867. 132p.
P4-S12600 — $20.00.

GUILD: Ancestry of Calvin Guild, Margaret Taft, James Humphreys & Rebecca Covell Martin, 1620-1890. By Howard R. Guild. 1891. 42p.
P4-S12595 — $10.00.

GUILFORD: Genealogy. By Helen Morrill Guilford. 1918. 68p.
P4-S12606 — $13.50.

GUILFORD: Family in America: pedigrees & genealogical notes of the Guilford & allied families. By Nathan Guilford. 1898. 69p. + charts
P4-S12601 — $16.00.

GUINNESS: Pedigree of the Magennis (Guinness) family of New Zealand & Dublin, Ireland. Richard Linn. 1897 58p.
P4-S12607 — $11.50.

GULICK: Descendants of Pieter Gulick, b. about 1689, d. 1774. By W.M. Huntley. 1959. 39p.
P4-S12608 — $10.00.

GULLICK: Gullicks & allied families, 1653-1948, with supplement to 1952 & index. By Eliza Haddon Brevoort. 1948-1953 261 + 44 + 47p.
P4-S12612 — $52.00.

GUNN: The Gunns. By Robt. R. Gunn. 1925. 171p.
P4-S12624 — $25.00.

GUNN: Complete family record: descendants of Reuben Gunn, Bernard Sweeney, Samuel Reaugh, Rev. James Dunn. By Benj. J. Gunn. 1891. 112p.
P4-S12618 — $17.50.

GUNNISON: A gen. of the desc. of Hugh Gunnison of Boston, MA, 1610-1876. By G.W. Gunnison. 1880. 222p.
P4-S12630 — $33.00.

GUNTHER: Family records, with notes on the families of Nagel, Schlossberger, Planer, Andrea, Urlsperger, Von Karpfen, McIntosh, etc. By Robert W.T. Gunther & A. Gunther. 1910. 110p.
P4-S12636 — $17.00.

GURLEY: History & genealogy of the Gurley family. A.E. Gurley. 1897. 285p. P4-S12642 — $42.50.

GUSEMAN: Abraham Guseman descendants. By Alta K. Allen. 1938. 46p., typescript. P4-S12643 — $10.00.

GUSLER: Partial history of the Gusler (Gossler) family, with notes on the Bennet & Wittmeyer families. By G. Gusler. 1954. 266p., typescript. P4-S12648 — $39.50.

GUSTIN: Ancestry of John S. Gustin & his wife Susan McComb, including an acct. of John Hubbard, 2nd husband of Elinor Shepherd. By S.A. Dewick. 1900. 136p. P4-S12654 — $22.00.

GUSTIN: Family, being the story of the Thomas Gustin branch of the family tree, 2nd ed. comp. by Lester C. Gustin. 1949. 128p. P4-S12666 — $17.50.

GUSTIN: Gang, being the story of the Thos. Gustin branch of the family tree By Lester C. Gustin. 1947. 88p. P4-S12660 — $18.00.

GUSTINE: Compendium. By G.C. Weaver. 1929. 339p. P4-S12672 — $54.00.

GUTHRIE: American Guthries & allied families: By Laurence R. Guthrie. 1933. 540p. P4-S12678 — $83.00.

GUTHRIE: Brief hist. of a branch of the Guthrie fam., By S. Guthrie. 1889. 62p. P4-S12679 — $12.50.

GUTHRIE: Records of the Guthrie family of PA, CT & VA, with ancestry of those who have intermarried with the fam. H.A. & E.G. Dunn. 1898. 170p. P4-S12696 — $25.50.

GUTHRIE: Henry Guthrie & John Lane Mason, their ancestors, descendants & collateral kin. By Mildred Murphy. 1953. 179p. P4-S12690 — $28.00.

GUTTERSON: The Gutterson family. By G.L. Gutterson, et al. 1927. 19p. P4-S12698 — $10.00.

GUY: Gen. record of William Guy. By A. Guy. 1898. 28p. P4-S12701 — $10.00.

GUYON: Etude genealogique sur Jean Guyon. Louis Guyon. 1927. 132p. P4-S12702 — $21.50.

GWATKINS: of Herefordshire: notes on families in Fownhope, Hereford-shire & other places, named Gwatkin. By E.M.G. 1914. 103p. P4-S12708 — $17.00.

GWIN: GWYN; History of the Gwin family (Gwin, Gwinn, Gwyn, Gwynn, Gwynne, Guin, Wynn, Wynne). By Jesse B. Gwin. 1961. 195p. P4-S12714 — $29.50.

H

HABERSHAM: History & gen. of the Habersham fam., also Clay, Stiles, Cumming, & other fam. By J.G.B. Bulloch. 1901. 228p. P4-S12720 — $37.50.

HADLEY: Notes on the Quaker fam. of Hadley. By C. Hadley. 1916. 59p. P4-S12729 — $12.00.

HADLEY: Gen. record of the desc. of Moses Hadley & Rebecca Page, of Hudson NH. By S.P. Hadley. 1887. 88p. P4-S12726 — $15.00.

HAFF: Gen. of Delbert James Haff & Wife Grace Isabel Barse. By D.J. Haff. 1936. 109p. P4-S12738 — $19.50.

HAGGARD: Genealogy & history of Haggard family in England & America, 1433-1899. By David A. Haggard. 1899. 136p. P4-S12744 — $22.00.

HAGGARD: History of the Haggard family in England & America, 1433 to 1899-1938. By Jennie H. Ray. 1938. 184p. P4-S12750 — $25.00.

HAGOOD: Meet your grandfather: sketch-book of the Hagood-Tobin family [of SC & VA]. By Gen. Johnson Hagood. 1946. 165p. P4-S12756 — $25.00.

HAILE: HAIL — HALE Family: descendants of Richar Haile of Swansea, MA (1640-1729). 1997. 374p. P4-S12757 — $54.00.

HAIN: History of the Hain family: descendants of George & Veronica Hain [settled in Berks & Lebanon Co. PA, 1723]. n.a. 1941. 88p. P4-S12762 — $17.00.

HAINES: Deacon Samuel Haines of Westbury, Wiltshire, Eng., & his desc. In America, 1635-1901. By A.M. & T.V. Haines. 1902. 400p. P4-S12783 — $51.50.

HAINES: Ancestry of Wm. Shipley Haines, with some account of the desc. of John & Joseph Haines & Col. Cowperthwait. By Wm. Francis Cregar. 1887. 85p. P4-S12780 — $16.50.

HAINES: Orig. papers relating to Samuel Haines & his desc. (Repr. NEHGR). By A.M. Haines. 1869. 29p. P4-S12769 — $10.00.

HAINES: Anc. of the Haines, Sharp, Collins & other fam.; comp. from notes of the late Geo. Haines, with some add. By R. Haines. 1902. 456p. P4-S12774 — $68.50.

HAINES: "The Clovercroft Chron-icles," 1314-1893. M.R. Haines. 1893. 347p. P4-S12768 — $53.50.

HAIRSTON: The Hairstons & Penns & their relations. By Elizabeth S. Hairston. 1940. 193p. P4-S12789 — $28.50.

HAKES: Family. H. Hakes. 1886. 87p. P4-S12798 — $17.50.

HAKES: Family. H. Hakes. 1889. 220p. P4-S12801 — $33.00.

HALE: HOUSE & related families, mainly of the CT River Valley. By Jacobus & Waterman. 1952. 914p. P4-S12846 — $109.00.

HALE: Documentary life of Nathan Hale, comprising all available official & private documents bearing on the life of the patriot . . . . By Geo. Dudley Seymour. 1941. 627p. P4-S12825 — $59.95

HALE: Desc. of Major Samuel Hale. By E. H. Smith. 1902. 123p. P4-S12813 — $18.50.

HALE: The Genealogy of John Hale, Jr. Roger Conant Hale. 2005. ix + 83p. P4-S12808 — $14.00.

HALE: Roots in Virginia: an account of Capt. Thomas Hale, VA frontiersman, his decendants. By Nathaniel C. Hale. 1948. 227p.
P4-S12834 — $35.00.

HALE: Family of CT. By S. Morris. 1907. 13p.
P4-S12809 — $10.00.

HALE: Ancestry & descendants of Joseph Hale, 5th in descent from Sam'l Hale of Hartford, CT, 1637 By Oscar F. Hale. 1909. 133p.
P4-S12807 — $21.00.

HALE: Descendants of Thomas Hale of DE, with an account of the Jamison & Green families. By Thos. H. Streets. 1913. 116p.
P4-S12819 — $17.00.

HALE: Family [of VA & TN]. By Edythe R. Whitley. 1934. 45p.
P4-S12811 — $10.00.

HALE: Genealogy of descendants of Thomas Hale of Walton, Eng., & of Newbury, MA. R. S. Hale. 1889. 427p.
P4-S12828 — $48.00.

HALEY: HEALY family ancestry of Ebenezer Haley, CA pioneer of 1850, with an acct. of his descendants By James B. Haley. 1964. 279p.
P4-S12858 — $42.50.

HALEY: The anc. of Charity Haley, 1755-1800, wife of Maj. Nicholas Davis of Limington, ME. By W. G. Davis, Jr. 1916. 91p.
P4-S12864 — $18.00.

HALEY: Thom. Haley of Winter Harbor & his desc. By W. G. Davis & A. Haley. 1930. 55p.
P4-S12853 — $11.00.

HALEY: Genealogical memoranda relating chiefly to to Haley, Piper, Neal & Ricker families of ME & NH. By John W. Hayley. 1900. 115p.
P4-S12852 — $19.50.

HALL: KNAPP Family history. By Leona Hall. 1911. 92p.
P4-S12891 — $17.50.

HALL: Series of sketches of the lin. anc. of the children of Sam'l Holden Parsons Hall & his wife Emeline Bulkeley of Binghamton, NY. By C. Hall. 1896. 517p.
P4-S12915 — $81.00.

HALL: Family of New England, genealogy & biography. By D. Hall. 1883. 800p.
P4-S12879 — $98.50.

HALL: Fam. settled at the town of Medford, MA. By W. H. Whitmore. 12p.
P4-S12877 — $10.00.

HALL: Gen. notes relating to the families of Hon. Lyman Hall of GA; Hon. Samuel Holden Parsons Hall of Binghamton, NY; etc. By Theo. Parson Hall. 1886. 192p.
P4-S12876 — $29.00.

HALL: Ancestry & descendants of Amaziah Hall & Betsey Baldwin. By Edith Bartlett Sumner. 1954. 255p.
P4-S12870 — $39.00.

HALL: Memoranda rel. to the anc. & fam. of Sophia Fidelia Hall. By S.F.H. Coe. 1902. 231p.
P4-S12909 — $30.00.

HALL: Ancestry of a few of the descendants of Edward Hall of Rehobeth, MA, with intermarriages. n.d. 56p.
P4-S12892 — $11.00.

HALL: John Hall of Wallingford, CT, A monograph (with gen.) By J. Shepard. 1902. 61p.
P4-S12900 — $12.00.

HALL: Family history. By Mrs R.M. Green. 1907. 39p.
P4-S12893 — $10.00.

HALL: Genealogy. By Helen L. Hall. 1960. 294p.
P4-S12885 — $45.00.

HALL: History of the Hall family & allied lines. By Gladys H. Meier & Robert R. Martindale. 1959. 185p.
P4-S12897 — $28.00.

HALL: Family Records of Theodore Parsons Hall & Alexandrine Louise Godfrey, of "Tonnancour," Grosse Pointe, MI. Theodore Parsons Hall. 1892. vi + 186p.
P4-S12886 — $29.00.

HALLADAY: Family, 1650-1933. By V.A. Kraft-Nicholson. n.d. 102p.
P4-S12921 — $19.00.

HALLETT: Family: descendants of Richard Hallett of Dorset, England & Long Island, NY. Art Reierson. 1998. 96p.
P4-S12927 — $18.00.

HALLMAN: History of the Hallman family in Canada. H.S. Hallman. n.d. 109p.
P4-S12933 — $18.00.

HALLOCK: Brief sketch of the Hallock anc. J. M. Sherman. 1866. 17p.
P4-S12940 — $10.00.

HALLOCK: Descendants of Peter Hallock, who landed at Southold, LI, 1640. By L. Hallock. 1926. 749p.
P4-S12939 — $109.00.

HALLOWELL: PAUL Family history, incl. the ancestry of related families of Worth, Luken, Jarrett, Morris, Scull, Stokes, Heath & others. By M.P.H. Hough & A.H. Penrose. 1924. 16 + 189p.
P4-S12945 — $32.00.

HALLOWELL: Record of a branch of the Hallowell fam., incl. the Longstreth, Penrose & Norwood branches. By W. P. Hallowell. 1893. 246p.
P4-S12951 — $37.00.

HALSEY: Family; The book of ghosts: a search through 300 years for 512 fathers. H.D & F.R. Halsey. 1927. 201p.
P4-S12957 — $31.00.

HALSEY: Thomas Halsey of Herts., Eng. & Southampton, LI, 1591-1679, with his anc. to 8th & 9th gen. By J.L. & E.D. Halsey. 1895. 550p.
P4-S12960 — $79.00.

HALSTEAD: Genealogy of the Halstead family. J.H. Halstead. 1963. 71p.
P4-S12966 — $14.00.

HALSTEAD: Family history, 1827-1990. Betty W. Bacon. 1990. 136 + 32p.
P4-S12972 — $25.00.

HALSTEAD: Story of the Halsteads of the US, By Wm. L. Halstead. 1934. 115p.
P4-S12978 — $17.50.

HALSTED: Some descendants of Jonas Halsted (1610-82) & some allied families. By Laura A.D. Shoptaugh. 1954. 206p.
P4-S12984 — $31.00.

HAM: Genealogy of the Ham family & the Young family. By T.C. Ham. 1949. 87p.
P4-S12990 — $15.00.

HAMBLEN: Extr. from Gen. Notes of Barnstable Fam. 17p.
P4-S12991 — $10.00.

HAMBLETON: Gen. record of the Hambleton fam. desc. of James Hambleton of Bucks Co., PA, d. 1751. By C. J. Hambleton. 1887. 108p.
P4-S12996 — $17.00.

HAMILTON: Genealogy of the Hamilton family in America. By Charles Wm. Hamilton. 1933. 63p.
P4-S13011 — $12.50.

HAMILTON: Genealogical tables of the descendants of John Hamilton of "Locust Hill," Lexington, VA, B. 1789-d. 1825. By L. McCormack Goodhart. 1933. 39p. + charts
P4-S13003 — $10.00.

HAMILTON: Family records: descendants of John & Jane Hamilton, of Cayuga Co., NY. By Marion S. Cummings. 1940. 65p.
P4-S13026 — $13.00.

HAMILTON: John Hamilton, yeoman of Concord [MA]: sketches of ten generations of one branch of the Hamilton family in America (1658-1958) By Chas. W. Hamilton. 1958. 104p. typescript.
P4-S13038 — $17.50.

HAMILTON: Family of Charles Co., MD. By Maria Louis H. Kelley & Inez B. Cherault. 1930. 76p.
P4-S13020 — $15.00.

HAMILTON: The Hamiltons of Burnside, NC & their ancestors & descendnts. By Patrick H. Baskervill. 1916. 158p.
P4-S13044 — $23.00.

HAMILTON: Family in America. By W.M. Clemens. 30p.
P4-S13004 — $10.00.

HAMILTON: The Hamiltons of Waterborough (York Co., ME) their anc. & desc. S.K. Hamilton. 1912. 423p.
P4-S13050 — $66.50.

HAMILTON: Hamiltons of Ogden Center & their antecedents of Norwich, Colchester, Nova Scotia & the British Isles By James A. Hamilton. 1930. 60p.
P4-S13029 — $12.00.

HAMILTON: Genealogy of the descendants of Hugh Hamilton. By Jas. A. Hamilton. 1921. 97p.
P4-S13002 — $18.00.

HAMILTON: Genealogy of the Hamilton family from 1716-1894. By S. Hamilton. 1894. 133p.
P4-S13008 — $20.00.

HAMLETT: My Virginia kin, comprising the Hamlett, Witt, Giles, Wills, Eubank-Fortune, Mullenix, Lynchard, Talbot & Kight families By Blanche J. Baldridge. 1958. 240p.
P4-S13056 — $37.00.

HAMLIN: Hamlins of New Eng., desc. of James & Anna Hamlin. By S. M. Hamlin. 1936. 65p.
P4-S13071 — $13.00.

HAMLIN: Family; a gen. of Capt. Giles Hamlin of Middletown, CT, 1654-1900. By H.F. Andrews. 1900. 479p.
P4-S13065 — $61.00.

HAMLIN: Gen of James Hamlin of Barnstable, MA, eldest son of James Hamlin, the immigr., 1639-1902. By H.A. Andrews. 1902. 1411p.
P4-S13062 — $198.50.

HAMLIN: Eleazer Hamlin & his descendants: their homes. By Myra S. Hamlin. 1909. 40p.
P4-S13063 — $10.00.

HAMLIN: History of the Hamlin family, with gen. of early settlers of the name in Amer., 1629-1894. By H.F. Andrews. 1894. 130p.
P4-S13077 — $19.50.

HAMMER: The Hammers & allied families, with their fam. circles centering in Pendleton Co., WV. By E.B. Boggs. 1950. 176p.
P4-S13083 — $28.00.

HAMMOND: A hist. & gen. of the desc. of Wm. Hammond of London, Eng., & his wife, Elizabeth Penn, through their son, Benjamin By R. Hammond. 1894. 320p.
P4-S13098 — $40.00.

HAMMOND: History & genealogy of the Hammond fam. in Amer., vol I. By F. Hammond. 1902. 674p.
P4-S13086 — $98.00.

HAMMOND: History & genealogy of the Hammond fam. in Amer., vol II. By F.S. Hammond. 1904. 881p.
P4-S13089 — $119.00.

HAMMOND: Swanzey Hammond gen. By J. Hammond. 1890. 17p.
P4-S13090 — $10.00.

HAMPTON: Joseph Hampton & the PA Quakers. V. B. Hampton. 1940. 116p.
P4-S13110 — $22.50.

HAMPTON: Family narrative as printed in "History of Alleghen Valley," 1913. 1913. 50p.
P4-S13105 — $10.00.

HAMPTON: History: account of the PA Hamptons in America in the line of John Hampton, Jr., of Wrightstown By John H. Doan. 1911. 199p.
P4-S13104 — $30.00.

HAMRICK: Generations, being a genealogy of the Hamrick family. By S.C. Jones. 1920. 207p.
P4-S13116 — $30.00.

HAMRICK: & Other Families: Indian Lore [& genealogy], By Mayme H. Hamrick 1939. 144p.
P4-S13122 — $21.00.

HANAFORD: Family records of branches of the Hanaford, Thompson, Huckins, Prescott & allied families. By M. E. N. Hanaford. 1915. 345p.
P4-S13128 — $55.00.

HANCHETT: Family. By Junius T. Hanchett. 1957. 119p.
P4-S13134 — $17.00.

HANCOCK: Some descendants of John Hancock (1733-1802) of Goochland, Fluvanna & Patrick Cos., VA. By R.R. & W. Hancock. 1938 86p.
P4-S13140 — $19.00.

HANDERSON: A contribution to the gen. of the Handerson fam. By H. E. Handerson. 1885. 80p.
P4-S13146 — $14.00.

HANDY: Samuel Handy of Somerset Co., MD & some of his desc. By E. D. Neill. 1875. 8p.
P4-S13147 — $10.00.

HANDY: Desc. of Richard Handy of Sandwich, MA. E. M. Lewis. 1925. 14p.
P4-S13148 — $10.00.

HANES: The David Hanes family. By Louise E. Gallagher. 1960. 139 + 10p., typescript.
P4-S13158 — $23.00.

HANES: John Hanes (d. Tyler Co., VA, 1815) & some of his descendants. By Edith Foster. 1963. 101p., typescript.
P4-S13152 — $18.00.

HANEY: Haney fam. By J. L. Haney. 1930. 46p.
P4-S13159 — $9.00.

HANFORD: Desc. of Rev. Thomas Hanford of CT. A. C. Golding. 1936. 153p.
P4-S13164 — $27.50.

HANKS: New England branch of the Hanks family papers. By Caroline H. Hitchcock. 1938? 367p., typescript.
P4-S13170 — $56.00.

HANNA: The house of Hanna. By Sarah A. Hanna. 1906. 142p.
P4-S13176 — $22.00.

HANNA: A History of the Hanna Family. Being a Genealogy of the Desc. of Thomas Hanna & Elizabeth [Henderson] Hanna. Charles Elmer Rice. 1905. lxiii + 238p.
P4-S13177 — $45.50.

HANNAY: Genealogy of the Hannay family. By Wm. V. Hannay. 1913. 71p.
P4-S13182 — $14.00.

HANNUM: Genealogy of the Hannum fam. desc. from John & Margery Hannum By Curtis H. Hannum. 1911. 702p.
P4-S13188 — $99.00.

HANNUM: William Hannum of New England, & some desc. By W.H. Hannum. 1936. 67p.
P4-S13194 — $13.50.

HANSARD: CHRISTIAN Family history records, Volume I. By Annie W. Burns. n.d. 98 + 11p.
P4-S13200 — $18.00.

HAPGOOD: Family: desc. of Shadrach, 1656-1898. By W. Hapgood. Incl. suppl. 1898. 590p.
P4-S13206 — $74.50.

HAPGOOD: Genealogy (from "Gen. Reg. of Several Ancient Puritans"). By A. Morse. 1859. 36p.
P4-S13207 — $10.00.

HARBAUGH: Annals of the Harbough fam. in Amer., 1736-1856. By H. Harbough. 1856. 148p.
P4-S13212 — $30.00.

HARBAUGH: History; A directory, gen. & source book of fam. records. By C.B. & J.L. Cooprider. 1947. 441p.
P4-S13218 — $68.50.

HARDAWAY: Thomas Hardaway of Chesterfield County, VA & his Descendants. Sarah Donelson Hubert. 1906. 55p.
P4-S13219 — $11.00.

HARDENBERGH: Family: a gen. comp. By M. Miller. 1958. 520p.
P4-S13224 — $79.50.

HARDENBERGH: Hardenbergh, Leaves out of Ancestral Tablets. Theo. W. Welles. 1893. 97p.
P4-S13225 — $18.00.

HARDIN: HARDING of VA & KY; With supplement. By Dorothy Ford Wulfeck. 1963, 1965 126 + 41p.
P4-S13230 — $22.00.

HARDING: The Hardings in Amer. A gen. register of the desc. of John Harding of Eng. born 1567. By W. J. Harding. 1925. 209p.
P4-S13260 — $28.00.

HARDING: Our Harding family: record of the family & descendants of Sam'l Harding By Mary E.H. Baird. 1957. 179p., typescript.
P4-S13254 — $27.50.

HARDING: Four centuries of the Harding family, ancestry & descendants of Perry Green Harding, 1807-1885. By Veryl E. Harding. 1958. 129p.
P4-S13248 — $18.50.

HARDING: The Genealogy of the Desc. of Several Ancient Puritans, by the Names of Harding, Harnden & Brigham. Rev. Abner Morse. 1864. 92 + 98p.
P4-S13243 — $29.00.

HARDING: Ancestry of Addie Clark Harding, daughter of Abner Clark Harding, Jr., & Maud McCain. By Gladys R. McPherson. 1960. 165p.
P4-S13242 — $25.00.

HARDING: Family, 1929 ed. By Forrest C. Harding. 1929. 44p.
P4-S13239 — $10.00.

HARDING: Ancestry of President Harding & its relation to the Hardings of Wyoming Valley & Clifford, PA. Clara G. Miller. 1928. 50p.
P4-S13243 — $10.00.

HARDING: A narrative hist. of the Harding fam. A. K. Holt. 1904. 142p.
P4-S13236 — $21.00.

HARDING: The Hardings: genealogical register of the descendants of John Harding, born a.d. 1567. Wilbur J. Harding. 1907. 225p.
P4-S13266 — $34.00.

HARDING: Hardings of ME, M.L. Dunn. 1977? 207 + 25p; typescript.
P4-S13238 — $37.00.

HARDY: HARDIE; past & present. By H.C. & E.N. Hardy. 1935. 1322p.
P4-S13272 — $179.00.

HARDY: Family tree: collection of family records of ancestors & descendants of Eldad Hardy, 1777-1857. By Lynn L. Hardy. 1942. 509p.
P4-S13278 — $76.50.

HARDY: Record of one hundred years of the Hardy fam. By J. Hardy. 1877. 12p.
P4-S13273 — $10.00.

HARGITT: HADDOCK Centennial history & genealogy, including collateral lines of Gibson, Johnson, Lynas, Nowlin, Sutton, 1820-1920. By Chas. W. Hargitt. 1921. 80p.
P4-S13284 — $16.00.

HARGRAVE: Forebears" a family saga, with statistical chart & outline. By Helen G. Hargrave. 1967. 287p.
P4-S13296 — $42.50.

HARGRAVE: Brief history of the Quakers in England & VA, & the Hargrave family, 1634-1939. By Harry S. Hargrave. 1939. 81p.
P4-S13290 — $16.00.

HARKNESS: Some descendants of John & Margaret Harkness of Newton, MA. By Roscoe L. Ball. 1957. 55p., typescript.
P4-S13297 — $11.00.

HARLAN: Hist & Gen of the Harlan family, desc. of George & Michael Harlan who settled in Chester Co., PA, 1687. By A. H. Harlan. 1914. 1065p.
P4-S13302 — $159.50.

HARLEY: The Heiligh & Harley fam. By J. Witcraft. 1914. 31p.
P4-S13303 — $10.00.

HARLLEE: Kinfolks: a gen. and bio. record of Thomas & Elizabeth (Stuart) Harllee; Andrew & Agnes (Cade) Fulmore; etc., Three-volume set By William Curry Harllee. 1934-1937 (Reprinted by permission.) 3 vols; 3270p.
P4-S13308 — $295.00./set

HARLLEE: Index to KINFOLKS. By Wm. Curry Harllee. 1937. 303p.
P4-S13332 — $30.00.

HARLOE: KELSO Genealogy, of the descendants of John Wm. Harloe & James Kelso By Dr Chas. B. Harloe. 1943. 358p.
P4-S13338 — $55.00.

HARLOW: Fam. (Repr. NEHGR) By T. P. Adams. 1860. 7p.
P4-S13339 — $10.00.

HARMAN: HARMON Genealogy & biogr., with hist. notes, 19 BC to 1928 AD. By J. W. Harman. 1928. 471p.
P4-S13344 — $70.50.

HARMAN: Genealogy (So. branch) with biogr. sketches 1700-1924. By J. N. Harman, Sr. 1925. 376p.
P4-S13350 — $58.50.

HARMON: Souvenir of the Harmon Reunion, & special family record of Israel Harmon (III) & Frances M. Cooley Harmon, etc. By Israel Harmon III. 1911. 119p.
P4-S13365 — $18.50.

HARMON: A good inheritance: gen. records of ten generations of desc. of John Harmon of Scarboro, ME [with related families]. By Francis S. Harmon. 1960. 255p.
P4-S13356 — $39.50.

HARMON: The Harmons in the Revolution: Harmon soldiers of 1776, with genealogical notes in the first Harmon settlers By Wm. M. Clemens. 1913. 32p.
P4-S13360 — $10.00.

HARMON: Genealogy, comprising all branches in New Eng. By A. C. Harmon. 1920. 383p.
P4-S13359 — $59.50.

HARPER: Records of the Harper family. By Jane C. Ford. 1905. 61p.
P4-S13374 — $12.00.

HARPER: History of the descendants of Sam'l Harper, James Purdy & James Leeper, & other branches 1894. 82p.
P4-S13371 — $16.00.

HARRELL: John Harrell & desc. of SC (in Happy Heritage) By L. J. Cannon. 1943. 9p.
P4-S13372 — $10.00.

HARRINGTON: Early generations of the family of Robt. Harrington of Watertown, MA, 1634, & some of his desc. By Frederick L. Weis. 1958. 153p.
P4-S13383 — $24.00.

HARRINGTON: Manuscript of Harrington Family Gazetteer, By George H. Harrington. 1941. 878p., typescript.
P4-S13407 — $125.00.

HARRINGTON: Narrative history of the Harrington family in Worcester, MA. By Chas. H. Bouley. 1963. 77p.
P4-S13413 — $14.50.

HARRINGTON: Family in RI. By Eva H. Baker with Lucy D.H. Johnson. 1928? 105p., typescript.
P4-S13401 — $18.00.

HARRINGTON: General history of the Harrington, DeWolfe & Tremaine families, with a genealogical record of 1643-1938. Chas. T. Harrington. 1938. 137p.
P4-S13389 — $23.50.

HARRINGTON: Family in America. By E. Harrington. 1907. 127p.
P4-S13395 — $19.00.

HARRIS: Robert Harris & desc. with notices of Morey & Metcalf fam. By L. M. Harris. 1861. 56p.
P4-S13420 — $11.00.

HARRIS: Harris Genealogy. Gideon Dowse Harris. 1914. 107p.
P4-S13421 — $16.50.

HARRIS: Genealogy & biogr. sketches of the NJ branch of the Harris family in the US. By S. Keifer. 1888. 350p.
P4-S13425 — $55.50.

HARRIS: Gen. of the desc. of Nicholas Harris, 5th in descent from Thomas Harris of Providence RI etc. By Mrs T.H. Ham. 1904. 88p.
P4-S13431 — $17.50.

HARRIS: Edw. Harris & his anc. 1634-1820. By W. P. Johnston. 1899. 26p.
P4-S13422 — $10.00.

HARRIS: Family from A.D. 1630 in Two Lines. D.J. & N.D. Harris. 1909. 131p.
P4-S13437 — $24.00.

HARRIS: Josiah Harris, 1770-1845, E. Machias, ME: his ancestors & descendants in nine generations, with index. By H. Harris. 1903. 19 + 5p.
P4-S13423 — $10.00.

HARRIS: History of James Harris of New London, CT & his desc., 1640-1878. By N.H. Morgan. 1878. 239p.
P4-S13461 — $36.00.

HARRIS: Family: Thomas Harris in Ipswich, MA in 1636, & some of his descendants through seven generations. By Wm. S. Harris. 1883. 135p.
P4-S13443 — $21.00.

HARRIS: Genealogy [descendants of Asa Harris of MA & CT). By Laura Hindman. 1940. 138p., typescript.
P4-S13449 — $22.00.

HARRIS: Records with allied families of Claiborne, Gillison, Thompson, Whitsett [of SC]. By Maud C. Hays. 1953. 130p., typescript.
P4-S13455 — $19.00.

HARRIS: Harrises in Boston before 1700. By R. B. Jones. 30p.
P4-S13424 — $10.00.

HARRIS: Collateral ancestry of Stephen Harris (b. Sept. 4, 1798) & Marianne Smith Smith (b. April 2, 1805). By J.S Harris. 1908. 190p.
P4-S13419 — $28.00.

HARRIS: Record of the Harris family, descended from John Harris, b. 1680 in Wiltshire, England. By Jos. S. Harris. 1903. 135p.
P4-S13473 — $22.00.

HARRIS: Personal & family history of Charles Hooks Harris & Margaret Monk Harris [of GA]. By James C. Harris. 1911. 116p.
P4-S13467 — $17.00.

HARRISON: The Story of the "Dining Fork" [the history of the Harrisons of Harrison Co OH, from John Harrison]. By Joseph T. Harrison. 1927. 370p.
P4-S13500 — $33.50.

HARRISON: Settlers by the Long Grey Trail; some Pioneers to old Augusta Co., VA & their descendants By J. Houston Harrison. 1935. 666p.
P4-S13494 — $99.00.

HARRISON: Aris sonis focisque; a mem. of an Amer. fam., the Harrisons of Skimino. By F. Harrison. 1910. 437p.
P4-S13488 — $66.00.

HARRISON: Ancestry of Benj. Harrison, President of the US, 1889-1893 By Charles P. Keith. 1893. 101p.
P4-S13482 — $18.00.

HARRISON: Brief hist. of the first Harrisons of VA, desc. of Cuthbert Harrison (1600-1915) By H. T. Harrison. 1915. 40p.
P4-S13480 — $10.00.

HARRISON: Partial hist. of the Harrison fam. By W. Harrison. 53p.
P4-S13481 — $10.00.

HARRISON: A century & Half of the Isaac Harrison family, 1744-1899. By Ella W Harrison. 1892. 144p.
P4-S13479 — $24.00.

HARROUN: History of the Harroun family in America, seven generations: desc of Alexander Harroun of Colrain, MA, 1691-1784. By Ernest B. Comstock. 1940. 195p.
P4-S13506 — $29.00.

HARSH: ORWIG Genealogies, for descendants of Simon Harsch (1722-1807) . . . & Gottfried Orwig (1719-1804); By James R. Harsch. 1947. 58p., typescript.
P4-S13509 — $12.00.

HARSHMAN: Family, also spelled Hershman & Hersman, history & genealogy. By Chas. W. Harshman. 1932. 352p.
P4-S13518 — $49.50.

HARSTAD: Brief history of Valle, Saetersdal, Norway, & of some families from there (the Harstad). By Bjug A. Harstad 1930. 64p.
P4-S13524 — $13.00.

HART: Hart of My Heart: The Life of Reuben Hart. Roger A. Hart. 2003. xv + 147p.
P4-S13531 — $24.50.

HART: Genealogical history of Deacon Stephen Hart & his desc., 1632-1875. By A. Andrews. 1875. 606p.
P4-S13536 — $91.00.

HART: The desc. of Lewis Hart & Anne Elliott with add. gen. & hist. data on the fams. of Hart, Warner, Curtiss, etc. J.S. Torrance. 1923. 380p.
P4-S13578 — $59.50.

HART: Family; Genealogical narrative of the Hart family in the US. By Mrs Sarah Young. 1882. 82p.
P4-S13554 — $16.00.

HART: Genealogy hist. of Samuell Hartt from London, Eng. to Lynn, MA, 1640, & desc. to 1903, Nicholas, Isaac & others. J.H. Hart. 1903. 631p.
P4-S13542 — $95.00.

HART: Joseph Hart & his desc. By C. C. Hart. 1901. 124p.
P4-S13566 — $22.50.

HART: Edward Hart descendants & allied fmailies. By Clara Hart Kennedy. 1939. 239p.
P4-S13530 — $38.00.

HART: Record of the Hart family of Philadelphia, with a genealogy of the family By Thos. Hart. 1920. 304p., typescript.
P4-S13572 — $46.50.

HART: Family history: Silas Hart, his ancestors & desendants. By Wm. L. Hart. 1942. 198p.
P4-S13548 — $29.50.

HART: Hist of the Hart family of Warminster, Bucks Co., PA, to which is added the genealogy of the family, By W.W.H. Davis. 1867. 139 + 20p.
P4-S13560 — $25.00.

HARTER: Journal: the family of Johannes George & Eva Harter. By Byron E. Harter. 1982 (reprinted with permission). 362p.
P4-S13584 — $54.00.

HARTMAN: Johannes Hartman of Chester Co., PA & his descendants. By John M. Hartman. 1937. 92p.
P4-S13590 — $18.00.

HARTWELL: Family: account of the descendants of William Hartwell of Concord, MA, 1636-1895. By L.W. Densmore. 1895. 80p.
P4-S13596 — $16.00.

HARTWELL: The Hartwells of America, a gen. of all the Hartwell families of the US & Canada By John F. Hartwell. 1958. 2 vols. in 1, 201 + 234p.
P4-S13602 — $66.00.

HARVARD: John Harvard & his anc. By H.F. Waters. 1885. 46p.
P4-S13603 — $10.00.

HARVEY: The desc. of Elisha Harvey from 1719-1914. By J. W. Knappenberger. 1914. 44p.
P4-S13609 — $10.00.

HARVEY: Book, giving the gen. of certain branches of the Amer. fams. of Harvey, Nesbitt, Dixon & Jameson. By O.J. Harvey. 1899. 1057p.
P4-S13614 — $139.50.

HARVEY: Family tree of the five Harvey brothers: Thomas, Peter, Philip & Andrew Harvey of Skaneateles, NY. By Lester M. Harvey, Jr. 1955. 165p.
P4-S13608 — $26.50.

HARVEY: Anc. of Col. John Harvey of Northwood, NH. J. Treat. 1907. 47p.
P4-S13610 — $10.00.

HARWOOD: A gen. hist. of the Harwood fam. desc. from James Harwood By W. H. Harwood. 1879. 33p.
P4-S13621 — $10.00.

HARWOOD: A gen. hist. of the Harwood fam., desc. from Andrew Harwood, whose Eng. home was in Dartmouth, Devonshire By W.H. Harwood. 1911. 3rd ed. 155p.
P4-S13623 — $21.00.

HARWOOD: A gen. hist. of the Salem Harwoods, desc. of Henry & Elizabeth Harwood who settled in Charlestown, MA. W.H. Harwood. Vol. II. 1912. 75p.
P4-S13629 — $15.00.

HARWOOD: A gen. hist. of the Concord Harwoods, desc. of Nathaniel Harwood, son of John Harwood of London, England By W. H. Harwood. Vol. III. 1912. 129p.
P4-S13635 — $19.50.

HARWOOD: Genealogical & historical account of Harwoods, Henrys & Dotsons. By James B. Harwood. 1902. 130p.
P4-S13620 — $19.50.

HASBROUCK: Family in America, with European background. Kenneth E. Hasbrouck. 1961. 2 vols., 837p.
P4-S13641 — $115.00.

HASKELL: A short acct. of the desc. of William Haskell of Gloucester, MA (Repr. Essex Inst. Hist. Coll.) By U. G. Haskell. 1896. 62p.
P4-S13650 — $12.50.

HASKELL: Genealogy of Roger Haskell of Salem, MA to November 1925. By Geo. I. Randall. 1926. 99p.
P4-S13665 — $18.00.

HASKELL: The Haskell Family Anthology. Volume I. W.A. Haskell. 2003. 212p
P4-S13660 — $32.00.

HASKELL: The Haskell Family Anthology. Volume II. W.A. Haskell. 2004. 211p.
P4-S13661 — $32.00.

HASKELL: In Search of Ancestors: More Haskell Chronicles. Winthrop A. Haskell & Gertrude O. Haskell. 1990. 260p.
P4-S13662 — $39.00.

HASKELL: Chron. of the Haskell fam. By I. Haskell. 1943. 294p.
P4-S13659 — $44.00.

HASKIN: A brief hist. of Elkanah Haskin & desc. of his son Enoch, 1700-1890. By D. C. Haskin. 1890. 53p.
P4-S13666 — $10.00.

HASKINS: Isaac Haskins family history & genealogy, including that of his son-in-law Henry T. Peck, of Wakeman, OH, with supplement By Charles R. Green. 1911. 16p.
P4-S13667 — $10.00.

HASLER: Families & where they came from, By Helen H. Dempsey. 1946 382p.
P4-S13671 — $57.50.

HASSAM: Family. By J. T. Hassam. 1896. 11p.
P4-S13672 — $10.00.

HASSELBACH: History & gen. of the Hasselbach family, being a record of the John Peter, John Phillip, Regina Elizabeth & Elizabeth Margaret. By John C. Overmyer. 1910. 159p.
P4-S13677 — $26.00.

HASTINGS: Desc. of Finando Hastings (1863-1910). By Rachel Saul Tefft. 1999. 30p.
P4-S13684 — $10.00.

HASTINGS: Family; A chapter in family history. John McIlvene. 1907. 137p.
P4-S13689 — $22.00.

HASTINGS: Memorial. A gen. acct. of the desc. of Thomas Hastings of Watertown, MA, from 1634-1864. By L.N.H. Buckminster. 1866. 183p.
P4-S13692 — $25.50.

HASTINGS: Family record of Dr Seth Hastings, Sr, of Clinton, Oneida Co., NY. By Francis H. Hastings. 1899. 195p.
P4-S13693 — $29.50.

HATCH: Major Timothy Hatch of Hartford & his desc. By E. H. Fletcher. 1879. 36p.
P4-S13699 — $10.00.

HATCH: Gen & Hist. of the Hatch Fam: desc. of Thomas & Grace Hatch of Dorchester, Yarmouth & Barnstable, MA, Two-volume set. comp. By Hatch Gen. Society. 1925. 2 vols., 776p.
P4-S13701 — $78.00./set

HATCH: Philip Hatch of York Co., ME & some of his desc. By H. I. Hiday. 1949. 34p.
P4-S13700 — $10.00.

HATCH: Desc. of William Hatch of Scituate, MA. By P. Derby. 1874. 23p.
P4-S13702 — $10.00.

HATCH: Thomas Hatch of Barnstable & some of his desc. ("Soc. of Col. Wars in NJ"). By C. Pack. 1930. 363p.
P4-S13707 — $57.50.

HATCH: Branches of our family tree, with charts. By Lewis Hatch. 1938. 87 + 19p., charts, typescript.
P4-S13698 — $22.00.

HATFIELD: Descendants of Matthias Hatfield. Abraham Hatfield. 1954. 314p.
P4-S13713 — $48.00.

HATFIELD: Desc. of Joseph & Anna Hatfield of NJ & OH. By S.K. Stephenson. 1897. 12p.
P4-S13714 — $10.00.

HATFIELD: The Hatfields of Westchester: a gen. of the desc. of Thomas Hatfield, of New Amsterdam & Mamaroneck A. Hatfield. 1935. 222p.
P4-S13719 — $34.50.

HATHAWAY: Desc. of Simeon Hathaway, also containing some lin. of Breckenridge, Bingham, Cass, Hinsdill, etc. By E.H. Parks. 1957. 68p.
P4-S13725 — $13.50.

HATTIE: Hattie Family Memoirs: Acct of Fams Desc from Alexander Hattie. R.M. Hattie & J.H. Kirk. 1936. viii + 261p.
P4-S13726 — $40.00.

HAUGHEY: History of the Haughey & allied families, as represented by the descendants & the antecedents of Luke Haughey By Dr Wm. H. Haughey & Dr Wilfrid Haughey. 1917. 69p.
P4-S13731 — $14.00.

HAUPT: The Haupt Family in America. Rev. William Henry Haupt. 1925. 74p.
P4-S13732 — $14.00.

HAVEN: Gen. of desc. of Richard Haven of Lynn, etc. By J. Adams. Rev. ed. 1849. 104p.
P4-S13737 — $19.00.

HAVEN: Sgt. Richard Haven of Lynn & one line of his desc., with some coll. branches. By W. Haven. 1927. 104p.
P4-S13743 — $18.50.

HAVENS: AUSTIN Genealogy: descendants of Lauren Havens (1799-1876) & Charlotte Ranney (1801-55) & Charles G. Austin (1808-91) etc. By Esher D.L. Woodworth. 1956. 46p., typescript.
P4-S13750 — $10.00.

HAVENS: The Havens family in NJ, with additional notes on the Tilton, Fielder, Hance, Osborn, Davison, Cox & Gifford families By Henry C. Havens. 1933. 103 + 30p.
P4-S13749 — $22.50.

HAVERFIELD: A Genealogy & Brief History of the Haverfield Family of the United Sates. Dr. Wallace Taylor. 1919. 316p.
P4-S13752 — $47.50.

HAVILAND: LOUNSBURY — MOULINIER Genealogy & Memoirs. By M.B. Moulinier. n.d. 169p.
P4-S13755 — $25.00.

HAVILAND: Ancestors & descendants of William Haviland of Newport, RI & Flushing, Long Isl., 1658-1688. By Josephine C. Frost. 1914. 551p.
P4-S13761 — $82.50.

HAW: Genealogy of John Haw, 1821-1916. By Percy L. Climo. 1962. 47p.
P4-S13766 — $10.00.

HAWES: Richard Hawes of Dorchester, MA & some of his desc. By F. M. Hawes. 1932. 263p.
P4-S13773 — $39.50.

HAWES: Edmond Hawes of Yarmouth, MA, an emigrant to Amer. in 1635, his anc., & some of his desc. By J. W. Hawes. 1914. 231p.
P4-S13767 — $34.50.

HAWK: Early German Hawk Families of Westmoreland County, PA. Kenneth Hawk Slaker. 1990. 508 + 16p.
P4-S13744 — $79.00.

HAWKES: Gleanings relative to the fam. of Adam Hawkes, one of the early settlers of the third plantation of Mass. Bay, By N. M. Hawkes. 1887. 20p.
P4-S13776 — $10.00.

HAWKINS: Genealogy of the Hawkins family. By George G. Barnes, et al. 1928. 99p.
P4-S13785 — $17.00.

HAWKINS: Ancestral lines of Jennis Cowen (Hawkins) Robinson, through Hawkins, Satterly, Mills, et al. By M. Francis. 1935. 117p.
P4-S13779 — $19.50.

HAWKINS: Memoranda concerning some branches of the Hawkins family & connections. By John P. Hawkins. 1913. 137p.
P4-S13791 — $22.00.

HAWLEY: House of Hawley. 1909. 100 + 6p.
P4-S13792 — $19.00.

HAWLEY: Gen. of the Hawley fam. of Marblehead. By W.D. Hawley. 1st & 2nd ed. 1897. 24p.
P4-S13793 — $10.00.

HAWLEY: Hawley & Nason anc. By E. H. Everett. 1929. 78p.
P4-S13794 — $12.50.

HAWS: Family & their seafaring kin. By Capt. G.W. Haws. 1932 252p.
P4-S13803 — $38.00.

HAXTON: Genealogy. By Bertha W. Clark. 1956. 167p., typescript.
P4-S13809 — $25.00.

HAY: Hist of the progenitors & some SC Desc. of Col. Ann Hawkes Hay, with collateral gen., 500-1908 By C.J. Colcock. Revised edition, 1908, 1959. 288p.
P4-S13815 — $44.00.

HAYDEN: Records of the CT line of the Hayden family. By J.H. Hayden. 1888. 329p.
P4-S13836 — $51.00.

HAYDEN: Hayden Fam. Magazine, Vol. III, incl. hist., biogr., & fam. records. 1931. 202p.
P4-S13833 — $30.00.

HAYDEN: Above, vol IV. 1932. 206p.
P4-S13821 — $31.00.

HAYDEN: Above, Vol V. 1933. 133p.
P4-S13827 — $20.00.

HAYER: HYER Genealogy: "What we know about the Hayer (Hyer) family," Annie Hyer Kemp. 1954. 274p.
P4-S13842 — $43.00.

HAYES: HEES; John Henry Hees (Hase, Haise, Hayes) & his descendants, 1750-1982. By Mrs Mary Wilder Hayes & David W. Hayes. 1982. 422p.
P4-S13875 — $64.00.

HAYES: Family: Origin, History, Genealogy. By R.S. Hayes. 1928. 464p.
P4-S13863 — $69.50.

HAYES: Bicentennial gathering of desc. of Henry Hayes at Unionville, PA, with gen. data. 1906. 89p.
P4-S13848 — $14.00.

HAYES: John Hayes of Dover, NH: A book of his family, Two-volume set By K.F. Richmond 1936. 911p.
P4-S13869 — $129.50./set

HAYES: George Hayes of Windsor & his desc. By C.W. Hayes. 1883. 354p.
P4-S13857 — $45.00.

HAYES: Fam. of Windsor & Granby, CT (Repr. NEHGR). By C. W. Hayes. 1882. 6p.
P4-S13849 — $10.00.

HAYES: Descendants of Richard Hayes of Lyme, CT, through his son, Titus Hayes. By H.M. Weeks, 1904. 192p.
P4-S13854 — $30.00.

HAYFORD: Hist. of the Hayford fam., 1100-1900, its connections by the Bonney, Fuller & Phinney fam. By O. Hayford. 1901. 253p.
P4-S13878 — $33.00.

HAYNER: History of the Hayner family, the descendants of Johannes Haner, 1710-1966. By Jennie A. Hayner, M.B. Hayner & F.W. Hayner. 1966. 166p.
P4-S13884 — $25.00.

HAYNES: Anc. & desc. of John Russell Haynes (incl. Haines, Cotton, Bradstreet, Dudley, Hubbard, & Brainerd fam.) G. W. Burch. 1924. 151p.
P4-S13890 — $28.50.

HAYNES: Walter Haynes of Sutton Mandeville, Wiltshire, Eng., & Sudbury, MA & his desc., 1583-1928. By F. Haynes. 1929. 235p.
P4-S13896 — $35.00.

HAYNIE: Fam. of Northumberland Co., VA. By G. Torrence. 1949. 41p.
P4-S13897 — $10.00.

HAYNSWORTH: FURMAN & allied families (including ancestry & descendants of Sarah Morse Haynsworth). Hugh C. Haynsworth. 1942. 333p.
P4-S13902 — $51.00.

HAYS: Records & Roberts & allied families. By M.C. Hays. 1952. 128p., typescript.
P4-S13908 — $25.00.

HAYWARD: Centennial Gathering of the Hayward Family, with Address by George W. Hayward. 1879. 39p.
P4-S13909 — $10.00.

HAYWARD: James Hayward, b. Apr. 4, 1750, killed in the Battle of Lexington, Apr. 19, 1775, with gen. notes rel. to the Haywards. By W.F. Adams. 1911. 58p.
P4-S13910 — $11.00.

HAZARD: HASSARD Some account of the family of Hassard, By Henry B. Swanzy. 1903. 113p.
P4-S13914 — $19.00.

HAZARD: Outlines of the history & genealogy of the Hassards & their connections. Henry Hassard. 1858 74p.
P4-S13926 — $15.00.

HAZARD: Fam. of RI, 1635-1894. Being a gen. & hist. of the desc. of Thomas Hazard. By C.E. Robinson. 1895. 298p.
P4-S13920 — $39.50.

HAZELTON: Genealogical sketches of Robt. & John Hazelton & some descendants. W. Lapham. 1892. 368p.
P4-S13929 — $46.00.

HAZEN: Family in America; a genealogy. By T.E. Hazen. 1947. 1175p.
P4-S13941 — $149.00.

HAZEN: Genealogy of Sam'l & Elizabeth (Dewitt) Hazen & their descendants. Cora H. Oliver. 1937. 142p.
P4-S13935 — $22.00.

HEAD: Descent of Henry Head (1695-1770) in America. Idress Head Alvord. 1949. 681p.
P4-S13948 — $98.00.

HEAD: Family. By John H. Watts. 1963. 467p.
P4-S13947 — $72.00.

HEADLEY: Genealogical record of the descendants of Leonard Headley of Elizabethtown, NJ. By Rev. A.J. Fretz. 1905. 223p.
P4-S13953 — $34.00.

HEALY: History, revised. By Mrs Carl V. Carrier. 1968. 112p.
P4-S13959 — $16.00.

HEARD: History of the Heard family of Wayland, MA. By John H. Edwards. 1880. 61p.
P4-S13962 — $12.00.

HEARD: A Heard Family Record-Based History: The First Five Generations in America. J. Perkerson Poole. 2005. v + 1037p.
P4-S13960 — $150.00.

HEARNE: Brief history & genealogy of the Hearne family, 1066-1907. By W. T. Hearne. 1907. 755p.
P4-S13968 — $94.50.

HEATH: Gen. record of one branch of Heath, Clark & Cone fam. By D. Stilwell. 1905. 42p.
P4-S13970 — $10.00.

HEATH: Gravestone records, Mt. Abram Cem., Salem, ME. By H.C. & G.W. Whitmore. 1955. 3p.
P4-S13971 — $10.00.

HEATWOLE: History of the Heatwole family, from the beginning of the 17th century to the present time (1907). By Cornelius J. Heatwole. 1907. 274p.
P4-S13980 — $42.50.

HECKAMAN: HECKEMAN Family (1729-1990), include the Johann Adam Swank (1800-1990) families [with related fams.]. F.J. Deisch. 1990. 945p.
P4-S13986 — $134.50.

HEIGHAM: Pedigree of the Heigham family. By Chas. W. Heigham. 1876 110p.
P4-S13992 — $17.00.

HEINECKE: The genealogy of Adam Heinecke & Henry Vandersaal, from 1747-1881. By S. Heinecke. 1881. 81p.
P4-S14004 — $16.00.

HEINECKE: Gen of Adam Heinecke & Henry Vandersaal, 1747-1881, with a brief acct. of the author's travels. By Rev. Samuel Heinecke. 1881. 2nd ed., 302p.
P4-S13998 — $45.00.

HEINER: History of the Heiner family. By D.B. Heiner. 1929. 130p.
P4-S14010 — $19.50.

HEINTZ: Johannes Heintz (John Hines) & his descendants [emigr. from Prussia to PA in 1751]. By John C. Proctor. 1918. 111p.
P4-S14016 — $17.50.

HEINY: Family Record. By Thyrza Heiny. 1910. 156p.
P4-S14022 — $25.00.

HELMER: Family; Philip Helmer, the Pioneer, & his desc. By P.W. Williams. 1931-1932. 183p.
P4-S14028 — $27.50.

HELTERLINE: The Ancestry of Emily Gustin Helterline and Leo L. Helterline, Sr. Emily Gustin Helterline. 1969. 99p.
P4-S14029 — $16.00.

HELWIG: This is My Line. By Bette Jean K. Helwig. 1979. 214p.
P4-S14034 — $31.00.

HELWIG: This is My Line — Book II. Bette Jeanne Kilpatrick Helwig. 1992. vi + 88p.
P4-S14035 — $17.00.

HEMENWAY: Gen. record of one branch of the Hemenway fam. 1634-1880. By A. Hemenway. 1880. 92p.
P4-S14040 — $18.00.

HEMENWAY: The MA Hemenway fam., desc. of Ralph Hemenway of Roxbury 1634. By M. & C. Newton. 1912. 56p.
P4-S14041 — $11.00.

HEMENWAY: Ralph Hemenway of Roxbury, MA, 1634, & his descendants, Vol. I. By Clair A. Hemenway Newton. 1932. 163p.
P4-S14046 — $25.00.

HEMENWAY: Ralph Hemenway of Roxbury, MA, 1634, & his desc., with Dietz gen., Volume II By Clair A. Hemenway Newton. 1943. 152p.
P4-S14052 — $28.50.

HEMPLEMAN: History of the Hempleman Family in America, By Geo. Whiteley. 1912. 97p.
P4-S14058 — $18.00.

HEMPSTEAD: Diary of Joshua Hempstead, 1711-1758, with an acct of a journey made from New London to MD. 1901. 750p.
P4-S14064 — $112.50.

HENCH: Records of the annual Hench & Dromgold reunions, held in Perry Co., PA, 1897-1912. By L.D. Emig. 1913. 191p.
P4-S14070 — $28.50.

HENCKEL: The Henckel Family Records: Nos. 1-14. The Henckel Family Association 1926-1939 690 + 80p.
P4-S14071 — $95.00.

HENDERSHOT: Genealogy of the Hendershot Family in America. By A.E. Hendershot. 1961. 213p.
P4-S14076 — $33.00.

HENDERSON: Family Records. By J.M. Seaver. 32p.
P4-S14083 — $10.00.

HENDERSON: Chronicles, desc. of Alexander Henderson of Scotland. By J. N. McCue. 1915. 113p.
P4-S14094 — $22.50.

HENDERSON: Descendants of Robert Henderson of Hendersonville, PA (Mercer Co.), b. 1741 — d. 1810. By Oren V. Henderson. 1947. 329p.
P4-S14082 — $51.00.

HENDERSON: Anc. & desc. of Lt. John Henderson of Greenbriar Co., VA, 1650-1900. By J. L. Miller. 1902. 37p.
P4-S14089 — $10.00.

HENDERSON: Family record of the Henderson & Whiddon families [of GA] & their descendants By Wm. Henderson. 1926. 314p.
P4-S14088 — $47.00.

HENDRICK: History & Genealogy of Hendrick, McClain, Breen, Rutherford, Shuler, McAlester, Holcomb, etc. Jerry & Wincie Hendricks. 2004. 710p.
P4-S14101 — $99.50.

HENDRICK: Genealogy: Daniel Hendrick of Haverhill, MA, & his descendants By Chas. T. Hendrick. 1923. 699p.
P4-S14100 — $99.50.

HENDRICKSON: Notes on the Messenger & Hendrickson fam. & desc. By M. P. Ferris. 1916. 79p.
P4-S14106 — $16.00.

HENDRIX: Before You Were Born, The Story of Your Family 495-1985. Lonnie C. Hendrix. 1997, 2004. 282p.
P4-S14107 — $42.50.

HENKEL: Memorial; 1st series, #4, & 2nd series, #1-3. A. Stapleton. 155p.
P4-S14112 — $28.00.

HENRY: Rec. of desc. of Simon Henry (1766-1854) & Rhoda Parsons (1774-1847), his wife . . . By F.A. Henry. 1905. 65p.
P4-S14160 — $13.00.

HENRY: Descendants of Samuel Henry of Hadley & Amherst, MA, 1734-1790, & Lurana Cady, his wife. By W.H. Eldridge. 1915. 240p.
P4-S14124 — $36.00.

HENRY: The History of the Henry Family of "Flower Hill" Ireland & their Descendants. M. B. Henry & M. H. Miller. 1926. 206 + 40p.
P4-S14119 — $37.00.

HENRY: Memorial of Mrs. Adelaide L. Wright, with a hist. of the Henry & Hooker fam. 1718-1918. R. P. Wright. 17p.
P4-S14120 — $10.00.

HENRY: Genealogy of the Henry fam. By D.F. Henry. 1919. 67p.
P4-S14136 — $13.00.

HENRY: Hist. of the Henry fam (KY). By J. Henry. 1900. 125p.
P4-S14148 — $20.00.

HENRY: History of the Henry Family from its Beginnings in this Country to the Present. By John F. Henry. 1946. 140p.
P4-S14154 — $27.50.

HENRY: Genealogy of the Descendants of John Henry of Bern Twp., Ahtens Co., OH. By Heber H. Henry. 1922. 100p.
P4-S14130 — $18.00.

HENRY: Family Records. By J. Montgomery Seaver. 32p.
P4-S14155 — $10.00.

HENRY: Family history: descendants of James Henry Sr of CT. By Alan D. Henry. 1993. 193p.
P4-S14142 — $29.50.

HENRY: Descendants of Philip Henry, rev. ed. By James E. Jones. 1844, 1925 68p.
P4-S14118 — $14.00.

HENSHIE: History & genealogy of the Henshie Family in America & their Descendants. By Lura M. Henshie. 1928. 48p.
P4-S14161 — $10.00.

HENSON: The Henson Family & Related Lines. Dr. Robert & Connie Medford. 2004 1014p.
P4-S14162 — $152.00.

HEPBURN: Gen. & hist. of the Hepburn fam. of the Susquehanna Valley, with ref. To other fam. of the same name. J. P. Meginness. 1894. 185p.
P4-S14166 — $28.00.

HERKIMER: The Herkimers & Schuylers, an hist. sketch of the two fam., with gen. of the desc. of George Herkimer By P. S. Cowen. 1903. 147p.
P4-S14172 — $22.00.

HERR: Gen Record of Rev. Hans Herr & his direct lineal desc., from his birth A.D. 1639 to the present. By T.W. Herr. 1908, 785p.
P4-S14178 — $115.00.

HERRICK: A Gen. Register of the Name & Fam. of Herrick, from the Settlement of Henerie Hericke in Salem, MA, 1629-1846. By J. Herrick. 1846. 60p.
P4-S14181 — $12.00.

HERRICK: Genealogy: One Line of Desc. from James Herrick, who Settled at Southampton, L.I., about 1653; By H.C. Brown. 1950. 95p.
P4-S14190 — $18.50.

HERRICK: A Gen. Register of the Name & Family of Herrick, from the Settlement of Henerie Hericke in Salem, MA, 1629-1846, revised By L.C. Herrick. 1885. 527p.
P4-S14193 — $65.50.

HERRING: HERING — HARING Family of PA; Part F: Descendants of Conrad Horing, Immigrant, 1767. Calvin Adam Herring. 1966. 116p.
P4-S14200 — $17.50.

HERRING: Lineage & Tradition of the Harring, Conyers, Hendrick, Boddie, Perry, Crudup, Denson & Hilliard families. By R.H. Hendrick. 1916. 172p.
P4-S14199 — $27.00.

HERRON: Herron fam. of NY & OH. By G. Keeler. 7p.
P4-S14202 — $10.00.

HERSHBERGER: Descendants of Peter Hershberger & Elizabeth Yoder, 1810-1950. By Eli P. Hershberger. 1950. 141p.
P4-S14205 — $22.50.

HERSHEY: History & Records of the Hershey Family from the Year 1600. By Scott F. Hershey. 1913. 108p.
P4-S14217 — $18.00.

HERSHEY: Hershey Family Tree of Pennsylvania. Floyd R. & Kathryn G Mason 2002 374p.
P4-S14212 — $56.00.

HERSHEY: Family History. By Henry Hershey. 1929. 291p.
P4-S14211 — $45.00.

HERTZLER: Harzler Family History. By Silas Hertzler. 1952. 773p.
P4-S14229 — $99.50.

HERTZLER: Brief Bio Memorial of Jacob Hertzler, & a Complete Genealogical Family Register, 1730-1883. By J. Hertzler, Sr. 1885. 384p.
P4-S14223 — $59.50.

HERVEY: A Tree of Four Ancient Stocks: Fourfold Family History [Hervey, Huey, McCombs, McCuskey]. By W.H. McCuskey. 1916. 84p.
P4-S14235 — $15.50.

HESS: HIGBEE Genealogy [of NY & PA]. Wm. Emerson Babcock. 1909. 175p.
P4-S14259 — $26.00.

HESS: History of Balser Hess, 1747-1806 & His Descendants. Frank E. Hess. 1950. 144 + 30p.
P4-S14242 — $26.50.

HESS: Record of the Hess fam. from the First Immigrant. By J. H. Hess. 1880. 73p.
P4-S14241 — $15.00.

HESS: Genealogy of the Hess Family from the First Emigrant to this Country, Down to the Present Time. By John H. Hess. 1896. 258p.
P4-S14253 — $39.50.

HESS: Genealogy. 1964? 52p.
P4-S14243 — $11.00.

HESS: Gen Record of the Descendants of Nicholas Hess, Pioneer Immigrant, 50th Anniv. Ed. 1962. 310p.
P4-S14247 — $46.50.

HESSER: History of the Hesser Family, 1708-1945. By George E. Hesser. 1947. 249p.
P4-S14265 — $38.00.

HESTER: Hist & Gen of the Desc of John Lawrence Hester & Godfrey Stough, 1752-1905 (with add to 1908). By M.M. Hester. 1905-1908 323 + 43p.
P4-S14271 — $58.00.

HETRICK: Family, 1651-1055, Hist & Bio sketch of the Hedderich, Heddrick, Hedrick, Hetrick family. By Martha L. Hetrick. 1955. 165p.
P4-S14277 — $27.00.

HEVERLY: History of the Heverly Fam., incl. Other Spellings. By H. F. Mears. 1945. 340p.
P4-S14283 — $41.00.

HEWES: Lt. Joshua Hewes, a New Eng. Pioneer, & Some of his Desc. By E. Putnam. 1913. 673p.
P4-S14289 — $99.00.

HEWINS: Gen. (from "Gen. Reg. of Several Ancient Puritans"). By A. Morse. 1859. 12p.
P4-S14290 — $10.00.

HEWITT: Descendants of Capt. Thomas Hewitt of Stonington, CT [with additions & corrections]. By Virginia H. Watterson. 1996, 2000. 485 + 20p.
P4-S14295 — $89.50.

HEWSON: House of Hewetson or Hewson of Ireland. By John Hewetson. 1891 216p.
P4-S14301 — $32.00.

HEYDECKER: Genealogy of the Heydecker Family. By Christian T. Heydecker. 1925. 66p.
P4-S14307 — $13.00.

HEYDON: Heydons in Eng. & Amer., a Fragment of Fam. Hist. By W. B. Hayden. 1877. 46p.
P4-S14308 — $10.00.

HIATT: HIETT Genealogy & Family History, 1699-1949, John Hiett, Quaker — England to PA, c.1699 By Wm. P.Johnson. 1951. 1014p.
P4-S14313 — $135.00.

HIBBARD: Genealogy of the Hibbard Family; Desc. of Robert Hibbard of Salem, MA. By A.G. Hibbard. 1901. 428p.
P4-S14322 — $55.00.

HIBBARD: Supplements to the 1901 "Genealogy of the Hibbard Family." By Frederick A. Hibbard & Robert E. Patterson. 1991. 209p.
P4-S14328 — $31.00.

HIBBS: Hibbs Family. By M. & L. Sheppard. 1963. 7p.
P4-S14329 — $10.00.

HICKERNELL: Hickernell. Robert L. Laucks. 2004. 250p.
P4-S14335 — $37.50.

HICKERNELL: Sketches [descendants of David Hickernell of PA]. By Mabel G. Granquist. 1945. 53p., typescript.
P4-S14336 — $11.00.

HICKERNELL: The Hickernells of Lancaster & Lebanon Cos. [PA]. By Robt. L. Laucks. 2001. 72p.
P4-S14334 — $15.00.

HICKMAN: Genealogy of the Hickman Family, Beginning with Roger Hickman of Kent Co., DE. By Sylverster Hickman. 1907. 148p.
P4-S14340 — $22.00.

HICKOCK: The Hickock Family; excerpt from "The Families of Old Fairfield." 6p.
P4-S14341 — $10.00.

HICKOK: Gen: Descendants of William Hickoks of Farmington CT, with ancestry of Charles Nelson Hickok. By C.N. Hickok. 1938. 469p.
P4-S14343 — $72.00.

HICKOK: The Hickok Family in Burlington, VT. n.d. 4p.
P4-S14342 — $10.00.

HICKS: A Family Memorial; Hicks & Allied. By Ella Hicks Johnson. 1894. 56p.
P4-S14344 — $11.00.

HIESTER: Gen. of Hiester fam. By V. E. C. Hill. 1903. 64p.
P4-S14346 — $12.50.

HIGBY: Edward Higby & his Descendants. By C. D. Higby. 1927. 467p.
P4-S14355 — $69.75

HIGDAY: Family Trails Across America: Higday, Ridgeway, Gannaway, Benefield & allied lines. By Hamilton Higday. 1933. 87p.
P4-S14361 — $16.50.

HIGGINS: & Allied Families, Showing the Descent of Francis Eben Buckley. ANON. 1955? 247p., typescript.
P4-S14367 — $37.00.

HIGGINS: Richard Higgins, a Resident & Pioneer Settler at Plymouth & Eastham, MA & at Piscataway, NJ & his desc. By Katherine C. Higgins. 1918. 799p.
P4-S14376 — $99.00.

HIGGINS: Supplement to: "Richard Higgins, a Resident & Pioneer Settler at Plymouth & Eastham, MA" (1918) 1924. 216p.
P4-S14382 — $32.00.

HIGGINS: Jesse Higgins & David Higgins, Colonial Residents at Eastham, MA & Pioneer Settlers at West Eden, ME. comp. by Harvard DeLorraine Higgins. 1990. 200p.
P4-S14373 — $29.50.

HIGGINSON: SKELTON Migration to Salem in 1629. F.A. Gardner. 1915. 19p.
P4-S14383 — $10.00.

HIGGINSON: Descendants of the Rev. Francis Higginson. By T.W. Higginson. 1910. 84p.
P4-S14385 — $12.50.

HIGGINSON: The Higginsons in England & America, Pt. 1. By Eben Putnam. 1903. 38p.
P4-S14384 — $10.00.

HIGHLAND: The Highland, Patton, Maxwell, Earle, Morris Genealogies. By Scotland G. Highland. 1926. 78p.
P4-S14394 — $15.50.

HIGHLEY: A Short History of the Highley Family. Geo. N. Highley, MD. 1898. 31p.
P4-S14396 — $10.00.

HIGLEY: The Higleys & their Anc. By M. C. Johnson. 1896. 748p.
P4-S14397 — $93.00.

HILDEBRAND: Family Data. By A. B. Sartori. 37p.
P4-S14400 — $12.00.

HILDRETH: Genealogy & Biogr. Sketches of the Hildreth Fam., 1652-1840. By S. P. Hildreth. 1840. 339p.
P4-S14415 — $54.00.

HILDRETH: Early Hildreths of New England. By Arthur Hildreth. 1894. 60p.
P4-S14406 — $12.00.

HILDRETH: Origin & Gen. of the Hildreth Fam. of Lowell, MA. By P. Reade. 1892. 71p.
P4-S14421 — $14.00.

HILDRETH: Hildreth Family Assn: Gen. & Hist. Data Relating to Richard Hildreth, Cambridge & Chelmsford, MA & Thomas Hildreth of Long Island, NY. Alice Hildreth Prichard. 1925. 120p.
P4-S14416 — $20.00.

HILGENDORF: Family, Past & Present. Jane B. Burns. 2000. 35 + 21p.
P4-S14422 — $10.00.

HILGENDORF: Family of Germany & Chicago. By Bob Treat. 1993. 32p.
P4-S14423 — $10.00.

HILL: Family genealogy of Killingly, CT from Hill Diaries & Patient Records. By Edwin Allen Hill, MD. 1996. 54 + 420p.
P4-S14459 — $71.00.

HILL: Luke Hill of Windsor, CT & John Hill of Guilford, CT & their Desc. By R.D. Smyth. 1903. 8p.
P4-S14460 — $10.00.

HILL: John Hill of Dover in 1649, & some of his desc. By W. B. Lapham. 1889. 16p.
P4-S14461 — $10.00.

HILL: Diary of Dr Hill [of Killingly, CT]. Edwin Allen Hill, MD. 1996. 332p.
P4-S14427 — $32.50.

HILL: John Hill of Dorchester, MA, 1663, & 5 gen. of his desc. Also an acct. of the Hill fam. of Poundsford, Eng. By J.G. Bartlett. 1904. 103p.
P4-S14469 — $15.00.

HILL: Family Gen, extending a line of John Hill of Dorchester, MA, 1633-1993, including allied families. By Lauralee (Hill) Clayton & Mary Jean (Stark) Farnham. 1993. 395p.
P4-S14457 — $59.50.

HILL: Records of the John & Luke Hill fam. of New Eng. (extr. from the Bassett gen.) 1926. 10p.
P4-S14462 — $10.00.

HILL: Semi-centennial & History of the Hill. Rodger & Brodie Families. 1888. 81p.
P4-S14475 — $16.00.

HILL: Family History. By Dr Daniel B.H. Richards. 1927. 278p.
P4-S14463 — $42.00.

HILL: Gen. of the Hill Fam. from 1632, incl. a Biogr. Sketch of Joel Barlow, By M. Hill. 1879. 29p.
P4-S14458 — $10.00.

HILL: Ebenezer Hill, the Little Minister of Mason, NH: a Sketch & a Genealogy. C.E. & J.B. HIll. 1923. 82p.
P4-S14433 — $16.50.

HILL: Biographical Sketch & Genealogical Record of the Desc of Melanchthon Hill of CT, 1610-1895. By Francis C. Hill. 1895. 43p.
P4-S14464 — $10.00.

HILL: Gen. of the Hill, Dean, Pinckney, Austin, Barker, Anderson, Rhoades & Finch fams. By F. Couch. 1907. 124p.
P4-S14439 — $22.00.

HILL: Descendants of William Hill, of Fairfield, CT Who Came from Exeter, England, 1632 in Ship Williiam & Frances. Eva Loesa Hill Hosley. 1909. 55 + 16p.
P4-S14465 — $12.00.

HILL: Descendants of William Hill & His Wife Alethea Carmer. A.J. Bleecker. 1927. 113p.
P4-S14466 — $17.00.

HILLEGAS: Michael Hillegas & his Descendants. By Emma S. Whitney. 1891. 118p.
P4-S14481 — $19.00.

HILLES: HILLS Family in Ireland & Eng. (in Welch Gen.) By G. C. Weaver. 1932. 25p.
P4-S14488 — $10.00.

HILLES: Memorial of the Hilles Family, More Particularly of Samuel & Margaret Hill Hilles of Wilmington, DE. By Samuel E. Hilles. 1928. 239p.
P4-S14487 — $37.00.

HILLHOUSE: History & Genealogy coll. rel. to the desc. of Rev. James Hillhouse. M.P. Hillhouse. 1924. 694p.
P4-S14493 — $99.00.

HILLMAN: Anc. Chronological Record of the Hillman Fam., 1550-1905. By H.W. Hillman. 1905. 203p.
P4-S14499 — $27.00.

HILLS: Gen. data, anc. & desc. of William Hills, Eng. emigrant to New Eng. In 1632, & of Joseph Hills in 1638. By W. & T. Hills. 1902. 148p.
P4-S14505 — $24.00.

HILLS: Family in Amer.; the anc. & desc. of William Hills, 1632, Joseph Hills, 1638, & the great-grandsons of Robert Hills, 1794-1806 By W.S. Hills, ed. By T. Hills. 1906. 734 + 36p.
P4-S14508 — $93.00.

HILTON: Family Genealogy. By J. T. Hassam. 1896. 24p.
P4-S14509 — $10.00.

HINDS: History & Genealogy of the Hinds Family. By A. Hinds. 1899. 394p.
P4-S14514 — $61.00.

HINE: Genealogy & History of the Descendants of Thomas Hine, Milford, CT, 1640. By Robt. C. Hine. 1898. 239p.
P4-S14520 — $37.00.

HINMAN: Hist. of the Hinmans, with record of kindred fam. By A. V. Hinman. 1907. 75p.
P4-S14532 — $15.00.

HINMAN: Fam. rec. of the desc. of Sgt. Edw. Hinman of Stratford, CT, 1650. By R. Hinman 1856. 80p.
P4-S14526 — $16.00.

HINSDALE: Family Chronicle. By A. Hinsdale. 1883. 31p.
P4-S14536 — $10.00.

HINSDALE: Desc. of Robt. Hinsdale of Dedham, Medfield, Hadley & Deerfield, MA with acct. of the French fam. of De Hinnidal. By H. Andrews. 1906. 508p.
P4-S14535 — $64.00.

HINSHAW: HENSHAW Family. By W. Hinshaw & M. Custer. 1911. 66p.
P4-S14541 — $13.00.

HINSHAW: Thomas Hinshaw & Others. By J. E. Hinshaw. 1911. 49p.
P4-14542 — $10.00.

HITCHCOCK: The gen. of the Hitchcock fam., desc. from Matthias Hitchcock of East Haven, CT & Luke Hitchcock of Wethersfield, CT. By E. Hitchcock Sr., ed by D. Marsh. 1894. 563p.
P4-S14550 — $73.50.

HITCHCOCK: Gen of One Direct Line of the Hitchcock Family; Desc from Luke Hitchcock of Wethersfield, CT. Dr. Clarence H. Hitchcock. 1958. x + 151p.
P4-S14551 — $25.00.

HITCHCOCK: Gen. of Tidal Hitchcock & his Desc, with addition of genealogy of John Drennen Hitchcock. By Francis E. Hitchcock, addition By John H. Hitchcock. 1922, 1983. 22 + 40p.
P4-S14544 — $12.50.

HIXSON: HIXON of TN. J.E. Hixson & Z. Armstrong. 1955. ii + 94p.
P4-S14555 — $15.00.

For hardcover versions, see the order form on page v. To order, call 1-888-296-3447.

HOADLEY: History of the desc. of Wm. Hoadley of Branford, CT, together with some acct. of other fam. of the name. F.B. Trowbridge. 1894. 295p.
P4-S14556 — $44.00.

HOAG: Hoag gen., incl. desc. of Sara H. Sterns from John Hoag 1643-1728. 18p.
P4-S14560 — $10.00.

HOAGLAND: History & genealogy of the Hoagland family in Amer., 1638-1891. D.H. Carpenter. 1891. 276p.
P4-S14562 — $42.00.

HOAR: HOARD — HORR: Record of Descendants of Hezekiah Hoar, Taunton, MA. Norton T. Horr. 1907. 49p.
P4-S14563 — $10.00.

HOAR: Fam. in Amer. & its Eng. Anc; a compilation from collections made by George Frisbie Hoar, (Repr. NEHGR) By H. S. Nourse. 1899. 37p.
P4-S14564 — $10.00.

HOAR: Lineage & Family Records of Alfred Wyman Hoar & his Wife Josephne Jackson. 1898. 56p.
P4-S14565 — $11.00.

HOBART: Family in America: Twelve Generations. By D.M. Titus. 1943. 78p.
P4-S14568 — $16.00.

HOBART: Family of Hingham, MA. By E. Thayer. 1835. 9p.
P4-S14569 — $10.00.

HOBART: Descendants of Edmund Hobart of Norfolk, Eng., & Hingham, MA. 32p.
P4-S14570 — $10.00.

HOBART: Hist & Gen, 1632-1912, from Edmund Hobart, who . . . settled in Bear Cove (Hingham), MA in 1632. By Edwin D. Hobart. 1912. 105p.
P4-S14574 — $18.00.

HOBART: William Hobart, his Ancestors & Descendants. By L. Hobart. 1886. 193p.
P4-S14580 — $29.50.

HOBBS: Gen. of the Hobbs Family of MA. By G. Hobbs. 1855. 16p.
P4-S14582 — $10.00.

HOBGOOD: Desc. of Thomas Hobgood. Sidney Carey Arnold, Jr. 2001. 111p.
P4-S14581 — $16.00.

HOBLER: Preliminary collection of data & histories on the surname of Hobler (also Hoebler, Hobeler, Hoblar). By Herbert W. Hobler. 1954. 81p. typescript.
P4-S14586 — $16.00.

HOBSON: Fam. of Buxton, ME. By J. Bailey. 1875. 15p.
P4-S14593 — $10.00.

HOBSON: Descendants of Geo. & Elizabeth Hobson, VA, NC, OH & IN. Earl H. Davis. 1957. 322p., typescript.
P4-S14592 — $49.00.

HOCHSTEDLER: Descendants of Barbara Hochstedler & Christian Stutzman. By Rev. Harvey Hostetler. 1938. 1391p.
P4-S14598 — $155.00.

HOCHSTETLER: Descendants of Jacob Hochstetler, immigr. of 1736. By H. Hochstetler. 1912. 1191p.
P4-S14604 — $159.00.

HODGE: Genealogy from the first of the name in US, with a number of allied families. O.J. Hodge. 1900. 455p.
P4-S14610 — $70.00.

HODGES: Genealogical records of the Hodges fam. of New Eng., to Dec. 31, 1894. A.D. Hodges, Jr 1896. 566p.
P4-S14619 — $78.50.

HODGES: Gen. record of the Hodges fam. in New Eng., 1633-1853. By A. D. Hodges. 1853. 71p.
P4-S14616 — $13.50.

HODGKINS: Gen. of the Hodgkins fam. of ME. E. B. Hodgkins. 1927. 98p.
P4-S14625 — $19.50.

HODGMAN: Partial genealogy of the Hodgman family. By Fred C. Hodgman. 1916. 304p., typescript.
P4-S14631 — $46.00.

HODSDON: Gen. of desc. of Nicholas Hodsdon (Hodgdon) 1635-1904. By A. L. White. 1904. 164p.
P4-S14643 — $28.00.

HODSDON: "The Restless Ones:" a family history [of the Hodsdon family of MN]. Beatrice Morosco. 1963. 299p.
P4-S14637 — $45.00.

HOFF: Genealogy of Kevin Glade Hoff, descendant of Thomas Rowell who helped to found Salisbury, MA. By Kevin G. Hoff. 1996. 28p.
P4-S14644 — $10.00.

HOFFMAN: The Hoffmans of NC: gen. presentaion of the original Hoffmans who settled in NC. By Max E. Hoffman. 1938. 191p.
P4-S14667 — $28.00.

HOFFMAN: Some notes on the history of the Hoffman & Schermerhorn family in Canada. By Emma H. Bogart. 1922. 64p.
P4-S14661 — $13.00.

HOFFMAN: Our kin, being a history of the Hoffman, Rhyne, Costner, Rudisill, Best [& other families]. By Laban M. Hoffman. 1915. 589p.
P4-S14655 — $89.00.

HOFFMAN: Genealogy of the Hoffman fam.; desc. of Martin Hoffman, with biographical notes. comp. By E.A. Hoffman. 1899. 545p.
P4-S14649 — $70.00.

HOFFMAN: Eleven generations of Hoffmans in NY, descendants of Martin Hoffman, 657-1957, By Wm. W. Hoffman. 1957. 47p.
P4-S14656 — $10.00.

HOGE: Family of Hoge: a genealogy. By James H. Tyler. 1927. 141p.
P4-S14673 — $22.00.

HOISINGTON: American Hoisington family. By Harry Hoisington. 1934. 211p., typscript.
P4-S14679 — $32.00.

HOISINGTON: Family. By Harry Hoisington. 1930. 25p., typescript.
P4-S14680 — $10.00.

HOLBROOK: Family, 1560-1800. By Geo. O. Caleff & Marion P. Carter. 1935. 42p., typescript.
P4-S14686 — $10.00.

HOLBROOK: & Allied families. By A. Roberts Lord. 1942. 177p.
P4-S14685 — $28.00.

HOLBROOK: Family of Derby, CT. By Mary L. Holbrook. 1932. 97p.
P4-S14691 — $17.00.

HOLBROW: Some account of the family of Holbrow, anciently of Kingscote, Uley & Leonard STanley in Gloucestershire. By W.P.W. Phillimore. 1901. 45p.
P4-S14692 — $10.00.

HOLCOMB: Memories of Walter Holcomb of Torrington, CT with a few departures in genealogy, public records, etc. By W. Holcomb. 1935. 47p.
P4-S14698 — $10.00.

HOLCOMB: The Holcombs, some acct. of their origin, settlement & scatterment, etc., incl. 1st & 2nd Holcomb reunions, 1879 & 1886. 1887. 33p.
P4-S14699 — $10.00.

HOLCOMB(E): A gen., hist. & directory of the Holcomb(e)s of the world, incl. the ancient & modern Eng. branch, the Amer. branchs & others. J. Seaver. 1925. 283p. typescript.
P4-S14697 — $42.00.

HOLCOMBE: Our Banyan tree, The Holcombe Family. By Beulah W. Russon. 1961? xx + 571p.
P4-S14701 — $89.00.

HOLCOMBE: The Holcombes: Nation builders. By E.W. McPherson. 1947. 1346p.
P4-S14703 — $142.50.

HOLCROFT: Notes on the Family of Holcroft, with an Account of their Arms. J. Paul Rylands. 1877. 55p.
P4-S14704 — $10.00.

HOLDEMAN: Descendants: a compilation of genealogical & biogr. record of the descendants of Christian Holdeman, 1788-1846. By Edwin L. Weavern. 1937. 574p.
P4-S14709 — $87.00.

HOLDEN: Genealogy; ancestors & desc. of Richard & Justinian Holden, & of Randall Holden, 2-vol. set By E. Putnam. 1923-1926 2 vols., 985p
P4-S14715 — $137.00.

HOLDER: The Holders of Holderness. A hist. & gen. of the Holder fam. C. F. Holder. 1902. 358p.
P4-S14721 — $57.00.

HOLE: History of the Hole family in England & America. By Chas. Elmer Rice. 1904. 134p.
P4-S14727 — $21.00.

HOLL: SCHRANTS; History of the Holl-Schrants family, 1730-1891, or the descendants of Ephraim holl. By Henry C. Holl. 1891. 112p.
P4-S14733 — $19.00.

HOLLAND: JACKSON Record, with related Hoyle — Swofford history. By Pearl D. McCall. 1959. 334p.
P4-S14739 — $51.00.

HOLLAND: The Lancashire [England] Hollands. By Bernard Holland. 1917 16 + 357p.
P4-S14751 — $57.00.

HOLLAND: The Hollands of Paulding Co. (GA), 1800-1966. By J.H. Stucki & D.H. Herring. 1966. 65p., typescript.
P4-S14745 — $13.00.

HOLLES: Memorials of the Holles family, 1493-1656. By Gervase Holles. 1937 287p.
P4-S14763 — $45.00.

HOLLINGSWORTH: Desc. of Valentine Hollingsworth, Sr. By J.A. Stewart. 1925. 214p.
P4-S14769 — $32.00.

HOLLINGSWORTH: Family & collateral lines of Cooch-Gilpin-Jamar-Mackall-Morris-Stewart: early history & Cecil Co., MD. By Mary H. Jamar. 1944. 76p.
P4-S14775 — $15.00.

HOLLINGSWORTH: Hollingsworth gen. memoranda in the US, from 1682-1884. By W.B. Hollingsworth. 1884. 144p.
P4-S14781 — $21.50.

HOLLISTER: Family. By S. V. Talcott. 1916. 20p.
P4-S14797 — $10.00.

HOLLISTER: Anc. & desc. of Ashbel Hollister, By H. Hollister. 1885. 10p.
P4-S14798 — $10.00.

HOLLISTER: Family of Amer.; Lt. John Hollister of Wethersfield, CT & his desc. By L.W. Case. 1886. 805p.
P4-S14796 — $101.50.

HOLLON: Gen. of Hollon & rel. fam., early settlers of E. KY & their desc. By C. Hollon. 1958. 108p.
P4-S14802 — $18.00.

HOLLOWAY: AMISS — LEAVELL Family. ed. By L.C. Morrell. 1952. 62p.
P4-S14820 — $13.00.

HOLLOWAY: Genealogy of the Holloway families. By Olin E. Holloway. 1927. 462p.
P4-S14814 — $69.50.

HOLLOWAY: Colonial cousins [the Holloway family of York Co., VA] By G.E. Hopkins. 1940. 89p.
P4-S14808 — $18.00.

HOLLOWAY: William Holloway of Taunton, MA in 1637, & his descendants, 1586-1949. By E.H. Pendleton. 1950. 356p.
P4-S14826 — $55.00.

HOLLYMAN: Hollyman fam., a gen. & hist. rec. of the desc. of Christopher Hollyman of Isle of Wight Co., VA & rel. fam. By G. Holleman. 1953 ? 275p.
P4-S14827 — $41.00.

HOLMAN: The Holmans in America, concerning the desc. of Solaman Holman who settled in W. Newbury, MA in 1692-3 D.E. Holman. 1909. 45 + 195p.
P4-S14832 — $54.50.

HOLMES: Descendants of George Holmes in Americam By Gold J. Butler. 1928. 122p.
P4-S14838 — $21.00.

HOLMES: Family. By Sarah E. Holmes. 1943. 109p., typscript.
P4-S14844 — $17.00.

HOLMES: Letter of directions to his father's birthplace, by John Holmes, with notes & a genealogy. By D.W. Patterson. 1864. 76p.
P4-S14850 — $15.00.

HOLMES: Our Holmes ancestors [of NJ]. By Eileen Diggles Bruce. 1950. 90p., typescript.
P4-S14856 — $17.50.

HOLMES: The American family of Obadiah Holmes. By Col. J.T. Holmes. 1915. 247p.
P4-S14862 — $37.00.

HOLMES: The desc. of George Holmes of Roxbury, 1594-1908, to which is added the desc. of John Holmes of Woodstock, CT. By G.A. Gray. 1908. 432p.
P4-S14868 — $68.00.

HOLMES: Holmes Family. E. Delroy Holmes. (n.d.) 28p.
P4-S14839 — $10.00.

HOLMES: Displaced Cherokee: Come Home, Come Home. Tonya Holmes Shook. 1986. 292p.
P4-S14840 — $44.00.

HOLSTEIN: Swedish Holsteins in America, 1644-1892, with the families of DeHaven, Rittenhouse, Clay, etc. By Anna M. Holstein. 1892. 305p.
P4-S14874 — $46.00.

HOLT: Genealogical hist. of the Holt fam. in the US; particularly the desc. of Nicholas Holt of Newbury & Andover, MA. D.S. Durrie. 1864. 367p.
P4-S14883 — $47.50.

HOLT: First three generations of the Holt family in America. By the Holt Assoc. of Amer. 1930. 370p.
P4-S14880 — $58.50.

HOLT: Lines of descent from Nathaniel Holt of the third generation [from Wm. Holt]. By Frank L. Holt. 1933. 133p., typescript.
P4-S14889 — $26.00.

HOLTON: Genealogy of the descendants in America of Wm. Holton (1610-91) of Hartford, CT & Northampton, MA. By Rev. Edw. P. Holton. 1935. 158 + 27p., typescript.
P4-S14901 — $28.00.

HOLTON: Ancestry of Ezra Holton of Northfield, MA & Soperton, Ont., 1785-1824. By E.L. Moffat. 1953. 158p., typscript.
P4-S14895 — $25.00.

HOLTZCLAW: Family, 1540-1935. By B.C. Holtzclaw. 1936. 249p.
P4-S14907 — $39.50.

HOMER: Brief acct. of the fam. of Homer or de Homere of Ettingshall, Co. Stafford, Eng., & Boston, MA. By B. H. Dixon. 1889. 27p.
P4-S14902 — $10.00.

HOMMON: Family book, Including Aydelott, Bixler, Bush, Critchfield, Foster, Grimes, Hommon, Kitterman, Riley. By Joan Kay Hommon Kimball. 2002. 154p.
P4-S14909 — $25.00.

HONEYMAN: Family (Honyman, Hunneman, etc.) in Scotland & America, 1548-1908. By A.V.D. Honeyman. 1909. 345p.
P4-S14910 — $44.50.

HOOD: The Tunis Hood family: its lineages & traditions. By D.O. Hood. 1960. 602p.
P4-S14916 — $87.50.

HOOD: John Hood of Lynn, MA & some of his desc. (Repr. Essex Inst. Hist. Coll.) By J.H. Bosson. 1909. 46p.
P4-S14917 — $10.00.

HOOK: James Hook & Virginia Eller; family hist. & gen. J.W. Hook. 1925. 171p.
P4-S14922 — $29.00.

HOOKE: Humphrey Hooke of Bristol, & his family & descendants in England & America during the 17th cent. By F. Todd. 1938. 201p.
P4-S14928 — $31.00.

HOOKER: Descendants of Rev. Thomas Hooker, Hartford, CT, 1586-1908. By E. Hooker. 1909. 558p.
P4-S14931 — $70.00.

HOOPER: A biogr. sketch of eight gen. of Hoopers in Amer.; William Hooper, 1635, to Idolene Snow (Hooper) Crosby, 1883. By W.S. Crosby. 1906. 42p.
P4-S14938 — $10.00.

HOOPER: Genealogy, By C.H. Pope & T. Hooper. 1908. 321p.
P4-S14937 — $49.50.

HOPKINS: [Stephen] Hopkins of the Mayflower: portrait of a dissenter. By Margaret Hodges. 1972. 274p.
P4-S14943 — $31.00.

HOPKINS: of VA & related families. By Walter Lee Hopkins. 1931. 405p.
P4-S14955 — $61.50.

HOPKINS: One branch of the Hopkins fam. (from John Hopkins of Hartford 1633) By S. M. Hopkins. 1898. 6p.
P4-S14944 — $10.00.

HOPKINS: One branch of the Hopkins fam. (desc. of Stephen & Giles) By A. B. Raymond. 16p.
P4-S14945 — $10.00.

HOPKINS: John Hopkins of Cambridge, MA, 1634, & some of his descendants. By Timothy Hopkins. 1932. 936p.
P4-S14961 — $129.50.

HOPKINS: A chapter of Hopkins genealogy, 1735-1905. By E. Harrison. 1905. 396p.
P4-S14949 — $51.50.

HOPKINS: Stephen Hopkins of the Mayflower. Rev. B.F. De Costa. n.d. 8p.
P4-S14944 — $10.00.

HOPKINS: Notes on the Thomas Hopkins fam. of RI. By A. Holbrook. 1889. 19p.
P4-S14945 — $10.00.

HOPKINS: Family marriages. By W. M. Clemens. 1916. 48p.
P4-S14946 — $10.00.

HOPKINS: Stephen & Giles Hopkins, Mayflower desc., & some of their desc. By J. W. Hawes. 1915. 27p.
P4-S14947 — $10.00.

HORD: The Hord Family of VA. Rev. Arnold Harris Hord. 1915. 122 + 12p.
P4-S14968 — $21.00.

HORD: Genealogy of the Hord family. By A.H. Hord. 1898. 199p.
P4-S14967 — $33.00.

HORNBERGER: Gen. information regarding the families of Hornberger & Yingling, & related families of Eckert, Lenhart, et al. By Claude J. Rahn. 1951. 164p.
P4-S14973 — $28.00.

HORNER: History of the relationship & descendants of Jacob & Catherin Horner in the US, from 1777-1914. By Elias L. Horner. 1914. 169p.
P4-S14979 — $26.00.

HORSFORD: HOSFORD: Ye Horseforde booke; the Horsford — Hosford fam. in the US. 1936. 256p.
P4-S14985 — $38.50.

HORTON: Genealogy. Chronicles of the Descendants of Barnabas Horton of Southold, Long Isl., with Appendix & 1879 Addenda. George F. Horton. 335p.
P4-S15012 — $52.50.

HORTON: Genealogy & history, desc. of Richard & Nathaniel Horton of PA. By G.W. Alloway. 1929. 141p.
P4-S15009 — $25.00.

HORTON: The Hortons in America; corrected repr. of 1876 work by G.F. Horton. By A.H. Horton. 1929. 650p.
P4-S15018 — $87.50.

HORTON: Anc. & desc. of Isaac Horton of Liberty, NY. By B.B. Horton. 1912. 52p.
P4-S14992 — $11.00.

HORTON: Descendants of Thomas Horton. By A.J. Horton. 1912. 131p.
P4-S15003 — $22.00.

HORTON: Ancestors & descendants of Isaac Horton of Liberty, NY. By Byron B. Horton. 1946. 144p.
P4-S14991 — $23.00.

HORTON: Anc. of Horace Ebenezer & Emma (Babcock) Horton. By H. E. Horton. 1920. 117p.
P4-S14997 — $21.00.

HOSKINS: Some descendants of John Hoskins, who came from Plymouth, England, to America, in 1630. n.a. 1957. 28p.
P4-S15019 — $10.00.

HOSKINSON: Genealogy of one branch of the Hoskinson family; descendants of George Washington Hoskinson. By Alice H. Wooldridge. 1963. 185p.
P4-S15024 — $28.50.

HOSMER: Genealogy; The desc. of James Hosmer who emigrated to Amer. in 1635 & settled in Concord, MA. By G.L. Hosmer. 1928. 271p.
P4-S15036 — $42.00.

HOSMER: Ancestors & descendants of Josiah Hosmer, Jr, 1600-1902. By Geo. D.R. Hubbard. 1902. 101p.
P4-S15030 — $18.50.

HOTCHKISS: Fam. (Repr. NEHGR) By D.L. Jacobus. 1912-1913. 33p.
P4-S15037 — $10.00.

HOTTEL: History of the desc. of John Hottel (immigr. from Switzerland) & an authentic genealogical family register of ten generations By W.D. & L.M. Huddle. 1930. 1182p.
P4-S15042 — $165.00.

HOUGH: Genealogy [of PA], By Elmer Hough. 1936. 75p.
P4-S15048 — $15.00.

HOUGH: Early Hough families of Bucks Co., PA. By Wallace I. Hough. 1935. 17p.
P4-S15049 — $10.00.

HOUGHTON: Descendants of Capt. Wm. Houghton, 1774-1863, & Marilla Clay, 1780-1858 W.D. Love. 1953. 67p.
P4-S15054 — $14.00.

HOUGHTON: Genealogy; the desc. of Ralph & John Houghton of Lancaster, MA. J. Houghton. 1912. 608p.
P4-S15063 — $73.00.

HOUGHTON: Report to the Houghton Assoc., US, made by Columbus Smith, 1869, also several gen. of different branches of the fam. 1869. 60p.
P4-S15066 — $12.50.

HOUGHTON: Hist. & gen. of the Houghton fam. 1896. 100p.
P4-S15060 — $18.00.

HOUSE: BROWN Genealogy: some descendants of Wm. House (c.1642-1703/4) & George Brown (c. 1714-1770) & related families. By Charles Staver House. 1984. 681p.
P4-S15075 — $89.00.

HOUSEHOLDER: Householders of America: genealogy of Johannes Hausshalter, early inhabitant of MD & PA with families from PA & elsewhere By Bessie R. Rogers. 1948. 151p., typescript.
P4-S15081 — $24.50.

HOUSEMAN: Family of Westmoreland Co., PA. Harry H. Frazier. 1937. 171p.
P4-S15087 — $25.00.

HOUSER: Genealogy of the Houser, Rhorer, Dillman, Hoover families. By W.W. Houser, et al. 1910. 239p.
P4-S15093 — $37.50.

HOUSTON: Family in VA. By L.L. Campbell. 1956. 77p.
P4-S15111 — $16.00.

HOUSTON: Brief biographical accounts of many members of the Houston family, with genealogical table. By S.R. Houston.F 1882. 420p.
P4-S15099 — $65.50.

HOUSTON: & allied families: genealogical study with biographical notes. By Thomas H. Bateman. 1950. 683p.
P4-S15105 — $99.50.

HOVEY: Book, describing Eng. anc. & Amer. desc. of Daniel Hovey of Ipswich, MA. comp. by the Daniel Hovey Assoc. 1914. 487p.
P4-S15117 — $74.50.

HOW: Anc. & desc. of Jacob How(e) of Rowley, MA, Bridgton & Paris, ME. By F. Howe. 1905. 20p.
P4-S15118 — $10.00.

HOWARD: Desc. of Claiborne Howard, soldier of the American Revolution, including Barnard, Brindle, Campbell, etc . . . By G.W. Cook. 1960. 186p.
P4-S15135 — $29.50.

HOWARD: "The Lion & the Rose," the great Howard story: Norfolk line, 957-1646; Suffolk line, 1603-1917. By Ethel Richardson. 1922 2 vols. In 1, 615p.
P4-S15123 — $75.00.

HOWARD: Lin. Anc. of Ida Boydstun Welch through her mother Eoline F. Howard Boydstun. G. Weaver. 1929. 230p.
P4-S15156 — $34.50.

HOWARD: The House of Howard, Vols I & II. Gerald Brenan. 1907. 367 + 403p.
P4-S15130 — $118.00.

HOWARD: History of Isaac Howard of Foster, RI, & his desc. By D. Howard. 1901. 168p.
P4-S15144 — $25.00.

HOWARD: A gen. rec. embracing all known desc. in this country of Thomas & Susanna Howard. By J.C. Howard. 1884. 238p.
P4-S15150 — $31.50.

HOWARD: Descendants of John Howard of Bridgewater, MA, 1643-1903. By H. Howard. 1903. 330p.
P4-S15138 — $49.50.

HOWARD: Abraham Howard of Marblehead, MA & his desc. By Howard, Holden & Howard. 1897. 71p.
P4-S15129 — $14.00.

HOWE: Four brothers in the American Revolution: Timothy, Darius, Baxter & Bezaleel Howe with a partial list of their descendants. By Herbert B. Howe. 1957. 115p.
P4-S15168 — $19.00.

HOWE: Genealogy of John Howe of Sudbury & Marlborough, MA. By D. Howe; rev. By G.B. Howe. 1929. 564p.
P4-S15177 — $73.50.

HOWE: Family gathering, Harmony Grove, S. Framingham MA, 1871. By E. Nason. 1871. 46p.
P4-S15163 — $10.00.

HOWE: Col. Joseph How, York Co., SC, his descendants & his brothers. By Olga M.R. Whitley. 1960. 97p., typescript.
P4-S15162 — $19.00.

HOWE: Gen. of Abraham of Roxbury, James of Ipswich, Abraham of Marlborough Edward of Lynn, MS, with appendix. By D.W. & G.B. Howe. 1929. 655p.
P4-S15174 — $97.50.

HOWELL: A Memorial History & Genealogical Record of the John Howell & Jacob Stutzman Families. Jonathan S. Howell. 1922. 274p.
P4-S15182 — $41.00.

HOWELL: In the Name of Howell: gen. of the Howell & related families from Dda ap Cadell Hywel — King of Wales to the present (2000). By Jim Howell and Bob & Connie Medford. 2000. 735p.
P4-S15183 — $105.00.

For hardcover versions, see the order form on page v. To order, call 1-888-296-3447.

HOWES: Desc. of John & Mary Howes of Montgomery Co., MD. By J.J.W. Howes. 1946. 53p.
P4-S15190 — $10.50.

HOWES: Gen. of the Howes fam. in Amer. Desc. of Thomas Howes, Yarmouth, MA, 1637-1892. By J.C. Howes. 1892. 209p.
P4-S15189 — $31.00.

HOWISON: Hist. & biogr. sketch of the Howison fam. 6p.
P4-S15191 — $10.00.

HOWLAND: Heirs; being the story of a family & a fortune. By W.M. Emery. 1919. 492p.
P4-S15204 — $76.50.

HOWLAND: Brief gen. & bio. record of Charles Roscoe Howland, brothers & forebears. By Chas. R. Howland. 1946? 284p.
P4-S15198 — $44.50.

HOWLAND: Brief gen. & bio. history of Arthur, Henry & John Howland & their descendants. By F. Howland. 1885. 463p.
P4-S15192 — $59.00.

HOWLAND: John Howland, a Mayflower pilgrim. 1926. 65p.
P4-S15210 — $13.00.

HOWLAND: The Howlands in America. 1939. 77p.
P4-S15216 — $15.00.

HOXIE: Family: three centuries in America [with every name index by M.G.D. Hinnckley]. By Leslie R. Hoxie. 1950, 1960. 300 _ 140p.
P4-S15222 — $67.50.

HOYES: of MD. By Capt. Charles E. Hoye. 1942. 264p.
P4-S15228 — $39.50.

HOYLE: Gen. of Peiter Heyl (Hoyle) & his desc., 1100-1936, with intermarried families of Arnold, Bess, Byrd, Cansler, et al. By E.H. Rucker. 1938. 1539p.
P4-S15234 — $198.00.

HOYT: Gen. history of the Hoyt, Haight & Hight fam., with a list of the first settlers of Salisbury & Amesbury, MA. By D.W. Hoyt. 1871. 698p.
P4-S15240 — $104.50.

HOYT: Fam., a gen. hist. of John of Salisbury & David of Deerfield, & their desc. By D.W. Hoyt. 1857. 144p.
P4-S15252 — $25.00.

HOYT: Record of the Hoyt fam. meeting, 1866. D.W. Hoyt. 1866. 64p.
P4-S15261 — $12.50.

HOYT: Part I, Genealogy of Sam'l Hoyt (1762-1838) & Betsy Webb (1772-1819) of Stamford CT; Part II, genealogy of Polly Hoyt (1773-1840), later Polly Hoyt Ferris. By Rev. John W. Hoyt. 1939. 103p., typescript.
P4-S15258 — $18.00.

HOYT: Gen. of Charles Davenport Hoyt of Stamford, CT, seventh generation from Simon Hoyt. By John Wm. Hoyt. 1939 75p., typescript.
P4-S15246 — $15.00.

HUBBARD: THOMPSON mem'l; gen. record & hist. acct. of the anc. & desc. of Ebenezer Hubbard & Mary Thompson, his wife. By L.K. Stewart. 1914. 423p.
P4-S15276 — $66.50.

HUBBARD: Historical Sketch of Rev. John Hubbard of Meriden, CT, His Ancestors & Descendants. 1903. 106p.
P4-S15271 — $18.00.

HUBBARD: One thousand years of Hubbard hist., 866-1895. By E.W. Day. 1895. 512p.
P4-S15270 — $65.50.

HUBBELL: History of the Hubbell family, containing gen. records of the ancestors & Desc. of Richard Hubbell, 1086-1915. By Walter Hubbell. 1915. 406p.
P4-S15288 — $62.00.

HUBBELL: History of the Hubbell family, containing a gen. rec. By W. Hubbell. 1881. 478p.
P4-S15282 — $74.50.

HUBER: HOOVER Family history: bio. & gen. history of the desc. of Hans Huber from the time of his arrival in PA to the 11th generation. By Harry M. Hoover. 1928. 335p.
P4-S15294 — $49.00.

HUBRECHT: Genealogie van het Geslacht Hubrecht (IN DUTCH). By J.H. Scheffer. 1879. 95p.
P4-S15300 — $18.00.

HUCKINS: Huckins fam. Robert Huckins of the Dover combination & some of his desc. By H.W. Hardon. 1916. 195p.
P4-S15306 — $32.00.

HUDDLESON: Family. By Fanny Huddelson. 1950. 187 + 60p., typescript.
P4-S15312 — $27.00.

HUDDLESTON: Family tables. By Geo. Huddleston. 1933. 289p.
P4-S15318 — $44.00.

HUDSON: Hudsons of the Eastern Shore: original settlers in Northampton & Accomac Cos., VA & their descendants By M.F. Hudson. 1944. 88p., typescript.
P4-S15325 — $10.00.

HUDSON: Descendants of Jesse Hudson & related families. By Jewel. N. Hudson. 1957. 101p.
P4-S15324 — $17.00.

HUFFHINES: John Huffhines family history & genealogy. By Eulalia H.T. Connally. 1940. 90p.
P4-S15330 — $18.00.

HUFFMASTER: HOFFMEISTER Family records. By James T. Huffmaster. 1922. 86p.
P4-S15338 — $16.00.

HUFFORD: Family history, 1729-1909. By F.P. Hoffert. 1909. 269p.
P4-S15342 — $41.00.

HUGGINS: Desc. of Phillip Huggins. D.E. & K.D. Page. 2001. xlvi + 895p.
P4-S15343 — $112.00.

HUGHES: Family & connections, especially the Gass, Ward & Boze families. By W.J.L. Hughes. 1911. 164p.
P4-S15366 — $24.50.

HUGHES: & allied families. By D.D. & W.H. Hughes. 1879. 253p.
P4-S15360 — $41.00.

HUGHES: Ancestral journal of the Hughes families & their interlinks, [NC] By Thelma R. Johnson Nelson. 1994. 380p.
P4-S15348 — $57.00.

HUGHES: The Family of John Joseph Hughes & Mary Lennon Hughes & the Families of Their Siblings. Kathleen Aponick & Mary Paula Baumann. 2000. vi + 220p.
P4-S15355 — $37.00.

HUGHES: Family history including Hughes, Dalton, Martin, Henderson, all originally of VA & many kindred branches. Lucy H. Horton. 1922. 289p.
P4-S15354 — $45.00.

HUGHES: Family of Cape May Co., NJ, 1650-1950: gen. of the desc. of Humphrey Hughes of Long Isl., 1650. By Raymond F. Hughes. 1950. 265p.
P4-S15372 — $39.50.

HUGHES: Family records. By J.M. Seaver. 39p.
P4-S15371 — $10.00.

HUGHEY: From "Larimer, McMasters & Allied fams." 12p.
P4-S15373 — $10.00.

HUIDEKOPER: American ancestry of Frederic Louis Huidekoper & Reginald Shippen Huidekoper of Washington DC. By F.L. Huidekoper. 1931. 62p.
P4-S15378 — $13.00.

HULBERT: Genealogy, being an historical record of the descent of Kenneth Leaman Hulbert from Thomas Hurlbut of Wethersfield, CT. By Henneth L. Hulbert. 1949. 158p.
P4-S15384 — $25.00.

HULL: Family in America. By C.H. Weygant. 1913. 647p.
P4-S15390 — $81.00.

HULL: Records of some of the desc. of Richard Hull, New Haven, 1639-1662. By S.C. Clarke. 1869. 20p.
P4-S15388 — $10.00.

HULL: Rev. Joseph Hull & some desc. By A. Hull. 1904. 64p.
P4-S15393 — $12.50.

HULL: A record of the desc. of Richard Hull of New Haven, 260 years in America. P.F. Mason. 1894. 78p.
P4-S15387 — $15.50.

HUME: History of the Hume family: biographical & chronological record of the rise & progress of this ancient family . . . John R. Hume. 1903. 287 + 32p.
P4-S15414 — $49.00.

HUME: Memorial to Geo. Hume, Esq., Crown surveyor of VA & Washington's teacher of surveying, with notes on his life. By Edgar E. Hume. 1939. 99p.
P4-S15432 — $18.00.

HUME: Colonial Scottish Jacobite family: establishment in VA of a branch of the Humes of Wedderburn. By Edgar E. Hume. 1931. 163p.
P4-S15402 — $25.00.

HUME: Early American history of Hume & allied families. By W.E. Brockman. 1926. 217p.
P4-S15405 — $37.00.

HUME: History of the Hume, Kennedy & Brockman families in three parts. By Wm. E. Brockman. 1912. 272p.
P4-S15426 — $42.00.

HUMPHREVILLE: with collateral lines Beecher, Bristol, Brown, Bullard, Clark et al: ancestral records of Frances Amelia (Smith) Lewis. By Harriet S.L. Barnes. 1903. 56p.
P4-S15433 — $11.00.

HUMPHREY: THOMAS; Colonists of Carolina in the lindeage of Hon. W.D. Humphrey By Blanche H. Abee. 1938. 259 + 32p.
P4-S15474 — $44.00.

HUMPHREY: Dorchester & Weymouth, MA families of Humphrey. By Gilbert Nash. 1883. 275p.
P4-S15438 — $39.00.

HUMPHREYS: Families in Amer. (CT branches), vol I. By F. Humphreys. et al. 1883. 398p.
P4-S15444 — $51.50.

HUMPHREYS: Family in America, vol II. 1884. 437p.
P4-S15450 — $68.00.

HUMPHREYS: Genealogy: some descendants of John Humphreys of Chester Co. PA. By Allan S. Humphreys. 1954. 138p.
P4-S15468 — $22.00.

HUMPHREYS: Abstr. of wills & mem. concerning English Humphreys, coll. from the . . . record offices of Gt. Britain (add. to "Humphreys Gen.") 1887. 106p.
P4-S15462 — $18.00.

HUMPHRIES: Desc. of Charles Humphries of VA, Nathaniel Pope of VA, Reuben Brock I of Ireland, & Aaron Parker of VA. By J.D. Humphries. 1938. 63p.
P4-S15477 — $12.50.

HUNGERFORD: Thomas Hungerford of Hartford & New London, CT & some of his desc., with their Eng. anc. By F. P. Leach. 1924. 34p.
P4-S15490 — $10.00.

HUNGERFORD: Add. & corr. for above. By F.P. Leach. 1932. 60p.
P4-S15483 — $12.00.

HUNKINS: Genealogical records of Robert Hastings Hunkins family. By Hazen H. Hunkins. 1961. 54p.
P4-S15497 — $11.00.

HUNNEWELL: Hunnewell: Chiefly Six Generations in MA. James Frothingham Hunnewell. 1900. 47p.
P4-S15496 — $10.00.

HUNNINGS: Some notes on the families of Hunnings of So. Lincolnshire, London & Suffolk. By W.E. Foster. 1912 61p.
P4-S15489 — $12.00.

HUNSAKER: Desc. Of Hartmann Hunsaker. D.E. Page. 2003. xxiii + 437p.
P4-S15500 — $69.00.

HUNSICKER: Genealogical history of the Hunsicker family. By H.A. Hunsicker. 1911. 358p.
P4-S15498 — $56.50.

HUNT: Genealogy of the name & family of Hunt. By T. Wyman. 1862-1863 430p.
P4-S15513 — $55.50.

HUNT: Birthrights: gen. record of Canadian branches of Hunt, Scott, Ives & Farwell families By W.H. Hunt. 1957. 205p.
P4-S15510 — $31.00.

HUNT: Family records. By J.M. Seaver. 38p.
P4-S15505 — $10.00.

HUNT: A gen. hist. of the Robert & Abigail Pancoast Hunt fams. By C.C. Hunt. 1906. 202p.
P4-S15504 — $27.00.

HUNTER: Family of VA & connections, embracing portions of families of Alexander, Pearson, Chapman, Travers, Tyler, West, et al. By Sidney M. Culbertson. 1934. 299p.
P4-S15525 — $45.00.

HUNTER: Descendants of Dr James Hunter who came to Canada from Yorkshire, Eng., in the year 1822. By Edwin G. Hunter. 1925. 82p.
P4-S15519 — $16.00.

HUNTER: Family of VA. By S. M. Culbertson. 1934. 22p.
P4-S15520 — $10.00.

HUNTER: Family records. By W. M. Clemens. 1914. 17p.
P4-S15521 — $10.00.

HUNTER: Record of Hunter of Hunterson, Ayrshire, Scotland. By Mary Alice H. Bull. 1902. 95p.
P4-S15537 — $18.00.

HUNTER: Joseph Hunter & related families Beckwith, Bird, Medley, Phillips, Riley & Sikes of S.E. MO. By S.B. & M.A.M. Hunter. 1959. 374p.
P4-S15531 — $58.50.

HUNTING: HUNTTING; Descendants of Abraham Huntting, 6th in line from John Huntting, 1st of the name in America. By T.D. Huntting. 1910. 11p.
P4-S15541 — $10.00.

HUNTING: or Huntting fam. in Amer. By T. Huntting. 1888. 83p.
P4-S15540 — $16.50.

HUNTINGTON: Family in America; a gen. memoir of the known desc. of Simon Huntington, 1613-1915. 1915. 1205p.
P4-S15558 — $159.00.

HUNTINGTON: Family in America: supplement to the genealogical memoir published in 1915 1962. 628p.
P4-S15552 — $89.50.

HUNTINGTON: Genealogical memoir of the Huntington family in this country, desc. of Simon & Margaret Huntington. By E.B. Huntington. 1863. 428p.
P4-S15546 — $67.00.

HUNTLEY: John Huntley of Lyme, CT & his descendants. By H. F. Johnston. 1949. 72p.
P4-S15564 — $15.00.

HUNTLEY: John Huntley of Lyme, CT & his descendants. By Ivy H. Horn. 1953. 444 + 104p., typescript.
P4-S15570 — $79.00.

HUNTOON: HUNTON; The Hunttons of Colonial Kingston, NH. By Robert Jay Evans. 1984. 306p.
P4-S15582 — $39.50.

HUNTOON: Ancestors & desc. of the IA Huntoons. By Joe Crockett Huntoon, Jr. 1971. 169p.
P4-S15576 — $19.50.

HUNTOON: Philip Hunton & his desc. By D. Huntoon. 1881. 113p.
P4-S15588 — $17.00.

HURD: History & genealogy of the family of Hurd in the US; also a partial history of the New Eng. fams. of Heard & Hord. D.D. Hurd. 1910. 339p.
P4-S15591 — $44.00.

HURFF: History & genealogy of the Hurff family. By the Hurff Family Assoc. 1951. 465p.
P4-S15597 — $69.50.

HURLBUT: Genealogy. By C.G. Hurlburt. 1922. 69p.
P4-S15603 — $14.00.

HURLBUT: Some of the desc. of Samuel Hurlbut of Chatham, CT. By H. Hurlbut. 1861. 24p.
P4-S15604 — $10.00.

HURLBUT: Genealogy; A record of the descendants of Thomas Hurlbut of Saybrook & Wethersfield, CT. By H.H. Hurlbut. 1888. 545p.
P4-S15606 — $69.00.

HURRY: Memorial of the family of Hurry of Gt Yarmouth & of NY, with additions. Chas. John Palmer & Edmund A. Hurry. 1873, 1900. 102 + 30p.
P4-S15612 — $21.50.

HURRY: Memorials of the family of Hurry of Gt Yarmouth, Norfolk, & of America, Australia & So. Africa. By Thos. Hurry-Houghton with Margaret Hurry-Houghton. 1926 127p.
P4-S15618 — $19.00.

HUSE: Descendants of Abel Huse of Newbury (1602-1690). By H.P. Huse. 1935. 438p.
P4-S15624 — $68.50.

HUSTON: History of the Huston families & their descendants, 1450-1912, with a genealogical record. By E. R. Huston. 1912. 277p.
P4-S15630 — $42.00.

HUSTON: William Huston of Voluntown, CT, ca. 1720-1777, & some of his descendants, By Aimee H. Eck. 1950. 113p., typescript.
P4-S15636 — $18.00.

HUTCHINS: Hutchins gen. By C. Hutchins. 1885. 16p.
P4-S15643 — $10.00.

HUTCHINS: Genealogy of Thomas Hutchins of Salem, MA, with a history of allied families. By Jack R. Hutchins. 1972. 788p.
P4-S15642 — $106.50.

HUTCHINS: Our ancestral heritage: ancestors & descendants of Cicero Mordecai Hutchins & his wife Frances Carter Sawyer By Marvin C. Hutchins. 1961. 144p.
P4-S15648 — $22.00.

HUTCHINSON: Family of Laurens Co., SC & descendants. By Frederick McA. Hutchinson. 1947. 263p.
P4-S15654 — $41.00.

HUTCHINSON: A brief gen. of the desc. of William Hutchinson & Thomas Oliver. By W. H. Whitmore. 1865. 38p.
P4-S15655 — $10.00.

HUTCHINSON: A Brief Narrative of the Hutchinson Family: Sixteen Sons & Daughters of the "Tribe of Jesse." Joshua Hutchinson. 1874. 73p.
P4-S15656 — $14.00.

HUTCHINSON: The Hutchinson Farm. T.M. Hutchinson. 1899. 7p.
P4-S15653 — $10.00.

HUTCHINSON: A gen. of the Hutchinson fam. of Yorkshire, & of the Amer. branch of the fam. desc. from Richard Hutchinson of Salem, MA. By J. L. Chester. 1868. 33p.
P4-S15652 — $10.00.

HUTCHINSON: The Hutchinson fam.; or, the desc. of Bernard Hutchinson of Cowlam, Eng. By P. Derby. 1870. 107p.
P4-S15657 — $15.00.

HUTCHINSON: The book of brothers; the hist. of the Hutchinson fam. 1852. 48p.
P4-S15658 — $10.00.

HUTCHINSON: A brief sketch of the Hutchinson fam. of NH. By F. A. Hutchinson. 1896. 23p.
P4-S15659 — $10.00.

HUTCHINSON: Notes upon the anc. of William Hutchinson & Anne Marbury. By J. L. Chester. 1866. 24p.
P4-S15649 — $10.00.

HYDE: Several ancestral lines of Moses Hyde & his wife Sarah Dana By Harriette H. Wells. 1904. 114p.
P4-S15666 — $18.00.

HYDE: Genealogy; desc. from William Hyde of Norwich. By R.H. Walworth. 1864. 2 vols., 1446p.
P4-S15660 — $183.00.

HYDE: The Descendants of Andrew Hyde of Lenox, MA. Edith Drake Hyde. 1937. 58p.
P4-S15661 — $11.00.

HYDORN: Genealogy of the Hydorn, Nelson, York & other related lineages in America. By G.H. Gordon & Mary E. Hydorn. 1934. 51p., typescript.
P4-S15667 — $10.00.

HYNES: Our heritage: rec. of info. about the Hynes, Wait, Powers, Chenault, Maxet, Brewster, Starr & McIntosh families. L.P. Hynes. 1957. 93p.
P4-S15672 — $18.00.

HYNES: Our pioneer ancestors; record of available info. as to the Hynes, Chenault, Dunn, McKee, etc. By Riggs & Riggs. 1941. 207p.
P4-S15678 — $32.00.

HYSLOP: Biographical sketches of the Hyslop & Baird families. By Charles Hyslop. 1928. 52p.
P4-S15679 — $10.00.

I

IDE: Pennsylvania branch of the Ide family, ancestors & descendants of Nehemiah & Ezra Ide. By Silas C. Ide. 1940. 180p.
P4-S15684 — $27.50.

IDE: Simon Ide, with a genealogy of the Ide family. Flanders et al. 1931. 347p.
P4-S15690 — $55.00.

IDEN: Sons & daughters of Randall Iden: authentic history of the Iden family dating from 1280 a.d. to the present year, 1941 a.d. By V. Gilmore Iden. 1941. 100p.
P4-S15696 — $18.00.

IMBRIE: Genealogy of the Imbrie family of Western PA: descendants of James Imbrie, pioneer settler, & his wife Euphamia Smart. By A.M. Imbrie et al. 1953. 194p.
P4-S15702 — $31.00.

IMLAY: Family. By Hugh & Nella Imlay. 1958. 192p.
P4-S15708 — $29.50.

INGALLS: The Ingalls fam. in Eng. & Amer., in comm. of the 300th anniversary of the settlement of Lynn, MA. By E. & F. Ingalls. 1930. 84p.
P4-S15717 — $16.50.

INGALLS: Gen. & history of the Ingalls family in Amer., giving the desc. of Edmund Ingalls, who settled at Lynn, MA in 1629. By C. Burleigh. 1903. 324p.
P4-S15711 — $45.00.

INGERSOLL: Genealogy of the Ingersoll family in America, 1629-1925. By L. D. Avery. 1926. 596p.
P4-S15723 — $89.00.

INGERSOLL: The Ingersolls of Hampshire. A gen. hist. of the fam. from their settlement in Amer., line of John Ingersoll of Westfield, MA. By C.S. Ripley. 1893. 107p.
P4-S15729 — $18.00.

INGERSOLL: Richard Ingersoll & some of his desc. By A.W. Greeley. 1909. 21p.
P4-S15724 — $10.00.

INGHAM: Family, or Joseph Ingham & his descendants, 1639-1871. 1871. 59p.
P4-S15742 — $12.00.

INGLIS: The Family of Inglis of Auchindinny & Redhall. John Alexander Inglis. 1914. 236 + 30p.
P4-S15743 — $40.00.

INGOLDSBY: Genealogy: Ingoldsby, Ingalsbe, Inglesby & Englesby, from the 13th century to 1904. By Frederick W. Ingalsbe. 1904. 72p.
P4-S15747 — $14.00.

INGPEN: An ancient family: a genealogical study showing the Saxon origin of the family of Ingpen. By A.R. Ingpen. 1916 208p.
P4-S15753 — $33.50.

INGRAHAM: To the descendants of Timothy Ingraham: information respecting the Great Ingraham Estate, in Great Britain. G.R. Gladding. 1859. 80p.
P4-S15759 — $16.00.

INGRAM: Our Home Place: A Personal Account of Life as it Was for a Particular Farm Family in IA, from the early 1900s to mid-century. W.M. Edgerton. 1976. vi + 211p.
P4-S15757 — $24.00.

INGRAM: This is Our Heritage, The Ancestral History of Charles & Cora (Beard) Ingram. Gladys A. Ingram 1978. 278p.
P4-S15758 — $41.00.

INGRAM: Descendants of Winifred Nelms & Joseph Ingram [of VA & NC]. By M.K.L. Davis. 1950. 39p.
P4-S15756 — $10.00.

INNES: An acct. of the family of Innes, comp. By Duncan Forbes of Culloden (1698), with an appendix of Charters & Notes. 1864. 286p.
P4-S15765 — $45.00.

INNES: Family of George & Jessie MacQueen Innes. By Margaret I. Gregory. 1965. 29p., typescript.
P4-S75766 — $10.00.

IRBY: Part I: the Irbys of Lincolnshire. By Paul A. Irby. 1928 158p.
P4-S15771 — $24.50.

IRBY: Part II: the Irebys of Cumberland. By Paul A. Irby. 1929 160p.
P4-S15777 — $25.00.

IRELAND: Sketch of the Ireland fam. By J. Ireland. 1907. 41p.
P4-S15790 — $10.00.

IRELAND: Gen. of Ireland fam. in Eng., Ireland & Amer. By W. M. Taylor. 1863. 10p.
P4-S15791 — $10.00.

IRELAND: Some acct. of the Ireland fam. of Long Island 1644-1880. By J. N. Ireland. 1880. 51p.
P4-S15792 — $10.00.

IRISH: Ancestors & descendants of Asa Irish, 1620-1932. By Jennie J. Wight Howes. 1932. 62p.
P4-S15780 — $12.50.

IRISH: Descendants of John Irish the Immigrant, 1629-1963, & allied fams. By W.L. & S.B. Irish. 1964. 662p.
P4-S15795 — $95.00.

IRISH: Desc. of James Irish, 1710-1940, & allied fam. By J.J.W. Howes. 1941. 261p.
P4-S15789 — $43.00.

IRISH: Sketch of Gen. Jas. Irish of Gorham, ME with fam. records. By L. Oak. 1898. 70p.
P4-S15801 — $14.00.

IRVINE: The Irvines & their kin: a history of the Irvine family & their descendants. By L. Boyd. 1898. 115p.
P4-S15813 — $18.00.

IRVINE: The Irvines & their kin; History of the Irvine fam. & their descendants; also, sketches of their kindred. By L. Boyd. 1908. 432p.
P4-S15807 — $67.50.

IRVING: The Irvings, Irwins, Irvines or Erinveines, or any other spelling of the name, an old Scots border clan. By John B. Irving of Bonshaw. 1907 295 + many illustrations
P4-S15819 — $47.50.

IRVINS: DOAKS — LOGANS & McCampbells of VA & KY. By Margaret L. Morris. 1916. 121p.
P4-S15825 — $19.00.

IRWIN: Genealogy of that branch of the Irwin family in NY, founded in the Hudson River Valley by Wm. Irwin, 1700-1787. By R.S. Hosmer & M.T. Fielder. 1938. 258p.
P4-S15831 — $39.50.

ISAAC: Ancestry of Mary Isaac, c.1549-1613, wife of Thomas Appleton of Little Waldinfield, co. Suffolk, & mother of Samuel Appleton of Ipswich, MA. W.G. Davis. 1955. 400p.
P4-S15837 — $61.00.

ISBELL: Gen. of the Isbell fam. By M.I. Scott. 1929. 256p.
P4-S15849 — $38.50.

ISBELL: Isbell & Kingman fam., Robt. Isbell & Henry Kingman & their desc. By L. Kingman. 1889. 30p.
P4-S15844 — $10.00.

ISBELL: Descendants of Robert Isbell in America. By Edna W. Mason. 1944. 296p.
P4-S15843 — $45.00.

ISENBERG: An Historical Sketch & Genealogical Record of the Isenberg Family of PA. Rev. J.M.S. Isenberg. 1900. 84p.
P4-S15850 — $13.00.

ISHAM: The Ishams in England & Amer: 850 years of hist. & gen. By H.W. Brainard. 1938. 672p.
P4-S15861 — $98.50.

ISHAM: Genealogy: brief hist. of Jirah Isham of New London, CT & his desc., from 1670-1940. By M.A. Phinney. 1940. 179p.
P4-S15855 — $27.00.

IVES: Genealogy of the Ives family, incl. a hist. of the early settlements, By A.C. Ives. 1932. 321p.
P4-S15867 — $48.50.

IVEY: Family in the US. By Geo. Franks Ivey. 1941. 113p.
P4-S15873 — $19.00.

J

JACKSON: Proceedings of the sesquicent. gathering of the desc. of Isaac & Ann Jackson at Harmony Grove, Chester Co., PA. Comp. by the Publ. Comm. 1878. 372p.
P4-S15909 — $58.50.

JACKSON: History of the Jackson family of Hempstead, Long Isl., OH & IN: descendants of Robt. & Agnes Washburn Jackson. By O.B. Robbins. 1951. 356p.
P4-S15897 — $55.00.

JACKSON: Some Jackson desc. of Cambridge Village (Newton), MA, Extr. Hist. of Newton. 27p.
P4-S15886 — $10.00.

JACKSON: History of Ephraim Jackson, first ancestor to come to America, & his descendants, 1684-1960. By J. Cross. 1961. 398p.
P4-S15891 — $62.50.

JACKSON: Sixty years in Texas (sketches of the old pioneers of Dallas Co., especially the Jackson family). By Geo. Jackson. 1908. 2nd ed., 383p.
P4-S15921 — $34.50.

JACKSON: Record of descendants & families of Charles & Ann (Maltby) Jackson in the US, 1845-1950. comp. by the Jackson Assoc. 1950. 113p., typescript.
P4-S15915 — $17.00.

JACKSON: Nehemiah Jackson of Woodstock, CT & some of his desc. By R. L. Jackson. 10p.
P4-S15887 — $10.00.

JACKSON: John Jackson of Portsmouth. By R. Jackson. 7p.
P4-S15888 — $10.00.

JACKSON: Descendants & ancestors of Wm. Jackson & his wife Rachel Tomlinson Jackson. By Mayburt S. Riegel. 1940. 159p.
P4-S15885 — $24.50.

JACKSON: The Family History of Michael Jackson, Emigrant from Ireland, Citizen of Hartford, CT. Horace Mortimer Jackson. 1909, 1914. 121 + 17p.
P4-S15889 — $21.00.

JACKSON: A branch of the Jackson correlated fam., 1730-1911. By S. Jackson. 1911. 60p.
P4-S15876 — $12.50.

JACKSON: Hon. Jonathan Jackson & Hannah Tracy Jackson: their ancestors & descendants [with 1914 supplement]. E.C. & J.J. Putnam. 1907. 70 + 11p.
P4-S15903 — $16.00.

JACKSON: The William Jackson fam. history. By S. Jackson. n.d. 14p.
P4-S15890 — $10.00.

JACOB: Desc. of Richard Jacob of Ipswich. By W.G. Davis. 1940. 12p.
P4-S15922 — $10.00.

JACOBY: Descendants of Bartholomew Jacoby. By Helen E. Evard. 1955. 291p.
P4-S15927 — $45.00.

JACOBY: Family genealogy; rec. of the desc. of the pioneer Peter Jacoby of Bucks Co., PA. H.S. Jacoby. 1930. 680p.
P4-S15933 — $98.00.

JAGGER: GAGER Genealogy; Desc. of Jeremiah Jagger (Gager) of Watertown, MA, 1639; etc. By H.G. Gager. n.d. 11p.
P4-S15934 — $10.00.

JAMES: A VA genealogy: Thomas James (Clerk of Kingston Parish, 1783-1796), ancestry & desc., 1653-1961. By E.H. Ironmonger. 1961. 374 + 28p.
P4-S15939 — $59.50.

JAMES: Family History of Cyrus Rosser James & Annie Shield James of York Co., VA. A.W. James. 1955. 44p. Typescript.
P4-S15940 — $10.00.

JAMES: Ancestors & descendants of Capt. John James & Esther Denison of Preston, CT. Clara P. Ohler. 1912. 216p.
P4-S15945 — $32.00.

JAMES: William James (1771-1832) of Albany NY & his descendants, with notes on collateral lines. By K.B. Hastings. 1924. 53p.
P4-S15941 — $11.00.

JAMES: Descendants of William James. Sarah Jane McKenzie. 1997. 93p.
P4-S15951 — $16.50.

JAMESON: The Jamesons in America, 1647-1900. Gen. records & memoranda. E.O. Jameson. 1901. 615p.
P4-S15957 — $75.00.

JANES: Family. Genealogy & brief history of the desc. of Wm. Janes, the emig. ancestor of 1637. By F. Janes. 1868. 419p.
P4-S15963 — $66.00.

JAQUETT: Genealogy of the Jaquett fam. By E.J. Sellers. 1907. 226p.
P4-S15969 — $34.00.

JARVIS: Family, or, the desc. of the 1st settlers of the name in MA. By Jarvis, Jarvis & Wetmore. 1879. 347p.
P4-S15975 — $45.00.

JAUDON: Account of the Jaudon family. By E.J. Sellers. 1890. 24p.
P4-S15980 — $10.00.

JAY: Family of LaRochelle & NY province & state. L. J. Wells. 1938. 64p.
P4-S15978 — $12.50.

JAYNES: Family of Haywood Co., NC, history & genealogy. By Jim Howell. 2000. 103p.
P4-S15987 — $18.00.

JELKE: FRAZIER & allied fam., By L.E. DeForest. 1931. 64p.
P4-S15993 — $18.50.

JELLY: Fam. births & deaths, Salem, MA, 1820-40. 1p.
P4-S15994 — $10.00.

JENKINS: Jenkins fam. book. By R. E. Jenkins. 1904. 244p.
P4-S15996 — $32.50.

JENKINS: Genealogy. J.M. Seaver. 30p.
P4-S15997 — $10.00.

JENKS: Fam. of Newport, NH. By G. Jenks. 1888. 12p.
P4-S16003 — $10.00.

JENKS: Family of America, with supplement. By W.B. Browne. 1952, 1956. 739 + 55p.
P4-S16002 — $110.00.

JENKS: Family of England (supplement to Jenks Genealogy, 1952). By Meredith B. Colket. 1956. 55p.
P4-S16001 — $11.00.

JENNESS: JENNINGS Fam. From Hist. of Rye, NH. 1905. 17p.
P4-S16006 — $10.00.

JENNINGS: DAVIDSON & allied families: gen. list & hist. of the desc. of the immigrants John Jennings, Southampton NY, & John Davison, Augusta Co. VA. By Lillie P. White. 1944. 269p.
P4-S16008 — $42.50.

JENNINGS: Gen. history of the Jennings family in Eng. & Amer: Vol II, the American family. By W.H. Jennings. (V.I not publ.) 1899. 828p.
P4-S16014 — $99.00.

JEPSON: Hist. & Gen. of the desc. of John Jepson of England & Boston, through his son John's two sons Wm. & Micah, 1610-1917. By Norton W. Jipson. 1917. 130p.
P4-S16020 — $19.00.

JERVIS: PORTER & Other Allied Families [Pt. vii of Johnsonian Gleanings]. Aleyn L. Reade. 1935 266p.
P4-S16026 — $39.50.

JESSUP: Edw. Jessup of W. Farms, Westchester Co. NY, & his desc., with an app. of records of other Amer. fam. of the name. By H. Jesup. 1887. 465p.
P4-S16032 — $56.00.

JETER: The Jeter Family [From "Our Kin: Gens of Early Fams of Bedford Co, VA.] M.D. Ackerly & L.E.J. Parker. 1930. 154p.
P4-S16033 — $23.00.

JEWELL: Jewell register, desc. of Thomas Jewell of Braintree. By P. & J. Jewell. 1860. 104p.
P4-S16038 — $17.50.

JEWETT: Family year book of 1911-13. 1911-13. 56 + 183p.
P4-S16050 — $36.00.

JEWETT: Hist. & gen. of the Jewetts of Amer.; rec. of Edward Jewett of Bradford, Eng., & of his sons, settlers of Rowley, MA in 1639. By F. Jewett. 1908. 2 vols., 1216p.
P4-S16044 — $159.00.

JIPSON: A Short History of the Jipson Family. N.W. Jipson, MD. 1908. 24p
P4-S16060 — $10.00.

JIPSON: Gen. of the Jipson/Jepson/Gipson family of ME: descendants of Wm. Jepson (ca. 1695-1723) of Moywater, co. Mayo, Ireland. By Alan H. Hawkins. 1991. 328p.
P4-S16059 — $47.00.

JOCELYN: JOSLIN — JOSLYN — JOSSELYN Family. By Edith S. Wessler. 1962. 310p.
P4-S16065 — $47.50.

JOHNES: The Johnes fam. of Southampton, Long Island, 1629-1886. By E.R. Johnes. 1886. 46p.
P4-S16066 — $10.00.

JOHNSON: Records of the desc. of John Johnson of Ipswich & Andover, MA, 1635-1892; with an appendix By W.W. Johnson. 1892. 200p.
P4-S16152 — $30.00.

JOHNSON: Genealogy of the Johnson family [desc. Od Wm. Johnson, Colony of VA, 1714]. 1926 144p.
P4-S16107 — $23.00.

JOHNSON: The Johnsons & their kin, of Randolph, NC. By J.O. Shaw. 1955. 214p.
P4-S16176 — $33.50.

JOHNSON: Rev. Jacob Johnson of Wallingford, CT & Willkes-Barre, PA. By F.O. Johnson. 1904. 32p.
P4-S16072 — $10.00.

JOHNSON: Our Clan of Johnsons of Argyll. Mary Rebecca Watson Powers. 1940. 126 + 6p.
P4-S16073 — $20.00.

JOHNSON: Memorial, Jeremiah Johnson & Thazin Blanchard Johnson, his wife: James B. Johnson. 1895. 163p.
P4-S16164 — $25.00.

JOHNSON: Descendants of Wm. & John Johnson, Colonial Friends of VA, with index. By Lorand V. Johnson. 1942. 188 + 38p.
P4-S16089 — $35.00.

JOHNSON: Genealogy of the descendants of Capt. Edmund Johnson, ca. 1741-1812. By Edmund R. Johnson with Laurence A. Johnson. 1954. 82p.
P4-S16101 — $17.00.

JOHNSON: Ancestry of Fannie May Johnson, of Lynn & Somerville, MA, wife of Robert Temple Skerry. By Claudia E.S. Cridland. 2000. 550p.
P4-S16071 — $77.50.

JOHNSON: Genealogy, records of the descendants of David Johnson of Leominster, with 1896 supplement. By Wm. W. Johnson. 1876. 85 + 27p.
P4-S16149 — $17.50.

JOHNSON: Hannah Johnson & Olly Palmer, with some of their kinsfolk. By Jennie H. Porter. 1930. 83p.
P4-S16113 — $16.00.

JOHNSON: Genealogy from 1520 to 1908, relating especially to Capt. Edw. Johnson & the compiler's line of his descendants. By Byron B. Johnson. 1908. 20p.
P4-S16074 — $10.00.

JOHNSON: History & genealogy of one line of desc. from Capt. Edward Johnson, together with his Eng. anc., 1500-1914. By A. Johnson. 1914. 232p.
P4-S16119 — $38.00.

JOHNSON: The Ancestry of Grafton Johnson, With its Four Branches: The Johnson — The Holman — The Keen — The Morris. Damaris Knobe. 1924. 384 + 68p.
P4-S16075 — $69.50.

JOHNSON: Jacob Johnson of Harpswell, ME & his desc. By C. N. Sinnett. 1907. 132p.
P4-S16125 — $26.00.

JOHNSON: New Haven & Wallingford (CT) Johnsons (Repr. NEHGR). By J. Shepard. 1902. 11p.
P4-S16075 — $10.00.

JOHNSON: Genealogy: descendants of William, 1625, of Portsmouth, England [through Elkanah of RI]. By Art Reierson. 1998. 89p.
PA-S16158 — $17.50.

JOHNSON: Family: descendants of Elkanah Johnson of Wales & RI. By Art Reierson. 1998. 131p.
P4-S16143 — $23.00.

JOHNSON: Genealogy of Capt. John Johnson of Roxbury, MA, generations I to XIV. By F.L. Johnson; ed. By P.F. Johnson & A.J. Modern. 1951. 499p.
P4-S16095 — $76.50.

JOHNSON: Mahlon Johnson family of Littleton, NJ, ancestors & descendants. Mary B.J. Pease et al. 1931. 133p.
P4-S16170 — $19.50.

JOHNSON: Descendants of John Johnson (1761-1815). By Rachel Saul Tefft. 1999. 110p.
P4-S16083 — $18.50.

JOHNSON: Anc. of Sarah Johnson, wife of Joseph Neal, of Litchfield, ME. By W.G. Davis. 1960. 104p.
P4-S16077 — $17.50.

JOHNSON: Reunion of the Family of Edwin Johnson, North Greenfield, WI. 1888. 25p.
P4-S16076 — $10.00.

JOHNSON: Family & allied families of Lincolnshire, England, being the ancestry & posterity of Lawrence Johnson of Philadelphia, By Robt. W. Johnson & Lawrence J. Morris. 1934. xxiii + 455 + 52p.
P4-S16137 — $79.00.

JOHNSTON: Gen. record of Peter Johnston, with hist. of clan. By C.E. Johnston. 1900. 118p.
P4-S16182 — $18.00.

JOHNSTON: The Johnstons of Salisbury, with a brief suppl. concerning the Hancock, Strother, & Preston fam. By W.P. Johnston. 1897. 216p.
P4-S16188 — $29.50.

JOLLIFFE: Hist., gen. & biogr. acct. of the Jolliffe fam. of VA, 1652-1893. Also sketches of cognate fam. By W. Jolliffe. 1893. 245p.
P4-S16194 — $38.00.

JONES: SKIPPER — DAVIS Fam. of Eng., Wales & Amer. (primarily SC). 20p.
P4-S16201 — $10.00.

JONES: & related families: a gen. comp. & history, incl. Stubbs, Gifford, Johnson, Hawkins, Small, Hobson, Green & others. C.B. Jones. 1951. 436p.
P4-S16251 — $67.50.

JONES: Genealogy of the Jones family, the descendants of Benj. Jones, who immigrate from So. Wales more than 250 years ago. By Geo. R. Jones. 1912. 85p.
P4-S16242 — $16.00.

JONES: Peter & Richard Jones genealogies. By A.B. Fothergill. 1924. 363p.
P4-S16275 — $57.00.

JONES: History & genealogy of the anc. & desc. of Capt. Israel Jones By L.N. Parker. 1902. 303p.
P4-S16245 — $39.50.

JONES: Family of Long Island, desc. of Maj. Thomas Jones (1665-1726) & allied families. J.H. Jones. 1907. 435p.
P4-S16257 — $68.00.

JONES: A gen. of the fam. of Cereno Upham Jones of Weymouth, Nova Scotia (a desc. of Lewis Jones of Roxbury, MA, 1640) By M.E.R. Jones. 1905. 38p.
P4-S16202 — $10.00.

JONES: The name & fam. of Jones. comp. Media Research Bureau. 13p.
P4-S16203 — $10.00.

JONES: Capt. Roger Jones of London & VA. Some anc. & desc. with notice of other fam. By L. Jones. 1891. 296p.
P4-S16212 — $44.00.

JONES: Some of the desc. of Lewis & Ann Jones of Roxbury, MA through their son Josiah, & grandson James. By W. B. Trask. 1878. 83p.
P4-S16287 — $14.00.

JONES: Desc. of Joel Jones, of MA & PA, 1764-1845. By E. Smith. 1925. 414p.
P4-S16218 — $65.00.

JONES: Fam. of Liberty & McIntosh Cos., GA, extr. from the Habersham gen. 1901. 13p.
P4-S16207 — $10.00.

JONES: Saybrook branch of the fam. of Deputy Gov. William Jones of New Haven. By E.A. Hill. 1895. 6p.
P4-S16208 — $10.00.

JONES: Genealogy, being a record of the descendants of Hugh Jones of Salem, MA, emigrant from Wincanton, England, 1635-1931. By Myrtle B. Clark. 1931. 219p.
P4-S16263 — $33.00.

JONES: Leaves from a family tree, being random records, letters & traditions of the Jones, Stimson & Clarke families L. Diman. 1941. 121p.
P4-S16269 — $19.00.

JONES: Family record of the Jones family, of Milford MA & Providence RI, with ancestry & family of Lorania Carrington Jones. G.F. Jones. 1884. 182p.
P4-S16224 — $28.00.

JONES: A genealogical history [Jones family of Roanoke, VA]. By Col. Cadwallader Jones. 1899. 75p.
P4-S16200 — $15.00.

JONES: Gen. notes: Jos. & Lydia Robert Jones of Gwynedd, Philadelphia Co., PA; John & Mary Stall Jones of Vincenet Twp., Chester Co., PA By George Keiter Miles. 1910. 67p.
P4-S16230 — $13.50.

JONES: Genealogy of David Jones. By E.M. Beales. 1903. 184p.
P4-S16236 — $25.00.

JONES: Thos. Jones of Dorchester, MA, 1635, & some of his descendants. By John L. Woodcock. 1914. 52p.
P4-S16209 — $11.00.

JONES: Records; Nathaniel & Rachel Bradford Jones, Ipswich, MA & some desc. By A. Caldwell. 7p.
P4-S16210 — $10.00.

JONES: Ancestors of my daughters [desc. from Pierpont Edwards Jones] By Nathan Henry Jones. 1914. 152p.
P4-S16206 — $24.00.

JORDAN: Memorial. Family records of the Rev. Robert Jordan & his descendants in America. T.F. Jordan. 1882. 495p.
P4-S16293 — $77.00.

JOY: A brief history of the Joy family. By One of Them (C. C. Joy Dyer). 1876. 37p.
P4-S16297 — $10.00.

JOY: Thomas Joy & his desc. By J. R. Joy. 1900. 225p.
P4-S16296 — $30.00.

JOY: Eng. anc. & royal desc. of the Joy fam. of Amer. By A.A.G. 13p.
P4-S16298 — $10.00.

JUDD: Philip Judd & his descendants. By Caroline J. McDowell. 1923. 291p.
P4-S16302 — $44.00.

JUDD: Thos. Judd & his desc. By S. Judd. 1856. 112p.
P4-S16305 — $17.00.

JUDY: History & genealogy of the Judy-Judah-Tschudy-Tschudin-Shudi By Marion P. Carlock. 1954. 576p.
P4-S16311 — $86.00.

JUNKINS: The desc. of Robert Junkins of York Co., ME. By H. A. Davis. 1938. 197p.
P4-S16317 — $30.00.

K

KAGY: History of the Kagy relations in America, from 1715-1900. By F. Keagy. 1899. 675p.
P4-S16320 — $85.50.

KAMPF: Desc. of Ulrich Kampf. D.E. Page. 2004. xx + 371p.
P4-S16322 — $59.00.

KANDEL: Genealogy of the descendants of Peter & Elizabeth Drushel Kandel, 1783-1942. By W.E. Kandel. 1942. 120p.
P4-S16326 — $21.00.

KAPPUS: Descendants of John Kappus & Mary Ann Hiltman of Prussia & the US. By Lillie Kappus. 1987. 110p.
P4-S16332 — $17.50.

KASPER: Some of Lewis Kasper's Kin. A.M. Prichard. 1946. 30 + 2p.
P4-S16333 — $10.00.

KASSON: Genealogy of the Kasson family in the US & Ireland. By Geo. F. Kasson. 1882. 51p.
P4-S16334 — $10.00.

KASTNER: CASTNER Fam. of PA. By S. Castner. 1901. 31p.
P4-S16335 — $10.00.

KATHAN: Hist. of Capt. John Kathan of Dummerston, VT. By D. L. Mansfield. 1902. 147p.
P4-S16338 — $28.50.

KAUFMAN: Peter Kaufman & Freni Strrausz Kaufman family record, 1844-1963. By E.G. Kaufman. 1963. 100p.
P4-S16344 — $18.00.

KAVANAUGH: The Ancient House of Kavanaugh. Anna T. Poynter Kavanaugh. n.d. 77p.
P4-S16339 — $12.00.

KEARNEY: Descendants of Cornelius Kearney. Sidney Carey Arnold, Jr. 2001. 96p.
P4-S16345 — $17.00.

KEARNS: Family history & a list of the desc. of John Kearns & his wife Margaret Groughbrough. By R. Kearns. 1909. 66p.
P4-S16347 — $12.00.

KEARSLEY: Desc. of Jonathan Kearsley, 1718-1782, & his wife Jane, 1720-1801 (from Scotland). By Elmer L. White. 1900. 86p.
P4-S16356 — $16.00.

KEATING: FORBES families & reminiscences of C.A. Keating, a.d. 1758-1920. By C.A. Keating. 1920. 175p.
P4-S16362 — $26.50.

KEATOR: Three centuries of the Keator family in America, with addendum. By Alfred D. Keator. 1955, 1961. 351 + 40p.
P4-S16368 — $59.50.

KECK: Gen. rec. of the Keck fam., By Keck & Grasselli. 1905. 66p.
P4-S16371 — $12.50.

KECK: Family, with special reference to the descendants of Michael Keck, who came to OH in 1806. By John M. Keck. 1926. 80p.
P4-S16380 — $15.50.

KEDZIE: Kedzies & their relatives. By A.S. & F.S. Kedzie. 1882. 96p.
P4-S16386 — $18.00.

KEELER: Desc. of Wm. Shilling Keeler. D. Page. 2005. xii + 194p.
P4-S16393 — $40.00.

KEELER: Ancestors of Evelyn Wood Keeler, wife of Willard Underhill Taylor. Josephine C. Frost. 1939. 630p.
P4-S16392 — $95.00.

KEELER: Genealogical records of the Keeler family, 1726-1924. By Joseph B. Keeler. 1924. 79p.
P4-S16398 — $15.00.

KEEN: KYN; Descendants of Joram Kyn of New Sweden. By G.B. Keen. 1913. 318p.
P4-S16416 — $48.00.

KEEN: KYN, Descendants of Joram Kyn, founder of "Upland — New Sweden" (now Chester, PA). 1878-1882. 243p.
P4-S16422 — $39.50.

KEEN: One line of the Keen fam. of Eng. & New Eng. 5p.
P4-S16405 — $10.00.

KEEN: Genealogy of the Keen family of Wayne Co., IL. H. T. Keen. 1965. 132p.
P4-S16404 — $19.00.

KEENE: KEAYNE — KEENE[E] — KEENEY — Kinne(y)-Kenney & allied families. By F.L.K. Robertson. 1942. 183p.
P4-S16428 — $27.00.

KEENE: Family history & genealogy. By E. Jones. 1923. 343p.
P4-S16434 — $54.50.

KEEP: John Keep of Longmeadow, MA, 1660-1676, & his desc. By F. E. Best. 1899. 263p.
P4-S16437 — $34.50.

KEESE: Fam. hist. & gen. 1690-1911. By W.T. Keese. 1911. 48p.
P4-S16435 — $10.00.

KEIGHLEY: Family (reprinted from "Yorkshire Archaelogical Jrnl."). By W. Paley Baildon. n.d. 109p.
P4-S16443 — $16.50.

KEIM: & Allied families in America & Europe. DeB. Randolph Keim. 1899. 736p.
P4-S16449 — $109.00.

KEIM: Acct. of the Keim fam. By H. M. Keim. 1874. 26p.
P4-S16450 — $10.00.

KEITH: Historical Account of the Noble Family of Keith up to 1745. P. Buchan. 1820. xii + 156p.
P4-S16456 — $25.95

KEITH: A gen. of the desc. of Benj. Keith through Timothy, son of Rev. James Keith. By Z. Keith. 1889. 114p.
P4-S16455 — $17.00.

KELKER: Gen. record of the family of Koelliker of Herrliburg, District Meilen, Canton Zurich, Switzerland . . . By J.J. Hess & R.F. Kelker. 1883. 132p.
P4-S16461 — $24.00.

KELLER: Descendants of Henry Keller of York Co., PA, & Fairfield Co., OH. By E. Shumaker, et al. 1924. 594p.
P4-S16422 — $89.50.

KELLER: History of the Keller fam. By E. Keller. 1905. 192p.
P4-S16473 — $29.50.

KELLER: The Kellers of Hamilton Twp. [PA]. By David H. Keller. 1922. 133p.
P4-S16479 — $21.00.

KELLEY: Genealogy; David O'Killia the immigrant of Old Yarmouth, MA, with his descendants & allied families By Eunice K. Randall. 1962. 818p.
P4-S16491 — $115.00.

KELLEY: Gen. history of the Kelley family, desc. from Joseph Kelley of Norwich, CT. By Hermon A. Kelley. 1897. 122 + 15p.
P4-S16485 — $21.00.

KELLEY: Reminiscences of New Hampton; also a gen. sketch of the Kelley & Simpson families. By Frank H. Kelley. 1929. 147p.
P4-S16497 — $19.50.

KELLOGG: Kelloggs of Colchester. By J. H. Perrin. 1894. 6p.
P4-S16501 — $10.00.

KELLOGG: Gen. items of the Kellogg family (Repr. NEHGR). By D. O. Kellogg. 1858-1860 14p.
P4-S16502 — $10.00.

KELLOGG: A supplement, containing notes on the families of Terry, White, & Woodbury. 1899. 45p.
P4-S16503 — $10.00.

KELLOGG: Notes on some of the descendants of Joseph Kellogg of Hadley. By J.P. Kellogg. 1898. 27p.
P4-S16504 — $10.00.

KELLOGG: The Kelloggs in the old world & the new, 3-volume set. By T. Hopkins 1903. 3 vols., 897 + 848 + 321p.
P4-S16500 — $255.00./set.

KELLY: Early Southwest Virginia families of Kelly, Smyth, Buchanan, Clark & related families of Edmonson, Keys, Beattie, etc. By Elizabeth Kelly Allison. 1960. 135p.
P4-S16548 — $21.00.

KELLY: Genealogy of the Kelly family. By T. M. Owen. 1900. 7p.
P4-S16507 — $10.00.

KELLY: History of James & Catherine Kelly & their descendants, By Richard T. Kelly. 1900. 114p.
P4-S16524 — $19.00.

KELLY: A gen. account of the descendants of John Kelly of Newbury, MA. G.M. Kelly. 1886. 178p.
P4-S16506 — $28.50.

KELLY: Ancestors & desc. of Seth Kelly, 1762-1850, of Blackstone, MA. By W. P. Kelly. 1937. 71p.
P4-S16512 — $14.00.

KELSEY: Fam. of New Eng. (extr. Bassett gen.). 1926. 6p.
P4-S16528 — $10.00.

KELSEY: Genealogy of the desc. of Wm. Kelsey, who settled at Cambridge MA in 1632; etc, vol I. By Claypool, Clizbee & Kelsey. 1928. 295p.
P4-S16530 — $47.00.

KELSEY: Genealogy of the desc. of Wm. Kelsey, who settled at Cambridge MA in 1632; etc, vol II. By Claypool, Clizbee & Kelsey. 1929. 424p.
P4-S16536 — $50.00.

KELSEY: Genealogy of the desc. of Wm. Kelsey, who settled at Cambridge MA in 1632; etc, vol III. By Claypool, Clizbee & Kelsey. 1947. 1018p.
P4-S16533 — $139.00.

KELSEY: Desc. of John Kelsey of Harvard & Shirley, MA. J. W. Kelsey. 3p.
P4-S16529 — $10.00.

KEMMERER: Two centuries of Kemmerer fam. hist., 1730-1929. By W. A. Backenstoe. 1929. 152p.
P4-S16542 — $27.00.

KEMP: The New England Kemps. By A.J. Weise. 1904. 193p.
P4-S16548 — $31.00.

KEMPER: Gen. of the Kemper family in the US: descendants of John Kemper of VA. By W.M. Kemper & H.L. Wright. 1899. 267p.
P4-S16554 — $41.00.

KENDALL: GELETTE Family history; The Kendall, Gelette & Ellis families of MN, from 1860. By W.W. Denny. 1994. 112p.
P4-S16560 — $19.00.

KENDALL: Memorial of Josiah Kendall, one of the first settlers of Sterling, MA & some of his anc. & of his desc. By O. Kendall. 1884. 153p.
P4-S16566 — $23.00.

KENDALL: Mem'l of Sam'l Reed & Matilda Thomas Kendall, & of their ancestors & of their descendants. By Ralph R. Kendall. 1936. 45p.
P4-S16561 — $10.00.

KENDALL: The Kendalls of Austrey, Twycross & Smithsby: a family history. By Henry John Broughton Kendall. 1909 64p.
P4-S16572 — $13.00.

KENDALL: Family record, descendants of Edward Kendall of Westminster, MA. E. S. Kendall. 1880. 11p.
P4-S16562 — $10.00.

KENDALL: Family in America. By W.M. Clemens. 1919. 24p.
P4-S16563 — $10.00.

KENDERDINE: The Kenderdines of America: Being a Gen. & Hist. Account of the Desc. of Thomas Kenderdine, of Montgomery Shire, Wales. Thaddeus Stevens Kenderdine. 1901. 275 + 27p.
P4-S16573 — $46.00.

KENFIELD: History: some lines of descent from William Canfield of Northampton, MA. By Earl P. Crandall. 1993. 125p.
P4-S16578 — $19.50.

KENNAMER: Family. By John R. Kennamer & Lorrin G. Kennamer. 1924. 375p.
P4-S16584 — $58.00.

KENNAN: Gen. of the Kennan fam. By T.L. Kennan. 1907. 134p.
P4-S16590 — $20.00.

KENNEDY: Hist. & gen. acct. of the principal fams. of the name of Kennedy, with notes & illus. R. Pitcairn. 1830 218p.
P4-S16602 — $34.50.

KENNEDY: History of the descendants of Wm. Kennedy & his wife Mary of Marion Henderson,1730-1880 By Elias D. Kennedy. 1881. 86p.
P4-S16608 — $17.00.

KENNEDY: Some descendants of Andrew Kennedy & Margaret (Peggy) Hatfield, 1824-1989. By Genevieve Curran Kennedy. 1989. 302p.
P4-S16614 — $49.50.

KENNEDY: Family records. By J. Montgomery Seaver. 1929. 34p.
P4-S16597 — $10.00.

KENNEDY: Early American history; Kennedy & allied families. By W. E. Brockman. 1926. 71p.
P4-S16596 — $14.00.

KENT: Gen. of the different families bearing the name of Kent in the US, their possible English ancestry, 1295-1898. By L.V. Briggs. 1898. 346p.
P4-S16626 — $44.00.

KENT: Letters & other papers of Daniel Kent, Emigrant & Redemptioner By E.L. Barnard. 1904. 135p.
P4-S16632 — $25.00.

KENT: Descendants of Absalom Kent of Eng. & VA. By A.S. Kent. 1933. 101p.
P4-S16620 — $19.00.

KENYON: American Kenyons: History of Kenyons & English connections of American Kenyons; By H.N. Kenyon. 1935. 285p.
P4-S16638 — $44.50.

KENYON: Genealogy of the family of Nathaniel Kenyon. By Byron M. Herrington. 1961. 90p., typescript.
P4-S16644 — $18.00.

KERFOOT: KEARFOTT & allied families in America. By R.R. Kearfott. 1948. 170p.
P4-S16650 — $28.00.

KERLEY: & allied fam. of the South. By W.C. Carley. 1945. 128p.
P4-S16656 — $25.00.

KERR: Joseph Kerr of Ballygoney & his descendants. By Mary Alice K. Arbuckle. 1904. 188p.
P4-S16662 — $28.00.

KERR: Clan of NJ, beginning with Walter Kerr of Freehold & ending with other related lines. By Wm. C. Armstrong. 1931. 196p.
P4-S16668 — $29.50.

KETCHAM: Genealogy of the Ketcham & Kutch families: twelve & eight generations respectively. By Melcherd H. Kutch. 1939. 207p.
P4-S16674 — $29.50.

KETCHAM: Family: descendants of John Ketcham & his wife Sarah Matthews of Mt Hope Twp., Orange Co., NY. By Electa K. Penney. 1954. 62 + 48p.
P4-S16680 — $19.00.

KETEL: Family, also Ketel, Kettel, Kittelle & Kittle. By Sumner E.W. Kittelle. 1946. 67p.
P4-S16686 — $14.50.

KETTENRING: Kettenring Family. H.H. Catron. 1966. 720p.
P4-S16688 — $105.00.

KETTERMAN: Family history. By L.C. Ketterman. 1985. 380p.
P4-S16692 — $59.00.

KEY: & allied families. By J.C. Lane. 1931. 495p.
P4-S16698 — $74.25

KEYES: Gen. & history if the related Keyes, North & Cruzen families, with a sketch of the early Norths of England. Millard F. Stipes. 1914. 321p.
P4-S16704 — $49.00.

KEYES: Gen. of Robert Keyes of Watertown, MA, 1633, Solomon Keyes of Newbury & Chelmsford, MA, 1653, & descendants. A. Keyes. 1880. 326p.
P4-S16707 — $41.50.

KIDDER: Genealogy of the Kidder family, comprising the desc. in the male line of Ensign James Kidder, 1626-1676, of Cambridge & Billerica, MA By M.H. Stafford. 1941. 750p.
P4-S16713 — $109.00.

KIDDER: Hist. of the Kidder fam., 1320-1676, incl. the biogr. of our emigr. anc. James Kidder F. Kidder. 1886. 174p.
P4-S16716 — $26.50.

KILBOURN: History & antiquity of the name & family of Kilbourn (in various orthographies). By P. Kilbourne. 1856. 444p.
P4-S16719 — $57.50.

KILBOURNE: Descendants of Jonathan Richmond Kilbourne & Mary Martin Kilbourne. By Ronald R. Kilbourne. 1997. 74p.
P4-S16725 — $15.00.

KILGORE: Charles Kilgore of King's Mountain: A New History of The Kilgore Family. Hugh M. Addington. 1935. 154 + 30p.
P4-S16727 — $27.95

KILGORE: Family, desc. of Joseph Kilgore of Scotland & York, ME, 1690-1888. 5p.
P4-S16728 — $10.00.

KILLAM: Genealogy of the Killam family of Essex Co., MA. By S. Perley. 1913. 29p.
P4-S16733 — $10.00.

KILMER: History of the Kilmer family in Amer. By C.H. Kilmer. 1897. 214p.
P4-S16737 — $28.00.

KIMBALL: WESTON Memorial, the American anc & desc. of Alonzo & Sarah (Weston) Kimball of Green Bay, WI. By Wm. Herbert Hobbs. 1902. 103p. + chart
P4-S16746 — $19.00.

KIMBALL: The Lt. Moses & Jemima Clement Kimball fam. By P. K. Skinner. 1941. 138p.
P4-S16764 — $20.50.

KIMBALL: History of the Kimball family in America, 1634-1897; also anc. of the Kemballs or Kemboldes of Eng. By L.A. Morrison & S.P. Sharples. 1897. 1278p.
P4-S16740 — $151.00.

KIMBALL: The Joseph Kimball family: gen. memoir of the ascendants & descendants of Joseph Kimball of Canterbury, NH. J. Kimball. 1885. 103p.
P4-S16758 — $18.00.

KIMBALL: Record of the family of Levi Kimball & some of his descendants. L. Darbee. 1861, rev. 1913. 173p.
P4-S16752 — $25.75

KIMBALL: Family book; includes Allgood, Curtis, Kimballs in IN & NE, Roberts, Wendell & Deutsch. By Joan Hommon Kimball. 2002. 67p.
P4-S16766 — $14.00.

KIMBER: Gen. hist. of the desc. of Richard Kimber of Grove, Berks., Eng. By S.A. Kimber. 1894. 91p.
P4-S16770 — $17.50.

KIMBERLY: Genealogy of the Kimberly family. By Donald L. Jacobus. 1950. 176p
P4-S16776 — $27.00.

KIMBLE: Genealogy of Jacob Kimble of the Paupack Settlement, Wayne & Pike Co., PA & his descendants By Mr & Mrs J.H. Scheider & Howard Kimble. 1952. 53p.
P4-S16777 — $11.00.

KINCHELOE: McPHERSON & Related Families. Their Genealogies & Biographies, Lewin Dwindell McPherson. 1951. 509p.
P4-S16784 — $76.50.

KING: Clement King of Marshfield, MA, 1668, & his descendants. By G.A. Morrison, Jr. 1898. 65p.
P4-S16785 — $13.00.

KING: Family: brief gen. history of Dr Robert King, a settler of Blanford, Berkshire Co., MA. By Sylvester M. King. 1883. 59p.
P4-S16806 — $12.00.

KING: Genealogy of the King family. By the American Heraldic Society. 1930. 199p. typescript.
P4-S16797 — $29.50.

KING: Genealogy of Jacob King (Konig) & Matheus King (Konig) 0f Northampton Co, PA. By Wilbur L. King. 1951. 119p.
P4-S16791 — $18.00.

KING: United King [family] book, 1820-1960 [descendants of Thos. King of SC]. By Guy L. King. 1960. 141p.
P4-S16821 — $27.00.

KING: Children of William & Dorothy King of Salem. H. F. Waters. 1880. 7p.
P4-S16798 — $10.00.

KING: Fam. of Suffield, CT. By E. J. Cleveland. 1892. 6p.
P4-S16799 — $10.00.

KING: Family of Suffield, CT, its Eng. anc., 1389-1662, & Amer. desc., 1662-1908. By C. King. 1908. 655p.
P4-S16803 — $63.50.

KING: Fam. of Yorkshire & GA, extr. from the Habersham gen. 1901. 10p.
P4-S16800 — $10.00.

KING: Genealogy & its branches Moultons, Sedgwicks & Shaws, & their descendants By Harvey B. King. 1897. 142p.
P4-S16815 — $24.00.

KINGMAN: Desc. of Henry Kingman. Some early gen. of the Kingman fam. By B. Kingman. 1912. 102p.
P4-S16827 — $15.00.

KINGSBURY: Genealogy of the desc. of Henry Kingsbury of Ipswich & Haverhill, MA. By F.J. Kingsbury & M.K. Talcott. 1905. 732p.
P4-S16836 — $92.00.

KINGSBURY: Gen. rec. of the early Eng. anc. to Amer., & lines of desc. to Nathaniel Kingsbury of Keene, NH & desc. of three daughters By F.B. Kingsbury. 1904. 63p.
P4-S16830 — $12.50.

KINGSBURY: Pendulous edition of Kingsbury genealogy, gathered by Rev. Addison Kingsbury. comp. by Jos. Addison Kingsbury. 1901. 258p.
P4-S16842 — $39.50.

KINNE: Genealogy of Henry & Ann Kinne, pioneers of Salem, MA. By Florance K. Robertson. 1947. 218p.
P4-S16848 — $33.50.

KINNE: History & genealogy of a branch of the family of Kinne. By Emerson Kinne. 1881. 96p.
P4-S16854 — $18.00.

KINNEAR: The Kinnears & their kin; A mem. vol. of hist., biogr. & gen. By White & Maltby. 1916. 596p.
P4-S16860 — $89.00.

KINNEY: Bible records. 2p.
P4-S16873 — $10.00.

KINNEY: Some VA families, being gen. of the Kinney, Stribling, Trout, McIlhany & other families of VA. By Hugh M. McIlhany. 1903. 274p.
P4-S16872 — $35.00.

KINNICK: Family; Gen. history of the Kinnick family in America: desc. of John Kinnick & Ann Kinnick of Davie Co., NC. By Nettie E.K. Waggener. 1953. 355p.
P4-S16878 — $55.00.

KINSEY: A History of Jacob Kinsey (Kintzy) & his descendants. By Wm. Kinsey. 1934. 202p.
P4-S16884 — $33.50.

KINSEY: A family history. By G.S. Kinsey. 35p.
P4-S16883 — $10.00.

KINSLAND: The Kinslands & related lines. By Robert & Connie Medford & Jean P. Warren. 2000. 360p.
P4-S16890 — $55.00.

KINSMAN: Genealogy of Robert Kinsman of Ipswich, MA. By T.F. Waters. 1909. 15p.
P4-S16897 — $10.00.

KINSMAN: Gen. record of the desc. of Robt. Kinsman of Ipswich, MA, 1624-1875. By L.W. Stickney. 1876. 258p.
P4-S16896 — $39.50.

KINTER: KINDER/KINTER Family of No. America & the Connection to Ireland, Scotland, England, Germany & the Netherlands. By Wm. P. Kinter. 1998. 329p.
P4-S16902 — $49.50.

KIP: Hist. notes of fam. of Kip of Kipsburg & Kips Bay, NY. By W.I. Kip. 1871. 49p.
P4-S16909 — $10.00.

KIP: History of the Kip family in America. By Kip & Hawley. 1928. 462p.
P4-S16908 — $71.00.

KIRBY: The Kirbys of New Eng. A hist. of the desc. of John Kirby of Middletown, CT & of Joseph Kirby of Hartford, CT, etc. By M. E. Dwight. 1898. 455p.
P4-S16911 — $57.00.

KIRBY: A Three Family Genealogy: A Hist. & Gen. Record of the Kirby Family, the Durkee Family & the Walker Family. John Walker Kirby. 1944. 92 + 6p.
P4-S16912 — $15.00.

KIRK: Genealogy of the descendants of John Kirk, 1660-1705. M. S. Roberts, ed. By G. Cope. 1912-1913. 729p.
P4-S16917 — $99.50.

KIRK: Hist. gen. of the Kirk fam., as established by Roger Kirk, who settled at Nottingham, Chester Co., PA, C. 1714, By C. H. Stubbs. 1872. 252p.
P4-S16923 — $31.00.

KIRKBRIDE: Brief hist. of Kirkbride fam., with specific reference to desc. of David Kirkbride 1775-1830. By S. A. Kirkbride. 1913. 64p.
P4-S16926 — $12.50.

KIRKPATRICK: Capt. John Kirkpatrick of NJ, 1739-1822, & his sisters Mrs Jos. Linn & Mrs Stephen Roy. By Wm. C. Armstrong. 1927. 81p.
P4-S16935 — $16.00.

KIRTLAND: or Kirkland fam. (Repr. NEHGR). 20p.
P4-S16936 — $10.00.

KISSAM: Family in America, from 1644-1825. By Edw. Kissam. 1892. 93p.
P4-S16941 — $18.00.

KISTLER: Kistler fam., desc. from George Kistler, Jr. of Berks Co., PA. By F. K. Sprague. 1944. 47p.
P4-S16948 — $10.00.

KITCHEL: and his descendants, from 1604-1879. By H.D. Kitchel. 1879. 80p.
P4-S16953 — $16.00.

KITCHEL: John Kitchel & Esther Peck, their ancestors, descendants & some kindred families. By Geo. C. McCormick. 1913. 136p.
P4-S16949 — $21.00.

KITE: Kite fam. By V. A. Kite. 122p.
P4-S16959 — $23.50.

KITTREDGE: Family in America. By M.T. Kittredge. 1936. 215p.
P4-S16965 — $32.50.

KLEIN: George Klein, Sr., family record. By Floyd R. & Kathryn G. Mason. 1997. 143p.
P4-S16971 — $21.50.

KLINE: Klan [of NJ]. 1960. 173p.
P4-S16977 — $26.50.

KLING: Genealogical history of John Ludwig Kling & his descendants, 1755-1924. Margaret E. Kling. 1924. 145p.
P4-S16983 — $23.00.

KLOPFENSTEIN: Family record: chronology of the descendants of Michael Klopfenstein, 1757-1925. By John Henry Klopfenstein. 1926. 68p.
P4-S16989 — $14.00.

KNAPP: Nicholas Knapp genealogy. By Alfred A. Knapp. 1953. 900p.
P4-S16998 — $119.50.

KNAPP: Supplement to Nicholas Knapp genealogy. By Alfred A. Knapp. 1956. 105p., typescript.
P4-S17004 — $19.00.

KNAPP: Fam. in Amer; A gen. of the desc. of Wm. Knapp, who settled in Watertown MA in 1630, incl. a pedigree of Hiram Knapp. By A. Knapp. 1909. 76p.
P4-S16992 — $15.00.

KNAUSS: Hist. & gen. of the Knauss family in America, tracing back the records to Ludwig Knauss to the year 1723. By James O. Knauss & Tilghman J. Knauss. 1915. 242p.
P4-S17010 — $37.50.

KNAUSS: Genealogy: Lukas Knauss (1633-1713) of Dudelsheim, Germany, & his American descendants. By Wilbur L. King. 1930. 239p.
P4-S17016 — $36.50.

KNAVE: Henry & Margaret Knave of PA & Rockingham Co., VA. By Floyd R. & Kathryn G. Mason. 2002. 155p.
P4-S17022 — $23.00.

KNEELAND: Seven centuries in the Kneeland fam. S. F. Kneeland. 1897. 583p.
P4-S17025 — $74.00.

KNEISLY: Kneisly gen. By H. Kneisly. 1932. 46p.
P4-S17026 — $10.00.

KNEPPER: Gen. of Knepper fam. of US, 1681-1911. M. Knepper. 1911. 132p.
P4-S17037 — $22.50.

KNICKERBACKER: VIELE; Sketches of allied families, to which is added an appendix containing family data. By K.K. Viele. 1916. 134p.
P4-S17037 — $22.50.

KNIGHT: Statistics & story of the descendants of Elijah & Enice Knight, 1804-1960. Harriet C. Moore. 1961. 126p.
P4-S17055 — $19.50.

KNIGHT: Jesse Knight family: Jesse Knight, his forebears & family. By Jesse Wm. Knight. 1941. 140p.
P4-S17049 — $25.00.

KNIGHT: History of the Knight Association, with genealogy. 1915. 102p.
P4-S17043 — $17.50.

KNIGHT: Family. By J. C. Martindale. 1911. 16p.
P4-S17044 — $10.00.

KNISELY: WOLF — NORRIS — McCOY Families. J.C. Knisely. 1923. 81p.
P4-S17061 — $16.00.

KNOWLES: Fam. of Eastham, MA. By C. T. Libby. 72p.
P4-S17067 — $14.00.

KNOWLTON: Family in England & No. America. Wm. P. Kinter. 1998. 60p.
P4-S17079 — $12.00.

KNOWLTON: Errata & addenda; with a complete index to both books. By G. H. Knowlton. 1903. 239p.
P4-S17073 — $36.00.

KNOWLTON: History & genealogy of the Knowltons of England & America. C. H. W. Stocking. 1897. 610p.
P4-S17076 — $77.50.

KNOX: Genealogical memoirs of John Knox, & of the family of Knox. By Charles Rogers. 1879. 184p.
P4-S17088 — $28.00.

KNOX: William Knox of Blandford, MA, a record of the births, marriages & deaths of some of his desc. By N. Foote. 1926. 302p.
P4-S17100 — $48.50.

KNOX: Fam.; Gen. & biogr. sketch of the desc. of John Knox of Rowan Co., NC & others. H. Goodman. 1905. 266p.
P4-S17094 — $35.00.

KOCH: Thirty ancestors of Richard Henry Koch (Koch, Neufang, Bock, Bolich, Beck, et al). By R.H. Koch. 1939. 327p.
P4-S17106 — $49.50.

KOINER: Historical sketch of Michael Keinadt & Margaret Diller, his wife By A.K., A.T. & E.T. Koiner. 1893. 171p.
P4-S17112 — $27.50.

KOINER: Supplement only. 1941. 34p.
P4-S17113 — $10.00.

KOLB: KULP — CULP Family. comp. by the History Committee. 1936. 110p.
P4-S17130 — $22.00.

KOLB: Gen. history of the Kolb, Kulp or Culp family & its branches in America, with bio. Sketches of descendants Dan'l K. Cassel. 1895. 584p.
P4-S17124 — $88.50.

KOLB: Dielman Kolb & his desc., 1648-1880, (in Custer gen.) By A. W. Storer. 60p.
P4-S17115 — $12.00.

KOLLOCK: Gen. of the Koolock fam. of Sussex Co., DE, 1657-1897. By E.J. Sellers. 1897. 76p.
P4-S17136 — $15.00.

KOPPES: Chronological outline & geographical directory of the Koppes family. By C.W. Koppes. 1917. 85p. **P4-S17142 — $16.00.**

KORSBOEN: Desc. of Selected Fams: Korsboen [Holt, Hunders], Pfoerter [Fadner, Beyel]. Lawrence T. Fadner. 2005. 388p. **P4-S17143 — $58.00.**

KOTHE: Biographical & other material related to the Kothe family, 1748-1891. By W. Kothe. 1961. 74p. **P4-S17148 — $15.00.**

KRATZ: A brief hist. of John Valentine Kratz, & a complete gen. fam. register. By A. J. Fretz. 1892. 315p. **P4-S17154 — $41.50.**

KREGEL: Genealogy of Peter Kregel of Grambow, Prov. of Pommern, Germany, & his descendants By John H. Schneider. 1941. 52p. **P4-S17155 — $10.50.**

KREKLER: & Related families. By Bessie K. Schafer. 1963. 35p. **P4-S17156 — $10.00.**

KRESS: Family history [of Germany, with an American line]. By K.F. von Frank zu Dofering, American genealogy By C.R. Roberts. 1931 (Austria) 770p. **P4-S17160 — $135.00.**

KRUMBEIN: Gen. of the Krumbein, Grumbine & Crumbine family, with a history of Leonard Krumbein By Clinton b. Krumbine. 1918. 265p. **P4-S17166 — $39.50.**

KUNDERS: Some scraps of history regarding Thomas Kunders & his children By H. Conrad. 1891. 128p **P4-S17172 — $21.00.**

KUYKENDALL: Family, since its settlement in Dutch NY in 1646, with genealogy. By Geo. B. Kuykendall. 1919. 665p. **P4-S17178 — $99.00.**

KYLE: Partial hist. of Kyle, Kile, Coyle fam. in Amer. O. M. Kile. 1958. 186p. **P4-S17184 — $35.00.**

L

LABAR: Labar Patchworks: William LaBar, 1709-1761 & His Descendants. Phyllis Parmley 1988. iv + 383p. **P4-S17185 — $58.00.**

LABAREE: History of the desc. of Peter Labaree, Charlestown, NH. By Jane Labaree. 1912. 89p. **P4-S17190 — $18.00.**

LACY: The roll of the house of Lacy. Pedigrees, mil. memoirs & synoptical hist. of the ancient & illustrious fam. of deLacy . . . By deLacy-Bellingari. 1928. 417p. **P4-S17196 — $65.00.**

LADD: Family; Descendants of Daniel of Haverhill, MA, Joseph of Portsmouth, NH; John of Burlington, NJ; John of Charles City Co., VA. By W. Ladd. 1890. 425p. **P4-S17199 — $57.00.**

LADUE: Ancestors & descendants of Sarah Eleanor Ladue. By Mrs Grant Rideout. 1930. 390p. **P4-S17205 — $59.50.**

LaFLECHE: La genealogie des familles Richer de la Fleche et Hamelin, avec notes historiques sur Sainte Anne de la Perade, les Grondines, etc. par F.L. Desauliers. 1909. IN FRENCH. 241p. **P4-S17211 — $37.50.**

LaFOLLETTE: History of the La Follette family in America. By John H. LaFollette. 1898. 84p. **P4-S17217 — $16.00.**

LAIN: Descendants of Wm. Lain & Keziah Mather, with her lineage from Rev. Richard Mather, By Beatrice L. Sheehan. 1957. 311p.

P4-S17223 — $47.00.

LAKE: Genealogy of the Lake family of Great Egg Harbor, NJ, desc. from John Lake of Gravesend, L. I. By A. Adams & S. Risley. 1915. 386p. **P4-S17229 — $60.00.**

LAKE: A Personal Narrative of Some Branches of the Lake Family in America. Devereux Lake. 1937. vi + 256p. **P4-S17230 — $38.50.**

LAKIN: The Lakin Family, Desc of Abraham Lakin & Martha Lee Lakin of Prince George's Co., MD. David V. Agricola, MD. 1989. xii + 154p. **P4-S17231 — $25.00.**

LAMAR: History of the Lamar or Lemar fmaily in Aermica. By Harol D. LeMar. 1941. 338 + 86p. **P4-S17235 — $64.50.**

LAMAR: Genealogy & history, a branch of the family of Lamar By Edward Mays. 1935. 74p. **P4-S17241 — $15.00.**

LAMB: MERRILL Family: "Lest our children forget," By Harriet J. Stradling. 1960. 300p. **P4-S17253 — $46.00.**

LAMB: Genealogical sketch of the Lamb family. Fred W. Lamb. 1903. 7p. **P4-S17248 — $10.00.**

LAMB: My North Carolina heritage, vol. 3: Descendants of Henry & Elizabeth Lamb of NC, a Quaker family legacy. By Marshall L. Styles. 2000. 525p. **P4-S17259 — $78.50.**

LAMB: Genealogy of the Lamb, Rose & others. By Dan'l S. Lamb. 1904. 100p. **P4-S17247 — $19.00.**

LAMB: Family marriages. By W. M. Clemens. 1916. 40p. **P4-S17249 — $10.00.**

LAMB: The Lambs of MN. By Harold E. Lamb. 24p. **P4-S17250 — $10.00.**

LAMB: Nathan Lamb of Leicester, MA, his anc. & desc. By C. F. Lamb. 1930. 96p. **P4-S17265 — $19.00.**

LAMBERT: The Lambert fam. of Salem, MA & the wife of Thomas Lord of Hartford, CT (Repr. Essex Inst. Hist. Coll.) By H. W. Belknap. 1918. 48p. **P4-S17266 — $10.00.**

LAMBERT: Roger Lambert & his desc. By I. Lambert. 1933. 61p. **P4-S17268 — $12.50.**

LAMBORN: Genealogy of the Lamborn fam., with extr. from hist., biog., anecdotes. S. Lamborn. 1894. 487p. **P4-S17277 — $62.00.**

LAMONT: ELDREDGE Family records. By B.E. Lamont. 1948. 334p. **P4-S17283 — $53.00.**

LAMPTON: Sketch of the Lampton fam. in Amer., 1740-1914. By C. Keith. 1914. 59p. **P4-S17286 — $12.00.**

LAMSON: Descendants of William Lamson of Ipswich, MA, 1634-1917. By W. Lamson. 1917. 414p.
P4-S17295 — $65.00.

LAMSON: Memorial of Elder Ebenezer Lamson of Concord, MA, his anc. & desc., 1635-1908. By O. & F. Lamson. 1908. 125p.
P4-S17301 — $19.00.

LANCASTER: Family of MD & KY: hist. of English ancestry, emigr. to the Col. of MD, Pioneers of KY. By Samuel Lancaster. n.d. 200p.
P4-S17313 — $32.50.

LANCASTER: Family. Thomas & Phebe Lancaster of Bucks Co. PA & their descendants, 1711-1902. By H.L. Lancaster. 1902. 302p.
P4-S17319 — $39.50.

LANCASTER: Joseph Lancaster of Amesbury & some of his desc. By J. S. Ware. 1933. 125p.
P4-S17307 — $20.00.

LANDIS: Fam. of Lancaster Co. By D.B. Landis. 1888. 90p.
P4-S17325 — $17.50.

LANDIS: Report of the 31st reunion of the Landis-Landes families held at Perkasie Park, Perkasie, Bucks Co., PA, 8/19/50. 1950. 65p.
P4-S17331 — $13.00.

LANDON: Genealogy: French & English home & ancestry, with some acct. of the descendants of James & Mary Vaill Landon in Amer. By J.O. Landon. 1928. 402p.
P4-S17337 — $62.50.

LANE: LAYNE — LAIN Genealogy, being a compilation of names & historical information of male descendants of 16 branches F.B. Layne. 1962. 336p.
P4-S17358 — $52.00.

LANE: Mem. relating to the Lane, Reyner, & Whipple fam., Yorkshire & MA. By W.H. Whitmore. 1857. 24p.
P4-S17344 — $10.00.

LANE: & a Cast of Thousands: Hist. of the Lane Family of Canada & the US, from their Arrival in 1819 to the Present. James K. Raywalt. 1989. 751p.
P4-S17343 — $89.50.

LANE: Genealogy. By Chapman & Fitts. 3 vols. 1891-1902. 1034p.
P4-S17352 — $105.00.

LANE: Families of the MA Bay Colony [memorial address at family reunion]. By James P. Lane. 1886. 58p.
P4-S17346 — $12.00.

LANG: Gen. of the first five generations in America of the Lang family, descendants of Robert Lang, of the Isle of Shoals & Sagamore Creek By Howard P. Moore. 1935. 91p.
P4-S17364 — $18.00.

LANGDON: John Langdon of Portsmouth, NH (Rambles about Portsmouth) By C. Brewster. 1873. 5p.
P4-S17365 — $10.00.

LANGDON: Gen. matter rel. to the late Rev. Samuel Langdon & his wife Elizabeth Brown, anc. & desc. 4p.
P4-S17366 — $10.00.

LANGLEY: Wm. Langley & his desc. By C.H. Wight. 16p.
P4-S17368 — $10.00.

LANSDALE: Two colonial families, the Lansdales of MD & the Luces of New England. By Maria H. Lansdale. 1938. 103p.
P4-S17382 — $19.00.

LANSING: Family: a gen. of the desc. of Gerrit Frederickse Lansing, who came to America from Hasselt, Province of Overijssell, Holland By Claude G. Munsell. 1916. 114p.
P4-S17388 — $21.00.

LANTZ: Family record, being a brief acct. of the Lantz fam. in the US. By Jacob W. Lantz. 1931. 265p.
P4-S17394 — $41.50.

LAPHAM: Lapham fam. register; or, records of some of the desc. of Thomas Lapham of Scituate, MA in 1635. By W. B. Lapham. 1873. 31p.
P4-S17401 — $10.00.

LAPHAM: Concerning John Lapham & some of his descendants. By M.W. Perkins. 1948? 67p.
P4-S17400 — $13.50.

LAPHAM: History & genealogy of the Lapham, Wells, Storle & Johnson families. By O. Lapham. 1934. 29p.
P4-S17402 — $10.00.

LAPHAM: Family in America: 13,000 descendants, incl. desc. of John (Devonshire, Eng. to Providence, RI, 1673) & Thomas (Kent, Eng. to Scituate, MA, 1634) By B.B.B. Aldridge. 1953. 552p.
P4-S17406 — $85.00.

LARIMER: McMASTERS & allied families. By R. Mellon. 1903. 196p.
P4-S17418 — $26.50.

LARY: Family genealogy: Daniel Lary of NH & his descendants. By Carleton E. Fisher. 1977. 83p.
P4-S17418 — $16.50.

LASH: History of the descendants of Jacob Lash, since 1740, & of John Brannum, since 1776. By Dorothy S. Lathrop. 1939? 63p.
P4-S17424 — $13.50.

LASHER: Genealogy. C. Rich. 1904. 270p.
P4-S17430 — $40.00.

LATHAM: Gen. of Latham-Hill-Montfort-Littlejohn- McCulloch-Campbell-Brownrigg fam. By W. Bailey 1899. 66p.
P4-S17433 — $12.50.

LATHROP: Gen memoir of the Lo-Lathrop fam. The desc. of Rev. John Lathrop of Scituate & Barnstable, MA. By E. B. Huntington. 1884. 464p.
P4-S17445 — $58.00.

LATHROP: Ancestors & descendants of Francis Lathrop, 1545-1992. By Lois Roberta Cook White. 1992. 82p.
P4-S17442 — $16.50.

LATIMER: A brief history & gene-alogy of George Griswold Latimer. By Madison C. Bates. 1919. 56p.
P4-S17446 — $11.00.

LATOURETTE: Annals in America. By Lyman E. Latourette. 1954. 132p.
P4-S17451 — $22.00.

LAUBACH: Hist. & gen. of one branch of the Laubach family, from the time of their arrival in America until the Present Time. By harvey H. Laubach. 1940. 93p.
P4-S17457 — $19.00.

LAUCKS: Family in PA. By Robert L. Laucks. 2001. 123p.
P4-S17463 — $21.00.

LAUDER: Notes on hist. references to the Scottish fam. of Lauder. By J. Young. 1884. 154p.
P4-S17469 — $21.00.

LAUDERDALE: The Lauderdales of Scotland & America, 1056-1936. By Chas. J. Lauderdale. 1937. 91p.
P4-S17475 — $18.00.

LAUFFER: A gen. chart of the desc. of Christian Lauffer, the pioneer. By J. A. Lauffer. 1906. 188p.
P4-S17481 — $35.00.

LAUGHLIN: History, 1807-1912, prepared for the reunion held at Bellecenter, OH, 1912. By John W. Laughlin. 1912. 123p.
P4-S17493 — $21.00.

LAUGHLIN: Hist., 1807-1907. By J.W. Laughlin. 1907. 64p.
P4-S17494 — $12.50.

LAUGHTER: Family genealogy. By Douglas Laughter. n.d. 175p.
P4-S17499 — $27.00.

LAVOCAT: Family in America, from 1845-1929. Matilda V. Baillif. 1929. 153p.
P4-S17505 — $24.00.

LAWRENCE: Descendants of Maj. Sam'l Lawrence of Groton, MA with some mention of allied families. By R. Lawrence. 1904. 355p.
P4-S17514 — $44.00.

LAWRENCE: A Diary & Remi-niscences Life & Times of William Van Duzer Lawrence. W.V.D. Lawrence. 1922. 234p.
P4-S17512 — $35.00.

LAWRENCE: Gen. memoir of the families of Lawrences, with a direct male line from Sir Robert Lawrence of Lancashire, a.d. 1199 By Mercy Hale. 1856. 20p.
P4-S17513 — $10.00.

LAWRENCE: Genealogical notices of the Lawrence family. 1867. 32p.
P4-S17515 — $10.00.

LAWRENCE: Family of Lawrence-Goss-Pomroy. J. Lawrence. 1881. 92p.
P4-S17526 — $17.50.

LAWRENCE: Gen. of the family of John Lawrence of Wisset, Suffolk, Eng. & of Watertown & Groton, MA. By J. Lawrence. 1869. 332p.
P4-S17535 — $43.00.

LAWRENCE: Genealogical memoir of the family of John Lawrence of Watertown, 1636 By John Lawrence. 1847. 64p.
P4-S17532 — $13.00.

LAWRENCE: Mem. of Robt. Lawrence, Robt. Bartlett, & their desc. By H.B. Lawrence. 1888. 223p.
P4-S17556 — $29.00.

LAWRENCE: Hist. gen. of the Lawrence fam., 1635-1858. By T. Lawrence. 1858. 240p.
P4-S17538 — $32.00.

LAWRENCE: Hist. sketches of some members of the Lawrence fam. By R.M. Lawrence. 1888. 215p.
P4-S17544 — $32.00.

LAWRENCE: The Newbold Lawrence family: Echoes from the past [family history, stories, letters, etc]. Caroline T. Lawrence. 1931. 176p.
P4-S17562 — $25.00.

LAWRENCE: The Mystery Solved: Facts Relating to the "Lawrence-Townley" & "Chase-Townley" Marriage. F.A. Hill. 1888. 94p.
P4-S17533 — $14.00.

LAWRENCE: St Albans origin of John Lawrence of New Amsterdam, Thomas Lawrence of Newtown, L.I., Wm. Lawrence of Flushing, l.I. By Consuelo Furman. 1955. 51p., typescript.
P4-S17563 — $10.00.

LAWRENCE: Divine covenant fulfilled in the ancestral family history of the Lawrence-Hughes & Eldredge gene-rations of Cape May Co., NJ. By Daneil L. Hughes. 1891. 161p.
P4-S17520 — $24.00.

LAWRENCE: An historic family: the Lawrences & associated families. By James Reed Lawrence, Jr. 1999. 430p.
P4-S17511 — $65.00.

LAWRENCE: History of the Lawrence-Townley & Chase-Townley estates in England By James Usher. 1883. 110p.
P4-S17550 — $19.50.

LAWSON: CHESTER Genealogy. comp. By Altshuler Gen. Svc. 1946. 50p.
P4-S17564 — $10.00.

LAY: Desc. of Robert Lay of Saybrook, CT (Repr. NEHGR) E. A. Hill. 1908. 12p.
P4-S17565 — $10.00.

LAYNE: Genealogy. By F.B. Layne. 1953. 251p.
P4-S17568 — $39.00.

LAZELL: John Lazell of Hingham, MA & some desc. (repr. NEHGR) By T. S. Lazell. 107p.
P4-S17574 — $18.00.

Le MAITRE: Connecting With Our Past: A Genealogy of Descendants of Claude Le Maitre. Philip D. Delamarter. 2002. 2 vols., 1360 + 29p.
P4-S17575 — $175.00.

LE VAN: Genealogical Record of the Le Van Family; Descendants of Daniel Le Van and Marie Beau. Warren Patten Coon. 1927. 356p.
P4-S17576 — $53.00.

LEA: Ancestry & posterity of John Lea of Christian Malford, Wilts., Eng., & PA, 1503-1906. By J.H. & G.H. Lea. 1906. 611p.
P4-S17580 — $91.50.

LEACH: Lawrence Leach of Salem, MA & some of his desc. By L.P. Leach. 1924-6. 344p.
P4-S17586 — $55.00.

LEADBETTER: Records. By J. E. Ames. 1917. 317p.
P4-S17592 — $49.50.

LEAKE: Families of Va., Vol. I: the Leake family & connecting lines. By Geo. W. Chappelear. 1932. 84p.
P4-S17598 — $17.00.

LEARNED: Fam. (Learned, Larned, Learnard, Lannard, & Lerned), being desc. of Wm. Learned who was of Charlestown, MA in 1632. By W.L. Learned. 2nd ed., 1898. 510p.
P4-S17604 — $78.00.

LEAS: Genealogy. By Fay W. Leas. 1930. 52p.
P4-S17581 — $11.00.

LEAS: Genealogy. By Fay W. Leas. 1950. 166p.
P4-S17610 — $24.00.

LEATHERS: Edward Leathers & his desc. (Repr. Dover Inquirer) By A. H. Quint. 1891. 13p.
P4-S17611 — $10.00.

LEAVELL: Genealogy of the Nine Leavell Brothers of Oxford, MS Comp by Charlotte Henry Leavell 1957. xiii + 185 + 40p.
P4-S17612 — $35.95

LEAVENS: Name, incl. Levings, 1632-1903. By P. Leavens. 1903. 152p.
P4-S17613 — $23.00.

LEAVENS: Name, its origin & track thru New Eng. to Northern VT. By P.F. Leavens. 1889. 29p.
P4-S17614 — $10.00.

LEAVENWORTH: A genealogy of the Leavenworth family in the US, - 1873. 376p.
P4-S17619 — $58.50.

LEAVITT: The Leavitts of Amer: a comp. of five branches & gleanings from New Eng. to CA & Canada. By C.G. Steer. 1924. 254p.
P4-S17625 — $39.50.

LeBARON: Desc. of Francis Le Baron of Plymouth, MA. By M. Le Baron Stockwell. 1904. 521p.
P4-S17631 — $81.50.

LECHMERE: Hanley Castle & the House of Lechmere. 1883 79p.
P4-S17637 — $16.00.

LeCONTE: History & Genealogy, with particular reference to Guillaume LeConte of New Rochelle & NY, & his descendants. By Richard LeConte Anderson. 1981. 2 vols., 1350p.
P4-S17643 — $159.00.

LEE: Gathering of the desc. & kinsmen of John Lee, one of the early settlers of Farmington, CT. By W.W. Lee. 1885. 128p.
P4-S17649 — $19.50.

LEE: John Lee of Farmington, Hartford Co. CT, & his descendants, 1634-1897. L. & S.F. Lee. 1897, 2nd ed. 572p.
P4-S17667 — $87.00.

LEE: Family of Marblehead (Repr. Essex Inst. Hist. Coll.) By T.A. Lee. 1916. 152p.
P4-S17685 — $22.50.

LEE: Genealogy. By Jonathan N. Smith. 1998. 37p.
P4-S17650 — $10.00.

LEE: John Lee of Farmington, Hartford Co., CT & his desc. By S.M. Lee. 1878. 182p.
P4-S17673 — $27.00.

LEE: John Lee of Agawam (Ipswich), MA, 1634-1671, & his desc. of the name of Lee. By W. Lee. 1888. 506p.
P4-S17661 — $78.00.

LEE: Family of Hounsfield, NY & related fam. By W.J. Coates. 1941. 102p.
P4-S17679 — $19.00.

LEE: Desc. of John Lee (Repr. NEHGR). By S. Lee. 1874. 9p.
P4-S17651 — $10.00.

LEE: of Va. (Repr. NEHGR) By J.H. Lea. 1892. 23p.
P4-S17652 — $10.00.

LEE: of VA, 1642-1892; biogr. & gen. sketches of the desc. of Col. Richard Lee, with brief notices of rel. fams. of Allerton, Armistead, etc. By E.J. Lee. 1895. 586p.
P4-S17691 — $74.00.

LEE: Genealogical history of the Lee family of VA & MD, from A.D. 1300 to A.D. 1866, with notes & illustrations. 1868. 114p.
P4-S17655 — $21.00.

LEE: Edw. & John Lee of Guilford, CT (Repr. NEHGR) By R.D. Smyth. 1899. 7p.
P4-S17653 — $10.00.

LEEDS: A NJ fam.; its beginning & a branchlet. By C.L. Humeston. 1900. 20p.
P4-S17692 — $10.00.

LEESE: The Lawrence Leese family: two centuries in America (1741-1941). By Charles Leese. 1941. 214p.
P4-S17697 — $34.00.

LEETE: Desc. of William Leete, one of the founders of Guilford, CT, President of the Fed. of Colonies, & governor of New Haven & CT Colonies. By E. Leete. 2nd ed., 1934. 408p.
P4-S17703 — $63.50.

LEETE: Family of William Leete, one of the first settlers of Guilford, CT & gov. of the New Haven & CT Colonies. By E. Leete. 1884. 168p.
P4-S17709 — $26.00.

LeFEVRE: The PA LeFevres. By George N. LeFevre, with Franklin D. LeFevre. 1952. 256p.
P4-S17715 — $38.00.

LEFFERTS: Gen. of the Lefferts fam., 1650-1878. By T.G. Bergen. 1878. 172p.
P4-S17718 — $26.50.

LEFFINGWELL: 1637-1897. The Leffingwell rec. A gen. of desc. of Lt. Thomas Leffingwell, a founder of Norwich, CT. By A. & C. Leffingwell. 1897. 263p.
P4-S17721 — $39.00.

LEFTWICH: TURNER Families of VA & their connections. By W.L. Hopkins. 1931. 368p.
P4-S17727 — $58.50.

LEGARE: Biogr. sketches of Huguenot Solomon Legare; also his fam. extending to the 4th gen. of his desc. By E.C.K. Fludd. 1886. 144p.
P4-S17733 — $20.00.

LEGH: Family of England: The House of Lyme, from its foundation to the end of the 18th century. By Lady Newton. 1917. 423p.
P4-S17745 — $64.00.

LEGH: History of the House of Lyme, in Cheshire, compiled from documents of the Legh familyof that house, & from other sources. By W. Beamont. 1876 208p.
P4-S17739 — $36.50.

LEHMAN: Brief hist of the Lehman family & gen. register of the desc. of Peter Lehman of Lancaster Co., PA. By H.L. Spessard. 1961. 136p.
P4-S17757 — $21.00.

LEHMAN: Abraham P. & Elizabeth Lehman & descendants, a family history from Mar., 1819 to Dec., 1964. By Elma & Paul Bixler. 1964. 338p.
P4-S17751 — $52.00.

LEIBENSPERGER: History & genealogy of the Leibensperger family; desc. of John George Leiptersberger & Catharine [his wife]. By Elmer L. Leibensperger. 1943. 563p.
P4-S17763 — $84.00.

LEIBY: Genealogy: ancestors & descendants of Dameil L.& Mary Steigerwalt Leiby, By a Family Committee. 1956. 64p.
P4-S17769 — $13.00.

LEIGHTON: Gen; An acct. of the desc. of Capt. Wm. Leighton of Kittery, ME; with collateral notes rel. to other fam. of York Co. & its vicinity. By T.F. Jordan. 1885. 136p.
P4-S17778 — $19.00.

LEIGHTON: Gen. sketch of Dover, NH, branch of Leighton fam. By W. L. Leighton. 1940. 31p.
P4-S17776 — $10.00.

LEIGHTON: Memorials of the Leightons of Ulishaven, Forfarshire, & other Scottish families of the name, a.d. 1260-1518 By Clarence F. Leighton. 1912. 126 + 56p.
P4-S17784 — $27.00.

LEIGHTON: Ancestors & desc. of George Leighton & Jean Guthrie who lived in West Ogil, Tannadice Parish Margaret K. Bowman, David T. Leighton & Helen M. Leighton. 1997. 718p.
P4-S17775 — $105.00.

LELAND: Magazine; or, a gen. record of Henry Leland & his desc., 1653-1850. By S. Leland. 1850. 279p.
P4-S17787 — $36.00.

LEMEN: History of the Lemen family of IL, VA & elsewhere, in two parts By Frank B. Lemen. 1898. 644p.
P4-S17793 — $99.50.

LEMING: Family history & genealogy. By Sam K. Leming. 1947. 138p.
P4-S17799 — $21.00.

LEMON: Brief hist. of the Lemon fam. By J. Yeager. 1912. 19p.
P4-S17794 — $10.00.

LENT: Hist. of the Lent (van Lent) fam. in the US, gen. & biogr., 1638-1902. By N.B. Lent. 1903. 171p.
P4-S17802 — $23.50.

LENZ: Family; History of the American branch established at Stone Arabia, NY in 1854. E.E. Lenz. 1937. 187p.
P4-S17808 — $31.00.

LEONARD: Stephen Banks Leonard of Owego, Tioga Co., NY. By W.A. Leonard. 1909. 342p.
P4-S17826 — $54.00.

LEONARD: Annals of the Leonard family By F. Koster. 1911. 226p.
P4-S17811 — $34.00.

LEONARD: Memoirs of the Leonard, Thompson & Haskell fams., with coll. fams. By C. Goodenough. 1928. 344p.
P4-S17820 — $54.50.

LEONARD: Memorial: genealogy, history, & biogr. of Solomon Leonard, 1637, of Duxbury & Bridgewater, MA & some of his desc. By M. Leonard. 1896. 454p.
P4-S17814 — $50.00.

LEROUX: Jacques LeRoux, The French Huguenot. E.D. Champine. 1939. 100 + 14p.
P4-S17827 — $17.00.

LeSAGE: Memorial de Familles: Genealogie LeSage, Genealogies Martin & Hamelin. 1910. xvi + 228p.
P4-S17828 — $37.00.

LESLEY: Life & letters of Peter & Susan Lesley, 2-volume set. 1909. 2 vols., 526 + 562p.
P4-S17835 — $119.50./set

LESLIE: The Leslies of Tarbert, Co. Kerry, & their forebears. By P.L. Pielou. 1935. 224p.
P4-S17847 — $33.50.

LESLIE: Historical records of the family of Leslie, from 1067-1869, collected from public records & authentic private sources. By Col. Leslie, K.H. 1869 3 vols. in 2 books, 430 + 681p.
P4-S17841 — $134.50.

LeSTRANGE: Records; A chronicle of the early LeStranges of Norfolk [England] & the March of Wales, 1100-1310. By H. LeStrange. 1916 407p.
P4-S178353 — $61.00.

LETHAM: LEATHAM Family book of remembrance: the story of Robert Letham & his wife Janet Urquhart By Louis S. Leatham. 1955. 1072p.
P4-S17859 — $135.00.

LEVEGOOD: Genealogy of the Levegood, Levergood, Livengood [et al] family, American for over two centuries, rev. ed. By Lynne L. Levegood. 1935. 64p., typescript.
P4-S17862 — $12.50.

LEVERETT: A memoir, biogr. & gen., of Sir John Leverett, governor of MA, 1673-9 & one of the fam. generally. By C.E. Leverett. 1856. 203p.
P4-S17871 — $30.50.

LEVERETT: A gen. memoir of the fam. of Elder Thomas Leverett of Boston. By N.B. Shurtleff. 1850. 20p.
P4-S17872 — $10.00.

LEVERING: Family history & genealogy. By J. Levering. 1897. 975p.
P4-S17877 — $135.00.

LEVERING: Family, or a gen. acct. of Wigard & Gerhard Levering, two of the pioneer settlers of Roxborough Twp., Phila. Co. (PA) & their desc. By H. Jones. 1858 203p.
P4-S17883 — $31.00.

LEVETT: Christopher Levett of York, the pioneer colonist in Casco Bay. By James Phinney Baxter. 1893. 166p.
P4-S17889 — $25.00.

LEWEN: History & Pedigree of the Family of Lewen of Durham, Northumberland & Scarborough. 1919. 354 + 38p.
P4-S17890 — $59.00.

LEWIS: GRISELL: Record of the Lewis & Grisell Families. comp. by M.M. Lewis & J.G. Emmons. 1903. xv + 478p.
P4-S17896 — $74.00.

LEWIS: Randall Lewis of Hopkinton, RI, & Delaware Co., NY & some desc. By F. & E. Lewis. 1929. 200p.
P4-S17925 — $33.00.

LEWIS: Records of the Lewis, Meriwether & Kindred Families; Genealogical Records of Minor, Davis, Wells, Gilmer & Clark Families. comp. by Lottie Wright Davis. 1951. 167 + 21p.
P4-S17897 — $29.00.

LEWIS: of Warner Hall: the hist. of a fam. incl. the gen. of the male & female lines, biogr. sketches of its members, & their desc. By M.E. Sorley. 1935. 887p.
P4-S17919 — $132.50.

LEWIS: Genealogy of the Lewis & kindred families. By J.M. McAllister & L.B. Tandy. 1906. 416p.
P4-S17901 — $65.00.

LEWIS: Genealogy of the Lewis fam. in Amer, primarily VA. By W.T. Lewis 1893. 458p.
P4-S17907 — $58.00.

LEWIS: Edmund Lewis of Lynn, MA & some of his desc. G.H. Lewis. 1908. 181p.
P4-S17895 — $27.00.

LEWIS: Wm. Lewis of Stoke-by-Nayland, Eng., & some of his anc. & desc., By I. Lewis. 1932. 106p.
P4-S17931 — $20.00.

L'HOMMEDIEU: L'Hommedieu Genealogy, Two-volume set By Wm.A. & P.H. L'Hommedieu. 1951 2 vols., 930p.
P4-S17938 — $120.00.

LIBBY: Family in America, 1602-1881. By C.T. Libby. 1882. 628p.
P4-S17949 — $79.50.

LICHTENWALNER: LICHTENWALTER Family History, 1700-1950. 1950. 424 + 77p.
P4-S17955 — $76.00.

LICHTENWALNER: Family history. Charles Lichtenwalner, et al. 1900. 198p.
P4-S17961 — $32.00.

LIDDLE: Genealogy of the Liddle family [descendants of John & Robert Liddle who emigrated from Scotland & settled in NY]. By Martha L. Gifford. 1922 72p.
P4-S17967 — $14.50.

LIGHT: The Light Genealogy in
America. By Moses Light. 1896. 38p
P4-S17968 — $10.00.

LIGON: Family & connections, vol I.
By W.D. Ligon, Jr. 1947. 943p.
P4-S17973 — $134.50.

LIGON: Family & Connections, vol
II. 1957. 232p.
P4-S17979 — $35.00.

LILLARD: A Short History of Thomas
Madison Lillard & Mary Bright
Lillard, of Boyle Co., KY. By John T.
Lillard. 1890. 79 + 23p.
P4-S17980 — $16.00.

LILLIE: Major John Lillie, 1755-1801.
The Lillie family of Boston, 1663-1896.
By E.L. Pierce. 1896. Rev. ed. 122p.
P4-S17985 — $18.00.

LILLY: Genealogical & Biographical
Record Concerning Mehitable (Reed)
Lilly & George Lilly. By Worrall
Dumont Prescott. 1959. 644 + 74p.
P4-S17987 — $108.00.

LINCOLN: The ancestry of Abraham
Lincoln. By J. Lea & J. Hutchinson.
1909. 310p.
P4-S18006 — $40.00.

LINCOLN: Notes on the Lincoln
fam. of MA, with some acct. of the
fam. of Abraham Lincoln (Repr.
NEHGR) By S. Lincoln. 1865. 10p.
P4-S17989 — $10.00.

LINCOLN: Some descendants of
Stephen Lincoln of Wymondham,
Eng.; Edmund Larkin of Eng.;
Thomas Oliver of Bristol, Eng.; etc. By
W.E. Lincoln. 1930. 322p.
P4-S17994 — $49.50.

LINCOLN: Stephen Lincoln of
Oakham, MA, his anc. & desc. By J.E.
Morris. 1895. 109p.
P4-S18000 — $18.00.

LINCOLN: The Lincoln Family &
Branches of Wareham, MA.
J.M. Lincoln. 1899. 124p.
P4-S17990 — $19.00.

LINCOLN: History of the Lincoln
fam.; an acct. of the desc. of Samuel
Lincoln of Hingham, MA, 1637-1920.
By W. Lincoln. 1923. 728p.
P4-S17988 — $90.00.

LINDLEY: History of the Lindley-
Lindsley-Linsley families in America,
1639-1930. By John M. Lindly. 1924,
1930. 2 vols., 584 + 599p.
P4-S18013 — $89.50./vol.

LINDSAY: History of the Lindsay
Family. E.J. Lindsay. 1925. 292 + 30p.
P4-S18017 — $48.50.

LINDSAY: The Lindsays of Amer. A
gen. narrative & fam. record. By M.I.
Lindsay. 1889. 293p.
P4-S18018 — $36.00.

LINDSEY: Book of Remembrance.
By Vaughn H. Rowley. 1963. 248p.
P4-S18024 — $37.50.

LINK: Family: antecedents &
descendants of John Jacob Link, 1417-
1951 By Paxson Link. 1951. 872 + 44p.
P4-S18030 — $120.00.

LINN: History of a fragment of the
Clan Linn & a genealogy of the Linn
& related families. By George W. Linn.
1905. 204p.
P4-S18048 — $31.00.

LINN: Genealogical history of the
family of Wm. Linn, who came from
Belfast, Ireland, in 1771. By Margarett
V. Hull. 1932. 146p.
P4-S18042 — $25.00.

LINN: Descendants of George Linn.
By Evangeline L. Halleck. 1941. 227p.
P4-S18036 — $34.00.

LINSCOTT: Family in ME, By C.N.
Sinnett. 1922. 14p.
P4-S18049 — $10.00.

LINTHICUM: Linthicum & Allied.
M.P. Badger. 1934. 189 + 48p.
P4-S18050 — $36.00.

LINZEE: The Lindeseie & Limesi
fam. of Gr. Britain, incl. the probates
at Somerset House, London, from
1300-1800 By J.W. Linzee. 1917. 2 vols.,
531 + 594p.
P4-S18054 — $135.00.

LIPPINCOTT: The Lippincotts in
England & America.
ed. from the papers of J.S. Lippincott.
n.d. 43p.
P4-S18055 — $10.00.

LITCHFIELD: Family in Amer., Part
1, nos. 1-5 in one vol. By W.J. Litchfield.
1901-1906. 384p.
P4-S18060 — $59.00.

LITTIG: Descendants of Peter Littig,
Godfrey Rogge & others. By M.D.
Littig et al. 1944. 40p.
P4-S18061 — $10.00.

LITTLE: Descendants of William
Little, Jr. & Allied Families.
Harriet F. Little. 1958. vi + 785p.
P4-S18064 — $111.00.

LITTLE: Descendants of George
Little who came to Newbury, MA in
1640. By G.T. Little. 1882. 638p.
P4-S18063 — $80.00.

LITTLE: Genealogy of the Little
family. Descendants of George Little,
who came to Newbury, MA, in 1640.
By G.T. Little. 1877. 82p.
P4-S18069 — $16.50.

LITTLEFIELD: Mem. rel. to the
Littlefields, esp. to the desc. of
Edmund who founded the MA branch
of the fam. in 1690 at Braintree. By G.
Littlefield. 1897. 80p.
P4-S18075 — $16.00.

LITTLETON: John Littleton of
Accomoack Co., VA, his family &
descendants. Brian J.L. Berry. 1999. 94p.
P4-S18081 — $18.00.

LIVERMORE: Family of America. By
W.E. Thwing. 1902. 479p.
P4-S18087 — $64.50.

LIVEZEY: Family: a genealogical &
historical record. C.H. Smith. 1934. 440p.
P4-S18093 — $68.00.

LIVEZEY: Supplement, 1944-1954.
C.A. Livezey. 1955. 50p.
P4-S18094 — $10.00.

LIVEZEY: Supplement, 1954-1964. By
C.A. Livezey. 1964. 85p.
P4-S18099 — $17.00.

LIVINGS: Genealogy of Richard &
Rachael Livings, American Premo-
genitors. Sarah Livings & David R.
Moulton Branch. Earl Alexander Mac
Lennan. 1927. 15p.
P4-S18100 — $10.00.

LIVINGSTON: The Livingstons of
Livingston Manor; the hist. of the
branch which settled in NY with an
acct. of Robert Livingston of Albany
By E.B. Livingston. 1910. 623p.
P4-S18111 — $75.50.

LIVINGSTON: Family in America &
its Scottish Origins. By Florence van
Rensselaer, 1949. 413p.
P4-S18105 — $63.00.

LLOYD: Genealogical notes relating to the families of Lloyd, Pemberton, Hutchinson, Hudson & Parke. By J.P. Parke & T. Ward. 1898. 89p.
P4-S18123 — $18.00.

LLOYD: Manuscripts; Welsh records from the collection of the late Howard Williams Lloyd. 1912. 437p.
P4-S18129 — $68.00.

LLOYD: A rec. of the desc. of Robert Lloyd, who came from Wales & settled in the Welsh Tract at Merion, PA about 1684. By R.L. Lloyd. 1947. 119p.
P4-S18117 — $19.50.

LOAR: The Loar Genealogy with Cognate Branches. By Emma Loar Gaddis. 1949. xii + 388p.
P4-S18135 — $59.50.

LOBDELL: Simon Lobdell--1646 of Milford, CT & his desc.; Nicholas Lobden (Lobdell)—1635 of Hingham, MA & some desc. J. Lobdell. 1907. 425p.
P4-S18138 — $66.50.

LOCKE: Book of the Lockes: a gen. & hist. record of desc. of Wm. Locke of Woburn, with appendix By J.G. Locke. 1853. 406p.
P4-S18141 — $52.00.

LOCKE: History & genealogy of Capt. John Locke, 1627-96, of Portsmouth & Rye, NH, & his descendants By A.H. Locke. 1916. 730 + 33p.
P4-S18147 — $109.50.

LOCKWOOD: Descendants of Robert Lockwood, colonial & Rev. history of the Lockwood fam. in Amer. from A.D. 1630. By F.A. Holden & E.D. Lockwood. 1889. 909p.
P4-S18150 — $134.00.

LOESCH: Desc of Balthaser & Susanna Loesch. By W. Lesh. 1914. 68p.
P4-S18156 — $13.50.

LOGAN: Family of KY. By T.M. Green. 115p.
P4-S18162 — $19.00.

LOGAN: History of the Logan Family. G.J.N. Logan Home. 1934. 250 + 74p.
P4-S18163 — $49.00.

LOMAX: Genealogical & Historical Sketches of the Lomax Family. Joseph Lomax. 1894. 264+104p.
P4-S18164 — $55.00.

LOMEN: Genealogies of the Lomen (Ringstad), Brandt & Joys families. By G.J. Lomen. 1929. 361p.
P4-S18168 — $55.50.

LONDON: Two hundred years of the London family in America, By O.L. Cox. 1976. 400p.
P4-S18174 — $59.50.

LONG: Benjamin Long & Mary Hershe Long, from A.D. 1810 to A.D. 1935. By Benj. F. Thomas, and Josephine R. Rogers Sr and Josephine R. Rogers, Jr. 1935. 64p.
P4-S18180 — $13.00.

LONG: Biographical sketch of Enoch Long, an Illinois pioneer [with genealogy]. By Harvey Reid. 1884. 134p.
P4-S18186 — $19.00.

LONG: History of the Long family of PA. By W.G. Long. 1930. 365p.
P4-S18192 — $56.00.

LONG: Longs of Charlestown & Nantucket, MA. H.P. Long. 1926. 28p.
P4-S18181 — $10.00.

LONGACRE: History of the Longacre-Langaker-Longenecker family, Publ. for the committee. 1902. 310p.
P4-S18198 — $40.00.

LONGLEY: Descendants of William Longley of Lynn, MA in 1635. By A. Longley. 1916. 10p.
P4-S18199 — $10.00.

LONGLEY: A Rec. of the Longley Families of Shirley, MA. 1884. 50p.
P4-S18200 — $10.00.

LONGYEAR: Descendants of Jacob Longyear of Ulster Co., NY. By Edmund J. Longyear. 1942. 622p.
P4-S18204 — $89.00.

LOOMIS: Descendants of Joseph Loomis in Amer. & his antecedents in the Old World. By E.S. Loomis. 1908. 859p. Rev. ed.
P4-S18213 — $77.50.

LOOMIS: Desc. (by female branches) of Joseph Loomis, who came from Braintree, Eng., in 1638 & settled in Windsor, CT in 1639. By E. Loomis. 1880. 2 vols., 1132p.
P4-S18210 — $149.00.

LOOS: Fam. genealogy, 1535-1958. By S.L. Bast. 1959. 245p.
P4-S18219 — $37.00.

LORD: Ancestors & descendants of Lt. Tobias Lord. C. Lord. 1913. 263p.
P4-S18225 — $42.00.

LORD: Certain members of the Lord family who settled in New York City in the early 1800's, desc. of Thomas Lord of Hartford, CT. By Kenneth Lord. 1945. 92p.
P4-S18231 — $18.00.

LORD: History of the descendants of Nathan Lord of ancient Kittery, ME. By C.C. Lord. 1912. 218p.
P4-S18237 — $33.00.

LORING: Genealogy. By C.H. Pope, with K.P. Loring. 1917. 443p.
P4-S18243 — $68.50.

LOTHROP: Anc. & desc. of Daniel Lothrop, Sr., 1545-1901. By G.D.R. Hubbard. 1901. 37p.
P4-S18256 — $10.00.

LOTT: Fam. in Amer., incl. allied fam. Cassell, Davis, Graybeal, Haring, etc. By A. Phillips. 1942. 179p.
P4-S18261 — $29.00.

LOUCKS: Genealogy of the Loucks family, beginning with Johann Dietrich Loucks & his descendants in direct line to Joseph Louck By E.M. McBrier. 1940. 22 + 295p.
P4-S18267 — $48.50.

LOUD: Gen. rec. of the desc. of Caleb Loud, child of Francis Loud & Onner Prince Loud. By W. Loud. 1889. 83p.
P4-S18273 — $14.50.

LOUGHRY: Brief genealogy of the Loughry family of PA. By J.A. Jewett. 1923. 85p.
P4-S18279 — $17.00.

LOVE: LOOMIS Fam. hist. By B.W. Loomis. 1963. 127p.
P4-S18285 — $20.00.

LOVE: Gen. of Thomas Love of NC & TN & his brothers, Robert & James. By R.A. Love. 1955. 47p.
P4-S18286 — $10.00.

LOVEJOY: Genealogy, with biogr. & hist., 1460-1930. C.E. Lovejoy. 1930. 470p.
P4-S18288 — $62.50.

LOVELAND: Genealogy of the Loveland fam. in the US, 1635 to 1892, containing the desc. of Thomas Loveland of Wethersfield, CT, 3-vol. set. J.B. & G. Loveland. 1892. 3 vols., 838p.
P4-S18294 — $125.50.

LOVELL: Biographical genealogy of the Lovell family in England & America. By L. Rhodes & T.G. Rhodes. 219p.
P4-S18300 — $33.50.

LOVEWELL: The expeditions of Capt. John Lovewell & his encounters with the Indians, with a bio. sketch of Capt. Lovewell. Frederic Kidder. 1865. 123p.
P4-S18306 — $19.00.

LOWE: The anc. of the John Lowe fam. circle & their desc. By E.M. Merriam. 1901. 189p.
P4-S18309 — $25.00.

LOWE: A Genealogical Quest. William G. Low 1908. 21p.
P4-S18308 — $10.00.

LOWELL: Historic genealogy of the Lowells of Amer. from 1639-1899. By D.R. Lowell. 1899. 878p.
P4-S18315 — $85.00.

LOWER: Some acct. of the Lower family in America, desc. of Adam Lower, who settled in Williamsport PA in 1779. By J.L. Lower. 1913. 144p.
P4-S18321 — $25.00.

LOWNDES: Family of SC, By G.B. Chase. 1876. 38p.
P4-S18322 — $10.00.

LOWREY: Hist.-gen. sketch of Col. Thomas Lowrey & Esther Fleming, his wife. By H. Race. 1892. 16p.
P4-S18323 — $10.00.

LOWRY: The Lowrys; Robert & Mary Lowry & children (6 gen.) By L. & H. Lowry. 1921. 118p.
P4-S18327 — $20.00.

LUCAS: Genealogy. A. Kemp. 1964. 495p.
P4-S18333 — $75.50.

LUCH: Desc. of Vasil Luch. By Rachel Saul Tefft. 1996. 11p.
P4-S18334 — $10.00.

LUDDINGTON: William Luddington of Malden, MA & East Haven, CT & his desc. By J. Shepard. 1904. 13p.
P4-S18335 — $10.00.

LUDLOW: ROSS Gen. The Anc of Lydia Ludlow & Ogden Ross. D.B. Brode. 1932. 126p.
P4-S18336 — $19.00.

LUDWIG: Gen. Sketch of Jos. Ludwig, b. in Germany in 1699, & his wife & fam., who settled at "Broad Bay," Waldoboro, 1753. By M.R. Ludwig. 1866. 223p.
P4-S18339 — $29.50.

LUKIN: Gen. notes & pedigrees of the Lovekyn- Luckyn-Lukin fam. in Eng. By A.T. Tudor-Craig. 1932. 58p.
P4-S18340 — $11.50.

LUM: Genealogy of the Lum family. By Edward H. Lum. 1927. 270p.
P4-S18345 — $42.50.

LUMAS: Edw. Lumas of Ipswich, MA & some desc. By G. Lewis, E. Loomis & C. Lummus. 1917. 43p.
P4-S1818346 — $10.00.

LUNDY: Family & their desc. of what-soever surname, with biogr. sketch of Benj. Lundy. W.C. Armstrong. 1902. 485p.
P4-S18351 — $62.00.

LUNT: History of the Lunt family in Amer. By T. Lunt. 1913. 306p.
P4-S18363 — $49.00.

LUNT: Ancestry of Abel Lunt, 1769-1806, of Newbury, MA. By W.G. Davis. 1963. 269p.
P4-S18357 — $42.00.

LYBARGER: History of the Lybarger family. By D.F. Lybarger. 1921. 101p.
P4-S18369 — $19.00.

LYFORD: Frances Lyford of Boston & Exeter, & some desc. By W.L. Welch. 1902. 88p.
P4-S18375 — $17.50.

LYLE: Family: ancestry & posterity of Matthew, John, Daniel & Samuel Lyle, pioneer settlers in VA. By O.K. Lyle. 1912. 361p.
P4-S18381 — $55.00.

LYLE: The Lyles of Washington Co., PA, Being an Acct. of the Origin, Migrations & Generations of the Family. Alvin Dinsmore White. 1963. 343p.
P4-S18387 — $53.00.

LYMAN: Saga, a family history. A.A. Rouberg. 1951 206p.
P4-S18391 — $33.50.

LYMAN: Proceedings at the reunion of the Lyman fam. held at Mt. Tom & Springfield, MA, 1871. 1871. 60p.
P4-S18393 — $12.50.

LYMAN: Genealogy of the Lyman family in Gr. Britain & Amer.; the anc. & desc. of Richard Lyman, from High Ongar in Eng., 1631. L. Coleman. 1872. 549p.
P4-S18390 — $67.50.

LYNCH: Record, containing a biographical sketches of men of the name Lynch, 16th to 20th century By E.C. Lynch. 1925. 154p.
P4-S18408 — $25.00.

LYNCH: Families of the southern states: lineages & court records. By L.D. Hines. 1966. 373p.
P4-S18402 — $58.50.

LYNDE: The diaries of Benj. Lunde & of Benj. Lynde, Jr., with an appendix. ed. by F. Oliver. 1880. 267p.
P4-S18414 — $40.00.

LYNN: Gen. of Colonel Andrew Lynn Jr. and Mary Ashercraft Johnson & Their Descendants. Eliza B. Lynn. 1912. 78p. + charts
P4-S18415 — $29.00.

LYON: Mem,; NY fam., desc. from the immigr. Thomas Lyon, of Rye. ed. By Miller & Lyons. 1907. 539p.
P4-S18420 — $70.00.

LYON: Mem: fams. of CT & NJ, incl. recs. of the immigr. Richard Lyon of Fairfield, Henry Lyon of Fairfield. By Lyon, Johnson & Lyons. 1907. 453p.
P4-S18417 — $58.00.

LYON: Memorial, MA fam., incl. desc. of the immigr. Wm. Lyon of Roxbury, Peter & Geo. of Dorchester By Lyon, Lyon & McPike. 1905. 491p.
P4-S18426 — $62.50.

M

MacCARTHY: The MacCarthys of Munster: the story of a great Irish sept. By Sam'l Trant McCarthy. 1922/1997. 567p.
P4-S18422 — $75.00.

MacCUBBIN: Fam. (in "Col. Fams. of the US"). 1914. 8p.
P4-S18430 — $10.00.

MacDONALD: McDONALD Family records. J. Montgomery Seaver. 1940 51p.
P4-S18431 — $11.00.

MACDONOUGH: HACKSTAFF Ancestry. R. Macdonough. 1901. 526 + 82p.
P4-S18432 — $91.00.

MacGREGOR: Partial genealogy of the Rev. James MacGregor family of Londonderry NH. n.d. 3p.
P4-S18433 — $10.00.

MacINTYRE: JOHNSTON Alliance. By James K. Raywalt. 1994. 178p. **P4-S18438 — $28.00.**

MACK: Genealogy; desc. of John Mack of Lyme, CT, with appendix By S. Martin. 1903. 1788p. **P4-S18450 — $219.00.**

MACK: Gen. records of the desc. of David Mack to 1879. By S. Smith & C.S. Smith. 1879. 81p. **P4-S18444 — $15.00.**

MacKENZIE: History of the MacKenzies, with gen. of the principal fams. of the name. By A. MacKenzie. 1894 663p. **P4-S18456 — $83.00.**

MACKINTOSH: Gen Collections House & Clan of Mackintosh. W. Macfarlane. (n.d.) 264 + 5p. **P4-S18451 — $40.00.**

MACLAY: Family; From Hunter Family of VA. By Sidney M. Culbertson. 1934. 10p. **P4-S18463 — $10.00.**

MACLAY: Memorial, sketching the lin., life & obsequies of Hon. Wm. B. Maclay. By O.B. Judd. 1884. 192p. **P4-S18462 — $28.75**

MACLEAN: Historical & genealogical account of the Clan MacLean, First Settlement at Castle Duart, in the Isle of Mull, to the Present Period [1838]. By "A Seneachie." 1838. 358p. **P4-S18474 — $54.00.**

MacLEAN: Brief history of the ancestry & posterity of Allan MacLean, 1715-1786, New England. By Mary MacL. Hardy. 1905. 80p. **P4-S18468 — $16.00.**

MacLEOD: Hist., with the gen. of the principal fam. of the name [in Scotland]. By A. MacKenzie. 1889. 463p. **P4-S18480 — $71.00.**

MacLEOD: Short sketch of their clan, history, folk-lore, tales & biographical notices of some eminent clansmen. By R.C. MacLeod. 1906 118p. **P4-S18486 — $19.50.**

MacMASTER: The History of MacMaster — McMaster Family. F.H. McMaster. 1926. 142 + 16p. **P4-S18487 — $24.00.**

MacMILLAN: The MacMillans & their septs. By S. MacMillan. 1952 126p. **P4-S18492 — $21.00.**

MacNEIL: The Clan MacNeil (Clann Niall) of Scotland. By the MacNeil of Barra. 1923. 227p. **P4-S18498 — $34.00.**

MACOMB: Fam. record, being an acct. of the fam. since the settlement in America. By H. Macomb, rev. By P. McComb. 1917. 206p. **P4-S18504 — $32.00.**

MACOMBER: Genealogy. By E.S. Stackpole. 1908 252p. **P4-S18510 — $38.00.**

MacQUEEN: MacQueens of Queensdale: A Biography of Col. James MacQueen. A.B. MacElyea. 1916. 261p. **P4-S18517 — $39.00.**

MacQUEEN: The MacQueens, being a brief hist. of the origin of the MacQueen fam. By J.A. Nydegger. 1928. 111p. **P4-S18516 — $18.50.**

MACRAE: History of the Clan Macrae, with genealogies. By A. Macrae. 1899 22 + 442p. **P4-S18522 — $71.00.**

MACY: Genealogy of the Macy family, 1635-1868. By S. Macy. 1868. 457p. **P4-S18525 — $58.00.**

MADDY: US Maddys: an account of the family in England & the descendants of William Maddy of Fairfax of Fairfax Co., VA. Olive Maddy. 1950. 280p. **P4-S18531 — $44.00.**

MAGEE: Desc. from John Magee of Clarion Co., PA (in Frampton Gen.) By I. Wrightnour. 8p. **P4-S18538 — $10.00.**

MAGEE: Fam. of James Magee of Ireland & Venango Co., PA (in Siggins Gen.) By E. White. 1918. 20p. **P4-S18539 — $10.00.**

MAGENNIS: Origin & history of the Magennis family, with sketches of the Keylor, Swisher, Marchbank & Bryan families. John F. Meginness. 1891. 245p. **P4-S18537 — $37.00.**

MAGILL: McGILL Genealogy, from the 1700's. Eunice Parr McGill. 1963. 57p. **P4-S18540 — $11.50.**

MAGILL: Magill Family Record. R.M. Magill. 1907. 244 + 20p. **P4-S18541 — $40.00.**

MAIKE: RAYWALT — FUTH — CZIRR. James K. Raywalt. 1992. 141p. **P4-S18543 — $25.00.**

MAIN: MAINE Fam. of Stonington, CT. By A. Aspinall. 1911. 57p. **P4-S18546 — $12.00.**

MAJOR: The Majors & Their Marriages. J.B. Cabell. 1915. 188p. **P4-S18544 — $28.00.**

MAKEPEACE: The gen. of the Makepeace fams. in the US, 1637-1857, By W. Makepeace. 1858. 107p. **P4-S18552 — $15.00.**

MALBONE: Godfrey Malbone's arm. silver, data on the Malbone fam. of Newport, RI. By R. Bowen. 1950. 27p. **P4-S18553 — $10.00.**

MALLET: John Mallet, the Huguenot, & his desc., 1694-1894. By A.S. Mallett. 1895. 342p. **P4-S18558 — $43.00.**

MALLET: La Famille Mallet. A. Choisy. 1930. 160 + 118p. **P4-S18559 — $39.00.**

MALLETT: Ancestors & Descendants of Colonel Peter Mallett, 1744-1805. Alice Collier Clark. 2002. 855 + 6p. **P4-S18560 — $131.00.**

MALLINSON: Two founders of Rowley, MA, Jewett & Mallinson. By T.E. Hazen. 1940. 15p. **P4-S18561 — $10.00.**

MALLORY: Genealogy of the Mallorys of VA. H.R. Mallory. 1954. 65p. **P4-S18564 — $13.00.**

MALONE: Jeremiah Dumas Malone, a genealogical outline. By E.E. Malone. 1949. 159p. **P4-S18570 — $25.00.**

MALTBY: MOREHOUSE Family: a list of pedigrees with genealogical notes. 1895. 157p. **P4-S18582 — $25.00.**

MALTBY: MALTBIE Family history. By D.M. Verril. 1916. 435p. **P4-S18576 — $68.00.**

MALTBY: Family of MA. By Art Reierson. 1998. 374p. **P4-S18588 — $58.00.**

MAN: Family. R.W. Lloyd. 1923. 24p. **P4-S18589 — $10.00.**

MANLY: Family: account of the descendants of Capt. Basil Manly of the Revolution, & related families. By Louise Manly. 1930. 351p.
P4-S18594 — $54.50.

MANN: Chronological records of the English Mann. By J.B. Mann. 1874. 95p.
P4-S18600 — $19.00.

MANN: Rec. of the Mann fam; Gen. of the desc. of Richard Man of Scituate, MA. By G. Mann. 1884. 251p.
P4-S18609 — $36.50.

MANN: John Washington Mann, Jr. By Marteal Wells. 2001 291p.
P4-S18606 — $45.00.

MANN: Fam.; Va. Co. records (in Valentine Papers). E.P. Valentine 1927. 26p.
P4-S18601 — $10.00.

MANNING: Notes on the Manning fam. of Co. Kent, Eng. With add. notes on the Waters, Proctor & Whitfield fam. (Repr. NEHGR) By H.F. Water. 1897. 35p.
P4-S18611 — $10.00.

MANNING: Gen. & biogr. history of the Manning family of New Eng. & desc. from settlement in America to present time. By W.H. Manning. 1902. iv + 865 + 36p.
P4-S18615 — $136.00.

MANNING: Our Kin [Manning & allied families]. W.H. Manning, Jr., & Edna Anderson Manning. 1958. 1601 + 77p.
P4-S18610 — $175.00.

MANSFIELD: The desc. of Richard & Gillian Mansfield, who settled in New Haven, 1639 By H. Mansfield. 1885. 198p.
P4-S18621 — $26.50.

MANTON: Record of the Manton family, 1750-1914. By Edw. Manton. 1914. 46 + 8p.
P4-S18623 — $11.00.

MAPES: The Mapes Family. S.H. Mapes. 1909. 116 + 64p.
P4-S18624 — $27.00.

MARCY: The Marcy fam. By C.D. Paige. 1902. 16p.
P4-S18625 — $10.00.

MARCY: Record of the Marcy fam. By O. Marcy. 1875. 15p.
P4-S18626 — $10.00.

MARGESON: & Related fams. By H.M. Spinney. 95p.
P4-S18627 — $18.00.

MARIS: Fam. in the US Rec. of the desc. of Geo. & Alice Maris, 1683-1885. By G. & A.M. Maris. 1885. 279 + 33p.
P4-S18630 — $36.00.

MARKHAM: Hist of the Markham Family. David F. Markham 1854. 116 + 12p.
P4-S18631 — $20.00.

MARSH: Gen. of the Marsh fam. Outline for five gen., with accts. of the 3rd fam. reunion at Lake Pleasant in 1886. ed. by D.W. Marsh. 1886. 60p.
P4-S18643 — $12.00.

MARSH: Genealogy, giving several thousand desc. of John Marsh of Hartford, CT, 1636-1895. By D. Marsh. 1895. 585p.
P4-S18642 — $65.50.

MARSH: Gen. of the fam. of Geo. Marsh, who came from Eng. in 1635 & settled in Hingham, MA. By E.J. Marsh. 1887. 229p.
P4-S18633 — $30.00.

MARSH: Gen. of the John Marsh of Salem, & his desc., 1633-1888, By L. Marsh, rev. By D. Marsh. 1888. 283p.
P4-S18636 — $36.00.

MARSHALL: The Marshall Family — Hist of Desc of William Marshall. O.S. Marshall. 1884. 245p.
P4-S18649 — $37.00.

MARSHALL: Family, or a gen. chart of the desc. of John Marshall & Elizabeth Markham, his wife. By W.M. Paxton. 1885. 415p.
P4-S18651 — $53.00.

MARSHALL: Fam. record, with Haskell, Boutwell, Barrett, & allied fam. By F.B. Kingsbury. 1913. 103p.
P4-S18648 — $15.00.

MARSTON: Marston Eng. anc. with some acct. of the Amer. immigrants of the name. By M.L. Holman. 1929. 41p.
P4-S18655 — $10.00.

MARSTON: Genealogy, in two parts. By N.W. Marston. 1888. 607p.
P4-S18654 — $85.00.

MARSTON: Memoirs of the Marstons of Salem, with a brief gen. of some of their desc. (Repr. NEHGR) By J.L. Watson. 1873. 48p.
P4-S18656 — $10.00.

MARTIN: PRICE. Distaff Descent. M.W.M. Rivinus. 1943. 485p.; typscript.
P4-S18661 — $106.00.

MARTIN: Peter Martin, 1741-1807, A Revolutionary Soldier of VA, buried in Shelby Co., KY. By Marjorie Ann M. Souder. 1989 (repr. by permission). 464p.
P4-S18693 — $69.50.

MARTIN: Descendants of John Martin of Brunswick and Old Bristol, ME. By Kenneth Alton Clark. 1993. 81p.
P4-S18660 — $16.00.

MARTIN: Family Records. By J. Montgomery Seaver. 1929. 59p.
P4-S18678 — $12.00.

MARTIN: The House of Martin. W.G. Willis Watson. 1906. xii + 146 + 8p.
P4-S18662 — $25.00.

MARTIN: Record of the descendants of Alfred Martin, late of Floyd, Oneida Co., NY. By Andeline E. Hicks. With 1996 addendum & index By Martin H. Irons. 1912. 34 + 4p.
P4-S18664 — $10.00.

MARTIN: Gen. notices & hist. of the Martin fam. of New Eng., who settled at Weymouth & Hingham in 1635, with acct. of their desc. By H. Martin. 1880. 358p.
P4-S18663 — $46.50.

MARTIN: Martin & Allied Families: Bogan, Farrar, Truit, Smith, Saxon, Hay, Cheney, Grubbs, Pope, Curry, Watson, Swann, Birch, King, Pruett & Other Branches. Lillie Martin Grubbs 1946. 306 + 16p., 5 charts
P4-S18665 — $59.95

MARTIN: Genealogy; Desc. of Lt. Samuel Martin of Wethersfield, CT. By T.A. Hay. 1911. 291p.
P4-S18687 — $46.50.

MARTIN: Family [of Ireland, US & Canada]. By G.C. Martin. 1914. 144p.
P4-S18675 — $25.00.

MARTIN: Genealogy of the Martin family. By C.W. Francis. 1918. 319p.
P4-S18669 — $46.50.

MARVIN: Gen. sketch of the desc. of Reinold & Matthew Marvin, who came to New Eng. in 1635. By T.R. Marvin. 1848. 56p.
P4-S18703 — $11.00.

MARVIN: Desc. of Reinold & Matthew Marvin of Hartford, CT, 1638 & 1635, sons of Edw. Marvin of Gt. Bentley, Eng. By G. & W. Marvin. 1904. 659p.
P4-S18696 — $89.50.

MARVIN: Eng. anc. of Reinold & Matthew Marvin of Hartford, CT, 1638. By W.T.R. Marvin. 1900. 184p.
P4-S18702 — $27.50.

MASKELL: Thomas Maskell of Simsbury, CT, his son Thomas Maskell of Greenwich, NJ & Some of their descendants. comp. by Frank D. Andrews. 1927. 38p.
P4-S18704 — $10.00.

MASON: MILLER; John Mason & Mary Ann Miller of VA. By Floyd R. Mason. 1986. 367p.
P4-S18735 — $55.00.

MASON: Capt. John Mason, founder of NH . . . with letters & other hist. documents, with a memoir by C.W. Tuttle. Ed. by J.W. Dean. 1887. 491p.
P4-S18714 — $64.00.

MASON: Descendants of Capt. Hugh Mason in America. By E.W. Mason. 1937. 867p.
P4-S18720 — $109.00.

MASON: Ancestors & descendants of Elisha Mason, Litchfield, CT, 1759-1858, & his wife Lucretia Webster, 1766-1853. By G.W. Mason. 1911. 120p.
P4-S18708 — $23.00.

MASON: Fam.; some of the desc. of Major John Mason (Repr. NEHGR) By R.H. Walworth. 1861-1863 28p.
P4-S18709 — $10.00.

MASON: A record of the desc. of Robert Mason, of Roxbury, MA. By W.L. Mason. 1891. 39p.
P4-S18710 — $10.00.

MASON: Enoch & Elizabeth Mason, their ancestry & descendants. By S.S. Mason. 1911. 91p.
P4-S18726 — $18.00.

MASON: Gen. of the Sampson Mason fam. By A.H. Mason. 1902. 288p.
P4-S18729 — $37.00.

MASSENGILL: The Massengills, Massengales & Variants, 1472-1931. S.E. Massengill, MD. 1931. 966p.
P4-S18736 — $115.00.

MATHER: Diary of Cotton Mather, Vol. I, 1681-1709. 604p.
P4-S18738 — $65.00.

MATHER: Diary of Cotton Mather, Vol. II, 1709-1724. 860p.
P4-S18740 — $89.50.

MATHER: Lineage of Rev. Richard Mather. By H. Mather. 1890. 540p.
P4-S18744 — $68.00.

MATHER: Family; From Hist. of Windsor, CT, 1892. 13p.
P4-S18745 — $10.00.

MATHESON: History of the Mathesons, with gen. of the var. branches [in Scotland]. By A. MacKenzie. 1882. 72p.
P4-S18750 — $15.00.

MATHESON: History of the Mathesons, with Genealogies of the Various Families. Alexander MacKenzie. 1900. 201p.
P4-S18751 — $32.00.

MATHEWS: Family descendants, from Canada to Cleveland & all over the country [some descendants of Amasi Mathews, b. 1794]. By Robert C. Hitchcock. 2002. 102p.
P4-S18760 — $19.50.

MATLACK: Col. Timothy Matlack, Patriot & Soldier, Haddonfield NJ. By Dr A.M. Stackhouse. 1910. 105p.
P4-S18756 — $19.00.

MATTESON: Mattesons in Amer: orig. records of early Matteson pioneers. By P. Matteson. 1960. 42p.
P4-S18761 — $10.00.

MATTHEWS: PAGE — WILSON — DEAN — BARTLETT & related families. By Kermit Dean Matthews. 1993. 290p.
P4-S18762 — $45.00.

MATTOON: A genealogy of the descendants of Philip Mattoon of Deerfield, MA. By L.G. Mattoon & D.P. Mattoon. 1965. 263 + 59 + 17p.
P4-S18768 — $52.50.

MAULL: John Maull (1714-1753) of Lewes, Dela: a gen. of his desc. in all branches. By B. Maull. 1941. 241 + 39p.
P4-S18774 — $43.00.

MAULSBY: Gen. of the Maulsby fam. for five generations, 1699-1902. By C.M. Payne. 1902. 147p.
P4-S18780 — $20.00.

MAURAN: Memorials of the Mauran family. By J.E. Mauran & J.C. Stockbridge. 1893. 171p.
P4-S18786 — $29.50.

MAURY: Memoirs of a Huguenot family, translated & Compiled from the orig. autobio. of the Rev. James Fontaine & Other family manuscripts. By Ann Maury. 1872. 512p.
P4-S18792 — $45.00.

MAUZY: Gen Rec of Desc of Henry Mauzy; with Desc of Jacob Kisling. R. Mauzy. 1911. 127p.
P4-S18793 — $19.00.

MAVERICK: Remarks on the Maverick fam. & the anc. of Gov. Simon Bradstreet. By I.J. Greenwood. 1894. 8p.
P4-S18794 — $10.00.

MAXSON: Family of RI. By Johnston & Jones. 68p.
P4-S18798 — $13.00.

MAXSON: Fam. of MA, RI & NY. By W. & M. Brown. 1940. 22p.
P4-S18799 — $10.00.

MAXSON: Family: descendants of John Maxson & wife Mary Mosher of Westerly, RI, With modern indexes by Jane H. Maxson. By Walter L. Brown. 1954. 256 + 35p.
P4-S18804 — $45.00.

MAXWELL: History & genealogy, including allied families. By Houston, Blaine & Mellette. 1916. 642p.
P4-S18810 — $96.50.

MAXWELL: Family in ME. By C. N. Sinnett. 1923. 10p.
P4-S18810 — $10.00.

MAY: Gen. of desc. of John May who came from Eng. to Roxbury in Amer., 1640. By S. May, et al. 1878. 212p.
P4-S18822 — $31.50.

MAY: Charles May & his descendants, who settled at Mays Cross Roads in Old Edgefield Co., SC. 1956. 287p.
P4-S18816 — $43.00.

MAYER: Memoir & gen. of the MD & PA fam. of Mayer. By B. Mayer. 179p.
P4-S18828 — $27.00.

MAYHAM: Family, 1795-1950: family of Henry Maham of Blenheim Hill, Schoharie Co., NY. By G. Raymond. 1950. 63p.
P4-S18831 — $12.50.

MAYHUGH: of VA & KY & allied fam. By M. Thompson 1957. 100p.
P4-S18840 — $19.50.

MAYNARD: John Maynard of Sudbury, MA & desc. By W.E. Gould. 1914. 38p.
P4-S18847 — $10.00.

MAYNARD: Brief memoir of Maynard fam., etc. By C.P. Stevens. 1916. 64p.
P4-S18846 — $13.00.

MAYO: Noah Mayo of Harpsell, ME & desc. By C.N. Sinnett. 1923. 4p.
P4-S18823 — $10.00.

MAYS: Gen of the Mays Family. S.E. Mays. 1929. 288 + 56p.
P4-S18824 — $52.00.

McAFEE: SKILES - LIEBMANN Memorial. The Hist of Three American Soldiers. A.G. Liebmann. 1929. 144p.
P4-S18847 — $22.00.

McALEER: The Surname McAleer. G. McAleer. 1909. 103 p.
P4-S18848 — $17.00.

McALLISTER: Family records, comp. for the desc, of Abraham Addams McAllister & his wife Julia Ellen (Stratton) McAllister of Covington, VA. By J. Gray McAllister. 1912. 88p.
P4-S18864 — $17.50.

McALLISTER: Descendants of Archibald McAllister of W. Pennsboro Twp., Cumberland Co., PA, 1730-1898. By Mary C. McAllister. 1898. 93 + 12p.
P4-S18858 — $19.50.

McARTHUR: BARNES Ancestral lines. By Selim W. McArthur. 1964. 221p.
P4-S18870 — $34.00.

McCALL: TIDWELL & allied families. By E.T. McCall. 1931. 672p.
P4-S18879 — $99.00.

McCALLISTER: Gen. Record of the Desc. of Col. Alexander McAllister of Cumberland Co., NC; Also of Mary & Isabella McAllister. Rev. D.S. McAllister. 1900. 244p.
P4-S18877 — $37.00.

McCALLUM: Family & desc. of Duncan McCallum; colonial ancestors of the John McCallum branch, & other allied lines. I.F. Johnson. 1957. 77p.
P4-S18888 — $15.00.

McCALLUM: David McCallum & Isabel Sellars: their antecedents, descendants & collateral relatives. By L. Farrell & F.J.H. Hooker. 1949. 234p.
P4-S18882 — $37.50.

McCANDLESS: with Ref. Sketch of Erin & Alban. S.A. McCandless. 1918. xiv + 185p.
P4-S18889 — $30.00.

McCANDLISH: BLACK Family history. By Elizabeth Black. 1935. 201p.
P4-S18894 — $30.00.

McCARTY: Thomas McCarty of Northampton Co., PA & some desc. (in Lancaster fam.). By H. Lancaster. 1902. 63p.
P4-S18897 — $12.50.

McCLANAHAN: McClanahan fam., desc. of Robert of Ireland & VA. By H. White. 1894. 43p.
P4-S18895 — $10.00.

McCLARY: Four gen. of the McClary fam. from Andrew McClary of Ulster, 1726. By H.P. McClary. 1896. 52p.
P4-S18896 — $10.00.

McCLAUGHRY: Genealogy of the MacClaughry family: a Scoto-Irish family from Galloway, Scotland, & emigr. to NY in 1765. By C.C. McClaughry. 1913. 459p.
P4-S18906 — $71.00.

McCLELLAND: HARPER: Settlers in the Wabash Valley, 1774-1954. Eliza H. Brevoort. 1955. 162 + 8p.
P4-S18907 — $25.50.

McCLENAHAN: The John McClenahan folk: biography & genealogy. J.M. Henderson. 1911. 125p.
P4-S18912 — $19.00.

McCLUNG: Gen.; a gen. & biogr. record of the McClung fam. from the time of their emigration to the year 1904. By W. McClung. 1904. 296p.
P4-S18918 — $44.00.

McCLURE: Family Genealogy. By J.A. McClure. 1914. 232p.
P4-S18924 — $35.00.

McCLURE: Family Records. By W.M. Clemens. 1914. 14p.
P4-S18925 — $10.00.

McCONNELL: Marriages & gen; Anc., desc. & marr. of a VA fam. By H. M. Addington. 1929. 36p.
P4-S18926 — $10.00.

McCORMICK: Family record & biogr. By L.J. McCormick. 1896. 490p.
P4-S18927 — $76.50.

McCOY: Wm. McCoy & his desc. Also a hist. of the fam. of Alexander McCoy. By L. McCoy. 1904. 204p.
P4-S18939 — $31.50.

McCUE: The McCues of the Old Dominion. J.N. McCue. 1912. 272 + 64p.
P4-S18940 — $50.00.

McCULLOUGH: Gen. of the McCullough fam. & other sketches. By J. McCullough. 1912. 100p.
P4-S18945 — $18.50.

McCURDY: From "Larimer, McMasters & Allied fams." 9p.
P4-S18946 — $10.00.

McCUTCHEON: (Cutcheon) fam. Records; Allied fam. of McClary, Tripp, Brown & Critchett. By F. McKee. 1931. 352p.
P4-S18951 — $55.00.

McDANIEL: Family Record. By C.G. Harris. 1929. 161p.
P4-S18957 — $28.50.

McDANIEL: Desc. of Geo. McDaniel & Margaret Goff of King Wm. Co., VA (in Rucker gen.) By S. Wood. 1932. 22p.
P4-S18958 — $10.00.

McDILL: McDills in America: Hist of Desc of John McDill & Janet Leslie of County Antrim, Ireland. comp by R.M. Woods & I.G. Woods. 1940. xiv + 210p.
P4-S18959 — $34.00.

McDONALD: Alexander McDonald of New Inverness, GA. D.H. Redfearn. 1954. 117 + 24p.
P4-S18961 — $30.00.

McDONALD: Bryan McDonald & Family, Settlers on Red Clay Creek, Mill Creek, Newcastle Co., DE. F.V. McDonald. 1879. 65p.
P4-S18960 — $10.00.

McDONALD: Family Portraits. Tanny McDonald. 2004. 161p.
P4-S18962 — $24.50.

McDONOUGH: HACKSTAFF Ancestry. R. Macdonough. 1901. 538p.
P4-S18963 — $79.00.

McELROY: Scotch-Irish McElroys in America, a.d. 1717 — a.d. 1900. By J.M. McElroy. 1901. 183p.
P4-S18975 — $28.00.

McELWEE: Gen of William McElwee, II of Clarks Fork of Bullocks Creek, York Co., SC. Col P.G. McElwee. 1959. 227 + 47p.
P4-S18976 — $41.00.

McEWEN: Descendants of William McEwen (1775-1840). By Rachel Saul Tefft. 1997. 113p.
P4-S18981 — $18.00.

McFADDEN: William H. McFadden family. By Marteal Wells. 1999. 277p.
P4-S18987 — $42.00.

McFADDIN: McFaddin, 1730-1930. By A.L. Blanding, et al. 1931. 99p.
P4-S18993 — $19.00.

McFARLAN: Our kindred: MacFarlan & Stern fams. of Chester Co., PA & New Castle Co., DE. C. Stern. 1885. 179p.
P4-S18999 — $24.00.

McFARLAND: KILGORE. The Book of the Generations of Wm. McFarland & Nancey Kilgore. J. McFarland. 1913. 110p.
P4-S19000 — $17.00.

McFARLAND: Desc. of Daniel McFarland, one of the Scotch Presbyterians, who settled in Worcester, MA. E.B. Crane. 1907. 28p.
P4-S19001 — $10.00.

McFARLAND: Gen. of the McFarland fam. of Hancock Co., ME. By D.Y. Mcfarland. 1910. 58p.
P4-S19002 — $12.00.

McFARLANE: Hist. of Clan MacFarlane, MacFarlan, MacFarland, MacFarlin. By C.M. Little. 1893. 254p.
P4-S19011 — $38.00.

McGAFFEY: Genealogical history of the McGaffey family, incl. also the Fellows, Ethridge & Sherman families. By G.W. McGaffey. 1904. 145p.
P4-S19017 — $23.50.

McGAVOCK: Family: gen. hist. of James McGavock & his descendants, from 1760-1903. Robert Gray. 1903. 175p.
P4-S19023 — $28.00.

McGILL: Family: Celtics, Ulstermen & Amer. pioneers: hist., heraldry, & trad. By A. McGill. 1910. 345p.
P4-S19029 — $44.00.

McGINNESS: SCOTT Families. S.W. McGinness & M.R. Ford. 1892. 299p.
P4-S19030 — $45.00.

McGUIRE: Fam. in VA (Irish anc.) By W.G. Stannard. 1926. 126p.
P4-S19035 — $25.00.

McHENRY: Hist. of the McHenry fam. of Garrett Co., MD. C.E. Hoye. 5p.
P4-S19036 — $10.00.

McILHANY: Family; From "Some VA Families," by H.M. McIlhany (1903). 1903 43p.
P4-S19037 — $10.00.

McILHENNY: KING Families of Adams Co., PA. J.A. Himes. n.d. 162p.
P4-S19038 — $24.00.

McINTIRE: Family: desc. of Micum Mecantire of York Co., ME. By H.A. Davis. 1939. 251p.
P4-S19059 — $39.50.

McINTIRE: Desc. of Micum McIntire, a Scot. Highlander deported by Cromwell & settled at York, ME about 1668. R.H. McIntire. 1940. 158p.
P4-S19047 — $23.50.

McINTIRE: Anc. of Robert H. McIntire & Helen A. McIntire. R.H. McIntire. 1950. 447p.
P4-S19048 — $67.00.

McINTIRE: Desc. of Philip McIntire, a Scot. Highlander deported by Cromwell & settled at Reading, MA, about 1660. By R. McIntire. 1941. 218p.
P4-S19053 — $32.50.

McINTOSH: Family History of McIntosh of NC. By M.L. and A.A.M. McIntosh. n.d. 17p., typescript.
P4-S19060 — $10.00.

McKAY: Gen of the McKay Family — Desc of Elkenny McKay. Dr. J.A. McKay. 1896. 72p.
P4-S19066 — $11.00.

McKAY: Gen. of Hugh McKay & his Desc. By W. Kean. 1895. 76p.
P4-S19065 — $15.00.

McKEAN: Genealogies, from the Earliest Settlement of McKeans or McKeens in America to the Present Time, 1902 By Cornelius McKean. 1902. 213 + 106p.
P4-S19077 — $48.00.

McKEAN: Gen. of the McKean Fam. of PA, with biogr. of the Hon Thomas McKean. By R. Buchanan. 1890. 288p.
P4-S19071 — $37.00.

McKEE: Hist. of Desc. of David McKee. By J. McKee. 1892. 112p.
P4-S19083 — $22.50.

McKELVEY: Story of the McKelveys in America, Including Hist. & Biogr. Sketches in Genealogical Arrangement, By E.J.McK. Mabon. 1928. 88p.
P4-S19089 — $18.00.

McKINLEY: The Scotch Anc. of William McKinley, president of the US. By E.A. Claypool. 1897. 46p.
P4-S19090 — $10.00.

McKINNEY: History of the Families of McKinney-Brady-Quigley. By B.M.H. Swope. 1905. 326p.
P4-S19095 — $49.50.

McKINSTRY: Gen. of the McKinstry Fam., with Essay on the Scot-Irish immigr. to Amer. W. Willis. 1866. 46p.
P4-S19096 — $10.00.

McMASTERS: John McMasters of York Co., PA & some Desc., (in Larimer & allied fam.) By R. Mellon. 1903. 8p.
P4-S19097 — $10.00.

McMATH: Memorials of the McMath Family. F.M. McMath. 1898. xviii + 240 + 50p.
P4-S19102 — $46.00.

McMATH: Collections for a History of the Ancient Family of McMath. By F.M. McMath. 1937. 272p.
P4-S19101 — $43.00.

McMILLAN: McMillan Gen & History: Desc. of John McMillan & Wife Mary Arnott. W.F. McMillan & C.E. McMillan. 1908. 353 + 76p.
P4-S19103 — $65.00.

McNAIR: McNEAR — McNEIR Gen. By J.B. McNair. 1923. 322p.
P4-S19107 — $48.50.

McNAIR: Supplement to McNair — McNear 1923 J.B. McNair. 1928. 349p.
P4-S19125 — $52.25

McNAIR: McNEAR — McNEIR Gen. By J.B. McNair. 1955. 457p.
P4-S19113 — $71.00.

McNAIR: Supplement to above. By J.B. McNair. 1960. 314p.
P4-S19119 — $46.50.

McNARY: Family, with Fam. Trees & Hist. 1907. 175p.
P4-S19131 — $31.00.

McNEAL: A History & Genealogy of Some of the Descendants of Colonel John McNeal, 1680-1765. Wm. H. McNeal. 1936. 91p.
P4-S19132 — $28.00.

McNEAR: The William McNear Family, 1770-1990. By John David McNair. 1990. 63p.
P4-S19137 — $13.00.

McNEILL: Beginning in Belfast: Descendants of Sampson Stuart McNeill. Carolyn Chapman. 1995. 86p.
P4-S19143 — $18.50.

McPIKE: Tales of our Forefathers, & Biogr. Annals of Fam. Allied to those of McPike, Guest & Dumont. By E. F. McPike. 1898. 181p.
P4-S19149 — $27.00.

McQUISTON: McCUISTON — McQUESTEN Families, 1620-1937. By L.B. McQuiston. 1937. 750p.
P4-S19155 — $109.00.

McSPADDEN: "Way Back When ... " [Descendants of Samuel McSpadden of TN & Related Families] By Anna B. McSpadden. 1980. 160p.
P4-S19161 — $24.00.

McWHORTER: History of the Henry McWhorter family of NJ and WV. By Minnie S. McWhorter. 1948. 248p.
P4-S19167 — $39.00.

McWILLIE: CUNNINGHAM Families. By R.B. Johnson. 1914. 219p.
P4-S19173 — $33.50.

MEAD: CLARK Genealogy. By Eva Mead Firestone. 1946. 84 + 88p.
P4-S19182 — $26.00.

MEAD: Hist. & Gen. of the Mead family of Fairfield Co., CT, Eastern NY, Western VT & Western PA, from 1180-1900. By S.P. Mead. 1901. 480p.
P4-S19176 — $75.00.

MEAD: Index to above. (May be ordered bound with above). 1907. 73p.
P4-S19178 — $12.00.

MEAD: Mead Relations — Mead, Brown, Powell, Keyser, Kelly, Trumbo, Austin, Toler, Prichard. A.M. Prichard. 1933. iv + 265p.
P4-S19177 — $40.50.

MEADE: Andrew Meade of Ireland & VA. P.H. Baskervill 1921. xv + 170 + 42p.
P4-S18183 — $34.00.

MEANS: Robert Means & Desc. By C. N. Sinnett. 1929. 14p.
P4-S19184 — $10.00.

MEARS: Some Desc. of John & Lucy (Rockwell) Mears of Windsor, CT. By H. Healy. 1960. 116p.
P4-S19188 — $22.50.

MEEK: Meek Gen., with sketches of Adam Meek & his Desc., 1640-1902. By H. Meek. 1902. 54p.
P4-S19189 — $10.00.

MEHARRY: Hist of the Meharry Family in America — Desc of Alexander Meharry I. Committee. 1925. 384p.
P4-S19190 — $58.00.

MEIGS: Record of the desc. of Vincent Meigs, who came from Dorsetshire, Eng., to Amer. about 1635. By R.J. Meigs. 2nd ed. 1934. 230p.
P4-S19194 — $34.50.

MELLICK: Moelich-Malick-Mellick gen., extr. from "Story of an Old Farm." By A.D. Mellick. 1889. 85p.
P4-S19200 — $17.00.

MELVIN: Genealogy, From "Palmer Groups," By Emily W. Leavitt. 1901-1905. 124p.
P4-S19206 — $21.00.

MENDELSSOHN: Die familie Mendelssohn, 1729-1847; Vol. II, 1836-1847 (letters of Felix & Fanny Mendelsohn, IN GERMAN). By S. Hensel. 1898 400p.
P4-S19212 — $61.00.

MENDENHALL: PENNELL Fam. of Eng. & PA (in Heacock hist.) By R. L. Heacock. 1950. 9p.
P4-S19213 — $10.00.

MENUEZ: MENUEY Family: Jean Menuez & One Line of his Desc., and Dominique Prudhon & some of his desc. By Mary Ann Menuey Thies. 1995. 2 vols., 1516p.
P4-S19218 — $199.00.

MERCER: GARNETT; Gen. of the Mercer-Garnett Family of Essex Co., VA. By James M. Garnett. 1910. 63p.
P4-S19224 — $13.00.

MERIAM: Some Meriams & their Connection with other Fam. By R.N. Meriam. 1888. 52p.
P4-S19225 — $10.00.

MERIWETHER: Lineage of the Meriwethers & the Minors. M.Meriwether. 1895. v + 230 + 30p.
P4-S19237 — $40.00.

MERIWETHER: The Meriwethers & Their Connections. A Fam. Record Giving the Gen. of the Meriwethers in America. By L. H. A. Minor. 1892. 180p.
P4-S19236 — $24.00.

MERRIAM: Genealogy in England & America. By C. Pope. 1906. 515p.
P4-S19239 — $69.50.

MERRIAM: Family of Merriam of MA. By W. Appleton. 1892. 15p.
P4-S19238 — $10.00.

MERRICK: Genealogy of the Merrick-Merick-Myrick family of MA, 1636-1902. By G.B. Merrick. 1902. 502p.
P4-S19242 — $63.00.

MERRILL: A Merrill Memorial: An Account of the Descendants of Nathaniel Merrill, and Early Settler of Newbury, MA. Samuel Merrill. 1928. 730p.
P4-S19249 — $109.50.

MERRILL: A Contr. to the Gen. of the Merrill Fam. in Amer.; Being a Particular Record of the Anc. of Hamilton Wilcox Merrill. By F. Merrill. 1899. 20p.
P4-S19250 — $10.00.

MERRILL: James Merrill of New Gloucester & Lee, ME. By C. N. Sinnett. 21p.
P4-S19251 — $10.00.

MERRILL: Gen. publ. in 1864, as appendix to his book "My Wife & My Mother; Anc. of Frances E. Merrill & Naomi Humphrey." By H. Barbour. 1885. 84p.
P4-S19248 — $16.00.

MERRIMAN: Reunion of Descendants of Nathaniel Merriman at Wallingford, CT, 1913, with a Merriman Genealogy for Five Generations. By Donald L. Jacobus. 1914. 186p.
P4-S19254 — $29.50.

MERRITT: Revised Merritt Record. By D. Merritt. 1916. 204p.
P4-S19263 — $33.50.

MERRITT: Genealogy of the Somersetshire Family of Meriet [Merritt] B.W. Greenfield. 1914. 131p.
P4-S19260 — $24.00.

MERROW: Henry Merrow of Reading, MA & his desc. Named Marrow, Marrow & Merry. By O.E. Merrow. 1954. 659p.
P4-S19269 — $98.00.

MERRYMAN: Walter Merryman of Harpswell, ME & his Desc. By C. N. Sinnett. 1905. 123p.
P4-S19275 — $17.50.

MERWIN: Miles Merwin, 1772-1859; his Anc. & Desc. By C.G. Newton. 1903. 87p.
P4-S19287 — $17.50.

MERWIN: Miles Merwin, 1623-1697, & one branch of his desc. By C.G. Newton. 1909. 105p.
P4-S19281 — $19.00.

MESICK: Mesick Gen. J.F. Mesick. 46p.
P4-S19288 — $10.00.

MESSER: The Messers of Western Carolina & East Tennessee. By R.J. & C.R. Medford. 2001 932p.
P4-S19293 — $120.00.

MESSERVY: Genealogie de la famille Messery. In French with English addendum, 108 + 19p.
P4-S19299 — $18.50.

MESSINGER: Gen. of the Messinger Fam. By G. Messinger. 1863. 14p.
P4-S19300 — $10.00.

MESSINGER: Fam. in Eur. & Amer., by G. Messinger, With mem. of Hon. Daniel Messinger of Boston (Repr. NEHGR) By J. Dean. 1882. 12p.
P4-S19301 — $10.00.

METCALFE: Lineages (2nd ed.). By Howard H. Metcalfe. 1994 (reprinted by permission). 670p.
P4-S19305 — $99.50.

MEYER: MOYER; Genealogy of the Descendants of Christian & Hans Meyer (Moyer) & other Pioneers. By A.J. Fretz 1896. 739p.
P4-S19323 — $105.00.

MEYER: Genealogy of the Meyer Family. By H. Meyer. 1890. 131p.
P4-S19311 — $19.50.

MICHENER: The Micheners in America. Anna E. Shaddinger. 1958. 627p.
P4-S19324 — $94.00.

MICKLEY: Gen. of the Mickley Family of Amer., with Brief Gen. Rec. of the Michelet fam. of Metz. By M. Mickley. 1893. 182p.
P4-S19329 — $27.50.

MIDDLEBROOK: Register of the Middlebrook Family, Desc. of Joseph Middlebrook of Fairfield, CT. By L.F. Middlebrook. 1909. 411p.
P4-S19335 — $52.00.

MIEDEMA: Het Miedema-Boek ("The Miedema Book"); Genealogish overzicht van alle Friese geslchten Miedema, Deel I. By W.T. Vleer. IN FRISIAN. 1955. 96p.
P4-S19341 — $15.00.

MILES: John Miles of Concord, MA & his Desc. By J. M. Miles. 1920. 48p.
P4-S19348 — $10.00.

MILES: Genealogy of the Miles Family of Concord, MA. H.A. Miles. 1840. 12p.
P4-S19349 — $10.00.

MILES: Annals of Miles Anc. in PA & story of a Forged Will. By C.H. Banes. 1895. 182p.
P4-S19347 — $25.00.

MILK: History & Genealogy of the Milk-Milks Family. By Grace Croft, et al. 1952. 308p.
P4-S19353 — $47.00.

MILLER: Adam Miller & Barbara Koger Family Record of Massahhuten [today Elkton, VA]. By Floyd R. & Kathryn G. Mason. 2000. 268p.
P4-S19365 — $41.00.

MILLER: Matthias Miller & His Seventeen children, 2nd ed. By Floyd R. & Kathryn Garst Mason. 1996. 137p.
P4-S19366 — $21.00.

MILLER: Green Sea: Descendants of Joseph Miller. A.W. Miller. 1991. 194 + 12p.
P4-S19367 — $31.00.

MILLER: John Clarence Calhoun Miller Family, an appendix to Sketch of Miller & Calhoun-Miller Families (1927). By M. Miller Hayes. 1961. 56p.
P4-S19368 — $11.00.

MILLER: Sketch of Miller (English) & Calhoun-Miller (Scotch-Irish) families, with their Genealogy. By Florence McW. Miller. 1927. 196p.
P4-S19401 — $29.50.

MILLER: An Address Delivered Before the Miller Reunion at N. Waldoboro, ME, Sept. 7, 1904, with Genealogy. Frank B. Miller. 1909. 47p.
P4-S19369 — $10.00.

MILLER: Desc. of Jacob Miller, b. Germany. C.P. Miller. 1932. 240 + 24p.
P4-S19370 — $39.00.

MILLER: Desc. of Capt. Joseph Miller of West Springfield, MA, 1698-1908. By C.S. Williams. 1908. 39p.
P4-S19372 — $10.00.

MILLER: The Michael Miller & Susanna Bechtol Family Record. Floyd R. & Kathryn G. Mason. 1993. iii + 1061p.
P4-S19407 — $137.00.

MILLER: Genealogy of the Family of Millers, from 1570-1925. By Frank E. Miller. 1925. 378p.
P4-S19377 — $58.00.

MILLER: History & Genealogy of the Family of Miller, Woods, Harris, Wallace, Maupin, Oldham, Kavanaugh & Brown, & Others. By W.H. Miller. 1906. 855p.
P4-S19383 — $118.00.

MILLER: Anc. of Sarah Miller of ME. By W. Davis. 1939. 93p.
P4-S19371 — $17.50.

MILLER: The Millers of Millerburg & their Desc. J. B. Nicklin Jr. 1923. 514p.
P4-S19413 — $79.50.

MILLETT: Family in England, ca. 1500-1934. 1934. 32p.
P4-S19414 — $10.00.

MILLIGAN: The House of Milligan. J.C.K. Milligan. 1930. 213p.
P4-S19415 — $32.00.

MILLIKEN: History of the Families Millingas & Millanges of Saxony & Normandy, etc G.T. Ridlon. 1907. 882p.
P4-S19419 — $106.00.

MILLIS: Millis & Allied Fam. By F. Millis. 1944. 64p.
P4-S19422 — $12.50.

MILLS: COPE & Related Families of GA. By T.H. Goddard & J.H. Goddard, Sr. 1962. 326p.
P4-S19437 — $51.00.

MILLS: Family Marriages. By W. M. Clemens. 1916. 52p.
P4-S19432 — $10.00.

MILLS: Family of Capt. John Mills of Medway & Sherburn, MA & Amherst, NH. By W.C. Hill. 1942. 136p.
P4-S19443 — $21.00.

MILLS: Andrew Mills & his Descendants, with Genealogies of Related Families. By E.M.L. Taylor. 1944. 150p.
P4-S19431 — $23.00.

MILLS: My North Carolina Heritage, Volume 5. Col. Ambrose Mills, a Soldier in the King's army during the American Revolution. By Marshall L. Styles. 1995. 221p.
P4-S19449 — $34.00.

MILTON: Desc. of Elisha Milton, Sr. D.E. Page. 2002. xxvi + 411p.
P4-S19453 — $70.00.

MINEAR: Descendants of John Minear (1732?-1781), By C.J. Maxwell. 1948. 232p.
P4-S19455 — $36.50.

MINER: One Branch of the Miner Fam., with Extensive notes on the Wood, Lounsberry, Rogers & 50 other allied fam. of CT & L.I. By L.M. Selleck. 1928. 275p.
P4-S19461 — $41.00.

MINOT: Genealogical Record of the Minot fam. in Amer. & Eng. By J. G. Minot. 1897. 55p.
P4-S19462 — $10.50.

MISBACH: Our Home Place. A Personal Account of Life as it was for a Particular Farm Family in IA, from the early 1900s to Mid-century. Wanda Misbach Edgerton. 1976. 211p.
P4-S19463 — $24.00.

MITCHELL: Record. By C.B. Mitchell. 1925. 183p.
P4-S19473 — $27.00.

MITCHELL: Families of Haywood Co., NC. Marshall L. Styles. 2002. 134p.
P4-S19478 — $22.50.

MITCHELL: Family Magazine, Genealogical, Historical & Biographical. 1916-1917 96p.
P4-S19467 — $18.00.

MITCHELL: Family Records. By J.M. Seaver. 41p.
P4-S19468 — $10.00.

MITCHELL: David & Margaret Mitchell; Emigrants from Ulster, Ireland. J. Mitchell. 1907. 241p.
P4-S19469 — $36.00.

MITTONG: Gen of the Mittong Family. B.F. Wilson. 1926. 187 + 41p.
P4-S19480 — $34.00.

MOFFAT: Genealogies: Descent from Rev. John Moffat of Ulster Co. NY. By R. Burnham Moffat. 1909. 158p.
P4-S19491 — $24.50.

MOFFAT: Descendants of John Moffat (1770-1845): Four Sons, One Grandson, Scotland to No. America. By Charles Moffat. 2001. 162p.
P4-S19479 — $25.00.

MOFFAT: Moffatana Bulletin, Gen. Notes on Moffat. 1907-1915 44p.
P4-S19486 — $10.00.

MOFFAT: Family Histories of Moffat, Crangle, Pierson, Angel, Lichtenwalter, McNeelan. By Charles & Norma Moffat. 1990. 168p.
P4-S19485 — $27.00.

MOHLER: Ludwig Mohler & his Desc. 1696-1921. By C. G. Dunning. 1921. 63p.
P4-S19494 — $12.50.

MOLYNEUX: History, Genealogy & Biogr. of the Molyneux family. By N.Z. Molyneux. 1904. 370p.
P4-S19503 — $58.00.

MONNET: Family Genealogy, an Emphasis of a Noble Huguenot Heritage, Somewhat of the first immigrant, Isaac & Pierre Monnet. By O.E. Monnette. 1911. 1245p.
P4-S19509 — $169.00.

MONRO: The Monros of Auchinbowie & Cognate Families. By John Alexander Inglis. 1911. 219p.
P4-S19515 — $34.00.

MONROE: Ancestors & Descendants of Albert Nelson Monroe of Swansea & Brighton, MA (1819-1902). By Estelle W. Wait. 1958. 30p.
P4-S19516 — $10.00.

MONSON: The Portsmouth, NH Race of Monsons, Munsons, Mansons; Richard Monson & desc. By M.A. Munson. 1910. 89p.
P4-S19521 — $18.50.

MONTAGUE: Hist. & Gen. of the Montague Fam. of Amer., Desc. from Richard Montague of Hadley, MA & Peter of Lancaster Co., VA. By G.W. & W.L. Montague. 1886. 785p.
P4-S19539 — $117.50.

MONTAGUE: History & Genealogy of Peter Montague, of Nansemond & Lancaster Cos., VA & his Desc., 1621-1894. By G. W. Montague. 1894. 494p.
P4-S19533 — $77.00.

MONTAGUE: Meeting of the Montague Fam. at Hadley, MA, 1882. ed. By R. Montague. 1882. 107p.
P4-S19545 — $19.00.

MONTAGUE: Cowdray: The History of a Great English House [seat of the Montagues, with some genealogy]. By Juie Ann E. Roundell. 1884. 178p.
P4-S19527 — $25.00.

MONTGOMERY: Genealogical History of the Montgomerys & their Descendants. By D.B. Montgomery. 1903. 436p.
P4-S19557 — $67.50.

MONTGOMERY: Genealogical History of the Family of Montgomery, incl. the pedigree chart. By T.H. Montgomery. 1863. 170p.
P4-S19551 — $35.00.

MONTGOMERY: Family Magazine, Genealogical, Historical & Biographical. Ed. by Wm. M. Clemens 1915-1917 2 vols. in 1 book, 128 + 96p.
P4-S19563 — $39.50.

MONTGOMERY: History of the Descendants & Connections of William Montgomery & James Somerville. F. Montgomery. 1897. 52p.
P4-S19552 — $10.00.

MONTGOMERY: Origin & Hist. of the Montgomerys: Comtes de Montgomery, Ponthieu, Alencon & LaMarche; etc. By B.G. de Montgomery. 303p.
P4-S19575 — $47.50.

MONTGOMERY: Genealogy (desc. of Elias). By C.G. Hurlburt. 1926. 66p.
P4-S19569 — $13.50.

MONTROSS: A Family History: Pierre Montras & his Descendants, a Record of 300 years of the Montras-Montross-Montrose-Montress family John W. Taylor & Eva Taylor. 1958. 861p.
P4-S19581 — $115.00.

MOOAR: MOORS Gen; Abraham Mooar of Andover & his Desc., By G. Mooar. 1901. 97p.
P4-S19587 — $19.00.

MOOD: Family Album: An Acct. of the Moods of Charleston, SC & Connected Families. By T.McA. Stubbs. 1943. 246p.
P4-S19593 — $39.50.

MOODY: Descendants of Levi Moody & Rebecca Wages (b. 1801, Darlington Co. SC & b. 1811, SC). By Chaplain Dan Franklin. 1993. 247p.
P4-S19599 — $41.00.

MOOR: Descendants of Ensign John Moor of Canterbury, NH, b. 1696 — d. 1786. By H.P. Moore. 1918. 370p.
P4-S19605 — $57.00.

MOORE: A History of Col. James Moore of the Revolutionary Army. Comp by G. Heide Norris 1893. 57p.
P4-S19612 — $10.00.

MOORE: Family History, 1599-1962. By A.L. Moore. 1962. 42p.
P4-S19613 — $10.00.

MOORE: Rev. John Moore of Newtown, L.I., & Some of his Desc. By J.W. Moore. 1903. 541p.
P4-S19659 — $68.00.

MOORE: Genealogy of the Moore Family of Londonderry & Peterborough, NH, 1648-1924. By Geo. W. Moore. 1925. 109p.
P4-S19623 — $18.00.

MOORE: Reminiscences of the Moore family, descended from James Moore, who settled in Belle Fontaine, in the State of Illinois in 1782. By Capt. J.M. Moore. 1882. 72p.
P4-S19653 — $15.00.

MOORE: Memorial of Ransom Baldwin Moore & Allied Fams. By W.B. Towne. 1920. 138p.
P4-S19629 — $22.50.

MOORE: Ancestry of Sharpless & Rachel (Roberts) Moore, with their direct anc., to & incl. 36 first or immigrant anc. B.M. Haines. 1937. 214p.
P4-S19617 — $33.50.

MOORE: Proceedings of the Centennial Reunion of the Moore family, held at Belleville, IL, 1882. By Dr D.N. Moore & McCabe Moore. 1882. 82p.
P4-S19647 — $17.00.

MOORE: Family Records. By J.M. Seaver. 89p.
P4-S19641 — $17.50.

MOORE: & Allied families: Anc. of Wm. Henry Moore. By L.E. & A.L. de Forst. 1938. 744p.
P4-S19635 — $93.00.

MOORE: Ancestors & Descendants of Andrew Moore, 1612-1897. By J.A.M. Passmore. 1897. 2 vols; 1599p.
P4-S19611 — $179.00.

MORAN: Family: 200 Years in Detroit. By J.B. Moran. 1949. 152 + 32p.
P4-S19677 — $28.00.

MORAN: Descendants of Franklin Peirce Moran & Mary Adelaide Snyder Moran, with Family Tree of Early Moran Ancestors. 1991. 373p.
P4-S19665 — $59.00.

MORAN: Family. Part I, descendants of Hezekiah, Robert Milton, Franklin Pierce Moran & Alice Grace Moran Wright; Part II, Services of George Brinton McClellan for the Preservation of the Union. Pt. I By Evelyn Wright Brown, Pt. II By Alice "Grace" Moran Wright. 1997, 2004. 171 + 198 + 217p.
P4-S19671 — $87.00.

MORE: History of the More Family, & an Account of their Reunion in 1890, with a Genealogical Record. By David Fellows More. 1893. 409p.
P4-S19689 — $63.00.

MORE: Chronicles of the More Family. ed By Grace Van Dyke More. 1955. 424p.
P4-S19683 — $63.50.

MOREHEAD: Family of NC & VA. By J. Morehead. 1921. 147p.
P4-S19695 — $24.00.

MOREHEAD: Family Redords of The "Moorhead" Turner, Elliott, Warder, Morris, Hooe, Shotwell, Nebeker, Russell Families. C. R. Morehead. 1912. 80p.
P4-S19696 — $12.00.

MOREHOUSE: Anc. & Desc. of Gershom Morehouse, Jr., of Redding, CT, a capt. in the Amer. Rev. By C. Morehouse. 1894. 40p.
P4-S19697 — $10.00.

MOREY: Gen. of one Branch of Morey Fam. 1631-1890. By E.W. Leavitt. 1890. 36p.
P4-S19698 — $10.00.

MORGAN: A History of the Descendants of Henry Oscar Morgan & Ellen Jane Mandigo. By James K. Raywalt. 1991. 203p.
P4-S19707 — $29.00.

MORGAN: "Limbus Patrum Morganiae at Glamorganiae": Gen. of the Older Gams. of Lordships Morgan & Glarmorgan. By G.T. Clark. 1886. 620p.
P4-S19701 — $79.00.

MORGAN: History of that Branch of the Morgan Fam. beginning with James of New London. By C.W. Morgan. 1911. 93 + 7p.
P4-S19713 — $15.00.

MORGAN: Hist. of the Desc. of David Morgan in Amer. Gen. Traced through the Morgan & Howard fam. By W.A. Daily. 1909. 11p.
P4-S19702 — $10.00.

MORGAN: Francis Morgan: An Early VA Burgess & Some Desc. comp by A.N. Sims from notes of W.O.N. Scott. 1920. 194 + 11p.
P4-S19703 — $31.00.

MORGAN: Fam. of Morgan, Stanley & Blatchley. A.S. Blatchley. 1929. 43p.
P4-S19704 — $10.00.

MORGAN: Gen; A hist. of James Morgan of New London, CT & his desc., 1607-1869. By N.H. Morgan. 1869. 281p.
P4-S19719 — $42.00.

MORR: MYERS; Supplement of the Genealogies of the Morr & Myers Families, By Ralph B. Morr. 1971. 630p.
P4-S19725 — $89.00.v

MORR: Gen of the Morr Family. C.F. Moyer & M.E. Morr. 1896. 294p.
P4-S19724 — $44.00.

MORRELL: The Anc. of Daniel Morrell of Hartford, with his Desc. & Some Contemporary Fam. By F.V. Morrell. 1916. 132p.
P4-S19731 — $21.00.

MORRILL: Kindred in Amer; An Acct. of the Desc. of Abraham Morrill of Salisbury, MA, 1632-1662. By A.M. Smith. 1914-1931. 2 vols.
P4-S19737 — $89.00.

MORRILL: Amer. Anc. of Benj. Morrill & his Wife Miriam Pecker Morrill, of Salisbury, MA & their Desc. to 1901. H.E. Morrill. 1903. 21p.
P4-S19738 — $10.00.

MORRIS: Family of Phila.; Desc. of Anthony Morris, 1654-1721, 3-vol. set By R.C. Moon 1898. 3 vols., 1257p.
P4-S19743 — $200.00.

MORRIS: Ephraim & Pamela (Converse) Morris, their Anc. & Desc. By T.S. Morris. 1894. 207p.
P4-S19767 — $31.00.

MORRIS: Memorial of the Desc. of Amos Morris of East Haven, CT. By E. Hart & O. Street. 1853. 103p.
P4-S19785 — $19.00.

MORRIS: Genealogical & Hist. Reg. of the Desc. of Edw. Morris of Roxbury, MA & Woodstock, CT. By J.F. Morris. 1887. 423p.
P4-S19779 — $66.50.

MORRIS: First Supplement, vol IV. 1908. 210p.
P4-S19773 — $38.00.

MORRIS: Second Supplement, vol V. 1909. 295p.
P4-S19745 — $49.00.

MORRIS: Genealogy. J.M. Seaver. 51p.
P4-S19744 — $10.00.

MORRIS: Family of Western CT. By D.L. Jacobus. 1917. 15p.
P4-S19746 — $10.00.

MORRIS: My North Carolina Heritage, Vol. 4, Zebedee William Morris of Montgomery Co., NC By Marshall L. Styles. 2nd ed. 1996. 385p.
P4-S19797 — $59.00.

MORRISON: Genealogy of the Descendants of John Morrison & Prudence Gwyn. By G.H. Morrison. 1907. 31p.
P4-S19804 — $10.00.

MORRISON: History of the Morison or Morrison family; a Complete History of Most Settlers of Londonderry, NH, of 1719 & their Desc By L.A. Morrison. 1880. 468p.
P4-S19803 — $59.50.

MORSE: Memorial of the Morses. By Abner Morse. 1850. 250p.
P4-S19815 — $39.00.

MORSE: Descendants of Samuel G. Morse of Worthington, MA. By Harriet M. Weeks. 1906. 56p.
P4-S19810 — $11.50.

MORSE: Memorial of the Family of Morse. By H.D. Lord. 1896. 556p.
P4-S19809 — $87.00.

MORSE: Genealogy; Rev. of the Mem. of the Morse Fam., by Abner Morse, 1850. By Morse & Leavitt. 1903-1905. 2 vols., 596p.
P4-S19818 — $90.00.

MORSE: Desc. & Relatives of Lt. Benjamin Clarke Morse. L.T. Fadner. 2006. 29p.
P4-S19811 — $10.00.

MORSE: The Morse Record. A History of the Proceedings of The Morse Society in Annual Meeting, December 4, 1895 . . . 1895. 44p.
P4-S19812 — $10.00.

MORTON: Family Tree: Chauncy Morton & Betsy Pike: their Ancestry & Descent. John N. Morton. 1947. 125p.
P4-S19830 — $23.00.

MORTON: The Mortons & their Kin: a Genealogy & a Source Book. By D. Morton. 1920. 899p.
P4-S19836 — $119.00.

MORTON: George Morton of Plymouth Col. & some of his Desc. By J.K. Allen. 1908. 46p.
P4-S19831 — $10.00.

MORTON: Mem. Relating to the Anc. & Fam. of Hon. Levi Parsons Morton, V.P. of the US (1889-1893). By J.G. Leach. 1894. 198p.
P4-S19824 — $31.50.

MORTON: Family Record from 1668-1881 (settled Hatfield, MA) By C. Morton. 1881. 48p.
P4-S19832 — $10.00.

MORTON: The Stem of Morton: Collection of Genealogical Notes Respecting the Family of Morton. 1895 311p.
P4-S19842 — $47.50.

MORTON: Genealogy of the Morton Family, with Related Genealogies. By W.M. Morton. 1930. 47p.
P4-S19833 — $10.00.

MOSELEY: Gen. of Moseley Fam., Sketch of one Branch. By E.S. Moseley. 1878. 56p.
P4-S19843 — $11.50.

MOSES: Hist. Sketches of John Moses of Plymouth, Portsmouth, Windsor & Simsbury. By Z. Moses. 1890. 138p.
P4-S19854 — $23.50.

MOSHER: Orig. & hist. of Mosher Fam., & Gen. of One Branch of the Fam., 1660-1898. W. Mosher. 1898. 44p.
P4-S19855 — $10.00.

MOSSER: Mosser/Musser Family. Anita L. Mott. 1999. 227 + 22p.
P4-S19856 — $37.50.

MOTLEY: John Lothrop Motley. A Memoir. Oliver Wendell Holmes. 1889. 285p.
P4-S19859 — $42.50.

MOTT: HOPPER — STRIKER Fam. By H.S. Mott. 1898. 18p.
P4-S19861 — $10.00.

MOTT: Anc. & desc. of Adam & Anne Mott. T. Cornell. 1890. 419 + 76p.
P4-S19860 — $74.00.

MOTT: James Mott of Dutchess Co., NY & his desc. E.D. Harris. 1911. 62p.
P4-S19863 — $12.50.

MOULTON: Hist. of the Moulton fam; Rec. of the desc. of James Moulton of Salem & Wenham, MA, 1629-1905. E. & H. Moulton. 1905. 56p.
P4-S19873 — $11.00.

MOULTON: A Gen. Register of Some of the Desc. of John Moulton of Hampton, & of Joseph of Portsmouth. By T. Moulton. 1873. 44p.
P4-S19874 — $10.00.

MOULTON: Annals. By H.W. Moulton, ed. By C. Moulton. 1906. 454p.
P4-S19872 — $70.00.

MOULTON: Some Desc. of John & William Moulton of Hampton, NH, 1592-1892. By A.F. Moulton. 1892. 99p.
P4-S19878 — $19.00.

MOUNT: History & Gen. Record of the Mount & Flippin fams. By J.A. Mount. 1954. 120p.
P4-S19884 — $21.00.

MOWER: Genealogy, 1690-1897. By E. Mower. 11p.
P4-S19897 — $10.00.

MOWER: Ancestors & desc. of Hannah (Haile) Mower (1780-1855), including the Bowen, Breck, Bullock, etc . . . By Lyman & Karen Hoiriis Mower. 1997. 343p.
P4-S19890 — $52.00.

MOWER: Fam. hist.; a Gen. Rec. of the ME Branch of this Fam. By W.L. Mower. 1923. 251p.
P4-S19896 — $37.50.

MOWER: Richard Mower of Lynn & Some of his Desc. E.L. Smith. 1904. 16p.
P4-S19891 — $10.00.

MOWER: Ancestry of Calvin Robinson Mower (1840-1927) Including the families of Berry, Bigelow, Bowen, Breck, etc. . . . Lyman Mower. 2004. 697 + 8p.
P4-S19892 — $99.00.

MOWRY: Descendants of Nathaniel Mowry of RI. By W. Mowry. 1878. 343p. **P4-S19914 — $54.50.**

MOWRY: Supplement to The descendants of Nathaniel Mowry of RI. By Wm. A. Mowry. 1900. 95p. **P4-S19926 — $19.00.**

MOWRY: Desc. of John Mowry of RI. By W.A. Mowry. 1909. 292p. **P4-S19908 — $44.00.**

MOWRY: A Fam. Hist. Richard Mowry of Uxbridge, MA, his anc. & his desc. By W.A. Mowry. 1878. 239p. **P4-S19902 — $36.00.**

MOYER: Gen of the Moyer Family. Rev. A.J. Fretz. 1909. 186p. **P4-S19927 — $28.00.**

MUDD: The Mudd Family of the US, Revised edition. Richard D. Mudd. 1951, 1971 2 vols., xi + 1835p. **P4-S19928 — $275.00.**

MUDGE: Memorials: Being a Gen., Biogr. & Hist. Acct. of the Name of Mudge in America, 1638-1868. By A. Mudge. 1868. 457p. **P4-S19932 — $56.00.**

MULFORD: Gen. of Fam. of Mulford. By W.R. Mulford. 10p. **P4-S19933 — $10.00.**

MULLICA: Eric Mullica & His Descendants. C.J. Werner. 1930. 117p. **P4-S19934 — $18.00.**

MULLIKIN: Mullikins of MD. E.H. Baker. 1932. 204 + 30p. **P4-S19935 — $35.00.**

MUMFORD: Memorial: Being the Story of the New Eng. Mumfords from the Year 1655 to the Present Time. By J.G. Mumford. 1900. 279p. **P4-S19938 — $42.00.**

MUNCY: Decendants of Francis Muncy I, with Genealogy of Allied Families. By M.E. Shaw. 1956 357p. **P4-S19944 — $49.50.**

MUNDY: Nicholas Mundy & Desc. who Settled in NJ in 1665. By E.F. Mundy. 1907. 160p. **P4-S19950 — $24.50.**

MUNGER: Book; Something of Mungers, 1639-1914, Incl. Some who Mistakenly Write the Name Monger & Mongor, By J.B. Munger. 1915. 634p. **P4-S19953 — $81.00.**

MUNRO: History of the Munros of Fowlis, with Gen. of the Principal Fams. of the Name. By A. MacKenzie. 1908 632p. **P4-S19959 — $95.00.**

MUNRO: Sketch of the Munro Clan; Also of William Munro Who, Deported from Scotland, Settled in Lexington, MA. By J.P. Munroe. 1900. 80p. **P4-S19965 — $16.00.**

MUNROE: Genealogy. By J.G. Locke. 1853. 15p. **P4-S19966 — $10.00.**

MUNSELL: An Hist. & Gen. Acct. of the Ancient Fam. of Maunsell-Mansell-Mansel. By W.W. Mansell. 1850 88p. **P4-S19977 — $17.50.**

MUNSELL: Gen. of the Windsor Fam. of Munsell. F. Munsell. 1880. 6p. **P4-S19972 — $10.00.**

MUNSELL: A Gen. of the Munsell Fam. (Munsill, Monsell, Maunsell) in America. By F. Munsell. 1884. 130p. **P4-S19971 — $21.50.**

MUNSEY: HOPKINS: Being the Anc. of Andrew Chauncey Munsey & Mary Jane Merrill Hopkins. By D.O.S. Lowell. 1920. 233p. **P4-S19983 — $36.00.**

MUNSON: Trad. Concerning the Origin of the Amer. Munsons. By M.A. Munson. 1897. 6p. **P4-S19990 — $10.00.**

MUNSON: Record, 1637-1887; Gen. & Biogr. Acct. of Capt. Thomas Munson (pioneer of Hartford & New Haven) & his Desc. By M. Munson. 1895. 2 vols., 1263p. **P4-S19989 — $169.00.**

MURDOCH: Along the Susquehanna; Desc. of Robert Murdoch. By L. Russell. 1917. 9p. **P4-S19991 — $10.00.**

MURDOCK: Robert Murdock of Roxbury, MA & Some of his Descendants By Jos. B. Murdock. 1925. 274p. **P4-S19995 — $44.00.**

MURPHY: Family; Genealogy, History & Biography By M.W. Downes. 1909. 363p. **P4-S20001 — $57.50.**

MURRAY: WILSON. Murray-Wilson. S.W. Murrary. 1900. 164 + 20p. **P4-S20008 — $28.00.**

MURRAY: CONWELL Genealogy & Allied Families. By M.L. Lawrence & G.L. Lombard. 1938. 115p. **P4-S20019 — $19.50.**

MURRAY: Descendants of Jonathan Murray of E. Guilford, CT. By W.B. Murray. 1956. 385p. **P4-S20007 — $61.50.**

MURRAY: Echoes in Time: The Murray, Connor & Moorer Families of SC. By G. Monroe Black. 1997. 399p. **P4-S20013 — $59.00.**

MURRAY: Jonathan Murray of E. Guilford, CT & some of his desc. By W.B. Murray. 1948. 8p. **P4-S20009 — $10.00.**

MURRAY: Letters of James Murray, Loyalist. 1901. 324p. **P4-S20010 — $42.00.**

MUSGRAVE: Notes on the Ancient Family of Musgrave of Musgrave, Westmorland [England], & its Various Branches By Percy Musgrave. 1911. 351p. **P4-S20025 — $49.50.**

MUSSER: Desc. of Sam'l Musser (1812-96). By Rachel Saul Tefft. 1999. 15p. **P4-S20026 — $10.00.**

MUTCH: Genealogy of the Mutch Family. By James R. Mutch. 1929. 94p. **P4-S20031 — $18.00.**

MYGATT: Hist. Notice of Joseph Mygatt of Cambridge, with a Record of his Desc. By F.T. Mygatt. 1853. 116p. **P4-S20034 — $20.00.**

N

NASH: Gen Rec of the Desc of William Nash of Bucks Co, PA. A.J. Fretz. 1903. 136p.
P4-S20038 — $20.00.

NASH: Fifty Puritan Anc., 1628-1660; Gen. Notes, 1560-1900. By E.T. Nash. 1902. 194p.
P4-S20037 — $33.00.

NASH: Fam., from Thomas Nash, 1638. By Nash & Noble. 1850. 16p.
P4-S20039 — $10.00.

NASH: The Nash Family Updated: Descendants of Thomas Nash of New Haven, CT, circa 1640. Deborah Lee Rothery. 2003. xxxviii + 2732p.
P4-S20040 — $275.00.

NASH: Family, or Records of the Desc. of Thomas Nash of New Haven, CT, 1640. S. Nash. 1853. 304p.
P4-S20043 — $48.50.

NAVARRE: Or, Researches After the Desc. of Robert Navarre, Whose Anc. are the Noble Bourbons of France. By C. Denissen. 1897. 418p.
P4-S20049 — $66.00.

NEAL: Anc. of Joseph Neal, 1769-c.1835, of Litchfield, ME, Incl. Hall, White, Rogers, Tilden, Twisden, etc. By W.G. Davis. 1945. 145p.
P4-S20055 — $23.50.

NEAL: Record; a List of the Desc. of John Neale, Early Settler of Salem, MA. By T.A. Neal. 1856. 30p.
P4-S20056 — $10.00.

NEAL: Descendants of John & Emma Neal. By R.T. Rowe. 1974. 68p.
P4-S20061 — $14.00.

NEAL: Family, By Emma E. Brigham. 1938. 378p.
P4-S20067 — $57.00.

NEALE: Charter & Records of Neales of Berkley, Yate & Corsham [England]. By John A. Neale. 1906 263p.
P4-S20073 — $41.00.

NEEDHAM: Desc. of John Needham of Braintree, MA & Boston 1669-75, 1675-89. By R.F. Needham. 1934. 18p.
P4-S20080 — $10.00.

NEEDHAM: Needhams of Wales, MA & Stafford, CT. By G.O. Chapman. 1942. 93p.
P4-S20079 — $20.00.

NEFF: Memorial of the Neff Family. E.E. Neff, MD. 1931. xiv + 132p.
P4-S20086 — $22.00.

NEFF: A Chronicle, Together with a Little Romance, Regarding Rudolf & Jacob Naf, of Frankford, PA & their Desc. By E. C. Neff. 1886. 352p.
P4-S20085 — $55.50.

NEFF: Addenda. 1899. 35p.
P4-S20087 — $10.00.

NEIL: From Generation to Generation: The Gens of Neil, Tillinghaste, Mallon, Slayton, Bargar & Chapin. J.E.S. Neil. 1915. 131p.
P4-S20090 — $20.00.

NEILL: John Neill of Lewes, DE, 1739, & his Descendants. By Edw. D. Neill. 1875. 127p.
P4-S20091 — $21.00.

NELL: Nell Family in the US. By R. B. Nell. 1929. 104p.
P4-S20097 — $19.00.

NELSON: Desc. of John Nelson & his Children, & Notes on the Fam. of Tailer & Stoughton. T. Prime. 1894. 61p.
P4-S20100 — $12.00.

NELSON: Anthony Nelson, 17th cent. PA & NJ & Some of his Desc. By E.G. Van Name. 1962. 53p.
P4-S20110 — $11.00.

NELSON: Descendants of John Nelson, Sr. — Mary Toby, Stafford Co., VA, 1740-1959, with Related Families. Olive N. Gibson. 1959. 350p.
P4-S20109 — $54.00.

NELSON: Family Record of the Desc. of Thomas Nelson & Joan, His Wife, by One of Them. 1868. 32p.
P4-S20111 — $10.00.

NELSON: Family Records. By J.M. Seaver. 31p.
P4-S20112 — $10.00.

NELSON: The Descendants of Henry Nelson, Sr. & Related Families. Charles D. Nelson. 2005. 229p.
P4-S20113 — $35.00.

NESBIT: Genealogy of the Nesbit, Ross, Porter, Taggart fam. of PA. By B.T. Hartman. 1929. 242p.
P4-S20115 — $36.00.

NEVILLE: Family of Eng. & the US. By W.E.N. Wilson. 1964. 115p.
P4-S20121 — $19.00.

NEVIN: Genealogica (some desc. of Daniel Nevin, Cumberland Valley, PA, 1770). By John D. Nevin. 1919-1929 2 vols. in 1, 435p.
P4-S20127 — $65.00.

NEVIUS: Joannes Nevius, Schepen & 3rd Secretary of New Amsterdam, & his desc., 1627-1900. By A. Van Doren Honeyman. 1900. 732p.
P4-S20139 — $99.00.

NEWBAKER: Gen. Record of the Desc. of Andrew Newbaker of Hardwick Twp., Warren Co., NJ, with hist. & biogr. sketches. A.J. Fretz. 1908. 42p.
P4-S20140 — $10.00.

NEWBERG: A Swedish Ancestry: The Newberg & Magnuson Families. By James K Raywalt. 1993. 192p.
P4-S20145 — $29.50.

NEWBERRY: Family of Windsor, CT in the line of Clarinda (Newberry) Goodwin of Hartford, CT, 1634-1866. By F.F. Starr. 1898. 70p.
P4-S20151 — $13.50.

NEWCOMB: Gen. Memoir of the Newcomb Fam. Containing Records of Nearly Every Person of the Name in America from 1635-1874. By J.B. Newcomb. 1874. 600p.
P4-S20160 — $76.00.

NEWCOMB: Andrew Newcomb, 1618-1686, & his Desc: a rev. ed. of "Gen. Mem." of the Newcomb fam. (1874). By B.M. Newcomb. 1923. 1021p.
P4-S20154 — $144.50.

NEWCOMER: Biographical Sketch of Benj. Franklin Newcomer. By Waldo Newcomer. 1902. 93p.
P4-S20166 — $17.00.

NEWELL: Descendants of Thomas Newell (1730-1803). By Rachel Saul Tefft. 1997. 180p.
P4-S20172 — $29.00.

NEWELL: Thomas Newell, Who Settled in Farmington, CT, 1632, & his Descendants. By M.A. Hall. 1878. 268p.
P4-S20178 — $40.00.

NEWHALL: The Record of My Anc. By C.L. Newhall. 1899. 222p.
P4-S20181 — $33.00.

NEWHOUSE: The Newhouse Familiy. J.R. Newhouse. 1915. 116p.
P4-S20182 — $17.00.

For hardcover versions, see the order form on page v. To order, call 1-888-296-3447.

NEWLOVE: Family Tree [Canadian Descendants of Newlove Family of Yorkshire, Eng.], By Thomas V. Newlove. 1971. 248p.
P4-S20187 — $39.00.

NEWMAN: Desc. of Samuel Newman of Rehoboth, MA. By S.C. Newman. 1860. 14p.
P4-S20183 — $10.00.

NEWTON: Rev. Roger Newton, Deceased 1683 & One Line of His Descendants & Abner Newton, 1764-1852, Ancestors & Descendants. By Caroline G. Newton. 1912. 280p.
P4-S20208 — $44.00.

NEWTON: Hist. of the Newton Fam. of Col. Amer., with Amer. Hist. of Fam. Interest Not Obtainable Elsewhere, Volume I By C.A. Newton. 1927. 96p.
P4-S20193 — $16.00.

NEWTON: Memoirs of Erastus & Julia Newton & Genealogical Records of the Newton & Hatch Families. By R.G. Newton. 1882. 187p.
P4-S20199 — $27.50.

NEWTON: Gen. Notes on Desc. of Thomas Newton of Fairfield, CT, by N. Lull; & Henry Wallbridge of Preston, CT. W. Wallbridge. 1896. 39p.
P4-S20200 — $10.00.

NEWTON: Being a Record of the Desc. of Richard Newton of Sudbury & Marlborough, MA, 1638. By E.N. Leonard. 1915. 880p.
P4-S20202 — $109.00.

NICHOLLS: Sergeant Francis Nicholls of Stratford, CT, 1639, & the Desc. of his Son Caleb Nicholls. By W. Nicholls. 1909. 101p.
P4-S20214 — $16.00.

NICHOLS: Anc. of Willard Atherton Nichols, Who Participated in the Civil & Military Affairs of the American Colonies. By W. A. Nichols. 1911. 64p.
P4-S20220 — $15.00.

NICHOLS: Family in America. By L.N. Nichols. 1919. 16p.
P4-S20221 — $10.00.

NICHOLS: Richard Nichols, the Immigrant. George E. Nichols. 1929. 46p.
P4-S20222 — $10.00.

NICHOLSON: ADAMS; Historical Data of the Nicholson Adams & Allied Families. Mrs J.L. Mims. 1944. 68p.
P4-S20226 — $14.00.

NICKOLS: Historical & Genealogical Sketch of the Nickols-Thomas Family in OH. Robert F. Bartlett. 1909. 16p.
P4-S20227 — $10.00.

NICOLET: Desc. of Jules Auguste Nicolet (1834-1912) of Neuchatel, Switzerland, who settled in Alton, IL. By H.F. Kershner. 1969. 50p.
P4-S20228 — $11.00.

NIVEN: The Family of Niven, with Biographical Sketches [& the Voyages, Letters & Diaries of Capt. John Niven]. John Niven. 1960. 252p.
P4-S20232 — $37.00.

NOBLE: DOUGHERTY. Descendants & Antecedents of Milton Bird & Leonora Dougherty Noble. By M. Birdie Noble Feiner. 1961. 398p.
P4-S20241 — $61.00.

NOBLE: Christopher Noble of Portsmouth, NH & some of his Desc. By F.A. Davis. 45p.
P4-S20236 — $10.00.

NOBLE: Hist. & Gen. of the Fam. of Thomas Noble, of Westfield, MA, with Gen. Notes of Other Fam. By the Name of Noble. By L.M. Boltwood. 1878. 870p.
P4-S20235 — $108.50.

NORRIS: Family of MD. By T.M. Myers. 1916. 119p.
P4-S20259 — $22.50.

NORRIS: Lineage & Biography of the Norris Family in Amer., from 1640-1892. By L.A. Morrison. 1892. 207p.
P4-S20253 — $31.00.

NORRIS: Jonathan & Tamesin Norris of ME, their Anc. & Desc. By H.M. Norris. 1906. 60p.
P4-S20244 — $12.00.

NORTH: An Acct. of the Celebration of the Diamond Wedding of Frederick & Harriet North, with Gen. By F.A. North. 1890. 64p.
P4-S20265 — $16.00.

NORTH: Records of the North fam. in Cont. of the Fam. hist. F.A. North, (1890-1918). By L.B. Deming. 17p.
P4-S20266 — $10.00.

NORTH: John North of Farmington, CT & his desc., with an acct. of other North fams. By D. North. 1921. 334p.
P4-S20268 — $46.50.

NORTHEND: Desc. of Ezekiel Northend of Rowley, MA. By W.D. Northend. 1874. 16p.
P4-S20270 — $10.00.

NORTHRUP: NORTHROP Gen.; Rec. of the Known Desc. of Joseph Northrup, an orig. settler of Milford, CT in 1639. A.J. Northrup. 1908. 473p.
P4-S20274 — $74.00.

NORTHRUP: Gen. (Repr. NEHGR). By A.J. Northrup. 1889. 13p.
P4-S20275 — $10.00.

NORTON: The Norton-Lathrop-Tolles-Doty Ancestry & Wright-Briggs-Cogswell-Dudley Ancestry. J.E. Norton. 1935. 187 + 7p.
P4-S20276 — $29.00.

NORTON: Rev. John Norton of Middleton (Repr. NEHGR). By Z.S. Eldredge. 1899. 5p.
P4-S20277 — $10.00.

NORTON: The desc. of Thomas Norton of Guilford, CT (Repr. NEHGR). By R.D. Smyth. 1900. 8p.
P4-S20278 — $10.00.

NORTON: Desc & Anc of Charles Norton, of Guilford, CT. Albert B. Norton. 1856. 26p.
P4-S20279 — $10.00.

NORWALK: Paternal Ancestry of Alexandra Leah Aschheim Feld: Gen. of the Norwalk, Eilenberg, Heilperin, Gutman & Kronenberg families By Jay Norwalk. 1997. 99 + 29p.
P4-S20286 — $21.00.

NOTHSTEIN: First Nothstein Family History, 1750-1950 [desc. of Peter Nothstein of PA]. n.a. 1950. 119 + 26p.
P4-S20292 — $22.50.

NOURSE: James Nourse & His Desc. By M.C.N. Lyle. 1897. 167p.
P4-S20298 — $22.50.

NOWLIN: STONE Gen: Record of the desc. of James Nowlin, who came to Pittsylvania Co., VA, from Ireland about 1700. James E. Nowlin. 1916. 548p.
P4-S20304 — $82.00.

NOYES: GILMAN Ancestry; Being a Series of Sketches, With a Chart of the Anc. of Charles Phelps Noyes & Emily H. (Gilman) Noyes, his Wife. By C.P. Noyes.F 1907. 478p.
P4-S20331 — $75.00.

NOYES: Gen. Record of Some of the Noyes Desc. of James, Nicholas & Peter Noyes, Vol I. By H. & H. Noyes. 1904. 575p.
P4-S20310 — $89.00.

NOYES: Gen. Record of Some of the Noyes Desc of James, Nicholas & Peter Noyes. Vol II. H & H. Noyes 1904. 437p.
P4-S20316 — $65.50.

NOYES: Pedigree, (Repr. NEHGR). By J.A. Noyes. 1899. 11p.
P4-S20311 — $10.00.

NOYES: Desc. of Rev. Wm. Noyes, b. Eng. 1568, in Direct Line to Laverne Noyes Giffem & Frances Noyes Giffen, Incl. Allied Fams. 1900. 115p.
P4-S20325 — $16.50.

NOYES: A Gen. Acct. of the Noyes Fam., Together with the Dike fam., & Fuller & Edson Fam. J. Noyes. 1861. 13p.
P4-S20312 — $10.00.

NOYES: Record of a branch of the desc. of Rev. James Noyes, Newbury, 1634-1656. By H.N. Noyes. 1889. 32p.
P4-S20313 — $10.00.

NUCKOLLS: First Virginia Nuckolls & Kindred, Book II, Sponsored by Nuckolls Worldwide Kindred Soc. 2000. 920p.
P4-S20337 — $125.00.

NULL: OHLER; Descendants of Jacob Null & Lucy Ohler. By Rachel Saul Tefft. 1997. 103p.
P4-S20343 — $16.00.

NUNN: Sketch of John Milton Nunn & Sally Heiston Nunn, Their Anc. & Desc. By C. & H. Nunn. 1939. 64p.
P4-S20349 — $13.00.

NUNN: My Grandmother's Name Was Clyde. Gen. of the Ancestors & Desc. of Evelyn Clyde Nunn & Robert Steele McCormick. Mary Marie McCormick Spainhour. 2003. 441p.
P4-S20350 — $66.00.

NUTTING: Nutting Genealogy. J.K. Nutting. 1908. 278p.
P4-S20359 — $42.00.

NUTTING: Gen of Desc of John Nutting of S. Amherst, MA. W.M. Nutting 1929. 340 + 54p.
P4-S20360 — $59.00.

NUTTING: Gen. A record of Some of the Desc. of John Nutting of Groton, MA. By J.K. Nutting. 1908. 278p.
P4-S20358 — $36.50.

NYCE: The Abraham & Leanna (Godshall) Nyce Family: Their Ancestors & Descendants. By Gladys P.N. Mease & Gwendolyn P.N. Hartzel. 1986. 109p.
P4-S20364 — $19.50.

NYDEGGER: Nydegger Family Chronicles. J.A. Nydegger. 1930. 123 + 18p.
P4-S20365 — $21.00.

NYE: Genealogy of the Nye Family. By G. Nye & F. Best, ed. By D.F. Nye. 1907. 704p.
P4-S20370 — $89.00.

O

OAKLEAF: Desc. of Benjamin Peter Oakleaf. A. Chittenden. 2006. 73p.
P4-S20375 — $11.00.

OAKS: OAKES Fam. Reg., Nathaniel Oak of Marlboro, MA & 3 Gen. of His Desc. By H.L. Oak. 1906. 90p.
P4-S20376 — $18.50.

OATLEY: The Oatley Family in America & Their Descendants. H.J. Oatley. 1970. 865p.
P4-S20377 — $142.00.

OBERHOLTZER: Gen. Rec. of the Desc. of Marton Oberholtzer, with Hist. & Biogr. By A.J. Fretz. 1903. 254p.
P4-S20382 — $33.00.

OBERHOLTZER: Some Account of Jacob Oberholtzer Who Settled, About 1719, in Franconia Twp., Montgomery Co., PA & of some descendants By Elisha S. Loomis. 1931. 412p.
P4-S20388 — $61.00.

OBERWINDER: Die Familie Oberwinder: Gen. Encyclopedia of the Family Connections of Richard Maria Wilhelm Oberwinder. By Howard Metcalf. 1999. 146p.
P4-S20394 — $24.00.

O'BRIAN: Brian O'Brian of Berks Co., PA & Cornelius O'Bryan of Rockingham Co., VA & their desc. By M.J. O'Brien. 1928. 18p.
P4-S20395 — $10.00.

O'BRIEN: PA O'Briens in Land Records & in Col.& Rev. Wars. By M.J. O'Brien. 1928. 15p.
P4-S20396 — $10.00.

O'BRIEN: The O'Briens of Machias, ME. Patriots of the American Revolution, Together with a Sketch of the Clan O'Brien. By Sherman & Murray. 1904. 87p.
P4-S20406 — $16.50.

O'BRIEN: Historical Memoir of the O'Briens, with Notes, Appendix & a Gen. Table of Their Several Branches. By Johm O'Donoghue. 1860 551p.
P4-S20400 — $79.00.

O'DALY: Hist of the O'Dalys; The Story of the Ancient Irish Sept the Race of Dalach of Corca Adaimh. comp By E.E. O'Daly. 1937. 546 + 30p.
P4-S20407 — $92.00.

ODELL: Genealogy in the US & Canada (1635-1935); Ten Gen. in Amer. in Direct Line. By M.A.L. Pool. 1935. 123p.
P4-S20412 — $21.00.

ODIORNE: Gen. of the Odiorne fam., with Notices of Other Fam. Connected Therewith. By J.C. Odiorne. 1875. 232p.
P4-S20418 — $33.00.

OGDEN: PRESTON gen; Anc. & desc. of Capt. Benj. Stratton Ogden & his wife Nancy (Preston) Ogden. By Stone & Powell. 1914. 31p.
P4-S20425 — $10.00.

OGDEN: Quaker Ogdens in Amer; David Ogden of Ye Goode Ship "Welcome" & His Desc., 1682-1897. By C. Ogden. 1898. 245p.
P4-S20433 — $32.00.

OGDEN: Ogdens of So. Jersey; The desc. of John Ogden of Fairfield, CT & New Fairfield, NJ, b. 1673; d. 1745. W.O. Sheeler & E.D. Halsey. 1894. 36p.
P4-S20426 — $10.00.

OGDEN: Family Hist. in the Line of Lt. Benjamin Ogden of NY (1735-1780) & His Wife, Rachel Westervelt. By A. Vermilve. 1906. 119p.
P4-S20424 — $18.00.

OGDEN: Family in America (Elizabeth-town branch) & their Eng. anc. John Ogden, the Pilgrim, & his desc., 1640-1906; By W.O. Wheeler. 1907. 526p.
P4-S20430 — $79.50.

OGLE: BERTRAM; Ogle & Bothal: history of the Baronies of Ogle, Bothal & Hepple, & of the families of Ogle & Bertram. Sir Henry Ogle. 1902 426 + 70p.
P4-S20442 — $75.00.

OGLE: The English origin of John Ogle, first of the name in DE. By F.H. Hibbard & S. Parks 1967. 47p.
P4-S20443 — $10.00.

OKELY: A Pedigree & Family History, John Okely of Bedford, England. 1899. 91 + 10p.
P4-S20444 — $15.00.

OLCOTT: Fam. of Hartford, CT, in the Line of Eunice Olcott Goodwin, 1639-1807. By F. Starr. 1899. 84p.
P4-S20451 — $16.50.

OLCOTT: Descendants of Thomas Olcott, One of the First Settlers of Hartford CT. By Nathaniel Goodwin. 1845. 63p.
P4-S20446 — $13.00.

OLCOTT: The Desc. of Thomas Olcott, One of the First Settlers of Hartford, CT. By N. Goodwin. Rev. By H. Olcott 1874. 124p.
P4-S20457 — $18.50.

OLDFATHER: Gen of the Oldfather Family. R.A. Longman. 1911. 220p.
P4-S20458 — $33.00.

OLDS: The Olds (Old, Ould) Family in England & America. E.B. Olds. 1915. 359p.
P4-S20459 — $54.00.

OLIN: Biogr. Sketches & Records of the Ezra Olin Fam. G.S. Nye. 1892. 441p.
P4-S20466 — $68.50.

OLIN: A Complete Record of the John Olin Fam., 1678-1893. By C.C. Olin. 1893. 234p.
P4-S20460 — $30.00.

OLIVER: Hist. of the Oliver, Vassall & Royall Houses in Dorchester, Cambridge & Medford, (Repr. Gen. Magazine) By R. T. Jackson. 1907. 17p.
P4-S20467 — $10.00.

OLIVER: Gen. of Desc. of Thomas Oliver, of Bristol, Eng., & of Boston, New Eng., in Direct Line of Rev. Daniel Oliver. By H. K. Oliver. 1868. 7p.
P4-S20468 — $10.00.

OLIVER: Anc. of Mary Oliver 1640-1698, Wife of Sam'l Appleton of Ipswich, MA. W. Appleton 1867. 29p.
P4-S20469 — $10.00.

OLMSTEAD: Abridged Gen. of Olmstead Fam. of New Eng. By E.L. Thomas. 1869. 30p.
P4-S20470 — $10.00.

OLMSTEAD: Desc. of Capt. Richard Olmstead of Fairfield, CT (Repr. NEHGR). By F.S. Hammond. 1905. 6p.
P4-S20471 — $10.00.

OLMSTED: Gen. of the Olmsted Fam. in Amer; The desc. of James & Richard Olmsted, 1632-1912. By H.K. Olmsted, rev. By G.K. Ward. 1912. 539p.
P4-S20472 — $82.00.

OLNEY: Gen of the Descs of Thomas Olney, an Original Proprietor of Providence, RI, Who Came from England in 1635. By J.H. Olney. 1889. 298p.
P4-S20475 — $44.50.

OLOFSSON: Know Desc of Carl Olofsson. 1953. 69 + 24p.
P4-S20476 — $14.00.

O'MEAGHERS: Some Hist. Notices of the O'Meaghers of Iberrin. By J.C. O'Meagher. 1890. 216p.
P4-S20481 — $32.00.

OMOHUNDRO: Genealogical Record: The Omohundro & Allied Families in America By Malvern H. Omohundro. 1951. 1287p.
P4-S20487 — $159.00.

ONDERDONK: Genealogy of the Onderdonk Family in America. By E. & A. Onderdonk. 1910. 374p.
P4-S20493 — $58.50.

ONG: The Ong Family of America. A.R. Ong. 1906. 171 + 59p.
P4-S20494 — $35.00.

OOTHOUT: Fam., extr. from Gen. Notes of NY & New Eng. Fam. By S.V. Talcott. 1883. 15p.
P4-S20495 — $5.00.

OPDYKE:Genealogy, containing the Opdyck-Opdycke -Updike Amer. Desc. of the of the Wesel & Holland fams. (does not include illustrations published with some original copies), By C.W. Opdyke. 1889. 499p.
P4-S20499 — $77.50.

ORMSBY: Short acct. of fam. of Ormsby of Pittsburgh, PA. By O.O. Page. 1892. 48p.
P4-S20500 — $10.00.

O'ROURKE: An Irish Odyssey: History of the Family O'Rourke. By Stephen Vincent O'Rourke, 1999. 162p.
P4-S20505 — $24.50.

ORTON: Acct. of Azaraih Orton of Farmington, IL, & desc. By E. Orton. 1900. 23p.
P4-S20509 — $10.00.

ORTON: An acct. of the desc. of Thomas Orton of Windsor, CT, 1641. By E. Orton. 1896. 220p.
P4-S20508 — $29.50.

ORVIS: A hist. of the Orvis fam. in Amer. By F.W. Orvis. 1922. 203p.
P4-S20514 — $30.00.

OSBORN: Gen. of Osborn fam., 1755-1891. By H. Runyan. 1891. 11p.
P4-S20515 — $10.00.

OSBORNE: Thomas Osborne of Ashford, Kent, England & some of his American descendants. By Daniel J. Weeks. Rev. ed., 1994. 32p.
P4-S20516 — $10.00.

OSGOOD: Gen. of the desc. of John, Christopher & William Osgood who settled in New England early in the 17th century. By I. Osgood. 1894. 491p.
P4-S20517 — $62.00.

OSWALD: The Desc of Henry Oswald. comp by C. E. C. Oswald. 1907. 106 + 30p.
P4-SS20518 — $20.00.

OTIS: A gen. memoir of the fam. of Richard Otis, & collaterally of the fam. of Baker, Varney, Waldron (& others). By H.N. Otis. 1851. 50p.
P4-S20524 — $10.00.

OTIS: Gen & Hist Memoir of the Otis family in America W.A. Otis. 1924. 729p.
P4-S20523 — $109.00.

OTIS: Some of the desc. of Ephraim Otis & Rachel (Hersey) Otis of Scituate, MA. By R.L. Weis. 1943. 74p.
P4-S20529 — $15.00.

OVERMYER: Overmyer History & Genealogy. B.B. & J.C. Overmyer. 1905. 336 + 72p.
P4-S20530 — $61.00.

OWEN: Isaac Owen of Hebron, CT & some desc. (Repr. NEHGR). By C.J. Huyck. 10p.
P4-S20536 — $10.00.

OWEN: John Owen of Windsor, CT & some desc. 31p.
P4-S20537 — $10.00.

OWEN: Family Records. By J. Montgomery Seaver. 1929. 34p.
P4-S20538 — $10.00.

OWEN: Gen. of Several allied families: Frazer, Owen, Bessellieu, Carter, Shaw, et al. Charles Owen Johnson. 1961. 543p.
P4-S20541 — $83.50.

OWEN: Descendants of John Owen of Windsor, CT (1622-1699). By R.D. Owen. 1941. 535p.
P4-S20535 — $83.00.

OWENS: BYRNES. Gen Rec of the Owens Family with Sketches of the Byrnes Kindred. E.W. Owens. n.d. 196p.
P4-S20542 — $29.00.

OWSLEY: Gen. facts of the Owsley family in England & America, from the time of the "Restoration" to the present. Harry Bryan Owsley. 1890. 164p.
P4-S20547 — $24.50.

P

PACKARD: Celebration of the 250th anniversary of the landing of Samuel Packard in in this country, Aug. 10, 1638, held at Brockton, MA. Issued by Packard Mem. Assoc. 1888. 72p.
P4-S20553 — $14.00.

PAGE: Carolina Pages: A Compilation of Gen. Information on Page Families in the Carolinas Beginning in 1521 to Present Time. By Robert E. Page III. 1990. 293p.
P4-S20559 — $45.00.

PAGE: Gen. registers of ancestors & desc. of . . . Lemuel Page & Polly Paige, Peter Joslin & Sarah Kidder . . . By Luke J. Page. 1887. 155p.
P4-S20565 — $25.00.

PAGE: Hist. & Description of the Great Page Estate. C. Page. 1917. 31p.
P4-S20560 — $10.00.

PAGE: Desc. from Nicholas Page of Eng. By C. Peirson. 1915. 18p.
P4-S20561 — $10.00.

PAGE: Story of our forebears: Page, Bradbury, Fessenden & Perley fams. By R.P. Reed. 1903. 154p.
P4-S20589 — $20.00.

PAGE: Hist. & gen. of the Page fam. from 1257 to the present, with a brief hist. & gen. of the allied fams. Nash & Peck. By C.N. Page. 1911. 143p.
P4-S20583 — $21.00.

PAGE: Gen., an error corrected. By L.B. Chase. 6p.
P4-S20562 — $10.00.

PAGE: Some Desc. of Exolheath Page of Goochland Co., VA. D.E. Page. 2005. xxxv + 815p.
P4-S20563 — $105.00.

PAGE: Gen. of the Page family in VA, also a condensed acct. of the Nelson, Walker, Pendleton & Randolph fams. By R.C.M. Page, 2nd ed., 1893. 275p.
P4-S20571 — $45.00.

PAGE: Wisconsin Page Pioneers & kinfold. By Turner, Turner & Sayre. 1953. 485p.
P4-S20601 — $74.50.

PAIGE: Record of the Paige fam. By E.R. Page. 1904. 14p.
P4-S20602 — $10.00.

PAINE: Ancestors & descendants of David Paine & Abigail Shepard of Ludlow, MA, 1463-1913. compiled By C.P. Ohler. 1913. 252p.
P4-S20607 — $39.50.

PAINE: Gen. notes on the Paine fam. of Worcester, MA. N. Paine. 1878. 27p.
P4-S20608 — $10.00.

PAINE: Genealogy, Ipswich branch. By A.W. Paine. 1881. 184p.
P4-S20628 — $27.50.

PAINE: Hist. of Samuel Paine, Jr, 1778-1861, & his wife Pamela Chase Paine, 1780-1856, Randolph, VT & their anc. & desc. A. Paine. 1923. 218p.
P4-S20619 — $35.00.

PAINE: The discovery of a grandmother. Glimpses into the homes & lives of eight gen. of an Ipswich — Paine fam. By H.H. Carter. 1920. 343p.
P4-S20634 — $54.00.

PAINE: Family records. A journal of gen. & biogr. info. Respecting the American family of Payne, Paine, Payn, etc. By H. D. Paine. 1880-1883 2 Vols. in 1, 522p.
P4-S20622 — $62.50.

PAINE: Family of Robert Treat Paine, signer of the Declaration of Independence, incl. maternal lines. By S.C. Paine & C.H. Pope. 1912. 336p.
P4-S20613 — $53.50.

PAINTER: The Painter fam., with notes on the Lamberton fam. (Repr. NEHGR) By D.L. Jacobus. 1914. 14p.
P4-S20635 — $10.00.

PALGRAVE: Fam. memorials. By C. & S. Parker. 1878. 208p.
P4-S20637 — $31.00.

PALMER: Families in America, Vol. I: Lt Wm. Palmer of Yarmouth, MA & his descendants of Greenwich, CT. By Horace W. Palmer. 1966. 889p.
P4-S20673 — $125.00.

PALMER: Families in America, Vol. III: Wm. Palmer of Plymouth & Duxbury, MA. By Horace W. Palmer. 1973. 231p.
P4-S20679 — $34.00.

PALMER: TRIMBLE Gen. record of the desc. of John & Mary Palmer of Concord, Chester (now Delaware) Co., PA in two divisions. Palmer & Trimble By L. Palmer. 1910. 725 + 398p.
P4-S20655 — $159.00.

PALMER: Some desc. of William Palmer of Watertown, MA & Hampton, NH. By W.L. Palmer. 1914. 4p.
P4-S20644 — $10.00.

PALMER: Gen. record of the desc. of John & Mary Palmer of Concord, Chester (now Delaware) Co., PA. By L. Palmer. 1875. 474p.
P4-S20667 — $74.00.

PALMER: Brief gen. hist. of the anc. & desc. of Dea. Stephen Palmer of Candia, NH. By F. Palmer. 1886. 106p.
P4-S20661 — $20.00.

PALMER: From Groups of Palmer families, from Walter Palmer of Charlestown & Rehoboth, MA & Stonington, CT. By Emily W. Leavitt. 1901. 240p.
P4-S20685 — $36.00.

PALMES: Branches of the Palmes Family Tree; Palmes, Hart, Marrone, Prosser, Huffman. Linda M. Marrone. 2004. 80p.
P4-S20686 — $15.00.

PAQUET: La Paroisse De Saint-Nicolas La Famille Paquet et les Familles Alliees. Hormisdas Magnan. 1918. 334 + 44p.
P4-S20689 — $57.00.

PARDEE: Genealogy of One Line of the Pardee Family. Aaron Pardee. 1896. 70p.
P4-S20692 — $14.00.

PARDEE: Genealogy. By D.L. Jacobus. 1927. 701p.
P4-S20691 — $105.00.

PARISH: John Parish of Groton, MA & some desc. (Repr. NEHGR) By R. Parish. 1909. 9p.
P4-S20696 — $10.00.

PARK: Biogr. sketch of the Park fam. of Washington Co., PA. By W.J. Park. 1880. 121p.
P4-S20697 — $24.00.

PARK: Genealogy, relating to descendants of John B. Park, 1794-1891, of Wells VT, Moriah NY & Trumbull Co. OH. By C.A. Harrington, with D.H. Richeson. 1967. 36p.
P4-S20698 — $10.00.

PARK/E/S: & Bunch on the trail west, with allied families Benton, Duvall, Foster, Greenwell, Jones, Loveless & Tally, revised edition. By Alice C. Park. 1982. 488p.
P4-S20703 — $74.50.

PARKE: Gen. of the Parke fam. of CT, incl. Robert Parke of New London, Edward Parks of Guilford, & others. By F.S. Parks. 1906. 333p.
P4-S20712 — $43.00.

PARKE: Supplement to the Parke families of CT. By F.S. Parks. 1934. 97p.
P4-S20718 — $19.00.

PARKE: Genealogy of the Parke families of MA; incl. Richard of Cambridge, Wm. of Groton, & others. By F.S. Parks. 1909. 263p.
P4-S20709 — $43.00.

PARKER: History of Peter Parker & Sarah Ruggles of Roxbury, MA, & their anc. & desc. J.W. Linzee. 1913. 609p.
P4-S20736 — $89.50.

PARKER: Desc. of Parker fam. of Cambridge Village (Newton) MA, extr. from Hist. of Newton. 6p.
P4-S20727 — $10.00.

PARKER: Genealogical & biogr. notes of John Parker of Lexington & his desc., showing his earlier anc. in America By T. Parker. 1893. 528p.
P4-S20724 — $68.00.

PARKER: Glances at the anc. of John Parker (b. 1807, d. 1891), By H.P. Ward. 1895. 16p.
P4-S20726 — $10.00.

PARKER: Gleanings from Col. & American records of Parker & Morse families, 1585-1915. By Wm. T. Parker. 1915. 62p.
P4-S20730 — $13.00.

PARKER: Gleanings from Parker records, 1271-1893. W.T. Parker. 1894. 51p.
P4-S20731 — $10.00.

PARKER: Lineage of Malcolm Metzger Parker from Johannes DeLang. By Dr I.H. DeLong. 1926. 62p.
P4-S20742 — $13.00.

PARKER: Family records. Parker-Pond-Peck, 1636-1892. By E.P. Parker. 1892. 51p.
P4-S20732 — $10.00.

PARKER: in America, 1630-1910, genealogy, biography & history. By A. Parker. 1911. 608p.
P4-S20748 — $81.00.

PARKER: Index to all Parker names in "Parker in Amer.," by A.G. Parker (1910). Comp. by R. Lee. 1970. 51p.
P4-S20725 — $10.00.

PARKHURST: John Parkhurst, his anc. & desc. G. H. Parkhurst. 1897. 51p.
P4-S20749 — $10.00.

PARKS: Rufus Parks Pedigree: 17 centuries of one family's ancestry. By Brian J.L. Berry. 1898 (Reprinted by permission.) 166p.
P4-S20754 — $29.00.

PARLEE: & related families. By Helen Spinney. n.d. 69 + 34p.
P4-S20760 — $15.00.

PARLIN: Genealogy, the desc. of Nicholas of Cambridge, MA. By F.E. Parlin. 1913. 289p.
P4-S20766 — $43.00.

PARMELEE: The desc. of John Parmelee (Repr. NEHGR). By R.D. Smyth. 1899. 6p.
P4-S20767 — $10.00.

PARR: Parr connections (in record of Wm. Weaver) R.I. Weaver. 1925. 36p.
P4-S20768 — $10.00.

PARRISH: Family, incl. the allied families of Belt, Boyd, Cole-Malone, Clokey, Garrett, Merryman, Parsons, Price & Tipton. Boyd & Gottschalk 1935. 413p.
P4-S20784 — $63.00.

PARRISH: A comp. of the available records covering direct desc. of Henry, Joel, Ansel & Absolom, sons of Henry Parrish (1740) J.T. Parrish. 1948. 410p.
P4-S20772 — $64.00.

PARRISH: Family (Phila.) incl. the related fams. of Cox, Dillinger, Roberts, Chandler, Mitchell, Painter & Pusey. By Wharton & Parrish. 1925. 336p.
P4-S20778 — $53.50.

PARSHALL: Family, A.D. 870-1913: Collection of historical records & notes to accompany the Parshall Pedigree. By Horace F. Parshall. 1915. 185p.
P4-S20796 — $28.00.

PARSHALL: History of the Parshall family, 1066 to the close of the 19th cent. By J.C. Parshall. 1903. 309p.
P4-S20790 — $41.00.

PARSHALL: James Parshall & desc. By J. Parshall. 1900. 42p.
P4-S20791 — $10.00.

PARSONS: The house of Cornet Jos. Parsons, together with the houses of a line of his descendants & their allied families. 1941 (?) 22 + 27p.
P4-S20803 — $10.00.

PARSONS: Desc. of Jeffrey Parsons of Gloucester, MA. Vol. I, generations 1-5. Mary H. Sibbalds. 2003. 390p.
P4-S20809 — $55.00.

PARSONS: Desc of Jeffery Parsons of Gloucester, MA. Vol. II, Generations 6-7. M.H. Sibbalds. 2006. 511 + 31p.
P4-S20804 — $79.00.

PARSONS: Parsons' Family Hist & Record. V. P. MacCabe. 1913. 294 + 40p.
P4-S20805 — $50.00.

PARSONS: Gen. record of the fam. of Parsons & Leonard of W. Springfield, MA. By S. Parsons. 1867. 36p.
P4-S20806 — $10.00.

PARSONS: Family: descendants of Cornet Joseph Parsons, Springfield 1636 — Northampton 1655. By H. Parsons. 1912-1920 2 vols., 1223p
P4-S20802 — $169.00.

PARSONS: Eli Parsons of Enfield, CT & his Brother, Thomas Parsons. J.A. Parsons. 1924. 128 + 22p.
P4-S20807 — $23.00.

PARTHEMORE: Gen. of the Parthemore fam., 1744-1885. By E.W.S. Parthemore. 1885. 250p.
P4-S20808 — $37.50.

PARTRIDGE: Desc. of John Partridge of Medfield, MA. By G.H. Partridge. 1904. 46p.
P4-S20815 — $10.00.

PARTRIDGE: Desc. of George Partridge of Duxbury, MA. By G.H. Partridge. 1915. 46p.
P4-S20816 — $10.00.

PARTRIDGE: William Partridge of Medfield & his desc., By G.H. Partridge. 1909. 10p.
P4-S20817 — $10.00.

PATCH: Quinton Patch of CT & his descendants, 1727-1951, supplement. Mary D. Tellefson. 1951. 48p., typescript.
P4-S20819 — $10.00.

PATCHEN: History & genealogy of the Patchin-Patchen family. By Grace P. Leggett. 1952. 1076p.
P4-S20814 — $145.00.

PATTEN: Anc. of James Patten of Kennebunkport, ME. By W.G. Davis. 1941. 113p.
P4-S20821 — $22.50.

PATTEN: Gen of the Pattens from the North of Ireland. H.P. Moore. 1939. 194 + 10p.
P4-S80822 — $31.00.

PATTEN: Gen. William Patten of Cambridge, 1635, & his desc. By T.W. Baldwin. 1908. 300p.
P4-S20823 — $38.50.

PATTERSON: PATTISON Family association, books 1-3: collection of genealogical records. Norman G. Patterson. 1963-65 215 + 213 + 202p; typescript.
P4-S20847 — $89.00.

PATTERSON: Graham Patterson of Portage, NY, his ancestry & descendants. By Norman G. Patterson. 1961. 53p., typescript.
P4-S20830 — $11.00.

PATTERSON: James Patterson of Conestoga Manor, & his descendants. By Edmund H. Bell & Mary H. Colwell. 1925. 313p.
P4-S20841 — $48.50.

PATTERSON: Genealogy of the Patterson, Wheat & Hearn fams. By R.E.H. Randle. 1926. 261p.
P4-S20835 — $41.00.

PATTERSON: "Concerning the Forefathers," being a memoir, with personal narrative & letters; Col. Robt. Patterson & Col. John Johnston By Charlotte R. Conover. 1902. 432 + 22p.
P4-S20829 — $69.00.

PAUL: Joseph Paull of Ilminster, Somerset, Eng. & some descendants who have resided in Philadelphia. By H.N. Paul. 1933. 157p.
P4-S20865 — $24.00.

PAUL: Ancestry of Katharine Choate Paul. By E.J. Paul. 1914. 386p.
P4-S20853 — $60.00.

PAULL: IRWIN: A family sketch. By E.M. Paul. 1915. viii + 198p.
P4-S20871 — $32.50.

PAXTON: The Paxtons: their origin in Scotland & migr. through Eng. & Ireland to the Col. of Pa., whence they moved South & West. By W. Paxton. 1903. 485p.
P4-S20877 — $76.50.

PAYNE: Thomas Payne of Salem & his desc., the Salem branch of the Paine fam. By N.E. Paine. 1928. 184p.
P4-S20889 — $27.50.

PAYNE: The Paynes of VA. Brooke Payne. 1937. xii + 543p.
P4-S20884 — $83.50.

PAYNE: The Paynes of Hamilton: a gen. & biogr. record. By A.F.P. White. 1912. 245p.
P4-S20883 — $39.50.

PAYNE: Genealogy of the families of Payne & Gore. By W.H. Whitmore. 1875. 30p.
P4-S20885 — $10.00.

PEABODY: (Paybody, Pabody, Pabodie) genealogy. By S. Peabody. 1909. 614p.
P4-S20901 — $92.00.

PEABODY: A gen. of the Peabody fam., with a partial record of the R. branch. By C.M. Endicott. 1867. 65p.
P4-S20895 — $13.00.

PEABODY: A gen. of the desc. of Moses & Hannah (Foster) Peabody. By M.E. Perley. 1904. 47p.
P4-S20896 — $10.00.

PEARCE: Pearce gen.; being the record of the posterity of Richard Pearce, an early inhabitant of Portsmouth, RI. By F.C. Pierce. 1888. 150p.
P4-S20904 — $22.50.

PEARL: Some of John Pearl's desc. By A.H. Dow. 1901. 33p.
P4-S20905 — $10.00.

PEARSALL: History & genealogy of the Pearsall family in England & America, Three-volume set By C.E. Pearsall. 1928. 3 vols., 1806p.
P4-S20910 — $275.00./set

PEARSON: Crispin Pearson of Bucks, Co., PA, 1748-1806. By A.P. Darrow. Ed. by W.C. Armstrong. 1932. 166p.
P4-S20934 — $25.00.

PEARSON: family; From Hunter Family of VA. By Sidney M. Culbertson. 1934. 21p.
P4-S20935 — $10.00.

PEASE: Pease fam. of Eng. & New Eng. By F. Pease. 1849. 34p.
P4-S20941 — $10.00.

PEASE: New Hampshire branch of the Pease family, search for the ancestors of Patty Pease who married John Pickering of Barnstead, NH By L.S. Cox. 1946. 64p.
P4-S20940 — $13.00.

PEASE: Gen.-hist. rec. of desc. of John Pease, Sr., last of Enfield, CT. By Fiske & Pease. 1869. 401p.
P4-S20943 — $62.50.

PEASE: The early hist. of the Pease fam. in Amer. By A.S. Pease. 1869. 96p.
P4-S20949 — $18.50.

PEASLEES: The Peaslees & others of Haverhill, MA & vicinity, By E.A. Kimball. 1899. 72p.
P4-S20955 — $15.00.

PECK: The Book of Pecks. By Herbert W. Peck. 1954 232p. + charts
P4-S20962 — $65.00.

PECK: A gen. acct. of the desc. in the male line of Wm. Peck, one of the founders in 1638 of the Col. of New Haven, CT. By D. Peck. 1877. 253p.
P4-S20961 — $38.00.

PECK: Genealogical history of the desc. of Joseph Peck, who emigr. in 1638. Also an appendix. By I. Peck. 1868. 443p.
P4-S20964 — $56.50.

PECKHAM: Genealogy; English ancestry & Amer. desc. of John Peckham of Newport, RI, 1630. By S. Peckham. 1922 602p.
P4-S20973 — $91.00.

PEDDICORD: Kelion Franklin Peddicord of Quirk's Scouts, Morgan's Kentucky Cavalry,. India W.P. Logan. 1908. 170 + 8p.
P4-S20974 — $27.00.

For hardcover versions, see the order form on page v. To order, call 1-888-296-3447.

PEDEN: The Pedens of America: Being a Summary of the Peden, Alexander, Morton, Morrow Reunion, 1899. John Peden & Margaret McDill. 1900. 303 + 29p.
P4-S20975 — $50.00.

PEDRICK: A Genealogical & Biographical Record of the Pedrick Family of NJ, 1675-1938. Hubert B. Shoemaker. 1938. xix + 341p.
P4-S20976 — $54.00.

PEEBLES: Peebles, ante 1600-1962. By Anne Bradbury Peebles. 1962. 191p.
P4-S20979 — $27.50.

PEERY: A branch of the Peery family tree: ancestors & descendants of James Peery who came to DE About 1730. By Lynn Perry. 1931. 125p.
P4-S20985 — $19.50.

PEFFLEY: PEFFLY — Pefley families in America, & allied families, 1729-1938. By M.M. & E.C. Frost. 1938. 245 + 30p.
P4-S20991 — $43.50.

PEIRCE: Solomon Pierce fam. gen., with a rec. of his desc., also an app. with the anc. of Solomon & his wife Amity Fessenden. M. Bailey. 1912. 190p.
P4-S21009 — $28.50.

PEIRCE: Fam. rec., 1687-1893; New ed. rev. with notices of related fam. Hardy, Grafton, Gardener, Dawes, Lathrop,etc . . . E.W. West. 1894. 101p.
P4-S21003 — $19.50.

PEIRCE: Family of the old colony; or the lineal desc. of Abraham Peirce, who came to Amer. as early as 1623. By E.W. Peirce. 1870. 510p.
P4-S20997 — $65.00.

PEIRCE: The record of John Pers of Watertown, MA, who came from Norwich, Eng., with notes on the hist. off Peirce, Pierce, Pearse, etc. By F.C. Peirce. 1880. 283p.
P4-S20998 — $42.00.

PELHAM: Herbert Pelham, his anc. & desc. (Repr. NEHGR) By J.L. Chester. 1879. 11p.
P4-S21010 — $10.00.

PELHAM: Some Early Pelhams. Mrs. Arthur Pelham. 1931. xi + 285 + 52p.
P4-S21011 — $52.00.

PELT: A genealogical history of the Pelt family branch of the Van Pelt family tree. Chester H. Pelt, Sr. 1992. 140p.
P4-S21015 — $22.00.

PELTON: Gen. of the Pelton family in America, desc. of John Pelton, who settled in Boston about 1630-1632. By J.M. Pelton. 1892. 722p.
P4-S1021 — $91.00.

PEMBER: Thomas Pember of New London, CT & desc. 1916. 13p.
P4-S21028 — $10.00.

PEMBER: John Pember: the history of the Pember family in America. By C.P. Hazen 1939. 342p.
P4-S21027 — $52.00.

PEMBERTON: The records of the Pemberton fam. O.S. Babcock. 1890. 26p.
P4-S20129 — $10.00.

PENCE: Hist. of Judge John Pence & desc. By K. Pence. 1912. 126p.
P4-S21033 — $25.00.

PENDARVIS: Genealogy of the Pendarvis-Bedon Families of SC, 1670-1900. comp by James Barnwell Heyward. 1905. 221p.
P4-S21034 — $33.00.

PENDLETON: Brian Pendleton & His Massachusetts, 1634-1681. Everett Hall Pendleton. 1951. 294p.
P4-S21040 — $44.00.

PENDLETON: Early New England Pendletons, with some account of the three groups who took the name Pempleton By Everett H. Pendleton. 1956. 354p.
P4-S21045 — $52.00.

PENDLETON: Later New England Pendletons: record of the Pendleton family from the 7th to 12th generations. By Everett H. Pendleton. 1966. 504p.
P4-S21051 — $75.00.

PENDLETON: Brian Pendleton & his desc., 1599-1910, with some acct. of the Pembleton fams. & notices of other Pendletons. By E.H. Pendleton. 1910. 871p.
P4-S21039 — $107.50.

PENFIELD: Gen. of the desc. of Samuel Penfield, with a supp. of Dr Levi Buckingham Line and the Gridley, Dwight, Burlingham, etc. By Florence B. Penfield. 1963. 320p.
P4-S21057 — $49.50.

PENFIELD: Ancestry of Annie Frances Penfield (1853-1936), the wife of Calvin Robinson Mower (1840-1927) By Lyman Mower & Karen Hoiriis Mower. 2002. 712p.
P4-S21060 — $99.50.

PENGRY: A gen. record of the desc. of Moses Pengry of Ipswich, MA. By W.M. Pingry. 1881. 186p.
P4-S21063 — $28.00.

PENHALLOW: Mem. of the Penhallow fam.; with copies of letters & papers of an early date (Repr. NEHGR) By P.W. Penhallow. 1878. 22p.
P4-S21064 — $10.00.

PENN: Family of VA. By W. M. Clemens. 1915. 16p.
P4-S21070 — $10.00.

PENN: Gen. gleanings contributory to a hist. of the fam. of Penn (Repr. Penn. Mag.) By J. H. Lea. 1890. 51p.
P4-S21071 — $10.00.

PENN: Family of Wm. Penn., founder of PA, anc. & desc. By H.M. Jenkins. 1899. 270p.
P4-S21069 — $34.00.

PENNELL: Pennell fam. of Eng. in Welsh records (in Lloyd manuscripts) By H.W. Lloyd. 1912. 7p.
P4-S21072 — $10.00.

PENNEY: A gen. record of the desc. of Thomas Penney of New Gloucester, ME. By J.W. Penney. 1897. 167p.
P4-S21075 — $25.00.

PENNINGTON: Fam. of CT & NJ (Repr. NEHGR) By A.C. Pennington. 1871. 11p.
P4-S21080 — $10.00.

PENNOCK: The Pennocks of Primitive Hall. By George Valentine Massey II. 1951. 139p.
P4-S21075 — $22.50.

PENNYPACKER: The Pennypacker reunion, October 4, 1877. By S.W. Pennypacker. 1878. 55p.
P4-S21082 — $10.50.

PENROSE: History of the Penrose Family of Philadelphia. J.G. Leach. 1903. 230p.
P4-S21083 — $35.00.

PEPPERRELL: in America. By C.H.C. Howard. 1906. 110p.
P4-S21087 — $20.50.

PEPYS: Genealogy of the Pepys Family, 1273-1887. By Walter C. Pepys. 1887. 102p.
P4-S21093 — $19.00.

PERCY: History of the house of Percy, from the earliest times down to the present century, 2-vol. set By Gerald Brenan. 1902 2 vols., 393 + 495p + charts
P4-S21111 — $129.00.

PERKINS: Formerly of Hillmorton. By Paul H. Daigle. 1997. 385p.
P4-S21132 — $58.50.

PERKINS: Descendants of Edward Perkins of New Haven, CT. By C.E. Perkins. 1914. 135p.
P4-S21123 — $21.00.

PERKINS: Fam. in olden times. Contents of a series of letters. By M. Parkyns, ed. By D. Perkins. 1916. 88p.
P4-S21144 — $18.00.

PERKINS: History of Ufton Court & the Parish of Ufton (Co. of Berks [Eng.]) & of the Perkins family. By A. Mary Sharp. 1892 276p.
P4-S21138 — $43.50.

PERKINS: "Gentleman" John Perkins. By Wm. W. Scott. 1920. 88p.
P4-S21117 — $19.00.

PERKINS: Fam. in the US in 1790. By D.W. Perkins. 1911. 48p.
P4-S21118 — $10.00.

PERKINS: Family of John Perkins of Ipswich, MA. By G.A. Perkins. 1889. 499p.
P4-S21126 — $50.00.

PERKINS: Family of CT. By F.B. Perkins. 1860. 8p.
P4-S21119 — $10.00.

PERKINS: English Origins of Six Early Colonists by the Name of Perkins. P.P. Mortensen. 1998. 104p.
P4-S21120 — $16.00.

PERLEY: History & genealogy of the Perley family. M.V.B. Perley. 1906. 770p.
P4-S21150 — $115.50.

PERRIN: Gen. of the Perrin fam. By Lapham & Bowen. 1878, 1942. 20p.
P4-S21157 — $10.00.

PERRIN: Gen. of the Perrin fam. By G. Perrin. 1885. 224p.
P4-S21162 — $34.00.

PERRIN: Daniel Perrin, "The Huguenot," & his desc. in America of the surnames Perrine, Perine, & Prine, 1665-1910. By H.D. Perrine. 1910. 553p.
P4-S21156 — $69.00.

PERRY: Incomplete history of the descendants of John Perry of London, 1604-1955. By Bertram Adams. 1955. 738p.
P4-S21174 — $105.00.

PERRY: Desc. of Eber Spencer Perry. By Rachel Saul Tefft. 1999. 14p.
P4-S21169 — $10.00.

PERRY: Descendants of James Newton Perry. By Rachel Saul Tefft. 1997. 44p.
P4-S21170 — $10.00.

PERRY: Desc. of Nathan Arista Perry (1846-1927). Rachel Saul Tefft. 1999. 162p.
P4-S21168 — $22.50.

PERRY: Desc. of Lucius Henry Perry (1843-1924). Rachel Saul Tefft. 1999. 33p
P4-S21171 — $10.00.

PERRY: Our Perry family in ME; its ancestors & descendants. By C.N. Sinnett. 1911. 127p.
P4-S21180 — $19.00.

PERRY: Some of the ancestors of Oliver Hazard Perry of Lowell, MA, Pt. 1, Perry ancestry, Pt. 2, Moseley ancestry. Mrs F.W. Brown. 1911. 32 + 28p.
P4-S21189 — $12.00.

PERRY: Perrys of RI & tales of Silver Creek, the Bosworth-Perry homestead, By C.B. Perry. 1913. 115p.
P4-S21186 — $23.00.

PERSHING: Family in America; A collection of hist. & gen. data. By E. Pershing. 1924. 434p.
P4-S21198 — $68.00.

PESHINE: Family in Europe & America: notes & sugg. for a gen. tree from the beginning of the 14th century to the present day By John H.H. Peshine. 1916. 109p.
P4-S21204 — $19.00.

PETERS: Conrad Peters & wife Clara Snidow: their descendants & ancestry. By O.E. Peters. n.d. 229p.
P4-S21210 — $35.00.

PETERS: & Their allied families of Flat Rock, MI. Janet Egler. 1999. 182p.
P4-S21216 — $27.00.

PETERS: of New England. A genealogy & family history. By E. & E. Peters. 1903. 470p.
P4-S21228 — $59.00.

PETERS: Lineage. Five gen. of the desc. of Dr. Charles Peters of Hempstead. By M. Flint. 1896. 175p.
P4-S21222 — $26.00.

PETERSON: Family of Duxbury, MA (Repr. NEHGR). W.B. Browne. 1916. 26p.
P4-S21235 — $10.00.

PETERSON: History & gen. acct. of the Peterson family: gen. rec. & sketches of the desc. of Lawrens Peterson & Nancy Jones-Peterson By W.H., S.J. & C.E. Peterson. 1926. 372p.
P4-S21228 — $59.00.

PETTINGELL: Genealogy. By J.M. Pettengell & C. Pope. 1906. 596p.
P4-S21240 — $89.00.

PETTIT: The Pettit Family in America, Including the Maternal Gen of the Desc of Joseph & Hannah Hussey Pettit. Asahel H. Pettit. 1906. xxii + 183p.
P4-S21241 — $31.00.

PETTUS: Family [in England & VA]. By Pocahontas H. Stacy. 1957. 67p.
P4-S21246 — $14.00.

PFEIFFER: Gen. of Dr. Francis J. Pfeiffer, Phila., PA & his desc., 1734-1899. By E. Sellers. 1899. 67p.
P4-S21258 — $14.00.

PHARR: Pharrs & Farrs, With Other Descendants from Five Scotch-Irish Pioneers in America. Henry Newton Pharr. 1955. xii + 604p.
P4-S21263 — $92.00.

PHELPS: Gen. & Short hist. narrative of one branch of the George Phelps family. 1897. 192p.
P4-S21270 — $29.50.

PHELPS: The Wm. A. Phelps family: life of Wm. Addison Phelps & Mary Jane Lippitt Phelps — their ancestors — their descendants. L.L. Krug. 1961. 191p.
P4-S21276 — $27.00.

PHELPS: Family of America & their English ancestry. By Phelps & Servin. 1899. 2 vols., 1865p.
P4-S21264 — $235.00.

PHILBRICK: A gen. of the Philbrick & Philbrook fam., desc. from the emigrant, Thomas Philbrick, 1583-1667. By J. Chapman. 1886. 202p.
P4-S21282 — $30.00.

PHILLIPS: Family of Eng. & New Eng., 1593-1877. E. Salisbury. 1885. 43p.
P4-S21289 — $10.00.

PHILLIPS: Brief history of the Phillips family, beginning with the emigration from Wales . . . Harry Phillips. 1935. 261p.
P4-S21288 — $42.00.

PHILLIPS: History of Richard & Francina [Hart] Phillips & Their Descendants. Comp. by Henry Hackenbracht. 1951. 305p.
P4-S21290 — $46.00.

For hardcover versions, see the order form on page v. To order, call 1-888-296-3447.

PHILLIPS: Desc. of Hiram & Mary Phillips, with anc. of John Solomon Ginther [& rel. Stocker, Hass & Heller fams.]. By E.M. Firestone & J.E. Stewart. n.d. 44p.
P4-S21292 — $10.00.

PHILLIPS: Gen; Incl. the fam. of Geo. Phillips, first minister of Watertown, MA, 1630 to present. By A. Phillips. 1885. 245p.
P4-S21291 — $31.50.

PHILLIPS: Family of John Phillips, Sr. of Duxbury & Marshfield. By A. Ames. 1903. 43p.
P4-S21293 — $10.00.

PHINIZY: The Phinizy Family in America. Ferdinand P. Calhoun. 1925. 176 + 90p.
P4-S21294 — $40.00.

PHINNEY: Gen. brief hist. of Ebenezer Phinney of Cape Cod & his desc., 1637-1947. By M.A. Phinney. 1948. 146p.
P4-S21297 — $22.00.

PHIPPS: The anc. & desc. of John Phipps of Sherborn, 1757-1847, abr. from the Phipps gen. F. Weis. 1924. 24p.
P4-S21298 — $10.00.

PHOENIX: The desc. of John Phoenix, an early settler in Kittery, ME. By S. W. Phoenix. 1867. 59p.
P4-S21300 — $12.00.

PICKEL: Anc. & desc. of Sherwood & Pickel fam., U.E. Loyalists, in Canada. By W.U. Pickel. 1948. 62p.
P4-S21306 — $12.50.

PICKERING: Supplement to below. 1884. 28p.
P4-S21316 — $10.00.

PICKERING: Gen. data respecting John Pickering of Portsmouth, NH & his desc. By R.H. Eddy. 1884. 36p.
P4-S21317 — $10.00.

PICKERING: Genealogy; acct. of the first three gen. of the Pickering fam. of Salem, MA, Three-volume set By Ellery & Bowditch. 1897. 3 vols., 1284p.
P4-S21315 — $176.00.

PIERCE: Seven Pierce families: record of births, deaths & marriages of the first seven generations of Pierces in America By H.C. Pierce. 1936. 48 + 324p.
P4-S21336 — $57.50.

PIERCE: Genealogy, #IV; record of the posterity of Capt. Michael, John, & Capt. Wm. Pierce, who came to this country from England. By F.C. Pierce. 1889. 441p.
P4-S21327 — $68.50.

PIERCE: Pierce Genealogy: Being a Partial Record of the Posterity of Richard Pearse. C. G. Hurlburt. 1927. 220 + 20p.
P4-S21328 — $36.00.

PIERCE: Genealogy. Record of the posterity of Thomas Pierce, early inhabitant of Charlestown. By F.B. Pierce, 1882. 369p.
P4-S21330 — $47.00.

PIERPONT: Gen. & connecting lines; Particularly Rev. John Pierpont of Hollis St. Church, Boston. By M.P. Barnum & A.E. Boardman. 1928. 42p.
P4-S21343 — $10.00.

PIERPONT: The Pierponts of No. Haven, CT, (Repr. NEHGR). By D.L. Jacobus. 1921. 11p.
P4-S21344 — $10.00.

PIERREPONT: Gens; Esp. the line from Hezekiah Pierpont, son of Rev. James Perpont of New Haven. By H.M. Pierpont. 1913. 211p.
P4-S21348 — $32.00.

PIERSON: Desc. of Stephen Pierson of Suffolk Co., Eng. & New Haven & Derby, CT. By F. Pierson. 1895. 33p.
P4-S21355 — $10.00.

PIERSON: Pierson gen. record. By L.B. Pierson. 1878. 106p.
P4-S21354 — $19.00.

PIETY: Partial history of James Duncan Piety, his forebears & descendants, 1796-1948. By W.P. Morgan. 1948. 150p.
P4-S21360 — $23.00.

PILLSBURY: Ancestry of Chas. Stinson Pillsbury & John Sargent Pillsbury, Two-volume set By M.L. Holman. 1938. 2 vols, 1212p.
P4-S21366 — $182.00.

PILLSBURY: Account of the proceedings at the reunion of the Pillsbury family at Newburyport, MA, 1891. 1891. 16p.
P4-S21367 — $10.00.

PILLSBURY: Notes on the Pillsburys of Leck, Co. Stafford, Eng., (Repr. Essex Inst. Hist. Coll.) By Getchell & Putnam. 1895. 24p.
P4-S21368 — $10.00.

PILLSBURY: Family; being a hist. of William & Dorothy Pillsbury (or Pilsbery) of Newbury in New Eng., & their desc. to the 11th gen. By D.B. Pilsbury & E.A. Getchell. 1898. 336p.
P4-S21372 — $43.50.

PINKHAM: Richard Pinkham of old Dover, NH & his desc. By C.N. Sinnett. 1908. 308p.
P4-S21384 — $48.50.

PIPER: The Piper-Wiberg Family: A Personal Study of the Ancestors of Fred Mosher Piper and Grace Amelia Wiberg. Monte R. Piper. 2003. 211 + 16p.
P4-S21391 — $34.00.

PIPER: Gen. of Elisha Piper, of Parsonfield, ME & his desc. H. Piper. 1889. 121p.
P4-S21390 — $17.50.

PIPER: Gen. of the fam. of Solomon Piper of Dublin, NH. S. Piper. 1849. 20p.
P4-S21392 — $10.00.

PIRKLE: The Pirkles & Their Descendants in the US. John A. Cagle. 1933. 165 + 37p.
P4-S21394 — $30.50.

PITCAIRN: The History of the Fife Pitcairns. Constance Pitcairn. 1905. xviii + 533 + 86p.
P4-S21395 — $96.00.

PITKIN: Family of America: gen. of the desc. of William Pitkin, the Progenitor of the family in the country By A.P. Pitkin. 1887. 325p.
P4-S21393 — $49.00.

PITMAN: Desc. of John Pitman, first of the name in RI. By C.M. Thurston. 1868. 48p.
P4-S21400 — $10.00.

PITMAN: History & pedigree of the family Pitman of Dunchideock, Exeter, & collaterals. C.E. Pitman. 1920 181p.
P4-S21399 — $27.50.

PITTIS: Genealogy; The Pittis family in England & America, 464 years, 16 generations, 1480-1944, with allied families. Margaret B. Pittis. 1945. 315p.
P4-S21405 — $49.50.

PITTS: Memoir of the lives & services of James Pitts & sons John, Samuel & Lendall during the Amer. Rev., 1760-1780. By D. Goodwin, Jr. 1882. 69p.
P4-S21411 — $13.00.

PLAISTED: Lt. Roger Plaisted of Kittery, ME & some of his desc. By M.F. King. 1904. 66p.
P4-S21417 — $13.00.

PLANT: The House of Plant of Macon, GA, with genealogies & hist. notes. By G.S. Dickerman. 1900. 259p.
P4-S21423 — $33.50.

PLATT: Genealogy in America, from the arrival of Richard Platt in New Haven, CT in 1638. By Charles Platt, Jr. 1963. 453p.
P4-S21429 — $71.00.

PLATT: Lineage; Genealogical research & record, By G.L. Platt. 1891. 398p.
P4-S21435 — $51.50.

PLAXCO: ROBINSON: Being an Account of Two of the Ancient Presbyterian Families of Upper SC. SB Mendenhall & WB White Jr. 1958. xviii + 160p
P4-S21436 — $27.00.

PLEASANTS: Pleasants & Allied Families. Norma Carter Miller & George Lane Miller, PhD 1980. vi + 423p.
P4-S21437 — $64.50.

PLIMPTON: A gen. & hist. notices of the fam. of Plimpton or Plympton in Amer., & of Plumpton in Eng. By L. B. Chase. 1884. 240p.
P4-S21438 — $32.00.

PLOWMAN: Register of Plowmans in Amer . . . . & extr. from Eng. & Amer. records. By B.H.F. Plowman. 1901. 90p.
P4-S21444 — $17.50.

PLUMB: The Plumbs, 1635-1800. By H. B. Plumb. 1893. 2nd ed. 102p.
P4-S21450 — $19.00.

PLUMER: Gen; Francis Plumer, who settled at Newbury, MA & some desc. By S. Perley. 1917. 259p.
P4-S21453 — $39.00.

PLUMMER: Genealogical record of compiler's branch of Plummer fam. By J.P. Thurston. 1885. 22p.
P4-S21454 — $10.00.

PLUMMER: System of gen. enumeration; Lin. of Francis Plumer, Newbury MA, 1635. By A. Plummer. 1904. 64p.
P4-S21456 — $12.50.

PLUNKETT: Ten thousand Plunketts: By E.P. Ivy. 1969. 528p.
P4-S21465 — $75.00.

PLYDREN: DUMMER fam., 1100-1884. By E. Salisbury. 1885. 70p.
P4-S21466 — $14.00.

POAGE: The Desc of Robert & John Poage, Pioneer Settlers in Augusta Co, VA. R.B. Woodworth. 1954. 1184p.
P4-S21470 — $178.00.

POCAHONTAS: Alias Matoaka, & Her Desc. Through Her Marriage at Jamestown, VA, with John Rolfe, Gentleman. By W. Robertson. 1887. 84p.
P4-S21469 — $10.00.

POE: Origin of the early hist. of the fams. of Poe, with full pedigrees of the Irish branch of the fams. & a discussion of the true anc. of Edgar Allen Poe. By E.T. Bewley. 1906. 88pp.
P4-S21471 — $16.00.

POLING: History & genealogy of the Poling family [of NJ, VA, MD]. By Clerissa H. Tatterson. 1978. 453p.
P4-S21477 — $68.50.

POLK: Family & Kinsmen. By Wm. Harrison Polk. 1912. 742 + 26p.
P4-S21483 — $115.00.

POLLARD: Family in New England: descendants of Wm. Pollard of Warwickshire & Thos. Pollard of Billerica. By S. Pollard. 1902. 8p.
P4-S21484 — $10.00.

POLLARD: The History of the Pollard Family of America. M.J. Pollard. 1961. 2 vols., 389 + 606p.
P4-S21485 — $140.00.

POLLARD: Ancestry & descendants of Jonathan Pollard, 1759-1821, with records of allied families. By L.M. Underwood. 1891. 20p.
P4-S21488 — $10.00.

POLLOCK: A record of the desc. of John, James, Charles & Samuel Pollock, who emig. from Ireland to PA about 1750. By H.E. Hayden. 1884. 16p.
P4-S21487 — $10.00.

POLLOCK: Bio. sketch of Oliver Pollock, Esq., of Carlisle, PA, US Commercial agent, 1776-1884 By Horace E. Hayden. 1883. 59p.
P4-S21486 — $12.00.

POMEROY: Romance & history of Eltweed Pomeroy's ancestors in Normandy & England. By A.A. Pomeroy. 1909. 81p.
P4-S21519 — $16.00.

POMEROY: House of de la Pomerai: annals of the family By Edw. B. Powley. 1944. 144p.
P4-S21507 — $22.00.

POMEROY: Pomeroy, Part III. By A.A. Pomeroy. 1922. 342p.
P4-S21513 — $53.00.

POMEROY: History & Genealogy of the Pomeroy family & Collateral lines, England — Ireland — America 1958. 2 vols.,1454 + 56p.
P4-S21495 — $220.00.

POMEROY: Eltweed Pomeroy of Dorchester, MA & Windsor, CT & four gen. of his desc. (Repr. NEHGR). By W.W. Rodman. 1903. 8p.
P4-S21496 — $10.00.

POMEROY: History & genealogy of the Pomeroy family: collateral lines in family groups, Normandy, Great Britain & America . . . By Albert A. Pomeroy. 1912. 962p.
P4-S21501 — $139.50.

POMROY: Family of Selah Pomroy of Quebec & Northampton, MA. By J. Lawrence. 1881. 12p.
P4-S21520 — $10.00.

POND: Gen. records of Samuel Pond & his desc. By D.S. Pond. 1875. 126p.
P4-S21528 — $25.00.

POND: Ponds of Milford & Branford, CT. By N. Pond. 16p.
P4-S21523 — $10.00.

POND: A gen. record of Daniel Pond & his desc. By E.D. Harris. 1873. 210p.
P4-S21522 — $31.50.

POOLE: The hist. of Edward Poole of Weymouth, MA (1635) & his desc., By M.E. Poole. 1893. 164p.
P4-S21531 — $25.50.

POOR: POORE Family gatherings, 1881-1888 [with genealogy]. 1881-1899 442p.
P4-S21537 — $67.00.

POORE: Memorial & genealogy of John Poore: Ten generations, 1615-1880. By A. Poore. 1881. 332p.
P4-S21540 — $43.00.

POORMAN: Fam. of Bernard Poorman of PA & OH (in Snyder Gen.) By A.B. Grove. 1892. 31p.
P4-S21541 — $10.00.

POPE: Genealogy of Thomas Pope (1608-1683) & some of his desc. (Repr. NEHGR). By F.L. Pope. 1888. 22p.
P4-S21553 — $10.00.

POPE: Genealogy of Thomas Pope (1608-1683) & his descendants. By Worden, Langworthy & Burch. 1917. 143p.
P4-S21546 — $24.00.

POPE: Notice of some of the desc. of Joseph Pope of Salem. H. Wheatland. 14p.
P4-S21551 — $10.00.

POPE: History of the Dorchester Pope family, 1634-1888. With sketches of other Popes in England & America. By C. H. Pope. 1888. 340p.
P4-S21552 — $44.00.

PORTER: The Porter fam. Proceedings at the reunion of the desc. of John Porter, of Danvers, held at Danvers, MA, July 17th, 1895. 1897. 72p.
P4-S21582 — $14.00.

PORTER: Gen. of the desc. of Richard Porter, who settled at Weymouth, MA, 1635, & allied fam. J.W. Porter. 1878. 344p.
P4-S21570 — $54.50.

PORTER: The desc. of Moses & Sarah Kilham Porter of Pawlet, VT, with some notice of their anc. By J.S. Lawrence. 1910. 203p.
P4-S21576 — $26.50.

PORTER: Genealogies & Reminiscences: Porter, Grigsby, McNutt, McCheeney, Hamilton & McCormick Families; rev. ed. H.M. McCormick. 1897. 213 + 69p.
P4-S21556 — $32.00.

PORTER: Descendants of John Porter of Windsor, CT, 1635-1639, 2-vol. set H.P. Andrews. 1893 2 vols., 436 + 451p.
P4-S21561 — $105.00.

PORTER: A Porter pedigree, being an acct. of the anc. & desc. of Samuel & Martha (Perley) Porter of Chester, NH. By J. Porter. 1907. 161p.
P4-S21567 — $24.00.

PORTERFIELD: The Porterfields. By Frank B. Porterfield. 1948. 345p.
P4-S21588 — $54.00.

PORTSCHE: Our Portsche Ties. R.L. Mann. 1995. 843p.
P4-S21549 — $110.00.

POST: Family. By M.C. de T. Post. 1905. 352p.
P4-S21594 — $56.00.

POTTER: The New Haven, CT Potters (Repr. NEHGR). By J. Shepard. 1900. 7p.
P4-S21598 — $10.00.

POTTER: Genealogy of the Potter families & their desc. in Amer., with hist. & biographical sketches. By C.W. Potter. 1888. 300p.
P4-S21597 — $38.00.

POTTS: Our family record. By T.M. Potts. 1895. 434p.
P4-S21615 — $54.00.

POTTS: Hist. coll. relating to the Potts family in Gt. Brit. & Amer., with an hist-gen. of the desc. of David Potts By T.M. Potts. 1901. 735p.
P4-S21603 — $94.50.

POTTS: Mem. of Thomas Potts, Jr., who settled in PA, with an hist.-gen. acct. of his desc. to the 8th gen. By T.P. James. 1874. 430p.
P4-S21609 — $67.50.

POUND: KESTER fam; An acct. of the anc. of John Pound (b. 1735) & Wm. Kester (b. 1733) & a gen. record of all their desc. J.E. Hunt. 1904. 628p.
P4-S21621 — $94.00.

POWELL: History & Genealogy of the Thomas J. & Henrietta (Howells) Powell Family. W.D. Shirk. 1918. 202 + 62p.
P4-S21628 — $40.00.

POWELL: Family of Norfolk & Elizabeth City Cos., VA & their descendants, with notes & data on collateral families. 1961. 305p.
P4-S21645 — $46.00.

POWELL: Family records of the Powell & Griffiths (with poetry of John Powell). Rachel Powell. 1866. 119p.
P4-S21627 — $19.50.

POWELL: Long Island genealogies, being kindred desc. of Thomas Powell of Bethpage, Long Island, 1688 By Mary P. Bunker. 1895. 350p.
P4-S21633 — $48.00.

POWELL: Authentic gen. mem'l hist. of Philip Powell of Mifflin Co., PA & his desc. & others. J. Powell. 1880. 447p.
P4-S21639 — $57.00.

POWERS: BANKS anc; Charles Powers, 1819-1871, & his wife Lydia Ann Banks, 1829-1919. By W. Powers. 1921. 325p.
P4-S21651 — $48.75

POWERS: Family, gen. & hist. record of Walter Power & some desc. to the 9th generation. A.H. Powers. 1884. 199p.
P4-S21657 — $28.00.

PRATT: Phineas Pratt & some of his desc. A monograph. E.F. Pratt. 1897. 164p.
P4-S21660 — $24.50.

PRATT: Family; Gen. record of Mathew Pratt of Weymouth, MA & his American descendants, 1623-1889. By F.G. Pratt, Jr. 1890. 226p.
P4-S21678 — $34.00.

PRATT: A collection of some facts about some of the desc. of John Pratt of Dorchester, MA. n.d. 37p.
P4-S21682 — $10.00.

PRATT: Family; or, descendants of Lt. Wm. Pratt, one of the first settlers of Hartford & Saybrook. By F. Chapman. 1864. 421p.
P4-S21681 — $54.50.

PRATT: Sketch of the life of Samuel F. Pratt, with some acct. of the early hist. of the Pratt fam. By W.P. Letchworth. 1874. 211p.
P4-S21687 — $31.50.

PRATT: 1538-1900. The anc. & the desc. of John Pratt of Hartford, CT, By C.B. Whittelsey. 1900. 204p.
P4-S21666 — $30.50.

PREBLE: A gen. sketch of the Preble fam. resident in Portland, ME, 1850. By W.P. Preble. 1850. 28p.
P4-S21691 — $10.00.

PREBLE: Gen. sketch of the first three generations of Prebles in America; with an account of Abraham Preble the emigrant . . . By G. H. Preble. 1868. 340p.
P4-S21690 — $54.00.

PREBLE: John Preble of Machias (1771-1841) & his desc. By W. P. Jones. 1929. 32p.
P4-S21692 — $10.00.

PREHN: Journal of a genealogist, with ancestral wills, [includes Anderson, Bass, Elder, Gaddy,etc . . .) By Alyene E. Westall Prehn. 1980. 864p.
P4-S21696 — $115.00.

PRENTICE: History & genealogy of the Prentice-Prentiss families in New England, 1631-1883. By C.J.F. Binney. 1883. With 1995 index. 2nd ed. 476p.
P4-S21705 — $59.50.

PRENTICE: History & genealogy of the Prentice, Prentis & Prentiss families in New England from 1631-1883 (based on the 1883 Edition) By Linus Joseph Dewald. 1997. 551p.
P4-S21702 — $79.50.

PRESBREY: Wm. Presbrey of London, Eng., & Taunton, MA & his desc., 1690-1918. By J.W. Presby. 1918. 151p.
P4-S21711 — $22.50.

PRESCOTT: Memorial; Gen. memoir of the Prescott fam. in Amer. By W. Prescott. 1870. 667p.
P4-S21717 — $100.00.

PRESTON: Genealogy; tracing the hist. of the fam. from about 1040. ed. by L.A. Wilson & W.B. Preston. 1900. 376p.
P4-S21726 — $58.50.

PRESTON: Mem. of the Preston fam. By O. Brown. 1864. 26p.
P4-S21724 — $10.00.

PRESTON: Descendants of Roger Preston of Ipswich & Salem Village. By C.H. Preston. 1931. 355p.
P4-S21723 — $56.00.

PRESTON: Mem. of the Preston fam. By O. Brown. 1842. 16p.
P4-S21725 — $10.00.

PRICE: Family history. By J. Montgomery Seaver. 41p.
P4-S21733 — $10.00.

PRICE: Thomas Price (Pioneer in Posey Co., IN) & his descendants: history and genealogy. By John E. Cox. 1926. 129p.
P4-S21738 — $22.00.

PRICE: A Genealogy of the Descendants of Rev. Jacob Price, Evangelist — Pioneer. By G.F.P. Wanger. 1926. x+832p.
P4-S21732 — $124.50.

PRICE: Golden wedding of Benj. & Jane Price, with brief family record. n.a. 1867? 48p.
P4-S21736 — $10.00.

PRICHARD: Desc. of Wm. Prichard. By A. M. Prichard. 1912. 61p.
P4-S21741 — $12.00.

PRICHARD: Prichard Family: Hist & Gen of the Desc of James & Elizabeth Hughes Prichard of New Castle, KY. Martha Coleman Johnson. 1915. 230p.
P4-S21739 — $34.95

PRIEST: Family; Collection of data . . . concerning various branches of the Priest fam. By G.E. Foster. 1900. 549p.
P4-S21747 — $69.00.

PRIME: Some acct. of the Prime fam. of Rowley, MA, with notes on the fams. of Platts, Jewett, & Hammond. By T. Prime. 1887. 40p.
P4-S21754 — $10.00.

PRIME: The autobiography of an octogenarian, with the genealogy of his ancestors & sketches of their history. By Daniel N. Prime. 1873. 293p.
P4-S21759 — $44.00.

PRIME: Notes — genealogical, biographical & bibliographical — of the Prime family. By E.D.G. Prime. 1888. 118p.
P4-S21753 — $19.50.

PRINCE: The gen. of the Prince fam. from 1660-1899. F.A. Prince. 1899. 153p.
P4-S21765 — $23.00.

PRINCE: Princes. Record of our Ancestors: Containing a Complete List of All Persons by the Name of Prince. Frank A. Prince. 1898. 88p.
P4-S21766 — $15.00.

PRINCE: Desc. of Daniel Prince, born May 1st, 1755, By A. Prince. 1898. 11p.
P4-S21769 — $10.00.

PRINCE: Elder John Prince of Hull, MA; A memorial biogr. & gen. By G. Prince. 1888. 32p.
P4-S21767 — $10.00.

PRINCE: Genealogy of the Prince Family of Danvers. Eben Putnam. n.d 11p.
P4-S21768 — $10.00.

PRINDLE: Genealogy, embracing the desc. of Wm. Pringle, the first settler, & also the anc. & desc. of Zalmon Prindle, 1654-1906. By F.C. Prindle. 1906. 352p.
P4-S21771 — $46.50.

PRIOR: A little info. on the Prior-Pryor fam. By H.E. Pryor. 58p.
P4-S21774 — $12.50.

PROCTOR: Gen. of the desc. of Robert Proctor of Concord & Chelmsford, MA, with notes of some connected fam. By Mr. & Mrs. W.L. Proctor. 1898. 315p.
P4-S21780 — $46.50.

PROCTOR: Gathering in comm. of the 100th wedding anniversary of their progenitors Joseph Proctor & Elizabeth Epes... 1868. 46p.
P4-S21781 — $10.00.

PROUTY: Prouty (Proute) gen. By C.H. Pope. 1910. 247p.
P4-S21783 — $32.00.

PROVOST: Biogr. & gen. notes of the Provost fam. from 1545-1895. By A.J. Provost. 1895. 147p.
P4-S21789 — $20.00.

PROVOST: Provoost & Casson Bible records. 3p.
P4-S21790 — $10.00.

PRUDDEN: Rev. Peter Prudden & his descendants in America. By Horton R. Prudden. 1983. 2 vols., 1351p.
P4-S21807 — $155.00.

PRUDDEN: Peter Prudden: a story of his life at New Haven & Milford, CT with the gen. of some of his desc. By L.E. Prudden. 1901. 169p.
P4-S21801 — $25.00.

PRUITT: PREWITT Ancestors. Charles Raymond Dillon. 1960. 242p., typescript.
P4-S21799 — $37.00.

PUCKETT: Descendants of John and William Puckett of Henrico County, VA. Sidney Carey Arnold, Jr. 2004. 264p.
P4-S21899 — $40.00.

PUCKETT: Puckett points: fam. of Richard Puckett of Lunenburg Co., VA. By J.D. Gallaway. 1931. 39p.
P4-S21808 — $10.00.

PUFFENBERGER: Descendants of George Puffenberger, (1787-1850). By Rachel Saul Tefft. 1998. 60p.
P4-S21813 — $13.00.

PUFFER: Fam. of Puffer of MA. By W. Appleton. 1882. 9p.
P4-S21820 — $10.00.

PUFFER: Descendants of Geo. Puffer of Braintree, MA, 1639-1915. By C. Nutt. 1915. 376p.
P4-S21819 — $48.50.

PULFISER: Anc. & desc. of Jonathan Pulfiser of Poland & Sumner, ME. By W.E. Pulfiser. 1928. 71p.
P4-S21831 — $14.00.

PULLEYN: Pulleyns of Yorkshire. C. Pullein. 1915. 886p.
P4-S21832 — $124.00.

PUNCHARD: A tribute to the mem. of John Punchard; a sermon preached at his funeral, Feb. 16, 1857, & an appendix. By S.M. Worcester. 1857. 69p.
P4-S21837 — $14.00.

PURDY: Allied fams. of Purdy, Fauconnier [Falconer], Archer & Perrin. By A.F. Perrin & M.F.P. Meeker. 1911. 114p.
P4-S21843 — $16.50.

PURMORT: Genealogy, consisting of nineteen generations, nine in England, ten in America. By Chas. H. Purmort. 1907. 148p.
P4-S21849 — $21.00.

PUTNAM: The Hon. Samuel Putnam & Sarah (Gooll) Putnam, with a gen. record of their desc. (Repr. Danvers Hist. Coll.) By E.C. Putnam & H. Tapley. 1922. 42p.
P4-S21853 — $10.00.

PUTNAM: History of the Putnam family in Eng. & Amer. (incl. "Putnam Leaflets"). By E. Putnam. 1891-1908. 2 vols., 720p.
P4-S21852 — $99.00.

PUTNAM: Lineage: hist.-gen. notes concerning the Puttenham fam. in England, with lines of royal desc. By E. Putnam. 1907. 400p.
P4-S21855 — $51.00.

PUTNAM: Colonial Putnam fams. of the province of SC. C.P. Mehringer. 7p.
P4-S21856 — $10.00.

PYNCHON: Record of the Pynchon fam. in Eng. & Amer. By Pynchon & Adams. 1898. 24p.
P4-S21862 — $10.00.

Q

QUATTLEBAUM: Family history. By M.M. Quattlebaum. 1950. 280p.
P4-S21867 — $48.50.

QUICK: Genealogy of the Quick family in America (1625-1942). By A.C. Quick. 1942. 507p.
P4-S21873 — $77.50.

QUINBY: Rec. of line of desc. from Robert Quinby to Benj. Quinby (Quimby) & his desc. By S. Quimby 1910. 29p.
P4-S21877 — $10.00.

QUINBY: Genealogical history of the Quinby (Quimby) fam. in Eng. & Amer. By H.C. Quimby. 1915. 604p.
P4-S21876 — $94.00.

QUINBY: Genealogical History of the Quinby-Quimby fam. of Sandwich, NH. By H.C. Quimby. (vol. 2 of above) 1923. 533p.
P4-S21882 — $82.00.

QUINCY: Fam. in Eng. & Amer., 1559-1877, By Edward E. Salisbury. 1885. 81p.
P4-S21888 — $16.00.

R

RAGLAND: Gen. of the Ragland fam. & numerous other fam. of prominence in Amer. with whom they have inter-married. By M. Strong. 1928. 129p.
P4-S21894 — $21.00.

RAINBOROWE: Fam; (Repr. NEHGR) By H. Waters, with I.J. Greenwood. 1886. 16p.
P4-S1898 — $10.00.

RAMSDELL: Family; William Ramsdell genealogy, 2nd ed. By William Ramsdell. 1995. 68p.
P4-S21900 — $13.50.

RAMSEY: Ramsey Family History. J.C. Ramsey. 1933. 216p.
P4-S21901 — $33.00.

RAND: Gen. of the Rand fam. in the US. By F. Rand. 1898. 269p.
P4-S21903 — $35.00.

RANDALL: & Allied families: William Randall (1609-1693) of Scituate & his descendants with ancestral families. By F.A. Randall. 1943. 596p.
P4-S21924 — $89.00.

RANDALL: Genealogy of a branch of the Randall family, 1666-1879. By P.K. Randall. 289p.
P4-S21912 — $43.00.

RANDALL: Biographical history of Robert Randall & his desc., 1608-1909. By W. L. Chaffin. 1909. 267p.
P4-S21906 — $40.00.

RANDALL: Genealogy of the desc. of Stephen Randall & Elizabeth Swazey: 1624-1668. London, Eng.; 1668-1738, RI & CT; 1738-1906, Long Isl., NY. By S.M. Randall. 1906. 64p.
P4-S21918 — $13.00.

RANDOLPH: Brief Sketches of the Randolphs & Their Connections; Woodsons, Keiths, Strothers, Pleasants & Mayos. W.E. Railey. 1933. 157 + 27p.
P4-S21943 — $28.00.

RANDOLPH: Lineages, being the ancestry of Iris Patricia Follows from the time of the Saxon invasion of England; Volume I, the Southerners. By Howard Metcalfe. 1991. 500p.
P4-S21942 — $75.00.

RANDOLPH: Lineages, Volume II: the Northerners. Howard Metcalfe. 1993. 612p.
P4-S21948 — $85.00.

RANDOLPH: Lineages, Vol. III: pedigrees. Howard Metcalfe. 1993. 506p.
P4-S21954 — $76.00.

RANDOLPH: The Randolphs of VA: A comp. of the desc. of Wm. Randolph of Turkey Isl. & his wife Mary Isham of Bermuda Hundred. By R.I. Randolph. 1937 404p.
P4-S21960 — $62.50.

RANKIN: WHARTON family & their gen. By S. M. Rankin. 1931. 295p.
P4-S21966 — $44.00.

RANSOM: Descendants of Capt. Samuel Ransom. Capt. C.B. Sears. 1882. 234p.
P4-S21970 — $35.00.

RANSOM: Historical outline of the Ransom family of America, and genealogical records of the Colchester, CT branch. Wyllys C. Ransom. 1903. 408p.
P4-S21972 — $62.00.

RATHBONE: Index to Rathbone gen. comp. By M. Dale. 1966. 253p.
P4-S21978 — $26.00.

RATHBONE: Genealogy; A complete hist. of the Rathbone fam., from 1574 to date. By J.C. Cooley. 1898. 827p.
P4-S21971 — $104.00.

RAUCH: Book. By Rufus Wm. Rauch. 1977. 89p.
P4-S21987 — $17.50.

RAVENEL: Records: History & genealogy of the Huguenot family of Ravenel, of SC. By Henry E. Ravenel. 1898. 279p.
P4-S21993 — $43.00.

RAWLE: Records of the Rawle fam., coll. from the Nat'l Archives, parish reg. & other sources. By E.J. Rawle. 1898. 336p.
P4-S21999 — $43.00.

RAWLINGS: Notes relating to Rawlings, or Rollins, with notices of early settlers of the name in America By J.R. Rollins. 1870. 84p.
P4-S22005 — $16.50.

RAWSON: Family; A rev. mem. of Edward Rawson, Sec. of the Col. of Mass. Bay, 1650-1686. By E.B. Crane. 1875. 350p.
P4-S22017 — $55.00.

RAWSON: Memoir of Edward Rawson, with gen. notices of his desc. By S. S. Rawson. 1849. 148p.
P4-S22011 — $30.00.

RAWSON: Anc. of Edward Rawson. By E.B. Crane. 1887. 54p.
P4-S22012 — $10.00.

RAYMOND: Gen. of the Raymond fam. of New Eng. 1630 to 1886, with a hist. sketch of some of the Raymonds of early times. S. Raymond. 1886. 304p.
P4-S22041 — $39.00.

RAYMOND: Genealogy; Descendants of John & Wm. Raymond, By S.E. Raymond & L.H. Raymond. 1972. 886p.
P4-S22050 — $129.00.

RAYMOND: Descendants of Richard Raymond. Vol I, Part I. S.E. Raymond & Louvera H. Raymond. 1969. 227p.
P4-S22041 — $34.50.

RAYMOND: Descendants of Richard Raymond, Volume I, Part. II. S.E Raymond & L.H. Raymond. 1970. 340p.
P4-S22023 — $54.00.

RAYMOND: Descendants of Richard Raymond, Vol. I, Part III. S.E. Raymond & L. H. Raymond. 1971. 534p.
P4-S22029 — $82.00.

RAYMOND: Descendants of R. Raymond, Vol. I; Part IV. S.E. & L.H Raymond. 1972. 510p.
P4-S22035 — $76.00.

REA: Journal of Caleb Rea, written during the expedition against Ticonderoga (1758). By F. Ray. 1881. 10p.
P4-S22051 — $10.00.

READ: The Reads & their relatives, being an account of Col. Clemens & Madam Read of Bushy Forest, Lunenburg Co. VA. By Alice Read. 1930. 688p.
P4-S22074 — $99.50.

READ: Genealogy of the brothers & sisters & fam. & desc. of Israel, Abner, John, Polly, William, Wolcott, Lewis & Nathaniel Read. By H.M. Dodd. 1912. 301p.
P4-S22056 — $48.00.

READ: & Allied families of Read, Corbin, Luttrell, & Bywaters of Culpeper Co., VA. By A.M. Prichard. 1930. 292p.
P4-S22062 — $46.00.

READE: Descendants of Reade or Reed: William Reade & Mabel (Kendall), his wife; By F.L.S. Meadows, with J.M. Ames. 1937. 285p.
P4-S22075 — $44.00.

READE: Record of the Reades of Barton Court, Berkshire, with a short precis of other lines of the name. By C. Reade. 1899. 148p.
P4-S22068 — $23.50.

READING: Genealogical & Biographical Memorials of the Reading, Howell, Yerkes, Watts, Latham & Elkins families. By Josiah Granville Leach. 1898. 286 + 96p.
P4-S22080 — $57.50.

REDFEARN: History of the Redfearn family. D.H. Redfearn. Rev. ed., 1954. 376p.
P4-S22086 — $57.50.

REDFIELD: Genealogical hist. of the Redfield fam. in the US; a rev. & extension of the gen. tables comp. in 1839. By John H. Redfield 1860. 345p.
P4-S22092 — $55.00.

REDINGTON: John Redington of Topsfield, MA & some of his desc. By C.M.R. Carter. 11p.
P4-S22097 — $10.00.

REDINGTON: John Redington of Topsfield, MA & some of his descendants, with notes on the Wales family. By C.M.R. Carter. 1909. 86p.
P4-S22098 — $17.00.

REED: READ Lineage; Capt. John Reed of Providence, RI & Norwalk, CT & his desc. through his sons John & Thomas, 1660-1909. By E. Reed-Wright. 1909. 796p.
P4-S22122 — $109.00.

REED: Genealogy of the Reed (Reid) Family. Vol. I. A.H. Reed. 1963. 282p.
P4-S22141 — $42.00.

REED: Genealogy of the Reed (Reid) Family. Vol. II. A.H. Reed. 1963. 245p.
P4-S22135 — $37.00.

REED: History of the Reed family in Europe & America. J.W. Reed. 1861. 596p.
P4-S22116 — $89.00.

REED: Genealogy, desc. of Wm. Reade of Weymouth, MA, from 1635-1902. By J.L. Reed. 1901. 786p.
P4-S22143 — $95.00.

REED: History & genealogy of the Reed family: Johann Philib Ried, Rieth, Ritt, Rudt, etc., in Europe & America By W.H. Reed. 1929. 529p.
P4-S22110 — $81.50.

REED: Desc; Thirteen generations, including anc. & desc. of Paul Reed, 1605-1955, other desc. of his immig. ancestor Wm. Reade, b. 1609, Eng. By B.B. Aldridge. 1955. 139p.
P4-S22128 — $23.50.

REED: Family records. By J. Montgomery Seaver. n.d. 65p.
P4-S22140 — $13.00.

REEDER: Desc. of John Reeder & Elizabeth Fisher of Northumberland Co., PA (in Fisher gen.) 1890. 12p.
P4-S22144 — $10.00.

REEMSNYDER: The Family History of Herman Frederick Reemsnyder & His Desc. B.E. Reemsnyder, et al. 1908. 238p.
P4-S22145 — $36.00.

REESE: Genealogy of the Reese family in Wales and America from their arrival in America to the present time [1903]. By M.E. Reese. 1903. 322p.
P4-S22149 — $49.50.

REITZ: Family history & record book of the descendants of Johan Friedrich Reitz, the Pioneer, who landed at Philadelphia, PA. J.J. Reitz. 1930. 289p.
P4-S22155 — $44.50.

REMICK: Gen. of the Remick fam. By O.P. Remick. 1893. 7p.
P4-S22162 — $10.00.

REMICK: Gen., comp. from the mss. of Lt. Oliver Philbrick Remick for the Maine Hist. Soc. By W.L. Holman. 1933. 211p.
P4-S22161 — $34.50.

REMINGTON: Thomas Remington of Suffield, CT & some desc. By L. Dewey. 1909. 9p.
P4-S22162 — $10.00.

RENWICK: Renwick gen. By H.H. McIver. 1924. 23p.
P4-S22163 — $10.00.

REQUA: The fam. of Requa, 1678-1898. By A.C. Requa. 1898. 102p.
P4-S22167 — $15.00.

RESSEGUIE: Family; A hist. & gen. rec. of Alexander Resseguie of Norwalk, CT & four gen. of his desc. By J.E. Morris. 1888. 99p.
P4-S22173 — $19.50.

REUTTER: Letters & Papers Concerning the Family of Michael Reutter, Jr. 1762-1805. A.A. Ebersole & G. H. Duncan 1968. 89p.
P4-S22175 — $17.00.

REX: Anc. & desc. of George Rex, first of Eng. to PA in 1771. By L.F. Rex. 1933. 192p.
P4-S22179 — $31.50.

REXFORD: Gen. hist. & paternal line of desc. from Arthur Rexford of Eng. & CT. By J.D. Rexford. 1891. 77p.
P4-S22185 — $16.00.

REYNOLDS: RENNOLDS fam. of Eng. & VA, 1530-1948, being the hist. of Christopher Reynolds of Co. Kent, Eng. & his desc. in VA, etc. By S.F. Tillman. 1948. 255p.
P4-S22257 — $39.50.

REYNOLDS: Christopher Reynolds & his descendants. By S.F. Tillman. 1959. 464p.
P4-S22191 — $69.50.

REYNOLDS: Reports of Reynolds Fam. Assoc., incl. gen. notes. M.H. Reynolds. 1928. 117p.
P4-S22221 — $16.00.

REYNOLDS: Family Assoc. 39th & 40th annual report, with gen. & hist. collection. comp. by A. Rippier 1931. 139p.
P4-S22245 — $22.50.

REYNOLDS: Family records. By J.M. Seaver. 37p.
P4S-22192 — $10.00.

REYNOLDS: Anc. & desc. of Wm. & Eliz. Reynolds of North Kingstown, RI. By T.A. Reynolds. 1903. 42p.
P4-S22193 — $10.00.

REYNOLDS: Reynolds Fam Assn 30th Annual Report, 1892-1921. comp. by A.C. Rippier. 1921. 222p.
P4-S22194 — $33.00.

REYNOLDS: Family Assoc. 16th annual report. 1907. 53p.
P4-S22195 — $11.00.

REYNOLDS: Family Assoc. 31st annual report, with hist. collection. comp. By A. Rippier 1922. 280p.
P4-S22227 — $42.00.

REYNOLDS: Family Assoc. 37th annual report, with gen. & hist. collection. comp. by A. Rippier 1928. 67p.
P4-S22239 — $13.50.

REYNOLDS: Family Assoc. 44th — 46th annual report, with gen. & hist. collection. comp. by A. Rippier 1937. 94p.
P4-S22251 — $19.00.

REYNOLDS: History & desc. of John & Sarah Reynolds (1630?-1923), of Watertown, MA & Wethersfield, Stamford & Greenwich, CT. By M.H. Reynolds. 1924. 509p.
P4-S22203 — $79.50.

REYNOLDS: History & one line of decendants of Robert & Mary Reynolds (1630? — 1928) of Boston, with the Hyatt family of Princeton, NJ. By M.H. Reynolds. 1928. 92p.
P4-S22209 — $18.00.

REYNOLDS: History & some of the descendants of Robert & Mary Reynolds (1630? — 1931) of Boston, MA. comp. By M.H. Reynolds. 1931. 236p.
P4-S22215 — $37.50.

REYNOLDS: Genealogy of James & Deborah Reynolds of North Kingstown, RI & descendants. By Steve Roth. 1999. 3 vols, 1785 + 478p., Index.
P4-S22197 — $225.00.

REYNOLDS: Family Assoc. 33rd & 34th annual report, with gen. & hist. collection. comp.by A. Rippier 1925. 171p.
P4-S22233 — $27.50.

RHOADES: Anc. lin. of Nelson Osgood Rhoades & Francis (Brown) Rhoades. By N.O. Rhoades. 1920. 21p.
P4-S22258 — $10.00.

RHODES: Family in America: a genealogy & history, from 1497 to the present day. By Howard J. Rhodes. 1959. 525p.
P4-S22263 — $79.00.

RICE: By the name of Rice. An hist. sketch of Dea. Edmund Rice, the Pilgrim (1594-1663), & of his desc. By C.E. Rice. 1911. 99p.
P4-S22275 — $15.00.

RICE: "We Sought the Wilderness" (memoir of some desc. of Dea. Edmund Rice). C.S. Rice. 1949. 257p.
P4-S22269 — $39.50.

RICE: Gen. history of the Rice family & desc. of Dea. Edm. Rice, who came from Berkhamstead, Eng., & settled at Sudbury, MA in 1638. By A.H. Ward. 1858. 387p.
P4-S22281 — $52.00.

RICH: Richard Rich of Eastham on Cape Cod & some desc. (Repr. NEHGR). By E. Rich. 94p.
P4-S22293 — $18.00.

RICH: Gen. Desc. of Jonathan Rich. By G. Rich. 1892. 39p.
P4-S22288 — $10.00.

RICH: Joel Rich ancestors & descendants, from Dover NH, Cape Cod & Gorham ME to Jackson Plantation, Waldo Co. (1677-1993). By Frances Morton-Rich DeMars. 1993. 175p.
P4-S22287 — $29.50.

RICH: Early Rich hist. & anc. of Jonathan Rich, Jr., Ft. Covington, NY. By G. Rich. 1922. 48p.
P4-S22289 — $10.00.

RICHARDS: The Genealogy of the Descendants of Several Ancient Puritans, Thomas Richards of Dorchester, MA, b. ca. 1590. By A. Morse. 1861. 243p.
P4-S22299 — $38.50.

RICHARDSON: DePRIEST family. By R. Roller. 1905. 50p.
P4-S22301 — $10.00.

RICHARDSON: Memorial, comprising a full hist. & gen. of the posterity of the three brothers, Ezekiel, Samuel & Thomas Richardson, By J.A. Vinton. 1876. 959p.
P4-S22302 — $109.00.

RICHARDSON: Genealogical record of the families in the descending line of Samuel Richardson, b. England about 1610, through ten generations By Joseph Hammond. 1896. 22p.
P4-S22303 — $10.00.

RICHARDSON: Gen. biogr. study of the name & fam. of Richardson, 1720-1860. By J. Richardson. 1860. 30p.
P4-S22304 — $10.00.

RICHARDSON: Memorial supplement. By I. & F. Richardson. 1898. 34p.
P4-S22305 — $10.00.

RICHARDSON: Thomas Richardson of S. Shields, Durham Co., Eng. & desc. in the US. By M. Seaman. 1929. 241p.
P4-S22308 — $36.00.

RICHEY: Descendants. By C. Edelbute. n.d. 93p., typescript.
P4-S22314 — $18.00.

RICHMOND: Family records, Vol. I: MD, VA, New England, Ireland & Somerset. By H.I. Richmond. 1933 232p.
P4-S22320 — $37.00.

RICHMOND: Family records, Vol. II: the Richmonds alias Webb of Wiltshire, England. H.I. Richmond. 1933. 265p.
P4-S22326 — $42.00.

RICHMOND: Family records, Vol. III: Richmonds of Wiltshire, England. H.I. Richmond. 1933. 327p.
P4-S22332 — $49.50.

RICHMOND: Family, 1594-1896, & pre-American ancestry, 1040-1594. By J.B. Richmond. 1897. 633p.
P4-S22344 — $95.00.

RICKER: Records of some desc. of Georgve & Maturin Ricker, Dover, NH. By W.B. Lapham. 1877. 29p.
P4-S22345 — $10.00.

RICKERSON: The Diary of Achsa M. Tubbs-Rickerson, 1887-1901, Spring Creek, Warren Co., PA. 1996. 137p.
P4-S22351 — $19.00.

RICKERT: Desc. of Daniel Rickert & Barbara (Rosenberger) Rickert of PA. By A. Fretz. 1906. 13p.
P4-S22355 — $10.00.

RICKETSON: William Ricketson, William Ricketson, Jr., & their desc., Vol I. G.W. Edes. 1917. 127p.
P4-S22362 — $19.00.

RICKETSON: William Ricketson & his desc., Vol. 2. G.W. Edes. 1932. 658p.
P4-S22356 — $97.50.

RICKS: Gen. of the Ricks fam. of Amer. By G. S. Rix. 1908. 184p.
P4-S22365 — $25.00.

RICKS: History & genealogy of the Ricks family of America, (Rev. ed. of The Ricks Family of America, 1908) Descendants of Isaac Ricks comp. By Howard Ricks, et al. 1957. 767p.
P4-S22371 — $109.00.

RIDDELL: History of the ancient Ryedales & their desc. in Normandy, Gt. Brit., Ireland & Amer., 860-1914 By G.T. Ridlon 1884. 796p.
P4-S22374 — $98.00.

RIDDLE: REDDELL- RIDDELL Trail newsletters, Vol. I, no. 1 through Vol. VI, no. 3. By Nettie Lee Benson. 1980-1990 515p., typescript.
P4-S22380 — $78.00.

RIDDLE: The descendants of Edward Riddle (1758-1826) & Margaret McMillan (c.1769-c.1825). By Joan Riddle Giles. 2000. 830p.
P4-S22386 — $99.50.

RIDGWAY: Desc. of Ridgway-Ridgeway fam. in Eng. & Amer. By G. L. Ridgway. 1926. 130p.
P4-S22392 — $27.50.

RIGGAN: Descendants of Ira Riggan. Sidney C. Arnold, Jr. 2004. 400p.
P4-S22399 — $60.00.

RIGGS: Family of MD; a genealogical & historical record including several of the families in England. By J.B. Riggs. 1939. 534p.
P4-S22413 — $81.00.

RIGGS: Our pioneer ancestors, being a record of available information as to the Riggs, Baldridge, Agnew, Earle, Kirkpatrick, Vreeland & allied families. By H.E. Riggs. 1942. 230p.
P4-S22407 — $37.00.

RIGGS: Descendants of some of the sons of Isaac & Mary Riggs, who came to KY ca. 1790, from West. PA. By R.C. Rich. 1976. 209p., typescript.
P4-S22398 — $29.50.

RIGGS: Genealogy of the Riggs fam.; desc. of Edw. Riggs of Eng. & Roxbury MA (b 1590). By J. Wallace. 1901. 147p.
P4-S22401 — $21.00.

RIKER: RYKER fam. of NY (in Welch gen.). 1932. 27p.
P4-S22414 — $10.00.

RILAND: Three hundred years of a family living, being a history of the Rilands of Sutton Coldfield [England]. By the Rev. W.K.R. Bedford. 1889 175p.
P4-S22419 — $28.00.

RINEHART: The Old Home [one line of descent from Abraham Rinehart & Catherine Brower]. By C. White. n.d. 72p.
P4-S22425 — $15.00.

RING: The gen. of the desc. of Jere Foster Ring & Phebe Ellis of Weld, ME. By H.P. Ring. 1931. 43p.
P4-S22426 — $10.00.

RIPLEY: Gen. of part of the Ripley fam. By H. Ripley 1867. 48p.
P4-S22427 — $10.00.

RISING: James Rising of Suffield, CT & some of his desc. (Repr. NEHGR). By L.M. Dewey. 1909. 11p.
P4-S22429 — $10.00.

RISLEY: Family history, incl. records of some of the early English Risleys; a genealogy of the desc. of Richard Risley (1633) & (1636), By E.H. Risley. 1909. 318p.
P4-S22428 — $40.00.

RITTER: Versuch den Ursprung und die Genealogie der Rheinpfalzischen Familie Ritter. Norton T. Horr. 1912. 54p.
P4-S22430 — $10.00.

RIVES: Reliques of the Rives (Ryves), being hist. & gen. notes of the ancient fam. of Ryves of Co. Dorset & the Rives of VA. By J.R. Childs. 1929. 780p.
P4-S22434 — $109.00.

RIX: History & genealogy of the Rix fam. of Amer. By G. S. Rix 1906. 253p.
P4-S22440 — $38.00.

RIXEY: Genealogy, with ref. to the Morehead, Hunton, Gibbs, Hall, Thomas, Jones, Lewis, Chancellor, Pendleton & other allied fam. By R. Rixey. 1933. 436p.
P4-S22446 — $68.00.

ROACH: ROBERTS, Ridgeway & allied fams. By M. R. Fair. 1951 258p.
P4-S22452 — $41.50.

ROARK: Roarks of Ireland & pedigree of Nathan Roark fam. in US. By M.I. Roark. 1950. 64p.
P4-S22458 — $13.00.

ROBARDS: Hist. of the Robards fam. By B. Farrior. 1959. 74p.
P4-S22464 — $15.00.

ROBBINS: Robbins fam.; Nicholas Robbins of Duxbury & desc. By H. & E. Robbins. 15p.
P4-S22471 — $10.00.

ROBBINS: Recollections of my mother [Anne Jean Robbins Lyman]. By Susan I. Lesley. 1889. 505p.
P4-S22472 — $57.00.

ROBBINS: History of the Robbins family of Walpole, MA: desc. of William & Priscilla Robbins. By D.W. Robbins. 1949. 60 + 221p.
P4-S22470 — $42.50.

ROBERDEAU: Gen. of the Roberdeau fam., incl. a biogr. of Gen. Daniel Roberdeau of the Rev. army. By R. Buchanan. 1876. 196p.
P4-S22476 — $29.00.

ROBERTS: Desc. of John Roberts of Simsbury & Bloomfield, CT. By L.A. Roberts. 1888. 7p.
P4-S22483 — $10.00.

ROBERTS: Fam. of Simsbury, CT in the line of Capt. Samuel Roberts, 1742-1789. By F. Starr. 1896. 54p.
P4-S22484 — $10.00.

ROBERTS: Thomas Roberts fam. of Marathon, IA. 1960. 110p.
P4-S22494 — $25.00.

ROBERTS: Family. Genealogy of Joseph Roberts of Windham, ME, 18th century. Amorena Grant. n.d. 143p.
P4-S22488 — $24.00.

ROBERTS: Family history & ancestry: Roberts — Thompson — Dunham, Basking Ridge, NJ. By Stanley E. Harris, Jr. 2001. 278p.
P4-S22482 — $42.00.

ROBERTS: Wm. Roberts family of Schuylkill Twp., Chester Co., PA from "Early Friends' Families of upper Bucks." 18p.
P4-S22489 — $10.00.

ROBERTS: Family records. By J. Montgomery Seaver. 45p.
P4-S22490 — $10.00.

ROBERTS: Thomas Roberts family, from "Early Friends' Families of upper Bucks." 28p.
P4-S22491 — $10.00.

ROBERTSON: PURCELL & related families. Laura P. Robertson. 1926. 242p.
P4-S22506 — $38.00.

ROBERTSON: RUFF Entwined: Robertson — Ruff Family history. By Vonceil Rust Robertson. n.d. 407 + 87p.
P4-S22512 — $74.50.

ROBERTSON: Family records. By J.M. Seaver. 1928. 126p.
P4-S22518 — $19.50.

ROBERTSON: Gen. of the Robertson, Small & related fam. By A.R. Small. 1907. 258p.
P4-S22500 — $39.00.

ROBERTSON: Robertson & Related Families. Paul G. Robertson 2004. 189p.
P4-S22507 — $28.50.

ROBESON: History & gen. acct. of Andrew Robeson of Scotland, NJ & PA & of his desc., 1653-1916. By Robeson, Stroud & Osborne. 1916. 776p.
P4-S22524 — $109.00.

ROBINSON: Genealogy; Desc. of the Rev. John Robinson, pastor of the Pilgrims, Vol. I C.E. Robinson. 1928. 410p.
P4-S22560 — $64.00.

ROBINSON: Thomas Robinson & his descendants, rev. ed. By Thomas H. Robinson. 1902. 233p.
P4-S22572 — $36.00.

ROBINSON: Robinson fam. of York Co., VA (Extr. from Va. Gen.). 20p.
P4-S22531 — $10.00.

ROBINSON: Descendants of Rev. William Robinson. By Bertha S. Taylor. 1936. 71p.
P4-S22530 — $14.00.

ROBINSON: Memoir of the Rev. William Robinson of Southington, CT, with some acct. of his anc. in this country, By E. Robinson. 1859. 226p.
P4-S22536 — $34.00.

ROBINSON: Recollections of older times; Rowland Robinson of Narragansett & his unfortunate daughter, with gen. of the Robinson & Hazard fam. of RI. Also, gen. sketch of the Hazards of the middle states. By T. Hazard. 1879. 264p.
P4-S22542 — $40.00.

ROBINSON: Fam. Gen. & Hist. Assoc. (The Robinsons & their Kin Folk, 1st Series) Officers, constitution & by-laws. 1902. 104p.
P4-S22548 — $19.50.

ROBINSON: Fam. Gen. & Hist. Assoc., 2nd series. 1904. 80p.
P4-S22554 — $16.00.

ROBINSON: Colonial & rev. anc. Some acct. of the New Eng. desc. of Hamline Elijah Robinson. 1903. 6p.
P4-S22537 — $10.00.

ROBINSON: Ten Robinson Generations from Joseph Robinson & the Robinson Families of Orangeburg, SC & Rankin County, MS. Frank Allen Robinson. 1978. 164p.
P4-S22538 — $48.00.

ROBINSON: The Robinsons & their kin folk, 3rd series. By the Robinson Family Gen. & Hist. Assoc. 1906. 159p.
P4-S22566 — $25.50.

ROBY: Pedigree of Roby of Castle Donington, County Leicester. By H.J. Roby. 1907, 2nd ed. 69p.
P4-S22575 — $14.00.

ROCKEFELLER: Transactions of the Rockefeller Family Assn for the Five Years, 1905-1909, with genealogy, vol 1. 1910. 382p.
P4-S22590 — $59.00.

ROCKEFELLER: Transactions of the Rockefeller Family Assn. for the Five Years, 1910-1914, with gen, vol 2. 1915. 338p.
P4-S22596 — $46.50.

ROCKEFELLER: Transactions of the Rockefeller Fam. Assn for the Five Years, 1915-25, with Genealogy, vol 3. 1926. 294p.
P4-S22602 — $46.00.

ROCKEFELLER: Genealogy, vol 4.
Comp. by Henry O. Rockefeller. n.d. 401p.
P4-S22584 — $61.00.

**ROCKWELL: Family in Amer: gen.
rec., from 1630-1873.** By H.E. Rockwell.
1873. 224p.
P4-S22611 — $30.00.

**ROCKWELL: Genealogy of the fams.
of John Rockwell of Stamford, Ct, 1641,
& Ralph Keeler of Hartford, 1639.** By J.
Boughton. 1903. 615p.
P4-S22605 — $77.00.

**ROCKWELL: Rockwells of North
America: Descendants of William
Rockwell (1591-1640).** Mark S. Rockwell.
2004. 362p.
P4-S22606 — $54.50.

**ROCKWELL: Fam. in one line of
desc.** By F. Rockwell. 1924. 241p.
P4-S22617 — $36.00.

**ROCKWOOD: Hist. & gen. record of
the desc. of Timothy Rockwood, 1727-
1806.** By E.L. Rockwood. 1856. 152p.
P4-S22623 — $24.50.

RODMAN: Notes on Rodman gen.
By W.W. Rodman. 1887. 27p.
P4-S22627 — $10.00.

RODMAN: Fam. gen., 1620-1886. By
C.H. Jones. 1886. 291p.
P4-S22626 — $38.00.

ROE: Hist. records of an old fam. By
F. Roe 1890. 16p.
P4-S22628 — $10.00.

**ROGERS: TURFLER Family: a search
for anc.** By I.N. Williams. 1946. 120p.
P4-S22638 — $19.00.

**ROGERS: Gen. memoir of the fam. of
Rev. Nathaniel Rogers of Ipswich,
Essex Co., MA (Repr. NEHGR).** By
A. D. Rogers. 1851. 68p.
P4-S22633 — $10.00.

ROGERS: Family History. By J.M.
Seaver. 67p.
P4-S22650 — $14.00.

**ROGERS: John Rogers of Marshfield
(MA) & some of his desc.** By J.H.
Drummond. 1898. 221p.
P4-S22632 — $29.50.

**ROGERS: Family; From "Some VA
Families,"** H.M. McIhany 1903 35p.
P4-S22634 — $10.00.

**ROGERS: The anc. & desc. of Luke
Rogers & Sarah Wright Brown.** By
E.B. Leatherbee. 1907. 71p.
P4-S22635 — $14.00.

**ROGERS: Desc. of the Rev. Daniel
Rogers, of Littleton, MA (Repr.
NEHGR).** By J.W. Dean. 1885. 8p.
P4-S22636 — $10.00.

ROGERS: Hope Rogers & his desc.
By J.S. Rogers. 1901. 7p.
P4-S22637 — $10.00.

**ROGERS: James Rogers of New
London, CT & his descendants.** By J.S.
Rogers. 1902. 514p.
P4-S22629 — $65.50.

ROGERS: As it May Be. Bessie S.
Rogers. 1905. 83 + 10p.
P4-S22639 — $14.00.

**ROGERS: James Rogers of London-
derry, & James Rogers of Dumbarton.**
By J.H. Drummond. 1897. 12p.
P4-S22640 — $10.00.

ROHRBOUGH: Family. By F.W.
Rohrbough. 1962. 130p.
P4-S22656 — $26.00.

**ROLLINS: My North Carolina
Heritage, Volume 2: Rollins, Ealy,
Morgan & Smelser families [with
related families]** By Marshall L. Styles.
1999. 408p.
P4-S22662 — $62.00.

**ROLLINS: Record of fam. of the
name of Rawlins or Rollins in the US.**
By J.R. Rollins. 1874. 362p.
P4-S22665 — $46.00.

**ROMER: Hist. sketches of the
Romer, Van Tassel, & allied fam.** By
J.L. Romer. 1917. 159p.
P4-S22671 — $24.00.

**ROOME: Descendants of Peter
Willemse Roome.** P. Warner. 1883.
410p.
P4-S22677 — $64.00.

ROOSEVELT: Genealogy, 1649-1902.
By C.B. Whittlesey. 1902. 121p.
P4-S22683 — $18.00.

**ROOT: Genealogical records, 1600-
1870, comprising the history of the
Root & Roots family in America.** By
J.P. Root. 1870. 533p.
P4-S22689 — $68.00.

**ROPER: Family of Sterling &
Rutland.** By E. Roper. 1904. 473p.
P4-S22695 — $74.00.

**ROSE: Col. Wm. Rose of TN, his
ancestors & desc., 1034-1938.** By V.
Rose. 1939. 283p.
P4-S22701 — $45.00.

**ROSE: Rose & Allied Families: Corker,
Mason, Stark, Sanford & Their Kin.**
George H. Rose. 1973. xxii + 369p.
P4-S22702 — $59.00.

**ROSE: Genealogy, including descen-
dants of Israel Rose, Pioneer of WA &
OR with add. & corr.** By J.A.
Nunamaker. 1963. 71 + 9p.
P4-S22707 — $16.00.

**ROSEBOOM: 1630-1897, Brief history
of the ancestors & descendants of
John Rosebook (1739-1805) & Jess
Johnson (1745-1832).** By Catharine
Roseboom, Dr J. L. Roseboom, et al.
1897. 140p.
P4-S22713 — $21.00.

**ROSENBERGER: Genealogical
record of the descendants of Henry
Rosenberger of Franconia, Montgomery Co., PA.** Rev. A.J. Fretz. 1906. 335p.
P4-S22719 — $51.50.

**ROSENKRANS: ROSECRANS;
Glimpses through portals of the past
[descendants of Herman Hendrickzen
Rosenkrans & his wife Magdalena
Dircks of Norway** By Warren Rosecrans
Hedden, James Spencer Hedden, et al.
1921. 82p., typescript.
P4-S22725 — $16.50.

**ROSENKRANS: Family in Europe &
America.** By A. Rosenkrans 1900. 332p.
P4-S22728 — $43.50.

**ROSS: John Ross of Ipswich, MA,
Windham, CT & Wilkes-Barre, PA.** By
Ross & O'Brien. 1984. 5p.
P4-S22729 — $10.00.

**ROSS: Dr. Samuel Ross of Colerain,
MA, his anc. & desc.** D.C. MacBryde.
1934. 22p.
P4-S22730 — $10.00.

**ROSS: Gen. of the Ross fam., desc. of
Zebulon Ross (Scotland to Dover,
Dutchess Co., NY)** By Griffith &
Palston. 1885. 16p.
P4-S22731 — $10.00.

**ROSSITER: Rossiters of CT (Repr.
NEHGR).** 6p.
P4-S22735 — $10.00.

ROSSON: The Rosson Story. By S.
Jackson. 1959 24p.
P4-S22736 — $10.00.

ROTCH: Memorandum Written by William Rotch in the Eightieth Year of His Age. William Rotch. 1916. 90 + 30p.
P4-S22745 — $19.50.

ROTCH: The Rotches [biography & genealogy of the Rotch family of Nantucket & New Bedford, MA]. By J.M. Bullard. 1947. 583p.
P4-S22746 — $89.00.

ROTCH: Joseph Rotch in Nantucket & Dartmouth. J.M. Bullard. 1931. 32p.
P4-S22747 — $10.00.

ROTH: The family of Nicholas Roth, Amer. settlers from Germany, with information on assoc. families of Winters, Darnold & Keppler. By Steve Roth. 1992. 197p.
P4-S22752 — $29.50.

ROUND: ROUNDS genealogy; Desc. of John Round of Swansea, MA, who dies 1716, & Rounds families of undetermined relationship. By N.R. Nichols. 1928. 259p.
P4-S22758 — $39.00.

ROUSE: Zimmerman, Tanner, Henderson, McClure, Porter & allied fam. By E. R. Lloyd. 1932. 228p.
P4-S22764 — $30.00.

ROUSH: History of the Roush family in America, from its founding by John Adam Rausch in 1736 to the present [1928]. By L.L. Roush. 1928. 738p.
P4-S22770 — $109.00.

ROWELL: Biogr. sketch of Samuel Rowell & notices of some of his desc., with a gen. for seven gen., 1754-1898. By R. Rowell. 1898. 216p.
P4-S22776 — $32.50.

ROWLEE: Lt. Herman Rowlee (1746-1818), & his desc. W. Rowlee. 1907. 138p.
P4-S22782 — $21.00.

ROWLEY: Desc. of Moses Rowley of Cape Cod (c. 1715) H.S. Russell. 1908. 33p.
P4-S22784 — $10.00.

ROY: The Roy fam. of VA & KY. By N.R. Roy. 1935. 190p.
P4-S22788 — $28.50.

ROYALL: The New Eng. Royalls. By E.D. Harris. 1885. 27p.
P4-S22790 — $10.00.

ROYER: Genealogical records of the Royer family in America, or more especially those of Sebastian Royer's Family. By F.G. Francis. 1928. 654p.
P4-S22794 — $95.00.

ROYER: Hist. of Christopher Royer & his posterity, (in Gift, Kern, Royer Gen.) By A.K. Gift. 1909. 40p.
P4-S22795 — $10.00.

RUBY: Gen. of the Ruby fam. By A.S. Ruby. 1926. 27p.
P4-S22799 — $10.00.

RUCKER: Genealogy of the Rucker family, with Bush genealogy. By L.B. Rucker. 1963. 148p.
P4-S22800 — $24.00.

RUCKER: Family genealogy, with anc., desc., & connections. By S.R. Wood. 1932. 585p.
P4-S22806 — $87.50.

RUGG: Descendants of John Rugg. By E.R. Rugg. 1911 580p.
P4-S22812 — $89.00.

RUGGLES: Lineage: five generations. By H.S. Ruggles. 1896. 14p.
P4-S22815 — $10.00.

RUGGLES: The gen. of Thomas Ruggles of Roxbury, 1637, to Thomas Ruggles of Pomfret, CT & Rutland, VT. By F.L. Bailey. 1896. 44p.
P4-S22816 — $10.00.

RUGGLES: Evidences of the derivation of the Ruggles fam. of Eng. & Amer. from that of Ruggeley of Staffordshire, (Repr. NYGBR) H. S. Ruggles. 1894. 4p.
P4-S22818 — $10.00.

RUGGLES: Family of England & America. By Edw. Stoddard Ruggles. 1893. 232p.
P4-S22824 — $36.00.

RULISON: Gen. of the Rulison, Rulifson & allied fams. in Amer., 1689-1918. By H.F. Rulison. 1919. 216p.
P4-S22830 — $34.50.

RUNKLE: Family, being an acct. of the Runkles in Europe & their desc. in Amer. By B. Fisher. 1899. 366p.
P4-S22836 — $58.00.

RUNNELS: Genealogy of the Runnels & Reynolds family in Amer. By M. T. Runnels. 1873. 371p.
P4-S22842 — $58.50.

RUNYAN: Gen of the Runyans. 1891. 10p.
P4-S22844 — $10.00.

RUSLING: Family. By J.F. Rusling. 1907. 160p.
P4-S22848 — $24.00.

RUSS: Russ Family Genealogy IV. Herbert M. Russ 2004. 359p.
P4-S22850 — $54.00.

RUSSELL: Ancestors & descendants of Abel Russell, Rev. Soldier from Westford, MA & Fayetter (Starling Plantaion), ME. By A.J. Russell & S.R. Child. 1922. 40p.
P4-S22855 — $10.00.

RUSSELL: A Gen. Register of the desc. of Robert & Agnes (Leitch) Russell, emigrants to Benton Co., MN, & pioneer experiences. By N. & R. Flint. 1923. 44 + 20p.
P4-S22856 — $10.00.

RUSSELL: All Things Connected; Anc Search of the Russell, Little, Milton, Chase & Higgins Families. Edward M. Russell. 2006. 116p.
P4-S22857 — $18.00.

RUSSELL: William Russell & descendants, & the Russell family of VA. A.R. & L. des Cognets. 1960. 319p.
P4-S22866 — $46.50.

RUSSELL: Acct. of some desc. of John Russell, who came to Boston, 1635; with some sketches of the allied fam. of Wadsworth, Tuttle & Beresford. G.W. Russell, ed. By E.S. Welles. 1910. 318p.
P4-S22854 — $47.50.

RUSSELL: Desc. of Wm. Russell, Cambridge, MA, abt. 1640. By H.S. Russell. 1900. 52p.
P4-S22861 — $10.00.

RUSSELL: Desc. of John Russell of Woburn, MA. J.R. Bartlett. 1879. 212p.
P4-S22860 — $35.00.

RUST: Record of the Rust fam., embracing the desc. of Henry Rust, who came from Eng. & settled in Hingham, MA, 1634-1635. By A. D. Rust. 1891. 544p.
P4-S22878 — $84.00.

RUST: of VA, gen. & biographical sketches of the descendants of William Rust, 1654-1940. By E.M Rust. 1940. 42 + 462p.
P4-S22872 — $73.00.

RUST: The Rust fam., desc. of Henry Rust of Hingham, MA. By G.S. Brown. 1909. 9p.
P4-S22873 — $10.00.

RUTLEDGE: Fam. of the South. By J.T. Cupit. 1954. 45p.
P4-S22880 — $10.00.

RYDER: The life of Azubah Freeman Ryder, & a list of her immediate anc. & desc. By J. Ryder. 1888. 45p.
P4-S22882 — $10.00.

RYERSON: Gen. & hist. of the Knickerbocker fam. of Ryerson, Ryerse, Ryerss; also Martense fam.; all desc. of Martin & Adrisen Reyersz(en), of Holland. By A. Ryerson, 1916. 459p.
P4-S22884 — $69.50.

RYMES: Genealogy: Samuel Rymes of Portsmouth, N.H., & his descendants. comp. for C.E. Rymes. 1897. 13p.
P4-S22886 — $10.00.

S

SABIN: Fam. of Amer, The four earliest gen. By A. Titus, Jr. 1882. 11p.
P4-S22888 — $10.00.

SACKETT: The Sacketts of America, their anc. & desc., 1630-1907. By C. H. Weygant. 1907. 553p.
P4-S22893 — $70.00.

SACKETT: The family record [magazine]: the Sackett, Weygant & Mapes families, By C.H. Weygant. 1897. 148p.
P4-S22890 — $25.00.

SADOWSKI: DRANREB! An Autobiographical Memoir, The Greatest Generation Plus One or Baby Boomer Generation Minus One. Bernard S. Sadowski, PhD. 2003. 186p.
P4-S22896 — $24.00.

SADOWSKI: Complete genealogy: Sadowski lineage from the Polish village of Bogucin, 1880 to Present. By Bernard S. Sadowski. 2002. 165p.
P4-S22895 — $24.00.

SADOWSKI: Notes on gen. of Sadowski fam. A.C. Sandusky. 1937. 31p.
P4-S22897 — $10.00.

SAFFORD: The Ohio Valley Saffords, rev. & enlarged ed. By R.H. Smith & S.M. Culbertson. 1932. 240p.
P4-S22899 — $37.50.

SAGE: Desc. of David Sage of Middletown, CT, second branch. By H.K. Sage. 1951. 94p.
P4-S22905 — $18.50.

SAGE: Sage notes. By M.L. Holman. 1932. 13p.
P4-S22906 — $10.00.

SAGE: Gen. record of desc. of David Sage of Middletown, CT. By E.L. & C.H. Sage. 1919. 128p.
P4-S22911 — $25.00.

SAGE: Hist. of the Sage & Slocum fam. of Eng. & Amer., incl. allied fams. of Montague, Wanton (& others). By H. Whittemore. 1908. 95p.
P4-S22920 — $18.50.

SAGE: Genealogical Records of Descendants of David Sage, one of the 1st settlers of Middleton, CT, 1652. By E. Sage. 1878. 82p.
P4-S22917 — $16.50.

SAHLER: The gen. of the Sahlers of the US & of their kinsmen, the Grass fam. By L. Sahler. 1895. 38p.
P4-S22921 — $10.00.

SAINT CLAIR: Family of Gen. Arthur St. Clair. By J. Maginess. 1897. 32p.
P4-S22922 — $10.00.

SAINT JOHN: Gen.; desc. of Matthias of Dorchester, MA, 1634; of Windsor, CT, 1640 (& Wethersfield & Norwalk). By O. Alexander. 1907. 639p.
P4-S22923 — $79.00.

SALE: Root & branch of the Sale tree in America: an account of ten generations. By Dorothy S. Goodman. 1939. 116 + 28p.
P4-S22929 — $24.00.

SALISBURY: Family of Eng. & Amer. Edward Elbridge Salisbury. 1885. 118p.
P4-S22935 — $22.50.

SALTONSTALL: Anc. & desc. of Sir Richard Saltonstall, first assoc. of the Mass. Bay Col. & patentee of CT. By L. Saltonstall. 1897. 277p.
P4-S22938 — $41.50.

SAMPSON: Fam. (of PA & OH) By L.B. Sampson. 1914. 238p.
P4-S22944 — $35.50.

SAMPSON: Gen. mem. from the arrival of the Mayflower in 1620 to the present By J. A. Vinton. 1864. 140p.
P4-S22947 — $21.00.

SANBORN: Gen. of the Sanborn fam. (Repr. NEHGR). N. Sanborn. 1856. 21p.
P4-S22951 — $10.00.

SANBORN: Amer. & Eng. Sanbornes. By V.C. Sanborn. 1895. 25p.
P4-S22952 — $10.00.

SANBORN: Genealogy of the fam. of Sanborne or Sanborn in Eng. & Amer., 1194-1898. By V.C. Sanborn. 1899. 709p.
P4-S22950 — $88.00.

SANBORN: Notes on the English ancestry of the following American families: Samborne or Sanborn; By V.C. Sanborn. 1894. 16p.
P4-S22954 — $10.00.

SANBORN: Suppl.; Eng. anc. of the Amer. Sanborns. 1916. 24p.
P4-S22953 — $10.00.

SANDERS: Gen. of the Cortland Co., NY, branch of the Sanders fam. By J. Sanders. 1908. 111p.
P4-S22956 — $19.00.

SANFORD: Thomas Sanford, emigrant to New England.: anc., life & desc., 1632-4; also sketches of four other pioneer Sanfords & some desc., By Carlton E. Sanford. 1911. 2 vols., 768 + 840p.
P4-S22989 — $185.00.

SANDFORD: Robert Sandford & his wife Ann (Adams) Sandford, with some of their desc., 1650-1930. By J.S. Ware. 1930. 85p.
P4-S22962 — $17.50.

SANDS: Descendants of James Sands of Block Island, with notes on the Walker, Hutchinson, Ray, Guthrie, Palgrave, Cornell (& other) families. By Malcolm S. Wilson. 1949. 109p.
P4-S22968 — $19.00.

SANDS: Descent of Comfort Sands & of his children, with notes on the fam. of Ray, Thomas, Guthrie (& others) By T. Prime. 1886. 91p.
P4-S22974 — $18.00.

SANDS: James Sands of Block Isl., RI & some desc. 1912. 4p.
P4-S22969 — $10.00.

SANFORD: Gen.; the branch of Wm. of Madison, NY, of the 6th Amer. gen. By H. Sanford. 1894. 70p.
P4-S22986 — $13.50.

SANFORD: John Sanford & his desc. of RI colony. By P.F. Pierce. 12p.
P4-S22987 — $10.00.

SANTEE: Genealogy of the Santee family in America. By Ellis M. Santee. 1927. 211p.
P4-S22995 — $33.50.

SAPP: Hist. of the Sapp fam. By Sapp & Stanley. 1910. 102p.
P4-S23001 — $10.00.

SARCHET: Genealogy of the Sarchet family from the Island of Guernsey to Cambridge, OH, 1806. By C.P.B. & J.C. Sarchet. 1936. 14p.
P4-S23003 — $10.00.

SARGEANT: Genealogy of the Sargeant family: the desc. of Wm. of Malden, MA. A. A. Sargent. 1858. 108p.
P4-S23007 — $19.00.

SARGENT: Early Sargents of New Eng. By W. Sargent. 1922. 53p.
P4-S23014 — $10.00.

SARGENT: Hugh Sargent of Courteenhall, Northants., & desc. in Eng.; Wm. Sargent of Malden, New Eng., & desc. in Amer. By J. Sargent. 1895. 218p.
P4-S23013 — $33.00.

SARGENT: Supplement to the 1895 Sargent genealogy. By Edward R. Sargent. 1925. 16p.
P4-S23015 — $10.00.

SARGENT: Record. William Sargent of New Eng., with his desc. & their intermarriages, & other Sargent branches. Edwin E. Sargent. 1899. 331p.
P4-S23016 — $49.50.

SARTAIN: Annals of the Sartain tribe, 1557 to 1886. By John Sartain. 1886. 77p.
P4-S23022 — $16.00.

SAUL: Descendants of Wm. Elmer Saul (1866-1929). By Rachel Saul Tefft. 1999. 20p.
P4-S23029 — $10.00.

SAUL: Desc. of Samuel Saul (1801-90). By Rachel Saul Tefft. 1998. 174p.
P4-S23034 — $28.00.

SAUL: Desc. of Wm. Saul (1834-88). By Rachel Saul Tefft. 1999. 69p.
P4-S23040 — $15.50.

SAUL: Desc. of Geo. Saul, Jr., (1845-1924). By Rachel Saul Tefft. 1998. 100p.
P4-S23028 — $22.00.

SAUNDERS: Founders of the Mass. Bay Colony. By S.S. Smith. 1897. 372p.
P4-S23049 — $48.00.

SAUNDERS: William Saunders & Sarah Flagg Saunders, late of Cambridge, with their family record & gen. 1872. 39p.
P4-S23047 — $10.00.

SAUNDERS: "Old Tobe": some lines of descent of Tobias Saunders of Westerly, RI. By Earl P. Crandall. 1995. 334p.
P4-S23046 — $48.00.

SAVAGE: Fam. of John Savage of Middletown, CT, 1652. By J.F. Savage. 1894. 25p.
P4-S23051 — $10.00.

SAVAGE: Suppl. to above. 1898. 13p.
P4-S23050 — $10.00.

SAVARY: A gen. & biogr. record of the Savery fam. (Savory, Savary), & of the Severy fam., (Severit, Savery, Savory) By A. W. Savary. 1893. 286p.
P4-S23055 — $43.00.

SAVERY: Supplement. By A.W. Savary. 1905. 58p.
P4-S23056 — $11.00.

SAVORY: Gen. sketch of some desc. of Robert Savory of Newbury, 1656. By F.W. Lamb. 1904. 16p.
P4-S23057 — $10.00.

SAWIN: Summary notes concerning John Sawin & his posterity. By T.E. Sawin. 1866. 48p.
P4-S23058 — $10.00.

SAWYER: Descendants of Betfield Sawyer of Hill, NH: continuation of the work of Roland Douglas Sawyer. By Jay Norwalk. 1995. 98p.
P4-S23061 — $18.00.

SAWYER: Sawyers in Amer., or a hist. of the immig. Sawyers who settled in New Eng. By A. Carter. 1883. 120p.
P4-S23079 — $18.00.

SAWYER: Family of Elliotsville (Piscataquis Co., ME): descendants of James Sawyer of Gloucester, MA & their kinfolk, the Drakes. By Fred E. Sawyer. 1960-1961. 98p.
P4-S23073 — $19.00.

SAWYER: Genealogical index of the Sawyer families of New England prior to 1900. By Fred E. Sawyer. 1983. 394p.
P4-S23067 — $39.50.

SAYLER: A hist. of the Sayler fam., being a coll. of gen. notes relative to Daniel of Frederick Co., MD, who came to Amer. 1725-1730, & his desc. By J.L. Sayler. 1898. 164p.
P4-S23085 — $28.00.

SAYLES: Country: a social history, 1600-1986, & some descendants of John & Mary (Williams) Sayles of Providence, RI. By Judith A. Hurst. 1986. Reprinted by permission. 319p.
P4-S23091 — $47.50.

SAYRE: Family: lineage of Thomas Sayre, a founder of Southampton. By Theodore M. Banta. 1901. 774p.
P4-S23097 — $116.00.

SAYWARD: Family; being the hist. & gen. of Henry Sayward of York, ME & his descendants. C. Sayward 1890. 183p.
P4-S23103 — $26.50.

SCARRITT: Gen. hist. of the Scarritt clan in America, By R.E. Pearson. 1938-1948 2 V. in 1, 265p.
P4-S23109 — $40.00.

SCHAEFFER: Memoirs & reminiscences together with the sketches of the early history of Sussex Co. NJ. By William M. Johnson. 1907. 187p.
P4-S23115 — $29.50.

SCHALL: Historical acct. of the Schall/Shaull family. By J.L.S. Lutz. 1968. 468p.
P4-S23121 — $73.50.

SCHAUFFLER: Chronicle; Roster & biographical sketches of the Schauffler family in America: By R.M. Schauffler. 1951. 121p.
P4-S23127 — $22.00.

SCHELL: Desc. of John Christian Schell & John Schell of NY. By C. Denissen. 1896. 98p.
P4-S23133 — $18.00.

SCHENBECK: SHANEBECK — SHANBECK Family record, 1798-1959. By Safara Shanebeck. 1959. 142p.
P4-S23139 — $25.00.

SCHENK: The Rev. William Schenk, his anc. & his desc. By A.D. Schenck. 1883. 163p.
P4-S23145 — $25.00.

SCHERMERHORN: Family Dutch Connection. By K.C. Koster. 1995. 43p.
P4-S23147 — $10.00.

SCHERMERHORN: Genealogy & family chronicles. By R. Schermerhorn, Jr. 1914. 425p.
P4-S23151 — $66.50.

SCHOFER: Johan Georg Schofer family history, containing records of antecedents in Europe, acct. of the migration to America in 1832. By H.M. Schofer. 1934. 180p.
P4-S23157 — $29.50.

SCHOFF: The desc. of Jacob Schoff, who came to Boston in 1752 & settled in Ashburnham in 1757. By W.H. Schoff. 1910. 163p.
P4-S23163 — $24.50.

SCHOLL: SHOLL — SHULL Genealogy, the colonial branches. By J.W. Scholl. 1930. 910p.
P4-S23175 — $127.50.

SCHOLL: Desc. of John Peter Scholl & his wife Anna A. D. Scholl, & gen. fam. hist. with a sketch of Philip Scholl & desc. A.G. Scholl. 1903. 87p.
P4-S23169 — $15.00.

SCHOPPE: Family gen., 1782-1932. By M.C. Schoppe. 1932. 208p.
P4-S23181 — $31.00.

SCHOTTLER: SHETTLER: Memorial history of Daniel Schottler, Sr & his father-in-law Cristian Schwartzendruker, Sr, & Jacob & Rebecca Kauffman By S.D. Guengerich. 1919. 119p.
P4-S23187 — $19.00.

SCHRAMM: Fam. in Germany & US. By A. Schramm. 1938. 18p.
P4-S23189 — $10.00.

SCHULER: BOBENMYER Clan book, 1758-1917, 2nd ed. By A.B. Schuyler 1917. 166p.
P4-S23193 — $24.00.

SCHUREMAN: The Schuremans of NJ, 2nd ed. By Richard Wynkoop. 1902. 142p.
P4-S23199 — $24.00.

SCHWENK: Genealogy of the Schwenk family. E.S. & J.K. Schwenk. 1929. 282p.
P4-S23205 — $44.50.

SCHWENKFELDER: Genealogical rec. of the Schwenkfelder families, seekers of religious liberty who fled from Silesia to Saxony, & thence to PA in 1731-1737. 1923. 2 vols., 1752p.
P4-S23211 — $215.00.

SCOTT: The Scott fam. of Shrewsbury, NJ, being the desc. of Wm. Scott & Abigail Tilton Warner, with sketches of rel. fam. By A. Cole. 1908. 73p.
P4-S23253 — $14.00.

SCOTT: Hugh Scott, an immigr. of 1670, and his desc. By J. Scott. 1895. 314p.
P4-S23229 — $47.50.

SCOTT: Genealogy. By M.L. Holman. 1919. 410p.
P4-S23241 — $63.50.

SCOTT: The Scotch-Irish & Charles Scott's desc. & related fam. By O.C. Scott. 1917. 115p.
P4-S23247 — $23.50.

SCOTT: Desc. of William Scott of Hatfield, MA, 1668-1906, & of John Scott of Springfield, MA, 1659-1906. By O.P. Allen. 1906. 220p.
P4-S23217 — $33.00.

SCOTT: Fam. of Scotland & Stafford Co., VA. 86p.
P4-S23235 — $17.00.

SCOTT: Hist. of the Scott fam. By H. Lee. 1919. 117p.
P4-S23223 — $20.00.

SCOVELL: Arthur Scovell & his desc. in Amer., 1660-1900. By J.M. Holley & H.W. Brainard. 1941. 285p.
P4-S23259 — $45.50.

SCOVILLE: Family records. By C.R. Eastman. 1910. 75p.
P4-S23265 — $15.00.

SCOVILLE: Survey of the Scovill(e)s in Eng. & Amer., 700 yrs of hist. & gen. By H. Brainerd. 1915. 586p.
P4-S23271 — $89.00.

SCRANTON: Genealogical register of descendants of John Scranton of Guilford, CT, who died in the year 1671. By E. Scranton. 1855. 104p.
P4-S23277 — $17.00.

SEAMAN: Family in America, as descended from Capt. John Seaman of Hempstead, Long Isl. By Mary T. Seaman. 1928. 338p.
P4-S232389 — $52.00.

SEAMAN: History of the Seaman family in PA, with genealogical tables, By G.S. Seaman. 1911. 135p.
P4-S23283 — $22.00.

SEAMANS: Family in Amer. as desc. from Thomas Seamans of Swansea, MA, 1687. Lawton & Brown. 1933. 299p.
P4-S23295 — $44.50.

SEARIGHT: A rec. of the Searight fam., est. in Amer. By Wm. Searight, who came to Lancaster Co., PA ca 1740; with acct. of his desc. By J.A. Searight. 1893. 242p.
P4-S23301 — $38.50.

SEARLE: Collection of historical memorials relating to the Searle families of Great Britain & America By Stannard Warne. 1897 73p.
P4-S23307 — $15.00.

SEARS: The desc. of Richard Sares (Sears) of Yarmouth, MA, 1638-1888, with some notices of other fam. By the name of Sears. By S. May. 1890. 676p.
P4-S23316 — $98.00.

SEARS: Some Doubts Concerning The Sears Pedigree. Samuel Pearce May. 1886. 10p.
P4-S23314 — $10.00.

SEARS: Genealogy & biogr. sketches of the anc. & desc. of Richard Sears, the Pilgrim. By E.H. Sears. 1857. 96p.
P4-S23313 — $17.50.

SEATON: Family, with gen. & biogr. By O.A. Seaton. 1906. 441p.
P4-S23322 — $68.50.

SEATON: Seatons of Western PA. By J.S. Crosby. 1945. 63p.
P4-S23325 — $12.50.

SEAVER: Family — Genealogy of Robert Seaver of Roxbury, MA, & Some Descendants. By Wm. B. Trask. 1872. 52p.
P4-S23326 — $11.00.

SEBOR: Descendants of Jacob Sebor, 1709-1793, of Middletown, CT. By H. Beach. 1923. 109p.
P4-S23334 — $19.00.

SEELY: Ancestors of Daniel James Seely & Charlotte Louisa Vail, with desc. By W.P. Bacon. 1914. 185p.
P4-S23340 — $29.50.

SELDEN: Seldens of VA & allied families. M. Kennedy 1911. 2 vols., 1363p.
P4-S23358 — $171.00.

SELDEN: & kindred of VA. By E.M. Selden. 1941. 224p.
P4-S23352 — $35.00.

SELDEN: Ancestry; a family history. By G.S. Selden. 1931. 523p.
P4-S23346 — $81.50.

For hardcover versions, see the order form on page v. To order, call 1-888-296-3447.

SELFE: Some Descendants of Old Rober Selfe (Abt. 1625-Unk). Annie Self Arnold 2004. 283p.
P4-S23399 — $42.50.

SEMPLE: Genealogical hist. of the fam. Semple from 1214-1888. By W.A. Semple. 1888. 60p.
P4-S23367 — $12.00.

SENSINEY: Sensineys of Amer. (incl. Senseny, Sensenig, etc.) By B. Sensening. 1943. 159p.
P4-S23376 — $24.00.

SESSIONS: Materials for a hist. of the Sessions fam. in Amer., the desc. of Alexander Sessions of Andover, MA, 1669. By F.C. Sessions. 1890. 252p.
P4-S23382 — $37.50.

SETON: Setons of Scotland & America: An Old Family. By M. Seton. 1899. 438p.
P4-S23388 — $68.00.

SEVERANS: Genealogical History. By J.L. Severance. 1893. 91p.
P4-S23391 — $15.00.

SEWALL: Fam. of Eng. & Amer., 1624-1857. By Edward Elbridge Salisbury. 1885. 75p.
P4-S23397 — $15.00.

SEWALL: Thomas Sewall; some of his anc. & all of his desc: a gen. By H.S. Webster. 1904. 20p.
P4-S23396 — $10.00.

SEWARD: Desc. of Lt. Wm. Seward of Guilford, CT (Repr. NEHGR). By R.D. Smyth. 1898. 7p.
P4-S23404 — $10.00.

SEWARD: Obadiah Seward of Long Isl., NY & his desc. By F.W. Seward, Jr 1948. 288p.
P4-S23403 — $44.00.

SEWELL: Sewells in the New World. By Sir H.L. Duff. 1924 122p.
P4-S23409 — $22.00.

SEWELL: The Sewells of the Isle of Wight [England], with an acct. of some of the families connected by marriage. M.C. Owen. 1900 188 + 16p.
P4-S23415 — $32.00.

SEYDEL: Johann Michel Seydel & descendants, 1773-1959. By Ed Seydel. 1959 185p.
P4-S23421 — $26.00.

SEYMOUR: History of the Seymour family; Desc. of Richard of Hartford, CT, for six generations. By Donald Lines Jacobus. 1939. 662p.
P4-S23427 — $99.50.

SEYMOUR: Richard Seymour of Hartford & Norwalk, CT & some desc. (Repr. NEHGR), By S. Morris. 1918. 39p.
P4-S23429 — $10.00.

SEYMOUR: Supplement to Records of Griswold, Crane, Paddock, Howes, Smith & Russell Families. Anna Russell Vance. n.d. 23p.
P4-S23428 — $10.00.

SEYMOUR: A record of the Seymour fam. in the Rev. By M.W. Seymour. 1912. 40p.
P4-S23430 — $10.00.

SEYMOUR: Fam. (repr. from Morris gen., 1894). 1900. 12p.
P4-S23431 — $10.00.

SHAFER: HUSTON family history. By Francis M. Marvin. 1951. 470p.
P4-S23433 — $72.00.

SHAKESPEARE: "Shakespeareana Genealogica": Pt. I, identification of the dramatis personae in the hist. plays, from King John to Henry VIII. By G.R. French. 1869. 546p.
P4-S23439 — $81.00.

SHALLENBERGER: Volume I: Shallenbergers of Echo Mountain: genealogy of Hans Jung Schallenberger, his son Jacob Shallenberger, & his descendants. By Martin J. Shallenberger. 1995. 465p.
P4-S23457 — $67.50.

SHALLENBERGER: Volume II. Descendants of Ulrich Schellenberger of Lancaster Co., PA. Martin Shallenberger, 1996. 416p.
P4-S23451 — $62.50.

SHANKS: Some anc. & desc. of James Shanks of Huron Co., OH. By H.S. Blaine. 1951. 82p.
P4-S23463 — $16.00.

SHANNON: Genealogy; genealogical record & memorials of one branch in America. By G. Hodgdon. 1905. 609p.
P4-S23469 — $73.00.

SHAPLEY: Westward, the American Shapleys: the family & Descendants of David Shapley, a 17th-century Marblehead, MA. By Brian J.L. Berry. 1987. Reprinted by permission. 466p.
P4-S23481 — $69.50.

SHAPLEY: The Shapleigh, Shapley & Shappley families: a comprehensive genealogy, 1635-1993. By Brian J.L. Berry. 1993. Repr. by permission. 534p.
P4-S23475 — $79.50.

SHARP: The Sharps of Chester Co., PA & abstracts of records in Gt. Britain. By W.C. Sharpe. 1903. 36p.
P4-S23483 — $10.00.

SHARP: Fam., desc. of Wm. & Thomas of Evesham, NJ (Extr. from Haines Gen.) 1902. 46p.
P4-S23484 — $10.00.

SHARPE: Genealogy & miscellany. By W.C. Sharpe. 1890. 178p.
P4-S23499 — $29.00.

SHARPE: Records of the Sharpe fam. in Eng. & Amer. from 1580-1870. By W.C. Sharpe. 1874. 34p.
P4-S23488 — $10.00.

SHARPE: Family Magazine, Vol. I., nos. 1-32. 1893-1896 212p.
P4-S23493 — $34.50.

SHARPE: Mary Alice Sharpe Yalden Thomson & Alexander Beatty Sharpe, Jr: Carter, Sharpe & allied fams. By E.E.B. Jones. 1940. 311p.
P4-S23487 — $48.50.

SHARPLESS: Gen. of the Sharpless fam., desc. from John & Jane Sharples, settlers near Chester, PA, 1682. By G. Cope. 1887. 1349p.
P4-S23505 — $178.00.

SHATSWELL: Shatswells of Ipswich. By A. Caldwell. 15p.
P4-S23506 — $10.00.

SHATTUCK: Memorials of the desc. of Wm. Shattuck, the progenitor of the fam. In Amer. that borne his name. By Lemuel C. Shattuck. 1855. 419p.
P4-S23508 — $66.00.

SHAW: Our Shaw family history. By Mary Shaw Holt. 2001. 313p.
P4-S23514 — $46.50.

SHAW: Brief history of the Shaw family. Christian Bailey Shaw. 1939. 111p.
P4-S23510 — $19.00.

SHAW: Records; A mem. of Roger Shaw, 1594-1661. H.F. Farwell. 1904. 435p.
P4-S23520 — $55.00.

SHAW: Rec. (MA Soldiers & Sailors of Rev. War) 1906. 48p.
P4-S23511 — $10.00.

SHAWAN: Family historical notes, 1744-1926, including a sketch of the Foster & Holmes families. By J.A. Shawan. 1926 34p.
P4-S23522 — $10.00.

SHEAFF: Genealogical record of the Sheaff family in America, 1752-1941. By Sarah A.S. Collingwood. 1941. 22p., typescript.
P4-S23523 — $10.00.

SHEAFFE: Fam. of Eng. & Amer. (extr. Bassett gen.) 1926. 6p.
P4-S23524 — $10.00.

SHEARER: AKERS fam., with "the Bryan line" through the seventh gen. By J. W. Shearer. 1915. 171p.
P4-S23526 — $25.50.

SHEARMAN: SHERMAN Fam., extr. from Gen. Notes of NY & New Eng. Fam. By S.V. Talcott. 1883. 41p.
P4-S23527 — $10.00.

SHED: Daniel Shed genealogy; anc. & desc. of Daniel Shed of Braintree, MA, 1327-1920. By F.E. Shedd, with J.G. Bartlett. 1921. 812p.
P4-S23529 — $119.50.

SHEDD: Daniel Shed gen.; appendix, 1921-1931. 1931. 29p.
P4-S23530 — $10.00.

SHEETS: Desc. of Joseph Sheets (1812-1900), By Rachel Saul Tefft. 1999. 156p.
P4-S23535 — $25.00.

SHEETS: Descendants of Yost Sheets. By Rachel Saul Tefft. 1997. 100p.
P4-S23541 — $17.50.

SHELDON: Sheldons of Derbyshire, Eng. & Israel Sheldon of New Eng. By J.G. Bartlett. 24p.
P4-S23542 — $10.00.

SHELTON: Shelton County: A Genealogy of Pittsylvania County's Largest Family. A. Miller. 1994. 142p.
P4-S23548 — $21.00.

SHELTON: A history of the Shelton family of England & America. By M.C. Whitaker. 1941. 275p.
P4-S23547 — $43.00.

SHEPARD: Desc. of Edw. Shepard, mariner, Cambridge, MA, 1639, (Repr. NEHGR). By J. Shepard. 1878. 9p.
P4-S23558 — $10.00.

SHEPARD: Gen. of Wm. Shepard of Fossecut, North- ants., Eng., & some desc. By G. Shepard. 1886. 63p.
P4-S23550 — $12.50.

SHEPARD: Ralph Shepard, Puritan. By R.H. Shepard. 1893. 50p.
P4-S23559 — $10.00.

SHEPPARD: Genealogy of the Allen Sheppard fam. (desc. of John Sheppard, Cohansey NJ, 1600s) 1950. 126p.
P4-S23559 — $19.00.

SHERMAN: Anc. of Rev. John Sherman & Capt. John Sherman. By C.A. White. 1897. 9p.
P4-S23566 — $10.00.

SHERMAN: Genealogy, incl. family of Essex, Suffolk & Norfolk, Eng. By T.T. Sherman. 1920. 490p.
P4-S23592 — $76.50.

SHERMAN: Directory: an alphabetical listing of over 25,000 Shermans with known vital records & relationships. John H. Sherman. 1991. 4 vols., 2874p.
P4-S23589 — $299.00.

SHERRARD: Family of Steubenville, (together with letters, records & genealogies of related families, ed. By Thos. J. Sherrard). By Robt. A. Sherrard. 1890. 409p.
P4-S23598 — $63.00.

SHERRILL: Desc. of Samuel Sherrill of Easthampton, NY. By C.H. Sherrill. 1894. 132p.
P4-S23604 — $25.00.

SHERWOOD: Thomas Sherwood of Fairfield, CT & desc. By M.B. Carlson. 1950. 92p.
P4-S23610 — $19.00.

SHERWOOD: Daniel L. Sherwood & his Paternal Ancestors. A. Sherwood. 1929. 390 + 66p.
P4-S23611 — $68.00.

SHIFLET: The Shiflets of GA. By Marteal Wells. 1996. 283p.
P4-S23616 — $43.00.

SHILLABER: Rec. of proceedings at the 1st gathering of desc. of John Shillaber at the Old Homestead, Peabody MA, 1877. 1877. 48p.
P4-S23618 — $10.00.

SHIMER: History & genealogy of the Shimer family in America, vols. 1-6. By Allen R. Shimer. 1908-1932 704p.
P4-S23622 — $105.00.

SHINGLER: Genealogy of the Shingler family of SC. By Edw. M. Shingler. 1950. 110p.
P4-S23628 — $18.00.

SHINKLE: The Shinkle Genealogy, Comprising the Descendants of Philipp Carl Schenckel, 1717-1897. Louisa J. Abbott & Charles L. Abbott. 1897. 348p.
P4-S23630 — $52.00.

SHINN: History of the Shinn family in Europe & Amer. J.H. Shinn. 1903. 434p.
P4-S23634 — $55.00.

SHIPLEY: SHEPLEY; Our family (Allen, Hitchcock, Rutledge, Shepley). By Shepley & Allen. n.d. 89p.
P4-S23646 — $18.00.

SHIPLEY: The Shipleys of MD: a genealogical study. prepared by committee 1937. 281p.
P4-S23640 — $44.00.

SHIPPEN: Genealogy of the descendants of Dr Wm. Shippen, the Elder, of Phildelphia, member of the Continental Congress. By Roberdeau Buchanan. 1877. 16p.
P4-S23647 — $10.00.

SHOBE: Genealogy of the Shobe, Kirkpatrick & Dilling fams., rev. 1950 ed. F.D. Shobe. 1919/1950. 182 + 19p.
P4-S23652 — $31.00.

SHOEMAKER: Family. By T.H. Shoemaker. 1893. 112p.
P4-S23658 — $21.00.

SHOEMAKER: The Michael Shoemaker book (Schumacher). By Wm. T. Blair. 1924. 995p.
P4-S23664 — $129.50.

SHOTWELL: Annals of our Col. ancestors & their descendants; or, our Quaker forebears, & their posterity. By A.M. Shotwell. 1895-1897. 291p.
P4-S23670 — $44.00.

SHOVE: An English ancestry: an acct. of the ancestry of Edward Melvin Shove & his siblings. By James K. Raywalt. 1992. 149p.
P4-S23676 — $21.00.

SHOVER: Shover's Journey from Erlinbach, Germany to Beeler, Kansas & Beyond. Gary E. Shover. 2004. 169p. P4-S23677 — $26.00.

SHRECK: The Shreck gen., the fam. of Paul & Bethany Shreck, 1771-1954, By C. May. 1954. 56p. P4-S23680 — $11.00.

SHREVE: Genealogy & history of the Shreve family from 1641. By L.P. Allen. 1901. 672p. P4-S23682 — $83.00.

SHRIVER: Anc. of Susannah Shriver Gordon. By D. Gordon. 9p. P4-S23684 — $10.00.

SHUEY: Hist. of the Shuey fam. in Amer., from 1732-1876. By D.B. Shuey. 1876. 279p. P4-S23694 — $35.50.

SHUEY: History of the Shuey family in America, 1732-1919. By D.B. Shuey. 1919. 381p. P4-S23688 — $58.00.

SHUFELT: Sarah's People: The Sufelts, Wilbores, Martins, Jenneys & Other Allied Families. Sandra Kling & Christine Enoch. 2004. 341p. P4-S23696 — $51.00.

SHUFORD: A hist. sketch of the Shuford fam. J.H. Shuford. 1902. 156p. P4-S23700 — $27.50.

SHULTZ: Genealogy of the Shultz, Cupp, Weyand & Pisel families which have descended from Michael Shultz. By Charles R. Shultz. 1943. 205p. P4-S23706 — $32.00.

SHUMAN: George Shuman family; gen. & hist. from arrival in Amer. in 1760-1913. By W. C. Shuman. 1913. 341p. P4-S23712 — $54.00.

SHUMWAY: Genealogy of the Shumway family in the US. By Asahel A. Shumway. 1909. 478p. P4-S23718 — $75.00.

SHURTLEFF: Descendants of William Shurtleff of Plymouth & Marshfield, MA. By B. Shurtleff. 1912. 2 vols., 758 + 738p. P4-S23724 — $165.00.

SHURTLEFF: Descendants of William Shurtleff — 1976 Rev. Ed. Roy L. Shurtleff 1976. 2 vols., 1325p. P4-S23725 — $187.00.

SIGGINS: Genealogical gleanings of Siggins & other PA fams. By White & Maltby. 1918. 726p. P4-S23730 — $99.50.

SIGOURNEY: Genealogy of the Sigourney Family. Henry H.W. Sigourney. 1857. 31p. P4-S23732 — $10.00.

SILL: Family; Old Silltown: something of its hist. & people, being principally a brief acct. of the early gen. of the Sill family. By S. S. Burt. 1912. 148p. P4-S23742 — $22.00.

SILL: Gen. of desc. of John Sill of Cambridge. By G.G. Sill. 1859. 108p. P4-S23736 — $17.50.

SILVESTER: Richard Silvester of Weymouth, MA & some desc. (Repr. NEHGR). By A.H. Silvester. 71p. P4-S23748 — $14.00.

SIMMONDS: John & Susan Simmonds & some of their desc. with related anc. lines. By F.W. Simmonds. 1940. 222p. P4-S23754 — $33.00.

SIMMONS: Hist. of the Simmons fam., from Moses Simmons (Symonson), ship Fortune, 1621. By L. Simmons. 1930. 315p. P4-S23766 — $49.00.

SIMMONS: History of our Simmons family through ten generations, & brief sketches of allied fams. of Bartlett, Moore & Mann. By M.E. Simmons. 1936. 244p. P4-S23760 — $38.50.

SIMONS: Thomas Grange Simons III, his forebears & relations. By Robt. B. Simons. 1954. 211p. P4-S23773 — $29.50.

SIMONTON: Family history — genealogical, historical & biographical — of the Simonton & related families. By Wm. Simonton. 1900. 199p. P4-S23778 — $31.00.

SIMPSON: Gen. of original Simpson fam. of York & Hancock Cos., ME. By J.S. Emery. 1891. 51p. P4-S23785 — $10.00.

SIMPSON: History of the Rev. John Simpson (1793-1860) & his descendants. By Wm. P. Kinter. 1998. 90p. P4-S23784 — $17.50.

SIMPSON: Simpsons of Rye Top, Cumberland Val., PA. By E.S. Bladen. 1905. 34p. P4-S23786 — $10.00.

SIMRALL: Book of Simrall: stories & notes on family history. By F.S. Riker. 1927. 198p. P4-S23790 — $31.00.

SIMS: Gen. of the Sims fam. By McClure & Nichols. 16p. P4-S23791 — $10.00.

SINCLAIR: Genealogy of Prince Henry Sinclair. By H.S. "Pete" Cummings, Jr. 1998. 417p. P4-S23796 — $64.50.

SINCLAIR: The Sinclairs of England. 1887. 414p. P4-S23805 — $61.00.

SINCLAIR: History of the Sinclair family in Europe & Amer. for 1100 years. By L.A. Morrison. 1896. 453p. P4-S23799 — $68.50.

SINCLAIR: The Saint Clairs of the Isles; Being a History of The Sea Kings of Orkney & Their Scottish Successors of the Sirname of Sinclair. Roland W. Saint-Clair. 1898. viii + 558p. P4-S23800 — $85.00.

SINGLETARY: Gen. of the Singletary-Curtis fam. [comp. from rec. from MA, NY, SC & others], By L. Singletary-Bedford. 1907. 115p. P4-S23811 — $19.50.

SINGLETON: The Singletons & interrelated families. By Dorothy Singleton Blue. 1992. 100p. P4-S23817 — $19.00.

SINNETT: Genealogy: Michael Sinnett of Harpswell, ME, his ancestry & descendants. By Charles N. Sinnett. 1910. 137p. P4-S23823 — $19.50.

SINNOTT: ROGERS, Coffin, Corlies, Reeves, Bodine & allied fams. By M.E. Sinnott. 1905. 278p. P4-S23829 — $36.00.

SISK: Book of Ages. By Charleta J. Dunn. 1998. 1173 + 400 charts P4-S23835 — $159.00.

SISSON: Yankee heritage: a Sisson ancestry [with 257 connecting lines]. By Brian J.L. Berry. 1991. Reprinted by permission. 549p. P4-S23841 — $83.00.

SISSON: Luther Sisson of Easton, MA, his anc. & desc. By A.A. Wood. 1909. 13p.
P4-S23842 — $10.00.

SIZER: A History of Antonio De Zocieur who changed his name to Anthony Sizer. L.H. Holch. 1941. 489p.
P4-S23846 — $73.00.

SKELTON: The Skeltons of Paxton, Pawhatan Co., VA, incl. sketches of the fams. of Skelton, Gifford & Crane. By P.H. Baskervil. 1922. 119p.
P4-S23847 — $22.00.

SKERRY: Some Descendants of Patrick Skerry of Halifax & New Ross, Nova Scotia. Claudia E. Cridland. 2003. 92p.
P4-S23848 — $19.50.

SKIDMORE: A Genealogical & Biographical Records of the Pioneer Thomas Skidmore, Scudamore, of the MA & CT Colonies in New England, & of Huntington By Emily C. Hawley. 1911. 359p.
P4-S23853 — $57.50.

SKIFF: Desc. of James Skiff of London, Eng. & Sandwich, MA. By F.L. Pierson. 1895. 24p.
P4-S23855 — $10.00.

SKILTON: Dr. Henry Skilton & descendants. By J. Skilton. 1921. 412p.
P4-S23859 — $65.00.

SKINNER: Fam. of Marblehead. By E.E. Dana. 1900. 10p.
P4-S23865 — $10.00.

SKINNER: Lt. John Skinner of the Continental Army, (Repr. NEHGR). By Z.S. Eldredge. 1899. 5p.
P4-S23866 — $10.00.

SKIPWITH: The Skipwiths of Amer., desc. of the Baronets of Prestwould. By F. Skipwith. 1878. 8p.
P4-S23870 — $10.00.

SLACK: Family, more particularly an acct. of the family of Eliphalet Slack & his wife Abigail Cutter: their ascendants, descendants & relations. By W.W. Slack. 1930. 252p.
P4-S23871 — $39.50.

SLADE: Wm. Slade of Windsor, CT & his desc. By T.B. Peck. 1910. 205p.
P4-S23877 — $30.50.

SLAFTER: Memoirs of John Slafter, with a gen. acct. of his desc. By E.F. Slafter. 1869. 165p.
P4-S23883 — $25.00.

SLATE: Wm. Slate of Windham & Mansfield, CT & some desc. By G.O. Chapman. 1941. 33p.
P4-S23885 — $10.00.

SLAUGHTER: Desc. of Robert Slaughter & Frances Ann Jones. By l.P. DuBellet. 1907. 19p.
P4-S23888 — $5.00.

SLAYMAKER: History of the Slaymaker family, Rev. Ed. By Henry C. Slaymaker. 1909, 1969. ix + 325p.
P4-S23889 — $49.50.

SLAYTON: History of the Slayton family, biogr. & gen. By A.W. Slayton. 1898. 322p.
P4-S23895 — $49.50.

SLEIGHT: Sleights of Sag Harbor. Harry D. Sleight. 1929. xii + 306p.
P4-S23900 — $48.00.

SLOCUM: A short history of the Slocums, Slocumbs & Slocombs of Amer., gen. & biogr., 1637-1881. By Charles E. Slocum. 1882. 644p.
P4-S23901 — $96.50.

SLOCUM: Volume II: Supplement to "A Short History of the Slocums &, Slocombs of America; Genealogy & Biography, 1637-1881. Charles E. Slocum. 1908. 549p.
P4-S23907 — $86.00.

SLONAKER: A History & Genealogy of the Slonaker Descendants in America. 1941. 732p.
P4-S23908 — $110.00.

SLOSSON: A gen. memoir of Nathaniel Slosson of Kent, CT & his desc., 1696-1872, with Nathan Slosson's desc. to 1896. By D.W. Patterson. 1896 38p.
P4-S23909 — $10.00.

SMALL: Descendants of Edw. Small of New Eng. & allied fam., & tracings of Eng. ancestry. By L. Underhill. 2nd ed. 1934. 3 vols., 1835p.
P4-S23913 — $259.00.

SMATHERS: The Smathers Family & Related Lines. Dr. Robert J. Medford. 2004. 850 + 6p.
P4-S23914 — $120.00.

SMEDLEY: Genealogy of the Smedley fam. desc. from Geo. & Sarah Smedley, settlers in Chester Co., PA, with brief notices of other fam. By G. Cope. 1901. 1011p.
P4-S23919 — $144.00.

SMELTZER: Irish-Palatine Smeltzers Around the World, with Early German Smelsers in Canada. M.R. Smeltzer. 1987. viii + 192p.
P4-S23920 — $30.00.

SMELTZER: The Smeltzers of Kilcooly & Their Irish-Palatine Kissing Cousins. Marjorie R. Smeltzer. 1981. 198p.
P4-S23921 — $30.00.

SMITH: Jesse Smith, his ancestry & descendants. By L. Smith. 1909. 187p.
P4-S23979 — $30.00.

SMITH: Collateral lines & Mayflower connections. H.S.L. Barnes. 1910. 51p.
P4-S23932 — $10.00.

SMITH: Genealogy of Consider Smith of New Bedford, with allied fam. of Mason & Thwing. L. T. Smith. 1915. 26p.
P4-S23933 — $10.00.

SMITH: Grant & Irons families of NJ Shore counties, including the related families of Willets & Birdsall. By J.W. Hook. 1955. 280p.
P4-S23967 — $47.50.

SMITH: The Smith & the Chamberlains; also the Wilsons, Walters, Warfields, Van Sitterts. By Clifford E. Smith. 1941. 184p.
P4-S24027 — $29.50.

SMITH: Family, being a popular acct. of most branches of the names — however spelt — from the 14th cent., with numerous pedigrees. By C. Reade. (Publ. in England) 1904. 324p.
P4-S24021 — $49.50.

SMITH: Ancestry of Hiram Smith & his wife Sarah Jane Bull. By J.G. Frost. 1927. 30p.
P4-S23980 — $10.00.

SMITH: Family tree book, genealogical & biographical, listing the relatives of Gen. William Alexander Smith & of W. Thomas Smith. comp. By W. Thomas Smith. 1922. 304p.
P4-S24015 — $47.00.

SMITH: Matthew Smith of Martha's Vineyard & Readfield, ME & desc. By F.M. Ames. 1925. 8p.
P4-S23981 — $10.00.

SMITH: Genealogical hist. of the desc. of the Rev. Nehemiah Smith of New London Co., CT with mention of his brother John & nephew Edward, 1638-1888. By H.A. Smith. 1889. 320p.
P4-S23949 — $49.00.

SMITH: Genealogy of family of Wm. Smith of Petersborough, NH. By Leonard & Smith. 1852. 24p.
P4-S23942 — $10.00.

SMITH: John Smith of Alabama, his anc. & desc. M.O. McDavid. 1948. 189p.
P4-S23985 — $23.00.

SMITH: John Smith of Milford, New Haven col., 1640, & some desc. (Repr. NEHGR). By R.A. Smith. 1891. 6p.
P4-S23966 — $10.00.

SMITH: Complete genealogy of the descendants of Matthew Smith of East Haddam, CT with mention of his ancestors, 1637-1890. By Sophia S. Martin. 1890. 269p.
P4-S23943 — $42.00.

SMITH: Nathaniel Smith of VT. Gary V. Smith. 1985. xii + 154p.
P4-S24011 — $25.00.

SMITH: Genealogy of the descendants of Robert Smith, who settled near Castle Shannon, Washington Co., now Allegheny Co. PA, 1772 By E.U. Smith. 1923. 311p.
P4-S23961 — $47.50.

SMITH: History & genealogy of the Smiths of "Big Spring Plantation," Frederick Co., VA, with a chron. of the Drugan & Carnahan fams. of PA & OH. By B.T. Hartman. 1929. 101p.
P4-S23973 — $18.00.

SMITH: Our Immigrant Ancestors from Scotland; George Smith & His wife, Mary Baird and their Desc. Alice Crandall Park. 2002. xii + 209p.
P4-S23956 — $34.00.

SMITH: Reunion of the Desc of William Smith held in Peterborough, NH, August 10, 1904. Smith Family. 1906. 176 + 12p.
P4-S23957 — $28.00.

SMITH: Wills of the Smith families of NY & Long Isl., 1664-1794, with gen. & hist. notes. By William S. Pelletreau. 1898. 151p.
P4-S24030 — $27.50.

SMITH: Genealogy & reminiscences of Wm. Smith & fam. By M.T. Smith. 1884. 86p.
P4-S23955 — $15.00.

SMITH: Lt. Samuel Smith; his children & one line of desc. & related fams. By J.W. Hook. 1953. 381p.
P4-S23991 — $59.50.

SMITH: The Home of the Smith Family in Peterborough, NH, 1749-1842. J. Smith. 1900. 202 + 34p.
P4-S23958 — $35.00.

SMITH: Notes & illustrations concerning the fam. hist. of James Smith of Coventry [England], (1731-1794), & his desc. By Lady Durning-Lawrence. 1912 156p.
P4-S23997 — $24.00.

SMITH: A mem'l of Rev. Thomas Smith & his desc: a full gen. record, 1707-1895. By S.A. Smith. 1895. 146p.
P4-S23931 — $23.00.

SMITH: The name & fam. of West. comp. By the Media Research Bureau. 10p.
P4-S23959 — $10.00.

SMITH: Francis West of Duxbury, MA & some desc. (Repr. NEHGR). By E.E. Cornwall. 1906. 10p.
P4-S23960 — $10.00.

SMITH: Prominent Rhode Island "Smiths" (extr. from "Representative Men & Old Families of R.I.") 1908. 88p.
P4-S24003 — $17.50.

SMITH: Chaplain Smith & the Baptists; or, Life, Journals, Letters & Addresses of the Rev. Hezekiah Smith of Haverhill, 1747-1805. By Reuben Aldridge Guild. 1885. 429p.
P4-S24010 — $65.00.

SMITH: Family of PA, Johann Friederich Schmidt, 1746-1812. By J.B. Nolan. 1932. 203p.
P4-S24009 — $35.00.

SMOCK: Gen. notes on the Smock fam. in Amer. By J.C. Smock. 1922. 47p.
P4-S24031 — $10.00.

SMYTH: Ralph Smyth of Hingham, MA. By T. Smyth. 1872. 8p.
P4-S24032 — $10.00.

SMYTH: Ralph Smyth of Hingham & Eastham, MA & His Desc. Dr. Dwight Smith. 1913. 174 + 5p.
P4-S24033 — $27.00.

SMYTHE: Desc. of Rev. Robert Smythe. D.E. Page. 2002. xii + 167 p.
P4-S24034 — $29.00.

SNELL: Thomas Snell (1625-1725) of Bridgewater, MA & some desc. By H.P. Long. 1958. 8p.
P4-S24035 — $10.00.

SNIDER: Solomon Snider (1778-1845) & desc. from Burris Dial book. By W.A. Dial. 15p.
P4-S24037 — $10.00.

SNIDER: Desc. of Jonas Snider & Anna Hostutter Snider, Shelby & Spencer Co., KY. J. Franklin. 1950. 18p.
P4-S24038 — $10.00.

SNIVELY: Genealogical Memoirs, 1659-1882. By W.A. Snively. 1883. 77p.
P4-S24036 — $14.00.

SNODDY: Fam. hist. & gen. of Jas. Snoddy of PA. By Sanders & Walton. 1959. 28p.
P4-S24041 — $10.00.

SNODDY: The John Snoddy & Related Families of PA. Mary M. McCormick Spainhour. 2004. 216p
P4-S24040 — $32.50.

SNODGRASS: Family. By S.C. Scott. 1928. 95p.
P4-S24042 — $19.00.

SNOW: ESTES Ancestry. By N.E. Snow & M. Jillson. 1939. 667 + 436p.
P4-S24060 — $149.00.

SNOW: Wm. Snow fam. who landed at Plymouth in 1635. By E.H. Snow. 1908. 64p.
P4-S24069 — $12.50.

SNOW: Genealogy, desc. of Nicholas Snow of Plymouth colony. By M. Alden. 1897. 24p.
P4-S24049 — $10.00.

SNOW: History of the family of Benj. Snow, a desc. of Richard Snow of Woburn, MA. By O. Wilcox. 1907. 385p.
P4-S24066 — $61.50.

SNOWBERGER: Forty North: Lineages of some early settlers along the 40th parallel, being the ancestry of Barbara Lenore Snowberger. By Howard H. Metcalfe. 1997. 1074p.
P4-S24078 — $139.50.

SOLLEY: Thomas Solley & his desc. By G. W. Solley. 1911. 217p.
P4-S24084 — $32.50.

SOLOMON: Gen. of Ezekiel Solomon desc., 1735-1900, (in Zaccheus Patterson desc.) By E.P. Gundry. 1957. 13p.
P4-S24083 — $10.00.

SONNICHSEN: Family History of Charles Leland Sonnichsen & Augusta Pauline (Jones) Sonnichsen/ Schwidetzky. Philip Sonnichsen. 2003. 204p.
P4-S24086 — $34.00.

SORRELLS: Family pioneers of Old Buncombe Co., NC: Desc of Joseph & Mille Sorrells, from 1760-2002. By Marshall L. Styles. 2002. 265p.
P4-S24085 — $39.50.

SOULE: Joseph Soule of Fairfield, VT & some desc. (Repr. NEHGR). By G.H. Doane. 18p.
P4-S24088 — $10.00.

SOULE: Contribution to the history, biogr. & gen. of the family named Sole, Solly, Soule, Sowle, Soulis. By G.T. Ridlon, Sr. 1926. 2 vols., 1180p.
P4-S24087 — $177.00.

SOUTHERLAND: Notes on the Southerland, Latham & allied families: register of the ancestors of Imogen Southerland Voorhees. By Edward K. Voorhees. 1932. 137p.
P4-S24093 — $23.00.

SOUTHGATE: Monographs on the Southgate fam. of Scarborough, ME; anc. & desc. By L. Chapman. 1907. 68p.
P4-S24099 — $14.00.

SOUTHWICK: Genealogy of desc. of Lawrence & Cassandra Southwick of Salem, MA. Caller & Ober. 1881. 616p.
P4-S24102 — $79.50.

SOUTHWORTH: Genealogy of the Southworths (Southards), desc. of Constant Southworth, with a sketch of the fam. in Eng. J.G. Webber. 1905. 492p.
P4-S24108 — $76.50.

SOUTHWORTH: Genealogical data. By G.S. Southworth. 1957. 5p.
P4-S24109 — $10.00.

SPACH: Descendants of Adam Spach: autobiography & memoirs of Adam Spach & his wife. A.L. Fries. 1924. 202p.
P4-S24114 — $37.00.

SPAID: Genealogy; from the first of the name in this country to the present times, with a number of allied fams. & many hist. facts. A.T. Secrest. 1922. 403p.
P4-S24120 — $62.50.

SPALDING: Memorial; a gen. hist. of Edw. Spalding of VA & MA Bay, & his desc. By C. W. Spalding 1897. 1276p.
P4-S24138 — $151.00.

SPALDING: Memorial: genealogical history of Edward Spalding of Mass. Bay, & his descendants, By S.J. Spalding. 1872. 619p.
P4-S24132 — $91.00.

SPALDING: Memorial & personal reminiscences, by P. Spalding, & life & selected poems of Caroline A. Spalding. By G.B. Spalding & P. Spalding. 1887. 324p.
P4-S24126 — $49.50.

SPARE: Family; Leonard Spare & his desc. Spare Fam. Assoc. 1931. 323p.
P4-S24144 — $48.50.

SPARHAWK: Fam. of Nathaniel Sparhawk of Cambridge (Repr. NEHGR). By W.S. Appleton. 1865. 3p.
P4-S24157 — $10.00.

SPARHAWK: Materials for a gen. of the Sparhawk fam. in New Eng. (Repr. Essex Inst. Hist. Coll.) By C.H.C. Howard. 1892. 113p.
P4-S24156 — $18.00.

SPEAR: Ancestry of Annis Spear, 1775-1858, of Litchfield, ME. By W.G. Davis. 1945. 170p.
P4-S24162 — $25.50.

SPEARE: Family, from 1642: Gene-alogical Records of Certain Branches. By C. L. Speare. 1938. 294p.
P4-S24168 — $46.00.

SPEED: Records & Memoirs of the Speed fam. By T. P. Speed. 1892. 206p.
P4-S24174 — $31.00.

SPEER: Reminiscences of the Speer family. John Grove Speer. 1900. 185 + 49p.
P4-S24175 — $35.00.

SPEER: Ten generations of George Speer, 1642-1942: three centuries of American life. By R.C. Speer. 1942 205p.
P4-S24180 — $33.50.

SPEICHER: History of the Speicher, Spicher, Spyker familiy. By P.I. Speicher. 1961. 51p.
P4-S24181 — $10.00.

SPELMAN: The English Ancestry & American Descendants of Richard Spelman of Middletown, CT, 1700. By F. C. Barbour. 1910. 559p.
P4-S24186 — $86.00.

SPENCER: Genealogical sketch of desc. of Samuel Spencer of PA. By H.M. Jenkins. 1904. 253p.
P4-S24192 — $39.00.

SPENCER: The Maine Spencers. A hist. & gen., 1596-1898. By W.D. Spencer. 1898. 247p.
P4-S24195 — $32.00.

SPENCER: The Spencers of the Great Migration: Vol. I, 1300-1783, A.D: history & genealogy of the five Spencer siblings of Bedfordshire who came to New England By Jack T. & Edith W. Spencer. 1997. 477p.
P4-S24201 — $72.00.

SPENGLER: The annals of the families of Caspar, Henry, Baltzer & George Spengler, who settled in York Co. (PA) respectively in 1729, 1732, 1732, & 1751. E.W. Spangler. 1896. 604p.
P4-S24207 — $91.00.

SPICER: Hist. of the desc. of Peter Spicer, landholder in New London, CT, as early as 1666, & others of the name, with short accts. of allied fams. By S.S. & S.B. Meech. 1911. 610p.
P4-S24216 — $77.00.

SPICER: A supplement to "The desc. of Peter Spicer" (1911), containing add. & corr. Susan B. Meech. 1923. 269p.
P4-S24213 — $42.00.

SPLAWN: Genealogy of the Splawn & Collins family, 1600-1960. By Jennie L. Splawn. 1960. 86p.
P4-S24222 — $17.00.

SPOFFORD: A fam. record of the desc. of John Spofford, who emigr. from Eng. & settled at Rowley, MA in 1638. By J. Spofford. 1869. 128p.
P4-S24225 — $19.00.

SPOFFORD: Genealogical record, incl. two genealogies in the female lines of desc. of John Spofford & Elizabeth Scott, who settled at Rowley, MA. By J. Spofford 1888. 502p.
P4-S24231 — $78.00.

SPOONER: Records of Wm. Spooner of Plymouth, MA & his desc., vol I. By T. Spooner. 1883. 694p.
P4-S24240 — $88.00.

SPOONER: Mem. of Wm. Spooner, 1637, & of his desc. to the 3rd gen., of his gr-grandson, Elnathan Spooner, & of his desc. to 1871. By T. Spooner. 1871. 242p.
P4-S24237 — $36.00.

For hardcover versions, see the order form on page v. To order, call 1-888-296-3447.

SPOONER: Brief sketch of the anc. of Alden Spooner, late of Brooklyn, NY, with record of his desc. to Aug. 1909. By A.S. Huling. 1909. 28p.
P4-S24238 — $10.00.

SPOOR: Family in America: record of the known descendants of Jan Wybesse Spoor, who migrated from Holland & Settled in the Hudson River Valley By Marie A. Underwood. 1901. 165p.
P4-S24246 — $24.50.

SPOOR: The Spoor fam. (alias Wybesse) of NY State. ed. By H.F. Johnston. 54p.
P4-S24247 — $10.00.

SPOTSWOOD: Gen. of the Spotswood fam. in Scotland & VA. By C. Campbell. 1868. 44p.
P4-S24257 — $10.00.

SPRAGUE: The Ralph Sprague genealogy. By E.G. Sprague. 1913. 322p.
P4-S24267 — $49.50.

SPRAGUE: Honorable Seth Sprague of Duxbury, Plymouth Co., MA: his descendants down to the 6th generation, with his reminiscences, By W.B. Weston. 1915. 134 + 26p.
P4-S24258 — $25.00.

SPRAGUE: The Spragues of Malden, MA. By G.W. Chamberlain. 1923. 325p.
P4-S24273 — $48.50.

SPRAGUE: Gen. of the Spragues in Hingham, counting from Wm. Sprague, one of the 1st planters in MA who arrived at Naumkeag from Eng. in 1628. By H. Sprague. 1828. 68p.
P4-S24249 — $12.50.

SPRAGUE: Genealogy (in part) of the Sprague families in America, as descended from Edward Sprague of England, from 1614, with the desc. of Edward Sprague By Augustus Brown Reed Sprague. Rev. ed., 1905. 49+10p.
P4-S24268 — $11.50.

SPRAGUE: Family in America. By W.V. Sprague. 1913. 578p.
P4-S24261 — $87.00.

SPRAGUE: Part of the 1940-1 Supplement to "Sprague families in America" (1913), Francus Sprague of Duxbury, MA. W.V. Sprague. 1941. 35p., typescript.
P4-S24262 — $10.00.

SPRINGER: Genealogy. By I.E. Springer. 1909. 38p.
P4-S24275 — $10.00.

SPRINGER: A genealogical table & hist. of the Springer fam. in Europe & N. America, Vol. I By M. Springer 1917. 154p.
P4-S24276 — $25.00.

SPRINGER: Another Look at der Springer: An Essay on the Ancestry of the Springer Family. Ronald L. Frampton. 1997. 41p.
P4-S27278 — $10.00.

SROUF: Fam. of IL: Bible record & letter from OH relative dated 1860 to IL Sroufs. 9p.
P4-S24281 — $10.00.

STAATS: Genealogy of the Staats Family. Harold Staats. 1921. 256 + 8p.
P4-S24277 — $40.00.

STACKHOUSE: The Stackhouse Family. William R. Stackhouse & Walter F. Stackhouse. 1935. 241 + 6p.
P4-S24283 — $37.00.

STACKPOLE: History & genealogy of the Stackpole family. By Everett S. Stackpole. 1920. 2nd ed. 352p.
P4-S24282 — $55.50.

STAEHLING: Family tree, 1598-1939. By W.E. Staehling. 1939. 37p.
P4-S24285 — $10.00.

STAFFORD: A contrib. to the gen. of the Stafford fam. in Amer. By H.M. Benedict. 1870. 27p.
P4-S24286 — $10.00.

STAGER: RUDY; "Freaundschaft," facts, incidents & tradition relating to the Stager-Rudy families & lineage, beginning with 1717. 1912. 144p.
P4-S24288 — $23.00.

STANDISH: The families of Standish of Standish, Lancashire, England; & Standish of Duxbury, Arley, Ormskirk, Gathurst, Croston, Park Brook & Wantage Frederick L. Weis. 1959. 77p.
P4-S24297 — $15.00.

STANDISH: Standishes of America. By M. Standish. 1895. 153p.
P4-S24291 — $30.00.

STANDISH: Some recent investigations concerning the ancestry of Capt. Miles Standish. By T.C. Porteus. 1914. 34p.
P4-S24292 — $10.00.

STANFIELD: History of the Stanfield family. O.C. Stanfield. 1961. 71 + 43p.
P4-S24303 — $19.50.

STANHOPE: Jonathan Stanhope of Sudbury, MA & some descendants. By G.O. Stanhope. 1941. 31p.
P4-S24304 — $10.00.

STANLEY: Family of America as descended from John, Timothy & Thomas Stanley of Hartford, CT, 1636. By I.P. Warren. 1887. 352p.
P4-S24309 — $55.50.

STANTON: A record, Genealogical, Biographical, statistical, of Thomas Stanton of CT & his desc., 1635-1891. By W.A. Stanton. 1891. 613p.
P4-S24312 — $92.00.

STANTON: Our ancestors, the Stantons. By W.H. Stanton. 1912. 649p.
P4-S24318 — $94.50.

STANTON: Lineage of the Stanton fam. (Geo. Stanton, NY, 1698), extr. "Olde Ulster." By W. Macy. 34p.
P4-S24317 — $10.00.

STANWOOD: History of the Stanwood family in Amer. By E.S. Bolton. 1899. 317p.
P4-S24324 — $47.50.

STAPELTON: The Stapeltons of Yorkshire. H.E. Chetwynd-Stapylton. 1897. 333 + 15p.
P4-S24325 — $52.00.

STARBIRD: Genealogy of the Starbird-Starbard family. By A.A. Starbird. 1942 179p.
P4-S24330 — $27.00.

STARIN: Fam. in Amer; Desc. of Nicholas Ster (Starin), one of the early settlers of Ft. Orange (Albany, NY). By W.L. Stone. 1892. 233p.
P4-S24342 — $35.00.

STARING: Family: records of early generations of hardy Pioneers who settled at German Flatts, now Herkimer, 1722-25. By Hubert W. Hess. 1929. 28p
P4-S24343 — $10.00.

STARK: A Life of Gen John Stark of NH. H.P. Moore. 1949. 539p.
P4-S24349 — $81.00.

STARK: Family of General John Stark, 1728-1822, of NH. By Jane Elizabeth Stark Maney. 2002. 442p.
P4-S24350 — $69.00.

STARK: Aaron Stark fam., seven gen. of the desc. of Aaron Stark of Groton, CT. By C. Stark. 1927. 148p.
P4-S24348 — $24.00.

STARKEY: The Starkeys of New England & allied families. By E.W. Leavitt. 1910. 149p.
P4-S24354 — $24.00.

STARKIE: Starkie fam. of Eng., By J.P. Rylands. 1880. 18p.
P4-S24351 — $10.00.

STARKWEATHER: A brief gen. hist. of Robert Starkweather of Roxbury & Ipswich, MA, who was the original Amer. anc., & of his desc. in various lines, 1640-1898. By C.L. Starkweather. 1904. 356p.
P4-S24360 — $56.00.

STARLING: Genealogy & family memorial [of Starling, Sullivant & related fams.]. Joseph Sullivant. 1874. 375p.
P4-S24366 — $58.50.

STARR: Early Starrs in Kent & New England. By H.S. Ballou. 1944. 141p.
P4-S24372 — $25.00.

STARR: History of the Starr family of New Eng., from Comfort Starr of Ashford, Co. Kent, Eng., who emigr. to Boston (1635). B. P. Starr. 1879. 587p.
P4-S24375 — $89.00.

START: Genealogical record of the Start family in America. By Wm. A. Start 1894. 30p.
P4-S24380 — $10.00.

STAUFFER: Genealogical record of the desc. of Henry Stauffer & other Stauffer pioneers. By A. J. Fretz. 1899. 371 + 104p.
P4-S24381 — $55.00.

STEARNS: Memoirs of the Stearns fam. incl. records of many desc. By W.E. Stearns. 1901. 173p.
P4-S24396 — $23.50.

STEARNS: Genealogy & memoirs of Isaac Stearns & his desc. By A.V. Wagenen. 1901. 746p.
P4-S24390 — $97.50.

STEARNS: Genealogy & memoirs of Charles & Nathaniel Stearns, & their desc. By A.V. Wagenen. 1901. 531p.
P4-S24387 — $83.00.

STEARNS: Gen. of the Stearns, Lanes, Holbrook & Warren fam. By M.L. Brook. 1898. 59p.
P4-S24388 — $10.00.

STEBBINS: Genealogy. By R.S. Greenlee. 1904. 2 vols., 1386p.
P4-S24405 — $176.00.

STEBBINS: Genealogy & hist. of some Stebbins lines to 1953. By J.A. Stebbins. 1957 190.
P4-S24402 — $29.00.

STEDMAN: Fam., (Repr. NEHGR) By G. Chandler. 1860. 6p.
P4-S24407 — $10.00.

STEELE: Archibald Steele & desc. By N. C. Steele. 1900. 143p.
P4-S24411 — $21.50.

STEELE: Gen of the Desc of James Steele & his Wife Mary. D.M. Steele. 1919. 338p.
P4-S24412 — $51.00.

STEELE: Family; Genealogical hist. of John & George Steele (settlers of Hartford, CT, 1635-6), & their desc.; By D.S. Durrie. 1862. 161 + 5p.
P4-S24414 — $25.00.

STEELMAN: Jonathan & Hannah Steelman family. By Sarah R. Lawyer. 1952. 106p.
P4-S24420 — $18.50.

STEEN: The Steen Family in Europe & America. Moses D.A. Steen. 1917 741p.
P4-S24421 — $111.00.

STEERE: A record of the desc. of John Steere, who settled in Providence, RI about 1660; with some acct. of the Steeres of Eng. By J.P. Root. 1890. 224p.
P4-S24426 — $38.00.

STEGGALL: Family in America: John Steggall & some of his descendants, with brief information on the families of Baldry & Hasner. By Mary Ann [Menuey] Thies. 1993. 280p.
P4-S24432 — $39.50.

STEIN: The Steins of Muscatine [IA.]: a fam. chronicle. By S.G. Stein. 1961. 53p.
P4-S24433 — $11.00.

STEINER: Genealogy of the Steiner family in Germany & America, especially the descendants of Jacob Steiner. L.H. & B.C. Steiner. 1896. 99p.
P4-S24438 — $19.00.

STEPHENS: STEVENS Genealogy: lineage from Henry Stephens or Stevens of Stonington, CT, 1668. By Plowdon Stevens. 1909. 358p.
P4-S24444 — $54.00.

STEPHENS: John Stephens of Guilford, CT & his desc. (Repr. NEHGR). By R.D. Smyth. 1902. 6p.
P4-S24445 — $10.00.

STEPHENS: Family with collateral branches (Vol. I of The American Genealogical Record). By Edward S. Clark. 1892. 185p.
P4-S24450 — $29.50.

STEPHENSON: Kinsmen; [Stephenson family of Cottingham, Yorkshire; Canada; US]. By Wesley Petty. 1918. 67p.
P4-S24453 — $12.50.

STERLING: Genealogy. By A.M. Sterling. 1909. 2 vols., 1418p.
P4-S24468 — $194.00.

STERLING: Charles Sterling of Wilton, CT & his descendants. By William G. Sterling. 1993. 70p. + charts
P4-S24462 — $15.00.

STERRETT: The Sterrett Genealogy: Families of PA, VA, Canada & Others. Comp by T. W. Sterrett. 1930. vii + 284p.
P4-S24469 — $49.00.

STETSON: Kindred of America (# 1 & 2). 1907-1908 39 + 23p.
P4-S24480 — $13.50.

STETSON: Kindred of America (# 3 & 4). comp. By G.W. & N.M. Stetson. 1912, 1914 45 + 147p.
P4-S24486 — $29.50.

STETSON: Genealogical & biographical sketch of name & fam. of Stetson 1634-1847. J.S. Barry. 1847. 116p.
P4-S24474 — $22.00.

STETSON: The Descendants of Cornet Robert Stetson of Scituate, MA. Stetson Kindred of America. 1933. 159p
P4-S24475 — $24.00.

STETSON: Stetson Genealogy 5th-7th generations. Stetson Kindred of America. 1955. 331p.
P4-S24476 — $50.00.

STEVENS: Gen; Some desc. of the Fitz Stevens fam. in Eng. & New Eng. By C.E. Stevens. 1904. 93p.
P4-S24510 — $17.00.

STEVENS: Erasmus Stevens, Boston, MA, 1674-1690, & his desc. By E.R. Stevens 1914. 116p.
P4-S24498 — $17.00.

STEVENS: Genealogy of the Stevens fam. 1635-1891. F.S. Stevens. 1891. 63p.
P35447500 — $12.50.

STEVENS: Genealogy; Embracing branches of the family descended from Puritan anc., 1650 to present. By E. Barney. 1907. 319p.
P4-S24516 — $41.50.

STEVENS: Genealogy of the Stevens & Tripp & allied families, from 1520-1906. Mary Stevens Ghastin. 1906. 48p.
P4-S24499 — $10.00.

STEVENS: Genealogy of the lineage desc. of John Steevens, who settled in Guilford, CT in 1645. By C.S. & C.W. Holmes. 1906. 162p.
P4-S24504 — $26.00.

STEVENSON: Thomas Stevenson of London, Eng., & his desc. By J.R. Stevenson. 1902. 181p.
P4-S24528 — $27.00.

STEVENSON: Descendants of Edw. & Mary Stevenson of Baltimore Co., MD. By Robert Barnes. 1966. 75p., typescript.
P4-S24522 — $15.00.

STEWART: A Narrative Gen of the Stewarts of Sequatchie Valley, TN & Allied Families. Mary Stewart Blakemore. 1960. xvi + 227p.
P4-S24535 — $39.00.

STEWART: Family records. By J.Montgomery Seaver. 62p.
P4-S24543 — $12.50.

STEWART: Col. George Steuart & his wife Margaret Harris: their anc. & desc., with appendixes of rel. fams. By R. Stewart. 1907. 522p.
P4-S24534 — $79.50.

STEWART: Gen. & biogr. of the desc. of Walter Stewart of Scotland, & of John Stewart who came to Amer. in 1718 & settled in Londonderry, NH. By B.F. Severance. 1905. 226p.
P4-S24540 — $34.00.

STEWART: The Stewarts of Coitsville: hist. of Robert & Sarah Stewart of Adams Co., PA & their desc. 1899. 198p.
P4-S24552 — $27.50.

STICHTER: Gen. of the Stichter fam., 1189-1902. By J. & J.L. Stichter. 1902. 42p.
P4-S24619 — $10.00.

STICKNEY: Family; genealogy of the desc. of Wm. & Elizabeth, 1637-1869. By M.A. Stickney. 1869. 534p.
P4-S24558 — $83.00.

STILES: Hist. of the KY-MO Stiles, with a sketch of NJ & other kindred. By L.S. Pence. 1896. 47p.
P4-S24571 — $10.00.

STILES: My North Carolina heritage, Volume I: Benj. & John Stiles of Western NC. By Marshall L. Stiles. 3rd ed., 1996. 399p.
P4-S24564 — $59.50.

STILES: From the Wyoming Valley of PA to the Platte Val. of NE: history & genealogy of the family of Mary Elizabeth Stiles, 1630-1941. By Rev. Leopold H. Hoppe. 1995. 313p.
P4-S24582 — $47.50.

STILES: Family in America; Gen. of the MA fam., & the Dover, NH fam. By M.S. Guild. 1892. 689p.
P4-S24570 — $86.00.

STILES: Contributions towards a gen. of the (MA) fam. of Stiles, desc. from Robert, of Rowley, MA, 1659-1860. By H.R. Stiles. 1863. 48p.
P4-S24568 — $10.00.

STILES: Family in America; Gen. of the CT family, also the CT-NJ fam., 1720-1894, & the southern (or Bermuda- GA) fam., 1635-1894. By Henry R. Stiles. 1895. 794p.
P4-S24567 — $119.00.

STILLWELL: Family; desc. of Nicholas Stillwell. 9p.
P4-S24589 — $10.00.

STILLWELL: History of Capt. Richard Stillwell, son of Lt. Nicholas Stillwell, & his desc. By J. Stillwell. 1930. 285p.
P4-S24588 — $46.00.

STILLWELL: Notes on desc. of Nicholas Stillwell; anc. of the fam. in Amer. By W. Stillwell. 1883. 62p.
P4-S24591 — $12.50.

STILWELL: Hist. & gen. record of one branch of the Stilwell fam. By D. Stilwell. 1914. 94p.
P4-S24606 — $17.00.

STILWELL: Early memoirs of the Stilwell family, compr. the life & times of Nicholas Stilwell, with acct. of his brothers John & Jasper. By B.M. Stilwell. 1878. 289p.
P4-S24600 — $46.50.

STIMPSON: Stimpson fam. of Charlestown, MA (Repr. NEHGR). By C.C. Whittier. 1905. 25p.
P4-S24613 — $10.00.

STIMPSON: Gen. of the Stimpson fam. of Charlestown, MA & allied lines, By C.C. Whittier. 1907. 206p.
P4-S24612 — $31.00.

STIRLING: The Stirlings of Keir & their family papers. By William Fraser. 1858 70 + 622p.
P4-S24618 — $99.50.

STOCKING: Fam. of Geo. Stocking, (Repr. NEHGR). By E.E. Cornwall. 1896. 8p.
P4-S24625 — $10.00.

STOCKING: Ancestors & Desc. of Geo. Stocking, founder of the Amer. fam. By C.H.W. Stocking. 1903. 205p.
P4-S24624 — $31.00.

STOCKTON: Stockton Family of NJ & Others. T.C. Stockton, MD. 1911. xxviii + 350 + 84p.
P4-S24628 — $69.00.

STOCKWELL: The Stockwell fam. By Brown & Chestnut. 1950. 17p.
P4-S24629 — $10.00.

STODDARD: SUDDUTH papers. By M.S. Stoddard. 1959-1960. 281p.
P4-S24654 — $45.00.

STODDARD: John Stoddard of New London, CT & his desc. By Stoddard & Shappee. n.d. 96p.
P4-S24636 — $19.50.

STODDARD: Family, being some account of some of the descendants of John Stodder of Hingham, MA. By F.R. Stoddard, Jr. 1912. 148p.
P4-S24660 — $23.00.

STODDARD: Some of the ancestsors of Rodman Stoddard, of Woodbury, CT & Detroit, MI. E. Deacon. 1893. 86p.
P4-S24648 — $16.50.

STODDARD: John Stoddard of Wethersfield, CT & his desc., 1642-1872. By D.W. Patterson. 1873. 96p.
P4-S24642 — $19.00.

STODDARD: Anthony Stoddard & his desc. C. & E. Stoddard. 1865. 95p.
P4-S24630 — $18.50.

STODDARD: Ralph Stoddard of New London & Groton, CT & desc: a genealogy. By E.W. Stoddard. 1872. 14p.
P4-S24643 — $10.00.

STOKES: Genealogy of the Stokes family, desc. from Thomas & Mary Stokes, who settled in Burlington Co., NJ. By Haines & Stokes. 1903. 342p.
P4-S24666 — $44.50.

STOKES: Notes on my Stokes ancestry. By J. Stokes. 1937. 61p.
P4-S24669 — $12.00.

STOKES: Descendants of Capt. Jonathan Stokes of Branford, CT. By E.A. Hill. n.d. 11p.
P4-S24667 — $10.00.

STOLLSTEIMER: Christian & Amanda: the life & times of a pioneer family of the San Juan Country, CO, with maps, photos & genealogy. By Robert S. Stollsteimer & Dorothy Causey. 1996. 132p.
P4-S24678 — $19.50.

STONE: Ancestors & desc. of Dea. Simon Stone of Watertown, MA, 1320-1926. By J.G. Bartlett. 1926. 811p.
P4-S24714 — $105.00.

STONE: Simon & Joan Clarke Stone of Watertown, MA, & three gen. of their desc. By D. Brown. 1899. 8p.
P4-S24685 — $10.00.

STONE: Souvenir of a part of the desc. of Gregory & Lydia Cooper Stone, 1634-1892. J.L. Stone. 1892. 78p.
P4-S24693 — $14.50.

STONE: Family History. By J.Montgomery Seaver. 59p.
P4-S24696 — $12.00.

STONE: Ancestors & desc. of Dea. Gregory Stone of Cambridge, MA, 1320-1917. By J.G. Bartlett. 1918. 913p.
P4-S24708 — $107.00.

STONE: The fam. of John Stone, one of the first settlers of Guilford, CT. By W.L. Stone. 1888. 192p.
P4-S24705 — $29.00.

STONE: Book II, of the fam. of John Stone, one of the first settlers of Guilford, CT; also names of all the desc. of Russell, Bille, Timothy & Eber Stone. By T.L. Stone. 1898. 360p.
P4-S24687 — $57.00.

STONE: Anc. of Sarah Stone, wife of James Patten of Arundel (Kennebunkport) ME. By W. Davis. 1930. 158p.
P4-S24684 — $23.50.

STORER: Annals of the Storer fam., together with notes on the Ayrault fam. By Malcolm Storer. 1927. 107p.
P4-S24720 — $18.50.

STORER: Family, 1725-1965. By Mahlon A. Storer. 1965. 214p.
P4-S24726 — $34.00.

STORKES: English Storkes in Amer. By C.A. Storke 1935. 224p.
P4-S24732 — $34.00.

STORRS: Family: genealogical & other memoranda. By C. Storrs. 1886. xv + 552p.
P4-S24738 — $84.00.

STORY: Elisha Story of Boston & some of his desc. By P. Derby & F.A. Gardner. 1915. 28p.
P4-S24743 — $10.00.

STOUFFER: Genealogical Memoranda, a.d. 1630-1903. By K.S. Snively. 1903. 104p.
P4-S24744 — $19.00.

STOUT: & Allied families. By H.F. Stout. 1951. xxii + 889p.
P4-S24750 — $129.50.

STOUT: Hosea Stout: Utah's Pioneer Statesman. Wayne Stout. 1953. vi + 304p.
P4-S24751 — $46.50.

STOVER: Genealogy, biography & history: a genealogical record of the desc. of William Stover, Pioneer, & other Stovers. B.E. Hughey. 1936. 249p.
P4-S24756 — $39.50.

STOWE: Genealogy of the Stowe family of New England. from the mss. of A.G. Stanley. 44p.
P4-S24757 — $10.00.

STOWELL: A record of the desc. of Sam'l Stowell of Hingham, MA. By W.H.H. Stowell. 1922. 980p.
P4-S24762 — $139.00.

STRACHAN: WISE Memorials of the Scottish Families of Strachan & Wise. Rev. Charles Rogers. 1877. 125p.
P4-S24763 — $19.00.

STRANAHAN: Gen. of the Stranahan, Josselyn, Fitch & Dow fam. in N. Amer. H.R. Stiles. 1868. 126p.
P4-S24768 — $19.00.

STRANG: The Strang Gen: Desc of Daniel Streing of New Rochelle, NY. Josephine C. Frost. 1915. vi + 192p.
P4-S24773 — $30.00.

STRANGE: Extraneus Book V: Strange of Eastern America. John R. Mayer. 1995 380p.
P4-S24775 — $57.00.

STRANGE: Extraneus, Book IX: Strange of Balcaskie & the clans outlandish Strang & Stronge, Strangus de Caledonia et Hibernia et America, second ed. By John R. Mayer. 1986, 1998. 820p.
P4-S24780 — $99.50.

STRANGE: Extraneus, Book X: The Annals Quinquepartite of Strange Lives. J.R. Mayer 1994. 256p.
P4-S24776 — $38.50.

STRANGE: Biogr. & hist. sketches of the Stranges of Amer. & across the seas. By A.T. Strange. 1911. 137p.
P4-S24774 — $22.50.

STRANGE: The Alloway Strange Family. John R. Mayer. 1994. xxiv + 256p.
P4-S24777 — $42.00.

STRASSBURGER: Family & allied families of PA, being the ancestry of Jacob Andrew Strassburger, Esquire, of Montgomery Co. PA. By R.B. Strassburger. 1922. 520p.
P4-S24786 — $76.50.

STRATTON: A book of Strattons; being a coll. of Stratton records from Eng. & Scot., & a gen. hist. of the early col. Strattons in Amer., with five gen. of their desc. By H.R. Stratton. 1908-1918 2 vols., 910p.
P4-S24789 — $129.00.

STRAW: Some genealogies & family records. By A.Y. Straw. 1931. 292p.
P4-S24795 — $46.00.

STREET: Genealogy. By H.A. & M.A. Street. 1895. 551p.
P4-S24798 — $69.50.

STREETER: A gen. hist. of the desc. of Stephen & Ursula Streeter of Gloucester, MA, 1642, with an acct. of the Streeters of Goudherst, Eng. By M. Streeter 1896. 360p.
P4-S24801 — $42.00.

STRETCHER: Allied families of DE: Stretcher, Fenwick, Davis, Draper, Kipshaven, Stidham. By E.E. Sellers. 1901. 171p.
P4-S24807 — $28.00.

STRICKLAND: Early history of Stricklands of Sizergh, with some acct. of the allied families d'Eyncourt, Fleming, Greystoke & Dunbar. By S.H.L. Washington. 1942. 100p.
P4-S24819 — $19.00.

STRICKLAND: Genealogical Memoirs of the Family of Strickland of Sizergh. Henry Hornyold. 1928. 330 + 60p.
P4-S24820 — $59.00.

STRICKLAND: The Stricklands of Sizergh Castle: records of 25 generations of a Westmoreland [England] family, with The Ancestry of Elizabeth D'eyncourt. By Daniel Scott. 1908 293p.
P4-S24825 — $46.50.

STRICKLER: Forerunners. History or gen. of the Strickler family. By H.M. Strickler. 1925. 440p.
P4-S24831 — $68.50.

STROBRIDGE: Genealogy; Strobridge Morrison or Morison Strawbridge. M.S.P. Guild. 1891. 318p.
P4-S24837 — $47.50.

STRONG: History of the desc. of Elder John Strong of Northampton, MA. B.W. Dwight. 1871. 2 vols., 1649p.
P4-S24840 — $199.50.

STRONG: The Strongs of Strongville: descendants of John Stoughton Strong & Eliphalet Strong, suppl. to "Hist. of the Strong Family," by Benj. W. Dwight. By Albert Strong. 1931. 91p.
P4-S24846 — $18.00.

STROTHER: Wm. Strother of VA & desc. By T. Owen. 1898. 25p.
P4-S24847 — $10.00.

STROUD: Family hist., desc. of Capt. Richard Stroud of New London, CT. By H.D. Lowell. 1934. 40p.
P4-S24853 — $10.00.

STROUD: The Strode & Stroud families in England & America. By James S. Elston. 1949-1976. 4 vols., 123 + 165 + 144 + 31p.
P4-S24852 — $66.00.

STROUD: The Strouds. A colonial fam. of Eng. desc. A.B. Stroud. 1918. 263p.
P4-S24858 — $39.50.

STUART: Some account of the Stuarts of Aubigny, in France, 1422-1672. By Elizabeth Cust. ? 130p.
P4-S24870 — $24.00.

STUART: Gen. hist. of the Duncan Stuart fam. in Amer. By J.A. Stuart. 1894. 183p.
P4-S24864 — $29.50.

STUART: Family of Coshocton, volume 2, By Curtiss N. Stuart. 2002. 821p.
P4-S24876 — $115.00.

STUBBS: Descendants of John Stubbs of Cappahosic, Gloucester Co., VA, 1652. By W.C. Stubbs. 1902. 116p.
P4-S24882 — $19.50.

STUBBS: Henry Stubbs Family of Lake Minnetonka. Daniel Philip Stubbs 1997 305 + 102p.
P4-S24883 — $53.50.

STUKEY: Genealogy of the Stukey, Ream, Grove, Clem & Denniston families. By E.L. Denniston. 1939. 591p.
P4-S24888 — $89.50.

STURGEON: A genealogical history of the Sturgeons of N. Amer. By C.T. McCoy. 1926. 239 + 46p., index.
P4-S24894 — $39.50.

STURGES: COLEMAN fam. gen. By A.W. Sturges. 1898. 16p.
P4-S24901 — $10.00.

STURGES: Sturges fam. of ME. By A.W. Sturges. 1900. 41p.
P4-S24902 — $10.00.

STURGES: Solomon Sturges & desc. By E. Buckingham. 1907. 84p.
P4-S24900 — $16.50.

STURGIS: From Books & Papers of Russell Sturgis. Julian Sturgis. 272 + 12p.
P4-S24907 — $42.95

STURGIS: Edw. Sturgis of Yarmouth, MA, 1613-1695, & his desc. ed. By R.F. Sturgis. 1914. 88p.
P4-S24906 — $18.00.

STURROCK: From Scotland to Texas: descendants of William Sturrock & Ann Swan. By Jeanne Branson Sturrock. 1992. 380p.
P4-S24912 — $57.00.

STURTEVANT: Family of WI. By John L. Sturtevant. 1934. 39p.
P4-S24914 — $10.00.

SULLIVAN: The Sullivan fam. of Sullivan, ME with some acct. of the town. By J. Emery. 1891. 22p.
P4-S24922 — $10.00.

SULLIVAN: Materials for a hist. of the fam. of John Sullivan of Berwick, New Eng., & of the O'Sullivans of Ardea, Ireland. T.C. Amory. 1893. 151p.
P4-S24921 — $26.00.

SULLIVAN: Royal ancestry of John Sullivan, b. 1690 in Ardea, Kerry, Ireland, emigr. to Berwick, ME, 1723; In "Ancestral fams. of Sturges Belsterling Schley," By Charles S. Belsterling. 1940. 157 + 65p; typescript.
P4-S24927 — $34.00.

SUMNER: Rec. of the desc. of Wm. Sumner of Dorchester, MA, 1636. By W.S. Appleton. 1879. 209p.
P4-S24936 — $31.50.

SUMNER: Record of descendants of Wm. Sumner of Dorchester, MA; additional notes & corrections to orig. 1879 gen. W.S. Appleton. 1881-1902. 40p.
P4-S24937 — $10.00.

SUMNER: Memoir of Increase Sumner, gov. of MA, by W.H. Sumner, with a gen. of the Sumner fam. By W.B. Trask. 1854. 70p.
P4-S24933 — $14.00.

SUPPLEE: DeHAVEN fam. hist. By I.D. Conard. 20p.
P4-S24940 — $10.00.

SURDAM: Genealogy of the Surdam family. By C.E. Surdam. 1909. 266p.
P4-S24942 — $40.00.

SURGES: McKAY; History of the Surges-McKay families; also allied fams. Pflueger, Reibel, Bouville, Beaune. By J.R. Crossman. 1991. 60p.
P4-S24948 — $13.50.

SUTCLIFFE: A gen. of the Sutcliffe-Sutliffe fam. in Amer. from before 1661-1903. The desc. of Nathaniel Sutcliffe. By B.H. Sutcliffe. 242p.
P4-S24954 — $36.50.

SUTHERLAND: Sutherland records. By D. Merritt. 1918. 76p.
P4-S24960 — $15.00.

SUTLIFF: A history of the American & Puritanical family of Sutliff or Sutliffe, spelled Sutcliffe in England. By S.M. Sutliff, Jr 1909. 199p.
P4-S24966 — $31.00.

SUTPHEN: Fam. gen. & biogr. notes. By L.L. DeBoar. 1926. 132p.
P4-S24972 — $27.50.

SUTTON: The Suttons & related lines (some descendants of John of Attleborough, England, & Hingham, MA). By Robert & Connie Medford, & Bruce D. Sutton. 2000. 965p.
P4-S24978 — $115.00.

For hardcover versions, see the order form on page v. To order, call 1-888-296-3447.

SWAIN: & allied families. By W.C. Swain. 1896. 137p.
P4-S24984 — $20.50.

SWAIN: Family, Jeremiah Swain of Reading, MA & desc. By W.C. Swain. 1896. 52p.
P4-S24991 — $10.00.

SWALLOW: Genealogy of the Swallow fam., 1666-1910, By Baker, North & Ellis. 1910. 217p.
P4-S24990 — $34.50.

SWAN: Dana H. Swan: His Ancestors & His Descendants. Rowena Otta Swan. 1994. vi + 186p.
P4-S24997 — $29.00.

SWAN: Ancestors of Alden Smith Swan & his wife Mary Althea Farwell. By J.C. Frost. 1923. 264p.
P4-S24996 — $39.50.

SWANDER: History of the Swander family. Rev. John I. Swander. 1899. 143p.
P4-S25002 — $23.00.

SWARTLEY: Genealogical record of the descendants of the Swartley family of Bucks & Montgomery Cos., PA. By Rev. A.J. Fretz. 1906. 81p.
P4-S25008 — $16.00.

SWASEY: Genealogy of the Swasey family. By B.F. Swasey. 1910. 525p.
P4-S25014 — $66.50.

SWAYNE: Descendants of Francis Swayne & others. By Norman Walton Swayne. 1921. 154p.
P4-S25020 — $22.00.

SWEARINGEN: Fam. register of Gerret van Sweringen & desc. By H.H. Swearingen. 1894. 2nd ed. 85p.
P4-S25026 — $17.00.

SWEET: Silas Sweet of New Bedford, MA & Bradford, VT & his desc. By C. Johnson. 1898. 21p.
P4-S25027 — $10.00.

SWEETSER: Seth Sweetser & descendants. P.S. Sweetser. 1938. 427p.
P4-S25032 — $65.00.

SWETT: Swett gen., desc. of John Swett of Newbury, MA. By Everett S. Stackpole. 123p.
P4-S25038 — $18.50.

SWETT: Mem. of the Swett family. By J. Thornton. 1851. 26p.
P4-S25039 — $10.00.

SWIFT: Family: hist. notes. comp. by K.W. Swift. 1955. 170p.
P4-S25044 — $28.00.

SWIFT: William Swift of Sandwich & some of his descendants, 1637-1899. By G.H. Swift. 1900. 165 + 15p.
P4-S25047 — $29.00.

SWINERTON: Job Swinerton of Salem Village [now Danvers] & some descendants. By H.S. Tapley. 14p.
P4-S25048 — $10.00.

SWING: Events in the life & hist. of the Swing fam. G.S. Swing. 1889. 398p.
P4-S25053 — $61.00.

SWINGLE: History of the Swingle family. Mrs C.F. Martzolff. 1925. 212p.
P4-S25059 — $33.00.

SWITZER: Hortense Lillian Switzer of Townshend & Brattleboro, VT, wife of Wm. Thatcher Bruce, Jr., her ancestors & some of her descendants. By Claudia E.S. Cridland. 2000. 81p.
P4-S25060 — $16.00.

SWOPE: History of the Swope Family, 1678-1896. Comp by G.E. Swope. 1896. vi + 390p.
P4-S25061 — $59.95

SYDNEY: SMITH & Clagett-Price Genealogy, with the Lewis, Montgomery, Harrison, Hawley, Moorhead, Rixey, et al. Lucy M. Price. 1927. 324p.
P4-S25065 — $49.50.

SYLVESTER: Fam. in ME. By C.N. Sinnett. 1922. 19p.
P4-S25068 — $10.00.

SYMMES: The Symmes mem. By J.A. Vinton. 1873. 184p.
P4-S25071 — $27.50.

T

TABER: Descendants of Jos. & Philip, sons of Philip Taber from RI & CT & Long Isl. By A.A. Wright & A.H. Wright. 1952. 86p.
P4-S25077 — $17.00.

TABER: Genealogy; descendants of Thomas, son of Phillip Taber. By G.L. Randall. 1924. 518p.
P4-S25083 — $81.50.

TAFT: The Taft Kin (Repr. Boston Evening Transcript) A. Titus. 1909. 8p.
P4-S25090 — $10.00.

TAFT: Taft fam. gathering: proceedings at the meeting of the Taft Fam. At Uxbridge, MA, 1874. 1874. 103p.
P4-S25089 — $19.00.

TAGGART: Gen. of Taggart fam. of PA. (in Nesbit Gen.) By B.T. Hartman. 1929. 79p.
P4-S25095 — $16.00.

TAINTER: Hist. & gen. of the desc. of Jospeh Taynter, who sailed from England, Apr. 1638, & settled in Watertown, MA. By D.W. Tainter. 1859. 94p.
P4-S25101 — $18.00.

TALBOT: The Eng. anc. of Peter Talbot of Dorchester, MA. By J.G. Bartlett. 1917. 116p.
P4-S25107 — $19.50.

TALCOTT: Pedigree in Eng. & Amer. from 1558-1876. S.V. Talcott. 1876. 316p.
P4-S25113 — $49.50.

TALIAFERRO: TOLIVER Family records. By N.W. Sherman. 1960. 242p.
P4-S25119 — $33.50.

TALIAFERRO: Family history, 1635-1899, By Charles Taliaferro. Transcribed By John K. Ellis II. 1899, 1995. 154p.
P4-S25125 — $25.00.

TALLEY: A hist. of the Talley fam. on the Delaware & their desc. from 1686. By G. A. Talley. 1899. 252p.
P4-S25131 — $38.00.

TALLMAN: The Hon. Peleg Tallman, 1764-1841. His anc. & desc. By W.M. Emery. 1935. 260p.
P4-S25137 — $39.00.

TALMADGE: TALLMADGE & Talmage genealogy; descendants of Thomas Talmadge of Lynn, MA, with an appendix incl. other fam. By A. Talmadge. 1909. 385p.
P4-S25143 — $60.00.

TANKERSLEY: Gen. of Tankersley fam. in US. C.W. Tankersley. 1895. 31p.
P4-S25145 — $10.00.

TANNAHILL: Genealogical History of the Tannahills, Tannehills & Taneyhills. James B. Tannehill. n.d. ix + 213p.
P4-S25147 — $34.00.

TANNER: William Tanner of North Kingstown, RI, & his desc. By Rev. G.C. Tanner. 216p.
P4-S25155 — $32.00.

TANNER: Desc of John Tanner, b. August 15, 1778 at Hopkintown, RI Comp by Maurice Tanner. 1942. 698p.
P4-S25150 — $105.00.

TANNER: William Tanner Sr. of So. Kingstown, RI & his desc. By G.C. Tanner. 1910. 516p.
P4-S25158 — $79.50.

TANNER: Gen. of the desc. of Thomas Tanner, Sr., of Cornwall, CT, with brief notes of several allied fam. By Rev. E. Tanner. 1893. 129p.
P4-S25149 — $19.00.

TAPLEY: Genealogy of the Tapley family. By H. Tapley. 1900. 275p.
P4-S25164 — $41.00.

TAPPAN: TOPPAN; Anc. & desc. of Abraham Toppan of Newbury, MA, 1606-1672. By D. Tappan. 1915. 169p.
P4-S25170 — $25.00.

TAPPAN: A sketch of the life of Rev. Daniel Dana Tappan, with an acct. of the Tappan fam. By his children. 1890. 28p.
P4-S25171 — $10.00.

TAPPAN: The fam. records of James & Nancy Dunham Tappan, of the 4th gen., formerly of Woodbridge, Middlesex Co., NJ. By P.B. Good. 1884. 136p.
P4-S25176 — $23.00.

TARLETON: Family. By Charles William Tarleton. 1900. 244p.
P4-S25182 — $36.50.

TARLETON: Records, containing the descendants of the three brothers John, Jeremiah & Caleb Tarleton of WV. By Carrie T. Goldsborough & Anna Goldsborough Fisher. 1950. 214p.
P4-S25188 — $32.00.

TATE: Family of Haywood Co., NC, history & genealogy. By Jim Howell. 2001. 293p.
P4-S25194 — $45.00.

TAYLOR: Family hist. of Anthony Taylor of Hampton, NH & some desc., 1635-1935. By H.M. Taylor, 1935. 530p.
P4-S25218 — $79.50.

TAYLOR: A friendly heritage along the Delaware: the Taylors of Washington Crossing & Some allied families in Bucks County. By Arthur E. Bye. 1959. 258p.
P4-S25206 — $35.00.

TAYLOR: Anthony Taylor of Hampton, NH: Additions. By H.M Taylor. 1945. 134p.
P4-S25206 — $23.50.

TAYLOR: Family records. By J. Montgomery Seaver. 1994. 80p.
P4-S25230 — $16.00.

TAYLOR: Hist. of John Taylor of Hadley, MA & the gen. of his desc. By Rev. E. Taylor. 1903. 111p.
P4-S25224 — $19.50.

TAYLOR: Desc. of John Taylor of Hadley ; Supplement to 1903 edition. By F.L. Taylor. 1922. 40p.
P4-S25201 — $10.00.

TAYLOR: Desc. of Robt. Taylor of PA. By A. Justice. 1925. 113p.
P4-S25212 — $22.00.

TEACHOUT: Fam. of Abraham Teachout of Herkimer Co., NY & some desc. (in Coates, Wilcox, Teachout Gen.). J.E. Snow. 1901. 24p.
P4-S25240 — $10.00.

TEALL: Gen. records in Eng. & Amer. By E. Dunn. 1926. 59p.
P4-S25233 — $12.50.

TEFFT: Desc. of Wm. V.B. Tefft (1821-98). Rachel Saul Tefft. 1998. 17p.
P4-S25243 — $10.00.

TEFFT: Desc. of Gardner Rowland Tefft (1824-72). By Rachel Saul Tefft. 1999. 178p.
P4-S25242 — $25.00.

TEFFT: Descendants of John Tefft, 1614-1676. Rachel Saul Tefft. 1997. 469p.
P4-S25248 — $71.50.

TEFFT: Descendants of Lorin Palmer Tefft (1828-68). Rachel Saul Tefft. 1999. 10p.
P4-S25249 — $10.00.

TEFFT: Partial record of the descendants of John Tefft, or Portsmouth, RI, & the nearly complete record of the desc. of John Tifft of Nassau, NY. By M.E.M. Tifft. 1896. 159p.
P4-S25254 — $25.00.

TELLMAN: Family hist., By Jean Tellman Ketterman. 1986. 88p.
P4-S25260 — $17.00.

TEMPLE: Some Temple pedigrees: gen. of the known desc. of Abraham Temple, who settled in Salem, MA in 1636 [& some connected fams.]. By L. D. Temple. 1900. 316p.
P4-S25290 — $47.50.

TEMPLE: Some account of the Temple family. By Temple Prime. 1887. 100p.
P4-S25266 — $18.00.

TEMPLE: Some account of the Temple Family, 2nd ed. Temple Prime. 1894. 111p.
P4-S25278 — $19.50.

TEMPLE: Some account of the Temple Family, 3rd ed. Temple Prime. 1896. 146p.
P4-S25284 — $22.00.

TEMPLE: Some account of the Temple Family, 4th ed. Temple Prime. 1899. 77p.
P4-S25272 — $16.00.

TEMPLE: The name & fam. of Temple. comp. by the Media Research Bureau. 8p.
P4-S25285 — $10.00.

TEMPLETON: & allied fam. A gen. hist. & fam. record. By Y.T. Clague. 1936. 169p.
P4-S25302 — $25.50.

TEMPLETON: John Templeton of Iredell Co., NC & related families of Handly, Marks, Folk, PIlcher, Colyar, Bate & Beall. Jay Norwalk. 1997. 578p.
P4-S25296 — $85.00.

TEN BROECK: Ten Broeck Genealogy: Being the Records & Annals of Dirck Wesselse Ten Broeck of Albany. Emma T.B. Runk. 1897. x + 277 + 69p.
P4-S25303 — $53.50.

TENNANT: Genealogy of the Tennant fam: anc. & desc. through many generations. A.M. Tennant et al. 1915. 356p.
P4-S25308 — $44.00.

TENNEY: Gen. of the Tenney fam. & the Kent fam. H.A. Tenney. 1875. 76p.
P4-S25314 — $15.00.

TENNEY: Family; desc. of Thomas Tenney of Rowley, MA, 1638-1904. By M.J. Tenney. 1904. 691p.
P4-S25317 — $99.50.

TERRELL: Richmond, William & Timothy Terrell, Col. Virginians. By C.J.T. Barnhill. 1934. 339p.
P4-S25323 — $54.00.

TERRELL: Terrell Genealogy. Comp by Emma Dicken. 1952. 315 + 15p.
P4-S25324 — $49.50.

TERRILL: Gen. of Terrell fam. By C.M. Terrell. 1906. 8p.
P4-S25325 — $10.00.

TERRILL: Gen. line of Tyrrell, Terrell, Terrill fam. of VA & TX. By R.L. Terrell. 1934. 11p.
P4-S25326 — $10.00.

TERRY: Notes of Terry family in the US, Mainly desc. from Samuel of Springfield, MA, but including some desc. from Stephen of Windsor, CT. By S. Terry. 1887. 351p.
P4-S25332 — $44.50.

THACHER: An old fam.; Amer. desc. of Peter Thacher of Salisbury, MA. 1882. 48p.
P4-S25333 — $10.00.

THARP: History of Thomas Tharp & Elizabeth Withers & John Tharp & Mary Webster: MD, PA, OH, IN & Westward Bound, 1712-1844. By Marjorie K. Starr. 1998. 444p.
P4-S25338 — $67.50.

THAYER: Memorial of the Thayer name, from the Mass. Colony of Weymouth & Braintree. By Bezaleel Thayer. 1874. 708p.
P4-S25350 — $99.00.

THAYER: Genealogy of Ephraim & Sarah Thayer with their 14 children, from the time of their marriage to 1835. By E. Thayer. 1835. 97p.
P4-S25344 — $18.00.

THOMAS: Gen. records & sketches of the desc. of Wm. Thomas of Hardwick, MA. By A.R. Thomas. 1891. 232p.
P4-S25362 — $35.00.

THOMAS: Book, giving the gene-alogy of Sir Rhys ap Thomas, K.G., the Thomas family descendants from him, & some allied families. By L.B. Thomas. 1896. 648p.
P4-S25374 — $97.00.

THOMAS: Genealogical notes, contain-ing the pedigree of the Thomas family of MD. By L.B. Thomas. 1877-1878 197 + 55p.
P4-S25356 — $39.00.

THOMAS: Fam. of Talbot Co., MD. By R.P. Spencer. 1914. 40p.
P4-S25357 — $10.00.

THOMAS: Seth Thomas, Clockmaker, & some of his desc. By Atwater & Orcutt. 3p.
P4-S25358 — $10.00.

THOMPSON: Genealogy of Gordon Thompson & Jane Clemens Thompson. By D.G. Thompson. 1940. 82p.
P4-S25380 — $16.00.

THOMPSON: Genealogy: descen-dants of Wm. & Margaret Thomson, first settled in that part of Windsor, CT, now E. Windsor & Ellington, 1720-1915. Mary A. Elliott. 1915. 518p.
P4-S25401 — $76.50.

THOMPSON: Notes on the Thompson fam. (Repr. NEHGR), By D.L. Jacobus. 1912. 14p.
P4-S25396 — $10.00.

THOMPSON: Thompson Lineage with Mention of Allied Fams. W.B. Thompson. 1911. 131p.
P4-S25393 — $20.00.

THOMPSON: Rec. of the David & Thomas Thompson fam. of New Eng. (extr. Bassett gen.) 1926. 21p.
P4-S25394 — $10.00.

THOMPSON: Hist. of the Thompson fam. from 1637-1860. By A.A. Thompson. 1865. 13p.
P4-S25397 — $10.00.

THOMPSON: Mem. of James Thompson of Charlestown, MA, 1630-1643, & Woburn, MA, 1642-1682, & his desc. By Rev. L. Thompson. 1887. 246p.
P4-S25392 — $31.00.

THOMPSON: Our Thompson fam. in ME, NH & & the West. By C.N. Sinnett. 1907. 293p.
P4-S25395 — $38.00.

THOMPSON: Hist. of the Thompson fam. of Eng. & NY. By G. Thompson. 1937. 87p.
P4-S25386 — $17.50.

THOMSON: Descendants of John Thomson, Pioneer Scotch Covenanter: gen. notes on all known desc. of John Thomson of Scotland, Ireland & Pa. By A.S. McAllister. 1917. 357p.
P4-S25407 — $59.50.

THORNBURG: Family of Randolph Co., IN. Thornburg & Weiss. 1959. 60p.
P4-S25410 — $12.00.

THORNDIKE: Descendants of John Thorndike of Essex Co., MA. By M.H. Staffod. 1960. 349p.
P4-S25419 — $54.00.

THORNE: Eight gen. from Wm. Thorne of Dorset, Eng. & Lynn, MA. By Middleton & Taylor. 1913. 10p.
P4-S25420 — $10.00.

THORNTON: Fam. of James Thornton. By C. T. Adams. 1905. 34p.
P4-S25421 — $10.00.

THORNTON: The Dozier Thornton line. By J. Thornton. 1957. 52p.
P4-S25422 — $10.00.

THROCKMORTON: A Genealogical and Historical Account of the Throck-morton Family in England & US. W. Wickliffe Throckmorton. 1930. viii + 503p.
P4-S25423 — $77.00.

THROOPE: William Throope & Adrian Scrope: the family tradition, hsitory of the Scrope family & barony of Bolton [etc.], with addendum. By Evelyn F. Knudson. 1943. 73 + 8p.
P4-S25425 — $16.00.

THURBER: Desc. of John Thurber. By A. Thurber, Jr. 1954. 39p.
P4-S25426 — $10.00.

THURSTON: Genealogy of Charles Thurston & Rachel Pitman & desc. By C. M. Thurston. 1865. 80p.
P4-S25443 — $16.00.

THURSTON: Descendants of Edw. Thurston, the first of the name in the colony of RI. By C. Thurston. 1868. 70p.
P4-S25437 — $14.00.

THURSTON: Genealogy, 1665-1892. By B. Thurston. 1892. 760p.
P4-S25446 — $94.00.

THURSTON: Ancestry of Walter M. Thurston, giving some acct. of the fam. of Carroll, De Beaufort (& others). By J.H. & W.M. Thurston. 1894. 95p.
P4-S25431 — $18.50.

THWING: A Genealogy, Biography & Historical Account of the family. By W.E. Thwing. 1883. 216p.
P4-S25452 — $32.00.

TIBBETTS: Henry Tibbetts of Dover, NH & some of his descendants. By M.T. Jarvis. 1937-1941 821p.
P4-S25458 — $117.00.

TICE: Families in Amer: Theis, Thyssen, Tyssen, Deis, vol I. By J.S. Elson. 1947. 320p.
P4-S25464 — $49.50.

TICHENOR: A part. hist. of the Tichenor fam. in Amer., desc. of Martin Techenor of CT & NJ, & a complete gen. of the branch of the fam. desc. from Isaac Tichenor By R.B. Teachenor. 1918. 32p.
P4-S25465 — $10.00.

TIERNAN: & other families. By Charles B. Tiernan. 1901. 466p.
P4-S25470 — $69.50.

TIERNAN: Family in MD. By Charles B. Tiernan. 1898. 222p.
P4-S25476 — $33.50.

TIFFANY: The Tiffanys of America, History & Genealogy. Nelson Otis Tiffany. 1901. 254 + 90p.
P4-S25483 — $52.00.

TIFFANY: Tiffany fam. gen. By E.F. Wright. 1904. 92p.
P4-S25482 — $20.00.

TILGHMAN: TILLMAN Family, 1225-1945. By Stephen F. Tillman. 1946. 473 + 19p.
P4-S25494 — $66.00.

TILLEY: Gen. of the Tilley fam. By R.H. Tilley. 1878. 79p.
P4-S25500 — $16.00.

TILLINGHAST: The Founder of the Tillinghast Family in the US. John Gifford Tillinghast. 1889. 31p.
P4-S25501 — $10.00.

TILLISCH: Ancestry of Gudrun Margarethe Tillisch (1870-1949), the wife of Frank Henry Kimball, MD (1855-1926), including allied families—rev. ed. By Lyman & Karen H. Mower. 2000. 615p.
P4-S25506 — $89.50.

TILLMAN: "Spes Alit Agricolam" (Hope sustains the farmer); the years 1225-1961 of the Tilghman (Tillman) & allied fam. By S. Tillman. 1962. 320p.
P4-S25512 — $49.50.

TILSON: Genealogy from Edmund Tilson at Plymouth, New Eng., 1638-1911. By M. Tilson. 1911. 610p.
P4-S25518 — $91.50.

TILTON: Kenneth Tilton of Dover Twp, NJ. J.O. Brown. 2005. 232p.
P4-S25525 — $35.00.

TILTON: Anc. of Phoebe Tilton, 1775-1847, wife of Capt. Abel Lunt of Newburyport, MA. By W. Davis. 1947. 257p.
P4-S25524 — $38.50.

TILTON: Hist. of the Tilton fam. in Amer. By F.T. Tilton. Vol. I, nos. 1-8. 1927-1930. 256p.
P4-S25527 — $33.00.

TINGLEY: Family, being a rec. of the desc. of Samuel Tingley of Malden, MA in the male & female lines. By R.M. Tingley. 1910. 894p.
P4-S25533 — $127.50.

TINGLEY: Some Anc Lines; Guilford Solon Tingley & His Wife Martha Pamela Meyers. R.M. Tingley. 1935. 465 + 42p.
P4-S25534 — $76.00.

TINKER: Family: ancestors & descendants of Joseph Wescot Tinker, Ellsworth ME, 1791-1868, a descendant of John Tinker of Boston. By Frederick J. Libbie. 1900. 36p.
P4-S25536 — $10.00.

TINKHAM: A biographical index, compiled from public records, personal recollections, & assorted family histories, revised ed. By Kenneth Ira Tinkham. 2003. xviii + 429p.
P4-S25539 — $59.00.

TIPPIN: Anc. of Tippin fam. of KY, with Mayfield anc. J.J. Tippin. 1940. 38p.
P4-S25540 — $10.00.

TISDALE: Gen. of Israel Tisdale & his desc. By E. F. Tisdale. 1909. 82p.
P4-S25545 — $16.50.

TISDALE: Supplement to "A family register," genealogy of Col. Israel Tisdale & his descendants. By E.F. Tisdale. 1920. 14p.
P4-S25546 — $10.00.

TITUS: Some notes on Titus fam. of MA & CT. ed. By H. F. Johnston. 6p.
P4-S25547 — $10.00.

TOBEY: TOBIE — TOBY genealogy; Thomas of Sandwich & James of Kittery, & their descendants. R. Tobey & Charles Henry Pope 1905. 350p.
P4-S25548 — $46.50.

TODD: The Todds, the Wheelers, "et id genus omne" Thomas Todd. 1909. 64p.
P4-S25558 — $12.50.

TODD: Descendants of Joseph Todd of Eling. Glenda F. Dobbs. 2003. 601p.
P4-S25559 — $79.00.

TODD: Genealogy; register of the descendants of Adams Todd, of the names Todd, Whetten & twenty-six others. By R. H. Greene. 1867. 160p.
P4-S25563 — $26.00.

TODD: Family in America, or the desc. of Christopher Todd, 1637-1919. By J.E. Todd. 1920. 721p.
P4-S25557 — $108.00.

TOLMAN: The Needham, MA branch of the Tolman fam. By A.M. Pickford. 1894. 29p.
P4-S25564 — $10.00.

TOMKINS: TOMPKINS genealogy. By R.A. & C.F. Tompkins. 1942. 720p.
P4-S25569 — $99.50.

TOMLINSON: A Story of the Family Tomlinson/Tomlonson. John Dean Tomlonson. 2003. 318p.
P4-S25576 — $50.00.

TOMLINSON: Henry Tomlinson & desc. in Amer. & a few add. Tomlinson branches. By S. Orcott. 1891. 244p.
P4-S25575 — $36.50.

TOMPKINS: Records of the ancestors & kindred of the children of Edward Tompkins, Sr., late of Oakland, CA, with appendix. By E. Tompkins, Jr. 1893. 65p.
P4-S25581 — $13.00.

TONG: TONGE — TONGUE & Allied families, 2nd ed. 1974. 201p.
P4-S25593 — $32.00.

TONGUE: Record of the descendants of Levi Nelson Tongue & Adeline Sutton Morse, with information concerning their ancestors. By Earl W. Hauer. 1949. 162p., typescript.
P4-S25599 — $25.00.

TONNANCOUR: La Famille Godefroy de Tonnancour. Pierre-Georges Roy 1904. 128p.
P4-S25600 — $20.00.

TOPHAM: Topham fam. Bible records. By E.P. Bassett. 1945. 5p.
P4-S25601 — $10.00.

TOPPAN: The Toppans of Toppan's Lane (Newbury, MA), their desc. & relations. By J. Coffin. 1862. 28p.
P4-S25602 — $10.00.

TORRENCE: & Allied families. By Robert M. Torrence. 1938. 559p.
P4-S25605 — $85.00.

TORREY: A contribution towards a gen. of all Torreys in Amer., showing the desc. from William Torrey of Eng., 1557, to Abner Torrey of Weymouth, MA. By D. Torrey. 1890. 210p.
P4-S25608 — $31.50.

TORREY: Families & their children in Amer., vol I. F.C. Torrey. 1924. 396p.
P4-S25614 — $58.50.

TORREY: Fams. & their children in Amer, vol II. F.C. Torrey. 1929. 488p.
P4-S25620 — $76.50.

TOTMAN: John & Thomas Totman (Tatman) & their desc., By R. N. Meriam. 1895. 31p.
P4-S25621 — $10.00.

TOUSEY: Tousey fam. in Amer. By T.C. Rose. 1916. 137p.
P4-S25626 — $27.50.

TOWER: Genealogy. An acct. of the desc. of John Tower of Hingham, MA. By C. Tower. 1891. 701p.
P4-S25629 — $87.50.

TOWLE: Descendants of Jonathan Towle, 1747-1822, of Hampton & Pittsfield, NH. A. Towle et al. 1903. 312p.
P4-S25629 — $49.00.

TOWNE: Letters & diary of Laura M. Towne, written from the Sea Islands of SC, 1862-1884. 1912. 310p.
P4-S25642 — $29.00.

TOWNE: Anc. of Lieutenant Amos Towne of Kennebunkport, ME. By W.G. Davis. 1927. 81p.
P4-S25641 — $16.00.

TOWNE: Maternal lines of William Towne descendants. By B.J. Schmidt Bragg & Dawn Robinson 1997. 156p.
P4-S25656 — $24.50.

TOWNE: Descendants of William Towne, who came to Amer. about 1630 & settled in Salem, MA. By E. E. Towne. 1901. 379p.
P4-S25644 — $48.50.

TOWNE: Family memorial. By E. E. Hubbard. 1880. 130p.
P4-S25662 — $19.50.

TOWNER: Genealogy of the Towner fam; The desc. of Richard Towner who came from Sussex Co., Eng. to Guilford, CT before 1685. By J.W. Towner. 1910. 269p.
P4-S25668 — $43.00.

TOWNSEND: TOWNSHEND, 1066-1909: The History, Genealogy & Alliances of the English & American House of Townsend. By Margaret Townsend. 1909. 125p.
P4-S25680 — $21.00.

TOWNSEND: A memorial of John, Henry & Richard Townsend & their descendants (with 1969 Index). By W.A. Townsend. 1865. 233 + 60p.
P4-S25674 — $47.00.

TOWNSEND: Notes on the Townsend family. By H. Waters. 1883. 43p.
P4-S25675 — $10.00.

TOWNSEND: A short hist. of the Eng. Townsends. M.I. Townsend. 1871. 8p.
P4-S25676 — $10.00.

TOWNSEND: English Townsends; Tancred Crusaders; Townsends of Watertown, MA; Townsends of Hebron, CT & Hancock, MA. By M.I. Townsend. 1899. 37p.
P4-S25677 — $10.00.

TOWNSHEND: Townshend fam. of Lynn, in Eng. & New Eng. By C. H. Townshend. 1884. 138p.
P4-S25686 — $17.50.

TOWNSHEND: Fam. (Repr. NEHGR). By C. Townshend. 1875. 15p.
P4-S25687 — $10.00.

TRACY: Tracy Genealogy: Anc & Desc of Thomas Tracy of Lenox, MA. M.L. Griswold. 1900. 230 + 74p.
P4-S25699 — $46.00.

TRACY: Genealogy, being some descendants of Stephen Tracy of Plymouth Colony, 1623; also ancestral sketches & chart. By Sherman W. Tracy. 1936. 242p.
P4-S25704 — $37.00.

TRACY: The anc. of Lt. Thomas Tracy of Norwich, CT. By C.S. Ripley. 1895. 100p.
P4-S25698 — $19.00.

TRACY: Ancestry & desc. of Lt. Thomas Tracy of Norwich, CT, 1660. By E.E. Tracy. 1898. 294p.
P4-S25692 — $44.00.

TRAVERS: Family; From Hunter Family of VA. By Sidney M. Culbertson. 1934. 10p.
P4-S25711 — $10.00.

TRAVERS: Desc. of Henry Travers of Eng. & Newbury, MA. By N. H. Daniels. 1903. 147p.
P4-S25710 — $25.00.

TRAYNE: John Trayne & some desc., especially Charles Jackson Train, USN. By S.T. Hand. 1933. 198p.
P4-S25716 — $29.50.

TRAYWICK: Decandants of Robarde Traywick. By Sidney Carey Arnold, Jr. 2001. 100p.
P4-S25718 — $18.00.

TREADWAY: Edward Treadway & His Descendants (News Letters No. 3-11). 1935-1943 148p.
P4-S25722 — $24.00.

TREADWELL: Down seven gen; A rescript of Treadwell & Platt gen. By A. C. Maltbie. 1883. 36p.
P4-S25723 — $10.00.

TREAT: The Cavalry Saber: Benj. Treat & Joseph Brown Civil War History & Legacy. Bob Treat. 1993. 62p.
P4-S25728 — $12.50.

TREAT: Family in America, 1622 — 1992 (line of Benjamin Franklin Treat). By Bob Treat. 1992. 70p.
P4-S25737 — $14.00.

TREAT: The Benjamin Franklin Treat (of Coopersville, MI), branch of the family tree. By Bob Treat. 1990. 10p.
P4-S25726 — $10.00.

TREAT: The Treat/Trott fam. of Eng. & New Eng. (extr. from the Bassett gen.) 1926. 10p.
P4-S25727 — $10.00.

TREAT: Genealgy of Trott, Tratt & Treat for 15 gen. & 450 years in Eng. & Amer., By J. H. Treat. 1893. 649p.
P4-S25725 — $80.00.

TREDWAY: History of the Tredway family. By W.T. Tredway. 1930. 14 + 400 + 18p.
P4-S25743 — $65.00.

TREE: Some accounts of the Tree fam. & its connections in Eng. & Amer. By J. Leach. 1908. 116p.
P4-S25749 — $18.00.

TREGO: Hist. acct. of the Trego fam. By A. Shertzer. 1884. 144p.
P4-S25755 — $28.50.

TRELOAR: Genealogy; Tree of Treloar. Orson Lee Treloar. 1962 309p.
P4-S25761 — $47.50.

TREMAN: TRUMAN Hist. of the Treman, Tremaine, Truman fam. in Amer., with the rel. fams. of Mack, Dey, Board & Ayers. By Treman & Poole. 1901. 2 vols., 2129p.
P4-S25779 — $260.00.

TRENHAILE: Genealogy & history of the descendants & ancestors of George Trenhaile (1812-78) & Mary Stephens (Stevens) (1814-78) of England. By Fred E. Sawyer. 1944. 65p.
P4-S25791 — $13.00.

TRENHOLME: in Yorkshire, with some notes on the Trenholms family. By Edward C. Trenholme. n.d. 96p.
P4-S25785 — $18.00.

TRICKEY: Gen. of the Trickey fam. By W.D. Trickey. 1930 22p.
P4-S25793 — $10.00.

TRIPP: Gen. record of Augustus Tripp of Lanesboro, MA. By G.A. Tripp. 1914. 11p.
P4-S25798 — $10.00.

TRIPP: Genealogy: desc. of James, son of John Tripp. By G. L. Randall. 1924. 264p.
P4-S25797 — $39.50.

TRIPP: Wills, Deeds & Ways, with Key to Tripp desc. via New England & also NY. Comp. by Valentine Research Bureau. 1932. 196p.
P4-S25803 — $29.50.

TROWBRIDGE: Genealogy: hist. of the Trowbridge fam. in Amer. By F.B. Trowbridge. 1908. 848p.
P4-S25824 — $150.00.

TROWBRIDGE: Family; or, the desc. of Thomas Trowbridge, one of the first settlers of New Haven, CT. By F.W. Chapman. 1872. 461p.
P4-S25818 — $71.00.

TRUBEE: Hist. of the Trubee fam. 1275-1894. By H. T. Carlick. 1894. 151p.
P4-S25830 — $30.00.

TRUEBLOOD: Ancestors of Thomas Trueblood from England to Illinois. K.J. Trueblood. 2006. vi + 455p.
P4-S25831 — $69.00.

TRUMBULL: Contributions to a Trumbull gen., from gleanings in Eng. fields. By J.H. Lea. 1895. 27p.
P4-S25832 — $10.00.

TUCK: Tuck gen. Robert Tuck of Hampton, NH & his desc., 1638-1877. By J. Dow. 1877. 146p.
P4-S25836 — $25.00.

TUCKER: Genealogy of the Tucker family, from various authentic sources. By E. Tucker. 1895. 414p.
P4-S25842 — $65.00.

TUCKER: Genealogy. A record of Gilbert Ruggles & Evelina Christina (Snyder) Tucker, their anc. & desc. By T.S. Morris. 1901. 305p.
P4-S25848 — $48.50.

TUCKER: Anc. & desc. of Jireh Tucker of Royalton, VT. By E. A. Bliefling. 1927. 24p.
P4-S25843 — $10.00.

TUCKER: Gen. & hist. acct. of desc. of Henry Tucker. By G. H. Tucker. 1851. 45p.
P4-S25844 — $10.00.

TUDOR: Genealogy. ed. By W. Tudor. 1896. 17p.
P4-S25849 — $10.00.

TULEY: Fam. Memoirs; Hist., biogr., & gen. story of the Tuleys & the Floyd fam. connections in VA, KY & IN. By W.F. Tuley. 1906. 75p.
P4-S25854 — $15.00.

TULL: Biographical Sketch of the life of John Porter Tull & his descendants, 1796-1942. James Porter Tull. xv + 170p.
P4-S25855 — $28.50.

TULLY: Family of Saybrook, CT. By S.H. Parsons. 1849. 8p.
P4-S25856 — $10.00.

TUNNELL: Genealogy of the Tunnell family of DE. By James M. Tunnell, Jr. 1954. 100p.
P4-S25860 — $19.50.

TUPPER: Thomas Tupper & his desc. By F.W. Tupper. 1945. 71p.
P4-S25866 — $14.00.

TURNER: BANKS; Pioneer families of western NC: descendants of Joseph & Mary Tyrner. By Marshall L. Styles. 2002. 571p.
P4-S25877 — $85.00.

TURNER: Fam. of CT (extr. Bassett gen.) 1926. 9p.
P4-S25876 — $10.00.

TURNER: Genealogy of the desc. of Humphrey Turner, with fam. records. By J. Turner. 1852. 64p.
P35715000 — $12.50.

TURNER: Family Magazine: genealogical, historical & biographical, Vols. 1 & 2, 1916-1917 95p.
P4-S25875 — $18.00.

TURNER: Historical Sketch of the Family of Thomas Turner, Eldest Son of Richard Turner, One of the First Settlers of Whitefield, ME. Eglantine Turner Preble. 1894. 12p.
P4-S25874 — $10.00.

TURNLEY: The Turnleys: a brief record, biographic & narrative, of some Turnleys in the US & Europe. ByP.T. Turnley. 1905. 298p.
P4-S25881 — $46.50.

TUTHILL: Family Meeting of Desc. of John Tuthill of Southold, NY. Tuthill Family. 1867. 60p.
P4-S25882 — $10.00.

TUTTLE: — TUTHILL; One branch of the Eli Tuthill family of Liberty Twp. of Michigan, descendants of the Tuthill family of Southold & Orient, Long Isl., 1640. By Jean L. LaPorte. 1992. 107p.
P4-S25896 — $15.00.

TUTTLE: — TUTHILL Lines in America. By Alva M. Tuttle. 1968. 726p.
P4-S25890 — $95.00.

TUTTLE: Descendants of Wm. & Elizabeth Tuttle, who came from old to New Eng. In 1635, & settled in New Haven in 1639. By G. F. Tuttle. 1883. 814p.
P4-S25884 — $95.00.

TWEED: Sketch of the James Tweed fam. of Wilmington, MA. By B. Walker. 1887. 30p.
P4-S25900 — $10.00.

TWINING: Desc. of Wm. Twining, Sr., of Eastham, MA, with notes of Eng., Welsh & Nova Scotia fams. of the name. By T.J. Twining. 1905. Rev. ed. 264p.
P4-S25905 — $33.50.

TWITCHELL: Gen. of the Twitchell fam. record of the desc. of the Puritan, Benjamin Twitchell, Dorchester, Lancaster, Medfield, & Sherborn, MA, 1632-1927. By R.E. Twitchell. 1929. 768p.
P4-S25911 — $115.00.

TYER: Gen. & biogr. record of one branch of Tyer fam., desc. from John Tyer. By E.T. Savery. 1894. 35p.
P4-S25912 — $10.00.

TYLER: Genealogy; Descendants of Job Tyler of Andover, MA, 1619-1700. By W.I.T. Brigham. 1912. 2 vols., 891p.
P4-S25914 — $124.00.

TYLER: Family; From Hunter Family of VA. Sidney M. Culbertson. 1934. 10p.
P4-S25915 — $10.00.

TYLER: Letters & Times of the Tylers. Lyon G. Tyler. 1884-1897. 3 vols., 633 + 736 + 234p.
P4-S25916 — $120.00.

U

UHLER: Gen., 1735-1901. By G.H. Uhler. 1901. 35p.
P4-S25919 — $10.00.

UNDERHILL: Burying ground: Acct. of a parcel of land . . . at Locust Val., Long Island . . . known as the Underhill Burying Ground. comp. by D.H. & F.J. Underhill. 1924 79p.
P4-S25926 — $16.00.

UNDERHILL: Genealogy, Volumes I-IV. 1932. 4 vols. in 2, 658 + 802p.
P4-S25920 — $185.00.

UNDERWOOD: Families of America. L.M. Underwood. 1913. 809p.
P4-S25941 — $107.50.

UPHAM: Hist. & biogr. sketch of the Upham fam. 5p.
P4-S25948 — $10.00.

UPHAM: The desc. of John Upham of MA, who came from Eng. in 1635 & lived in Weymouth & Malden. By F.K. Upham. 1892. 573p.
P4-S25962 — $72.00.

UPHAM: Gen. & fam. hist. of the Uphams of Castine, ME & Dixon, IL, with gen. notes of Brooks, Kidder & other fam. By F. K. Upham. 1887. 68p.
P4-S25947 — $14.00.

UPHAM: The name & fam. of Upham. comp. by Media Research Bureau. 6p.
P4-S25949 — $10.00.

UPHAM: Notices of John Upham & desc. By A. Upham. 1845. 92p.
P4-S25959 — $18.00.

UPSHAW: Drury Upshaw of VA & some of his desc. By B. Selleck. 17p.
P4-S25961 — $10.00.

UPSHUR: Hitherto above reproach: the life of Dr Thomas Harold Wilson Upshur. Peyton F. Carter III 2003. 106p.
P4-S25960 — $19.00.

UPSON: Family in America. comp. by the Upson Family Assoc. 1940. 624p.
P4-S25968 — $94.00.

UPTON: Memorial; Genealogical rec. of the desc. of John Upton, of N. Reading, MA, with short gen. of the Putnam, Stone & Bruce fam. By J.A. Vinton. 1874. 556p.
P4-S25977 — $69.50.

UPTON: Family Records: being genealogical collections for an Upton fam. hist. By W. H. Upton. 1893. 534p.
P4-S25974 — $83.00.

UPTON: Gleanings from Upton fam. records. By P. E. Hamilton. 1916. 31p.
P4-S25975 — $10.00.

URANN: Urann fam. of New Eng. By C. C. Whittier. 1910. 59p.
P4-S25980 — $12.00.

URBANIK: Complete genealogy: Urbanik lineage from the Polish village of Zdziary in the former Calicia Partition, 1850 to Present. By Bernard S. Sadowski. 2002. 151p.
P4-S25984 — $24.00.

USHER: A brief gen. of the Usher fam. of New Eng. By W. H. Whitmore. 1869. 11p.
P4-S25990 — $10.00.

USHER: Memorial sketch of Roland Greene Usher, 1823-1895, to which is added a gen. of the Usher Fam. in New Eng., 1638-1895, By E.P. Usher. 1895. 160p. P4-S25989 — $25.00.

UTTER: Nicholas Utter of Westerly, RI, & a few of his descendants. By Katharine M.U. Waterman, & G.B. & W.B. Utter. 1941. 176p.
P4-S25995 — $27.50.

UTTERBACK: History & Genealogy of the Utterback family in America, 1622-1937. Wm. I. Utterback. 1937. 470p.
P4-S26001 — $72.00.

V

VAIL: Genealogy of the Vail family, desc. from Jeremiah Vail, at Salem, MA, 1639. By H.H. Vail. 1902. 371p.
P4-S26013 — $58.00.

VAIL: Genealogy of some of the Vail family, descended from Thomas Vail at Salem, MA, 1640, together with collateral lines. By William Penn Vail. 1937. 592p.
P4-S26007 — $89.50.

VAIL: Moses Vail of Huntington, L.I.; his desc. from Joseph Vail, son of Jeremiah of Salem, MA, 1640, with coll. lines. By W.P. Vail. 1947. 524p.
P4-S26019 — $81.50.

VALENTINE: The Valentines in Amer., 1644-1874. By T. W. Valentine. 1874. 254p.
P4-S26025 — $38.00.

VAN ALSTYNE: Lambert Janse Van Alstyne & some of his desc. By L. Van Alstyne. 1897. 142p.
P4-S26037 — $30.00.

VAN BENSCHOTEN: Desc. of Dorr Kellogg Van Benschoten, b. 1853. By Rachel Saul Tefft. 1999. 19p.
P4-S26042 — $10.00.

VAN BENTHUYSEN: Genealogy; Desc. of Paulus Martense Van Benthuysen, who settled in Albany, NY, male & female lines. By A.S. Van Benthuysen. 1953. 592p.
P4-S26043 — $89.50.

VAN BRUNT: Genealogy of the Van Brunt family of NY, 1653-1867. By T.G. Bergen. 1867. 79p.
P4-S26049 — $16.50.

VAN BUNSCHOTEN: Descendants of Theunis Eliasen Van Bunschoten. By Rachel Saul Tefft. 1997. 80p.
P4-S26055 — $16.00.

VAN BUNSCHOTEN: Concerning the Van Bunschoten or Van Benschoten Family in America. W.H. Van Benschoten. 1907. 813 + 117p.
P4-S26056 — $139.50.

VAN BUREN: History of Cornelis Maessen Van Buren, who cam from Holland to the New Netherlands in 1631, & his desc. By H.C. Peckham. 1913. 431 + 84p.
P4-S26061 — $66.00.

VAN CLEEF: History of Jan Van Cleef of New Utrecht, L.I., NY & some desc. By M.E. Poole. 1909. 14p.
P4-S26062 — $10.00.

VAN CULEMBORG: Allied ancestry of the Van Culemborg family of Culemborg, Holland, being the ancestry of Sophia Van Culemborg. By Edwin J. Sellers. 1913. 161p.
P4-S26067 — $25.00.

VAN CUREN: Van Keulen/Van Keuren/Van Kuren/Van Curen: a family history, with corrections & index. By D.G. Van Curen. 1998, 2001. 141 + 26p.
P4-S26073 — $27.00.

VAN DER SLICE: & Allied families. H. Vanderslice & H.N. Monnett. 303p.
P4-S26079 — $46.00.

VAN DER VEER: A Genealogy of this Branch of The Van Der Veer Family in America; A Genealogy of this Branch of The Conover Family in America. John J. Van Der Veer. 1912. 56 + 26 + 32p.
P4-S26080 — $17.00.

VAN DEUSEN: VAN DEURSEN family. By A. H. Van Deusen. 1912. 2 vols in 1, 915p.
P4-S26091 — $129.00.

VAN DEUSEN: Abraham Van Deusen & many of his desc., with biogr. notes. By C.B. Benson. 1901. 182p.
P4-S26085 — $27.50.

VAN DEVENTER: Family. By Christobelle Van Deventer. 1943. 257p.
P4-S26092 — $37.50.

VAN DOORN: Family (Van Dorn, Van Doren, etc.) in Holland & Amer., 1088-1908. By A.Van Doorn Honeyman. 1909. 765p.
P4-S26097 — $109.00.

VAN EVERY: Records of the Van Every family, United Empire Loyalists, NY state, 1653-1784, Canada, 1784-1947. Mary B. Pierson. 1947. 131p.
P4-S26103 — $24.50.

VAN HECKE: & Allied ancestry: anc. of Josina Van Heck, wife of Roeland de Carpentier, grandparents of Maria de Carpentier, wife of Jean Paul Jaquet By E. J. Sellers. 1933. 154p.
P4-S26109 — $25.00.

VAN HEUSEN: Branch of Van Heusen fam. of Albany, NY. 8p.
P4-S26110 — $10.00.

VAN HOOK: Descendants of Arent Isaacszen Van Hoeck, immigrant to New Amsterdam. By Matthew Van Hook. 1998. 260p.
P4-S26115 — $39.50.

VAN HOOSEAR: Genealogy of the Van Hoosear fam., desc. of Rinear Van Hoosear, an officer in the Rev. Army. By D. VanHoosear. 1902. 96p.
P4-S26121 — $20.00.

VAN HORN: Family history. By Francis M. Marvin. 1929. 464p.
P4-S26127 — $69.50.

VAN HORNE: Brief acct. of desc. of Capt. Cornelius VanHorne of White House, Hunterton Co., NJ. By M. Van Horne. 18p.
P4-S26134 — $10.00.

VAN HORNE: An hist. record of VanHorne family in Amer., By A. VanHorne. 1888. 80p.
P4-S26133 — $16.00.

VAN HOUTEN: Desc of Reolof Van Houten of 1638. Herbert S. Ackerman. 1945. 390p
P4-S26135 — $58.95

VAN KLEECK: Family of Pough-keepsie, NY. F. Van Kleeck. 1900. 59p.
P4-S26136 — $12.00.

VAN NORDEN: Family, 1623-1925. By T. Van Norden. 1923. 74p.
P4-S26145 — $15.00.

VAN PATTEN: Genealogical record of Van Patten fam., 1641-1922. 1922. 27p.
P4-S26146 — $10.00.

VAN PELT: Van Pelt Genealogy: NC Origins. Michael P. & Malcolm P. Pelt. 2004. 2 vols in 1, 246 + 281p.
P4-S26152 — $79.00.

VAN PELT: Genealogy of the Van Pelt family. By E. Smith. 1913. 251p.
P4-S26151 — $29.75

VAN SICKLE: Descendants of Fernenandus Van Sycklin, b. about 1635-d. about 1712, retyped and indexed by R.S. Tefft By John Waddell Van Sickel. 1880, 1998 227p.
P4-S26152 — $34.00.

VAN SICKLE: Descendants of Isaac Van Sickle. Rachel Saul Tefft. 1997. 25p.
P4-S26153 — $10.00.

VAN VALKENBURG: Descendants of Francis Van Valkenburg (1810-1895). By Rachel Saul Tefft. 1996. 110p.
P4-S26157 — $18.00.

VAN VALKENBURG: Desc. of Geo. Benj. Van Valkenburg I (1875-1950). By Rachel Saul Tefft. 1999. 42p.
P4-S26158 — $10.00.

VAN VECHTEN: Genealogical rec. of the Van Vechtens from 1638-1896. By P. Van Vechten, Jr. 1896. 117p.
P4-S26163 — $22.00.

VAN VOORHEES: Gen of the Van Voorhees family in America, or the Desc of Steven Coerte Van Voorhees. By Elias W. Van Voorhis. 1888. 380p.
P4-S26169 — $59.50.

VAN VOORHEES: Condensed Gen. of Van Voorhees family; Supplement to Van Voorhees (1888). E.W. Van Voorhis 1932. 31p.
P4-S26170 — $10.00.

VAN VOORHIS: Notes on the Ancestry of Maj. Wm. Roe Van Voorhis of Fishkill, Duchess Co., NY. By E.W. Van Voorhis. 1881. 239 + 22p.
P4-S26175 — $29.75

VAN WAGENEN: Gen. of Van Wagenen fam. 1650-1884. By G. Van Wagenen. 1884. 83p.
P4-S26181 — $17.50.

VAN WINKLE: Genealogy of the Van Winkle family: account of its origin & settlement in this county with data, 1630-1913. Daniel Van Winkle. 1913. 433p.
P4-S26187 — $66.50.

VAN WYCK: Desc of Cronelius Barentse Van Wyck & Anna Polhemus. A. Van Wyck. 1912. 508 + 160p.
P4-S26188 — $100.00.

VANDERLIP: Vanderlip, Van Derlip, Vander Lippe family in America, also including some account of the Von der Liipe fam. of Lippe, Germany By C.E. Booth. 1914. 188p.
P4-S26193 — $29.00.

VARNUM: The Varnums of Dracut, MA; Hist. of Geo. Varnum, his son Samuel & grandsons Thomas, John & Joseph, & their desc. By J.M. Varnum. 1907. 314p.
P4-S26205 — $49.50.

VASSALL: Notes on Colonel Henry Vassall (1721-1769), His wife Penelope Royall, His house at Cambridge & his slaves Tony & Darby. Samuel Francis Batchelder. 1917. 85 + 18p.
P4-S26206 — $17.00.

VASSALL: Vassalls of New Eng. & their immediate desc. By E.D. Harris. 1862. 26p.
P4-S26207 — $10.00.

VAUGHAN: The Vaughans in Wales & America: A search for the Welsh anc. of William Vaughan (1750-1840). James E. Vaughan. Rev. ed., 1992. 270p.
P4-S26229 — $43.00.

VAUGHAN: Reminiscences & gen. record of the Vaughan fam. of NH, by G. Hodgdon, Suppl. By an acct. of the Vaughans of South Wales. By T.W. Hancock. 1918. 179p.
P4-S26223 — $27.00.

VAUGHAN: Reminiscences of the Vaughan fam., & more particularly of Benjamin Vaughan, Ll.D., with a few additions, a gen. & notes. By J.H. Sheppard. 1865. 40p.
P4-S26218 — $10.00.

VAUGHAN: Abraham Vaughan of KY & desc., a fam. tree. By N.V. Ragland. 55p.
P4-S26219 — $10.00.

VAUGHAN: Pioneers: William & Fereby Vaughan of Russell Co., VA & their descendants. By Lewis E. Vaughan. 1979. 359p.
P4-S26217 — $42.00.

VAWTER: The Vawter Family in America, with Allied Families of Branham, Crawford, Wise, Lewis, Stribling, Glover & Moncrief. Grace Vawter Bicknell. 1905. 442 + 18p.
P4-S26230 — $69.00.

VEACH: Amer. lin. Veach & Stover fam. By R.S. Veach. 1913. 134p.
P4-S26235 — $26.50.

VEBLEN: Gen.; an acct. of the Norwegian anc. of the Veblen fam. in Amer., which was founded by Thomas A. Veblen & his wife Kari Bunde. By A. Veblen. 1925. 156p.
P4-S26241 — $23.00.

VEEDER: Genealogical record of the Veeder family. V. A. Leonard 1937. 351p.
P4-S26247 — $55.00.

VENABLE: Venables of VA. By E. M. Venable. 1925. 228p.
P4-S26253 — $40.00.

Ver PLANCK: History of Abraham Isaacse Ver Planck & his male descendants in America. By Wm. E. Ver Planck. 1892. 304p.
P4-S26259 — $47.00.

VERDERY: The Verderys of Georgia, 1794-1942 a.d., a genealogical history of the American descendants of Jean Jaques de Verdery By Emily Prather. 1942. 236p.
P4-S26265 — $35.00.

VERNON: Family records: descendants of Robert Vernon (1682). By John V. & Laureen E. Winterton. 1995. 125p.
P4-S26271 — $19.50.

VESTAL: Gen. of Vestal fam. 1893. 5p.
P4-S26273 — $10.00.

VIALL: John Viall of Swansey, MA & some of his desc. By D. Jillson. 37p.
P4-S26279 — $10.00.

VIETS: Gen. of the Viets fam. with biogr. sketches. Dr. John Viets of Simsbury, CT, 1710, & his desc. By F.H. Viets. 1902, 1990. 228p.
P4-S26283 — $34.50.

VILAS: Gen. of desc. of Peter Vilas. By C. Vilas. 1875. 221p
P4-S26289 — $36.00.

VINCENT: Fam. of Vincent, hist., gen., & biogr. notices. B. Vincent. 158p.
P4-S26295 — $30.00.

VINTON: Memorial, comprising a genealogy of the desc. of John Vinton of Lynn, 1648. By J.A. Vinton. 1858. 554p.
P4-S26304 — $68.00.

VISSCHER: Family. 6p.
P4-S26305 — $10.00.

VOGT: & Allied families, gen. & bio. [one line of descent from August Jacob Wilhelm "William" Vogt of WV]. 1926. 57p.
P4-S26306 — $11.00.

VORCE: Genealogical & historical record of the Vorce family in America, with notes of allied families. By C.M. Vorce. 1901. 110p.
P4-S26310 — $22.00.

VOSE: Robert Vose & his descendants. By Eleanor F. Vose. 1932. 725p.
P4-S26316 — $99.50.

VOUGHT: Vought fam., desc. of Simon & Christina Vought. By W. Ver Planck. 1907. 27p.
P4-S26318 — $10.00.

VREELAND: Hist. & gen. of the Vreeland fam. N.G. Vreeland. 1909. 323p.
P4-S26322 — $48.50.

VROOMAN: Family in Amer: desc. of Hendrick Meese Vrooman, who came from Holland to Amer. in 1664. By G.V. Wickersham & E.B. Comstock. 1949. 341p.
P4-S26328 — $53.00.

W

WADE: Family, Monongalia Co., VA, now WV. By F. Brand. 1927. 486p.
P4-S26334 — $76.00.

WADE: Genealogy; Account of the origin of the name, pedigrees of famous Endglishmen of the name; a genealogy of the family in MA & NJ. By S.C. Wade. 1900. 384p.
P4-S26340 — $59.50.

WADE: Index to the 1900 Wade gen. 49p.
P4-S26335 — $10.00.

WADHAM: Genealogy, preceded by a sketch of the Wadham fam. in Eng. By H.W.W. Stevens. 1913. 652p.
P4-S26346 — $97.50.

WADSWORTH: Abiah Wadsworth & his family. By C. Douglas Wadsworth. 1979. 502p.
P4-S26358 — $75.00.

WADSWORTH: 250 years of the Wadsworth fam. in Amer., an acct. of the reunion at Duxbury, MA & a gen. register. H.A. Wadsworth. 1883. 257p.
P4-S26352 — $34.50.

WADSWORTH: Moses Wadsworth & Hannah Stevens, their Ancestral Lines & Their Descendants. Mary Wadsworth Jones. 1941. 202 + 10p.
P4-S26353 — $32.00.

WAGAMAN: reunion, with gen. notes. By P. Wagaman. 1941. 19p.
P4-S26360 — $10.00.

WAGENSELLER: Hist. of the Wagenseller fam. in Amer. with kindred branches. By G. W. Wagenseller. 1898. 225p.
P4-S26364 — $34.00.

WAGGONER: Charles C. Waggoner, Auglaize Co., Ohio, 1805-1879 & allied families of Layton, Bitler, Heidrick, Brakney, Hague, Bayliff. By Charles & Norma Moffat. 1989. 86p.
P4-S26370 — $18.00.

WAGLE: John Wagle gen. By L. A. Duermyer. 1947. 50p.
P4-S26371 — $10.00.

WAINWRIGHT: Those who came before us: Wainwrights, Mayhews, Stuyvesants & others. By J.Mayhew Wainwright. 203p.
P4-S26376 — $32.00.

WAIT: A gen. sketch of a branch of the Wait or Waite fam. of Amer. By D.B. Waite. 1893. 28p.
P4-S26380 — $10.00.

WAIT: Records of the desc. of Thomas Wait of Portsmouth, RI. By J. C. Wait. 1904. 58p.
P35796000 — $12.50.

WAITE: Family of Boston, MA. By H.E. Waite. 1877. 4p.
P4-S26392 — $10.00.

WAITE: Family of Malden, MA. By D. P. Corey. 1878. 9p.
P4-S26393 — $10.00.

WAITE: Family of Malden, MA. By Deloraine P. Corey. 1913. 129p.
P4-S26391 — $19.50.

WAKEFIELD: Memorial: an hist., gen., & biogr. register of the name & fam. By H. Wakefield. 1897. 367p.
P4-S26394 — $45.00.

WAKEMAN: Genealogy, 1630-1899. Hist. of the desc. of Sam'l Wakeman of Hartford, CT & of John Wakeman, treas. of New Haven col. By R. Wakeman. 1900. 438p.
P4-S26400 — $68.00.

WALCOTT: History & genealoy of the American family of Walcott & notes of Eng. Walcotts. By A. Walcott. 1925. 288p.
P4-S26406 — $43.00.

WALCOTT: Wm. Walcott of Salem Village, MA & some of his desc. By H.S. Tapley. 16p.
P4-S26407 — $10.00.

WALDO: Descendants of Cornelius Waldo, with related lines & ancestry for 1-25 years, 970-1995 [a continuation of the 1883 & 1943 Waldo genealogies]. By George S. Waldo. 1996. 339p.
P4-S26427 — $49.00.

WALDO: Genealogy of the Waldo fam.; a records of the desc. of Cornelius Waldo of Ipswich, MA, from 1647 to 1900. By W. Lincoln. 1902 2 vols., 542 + 578p.
P4-S26415 — $149.00.

WALDO: Continuation of the Waldo Genealogy, 1900-1943. By C.S. Waldo. 1943. 295p.
P4-S26421 — $46.50.

WALDO: Genealogy & biogr. of the Waldos of Amer., from 1650-1883. By J.D. Hall, Jr. 1883. 145p.
P4-S26433 — $24.00.

WALDRON: Gen. of Fredk. Waldron from settlement of New Amsterdam thru the Waldrons, Whitneys & Rigges. By F.H. Waldron. 1909. 32p.
P4-S26438 — $10.00.

WALDRON: John Waldron of Dover, NH & his desc. A.H. Quint. 1879. 10p.
P4-S26439 — $10.00.

WALES: One line from Nathaniel of Dorchester, MA, 1636 (extr. "Gen. of Fourteen fams. of Early New Eng."). By E. Thayer. 1835. 9p.
P4-S26440 — $10.00.

WALES: Gen. of desc. of Timothy Wales of CT. W.H. Whitmore. 1875. 56p.
P4-S26436 — $12.00.

WALKER: Lewis Walker of Chester Valley & his desc., 1686-1896. By P.W. Streets. 1896. 446p.
P4-S26451 — $69.50.

WALKER: Walkers of Yesterday From Deputy Governor Richard Walker of Lynn, Reading, (Wakefield) & Boston to Captain Solomon Walker of Woolwich, ME. Ernest George Walker. 1937. xiii +266p.
P4-S26452 — $26.00.

WALKER: Memorial; Walkers of Old Plymouth Col. embracing gen. sketches of James of Taunton, Philip of Rehoboth, etc. & their descendants By J. Walker. 1861. 479p.
P4-S26454 — $75.00.

WALKER: Gen. of the desc. of John Walker of Wigton, Scotland, with records of a few allied fam. By E. S. White. 1902. 752p.
P4-S26445 — $91.00.

WALLACE: — BRUCE & closely related families, history & genealogy. By James Wallace. 1930. 389p.
P4-S26472 — $59.50.

WALLACE: Genealogy of Wallace fam. of PA. By J. Wallace. 1902. 60p.
P4-S26463 — $12.50.

WALLACE: The Book of Wallace. Charles Rogers. 1889. 2 vols, 322 + 362p.
P4-S26461 — $103.00.

WALLACE: Genealogical Data Pertaining to Descendants of Peter Wallace & Elizabeth Woods, His Wife. By G. S. Wallace. 1938. 426 + 22p.
P4-S26462 — $67.00.

WALLBRIDGE: Desc. of Henry Wallbridge who married Anna Amos, Dec. 25 1688, at Preston, CT. By W. G. Wallbridge. 1898. 369p.
P4-S26478 — $58.00.

WALLEY: Fam. in Eng. & Amer., 1616-1877. By E. Salisbury. 1885. 11p.
P4-S26480 — $10.00.

WALLIN: The Michigan Wallins: a history, from Stratford-on-Avon, 1791, to Wallinwood-on-the- Grand, 1933. By Van A. Wallin. 1933. 129p.
P4-S26484 — $22.00.

WALSH: The name & the arms. By Frankford. 1910. 9p.
P4-S26485 — $10.00.

WALSH: Record of Hugh Walsh's fam. By W. Walsh. 1903. 21p.
P4-S26486 — $10.00.

WALTHALL: Walthall fam. By E. T. Walthall. 1906. 33p.
P4-S264488 — $10.00.

WALTMAN: The house of Waltman & its allied fam. L.S. LaMance. 1928. 278p.
P4-S26490 — $40.00.

WALTON: Walton fam. By J. C. Martindale. 1911. 12p.
P4-S26497 — $10.00.

WALTON: Fam. records, 1598-1898, with inter-marriages with Oakes & Satons, & the Proctor fam., By J.P. Walton. 1898. 88p.
P4-S26496 — $18.00.

WALTZ: Fam. hist. & gen. record, desc. of Fred. Waltz. By L. Waltz. 1884. 128p.
P4-S26502 — $26.00.

WALWORTH: Walworths of Amer., five chapters of fam. hist., with additional chapters of gen. By C.A. Walworth. 1897. 202p.
P4-S26508 — $40.00.

WAMPLER: Family record: John Wampler & Magdalena Garber of MD & VA. By Floyd R. & Kathryn G. Mason. 1997. 384p.
P4-S26514 — $54.00.

WANNAMAKER: The Wannamaker, Salley, Mackay & Bellinger Families. J. Skottowe Wannamaker. 1937. 485p.
P4-S26515 — $73.00.

WANTON: Hist. of the Wanton fam. of Newport, RI. J. R. Bartlett. 1878. 152p.
P4-S26517 — $29.00.

WANZER: History of the Wanzer Family in America, from the Settlement in New Amsterdam, NY, 1642-1920. By William David Wanzer. 1920. 121 + 32p.
P4-S26523 — $25.00.

WARBASSE: History: a study in the sociology of heredity in two parts. By James P. Warbasse. 1954. 226p.
P4-S26529 — $34.00.

WARBURTON: Gen. of John Warburton & desc. By Pennington & Warburton. 1913. 21p.
P4-S26530 — $10.00.

WARD: Desc. of John Ward, son of Wm. Ward of Sudbury, MA. Extr. from Hist. of Newton. 11p.
P4-S26554 — $10.00.

WARD: Andrew Warde & his desc., 1597-1910, being a comp. of facts relating to one of the oldest New Eng. fam., & embracing many fam. of other names. By G.K. Ward. 1910-1911 Rev. ed. 626p.
P4-S26535 — $76.00.

WARD: The life of Dr Isaac Blowers Ward (1800-1843) & his wife Ann Vines (1803-1852), together with some accounts of their near relatives . . . By Harry Parker Ward. 1900. 251p.
P4-S26541 — $38.00.

WARD: William Ward genealogy: history of the desc. of Wm. Ward of Sudbury, MA, 1638-1925. By C. N. Martyn. 1925. 767p.
P4-S26562 — $94.50.

WARD: Family; Descendants of Wm. Ward who settled in Sudbury, MA in 1639, with an appendix of the names of families that have intermarried with them. By A. Ward. 1851. 265p.
P4-S26559 — $35.00.

WARD: Thomas Ward & his descendants. By Frank A. Ward. 1963. 160p., typescript.
P4-S26550 — $25.00.

WARD: Skeletons in Our Closet: Pilgrims, Witches & a Revolutionary War General, Artemas Ward Genealogy. Robert E. La Flamme & Richard Shyllberg. 1997. 158p.
P4-S26542 — $24.00.

WARDELL: Brief history of Wardell family, 1734-1910. By G.P. Smith. 1910. Rev. ed. 104p.
P4-S26568 — $20.00.

WARDEN: Ancestors, kin & desc. of John Warden & Narcissa Davie Warden, with rec. of some other branches of Warden fam. in Amer. By W. A. Warden. 1901. 256p.
P4-S26574 — $38.00.

WARDWELL: Sketches of anc. of Solomon Wardwell, with desc. of sons Ezra & Amos Wardwell. By E. Stay. 1905. 22p.
P4-S26575 — $10.00.

WARE: Genealogy: Robert Ware of Dedham, MA & his lineal desc. By E. Ware. 1901. 335p.
P4-S26577 — $53.50.

WARE: Gen. of the Ware fam., desc. of Robert Ware of Dedham. By W.B. Trask. 1852. 8p.
P4-S26578 — $10.00.

WARFIELD: Warfield fam. of MD. By J.D. Warfield. 1898. 81p.
P4-S26583 — $16.50.

WARNE: Genealogy of the Warne family in Amer., principally the desc. of Thomas Warne, 1652-1722, a proprietor of East N.J. G. Lobaw. 1911. 701p.
P4-S26589 — $99.00.

WARNER: Sir Thomas Warner, pioneer of the West Indies: a chronicle of his family. By A. Warner. 1933 174p.
P4-S26598 — $26.00.

WARNER: Descendants of Andrew Warner. By L.C. Warner & J.G. Nichols. 1919. 804p.
P4-S26592 — $115.00.

WARNER: The posterity of Wm. Warner, one of the early settlers of Ipswich, MA. By E. Warner. 1866. 11p.
P4-S26593 — $10.00.

WARREN: JACKSON & allied fams., being the anc. of Jesse Warren & Betsey Jackson. B.W. Davis. 1903. 207p.
P4-S26622 — $32.50.

WARREN: CLARKE gen., a rec. of persons rel. within the 6th degree to the children of Samuel Dennis Warren & Susan Clarke. By C.W. Huntington. 1894. 238p.
P4-S26631 — $36.00.

WARREN: History & gen. of the Warren family in Normandy, Gt. Britain & Ireland, France, Holland, US, etc., By T. Warren. 1902. 494p.
P4-S26616 — $77.50.

WARREN: Genealogy of the desc. of James Warren, who was in Kittery, ME, 1652-1656. O. Warren. 1902. 138p.
P4-S26604 — $20.50.

WARREN: Some desc. of Arthur Warren of Weymouth, Mass. Bay col. By W. Foster. 1911. 209p.
P4-S26625 — $28.50.

WARREN: Gen. of the Warren fam., from Richard, who came in the Mayflower in 1620-1872. 1874. 7p.
P4-S26626 — $10.00.

WARREN: Richard Warren of the Mayflower, & some desc. (Repr. NEHGR). W. A. Roebling. 1901. 18p.
P4-S26627 — $10.00.

WARRINER: Fam. of New Eng. Origin, hist. & gen. of Wm. Warriner of Springfield, MA & his desc. 1638-1898. By E. Warriner. 1899. 287p.
P4-S26640 — $43.00.

WARRINER: Colonial [New England] & Euro. anc. of Julia Adelaide Warriner (1853-1883). By Richard L. Dickson. 1991. 123p.
P4-S26637 — $19.50.

WARTENBE: Genealogy: ancestors & descendants of William & Catherine (White) Wartenbe of NJ, VA & OH. By Mary Esther Ford. 1987. 210p.
P4-S26646 — $32.00.

For hardcover versions, see the order form on page v. To order, call 1-888-296-3447.

WASHBURN: Genealogical notes of the Washburn fam. with a brief sketch of the fam. in Eng., containing a full rec. of the desc. of Israel Washburn of Raynham. J.C. Washburn. 1898. 104p.
P4-S26655 — $18.00.

WASHBURN: Ebenezer Washburn; his anc. & desc., with some connected fam. A fam. story of 700 years. By G. T. Washburn. 1913. 224p.
P4-S26652 — $33.50.

WASHBURN: Some notes on the Evesham branch of the Washburne fam. By E. Barnard. 1914. 60p.
P4-S26658 — $12.00.

WASHBURN: Washburn Family Foundations in Normandy, England & America. M.T.R. Washburn. 1953. 189 + 45p.
P4-S26656 — $35.00.

WASHBURN: The Richard Washburn family genealogy; a family history of 200 years, with some connected families. By Ada C. Haight, 1937. 1271p.
P4-S26667 — $139.50.

WASHINGTON: Experimental pedigree of the desc. of Lawrence Washington, 1635-1677, of VA (Repr. from his VA gen.) By H. E. Hayden. 1891. 6p.
P4-S26674 — $10.00.

WASHINGTON: Pedigree & hist. of the Washington fam., derived from Odin, founder of Scandinavia, B.C. 70, down to Gen. Geo. Washington. By A. Welles. 1879. 420p.
P4-S26673 — $66.00.

WASHINGTON: An examination of the Eng. anc. of Geo. Washington; the evidence to connect him with the Washingtons of Sulgrave & Brington, (Repr. NEHGR). H.F. Waters. 1889. 53p.
P4-S26675 — $10.50.

WATERHOUSE: The families of Jacob Waterhouse, 1605-1676. By Jerry E. Waterous. 1993. 228p.
P4-S26679 — $34.00.

WATERHOUSE: Ancestry of Joseph Waterhouse, 1754-1837, of Standish, ME. By W.G. Davis. 1949. 144p.
P4-S26679 — $21.00.

WATERHOUSE: Waterhouse & other fam. of Stroudwater Village (near Portland) ME. By L. B. Chapman. 1906. 31p.
P4-S26680 — $10.00.

WATERMAN: Descendants of Robert Waterman of Marshfield, MA, through seven generations, vol I. By Donald Lines Jacobus. 1939. 818p.
P4-S26703 — $109.00.

WATERMAN: Descendants of Robert Waterman of Marshfield, MA, from 7th generation, vol II. By Waterman & Jacobus. 1942. 784p.
P4-S26697 — $88.50.

WATERMAN: Desc. of Richard Waterman of Providence, RI, with records of many other family groups of the Waterman name, vol III. By Jacobus & Waterman. 1954. 808p.
P4-S26691 — $108.00.

WATERS: A gen. hist. of the Waters & kindred fam. P. B. Waters. 1902. 189p.
P4-S26709 — $28.00.

WATERS: Anc. of Waters fam. of Marletta, OH. By W. Waters. 1882. 32p.
P4-S26710 — $10.00.

WATERS: Gen. hist. of Abel Waters of Sutton, MA. By M. & E. Waters. 15p.
P4-S26711 — $10.00.

WATKINS: Watkins fam. of NC, desc. of Levin Watkins (to AL & MS) By W. B. Watkins. 85p.
P4-S26715 — $17.50.

WATKINS: Catalogue of Thomas Watkins of Chickahomony in VA. By F. N. Watkins. 1899. 50p.
P4-S26716 — $10.00.

WATSON: KITTREDGE, Broadwell & allied families, gen. & biogr. comp. for Mrs T.J Watson. 1961. 89p.
P4-S26745 — $18.00.

WATSON: John Watson of Hartford, CT & his desc.; a gen. By T. Watson. 1865. 47p.
P4-S26722 — $10.00.

WATSON: "Of sceptred race" (Watson gen.). A. Watson. 1910. 389p.
P4-S26721 — $60.00.

WATSON: Gen. (Repr. NEHGR) By W.R. Deane. 1864. 5p.
P4-S26723 — $10.00.

WATSON: History & genealogy of the Watson family, descendants of Matthew Watson who came to America in 1718. J.D. & A.A. Bemis. 1894. 163p.
P4-S26733 — $27.00.

WATSON: Exploring life: the autobiography of Thomas A. Watson. Thomas A. Watson. 1926. 315p.
P4-S26727 — $39.00.

WATTLES: Autobiography of Gurdon Wallace Wattles, with genealogy. By G.W. Wattles. 1922. 268p.
P4-S26751 — $42.00.

WATTS: Watts (Watt) in NY & Scotland, also Watter, Wattys, Wathes, etc. in Eng., By A. Welles. 1898. 48p.
P4-S26747 — $10.00.

WAY: Geo. Way & his desc. 1628-1821. By C. Way. 1887. 23p.
P4-S26755 — $10.00.

WAYNE: Eng. anc. of the Wayne fam. of PA. By E. J. Sellers. 1927. 56p.
P4-S26754 — $12.00.

WEARN: The Descendants of Richard & Henrietta Wearn. Cornelia Wearn Henderson. 76p.
P4-S26762 — $14.50.

WEATHERBY: Genealogy, 1682-1936. By George W. Weatherby, Jr. 1936. 110p.
P4-S26763 — $19.50.

WEATHERS: Preserving the Past: Volume II. Weathers/Wethers/ Withers Family and Allied Families Hunter, Clark, McClendon & Ball. Bertha Irene Keller. 1990. 516p.
P4-S26764 — $77.50.

WEAVER: Record of Wm. Weaver & his desc. of Illinois. By R. I. Weaver. 1925. 106p.
P4-S26775 — $20.00.

WEAVER: Fam. of New York City. By I.J. Greenwood. 1893. 13p.
P4-S26770 — $10.00.

WEAVER: The name & fam. of Weaver. comp. by the Media Research Bureau. 16p.
P4-S26771 — $10.00.

WEAVER: Family marriages. By W. M. Clemens. 1916. 32p.
P4-S26772 — $10.00.

WEAVER: History & genealogy of a branch of the Weaver family. By Lucius E. Weaver. 1928. 743p.
P4-S26769 — $105.00.

WEBB: Anc. & desc. of Nancy Allyn (Foote) Webb, Rev. Edw. Webb, & Joseph Wilkins Cooch. By M.E.W. Cooch. 1919. 157p.
P4-S26781 — $25.00.

WEBB: Anthony Webb of Eng. & some of his desc. (in gen. mem.) By R. Waters. 1878. 20p.
P4-S26782 — $10.00.

WEBB: Gen. notes of the Webb fam. (Repr. Essex Inst. Hist. Coll.) By E. S. Webb. 1880. 24p.
P4-S26783 — $10.00.

WEBB: Our Webb kin of Dixie: a family history, with supplement A. By Wm. James Webb, et al. 1940. 205P.
P4-S26787 — $32.00.

WEBBER: Richard Webber fam., gen. from the first settlement in Amer. By L. Washburn. 1909. 25p.
P4-S26788 — $10.00.

WEBBER: Desc. of Andrew Webber 1763-1845. By L. Webber. 1897. 55p.
P4-S26789 — $11.00.

WEBBER: Gen. sketch of desc. of several branches of the Webber fam., who came to NY & New Eng. in the early part of the 17th cent. By A. Button. 1878. 42p.
P4-S26790 — $10.00.

WEBSTER: History & genealogy of the Gov. John Webster fam. of CT. By W.H. & M.R. Webster. 1915. 2 vols., 833 + 827p.
P4-S26805 — $209.00.

WEBSTER: Gen. of some desc. of John Webster of Ipswich, MA, in 1635. By Lapham & Webster. 1884. 14p.
P4-S26794 — $10.00.

WEBSTER: Genealogy of one branch of the Webster family, from Thomas Webster of Ormesby, Co. Norfolk, Eng. By P. Webster. 1894. 45p.
P4-S26795 — $10.00.

WEBSTER: Some of the descendants of John Webster of Ipswich, MA, 1634. By J. C. Webster. 1912. 92p.
P4-S26808 — $18.50.

WEBSTER: Henry and Charity Webster Family Record of VA. Floyd R. & Kathryn G. Mason. 2004. 89p.
P4-S26796 — $13.50.

WEEKES: Genealogy of the family of Geo. Weekes, of Dorchester, MA, 1635-1650, with some info. in regard to other fam. of the name By Robert D. Weeks. 1885. 468p.
P4-S26814 — $59.00.

WEEKES: Genealogy of the family of George Weekes, of Dorchester, MA. [part II]. Robt. D. Weekes. 1892. 174 + 27p.
P4-S26815 — $30.50.

WEEKS: — WICKES Families: John Wickes & Wm. Weeks & some of their American descendants. By Daniel J. Weeks. 1998. 135p.
P4-S26826 — $21.00.

WEEKS: Leonard Weeks of Greenland, NH & desc., 1639-1888, with early records of fam. connected. By J. Chapman. 1889. 202p.
P4-S26820 — $25.50.

WEIKERT: History of the Weikert family from 1735-1930. By E. L. Weikert, Jr. 1930. 357p.
P4-S26832 — $57.00.

WEIMER: Biographical sketches & family records of the Gabriel Weimer & David Weimer families. By L.C. Potts. 1936. 270p.
P4-S26838 — $42.50.

WEIS: The anc. & desc. of Daniel Weis, "Gentleman — at — Arms," 1629. By F.L. Weis. 1927. 45p.
P4-S26840 — $10.00.

WEISER: Family. By H. M. Richards. 1924. 115p.
P4-S26844 — $21.00.

WEITZEL: Memorial hist. & gen. record of desc. of Paul Weitzel of Lancaster, PA, 1740, By H. Hayden. 1883. 81p.
P4-S26850 — $17.00.

WELCH: An Overland Trip from Iowa to California in 1854. A Narrative Memoir. John Allen Welch. 1920. 131p
P4-S26857 — $21.00.

WELCH: & allied families. By G. C. Weaver. 1932. 312p.
P4-S26862 — $48.00.

WELCH: Philip Welch of Ipswich, MA & his desc. By A.M. Welch. 1947. 354p.
P4-S26856 — $56.00.

WELD: Hist. of the Weld fam., from 1632-1878. By C. W. Fowler. 1879. 64p.
P4-S26868 — $13.50.

WELLES: 1989 Index only; Comp. by Welles Fam. Reseach Assoc., 1989. 1989. 26p.
P4-S26881 — $10.00.

WELLES: Hist. of the Welles fam. in Eng. & Normandy, with the derivation from their progenitors of some desc. in the US. By Albert Welles. Incl. 1989 index. 1876. 317 + 26p.
P4-S26880 — $49.50.

WELLES: Diary of Gideon Welles, Secretary of the Navy under Lincoln & Johnson, Vol. I, 1861-1864. 549p.
P4-S26871 — $62.50.

WELLES: Diary of Gideon Welles, Secretary of the Navy under Lincoln & Johnson, Vol. II, 1864-1866. 653p.
P4-S26874 — $72.50.

WELLES: Diary of Gideon Welles, Secretary of the Navy under Lincoln & Johnson, Vol. III, 1867-1869. 671p.
P4-S26877 — $75.00.

WELLES: Hist of the Welles fam.in England, with their derivation in this country from Gov. Thomas Welles of CT. By Welles & Clements. 1874. 127p.
P4-S26886 — $21.50.

WELLINGTON: A few facts concerning Roger Wellington & some of his desc. By A. W. Griswold. 1892. 26p.
P4-S26890 — $10.00.

WELLMAN: Gen. & hist. of the Wellmans of New Eng. By J. Wellman. 1867. 66p.
P4-S26898 — $13.00.

WELLMAN: Descendants of Thomas Wellman of Lynn, MA. By J. W. Wellman. 1918. 596p.
P4-S26892 — $89.00.

WELLS: Gen. of Wells fam. of Wells, ME. By C. Wells 1874. 81p.
P4-S26928 — $16.50.

WELLS: "Inherited genes," including families: Wells. Price, Sharpe, Alexander, McKnight, Wallace, Holy, Costner et al. By Bobbie Wells Moffat. 2000. 367p.
P4-S26904 — $52.00.

WELLS: Patriot ancestors: John Wells, John Lattimore, Davis Stockton, Thomas Stockton, Michael Peeler, William Hill Sr [& Jr], John Hoyl, Hanchrist Carlock. By Bobbie W. Moffat. 2000. 384p.
P4-S26934 — $48.00.

WELLS: Family. By D.W. Norris & H.A. Feldmann. 1942. 437p.
P4-S26946 — $66.50.

WELLS: Anc. & desc. of Col. Daniel Wells (1760-1815) of Greenfield, MA. By S.C. Wells. 65p.
P4-S26916 — $13.00.

WELLS: Wm. Wells of Southold & his desc., 1638-1878. C.W. Hayes. 1878. 300p.
P4-S26958 — $49.50.

WELLS: William Wells & descendants, 1755-1909. By F. Wells. 1909. 117p.
P4-S26952 — $21.50.

WELLS: Gen. of the Wells fam. & fams. related. By G.W. Wells-Cushing. 1903. 205p.
P4-S26922 — $32.00.

WELLS: Thomas & Abigail Wells, Ipswich, MA & some of their desc. By A. Caldwell. 8p.
P4-S26905 — $10.00.

WELLS: A southern Wells family. By Marteal Wells. 1997. 219p.
P4-S26910 — $31.00.

WELLS: The big Wells family [of KY]. By Joseph William Wells. 1957. 95p.
P4-S26940 — $17.50.

WENDELL: Fam. of Holland & Amer. By E. Salisbury. 1885. 15p.
P4-S26960 — $10.00.

WENDELL: Direct anc. of the late Jacob Wendell of Portsmouth, NH, with sketch of New Netherland settlement 1614-1664. J. Stanwood. 1882. 49p.
P4-S26961 — $10.00.

WENSEL: Descendants of John Wensel (1821-1896). By Rachel Saul Tefft. 1996. 83p.
P4-S26964 — $16.50.

WENTWORTH: Genealogy, Eng. & Amer., in 3 vols. By J. Wentworth. 1878. 3 vols., 711 + 728 + 803p.
P4-S26988 — $250.00.

WENTZ: Rec. of desc. of Johann Jost Wentz. By R. Wentz. 1884. 89p.
P4-S26994 — $18.00.

WESLEY: Memorials of the Wesley family, including biographical & historical sketches of all the members of the family for 250 years By George J. Stevenson. 1896. 562p.
P4-S27000 — $87.00.

WESSELS: Genealogical Notes Relating to Warner Wessels & his Descendants. J.G.B Bullock & Arthur Adams. 1913. 15p.
P4-S27002 — $10.00.

WEST: Family; From Hunter Family of VA. Sidney M. Culbertson. 1934. 10p.
P4-S27007 — $10.00.

WEST: Family of Boston & Taunton, MA & allied fam. (Repr. NEHGR). By G.W. Jackson. 6p.
P4-S27008 — $10.00.

WEST: Family register; important lines traced, 1326-1928. By L.B. Stone. 1928. 493p.
P4-S27006 — $77.00.

WESTCOTT: History & genealogy of the anc. & desc. of Stukely Westcott, one of thirteen orig. props. of Providence Plantation & Col of RI. By R.L. Whitman. 1932. 435p.
P4-S27012 — $66.50.

WESTCOTT: Book of Appendices to Volume I. By Roscoe L. Whitman. 457p.
P4-S27018 — $69.00.

WESTERVELT: Gen. of Westervelt fam. Westervelt & Dickinson. 1905. 175p.
P4-S27024 — $25.00.

WESTON: In memoriam: my father & mother, Hon. Gershom Bradford Weston & Deborah Brownell Weston of Duxbury, MA. By Edmund Brownell Weston. 1916. 93p.
P4-S27030 — $18.00.

WESTON: Desc. of Edm. Weston of Duxbury, MA, for five gen. (Repr. NEHGR). By T. Weston, Jr. 1887. 23p.
P4-S27031 — $10.00.

WESTON: The Revolution: Life of Hannah Weston, with a brief history of her ancestry. George W. Drisko. 1903. 138p.
P4-S27036 — $18.00.

WESTON: Thomas Weston & his fam. (Repr. NEHGR). By C. Johnston. 1896. 5p.
P4-S27034 — $10.00.

WETMORE: Family of America & its Collateral Branches. By James C. Wetmore. 1861. xii + 672p.
P4-S27048 — $102.00.

WEYERBACHER: Descendants of Hans Otto Weyerbacher (1640-1714). By Rachel Saul Tefft. 1997. 74p.
P4-S27054 — $15.00.

WHALEY: English records of the Whaley family & its branches in Amer. By S. Whaley. 1901. 234p.
P4-S27060 — $36.50.

WHARTON: Genealogy of the Wharton family of Philadelphia, 1664-1880. By Anne H. Wharton. 1880. 135p.
P4-S27069 — $21.00.

WHEAT: Wheat Genealogy: Descendants of Moses Wheat of Concord, MA & Francis Wheat of MD. Silas Carmi Wheat. 1960. 439p.
P4-S27079 — $66.00.

WHEAT: A hist. of the Wheat fam. in Amer., with a brief acct. of the name & fam. in Eng. & Normandy, Volume I By S.C. Wheat. 1902. 122p.
P4-S27078 — $22.00.

WHEATLEY: Gen. of Wheatley-Wheatleigh fam; Hist. of the fam. in Eng. & Amer. H. Wheatley. 1902. 154p.
P4-S27084 — $25.00.

WHEELER: WARREN fam., desc. of George Wheeler of Concord 1638, & John Warren of Boston 1630. By H. Wheeler. 1892. 121p.
P4-S27120 — $25.00.

WHEELER: Gen. of a branch of the Wheelers. By G. Wheeler. 1908. 61p.
P4-S27093 — $12.00.

WHEELER: Notes from "The Wheeler Fam. in Amer.," together with Notes on the desc. of Elisha Wheeler of Sudbury, MA. 1930 506p., typescript.
P4-S27114 — $77.00.

WHEELER: Notes from "The Wheeler Fam. in Amer.," together with Notes on the desc. of Elisha Wheeler of Sudbury, MA. Outline of fams. & index. 1942 159p.
P4-S27103 — $24.00.

WHEELER: Family of Rutland, MA & some of their anc. By D. M. Wheeler. 1924. 137p.
P4-S27126 — $24.00.

WHEELER: Gen. of some of the desc. of Obadiah Wheeler of Concord, & Thomas Thaxter of Hingham. By H.M. Wheeler. 1898. 74p.
P4-S27102 — $15.00.

WHEELER: Amer. anc. of the children of Joseph & Daniella Wheeler of whom we have records. By J. & D. Wheeler. 1896. 24p.
P4-S27104 — $10.00.

WHEELER: Genealogy & encyclopedic history of the Wheeler fam. in Amer., comp. By the Amer. College of Gen. dir. by A.G. Wheeler. 1914. 1273p.
P4-S27090 — $169.00.

WHEELOCK: Fam. of Calais, VT: their Amer. ancestry & desc. By M.W. Waite. 1940. 175p.
P4-S27132 — $26.00.

WHEELWRIGHT: Memoir of John Wheelwright. C.H. Bell. 1876. 148p.
P4-S27135 — $26.00.

WHEELWRIGHT: A frontier fam. By E.M. Wheelwright. 1894. 35p.
P4-S27136 — $10.00.

WHIDDEN: Gen. record of Antigonish, Nova Scotia, Whidden fam. By D.G. Whidden. 1930. 24p.
P4-S27140 — $10.00.

WHIPPLE: — WRIGHT & Allied families (Whipple-Wright, Wager, Ward-Pell, McLean-Burnett families), with record of allied families. By Charles H. Whipple. 1917. 117p.
P4-S27156 — $22.00.

WHIPPLE: Gen. notes of the Whipple-Hill fam., with fragmentary records of other fam. By J.W. Hill. 1897. 106p.
P4-S27144 — $20.00.

WHIPPLE: Hist. of the Whipples, desc. of John & Sarah of RI. By B., M. & J. Whipple. 1923. 7p.
P4-S27152 — $10.00.

WHIPPLE: Brief gen. of the Whipple fam. By J. A. Boutelle. 1857. 36p.
P4-S27153 — $10.00.

WHIPPLE: The John Whipple House in Ipswich, MA & the people who have owned & lived in it, By T.F. Waters. 1915. 55p.
P4-S27151 — $11.00.

WHIPPLE: Partial list of the descendants of Matthew Whipple, the Elder, of Bocking, Essex Co., England. Comp. by Henry B. Whipple. 1965, 1969. 2 vols. in 1, 197 + 184p.
P4-S27150 — $57.00.

WHIPPLE: Brief gen. of Whipple fam. who settled in RI. By H. E. Whipple. 1873. 63p.
P4-S27135 — $12.50.

WHITCHER: Desc. of Chase Whitcher of Warren, NH, fourth in desc. from Thomas Whittier of Salisbury (Haverhill), MA. By W. F. Whitcher. 1907. 135p.
P4-S27162 — $20.00.

WHITCOMB: Family in America, a biogr. genealogy. By C. Whitcomb. 1904. 621p.
P4-S27168 — $78.00.

WHITE: Gen. rec. of the fam. of White. By J. White. 1878. 44p.
P4-S27175 — $10.00.

WHITE: A brief acct. of the fam. of White & Clarke, By J. C. White. 1915. 37p.
P4-S27224 — $10.00.

WHITE: 1632-1892. Mem. of Roderick White & his wife Lucy Blakeslee, of Paris Hill, NY, with some acct. of their Amer. anc. A. C. White. 1892. 32p.
P4-S27176 — $10.00.

WHITE: Your fam: an informal acct. of the anc. of Allen Kirby White & Emma Chambers White [incl. White, Allen, Chambers, Hayes fams.]. By E. White. 1941. 196p.
P4-S27294 — $32.00.

WHITE: Anc. chronological record of the Wm. White fam., from 1607-8 to 1895. By T. & S. White. 1895. 393p.
P4-S27276 — $61.00.

WHITE: Norman White, his ancestors & descendants. By Erskine N. White. 1905. 155p.
P4-S27240 — $25.00.

WHITE: Anc. of John Barber White & of his desc. By A. L. White. 1913. 355p.
P4-S27204 — $56.00.

WHITE: The Nicholas White fam., 1643-1900. By T. J. Lothrop. 1902. 493p.
P4-S27252 — $63.00.

WHITE: Descendants of Wm. White, of Haverhill, MA Gen. notices by D. A. White, 1863; additional gen. & biogr. notices. A. F. Richards. 1889. 80p.
P4-S27216 — $16.50.

WHITE: Genealogy of descendants of John White of Wenham & Lancaster, MA, Four-volume set By A.L. White. 1900-1909 2819p.
P4-S27174A — $365.00./set

WHITE: Genealogy of descendants of John White of Wenham & Lancaster, MA, 1638-1900, vol I. By A.L. White. 1900. 931p.
P4-S27174 — $120.00.

WHITE: Genealogy of descendants of John White of Wenham & Lancaster, MA, 1638-1903, vol II. By A.L. White. 1903. 924p.
P4-S27180 — $120.00.

WHITE: Genealogy of descendants of John White of Wenham & Lancaster, MA, 1638-1905, vol III. By A.L. White. 1905. 754p.
P4-S27186 — $110.00.

WHITE: Genealogy of descendants of John White of Wenham & Lancaster, MA, 1638-1909, vol IV. By A.L. White. 1909. 210p.
P4-S27192 — $35.00.

WHITE: The White genealogy; A history of the desc. of Matthew & Elizabeth (Given) White of Co. Tyrone, Ireland, & Albany, NY VOL. I: The line of Joseph & Elizabeth (White) Strain By Harold Putnam White, Jr. 1988. 236p.
P4-S27264 — $35.00.

WHITE: The White gen; A hist. of the desc. of Matthew & Elizabeth (Given) White VOL. II: The line of William & Laura (Putnam) White. By Harold Putnam White, Jr. 1988. 234p.
P4-S27223 — $35.50.

WHITE: Above, VOL. III: The line of John G. & Hannah (Putnam) White. 1989. 370p.
P4-S27270 — $53.50.

WHITE: Genealogy, Vol. IV: the lines of Andrew & Lillia (Risk) White; Rev. James & Rebecca (White) Martin, Descendants of Matthew & Elizabeth (Given) White. By Harold P. White, Jr 1990. 253p.
P4-S27282 — $39.00.

WHITE: Samuel White & his Father Judge Thomas White. An Almost Forgotten Senator. Henry C. Conrad 1903 17p.
P4-S27241 — $10.00.

WHITE: Descendants of Thomas White, Sudbury, MA, 1638. By E.W. Ford. 1952. 93p.
P4-S27210 — $17.00.

For hardcover versions, see the order form on page v. To order, call 1-888-296-3447.

WHITE: Memoirs of Elder John White, one of the first settlers of Hartford, CT & of his desc. By A. S. Kellogg. 1860. 340p.
P4-S27234 — $54.00.

WHITE: The White Family, Desc of Jesse White & Elizabeth Wells from 1762. W.W. & H. Johnston. 1995. vii + 165p.
P4-S27242 — $26.00.

WHITE: "From the Dim & Misty past:" genealogy of the White family [descendants of Alexander White, b. Ireland & emigrated to PA in 18th century]. By L.B. White. 1944. 50p.
P4-S27243 — $10.00.

WHITE: Genesis of the White fam: A rec. of the White fam. beginning in 900 at the time of its Welsh origin when the name was Wynn. By E.S. White. 1920. 346p.
P4-S27228 — $55.00.

WHITE: Genealogy of the White family By Jennett Nichols-Vanderpool. 1899. 104p.
P4-S27222 — $18.00.

WHITE: Records of the fam. of Nicholas & Robert White of New Eng. (extr. from the Bassett gen.) 1926. 10p.
P4-S27225 — $10.00.

WHITE: Some White Family History. A.K. White. 1948. 432p.
P4-S27226 — $65.00.

WHITE: Genealogy; Thomas Allen White & his descendants. By Diane B. Middlebrooks. 1989. 304p.
P4-S27288 — $45.00.

WHITE: The desc. of Thomas White of Marblehead, & Mark Haskell of Beverly, MA, with brief notice of the Coombe fam. By P. Derby. 1872. 82p.
P4-S27246 — $16.75

WHITE: The White Family: Descendants of Jesse White & Elizabeth Wells, from 1762. W.W. & H. Johnston. 1997. 107p.
P4-S27227 — $16.00.

WHITEHEAD: John Whitehead of New Haven & Branford, CT (Repr. NEHGR) By J. Shepard. 1902. 7p.
P4-S27300 — $10.00.

WHITEHURST: The Whitehurst Family of Princess Anne Co, VA & Pitt Co, NC. Diane Whitehurst Collins. 2004. 546p.
P4-S27302 — $84.00.

WHITIN: Family hist. notes. By K.W. Swift. 1955. 216p.
P4-S27306 — $32.00.

WHITING: Nathaniel Whiting of Dedham, MA, 1641, & five generations of his desc. By T.S. Lazell. 1902. 80p.
P4-S27318 — $16.00.

WHITING: Mem. of Rev. Sam'l Whiting & his wife Elizabeth St John; with ref. To some of their Eng. anc. & Amer. desc. By W. Whiting. 2nd ed. 1873. 334p.
P4-S27312 — $53.00.

WHITMAN: Mem. of John Whitman & his desc. By E. Whitman. 1832. 44p.
P4-S27325 — $10.00.

WHITMAN: History of the desc. of John Whitman of Weymouth, MA. By C.H. Farnam. 1889. 1261p.
P4-S27324 — $157.00.

WHITMORE: Record of desc. of Francis Whitmore of Cambridge. By W. H. Whitmore. 1855. 24p.
P4-S27331 — $10.00.

WHITMORE: Notes on the Whitmores of Madeley, Eng., & the Farrars & Brewers of Essex Co., MA. By W. H. Whitmore. 1875. 47p.
P4-S27332 — $10.00.

WHITMORE: Whitmore gen., record of desc. of Francis Whitmore of Cambridge. By J. Purdy. 1907. 158p.
P4-S27330 — $30.00.

WHITNEY: Descendans of John Whitney, who came from London, Eng. to Watertown, MA in 1635. By F. C. Pierce. 1895. 692p.
P4-S27363 — $85.00.

WHITNEY: Family of CT & its affiliations, being an attempt to trace the desc. of Henry Whitney, from 1649, to which is prefixed some acct. of the Whitneys of Eng. By S.W. Phoenix. 1878. 3 vols., 2766p.
P4-S27354 — $335.00.

WHITNEY: The American Ancestry of Imogene Whitney. R.R. Willoughby. 1935. 41p.
P4-S27406 — $10.00.

WHITNEY: The Whitneys: England to America, 1635. By Eleanor M. [Whitney] Crouch. 2002. 109 + 20p.
P4-S27365 — $19.50.

WHITNEY: Anc. of John Whitney, who emigrated from London in 1635, & settled in Watertown, MA, the first of the name in Amer. By H. Melville. 1896. 313p.
P4-S27360 — $38.50.

WHITON: Whiton fam. in Amer. The desc. of Thomas Whiton (1635) By A.S. Whiton. 1932. 258p.
P4-S27369 — $39.00.

WHITTELSEY: Genealogy of the Whittelsey-Whittlesey family. By C.B. Whittelsey. 1898. 414p.
P4-S27375 — $53.00.

WHITTEMORE: A gen. of several branches of the Whittemore fam., incl. the original Whittemore fam. of Hitchin, Herts., Eng., & a brief lineage of other branches. By B.B. Whittemore. 1890. 106p.
P4-S27381 — $20.00.

WHITTEMORE: Gen. of several branches of the Whittemore fam. By B.B. Whittemore. 1893. 132p.
P4-S27393 — $25.00.

WHITTEMORE: Anc. of Rev. Wm. Howe Whittemore, Bolton, CT, 1800 — Rye, NY, 1885, & of his wife Maria Clark, NY, 1803 — Brooklyn, 1886. By W.P. Bacon. 1907. 124p.
P4-S27387 — $22.50.

WHITTEMORE: Whittemore fam. of Fitzwilliam, NH. By L.W. Rhodes. 1923. 9p.
P4-S27382 — $10.00.

WHITTIER: Gen. of two branches of the Whittier fam., from 1620-1873. By D. B. Whittier. 1873. 22p.
P4-S27398 — $10.00.

WHITTIER: Notes on the Eng. anc. of the Whittier & Rolfe fam. of New Eng. By C. Whittier. 1912. 14p.
P4-S27397 — $10.00.

WHITTIER: Descendants of Thomas Whittier & Ruth Green of Salisbury & Haverhill, MA. C. Whittier. 1937. 594p.
P4-S27399 — $89.00.

WHITTLESEY: Mem. of the Whittlesey fam. in the US (The Whittlesey Assn. pubn.) 1855. 131p.
P4-S27405 — $23.00.

WIARD: Family. By G.K. Collins &
W.W. Wiard. 1912. 61p.
P4-S27408 — $12.00.

WIARD: Wiard Family, 1062-1941.
Louis Wiard. 1941. 158p.
P4-S27409 — $26.00.

**WICKER: The New Wicker — Whicker
Family, rev. & enlarged.** By Richard
Fenton Wicker, Jr. 1989, 1997. 839p.
P4-S27417 — $99.00.

**WICKHAM: Ancestors of James
Wickham & his wife Cora Prudence
Billard.** By J.C. Frost. 1935. 207p.
P4-S27423 — $32.50.

**WICKWARE: Gen. of the Wickware
fam., containing an acct. of the origin
& early hist. of the name & fam. in
England; the rec. of John Wickware.**
By A.M. Wickwire. 1909. 283p.
P4-S27429 — $37.50.

**WIERMAN: History of the Wierman
family: Wierman memories.** By Maude
W. Kennedy. 1952. 40p.
P4-S27430 — $10.00.

**WIGGIN: Family; Copy of a record by
Wm. H. Wiggin.** 21p.
P4-S27436 — $10.00.

**WIGGIN: Family [biography, gene-
alogy].** By J.H. Wiggin. 1888. 148p.
P4-S27435 — $22.50.

**WIGHT: The Wights. Thomas Wight
of Dedham & Medfield, & his desc.,
1635-1890.** By W. W. Wight. 1890. 368p.
P4-S27447 — $58.00.

**WIGHT: Mem. of Thomas Wight of
Dedham, with gen. notices of his
desc., 1637-1840.** D.P. Wight. 1848. 119p.
P4-S27441 — $27.50.

**WIGHTMAN: George Wightman of
Quidnessett, RI (1632-1721/2) & desc.,
incl. Waitman, Weightman, Whiteman,
Whitman.** M.R. Whitman. 1939. 486p.
P4-S27453 — $73.50.

**WILBUR: Gen. record of the Wilbur
fam.** By A. Wilbur. 1871. 89p.
P4-S27495 — $18.50.

**WILBUR: The Wildbores in Amer: a
fam. tree.** comp. by J.R. Wilbor & B.F.
Wilbour. Rev. ed. 1933-1938 5 vols., 1513p.
P4-S27489 — $199.00./set

**WILCOX: WILCOXSON & allied
fams. (Willcockson, Wilcoxen,
Wilcox).** By D.F. Wulfeck. 1938. 505p.
P4-S27519 — $77.00.

**WILCOX: — WILCOXSON; Desc. of
William Wilcoxson, Vincent Meigs &
Richard Webb.** By Reynold Webb
Wilcox. 1893, 83p.
P4-S27498 — $12.50.

WILCOX: Family (Repr. NEHGR)
By W.H. Whitmore. 1875. 5p.
P4-S27520 — $10.00.

**WILCOX: Daniel Wilcox of Ports-
mouth, RI & desc.** H.F. Johnston. 36p.
P4-S27521 — $10.00.

WILCOX: Edw. Wilcox of RI & desc.
By H. Johnston. 134p.
P4-S27507 — $25.00.

**WILCOX: John Wilcox of Hartford,
CT & desc.** H.F. Johnston. 1948. 52p.
P4-S27522 — $10.00.

**WILCOX: William Wilcox of
Cambridge.** 1880 8p.
P4-S27508 — $10.00.

**WILCOX: William Wilcox of Stratford,
CT & desc.** By H.F. Johnston. 138p.
P4-S27525 — $26.00.

**WILDER: Book of the Wilders. The
hist. from 1497 in Eng., the emigration
of Martha, a widow, & her fam. to Mass.
Bay in 1638, her fam. to 1875 with a
gen. table.** Rev. M. Wilder. 1878. 410p.
P4-S27528 — $50.00.

WILDES: Fam. of Essex Co., MA. By
W. Davis. 1906. 61p.
P4-S27531 — $12.00.

**WILDRICK: John Wildrick of New
Jersey, 1707-1793; genealogy of the
descendants of his son George Wildrick.**
By W.Clinton Armstrong. 1933. 67p.
P4-S27540 — $14.00.

**WILFORD: WILLIFORD Family
treks into America.** By Eudie P.W. Neel.
1959. 437 + 94p.
P4-S27546 — $84.00.

**WILKIN: Robert Wilkin (1766-1835) &
Mary (Hyde) Wilkin, their parents &
descendants.** By F. McIntyre & L.M.
Wilkin. 1962 802p.
P4-S27552 — $115.00.

**WILKINS: Fam. of Bray Wilkins,
patriach of Will's Hill of Salem
(Middleton), MA.** W. Hill. 1943. 213p.
P4-S27558 — $32.00.

**WILKINSON: Mem. of the Wilkinson
fam. in Amer. Gen. sketches of Lawrence
of Providence, RI, Edw. of New
Milford, CT, John of Attleborough,
MA.** By I. Wilkinson. 1869. 589p.
P4-S27570 — $89.00.

**WILKINSON: Gen. of Wilkinson &
kindred fams. (southern branch).** By
M.M. Wilkinson. 1949. 546p.
P4-S27564 — $82.50.

**WILLARD: Genealogy: sequel to
Willard memoir, by Willard &
Walker,** ed. & compl. By Charles Henry
Pope. 1915. 776p.
P4-S27576 — $93.50.

**WILLARD: Memoir, or life & times of
Maj. Simon Willard, with notices of
three gen. of his desc., & two coll.
branches in the US.** By J. Willard. 1858.
484p.
P4-S27582 — $72.75

**WILLARD: Memorial to Henry
Augustus Willard & Sarah Bradley
Willard.** H.K. Willard. 1925. 376 + 40p.
P4-S27575 — $63.00.

**WILLCOMB: Genealogy of the
Willcomb fam. of New Eng. (1665-
1902), together with a condensed hist.
of the town of Ipswich, MA.** By O.C.
Willcomb. 1902. 302p.
P4-S27588 — $48.00.

WILLCOX: Willcox & allied families.
By J. Willcox. 1911. 139p.
P4-S27594 — $23.00.

**WILLEY: Isaac Willey of New London,
CT & his desc.** By H. Willey. 1888. 189p.
P4-S27600 — $28.00.

**WILLIAMS: MURPHY Records &
related families, of VA, NC, etc.** By
Robert M. Williams. 1949. 372p.
P4-S27686 — $55.00.

**WILLIAMS: Anc. of Lawrence
Williams. Pt. I, anc. of his father,
Simon Breed Williams; Pt. II, anc. of
his mother, Cornelia Johnston.** By C.
Williams. 1915. 291p.
P4-S27606 — $43.50.

**WILLIAMS: Life, anc. & desc. of
Robert Williams of Roxbury, MA,
1607-1693, with biogr. sketches.** By H.
Williams. 1934. 216p.
P4-S27636 — $33.00.

WILLIAMS: Desc. of John Williams, of Newbury & Haverhill, MA, 1600-1674. By Cornelia & Anna P. Williams. 1925. 179p.
P4-S27612 — $28.50.

WILLIAMS: Chronicle; Desc. of Thomas Williams of Sullivan Co., NY & Jefferson Co., PA, incl. rel. fams. By F.H. Ehrig. 1969. 198p.
P4-S27684 — $29.50.

WILLIAMS: Hist. & biogr. sketch of the Williams fam. of MA, CT, RI, NJ, PA & MD. 46p.
P4-S27607 — $10.00.

WILLIAMS: Bible records. 4p.
P4-S27608 — $10.00.

WILLIAMS: Roger Williams of Providence, RI & desc. By Bertha W. Anthony & Harriett W. Weeden. 1949, 1966 2 vols., 433p.
P4-S27648 — $64.00.

WILLIAMS: Genealogy of Williams families: Wm. Williams of New London Co., Groton & Ledyard CT, & Emanuel Williams of Taunton MA. By J.O. Williams. 1938. 215p.
P4-S27630 — $34.00.

WILLIAMS: Desc. of Veach Williams of Lebanon, CT. A.H. Wright. 1887. 186p.
P4-S27618 — $30.00.

WILLIAMS: The families of Joshua Williams of Chester Co. PA & John McKeehan of Cumberland Co. PA, with some allied families. By Bessie P. Douglas. 1928. 504p.
P4-S27660 — $76.00.

WILLIAMS: The Groves & Lappan (Monaghan Co., Ire.) Acct. of a pilgrimage thither, in search of the gen. of the Williams fam. By J. Williams. 1889. 68p.
P4-S27672 — $13.50.

WILLIAMS: Gen. notes of the Williams & Gallup fam., esp. rel. to the children of Caleb & Sabra Gallup Williams, desc. of Robert Williams of Roxbury. By C.F. Williams. 1897. 136p.
P4-S27624 — $20.50.

WILLIAMS: Richard Williams of Taunton & his connection with the Cromwell fam. By J.H. Drummond. 1897. 4p.
P4-S27609 — $10.00.

WILLIAMS: Gen. of Samuel Williams of Grafton, NH, 5th in desc. from Richard of Taunton. J.H. Drummond. 1899. 20p.
P4-S27610 — $10.00.

WILLIAMS: The anc. & desc. of Ezekiel Williams of Wethersfield, 1608-1907. M.D.W. McLean. 1907. 92p.
P4-S27654 — $18.50.

WILLIAMS: The gen. & hist. of the fam. of Williams in Amer., more particularly of the desc. of Robert Williams of Roxbury. By S.W. Williams. 1847. 424p.
P4-S27666 — $66.50.

WILLIAMSON: Alden Williamson genealogy: gen. record of Alden Williamson's family in Pike, Martin, Floyd, Johnson, Lawrence & Boyd Counties in KY. By Joseph W. Alley. 1962. 254p.
P4-S27690 — $39.00.

WILLIAMSON: Timothy Williamson of Marshfield, MA (Repr. NEHGR). By G.W. Edes. 132p.
P4-S27702 — $22.50.

WILLIAMSON: Gen. records of Williamson fam. in Amer. By J.A. Williamson. 1896. 26p.
P4-S27691 — $10.00.

WILLIAMSON: The Williamson & Cobb fam. in the lines of Caleb & Mary (Cobb) Williamson of Barnstable, MA & Hartford, CT. By F.F. Starr. 1896. 66p.
P4-S27693 — $12.50.

WILLIFORD: Willford & Allied Families. W.B. Williford. 1961. 284p.
P4-S27704 — $43.00.

WILLIS: Genealogy. N. Willis. 1863. 8p.
P4-S27709 — $10.00.

WILLIS: WYLLYS Family of CT By M.K. Talcott. 1883. 5p.
P4-S27710 — $10.00.

WILLIS: The House of Willis, With Allied Families Willingham, Baynard, Wright & Harper. Anne W. Willis. 1946. xiv + 207 + 42p.
P4-S27711 — $39.95

WILLIS: History of the Willis family of New Eng. & NJ, & their anc., to which is added a hist. of the fam. of John Howard of Richmond, VA. By C. & F. Willis. 1917. 352p.
P4-S27708 — $52.75

WILLIS: Records of the Willis family of Haverhill, Portland & Boston. By P. Willis. 1908. 2nd ed. 130p.
P4-S27714 — $22.50.

WILLIS: Sketch of the Willis fam., Fredericksburg branch. By B.C. Willis. 1909. 116p.
P4-S27726 — $22.50.

WILLIS: Sketch of the Willis family of VA & of their kindred in other states, with brief biographies of the Reades, Warners, Lewises, Byrds, Carters, etc., By B.C. Willis & R.H. Willis. 1898. 160p.
P4-S27720 — $25.00.

WILLISTON: Jos. Williston & Jos., Jr., 1667-1747, & the desc. of Rev. Noah Williston, with allied branches, 1734-1912. By A. Williston. 1912. 28p.
P4-S27730 — $10.00.

WILLITS: Anc. & desc. of James & Ann Willits of Little Egg Harbor, NJ. By A.C. Willits. 1898. 30p.
P4-S27731 — $10.00.

WILLOUGHBY: Suggestions & inquiries respecting the anc. of Col. Wm. Willoughby. E. Salisbury. 1885. 11p.
P4-S27732 — $10.00.

WILLOUGHBY: Family of New England. By I.J. Greenwood. 1876. 15p.
P4-S27733 — $10.00.

WILLS: Family: Desc. of Daniel who emigr. to Burlington, NJ in 1677, Extr. Haines gen. 1902. 52p.
P4-S27734 — $10.00.

WILMOT: Fam. of New Haven, CT. By D.L. Jacobus. 1905. 7p.
P4-S27735 — $10.00.

WILSON: Early history of the Wilson family of Kittery, ME. By F.A. Wilson. 1898. 98p.
P4-S27738 — $19.00.

WILSON: Genealogy of the Family of Nathaniel Wilson of Kittery, ME, b. 1760, d. 1841. By F.A. Wilson. 1894. 25p.
P4-S27739 — $10.00.

WILSON: Genealogy of the Wilson-Thompson families, being an acct. of the desc. of John Wilson of Co. Antrim., Ireland, whose two sons, John & Wm. By the Wilson-Thompson Fam. Assoc. 1916. 381p.
P4-S27744 — $57.50.

WILSON: Genealogy of the family of Elihu Parsons Wilson of Kittery, ME, b. 1769, d. 1834. By F. Wilson. 1894. 38p. P4-S27740 — $10.00.

WILTSEE: Genealogy & psych. memoir of Philippe Wiltsee & his desc., with hist. intro. referring to the Wiltsee nation & its colonies, Part I By J. Wiltsee, Sr. 1908. 304p. P4-S27750 — $48.50.

WINBORNE: The Winborne Family/ The Winbornes of Old. Benj. B. Winborne. 1905, 1911 215 + 40p. P4-S27769 — $38.50.

WINCHELL: Genealogy. Those born to the Winchell name in Amer. since 1635, with the orig. & hist. of the name in Eng. & notes on the Wincoll fam. By N. & A. Winchell. 1917. 2nd ed. 566p. P4-S27756 — $87.00.

WINCHESTER: Winchester Notes. By F. Winchester. 1912. 375p. P4-S27768 — $58.50.

WINCHESTER: John Winchester of New Eng. & some of his desc. By H.W. Cunningham. 1925. 139p. P4-S27762 — $21.00.

WINCHESTER: John Winchester & one line of his desc. By G.R. Presson. 1897. 45p. P4-S27763 — $10.00.

WINDER: Winders of America: John of NY, 1674-5; Thomas of NJ, 1703-34; John of MD, 1665-98. By R.W. Johnson. 1902. 112p. P4-S27774 — $19.50.

WINE: Family in Amer., First Section. By J.D. Wine. 1952. 560p. P4-S27780 — $86.00.

WING: History & gen. reg. of John Wing of Sandwich, Ma. & his desc., 1662-1881. By Rev. C. Wing. 1881. 340p. P4-S27783 — $43.00.

WING: The Sermons of Rev. John Wing: Sermon V: "The Crown Conjugall." Rev. John Wing. 196p. P4-S27784 — $38.00.

WING: The Sermons of Rev. John Wing. Sermon I: Chronological Table & "Abel's Offering." Rev. John Wing. 176p. P4-S27786 — $35.00.

WING: The Sermons of Rev. John Wing, Sermon II: "The Best Merchandise." Rev. John Wing. 226p. P4-S27785 — $43.00.

WING: The Sermons of Rev. John Wing; Sermon III: "The Saint's Advantage." Rev. John Wing. 112p. P4-S27788 — $26.00.

WING: The Sermons of Rev. John Wing; Sermon IV: "Jacob's Staff" [parts 1-3]. Rev. John Wing. 386p. P4-S27787 — $67.00.

WINGATE: Family History of the Wingate fam. in Eng. & Amer. with gen. tables. C.E. Wingate. 1886. 293p. P4-S27789 — $44.00.

WINSLOW: Gen. of Edw. Winslow of the Mayflower & his desc., from 1620-1865. By M.W. Bryant. 1915. 150p. P4-S27795 — $25.00.

WINSLOW: Memorial. Family records of the Winslows & their desc. in America, with English ancestry as far as known. By D.P. & F.K. Holton. 1877-1888. 2 vols., xvi + 658 + 529 + 13p. P4-S27801 — $182.00.

WINSOR: Winsor Family. By W.P. Eddy. 2p. P4-S27802 — $10.00.

WINSOR: Gen. acct. of ancient Winsor fam. in U. S., By O. Winsor. 1847. 13p. P4-S27803 — $10.00.

WINSTON: Winston of VA & Allied Families. By C. Torrence. 1927. 501p. P4-S27807 — $78.00.

WINTERMUTE: Family History. By J.B. Wintermute. 1900. 335p. P4-S27813 — $53.00.

WINTHROP: BABCOCK; Ancestors of Henry Rogers Winthrop & his wife Alice Woodward Babcock. By Josephine C. Frost. 1927. 595p. P4-S27843 — $89.50.

WINTHROP: Life & letters of John Winthrop: Volume I, 1588-1630, Vol. II, 1630-1649. With genealogical information. 1864, 1867. 2 vols., 452 + 483p. P4-S27825 — $105.00./set

WINTHROP: A short acct. of the Winthrop fam. By R.C. Winthrop, Jr. 1887. 16p. P4-S27820 — $10.00.

WINTHROP: Evidences of the Winthrops of Groton, Co. Suffolk, Eng. & of fams. With whom they intermarried. By J. Muskett & R. Winthrop. 1894-1896. 176p. P4-S27819 — $26.00.

WINTHROP: Genealogy: descendants of William Wynethorpe, 1400, Wynethorpe, England. By Art Reierson. 1998. 233p. P4-S27837 — $36.00.

WINTHROP: Some acct. of the early gen. of the Winthrop fam. in Ireland. By R.C. Winthrop, Jr. 1883. 24p. P4-S27826 — $10.00.

WIREBAUGH: Desc. of John Wirebaugh (1821-96). By Rachel Saul Tefft. 1999. 140p. P4-S27849 — $22.00.

WISDOM: Family. By George W. Wisdom. 1910. 231p. P4-S27855 — $30.00.

WISE: Col. John Wise of England & VA, 1617-1695: his anc. & desc. By J.C. Wise. 1918. 355p. P4-S27861 — $56.00.

WISWALL: A Wiswall line, ten gen. in desc. from Thomas Wiswall of Dorchester, 1635. By C. Wiswall. 1925. 59p. P4-S27864 — $12.00.

WITHAM: Witham Family. By E. W. Salkeld. 6p. P4-S27866 — $10.00.

WITHERELL: History & Genealogy of the Witherell/Wetherell/Witherill family of New England: some desc. of Rev. Wm. Witerell (ca.1600-84) of Scituate. By Peter C. Witherell & Edwin R. Witherell. 1976. 742p. P4-S27873 — $99.00.

WITT: Genealogy. By F.W. Balcomb. 1943. 40p. P4-S27877 — $10.00.

WITT: One line, from John Witt of Lynn, 1646 (extr. "Stevens & Miller Gen."). By M.L. Holman. 3p. P4-S27878 — $10.00.

WITTER: Some records of the Witter fam. of CT. (Repr. NEHGR) By I.M. Strobridge. 1927. 6p. P4-S27886 — $10.00.

WITTER: Descendants of Wm. Witter of Swampscott, MA, 1639-1659. By G. Washburn, ed. M.T. Washburn. 1929. 394p. P4-S27885 — $61.00.

WOLCOTT: Genealogy; Family of Henry Wolcott, one of the first settlers of Windsor, CT. C. C. Wolcott. 1912. 480p. P4-S27891 — $56.50.

WOLCOTT: Family. (Repr. NEHGR) 1847. 6p.
P4-S27892 — $10.00.

WOLFF: A Centennial Memorial of Christian & Anna Maria Wolff, with Brief Records of Their Children & Relatives. G. W. Fahnestock. 1863. 112p.
P4-S27897 — $21.00.

WOLLAM: Descendants of Jacob Wollam, Sr. (1715-1778). By Rachel Saul Tefft. 1997. 151p.
P4-S27903 — $24.00.

WOOD: Family, from "Family Sketches." By J.R. Wood. 1870. 34p.
P4-S27910 — $10.00.

WOOD: The first hundred years of Lake Co., Indiana, as lived & acted by Bartlett Woods & family & Sam B. Woods & family. By Sam B. Woods. 1936. 418p.
P4-S27933 — $59.50.

WOOD: Family, Sackville, N.B., being a gen. of the line of Thomas Wood of Rowley, MA, b. about 1634, to Josiah Wood of Sackville, N.B., b. in 1843. By J.A. Kibble. 1904. 46p.
P4-S27911 — $10.00.

WOOD: Descendants of the brothers Jeremiah & John Wood, By W.S. Wood. 1885. 292p.
P4-S27909 — $38.50.

WOOD: Descendants of twin brothers John & Benj. Wood. By J.A. Wood. 1902. 187p.
P4-S27915 — $28.00.

WOOD: Genealogy of the lineal descendants of Wm. Wood who settled in Concord, MA in 1638, containing also rev. & other records. By C.W. Holmes. 1901. 365p.
P4-S27921 — $57.50.

WOOD: Genealogy of one branch of the Wood family, 1638-1870. By T.W. Valentine. 1871. 26p.
P4-S27912 — $10.00.

WOOD: Yorkshire to Westchester: chronicle of the Wood family. By H.B. Howe. 1948. 290p.
P4-S27945 — $45.00.

WOOD: Genealogy & other family sketches; Gen. memoranda of a branch of the Wood family in England & America, Also sketches of related families. Leland N. Wood. 1937. 130p.
P4-S27939 — $25.00.

WOOD: The anc. & desc. of Ebenezer Wood of W. Gouldsborough, ME. By E. Wood. 90p.
P4-S27927 — $18.00.

WOODBRIDGE: Records: an acct. of the desc. of the Rev. John Woodbridge of Newbury, MA. L. Mitchell. 1883. 272p.
P4-S27957 — $35.00.

WOODBRIDGE: Genealogy of the Woodbridge family. By M. Talcott. 1878. 5p.
P4-S27958 — $10.00.

WOODBURY: Annals of the Clan: a story for desc. of Francis Woodbury. By A.K. Woodbury. 1932. 102p.
P4-S27963 — $19.00.

WOODBURY: A Sketch of John Page Woodbury. C.J.H. Woodbury. 1911. 10p.
P4-S27964 — $10.00.

WOODBURY: John Woodbury & some desc. (Repr. Essex. Inst. Hist. Coll.) By P. Derby. 1900. 24p.
P4-S27965 — $10.00.

WOODBURY: Gen. sketches of the Woodbury fam., its intermarriages & connections. By C.L. Woodbury, ed. By E. Woodbury. 1904. 251p.
P4-S27969 — $37.50.

WOODCOCK: John Woodcock of Rehobeth, MA, 1647, & some desc. By J.L. Woodcock. 1913. 144p.
P4-S27981 — $20.00.

WOODCOCK: History of the Woodcock Family, 1692-1912. By W.L. Woodcock. 1913. 62p.
P4-S27972 — $12.00.

WOODCOCK: Family Notes. By H. R. Guild. 8p.
P4-S27982 — $10.00.

WOODHULL: Genealogy: The Woodhull Family in England & America. By Mary G. Woodhull & Francis Bowles Stevens. 1904. 366 + 56p.
P4-S27987 — $65.00.

WOODLING: Biographical History & Genealogy of the Woodling Family. By C.A. Fisher. 1936. 43p.
P4-S27990 — $10.00.

WOODMAN: List of some desc. of Edward Woodman who settled at Newbury, MA, 1635. J. Coffin. 1855. 12p.
P4-S27994 — $10.00.

WOODMAN: The Woodmans of Buxton, ME. C. Woodman 1874. 131p.
P4-S27993 — $19.50.

WOODRUFF: Matthew Woodruff of Farmington, CT, 1640, & 10 gen. of his desc. By Mackenzie, Stewart & Woodruff. 1925. 29p.
P4-S27998 — $10.00.

WOODRUFF: The Woodruffs of NJ, Who Came from Fordwich, Kent, Eng., by way of Lynn, MA & Southampton, L.I.; rev. ed. By F.E. Woodruff. 1909. 143p.
P4-S27999 — $21.50.

WOODS: McAFEE Memorial, containing an account of John Woods & James McAfee of Ireland, & their descendants in America By Rev. Neander M. Woods. 1905. 503p. + maps
P4-S28011 — $79.00.

WOODS: The first hundred years of Lake Co., IN as lived & acted by Bartlett Woods & family & Sam B. Woods & family. By Sam B. Woods. 1936. 418p.
P4-S28005 — $59.50.

WOODSON: Historical Genealogy of the Woodsons & Their Connections. Comp. by Henry M. Woodson. 1915. 760 + 148p.
P4-S28012 — $136.95

WOODWELL: Matthew Woodwell of Salem, MA & his Desc. (Essex Inst. Hist. Coll.). By W. Woodwell. 1910. 21p.
P4-S28014 — $10.00.

WOODWORTH: From the Old Colony of New Plymouth to NE, 1620-1920: Hist & Gen of the family of Mildred Woodworth. By L.H. Hoppe. 1992. 248p.
P4-S28023 — $37.50.

WOODWORTH: Desc. of Walter Woodworth of Scituate, MA. By E.B. Woodworth. 1901. 70p.
P4-S28017 — $14.00.

WOODY: Family: Descendants of Richard Woody of England & MA. By Art Reierson. 1998. 329p.
P4-S28029 — $49.50.

WOOLSEY: Fam. records, being some acct. of the anc. of my father & mother Charles W. Woolsey & Jane Eliza Newton. E. W. Howland. 1900. 270p.
P4-S28041 — $40.00.

WOOLSEY: Genealogy: descendants of Cardinal Robert Wulcy, 1440, Ipswich, England. By Art Reierson. 1998. 171p.
P4-S28047 — $25.00.

WOOLSEY: Family of George Wood Woolsey & Sarah Nelson Woolsey. By Hester Woolsey Brewer. 1940. 134p.
P4-S28035 — $22.00.

WOOLWORTH: The desc. of Richard & Hannah Huggins Woolworth, who landed at Newbury, MA, 1678, removed to Suffield, CTin 1685. By C.R. Woolworth, assisted By J.L. Kimpton. 1893. 209p.
P4-S28053 — $31.00.

WOOSTER: Genealogy of the Woosters in America: Desc. from Edw. Wooster, of CT. By D. Wooster. 1885. 139p.
P4-S28059 — $22.50.

WOOSTER: Edward Wooster of Derby, CT & some of his descendants. By D.L. Jacobus. 21p.
P4-S28060 — $10.00.

WOOTEN: We all become forefathers . . . Genealogies of the Wooten, Boykin, Whitaker & Broadhurst families. By David Robert Wooten. 1993. 326 + 46p.
P4-S28065 — $49.50.

WORCESTER: Desc of Rev. Wm. Worcester, with a brief notice of the CT Wooster Family, pub. in 1856. By J.F. Worcester, rev. By S.A. Worcester. 1914. 292p.
P4-S28071 — $43.50.

WORCESTER: The Worcester fam.; or, the desc. of Rev. Wm. Worcester, with a brief notice of the CT Wooster fam., By J. F. Worcester. 1856. 112p.
P4-S28077 — $21.00.

WORDEN: Some Records of Persons by the Name of Worden. By O. N. Worden. 1868. 160p.
P4-S28083 — $24.00.

WORTHINGTON: The Genealogy of the Worthington Family. By G. Worthington. 1894. 489p.
P4-S28089 — $76.00.

WRAY: History of the Wrays of Glentworth, 1523-1852, Vol. I. Charles Dalton. 1880. 259 + 12p.
P4-S28090 — $41.00.

WRIGHT: Wright Family of CT. By S.V. Talcott. 1912. 20p.
P4-S28108 — $10.00.

WRIGHT: Gen. & bio. notices of desc. of Sir John Wright of Kelvedon Hall, Essex, England; in America, Thomas Wright of Wethersfield CT. By Curtis Wright. 1915. 321p.
P4-S28107 — $49.50.

WRIGHT: The Wright Ancestry of Caroline, Dorchester, Somerset & Wicomico Cos., MD. By C.W. Wright. 1907. 218p.
P4-S28131 — $34.00.

WRIGHT: Colonial Families & their Descendants: Wright & Others. By M.B. Emory. 1900. 255p.
P4-S28095 — $42.00.

WRIGHT: Descendants of Owen Wright & Letitia Dow (Collins) Wright; James Wright & 1) Lydia E. (Sorrels) Wright & 2) Anna L. (Davenbrock) Wright. By Evelyn W. Brown & Opal W.R. Sikes. 1991-1992 870 + 200p.
P4-S28101 — $119.50.

WRIGHT: Family, a genealogical record from 1740 to 1914 of the descendants of Peter Wright, 1740-1821. By Fred Philo Wright. 1914. 35p.
P4-S28109 — $10.00.

WRIGHT: Genealogy of Lt. Abel Wright of Springfield, MA, (Repr. NEHGR) By S. Wright. 1881. 9p.
P4-S28110 — $10.00.

WRIGHT: Family Memorial. By A. E. Mathews. 1886. 42p.
P4-S28111 — $10.00.

WRIGHT: Peter Wright: A Family Record. By E. Wright. 1939. 146p.
P4-S28125 — $25.00.

WRIGHT: Hist. of the Wright fam., who are desc. of Samuel (1722-1789), of Lenox, MA, with lin. back to Thomas (1610-1670), of Wethersfield, CT. W.H. Wright & G.W. Ketcham. 1913. 235p.
P4-S28113 — $35.00.

WRIGHT: Peter Wright & Mary Anderson, a Family Record: Genealogy of Their Descendants & Those of Cecelia Anderson, Who Married Daniel Neall. E. N. Wright. 1947. 198p.
P4-S28119 — $29.50.

WURTS: Genealogical record of the Wurts family: descendants of Rev. Johannes Conrad Wirz, who came to America from Zurich, Switzerland, in 1734; By C.P. Wurts. 1889. 91p.
P4-S28143 — $18.00.

WYATT: Genealogy of the Wyatt Family. By A.H. Wyatt. 1921. 35p.
P4-S28144 — $10.00.

WYNKOOP: Wynkoop Genealogy in the US. By R. Wynkoop. 1904. 254p.
P4-S28155 — $41.50.

WYNKOOP: Wynkoop Genealogy in the US. By R. Wynkoop. 1878. 130p.
P4-S28149 — $25.00.

Y

YALE: Genealogy & History of Wales (with biographies). By Rodney Horace Yale. 1908. 597 + 25p.
P4-S28167 — $91.00.

YALE: Family: Descendants of David Yale. By E. Yale. 1850. 201p.
P4-S28161 — $30.00.

YANCEY: Descendants of Jackson M. Yancey & Elizabeth B. Goode, his wife. By Lloyd R. Garrison. 1962. 134p.
P4-S28173 — $22.00.

YAPLE: The Yaple Family in America: Ancestors & Descendants of 1753 Immigrant Philip Henry Yaple. Doris Yaple Gates & Roland W. Yaple. 1990. xvi + 552p.
P4-S28174 — $85.00.

YAPLE: History & Genealogy of the Yaple Family. Grace Vandervort Crowe & Flora Yaple. 1977. 247p.
P4-S28175 — $37.00.

YARDLEY: Family Genealogy, 1402-1881. By T. Yardley. 1881. 257p.
P4-S28179 — $38.50.

YARNALL: Partial Genealogy of the Name Yarnall-Yarnell, 1683-1970. By Harry H. & Ruth Brookman Yarnell. 1970. 507p.
P4-S28185 — $75.00.

YATES: Book: Wm. Yates & his desc; Hist. & gen. of Wm. Yates (1772-1868), of Greenwood, ME & his wife Martha Morgan. By E. Yates. 1906. 51p.
P4-S28192 — $10.00.

YATES: Memorials of a family in Eng. & Va., 1771-1851: Yates, Orfeur, Aglionby, Musgrave fams. By A.E. Terrill. 1887. 383p.
P4-S28191 — $59.00.

YEAGER: Brief Hist. of the Yeager, Buffington, Creighton, Jacobs, Lemon, Hoffman & Woodside Fam. & their Coll. Kindred of PA. By J. Yeager. 1912. 278p.
P4-S28197 — $43.00.

YEAGER: History of the Yeager Family of PA. By J. Yeager. 110p.
P4-S28203 — $22.50.

YEAMANS: YEAOMANS - YOUMANS Genealogy. By G.S. Youmans. 1946. 127p.
P4-S28209 — $25.00.

YERKES: Chronicle of the Yerkes fam., with notes on the Leech & Rutter fam. By J. G. Leach. 1904. 274p.
P4-S28215 — $41.00.

YNTEMA: Family of Hessel P. Yntema, Frisian immigrant to Michigan, 1847. By Mary E. Yntema. 1958. 72p.
P4-S28221 — $15.00.

YODER: Descendants of Jacob Yoder. By D. A. Hostetler. 1951. 105p.
P4-S28227 — $19.00.

YORK: The York Family. By W.M. Sargent. 22p.
P4-S28228 — $10.00.

YOUNG: JUNG Families of the Mohawk Valley, 1710-1946. By Clifford M. Young. 1947. 354p.
P4-S28245 — $55.00.

YOUNG: The History of Noah Young & Alice Driskell Young: The Driskell Ancestors & Young Descendants. Janelle Young Rogols. 2003. 351 p.
P4-S28234 — $53.00.

YOUNG: Robert John Young & Daisie Frances Denton; Ancestral notes & some descendants. By R.M. Young-Widdifield. 1961. 160 + 34p.
P4-S28239 — $31.00.

YOUNG: Family History. By J. Montgomery Seaver. 48p.
P4-S28240 — $10.00.

YOUNG: Our Young family in America. Edward .H. Young. 1947. 315p.
P4-S28233 — $48.00.

YOUNGS: Vicar Christopher Yonges, his anc. in Eng. & his desc. in America. By S. Youngs, Jr. 1907. 385p.
P4-S28254 — $48.00.

YOUNGS: Thomas Youngs of Oyster Bay & his desc. Rev. C. Youngs. 1890. 142p.
P4-S28251 — $21.00.

Z

ZABRISKIE: A 301-year history of the descendants of Albrecht Zabrowoskij (ca. 1638-1711) of Bergen County, N.J. George O. Zabriskie. 1963. 2 vols., 1950p.
P4-S28260 — $225.00.

ZAHNISER: The Zahnisers: A History of the Family in America. By Kate M. & Charles Reed Zahniser. 1906. 218p.
P4-S28266 — $33.00.

ZIEGLER: Family Record: Complete Record of the Ziegler Fam from our ancestor, Philip Ziegler, born in Bern, Switzerland, in 1734, to 7th & 8th generations. By J. Ziegler and D. Ziegler. 1906. 118p.
P4-S28278 — $21.00.

ZIEGLER: Family Record: Ziegler, Zeigler & Zigler. By Floyd R, & Kathryn G. Mason. 1999. 672p.
P4-S28272 — $94.50.

ZIMMERMAN: WATERS & Allied Fams. By D.E.Z. Allen. n.d. 162p.
P4-S28290 — $26.00.

ZIMMERMAN: Johan Jost Zimmerman & related genealogies of Roth, Yaggy, Schlunegger, Bratton, Cochlin, Elliott, Campbell & McCullough. By Jay Norwalk. 1998. 664p.
P4-S28284 — $97.00.

ZINK: Families in America, incl. many of the Archer, Colglazier, Marshal, Martin, Perisho, Seaton & Zimmerly fams. By D.Z. Kellogg. 1933. 385p.
P4-S28296 — $61.00.

ZULLMAN: ZOLLMAN — ZOLMAN Families: US Desc of Johannes Zullman of Mensfelden, Germany. By Art Reierson. 1998. 562p.
P4-S28302 — $84.00.

ZUMBRUN: Family of Switzerland & Montgomery Co., MD. By Art Reierson. 1998. 422p.
P4-S028308 — $65.00.

LOCAL
HISTORIES

CANADA

Canada — general

CYCLOPEDIA OF CANADIAN BIOGRAPHY, Being Chiefly Men of the Time: Collection of Persons Distinguished in Professional & Political Life; Leaders in the Commerce & Industry of Canada; & Successful Pioneers. Ed. By Geo. MacLean Rose. 1886. 807p.
P5-CN0026 — $82.50.

HISTORY OF THE COUNTIES OF ARGENTEUIL, QUEBEC & PRESCOTT, ONTARIO. By C. Thomas. 1896. 665 + 24p.
P5-CAN0004 — $69.00.

NORMAN PEOPLE & Their Existing Descendants in the British Dominions & the U.S.A. 1874. xvi + 484p.
P5-GR0211 — $49.50.

OLD UNITED EMPIRE LOYALISTS LIST. 1885. 344p.
P5-CN0016 — $20.00.

THE CHIGNECTO ISTHMUS & ITS FIRST SETTLERS. By Howard Trueman. 1902. 268p.
P5-NB0001 — $32.00.

New Brunswick

ANNALS OF CALAIS, ME AND ST. STEPHEN, NEW BRUNSWICK By Rev. I.C. Knowlton 1875. 208p.
P26590000 — $39.00.

Nova Scotia

HISTORY OF NOVA SCOTIA, 3-vol. set in 2 books. By David Allison. 1914. 3 vols. in 2, 940 + 700p.
P5-NS0006 — $163.50/set.

HISTORY OF NOVA SCOTIA, Vols. I & II. David Allison. 1914. 940p.
P5-NS0006A — $99.00.
HISTORY OF NOVA SCOTIA, Vol. III. By David Allison. 1914. 700p.
P5-NS0006B — $75.00.

LOYALISTS & LAND SETTLEMENTS IN NOVA SCOTIA. Comp. by M. Gilroy & D.C. Harvey. 1937. 154p.
P5-NS0005 — $15.00.MILITARY

OPERATIONS IN EASTERN MAINE & NOVA SCOTIA During the Revolution. By Frederic Kidder. 1867. 336p.
P5-ME0135 — $43.00.

HISTORY OF THE CO. OF ANNAPOLIS, including Old Port Royal & Acadia, with Genealogical Sketches of its Early English Settlers & their Families. By W.A. Calnek. 1897. 682p.
P5-NS0002 — $72.00.

HISTORY OF THE COUNTY OF ANTIGONISH. By Rev. D.J. Rankin. 1919. 390p.
P5-NS0008 — $45.00.

HISTORY OF BARRINGTON TWP. & Vicinity, Shelbourne Co., 1604-1870, with a Biogr. & Gen. Appendix. By E. Crowell. 1870. 610p.
P5-NS0003 — $63.00.

HISTORY OF DIGBY COUNTY, NOVA SCOTIA, CANADA By A. Hill 1901. 115p.
P28557000 — $26.00.

HISTORY OF GRAND-PRE, Home of Longfellow's Evangeline. By John Frederic Herbin. . 168p., 4th ed.
P5-NS0007 — $26.00.

HISTORY OF KING'S CO. Heart of the Acadian Land. Giving a sketch of the French and their expulsion, and a history of the New England planters who came in their stead, with many genealogies. By Arthur W. H. Eaton 1910. 898p.
P5-NS0004 — $89.00.

LUNENBURGH, or the Old Eastern District, its Settlement and Early Progress, with Personal Recollections of the Town of Cornwall from 1824. J.F. Pringle. 1890. 423p.
P5-CN0022 — $48.00.

HISTORY OF THE COUNTY OF LUNENBURG. 2nd ed. By Mather Byles DesBrisay. 1895. 586p.
P5-CN0019B — $64.00.

HISTORY OF QUEENS COUNTY, Nova Scotia. James F. More. 1873. 255p.
P5-NS0001 — $35.00.

YARMOUTH, NOVA SCOTIA: A Sequel to Campbell's History. By George S. Brown. 1888. 524p.
P5-CAN0002 — $55.00.

Ontario

ONTARIAN FAMILIES: Genealogies of United Empire Loyalist & other Pioneer Families of Upper Canada, 2-vol. set. By Edw. M. Chadwick. 1895-1898. 2 vols., 203 + 194p.
P5-ON0003B — $43.00/set.

ONTARIAN FAMILIES . . ., Vol. I. By Edw. M. Chadwick. 1895-1898. 203p
P5-ON0003B1 — $25.00.

ONTARIAN FAMILIES . . ., Vol. II. By Edw. M. Chadwick. 1895-1898. 194p.
P5-ON0003B2 — $25.00.

PIONEER LIFE ON THE BAY OF QUINTE, including Genealogies of Old Families & Biographical Sketches of Representative Citizens. 1904. 1005p.
P5-PQ0005 — $99.50.

STORY OF DUNDAS, Being a History of the Co. of Dundas, 1784 to 1904. With portraits & illustrations. By J. Smyth Carter. 1905. 462p.
P5-CN0019A — $51.00.

HISTORY OF THE COUNTY OF GREY. By E.L. Marsh. 1931. 487p.
P5-ON0005 — $54.00.

HISTORY OF LEEDS & GRENVILLE, ONTARIO, from 1749 to 1879, with Illustrations & Biographical Sketches of Some of its Prominent Men & Pioneers. By Thad W.H. Leavitt. 1879. 200p.
P5-CN0020 — $34.00.

HISTORY OF THE COUNTIES OF LENNOX & ADDINGTON. By Walter S. Herrington. 1913. xii + 426p.
P5-ON0001 — $45.00.

PIONEER SKETCHES OF LONG POINT SETTLEMENT, or Norfolk's Foundation Builders & Their Family Genealogies. By E.A. Owen. 1898. 578p.
P5-CN0023 — $61.50.

HISTORY OF EAST OXFORD TOWNSHIP. By Ken Peers. 1967. 80p
P5-ON0100 — $15.00.

Ontario cont.

TORONTO: Past and Present: Historical and Descriptive. By Rev. Henry Scadding. 1884. 378p.
P5-CAN0001 — $38.00.

LIFE AND TIMES OF JOSEPH GOULD: Reminiscences of Sixty Years of Active Political and Municipal Life. [ONTARIO, UXBRIDGE]. W.H. Higgins. 1887. 304p.
P5-ON0002 — $39.50.

COMMEMORATIVE BIOGRAPH-ICAL RECORD OF THE COUNTY OF YORK, Containing Biographical Sketches of Prominent & Representative Citizens & Many of the Early Settled Families. 1907. 673p.
P5-ON0003A — $72.50.

Quebec

HISTORY OF THE EASTERN TOWNSHIPS, Prov. of Quebec, Civil & Descriptive, in Three Parts. By Mrs C.M. Day. 1869. 475p.
P5-CN0024 — $54.00.

RECHERCHES GENEALOGIQUE sur les Famillies Gravel, Cloutier, Bruneau, et al. By F.L Desaulniers. 1902. 197p
P5-PQ0004 — $21.00.

SIEGE OF QUEBEC & THE BATTLE OF THE PLAINS OF ABRAHAM, Volumes I-VI. By A. Doughty & G.W. Parmelee. 1901-2. 6 vols; 352 + 376 + 408 + 316 + 374 + 354p.
P5-CAN0003 — $275.00/set.

SIEGE OF QUEBEC & THE BATTLE OF THE PLAINS OF ABRAHAM, Vol. I. 1901-2. 352p.
P5-CAN0003A — $50.00.

SIEGE OF QUEBEC & THE BATTLE OF THE PLAINS OF ABRAHAM, Vol. II. 1901-2. 376p.
P5-CAN0003B — $50.00.

SIEGE OF QUEBEC & THE BATTLE OF THE PLAINS OF ABRAHAM, Vol. III. 1901-2. 408p.
P5-CAN0003C — $50.00.

SIEGE OF QUEBEC & THE BATTLE OF THE PLAINS OF ABRAHAM, Vol. IV. 1901-2. 316p.
P5-CAN0003D — $50.00.

SIEGE OF QUEBEC & THE BATTLE OF THE PLAINS OF ABRAHAM, Vol. IV. 1901-2. 316p.
P5-CAN0003D — $50.00.

SIEGE OF QUEBEC & THE BATTLE OF THE PLAINS OF ABRAHAM, Vol. V. 1901-2. 374p.
P5-CAN0003E — $50.00.

SIEGE OF QUEBEC & THE BATTLE OF THE PLAINS OF ABRAHAM, Vol. VI. 1901-2. 354p.
P5-CAN0003F — $50.00.

NOTES HISTORIQUE SUR LA PAROISSE de St Guillaume D'Upton. By F.L Desaulniers. 1905. 143p
P5-PQ0003 — $19.00.

FOREST & CLEARINGS: History of Stanstead Co., Prov. of Quebec, with Sketches of More Than 500 Families. By B.F. Hubbard. 1874. 367p.
P5-PQ0001 — $44.50.

FORESTS & CLEARINGS: HISTORY OF STANSTEAD CO., Prov. of Quebec, with Sketches of More than Five Humdred Families. Comp. by B.F. Hubbard. 1874. 367p.
P5-CAN0025 — $44.00.

LES VIELLES FAMILLES D'YAMACHICHE [in French], 2-vol. set. By F.L Desaulniers. 2 vols., 242 + 303p.
P5-PQ0002 — $50.00/set.

LES VIELLES FAMILLES D'YAMACHICHE, Vol. I. 242p.
P5-PQ0002A — $27.50.

LES VIELLES FAMILLES D'YAMACHICHE, Vol. 2. 303p.
P5-PQ0002B — $27.50.

EUROPE

Belgium

THE BELGIANS: First Settlers in New York & in the Middle States, with a Review of the Events which Led to their Immigration. By Henry G. Bayer. 1925. 373p.
P5-BG0001 — $39.50.

England

[HOTTEN'S] ORIGINAL LISTS OF PERSONS OF QUALITY: Emigrants, Religious Exiles, Political Rebels . . . & Others who Went from Great Britain to the American Plantations, 1690-1700. By J.C. Hotten. 1874. 580p.
P5-HT0001 — $49.00.

AMERICAN COLONISTS IN ENGLISH RECORDS. 1st & 2nd series in 1 vol. G. Sherwood. 1932-3. 216p.
P5-GR0031 — $19.95.

BURKE'S DORMANT, ABEYANT, FORFEITED & EXTINCT PEER-AGES of the British Empire. By B. Burke. 1883. 642p.
P5-BU0001 — $55.00.

BURKE'S EXTINCT & DORMANT BARONETCIES of England, Ireland & Scotland. By J. & J.B. Burke. 1841. 644p.
P5-BU0002 — $54.50.

BURKE'S FAMILY RECORDS. By Ashworth P. Burke. 1897. 709p.
P5-BU0003 — $72.00.

ENGLISH ANCESTRY & HOMES OF THE PILGRIM FATHERS who Came to Plymouth in the "Mayflower" in 1620, the Fortune" in 1621, & the "Anne" & "Little James" in 1623. By Charles Edw. Banks. 1929. 187p.
P5-GR0016 — $21.50.

FAIRBAIRN'S CRESTS of the Leading Families in Great Britain & Ireland, & their Kindred in other Lands. Comp. by J. Fairbairn. 1841. 2 vols. in 1. 137 + 605p.
P5-HR0001 — $75.00.

GENEALOGICAL GLEANINGS IN ENGLAND: Abstracts of Wills Related to Early American Families with Genealogical Notes & Pedigrees Constructed from Wills & other Records. With New Series. 2-vol. set By Henry F. Waters. 1901, 1907. 2 vols., 1760p.
P5-WA0001B — $125.00/set.

GENEALOGICAL GLEANINGS IN ENGLAND . . ., Vol. I. 1901.
P5-WA0001BA — $68.50.

GENEALOGICAL GLEANINGS IN ENGLAND . . ., Vol. II. 1907.
P5-WA0001BB — $68.50.

HISTORIC PEERAGE OF ENGLAND . . . The origin, Descent & Present [1857] State of Every Title of Peerage which has Existed [in England] Since the Conquest. By Wm. Courthope. 1857. 610p.
P5-GB0004 — $67.00.

KEY TO ANCIENT PARISH REGISTERS OF ENGLAND & WALES. By A.M. Burke. 1906. 163p.
P5-GR0018 — $19.95.

THE ENGLAND & HOLLAND OF THE PILGRIMS. By H.M. & D. Martin. 1906. 673p.
P5-GR1460 — $65.00.

HISTORY OF THE COUNTY OF AYR, with a Genealogical Account of the Families of Ayrshire, Vol. I. By James Paterson. 1857. 463p.
P5-GB0003 — $51.00.

ROLL OF BATTLE ABBEY. Comp. by J.B. Burke. 1848. 127p.
P5-GR0010B — $17.50

REGISTERS OF BRUTON, CO. SOMERSET. Vols. I & II. 1911. 284 + 415p
P5-ENG0005 — $70.00/set.

REGISTERS OF BRUTON, CO. SOMERSET. Vol. I. 1911. 284p.
P5-ENG0005A — $40.00.

REGISTERS OF BRUTON, CO. SOMERSET. Vol. II. 1911. 415p.
P5-ENG0005B — $35.00.

HISTORY OF THE HUNDRED OF CARHAMPTON, in the County of Somerset. James Savage. 1830. 662p.
P5-GR0011A — $72.00.

HISTORY OF GREAT YARMOUTH, 2 vols. By Henry Manship. 1856. 2 vols., 435 + 388p.
P5-GB0008 — $90.00/set.

HISTORY OF GREAT YARMOUTH, Vol. I. 1856. 435p
P5-GB0008A — $51.00.

HISTORY OF GREAT YARMOUTH, Vol. II. 1856. 388p
P5-GB0008B — $46.00.

REGISTERS OF HASLEMERE, CO. SURREY. 1906. 360p.
P5-ENG0006 — $38.00.

PARISH OF HEMINGBROUGH IN THE COUNTY OF YORK. By Thomas Burton. 1888. 418p. + 8 charts.
P5-ENG0003 — $47.00.

LINCOLN MARRIAGE LICENCES. An Abstract of the Allegation Books Preserved by the Registry of the Bishop of Lincoln, 1598-1628. 1888. 163p.
P5-GB0009 — $19.50.

REGISTERS OF MICKLEOVER [1607-1812] AND OF LITTLEOVER [1680-1812], CO. DERBY. 1909. 295p.
P5-ENG0004 — $34.00.

HISTORY OF OXFORDSHIRE. By J. Meade Falkner. 1899. 327p.
P5-GR0005A — $39.50.

MARRIAGES AT ST. ANDREWS, PLYMOUTH, 1581-1837. (Vol. II, Devon Parish Registers). 1915. 166p.
P5-GB0010 — $25.00.

FOUNDERS OF NEW PLYMOUTH, THE PARENT COLONY OF NEW ENGLAND: Collections Concerning the Church or Congregation of Protestant Separatists Formed at Scrooby in No. Nottinghamshire. By J. Hunter, 1854. 205p.
P5-GR0006 — $32.00.

REGISTER OF SELATTYN, SHROPSHIRE. 1906. 417p.
P5-ENG0001 — $50.50.

WEDMORE [SOMERSET] PARISH REGISTERS, 1561-1812. 1890. 3 vols. in 2, 380 + 151 +367p.
P5-GB0001 — $89.50/set.

REGISTERS OF STRATFORD-ON-AVON, County Warwick. 1905. 194p.
P5-ENG0002 — $29.00.

TRENHOLME IN YORKSHIRE, with Some Notes on the Trenholme Family. By Edw. C. Trenholme. 96p.
P5-GB0002 — $18.00.

France

FAMILY NAMES OF HUGUENOT REFUGEES TO AMERICA. From "Constitution of the Huguenot Society of America." Comp. by Mrs J. Lawton. 1901. 20p.
P5-FR0020 — $10.00.

FRENCH BLOOD IN AMERICA. By L.J. Fosdick. 1906. 448p.
P5-FR0001 — $49.50.

HISTORY OF HUGUENOT EMIGRATION TO AMERICA. By Charles W. Baird. 1885. 2 vols. in 1, 353 + 448p.
P5-FR0021 — $79.00.

NORMAN PEOPLE & Their Existing Descendants in the British Dominions & the U.S.A. 1874. xvi + 484p.
P5-GR0211 — $49.50.

THE FALAISE ROLL, Recording Prominent Companions of Wm., Duke of Normandy at the Conquest of England. With add. & corr. By Crispin & Macary. 1938. 258p.
P5-GR0210 — $30.00.

Germany

GERMAN ALLIED TROOPS IN THE NORTH AMERICAN WAR OF INDEPENDENCE, 1776-1783. Trans. by M. Von Eelking. 1893. 360p.
P5-GE0001 — $39.00.

SIMMENDINGER REGISTER. True & Authentic Register of Persons still Living who, in the Year 1709, Journeyed from Germany to America. Comp. by Ulrich Simmendinger in 1717. 1934. 20p.
P5-GE0004 — $10.00.

THE HESSIANS and the Other German Auxiliaries of Great Britain in the Revolutionary War. By Edward J. Lowell. 1884. 328p.
P5-GE0002 — $42.00.

Ireland

FAIRBAIRN'S CRESTS of the Leading Families in Great Britain & Ireland, & their Kindred in other Lands. Comp. by J. Fairbairn. 1841. 2 vols. in 1. 137 + 605p.
P5-HR0001 — $75.00.

INDEX TO THE PREROGATIVE WILLS OF IRELAND, 1536-1810. By Sir Arthur Vicars. 1897. 512p.
P5-IR6060 — $55.00.

IRELAND CENSUS OF 1851: General Alphabetical Index to the Townlands & Towns, Parishes & Baronies of Ireland, Based on the Census of Ireland for the Year 1851. 1861. 968p.
P5-IR0062 — $95.00.

IRISH PEDIGREES, Or the Origin & Stem of the Irish Nation, 2-vol. set. J. O'Hart. 1915. 2 vols., 912 + 948p.
P5-IR0001 — $189.00/set.

IRISH PEDIGREES, or the Origin & Stem of the Irish Nation, Vol. I. 1915. 912p.
P5-IR0001A — $89.00.

IRISH PEDIGREES, or the Origin & Stem of the Irish Nation, Vol. II. 1915. 948p.
P5-IR0001B — $89.00.

RETURN OF OWNERS OF LAND OF ONE ACRE AND UPWARDS, in the Several Counties, Counties of Cities, and Counties of Towns in Ireland, Showing the names of such owners arranged alphabetically, their addresses, etc. 1876. 323p.
P5-IR0004B — $29.95.

TOPOGRAPHICAL DICTIONARY OF IRELAND, Comprising the Several Counties, Cities, Borough, Corporate, Market & Post Towns, Parishes & Villages, with History & Statistics, 2-vol. set. By S. Lewis. 1837. 2 vols, 675 + 737p.
P5-IR0004A — $135.00/set.

TOPOGRAPHICAL DICTIONARY OF IRELAND . . ., Vol. I. 1837. 675p
P5-IR0004AB — $70.00.

TOPOGRAPHICAL DICTIONARY OF IRELAND . . ., Vol. II. 1837. 737p.
P5-IR000AC — $70.00.

TOPOGRAPHICAL DICTIONARY OF IRELAND, Comprising the Several Counties, Cities, Boroughs . . . Parishes & Villages, with Historical & Statistical Descriptions. Vol. I, A-G, Vol. II, H-end. By Samuel Lewis. 1837. 2 vols., 675 + 737p.
P5-IR0002 — $129.50/set.

TOPOGRAPHICAL DICTIONARY OF IRELAND . . ., Vol. I, A-G. 1837. 675p
P5-IR0002A — $69.50.

TOPOGRAPHICAL DICTIONARY OF IRELAND . . ., Vol. II, H-end. 1837. 737p
P5-IR0002B — $69.50.

TOWNLANDS IN POORLAW UNIONS: Reprints of Poor Law Union Pamphlets of the General Registrars Office, with an Introduction and Six Appendices Relating to Irish Genealogical Research. Duchess of Cleveland 1889. 1314p.
P28560000 — $418.00.

TOWNLANDS IN POOR LAW UNIONS: Reprints of Poor Law Union Pamphlets of the General Registrar's office, with an Introduction & Six Appendices Relating to Irish Genealogical Research. Comp. & ed. by George B. Handran. 1997. 613p.
P5-IR0010 — $67.00.

CHURCH & PARISH RECORDS of the United Diocese of Cork, Cloyne, and Ross. By Rev. J.H. Cole. 1903. xxvi + 347p.
P5-IRE0001 — $43.00.

Norway

NORIFTE SETTLEMENTERS [NORWEGIAN SETTLERS], en Overfigt over den Norifte Indvandring til og Bebyggelfe af Umerifas Nurdveften fra Umeritas Opdagelfe til Indianerfrigen i dveften. IN NORWEGIAN. By Hjalmar Rued Holand. 1909. 603p.
P5-NW0001 — $65.00.

Russia

THE DOUKHOBORS, Their History in Russia, Their Migration to Canada. By Joseph Elkinton. 1903. 336p,
P5-RU0001 — $39.50.

Scotland

GREAT HISTORIC FAMILIES OF SCOTLAND. By James Taylor. 1887. 410 + 431p.
P5-SL0003A — $79.50.

ORDNANCE GAZETEER OF SCOTLAND: A Graphic and Accurate Description of Every Place in Scotland, 3-vol. set. 1902. 3 vols., 1762p.
P5-SL0003B — $155.00/set.

ORDNANCE GAZETEER OF SCOTLAND . . ., Vol. I. 1902.
P5-SL0003B1 — $57.00.

ORDNANCE GAZETEER OF SCOTLAND . . ., Vol. II. 1902.
P5-SL0003B2 — $57.00.

ORDNANCE GAZETEER OF SCOTLAND . . ., Vol. III. 1902.
P5-SL0003B3 — $57.00.

SCOTCH-IRISH PIONEERS in Ulster & America. By C.K. Bolton. 1910. 398p.
P5-SL0002 — $44.00.

SCOTS & SCOTS' DESCENDANTS in America. 1917. 390p.
P5-SC0002 — $35.00.

SCOTTISH FAMILY HISTORIES Held in Scottish Libraries. By J.P.S. Ferguson. 1960. 194p.
P5-SL0001 — $29.00.

SCOTTISH FAMILY HISTORY: Guide to Works of Reference on the History & Genealogy of Scottish Families. Margaret Stuart. 1930. 386p.
P5-SL0050 — $35.00.

Sweden

VIKING ODYSSEY TO THE NEW WORLD: from Ancient Sweden to Alabama, via Norway, Normandy, England, Scotland, Va., N.C. & Georgia. By James J. Blue. 1992. 183p.
P5-SW0003 — $25.00.

UNITED STATES

United States — General

[HOTTEN'S] ORIGINAL LISTS OF PERSONS OF QUALITY: Emigrants, Religious Exiles, Political Rebels . . . & Others Who Went from Great Britain to the American Plantations, 1690-1700. 1874. 580p.
P5-HT0001 — $49.00.

HEADS OF FAMILIES at the First Census of the U.S. taken in the Year 1790. 1908. 308p.
P5-NY0020 — $30.00.

["MUNSELL'S INDEX"] INDEX TO AMERICAN GENEALOGIES & TO GENEALOGICAL MATERIAL CONTAINED IN ALL WORKS such as Town Histories, County Hist., Local Hist., Historical Society Publications, Biogr., Hist. Periodicals & Kindred Works. 5th ed. rev. & enlarged. 2 vols. in 1. 1900, 1908. 352 + 107p.
P5-MU0001 — $45.00.

NORMAN PEOPLE & their Existing Descendants in the British Dominions & the U.S.A. 1874. xvi + 484p.
P5-GR0211 — $49.50.

AMERICAN MARRIAGE RECORDS BEFORE 1699. With supplement from "Genealogical Magazine." By W.M. Clemens. 1926, 1929, 1930. 229p.
P5-GR0026 — $24.50.

AMERICAN COLONISTS IN ENGLISH RECORDS. 1st & 2nd series in 1 vol. By G. Sherwood. 1932-3. 216p.
P5-GR0031 — $19.95.

HISTORY BRIEF OF AMERICA, Years 1492-1986. The Importance of the George Yarmouth Voyage to the Gulf of Maine in the Year of 1605. By Rundlette K. Palmer. 1986. 246p.
P5-MISC0006 — $36.00.

MARRIAGE NOTICES FOR THE WHOLE U.S., 1785-94. By C.K. Bolton. 1900. 139p.
P5-GR0011B — $19.50.

PROMINENT FAMILIES OF THE UNITED STATES. By A.M. Burke. 1908. 510p.
P5-US0001 — $45.00.

United States — Middle Atlantic

REVOLUTION ON THE UPPER OHIO (RIVER), 1775-1777 By A. Williams 1984. 96p.
P28475200 — $20.00.

United States — Midwest

DES MOINES, the Pioneer of Municipal Progress and Reform of the Middle West, Together with the History of Polk Co., vol. I. By Johnson Brigham. 1911. 746p.
P5-IA0024A — $73.00.

United States — New England

DIRECTORY OF ANCESTRAL HEADS OF NEW ENGLAND FAMILIES, 1630-1700. By F.R. Holman. 1923. 274p.
P5-GR0017 — $29.00.

FOUNDERS OF NEW PLYMOUTH, THE PARENT COLONY OF NEW ENGLAND: Collections Concerning the Church or Congregation of Protestant Separatists Formed at Scrooby in No. Nottinghamshire. By J. Hunter, 1854. 205p.
P5-GR0006 — $32.00.

GENEALOGICAL NOTES ON THE FOUNDING OF NEW ENGLAND: My Ancestors Part in the Undertaking. By Ernest Flagg. 1926. 440p.
P5-GR0102 — $39.95.

NEW ENGLAND FAMILIES, GENEALOGICAL & MEMORIAL: Record of the Achievements of Her People in the Making of Commonwealth & the Founding of a Nation, Vols. I — III. 1916. 1259p.
P5-NEG002 — $126.00.

NEW ENGLAND FAMILIES, GENEALOGICAL & MEMORIAL, Vol.s IV & V. 874p.
P5-NEG003 — $92.50.

NEW ENGLAND FAMILY HISTORY. 1908. 866p.
P5-NEG005 — $89.50.

ONE HUNDRED & SIXTY ALLIED FAMILIES. By J.O. Austin. 1893. 288p.
P5-RI0006 — $36.00.

PLANTERS OF THE COMMONWEALTH: Study of the Emigrants & Emigration in Colonial Times . . . Lists of Passengers to Boston & the Bay Colony, the Ships which Brought Them, Their English Homes & the Places of Their Settlement in Mass., 1620-1640. Charles Edw. Banks. 1930. 231p.
P5-GR0015 — $29.50.

"SAVAGE'S DICTIONARY" GENEALOGICAL DICTIONARY OF THE FIRST SETTLERS OF NEW ENGLAND, Showing Three Generations of Those who Came Before May, 1692, on the Basis of Farmer's Register. With genealogical cross-index. 4-vol. set. By J. Savage. 1860-1862. 4 vols., 2541 + 38p.
P5-NEG001 — $145.00/set.

"SAVAGE'S DICTIONARY" . . ., Vol. I. 1860-1862.
P5-NEG001A — $39.50.

"SAVAGE'S DICTIONARY" . . ., Vol. II. 1860-1862.
P5-NEG001B — $39.50.

"SAVAGE'S DICTIONARY" . . ., Vol. III. 1860-1862.
P5-NEG001C — $39.50.

"SAVAGE'S DICTIONARY". . ., Vol. IV. 1860-1862.
P5-NEG001D — $39.50.

RESULT OF RESEARCHES AMONG THE BRITISH ARCHIVES for Information Relative to the Founders of New England, made in the Years 1858-60. By S.G. Drake. 1860. 143p.
P5-GR0019 — $22.50.

SHIPS' LOCATOR: A Reference to over 2,000 Ships, Schooners, and Other Vessels of Nineteenth-Century New England and the Atlantic Seaboard, with a Separate Index to more than a Thousand Vessel Masters. By Robert Moseley Jackson, Jr. 1998. 348p.
P5-EM0001 — $32.50.

New England cont.

TERCENTENARY OF NEW ENGLAND FAMILIES, 1620-1922: Record of Achievements of her People in the Making of Commonwealths & the Founding of a Nation [with many illustrations]. 1922. 256p. **P5-NEG004 — $45.00.**

TOPOGRAPHICAL DICTIONARY OF 2885 ENGLISH EMIGRANTS TO NEW ENGLAND, 1620-1650. By Charles E. Banks. 1937. 295p. **P5-GR0025 — $37.00.**

WARNING OUT IN NEW ENGLAND, 1656-87. By Josiah H. Benton. 1911. 131p. **P5-SO0001 — $17.50.**

WINTHROP FLEET of 1630: An Account of the Vessels, the Voyage, the Passengers & their English Homes. Chas. Edw. Banks. 1930. 119p. **P5-GR0038 — $17.50.**

United States — Northwest

FIFTY YEARS IN THE NORTHWEST, with an Introduction and Appendix containing Reminiscences, Incidents and Notes. By W.H.C. Folsom. 1888. 763p. **P5-WI0013B — $77.00.**

United States — South

KEY TO SOUTHERN PEDIGREES, Being a Comprehensive Guide to the Colonial Ancestry of Families in Virginia, Maryland, Georgia, No. & So. Carolina, Ky., Tenn., W. Va. & Alabama. 1910-1. 81p. **P5-SS0010 — $16.00.**

Alabama

ALABAMA: Her History, Resources, War Record & Public Men, from 1540 to 1872. With biographical sketches of early settlers. W. Brewer. 1872. 712p. **P5-AL0004 — $76.50.**

ANNALS OF NORTHWEST ALABAMA, Including a Reprint of Nelson F. Smith's "History of Pickens County (1856)." By Carl Elliott. 1958. 2 vols. in 1, 240 + 288p. **P5-AL0008 — $57.00.**

EARLY SETTLERS OF ALABAMA. By J.E. Saunders. With Notes & Gen. by E.S.B. Stubbs. 1899. 530p. **P5-AL0001 — $42.00.**

HISTORY OF ALABAMA, & Incidentally of Georgia & Mississippi from the Earliest Period. 2nd edition. 2-vol. set By Albert J. Pickett. 1851. 377 + 445p. **P5-AL0005 — $87.00/set.**

HISTORY OF ALABAMA . . ., Vol. I. By Albert J. Pickett. 1851. 377p. **P5-AL0005A — $46.00.**

HISTORY OF ALABAMA . . ., Vol. II. By Albert J. Pickett. 1851. 454p. **P5-AL0005B — $46.00.**

HISTORY OF THE FIRST REGIMENT, Alabama Volunteer Infantry CSA. By Edward Young McMorries. 1904. 142p. **P5-AL0003 — $25.00.**

MEMORIAL RECORD OF ALABAMA, 2-vol. set. 1893. 2 vols., 1144 + 1100p. **P5-AL0015 — $200.00/set.**

MEMORIAL RECORD OF ALABAMA, Vol. I. 1893. 1144p. **P5-AL0015A — $105.00.**

MEMORIAL RECORD OF ALABAMA, Vol. II. 1893. 1100p. **P5-AL0015B — $105.00.**

REVOLUTIONARY SOLDIERS IN ALABAMA, Being a List of Names, comp. from Authentic Sources, of Soldiers of the Amer. Rev. who Resided in the State of Alabama. By T.H. Owens. 1911. 131p. **P5-AL0010B — $22.00.**

VIKING ODYSSEY TO THE NEW WORLD: from Ancient Sweden to Alabama, via Norway, Normandy, England, Scotland, Va., N.C. & Georgia. By James J. Blue. 1992. 183p. **P5-SW0003 — $25.00.**

HISTORY OF BUTLER COUNTY, from 1815 to 1885, with Sketches of Some of Her Most Distinguished Citizens & Glances at her Rich & Varied Resources. By John Buckner Little. 1885. 256p. **P5-AL0006 — $34.00.**

HISTORY OF CLARKE COUNTY. By John Simpson Graham. 1923. 351p. **P5-AL0007 — $43.50.**

HISTORY OF CONECUH COUNTY, Embracing a Detailed Record of Events from the Earliest Period to the Present [1881]; Biographical Sketches of those who have been Most Conspicuous in the Annals. By Rev. B.F. Riley. 1881. 233p. **P5-AL0011A — $31.50.**

DEKALB COUNTY MARRIAGE INDEX, 1916-1925. Trans. & comp. by Dorothy Smith Duff. 2002. 185p. **P5-AL0013 — $25.00.**

DISTINGUISHED MEN, WOMEN & FAMILIES OF FRANKLIN COUNTY. By Robert L. James. 112p. **P5-AL0009 — $18.00.**

JEFFERSON COUNTY & BIRMINGHAM: Historical & Biographical. 1887. 595p. **P5-AL0002 — $64.50.**

COLONIAL MOBILE: An Historical Study Largely from Original Sources, of the Alabama-Tombigbee Basin & the Old South West, from the Discovery of Spiritu Santo in 1519 until the Demolition of Ft. Charlotte in 1821. By Peter J. Hamilton. 1910. 594p. **P5-AL0010A — $64.00.**

PERRY COUNTY CEMETERY RECORDS. 110p., typescript. **P5-AL0011B — $17.00.**

RUSSELL COUNTY IN RETROSPECT. A.K. Walker. 1951. 423 + 118p. **P5-AL0014 — $54.00.**

HISTORY OF WALKER COUNTY, its Towns & its People. By John Martin Dombhart. 1937. 382p. **P5-AL0012 — $44.50.**

Arizona

HAND-BOOK OF ARIZONA: Its Resources, History, Towns, Mines, Ruins & Scenery. By Richard J. Hinton. 1878. 431 + 101 + 43p., map.
P5-AZ0002 — $61.00.

HISTORY OF ARIZONA TERRI-TORY, Showing its Resources & Advantages with Illustrations Descriptive of its Scenery, Residences . . . 1884. 324p., map.
P5-AZ0002A — $39.50.

HISTORY OF ARIZONA, 4-vol. set. By Ward R. Adams, et al. 1930. 4 vols., 525 + 531 + 615 + 622p.
P5-AZ0001A — $199.00/set.

HISTORY OF ARIZONA, Vol. I. By Ward R. Adams, et al. 1930. 525p.
P5-AZ0001AB — $55.00.

HISTORY OF ARIZONA, Vol. II. By Ward R. Adams, et al. 1930. 531p.
P5-AZ0001AC — $55.00.

HISTORY OF ARIZONA, Vol. III. By Ward R. Adams, et al. 1930. 615p.
P5-AZ0001AD — $55.00.

HISTORY OF ARIZONA, Vol. IV. By Ward R. Adams, et al. 1930. 622p.
P5-AZ0001AE — $55.00.

WHO'S WHO IN ARIZONA, Vol. I (all published). Biographical sketches of approx. 400 prominent Arizonans, with history of the territory and state. By Jo Conners. 1913. 820p.
P5-AZ0001B — $87.00.

Arkansas

PICTORIAL HISTORY OF ARKANSAS From Earliest Times to the Year 1890: Full & Complete Account...; Also extended History of Each County... & of the Principal Cities & Towns; Together with Biographical Notices of Distinguished & Prominent Citizens. By Fay Hempstead. 1890. 1240p.
P5-AR0002 — $119.00.

PIONEERS & MAKERS OF ARKANSAS. J.H. Shinn. 1908. 423p.
P5-AR0001 — $44.50.

HISTORY OF BAXTER COUNTY, 1873-1973. Mary Ann Messick. 1973. 506p.
P5-AR0003 — $54.00.

HISTORY OF BENTON, WASH-INGTON, CARROLL, MADISON, CRAWFORD, FRANKLIN & SEBASTIAN COUNTIES, from the Earliest Time to [1889]. 1889. 1379p.
P5-AR0011 — $129.00.

HISTORY OF CRAIGHEAD COUNTY. With genealogies. By Harry Lee Williams. 1930. 654p.
P5-AR0004 — $71.50.

HISTORY OF CRAWFORD COUNTY. Clara B. Eno. 1951. 499p.
P5-AR0007 — $54.50.

HISTORY OF GREENE COUNTY. By Vivian Hansborough. 1946. 201p.
P5-AR0009 — $31.00.

HISTORY OF IZARD COUNTY. By Karr Shannon. 1947. 158p.
P5-AR0010 — $17.00.

HISTORY OF NEWTON COUNTY. By Walter F. Lackey. 1950. 432p.
P5-AR0005 — $49.00.

REMINISCENT HISTORY OF THE OZARK REGION, Containing a Condensed General History, a Brief Descriptive History of Each County, & Numerous Biographical Sketches of Prominent Citizens of Such Counties. 787p.
P5-AR0006 — $83.50.

HISTORY OF RANDOLPH COUNTY. With family sketches. By Lawrence Dalton. 1946. 359p.
P5-AR0008 — $44.00.

California

GLIMPSES OF CALIFORNIA & THE MISSIONS. By Helen Hunt Jackson. 1902. 292p.
P5-CA0034 — $39.50.

HISTORICAL & BIOGRAPHICAL RECORD OF SOUTHERN CALIFORNIA, Containing a History of Southern California from its Earliest Settlement to the Opening Year of the 20th Century; Also Containing Biographies of Well-Known Citizens . . . By J.M Guinn. 1902. 1295p.
P5-CA0025 — $124.50.

HISTORY OF THE STATE OF CALIFORNIA & BIOGRAPHICAL RECORD OF COAST COUNTIES: Historical Record of the State's Marvelous Growth from its Earliest Settlement to the Present Time [1904]. Prof. J.M. Gunn. 1904. 1418p.
P5-CA0022 — $135.00.

MEMOIRS & GENEALOGY OF REPRESENTATIVE CITIZENS OF NORTHERN CALIFORNIA, Including biographies of many of those who have passed away. 1901. 831p.
P5-CA0023 — $87.00.

OVERLAND STAGE TO CALI-FORNIA: Personal Reminiscences & Authentic History of the Great Overland Stage Line & Pony Express from the Missouri River to the Pacific Ocean. By Frank A. Root & William E. Connelley. 1901. 631p.
P5-CO0001 — $65.00.

PIONEER REGISTER & INDEX, 1542-1848. H.H. Bancroft. 1884-90. 370p.
P5-CA0001 — $39.50.

RECORDS OF CALIFORNIA MEN IN THE WAR OF THE REBELLION, 1861 to 1867. Comp. by Richard H. Orton. 1890. 887p.
P5-CA0035 — $89.00.

HISTORY OF ALAMEDA COUNTY, including . . . the Early History & Settlement; a Full Political History; Separate History of Each Township; and Incidents of Pioneer Life. J.P. Munro-Fraser. 1883. 1001p.
P5-CA0010 — $99.50.

PAST & PRESENT OF ALAMEDA COUNTY, 2-vol. set. 1914. 2 vols., 463 + 594p.
P5-CA0002 — $99.50/set.

PAST & PRESENT OF ALAMEDA COUNTY, Vol. I. 1914. 463p.
P5-CA0002A — $53.00.

PAST & PRESENT OF ALAMEDA COUNTY, Vol. II. 1914. 594p.
P5-CA0002B — $53.00.

COLUSA COUNTY: Its History Traced from a State of Nature through the Early Period of Settlement & Development to the Present Day [1891]. With biographical sketches . . . By Justus H. Rogers. 1891. 473p.
P5-CA0013 — $51.50.

California, cont.

HISTORY OF COLUSA & GLENN COUNTIES, with Biographical Sketches of Leading Men & Women of the Counties. Charles Davis McComish & Rebecca T. Lambert. 1918. 1074p.
P5-CA0012 — $99.50.

HISTORY OF CONTRA COSTA COUNTY, with Biographical Sketches of Leading Men & Women of the County . . . from the Early Days to [1926]. 1926. 1102p.
P5-CA0003 — $109.00.

MEMORIAL & BIOGRAPHICAL HISTORY OF THE COUNTIES OF FRESNO, TULARE & KERN. 1892. 822p.
P5-CA0004 — $86.50.

HISTORY OF IMPERIAL COUNTY. 1918. 526p.
P5-CA0026 — $57.00.

FAIRFIELD'S PIONEER HISTORY OF LASSEN COUNTY . . . from the Beginning of the World . . . to 1870. By Asa Merrill Fairfield. 1916. 506p.
P5-CA0014 — $57.00.

HISTORY OF LONG BEACH & VICINITY, 2-vol. set. By Walter H. Case, with history by Jane E. Harnett. 1927. 2 vols., 684 + 712p.
P5-CA0027 — $137.00/set.

HISTORY OF LONG BEACH & VICINITY, Vol. I. 1927. 684p.
P5-CA0027A — $74.00.

HISTORY OF LONG BEACH & VICINITY, Vol. II. 712p.
P5-CA0027B — $74.00.

HISTORY OF LOS ANGELES COUNTY. 1880. 192p. + 200 illus.
P5-CA0050 — $55.00.

HISTORY OF LOS ANGELES COUNTY. With Selected Biography of Actors & Witnesses in the Period of the County's Greatest Growth & Achievement, 3-vol. set. 1923. 3 vols., 505 + 535 + 551p.
P5-CA0029 — $149.50/set.

HISTORY OF LOS ANGELES COUNTY . . ., Vol. I. 1923. 505p.
P5-CA0029A — $57.00.

HISTORY OF LOS ANGELES COUNTY . . ., Vol. II. 1923. 535p.
P5-CA0029B — $57.00.

HISTORY OF LOS ANGELES COUNTY . . ., Vol. III. 1923. 551p.
P5-CA0029C — $57.00.

ILLUSTRATED HISTORY OF LOS ANGELES CO., Containing a History of Los Angeles Co. from Earliest Period of its Occupancy to [1889], together with . . . Profuse Illustrations . . . & Biographical Mention of Pioneers & Prominent Citizens. 1889. 835p.
P5-CA0028 — $87.00.

STORY OF EARLY MONO COUNTY: Its Settlers, Gold Rushes, Indians, Ghost Towns. Ella M.Cain. 1964. 166p.
P5-CA0044 — $31.00.

HISTORY OF MONROVIA. By John L. Wiley. 1927. 291p.
P5-CA0036 — $37.00.

HISTORY OF NAPA & LAKE COUNTIES, Comprising their Geography, Geology, Topography . . . also Extended Sketches of the Milling, Mining, Pisciculture & Wine Interests. With biographical sketches. By Lyman L. Palmer. 1881. 600 + 291p.
P5-CA0021 — $92.50.

HISTORY OF THE STATE OF CALIFORNIA & BIOGRAPHICAL RECORD OF OAKLAND & ENVIRONS. Also Containing Biographies of Well-Known Citizens of Past & Present. By J.M Guinn. 1907. 2 vols. in 1, 858p.
P5-CA0030 — $89.50.

DIRECTORY OF THE COUNTY OF PLACER for the Year 1861, Containing a History of the County & of the Different Towns in the County; with the Names of Inhabitants . . . Comp. by Steele, Bull & Houston. 1861. 208p.
P5-CA0041 — $24.50.

HISTORY OF SACRAMENTO VALLEY, 3-vol. set By Major J.W. Woolridge. 1931. 3 vols., 508 + 474 + 415p.
P5-CA0024 — $139.00/set.

HISTORY OF SACRAMENTO VALLEY, Vol. I. 1931. 508p.
PS-CA0024A — $48.00.

HISTORY OF SACRAMENTO VALLEY, Vol. II. 1931. 474p.
P5-CA0024B — $48.00.

HISTORY OF SACRAMENTO VALLEY, Vol. III. 1931. 415p.
P5-CA0024C — $48.00.

ANNALS OF SAN FRANCISCO . . . with Biographical Memoirs of Some Prominent Citizens. 1855. 824p.
P5-CA0016 — $86.50.

SAN FRANCISCO: A History of the Pacific Coast Metropolis. By John Philip Young. 1912. 2 vols., xxx + 969p.
P5-CA0017 — $99.50.

HISTORY OF SANTA BARBARA & VENTURA COUNTIES, with Illustrations & Biographical Sketches of its Prominent Men & Pioneers. 1883. 477p.
P5-CA0015 — $51.50.

HISTORY OF SANTA CLARA CO.. Together with Early History & Settlements . . . Names of Original Spanish & American Pioneers; Separate Histories of Earch Township; also Incidents of Pulic Life & Biographical Sketches of Early & Prominent Settlers & [citizens]. 1881. 798p.
P5-CA0031 — $84.00.

HISTORY OF SOLANO & NAPA COUNTY. Vol. II, Biographical. 1926. 495p.
P5-CA0020 — $54.50.

HISTORY OF SONOMA CO., including its Geology, Topography, Mountains, Valleys & Streets, together with a Full & Particular Record of the Spanish Grants, its Early History & Settlements . . . Histories of Each Twp . . . & Biogr. Sketches of Early & Prominent Settlers. 1880. 709p.
P5-CA0032 — $77.00.

HISTORY OF SONOMA COUNTY, 2-vol. set. By Honoria Tuomey. 1926. 2 vols., 784 + 958p.
P5-CA0040 — $159.50/set.

HISTORY OF SONOMA COUNTY, Vol. I. 1926. 784p.
P5-CA0040A — $85.00.

HISTORY OF SONOMA COUNTY, Vol. II. 1926. 958p.
P5-CA0040B — $85.00.

HISTORY OF SONOMA COUNTY, with Biographical Sketches of Leading Men & Women of the County . . . from the Early Days to the Present Time [1911]. By Tom Gregory. 1911. 1122p.
P5-CA0039 — $109.50.

HISTORY OF SONOMA COUNTY: Its People and Resources. 1937. 443 + 384 + 35p.
P5-CA0037 — $89.50.

ILLUSTRATED HISTORY OF SONOMA COUNTY, Containing a History of the County of Sonoma from the Earliest Period of its Occupancy to [1889]. With biographical sketches. 1889. 737p.
P5-CA0038 — $78.50.

HISTORY OF STANISLAUS COUNTY, with Illustrations Descriptive of its Scenery, Farms, Residences, Public Buildings, etc., with Biographical Sketches of Prominent Citizens. 1881. 254p.
P5-CA0019 — $35.00.

HISTORY OF TUOLUMNE COUNTY. With biographies. By Herbert O. Lang (?) 1882. 509 + 48p.
P5-CA0018 — $59.50.

HISTORY OF YOLO COUNTY, Its Resources & Its People. 1940. 18 + 579p.
P5-CA0043 — $62.00.

HISTORY OF YOLO COUNTY, with Biographical Sketches of the Leading Men & Women. By Tom Gregory, et al. 1913. 12 + 889p.
P5-CA0046 — $89.50.

YOLO COUNTY, WESTERN SHORE GAZETTEER, Giving a Brief History . . . [with Business & Personal Directory]. Comp. by C.P. Sprague & H.W. Atwell. 1870. 602p.
P5-CA0033 — $64.50.

Colorado

HISTORY OF THE ARKANSAS VALLEY, Illustrated with bio. sketches. 1881. 889p.
P5-CO0003 — $93.50.

HISTORY OF CLEAR CREEK & BOULDER VALLEYS, Containing a Brief History of the State of Colorado from its Earliest Settlement to [1880]; a History of Gilpin, Clear Creek, Boulder & Jefferson Counties; & Biographical Sketches. 1880. 711p.
P5-CO0004 — $77.00.

OVERLAND STAGE TO CALIFORNIA [Denver, Colo.]: Personal Reminiscences & Authentic History of the Great Overland Stage Line & Pony Express from the Missouri River to the Pacific Ocean. Frank A. Root & William E. Connelley. 1901. 631p.
P5-CO0001 — $65.00.

PORTRAIT & BIOGRAPHICAL RECORD OF DENVER & VICINITY, Containing Portraits & Biographies of Many Well Known Citizens . . . 1898. 1306p.
P5-CO0005 — $126.50.

BRIEF HISTORY OF LOGAN COUNTY, with Reminiscences by Pioneers. Comp. by Emma B. Conklin. 1928. 354p.
P5-CO0002 — $47.00.

PIONEER BOOK OF WASHINGTON COUNTY. Prepared & published by Washington Co. Museum Assoc. 1959. 392p.
P5-CO0006 — $46.00.

Connecticut

BOUNDARY DISPUTES OF CONNECTICUT. By Clarence Winthrop Bowen. 1882. 90p.
P5-CT0328 — $16.00.

CATALOGUE OF CONNECTICUT VOLUNTEER ORGANIZATIONS: An Extensive List of Infantry, Cavalry, and Artillery in the Service of the United States, 1861-1865. 1869. 936p
P26482500 — $141.00.

CATALOGUE OF THE NAMES OF THE EARLY PURITAN SETTLERS of the Colony of Connecticut, with the Time of their Arrival in the Country & Colony. By Royal R. Hinman. 1852. 884p.
P5-CT0136 — $87.50.

COLLECTIONS OF THE CONNECTICUT HISTORICAL SOCIETY, VOL. 9, INCLUDING THE ROLLS OF CT MEN IN THE FRENCH AND INDIAN WAR, 1755-1762. 1903. x + 354p.
P26474700 — $61.00.

CONNECTICUT SOLDIERS IN THE FRENCH & INDIAN WAR: Bills, Receipts & Documents. By Frank D. Andrews. 1925. 41p.
P5-CT0329 — $10.00.

CONNECTICUT SOLDIERS IN THE PEQUOT WAR OF 1637. By James Shepard 1913. 32p.
P26477500 — $26.00.

EARLY CONNECTICUT HOUSES: An Historical & Architectural Study. By Norman M. Isham & Albert F. Brown. 1900. 303p.
P5-CT0327 — $39.00.

EARLY CONNECTICUT MARRIAGES, as Found on Ancient Church Records Prior to 1800. By F.W. Bailey, with add. & corr. 1896-1906. 7 vols. in 1, 994p.
P5-CT0230 — $59.00.

EARLY PURITAN SETTLERS OF THE COLONY OF CONNECTICUT. 1852. 894p.
P26474500 — $135.00.

GAZETTEER OF THE STATES OF CONNECTICUT & R.I. Consisting of Two Parts: I, Geogr. & Statistical Desc. of Earch State; II, General Geogr. View of Each County, & a Minute & Ample Topographical Desc. of Each Town, Village, etc. By J. Pease & J. Niles. 1819. 339p.
P5-CT0061 — $35.00.

GENEALOGICAL & FAMILY HISTORY OF THE STATE OF CONNECTICUT: Record of the Achievements of her People in the Making of a Commonwealth & the Founding of a Nation, 4-vol. set. Ed. by Wm. Richard Cutter, et al. 1911. 4 vols., 2208p.
P5-CT0330 — $219.00/SET.

GENEALOGICAL & FAMILY HISTORY OF THE STATE OF CONNECTICUT . . ., Vol. I. 1911.
P5-CT0330A — $57.50.

For hardcover versions, see the order form on page v. To order, call 1-888-296-3447.

Connecticut, cont.

GENEALOGICAL & FAMILY HISTORY OF THE STATE OF CONNECTICUT . . ., Vol. II. 1911.
P5-CT0330B — $57.50.

GENEALOGICAL & FAMILY HISTORY OF THE STATE OF CONNECTICUT . . ., Vol. III. 1911.
P5-CT0330C — $57.50.

GENEALOGICAL & FAMILY HISTORY OF THE STATE OF CONNECTICUT . . ., Vol. IV. 1911.
P5-CT0330D — $57.50.

GENEALOGICAL NOTES, or, Contributions to the Family Hist. of Some of the First Settlers of Conn. & Mass. By N. Goodwin. 1856. 372p.
P5-CT0260 — $39.00.

GEOGRAPHIC DICTIONARY OF CONN. & R.I. H. Gannett. 1894. 98p.
P5-CT0060 — $18.50.

HEADS OF FAMILIES IN THE FIRST CENSUS OF THE U.S., taken in the Year 1790: Connecticut. 1908. 227p.
P5-CT0056 — $29.00.

HISTORY OF CONNECTICUT, VOL. I By G.H. Hollister 1855. 506p.
P26474800 — $81.00.

INDIANS OF THE HOUSATONIC & NAUGATUCK VALLEYS. By Samuel Orcutt. 1882. 220p.
P5-CT0326 — $34.50.

LISTS AND RETURNS OF CONNECTICUT MEN IN THE REVOLUTION. By the Connecticut Historical Society 1909. 489p.
26474700 — $78.00.

PUBLIC RECORDS OF THE COLONY OF CONNECTICUT, from 1665 to 1678, with the Journal of the Council of War, 1675 to 1678. J.H. Trumbull. Vol. II of a series. 1854. 610p.
P5-CT0262 — $59.00.

RECORD OF CONNECTICUT MEN in the Military & Naval Service during the War of the Revolution, 1775-1783. 1889. 777p.
P5-CT0141 — $79.50.

RECORD OF CONNECTICUT MEN in the Regular Army & the Militia in the War of 1812 & Mexican War. 1889. 180p.
P5-CT0143 — $22.50.

RECORD OF CONNECTICUT MILITIA in the War of 1812. 1889. 180p.
P5-CT0300 — $32.50.

RECORD OF SERVICE OF CONNECTICUT MEN in the Army and Navy of the United States, During the War of the Rebellion. 1889. 1071p.
P5-CT0315 — $105.00.

RECORDS OF SERVICE OF CONNECTICUT MEN IN THE WARS: Includes records of service-men in the Revolutionary War, the War of 1812 and the Mexican War. 1889. 959p.
P26480000 — $144.00.

INSCRIPTIONS FROM ASHFORD CEMETERIES. By Grace O. Chapman & Emily J. Chism. 1942. 220p.
P5-CT0331 — $23.00.

GENEALOGICAL DATA FROM AVON CEMETERIES. Comp. by Lucius B. Barbour. 1932. 45p., typescript.
P5-CT0332 — $10.00.

BARKHAMSTED & ITS CENTENNIAL, 1879, to which is added an Historical Appendix. By Wallace Lee. 1881. 178p.
P5-CT0284 — $29.50.

CATALOG OF BARKHAMSTED MEN Who Served in the Various Wars, 1775-1865. By Wm. Wallace Lee. 1897. 100p.
P5-CT0333 — $17.50.

GENEALOGICAL DATA FROM BERLIN CEMETERIES. Comp. by Lucius B. Barbour. 1915-1932. 80p., typescript.
P5-CT0334 — $15.00.

HISTORY OF BERLIN. By C.M. North. 1916. 294p.
P5-CT0001 — $38.00.

BETHANY & ITS HILLS: Glimpses of the Town of Bethany as it was Before the Railroads & the Fire.. By Eliza J. Lines. 1905. 65p.
P5-CT0336 — $13.00.

GENEALOGICAL DATA FROM BLOOMFIELD CEMETERIES. 1932. 24p.
P5-CT0335 — $10.00.

INSCRIPTIONS FROM THE CEMETERIES OF THE TOWNS OF BOLTON & VERNON. 1905-1907. 70p.
P5-CT0337 — $13.50.

GENEALOGICAL DATA FROM BRANFORD CEMETERIES. Comp. by Lucius B. Barbour. 1932. 66p., typescript.
P5-CT0338 — $13.00.

HISTORY OF BRIDGEPORT & Vicinity, 2-vol. set. 1917. 1234p.
P5-CT0107 — $109.00.

HISTORY OF BRIDGEPORT & Vicinity, Vol. II. 1917.
P5-CT0107B — $58.00.

THE STANDARD'S HISTORY OF BRIDGEPORT. Comp. by George C. Waldo, Jr. 1897. 203p.
P5-CT0204 — $32.00.

BRISTOL, Connecticut ("In Olden Time New Cambridge"), which includes Forestville. By F.C. Norton, et al. 1907. 711p.
P5-CT0281 — $74.50.

GENEALOGICAL DATA FROM BRISTOL CEMETERIES. Comp. by Lucius B. Barbour. 1932. 130p., typescript.
P5-CT0339 — $19.00.

HISTORY OF BRISTOL. By Epaphroditus Peck. 1932. 362p.
P5-CT0221 — $41.00.

ANNALS OF BROOKFIELD, Fairfield County. With genealogies. By Emily C. Hawley 1929. 656p.
P5-CT0207 — $68.00.

BURLINGTON EPITAPHS. By Lucius B. Barbour. 1932. 32p.
P5-CT0340A — $10.00.

BURLINGTON: Historical Address Delivered at the Centennial Celebration. Epaphroditus Peck. 1906. 38p.
P5-CT0423 — $10.00.

RECORDS OF THE CONGREGATIONAL CHURCH IN CANTERBURY, 1711-1844. 1932. 217p.
P5-CT0341 — $22.50.

GENEALOGICAL HISTORY, with Short Sketches & Family Records of the Early Settlers of West Simsbury, now Canton. Abiel Brown. 1856. 151p.
P5-CT0413 — $19.00.

HISTORY OF CHESHIRE FROM 1694 to 1840, including Prospect, which as Columbia Parish, was a Part of Cheshire until 1829. By Joseph P. Beach. 1912. 574p.
P5-CT0277 — $61.50.

OLD HISTORIC HOMES OF CHESHIRE, with an Account of the the Early Settlement of the Town, etc. Comp. by Edwin R. Brown. 1895. 138p.
P5-CT0342 — $25.00.

CLINTON EPITAPHS. By Lucius B. Barbour. 1931. 58p.
P5-CT0343 — $12.00.

HISTORY OF COLEBROOK, & Other Papers. By Irving E. Manchester. 1935. 208p.
P5-CT0425 — $29.50.

HISTORICAL RECORD OF THE TOWN OF CORNWALL, Litchfield Co., By Theodore S. Gold. 1877. 339p.
P5-CT0280A — $38.50.

HISTORY OF CORNWALL: A Typical New England Town. By Edward Comfort Starr. 1926. 547p.
P5-CT0108A — $58.00.

TOWN OF CORNWALL By Theodore S. Gold. 1904. 23 + 35 + 489p.
P26487500 — $129.00.

BIRTHS, MARRIAGES, BAPTISMS & DEATHS, from the Records of the Town & Churches in Coventry, 1711-1844. Comp. by Susan Whitney Dimock. 1897. 301p.
P5-CT0345 — $37.00.

HISTORY OF DANBURY, 1684-1896. By S.B. Hill from research by James Montgomery Bailey. 1896. 583p.
P5-CT0109 — $59.50.

HISTORICAL MEMOIR OF THE WEST OR BROOKLYN SIDE, Danielson, Connecticut: A specimen of Village Annals or Common-Place Local History. With 1996 index by Marcella Pasay. By H.V. Arnold. 1906. 164 + 9p.
P5-CT0346 — $21.50.

HISTORY OF DANIELSON to the Year 1882. With 1996 index by Marcella Pasay. 1905. 228 + 9p.
P5-CT0347 — $27.00.

HISTORY OF THE OLD TOWN OF DERBY, 1642-1880, with Biogr. & Gen. By S. Orcutt & A. Beardsley. 1880. 843p.
P5-CT0002 — $89.00.

INSCRIPTIONS FROM THE GRAVESTONES OF DERBY, with add. & corr. . 31p.
P5-CT0003 — $10.00.

TOWN RECORDS OF DERBY, 1655-1710. Comp. by Nancy O. Phillips. 1901. 496p.
P5-CT0348A — $54.50.

DURHAM [CEMETERY] INSCRIPTIONS. n.d. 75p.
P5-CT0348B — $14.00.

HISTORY OF DURHAM, from its First Grant of Land in 1662 to 1866. By W.C. Fowler. 1866. 460p.
P5-CT0100 — $49.00.

RECORDS OF THE CONGREGATIONAL CHURCH IN TURKEY HILLS, Now the Town of East Granby, 1776-1858. By Albert C. Bates. 1907. 158p.
P5-CT0350 — $19.50.

RECORDS OF THE SOCIETY OR PARISH OF TURKEY HILLS, now the Town of East Granby, 1737-1791. By Albert C. Bates. 1901. 78p.
P5-CT0349 — $15.50.

HISTORY OF ENFIELD . . . from the Beginning to 1850, together with Graveyard Inscriptions and those Hartford, Northampton & Springfield Records which Refer to the People of Enfield, 3-vol. set. 1900. 2652p.
P5-CT0280B — $225.00/SET.

HISTORY OF ENFIELD . . ., Vol. I. 1900.
P5-CT0280BA — $89.50.

HISTORY OF ENFIELD . . ., Vol. II. 1900.
P5-CT0280BB — $89.50.

HISTORY OF ENFIELD . . ., Vol. III. 1900.
P5-CT0280BC — $89.50.

INSCRIPTIONS OF THE TOWN OF ESSEX [cemeteries]. 1907-1909. 132p.
P5-CT0353 — $17.50.

ABSTRACT OF PROBATE RECORDS AT FAIRFIELD, County of Fairfield, 1648-1750. By Spencer P. Mead. 1929. 363p., typescript.
P5-CT0356 — $39.50.

BLACK ROCK, Seaport of Old Fairfield, 1644-1870. By Cornelia P. Lathrop. 1930. 214p.
P5-CT0316 — $34.00.

FAIRFIELD ANCIENT & MODERN, 1639-1909: Brief Account, Historic & Descriptive, of a Famous Connecticut Town. By Frank S. Child. 1909. 73p.
P5-CT0355 — $15.00.

HISTORY & GENEALOGY OF THE FAMILIES OF OLD FAIRFIELD, 2-vol. set. By D.L. Jacobus. 1930-1932. 2 vols., 2051p.
P5-CT1370 — $139.00/the set.

HISTORY & GENEALOGY OF THE FAMILIES OF OLD FAIRFIELD, Vol. I. 1930-1932.
P5-CT1370A — $75.00.

HISTORY & GENEALOGY OF THE FAMILIES OF OLD FAIRFIELD, Vol. II. 1930-1932.
P5-CT1370B — $75.00.

HISTORY OF FAIRFIELD, Vol. I: 1639-1818. By Elizabeth H. Schenk. 1889. 423p.
P5-CT0004 — $47.00.

HISTORY OF FAIRFIELD, Vol. II: 1700-1800. 1905. 538p.
P5-CT0005 — $59.00.

HISTORY OF FAIRFIELD. Genealogies only, Vol. I. 103p.
P5-CT0021 — $15.00.

HISTORY OF FAIRFIELD. Genealogies only, Vol. II. 80p.
P5-CT0022 — $12.00.

INSCRIPTIONS FROM THE GRAVEYARDS, Arranged with Notes & Index [FAIRFIELD]. By Francis F. Spies. 1934. 180p.
P5-CT0354 — $23.50.

Connecticut, cont.

OLD BURYING GROUND OF FAIRFIELD: Memorial of Many Early Settlers & Transcript of the Inscriptions & Epitaphs on the Tombstones found in the Oldest Burying Ground in Fairfield. By K.E. Perry. 1882. 241p.
P5-CT0035 — $29.50.

AN OLD NEW ENGLAND TOWN: Sketches of Life, Scenery, Character [FAIRFIELD]. By Frank Samuel Child. 1895. xvi + 230p.
P5-CT0289 — $32.50.

COMMEMORATIVE BIOGRAPH-ICAL RECORD OF FAIRFIELD COUNTY, Containing Biographical Sketches of Prominent & Repre-sentative Citizens, & of Many of the Early Settled Families. 1899. 1348p.
P5-CT0163 — $125.00.

HISTORY OF FAIRFIELD COUNTY, 1639-1928, 3-vol. set. By Lynn Winfield Wilson. 1929. 3 vols., 699 + 615 + 629p.
P5-CT0205-6 — $175.00/set.

HISTORY OF FAIRFIELD COUNTY, 1639-1928, Vol. I. 1929. 699p.
P5-CT0205-6A — $66.00.

HISTORY OF FAIRFIELD COUN-TY, 1639-1928, Vol. II. 1929. 615p.
P5-CT0205-6B — $66.00.

HISTORY OF FAIRFIELD COUNTY, 1639-1928, Vol. III. 1929. 629p.
P5-CT0205-6C — $66.00.

HISTORY OF FAIRFIELD COUNTY, with Illustrations & Biographical Sketches of its Prom-inent Men & Pioneers. 1881. 847p.
P5-CT0023 — $89.00.

FARMINGTON PAPERS [Histori-cal sketches]. Julius Gay. 1929. 338p.
P5-CT0427 — $41.50.

FARMINGTON, THE VILLAGE OF BEAUTIFUL HOMES: Photo-graphic Reproductions Illustrating Every Home in the Town; Prominent People Past & Present; All of the School Children; Local Antiques, etc. 1906. 213p.
P5-CT0358 — $32.50.

GENEALOGICAL DATA FROM FARMINGTON CEMETERIES. By Lucius B. Barbour. 1914-1932. 63p.
P5-CT0357 — $12.50.

CELEBRATION OF THE 150th ANNIVERSARY of the Organization of the Congregational Church & Society in Franklin, 1868. 1869. 151p.
P5-CT0286 — $19.50.

GLASTENBURY FOR TWO HUNDRED YEARS: A Centennial Discourse, May 18th, 1853. By Alonzo B. Chapin. 1853. 252p.
P5-CT0282 — $34.50.

GLASTONBURY CEMETERY INSCRIPTIONS. 1914. 92p.
P5-CT0359 — $18.50.

INSCRIPTIONS FROM GRAVE-STONES IN GLASTONBURY. Comp. by Dewey & Barbour. 101p.
P5-CT0006 — $15.00.

GOSHEN MARRIAGES, 1740-1896. From History of Goshen. 22p.
P5-CT0007 — $10.00.

HISTORY OF THE TOWN OF GOSHEN, with Genealogies & Biographies. Based upon the records of Dea. L.M. Norton. By A.G. Hibbard. 1897. 602p.
P5-CT0029 — $63.50.

INSCRIPTIONS FROM THE GRAVEYARDS, with Notes & an Index [GREENFIELD HILLS]. By Francis F. Spies. 1934. 227p.
P5-CT0360 — $25.00.

GREENWICH EPITAPHS: Inscrip-tions from Gravestones Arranged with Genealogical Notes & a List of Revolutionary Soldiers & Index. By Francis F. Spies. 1930-1931. 2 parts in 1, 170 + 298p.
P5-CT0361 — $47.00.

HISTORY OF GREENWICH, Fairfield Co., with Many Important Statistics. Daniel M. Mead. 1857. 318p.
P5-CT0200 — $39.00.

OTHER DAYS IN GREENWICH, or Tales & Reminiscences of an Old New England Town. F.A. Hubbard. 1913. 363p.
P5-CT0037A — $41.50.

YE HISTORIE OF YE TOWN OF GREENWICH, Co. of Fairfield and State of Conn., W ith Genealogical Notes on [many] Families. Revision & continuation of 1857 History of the Town of Greenwich, by Daniel M. Mead. By Spencer P. Mead. 1911. 768p.
P5-CT0264 — $77.50.

GRISWOLD--A HISTORY, Being a History of the Town of Griswold, from the Earliest Times to . . . World War in 1917. By Daniel L. Phillips. 1929. 456p.
P5-CT0317 — $49.00.

GROTON, 1705-1905. By Charles R. Stark. 1922. 444p.
P5-CT0363 — $49.50.

HISTORIC GROTON, Comprising Historic & Descriptive Sketches Pertaining to Groton Heights, Center Groton, Poquonnoc Bridge, Noank, Mystic & Old Mystic. By Local Writers. 1909. 101p.
P5-CT0362 — $15.00.

STONE RECORDS OF GROTON. By Frances M. Caulkins. 1903. 96p.
P5-CT0273 — $18.00.

GENEALOGICAL DATA FROM GUILFORD CEMETERIES. By Lucius B. Barbour. 1932. 104p.
P5-CT0364 — $15.00.

HISTORY OF GUILFORD, from its First Settlement in 1639. From the mss. of R.D. Smith. 1877. 219p.
P5-CT0033 — $35.00.

HISTORY OF THE PLANTATION OF MENUNKATUCK, & the Original Town of Guilford [incl. Madison]. By B.C. Steiner. 1897. 538p.
P5-CT0112 — $56.00.

PROCEEDINGS AT THE CELE-BRATION OF THE 250TH ANNIVERSARY of the 250th Anniversary of the Settlement of Guilford, 1639-1889. 1889. 288p.
P5-CT0288 — $39.50.

BY-GONE DAYS IN PONSETT-HADDAM, Middlesex Co.: A Story. By Rev. Wm. C. Knowles. 1914. 65p.
P5-CT0269 — $14.00.

HADDAM EPITAPHS. By Lucius B. Barbour. 1931. 82p.
P5-CT0365 — $15.00.

HISTORY OF THE TOWN OF HAMDEN, with an Account of the Centennial Celebration. 1888. 350p.
P5-CT0274 — $39.50.

COLONIAL HISTORY OF HARTFORD, Gathered from the Original Records. By William DeLoss Love. 1914. 369p.
P5-CT0135 — $41.50.

DIGEST OF THE EARLY CONNECTICUT PROBATE RECORDS: Hartford District, 1635-1750, 3-vol. set. Comp. by Charles Wm. Manwaring. 1904. 3 vols., 669 + 711 + 794p.
P5-CT0368 — $219.50/set.

DIGEST OF THE EARLY CONNECTICUT PROBATE RECORDS: Hartford District, 1635-1750, Vol. I. 1904. 669p.
P5-CT0368A — $75.00.

DIGEST OF THE EARLY CONNECTICUT PROBATE RECORDS: Hartford District, 1635-1750, Vol. II. 1904. 711p.
P5-CT0368B — $75.00.

DIGEST OF THE EARLY CONNECTICUT PROBATE RECORDS: Hartford District, 1635-1750, Vol. III. 1904. 794p.
P5-CT0358C — $75.00.

HISTORICAL CATALOG of the First Church in Hartford, 1633-1885 (includes members, births & bapts., marriages & deaths). 1885. 274p.
P5-CT0275 — $27.50.

COMMEMORATIVE BIOGRAPH-ICAL RECORD OF HARTFORD COUNTY, Containing Biographical Sketches of Prominent Men & Representative Citizens, & of Many of the Early Settled Families. 1901. 1591p.
P5-CT0366 — $149.00.

HISTORY OF HARTFORD COUNTY, 1633-1928, Being a Study of the Makers of the First Constitution & the Story of Their Lives, of Their Descendants & of All Who Have Come, 3 vol. set in 2 books. By Charles W. Burpee. 1928. 3 vols. in 2 books 1383 + 1368.
P5-CT0367 — $215.00/set.

HISTORY OF HARTFORD COUNTY, 1633-1928 . . ., Book I. 1928. 1383p.
P5-CT0367A — $125.00.

HISTORY OF HARTFORD COUNTY, 1633-1928 . . ., Book II. 1928. 1368p.
P5-CT0367B — $125.00.

MEMORIAL HISTORY OF HARTFORD COUNTY, 1633-1884. Vol. I, General county history; town & city of Hartford. Vol. II, History of individual towns in Hartford County. 1886. 2 vols., 704 + 569p.
P5-CT0208-9 — $119.50/set.

MEMORIAL HISTORY OF HARTFORD COUNTY, 1633-1884. Vol. I, General county history; town & city of Hartford. 1886. 704p.
P5-CT0208-9A — $71.00.

MEMORIAL HISTORY OF HARTFORD COUNTY, 1633-1884. Vol. II, History of individual towns in Hartford County. 1886. 569p.
P5-CT0208-9B — $57.50.

HISTORY OF HARTLAND, the 69th Town in the Colony of Connecticut. By Stanley A. Ransom. 1961. 189p.
P5-CT0318 — $29.00.

HISTORY OF HARWINTON. By R. Manning Chipman. 1860. 152p.
P5-CT0113 — $22.00.

HISTORY OF KENT, including Biographical Sketches of Many of its Present or Former Inhabitants. By Francis Atwater. 1897. 176p.
P5-CT0285 — $27.50.

DIARY OF DR HILL [Killingly, CT]. Edwin Allen Hill, MD. 1996. 332p.
P5-CT0369 — $42.50.

KILLINGSWORTH & CLINTON [CEMETERY] INSCRIPTIONS. Comp. by Glenn E. Griswold. 1936. 119p.
P5-CT0371 — $16.00.

EARLY LEBANON: AN HIS-TORICAL ADDRESS (1876) By Rev. Orlo D. Hine 1880. 176p.
P26474500 — $35.00.

LEBANON: Three Centuries in a Conn. Hilltop Town. By George M. Milne. 1986. 287p.
P5-CT0319 — $39.00.

HISTORY OF THE TOWN OF LEDYARD, 1650-1900. By Rev. J. Avery. 1901. 334p.
P5-CT0114 — $39.50.

HISTORICAL SKETCH OF LISBON, From 1786 to 1900. By Henry F. Bishop. 1903. 83p.
P5-CT0372 — $16.00.

GENEALOGICAL REGISTER OF THE INHABITANTS OF LITCH-FIELD, from the Settlement, 1720, to the Year 1800. By George C. Woodruff. 1900. 257p.
P5-CT0376 — $25.00.

HISTORIC LITCHFIELD, 1721-1907, Being a Short Account of the History of the Old Houses of Litch-field. By Alice T. Bulkeley. 1907. 37p.
P5-CT0373 — $10.00.

HISTORY OF THE TOWN OF LITCHFIELD, 1720-1920. By Alain C. White. 1920. 360p.
P5-CT0016A — $42.50.

LITCHFIELD & MORRIS INSCRIPTIONS: Record of Inscriptions Upon the Tombstones in the Towns of Litchfield & Morris. Transcribed by Charles T. Payne. 1905. 304p.
P5-CT0375 — $39.00.

LITCHFIELD BOOK OF DAYS: A Collation of the Historical, Biographical & Literary Reminiscences of Litchfield. Ed. by G.C. Boswell. 1900. 221p.
P5-CT0117 — $32.00.

SKETCHES & CHRONICLES OF THE TOWN OF LITCHFIELD. By Payne Kenyon Kilbourne. 1859. 265p.
P5-CT0015 — $34.50.

BIOGRAPHICAL HISTORY OF THE COUNTY OF LITCHFIELD, Comprising Biographical Sketches of Distinguished Natives & Residents of the County. By Payne Kenyon Kilbourne. 1851. 413p.
P5-CT0377 — $46.00.

BIOGRAPHICAL REVIEW: Biographical Sketches of the Leading Citizens of Litchfield Co. 1896. 670p.
P5-CT0379 — $71.00.

Connecticut, cont.

HISTORY OF LITCHFIELD COUNTY, with Illustrations & Biographical Sketches of its Prominent Men & Pioneers. By Robert M. Addington. 1881. 730p.
P5-CT0301 — $77.50.

HONOR ROLL OF LITCHFIELD COUNTY REVOLUTIONARY SOLDIERS. By Josephine E. Richards 1912. 233p.
P26479000 — $43.00.

LITCHFIELD COUNTY SKETCHES. By Newell Meeker Calhoun. 1906. 177p.
P5-CT0374 — $22.00.

BUCKLAND, the North West Section of Manchester. By Gladys S. Adams. 1995. 123p.
P5-CT0320 — $17.50.

HISTORY OF MANCHESTER. By Mathias Spiess & Percy W. Bidwell. 1924. 306p.
P5-CT0378 — $39.50.

BIRTHS, BAPTISMS, MARRIAGES AND DEATHS (MANSFIELD, CONNECTICUT). By Susan W. Dimock 1898. vi + 475p.
P26516000 — $77.00.

A CENTURY OF MERIDEN: an Historic Record & Pictorial Description of the Town of Meriden. By C.B. Gillespie & G.C. Munson. 1906. 1226p.
P5-CT0118 — $109.00.

RECOLLECTIONS OF A NEW ENGLAND TOWN [MERIDEN]. By "Faith" (Mrs Frances A. Breckenridge). 1899. 222p.
P5-CT0283 — $31.50.

HISTORY OF MIDDLEFIELD & LONG HILL. By Thomas Atkins. 1883. 175p.
P5-CT0380 — $28.50.

COMMEMORATIVE BIOGRAPHICAL RECORD OF MIDDLESEX COUNTY, Containing Biographical Sketches of Prominent & Representative Citizens & of Many of the Early Settled Families. 1903. 1001p.
P5-CT0381 — $99.50.

MIDDLETOWN UPPER HOUSES: A history of the North Society of Middletown, Connecticut, from 1650 to 1800, with Genealogical and Biographical Chapters on Early Families and a full Genealogy of the Ranney Family. By Charles Collard Adams. 1908. 847 + 156p.
P5-CT1366 — $99.50.

NATHAN STARR ARMS [MIDDLETOWN]. By Bernard P. Prue. 1999. 214p.
P5-CT0340B — $34.50.

HISTORY OF MILFORD, 1639-1939. 1939. xi + 204p.
P5-CT0426 — $31.00.

INSCRIPTION OF TOMBSTONES IN MILFORD. n.d. 69p.
P5-CT0160 — $15.00.

ONE HUNDRED YEARS: History of Morris, 1859-1959. Comp. by Laura C. Wiek. 1959. 250p.
P5-CT0211 — $33.00.

COLONIAL HISTORY OF THE PARISH OF MOUNT CARMEL, as Read in its Geologic Formations, Records & Traditions. By J. Dickerman. 1904. 109p.
P5-CT0279 — $17.50.

HISTORY OF WEST MYSTIC, 1600-1985. By Kathleen Greenhalgh. 1985. 248p.
P5-CT0321 — $37.00.

HISTORY OF NAUGATUCK. By Constance McL. Green. 1948. 331p.
P5-CT0510 — $39.50.

HISTORY OF NEW BRITAIN, with Sketches of Farmington & Berlin, 1640-1889. By David N. Camp. 1889. 534p.
P5-CT0276 — $56.00.

NEW CANAAN INSCRIPTIONS COPIED FROM GRAVESTONES . . . Arranged with Genealogical Notes & Record of Revolutionary Service. Francis F. Spies. 1930. 173p.
P5-CT0382 — $19.50.

CHRONICLES OF NEW HAVEN GREEN from 1638-1862: A Series of Papers Read Before the New Haven Colony Historical Society. By Henry T. Blake. 1898. 280 + 40p.
P5-CT1369 — $40.00.

FAMILIES OF ANCIENT NEW HAVEN, 9-vol. set By Donald Lines Jacobus. 1922-1932. 9 vols., 2369p.
P5-CT0140 — $139.50/set.

FAMILIES OF ANCIENT NEW HAVEN, Vol. I. 1922-1932.
P5-CT0140A — $27.00.

FAMILIES OF ANCIENT NEW HAVEN, Vol. II. 1922-1932.
P5-CT0140B — $27.00.

FAMILIES OF ANCIENT NEW HAVEN, Vol. III. 1922-1932.
P5-CT0140C — $27.00.

FAMILIES OF ANCIENT NEW HAVEN, Vol. IV. 1922-1932.
P5-CT0140D — $27.00.

FAMILIES OF ANCIENT NEW HAVEN, Vol. V. 1922-1932.
P5-CT0140E — $27.00.

FAMILIES OF ANCIENT NEW HAVEN, Vol. VI By Donald Lines Jacobus. 1922-1932.
P5-CT0140F — $27.00.

FAMILIES OF ANCIENT NEW HAVEN, Vol. VII By Donald Lines Jacobus. 1922-1932.
P5-CT0140G — $27.00.

FAMILIES OF ANCIENT NEW HAVEN, Vol. VIII. 1922-1932.
P5-CT0140H — $27.00.

FAMILIES OF ANCIENT NEW HAVEN, Vol. IX. 1922-1932.
P5-CT0140J — $27.00.

HISTORY OF THE COLONY OF NEW HAVEN to its Absorption into Conn., with Supp. History & Personnel of the Towns of Branford, Guilford, Milford, Stratford, Norwalk, Southold, etc. By Edw. E. Atwater, et al. 1902. 2 vols. in 1, 767p.
P5-CT0267 — $75.00.

MODERN HISTORY OF NEW HAVEN & Eastern New Haven County. 2-vol. set: Vol. I, Historical. Vol. II, Biographical. By Everett G. Hill. 1918. 2 vols., 436 + 907p.
P5-CT0212-3 — $129.00/set.

MODERN HISTORY OF NEW HAVEN & Eastern New Haven County. Vol. I, Historical. 1918. 436p.
P5-CT0212-3A — $47.50.

MODERN HISTORY OF NEW HAVEN & Eastern New Haven County. Vol. II, Biographical. 1918. 907p.
P5-CT0212-3B — $89.50.

NEW HAVEN VITAL RECORDS, 1649-1850. Part I. 1917. 599p.
P5-CT0037BA — $61.00.

NEW HAVEN VITAL RECORDS, 1649-1850. Part II. 1917. 690p.
P5-CT0037BB — $71.00.

NEW HAVEN VITAL RECORDS, 1649-1850. Parts I & II. 1917. 2 vols., 599 + 690p.
P5-CT0037B — $128.00/set.

RECORDS OF THE COLONY AND PLANTATION OF NEW HAVEN, 1638-1649. By Charles Hoadley 1857. vii + 547p
P26520080 — $88.00.

RECORDS OF THE COLONY OR JURISDICTION OF NEW HAVEN FROM MAY 1653 TO THE UNION. By Charles Hoadley. 1858. iv + 626p.
P26520090 — $98.00.

COMMEMORATIVE BIOGRAPH-ICAL RECORD OF NEW HAVEN COUNTY, CONNECTICUT con-taining Biographical Sketches of Prominent and Representative Cit-izens, and of Many of the Early Settled Families. 1902. 1563 + 744p.
P5-CT1367 — $195.00.

HISTORY OF NEW HAVEN COUNTY, Vol. I. 1892. 740p.
P5-CT0384A — $81.50.

HISTORY OF NEW HAVEN COUNTY, Vol. II. 1892. 827p.
P5-CT0384B — $81.50.

BATTLE OF GROTON HEIGHTS [NEW LONDON]: A Collection of Narratives, Official Reports, Records, etc., of the Storming of Ft. Griswold. Charles Allyn. 1882. 399p.
P5-CT0125 — $45.00.

FIRST CHURCH OF CHRIST, NEW LONDON, CONNECTICUT. By S. Leroy Blake 1900. 559p.
P26520300 — $88.00.

GENEALOGICAL DATA FROM CONNECTICUT CEMETERIES [New London]. By Lucius B. Barbour. 1933. 207p.
P5-CT0385 — $22.50.

HISTORY OF MONTVILLE, for-merly the North Parish of New London, 1640-1896 [with genealo-gies]. Henry A. Baker. 1896. 726 + 106p.
P5-CT0119A — $75.00.

HISTORY OF NEW LONDON, from its First Survey of the Coast in 1612, to 1860. F.M. Caulkins. 1895. 714p.
P5-CT0034 — $75.00.

MISCELLANEOUS HISTORY of New London, from the Records & Papers of the New London Historical Society. Incl. the early whaling industry of New London, famous old taverns, facts & reminiscence, and more. 1895. 110p.
P5-CT0272 — $15.00.

PICTURESQUE NEW LONDON & its environs — Groton — Mystic — Montville — Waterford. 1901. 192p.
P5-CT0101 — $32.00.

THE ROGERENES [NEW LONDON]: Some Hitherto Unpub-lished Annals Belonging to the Colo-nial History of Connecticut. With appendix of Rogerene writings. J.R. Bolles & Anna B. Williams. 1904. 396p.
P5-CT0064 — $42.50.

YE ANCIENT BURIALL PLACE OF NEW LONDON, CONNECTI-CUT. 1899. 40p.
P26520400 — $27.00.

GENEALOGICAL & BIOGRAPH-ICAL RECORD OF NEW LONDON COUNTY, Containing Biographical Sketches of Prominent & Represen-tative Citizens & Genealogical Rec-ords of Many of the Early Settled Families. 1905. 957p.
P5-CT0387 — $97.50.

HISTORY OF NEW LONDON COUNTY, with Biographical Sketches of Many of its Pioneers & Prominent Men. 1882. 768p.
P5-CT0055 — $79.00.

MODERN HISTORY OF NEW LONDON COUNTY, 3-vol. set. 1922. 3 vols. in 2, 619 + 535p.
P5-CT0386 — $119.50/set.

HISTORY OF THE TOWNS OF NEW MILFORD & BRIDGE-WATER, 1703-1882. [Incl. cemetery records & genealogies]. By S. Orcutt. 1882. 909p.
P5-CT0102 — $89.00.

TWO CENTURIES OF NEW MIL-FORD, with an Account of the Bi-Centennial Celebration. 1907. xii + 307p.
P5-CT0214 — $37.00.

EARLY ANNALS OF NEWINGTON. 1874. 204p.
P5-CT0103 — $29.00.

EARLY DAYS IN NEWINGTON, 1833-1836. Henry G. Little. 1937. 122p.
P5-CT0271 — $17.50.

NEWTOWN'S HISTORY, & Historical Ezra Kevan Johnson. With additional material. Includes gene-alogies. Jane Eliza Johnson. 1907. 365p.
P5-CT0119B — $41.00.

HISTORY OF NORFOLK, 1744-1900, Litchfield County. By J. Eldridge & T.W. Crissey. 1900. 648p.
P5-CT0120 — $67.00.

NORTH HAVEN ANNALS: History of the Town from its Settlement, 1680, to its First Centennial, 1886. By Sheldon B. Thorpe. 1892. 422p.
P5-CT0278 — $47.00.

NORTH HAVEN IN THE 19TH CENTURY: A Memorial. By Sheldon B. Thorpe. 1901. 207p.
P5-CT0388A — $29.00.

ANCIENT HISTORICAL REC-ORDS OF NORWALK. With genealogical register. 1865. 320p.
P5-CT0215 — $38.00.

COMPLETE COPY OF THE INSCRIPTIONS Found on the Monuments, Headstones, etc., in the Oldest Cemetery in Norwalk, Ct. Comp. by D.H. Van Hoosear. 1895. 47p.
P5-CT0270 — $10.00.

NORWALK AFTER TWO HUN-DRED FIFTY YEARS: Account of the Celebration of the 250th Anni-versary of the Charter of the Town, 1651- 1901. Includes historical sketches of churches, schools, old homes, institutions, eminent men, etc, along with military records. 1902. 387p.
P5-CT0265 — $44.00.

NORWALK CEMETERIES. By Lester Card. 1945. 152p.
P5-CT0389 — $21.00.

For hardcover versions, see the order form on page v. To order, call 1-888-296-3447.

Connecticut, cont.

NORWALK INSCRIPTIONS COPIED FROM GRAVESTONES . . . Arranged with Genealogical Notes & Record of Revolutionary Service, etc., in Three Parts. Francis F. Spies. 1931. 246 + 267 + 341p.
P5-CT0388B — $88.50/set.

NORWALK INSCRIPTIONS COPIED FROM GRAVESTONES . . ., Part I. 1931. 246p.
P5-CT0388BA — $32.00.

NORWALK INSCRIPTIONS COPIED FROM GRAVESTONES . . . Part II. 1931. 267p.
P5-CT0388BB — $32.00.

NORWALK INSCRIPTIONS COPIED FROM GRAVESTONES . . ., Part III. 1931. 341p.
P5-CT0388BC — $32.00.

NORWALK. Vol. I, with Supplement (all published). With genealogical register. By Rev. Charles M. Selleck. 1896. 482 + 43p.
P5-CT0390 — $59.00.

HISTORY OF NORWICH, from its Possession by Indians to 1866. With index. F.M. Caulkins. 1866. 704 + 42p.
P5-CT0104 — $75.00.

HISTORY OF NORWICH, from its Settlement in 1660 to January, 1845. By Fannie M. Caulkins. 1845. 359p.
P5-CT0392 — $45.00.

NORWICH MEMORIAL: Annals of Norwich, New London Co., in the Great Rebellion of 1861-5. By Malcolm McG. Dana. 1873. 395p.
P5-CT0391 — $47.00.

OLD HOUSES OF THE ANCIENT TOWN OF NORWICH, 1660-1800. With maps, illus., portraits & genealogies. By M.E. Perkins. 1895. 621p.
P5-CT0105 — $67.00.

VITAL RECORDS OF NORWICH, 1649-1848. Parts I & II. 1913. 1180p.
P5-CT0106 — $109.00.

INSCRIPTIONS FROM GRAVESTONES, Norwich Town. By George S. Porter. 1933. 171p.
P5-CT0400 — $21.00.

INSCRIPTIONS FROM GRAVESTONES AT OLD LYME, LYME & E. LYME. 68p.
P5-CT0008 — $10.00.

HISTORY OF OXFORD. Part First: Church Records, Births, Marriages, Deaths, etc.; Part Second: Sketches & Records. W.C. Sharpe. 1885. 184p.
P5-CT0394 — $28.50.

HISTORY OF THE TOWN OF OXFORD. By Norman Litchfield & Sabina Connolly Hoyt. 1960. 328p.
P5-CT0395 — $37.50.

HISTORY OF THE TOWN OF PLYMOUTH, with an Account of the Centennial Celebration & a Sketch of Plymouth, Ohio, Settled by Local Families. By F. Atwater. 1895. 447p.
P5-CT0032 — $51.00.

FOLKLORE & FIRESIDES OF POMFRET & HAMPTON, & Vicinity, By Susan Jewett Griggs. 1950. 161 + 118p.
P5-CT0126 — $36.00.

MONUMENTAL INSCRIPTIONS FROM WAPPAQUIAN BURIAL GROUND IN POMFRET, Copied in 1862. By Marian Chandler Holt. 1913. 150p., typescript.
P5-CT0396 — $19.50.

FIRST CONGREGATIONAL CHURCH OF PRESTON, 1698-1898, Together with Statistics of the Church taken from Church Records. 1900. 201p.
P5-CT0062 — $21.00.

HISTORY OF REDDING, from its First Settlement to the Present Time, with Notes on the Early Families. By C.B. Todd. 1880. 248p.
P5-CT0031 — $34.00.

HISTORY OF RIDGEFIELD, From its First Settlement to the Present Time. By Daniel W. Teller. 1878. 251p.
P5-CT0397 — $36.00.

IMPACT: HISTORICAL ACCOUNT OF THE ITALIAN IMMIGRANTS OF RIDGEFIELD. By Aldo P. Biagiotti. 1990. 345p.
P5-CT0161 — $42.50.

RIDGEFIELD IN REVIEW. By Sylvio A. Bedini with a foreward by Prof. Allan Nevins. 1958. 396p.
P5-CT0222 — $44.50.

HISTORICAL COLLECTIONS OF THE SALISBURY ASSOCIATION, with Vital Records to About 1770, Cemetery Records & a Brief Military History. 1916. 2 vols. in 1, 154 + 208p.
P5-CT0399 — $41.00.

SAYBROOK at the Mouth of the Connecticut River: the First One Hundred Years. By Gilman C. Gates. 1935. 246p.
P5-CT0322 — $36.50.

HISTORY OF SEYMOUR, with Biographies and Genealogies. By W.C. Sharpe. 1879. 244p.
P5-CT0202 — $35.00.

SEYMOUR, Past & Present. By Hollis A. Campbell, Wm. C. Sharpe & Frank G. Bassett. 1902. 613p.
P5-CT0323 — $68.00.

VITAL STATISTICS OF SEYMOUR. Comp. by W.C. Sharpe. 1883. 136p.
P5-CT0401 — $18.00.

BORN, MARRIED, AND DIED: A RECORD OF BIRTHS, MARRIAGES, AND DEATHS IN THE TOWN OF SHARON, CONNECTICUT, 1721-1879. 1897. 144p.
P26521400 — $30.00.

GENERAL HISTORY OF THE TOWN OF SHARON, Litchfield Co., From its First By Charles F. Sedgwick. 1898. 204p.
P5-CT0398 — $29.00.

SIMSBURY, Being a Brief Historical Sketch of Ancient & Modern Simsbury, 1642-1935. By John E. Ellsworth. 1935. 190p.
P5-CT0402 — $28.50.

SKETCHES & RECORDS OF SOUTH BRITAIN. By W.C. Sharpe. 1898. 167p.
P5-CT0011 — $25.00.

GENEALOGICAL DATA FROM SOUTHINGTON CEMETERIES. Comp. by Lucius B. Barbour. 1932. 117p., typescript.
P5-CT0403 — $18.00.

HISTORY OF SOUTHINGTON. By Francis Atwater. 1924. 549p.
P5-CT0263 — $57.50.

SKETCHES OF SOUTHINGTON: Ecclesiastical & Others. By Heman R. Timlow. 1875.
P5-CT0302 — $64.00.

For hardcover versions, see the order form on page v. To order, call 1-888-296-3447.

ABSTRACT OF CHURCH RECORDS OF THE TOWN OF STAMFORD, County of Fairfield, from the Earliest Records to 1850. By Spencer P. Mead. 1924. 499p., typescript.
P5-CT0404 — $53.50.

ABSTRACT OF PROBATE RECORDS FOR THE DISTRICT OF STAMFORD, County of Fairfield, 1729-1848, 2-vol. set. Spencer P. Mead. 1924. 2 vols., 425 + 503p., typescript.
P5-CT0405 — $95.00/set.

ABSTRACT OF PROBATE RECORDS FOR THE DISTRICT OF STAMFORD . . ., Vol. I. 1924. 425p., typescript.
P5-CT0405A — $52.00.

ABSTRACT OF PROBATE RECORDS FOR THE DISTRICT OF STAMFORD . . ., Vol. II. 1924. 503p., typescript.
P5-CT0405B — $52.00.

HISTORY OF STAMFORD From its Settlement in 1641 to 1868, including Darien. With modern index. By E.B. Huntington. 1868. 492 + 69p. Index, typescript.
P5-CT0012 — $57.00.

REGISTRATION OF BIRTHS, MARRIAGES & DEATHS OF STAMFORD FAMILIES. By Rev. E.B. Huntington. 1874. 139p.
P5-CT1368 — $25.00.

HISTORY OF THE FIRST CONGREGATIONAL CHURCH OF STONINGTON, 1674-1874, with the Report of Bi-Centennial Proceedings and Appendix containing Statistics of the Church. By R.A. Wheeler. 1875. 299p.
P5-CT0063 — $30.00.

HISTORY OF THE TOWN OF STONINGTON, County of New London, 1649-1900. By Richard Anson Wheeler. 1900. 754p.
P5-CT0013 — $69.50.

OLD HOMES IN STONINGTON, with Additional Chapters & Graveyard Inscriptions. By Grace Denison Wheeler. 1903. 336p.
P5-CT0129 — $41.50.

STONINGTON CHRONOLOGY, 1649-1949, Being a Year-by-Year Record of the American Way of Life in a Connecticut Town. By Williams Haynes. 1949. 151p.
P5-CT0220 — $25.00.

STONINGTON HOUSES: A Panorama of New England Architecture, 1750-1900. By John J. Trask. 1976 reprinted by permission. 120p.
P5-CT0266 — $29.95.

HISTORY OF STRATFORD, 1639-1939. By William H. Wilcoxson. 1939. 806p.
P5-CT0428 — $84.50.

HISTORY OF THE OLD TOWN OF STRATFORD & THE CITY OF BRIDGEPORT, Two-vol. set By S. Orcutt. 1886. 2 vols., 692 + 700p.
P5-CT0014 — $143.00/set.

HISTORY OF THE OLD TOWN OF STRATFORD AND THE CITY OF BRIDGEPORT, CONNECTICUT. By Rev Samuel Orcutt 1886. 2 vols., 1,393p
P26524900 — $220.00.

HISTORY OF THE OLD TOWN OF STRATFORD & THE CITY OF BRIDGEPORT, Vol. I. By S. Orcutt. 1886. 692p.
P5-CT0014A — $75.00.

HISTORY OF THE OLD TOWN OF STRATFORD & THE CITY OF BRIDGEPORT, Vol. II. By S. Orcutt. 1886. 700p.
P5-CT0014B — $75.00.

STRATFORD BURYING-PLACES. 131p.
P5-CT0017 — $14.00.

THE FIRST PLANTERS: The Original Settlers of Stratford. Extr. From above. 52p.
P5-CT0016B — $10.00.

DOCUMENTARY HISTORY OF SUFFIELD [now CT], in the Colony & Province of Mass. Bay in New England, 1660-1749. By Hezekiah Spencer Sheldon. 1879. 342p.
P5-CT0130 — $39.00.

ADDRESS DELIVERED BEFORE THE TOLLAND COUNTY HISTORICAL SOCIETY. By Loren P. Waldo. 1861. 148p.
P5-CT0406 — $18.50.

COMMEMORATIVE BIOGRAPHICAL RECORD OF TOLLAND & WINDHAM COUNTIES, Containing Biographical Sketches of Prominent & Representative Citizens & of Many of the Early Settled Families. 1903. 1358p.
P5-CT0407 — $129.50.

HISTORY OF TOLLAND COUNTY. By J.R. Cole. 1888. 992p.
P5-CT0122 — $99.50.

HISTORY OF TORRINGTON, from its First Settlement in 1737, with Biographies and Genealogies. By S. Orcutt. 1878. 817p.
P5-CT0024 — $87.00.

HISTORY OF UNION. Founded on material gathered by Rev. Charles Hammond. Harvey M. Lawson, et al. 1893. 509p.
P5-CT0324 — $57.00.

Cascades & Courage: the History of the Town of Vernon & the City of Rockville. By George S. Brookes. 1955. 529p.
P5-CT0131 — $55.00.

EARLY FAMILIES OF WALLINGFORD. Extr. from History of Wallingford, 1870. 363p.
P5-CT1365 — $29.50.

HISTORY OF WALLINGFORD, from its Settlement in 1670 to the Present, including Meridenm which was one of its Parishes until 1806, & Cheshire, which was Incorporated in 1780. By C.H.S. Davis. 1870. 956p.
P5-CT0025 — $97.00.

Inscription on All Stones Still Standing in Cemeteries in the Town of Washington. Comp. by Helen S. Boyd. 1948. 105p.
P5-CT0408 — $15.00.

ANCIENT BURYING-GROUNDS OF THE TOWN OF WATERBURY, Together with Other Records of Church and Town. Transcribed by K.A. Prichard. 1917. 338p.
P5-CT0026 — $38.00.

HISTORY OF WATERBURY & THE NAUGATUCK VALLEY, Three-vol. set By Wm. J. Pape. 1918. 3 vols., 444 + 583 + 641p
P5-CT0410 — $175.00/set.

204　　　　　　　　　　　　　　　　　　*Local Histories*

Connecticut, cont.

**HISTORY OF WATERBURY &
THE NAUGATUCK VALLEY,
Vol. I.** 1918. 444p.
P5-CT0410A — $65.00.

**HISTORY OF WATERBURY &
THE NAUGATUCK VALLEY,
Vol. II.** 1918. 563p.
P5-CT0410B — $65.00.

**HISTORY OF WATERBURY &
THE NAUGATUCK VALLEY,
Vol. III.** 1918. 641p.
P5-CT0410C — $65.00.

**HISTORY OF WATERBURY, with
an Appendix of Biography, Genealogy & Statistics.** By Henry Bronson.
1858. 583p.
P5-CT0132 — $59.00.

**PROPRIETORS RECORDS OF
THE TOWN OF WATERBURY,
1677-1761.** Transcribed by K.A.
Prichard. 260p.
P5-CT0027 — $34.00.

**TOWN & CITY OF WATERBURY,
from the Aboriginal Period to the
Year 1895, 3-vol. set.** Ed. by Joseph
Anderson. 1896. 884 + 560 + 820p.
P5-CT0409 — $209.00/set.

**TOWN & CITY OF WATERBURY
. . ., Vol. I.** 1896. 884p.
P5-CT0409A — $77.50.

**TOWN & CITY OF WATERBURY
. . ., Vol. II.** 1896. 560p.
P5-CT0409B — $77.50.

**TOWN & CITY OF WATERBURY
. . ., Vol. III.** 1896. 820p.
P5-CT0409C — $77.50.

WEST HARTFORD. By William H.
Hall. 1930. 267p.
P5-CT0429 — $39.00.

**HISTORY OF ANCIENT WEST-
BURY & PRESENT WATERTOWN,
from its Settlement to 1907.** 1907. 114p.
P5-CT0411 — $15.00.

**OLD BURYING GROUND OF
ANCIENT WESTBURY &
PRESENT WATERTOWN.**
1938. 145p.
P5-CT0412 — $19.00.

**HISTORY OF ANCIENT
WETHERSFIELD, 2-vol. set.** By
Henry R. Stiles. 1904. 995 + 946p.
P5-CT0018 — $185.00.

**HISTORY OF ANCIENT
WETHERSFIELD, Vol. I.** 1904.
995p.
P5-CT0018A — $99.00.

**HISTORY OF ANCIENT
WETHERSFIELD, Vol. II.** 1904.
946p.
P5-CT0018B — $99.00.

**RIVER TOWNS OF CONNECTI-
CUT: A Study of Wethersfield,
Hartford & Windsor.** By Charles M.
Andrews. 1889. 126p.
P5-CT0268 — $19.50.

**WETHERSFIELD & HER
DAUGHTERS, Glastonbury, Rocky
Hill, Newington. From 1634 to 1934.**
By Frances W. Fox, Jared B. Standish, L.
Wm. Ripley, et al. 1934. 123p.
P5-CT0414 — $16.50.

**ANNALS & FAMILY RECORDS
OF WINCHESTER.** By J. Boyd. 1873.
632p.
P5-CT0028 — $67.00.

**HISTORY OF ANCIENT
WINDHAM: Genealogy, Containing
a Genealogical Record of all of the
Early Families of Ancient Windham,
Embracing the Present Towns of
Windham, Mansfield, Hampton,
Chaplin & Scotland.** By Wm. L.
Weaver. 1864. 112p.
P5-CT0415 — $15.00.

**HISTORIC GLEANINGS IN
WINDHAM COUNTY.** By Ellen D.
Larned. 1899. 254p.
P5-CT0416 — $34.50.

**HISTORY OF WINDHAM
COUNTY, two vols.** By Ellen D.
Larned. 1874. 2 vols., 1181p.
P5-CT0133 — $113.00/set.

**HISTORY OF WINDHAM
COUNTY, Vol. I.** By Ellen D. Larned.
P5-CT0133A — $61.50.

**HISTORY OF WINDHAM
COUNTY, Vol. II.** By Ellen D.
Larned. .
P5-CT0133B — $61.50.

**HISTORY OF WINDHAM
COUNTY.**
Ed. by Richard M. Bayles. 1889. In two
parts, 1204p.
P5-CT0424 — $119.00.

**MODERN HISTORY OF
WINDHAM COUNTY: A Windham
County Treasure Book, Vol. I.** 1920.
P5-CT0218A — $90.00.

**MODERN HISTORY OF
WINDHAM COUNTY: A Windham
County Treasure Book, Vol. II.** 1920.
P5-CT0218B — $90.00.

**MODERN HISTORY OF
WINDHAM COUNTY: A Windham
County Treasure Book. Two-vol. set**
1920. 2 vols., 1827p.
P5-CT0218 — $175.00/set.

**CEMETERY INSCRIPTIONS IN
WINDSOR. With appendix contain-
ing Filley Records.** 1929. 178p.
P5-CT0417 — $21.50.

**HISTORY & GENEALOGY OF
ANCIENT WINDSOR, including E.
Windsor, S. Windsor, Bloomfield,
Windsor Locks & Ellington, 1635-
1891. 2-vol. set.** By Henry Stiles. 1859,
1892. 2 vols, 922 + 867p.
P5-CT0019-20 — $175.00/set.

**HISTORY & GENEALOGY OF
ANCIENT WINDSOR . . ., Vol. I.**
1859. 922p.
P5-CT0019-20A — $89.50.

**HISTORY & GENEALOGY OF
ANCIENT WINDSOR . . ., Vol. II.**
1892. 867p.
P5-CT0019-20B — $89.50.

**NEW HISTORY OF OLD WIND-
SOR.** By Daniel Howard. 1935. 428p.
P5-CT0418B — $47.00.

**SOME EARLY RECORDS &
DOCUMENTS OF AND RELAT-
ING TO WINDSOR, 1639-1703.** By
Edwin Stanley Welles. 1898, 1930. 227p.
P5-CT0134 — $29.50.

**HISTORICAL SKETCHES
[WINDSOR LOCKS].** By Jabez H
Hayden. 1915. 132p.
P5-CT0418A — $16.50.

**HISTORY OF THE TOWN OF
WOLCOTT, from 1731 to 1874.** By S.
Orcutt. 1874. 608p.
P5-CT0108B — $62.50.

**HISTORY OF ANCIENT
WOODBURY, Vols. I & II.** By W.
Cothren. 1854-1872. 2 vols., 1610p.
P5-CT0052 — $150.00/set.

HISTORY OF ANCIENT
WOODBURY, Vol. I. 1854-1872.
P5-CT0052 — $83.50.

HISTORY OF ANCIENT
WOODBURY, Vol. II. 1872.
P5-CT0052B — $83.50.

HOMES OF OLD WOODBURY.
Comp. by Old Woodbury Hist. Soc.
1959. 262p.
P5-CT0325 — $37.00.

HISTORY OF WOODSTOCK &
Genealogies of Woodstock Families,
8-vol. set. By Clarence W. Bowen &
Donald L. Jacobus & Wm. H. Wood.
1926-1943. 8 vols.
P5-CT0420 — The set: $499.00.

HISTORY OF WOODSTOCK &
Genealogies of Woodstock Families,
Vol. I. 1926-1943.
P5-CT0420A — $68.00.

HISTORY OF WOODSTOCK &
Genealogies of Woodstock Families,
Vol. II. 1926-1943.
P5-CT0420B — $68.00.

HISTORY OF WOODSTOCK &
Genealogies of Woodstock Families,
Vol. III. 1926-1943.
P5-CT0420C — $68.00.

HISTORY OF WOODSTOCK &
Genealogies of Woodstock Families,
Vol. IV.
P5-CT0420D — $68.00.

HISTORY OF WOODSTOCK &
Genealogies of Woodstock Families,
Vol. V.
P5-CT0420E — $68.00.

HISTORY OF WOODSTOCK &
Genealogies of Woodstock Families,
Vol. VI.
P5-CT0420F — $68.00.

HISTORY OF WOODSTOCK &
Genealogies of Woodstock Families,
Vol. VII. 1926-1943.
P5-CT0420G — $68.00.

HISTORY OF WOODSTOCK &
Genealogies of Woodstock Families,
Vol. VIII. 1926-1943.
P5-CT0420H — $68.00.

VITAL RECORDS OF
WOODSTOCK, 1686-1854. 1914. 622p.
P5-CT0419 — $67.00.

Delaware

GAZETTEER OF MARYLAND &
DELAWARE. H. Gannett. 1904. 84+15p.
P5-MD0008 — $15.00.

OLD DELAWARE CLOCK-
MAKERS. Henry C. Conrad. 1898. 34p.
P5-DE0004 — $10.00.

HISTORY OF LEWES. By Pennock
Pusey. 1903. 32p.
P5-DE0005 — $10.00.

RECORDS OF THE WELSH
TRACT BAPTIST MEETING,
Pencader Hundred, New Castle Co.,
Dela., 1701-1898, Parts I & II. 1904. 88
+ 147p.
P5-DE0006 — $25.00.

LITTLE KNOWN HISTORY OF
NEWARK & ITS ENVIRONS. By
Francis A. Cooch. 1936. 297p.
P5-DE0007 — $37.00.

CEMETERY RECORDS OF
SUSSEX COUNTY. Comp. by Millard
F. Hudson. 1926-30. 717+ 35p.,
typescript.
P5-DE0003 — $76.50.

CRANE HOOK CHURCH, Pre-
decessor of Old Swede's Church
[Wilmington]. By Pennock Pusey.
1895. 28p.
P5-DE0009 — $10.00.

RECORDS OF THE HOLY TRIN
(OLD SWEDES) CHURCH
[Wilmington] from 1697 to 1773.
Trans. by H. Burr, with abstr. of the
English records, 1773-1810. 1890. 772p.
P5-DE0001 — $79.50.

WILMINGTON: Three Centuries
Under Four Flags, 1609-1937. By Anna
T. Lincoln. 1937. 411p.
P5-DE0008 — $47.00.

Florida

FLORIDA GAZETTEER, Con-
taining Also a Guide to & Through
the State; Complete Official &
Business Directory, etc. 1971. 214p.
P5-FL0001 — $29.50.

HISTORY OF DUVAL COUNTY,
Including History of East Florida. By
Pleasant Daniel Gold. 1929. 234p.
P5-FL0006 — $31.00.

HISTORY OF DUVAL COUNTY;
also, Biographies of Men & Women
who have Done their Part in Making
Duval Co., Past & Present. By
Pleasant Daniel Gold. 1928. 693p.
P5-FL0005 — $74.50.

EVERGREEN CEMETERY
RECORDS, Jacksonville. 1946. 4 vols.
in 1, 834p., typescript
P5-FL0002 — $82.50.

POLK COUNTY CEMETERY
RECORDS. 1946. 223p.
P5-FL0007 — $25.00.

OLD SAINT AUGUSTINE, A Story
of Three Centuries. By Charles B.
Reynold. 1885. 144p.
P5-FL0003 — $21.00.

SAINT JOHN'S COUNTY CEM-
ETERY RECORDS. 1946. 138p.
P5-FL0008 — $19.00.

HISTORY OF ST PETERSBURG,
Historical & Biographical. By Karl H.
Grismer. 1924. 305p.
P5-FL0009 — $39.50.

GENEALOGICAL RECORDS OF
THE PIONEERS OF TAMPA &
Some Who Came After Them. By
Charles Harrison. 1915. 160p.
P5-FL0004 — $21.00.

HISTORY OF VOLUSIA COUNTY.
By Pleasant Daniel Gold. 1927. 168p.
P5-FL0010 — $21.50.

Georgia

HISTORIC GEORGIA FAMILIES.
By L.W. Rigsby. 1928. 258p.
P5-GA0001 — $34.50.

HISTORICAL COLLECTIONS OF
GEORGIA, Containing the Most
Interesting Facts, Traditions. Bio-
graphical Sketches, Anecdotes . . .
from the First Settlement to [1855].
By Rev. George White. 1855. 688+41p.
P5-GA0010 — $74.00.

Georgia, cont.

SKETCHES OF SOME OF THE FIRST SETTLERS OF UPPER GEORGIA of the Cherokees, & the Author. Revised edition. By J.E.D. Shipp. 1926. 458p.
P5-GA0004 — $49.50.

The History of the State of Georgia, 1850-1881. I.W. Avery. 1881. 754+ 80p.
P5-GA0031 — $78.00.

REPORT OF THE WISCONSIN MONUMENT COMM., Appointed to erect a Monument at Andersonville, Georgia. 1911. 296 + vii p.
P5-MISC0030 — $40.00.

HISTORY OF BALDWIN COUNTY. By Anna Maria Green Cook. 1925. 484p.
P5-GA0024 — $54.50.

OUR TODAYS & YESTERDAYS: A Story of Brunswick & the Coastal Islands. Revised ed. By Margaret Davis Cate. 1930. 302p.
P5-GA0020 — $38.00.

CARROLL COUNTY & HER PEOPLE. Priv. Joe Cobb. n.d. 149p.
P5-GA0005 — $21.00.

HISTORY OF CHARLTON COUNTY. With genealogical sketches. Alex. S. McQueen. 1932. 269p.
P5-GA0003 — $34.50.

HISTORY OF CLINCH COUNTY, Giving the Early History of the County Down to the Present [1916] . . . with Chapters on the Histories of Old Families of Clinch County . . . By Folks Huxford. 1916. 309p.
P5-GA0006 — $39.00.

HISTORY OF COLUMBUS, 1828-1928. With biographical sketches. By Nancy Telfair. 1929. 368 + 208p.
P5-GA0019 — $61.00.

HISTORY OF DODGE COUNTY. By Mrs. Wilton Philip Cobb. 1932. 258 + xiii p.
P5-GA0029 — $37.50.

HISTORY & REMINISCENCES OF DOUGHERTY COUNTY. Comp. by the Thronateeska Chapt., D.A.R. 1924. 411p.
P5-GA0026 — $62.50.

OFFICIAL HISTORY OF FULTON COUNTY. By Walter G. Cooper. 1934. 912p.
P5-GA0028 — $93.50.

HISTORY OF GORDON COUNTY. By Lulie Pitts. 1933. 480p.
P5-GA0023 — $54.00.

LOST ARCADIA, or the Story of My Old Community [with biographical sketches] [HEPHZIBAH]. By Walter A. Clark. 1909. 200p.
P5-GA0007 — $31.50.

HISTORY OF IRWIN COUNTY [including pioneer families, marriages records, etc.] By J.B. Clements. 1932. 539p.
P5-GA0021 — $59.00.

EARLY HISTORY OF JACKSON COUNTY: First Settlers, 1784; Formation & Boundaries to [1914]; Records of Talasee Colony; Struggles of the Colonies of Yamacutah, Groaning Rock; Ft Yargo; Stonethrow & Thomocoggan. By G.J.N. Wilson. 1914. 343p.
P5-GA0008 — $41.50.

HISTORICAL RECORD OF MACON & CENTRAL GEORGIA, Containing Many Interesting & Valuable Reminscences Connected with the Whole State, including Numerous Incidents & Facts Never Before Published & of Great Historic Value. By John C. Butler. 1879. 380p.
P5-GA0009 — $44.50.

SKETCHES OF RABUN COUNTY HISTORY, 1819-1948. By Andrew Jackson Ritchie. 1948. 503p.
P5-GA0011 — $55.00.

HISTORY OF ROME & FLOYD COUNTY, Including Numerous Incidents of More then Local Interest, 1540-1922, Vol. I (all published). By George Magruder Battey, Jr. 1922. 640p.
P5-GA0012 — $68.00.

HISTORICAL RECORD OF THE CITY OF SAVANNAH. By F.D. Lee & J.L. Agnew. 1869. 248p.
P5-GA0013 — $34.00.

SIEGE OF SAVANNAH By the Combined American & French Forces under the Command of Gen. Lincoln & the Count D'Estaing in the Autumn of 1779. 1866. 187p.
P5-GA0014 — $27.00.

HISTORY OF TROUP COUNTY. By Clifford L. Smith. 1933. 323p.
P5-GA0022 — $44.00.

HISTORY OF TURNER COUNTY. By John Ben Pate. 1933. 198p.
P5-GA0018 — $31.00.

HISTORY OF WALKER COUNTY, Vol. I. By James Alfred Sartain. 1932. 559p.
P5-GA0015 — $59.50.

HISTORY OF WARE COUNTY. By Laura Singleton Walker. 1934. 547p.
P5-GA0017 — $57.50.

HISTORY OF WASHINGTON COUNTY. Ella Mitchell. 1924. 173p.
P5-GA0016 — $28.00.

Idaho

HISTORY OF IDAHO, A Narrative Account of its Historical Progress, its People, & its Principal Interests, 3-vol. set. By Hiram T. French. 1914. 3 vols., 1320p.
P5-ID0001 — $125.00/set.

HISTORY OF IDAHO, A Narrative Account . . ., Vol. I. 1914.
P5-ID0001A — $49.50.

HISTORY OF IDAHO, A Narrative Account . . ., Vol. II. 1914.
P5-ID0001B — $49.50.

HISTORY OF IDAHO, A Narrative Account . . ., Vol. III. 1914.
P5-ID0001C — $49.50.

HISTORY OF IDAHO, The Gem of the Mountains, 4-vol. set. 1920. 4 vols., 894 + 1008 + 908 + 594p.
P5-ID0002 — $265.00/set.

HISTORY OF IDAHO, The Gem of the Mountains, Vol. I. 1920. 894p.
P5-ID0002A — $70.00.

HISTORY OF IDAHO, The Gem of the Mountains, Vol. II. 1920. 894p.
P5-ID0002B — $70.00.

HISTORY OF IDAHO, The Gem of the Mountains, Vol. III. 1920. 908p.
P5-ID0002C — $70.00.

HISTORY OF IDAHO, The Gem of the Mountains, Vol. IV. 1920. 594p.
P5-ID0002D — $70.00.

GOODING COUNTY Roots and Branches. Vols. I & II. By Gooding, ID, Book Committee. 1989-1990. 268 + 80 p.
P5-ID0003 — $39.00.

Illinois

BUGLE ECHOES: the Story of Illinois 47th Infantry. By Cloyd Bryner. 1905. 262p.
P5-IL0062 — $36.50.

GERMAN EMIGRANTS TO THE US, Series B, vol. I. By Dr. Heinz Marxkors. 2004. 137p.
P5-IL0242 — $26.00.

GERMAN EMIGRANTS TO THE US, Series B, vol. II. By Dr. Heinz Marxkors. 2004. 161p.
P5-IL0246 — $28.00.

GERMAN EMIGRANTS TO THE US, Series B, vol. III. By Dr. Heinz Marxkors. 2004. 358p.
P5-IL0247 — $45.00.

GERMAN EMIGRANTS TO THE US, Series B, vol. IV. By Dr. Heinz Marxkors. 2005. 262p.
P5-IL0252 — $36.00.

GERMAN EMIGRANTS TO THE US, series B, vol. V. By Dr. Heinz Marxkors. 2005. 130p.
P5-IL0255 — $25.00.

GERMAN EMIGRANTS TO US, Series B, vol. VI. By Dr. Heinz Marxkors. 2005. 197p.
P5-IL0256 — $32.00.

GERMAN EMIGRANTS TO THE US, Series B, vol. VII. By Dr. Heinz Marxkors. 2005. 257p.
P5-IL0257 — $37.00.

GERMAN EMIGRANTS TO THE US, Series B, vol. VIII. By Dr. Heinz Marxkors. 2005. 109p.
P5-IL0260 — $28.00.

GERMAN EMIGRANTS TO THE US, Series B, vol. IX. By Dr. Heinz Marxkors. 2005. 88p.
P5-IL0262 — $27.00.

GERMAN EMIGRANTS TO THE US, IL. Series B, vol. X. By Dr. Heinz Marxkors. 2005. 98p.
P5-IL0261 — $27.00.

GERMAN EMIGRANTS TO THE US, Series B, vol. XI. By Dr. Heinz Marxkors. 2005. 216p.
P5-IL0259 — $33.00.

HISTORICAL ENCYCLOPEDIA OF ILLINOIS & HISTORY OF HENDERSON COUNTY, 2-vol. set. Encyclopedia ed. by Bateman & Selby. 1911. 2 vols., 905p.
P5-IL0121 — $95.00/set.

HISTORICAL ENCYCLOPEDIA OF ILLINOIS & HISTORY OF HENDERSON COUNTY, Vol. I. 1911.
P5-IL0121A — $50.00.

HISTORICAL ENCYCLOPEDIA OF ILLINOIS & HISTORY OF HENDERSON COUNTY, Vol. II. 1911.
P5-IL0121B — $50.00.

HISTORICAL ENCYCLOPEDIA OF ILLINOIS, ed. by Bateman & Selby, & History of St Clair Co. Vol. I, Illinois. 616p.
P5-IL0009B1 — $62.50.

HISTORICAL ENCYCLOPEDIA OF ILLINOIS, ed. by Bateman & Selby, & History of St Clair Co., Vol. II, St Clair Co. 522p.
P5-IL0009B2 — $55.00.

HISTORICAL ENCYCLOPEDIA OF ILLINOIS. 1921. 635 + 87p.
P5-IL0081 — $71.00.

HISTORY OF SOUTHERN ILLINOIS: Narrative Account of its Historical Progress, its People & its Principal Interests, 3-vol. set. By Geo. Washington Smith. 1912. 3 vols., 1717p.
P5-IL0085 — $155.00/set.

HISTORY OF SOUTHERN ILLINOIS . . ., Vol. I. 1912.
P5-IL0085A — $64.50.

HISTORY OF SOUTHERN ILLINOIS . . ., Vol. II. 1912.
P5-IL0085B — $64.50.

HISTORY OF SOUTHERN ILLINOIS . . ., Vol. III. 1912.
P5-IL0085C — $64.50.

HISTORY OF THE SWEDES IN ILLINOIS, 2-vol. set. 1908. 2 vols., 933 + 684p.
P5-SW0001 — $139.00/set.

HISTORY OF THE SWEDES IN ILLINOIS, Vol. I. 1908. 933p.
P5-SW0001A — $78.00.

HISTORY OF THE SWEDES IN ILLINOIS, Vol. II. 1908. 684p.
P5-SW0001B — $65.00.

OUR 125TH REGIMENT ILLINOIS VOLUNTEER INFANTRY: Attention Batallion! By Robert M. Rogers. 1882. 226p.
P5-ILCW01 — $37.00.

RECORD OF THE SERVICES OF ILLINOIS SOLDIERS in the Black-Hawk War, 1831-2, and in the Mexican War, 1846-8, Containing a Complete Roster. Isaac H. Elliott. 1882. 343p.
P5-IL0084 — $51.50.

REVOLUTIONARY SOLDIERS BURIED IN ILLINOIS. By Harriet J. Walker. 1918. 184p.
P5-IL0082 — $22.50.

SETTLEMENT OF ILLINOIS, 1778-1830. By Arthur Clinton Boggess. 1908. 267p.
P5-IL0083A — $34.50.

U.S. BIOGRAPHICAL DICTION-ARY & PORTRAIT GALLERY OF EMINENT & SELF-MADE MEN, ILLINOIS VOLUME. 2-vol. set 1876. 2 vols., 798p. + many portraits
P5-IL0080 — $87.00.

U.S. BIOGRAPHICAL DICTION-ARY & PORTRAIT GALLERY . . ., Vol. I. 1876.
P5-IL0080A — $45.00.

U.S. BIOGRAPHICAL DICTION-ARY & PORTRAIT GALLERY . . ., Vol. II. 1876.
P5-IL0080B — $45.00.

HISTORY OF ADAMS COUNTY, Containing a History of . . . its Cities, Towns, etc.; Biographical Directory of its Citizens; Portraits of Early Settlers & Prominent Men; etc. 1879. 971p.
P5-IL0086 — $99.50.

Illinois, cont.

PORTRAIT & BIOGRAPHICAL RECORD OF ADAMS COUNTY, Containing Biographical Sketches of Prominent & Representative Citizens. 1892. 598p.
P5-IL0087 — $64.50.

HISTORY OF BLOOMINGTON & NORMAL, in McLean Co. By J.H. Burnham. 1879. 145p.
P5-IL0088 — $19.50.

FIRST HUNDRED YEARS, 1835-1936: Historical Review of Blue Island. By John H. Volp. 1935. 384p.
P5-IL0064 — $48.50.

HISTORY OF BOND & MONT-GOMERY COUNTIES, IL. 1882. 419 + 333p.
P5-IL0267 — $75.00.

HISTORY OF BOONE COUNTY. With biographical sketches. [Reprinted without Historical Encyclopedia of Ill., available separately]. 1909. 282p.
P5-IL0090 — $38.00.

PAST & PRESENT OF BOONE COUNTY, Containing a History of . . . its Cities, Towns, etc.; a Biographical Directory of its Citizens; Portraits of Early Settlers & Prominent Men; etc. 1877. 416p.
P5-IL0089 — $47.00.

PRAIRIE FARMER'S DIRECTORY of Brown and Schuyler Cos.: Complete Directory of the Farmers of Will & Southern Cook Cos., with Valuable Information . . .[and] Business Directory . . .[and] Valuable Statistics and General Information. 1918. 251p.
P5-IL10003 — $25.00.

BIOGRAPHICAL RECORD OF BUREAU, MARSHALL & PUTNAM COUNTIES. 1896. 727p.
P5-IL0091 — $77.00.

HISTORY OF BUREAU COUNTY. 1885. 710p.
P5-IL0035 — $74.00.

PAST & PRESENT OF BUREAU COUNTY, Together with Biographical Sketches of Many of its Prominent & Leading Citizens & Illustrious Dead. With 1986 every-name index by Jacquelyn G. Glavinick. George B. Harrington. 1906. 968 + 124p.
P5-IL0092 — $99.50.

REMINISCENCES OF BUREAU COUNTY, in Two Parts, with Illustrations. N. Matson. 1872. 401p.
P5-IL0016 — $44.00.

VOTERS & TAX-PAYERS OF BUREAU COUNTY, Containing also a Biographical Directory of its Tax-payers & Voters; History of the County & State; etc. 1877. 411p.
P5-IL0093 — $47.50.

SEMI-CENTENARIANS OF BUTLER GROVE TOWNSHIP, Montgomery Co.; also a Brief History of the Village of Butler. By Rev. T.E. Spilman. 1878. 143p.
P5-IL0094 — $19.00.

HISTORY OF THE CITY OF CAIRO. John M. Lansden 1910. 303p.
P5-IL0095 — $39.50.

CANTON: Its Pioneers & History: Contribution to the History of Fulton County. Alonzo M. Swan. 1871. 164p.
P5-IL0096 — $19.50.

HISTORY OF CARROLL COUNTY (reprinted without Historical Encyclopedia of Illinois, available separately). 1913. 325p.
P5-IL0207 — $43.00.

HISTORY OF CARROLL COUNTY, Containing a history of . . . its Cities, Towns, etc., & a Biographical Directory. 1878. 501p.
P5-IL0036 — $53.50.

HISTORY OF CASS COUNTY. With biographical sketches [reprinted without Historical Encyclopedia of Illinois]. 1915. 376p.
P5-IL0097 — $44.50.

HISTORY OF CHAMPAIGN COUN-TY. J.O. Cunningham. 1905. 435p.
P5-IL0058 — $47.00.

PRAIRIE FARMER'S DIRECTORY OF CHAMPAIGN COUNTY. Complete Directory of the Farmers of Champaign County; Breeders Directory; Business Directory. 1917. 266p.
P5-IL0042 — $25.00.

STANDARD HISTORY OF CHAM-PAIGN COUNTY: An Authentic Narrative of the Past, with Particular Attention to the Modern Era . . . with Family Lineage and Memoirs. 2-vol. set. 1918. 2 vols., 1072p.
P5-IL0059 — $109.00/set.

STANDARD HISTORY OF CHAMPAIGN COUNTY . . . , Vol. I. 1918.
P5-IL0059A — $59.50.

STANDARD HISTORY OF CHAMPAIGN COUNTY . . . , Vol. II. 1918.
P5-IL0059B — $59.50.

HISTORY OF THE EARLY SETTLEMENT OF CHEBANSE TOWNSHIP. Joseph Haigh. 1884. 60p.
P5-IL0098 — $12.00.

BIO. DICTIONARY & PORTRAIT GALLERY OF REP. MEN OF CHICAGO, Wisconsin and the World's Columbian Exposition. 1895. 609 + 386p.
P5-IL0267 — $99.00.

CHICAGO ANTIQUITIES, Comprising Original Items & Relations, Letters, Extracts & Notes Pertaining to Early Chicago, with Views, Portraits, etc. By Henry H. Hurlbut. 1881. 673p.
P5-IL0100 — $71.00.

HISTORY OF CHICAGO, from the Earliest Period to the Present Time, 3-vol. set. A.T. Andreas. 1885. 3 vols.
P5-IL0099 — $199.00/set.

HISTORY OF CHICAGO, from the Earliest Period . . ., Vol. I. 1885.
P5-IL0099A — $70.00.

HISTORY OF CHICAGO, from the Earliest Period . . ., Vol. II. 1885.
P5-IL0099B — $70.00.

HISTORY OF CHICAGO, from the Earliest Period . . ., Vol. III. 1885.
P5-IL0099C — $70.00.

HISTORY OF CHRISTIAN COUNTY. With biographical sketches [reprinted without Historical Encyclopedia of Illinois]. 1918. 412p.
P5-IL0101 — $49.50.

PORTRAIT & BIOGRAPHICAL RECORD OF CHRISTIAN COUNTY, Containing Sketches of Prominent & Representative Citizens. 1893. 459p.
P5-IL0205 — $51.00.

PRAIRIE FARMER'S RELIABLE DIRECTORY OF FARMERS AND BREEDERS, CHRISTIAN COUNTY, ILLINOIS. 1918. 215p.
P5-IL0233 — $33.50.

HISTORY OF CLARK COUNTY (Reprinted without Historical Encyclopedia of Illinois, available separately). 1907. 234p.
P5-IL0230 — $34.00.

COMMERCIAL HISTORY OF CLINTON COUNTY AND ITS THRIVING CITIES. 1913. 90p.
P5-IL0238 — $27.00.

HISTORY OF COLES COUNTY, Containing a History of the County, its Cities, Towns, &c; Portraits of Early Settlers & Prominent Men; etc. 1879. 699 + 10p.
P5-IL0181A — $76.50.

HISTORY OF COLES COUNTY. With biographical sketches. [Published without Encyclopedia of Illinois]. Charles Edw. Wilson. 1905. 270p.
P5-IL0102 — $39.00.

PORTRAIT & BIOGRAPHICAL ALBUM OF COLES COUNTY, Containing Portraits & Biographical Sketches of Prominent & Representative Citizens of the County. 1887. 580p.
P5-IL0215 — $63.00.

ALBUM OF GENEALOGY & BIOGRAPHY, Cook County, 9th ed. 1898. 766p.
P5-IL0104 — $83.00.

HISTORICAL ENCYCLOPEDIA OF ILLINOIS, Cook Co. ed., 2-vol. set. 1905. 2 vols., 1030p.
P5-IL0054 — $115.00/set.

HISTORICAL ENCYCLOPEDIA OF ILLINOIS, Cook Co. ed., Vol. I. 1905.
P5-IL0054A — $62.00.

HISTORICAL ENCYCLOPEDIA OF ILLINOIS, Cook Co. ed., Vol. II. 1905.
P5-IL0054B — $62.00.

HISTORY OF COOK COUNTY, Being a General Survey of Cook Co. History, including a Condensed History of Chicago & a Special Account of Districts Outside the City Limits, from the Earliest Settlement to the Present Time, 2-vol. set. 1909. 2 vols., 864+1011p.
P5-IL0105 — $165.00.

HISTORY OF COOK COUNTY, Being a General Survey of Cook Co. History, including a Condensed History of Chicago & a Special Account of Districts Outside the City Limits, from the Earliest Settlement to the Present Time, Vol. I. 1909. 864p.
P5-IL0105A — $70.00.

HISTORY OF COOK COUNTY, from the Earliest Period to the Present Time [1884]. With biograpical sketches. By A.T. Andreas. 1884. 888p.
P5-IL0103 — $91.50.

HISTORY OF CRAWFORD & CLARK COUNTIES. With biographical sketches. Every-name index. 1883. 470 + 374 + 114p.
P5-IL0106 — $87.00.

COUNTIES OF CUMBERLAND, JASPER & RICHLAND, Historical & Biographical. 1884. 839p.
P5-IL0228 — $85.00.

HISTORY OF THE SOMONAUK UNITED PRESBYTERIAN CHURCH Near Sandwich, De Kalb County, Illinois. By Jennie M. Patten. 1928. 373 + 70p.
P5-IL0243 — $46.00.

CENTENNIAL OF DECATUR & MACON COUNTY. By Mabel E. Richmond. 1930. 479p.
P5-IL0180 — $54.00.

PAST & PRESENT OF THE CITY OF DECATUR AND MACON COUNTY, History & Biographical. 1903. 884p.
P5-IL0065 — $91.50.

HISTORY OF DEERFIELD. By Marie Ward Reichelt. 1928. 215p.
P5-IL0108 — $24.50.

BIOGRAPHICAL RECORD OF DEKALB COUNTY. 1898. 562p.
P5-IL0107 — $61.00.

PAST & PRESENT OF DEKALB COUNTY, 2-vol. set By Prof. Lewis M. Gross. 1907. 2 vols., 596+608p.
P5-IL0211 — $119.00/set.

PAST & PRESENT OF DEKALB COUNTY, Vol. I. By Prof. Lewis M. Gross. 1907. 596p.
P5-IL0211A — $64.50.

PAST & PRESENT OF DEKALB COUNTY, Vol. II. By Prof. Lewis M. Gross. 1907. 608p.
P5-IL0211B — $64.50.

PORTRAIT & BIOGRAPHICAL ALBUM OF DEKALB COUNTY, Containing Portraits & Biographical Sketches of Prominent & Representative Citizens of the Counties. (Reprinted without biographies of Presidents & Governors). 1885. 721p.
P5-IL0212 — $79.00.

PRAIRIE FARMER'S DIRECTORY OF DeKALB COUNTY: Complete Directory of the Farmers of DeKalb Co., with Valuable Information about Each Farm . . ., Business Directory . . ., Valuable Statistic and General Information. 1917. 175p.
P5-IL0004 — $24.50.

HISTORY OF DeWITT COUNTY, with Biographical Sketches of Prominent Representative Citizens of the County, 2-vol. set 1910. 2 vols., 438 + 412p.
P5-IL0208 — $89.00/set.

HISTORY OF DeWITT COUNTY . . ., Vol. I. 1910. 438p.
P5-IL0208A — $46.50.

HISTORY OF DeWITT COUNTY . . ., Vol. II. 1910. 412p.
P5-IL0208B — $46.50.

PORTRAIT & BIOGRAPHICAL ALBUM OF DeWITT & PIATT COUNTIES, Containing Full-page Portraits & Biographical Sketches of Prominent & Representative Citizens of the Counties. 1891. 968p.
P5-IL0109 — $97.00.

HISTORY OF DU PAGE COUNTY. By Rufus Blanchard. 1882. 294 + 247p.
P5-IL0110 — $61.50.

HISTORY OF THE COUNTY OF DU PAGE, Containing an Account of its Early Settlement & Present Advantages & a Separate History of the Several Towns. C.W. Richmond & H.F. Vallette. 1857. 212p.
P5-IL0034A — $29.50.

PRAIRIE FARMER'S DIRECTORY OF DU PAGE AND NORTHERN COOK COUNTIES, ILLINOIS. 1918. 271p.
P5-IL10005 — $29.00.

For hardcover versions, see the order form on page v. To order, call 1-888-296-3447.

Illinois, cont.

HISTORY OF DWIGHT, from 1853 to 1894. Dustin & Wassell. 1894. 153p.
P5-IL0111 — $21.00.

COMBINED HISTORY OF EDWARDS, LAWRENCE & WABASH COUNTIES, with Illustrations Descriptive of their Scenery & Biographical Sketches of Some of Their Prominent Men & Pioneers, 1682-1883. 1883. 377p.
P5-IL0112 — $44.50.

HISTORY OF THE ENGLISH SETTLEMENT OF EDWARDS CO., Founded in 1817 & 1818. By G. Flower & E. Washburne. 1882. 402p.
P5-IL0001 — $42.50.

HISTORY OF EFFINGHAM COUNTY. Ed. by William Henry Perrin. 1883. 640p.
P5-IL0019A — $67.00.

ILLINOIS & EFFINGHAM COUNTY, Historical & Biographical. Vol. I, Encyclopedia of Illinois. Vol. II, Effingham County. Ed. by Newton Bateman & Paul Selby. 1910. 2 vols., 616 + 272p.
P5-IL0020 — $99.00/set.

ILLINOIS & EFFINGHAM COUNTY, Historical & Biographical, Vol. I: Encyclopedia of Illinois. Ed. by Newton Bateman & Paul Selby. 1910. 616p.
P5-IL0020A — $66.00.

ILLINOIS & EFFINGHAM COUNTY, Historical & Biographical, Vol. II: Effingham County. Ed. by Newton Bateman & Paul Selby. 1910. 272p.
P5-IL0020B — $33.00.

EVANSTON: Its Land & Its People. By Viola Crouch Reeling. 1928. 468p.
P5-IL0225 — $49.00.

HISTORY OF EVANSTON [with biographical sketches & a history of Northwester University]. 1906. 630p.
P5-IL0113 — $68.00.

HISTORY OF FAYETTE COUNTY. With biographical sketches. (Reprinted without Historical Encyclopedia of Illinois, available separately). 1910. 218p.
P5-IL0220 — $31.50.

HISTORY OF FORD COUNTY from its Earliest Settlement to 1908, with Biographical Sketches of Some Prominent Citizens of the County, 2-vol. set By E.A. Gardner. 1908. 2 vols., 877p.
P5-IL0114 — $94.00/set.

HISTORY OF FORD COUNTY . . ., Vol. I. 1908.
P5-IL0114A — $49.00.

HISTORY OF FORD COUNTY . . ., Vol. II. 1908.
P5-IL0114B — $49.00.

PRAIRIE FARMER'S DIRECTORY OF FORD COUNTY. Complete Directory of the Farmers of Ford County; Breeders Directory; Business Directory. 1917. 152p.
P5-IL0041 — $17.00.

HISTORY OF FULTON COUNTY [published without Historical Encyclopedia of Illinois]. With biographical sketches. 1908. 590p.
P5-IL0115 — $64.00.

HISTORY OF FULTON COUNTY. With biographies. 1879. 1090p.
P5-IL0066 — $109.00.

HISTORY OF GALLATIN, SALINE, HAMILTON, FRANKLIN & WILLIAMSON COUNTIES, from the Earliest Time to the Present; Together with Sundry & Interesting Biographical Sketches . . . 1887. 961p.
P5-IL0181B — $98.00.

GLEN ELLYN: THE STORY OF AN OLD TOWN. With genealogical sketches. By Ada Douglas Harmon, 1928. 208p.
P5-IL0021 — $29.50.

EARLY DAYS IN GREENBUSH, with Biographical Sletches of the Old Settlers. William L. Snapp. 1905. 195p.
P5-IL0025 — $26.00.

HISTORY OF GREENE & JERSEY COUNTIES, Together with Sketches of the Towns, Villages & Townships; ..Civil, Military & Political History; .. And Biographies of Representative Men. 1885. 1156p.
P5-IL0116 — 109.00.

PAST & PRESENT OF GREENE COUNTY. By Ed. Miner. 1905. 645p.
P5-IL0117 — $69.50.

HISTORY OF GRUNDY COUNTY, Containing a History from the Earliest Settlement to [1882]..Giving an Account of its Aboriginal Inhabitants; Early Settlement by Whites; Pioneer Incidents; . . . Biographical Sketchesl Portraits of Early Settlers, etc. 1882. 362 + 156p.
P5-IL0217 — $58.00.

PRAIRIE FARMER'S DIRECTORY OF GRUNDY & KENDALL COUNTIES: Complete Directory of the Farmers of Grundy & Kendall Cos..Breeders' Directory . . . [and] Business Directory. 1917. 224p.
P5-IL0018 — $25.00.

HISTORY OF HANCOCK COUNTY. By T.H. Gregg. 1880. 1036p.
P5-IL0202 — $105.00.

HISTORY OF HANCOCK COUNTY. With biographical sketches. [published without Historical Encyclopedia of Illinois]. 1921. 802p.
P5-IL0120 — $84.50.

PORTRAIT & BIOGRAPHICAL RECORD OF HANCOCK, McDONOUGH & HENDERSON COUNTIES, Containing Biographical Sketches of Prominent & Representative Citizens of the County. 1894. 602p.
P5-IL0019B — $66.50.

PRAIRIE FARMER'S DIRECTORY OF HANCOCK COUNTY: Complete Directory of Farmers . . .; Business Directory . . .; Valuable Statistics and General Information. 1918. 267p.
P5-IL0200 — $27.50.

HISTORY OF HENRY COUNTY, its Taxpayers & Voters, Containing also a Biographical Directory . . . 1877. 589p.
P5-IL0067 — $61.50.

HISTORY OF HENRY COUNTY, 2 vols. By Henry L. Kiner. 1910. 2 vols., 827 + 1073p.
P5-IL0122 — $169.00/set.

HISTORY OF HENRY COUNTY, vol. I. By Henry L. Kiner. 1910. 827p.
P5-IL0122A — $89.00.

HISTORY OF HENRY COUNTY, vol. II. By Henry L. Kiner. 1910. 1073p.
P5-IL0122B — $89.00.

PORTRAIT & BIOGRAPHICAL ALBUM OF HENRY COUNTY, Containing Full-page Portraits & Biographical Sketches of Citizens ... of the County. 1885. 834p.
P5-IL0013 — $85.00.

PRAIRIE FARMER DIRECTORY OF HENRY CO., IL. 1916. 167p.
P5-IL0266 — $27.00.

CENTENNIAL HISTORY OF THE VILLAGES OF IROQUOIS & MONTGOMERY, & the Twp. of Concord, 1818-1918. S. Ely. 1918. 142p.
P5-IL0003 — $17.00.

PAST & PRESENT OF IROQUOIS COUNTY, together with Biographical Sketches of Many of its Prominent & Leading Citizens & Illustrious Dead. Hist. by J.W. Kern. 1907. 741p.
P5-IL0123 — $79.50.

HISTORY OF JEFFERSON COUNTY. With biographical sketches. By John A. Wall. 1909. 618p.
P5-IL0124 — $66.00.

HISTORY OF JERSEY COUNTY. 1919. 673p.
P5-IL0047 — $69.50.

HISTORY OF JERSEYVILLE, 1822 to 1901. By Rev. Marshall M. Cooper. 1901. 245p.
P5-IL0045 — $34.50.

HISTORY OF JO DAVIESS COUNTY, Containing a History of ... its Cities, Towns, etc., & a Biographical Directory. 1878. 853p.
P5-IL0037 — $87.00.

HISTORY OF JOHNSON COUNTY. By Mrs P.T. Chapman. 1925. 502p.
P5-IL0224 — $54.50.

FORTY YEARS AGO! Contribution to the Early History of Joliet & Will County. Geo. Woodruff. 1874. 108p.
P5-IL0125 — $17.00.

BIOGRAPHICAL RECORD OF KANE COUNTY. 1898. 769p.
P5-IL0127 — $79.50.

COMMEMORATIVE PORTRAIT & BIOGRAPHICAL RECORD OF KANE & KENDALL COUNTIES, containing ... Portraits & Biographical Sketches of Prominent & Representative Citizens of Kane & Kendall Counties [published without section on Governors & Presidents]. 1888. 819p.
P5-IL0126 — $86.50.

HISTORY OF KANE COUNTY, Vol. I. By R. Waite Joslyn & Frank W. Joslyn. 1908. 868p.
P5-IL0128A — $93.50.

HISTORY OF KANE COUNTY, Vol. II. By R. Waite Joslyn & Frank W. Joslyn. 1908. 911p.
P5-IL0128B — $93.50.

PAST & PRESENT OF KANE COUNTY: History of the County — its Cities, Towns, etc.; Directory of its Citizens; Portraits of Early Settlers & Prominent Men. 1878. 821p.
P5-IL0210 — $88.50.

PRAIRIE FARMER'S RELIABLE DIRECTORY OF FARMERS AND BREEDERS, KANE COUNTY, ILLINOIS. 1918. 217p.
P5-IL0251 — $33.00.

HISTORY OF KENDALL COUNTY, from the Earliest Discoveries to the Present Time. By Rev. E.W. Hicks. 1877. 438p.
P5-IL0068 — $51.50.

KENILWORTH — The First Fifty Years. 1947. 116p.
P5-IL0034B — $16.00.

HISTORY OF KNOX COUNTY [reprinted without Historical Encyclopedia of Illinois, available separately]. 1899. 360p.
P5-IL0129 — $44.00.

HISTORY OF KNOX COUNTY, its Cities, Towns & People, 2-vol. set. By Albert J. Perry. 1912. 2 vols., 803 + 1154p.
P5-IL0130 — $165.00/set.

HISTORY OF KNOX COUNTY, its Cities, Towns & People, Vol. I. By Albert J. Perry. 1912. 803p.
P5-IL0130A — $85.00.

HISTORY OF KNOX COUNTY, its Cities, Towns & People, Vol. II. By Albert J. Perry. 1912. 1154p.
P5-IL0130B — $100.00.

HISTORY OF KNOX COUNTY, together with Sketches of the Cities, Villages & Townships; ... and Biographical Sketches. By Chas. C. Chapman & Co. 1878. 718p.
P5-IL0069 — $79.00.

HISTORY OF La SALLE COUNTY, 3-vol. set By Michael Cyprian O'Byrne. 1924. 3 vols. in 2, 495 + 653p.
P5-IL0070 — $109.50/set.

HISTORY OF La SALLE COUNTY, Book I. 1924. 495p.
P5-IL0070A — $58.00.

HISTORY OF La SALLE COUNTY, Book II. 1924. 653p.
P5-IL0070B — $62.00.

HISTORY OF La SALLE COUNTY ... and a Sketch of the Pioneer Settlers of Each Town to 1840, with an Appendix. By Elmer Baldwin. 1877. 552p.
P5-IL0026 — $58.00.

LIFE OF A WOMAN PIONEER, as Illustrated in the Life of Elsie Strawn Armstrong, 1789-1871; Part I, her Personal History; Part II, Short Accounts of Important Events in Pioneer Times. [LA SALLE CO.] By James Elder Armstrong. 1931. 124p.
P5-IL0131 — $18.00.

PAST & PRESENT OF LA SALLE COUNTY, Containing a History of the County, its Cities, Towns, etc., a Biographical Directory of its Citizens ... 1877. 653p.
P5-IL0046 — $67.00.

PRAIRIE FARMER'S RELIABLE DIRECTORY OF FARMERS AND BREEDERS: La Salle County, Illinois. 1917. 391p.
P5-IL0236 — $42.00.

HISTORY OF LAKE COUNTY. Ed. by John J. Halsey. 1912. 872p.
P5-IL0061 — $91.00.

PAST & PRESENT OF LAKE COUNTY, Containing a History of the County; its Cities, Towns, etc.; Biographical Directory of its Citizens; Portraits of Early Settlers & Prominent Men; etc. 1877. 501p.
P5-IL0133 — $57.00.

Illinois, cont.

PORTRAIT & BIOGRAPHICAL ALBUM OF LAKE COUNTY, Containing Full Page Portraits & Biographical Sketches of Prominent & Representative Citizens of the County. 1891. 785p.
P5-IL0132 — $81.50.

PRAIRIE FARMER'S DIRECTORY OF LAKE COUNTY. 1917. 140p.
P5-IL0232 — $28.00.

HISTORY OF LEE COUNTY, Together with Biographical Matter, etc. By Dr Cochran et al. 1881. 873p.
P5-IL0022 — $89.50.

PORTRAITS & BIOGRAPHICAL RECORD OF LEE COUNTY, Containing Biographical Sketches of Prominent & Representative Citizens. 1892. 854p.
P5-IL0134 — $89.50.

RECOLLECTIONS OF THE PIONEERS OF LEE COUNTY. 1893. 583p.
P5-IL0135 — $64.00.

WAR HISTORY OF LEE COUNTY, 1917-19: History of the Part Taken by the People of Lee Co. in the [First] World War. n.d. 271p.
P5-IL0009A — $27.00.

CENTENNIAL HISTORY OF LITCHFIELD, 1853-1953. Comp. by Litchfield Centennial, Inc. 1953. 208p.
P5-IL0034C — $19.50.

BIOGRAPHICAL RECORD OF LIVINGSTON & WOODFORD COUNTIES. 1900. 684p.
P5-IL0136 — $71.50.

BIOGRAPHICAL RECORD OF LOGAN COUNTY. 1901. 654p.
P5-IL0209 — $71.00.

HISTORY OF LOGAN COUNTY, Together with Sketches of its Cities, Villages & Towns . . .; Civil, Military & Political History . . .; and Biographies of Representative Citizens. 1886. 909p.
P5-IL0137 — $91.50.

HISTORY OF LOGAN COUNTY: A Record of its Settlement, Organization, Progress and Achievement, 2-vol. set. By Lawrence B. Stringer. 1911. 2 vols., 630 + 407p.
P5-IL0072 — $109.00.

HISTORY OF LOGAN COUNTY . . ., Vol. I. 1911. 630p.
P5-IL0072A — $64.00.

HISTORY OF LOGAN COUNTY . . ., Vol. II. 1911. 407p.
P5-IL0072B — $56.00.

PRAIRIE FARMER'S RELIABLE DIRECTORY OF FARMERS AND BREEDERS, MACAUPIN CO. 1919. 279p.
P5-IL0269 — $39.00.

HISTORY OF MACON COUNTY, from its Organization to 1876. With biographical sketches. By John W. Smith. 1876. 304p.
P5-IL0138 — $39.00.

HISTORY OF MACOUPIN COUNTY, with Illustrations . . . and Biographical Sketches of Prominent Men & Pioneers. 1879. 288p.
P5-IL0057 — $39.00.

PORTRAIT & BIOGRAPHICAL RECORD OF MACOUPIN COUNTY, Containing Biographical Sketches of Prominent & Representative Citizens. (Reprinted without biographies of Presidents and Governors.) 1891. 720p.
P5-IL0073 — $79.00.

CENTENNIAL HISTORY OF MADISON COUNTY & ITS PEOPLE, 1812 to 1912, 2-vol. set. 1912. 2 vols., 1208p.
P5-IL0140 — $129.00/set.

CENTENNIAL HISTORY OF MADISON COUNTY & ITS PEOPLE . . ., Vol. I. 1912.
P5-IL0140A — $65.00.

CENTENNIAL HISTORY OF MADISON COUNTY & ITS PEOPLE . . ., Vol. II. 1912.
P5-IL0140B — $65.00.

HISTORY OF MADISON COUNTY, with Biographical Sketches of many Prominent Men & Pioneers. 1882. 603p.
P5-IL0007 — $55.00.

PORTRAIT & BIOGRAPHICAL RECORD OF MADISON COUNTY, Containing Biographical Sketches of Prominent & Representative Citizens of the County. 1894. 548p.
P5-IL0216 — $61.50.

PAST & PRESENT OF MARSHALL & PUTNAM COUNTIES, with Biographical Sketches of Many Prominent & Leading Citizens & Illustrious Dead. By John S. Burt & W.E. Hawthorne. 1907. 511p.
P5-IL0206 — $58.00.

EARLY HISTORY OF MASCOUTAH, to and Including the Year 1850. By Herbert F. Lill. 1963. 184p.
P5-IL0141 — $29.00.

CENTENNIAL HISTORY OF MASON COUNTY, including a Sketch of the Early History of Illinois. Joseph Cochrane. 1876. 352p.
P5-IL0074 — $44.50.

HISTORY OF MASSAC COUNTY, with Life Sketches & Portraits. By O.J. Page. 1900. 383p.
P5-IL0142 — $46.50.

HISTORY OF McDONOUGH COUNTY, Its Cities, Towns & Villages, with Early Reminiscences, Personal Incidents & Anecdotes. By J.J. Clark. 1878. 692p.
P5-IL0005 — $69.50.

HISTORY OF McDONOUGH COUNTY, together with Sketches of the Towns, Villages, & Townships . . . & Biographies of Representative Citizens. 1885. 1158p.
P5-IL0023 — $109.00.

HISTORY OF McDONOUGH COUNTY. With biographical sketches. (Reprinted without Historical Encyclopedia of Illinois, available separately). 1907. 445p.
P5-IL0219 — $51.50.

BIOGRAPHICAL OF THE TAX-PAYERS & VOTERS OF McHENRY COUNTY, Containing Also . . . an Historical Sketch of the County, its Towns & Villages; Business Directory, etc. 1877. 352p.
P5-IL0143 — $41.50.

HISTORY OF MCHENRY CO., IL. 1885. 941 + 132p.
P5-IL0268 — $107.00.

HISTORY OF McHENRY COUNTY, Vol. I, History. 1922. 457p.
P5-IL0083B — $49.00.

HISTORY OF McHENRY COUNTY, Vol. II, Biographical. 502p.
P5-IL0082 — $52.00.

GOOD OLD TIMES IN McLEAN COUNTY, Containing Two Hundred & Sixty-One Sketches of Old Settlers & a Complete Historical Sketch of the Black Hawk War. By Dr E. Duis. 1874. 865p.
P5-IL0006 — $85.00.

HISTORY OF McLEAN COUNTY, Containing a History of the . . . Cities, Towns, etc..& Portraits of Early Settlers & Prominent Men. 1879. 1078p.
P5-IL0024 — $105.00.

HISTORY OF McLEAN COUNTY. By Jacob L. Hasbrouck. 1924. 1295p.
P5-IL0076 — $125.00.

HISTORY OF McLEAN COUNTY. With biographical sketches [published without Historical Encyclopedia of Illinois]. Ed. by Ezra M. Prince & John H. Burnham. 1908. 615p.
P5-IL0144 — $67.00.

PORTRAIT & BIOGRAPHICAL ALBUM OF McLEAN COUNTY, Containing Full Page Portraits & Biographical Sketches of Prominent & Representative Citizens. With history of McLean Co. Reprinted without the biogr. of U.S presidents & governors of Illinois. 1887. 1030p.
P5-IL0075 — $99.00.

MENARD, SALEM, LINCOLN Souvenir Album. By Illinois Woman's Columbian Club. 1893. 84p.
P5-IL0240 — $24.00.

PAST AND PRESENT OF MENARD COUNTY, ILLINOIS. Rev. R.D. Miller. 1905. 552 + 86p.
P5-IL0239 — $64.00.

PIONEERS OF MENARD & MASON COUNTIES . . . Including Personal Reminiscens of Abraham Lincoln & Peter Cartwright. By T.G. Onstot. 1902. 400p.
P5-IL0145 — $47.00.

HISTORY OF MERCER COUNTY. With biographical sketches. (Reprinted without Historical Encyclopedia of Illinois, available separately). 1903. 168p.
P5-IL0218 — $29.00.

PAST & PRESENT OF MERCER COUNTY, 2-vol. set By Isaac Newton Bassett. 1914. 2 vols., 535 + 582p.
P5-IL0146 — $119.00/set.

PAST & PRESENT OF MERCER COUNTY, Vol. I. 1914. 535p
P5-IL0146A — $61.00.

PAST & PRESENT OF MERCER COUNTY, Vol. II. 1914. 582p.
P5-IL0146B — $61.00.

HISTORICAL & BIOGRAPHICAL RECORD OF MONMOUTH & WARREN COUNTY. 1927. 2 vols. in 1, 565p.
P5-IL0148 — $63.00.

PORTRAIT & BIOGRAPHICAL RECORD OF MONTGOMERY & BOND COUNTIES, Containing Biographical Sketches of Prominent & Representative Citizens. 1882. 521p.
P5-IL0149 — $59.00.

HISTORY OF MORGAN COUNTY, Its Past & Present Containing a History of the County, its Cities, Towns, etc.; Biographical Directory of its Citizens; . . . Portraits of its Early Settlers, etc. 1878. 770p.
P5-IL0150 — $81.50.

AND SHE HELD FORTH HER HAND: History & Genealogy of Mount Pulaski & Surrounding Vicinity. Comp. by Emagene V. Green. 1961. 117 + 170p.
P5-IL0151 — $39.50.

MOUNT MORRIS: Past & Present. Illustrated History of the Village of Mt.Morris, Ogle County, Illinois. By H.G. Kable. 1938. 464p.
P5-IL0226 — $51.00.

HISTORY OF OGLE COUNTY, Containing a History of the County, its Cities, Towns, etc. With a Biographical Directory of its Citizens . . . and Portraits of Early Settlers & Prominent Men. 1878. 858p.
P5-IL0008A — $87.00.

HISTORY OF OGLE COUNTY, ILLINOIS. 1909. 457p.
P5-IL0221 — $51.50.

PRAIRIE FARMER'S RELIABLE DIRECTORY OF FARMERS AND BREEDERS: Ogle County. 1917. 217 + vi p.
P5-IL0231 — $24.00.

SKETCHES OF THE HISTORY OF OGLE COUNTY & the Early Settlement of the Northwest. 1859. 88p.
P5-IL0152 — $15.00.

150 YEARS ALONG THE FOX The History of Oswego Township, Illinois. By Roger Matile, et al. 1983. 191p.
P5-IL0237 — $38.50.

HISTORY OF PEORIA. By C. Ballance. 1870. 271p.
P5-IL0153 — $37.00.

PEORIA CITY & COUNTY: Record of Settlement, Organization, Progress & Achievement, 2-vol. set. By Col. James M. Rice. 1912. 2 vols., 905p.
P5-IL0155 — $97.00.

PEORIA CITY & COUNTY . . ., Vol. I. 1912.
P5-IL0155A — $51.50.

PEORIA CITY & COUNTY . . ., Vol. II. 1912.
P5-IL0155B — $51.50.

HISTORY OF PEORIA COUNTY [Published without the Historical Encyclopedia of Illinois]. With biographical sketches. 1902. 843p.
P5-IL0154 — $91.50.

PORTRAIT and BIOGRAPHICAL ALBUM OF PEORIA COUNTY, with Biographical Sketches of Prominent and Prepresentative Citizens. 1890. 990p.
P5-IL0055 — $99.50.

HISTORY OF PIATT COUNTY, . . . with a Brief History of Illinois from the Discovery of the Mississippi to the Present Time [1883]. By Emma C. Piatt. 1883. 643p.
P5-IL0044 — $69.50.

HISTORY OF PIKE COUNTY, together with Sketches of its Cities, Villages & Townships; . . . Civil, Military & Political History; ..and Biographies of Representative Citizens, with the History of Illinois. 1880. 965p.
P5-IL0156 — $99.50.

For hardcover versions, see the order form on page v. To order, call 1-888-296-3447.

Illinois, cont.

PORTRAIT & BIOGRAPHICAL ALBUM OF PIKE & CALHOUN COS, Containing Portraits & Biographical Sketches of Prominent & Representative Citizens of the Counties. (Reprinted without biographies of Presidents & Governors). 1891. 628p.
P5-IL0213 — $69.00.

PLANO: Birthplace of the Harvester, 1854-1954. 1954. 32p.
P5-IL0015 — $10.00.

SKETCHES OF THE EARLY SETTLEMENT & PRESENT ADVANTAGES OF PRINCETON, Including Valuable Statistics & a Brief Sketch of Bureau County & a Business Directory. By Isaac B. Smith. 1857. 96p.
P5-IL0157 — $17.50.

HISTORY & REMINISCENCES From the Records of Old Settlers' Union of Princeville & Vicinity, Vols. I-IV. Comp. by Old Settlers' Union Committee. 1912-29. 116 + 161 + 130 + 160p.
P5-IL0158 — $51.00.

RECORDS OF THE OLDEN TIME, or Fifty Years on the Prairies, Embracing Sketches of the Discovery, Exploration & Settlement of the Country & the Organization of the Counties of Putnam & Marshall, Biographies of Citizens, etc. By Spencer Ellsworth. 1880. 772p.
P5-IL0159 — $81.50.

HISTORY OF QUINCY & ITS MEN OF MARK, or Facts & Figures Exhibiting its Advantages & Resources, Manufacturers & Commerce. By Pat H. Redmond. 1869. 302p.
P5-IL0161 — $39.50.

QUINCY & ADAMS COUNTY: History & Representative Men, 2-vol. set. 1919. 2 vols., 1502p.
P5-IL0160 — $155.00/set.

QUINCY & ADAMS COUNTY: History & Representative Men, Vol. I. 1919.
P5-il0160A — $79.50.

QUINCY & ADAMS COUNTY: History & Representative Men, Vol. II. 1919.
P5-IL0160B — $79.50.

REMINISCENCES OF QUINCY, Containing Historical Events, Anecdotes, Matters Concerning Old Settlers; and Old Times. By Henry Asbury. 1882. 224p.
P5-IL0050 — $32.50.

COMBINED HISTORY OF RANDOLPH, MONROE & PERRY COS., with Illustrations Descriptive of their Scenery & Biographical Sketches of some of their Prominent Men & Pioneers. 1883. 504p.
P5-IL0077 — $55.00.

MARRIAGE RECORDS, Randolph Co., 1809-1870. Comp. by Mrs F.S. Torrens. 1948?. 95p., typescript
P5-IL0162 — $18.00.

PORTRAIT & BIOGRAPHICAL RECORD OF RANDOLPH, JACKSON, PERRY & MONROE COUNTIES, Containing Biographical Sketches of Prominent & Representative Citizens of the Counties [Published without the Biographies & Portraits of the Presidents of the US & Governors]. 1894. 694p.
P5-IL0163 — $74.00.

BIOGRAPHICAL & REMINISCENT HISTORY OF RICHLAND, CLAY & MARION COS. 1909. 608p.
P5-IL0164 — $65.00.

EARLY DAYS OF ROCK ISLAND [ILL.] & DAVENPORT [IA.]: The Narratives of J.W. Spencer (1872) & J.M.D. Burrows (1888). 1872, 1888, 1942. 315p.
P5-IL0053 — $39.50.

HISTORIC ROCK ISLAND COUNTY: History of the Settlement from the Earliest Known Period to the Present Time. Including biographies. 1908. 230 + 184p.
P5-IL0027 — $47.50.

HISTORY OF ROCK ISLAND COUNTY. With biographical sketches [published without Historical Encyclopedia of Illinois, available separately]. 1914. 735p.
P5-IL0201 — $75.00.

PAST & PRESENT OF ROCK ISLAND COUNTY, Containing a Hist. of the County, its Cities, Towns, etc., & a biographical Directory of its Citizens. 1877. 474p.
P5-IL0011 — $49.50.

PORTRAIT & BIOGRAPHICAL ALBUM OF ROCK ISLAND COUNTY, Containing Full-Page Portraits & Biographical Sketches of Citizens of the County. 1885. 818p.
P5-IL0012 — $84.50.

HISTORY OF ROCKFORD & Winnebago County, from the First Settlement in 1834 to the Civil War. By Charles A. Church. 1900. 386p.
P5-IL0166 — $47.00.

REMINISCENCES, Sporting & Otherwise, of Early Days in Rockford. By John H. Thurston. 1891. 117p.
P5-IL0165 — $18.50.

ROCKFORD TODAY: Historical, Descriptive, Biographical. By the Rockford Morning Star. 1903. 179p.
P5-IL0167 — $28.00.

HISTORY OF ROCKTON, Winnebago Co., 1820 to 1898. By Edson I. Carr. 1898. 200p.
P5-IL0168 — $31.50.

HISTORY OF SANGAMON COUNTY [reprinted without Historical Encyclopedia of Illinois]. **In two parts.** 1912. 2 parts, 1752p.
P5-IL0171 — $159.50/set.

HISTORY OF SANGAMON COUNTY [reprinted without Historical Encyclopedia of Illinois], **Part I.** 1912.
P5-IL0171A — $89.50.

HISTORY OF SANGAMON COUNTY [reprinted without Historical Encyclopedia of Illinois]. **Part II.** 1912.
P5-IL0171B — $89.50.

HISTORY OF SANGAMON COUNTY, Together with Sketches of its Cities, Villages & Townships . . . and Biographies of Prominent Persons. 1881. 1067p.
P5-IL0010 — $99.50.

HISTORY OF THE EARLY SETTLERS OF SANGAMON COUNTY. By John Carroll Power, with S.A. Power. 1876. 797p.
P5-IL0170 — $81.50.

PORTRAIT & BIOGRAPHICAL ALBUM OF SANGAMON COUNTY, Containing Portraits & Biographical Sketches of Prominent & Representative Citizens of the County. (Reprinted without biographies of Presidents & Governors). 1891. 680p.
P5-IL0214 — $73.50.

HISTORIC SKETCH and BIO-GRAPHICAL ALBUM of SHELBY COUNTY. 1900. 320p.
P5-IL0056 — $41.50.

HISTORY OF SHELBY & MOUL-TRIE COUNTIES, with Illustrations Descriptive of their Scenery & Biographical Sketches of Some of its Prominent Men & Pioneers, 1763-1881. 1881. 330p.
P5-IL0172 — $41.50.

PORTRAIT & BIOGRAPHICAL RECORD OF SHELBY & MOUL-TRIE COUNTIES, Containing Biographical Sketches of Prominent & Representative Citizens of the Counties, with Biographies of the Governors of Illinois & the Presidents of the U.S. 1891. 730p.
P5-IL0173 — $81.50.

PRAIRIE FARMER'S DIRECTORY OF SHELBY COUNTY. Complete Directory of the Farmers of Shelby County; Breeders Directory; Business Directory. 1918. 239p.
P5-IL0040 — $22.50.

HISTORY OF ST CLAIR COUNTY, with Illustrations Descriptive of its Scenery & Biographical Sketches of Some of its Prominent Men & Pioneers, 1686-1881. 1881. 385p.
P5-IL0169 — $44.00.

GERMAN EMIGRANTS IN ST. LIBORY, ILLINOIS, Series A, vol. I. By Dr. Heinz Marxkors. 2004. 101p,
P5-IL0241 — $23.00.

GERMAN EMIGRANTS TO ST. LIBORY, Series A, vol. II. By Dr. Heinz Marxkors. 2004. 112p.
P5-IL0258 — $23.00.

GERMAN EMIGRANTS IN ST. LIBORY, ILLINOIS, Series A, vol. III. By Dr. Heinz Marxkors. 2004. 99p.
P5-IL0244 — $22.00.

GERMAN EMIGRANTS IN ST. LIBORY, ILLINOIS, Series A, vol. IV. By Dr. Heinz Marxkors. 2005. 103p.
P5-IL0248 — $23.00.

GERMAN EMIGRANTS IN ST. LIBORY, ILLINOIS, Series A, vol. V. By Dr. Heinz Marxkors. 2005. 103p.
P5-IL0249 — $23.00.

GERMAN EMIGRANTS IN ST. LIBORY, ILLINOIS, Series A, vol. VI. By Dr. Heinz Marxkors. 2005. 92p.
P5-IL0250 — $22.00.

GERMAN EMIGRANTS TO ST. LIBORY, ILLINOIS, Series A, vol. VII. By Dr. Heinz Marxkors. 2005. 136p.
P5-IL0253 — $23.00.

GERMAN EMIGRANTS TO ST. LIBORY, ILLINOIS, Series A, vol. VIII. By Dr. Heinz Marxkors. 2005. 108p.
P5-IL0254 — $20.00.

STARK COUNTY & ITS PIONEERS. By Mrs E.H. Shallenberger. 1876. 328p.
P5-IL0028 — $37.50.

HISTORY OF STEPHENSON COUNTY, Containing a History of the County, its Cities, Towns, etc.. With biographies. 1880. 786p.
P5-IL0043 — $79.50.

PRAIRIE FARMER'S DIRECTORY OF STEPHENSON CO., IL. 1917. 195p.
P5-IL0263 — $23.00.

HISTORY OF TAZEWELL COUNTY, Together with Sketches of its Cities, Villages & Townships. 1879. 794p.
P5-IL0029 — $79.50.

PORTRAIT & BIOGRAPHICAL RECORD OF TAZEWELL & MASON COUNTIES, Containing Biographical Sketches of Prominent & Representative Citizens of the Counties. 1894. 712p.
P5-IL0174 — $77.50.

HISTORY OF VERMILION COUNTY, Together with Historic Notes on the Northwest. By H.W. Beckwith. 1879. 1041p.
P5-IL0030 — $99.50.

PRAIRIE FARMER'S DIRECTORY OF VERMILION COUNTY, ILLINOIS. 1918. 239p.
P5-IL10006 — $25.00.

ILLINOIS HISTORICAL, WABASH COUNTY BIOGRAPHICAL. 1911. 738p.
P5-IL0048 — $83.50.

PAST & PRESENT OF WARREN COUNTY, Containing a History of the County, its Cities, Towns, etc.; a Biographical Directory of its Citizens . . . With modern every-name index. 1877. 352 + 119p.
P5-IL0049 — $49.50.

PRAIRIE FARMER'S RELIABLE DIRECTORY OF FARMERS AND BREEDERS: Warren and Henderson Counties, Illinois. 1918. 327p
P5-IL0235 — $32.50.

PRAIRIE FARMER'S DIRECTORY OF WASHINGTON & CLINTON COUNTIES: Complete Directory of the Farmers of Washington & Clinton Cos., with Valuable Information . . . [and] Business Directory . . . [and] Valuable Statistics and General Information. 1918. 260p.
P5-IL0301 — $27.00.

HISTORY OF WAYNE & CLAY COUNTIES. 1884. 714p.
P5-IL0175 — $77.00.

BIOGRAPHICAL RECORD OF WHITESIDE COUNTY. 1900. 522p.
P5-IL0051 — $59.50.

HISTORY OF WHITESIDE COUNTY, from its Earliest Settlement to 1908. With biographical sketches of some prominent citizens, 2-vol. set By William A. Davis. 1908. 2 vol. set, 628 + 689p.
P5-IL0032 — $132.50/set.

HISTORY OF WHITESIDE COUNTY . . ., Vol. I. By William A. Davis. 1908. 628p.
P5-IL0032A — $69.00.

HISTORY OF WHITESIDE COUNTY, from its Earliest Settlement to 1908 . . ., Vol. II By William A. Davis. 1908. 689p.
P5-IL0032B — $69.00.

HISTORY OF WHITESIDE COUNTY, from its First Settlement to the Present Time, with Numerous Biographical & Family Sketches. 1877. 534p.
P5-IL0031 — $55.00.

Illinois, cont.

PORTRAIT AND BIOGRAPHICAL ALBUM OF WHITESIDE COUNTY, Containing Full-page Portraits & Biographical Sketches of Prominent & Representative Citizens of the County with . . . a History of the County, from its Earliest Settlement to the Present [1885]. 1885. 942p.
P5-IL0052 — $99.00.

PRAIRIE FARMER'S DIRECTORY OF WHITESIDE COUNTY, ILLINOIS. 1917. 162p.
P5-IL0008B — $20.00.

HISTORY OF WILL COUNTY. 1878. 995p.
P5-IL0033 — $97.50.

PAST & PRESENT OF WILL COUNTY. With biographical sketches, 2-vol. set. By W.W. Stevens. 1917. 2 vols., 854p.
P5-IL0176 — $90.00/set.

PAST & PRESENT OF WILL COUNTY, Vol. I. 1917.
P5-IL0176A — $47.00.

PAST & PRESENT OF WILL COUNTY, Vol. II. 1917.
P5-IL0176B — $47.00.

PRAIRIE FARMERS DIRECTORY OF WILL & SOUTHERN COOK COUNTIES: Complete Directory of the Farmers of Will & Southern Cook Cos., with Valuable Information . . . [and] Business Directory . . . [and] Valuable Statistics and General Information. 1918. 387p.
P5-IL10009 — $42.00.

HISTORY OF WILLIAMSON COUNTY, from the Earliest Times Down to the Present [1876]. By Mile Erwin. 1876. 286p.
P5-IL0014 — $35.00.

HISTORY OF WINNEBAGO COUNTY [Published without Historical Encyclopedia of Illinois, which is available separately]. 1916. 647p.
P5-IL0178 — $69.50.

HISTORY OF WINNEBAGO COUNTY, Its Past & Present, Containing a History of the County—its Cities, Towns, etc.; A Biographical Directory . . . Portraits of Early Settlers & Prominent Men; etc. 1877. 671p.
P5-IL0177 — $71.50.

PORTRAIT & BIOGRAPHICAL RECORD OF WINNEBAGO & BOONE COS., Containing Biographical Sketches of Prominent & Representative Citizens (reprinted without biographies of presidents). 1892. 1140p.
P5-IL0229 — $109.50.

HISTORY OF WOODFORD COUNTY: Concise History of the Settlement & Growth of Woodford County. By Roy L. Moore. 1910. 248p.
P5-IL0179 — $34.50.

PAST & PRESENT OF WOODFORD COUNTY. With biographical sketches. 1878. 660p.
P5-IL0078 — $72.00.

YATES CITY Community Centennial, 1957. 1957. 159p.
P5-IL0079 — $24.50.

Indiana

HISTORIC INDIANA, Being Chapters in the Story of the Hoosier State, from the Romantic Period of Foreign Exploration & Dominion through Pioneer Days, etc. By Julia H. Levering. 1919. 538p.
P5-IN0098 — $57.00.

HISTORY OF NORTHEAST INDIANA: Lagrange, Steuben, Noble & DeKalb Counties, 2-vol. set. 1920. 2 vols., 612 + 463p.
P5-IN0059 — $105.00/set.

HISTORY OF NORTHEAST INDIANA . . ., Vol. I. 1920. 612p.
P5-IN0059A — $62.50.

HISTORY OF NORTHEAST INDIANA. . ., Vol. II. 1920. 463p.
P5-IN0059B — $54.50.

HISTORY OF THE LAKE & CALUMET REGION OF INDIANA, Embracing the Counties of Lake, Porter & La Porte: An Historical Account of its People & Progress from the Earliest Times to [1927], 2-vol. set. 1927. 2 vols., 840 + 827p.
P5-IN0029 — $159.00.

HISTORY OF THE LAKE & CALUMET REGION OF INDIANA . . ., Vol. I. 1927. 840p.
P5-IN0029A — $84.00.

HISTORY OF THE LAKE & CALUMET REGION OF INDIANA . . ., Vol. II. 1927. 827p.
P5-IN0029B — $84.00.

INDIANA GAZETTEER, or Topographical Dictionary of the State of Indiana. 1850. 440p.
P5-IN0051C — $46.00.

INDIANA IN THE MEXICAN WAR. By Oran Perry. 1908. 496p.
P5-IN0103 — $55.00.

INDIANA IN THE WAR OF THE REBELLION. Part I, History; Part II, Statistics & Documents. By W.H.H. Terrell, Adj. General 1869. 2 parts, 466 + 372p.
P5-IN0065 — $86.50.

INDIANA IN THE WAR OF THE REBELLION, Part I: History. 1869. 466p.
P5-IN0065A — $46.00.

INDIANA IN THE WAR OF THE REBELLION, Part II: Statistics & Documents. 1869. 372p.
P5-IN0065B — $46.00.

INDIANA LAND ENTRIES, Vols. I & II. By Margaret R. Waters. 1948-9. 241 + 274p., typescript.
P5-IN0068 — $50.00.

INDIANA LAND ENTRIES, Vol. I. By Margaret R. Waters. 1948-9. 274p., typescript.
P5-IN0068A — $27.50.

INDIANA LAND ENTRIES, Vol. II. By Margaret R. Waters. 1948-9. 274p., typescript.
P5-IN0068B — $27.50.

LAND OF THE MIAMIS: Account of the Struggle to Secure Possession of the North West from the End of the Revolution until 1812. By Elmore Barce. 1922. 422p.
P5-IN0096 — $47.00.

NORTHWESTERN INDIANA, from 1800 to 1900: a View of our Region through the Nineteenth Century. By T.H. Ball. 1900. 570p.
P5-IN0061B — $61.00.

PIONEER HISTORY OF INDIANA, Including Stories, Incidents & Customs of the Early Settlers. By Col. Wm. M. Cockrum. 1907. 638p.
P5-IN0066 — $67.00.

STORY OF INDIANA & ITS PEOPLE. By Robert J. Aley & Max Aley. 1912. 317p.
P5-IN0099 — $36.50.

TRUE INDIAN STORIES, with Glossary of Indiana Indian Names. By Jacob Piatt Dunn. 1908. 320p.
P5-IN0067 — $39.50.

BIOGRAPHICAL & HISTORICAL RECORDS OF ADAMS & WELLS COUNTIES (reprinted without the section on U.S. presidents), 2-vol. set. 1897. 2 vols., 370 + 475p.
P5-IN0070 — $89.00/set.

BIOGRAPHICAL & HISTORICAL RECORDS OF ADAMS & WELLS COUNTIES, Vol. I: Adams County. 1897. 370p.
P5-IN0070A — $45.00.

BIOGRAPHICAL & HISTORICAL RECORDS OF ADAMS & WELLS COUNTIES, Vol. II: Wells County. 1897. 475p.
P5-IN0070B — $49.50.

SHORT, SHORT STORY OF ADAMS CO. French Quinn. 1936. 142p.
P5-IN0069 — $26.00.

STANDARD HISTORY OF ADAMS & WELLS COUNTIES: An Authentic Narrative of the Past, with an Extended Survey of Modern Developments in the Progress of the Town & Country. 1918. 2 vols. in 1, 985p.
P5-IN0005 — $98.50.

VALLEY OF THE UPPER MAUMEE RIVER, with Historical Account of Allen Co. & the City of Ft Wayne: the Story of its Progress from Savagery to Civilization, 2-vol. set. 1889. 2 vols., 498 + 509p.
P5-IN0062A — $99.50.

VALLEY OF THE UPPER MAUMEE RIVER . . ., Vol. I. 1889. 498p.
P5-IN0062A1 — $54.50.

VALLEY OF THE UPPER MAUMEE RIVER . . ., Vol. II. 1889. 509p.
P5-IN0062A2 — $54.50.

HISTORY OF BENTON COUNTY & HISTORIC OXFORD. By John Jesse Setlington Birch. 1928. 386p.
P5-IN0006 — $45.00.

PRAIRIE FARMER'S DIRECTORY OF BENTON AND WARREN COUNTIES, INDIANA. 1919. 271p.
P5-IN10010 — $28.00.

BOONE & CLINTON COUNTIES. A Portrait & Biographical Record of Boone & Clinton Counties, containing Biographical Sketches of Many Prominent & Representative Citizens. 1895. 908p.
P5-IN0008 — $89.00.

EARLY LIFE & TIMES IN BOONE COUNTY, from the First down to 1886, with Biographical Sketches of some of the Prominent Men & Women. Comp. by Samuel Harden & D. Spahr. 1887. 498p.
P5-IN0007 — $51.50.

PRAIRIE FARMER'S RELIABLE DIRECTORY OF FARMERS & BREEDERS, BOONE CO. 1920. 251p.
P5-IN10011 — $25.00.

RECOLLECTIONS OF THE EARLY SETTLEMENT OF CARROLL COUNTY. By Dr James Hervey Stewart. 1872. 372p.
P5-IN0051A — $41.50.

BIOGRAPHICAL & GENEALOGICAL HISTORY OF THE COUNTIES OF CASS, MIAMI, HOWARD & TIPTON, 2-vol. set. 1898 2 vols.; 1395p.
P5-IN0010 $135.00/set

BIOGRAPHICAL & GENEALOGICAL HISTORY OF THE COUNTIES OF CASS, MIAMI, HOWARD & TIPTON, Vol. I. 1898.
P5-IN0010A — $75.00.

BIOGRAPHICAL & GENEALOGICAL HISTORY OF THE COUNTIES OF CASS, MIAMI, HOWARD & TIPTON, Vol. II. 1898.
P5-IN0010B — $75.00.

HISTORY OF CASS COUNTY, from its Earliest Settlement to the Present Time [1913]; with Biographical Sketches & Reference to Biographies Previously Compiled, 2-vol. set. 1913. 2 vols.; 1207p.
P5-IN0009 — $109.00.

HISTORY OF CASS COUNTY . . ., Vol. II. 1913.
P5-IN0009B — $60.00.

PIONEER FAMILIES OF CLARK COUNTY, W.H. McCoy. 1947. 15p.
P5-IN0001 — $10.00.

COUNTIES OF CLAY & OWEN, Historical & Biographical. Ed. by Charles Blanchard, 1884. 966p.
P5-IN0011 — $95.00.

HISTORY OF CLINTON COUNTY, with Historical Sketches of Representative Citizens & Genealogical Records of Many of the Old Families. By Hon. Joseph Claybaugh. 1913. 982p.
P5-IN0012 — $97.00.

HISTORY OF CRAWFORD COUNTY. By Hazen H. Pleasant. 1926. 644p.
P5-IN0013 — $67.00.

HISTORY OF DEARBORN & OHIO COUNTIES, from their Earliest Settlement. With biographies. 1885. 1072p.
P5-IN0052 — $98.50.

HISTORY OF DEARBORN COUNTY, her People, Industries & Institutions, with Biographical Sketches of Representative Citizens & Genealogical Records of Old Families. 1915. 1072p.
P5-IN0014 — $99.00.

HISTORY OF DECATUR COUNTY: its People, Industries & Institutions. By Lewis A. Harding. 1915. 1216p.
P5-IN0015 — $109.00.

HISTORY OF DEKALB COUNTY, with Biographical Sketches of Representative Citizens and Genealogical Records of Old Families. 1914. 1004p.
P5-IN0016 — $97.00.

HISTORY OF DELAWARE COUNTY, 2-vol. set. Ed. by Frank D. Haimbaugh. 1924. 2 vols., 578 + 687p.
P5-IN0018 — $115.00.

HISTORY OF DELAWARE COUNTY, Vol. I. 1924. 578p.
P5-IN0018A — $65.00.

HISTORY OF DELAWARE COUNTY, Vol. II. 1924. 687p.
P5-IN0018B — $75.00.

Indiana, cont.

OUR COUNTY [DELAWARE CO.]:
Its History & Early Settlement by
Townships . . . with Reminiscences
of Pioneer Life, etc. By John S. Ellis.
1898. 195p.
P5-IN0071 — $31.00.

PORTRAIT & BIOGRAPHICAL
RECORDS OF DELAWARE &
RANDOLPH COUNTIES, Con-
taining Biographical Sketches of
Many Prominent & Representative
Citizens. 1894. 1445p.
P5-IN0017 — $135.00.

BIOGRAPHICAL & PICTORIAL
MEMOIRS OF ELKHART & ST
JOSEPH COUNTIES, Together with
Biographies of Many Prominent Men
of N. Indiana & of the Whole State.
1893. 777p.
P5-IN0020 — $79.50.

HISTORY OF ELKHART COUNTY,
Together with Sketches of its Cities,
Villages & Townships and . . . Biogra-
phies of Representative Citizens. With
the History of Indiana. 1881. 1181p.
P5-IN0019 — $109.00.

PIONEER HISTORY OF
ELKHART COUNTY, with
Sketches & Stories. By Henry S.K.
Bartholomew. 1930. 337p.
P5-IN0072 — $41.50.

TWENTIETH CENTURY
BIOGRAPHICAL RECORD OF
ELKHART COUNTY. 1905. 793p.
P5-IN0073 — $84.00.

GRAVESTONE RECORDS OF
SICKLER CEMETERY NEAR
ELSTON. By C.A. Perkins. 1929. 3p.
P5-IN0002 — $10.00.

HISTORY OF THE CITY OF
EVANSVILLE & VANDERBURG
COUNTY, 2-vol. set. By Frank M.
Gilbert. 1911. 2 vols., 416 + 431p.
P5-IN0074 — $89.00.

HISTORY OF THE CITY OF
EVANSVILLE & VANDERBURG
COUNTY, Vol. I. 1911. 416p.
P5-IN0074A — $47.00.

HISTORY OF THE CITY OF
EVANSVILLE & VANDERBURG
COUNTY, Vol. II. 1911. 431p.
P5-IN0074B — $47.00.

MAKING OF A TOWNSHIP, Being
an Account of the Early Settlement &
Subsequent Development of Fairmount
Twp., Grant Co., 1829-1917. 1917. 503p.
P5-IN0075 — $54.50.

HISTORY OF FORT WAYNE, from
the Earliest Known Accounts to the
Present Period [1868], with a Sketch
of the Life of General Anthony Wayne;
together with Short Sketches of . . .
the Early Pioneer Settlers of Ft. Wayne.
By Wallace A. Brice. 1868. 324 + 33p.
P5-IN0076 — $42.50.

HISTORY OF FOUNTAIN
COUNTY [and Montgomery Co.],
Together with Historic Notes on the
Wabash Valley. By H.W. Beckwith.
1881. 982p.
P5-IN0021 — $95.00.

PAST & PRESENT OF FOUNTAIN
AND WARREN COUNTIES,
INDIANA. 1913. 989 + 158p.
P5-IN0108 — $110.00.

FULTON COUNTY FOLKS Vol. I.
1974. 236 + 49p.
P5-IN10012 — $44.50.

BIOGRAPHICAL MEMOIRS OF
GRANT COUNTY, to which is
Appended a Comprehensive Compen-
dium of Nat'l Biography — Memoirs
of Eminent Men & Women in the
U.S. 1901. 895p.
P5-IN0102 — $92.50.

CENTENNIAL HISTORY OF
GRANT COUNTY, 1812 to 1912,
compiled from Records of the Grant
Co. Historical Society, Archives of
the County, Data of Personal
Interviews, & other Authentic Souces
of Local Information, 2-vol. set. 1914.
2 vols., 1429p.
P5-IN0104 — $135.00/set.

CENTENNIAL HISTORY OF
GRANT COUNTY . . ., Vol. I. 1914.
P5-IN0104A — $75.00.

CENTENNIAL HISTORY OF
GRANT COUNTY . . ., Vol. II. 1914.
P5-IN0104B — $75.00.

HISTORY OF GRANT COUNTY,
from the Earliest Time to [1886], with
Biographical Sketches, Notes, etc.,
together with an Extended History of
the Northwest, the Indiana Territory,
and the State of Indiana. 1886. 944p.
P5-IN0100 — $95.00.

HISTORY OF GREENE &
SULLIVAN COUNTIES, from the
Earliest Times to the Present,
together with Interesting Biograph-
ical Sketches. 1884. 824p.
P5-IN0053 — $85.00.

HISTORY OF THE FORMATION,
SETTLEMENT & DEVELOP-
MENT OF HAMILTON COUNTY,
from the Year 1818 to the Close of the
Civil War. By Augustus Finch Shirts.
1901. 370p.
P5-IN0022 — $39.50.

PRAIRIE FARMER'S RELIABLE
DIRECTORY OF FARMERS AND
BREEDERS: HAMILTON COUNTY,
INDIANA. 1919. 247p.
P5-IN0106 — $37.00.

BIOGRAPHICAL MEMOIRS OF
HANCOCK COUNTY, IN. 1902. 791
+ 56p.
P5-IN0109 — $89.00.

HISTORY OF HANCOCK
COUNTY, from its Earliest
Settlement by the "Pale Face" in
1818, down to 1882. By J.H. Binford.
1882. 536p.
P5-IN0024 — $57.00.

HISTORY OF HANCOCK
COUNTY: its People, Industries &
Institutions. With biographical
sketches of representative citizens &
genealogical records. 1916. 815p.
P5-IN0023 — $82.50.

HISTORY OF HENDRICKS
COUNTY, Together with Sketches
of its Cities, Villages & Towns;
..Civil, Military & Political History;
Portraits of Prominent Persons &
Biographies of Representative
Citizens. 1885. 755p.
P5-IN0077 — $79.40.

HAZZARD'S HISTORY OF
HENRY COUNTY, 1822-1906:
Military Edition, 2-vol. set By George
Hazzard. 1906. 2 vols., 1236p.
P5-IN0054 — $119.50.

HAZZARD'S HISTORY OF
HENRY COUNTY . . ., Vol. I. 1906.
P5-IN0054A — $62.50.

HAZZARD'S HISTORY OF
HENRY COUNTY . . ., Vol. II. 1906.
P5-IN0054B — $62.50.

HISTORY OF HENRY COUNTY, Together with Sketches of its Cities, Villages & Towns . . . and Biographies of Representative Citizens. With a condensed history of Indiana. By Edward Pleas. 1884. 912p.
P5-IN0026 — $89.50.

COUNTIES OF HOWARD & TIPTON, Historical & Biographical. 1883. 497 + 451p.
P5-IN0078 — $95.00.

HISTORY OF HUNTINGTON COUNTY from the Earliest Times to the Present, with Biopgrahical Sketches, etc. With a short history of Indiana. 1887. 883p.
P5-IN0027 — $89.00.

HISTORY & STATISTICAL SKETCH OF THE RAILROAD CITY [INDIANAPOLIS]: A Chronicle of its Social, Municipal, Commercial & Manufacturing Progress. W.R. Holloway. 1870. 390p.
P5-IN0004 — $42.50.

HISTORY OF INDIANAPOLIS & MARION COUNTY. By Berry R. Sulgrove. 1884. 665p.
P5-IN0003 — $75.00.

BIOGRAPHICAL AND HISTORICAL RECORD OF JAY AND BLACKFORD COUNTIES. 1887. 901p.
P5-IN0094 — $91.00.

HISTORICAL SKETCH OF JOHNSON COUNTY. By D.D. Banta. 1881. 170p.
P5-IN0081 — $26.50.

HISTORY OF JOHNSON COUNTY, from the Earliest Time to the Present, with Biographical Sketches, Notes, Etc. 1888. 918p.
P5-IN0080 — $94.50.

HISTORY OF JOHNSON COUNTY. By Elba L. Branigin. 1913. 863p.
P5-IN0079 — $89.50.

HISTORY OF KNOX & DAVIESS COUNTIES, from the Earliest Time to the Present; with Biographical Sketches, Reminiscences, Notes, etc. . . . with an Extended History of the Colonial Days of Vincennes, & its Progress . . . 1886. 914p.
P5-IN0063 — $94.50.

HISTORICAL & BIOGRAPHICAL RECORDS OF KOSCIUSKO COUNTY . . . with Personal Histories of Many of the Leading Families. 1887. 734p.
P5-IN0055A — $76.50.

COUNTIES OF LAGRANGE & NOBLE, Historical & Biographical. 1882. 441 + 502p.
P5-IN0056A — $95.00.

ENCYCLOPEDIA OF GENEALOGY & BIOGRAPHY OF LAKE COUNTY, with a Compendium of History, 1834-1904. By Rev. T.H. Ball. 1904. 674p.
P5-IN0028 — $69.50.

LAKE COUNTY, 1884: Account of the Semi-Centennial of Lake Co., with Historical Papers & Other Interesting Records. 1884. 488p.
P5-IN0082 — $51.50.

HISTORY OF LAPEL & FISHERSBURG, from Pioneer Days to August, 1938. By Edith V. Cascadden. 1938. 201p.
P5-IN0097 — $31.00.

HISTORY OF LAPORTE COUNTY & its Townships, Towns & Cities. Jasper Packard. 1876. 467p.
P5-IN0057 — $49.50.

HISTORY OF LaPORTE COUNTY. With biographies. Reprinted without general history of Indiana. 1880. 586p.
P5-IN0061A — $64.50.

HISTORY OF LAWRENCE, ORANGE & WASHINGTON COUNTIES, from the Earliest Time to the Present [1884], with . . . Biographical Sketches, etc. 1884. 937p.
P5-IN0030 — $94.00.

HISTORICAL SKETCHES & REMINISCENCES OF MADISON COUNTY. By John L. Forkner & Byron H. Dyson. 1897. 1038p.
P5-IN0055B — $99.50.

HISTORY OF MADISON COUNTY, from 1820 to 1874, Giving a General Review of Principal Events, Statistical & Historical Items. By Sam'l Harden. 1874. 411p.
P5-IN0084 — $47.00.

HISTORY OF MADISON COUNTY: A Narrative Account of its Historical Progress, its People, & Principal Interests. By John L. Forkner. 1914. 2 vols. in 1, 791p.
P5-IN0031 — $79.50.

HISTORY OF MIAMI COUNTY, from the Earliest Time to the Present [1887], with Biographical Sketches, Notes, etc. With a history of Indiana. 1887. 812p.
P5-IN0032 — $83.00.

HISTORY OF MIAMI COUNTY, Illustrated. John H. Stephens. 1876. 380p.
P5-IN0058 — $43.50.

HISTORY OF MICHIGAN CITY. By Rollo B. Oglesbee & Albert Hale. 1908. 201p.
P5-IN0062B — $29.50.

HISTORY OF MONTGOMERY COUNTY, together with Historic Notes on the Wabash Valley, Gleaned from Early Authors, Old Maps & Manuscripts . . . & other Authentic . . . Sources. By H.W. Beckwith. 1881. 607p.
P5-IN0085 — $65.00.

MONTPELIER HIGH SCHOOL ALUMNI ASSOCIATION: Blackford County, Indiana. By Judith Pugh Vancamp. 1996. 102 + 122p.
P5-IN0107 — $33.50.

COUNTIES OF MORGAN, MONROE & BROWN, Historical & Biographical. 1884. 800p.
P5-IN0033 — $79.50.

NEWTON COUNTY: Collection of Historical Facts & Personal Recollections Concerning Newton Co., from 1853 to 1911. John Ade. 1911. 314p.
P5-IN0086 — $39.50.

ALVORD'S HISTORY OF NOBLE COUNTY, INDIANA By Samuel E. Alvord 1902. 602 + 53p.
P5-IN10014 — $66.00.

HISTORY OF PARKE & VERMILLION COUNTIES, with Historical Sketches of Representative Citizens & Genealogical Records of Many Old Families. 1913. 816p.
P5-IN0034 — $83.00.

PERRY COUNTY, A History. By Thomas J. de la Hunt. 1916. 359p.
P5-IN0035 — $43.00.

Indiana, cont.

COUNTIES OF PORTER & LAKE,
Historical & Biographical. 1882. 771p.
P5-IN0087 — $81.50.

HISTORY OF PORTER COUNTY:
Narrative Account of its Historical
Progress, its People & its Principal
Interests, 2-vol. set. 1912. 2 vols., 881p.
P5-IN0095 — $92.00/set.

HISTORY OF PORTER COUNTY
. . ., Vol. I. 1912.
P5-IN0095A — $49.50.

HISTORY OF PORTER COUNTY
. . ., Vol. II. 1912.
P5-IN0095B — $49.50.

HISTORY OF POSEY COUNTY.
Edited by John C. Leffel. 1913. 401p.
P5-IN0036 — $44.00.

WEIK'S HISTORY OF PUTNAM
COUNTY. Jesse W. Weik. 1910. 785p.
P5-IN0037 — $79.50.

HISTORY OF THE TOWN OF
REMINGTON & Vicinity, Jasper Co.
Comp. by James H. Royalty. 1894. 271p.
P5-IN0038 — $35.00.

SAGA OF A HOOSIER VILLAGE
[ROANOKE]. E.M. Wasmuth. n.d. 147p.
P5-IN0088 — $26.00.

HISTORY OF RUSH COUNTY,
from the Earliest Time to the Present
[1888], with Biographical Sketches,
Notes, Etc. 1888 876p.
P5-IN0089 — $91.00.

HISTORY OF SPENCERVILLE. By
Dr. W.W. Carey. 1952. 125p.
P5-IN0064 — $17.00.

HISTORY OF SAINT JOSEPH
COUNTY, 2-vol. set. By Timothy
Edward Howard. 1907. 2 vols., 1157p.
P5-IN0039 — $109.00.

HISTORY OF SAINT JOSEPH
COUNTY, Vol. I. 1907.
P5-IN0039A — $60.00.

HISTORY OF SAINT JOSEPH
COUNTY, Vol. II. 1907.
P5-IN0039B — $60.00.

HISTORY OF ST JOSEPH COUNTY,
Together with Sketches of its Cities,
Villages & Townships; . . .Civil, Mili-
tary & Political History; Portraits of
Prominent Persons & Biographies of
Representative Citizens. 1880. 971p.
P5-IN0090 — $98.50

SWISS SETTLEMENT OF
SWITZERLAND COUNTY. By
Perret Dufour, with intro. by Harlow
Lindley. 1925. 446p.
P5-IN0040 — $49.00.

HISTORY OF EARLY TERRE
HAUTE, from 1816 to 1840. By
Blackford Condit. 1900. 198p.
P5-IN0091 — $29.50.

BIOGRAPHICAL HISTORY OF
TIPPECANOE, WHITE, JASPER,
NEWTON, BENTON, WARREN &
PULASKI COUNTIES. 2-vol. set.
1899. 2 vols., 1074p.
P5-IN0042 — $99.50.

BIOGRAPHICAL HISTORY OF
TIPPECANOE, WHITE, JASPER,
NEWTON, BENTON, WARREN &
PULASKI COUNTIES, Vol. I. 1899.
P5-IN0042A — $60.00.

BIOGRAPHICAL HISTORY OF
TIPPECANOE, WHITE, JASPER,
NEWTON, BENTON, WARREN &
PULASKI COUNTIES, Vol. II. 1899.
P5-IN0042B — $60.00.

BIOGRAPHICAL RECORD &
PORTRAIT ALBUM of TIPPE-
CANOE COUNTY. 1888. 825p.
P5-IN0041 — $84.50.

PRAIRIE FARMERS RELIABLE
DIRECTORY OF FARMERS AND
BREEDERS: TIPPECANOE
COUNTY, INDIANA. 1919. 247p.
P5-IN0105 — $37.00.

BRIEF HISTORY OF VAN
BUREN TOWNSHIP, Madison Co.
Edna O. Whitson. n.d. 305p., typescript.
P5-IN0092 — $36.50.

HISTORY OF VIGO COUNTY,
with Biographical Selections. By
Henry C. Bradsby. 1891. 1018p.
P5-IN0043 — $99.50.

COLONIAL HISTORY OF VIN-
CENNES under the French, British
& American Governments, from its
First Settlement to the Territorial
Administration of Gen. Wm. Henry
Harrison. By Judge Law. 1858. 157p.
P5-IN0093 — $21.50.

HISTORY OF THE CITY OF
VINCENNES, from 1702 to 1901. By
Henry S. Cauthorn. 1901. 220p.
P5-IN0060 — $32.00.

HISTORY OF WABASH COUNTY: A
Narrative Account of its Historical
Progress, its People & its Principal
Interests, 2-vol. set. 1914. 2 vols., 970p.
P5-IN0044 — $97.50.

HISTORY OF WABASH COUNTY
. . ., Vol. I. 1914.
P5-IN0044A — $57.50.

HISTORY OF WABASH COUNTY
. . ., Vol. II. 1914.
P5-IN0044B — $57.50.

COUNTIES OF WARREN,
BENTON, JASPER & NEWTON:
Historical & Biographical. By Weston
A. Goodspeed. 1883. 810p.
P5-IN0045 — $83.00.

HISTORY OF WARRICK,
SPENCER & PERRY COUNTIES,
from the Earliest Time to the Present, together with Interesting Biographical Sketches, etc. 1885. 837p.
P5-IN0051B — $86.00.

HISTORY OF WAYNE COUNTY,
from its First Settlement to the
Present Time, with Biographical &
Family Sketches. By Andrew W.
Young. 1872. 459p.
P5-IN0056B — $48.00.

HISTORY OF WAYNE COUNTY,
together with Sketches of its Cities,
Villages & Towns . . . and Biographies of Representative Citizens.
2-vol. set. 1884. 2 vols., 735 + 800p.
P5-IN0046A — $125.00.

HISTORY OF WAYNE COUNTY
. . ., Vol. I. 1884. 735p.
P5-IN0046A1 — $67.50.

HISTORY OF WAYNE COUNTY
. . ., Vol. II. 1884. 800p.
P5-IN0046A2 — $67.50.

HISTORY OF WAYNE, FAYETTE,
UNION & FRANKLIN COUNTIES,
2-vol. set. 1899. 2 vols., 1073p.
P5-IN0046B — $99.50.

HISTORY OF WAYNE, FAYETTE,
UNION & FRANKLIN COUNTIES,
Vol. I. 1899.
P5-IN0046B1 — $55.50.

HISTORY OF WAYNE, FAYETTE,
UNION & FRANKLIN COUNTIES,
Vol. II. 1899.
P5-IN0046B2 — $55.50.

MEMOIRS OF WAYNE CO. &
THE CITY OF RICHMOND, IN,
2-vol. set. 1912. 2 vols., 590 + 912p.
P5-IN0110 — $150.00.

MEMOIRS OF WAYNE CO. &
THE CITY OF RICHMOND, IN,
Vol. I. 1912. 590p.
P5-IN0110A — $65.00.

MEMOIRS OF WAYNE CO. &
THE CITY OF RICHMOND, IN,
Vol. II. 1912. 912p.
P5-IN0110B — $95.00.

COUNTIES OF WHITE &
PULASKI: Historical & Bio-
graphical. 1883. 772p.
P5-IN0048 — $79.50.

COUNTIES OF WHITLEY &
NOBLE: Historical & Biographical,
2 vols. 1882. 2 vols., 428 + 502p.
P5-IN0050 — $98.00.

COUNTIES OF WHITLEY &
NOBLE, vol. I. 1882. 428p.
P5-IN0050A — $55.00.

COUNTIES OF WHITLEY &
NOBLE, vol. II. 1882. 502p.
P5-IN0050B — $55.00.

HISTORY OF WHITLEY
COUNTY. By S.P. Kaler & R.H.
Maring. 1907. 861p.
P5-IN0049 — $88.00.

Iowa

JEWS OF IOWA: Complete History
& Accurate Account of their Religious, Social, Economical & Educational Progress on this State; History
of the Jews of Europe, North &
South America in Modern Times; &
a Brief History of Iowa. By Rabbi
Simon Glazer. 1904. 359p.
P5-IA0129 — $44.50.

LIST OF EX-SOLDIERS, SAILORS
& MARINES LIVING IN IOWA.
1886. 772p.
P5-IA0071 — $79.00.

OUR HOME PLACE. A personal
account of life as it was for a particular farm family in Iowa, from the
early 1900s to mid-century. By Wanda
Misbach Edgerton. 1976. 211 + vi p.
P5-IA0201 — $36.00.

HISTORY OF BENTON COUNTY
[with sketches of representative
men], 2-vol. set. 1910. 2 vols., 900p.
P5-IA0116 — $89.00.

HISTORY OF BENTON
COUNTY, Vol. I. 1910.
P5-IA0116A — $47.50.

HISTORY OF BENTON COUNTY,
Vol. II. 1910.
P5-IA0116B — $47.50.

HISTORY OF BENTON
COUNTY, Containing a History of
the County . . . and a Biographical
Birectory of its Citizens. 1878. 641p.
P5-IA0020 — $67.00.

PORTRAIT & BIOGRAPHICAL
ALBUM OF BENTON CO., Con-
taining Full Page Portraits & Biographical Sketches of Prominent &
Representative Citizens of the County.
1887. 424p.
P5-IA0144 — $47.50.

HISTORY OF BLACK HAWK
COUNTY & ITS PEOPLE, 2-vol.
set. 1915. 2 vols., 432 + 497p.
P5-IA0072 — $99.00/set.

HISTORY OF BLACK HAWK
COUNTY & ITS PEOPLE, Vol. I.
1915. 432p.
P5-IA0072A — $51.00.

HISTORY OF BLACK HAWK
COUNTY & ITS PEOPLE, Vol. II.
1915. 497p.
P5-IA0072B — $51.00

BIOGRAPHICAL RECORD OF
BOONE COUNTY. 1902. 664p.
P5-IA0022 — $68.00.

HISTORY OF BOONE COUNTY,
Containing a History of the County
. . . and a Biographical Directory of
its Citizens. 1880. 680p.
P5-IA0021 — $69.00

HISTORY OF BOONE COUNTY,
2-vol. set. 1914. 2 vols., 534 + 705p.
P5-IA0073 — $119.00/set.

HISTORY OF BOONE COUNTY,
Vol. I. 1914. 534p.
P5-IA0073A — $59.00.

HISTORY OF BOONE COUNTY,
Vol. II. 1914. 705p.
P5-IA0073B — $69.00.

HISTORY OF BUCHANAN
COUNTY & ITS PEOPLE. 2-vol.
set. By Harry Church & Katharyn J.
Chappell. 1914. 2 vols., 632 + 607p.
P5-IA0133 — $124.50.

HISTORY OF BUCHANAN COUN-
TY & ITS PEOPLE, Vol. I. 632p.
P5-IA0133A — $67.00.

HISTORY OF BUCHANAN COUN-
TY & ITS PEOPLE, Vol. II. 607p.
P5-IA0133A — $67.00.

HISTORY OF BUTLER &
BREMER COUNTIES, together
with Biographies . . . 1883. 1323p.
P5-IA0001 — $129.50.

BIOGRAPHICAL RECORDS OF
CALHOUN COUNTY. 1902. 585p.
P5-IA0117 — $62.00.

HISTORY OF CARROLL COUNTY,
A Record of Settlement, Organization, Progress & Achievement.
1912. 250p.
P5-IA0023 — $34.50.

COMPENDIUM OF HISTORY &
BIOGRAPHY OF CASS COUNTY:
Pioneer History — Patriotic War
Record — Detailed Twp. History,
with Sketches of Towns, Cities &
Prominent Citizens & Institutions —
Biographies of Old Settlers, etc.
1906. 576p.
P5-IA0118 — $61.50.

HISTORY OF CASS COUNTY,
Together with Sketches of its Towns,
Villages & Townships; Military &
Political History; Portraits of
Prominent Persons & Biographies of
Old Settlers & Representative
Citizens. 1884. 910p.
P5-IA0075 — $91.50.

HISTORY OF CEDAR COUNTY,
Containing a History of the County,
its Cities, Towns, etc. [with a] Biographical Directory. 1878. 729p.
P5-IA0061 — $77.00.

TOPICAL HISTORY OF CEDAR
COUNTY, 2-vol. set. 1910. 2 vols.,
516 + 919p.
P5-IA0076 — $139.50/set.

TOPICAL HISTORY OF CEDAR
COUNTY, Vol. I. 1910. 516p.
P5-IA0076A — $66.00.

Iowa, cont.

TOPICAL HISTORY OF CEDAR COUNTY, Vol. II. 1910. 919p.
P5-IA0076B — $88.00.

STORY OF CEDAR RAPIDS. By Janette S. Murray & Frederick G. Murray. 1950. 284p.
P5-IA0044 — $37.00.

HISTORY OF CERRO GORDO COUNTY . . . Containing Sketches of Representative Citizens, Vol. I. 1910.
P5-IA0136A — $43.50.

HISTORY OF CERRO GORDO COUNTY . . . Containing Sketches of Representative Citizens, Vol. II. 1910.
P5-IA0136B — $43.50.

HISTORICAL & REMINISCENCES OF CHICKASAW COUNTY. J.H. Powers. 1894. 332p.
P5-IA0002 — $39.00.

HISTORY OF CLAY COUNTY, Containing a History of the County, Towns, etc., A Biographical Directory of its Citizens, Early Incidents & Events; Growth & Development, etc. By W.S. Gilbreath. 1889. 272p.
P5-IA0119 — $37.00.

HISTORY OF CLAY COUNTY, from its Earliest Settlement to 1909. With biographical sketches. By Samuel Gillespie and James E. Steele. 1909. 682p.
P5-IA0056 — $74.00.

HISTORY OF CLAYTON COUNTY, from the Earliest Historical Times down to the Present. With genealogical & biographical records. 1916. 2 vols. in 1, 494 + 459p.
P5-IA0003 — $94.00.

HISTORY OF CLAYTON COUNTY, Together with Sketches of its Cities, Villages & Townships; . . . Civil, Military & Polical History; Portraits of Prominent Persons & Biographies of Representative Citizens. 1882. 1144p.
P5-IA0077 — $109.50.

HISTORY OF CLINTON COUNTY, IOWA, Containing a History of the County Its Cities, Towns, etc. . . 1879. 918p.
P5-IA0202 — $91.00.

BIOGRAPHICAL HISTORY OF CRAWFORD, IDA & SAC COUNTIES. 1893. 688p.
P5-IA0062 — $74.00.

HISTORY OF DALLAS COUNTY, Containing a History of the County, its Cities, Towns, etc.; a Biographical Directory of its Citizens; . . . Portraits of Early Settlers & Prominent Men; etc. 1879. 648p.
P5-IA0078 — $69.50.

PAST & PRESENT OF DALLAS COUNTY, together with Biographical Sketches of Many of its Prominent & Leading Citizens . . . By Robert F. Wood. 1907. 795p.
P5-IA0004 — $79.50.

DAVENPORT PAST & PRESENT, including the Early History & Personal & Anecdotal Reminiscences of Davenport, together with Biographies. By Franc B. Wilkie. 1858. 334p.
P5-IA0005 — $38.50.

EARLY DAYS OF ROCK ISLAND [ILL.] & DAVENPORT [IA.]: The Narratives of J.W. Spencer (1872) & J.M.D. Burrows (1888). 1872, 1888, 1942. 315p.
P5-IL0053 — $39.50.

HISTORY OF DAVENPORT & SCOTT COUNTY, 2 vols. By Harry E. Downer. 1910. 2 vols., 1035 + 1011p.
P5-IA0079 — $175.00/set.

HISTORY OF DAVENPORT & SCOTT COUNTY, vol. I. 1910. 1035p.
P5-IA0079A — $101.50.

HISTORY OF DAVENPORT & SCOTT COUNTY, vol. II. 1910. 1011p.
P5-IA0079B — $101.50.

BIOGRAPHICAL SOUVENIR OF THE COUNTIES OF DELAWARE & BUCHANAN, Containing Portraits & Biographies . . . of Many of the Prominent & Representative Citizens & Sketches of Many of the Early Settled Families of these Counties. 1890. 729p.
P5-IA0081 — $77.00.

HISTORY OF DELAWARE COUNTY & its People, 2 vol. set. 1914. 2 vols., 375 + 526p.
P5-IA0045 — $95.00/set.

HISTORY OF DELAWARE COUNTY & its People, Vol. I. 1914. 375p.
P5-IA0045A — $44.50.
HISTORY OF DELAWARE COUNTY & its People, Vol. II. 1914. 526p.
P5-IA0045B — $55.00.

HISTORY OF DELAWARE COUNTY, Containing a History of the County, its Cities, Towns, etc.; Biographical Sketches of Citizens; etc. 1878. 708p.
P5-IA0080 — $74.50.

DES MOINES, the Pioneer of Municipal Progress and Reform of the Middle West, Together with the History of Polk Co., vol. II. By Johnson Brigham. 1911. 1448p.
P5-IA0024B — $95.00.

JEWS OF DES MOINES: The First Century. Frank Rosenthal. 1957. 213p.
P5-IA0128 — $34.00.

BIOGRAPHICAL REVIEW OF DES MOINES COUNTY, Containing Biographical & Genealogical Sketches of Many of the Prominent Citizens of Today & also of the Past. 1905. 1107p.
P5-IA0082 — $109.00.

HISTORY OF DES MOINES COUNTY and Its People, 2 vols. By Augustine M. Antrobus. 1915. 2 vols., 556 + 537p.
P5-IA0025 — $105.00/set.

HISTORY OF DES MOINES COUNTY and Its People, vol. I. 1915. 556p.
P5-IA0025A — $55.00.

HISTORY OF DES MOINES COUNTY and Its People, vol. II. 1915. 537p.
P5-IA0025B — $55.00.

HISTORY OF DES MOINES COUNTY, its Cities, Towns, etc.; Biographical Directory of Citizens; . . . Portraits of Early Settlers & Prominent Men; etc. 1879. 723p.
P5-IA0084 — $77.00.

PORTRAIT & BIOGRAPHICAL ALBUM OF DES MOINES COUNTY, Containing Full Page Portraits & Biographical Sketches of Prominent & Representative Citizens of the County. 1888. 778p.
P5-IA0126A — $81.50.

HISTORY OF DICKINSON COUNTY, Together with an Account of the Spirit Lake Massacre and the Indian Troubles on the Northwestern Frontier. By R.A. Smith. 1902. 598p.
P5-IA0057 — $65.00.

For hardcover versions, see the order form on page v. To order, call 1-888-296-3447.

HISTORY OF DUBUQUE COUNTY, Being a General Survey of Dubuque County History, including a History of the City of Dubuque . . . from the Earliest Settlement to the Present Time [1911]. Ed. by Frank T. Oldt & P.J. Quigley. 1911. 943p.
P5-IA0006 — $95.00.

PORTRAIT & BIOGRAPHICAL RECORD OF DUBUQUE, JONES & CLAYTON COUNTIES, Containing Biographical Sketches of Prominent & Representative Citizens of the Counties. 1894. 557p.
P5-IA0127 — $61.00.

HISTORY OF FAYETTE COUNTY, Containing . . . a Biographical Directory of its Citizens. With modern every-name index. 1878. 758 + 80p.
P5-IA0028 — $79.50.

HISTORY OF FLOYD COUNTY, together with Sketches of its Cities, Villages & Townships; . . . Portraits of Prominent Persons & Biographies of Representative Citizens. 1882. 1148p.
P5-IA0143 — $109.00.

BIOGRAPHICAL HISTORY OF FREMONT & MILLS COUNTIES. 1901. 622p.
P5-IA0137 — $67.00.

BIOGRAPHICAL & HISTORICAL RECORD OF GREENE & CARROLL COS. 1887. 707p.
P5-IA0120 — $72.50.

PAST & PRESENT OF GREENE COUNTY, together with Biograpical Sketches of Many of its Prominent & Leading Citizens. By E.B. Stillman, et al. 1907. 664p.
P5-IA0008 — $69.50.

HISTORY OF HAMILTON, IOWA, two-vol. set By J.W. Lee. 1912. 2 vols., 452 + 482p.
P5-IA0142 — $95.00/set.

HISTORY OF HAMILTON, IOWA, Vol. I. By J.W. Lee. 1912. 452p.
P5-IA0142A — $49.50.

HISTORY OF HAMILTON, IOWA, Vol. II. By J.W. Lee. 1912. 482p.
P5-IA0142B — $49.50.

HISTORY OF HARDIN COUNTY, together with Sketches of its Towns, Villages & Twps. . .; Portraits of Prominent Persons; & Biographies of Representative Citizens. 1883. 984p.
P5-IA0140 — $98.50.

PAST & PRESENT OF HARDIN COUNTY. 1911. 1051p.
P5-IA0085 — $105.00.

HISTORY OF HARRISON COUNTY, its People, Industries & Institutions. With biographical sketches of representative citizens & genealogical records of many of the old families. By Charles W. Hunt, with W.L. Clark. 1915. 987p.
P5-IA0063 — $99.00.

HISTORY OF HARRISON COUNTY. 1891. 978 + 160p.
P5-IA0040A — $115.00.

HISTORY OF HENRY COUNTY, Containing a History of the County, its Cities, Towns, etc. With biographies. 1879. 637p. + 5p. index.
P5-IA0064 — $68.50.

HISTORY OF IOWA FALLS, 1900-1950. By L.A. Nichols. 1956. 365p.
P5-IA0042A — $43.50.

HISTORY OF JACKSON COUNTY, Containing a History of the County . . . and Biographical Sketches of its Citizens. 1879. 783p.
P5-IA0029 — $79.50.

THE JANESVILLIANS, 1849-1974. By Helen Maxine C. Leonard. 1974. 250p., typescript.
P5-IA0126B — $37.00.

HISTORY OF JASPER COUNTY . . . Its Cities, Towns, etc.; Biographical Directory of Citizens; . . . Portraints of Early Settlers & Prominent Men, etc. 1878. 674p.
P5-IA0138 — $72.00.

PAST & PRESENT OF JASPER COUNTY, 2-vol. set. By James B. Weaver. 1912. 2 vols., 752 + 613p.
P5-IA0027 — $129.50/set.

PAST & PRESENT OF JASPER COUNTY, Vol. I. 1912. 752p.
P5-IA0027A — $75.00.

PAST & PRESENT OF JASPER COUNTY, Vol. II. 1912. 613p.
P5-IA0027B — $62.50.

PORTRAIT & BIOGRAPHICAL RECORDS OF JASPER, MARSHALL & GRUNDY COUNTIES, Containing Biographical Sketches of Prominent & Representative Citizens . . . 1894. 678p.
P5-IA0009 — $69.50.

HISTORY OF JEFFERSON COUNTY, A Record of Settlement, Organization, Progress & Achievement, 2-vol. set. By Chas. J. Fulton. 1912-1914. 2 vols., 425 + 483p.
P5-IA0087 — $91.50/set.

HISTORY OF JEFFERSON COUNTY . . ., Vol. I. 1912-1914. 425p.
P5-IA0087A — $48.00.

HISTORY OF JEFFERSON COUNTY . . ., Vol. II. 1912-1914. 483p.
P5-IA0087B — $48.00.

HISTORY OF JEFFERSON COUNTY, Containing a History of the County, its Cities, Towns, etc., Biographical Directory of Citizens, etc. 1879. 604p.
P5-IA0122 — $64.00.

PORTRAITS & BIOGRAPHICAL ALBUM OF JEFFERSON & VAN BUREN COUNTIES, Containing Full Page Portraits & Biographical Sketches of Prominent & Representative Citizens of the County. 1890. 664p.
P5-IA0086 — $71.00.

HISTORY OF JOHNSON COUNTY, Containing a History of the County & its Townships, Cities & Villages from 1836 to 1882, together with Biographical Sketches of Many Enterprising Farmers, Merchants, Mechanics, Professional & Businessmen, etc. 1883. 966p.
P5-IA0141 — $98.00.

HISTORY OF JONES COUNTY, containing a History of the County, its Cities, Towns, etc., with Biographical Sketches of Citizens . . . 1879. 705p.
P5-IA0010 — $69.50.

Iowa, cont.

HISTORY OF JONES COUNTY,
Past & Present, 2-vol. set. By R.M.
Corbit. 1910. 2 vols., 742 + 662p.
P5-IA0030 — $135.00.

HISTORY OF JONES COUNTY,
Past & Present, Vol. I. 1910. 742p.
P5-IA0030A — $75.00.

HISTORY OF JONES COUNTY,
Past & Present, Vol. II. 1910. 626p.
P5-IA0030B — $67.50.

HISTORY OF KOSSUTH,
HANCOCK & WINNEBAGO
COUNTIES, together with Sketches
of their Cities, Villages & Townships,
. . . Military & Political History;
Portraits of Prominent Persons; &
Biographies of Representative
Citizens. 1884. 933p.
P5-IA0131 — $97.00.

HISTORY OF LEE COUNTY: A
History of the County, its Cities,
Towns; a Biographical Directory of
its Citizens, etc. 1879. 887p.
P5-IA0011 — $89.50.

STORY OF LEE COUNTY, 2-vol.
set. 1914. 2 vols., 371 + 467p.
P5-IA0135 — $87.50/set.

STORY OF LEE COUNTY, Vol. I.
1914. 371p.
P5-IA0135A — $46.00.

STORY OF LEE COUNTY, Vol. II.
1914. 467p.
P5-IA0135B — $46.00.

BIOGRAPHICAL RECORD OF
LINN COUNTY. 1901. 993p.
P5-IA0091 — $99.00.

HISTORY OF LINN COUNTY,
Containing a History of the County,
its Cities, Towns, etc.; Biographical
Sketches of Citizens; etc. 1878. 816p.
P5-IA0089 — $85.00.

HISTORY OF LINN COUNTY,
from its Earliest Settlement to the
Present Time, 2-vol. set. By Luther A.
Brewer & Barthinius L. Wick. 1911. 2
vols., 496 + 880p.
P5-IA0130 — $129.50/set.

HISTORY OF LINN COUNTY . . .,
Vol. I. 496p.
P5-IA0130A — $59.50.

HISTORY OF LINN COUNTY . . .,
Vol. II. 1911. 880p.
P5-IA0130B — $78.50.

PORTRAITS & BIOGRAPHICAL
ALBUM OF LINN COUNTY,
Containing Full Page Portraits &
Biographical Sketches . . . of
Prominent & Representative Citizens
of the County. 1887. 972p.
P5-IA0090 — $99.00.

HISTORY OF LOUISA CO, IA,
from Earliest Settlement to 1912, 2-
vol. set. By A. Springer 1911-1912. 2
vols; 540 + 564 + 93p.
P5-IA0204 — $119.00.

HISTORY OF LOUISA CO, IA
. . ., Vol. I. 1911-1912. 540p.
P5-IA0204A — $65.00.

HISTORY OF LOUISA CO, IA,
. . ., Vol. II. 1911-1912. 564 + 93p.
P5-IA0204B — $65.00.

PORTRAIT & BIOGRAPHICAL
ALBUM OF LOUISA COUNTY,
Containing Full Page Portraits &
Biographical Sketches of Prominent .
. . Citizens of the County. 1889. 658p.
P5-IA0031 — $67.00.

HISTORY OF MADISON
COUNTY, Containing a History of
the County, its Cities, Towns, etc.; a
Biographical Directory of its Citi-
zens; . . . Portraits of Early Settlers &
Prominent Men; etc. 1879. 657p.
P5-IA0092 — $71.00.

HISTORY OF MAHASKA COUNTY.
With biographies. 1878. 724p.
P5-IA0046 — $76.50.

PAST & PRESENT OF MAHASKA
COUNTY, together with Biographical Sketches of Many of its Prominent & Leading Citizens & Illustrious Dead. Manoah Hedge. 1906. 576p.
P5-IA0139 — $59.00.

PORTRAIT & BIOGRAPHICAL
ALBUM OF MAHASKA COUNTY,
Containing Full Page Portraits &
Biographical Sketches of Prominent
& Representative Citizens of the
County. 1887. 552p.
P5-IA0065 — $59.50.

PROUD MAHASKA [County], 1843-
1900. Semira Phillips. 1900. 383p.
P5-IA0012 — $42.50.

ROUSTABOUT'S HISTORY OF
MAHASKA COUNTY. By "Rousta-
bout" (Phil Hoffman). 1916. 102p.
P5-IA0013 — $12.00.

PAST & PRESENT OF MARSHALL
COUNTY, 2-vol. set (Vol. I: History;
Vol. II: Biography). By Judge Wm.
Battin & F.A. Moscrip. 1912. 2 vols., 672
+ 500p.
P5-IA0014 — $109.00/set.

PAST & PRESENT OF
MARSHALL COUNTY, Vol. I:
History. 1912. 672p.
P5-IA0014A — $69.00.

PAST & PRESENT OF
MARSHALL COUNTY, Vol. II:
Biography. 1912. 500p.
P5-IA0014B — $51.00.

HISTORY OF MITCHELL &
WORTH COUNTIES. 1884. 886p.
P5-IA0033 — $89.50.

HISTORY OF MONONA COUNTY,
Containing Portraits & Biographical
Sketches of Prominent & Represen-
tative Citizens of the County. With mod-
ern every-name index. 1890. 661 + 52p.
P5-IA0093 — $72.50.

HISTORY OF MONROE COUNTY,
Containing a History of the County,
its Cities, Towns, etc. With a biographical directory of citzens. 1878. 507p.
P5-IA0134 — $57.00.

ILLUSTRATED HISTORY OF
MONROE COUNTY: a Complete
Civil, Political & Military History of
the County, from its Earliest Period
down to 1896. With biographies. By
Frank Hickenlooper. 1896. 360p.
P5-IA0014 — $39.00.

HISTORY OF MONTGOMERY
COUNTY, Containing a History of
the County, its Cities, Towns, etc.; a
Biographical Directory of its Citi-
zens; . . . Portraits of Early Settlers &
Prominent Men; etc. 1881. 741p.
P5-IA0094 — $79.00.

HISTORY OF THE COUNTY OF
MONTGOMERY, from the Earliest
Days to 1906. By W.W. Merritt, Sr.
1906. 343p.
P5-IA0035 — $39.50.

CENTENNIAL HISTORY OF MT
VERNON, 1847-1947. 1948. 236p.
P5-IA0095 — $34.00.

HISTORY OF MUSCATINE COUNTY, a History of ... its Cities, Towns, etc.; Biographical Sketches of Citizens; Portraits of Early Settlers & Prominent Men; etc. 1879. 692p.
P5-IA0096 — $75.00.

HISTORY OF MUSCATINE COUNTY, from the Earliest Settlement to the Present Time [1911], 2-vol. set. 1911. 2 vols., 489 + 789p.
P5-IA0097 — $119.00/set.

HISTORY OF MUSCATINE COUNTY, from the Earliest Settlement to the Present Time [1911], Vol. I. 1911. 489p.
P5-IA0097A — $55.00.

HISTORY OF MUSCATINE COUNTY, from the Earliest Settlement to the Present Time [1911], Vol. II. 1911. 789p.
P5-IA0097B — $75.00.

SEMI-CENTENNIAL SOUVENIR OF NORTHWOOD, IA. 1907. 73p.
P5-IA0203 — $22.00.

HISTORY OF O'BRIEN COUNTY, from its Organization to the Present Time. By D.A.W. Perkins. 1897. 485p.
P5-IA0015 — $49.50.

PAST & PRESENT OF O'BRIEN & OSCEOLA COUNTIES, 2-vol. set. J.L.E. Peck, O.H. Montzheimer & Wm. J. Miller. 1914. 2 vols., 690 + 629p.
P5-IA0036 — $125.00/set.

PAST & PRESENT OF O'BRIEN & OSCEOLA COUNTIES, Vol. I. 690p.
P5-IA0036A — $65.00.

PAST & PRESENT OF O'BRIEN & OSCEOLA COUNTIES, Vol. II. 629p.
P5-IA0036B — $65.00.

HISTORY OF OSCEOLA COUNTY, from its Organization to the Present Time. D.A.W. Perkins. 1892. 267 + 27p.
P5-IA0016 — $37.50.

BIOGRAPHICAL HISTORY OF PAGE COUNTY, Containing ... Engravings of Prominent Citizens in Page County, with Personal Histories of Many of the Early Settlers & Leading Families; & a Concise History of the County, the Cities & Townships. 1890. 864p.
P5-IA0098 — $91.00.

HISTORY OF PAGE COUNTY, from the Earliest Settlement, in 1843, to the First Centennial of American Independence, 1876. By E. Miller. 1876. 114p.
P5-IA0066 — $19.50.

HISTORY OF PAGE COUNTY; also Biographical Sketches of Some Prominent Citizens of the County, 2-vol. set By W.L. Kershaw. 1909. 2 vols., 478 + 605p.
P5-IA0037 — $107.00/set.

HISTORY OF PAGE COUNTY; also Biographical Sketches ..., Vol. I. By W.L. Kershaw. 1909. 478p.
P5-IA0037A — $49.50.

HISTORY OF PAGE COUNTY; also Biographical Sketches ..., Vol. II. By W.L. Kershaw. 1909. 605p.
P5-IA0037B — $62.00.

HISTORY OF PALO ALTO COUNTY. By Dwight G. McCarty. 1910. 201p.
P5-IA0099 — $31.50.

SOUVENIR HISTORY OF PELLA, 1857-1022. Cyrenus Cole, et al. 1922. 344p.
P5-IA0100 — $41.50.

PIONEER HISTORY OF POCAHONTAS COUNTY, from the Time of its Earliest Settlement to the Present, including the Complete Hist. of Each Twp., Town & Important Business ... & Biographical Sketches of the Leading Citizens. By Robert E. Flickinger. 1904. xxiv + 909p.
P5-IA0017 — $94.00.

ANNALS OF POLK COUNTY & the City of Des Moines. By Will Porter. 1898. 1064p.
P5-IA0038 — $99.50.

CENTENNIAL HISTORY OF POLK COUNTY. 1876. 361p.
P5-IA0101 — $44.00.

PIONEERS OF POLK COUNTY & Reminiscences of Early Days, 2-vol. set. By L.F. Andrews. 1906. 2 vols., 456 + 472p.
P5-IA0039 — $94.50/set.

PIONEERS OF POLK COUNTY & Reminiscences of Early Days, Vol. I. By L.F. Andrews. 1906. 456p.
P5-IA0039A — $50.00.

PIONEERS OF POLK COUNTY & Reminiscences of Early Days, Vol. II. By L.F. Andrews. 1906. 472p.
P5-IA0039B — $50.00.

PORTRAIT & BIOGRAPHICAL ALBUM OF POLK COUNTY, Containing Full Page Portraits & Biographical Sketches of Prominent & Representative Citizens. (Reprinted without biographies of presidents & governors.) Lake City Pub.; 1890. 690p.
P5-IA0068 — $75.00.

BIOGRAPHICAL HISTORY OF POTTAWATTAMIE COUNTY, containing ... Engravings of Prominent Citizens of Pottawattamie County, with Personal Histories of Many of the Early Settlers & Leading Families. 1891. 712p.
P5-IA0102 — $77.00.

HISTORY OF POTTAWATTAMIE COUNTY, From the Earliest Historic Times to 1907, 2-vol. set. By Homer H. Field & Joseph R. Reed. 1907. 2 vols., 562 + 638p.
P5-IA0040B — $115.00/set.

HISTORY OF POTTAWATTAMIE COUNTY ..., Vol. I. 1907. 562p.
P5-IA0040B1 — $57.50.

HISTORY OF POTTAWATTAMIE COUNTY ..., Vol. II. 1907. 638p.
P5-IA0040B2 — $65.00.

HISTORY OF POWESHIEK COUNTY. With 2000 index compiled by Poweshiek Co. Hist. & Gen. Society. 1880. 975 + 10p.
P5-IA0041B — $95.00.

HISTORY OF POWESHIEK COUNTY: Record of Settlement, Organization, Progress & Achievement, 2-vol. set By Prof. L.F. Parker. 1911. 2 vols., 392 + 759p.
P5-IA0103 — $115.00/set.

HISTORY OF POWESHIEK COUNTY ..., Vol. I. 1911. 392p.
P5-IA0103A — $40.00.

HISTORY OF POWESHIEK COUNTY ..., Vol. II. 1911. 759p.
P5-IA0103B — $69.00.

For hardcover versions, see the order form on page v. To order, call 1-888-296-3447.

Iowa, cont.

BIOGRAPHICAL & HISTORICAL RECORD OF RINGGOLD & DECATUR COS., Containing Engravings of Prominent Citizens of the Counties, with Personal Histories of Many of the Leading Families & a Concise History of Ringgold & Decatur Counties & their Cities & Villages. 1887. 796p.
P5-IA0105 — $84.00

BIOGRAPHICAL & HISTORICAL RECORD OF RINGGOLD & UNION COUNTIES, . . . with Personal Histories of Many of the Leading Families, & a Concise History of Ringgold & Union Cos. & their Cities & Villages. 1887. 737p.
P5-IA0104 — $78.00.

HISTORY OF SCOTT COUNTY. 1882. 1265p.
P5-IA0042B — $119.50.

BIOGRAPHICAL HISTORY OF SHELBY & AUDUBON COUNTIES, . . . with Personal Histories of Many of the Leading Families, & a Concise History of Wayne & Appanoose Cos. & their Cities & Villages. 1889. 825p.
P5-IA0106 — $87.00.

PAST & PRESENT OF SHELBY COUNTY. By Edward S. White. 1915. 1511p.
P5-IA0107 — $145.00.

PAST & PRESENT OF SIOUX CITY & WOODBURY CO. [Biographical sketches of prominent citizens]. 1904. 826p.
P5-IA0123 — $85.00.

HISTORY OF TAMA COUNTY, its Cities, Towns & Villages, with Early Reminiscences, Personal Incidents & Anecdotes, & a Complete Business Directory of the County. By Sam'l D. Chapman. 1879. 296p.
P5-IA0108 — $39.00.

HISTORY OF TAMA COUNTY, Together with Sketches of their Towns, Villages & Townships; Portraits of Prominent Persons; & Biographies of Representative Citizens. 1883. 1081p.
P5-IA0124 — $105.00.

HISTORY OF TAMA COUNTY, 2-vol. set. By J.R. Caldwell. 1910. 2 vols., 1020p.
P5-IA0069 — $105.00.

HISTORY OF TAMA COUNTY, Vol. I. By J.R. Caldwell. 1910.
P5-IA0069A — $57.50.

HISTORY OF TAMA COUNTY, Vol. II. By J.R. Caldwell. 1910.
P5-IA0069B — $57.50.

HISTORY OF THE COMMUNITY OF TREYNOR. Comp. by Treynor Town & Country Club. 1961. 250p.
P5-IA0058 — $37.00.

HISTORY OF UNION COUNTY, from the Earliest Historic Times to 1908; also Biographical Sketches of Some Prominent Citizens of the County. By George A. Ise. 1908. 842p.
P5-IA0200 — $88.00.

HISTORY OF VAN BUREN COUNTY, Containing a History of the County, its Cities, Towns, etc.; Biographical Sketches of Citizens; etc. 1878. 606p.
P5-IA0109 — $67.00.

HISTORY OF WAPELLO COUNTY & Representative Citizens. 1901. 670p.
P5-IA0125 — $69.50.

BUCK-EYE PRAIRIE & THREE RIVERS COUNTY FOLK [WARREN CO.]: Genealogical Review, Chronological Recordings & Events of Early Iowa Pioneer Life. By Clyde F. Wright. 1945-1956. 3 vols. in 1, 216p.
P5-IA0111 — $22.50.

HISTORY OF WARREN COUNTY, Containing a History of the County, its Cities, Towns, etc., with a Biographical Directory of its Citizens . . . 1879. 800p.
P5-IA0018 — $79.50.

HISTORY OF WARREN COUNTY, from its Earliest Settlement to 1908, with Biographical Sketches of Some Prominent Citizens of the County. By Rev. W.C. Martin. 1908. 1000p.
P5-IA0110 — $101.50.

HISTORY OF WASHINGTON COUNTY, Containing a History of the County, its Cities, Towns, Biographical Directory of its Citizens, Portraits of Early Settlers and Prominent Men, etc. 1880. 702p.
P5-IA0146 — $73.50.

PORTRAIT & BIOGRAPHICAL ALBUM OF WASHINGTON COUNTY, with Full Page Portraits & Biographical Sketches of Prominent & Representative Citizens. 1887. 692p.
P5-IA0132 — $74.50.

BIOGRAPHICAL & HISTORICAL RECORD OF WAYNE & APPANOOSE COUNTIES, . . . with Personal Histories of Many of the Leading Families, & a Concise History of Wayne & Appanoose Cos. & their Cities & Villages. 1886. 746p.
P5-IA0112 — $79.00.

HISTORY OF WINNEBAGO COUNTY & HANCOCK COUNTY: A Record of its Settlement, Organization, Progress & Achievement. 2-vol. set. 1917. 2 vols., 353 + 566p.
P5-IA0113 — $95.00/set.

HISTORY OF WINNEBAGO COUNTY & HANCOCK COUNTY: A Record of its Settlement, Organization, Progress & Achievement, Vol. I. 1917. 353p.
P5-IA0113A — $40.00.

HISTORY OF WINNEBAGO COUNTY & HANCOCK COUNTY: A Record of its Settlement, Organization, Progress & Achievement, Vol. II. 1917. 353p.
P5-IA0113B — $40.00.

HISTORY OF WINNESHIEK & ALLAMAKEE COUNTIES. By W.E. Alexander. 1882. 739p.
P5-IA0114 — $78.00.

PAST & PRESENT OF WINNESHIEK COUNTY: A Record of Settlement, Organization, Progress & Achievement, 2-vol. set. Edwin C. Bailey. 1913. 2 vols., 354 + 580p.
P5-IA0070 — $99.00/set.

PAST & PRESENT OF WINNESHIEK COUNTY . . ., Vol. I. 1913. 354p.
P5-IA0070A — $39.50.

PAST & PRESENT OF WINNESHIEK COUNTY . . ., Vol. II. 1913. 580p.
P5-IA0070B — $62.00.

HISTORY OF THE COUNTIES OF WOODBURY & PLYMOUTH, including an Extended Sketch of Sioux City . . . with Biographies of Many of the Representative Citizens. By W.L. Clark, J.E. Norris, et al. 1890-1891. 1022p.
P5-IA0019 — $99.50.

HISTORY OF WRIGHT COUNTY, its People, Industries & Institutions. B.P. Birdsall. 1915. 1061p.
P5-IA0043 — $105.00.

YELLOW SPRING & HURON: A Local History Containing Sketches of All the People, Institutions & Events, from the Earliest Settlement to Date of Publication. By J.W. Merrill. 1897. 433p.
P5-IA0115 — $48.50.

ABANDONED AND SEMI-ACTIVE CEMETERIES. Comp. by Don L. Ford. 1985.
P5-KS0004 — $135.00.

Kansas

BIOGRAPHICAL HISTORY OF CENTRAL KANSAS, Embellished with Portraits of Many Well-Known People of this Section of the Great West, who Have Been or are Prominent in its History & Development, 2-vol. set. 1902. 2 vols., 1474p.
P5-KS0017 — $145.00/set.

BIOGRAPHICAL HISTORY OF CENTRAL KANSAS . . ., Vol. I. 1902.
P5-KS0017A — $75.00.

BIOGRAPHICAL HISTORY OF CENTRAL KANSAS . . ., Vol. II. 1902.
P5-KS0017B — $75.00.

GENEALOGICAL & BIOGRAPHICAL RECORD OF NORTH-EASTERN KANSAS. 1900. 755p.
P5-KS0018 — $79.50.

PORTRAIT & BIOGRAPHICAL RECORD OF SOUTHEASTERN KANSAS, Containing Biographical Sketches of Prominent & Representative Citizens of the Counties. 1894. 501p.
P5-KS0019 — $55.00.

OVERLAND STAGE TO CALIFORNIA [ATCHISON, KS]: Personal Reminiscences & Authentic History of the Great Overland Stage Line & Pony Express from the Missouri River to the Pacific Ocean. By Frank A. Root & William E. Connelley. 1901. 628p.
P5-KS0005 — $65.00.

BIOGRAPHICAL HISTORY OF BARTON COUNTY. 1912. 318p.
P5-KS0020 — $39.00.

HISTORY OF BOURBON COUNTY, to the Close of 1865. By T.F. Robley. 1894. 223p.
P5-KS0034 — $32.00.

SOME CEMETERIES OF BROWN COUNTY, with Supplements. Comp. by Don L. Ford. 1986. 319p.
P5-KS0001 — $48.00.

HISTORY OF BUTLER COUNTY. By V.P. Mooney. 1916. 869p.
P5-KS0002 — $87.00.

BIOGRAPHICAL HISTORY OF CLOUD COUNTY: Biographies of Representative Citizens, Illustrated with Portraits of Prominent People, etc. By Mrs E.F. Hollibaugh. n.d. 919p.
P5-KS0021 — $94.00.

DONIPHAN COUNTY CEMETERIES AND BURIAL SITES. Comp. by Don L. Ford. 1986. 194p.
P5-KS0003 — $28.00.

HISTORY OF GRANT COUNTY. R.R. Wilson & Ethel M. Sears. 1950. 278p.
P5-KS0014 — $34.00.

HUTCHINSON, A Prairie City in Kansas. By Willard Welsh. 1946. 166p.
P5-KS0015 — $27.00.

HISTORY OF LABETTE COUNTY & Representative Citizens. 1901. 825p.
P5-KS0032 — $86.00.

HISTORY OF LAWRENCE, from First Settlement to the Close of the Rebellion. By R. Cordley. 1895. 269p.
P5-KS0007 — $34.00.

EARLY HISTORY OF LEAVENWORTH, CITY & COUNTY. By Henry Miles Moore. 1906. 339p.
P5-KS0008 — $38.00.

PORTRAITS & BIOGRAPHICAL RECORD OF LEAVENWORTH, DOUGLAS & FRANKLIN COUNTIES, Containing Portraits, Biographies & Genealogies of Well Know Citizens of the Past & Present. 1899. 845p.
P5-KS0023 — $88.50.

LINN COUNTY, A History. By William Ansel Mitchell. 1928. 404p.
P5-KS0011 — $42.50.

"US" & "OUR NEIGHBORS": Historical Genealogical Directory of More than 3200 Men, Women & Children who Live about Lyndon, Osage Co. By C.R. Green. 1901. 39p.
P5-KS0024 — $10.00.

HISTORY OF MEADE COUNTY. By Frank S. Sullivan. 1916. 184p.
P5-KS0012 — $29.50.

HISTORY OF MONTGOMERY COUNTY By its Own People, Containing Sketches of our Pioneers.. & Biographies of their Worthy Sucessors . . . 1903. 852p.
P5-KS0025 — $89.00.

HISTORY OF NEMAHA COUNTY. By Ralph Tennal. 1916. 816p.
P5-KS0031 — $85.00.

HISTORY OF NEOSHO & WILSON COUNTIES, Containing Sketches of our Pioneers . . .; Biographies of their Worthy Successors & Portraits of Prominent People of the Counties, Past & Present. 1902. 932p.
P5-KS0027 — $97.00.

NESS, Western Co., Kansas, By Minnie Dubbs Millbrook. 1935. 329p.
P5-KS0033 — $39.50.

THE PEOPLE CAME: History of Osborne County, Kansas. By Osborne Co. Gen. Hist. Committee 1977. 584p.
P5-KS0035 — $58.00.

OLD SETTLERS' TALES, Pottawatamie & Nemaha Counties: Historical & Biographical Sketches of the Early Settlement & Settlers of Northeastern Pottawatomie & Southwestern Nemaha Cos., from Earliest Settlement to the Year 1877. By E.E. Crevecoeur. 1901-1902. 162p.
P5-KS0016 — $27.00.

Kansas, cont.

HISTORY OF REPUBLIC COUNTY,
Embracing a Full & Complete
Account of All the Leading Events in
its History from its First Settlement
Down to June 1, '01. By I.O. Savage.
1901. 323p.
P5-KS0028 — $41.50.

HISTORY OF SHAWNEE COUNTY
& REPRESENTATIVE CITIZENS.
1905. 628p.
P5-KS0029 — $68.00.

PORTRAIT & BIOGRAPHICAL
ALBUM OF WASHINGTON, CLAY
& RILEY COUNTIES, Containing
Full Page Portraits & Biographical
Sketches of Prominent &
Representative Citizens of the
Counties. 1890. 1233p.
P5-KS0030 — $119.50.

Kentucky

COLLINS' HISTORICAL
SKETCHES OF KENTUCKY,
Embracing Pre-Historic, Annals for
331 Years . . .; Incidents of Pioneer
Life; & Nearly Five Hundred Bio-
graphical Sketches of Distinguished
Pioneers, etc., 2-vol. set By Lewis
Collins. 1847, 1882. 2 vols., 683 + 804p.
P5-KY0024 — $149.50.

COLLINS' HISTORICAL
SKETCHES OF KENTUCKY . . .,
Vol. I. 1847. 683p.
P5-KY0024A — $79.50.

COLLINS' HISTORICAL
SKETCHES OF KENTUCKY . . .,
Vol. II. 1882. 804p.
P5-KY0024B — $79.50.

HISTORY OF KENTUCKY, 2-vol.
set. By the late Lewis Collins, rev. &
enlarged by Richard H. Collins. 1874. 2
vols., 683 + 804p.
P5-KY0022 — $149.00/set.

HISTORY OF KENTUCKY, Vol. I.
By the late Lewis Collins, rev. & enlarged
by Richard H. Collins. 1874. 683p.
P5-KY0022A — $80.00.

HISTORY OF KENTUCKY, Vol. II.
By the late Lewis Collins, rev. & enlarged
by Richard H. Collins. 1874. 804p.
P5-KY0022B — $80.00.

KENTUCKY PIONEERS & Their
Descendants. I.E. Fowler. 1951. 460p.
P5-KY0020 — $42.00.

MOUNTAIN PEOPLE OF
KENTUCKY: Account of the Present
[1906] Conditions with the Attitude of
the People toward Improvement. By
Wm. H. Haney. 1906. 196p.
P5-KY0025 — $27.00.

PIONEER LIFE IN KENTUCKY:
Series of Reminiscential Letters from
Daniel Drake, M.D., of Cincinnati to
His Children. Ohio Valley Historical
Series, No. VI. 1870. 263p.
P5-KY0026 — $35.00.

REVOLUTIONARY SOLDIERS IN
KY., Containing Roll of the Officers
of Va. Line who Rec'd Land
Bounties; a Roll of the Revolutionary
Pensioners in Ky.; List of the Ill.
Regiment who Served under George
Rogers Clark in the N.W. Campaign
& roster of Va. Navy. Comp. by
Anderson C. Quisenberry. 1895. 223p.
P5-KY0010 — $25.00.

BOONESBOROUGH, its Founding,
Pioneer Struggles, Indian Experi-
ences, Transylvania Days &
Revolutionary Annals, with Full
Historical Noets & Appendix. By
George W. Ranck. 1901. 286p.
P5-KY0027 — $36.00.

BRYAN STATION HEROES &
HEROINES, Being an Historical
Sketch of Bryan Station from 1779 to
1932, including . . . Sketches of the
Heroes & Heroines. By Virginia Webb
Howard. 1928-30. 168p.
P5-KY0042A — $22.00.

COUNTY OF CHRISTIAN, Historical
& Biographical. 1884. 2 vols. in 1, 640p.
P5-KY0003 — $67.00.

HISTORICAL RECORDS OF OLD
CRAB ORCHARD, Lincoln Co.,
Stanford. By Lucy K. McGhee. n.d.
117p., typescript.
P5-KY0028 — $17.00.

HISTORY OF CUMBERLAND
COUNTY. By J.W. Wells. 1947. 480p.
P5-KY0011 — $49.50.

CHRONICLES OF CYNTHIANA
& Other Chronicles. By Mrs L. Boyd.
1894. 259p.
P5-KY0029 — $34.00.

HISTORY OF DAVIESS COUNTY,
Together with Sketches of its Cities,
Villages & Political History . . . and
Biographies of Representative Citi-
zens. 1883. 870p.
P5-KY0004 — $89.50.

HISTORY OF ELIZABETHTOWN
& ITS SURROUNDINGS. By Samuel
Haycraft. 1869, 1921. 183p.
P5-KY0042B — $29.50.

RECORD OF MARRIAGES IN
FAYETTE COUNTY for the Period
of Years 1803 to 1851. By Annie A.B.
Bell. 1931. 138p., typescript.
P5-KY0030 — $21.00.

REVOLUTIONARY WAR PEN-
SIONS of Soldiers who Settled in
Fayette Co. Comp. by Annie Walker
Burns. 1936. 121p.
P5-KY0044 — $17.50.

HISTORY OF FRANKLIN
COUNTY. By L.F. Johnson. 1912. 286
+ 18p.
P5-KY0032 — $37.00.

HISTORY OF HENDERSON
COUNTY. By Edmund L. Sparling.
1887. 840p.
P5-KY0005 — $85.00.

JOHNSON COUNTY: History of
the County & Genealogy of its
People to the Year 1927, 2-vol. set.
Mitchel Hall. 1928. 2 vols., 552 + 708p.
P5-KY0007 — The set: $119.00/set.

JOHNSON COUNTY . . ., Vol. I:
History. By Mitchel Hall. 1928. 552p.
P5-KY0007A — $55.00.

JOHNSON COUNTY . . ., Vol. II:
Genealogy. By Mitchel Hall. 1928. 708p.
P5-KY0007B — $71.00.

HISTORY OF LEXINGTON: Its
Early Annals & Recent Progress,
including Biographical Sketches &
Personal Reminiscences of the
Pioneer Settlers, Notices of Promi-
nent Citizens, etc. By Geo. W. Ranck.
1872. 428p.
P5-KY0033 — $47.00.

HISTORY OF PIONEER LEXING-
TON, 1779-1806. By Charles R. Staples.
1939. 361p.
P5-KY0046 — $43.00.

LOUISVILLE'S FIRST FAMILIES: A Series of Genealogical Sketches. By Kathleen Jennings. 1920. 176p.
P5-KY0034 — $27.00.

MEMORIAL HISTORY OF LOUISVILLE, from its First Settlement to the Year 1896. With biographical sketches, 2-vol. set. 1896. 2 vols., 661 + 678p.
P5-KY0035 — $129.00/set.

MEMORIAL HISTORY OF LOUISVILLE . . ., Vol. I. 1896. 661p.
P5-KY0035A — $69.50.

MEMORIAL HISTORY OF LOUISVILLE . . ., Vol. II. 1896. 678p.
P5-KY0035B — $69.50.

HISTORY OF CITY OF LUDLOW. Judge John M. Hunnicutt. 1935. 93p.
P5-KY0047 — $16.00.

HISTORY OF MARSHALL COUNTY. By Leon Lewis Freeman & Edward C. Olds. 1933. 252 + 52 + 40p.
P5-KY0006 — $39.00.

HISTORY OF MUHLENBERG COUNTY. Otto A. Rothbert. 1913. 496p.
P5-KY0036 — $54.00.

OHIO COUNTY, KENTUCKY, in the Olden Days. A Series of old newspaper sketches of fragmentary history. By Harrison D. Taylor. 1926. 204 + 16p.
P5-KY0048 — $32.00.

HISTORY OF SHELBY COUNTY. By George L. Willis, Sr. 1929. 268p.
P5-KY0023 — $37.00.

RECORD OF MARRIAGES IN SHELBY COUNTY, for the Period of Years 1788 to 1851. By Annie W. Burns. 1932. 98p., typescript.
P5-KY0037 — $18.00.

RECORD OF THE PENSION ABSTRACTS, Revolutionary War Soldiers, War of 1812 & Indian Wars, who Settled in Warren County. By Annie A.B. Bell. 1935. 80p., typescript.
P5-KY0038 — $15.00.

EARLY AND MODERN HISTORY OF WOLFE COUNTY. Comp. by Wolfe Co. Women's Club. 1958. 340p.
P5-KY0021 — $41.50.

HISTORY OF WOODFORD COUNTY. W.E. Railey. 1938. 449p.
P5-KY0001 — $48.00.

MARRIAGES IN WOODFORD COUNTY, for the Period of Years 1788 to 1851. By Annie W. Burns. 1931. 32p., typescript.
P5-KY0039 — $7.00.

RECORD OF WILLS IN WOOD-FORD COUNTY, for the Period of Years 1788 to 1851. By Annie W. Burns. 1933. 88p., typescript.
P5-KY0040 — $16.50.

Louisiana

FLIGHT OF A CENTURY (1800-1900) IN ASCENSION PARISH. By Sidney A. Marchand. 1936. 237p.
P5-LA0002 — $34.50.

STORY OF ASCENSION PARISH. By Sidney A. Marchand. 1931. 193p.
P5-LA0001 — $31.00.

ACROSS THE YEARS [History of Donaldsonville, Louisiana.] By Sidney A. Marchand 1949. 204p.
P5-LA0003 — $32.00.

DONALDSONVILLE, Its Business-men, and Their Commerce at the Turn of the Century. By Henry A. Garon. 1976. 170p.
P5-LA0004 — $34.00.

Maine

ALPHABETICAL INDEX OF REVOLUTIONARY PENSIONERS LIVING IN MAINE. By Charles Alcott Flagg. 1920. 91p.
P5-ME0120 — $18.00.

ANNUAL REPORT OF THE LAND AGENT OF THE STATE OF MAINE, for the Year Ending Nov. 30, 1885. 1886. 65p.
P5-ME0108 — $13.00.

CRYING OVER A LOOK BACK TO THE WISCASSET, WATERVILLE & FARMINGTON RAILROAD. By Rundlette Kensell Palmer. 1996. 228p.
P5-ME0581 — $35.00.

GENEALOGICAL & FAMILY HIS-TORY of the State of Maine. 4-vol. set. 1909. 4 vols., 2283p., many portraits.
P5-ME0236A — $209.00/set.

GENEALOGICAL & FAMILY HIS-TORY of the State of Maine, Vol. I. 1909.
P5-ME0236A1 — $60.00.

GENEALOGICAL & FAMILY HIS-TORY of the State of Maine, Vol. II. 1909.
P5-ME0236A2 — $60.00.

GENEALOGICAL & FAMILY HIS-TORY of the State of Maine, Vol. III. 1909.
P5-ME0236A3 — $60.00.

GENEALOGICAL & FAMILY HIS-TORY of the State of Maine, Vol. IV. 1909.
P5-ME0236A4 — $60.00.

GENEALOGICAL DICTIONARY OF MAINE & NEW HAMPSHIRE. Noyes, Libby & Davis. 1928-39. 795p.
P5-ME0049 — $49.00.

HISTORY OF THE BAPTISTS IN MAINE. Henry S. Burrage. 1904. 497p.
P5-ME0127 — $56.00.

HISTORY OF THE FIRST MAINE CAVALRY, 1861-1865. By Edward P. Tobie. 1887. 735p.
P5-ME0128 — $77.00.

LEBANON, MAINE GENE-ALOGIES, 1750-1892. By George Walter Chamberlain. 1892. 214p
P26615000 — $40.00.

MAINE AT GETTYSBURG: Report of Maine Commissioners. Prepared by the Executive Comm. 1898. 602p.
P5-ME0129 — $67.00.

MAINE AT WORK IN 1861: A Directory of 17,000 Maine Residents & their Occupations & Businesses. Compiled by Robert M. Jackson, Jr. 1999. 334p.
P5-ME0268 — $39.50.

MAINE HISTORICAL AND GENEALOGICAL RECORDER MAGAZINE, VOL. I: 1884. viii + 215 + v p.
P26566000 — $42.00.

Maine, cont.

MAINE HISTORICAL AND GENEALOGICAL RECORDER MAGAZINE, VOL. II: 1885. vii + 268 + viii p.
P26566100 — $50.00.

MAINE HISTORICAL AND GENEALOGICAL RECORDER MAGAZINE, VOL. III: 1886. ix +294 + viii p.
P26566200 — $54.00.

MAINE HISTORICAL AND GENEALOGICAL RECORDER MAGAZINE, VOL. IV: 1887. viii + 304 + viii p.
P26566300 — $55.00.

MAINE HISTORICAL AND GENEALOGICAL RECORDER MAGAZINE, VOL. V: 1888. vi + 246 + viii p.
P26566400 — $46.00.

MAINE HISTORICAL AND GENEALOGICAL RECORDER MAGAZINE, VOL. VI. vii + 510 + viii p.
P26566500 — $84.00.

MAINE HISTORICAL AND GENEALOGICAL RECORDER MAGAZINE, VOL. VII: 1893. vii + 236 + viii p.
P26566600 — $45.00.

MAINE HISTORICAL AND GENEALOGICAL RECORDER MAGAZINE, VOL. VIII: 1895. vi + 252 + viii p.
P26566700 — $47.00.

MAINE HISTORICAL AND GENEALOGICAL RECORDER MAGAZINE, VOL. IX: 1898. 1898. xi + 384 p.
P26566800 — $65.00.

MAINE WILLS, 1640-1760: Also a list of the judges of probate, the registers of probate, explanation of contratcions, official certificates, and errata. 1887. 906p.
P26567000 — $137.00.

MAINE WORKING IN 1872: Directory to 15,000 Maine Residents & their Occupations & Businesses By Robert Moseley Jackson, Jr. 2000. 286p.
P5-ME0238A — $29.00.

MILITARY OPERATIONS IN EASTERN MAINE & NOVA SCOTIA During the Revolution. By Frederic Kidder. 1867. 336p.
P5-ME0135 — $43.00.

PIONEERS OF MAINE & NEW HAMPSHIRE, 1623 to 1660: Descriptive List Drawn from Records of the Colonies, Towns, Churches, Courts & other Contemporary Sources. By Charles Henry Pope. 1908. 252p.
P5-ME0054 — $24.50.

PIONEERS OF NEW FRANCE IN NEW ENGLAND [mostly Maine], with Contemporary Letters & Documents. By James P. Baxter. 1894. 450p.
P5-ME0107 — $48.00.

PIONEERS ON MAINE RIVERS, with Lists to 1651. Compiled from the Original Sources. By W.D. Spencer. 1930. 414p.
P5-ME0044 — $46.00.

REFERENCE LIST OF MANU-SCRIPTS Relating to the History of Maine [bibliographical]. Comp. by Elizabeth Rimg. 1938. 970p.
P5-ME0050 — $89.50.

HISTORY OF ALNA, MAINE. By Rundlette Kensell Palmer. 1979. 676 + 26p.
P5-ME0576 — $77.00.

HISTORY OF ANDROSCOGGIN COUNTY. 1891. 893p.
P5-ME0026 — $92.50.

HISTORY OF AROOSTOOK, Comprising Facts, Names & Dates Relating to the Early Settlement of all . . . Towns & Plantations of the County. Vol. I (no more published). By Edward Wiggin. 1922. 306 + 122p.
P5-ME0071 — $47.00.

HISTORY OF AUGUSTA, First Settlements & Early Days as a Town, Including the Diary of Mrs. Martha Moore Ballard (1785-1812). By Charles E. Nash. 1904. 612p.
P5-ME0159A — $65.00.

HISTORY OF AUGUSTA, From Earliest Settlement to the Present Time [1870], with Notes on the Plymouth Company & Settlements on the Kennebec, with Biographical Sketches & Genealogical Register. By James W. North. 1870. 990p.
P5-ME0136 — $99.00.

VITAL RECORDS OF AUGUSTA, MAINE, TO THE YEAR 1892, VOL. I: Births and Marriages [marriages end with the name McWalter]. Ethel ColConant 1933. 479p.
P26579500 — $77.00.

VITAL RECORDS OF AUGUSTA, MAINE, TO THE YEAR 1892, VOL. II: Marriages and Deaths. Ethel ColConant 1933. 479p.
P26579000 — $77.00.

ANNALS OF BANGOR, 1769-1882. (Extr. Hist. of Penobscot Co.) By John E. Godfrey. 1882. 304p.
P5-ME0039 — $38.00.

EAST BANGOR CEMETERY, E. Bangor, Penobscot County [oldest marked grave, 1833]. By Holman & Newman. 1943. 40p.
P5-ME0172A — $8.00.

SOME CEMETERIES NEAR BANGOR. Comp. by F.D. Williams Chapter DAR. 1942. 89p.
P5-ME0175A — $18.00.

HISTORY OF BATH. By Henry Wilson Owen. 1936. 575p.
P5-ME0121 — $63.00.

HISTORICAL DATES OF THE TOWN & CITY OF BATH, and Town of Georgetown, from 1604 to 1874. By Levi P. Lemont. 1874. 104p.
P5-ME0116 — $15.00.

HISTORY OF BATH & Environs, Sagadohoc Co., 1607-1895, with Illustrations. By Parker McCobb Reed. 1894. 526p.
P5-ME0058 — $55.00.

BELFAST VITAL RECORDS, VOL. I: Births. 1917. 213p.
P5-ME0137 — $24.50.

HISTORY OF THE CITY OF BELFAST, in the State of Maine, from its First Settlement in 1770 to 1875. Joseph Williamson. 1877. 956p.
P5-ME0139 — $94.50.

BELGRADE CEMETERIES. Comp. by M.R. & A.M. Whiting. 1937. 64p.
P5-ME0169 — $12.50.

BELMONT, Maine: the First Hundred Years. By Isabel Morse Maresh. 2002. 712 p.
P5-ME0575A — $69.50.

BURIAL INSCRIPTIONS OF BERWICK TO 1922. Comp. by W.D. Spencer. 1922. 133p.
P5-ME0002 — $15.00.

LIST OF REVOLUTIONARY SOLDIERS OF BERWICK. Comp. by W.D. Spencer. 1898. 18p.
P5-ME0001 — $10.00.

STORY OF BERWICK. 1963. 166p.
P5-ME0122 — $29.50.

HISTORY OF BETHEL (Formerly Sudbury, Canada), Oxford Co., 1768-1890, with a Brief Sketch of Hanover & Family Statistics. By Wm. B. Lapham. 1891. 688p.
P5-ME0140 — $69.50.

HISTORICAL SKETCHES OF BLUEHILL. R.G.F. Candage. 1905. 83p.
P5-ME0141 — $16.00.

FAMILY HISTORY OF THE BOOTHBAY REGION: Embracing Family Genealogies and Biographical Sketches from the First Permanent Settlement in 1730 to Recent Times. Francis B. Greene. 1932. 185p
P26579900 — $36.00.

HISTORY OF BOOTHBAY, SOUTHPORT & BOOTHBAY HARBOR, 1623-1905. With gene-alogies. Francis B. Greene. 1906. 693p.
P5-ME0051 — $59.00.

VITAL RECORDS OF BOWDOIN to the Year 1892. 3-vol. set. Vol. I, Births; Vol. II, Births & Deaths; Vol. III, Marriages. 1944-1945. 238 + 140 + 205p.
P5-ME0142 — $57.50/set.

VITAL RECORDS OF BOWDOIN to the Year 1892. Vol. I, Births. 1944-1945. 238p.
P5-ME0142A — $21.00.

VITAL RECORDS OF BOWDOIN to the Year 1892. Vol. II, Births & Deaths. 1944-1945. 140p.
P5-ME0142B — $21.00.

VITAL RECORDS OF BOWDOIN to the Year 1892. Vol. III, Marriages. 1944-1945. 205p.
P5-ME0142C — $21.00.

HISTORY OF THE TOWN OF BOWDOINHAM, 1762-1912. By Silas Adams. 1912. 295p.
P5-ME0143 — $37.00.

BREWER — ORRINGTON — HOLDEN — EDDINGTON: History and families. M.N. Thayer and Mrs E.W. Ames. 1962. 285 + 207p.
P5-ME0163A — $52.00.

BRIDGTON TOWN REGISTER, 1905 [Town History & Directory]. By Mitchell, Bean & Hartford. 1905. 109p.
P5-ME0144 — $17.50.

HISTORY OF THE TOWNS OF BRISTOL & BREMEN in the State of Maine, including the Pemaquid Settlement. By J. Johnston. 1873. 524p.
P5-ME0012 — $56.50.

VITAL RECORDS OF OLD BRISTOL AND NOBLEBORO, MAINE. By Christine Huston Dodge 1951. 780p
P26580000 — $119.00.

SKETCHES OF BROOKS HISTORY. By Seth W. Norwood. 1935. 454p.
P5-ME0112 — $48.50.

STORIES OF BROOKSVILLE. Coll. by Grace C. Limeburner. 1924. 81p.
P5-ME0060 — $16.00.

TRADITIONS & RECORDS OF BROOKSVILLE. Coll. by the Brooksville Hist. Soc. 1936. 132p.
P5-ME0003 — $18.50.

BROWNFIELD, DENMARK, HIRAM & PORTER TOWN REGISTER, 1907 [Town Histories & Directories]. Comp. by Mitchell, Davis & Daggett. 1907. 208p.
P5-ME0146 — $28.00.

HISTORY OF BROWNFIELD, Including Organization of the Town, Town Officers, Schools, MEetings Houses, Churches, Ministers. Comp. by Eli B. Bean. n.d. 165p.
P5-ME0145 — $21.00.

REMINISCENCES OF BROWN-FIELD: Short Sketches from the History of the Town. By Mrs E.A.G. Stickney. 1901. 69p.
P5-ME0147 — $14.00.

HANDBOOK OF BROWNVILLE HISTORY, with Records of its Cen-tennial Celebration, Incorporated 1824. Comp. by Susan Lewis. 1935. 122p.
P5-ME0148 — $17.50.

HISTORY OF BROWNVILLE, 1824-1924. 1924. 71p.
P5-ME0070 — $14.00.

HISTORY OF BRUNSWICK, TOPSHAM & HARPSWELL, including the Ancient Territory Known as Pejepscot. By Geo. A. Wheeler & Henry W. Wheeler. 1878. 959p.
P5-ME0200 — $94.00.

HISTORY OF BUCKFIELD, Oxford Co., from the Earliest Explorations to the Close of the Year 1900, By A. Cole & C.F. Whitman. 1915. 758p.
P5-ME0118 — $78.00.

ANNALS OF CALAIS, ME AND ST. STEPHEN, NEW BRUNSWICK. By Rev. I.C. Knowlton 1875. 208p.
P26590000 — $39.00.

CAMDEN HILLS: An Informal History of the Camden-Rockport Region. By Lew Dietz. 1947. 93p.
P5-ME0160A — $17.00.

HISTORY OF CAMDEN & ROCKPORT. By Reuel Robinson. 1907. 647p.
P5-ME0149 — $67.00.

SKETCHES OF THE HISTORY OF THE TOWN OF CAMDEN, incl. Incidental References to the Neighbouring Places & Adjacent Waters. By J.L. Locke. 1859. 267p.
P5-ME0019 — $32.00.

CANTON & DIXFIELD REG-ISTER, 1905. [Town Histories & Directories]. Comp. by Mitchell & Davis. 1905. 115p.
P5-ME0150 — $19.00.

HISTORY OF CAPE PORPOISE. By Melville C. Freeman. 1955. 107p.
P5-ME0124 — $24.50.

EARLY HISTORY OF CARIBOU, 1843-1895. Stella King White. 1945. 147p.
P5-ME0151 — $21.50.

CARMEL & HERMON TOWN REGISTER, 1904. [Town Histories & Directories]. Comp. by Mitchell, Carroll & Gastonguay. 1904. 120p.
P5-ME0152 — $19.00.

HISTORY OF CASTINE, PENOB-SCOT & BROOKSVILLE, including the Ancient Settlement of Pentagoet. George Augustus Wheeler. 1875. 401p.
P5-ME0065 — $42.50.

For hardcover versions, see the order form on page v. To order, call 1-888-296-3447.

Maine, cont.

CHERRYFIELD REGISTER, 1905 [Town History & Directory]. Comp. by Mitchell & Campbell. 1905. 92p.
P5-ME0153A — $17.50.

CLINTON & BENTON REGISTER, 1904. [Town Histories & Directories]. Comp. by Mitchell & Daggett. 1904. 131p.
P5-ME0154A — $21.00.

CLINTON VITAL RECORDS, Births, Marriages & Deaths. 1967. 357p.
P5-ME0100 — $38.00.

CORINNA RECORD BOOK [Cemetery Inscriptions]. Comp. by John E. Frost. 1963. 85p.
P5-ME0173A — $17.00.

THE LOST TOWN OF CORK. By M.J. O'Brien. n.d. 12p.
P5-ME0004 — $10.00.

CORNISH RECORD BOOK [cemetery inscriptions]. Comp. by John E. Frost. 1965. 97p.
P5-ME0273 — $19.00.

COUSINS & LITTLEJOHN'S ISLANDS, 1645-1893. By Katherine Prescott Kaster. n.d. 128p.
P5-ME0155 — $17.00.

BIOGRAPHICAL SKETCHES OF LEADING CITIZENS OF CUMBERLAND COUNTY. 1896. 707p.
P5-ME0156A — $72.00.

CUMBERLAND & NO. YARMOUTH REGISTER, 1904. [Town Histories & Directories]. Comp. by Mitchell, Russell & Strout. 1904. 100p.
P5-ME0157A — $17.00.

HISTORY OF CUMBERLAND COUNTY, with Illustrations & Biographical Sketches of Prominent Men & Pioneers. 1880. 456p.
P5-ME0009 — $51.00.

HISTORICAL SKETCH OF THE TOWN OF DEER ISLE, with Notices of its Settlers & Early Inhabitants. G.L. Hosmer. 1886. 292p.
P5-ME0021 — $35.00.

DOVER & FOXCROFT REGISTER, 1904 [Town Histories & Directories]. Comp. by Mitchell & Remick. 1904. 154p.
P5-ME0158A — $24.00.

HISTORY OF DRESDEN, MAINE. By Rundlette K. Palmer. 1979. 562 + 28p.
P5-ME0577 — $69.00.

HISTORY OF DURHAM, with Genealogical Notes. By E.S. Stackpole. 1899. 314p.
P5-ME0005 — $39.50.

EASTPORT & PASSAMAQUODDY: A Collection of Historical & Biographical Sketches. Comp. by William Henry Kilby. Incl. Weston's 1834 "History." 1888. 505p.
P5-ME0047 — $49.50.

CITY OF ELLSWORTH REGISTER, with Surry & Bluehill, 1908 [Town histories & directories]. By Lawton, Loring & Jordan. 1908. 252p.
P5-ME0160B — $34.50.

HISTORY OF ELLSWORTH. By Albert H. Davis. 1927. 244p.
P5-ME0266 — $34.50.

FAIRFIELD REGISTER, 1904 [Town history & directory]. Comp. by Mitchell & Cavis. 1904. 128p.
P5-ME0161A — $17.00.

STORY OF OLD FALMOUTH. By James Otis. 1901. 127p.
P5-ME0162A — $19.50.

VITAL RECORDS OF FARMING-DALE to the Year 1892. 1909. 96p.
P5-ME0258 — $18.00.

FARMINGTON TOWN REGISTER, 1902-3 [Town History & Directory]. Comp. by H.E. Mitchell. 1903. 126p.
P5-ME0163C — $21.50.

HISTORY OF FARMINGTON, Franklin Co., from the Earliest Explorations to the Present Time, 1776-1885. By Francis Gould Butler. 1885. 683p.
P5-ME0163B — $69.00.

FAYETTE & MOUNT VERNON REGISTER, 1903 [Town Histories & Directories]. Comp. by R.E. Mitchell. 1903. 112p.
P5-ME0165A — $19.00.

HISTORY OF FAYETTE. By Joseph H. Underwood. 1956. 174p.
P5-ME0164A — $27.50.

HISTORY OF FORT FAIRFIELD, & Biographical Sketches with Illustrations. By C.H. Ellis. 1894. 382p.
P5-ME0052 — $42.50.

OLD FOXCROFT: Traditions & Memories, with Family Records. By Mary Chandler Lowell, M.D. 1935. 262p.
P5-ME0158B — $34.00.

THREE CENTURIES OF FREEPORT. Florence G. Thurston & Harmon S. Cross. 1940. 254p.
P5-ME0160C — $34.00.

FRYEBURG, MAINE: An Historical Sketch. J.S. Barrows. 1938. 309p.
P5-ME0032 — $37.50.

GARDINER VITAL RECORDS, Part I: Births. 1914. 186p.
P5-ME0167A — $21.00.

HISTORY OF GARDINER, PITTSTON & WEST GARDINER, with a Sketch of the Kennebec Indians & New Plymouth Purchase, 1602-1852. By J.W. Hanson. 1852. 359p.
P5-ME0110 — $44.00.

VITAL RECORDS OF GARDINER to the Year 1892, Part II, Marriages & Deaths. 1915. 675p.
P5-ME0257 — $69.50.

HISTORY OF GARLAND. By L. Oak. 1911. 401p.
P5-ME0033 — $44.00.

VITAL RECORDS OF GEORGE-TOWN to the Year 1892, 3-vol. set. Ed. by Mary P. Hill. 1939, 1941, 1943. 3 v., 207 + 199 + 93p.
P5-ME0161B — $51.50/3 vols. in 1

VITAL RECORDS OF GEORGE-TOWN to the Year 1892, Vol. I. Ed. by Mary P. Hill. 1939. 207p.
P5-ME0161B1 — $20.00.

VITAL RECORDS OF GEORGE-TOWN to the Year 1892, Vol. II. Ed. by Mary P. Hill. 1941. 199p.
P5-ME0161B2 — $20.00.

VITAL RECORDS OF GEORGE-TOWN to the Year 1892, Vol. III. Ed. by Mary P. Hill. 1943. 93p.
P5-ME0161B3 — $15.00.

GORHAM & BUXTON TOWN REGISTER, 1905. [Town Histories & Directories]. Comp. by Mitchell, Daggett & Bassett. 1905. 222p.
P5-ME0170A — $27.50.

HISTORY OF THE TOWN OF GORHAM. Josiah Pierce. 1862. 239p.
P5-ME0169 — $31.50.

PUBLISHMENTS, MARRIAGES, BIRTHS & DEATHS from the Earlier Records of Gorham. Comp. by Marquis F. King. 1895. 215p.
P5-ME0171A — $25.00.

HISTORICAL RESEARCHES OF GOULDSBOROUGH. 1904. 108p.
P5-ME0168A — $17.00.

GRAY & NEW GLOUCESTER REGISTER, 1905 [Town Histories & Directories]. Comp. by Mitchell, Daggett, Weston & Reed. 1905. 110p.
P5-ME0172B — $18.00.

HISTORY AND GENEALOGY OF GREENBUSH. Eleanor M. Crouch and Joyce M. Sanborn. 2001. 269 + 95p.
P5-ME0237A — $45.00.

SESQUICENTENNIAL HISTORY OF THE TOWN OF GREENE, Androscoggin Co., 1775 to 1900, with Some Matter Extending to a Later Date. By Walter L. Mower. 1938. 578p.
P5-ME0114 — $59.50.

OLD HALLOWELL ON THE KENNEBEC. By Emma Huntington Nason. 1909. 359p.
P5-ME0173B — $44.00.

VITAL RECORDS OF HALLOWELL, to the Year 1892. 1924-1929. 6 vols. in 3.
P5-ME0174A — $97.00/set.

HAMPDEN REGISTER, 1904 [Town History & Directory]. Comp. by Mitchell & Johnson. 1904. 127p.
P5-ME0175B — $21.00.

HANCOCK, 1828-1928. By Alfred B. Crabtree & Hattie B. Martin. 1928. 90p.
P5-ME0177 — $18.00.

OLD HANCOCK COUNTY FAMILIES, Containing Genealogies of Familes Resident in Hancock County in 1933, whose Ancestors of their Surnames Settled in the Town in or Before 1790. By Wm. MacBeth Pierce. 1933. 133p.
P5-ME0176 — $18.50.

CENTENNIAL HISTORY OF HARRISON, Containing the Celebration of 1905 and Historical and Biographical Matter. Comp. & ed. by A. Moulton, H.L. Sampson & G. Fernald. 1909. 727p.
P5-ME0109A — $77.00.

EARLY SETTLERS OF HARRISON, with an Historical Sketch of the Settlement, Progress & Present Condition of the Town. By G.T. Ridlon. 1877. 138p.
P5-ME0178 — $17.50.

HARTLAND & ST ALBANS REGISTER, 1904 [Town Histories & Directories]. Comp. by Mitchell, Remick & Bean. 1904. 101p.
P5-ME0179 — $17.00.

HINCKLEY TOWNSHIP, or Grand Lake Stream Plantation. By Minnie Atkinson. 1920. 122p.
P5-ME0180 — $18.00.

HINSDALE, WALPOLE, WEST-MORELAND, WINCHESTER & CHESTERFIELD TOWN REGIS-TER, 1909 [Town Histories & Directories]. 1909. 150p.
P5-ME0181 — $22.00.

STORY OF HOULTON, from the Public Records & from the Experi-ence of its Founders, their Descen-dants, & Associates to the Present Time [1889]. Francis Barnes. 1889. 129p.
P5-ME0182 — $19.50.

STORY OF HOULTON. With supplement. By Cora M. Putnam. 1958. 423 + 8p.
P5-ME0184 — $47.00.

THE IRISHMAN: A Factor in the Development of Houlton; History of the Parish of St Mary's. By W.J. Thibabeau. n.d. 110p.
P5-ME0183 — $18.00.

HISTORY OF THE TOWN OF INDUSTRY, Franklin Co., from the Earliest Settlement in 1787 down to the Present Time [1893], Embracing the Cessions of New Sharon, New Vineyard, Anson & Stark, including the History & Genealogy of Many of the Leading Families . . . By Wm. C. Hatch. 1893. 852p.
P5-ME0271 — $88.00.

HISTORY OF ISLEBOROUGH, 1764-1892. By J.P. Farrow. 1893. 325p.
P5-ME0022 — $41.00.

HISTORY OF JAY, Franklin County. By Benjamin F. Lawrence. 1912. 93p.
P5-ME0185 — $18.00.

JONESPORT REGISTER [Town history & directory]. Comp. by Mitchell & Campbell. 1905. 112p.
P5-ME0272 — $19.50.

ILLUSTRATED HISTORY OF KENNEBEC COUNTY, 1625-1892, 2-vol. set. 1892. 2 vols., 600 + 673p.
P5-ME0010 — $122.50/set.

ILLUSTRATED HISTORY OF KENNEBEC COUNTY, 1625-1892, Vol. I. 1892. 600p.
P5-ME0010A — $65.00.

ILLUSTRATED HISTORY OF KENNEBEC COUNTY, 1625-1892, Vol. II. 1892. 673p.
P5-ME0010B — $65.00.

KENNEBEC VALLEY. By S.H. Whitney. 1887. 122p.
P5-ME0102 — $20.00.

KENNEBUNK RECORD BOOK [Cemetery Inscriptions]. By John Eldridge Frost. 1964. 238 + 12p.
P5-ME0167B — $25.00.

HISTORY OF KENNEBUNK, from its Earliest Settlement to 1890, including Biographical Sketches. By Daniel Remich. 1890. 580p.
P5-ME0053 — $58.00.

ARUNDEL (KENNEBUNKPORT, MAINE) RECORDS WITH INDEX. Compiled by Harold Clarke Durrell 1911. 109p.
P26578000 — $27.00.

HISTORY OF KENNEBUNK-PORT, from its First Discovery by Bartholomew Gosnold, 1602, to a.d. 1837. By Charles Bradbury. 1837. 338p.
P5-ME0048 — $39.50.

KENNEBUNKPORT REGISTER, 1904 [Town History & Directory]. Comp. by Mitchell & Campbell. 1904. 112p.
P5-ME0186 — $18.00.

For hardcover versions, see the order form on page v. To order, call 1-888-296-3447.

Maine, cont.

OLD KITTERY & HER FAMILIES.
By E.S. Stackpole. 1903. 822p.
P5-ME0027 — $86.00.

RECORD OF THE SERVICES OF THE COMMISSIONED OFFICES & Enlisted Men of Kittery & Eliot, who Served Their Country . . . in the Revolution, 1775-1783. By Lt Oliver P. Remick. 1901. 223p.
P5-ME0187 — $25.00.

LEBANON VITAL RECORDS, to the Year 1892. Vol. I, Births. Vol. III, Deaths. 1922. 168 + 149p.
P5-ME0188 — $39.00/set.

LEBANON VITAL RECORDS, to the Year 1892. Vol. I, Births. 1922. 168p.
P5-ME0188A — $20.00.

LEBANON VITAL RECORDS, to the Year 1892. Vol. III, Deaths. 1922. 149p.
P5-ME0188B — $20.00.

SOLDIERS OF THE AMERICAN REVOLUTION OF LEBANON. By George Walter Chamberlain. 1897. 48p.
P5-ME0189 — $10.00.

STORY OF AN OLD NEW ENGLAND TOWN: History of Lee. With genealogies. Comp. by Vinal A. Houghton. 1926. 248p.
P5-ME0171B — $35.00.

HISTORY OF THE TOWN OF LEEDS, Androscoggin Co., from its Settlement June 10, 1780. With many genealogies. By J.C. Stinchfield et al. 1901. 419p.
P5-ME0034 — $45.00.

PROBATE RECORDS OF LINCOLN COUNTY, 1760-1800. 1895. 368 + 53p.
P5-ME0256 — $47.00.

LINCOLNVILLE, NORTHPORT, BELMONT, MORRILL, SEARSMONT & WALDO TOWN REGISTER, 1907 [Town Histories & Directories]. Comp. by Mitchell, Lawton & Bryant. 1907. 175p.
P5-ME0190 — $27.50.

LISBON TOWN REGISTER, 1905 [Town History & Directory]. Comp. by Mitchell & Campbell. 1905. 117p.
P5-ME0191 — $19.50.

HISTORY OF LITCHFIELD, and an Account of its Centennial Celebration in 1895. 1897. 548p.
P5-ME0015 — $59.50.

EAST LIVERMORE & LIVERMORE REGISTER, 1903-4 [Town histories & directories]. By Mitchell & Daggett. 1904. 148p.
P5-ME0159B — $21.00.

HISTORY OF THE TOWN OF LIVERMORE, Androscoggin Co., from its Inception in 1735 & its Grant of Land in 1772, to its Organization & Incorporation in 1795 up to 1928. By Ira T. Moore. 1928. 275p.
P5-ME0192 — $34.00.

NOTES, HISTORICAL, DESCRIPTIVE & PERSONAL, OF LIVERMORE in Androscoggin (formerly in Oxford) County. 1874. 169p.
P5-ME0193 — $27.00.

NARRATIVE OF THE TOWN OF MACHIAS: the Old & the New, the Early & the Late. By G.W. Drisko. 1904. 589p.
P5-ME0020 — $64.00.

MACHIAS. Index of Surnames to George W. Drisko's "Narrative of the Town of Machias," above. Comp. by Wade F. Harmon. 1995. 93p.
P5-ME0109B — $18.00.

THE REVOLUTION: Life of Hannah Weston, with a Brief History of her Ancestry [MACHIAS]; also a Condensed History of Jonesborough, Machias & Other Neighboring Towns. By George W. Drisko. 1903. 138p.
P5-ME0174B — $18.00.

MADISON REGISTER, 1903 [Town History & Directory]. Comp. by Mitchell & Randall. 1903. 137p.
P5-ME0194 — $21.00.

PIONEERS OF MAGALLOWAY REGION, from 1820 to 1904. By Granville P. Wilson. 1918. 64p.
P5-ME0134 — $13.00.

MATINICUS ISLE, Its Story and Its People, in Two Parts: Pt. I, Historical; Pt. II, Genealogical. By Charles A.E. Long. 1926. 245p.
P5-ME0261 — $35.00.

MILBRIDGE REGISTER, 1905 [Town History & Directory]. By Mitchell & Campbell. 1905. 88p.
P5-ME0195 — $17.50.

MILO & BROWNVILLE TOWN REGISTER, 1905 [Town histories & directories]. Comp. by Mitchell, Daggett & Curtis. 1905. 120p.
P5-ME0196 — $16.00.

FORTUNATE ISLAND OF MONHEGAN: A Historical Monograph. By Charles Francis Jenney. 1922. 78p.
P5-ME0197 — $16.00.

MONHEGAN, THE CRADLE OF NEW ENGLAND. By Ida Sedgewick Proper. 1930. 275p.
P5-ME0154B — $37.00.

HISTORY OF MONMOUTH AND WALES. With genealogical appendix, 2-vol. set By Harry H. Cochrane. 1894. 2 vols., 1065p.
P5-ME0198 — $99.00/set.

HISTORY OF MONMOUTH AND WALES . . ., Vol. I. 1894.
P5-ME0198A — $53.00.

HISTORY OF MONMOUTH AND WALES . . ., Vol. II. 1894.
P5-ME0198B — $53.00.

MONMOUTH CEMETERIES. 1931. 2 vols. in 1, 34 + 32p.
P5-ME0170B — $10.00.

GENEALOGICAL HISTORY OF THE FAMILIES OF MORRILL. By Theoda M. Morse and Mr & Mrs Charkes White. 1957. 461p.
P5-ME0265 — $47.50.

HISTORY OF THE TOWN OF MORRILL in the County of Waldo & State of Maine. By Timothy W. Robinson. 1944. 253p.
P5-ME0199 — $32.00.

MOUNT DESERT: A History. By George E. Street. 1905. 370p.
P5-MEMD01 — $47.00.

STORY OF NEW SWEDEN, as Told at the Quarter Centennial Celebration of the Founding of the Swedish Colony in the Woods of Maine. 1896. 134p.
P5-ME0200 — $17.50.

HISTORY OF NEWCASTLE, MAINE. By Rundlette K. Palmer. 1979. 762 + 55p.
P5-ME0578 — $78.00.

EARLY DAYS of NORRIDGEWOCK. Henrietta Danforth Wood. 1933. 124 + 20p.
P5-ME0104 — $21.50.

HISTORY OF NORRIDGEWOCK AND CANAAN, MAINE By J. W. Hanson 1849. 372p.
P26520500 — $62.00.

NORRIDGEWOCK REGISTER, 1903. 1903. 89p.
P5-ME0103 — $15.00.

NORTH BERWICK RECORD BOOK [Cemetery Inscriptions]. By John Eldridge Frost. 1964. 101p.
P5-ME0168B — $15.00.

NORTH BERWICK REGISTER, 1904 [Town History & Directory]. By Mitchell & Campbell. 1904. 112p.
P5-ME0201 — $19.50.

OUR ISLAND TOWN, By Our Townspeople & Friends [NORTH HAVEN]. Prepared by Lillie S. Bousfield. n.d. 136p.
P5-ME0267 — $17.00.

HISTORY OF NORWAY, Comprising a Minute Account of its First Settlement . . . Interspersed with Historical Sketches, Narrative & Anecdote. David Noyes. 1852. 215p.
P5-ME0202 — $29.00.

HISTORY OF NORWAY, from the Earliest Settlements to the Close of the Year 1922. By Charles F. Whitman. 1924. 581p.
P5-ME0157B — $61.50.

OAKLAND REGISTER, 1903 [Town History & Directory]. Comp. by H.E. Mitchell. 1903. 115p.
P5-ME0203 — $19.50.

SKETCHES OF THE TOWN OF OLD TOWN, Penobscot Co., from its Earliest Settlement to 1879, with Biographical Sketches. By David Norton. 1881. 152p.
P5-ME0205 — $19.50.

OTISFIELD GENEALOGIES ONLY. 340p.
P5-ME0035 — $34.00.

OTISFIELD, HARRISON, NAPLES & SEBAGO TOWN REGISTER, 1906. [Town Histories & Directories]. Comp. by Mitchell & Davis. 1906. 169p.
P5-ME0207 — $24.00.

ANNALS OF OXFORD, from its Incorporation . . . in 1829 to 1850, with a Brief Account of the Settlement of Shepardsfield Plantation, now Hebron and Oxford, and Genealogical Notes from . . . Both Towns. Marquis F. King. 1903. 298p.
P5-ME0115 — $37.00.

OXFORD, HEBRON & MINOT REGISTER, 1906. [Town Histories & Directories]. Comp. by Mitchell & Davis. 1906. 142p.
P5-ME0208 — $22.00.

BIOGRAPHICAL REVIEW: Biographical Sketches of Leading Citizens of Oxford & Franklin Cos. 1897. 639p.
P5-ME0131 — $67.00.

HISTORY OF PARIS, from its Settlement to 1880, with a History of the Grants of 1736 & 1771, with Personal Sketches, a Copious Genealogical Register, & an Appendix. By Wm. B. Lapham & S.P. Maxim. 1884. 911p.
P5-ME0119 — $91.50.

PARIS REGISTER, 1906 [Town History & Directory]. Comp. by Mitchell & Davis. 1906. 154p.
P5-ME0209 — $23.50.

HISTORY OF THE FIRST CENTURY OF PARSONFIELD, Incorporated August 29, 1785. Includes genealogies. By a Committee of the Town. 1888. 499p.
P5-ME0023 — $57.00.

HISTORY OF PEAKS ISLAND & ITS PEOPLE; Also a Short History of House Island, Portland. By Nathan Gould. 1897. 75p.
P5-ME0210 — $15.00.

ANCIENT PEMAQUID: An Historical Review. By J. Wingate Thornton. 1857. 178p.
P5-ME0213 — $27.00.

HISTORY OF PEMAQUID, with Sketches of Monhegan, Popham & Castine. Arlita D. Parker. 1925. 226p.
P5-ME0156B — $31.50.

STORY OF PEMAQUID. By James Otis. 1902. 181p.
P5-ME0211 — $26.00.

TWENTY YEARS AT PEMAQUID: Sketches of its History & its Remains, Ancient & Modern. By J. Henry Cartland. 1914. 224p.
P5-ME0212 — $29.50.

GRAVESTONE INSCRIPTIONS, Penobscot. Comp. by Grace Limeburner. 1941-1942. 2 vols. in 1, 27 + 17p.
P5-ME0215 — $10.00.

VITAL STATISTICS FROM TOWN RECORDS, PENOBSCOT, 1787 to 1875. Comp. by Brooksville Hist. Soc. 1940. 217p.
P5-ME0262 — $29.00.

HISTORY OF PENOBSCOT COUNTY, with Illustrations & Biographical Sketches. 1882. 922p.
P5-me0575B — $92.00.

HISTORY OF PERU, in the County of Oxford, from 1789 to 1911. With residents and genealogies of the families. Hollis Turner. 1911. 313p.
P5-ME0061 — $37.00.

VITAL RECORDS OF PHIPPSBURG, to the Year 1892: Births, Marriages & Deaths. 1935. 431p.
P5-ME0216 — $47.00.

HISTORY OF PISCATAQUIS COUNTY, From its Earliest Settlement to 1880. By Rev. Amasa Loring. 1880. 304p.
P5-ME0217 — $39.50.

PISCATAQUIS BIOGRAPHY & FRAGMENTS. By John Francis Sprague. 1899. 102p.
P5-ME0218 — $15.00.

HISTORY OF PITTSTON, MAINE. By Rundlette K. Palmer. 1979. 747p.
P5-ME0579 — $78.00.

VITAL RECORDS OF PITTSTON, MAINE TO THE YEAR 1892. By Henry Sewall Webster. 1911. 387p.
P26627000 — $64.00.

TOWN REGISTER OF POLAND, RAYMOND & CASCO, 1906 [Town histories & directories.] Comp. by Mitchell & Davis. 1906. 141p.
P5-ME0219 — $19.00.

For hardcover versions, see the order form on page v. To order, call 1-888-296-3447.

Maine, cont.

PORTER AS A PORTION OF MAINE: Its Settlement, etc. By Thomas Moulton. 1879. 96p.
P5-ME0220 — $19.00.

PORTLAND & VICINITY. By Edw. H. Elwell. 1876. 142p.
P5-ME0028 — $35.00.

PRESQUE ISLE REGISTER, 1904 [Town History & Directory]. Comp. by Mitchell & Pettingill. 1904. 130p.
P5-ME0221 — $21.50.

PROSPECT Births, Marriages & Deaths, 1753 to 1871 (Marriages 1816-1832 not included). Comp. by Mrs E.H. Sweetser. 1934. 179p.
P5-ME0222 — $23.00.

OLD PROUTS NECK. By Augustus F. Moulton. 1924. 119p.
P5-ME0223 — $15.00.

RANDOLPH VITAL RECORDS TO THE YEAR 1892. 1910. 144p.
P5-ME0105 — $22.50.

REDFIELD REGISTER, 1903 [Town history & directory]. Comp. by H.E. Mitchell. 1903. 80p.
P5-ME0224A — $16.00.

RICHMOND REGISTER, 1904 [Town history of directory]. Comp. by Mitchell & Denning. 1904. 103p.
P5-ME0225A — $15.00.

ROCKPORT REGISTER, 1904 [Town History & Directory]. By Mitchell, Carroll & Pressey. 1904. 94p.
P5-ME0227A — $17.00.

HISTORY OF RUMFORD, OXFORD CO., from its First Settlement to the Present Time [1890]. William B. Lapham. 1890. 432p.
P5-ME0274 — $45.00.

FIRST BOOK OF RECORDS of the First Church in Pepperrellborough [now Saco, Maine]. Compiled by Rev. John Fairfield. 1914. 78p.
P5-ME0585 — $20.00.

FIRST BOOK OF RECORDS OF THE TOWN OF PEPPERELL-BOROUGH, Now the City of Saco. Includes births, marriages & daeaths to app. 1840. 1896. 299p.
P5-ME0228A — $35.00.

OLD TIMES IN SACO By Daniel E. Owen 1891. 172p.
P26632500 — $34.00.

SACO VALLEY SETTLEMENTS & FAMILIES, Historical, Biographical, Genealogical, Traditional & Legendary. G.T. Ridlon, Sr. 1895. 1224p.
P5-ME0062 — $95.00.

SHORES OF SACO BAY: Historical Guide to Biddeford Pool, Old Orchard Beach, Pine Point, Prout's Neck. By J.S. Locke. 1880. 107p.
P5-ME0204 — $15.00.

BIOGRAPHICAL REVIEW: Life Sketches of Leading Citizens of Sagadahoc, Lincoln, Knox & Waldo Cos. 1897. 422p.
P5-ME0130 — $47.00.

HISTORY OF SANFORD, 1661-1900. By Edwin Emery. 1901. 537p.
P5-ME0230A — $55.00.

GRANDFATHER TALES OF SCARBOROUGH. By Augustus F. Moulton. 1925. 209p.
P5-ME0232C — $29.00.

HISTORY OF SCARBOROUGH from 1633 to 1783. By Wm. S. Southgate. 1853. 238p.
P5-ME0162B — $36.50.

SCARBORO REGISTER, 1905 [Town History & Directory]. Comp. by Mitchell & Campbell. 1905. 95p.
P5-ME0231 — $17.00.

SEDGEWICK GRAVESTONE INSCRIPTIONS TO 1892. Comp. by Grace M. Limeburner. 1941. 44 + 41p.
P5-ME0233A — $15.50.
SEDGEWICK, Incorporated January 12, 1789: All Vital Statistics . . . [1789 to 1809]. Comp. by Grace M. Lime-burner. 1941. 55 + 29p.
P5-ME0224B — $15.00.

HISTORY OF ANCIENT SHEEP-SCOT & NEWCASTLE, Including . . . other Contiguous Places from Earliest Discovery to the Present Time, with the Genealogy of More than Four Hundred Families. By D.Q. Cushman. 1882. 458p.
P5-ME0040 — $48.00.

SKOWHEGAN ON THE KENNEBEC, 2-vol. set. By Louise Helen Coburn, et al. 1941. 2 vols., 1050p.
P5-ME0055 — $99.50/set.

SKOWHEGAN ON THE KENNEBEC, Vol. I. 1941.
P5-ME0055A — $52.00.

SKOWHEGAN ON THE KENNEBEC, Vol. II. 1941.
P5-ME0055B — $52.00.

RECORDS OF SOUTHPORT: Vital Records, Cemeteries, 1850 Census, Church Records. Comp. by J.J. Haskell & G. Lilly. 1937. 62p.
P5-ME0225B — $12.50.

TRADITIONS & RECORDS OF SOUTHWEST HARBOR & SOMESVILLE, Mt Desert Island. By Mrs. S.S. Thornton. 1938. 346p.
P5-ME0117 — $41.50.

SAINT GEORGE CHRONICLES, Containing an Historical Sketch from 1605 to 1932. Comp. by Jos. T. Simmons & Mabelle A. Rose. 1932. 78p.
P5-ME0229A — $15.50.

HISTORICAL SKETCH OF STOCKTON SPRINGS. By Faustina Hichborn. 1908. 133p.
P5-ME0132 — $19.50.

STORY OF STOCKTON SPRING. By Alice V. Ellis. 1955. 223p.
P5-ME0226 — $29.50.

SULLIVAN & SORRENTO Since 1760. With genealogies. By Lelia A.C. Johnson. 1953. 410p.
P5-ME0227B — $45.00.

HISTORY OF SWAN'S ISLAND. By H.W. Small, MD. 1898. 244p.
P5-ME0228B — $31.50.

HISTORY OF THOMASTON, ROCKLAND & SO. THOMASTON, from their First Exploration, a.d. 1605. With genealogies, 2-vol. set. By C. Eaton. 1865. 468 + 472p.
P5-ME0016 — $98.00/set.

HISTORY OF THOMASTON, ROCKLAND & SO. THOMASTON . . ., Vol. I. 1865. 468p.
P5-ME0016A — $52.00.

HISTORY OF THOMASTON, ROCKLAND & SO. THOMASTON . . ., Vol. II. 1865. 472p.
P5-ME0016B — $52.00.

THOMASTON REGISTER, 1904 [Town History & Directory]. By Mitchell & Gastonguay. 1904. 102p.
P5-ME0229B — $17.00.

VITAL RECORDS OF TOPSHAM, to the Year 1892, 2-vol. set. 1929. 2 vols., 214 + 402p.
P5-ME0260 — $77.50/set.

VITAL RECORDS OF TOPSHAM, to the Year 1892, Vol. I. 1929. 214p.
P5-ME0260A — $35.00.

VITAL RECORDS OF TOPSHAM, to the Year 1892, Vol. II. 1929. 402p.
P5-ME0260B — $50.00.

TURNER REGISTER, 1903-4 [history & town directory]. By Rev. B.V. Davis. 1904. 109p.
P5-ME0164B — $17.50.

HISTORY OF THE TOWN OF UNION, in the County of Lincoln, to the Middle ot the 19th Century, with a Family Register of the Settlers before the Year 1800 & their Descendants. By John Langdon Sibley. 1851. 540p.
P5-ME0230B — $56.00.

UNION, PAST & PRESENT: An Illustrated History of the Town of Union, from Earliest Times. 1895. 96p.
P5-ME0232A — $16.00.

HISTORY OF THE TOWN OF UNITY. By James B. Vickery III. 1954. 254p.
P5-ME0232B — $32.00.

HISTORY OF UNITY. By James R. Taber. 1916. 144p.
P5-ME0233B — $18.50.

VASSALBORO REGISTER, 1904 [Town History & Directory]. Comp. by Mitchell & Davis. 1904. 132p.
P5-ME0234 — $21.50.

VASSALBORO VITAL RECORDS. Comp. by J.J. Haskell. 1. 80 + 99p.
P5-ME0166B — $21.00.

VEAZIE CEMETERY, Veazie; Hews Cemetery & Abandoned Roadside Cemetery, Orono [cemetery inscriptions]. Comp. by F.D. Williams Chapter D.A.R. 1942. 88p.
P5-ME0165B — $15.00.

BRIEF HISTORICAL SKETCH OF THE TOWN OF VINALHAVEN, from its Earliest Known Settlement. 1900. 84p.
P5-ME0235 — $16.00.

HISTORY OF THE TOWN OF WALDOBORO. S.L. Miller. 1910. 281p.
P5-ME0007 — $37.00.

WALDOBORO VITAL RECORDS, 1773 to 1891. Comp. by Mrs W Colwell, Esther Gross & Georgiana Lilly. 1949-1950. 211 + 38p.
P5-ME0236B — $25.00.

ANNALS OF THE TOWN OF WARREN, in Knox Co., with the Early History of St George's, Broad Bay, & their Neighboring Settlements on the Waldo Patent. By Cyrus Eaton. 1877. 680p.
P5-ME0237B — $69.50.

HISTORY OF WATERFORD, Oxford County, Comprising Historical Address, Record of Families, Centennial Proceedings. By Henry P. Warren, et al. 1879. 371p.
P5-ME0063 — $42.00.

NOTES ON THE HISTORY OF WATERFORD. 1913. 87p.
P5-ME0238B — $16.50.

CENTENNIAL HISTORY OF WATERVILLE, KENNEBEC COUNTY, 1802-1902. 1902. 592p.
P5-ME0013 — $65.00.

CHRONOLOGY OF MUNICIPAL HISTORY and ELECTION STATISTICS, WATERVILLE, 1771-1908. 1908. 282p.
P5-ME0125A — $39.00.

HISTORY OF THE TOWN OF WAYNE, Kennebac Co., from its Settlement to 1898. With genealogies. By C.F. Leadbetter, C.E. Wing, et al. 1898. 354p.
P5-ME0056 — $42.00.

HISTORY OF WELLS & KENNEBUNK, from the Earliest Settlement to the Year 1820, at Which Time Kennebunk was Set Off and Incorporated, with Biographical Sketches. Edw. E. Bourne. 1875. 797p.
P5-ME0239 — $79.50.

VITAL RECORDS OF WEST GARDINER, to the Year 1892. 1913. 109p.
P5-ME0241 — $15.00.

HIGHLIGHTS OF WESTBROOK HISTORY. Comp. by Ernest R. Rowe, et al. 1952. 242p.
P5-ME0125B — $36.50.

51 YEARS FROM THE PLAINS [Whitefield, Maine]. By Rundlette K. Palmer. 1977. 300p.
P5-ME0583 — $42.00.

HISTORY OF WHITEFIELD, MAINE. By Rundlette K. Palmer. 1978. 1051p.
P5-ME0580 — $100.00.

LARGE PEEK FROM THE PLAINS: Partial History of Whitefield, Maine. By Rundlette K. Palmer. 1977. 778p.
P5-ME0582 — $77.00.

WHITEFIELD CEMETERIES IN 1977 from the Readable Remaining Stones. Rundlette K. Palmer. 1977. 338p.
P5-ME0584 — $46.00.

WILTON REGISTER, 1903-4 [Town History & Directory]. By Mitchell & Remick. 1904. 98p.
P5-ME0242 — $19.00.
SKETCHES OF THE HISTORY OF WINDHAM, 1734-1935: the Story of a Typical New England Town. Frederick H. Dole. 1935. 157p.
P5-ME0243 — $21.00.

WINDHAM IN THE PAST. With genealogical sketches. By Samuel T. Dole. 1916. 611p.
P5-ME0244 — $64.00.

WINDHAM IN THE WAR OF THE REBELLION, 1775-1783. By Nathan Gold. 1900. 16p.
P5-ME0254 — $10.00.

WINDHAM REGISTER, 1904 [Town History & Directory]. Comp. by Mitchell & Russell. 1904. 110p.
P5-ME0245 — $17.50.

WINSLOW REGISTER, 1904 [Town History & Directory]. By Mitchell & Davis. 1904. 103p.
P5-ME0246 — $17.50.

WINSLOW VITAL RECORDS, to the Year 1892: Births, Marriages & Deaths. 1937. 325p.
P5-ME0041 — $37.50.

AN OLD RIVER TOWN, Being a History of Winterport (Old Frankfort). With 1993 addendum. By Ada Douglas Littlefield. 1907. 249 + 50 + 11p.
P5-ME0064 — $32.50.

For hardcover versions, see the order form on page v. To order, call 1-888-296-3447.

Maine, cont.

**BRIEF HISTORY OF WINTHROP,
from 1764 to October, 1855.** By David
Thurston. 1855. 247p.
P5-ME0153B — $32.00.

**WINTHROP REGISTER, 1903-4
[Town History & Directory].** By
Mitchell & Remick. 1904. 99p.
P5-ME0247 — $18.00.

**WISCASSET IN
POWNALBOROUGH [history].** By
F.S. Chase. 1941. 640p.
P5-ME0030 — $67.00.

**HISTORY OF WOODSTOCK, with
Family Sketches and an Appendix.**
By Wm. B. Lapham. 1882. 315p.
P5-ME0263 — $37.50.

**WOODSTOCK, SUMNER &
BUCKFIELD TOWN REGISTER,
1905. [Town Histories & Direc-
tories].** Comp. by Mitchell & Davis.
1905. 222p.
P5-ME0249 — $26.50.

**ANCIENT NORTH YARMOUTH
& YARMOUTH, 1636-1936, A
History.** By Wm. Hutchinson Rowe.
1937. 427p.
P5-ME0126 — $47.00.

**YARMOUTH REGISTER, 1904
[Town History & Directory].** By
Mitchell & Remick. 1904. 112p.
P5-ME0250 — $19.50.

**ANCIENT CITY OF GORGEANA
& MODERN TOWN OF YORK,
From its Earliest Settlement to the
Present Time[1874]; Also its Beaches
& Summer Resorts.** By Geo. A.
Emery. 1874. 256p.
P5-ME0252 — $34.00.

**HANDBOOK HISTORY OF THE
TOWN OF YORK, From Early
Times to the Present [1914].** By Edw.
C. Moody. 1914. 251p.
P5-ME0253 — $34.00.

**HISTORY OF YORK, Successively
Known as Bristol (1632), Agamenticus
(1641), Gorgeana (1642) & York
(1652), 2-vol. set** By Charles Edw.
Banks. 1931-1935. 2 vols., 474 + 464p.
P5-ME0251 — $94.50/set.

HISTORY OF YORK . . ., Vol. I.
1931-1935. 474p.
P5-ME0251A — $50.50.

HISTORY OF YORK . . ., Vol. II.
1931-1935. 464p.
P5-ME0251B — $50.50.

NEW ENGLAND MINIATURE: A
History of York, Maine. By George
Ernst. 1961. 284p.
P5-ME0057 — $34.00.

**HISTORY OF YORK COUNTY,
with Illustrations and Biographical
Sketches of Prominent Men and
Pioneers.** 1880. 441p.
P5-ME0008 — $49.50.

Maryland

**BRITISH INVASION OF MARY-
LAND, 1812-1815.** By Wm. M. Marine.
1913. 519p.
P5-MD0019 — $52.00.

**COLONIAL, REVOLUTIONARY,
COUNTY & CHURCH RECORDS
from Original Sources, 2 vols.** By
G.M. Brumbaugh. 1915, 1928. 2 vols.,
513 + 688p.
P5-MD0050 — $75.00/set.

**COLONIAL, REVOLUTIONARY,
COUNTY & CHURCH RECORDS .
. ., vol. I.** 1915. 513p.
P5-MD0050A — $42.50.

**COLONIAL, REVOLUTIONARY,
COUNTY & CHURCH RECORDS .
. ., vol. II.** 1928. 688p.
P5-MD0050B — $45.00.

**FIRST PARISHES OF THE PROV-
INCE OF MARYLAND, Wherein
are given Historical Sketches of the
Ten Counties & Thirty Parishes in
the Provice.. in 1692.** By Percy G.
Skirven. 1923. 199p.
P5-MD0054 — $22.50.

**FOUNDERS OF MARYLAND, as
Portrayed in Manuscripts, Provincial
Records & Early Documents.** By Rev.
Edw. D. Neill. 1876. 193p.
P5-MD0022 — $22.50.

**GAZETTEER OF MARYLAND &
DELWARE.** H. Gannett. 1904. 84 + 15p.
P5-MD0008 — $15.00.

**GENEALOGICAL & MEMORIAL
ENCYCLOPEDIA OF THE STATE
OF MARYLAND: Record of the
Achievements of her People in the
Making of a Commonwealth & the
Founding of a Nation.** 1919. 2 vols. in
1, 756p.
P5-MD0023 — $81.00.

**HEADS OF FAMILIES at the First
Census of the U.S. Taken in 1790
[Maryland].** 1907. 189p.
P5-MD0001 — $19.50.

**HISTORY OF MARYLAND, Vols.
I–III.** By J. Thomas Scharf. 1879. 3
vols., 556 + 655 + 796p.
P5-MD0254 — $200.00/set.

HISTORY OF MARYLAND, Vol. I.
By J. Thomas Scharf. 1879. 556p.
P5-MD0254A — $66.00.

HISTORY OF MARYLAND, Vol. II.
By J. Thomas Scharf. 1879. 655p.
P5-MD0254B — $72.00.

**HISTORY OF MARYLAND, Vol.
III.** By J. Thomas Scharf. 1879. 796p.
P5-MD0254C — $80.00.

**HISTORY OF WESTERN MARY-
LAND, Being a History of Frederick,
Montgomery, Carroll, Washington,
Allegany and Garrett Cos., from the
Earliest Period to the Present Day,
including Biographical Sketches of
Representative Men, 2-vol. set.** By
J. Thomas Scharf. 1882. 2 vols., 1560p.
P5-MD0018 — $149.00/set.

**HISTORY OF WESTERN
MARYLAND. . ., Vol. I.** 1882.
P5-MD0018A — $84.00.

**HISTORY OF WESTERN
MARYLAND. . ., Vol. II.** 1882.
P5-MD0018B — $84.00.

**JEWS STRUGGLE FOR RELI-
GIOUS & CIVIL LIBERTY IN
MARYLAND.** By E. Milton Altfeld.
1924. 211p.
P5-MD0053 — $22.50.

**MARYLAND'S COLONIAL
EASTERN SHORE: Historical
Sketches of Counties & of Some
Notable Structures.** 1916. 204p.
P5-MD0021 — $31.00.

**PENNSYLVANIA-GERMAN IN
THE SETTLEMENT OF MARY-
LAND.** Daniel W. Nead. 1914. 304p.
P5-MD0024 — $39.50.

REVOLUTIONARY RECORDS OF MARYLAND. By G.M. Brumbaugh & M.R. Hodges. 1924. 96p.
P5-MD0003 — $10.00.

TERRA MARIA: or, Threads of Maryland Colonial History. By Edw. D. Neill. 1867. 260p.
P5-MD0020 — $34.50.

THE PENNSYLVANIA-GERMAN in the Settlement of Maryland. By Daniel Wunderlich Nead. 1914. 304p.
P5-MD10018 — $30.50.

HISTORY OF ALLEGANY COUNTY. 2-vol. set. By James W. Thomas & T.J.C Williams. 1923. 2 vols., 1290p.
P5-MD0025 — $131.00/set.

HISTORY OF ALLEGANY COUNTY, Vol. I. 1923.
P5-MD0025A — $69.50.

HISTORY OF ALLEGANY COUNTY, Vol. II. 1923.
P5-MD0025B — $69.50.

ANNALS OF ANNAPOLIS, Comprising Sundry Notices of that Old City from the First Settlements in 1649 to the War of 1812. By David Ridgely. 1841. 283p.
P5-MD0007 — $35.00.

ANNE ARUNDEL GENTRY: A Genealogical History of Twenty-two Pioneers of Anne Arundel County and their Descendants. By Harry Wright Newman. 1933. 668p.
P5-MD0017 — $71.50.

FOUNDERS OF ANNE ARUNDEL & HOWARD COS.: A Genealogical & Biographical Review from Wills, Deeds & Church Records. By J.D. Warfield. 1905. 543 + 56p.
P5-MD0006 — $49.00.

GENEALOGY & BIOGRAPHY OF LEADING FAMILIES OF THE CITY OF BALTIMORE & Baltimore County, Containing Portraits of Many Well Known Citizens of the Past & Present. 1897. 1061p.
P5-MD0026 — $109.00.

HISTORY OF BALTIMORE, City & County, from the Earliest Period to the Present Time, including Biographical Sketches of their Representative Men. By J. Thomas Scharf. 1881. 947p.
P5-MD0028 — $99.00.

THE MONUMENTAL CITY [BALTIMORE], its Past History & Present Resources. By George W. Howard. 1873. 874p.
P5-MD0027 — $91.00.

OLD BUCKINGHAM BY THE SEA on the Eastern Shore of Maryland. By I. Marshall Price. 1936. 252p.
P5-MD0055 — $34.50.

HISTORY OF CAROLINE COUNTY, from its Beginning, rev. ed. 1920. 345p.
P5-MD0029 — $44.00.

CECIL COUNTY: A Study in Local History. Alice E. Miller. 1949. 173p.
P5-MD0056 — $29.00.

HISTORY OF CECIL COUNTY & the Early Settlements around the Head of the Chesapeake Bay & on the Delaware River, with Sketches of Some of the Old Families. By G. Johnson. 1881. 548p.
P5-MD0009 — $55.00.

CHARLES COUNTY GENTRY: Genealogical History of Six Emigrants — Thos. Dent, John Dent, Richard Edelson, John Hanson, Geo. Newman, Humphrey Warren — who Settled in Charles Co., & their Descendants, Showing Emigrations to the South & West. Harry W. Newman. 1940. 321p.
P5-MD0030 — $41.50.

CHARLOTTE HALL: the Village, 1797-1997. J. Roy Guyther. 1997. 222p.
P5-MD10017 — $34.00.

HISTORY OF CUMBERLAND from the Time of the Indian Town Caiuctucuc in 1728, up to the Present Day [1878]. By Will H. Lowdermilk. 1878. 554p.
P5-MD0031 — $59.50.

REVISED HISTORY OF DORCHESTER COUNTY. By Elias Jones. 1925. 603p.
P5-MD0013 — $59.50.

HISTORY OF FREDERICK COUNTY, from the Earliest Settlements to the Beginning of the War Between the States, Continued from the Beginning of the Year 1861 Down to the Present [1910], 2-vol. set. By T.J.C. William, continued by Folger McKinsey. 1910. 663 + 940p.
P5-MD0032 — $155.00/set.

HISTORY OF FREDERICK COUNTY . . ., Vol. I. 1910. 663p.
P5-MD0032A — $75.00.

HISTORY OF FREDERICK COUNTY . . ., Vol. II. 1910. 940p.
P5-MD0032B — $97.00.

HISTORY OF GRACEHAM, Frederick County. By Rev. A.L. Oerter. 1913. 189p.
P5-MD0033 — $28.50.

HISTORY OF KENT COUNTY, 1630-1916. Fred G. Usilton. 1916. 250p.
P5-MD0034 — $34.50.

HISTORY OF LEITERSBURG DISTRICT, Washington Co., including its Original Land Tenure; First Settlement; Material Development; Biographical Sketches, etc. By Herbert C. Bell. 1898. 331p.
P5-MD0016 — $41.50.

MECHANICSVILLE: The Story of Our Village. By J. Roy Guyther, MD. 1994. 184p.
P5-MD10019 — $31.00.

HISTORIC MONTGOMERY COUNTY, Old Homes & History. By Roger B. Farquhar. 1952. 373p.
P5-MD0014 — $42.50.

OLD KENT, EASTERN SHORE OF MARYLAND: Notes Illustrative of Ancient Records of Kent Co. With hundreds of genealogies from the entire Eastern Shore. By G.A. Hanson. 1876. 383p.
P5-MD0005 — $35.00.

HISTORICAL SALISBURY, Including Historical Sketches of the Eastern Shore. By Charles J. Truitt. 1932. 227p.
P5-MD0057 — $31.50.

MEMOIRS OF A COUNTRY DOCTOR St. Mary's County Patients are Special Folks. By J. Roy Guther, MD. 1999. 116p.
P5-MD10020 — $27.00.

HISTORY OF TALBOT COUNTY, 1661-1861, 2-vol. set. Data collected by Sam'l Alexander Harrison. 1915. 2 vols., 649 + 555p.
P5-MD0015 — $119.00/set.

HISTORY OF TALBOT COUNTY, 1661-1861, Vol. I. 1915. 649p.
P5-MD0015A — $61.50.

Maryland, cont.

HISTORY OF TALBOT COUNTY,
1661-1861, Vol. II. 1915. 555p.
P5-MD0015B — $61.50.

HISTORY OF WASHINGTON
COUNTY, from the Earliest
Settlements to the Present Times,
including a History of Hagerstown.
With biographical records of repre-
sentative families. 2-vol. set. Thomas
J.C. Williams. 1906. 2 vols., 1347p.
P5-MD0011 — $125.00/set.

HISTORY OF WASHINGTON
COUNTY . . ., Vol. I. 1906.
P5-MD0011A — $67.50.

HISTORY OF WASHINGTON
COUNTY . . ., Vol. II. 1906.
P5-MD0011B — $67.50.

INSCRIPTIONS ON TOMB-
STONES IN CEMETERIES OF
WORCESTER COUNTY. Comp. by
Millard F. Hudson. 1944?. 227p., typescript.
P5-MD0058 — $25.00.

Massachusetts

MAYFLOWER DESCENDANTS &
THEIR MARRIAGES FOR TWO
GENERATIONS AFTER THE
LANDING. By J.T. Landis. 1922. 37p.
P5-GR0001 — $10.00.

SKETCHES OF THE OLD
INHABITANTS & Other Citizens of
Old Springfield of the Present
Century, & its Historic Mansions of
"ye olden tyme." With 124 illustra-
tions. Charles W. Chapin. 1893. 431p.
P5-MA0172 — $45.00.

ANNALS OF WITCHCRAFT IN
NEW ENGLAND & Elsewhere in
the U.S., from their First Settlement.
By Samuel G. Drake. 1869. 306p.
P5-MA0425 — $37.00.

CHRONICLES OF THE FIRST
PLANTERS OF THE COLONY OF
MASS. BAY FROM 1623 TO 1636. By
A. Young. 1846. 571p.
P5-MA0410 — $45.00.

EARLY MASSACHUSETTS
MARRIAGES, Prior to 1800, as
Found in Ancient Court Records.
1897-1914. 3 vols. in 1, 607p.
P5-MA0157 — $55.00.

FAMILIES OF THE PILGRIMS.
Comp. for the Mass. Soc. of Mayflower
Desc. by H.K. Shaw. 1956. 178p.
P5-MA0083 — $19.00.

GAZETTEER OF THE STATE OF
MASSACHUSETTS, with Numerous
Illustrations on Wood & Steel. By
Elias Nason. 1876. 576p.
P5-MA0518 — $59.00.

GENEALOGICAL & PERSONAL
MEMOIRS Relating to the Families
of Boston & Eastern Mass., Vol. I. 1908.
P5-MA0380A — $61.50.

GENEALOGICAL & PERSONAL
MEMOIRS Relating to the Families
of Boston & Eastern Mass., Vol. II.
1908.
P5-MA0380B — $61.50.

GENEALOGICAL & PERSONAL
MEMOIRS Relating to the Families
of Boston & Eastern Mass., Vol. III.
1908.
P5-MA0380C — $61.50.

GENEALOGICAL & PERSONAL
MEMOIRS Relating to the Families
of Boston & Eastern Mass., Vol. IV.
1908.
P5-MA0380D — $61.50.

GEOGRAPHIC DICTIONARY OF
MASS. By H. Gannett. 1894. 126p.
P5-MA0400 — $15.00.

HISTORICAL COLLECTIONS,
Being a General Collection of
Interesting Facts, Traditions . . .
Relating to the History & Antiquities
of Every Town in Mass., with Geogr.
Descriptions. With 200 engravings.
John Warner Barber. 1839. 624p.
P5-MA0401 — $65.00.

HISTORY OF THE CONNECTI-
CUT VALLEY in Massachusetts,
with Illustrations & Biographical
Sketches of Some of its Prominent
Men & Pioneers. Vol. I Hampshire
County; Vol. II Franklin & Hampden
Counties. Comp. by Nathaniel Bartlett
Sylvester et al. 1879. 1111p.
P5-MA0402 — $105.00/Set.

HISTORY OF THE CONNECTI-
CUT VALLEY . . ., Vol. I
Hampshire County. 1879.
P5-MA0402A — $57.50.

HISTORY OF THE CONNECTI-
CUT VALLEY . . ., Vol. II Franklin
& Hampden Counties. 1879..
P5-MA0402B — $57.50.

HISTORY OF THE FIRST REGI-
MENT (Mass. Infantry), from the
25th of May, 1861, to the 25th of May,
1864, including Brief References to
the Operations of the Army of the
Potomac. Warren H. Cudworth. 1866.
528p.
P5-MA0391 — $59.00.

HISTORY OF THE MILITARY
COMPANY OF MASSACHUSETTS,
Now Called the Ancient & Honor-
able Artillery Co. of Mass., 1637-1888,
4-vol. set. Oliver Ayr Roberts. 1895-
1901. 4 vols., 500 + 479 + 435 +512p.
P5-MA0574B — $189.00/set.

HISTORY OF THE MILITARY
COMPANY OF MASSACHUSETTS
. . ., Vol. I. 1895-1901. 500p.
P5-MA0574B1 — $52.00.

HISTORY OF THE MILITARY
COMPANY OF MASSACHUSETTS
. . ., Vol. II. 1895-1901. 479p.
P5-MA0574B2 — $52.00.

HISTORY OF THE MILITARY
COMPANY OF MASSACHUSETTS
. . ., Vol. III. 1895-1901. 435p.
P5-MA0574B3 — $52.00.

HISTORY OF THE MILITARY
COMPANY OF MASSACHUSETTS
. . ., Vol. IV. 512p.
P5-MA0574B4 — $52.00.

INDEX OF PIONEERS FROM
MASSACHUSETTS TO THE
WEST, Especially to the State of
Michigan. By C.A. Flagg. 1915. 86p.
P5-MI0001 — $10.00.

LIST OF FREEMEN OF MASSA-
CHUSETTS. By L. Paige. 1849. 40p.
P5-MA0243 — $9.00.

LIST OF PERSONS WHOSE
NAMES have been changed in
Massachusetts, 1780-1892. Comp. by
the Mass. Secretary of the Common-
wealth. 1893, 2nd ed. 522p.
P5-MA0148 — $49.50.

LOYALISTS OF MASSACHU-
SETTS, and the Other Side of the
American Revolution. By J.H. Stark.
1910. 509p.
P5-MA0276 — $54.00.

MASSACHUSETTS CIVIL LIST FOR THE COLONIAL & PROVINCIAL PERIODS, 1630-1774, Being a List of the Names & Dates of Appointment of All Civil Officers. By Wm. H. Whitemore. 1870. 172p.
P5-MA0390 — $21.00.

OLD INDIAN CHRONICLE, Being a Collection of Exceeding Rare Tracts Written and Published in the Time of King Philip's War by Persons Residing in the Country. By Samuel G. Drake. 1867. 333p.
P5-MA0297 — $43.50.

ORIGINAL NARRATIVES OF EARLY AMERICAN HISTORY: Narratives of the Witchcraft Cases, 1648-1706. 1914. 467 + xviii p.
P5-MA3002 — $54.50.

PIONEERS OF MASSACHUSETTS (1620-1650) By Charles Henry Pope. 1900. 550p.
P5-MA0350B — $32.50.

RECORDS OF MASSACHUSETTS, Vols. I-V, 5-vol. set. 1853-54. 5 vols.; 479 + 344 + 510 + 1165 +615p.
P5-MA3046 — $295.00/set.
RECORDS OF MASSACHUSETTS, Vol. I. 1853-54. 479p.
P5-MA3046A — $55.00.

RECORDS OF MASSACHUSETTS, Vol. II. 1853-54. 344p.
P5-MA3046B — $45.00.

RECORDS OF MASSACHUSETTS, Vol. III. 1853-54. 510p.
P5-MA3046C — $55.00.

RECORDS OF MASSACHUSETTS, Vol. IV. 1853-54. 1165p.
P5-MA3046D — $99.50.

RECORDS OF MASSACHUSETTS, Vol. V. 1853-54. 615p.
P5-MA3046E — $65.00.

RECORDS OF THE COURT OF ASSISTANTS OF THE COLONY OF THE MASSACHUSETTS BAY, 1630-1692, 3-vol. set. County of Suffolk; 1901-1928. 3 vols.
P5-MA0159A — $129.00/set.

RECORDS OF THE COURT OF ASSISTANTS OF THE COLONY OF THE MASSACHUSETTS BAY, 1630-1692, Vol. I. 1901-1928.
P5-MA0159A1 — $50.00.

RECORDS OF THE COURT OF ASSISTANTS OF THE COLONY OF THE MASSACHUSETTS BAY, 1630-1692, Vol. II. 1901-1928.
P5-MA0159A2 — $50.00.

RECORDS OF THE COURT OF ASSISTANTS OF THE COLONY OF THE MASSACHUSETTS BAY, 1630-1692, Vol. III. 1901-1928.
P5-MA0159A3 — $50.00.

RECORDS OF THE MASSACHUSETTS MILITIA IN THE WAR OF 1812-14. 1913. 448p.
P5-MA0514 — $51.00.

SOLDIERS IN KING PHILIP'S WAR, Containing Lists of Soldiers of Mass. Colony, who Served in the Indian Wars from 1620-77. Incl. sketches of principal officers & copies of ancient documents & records . . . By George M. Bodge. Third ed., 1906. 502p.
P5-MA0413 — $45.00.

ABINGTON, MASSACHUSETTS VITAL RECORDS TO THE YEAR 1850. 1912. 613p.
P26740000 — $88.00.

HISTORICAL SKETCH OF ABINGTON, Plymouth Co., with an appendix, By Aaron Hobart. 1839. 176 + 15p.
P5-MA0519 — $21.50.

HISTORY OF THE TOWN OF ABINGTON, Plymouth Co., from its First Settlement. By B. Hobart. 1866. 452p.
P5-MA0001 — $51.00.

ACTON, MASSACHUSETTS, VITAL RECORDS TO THE YEAR 1850. 1923. 311p.
P26475000 — $54.00.

HISTORY OF THE ACTON MINUTEMEN AND MILITIA COMPANIES, Vol. I (1754-1925). Charles R. Husbands 2003. 271 + vi p.
P5-MA2999 — $39.00.

HISTORY OF THE ACTON MINUTEMEN AND MILITIA COMPANIES, Vol. II (1917-1976). Charles R. Husbands. 2004. 344 + vi p.
P5-MA3011 — $47.00.

HISTORY OF THE TOWN OF ACTON. Harold R. Phalen. 1954. 471p.
P5-MA0351A — $51.50.

HISTORY OF THE TOWN OF ACUSHNET, Bristol Co. By Franklyn Howland. 1907. 398p.
P5-MA0362 — $44.50.

AMESBURY, MASSACHUSETTS, VITAL RECORDS TO THE YEAR 1850. 1913. 600p.
P26750000 — $94.00.

HISTORY OF AMESBURY, including the First Seventeen Years of Salisbury to Separation in 1654, & Merrimac from Incorporation in 1876. By J. Merrill. 1880. 431p.
P5-MA0002 — $47.00.

HISTORY OF THE TOWN OF AMHERST. Part I, General History of the Town; **Part II,** Town Meeting Records. Comp. by Carpenter and Morehouse. 1896. xxiii + 640 + 263p.
P5-MA0115 — $91.50.

ANDOVER, MASSACHUSETTS, VITAL RECORDS TO THE YEAR 1850. 1912. 391 + 575p.
P26760000 — $145.00.

HISTORICAL MANUAL OF THE SOUTH CHURCH IN ANDOVER, MASS. By George Mooar. 1859. 200p.
P5-MA3004 — $32.00.

HISTORICAL SKETCHES OF ANDOVER. S.L. Bailey. 1880. 650p.
P5-MA0005 — $68.00.

HISTORY OF ANDOVER from its Settlement to 1829. A. Abbot. 1829. 204p.
P5-MA0116 — $29.50.

RECORD OF ANDOVER DURING THE REBELLION. Comp. by Samuel Raymond. 1875. 232p.
P5-MA0363 — $25.00.

ARLINGTON, MASSACHUSETTS, VITAL RECORDS TO THE YEAR 1850. 1904. 162p.
P26765000 — $33.00.

HISTORY OF ARLINGTON, 1635-1879. By B. & W. Cutter. 1880. 368p.
P5-MA0007 — $41.00.

TOWN OF ARLINGTON, Past & Present: Narrative of Larger Events & Important Changes in the Village, Precinct & Town from 1637 to 1907. By Charles S. Parker. 1907. 331p.
P5-MA0364 — $39.50.

Massachusetts, cont.

**ASHBURNHAM, MASSACHU-
SETTS, VITAL RECORDS TO
THE YEAR 1850.** 1909. 215p.
P26766000 — $40.00.

**HISTORY OF ASHBURNHAM,
from 1734-1886, with a Genealogical
Register.** By E.S. Stearns. 1887. 1022p.
P5-MA0008 — $113.00.

**ASHFIELD, MASSACHUSETTS,
VITAL RECORDS TO THE YEAR
1850.** 1942. 273p.
P26766500 — $48.00.

**HISTORY OF THE TOWN OF
ASHFIELD, Franklin Co., from
settlement in 1742 to 1910.** By F. G.
Howes. 1910. 425p.
P5-MA0009 — $47.00.

**ATHOL, MASSACHUSETTS,
VITAL RECORDS TO THE YEAR
1850.** 1910. 230p.
P26770000 — $41.00.

HISTORY OF ATHOL. By William
G. Lord. 1953. 745p.
P5-MA0298A — $77.00.

**SKETCH OF THE HISTORY OF
ATTLEBORO, from its Settlement
to the Present Time.** By John Daggett.
1834. 136p.
P5-MA0117 — $22.00.

**SKETCH OF THE HISTORY OF
ATTLEBORO, from its Settlement
to the Present Time.** John Daggett, ed
by his daughter. 2nd ed. 1894. 788p.
P5-MA0118 — $79.50.

**ATTLEBOROUGH, MASSACHU-
SETTS, VITAL RECORDS TO
THE YEAR 1850.** 1900. 747p.
P27661500 — $115.00.

**AUBURN, MASSACHUSETTS,
VITAL RECORDS TO THE YEAR
1850.** 1900. 142p.
P27670000 — $30.00.

**HISTORY OF BARNSTABLE
COUNTY, 1620-1890.** 1890. 1010p. In
two parts.
P5-MA0365 — $105.00.

**MEMORIAL OF THE 100th ANNI-
VERSARY OF THE INCORPORA-
TION OF THE TOWN OF BARRE,
1874.** With historical discourse by
J.W. Thompson. 1875. 281p.
P5-MA0370 — $37.00.

**GLIMPSES OF OLD NEW
ENGLAND LIFE: Legends of Old
Bedford.** By Abram English Brown.
1892. 199p.
P5-MA0125 — $27.00.

**HISTORY OF THE TOWN OF
BEDFORD, from its Earliest
Settlement to the Year 1891, with a
Gen. Reg. of Old Families.** By Abram
English Brown. 1891. 164p.
P5-MA0119 — $35.00.

**HISTORY OF THE TOWN OF
BELLINGHAM, 1719-1919.** By
George F. Partridge. 1919. 221p.
P5-MA0371 — $34.50.

**HISTORY OF THE TOWN OF
BERKLEY.** By E. Sanford. 1872. 60p.
P5-MA0010 — $10.00.

**BIOGRAPHICAL REVIEW, Con-
taining Life Sketches of Leading
Citizens of Berkshire County.** 1899.
597p.
P5-MA0520 — $66.00.

**HISTORY OF BERKSHIRE
COUNTY, with Biographical
Sketches of its Prominent Men, 2-vol.
set.** 1885. 2 vols., 701 + 708p.
P5-MA0184 — $139.00/set.

**HISTORY OF BERKSHIRE
COUNTY, with Biographical
Sketches of its Prominent Men,
Vol. I.** 1885. 701p.
P5-MA0184A — $72.00.

**HISTORY OF BERKSHIRE
COUNTY, with Biographical
Sketches of its Prominent Men,
Vol. II.** 1885. 708p.
P5-MA0184B — $72.00.

**HISTORY OF THE TOWN OF
BERLIN, Worcester Co., from 1784
to 1895. Contains over 200 pages of
genealogies.** By William A. Houghton.
1895. 584p
P5-MA0406 — $59.00.

**HISTORY OF THE TOWN OF
BERNARDSTON, Franklin Co.,
1736-1900, with Genealogies.** By Lucy
Cutler Kellogg. 1902. 581p.
P5-MA0120 — $58.50.

**BEVERLY CEMETERY INSCRIP-
TIONS prior to 1800.** Extr. from the
Essex Antiquarian. 49p.
P5-MA0012 — $10.00.

**BEVERLY PRIVATEERS IN THE
AMERICAN REVOLUTION.** By
Octavius T. Howe. 1922. 112p.
P5-MA0521 — $16.50.

**BEVERLY, GARDEN CITY BY
THE SEA: an Historical Sketch of
the North Shore City..** By William C.
Morgan. 1897. 207p.
P5-MA0373 — $31.50.

**GENEALOGICAL HISTORY OF
THE ABBOTT STREET CEME-
TERY, BEVERLY, MASSACHU-
SETTS.** William C. Carlson 1998. 41p.
P5-MA10021 — $10.00.

**HISTORY OF BEVERLY, Civil &
Ecclesiastical, from its Settlement in
1630 to 1842.** Edwin M. Stone. 1843. 322p.
P5-MA0407 — $36.50.

**OLD PLANTERS OF BEVERLY
IN MASSACHUSETTS, and the
Thousand Acre Grant of 1635.** By
Alice G. Lapham. 1930. 133p.
P5-MA0477 — $19.50.

**RECORDS OF THE FIRST
CHURCH IN BEVERLY,
1667-1772.** 1905. 270p.
P5-MA0372 — $37.00.

**BILLERICA, MASSACHUSETTS,
VITAL RECORDS TO THE YEAR
1850.** 1908. 405p.
P26810000 — $63.00.

HISTORY OF BILLERICA. By H. A.
Hazen. 1883. 513p.
P5-MA0013 — $53.00.

**TAVERNS & TURNPIKES OF
BLANDFORD, 1733-1833.** Inter-
esting, well-illustrated social history.
By S. G. Wood. 1908. 351p.
P5-MA0311 — $39.00.

**BOLTON, MASSACHUSETTS,
VITAL RECORDS TO THE YEAR
1850.** 1910. 232p.
P26820000 — $42.00.

HISTORY OF BOLTON, 1738-1938.
Comp. by Esther K. Whitcomb, et al.
1938. 274p.
P5-MA0379 — $39.00.

**A REPORT OF THE RECORD
COMMISSIONERS OF THE CITY
OF BOSTON CONTAINING
BOSTON BIRTHS FROM A.D.
1700 TO A.D. 1800.** 1894. 379p.
P26826000 — $63.00.

For hardcover versions, see the order form on page v. To order, call 1-888-296-3447.

BOSTON RECORDS:The Statistics of the U.S. Direct Tax of 1798, as Assessed on Boston & the Names of the Inhabitants of Boston in 1790 as Collected for the 1st National Census. All properties are described and owners listed. 1890. 537p.
P5-MA0015 — $54.00.

CENTRAL BURYING GROUND OF BOSTON. 1917. 167p
P27705000 — $33.00.

GRAVEYARDS OF BOSTON. First vol.: Copp's Hill Epitaphs. By W. H. Whitmore. 1878. 116p.
P5-MA0014 — $12.50.

HISTORICAL CATALOGUE OF THE OLD SOUTH CHURCH (THIRD CHURCH), BOSTON. 1883. 370 + xv p.
P5-MA3001 — $44.50.

HISTORY & ANTIQUITIES OF BOSTON, from its Settlement in 1630 to the year 1770. Also, an Introductory History of the Discovery & Settlement of New England. By S. G. Drake. 1856. 840p.
P5-MA0175 — $85.00.

MEMORIAL HISTORY OF BOSTON, Including Suffolk Co., 1630-1880, 4-vol. set. 1880. 4 vols.
P5-MA0576 — $249.00/set.

MEMORIAL HISTORY OF BOSTON, Including Suffolk Co., 1630-1880, Vol. I. 1880.
P5-MA0576A — $67.50.

MEMORIAL HISTORY OF BOSTON, Including Suffolk Co., 1630-1880, Vol. II. 1880.
P5-MA0576B — $67.50.

MEMORIAL HISTORY OF BOSTON, Including Suffolk Co., 1630-1880, Vol. III. 1880.
P5-MA0576C — $67.50.

MEMORIAL HISTORY OF BOSTON, Including Suffolk Co., 1630-1880, Vol. IV. 1880.
P5-MA0576D — $67.50.

RAMBLES IN OLD BOSTON. Concentrates on the history and buildings of the old North End of Boston. By Edward G. Porter. Illus. by G. R. Tolam. 1887. 439p.
P5-MA0312 — $49.00.

REPORT OF THE RECORD COMMISSIONERS OF THE CITY OF BOSTON CONTAINING DORCHESTER BIRTHS, MARRIAGES, AND DEATHS TO THE END OF 1825. 1890. iv + 392p
P26827000 — $65.00.

REPORT OF THE RECORD COMMISSIONERS OF THE CITY OF BOSTON: BOSTON BIRTHS, BAPTISMS, MARRIAGES, AND DEATHS, 1630-1699. 1883. 288p
P26825000 — $50.00.

THE MANIFESTO CHURCH RECORDS OF THE CHURCH IN BRATTLE SQUARE [Boston]. Benevolent Fraternity of Churches 1902. 448p.
P27678500 — $73.00.

VITAL RECORDS, BOSTON, 1630-1699: Alphabetized Lists of Births, Baptisms, Marriages & Deaths, transcribed from document 130 — 1883. Trans. by John Newell Peirce. 2002. 358p.
P5-MA0575 — $35.00.

HISTORY OF BOURNE, from 1622 to 1937. Betsey D. Keene. 1937. 20 + 221p.
P5-MA0121 — $32.00.

BOXBORO. A New England Town & Its People, with Sketches & Illustrations. L. C. Hager. 1891. 218p.
P5-MA0018 — $31.00.

DWELLINGS OF BOXFORD, Essex County. By Sidney Perley. 1893. 272p.
P5-MA0381 — $39.50.

HISTORY OF BOXFORD, from its Settlement to 1875. S. Perley. 1880. 418p.
P5-MA0020 — $44.00.

HISTORY OF THE FIRST CONGREGATIONAL CHURCH [BOXFORD], 1702-1952. By Winnifrid C. Parkhurst. 1952. 114p.
P5-MA0522 — $19.00.

BOYLSTON, MASSACHUSETTS, VITAL RECORDS TO THE YEAR 1850. 1904. 124p.
P26830000 — $28.00.

MEMORIAL HISTORY OF BRADFORD, from the Earliest Period to the Close of 1882. By J. D. Kingsbury. 1883. 144p.
P5-MA0122 — $21.00.

BRAINTREE, MASSACHUSETTS, TOWN RECORDS, 1640-1793. 1886. 939p
P27710000 — $141.00.

HISTORY OF BRAINTREE (1639-1708), the north precinct of Braintree (1708-1792) & the town of Quincy (1792-1889). Charles Francis Adams. 1891. 365p.
P5-MA0356B — $44.00.

HISTORY OF OLD BRAINTREE & QUINCY, with a Sketch of Randolph & Holbrook. By W. S. Pattee. 1878. 660p.
P5-MA0250 — $66.00.

RECORDS OF THE TOWN OF BRAINTREE, 1640-1793. Includes government & vital records. 1886. 939p.
P5-MA0218 — $96.00.

[BAPTISMAL] RECORDS OF THE BREWSTER CONGREGATIONAL CHURCH, 1700-1792. 1911. 169p.
P5-MA0383 — $22.00.

BREWSTER SHIP MASTERS. By J. Henry Sears. 1906. 9 + 80p.
P5-MA0382 — $17.50.

BREWSTER, MASSACHUSETTS, VITAL RECORDS TO THE YEAR 1850. 1904. xi + 281p
P26836000 — $53.00.

BRIDGEWATER, MASSACHUSETTS, VITAL RECORDS TO THE YEAR 1850. 1916. 360 + 588p
P26840000 — $142.00.

HISTORY OF THE EARLY SETTLEMENT OF BRIDGEWATER, in Plymouth Co., including an Extensive Family Register. By Nahum Mitchell. 1897 & 1840. 424p.
P5-MA0419 — $44.50.

HISTORICAL BRIGHTON; An Illustrated History of Brighton & its Citizens. Contains much genealogical information. By J.P.C. Winship. 1899 & 1902. 2 vols. in 1, 240 + 222p.
P5-MA0024 — $47.00.

HISTORICAL CELEBRATION OF BRIMFIELD, 1701-1876. By Charles M. Hyde, et al. 1879. 487p.
P5-MA0026 — $54.00.

HISTORY OF BRISTOL COUNTY, MASSACHUSETTS: Vol. I. Edited by Frank Walcott Hutt 1924. 506p
P26665000 — $81.00.

Massachusetts, cont.

HISTORY OF BRISTOL COUNTY, MASSACHUSETTS: Vol. II. Edited by Frank Walcott Hutt 1924. 394p.
P26665100 — $65.00.

HISTORY OF BRISTOL COUNTY, MASSACHUSETTS: Vol. III. Edited by Frank Walcott Hutt 1924. 342p
P26665200 — $58.00.

OUR COUNTY AND ITS PEOPLE: Descriptive & Biographical Record of Bristol Co. Prepared for publ. by Fall River News & Taunton Gazette, with Alanson Borden. 1899. 1217pp.
P5-MA0123 — $115.00.

BROCKTON, MASSACHUSETTS, VITAL RECORDS TO THE YEAR 1850. 1911. 371p
P26850000 — $59.00.

HISTORY OF BROCKTON, Plymouth Co., 1656-1894. By Bradford Kingman. 1895. 814 + 122p.
P5-MA0384 — $96.50.

BROOKLINE: History of a Favored Town. Charles K. Bolton. 1897. 213p.
P5-MA0387 — $34.00.

BURIALS & INSCRIPTIONS IN THE WALNUT STREET CEMETERY, BROOKLINE, with Historical Sketches of the persons Buried There. By Harriet A. Cummings. 1920. 135p.
P5-MA0386 — $19.00.

HISTORICAL SKETCHES OF BROOKLINE. By H. F. Woods. 1874. 431pp.
P5-MA0204 — $43.00.

MUDDY RIVER & BROOKLINE RECORDS, 1634-1838. By the Inhabitants of Brookline. 1875. 703p.
P5-MA0385 — $76.00.
BURLINGTON, MASSACHUSETTS, VITAL RECORDS TO THE YEAR 1850. 1915. 100p
P26855000 — $44.00.

STORY OF BYFIELD, A New England Parish. J. L. Ewell. 1904. 344p.
P5-MA0029A — $38.00.

CAMBRIDGE, MASSACHUSETTS, DIRECTORY FOR 1863, No. XXII. 1873. 452 + 43p
P27730000 — $99.00.

EPITAPHS FROM THE OLD BURYING-GROUND OF CAMBRIDGE, with Notes. By Wm. T. Harris. 1845. 192p.
P5-MA0388 — $24.50.

HISTORY OF CAMBRIDGE, 1630-1877, with a Genealogical Register. By Lucius R. Paige. 1877. 731p.
P5-MA0338 — $79.00.

HISTORY OF CAMBRIDGE, 1630-1930, Supplement & Index, Comprising a Biog. & Genealogical Record of the Early Settlers & their Descendants; with References to their Wills & the Administration of their Estates in the Middlesex Co. Registry of Probate. By Mary Isabella Gozzaldi. 1930. 860p.
P5-MA0339 — $77.00.

RECORDS OF THE TOWN OF CAMBRIDGE, 1630-1703: The Records of the Town Meetings and the Selectmen, Comprising all of the First Vol. of Records and Being Vol. II of the Printed Records of the Town. 1901. 397p.
P5-MA0341 — $44.00.

CANTON AND STOUGHTON, MASSACHUSETTS, VITAL RECORDS TO THE YEAR 1850. 1896. 317p.
P26860000 — $52.00.

HISTORY OF THE TOWN OF CANTON, Norfolk County. By Daniel V. Huntoon. 1893. 666p.
P5-MA0523 — $71.00.

CAPE COD SERIES. History and Genealogy of the Mayflower Planters and First Comers to Ye Olde Colonies, 2-vol. set. By L. C. Hills 1936-1941. 2 vols., 177+284p.
P5-MA0240 — $49.00/set.

CAPE COD SERIES. History and Genealogy of the Mayflower Planters . . ., Vol. I. 1936-1941. 177p.
P5-MA0240A — $25.00.

CAPE COD SERIES. History and Genealogy of the Mayflower Planters . . ., Vol. II. 1936-1941. 284p.
P5-MA0240B — $32.50.

HISTORY OF CAPE COD (BARNSTABLE COUNTY), 2-vol. set. By Frederick Freeman 1858, 1869. 2 vols., 803 + 803p.
P26670000 — $245.00/set.

HISTORY OF CAPE COD (BARNSTABLE COUNTY), Vol. I. 1858. 803p.
P26670000A — $135.00.

HISTORY OF CAPE COD (BARNSTABLE COUNTY), Vol. II. 1869. 803p.
P26670000B — $135.00.

HISTORY OF CAPE COD: Annals of Barnstable Co., Including the District of Mashpee, 2-vol. set. By F. Freeman. 1858. 2 vols., 803+803p.
P5-MA0275 — $149.00/set.

HISTORY OF CAPE COD: Annals of Barnstable Co. . . ., Vol. I. 1858. 803p.
P5-MA0275A — $79.00.

HISTORY OF CAPE COD: Annals of Barnstable Co. . . ., Vol. II. 1858. 803p.
P5-MA0275B — $79.00.

HISTORY OF THE TOWN OF CARLISLE, 1754-1920. By Sidney A. Bull. 1920. 365p.
P5-MA0408 — $39.50.

CARVER, MASSACHUSETTS, VITAL RECORDS TO THE YEAR 1850. 1911. 179p
P26870000 — $35.00.

HISTORY OF THE TOWN OF CARVER. Henry S. Griffith. 1913. 366p.
P5-MA0314 — $40.00.

GENEALOGIES & ESTATES OF CHARLESTOWN, 1629-1818. Many families spent some time in Charlestown before moving on to settle permanently, and this book includes both permanent residents of Charlestown, and those families that stayed only a year or so. By Thomas Bellows Wyman. 1879. 1208p.
P5-MA0292 — $87.50.

HISTORY OF CHARLESTOWN By R. Frothingham, Jr. 1845. 368p.
P5-MA0033 — $37.00.

OLD CHARLESTOWN: Historical, Biographical, Reminiscent. By Thimothy T. Sawyer. 1902. 527p.
P5-MA0574a — $55.00.

RECORDS OF THE FIRST CHURCH OF CHARLESTOWN, MASSACHUSETTS, 1632-1789. 1880. xiii + 168p
P27735300 — $35.00.

HISTORY OF CHATHAM, Formerly the Constablewick or Village of Monomoit. With Numerous Genealogical Notes. By William C. Smith 1909-1917. 4 Vols. in 1, 400p.
P5-MA0323 — $42.00.

CHELMSFORD, MASSACHUSETTS, VITAL RECORDS TO THE YEAR 1850. 1914. 460p
P26910000 — $80.00.

HISTORY OF CHELMSFORD. By Wilson Waters. 1917. 893p. + maps.
P5-MA0573A — $89.50.

DOCUMENTARY HISTORY OF CHELSEA, including the Boston Precincts of Wimmisimmet, Rumney Marsh & Pullen Point, 1624-1824, 2-vol. set. By M. Chamberlain. 1908. 2 vols., 712 + 792p.
P5-MA0524 — $145.00/set.

DOCUMENTARY HISTORY OF CHELSEA . . ., Vol. I. 1908. 712p.
P5-MA0524A — $75.00.

DOCUMENTARY HISTORY OF CHELSEA . . ., Vol. II. 1908. 792p.
P5-MA0524B — $75.00.

THE BURNING OF CHELSEA. With numerous illustrations. By William M. Pratt. 1908. 149p.
P5-MA0126 — $24.50.

HISTORY OF THE TOWN OF CHESHIRE, Berkshire County. By Ellen M. Raynor & Emma L. Petitclerc. 1885. 219p.
P5-MA0409 — $28.00.

CHESTER, MASSACHUSETTS, VITAL RECORDS TO THE YEAR 1850. 1911. 256p
P26930000 — $44.00.

HISTORY OF THE TOWN OF MURRAYFIELD, Earlier known as Township No. 9 and Comprising the Present Towns of Chester & Huntington, the Northern Part of Montgomery, & the Southeast Corner of Middlefield, 1760-1783. By Alfred M. Copeland. 1892. 175p.
P5-MA0355A — $22.50.

HISTORY & GENEALOGY OF THE FAMILIES OF CHESTERFIELD, 1762-1962. Bicentennial Gen. Comm. 1962. 427 + 25p.
P5-MA0109 — $48.50.

HISTORY OF THE ORIGIN OF THE TOWN OF CLINTON, 1653-1865. By Andrew E. Ford. 1896. 696p.
P5-MA0127 — $69.50.

GENEALOGIES OF THE FAMILIES OF COHASSET. Supp. to History above. Comp. by G. L. Davenport et al. 1909. 631p.
P5-MA0129A — $65.00.

NARRATIVE HISTORY OF THE TOWN OF COHASSET. By E. Victor Bigelow. 1898. 561p.
P5-MA0291 — $56.50.

HISTORY OF COLRAIN, with Genealogies of Early Families. By Louise McClellan Patrie. 1974; reprinted by permission. 337 + 237p.
P5-MA0564 — $62.00.

CONCORD BIRTHS, MARRIAGES & DEATHS, 1635-1850. 1891. 496p.
P5-MA0038 — $50.00.

CONCORD IN THE COLONIAL PERIOD, Being a History of the Town of Concord from Earliest Settlement to the Overthrow of the Andros Government, 1685-1689. By Charles H. Walcott. 1884. 186p.
P5-MA0129B — $26.50.

GENEALOGIES OF SOME OLD FAMILIES OF CONCORD, MASSACHUSETTS: Vol. I. By Charles Edward Potter 1887. 143p
P27750000 — $30.00.

HISTORY OF CONCORD: Vol. I, Colonial Concord. By Alfred Sereno Hudson. 1904. 18 + 496 + 13p.
P5-MA0352a — $57.00.

HISTORY OF THE TOWN OF CONCORD, MIDDLESEX CO., from earliest settlement to 1832, and of the Adjoining Towns of Bedford, Acton, Lincoln & Carlisle. By L. Shattuck. 1834. 412p.
P5-MA0037 — $45.00.

MEMORIES OF CONCORD. By Mary Hosmer Brown. 1926. 111 + 16p.
P5-MA3031 — $24.00.

HISTORY OF CONWAY, 1767-1917. With genealogies. 1917. 343p.
P5-MA0392 — $41.00.

CHRONICLES OF DANVERS (Old Salem Village), 1632-1923. By Harriett Silvester Tapley. 1923. 283p.
P5-MA0353A — $39.00.

DANVERS. A Resume of her Past History & Progress. Contains over 200 pictures of people, homes, businesses & landmarks. 1899. 202p.
P5-MA0315 — $25.00.

HISTORY OF THE TOWN OF DANVERS, from its Early Settlement to 1848. J. W. Hanson 1848. 304p.
P5-MA0039 — $36.50.

REPORT OF THE COMMITTEE Appointed to Revise the Soldiers' Records [DANVERS]. Contains list of soldiers in the Rev. War, with biographical information; also, lists of soldiers from War of 1812, Mexican War, & militia. 1895. 165p.
P5-MA0130 — $19.50.

DARTMOUTH, MASSACHUSETTS, VITAL RECORDS TO THE YEAR 1850. 1929-1930. 314 + 576 + 82p.
P26960000 — $169.00.

HISTORY OF OLD DARTMOUTH from 1602 to 1676. Gladys B. Gifford. n.d. 25p., typescript.
P5-MA0525 — $10.00.

ALPHABETICAL ABSTRACT OF THE RECORD OF BIRTHS IN THE TOWN OF DEDHAM, MASSACHUSETTS, 1844-1890. 1894. 206p
P27762500 — $41.00.

DEDHAM HISTORICAL REGISTER Vols. I-XIV. 1890-1903. 14-vol. set

P5-MA0555 — $266.00/set.
DEDHAM HISTORICAL REGISTER Vol. I. 1890-1903.
P5-MA0555A — $20.00.

DEDHAM HISTORICAL REGISTER Vol. II. 1890-1903.
P5-MA0555B — $20.00.

DEDHAM HISTORICAL REGISTER Vol. III. 1890-1903.
P5-MA0555C — $20.00.

DEDHAM HISTORICAL REGISTER Vol. IV. 1890-1903.
P5-MA0555D — $20.00.

DEDHAM HISTORICAL REGISTER Vol. V. 1890-1903.
P5-MA0555E — $20.00.

DEDHAM HISTORICAL REGISTER Vol. VI. 1890-1903.
P5-MA0555F — $20.00.

Massachusetts, cont.

DEDHAM HISTORICAL REGISTER Vol. VII. 1890-1903. P5-MA0555G — $20.00.

DEDHAM HISTORICAL REGISTER Vol. VIII. 1890-1903. P5-MA0555H — $20.00.

DEDHAM HISTORICAL REGISTER Vol. IX. 1890-1903. P5-MA0555J — $20.00.

DEDHAM HISTORICAL REGISTER Vol. XI. 1890-1903. P5-MA0555L — $20.00.

DEDHAM HISTORICAL REGISTER Vol. XII. 1890-1903. P5-MA0555M — $20.00.

DEDHAM HISTORICAL REGISTER Vol. XIII. 1890-1903. P5-MA0555N — $20.00.

DEDHAM HISTORICAL REGISTER Vol. XIV. 1890-1903. P5-MA0555P — $20.00.

DEDHAM, MASSACHUSETTS, RECORD OF BAPTISMS, MAR-RIAGES, AND DEATHS, 1638-1845. 1888. 344p P27762000 — $60.00.

DEDHAM, 1635-1890: "Examples of things past." With 1996 index. By Robert B. Hanson. 1976. 250 + 23p. P5-MA0342 — $39.00.

HISTORICAL ANNALS OF DEDHAM, from its Settlement in 1635 to 1847. Herman Mann. 1847. 136p. P5-MA0459 — $22.50.

EPITAPHS IN THE OLD BURY-ING GROUND OF DEERFIELD. Comp. by Baker & Coleman. 1924. 49p. P5-MA0042 — $10.00.

HISTORY OF DEERFIELD, By G. Sheldon. 1895. 924 + 477p. P5-MA0217 — The set: $132.00.

HISTORY OF DIGHTON, The South Purchase, 1712. By Helen H. Lane. 1962. 263p. P5-MA0450 — $36.50.

RECORDS OF THE FIRST CHURCH AT DORCHESTER in New England, 1636-1734. 1891. 254 + 16p. P5-MA0526 — $27.50.

THE "MARY & JOHN": A STORY OF THE FOUNDING OF DOR-CHESTER, MA, 1630. Authoritative genealogical study on the passengers of the "Mary & John" and their descendants. Maude Pinney Kuhns. 1943. 254p. P5-MA0308 — $32.00.

DORCHESTER, MASSACHU-SETTS, VITAL RECORDS TO THE YEAR 1850. 1891, 1905. 392 + 288p P26970000 — $110.00.

HISTORY OF THE TOWN OF DORCHESTER. Comm. of the Dorchester Antiquarian & Hist. Soc. 1859. 671p. P5-MA0300 — $65.00.

ALLUM POND ESTATES [DOUGLAS]. By Harry Lee Barnes. 1922. 85p. P5-MA0512 — $16.50.

HISTORY OF THE TOWN OF DOUGLAS, From the Earliest Period to the Close of 1878. By William A. Emerson. 1879. 359p. P5-MA0131 — $39.00.

DOVER FARMS, in which is Traced the Development of the Territory from the First Settlement in 1640 to 1900. Frank Smith. 1914. 160p. P5-MA0132 — $22.50.

GENEALOGICAL HISTORY OF DOVER, Tracing all Families Previous to 1850 & Many Families that have Lived in the Town Since. By F. Smith. 1917. 298p. P5-MA0044 — $30.00.

NARRATIVE HISTORY OF DOVER as a Precinct, Parish, District & Town. F. Smith. 1897. 354p. P5-MA0043 — $42.00.

DRACUT, MASSACHUSETTS, VITAL RECORDS TO THE YEAR 1850. 1907. 302P P27000000 — $50.00.

DUNSTABLE, MASSACHUSETTS, VITAL RECORDS TO THE YEAR 1850. 1913. 238p P27005000 — $43.00.

DUNSTABLE, MASSACHUSETTS, VITAL RECORDS TO THE YEAR 1850. 1913. 238p P27005000 — $43.00.

EARLY GENERATIONS OF OLD DUNSTABLE: Thirty Families. By Ezra S. Steans. 1911. 103p. P5-MA0528 — $18.00.

HISTORY OF THE TOWN OF DUNSTABLE, from its Earliest Settlement to the Year 1873. By E. Nason 1877. 316p. P5-MA0045 — $39.00.

COPY OF THE OLD RECORDS OF THE TOWN OF DUXBURY, from 1642 to 1770, Made in the Year 1892. 1893. 348p. P5-MA0393 — $41.50.

DUXBURY, MASSACHUSETTS, VITAL RECORD TO THE YEAR 1850. 1917. 446p P27010000 — $68.00.

DUXBURY, MASSACHUSETTS, VITAL RECORD TO THE YEAR 1850. 1917. 446p P27010000 — $68.00.

HISTORIC DUXBURY IN PLYMOUTH COUNTY. By Laurence Bradford. 2nd ed. 1902. 128p. P5-MA0403 — $22.50.

HISTORY OF THE TOWN OF DUXBURY, with Genealogical Registers. Justin Winsor. 1849. 360p. P5-MA0133 — $39.50.

STORY OF DUXBURY, 1637-1937. 1937. 237p. P5-MA0404 — $29.00.

HISTORY OF EAST BOSTON, with Biographical Sketches of its Early Proprietors & an Appendix. By Wm. H. Sumner. 1858. 801p. P5-MA0480 — $84.50.

EAST BRIDGEWATER, MASSA-CHUSETTS, VITAL RECORDS TO THE YEAR 1850. 1917. 406p P27020000 — $63.00.

HISTORY OF EASTHAMPTON: Its Settlement & Growth, with a Gen. Record of Original Families. By P. W. Lyman. 1866. 194p. P5-MA0046 — $32.00.

HISTORY OF THE TOWN OF EASTON. Wm. L. Chaffin. 1886. 838p. P5-MA0529 — $87.00.

EDGARTOWN, MASSACHU-
SETTS, VITAL RECORDS TO
THE YEAR 1850. 1906. 276p.
P27030000 — $47.00.

HISTORY OF THE TOWN OF
ESSEX FROM 1634-1868, with
Sketches of the Soldiers in the War of
the Rebellion. By R. Crowell & D.
Choate. 1868. 488p.
P5-MA0179 — $49.00.

ESSEX ANTIQUARIAN: A Monthly
Magazine Devoted to the Biography,
Genealogy, History and Antiquities
of Essex County, Massachusetts.
VOL. I. 1897. 205 + 31p.
P5-MA3018 — $32.00.

ESSEX ANTIQUARIAN. VOL. II.
1898. 208 + 30p.
P5-MA3019 — $32.00.

ESSEX ANTIQUARIAN. VOL. III.
1899. 203 + 30p.
P5-MA3020 — $32.00.

ESSEX ANTIQUARIAN. VOL. IV.
1900. 201 + 26p.
P5-MA3021 — $32.00.

ESSEX ANTIQUARIAN. VOL. V.
1901. 201 + 22p.
P5-MA3022 — $32.00.

ESSEX ANTIQUARIAN. VOL. VI.
1902. 202 + 18p.
P5-MA3023 — $32.00.

ESSEX ANTIQUARIAN. VOL. VII.
1903. 202 + 10p.
P5-MA3024 — $31.00.

ESSEX ANTIQUARIAN. VOL.
VIII. 1904. 202 + 8p.
P5-MA3025 — $31.00.

ESSEX ANTIQUARIAN. VOL. IX.
1905. 202 + 10p.
P5-MA3026 — $31.00.

ESSEX ANTIQUARIAN. VOL. X.
1906. 202 + 22p.
P5-MA3027 — $32.00.

ESSEX ANTIQUARIAN. VOL. XI.
1907. 202 + 10p.
P5-MA3028 — $31.00.

ESSEX ANTIQUARIAN. VOL. XII.
1908. 201 + 8p.
P5-MA3029 — $31.00.

ESSEX COUNTY HISTORICAL
AND GENEALOGICAL REG-
ISTER, 1894. 1895. 300p.
p26677500 — $52.00.

HISTORY OF ESSEX COUNTY,
with Biographical Sketches of Many
Pioneers & Prominent Men. Comp.
by D.H. Hurd. 1888. 2 vols., 957 +
1173p.
P5-MA0530 — The set: $195.00.

MUNICIPAL HIST OF ESSEX CO,
MA, Four-vol. set
1922. 4 vols; 518 + 503 + 388 +302p.
P5-MA3047 — $171.00/set.

MUNICIPAL HIST OF ESSEX CO,
MA, Vol. I. 1922. 518p.
P5-MA3047A — $50.00.

MUNICIPAL HIST OF ESSEX CO,
MA, Vol. II. 1922. 503p.
P5-MA3047B — $50.00.

MUNICIPAL HIST OF ESSEX CO,
MA, Vol. III. 1922. 388p.
P5-MA3047C — $39.00.

MUNICIPAL HIST OF ESSEX CO,
MA, Vol. IV. 1922. 302p.
P5-MA3047D — $33.50.

PROBATE RECORDS OF ESSEX
COUNTY, 1635-1681, Vol. II, 1665-
1674. Ed. by George F. Dow 1918. 527p.
P26678100 — $84.00.

PROBATE RECORDS OF ESSEX
COUNTY, 1635-1681, Vol. III, 1675-
1681. Ed. by George F. Dow 1920. 501p.
P26678200 — $80.00.

PROBATE RECORDS OF ESSEX
COUNTY, 1635-1681. Vol. I, 1635-
1664. Ed. by George F. Dow 1916. 542p.
P26678000 — $86.00.

PROBATE RECORDS OF ESSEX
COUNTY, 1635-1681. Vol. I, 1635-
1664: Vol. II, 1665-1674; Vol. III, 1675-
1681, 3-vol. set. Edited by George F.
Dow 1916-1920.
P5-MA0217BH — $200.00/set.

RECORDS AND FILES OF THE
QUARTERLY COURTS of Essex
County. Complete record of wills,
inventories, vital records, court cases,
fines, depositions, etc., presented in
abstracted but with all "particulars"
needed for research. Each volume
indexed. 1911-1917.
P5-MA0451 — $325.00/set.

OLD-TIME FAIRHAVEN Erstwhile
Eastern New Bedford. By Charles
Augustus Harris. 1947. 342 + 238 + 254p.
P5-MA3005 — $85.00.

CENTENNIAL HISTORY OF
FALL RIVER, comprising a Record
of its Corporate Progress, 1656-1876,
with Sketches of its Manufacturing
Industries, Local & General Characteristics, etc. 1877. 252p.
P5-MA0394 — $37.00.

FALL RIVER & ITS INDUSTRIES:
an Historical & Statistical Record of
Village, Town & City, from . . . 1656
to the Present Time [1877], with . . .
Family Genealogies, etc. Frederick M.
Peck & Henry H. Earl. 1877. 280p.
P5-MA0567 — $38.00.

HISTORY OF FALL RIVER.
Comp. by Henry M. Fenner. 1911. 100p.
P5-MA0395 — $15.00.

HISTORY OF FALL RIVER. By
Henry M. Fenner, with Benj. Buffinton.
1906. 100p.
P5-MA0572 — $35.00.

EARLY HISTORY OF THE TOWN
OF FALMOUTH, Covering the
Time from its Settlement to 1812. By
Charles W. Jenkins. 1889. 125p.
P5-MA0396 — $19.00.

FITCHBURG IN THE WAR OF
THE REBELLION. By Henry A.
Willis. 1866. 282p.
P5-MA0559 — $38.00.

FITCHBURG, Past & Present. By
William A. Emerson. 1887. 38 + 312pp.
P5-MA0134 — $39.50.

HISTORY OF THE TOWN OF
FITCHBURG, Comprising also a
History of Lunenburg from its 1st
Settlement to the year 1764. By R. C.
Torrey. 1865. 128pp.
P5-MA0205 — $21.00.

HISTORY OF FLORENCE. With
biographies. 1895. 250p.
P5-MA0397 — $37.00.

FRAMINGHAM, MASSACHU-
SETTS, VITAL RECORDS TO
THE YEAR 1850. 1911. 474p
P27037000 — $77.00.

HISTORY OF FRAMINGHAM,
Incl. the Plantation, from 1640 to
1846. Also a Register of Inhabitants
before 1800, with Gen. Sketches. By
W. Barry. 1847. 456p.
P5-MA0048 — $48.50.

Massachusetts, cont.

HISTORY OF FRAMINGHAM, with a Genealogical Register. By J. H. Temple. 1887. 794p.
P5-MA0049 — $79.50.

HISTORY OF THE TOWN OF FRANKLIN, from its Settlement to the Completion of its 1st Century. 1878. 263p.
P5-MA0051 — $33.00.

RECORDS OF BIRTHS, MAR-RIAGES, AND DEATHS IN THE TOWN OF FRANKLIN, MASSA-CHUSETTS, 1778-1872. Ed. by Orestes T. Doe 1898. 232p.
P27785000 — $42.00.

HISTORY OF THE TOWN OF FREETOWN. 1902. 287p.
P5-MA0316 — $30.00.

HISTORY OF THE TOWN OF GARDNER, Worcester Co., from the Incorporation, 1785, to the Present Time. Wm. D. Herrick. 1878. 535p.
P5-MA0398 — $57.00.

GLOUCESTER Town and City Records Guide, incl. Related Material. Comp. by Archives Committee of Gloucester. 150p.
P5-MA0135 — $22.50.

GLOUCESTER, MASSACHU-SETTS, VITAL RECORDS TO THE YEAR 1850, Vol. I: Births. 1917. 805p
P27045000 — $127.00.

GLOUCESTER, MASSACHU-SETTS, VITAL RECORDS TO THE YEAR 1850, Vol. II: Marriages. 1923. 605p
P27045100 — $89.00.

GLOUCESTER, MASSACHU-SETTS, VITAL RECORDS TO THE YEAR 1850, Vol. III: Deaths. 1924. 338p.
P27045200 — $58.00.

HISTORY OF THE TOWN & CITY OF GLOUCESTER, Cape Ann. By James R. Pringle. 1892. 340p.
P5-MA0399 — $41.50.

HISTORY OF THE TOWN OF GLOUCESTER, incl. the Town of Rockport. John J. Babson. 1860. 610p.
P5-MA0321 — $64.50.

HISTORY OF THE TOWN OF GOSHEN, Hampshire Co., from 1761-1881, with family sketches. By H. Barrus. 1881. 262p.
P5-MA0052 — $33.50.

GRAFTON, MASSACHUSETTS, VITAL RECORDS TO THE YEAR 1850. 1906. 377p
P27050000 — $63.00.

HISTORY OF GRAFTON, Worcester Co., from Early Settlement by the Indians in 1647-1879, incl. gen. of 79 Older Families. F. C. Pierce. 1879. 623p.
P5-MA0053 — $69.50.

HISTORY OF GRANVILLE, MASSACHUSETTS, 1954-2004. The Granville Historical Society. 2004. 67p.
P5-MA3010 — $26.00.

HISTORY OF GRANVILLE. By Albion B. Wilson. 1954. 381p.
P5-MA0531 — $47.00.

GREAT BARRINGTON, MASSA-CHUSETTS, VITAL RECORDS TO THE YEAR 1850. 1904. 90p
P27065000 — $43.00.

HISTORY OF GREAT BARRING-TON, Berkshire Co. C. Taylor. 1882. 516p.
P5-MA0054 — $55.00.

HISTORY OF GREAT BARRING-TON, 1676-1882, Extended to 1922. Orig. by Charles J. Taylor, extended by George E. McLean. 1928. 620p.
P5-MA0411 — $59.50.

HISTORY OF GREENFIELD, 1682-1900, 2-vol. set. By F. M. Thompson. 1904. 2 vols., 1308p.
P5-MA0317 — $98.00/set.

HISTORY OF GREENFIELD, 1682-1900, Vol. I. 1904.
P5-MA0317A — $55.00.

HISTORY OF GREENFIELD, 1682-1900, Vol. II. 1904.
P5-MA0317B — $55.00.

HISTORY OF GREENFIELD, 1900-1929. Vol. 3 of "1904" set above. By Lucy C. Kellogg. 1931. 629p.
P5-MA0318 — $60.00.

HISTORY OF GREENFIELD, 1930-1953. Vol. 4 of "1904" set above. By C. S. Severance. 1954. 551p.
P5-MA0319 — $55.00.

BOUNDARY LINES OF OLD GROTON. Describes the "Groton Plantation," which includes all or part of Littleton, Shirley, Pepperell, Harvard, Ayer, Dunstable and Tyngsborough. S.A. Green. 1885. 103p.
P5-MA0464 — $10.00.

EARLY CHURCH RECORDS OF GROTON, 1706-1830, with a Register of Births, Deaths & Marriages, 1664-1830. Comp. by Samuel A. Green. 1896. 194 + 64p.
P5-MA0294 — $29.00.

EPITAPHS FROM THE OLD BURYING GROUND IN GROTON. Sam'l A. Green. 1878. 271p.
P5-MA0565 — $27.00.

GROTON During the Indian Wars. By S. A. Green. 1883. 214p.
P5-MA0176 — $25.00.

GROTON DURING THE REVO-LUTION, with an Appendix. By S. A. Green. 1900. 343p.
P5-MA0209 — $34.50.

GROTON HISTORICAL SERIES: A Collection of Papers Relating to the History of the Town of Groton, 4-vol. set. Samuel Abbot Green. 1887-1899. 4 vols., 490 + 471 + 489 + 520p.
P5-MA0452 — $189.00/set.

GROTON HISTORICAL SERIES: A Collection of Papers . . ., Vol. I. 1887-1899. 490p.
P5-MA0452A — $52.00.

GROTON HISTORICAL SERIES: A Collection of Papers . . ., Vol. II. 1887-1899. 471p.
P5-MA0452B — $52.00.

GROTON HISTORICAL SERIES: A Collection of Papers . . ., Vol. III. 1887-1899. 489p.
P5-MA0452C — $52.00.

GROTON HISTORICAL SERIES: A Collection of Papers . . ., Vol. IV. 1887-1899. 520p.
P5-MA0452D — $52.00.

HISTORY OF THE TOWN OF GROTON, incl. Pepperell & Shirley, from the First Grant of Groton Plantation in 1655. By Caleb Butler. 1848. 29 + 499p.
P5-MA0136 — $52.50.

For hardcover versions, see the order form on page v. To order, call 1-888-296-3447.

THREE MILITARY DIARIES KEPT BY GROTON SOLDIERS in different wars. 1901. viii + 133p.
P5-MA10028 — $19.00.

GEN. OF HADLEY FAMILIES, Embracing the Early Settlers of the Towns of Hatfield, South Hadley, Amherst & Granby. L. M. Boltwood. 1905. 205p.
P5-MA0242 — $21.00.

HISTORY OF HADLEY, incl. the Early History of Hatfield, South Hadley, Amherst & Granby. By Sylvester Judd. With Family Genealogies by L. M Boltwood. 1863. 709p.
P5-MA0137 — $72.50.

HALIFAX, MASSACHUSETTS, VITAL RECORDS TO THE YEAR 1850. 1905. 222p
P27067500 — $41.00.

BIOGRAPHICAL REVIEW: Biographical Sketches of the Leading Citizens of Hampden County. 1895. 1139p.
P5-MA0560 — $109.00.

HISTORY OF HAMPDEN COUNTY: Our County & its People, 3-vol. set. By Alfred M. Copeland. 1902. 3 vols., 505 + 521 + 573pp.
P5-MA0285 — $145.00/set.

HISTORY OF HAMPDEN COUNTY. . ., Vol. I. 1902. 505p.
P5-MA0285A — $52.50.

HISTORY OF HAMPDEN COUNTY. . ., Vol. II. 1902. 521p.
P5-MA0285B — $52.50.

HISTORY OF HAMPDEN COUNTY. . ., Vol. III. 1902. 573p.
P5-MA0285C — $52.50.

INDIAN DEEDS OF HAMPDEN COUNTY, Being Copies of All Land Transfers from the Indians Recorded in the Co. of Hampden. 1905. 194p.
P5-MA0425 — $22.50.

BIOGRAPHICAL REVIEW OF THE LEADING CITIZENS OF HAMPSHIRE COUNTY. 1896. 581p.
P5-MA0138 — $59.50.

HANOVER, MASSACHUSETTS, VITAL RECORDS TO THE YEAR 1850. 1898. 319p
P27068000 — $55.00.

HANOVER. First Congregational Church & Cemetery Records, 1727-1895. By L. V. Briggs. 1895. 216p.
P5-MA0110 — $23.00.

HISTORICAL SKETCHES OF THE TOWN OF HANOVER, with Family Genealogies. By John S. Barry. 1853. 448p.
P5-MA0333 — $46.50.

HISTORY OF THE TOWN OF HANOVER, with Family Genealogies, 2-vol. set. By Dwelley & Simmons. 1910. 2 vols., 291 + 474p.
P5-MA0532 — $79.50/set.

HISTORY OF THE TOWN OF HANOVER. . ., Vol. I. 291p.
P5-MA0532A — $35.00.

HISTORY OF THE TOWN OF HANOVER. . ., Vol. II. 474p.
P5-MA0532B — $50.00.

HISTORY OF HARDWICK, MASS. with a Gen. Reg. L. R. Paige. 1883. 555p.
P5-MA0187 — $59.50.

HARVARD, MASSACHUSETTS, VITAL RECORDS TO THE YEAR 1850. 1917. 326p
P27072500 — $56.00.

HISTORY OF THE TOWN OF HARVARD, 1732-1893. By Henry S. Nourse. 1894. 605p.
P5-MA0427 — $64.50.

HISTORY OF HARWICH, Barnstable Co., 1620-1900, including the Early History of that Part now Brewster. By Josiah Paine. 1937. 503p.
P5-MA0481 — $56.00.

HISTORY OF HATFIELD IN THREE PARTS, Incl. Gen. of the Families of the First Settlers. By D. W. & R. F. Wells. 1910. 536p.
P5-MA0055 — $57.00.

PAPERS CONCERNING THE ATTACK OF HATFIELD AND DEERFIELD BY A PARTY OF INDIANS FROM CANADA, SEPTEMBER 19, 1677. 1859. viii + 82p.
P27075000 — $43.00.

CHAPLAIN SMITH & THE BAPTISTS; or, Life, Journals, Letters & Addresses of the Rev. Hezekiah Smith of Haverhill, 1747-1805. Reuben Aldridge Guild. 1885. 429p.
P5-MA0533 — $47.00.

HAVERHILL, MASSACHUSETTS, VITAL RECORDS TO THE YEAR 1850. 1911. 827p
P27080000 — $128.00.

HISTORY OF HAVERHILL, from its First Settlement in 1640 to the Year 1860. By George W. Chase. 1861. 663 + xx p.
P5-MA0145A — $69.00.

HISTORY OF THE TOWN OF HAWLEY, Franklin Co., 1771-1951, with genealogies. By Louise Hale Johnson. 1953. 392p.
P5-MA10022 — $42.50.

HISTORY OF THE TOWN OF HAWLEY, Franklin Co., from 1771 to 1887. With family records & biographical sketches. By W. G. Atkins. 1887. 132p.
P5-MA0057 — $19.00.

HINGHAM: A Story of its Early Settlement & Life, its Ancient Landmarks, its Historic Sites & Buildings. 1911. 123p.
P5-MA0428 — $29.50.

HISTORY OF THE TOWN OF HINGHAM. 1893.
P5-MA0140 — $135.00.

TOWN OF HINGHAM IN THE LATE CIVIL WAR, with Sketches of its Soldiers & Sailors. By Fearing Burr & George Lincoln. 1876. 455p.
P5-MA0568 — $52.00.

HISTORY OF HOLDEN, 1667-1841. By Samuel C. Damon. 1841. 155p.
P5-MA10023 — $19.50.

HISTORY OF HOLDEN, 1684-1894. With genealogies. By David Foster Estes. 1894. 446p.
P5-MA0429 — $51.00.

HISTORY OF THE TOWN OF HOLLAND. M. Lovering. 1915. 745p.
P5-MA0058 — $77.00.

HOLLAND MILITARY LISTS from the French & Indian War Through the Civil War. Extr. from above. 58p.
P5-MA0059 — $12.00.

HOLLISTON, MASSACHUSETTS, VITAL RECORDS TO THE YEAR 1850. 1908. 358p
P27100000 — $57.00.

Massachusetts, cont.

**HOPKINTON, MASSACHU-
SETTS, VITAL RECORDS TO
THE YEAR 1850.** 1911. 462p
P27110000 — $70.00.

**HISTORY OF THE TOWN OF
HUBBARDSTON, from the Time its
Territory was Purchased of the
Indians in 1686 to the Present. With
the genealogy of residents.** By Rev. J.
M. Stowe. 1881. 383p.
P5-MA0142 — $42.50.

**HISTORY OF IPSWICH, ESSEX &
HAMILTON.** J.B. Felt. 1834. 304p.
P5-MA0061 — $35.00.

**IPSWICH ANTIQUARIAN
PAPERS, 1879-1885.** 1879. 239p
P27797500 — $43.00.

**IPSWICH IN THE MASS. BAY
COLONY, Vol. II. A History of the
Town from 1700 to 1917.** By T. F.
Waters. 1917. 837p.
P5-MA0336 — $84.00.

**IPSWICH IN THE MASS. BAY
COLONY. Pt. I — Historical, Pt. II
— Houses & Lands.** By T. F. Waters.
1905. 586p.
P5-MA0062 — $62.00.

**IPSWICH, MASSACHUSETTS,
VITAL RECORDS TO THE YEAR
1850. 2-vol. set.** 1910+1919. 404 +721
+ 52p
P27130000 — $164.00/set.

**JEFFREY'S NECK & the Way
Leading Thereto, with Notes on
Little Neck [Ipswich].** By Thomas
Franklin Waters. 1912. 94p.
P5-MA0177 — $10.00.

**MOMENTO MORI: An Accurate
Transcription of the [Memorials] in
the Town of Ipswich . . . from 1634 to
[1935].** Comp. by A. W. Johnson & R.
E. Ladd Jr. 1935. 264p.
P5-MA0289 — $25.00.

**DEATH RECORDS FROM THE
ANCIENT BURIAL GROUND AT
KINGSTON.** Trans. by T. S. Lazell.
1905. 31p.
P5-MA0306 — $10.00.

**KINGSTON, 1620-1876: Report of
the Proceedings & Exercises at the
150th Anniversary of the Incorporation of the Town. With historical
sketch.** 1876. 152p.
P5-MA0430 — $19.00.

**KINGSTON, MASSACHUSETTS,
VITAL RECORDS TO THE YEAR
1850.** 1911. 396p
P27140000 — $62.00.

**BIRTH, MARRIAGE AND DEATH
REGISTER, CHURCH RECORDS
AND EPITAPHS OF LANCASTER,
MA.** 1890. 508p.
P5-MA3017 — $51.00.

**EARLY RECORDS OF LANCASTER,
MASSACHUSETTS.** 1884. 364 + 9p.
P5-MA3012 — $38.00.

**HISTORY OF THE TOWN OF
LANCASTER, MASS., from the 1st
Settlement to the Present Time, 1643-
1879.** By A. P. Marvin. 1879. 798p.
P5-MA0198 — $81.00.

**MILITARY ANNALS OF
LANCASTER, 1740-1865. Includes
lists of soldiers who served in the Col.
& Rev. Wars for Berlin,
Bolton, Harvard, Leominster &
Sterling.** By H. S. Nourse. 1889. 402p.
P5-MA0021 — $44.50.

**HISTORY OF TOWN OF LANES-
BOROUGH, 1741-1905. With gene-
alogies.** Charles J. Palmer. 1905. 169p.
P5-MA0431 — $29.50.

**AUTHENTIC HISTORY OF THE
LAWRENCE CALAMITY, Embracing
a Description of the Pemberton Mill,
a Detailed Account of the Catastrophe
. . . Names of Killed & Wounded, etc.**
1860. 98p.
P5-MA0144 — $18.00.

**HISTORY OF LAWRENCE, with
Portraits & Biographical Sketches of
ex-Mayors to 1880, & other Distinguished Citizens.** H. A. Wadsworth.
1878. 179p.
P5-MA0143 — $24.50.

**LAWRENCE, UP TO DATE, 1845-
1895.** 1895. 172 + 87p.
P5-MA3045 — $27.00.

**LAWRENCE, YESTERDAY &
TODAY (1845-1918).** By Maurice B.
Dorgan. 1918. 263p.
P5-MA0414 — $32.50.

**CENTENNIAL CELEBRATION &
CENTENNIAL HISTORY OF
THE TOWN OF LEE.** Comp. by
C.M. Hyde & Alexander Hyde. 1878.
352p.
P5-MA0145B — $38.50.

**GRAVESTONE INSCRIPTIONS,
LEE, MASSACHUSETTS, in Three
Parts: 1773-1800, 1801-25, 1826-50;
Also Deaths Recorded 1775-1800 &
Marriages by Dr Hyde Prior to 1801.**
Comp. by D.M. Wilcox. n.d. 124p.
P5-MA0432 — $16.00.

**VITAL RECORDS OF LEE, 1777-
1801, from the Records of the Town
Congregation Church & Inscriptions
in the Early Burial Grounds [with
baptisms].** 1897. 108p.
P5-MA0433 — $18.00.
BRIEF HISTORY OF LEICESTER.
By Rev. A.H. Coolidge. 1890. 76p,
P5-MA0434 — $14.50.

**CELEBRATION OF THE 150TH
ANNIVERSARY OF THE ORG OF
THE TOWN OF LEICESTER.**
1871. 77p.
P5-MA3039 — $18.00.

**HISTORICAL SKETCH OF THE
TOWN OF LEICESTER, during the
First Century from its Settlement.**
Emory Washburn. 1860. 467p.
P5-MA0146 — $47.50.

**VITAL RECORDS OF LEICESTER,
MA to 1849.** 1903. 284p.
P5-MAVR — $29.00.

**LENOX and the Berkshire High-
lands.** R. DeWitt Mallary. 1902. 363p.
P5-MA0465 — $44.50.

**HISTORY OF LEOMINSTER, or
the Northern Half of the Lancaster
New Grant, from 1701 to 1852.** By D.
Wilder. 1853. 263p.
P5-MA0064 — $33.00.

**LEOMINSTER OF TODAY: Over
Two Hundred Choice Photographic
Views of its Churches, Public Build-
ings, Streets, Residences, Factories,
Reservoirs, Parks & Other Scenes of
Interest.** Comp. by Kate E. Nichols.
1900. 361p.
P5-MA0534 — $44.00.

LEOMINSTER TRADITIONS: Incidents, Anecdotes, Reminiscences, etc., Connected with the History of Leominster, Mass., & Vicinity. William A. Emerson. 1891. 99p.
P5-MA0286 — $18.00.

LEOMINSTER, MASSACHUSETTS, VITAL RECORDS TO THE YEAR 1850. 1911. 369p
P27150000 — $58.00.

THE LEOMINSTER BOOK: Recognition by the 20th Century of the Town's 19th Century Progress & its Makers. Wm. A. Emerson. 1901. 300p.
P5-MA0563 — $39.00.

HISTORY OF THE TOWN OF LEXINGTON, MIDDLESEX CO., from its 1st Settlement to 1868, 2-vol. set: Vol. I, History; Vol. II: Genealogy. By C. Hudson. Rev. & cont. to 1912 by Lexington Hist. Soc. 1913. 2 vols., 583p. + 897p.
P5-MA0562 — $148.75/set.

HISTORY OF THE TOWN OF LEXINGTON, MIDDLESEX CO . . . Vol. I, History. 1913. 583p.
P5-MA0562A — $65.00.

HISTORY OF THE TOWN OF LEXINGTON, MIDDLESEX CO. . . ., Vol. II: Genealogy. 1913. 897p.
P5-MA0562B — $95.00.

HISTORY OF THE TOWN OF LEXINGTON, MIDDLESEX CO., From its First Settlement to 1868, with a Genealogical Register. By C. Hudson. 1868. 745p.
P5-MA0065 — $77.00.

LEXINGTON EPITAPHS: A Copy of Epitaphs in the Old Burying Grounds of Lexington, Mass. By Francis H. Brown. 1905. 169p.
P5-MA0147 — $19.50.

LEXINGTON, MASSACHUSETTS, VITAL RECORDS TO THE YEAR 1850. 1898. 484p
P27151000 — $78.00.

LEXINGTON. Record of Births, Marriages & Deaths to Jan. 1, 1898.
P5-MA0066 — $58.00.

HISTORY OF LEYDEN, 1676-1959. By Wm. Tyler Arms, with Marsha E. Arms. 1959. 220p.
P5-MA0354A — $34.00.

ACCOUNT OF THE CELEBRATION BY THE TOWN OF LINCOLN, of the 150th Anniversary of its Incorporation, 1754-1904. With historical sketch & letters. 1904. 240p.
P5-MA0435 — $34.00.

LINCOLN, MASSACHUSETTS, VITAL RECORDS TO THE YEAR 1850. 1908. 179p
P27152000 — $35.00.

INDEX TO LITTLETON. From the Earliest Records in the Town Books, Begun in 1715.
P5-MA0069 — $18.00.

LITTLETON, MASSACHUSETTS, VITAL RECORDS TO THE YEAR 1850: Births and Deaths. 1900. 720p.
P27152500 — $13.00.
LITTLETON. From the Earliest Records in the Town Books, Begun in 1715. Births & Deaths; Some Marriages. 542p.
P5-MA0068 — $54.00.

CENTENNIAL CELEBRATION OF THE TOWN OF LONGMEADOW, October 17th, 1883, with Numerous Historical Appendices & Town Genealogy. By R. S. Storrs, et al. 1884. 321 + 97p.
P5-MA0149 — $43.50.

ILLUSTRATED HISTORY OF LOWELL & VICINITY. 1897. 881p.
P5-MA0150 — $89.50.

ILLUSTRATED HISTORY OF LOWELL. Rev. ed. by Charles Cowley. 1868. 235p.
P5-MA0295 — $29.50.

LOWELL, MASSACHUSETTS, VITAL RECORDS TO THE YEAR 1850, Vol. I: Births. 1930. 403p
P27153000 — $66.00.

LOWELL, MASSACHUSETTS, VITAL RECORDS TO THE YEAR 1850, Vol. II: Marriages. 1930. 543p
P27153100 — $86.00.

LOWELL, MASSACHUSETTS, VITAL RECORDS TO THE YEAR 1850, Vol. III: Marriages. 1930. 427p
P27153200 — $70.00.

LOWELL, MASSCHUSETTS, VITAL RECORDS TO THE YEAR 1850, Vol. IV: Deaths. 1930. 324p
P27153300 — $55.00.

HISTORY OF LUDLOW, with Biogr. Sketches of Leading Citizens, Reminiscences, Genealogies, Farm Hist., & an Acct. of the Centennial Celebration, 1874. By A. Noon, 2nd ed. rev. and enlarged. 1912. 592p.
P5-MA0214 — $63.00.

EARLY RECORDS OF THE TOWN OF LUNENBURG, including that Part which is Now Fitchburg, 1719-1764. [Town and selectmen's records; vital statistics]. Comp. by Walter A. Davis. 1896. 384p.
P5-MA0456 — $44.50.

INSCRIPTIONS FROM THE BURIAL GROUNDS OF LUNENBURG. Comp. by Marshall & Cox. 1902. 100p.
P5-MA0071 — $11.50.

PROPRIETORS' RECORDS OF THE TOWN OF LUNENBURG. By W.A. Davis. 1897. 374 + xii p.
P5-MA3036 — $49.00.

CENTENNIAL MEMORIAL OF LYNN, Embracing an Historical Sketch, 1629-1876. By James R. Newhall. 1876. 203p.
P5-MA0437 — $29.50.

EARLY HISTORY OF LYNN, MASSACHUSETTS By Obidiah Oldpath (Pseud. for James R. Newhall) 1890. 500p.
P27810000 — $80.00.

EARLY LYNN FAMS. INCL. LYNNFIELD, NAHANT, SAUGUS & SWAMPSCOTT: A Study from the Earliest Settlers Through the Rev. War. By Marcia Wilson Wiswall Lindberg. 2004. 978p.
P5-MA3009 — $98.00.

HISTORY OF LYNN, Essex Co., including Lynnfield, Saugus, Swampscott & Nahant, By A. Lewis & J. R. Newhall. 1865. 620p.
P5-MA0072 — $67.00.

HISTORY OF LYNN, Essex Co., Including Lynnfield, Saugus, Swampscott & Nahant (1883 Vol.). By James R. Newhall. 1883. 325p.
P5-MA0535 — $41.50.

HISTORY OF LYNN, including Nahant. By Alonzo Lewis. 1844. 278p.
P5-MA0440 — $38.00.

For hardcover versions, see the order form on page v. To order, call 1-888-296-3447.

Massachusetts, cont.

HISTORY OF LYNN. Vol. II, 1864-1893. 1897. 383p.
P5-MA0537 — $46.00.

IN LYNN WOODS with Pen & Camera. By Nathan Mortimer Hawkes. 1893. 104p.
P5-MA0441 — $15.00.

LIN: or, Notable People & Notable Things in the Early History of Lynn, the Third Plantaion of Massachusetts Colony [history & reminscences]. By Obadiah Oldpath. 1879. 500p.
P5-MA0536 — $54.00.

LYNN & SURROUNDINGS. By Clarence W. Hobbs. 1886. 161p.
P5-MA0439 — $28.00.
LYNN IN THE REVOLUTION. Comp. from notes gathered by Howard K. Sanderson. 1909. 503 + 50p.
P5-MA0152 — $55.00.

LYNN, MASSACHUSETTS, VITAL RECORDS TO THE YEAR 1850. 1905. 1,049p
P27155000 — $152.00.

SKETCHES OF LYNN, or the Changes of Fifty Years. By David N. Johnson. 1880. 490p.
P5-MA0438 — $55.00.

HISTORY OF LYNNFIELD, 1635-1785. Thomas B. Wellman. 1895. 283p.
P5-MA0252 — $37.50.

LYNNFIELD, MASSACHUSETTS, VITAL RECORDS TO THE YEAR 1850. 1907. 98p
P27155500 — $44.00.

BIRTHS, MARRIAGES, AND DEATHS IN THE TOWN OF MALDEN, MASSACHUSETTS, 1649-1850. Comp. by Deloraine P. Corey 1903. 393p.
P27157000 — $66.00.

HISTORY OF MALDEN, MASS., 1633-1785. By D. P. Corey. 1899. 870p.
P5-MA0199 — $89.00.

MEMORIAL OF THE CELEBRATION OF THE 250TH ANNIVERSARY OF THE INC. OF MALDEN. 1900. 340 + 102p.
P5-MA3038 — $44.00.

GENEALOGICAL HISTORY OF THE 1661 BURIAL GROUND MANCHESTER, MASS. By William C. Carlson. 2003. 98p.
P5-MA10024 — $13.00.

HISTORY OF THE TOWN OF MANCHESTER, 1645-1895. By Rev. D. F. Lamson. 1895. 26 + 425p.
P5-MA0153 — $47.50.

MANCHESTER-BY-THE-SEA. By Frank L. Floyd. 1945. 209p.
P5-MA0287 — $29.50.

MANSFIELD, MASSACHUSETTS, VITAL RECORDS TO THE YEAR 1850. 1933. 230p
P27195000 — $42.00.

GUIDE TO THE OLD BURYING HILL [MARBLEHEAD], Containing Many Quaint Inscriptions. By Frank L. Bessom. 1914. 40p.
P5-MA0442 — $10.00.

HISTORY & TRADITIONS OF MARBLEHEAD. By S. Roads Jr. Rev. Ed. 1897. 595p.
P5-MA0111 — $62.00.

MARBLEHEAD, MASSACHUSETTS, VITAL RECORDS TO THE YEAR 1850, Vol. I: Births. 1903. 564p
P27197100 — $89.00.

MARBLEHEAD, MASSACHUSETTS, VITAL RECORDS TO THE YEAR 1850, Vol. II: Deaths. 1903. 708p
P27197200 — $109.00.

OLD MARBLEHEAD SEA CAPTAINS & the Ships in Which They Sailed. Comp. by Benjamin J. Lindsey. 1915. 137p.
P5-MA0154 — $25.00.

HISTORICAL REMINISCENCES OF EARLY TIMES IN MARLBOROUGH, & Prominent Events from 1860 to 1910. By Ella A. Bigelow. 1910. 488p.
P5-MA0155 — $49.50.

HISTORY OF THE TOWN OF MARLBOROUGH, Middlesex Co., from its First Settlement in 1657 to 1861, with a Brief Sketch of the Town of Northborough and a Genealogy of the Families in Marlborough to 1800. By Charles Hudson. 1862. 544p.
P5-MA0455 — $61.50.

MARLBOROUGH BURIAL GROUND INSCRIPTIONS: Old Common, Spring Hill & Brigham Cemeteries. 1908. 218p.
P5-MA0073 — $29.00.

MARLBOROUGH, MASSACHUSETTS, VITAL RECORDS TO THE YEAR 1850. 1908. 404p
P27200000 — $62.00.

HISTORY OF MARSHFIELD, Vol. I. Lysander S. Richards. 1901. 238p.
P5-MA0156A — $31.50.

HISTORY OF MARSHFIELD, Vol. II. Lysander S. Richards. 1905. 245p.
P5-MA0156B — $31.50.

HISTORY OF MARTHA'S VINEYARD, 3-vol. set. By Charles Edward Banks 1911, 1925. 3 vols., 535 + 580 + 565p.
P5-MA0257A — $265.00/set.

HISTORY OF MARTHA'S VINEYARD, Vol I. 1911. 535p.
P27205100 — $90.00.

HISTORY OF MARTHA'S VINEYARD, Vol. II. 1911. 580p
P27205200 — $95.00.

HISTORY OF MARTHA'S VINEYARD, Vol. III. Genealogies. 1925. 565p.
P5-MA0257 — $90.00.

MATTAPOISETT & OLD ROCHESTER, Being a History of these Towns, & also in Part of Marion & a Portion of Wareham. Prep. under direction of Committee of Town of Mattapoisett. 3rd ed. 1907. 426p.
P5-MA0405 — $44.00.

BRIEF HISTORY OF THE TOWN OF MAYNARD. With genealogy. By William H. Gutteridge. 1921. 115p.
P5-MA0443 — $18.00.

HISTORY OF THE TOWN OF MEDFIELD, 1650-1886, with Genealogies . . . W. S. Tilden. 1887. 556p.
P5-MA0178 — $58.00.

MEDFIELD, MASSACHUSETTS, VITAL RECORDS TO THE YEAR 1850. 1903. 243p
P27210000 — $43.00.

HISTORY OF THE TOWN OF MEDFORD, Middlesex Co, from its 1st Settlement in 1630 to 1855. By C. Brooks, rev. by J. M. Usher. 1886. 592p. P5-MA0195 — $62.00.

MEDFORD IN THE REVOLUTION: Military History of Medford, Massachusetts, 1765-1783; also a List of Soldiers & Civil Officers with Genealogical & Biographical Notes. By Helen Tilden Wild. 1903. 67p. P5-MA0446 — $13.00.

MEDFORD PAST & PRESENT: 275th Anniversary of Medford, June, 1905. With many illustrations. 1905. 170p. P5-MA0445 — $31.00.

MEDFORD, MASSACHUSETTS, VITAL RECORDS TO THE YEAR 1850. 1907. 469p. P27220000 — $71.00.

REGISTER OF FAMILIES SETTLED AT THE TOWN OF MEDFORD. Comp. by W.H. Whitmore. 1855. 96p. P5-MA0444 — $17.00.

BIOGRAPHICAL SKETCHES OF PROMINENT PERSONS & The Genealogical Records of Many Early & Other Families in Medway, 1713-1886. By E. O. Jameson. 1886. 208p. P5-MA0183A — $28.00.

HANDBOOK OF MEDWAY HISTORY. Orion T. Mason. 1913. 116p. P5-MA3032 — $24.00.

HISTORY OF MEDWAY, 1713 to 1885. 1886. 534p. P5-MA0448 — $59.00.

MEDWAY. MASSACHUSETTS, VITAL RECORDS TO THE YEAR 1850. 1905. 345p P27221000 — $58.00.

MILITARY HISTORY OF MEDWAY, 1745-1885. Containing the Names of the Inhabitant Soldiers in the French & Indian Wars, the War of the Revolution, the War of 1812 . . . and the War for the Union. 1886. 110p. P5-MA0447 — $16.00.

HISTORY OF MELROSE, County of Middlesex. By Elbridge H. Goss. 1902. 508p. P5-MA0449 — $56.00.

ANNALS OF THE TOWN OF MENDON, from 1659 to 1880. Comp. by John G. Metcalf. 1880. 723p. P5-MA0159B — $72.00.

MENDON, MASSACHUSETTS, VITAL RECORDS TO THE YEAR 1850. 1920. 519p P27221500 — $83.00.

DESCRIPTIVE CATALOG OF MEMBERS OF THE 1ST CONGREGATIONAL CHURCH [MIDDLEBORO]. With Index to Surnames. Extr. from "200th Anniversary of 1st Cong. Church." 1895. 16p. P5-MA0298B — $10.00.

HISTORY OF THE TOWN OF MIDDLEBORO. By Thomas Weston. 1906. 724p. P5-MA0415 — $73.00.

HISTORY OF THE TOWN OF MIDDLEFIELD. Extensive chapter of genealogy is included. By E. C. & P. M. Smith. 1924. 662p. P5-MA0320 — $67.50.

ANCIENT MIDDLESEX [County], with Brief Biographical Sketches of the Men who have Served the County Officially since its Settlement. By Levi S. Gould. 1905. 336p. P5-MA0345 — $41.50.

HISTORY OF MIDDLESEX COUNTY, MASSACHUSETTS, containing Carefully Prepared Histories of Every City and Town in the County. By Samuel Adams Drake. 1880. 505 + 587p. P5-MA3015 — $110.00.

HISTORY OF MIDDLESEX COUNTY, with Biographical Sketches of Many of its Prominent Men & Pioneers, 3-vol. set. 1890. 3 vols., 769 + 886 + 877p. P5-MA0346 — $239.00/set.

HISTORY OF MIDDLESEX COUNTY . . ., Vol. I. 1890. 769p. P5-MA0346A — $89.00.

HISTORY OF MIDDLESEX COUNTY . . ., Vol. II. 1890. 886p. P5-MA0346B — $89.00.

HISTORY OF MIDDLESEX COUNTY . . ., Vol. III. 1890. 877p. P5-MA0346C — $89.00.

INDEX TO THE PROBATE RECORDS OF MIDDLESEX, MASSACHUSETTS, covering the years 1648-1871. Samuel H. Folsom 1914. 552p P26705000 — $87.00.

MIDDLETON, MASSACHUSETTS, VITAL RECORDS TO THE YEAR 1850. 1904. 143p P27221800 — $30.00.

HISTORY OF THE TOWN OF MILFORD, from its First Settlement, 2-vol. set. By A. Ballou. 1882. 2 vols., 511 + 646p. P5-MA0260 — $116.50/set.

HISTORY OF THE TOWN OF MILFORD . . ., Vol. I. 1882. 511p. P5-MA0260A — $60.00.

HISTORY OF THE TOWN OF MILFORD . . ., Vol. II. 1882. 646p. P5-MA0260B — $70.00.

MILFORD, 1880-1930: A Chronological List of Events for Fifty Years, with illustrations. 1930. 248p. P5-MA0246 — $29.50.

MILFORD, MASSACHUSETTS, VITAL RECORDS TO THE YEAR 1850. 1917. 378p P27240000 — $63.00.

CENTENNIAL HISTORY OF THE TOWN OF MILLBURY, including Vital Statistics, 1850-1899. 1915. 814p. P5-MA0422 — $81.50.

HISTORY OF MILTON, 1640-1887. Ed. by A. K. Teele. 1887. 668p. P5-MA0074 — $68.00.

MILTON, MASSACHUSETTS, VITAL RECORDS TO THE YEAR 1850. 1900. 258p P27250000 — $45.00.

SOME ANNALS OF NAHANT. By Fred A. Wilson. 1928. 412p. P5-MA0470 — $42.50.

FASCINATING OLD TOWN ON THE ISLAND IN THE SEA: Brief Historical Data & Memories of My Boyhood Days in Nantucket. Joseph E. C. Farnham. 2nd Ed. 1923. 319p. P5-MA0161 — $36.00.

HISTORY OF NANTUCKET County, Island & Town, Including Genealogies of the First Settlers. By Alexander Starbuck. 1924. 871p. P5-MA0160 — $75.00.

Massachusetts, cont.

HISTORY OF NANTUCKET . . .
First Settlement of the Island by the
English, together with the Rise and
Progress of the Whale Fishery, and
other Historical Facts . . . Obed Macy,
with William C. Macy. 1880; 2nd ed. 313p.
P5-MA0463 — $41.00.

HISTORY OF NATICK from its
First Settlement in 1651 to the Present
Time, with Notices of the First White
Families. Oliver N. Bacon. 1856. 261p.
P5-MA0056 — $34.50.

NATICK, MASSACHUSETTS,
VITAL RECORDS TO THE YEAR
1850. 1910. 249p
P27270000 — $50.00.

EPITAPHS FROM GRAVEYARDS, in
Wellesley, No Natick, & St Mary's
Churchyards in Newton Lower Falls,
with Genealogical & Biographical
Notes [Needham]. 1900. 241p.
P5-MA0162 — $24.00.

HISTORY OF NEEDHAM, MASS.,
1711-1911, incl. West Needham, now
Wellesley, to its Separation in 1881
with Some References to its Affairs to
1911. By G. K. Clark. 1913. 746p.
P5-MA0202 — $75.00.

HISTORICAL SKETCH OF THE
FRIENDS ACADEMY [NEW
BEDFORD]. 1876. 73 + 9p.
P5-MA3008 — $25.50.

HISTORY OF NEW BEDFORD &
VICINITY, 1602-1892. By L. B. Ellis.
1892. 731 + 175p.
P5-MA0268 — $91.50.

HISTORY OF NEW BEDFORD,
including a History of the Old
Township of Dartmouth & the
Present Townships of Westport,
Dartmouth & Fairhaven. By Daniel
Ricketson. 1858. 412p.
P5-MA0347 — $46.50.

HISTORY OF NEW BEDFORD, 3-
vol. set. 1918. 3 Vols; 1312p.
P5-MA3035 — $132.00/set.

HISTORY OF NEW BEDFORD,
Vol. I. 1918.
P5-MA3035A — $42.00.

HISTORY OF NEW BEDFORD,
Vol. II. 1918.
P5-MA3035B — $42.00.

HISTORY OF NEW BEDFORD,
Vol. III. 1918.
P5-MA3035C — $42.00.

WHALING MASTERS . . . The
whaling industry of New Bedford,
Nantucket, etc. Incl. a directory of
ship captains with home ports and a
"roll of honor" of whaling men.
Comp. & written by Fed. Writers Project of
Works Projects Admin. 1938. 314p.
P5-MA0416 — $35.00.

NEW BRAINTREE, MASSACHU-
SETTS, VITAL RECORDS TO
THE YEAR 1850. 1904. 163p
P27300000 — $33.00.

HISTORY OF NEW MARLBOR-
OUGH. Hadley K. Turner. 1944. 93p.
P5-MA0538 — $17.50.

HISTORY OF NEWBURY, 1635-
1902. By John J. Currier. 1902. 755p.
P5-MA0163 — $75.00.

SKETCH OF THE HISTORY OF
NEWBURY, NEWBURYPORT &
WEST NEWBURY, from 1635-1845.
By J. Coffin. 1845. 416p.
P5-MA0075 — $42.00.
NEWBURY, MASSACHUSETTS,
VITAL RECORDS TO THE YEAR
1850, 2-vol. set. 1911. 428 + 534p
P27310000 — $150.00.

NEWBURY, MASSACHUSETTS,
VITAL RECORDS TO THE YEAR
1850: Vol. I: Births. 1911. 428p
P27311100 — $69.00.

NEWBURY, MASSACHUSETTS,
VITAL RECORDS TO THE YEAR
1850, Vol. II: Marriages & Deaths.
1911. 534p
P27311200 — $81.00.

CITY OF NEWBURYPORT IN
THE CIVIL WAR . . . with Indi-
vidual Records of the Soldiers &
Sailors . . . also the War Records of
Many Natives & Residents of the
City, Credited to Other Places. By
George W. Creasey. 1903. 539p.
P5-MA0540 — $57.00.

HISTORY OF NEWBURYPORT,
1764-1909, 2-vol. set. By John J. Currier.
1905, 1909. 2 vols., 766 + 679p.
P5-MA0356A — $145.00/set.

HISTORY OF NEWBURYPORT,
1764-1909, Vol. I. 1905. 766p.
P5-MA0356A1 — $74.50.

HISTORY OF NEWBURYPORT,
1764-1909, Vol. II. 1909. 679p.
P5-MA0356A2 — $74.50.

HISTORY OF NEWBURYPORT,
from the Earliest Settlement of the
Country to the Present Time [1854],
with a Biographical Appendix. By
Mrs E. Vale Smith. 1854. 414p.
P5-MA0349 — $47.00.

HISTORY OF THE MARINE
SOCIETY OF NEWBURYPORT,
from its Incorporation in 1772-1906.
With complete roster & narrative of
the important events in the lives of its
members. Comp. by Capt. W. H. Bayley
et al. 1906. 506p.
P5-MA0164 — $49.50.

LIFE OF LORD TIMOTHY
DEXTER; with Sketches of . . . his
Associates; Including his own
Writings, "Dexter's Pickle for the
Knowing Ones," etc. [Newburyport].
By Samuel L. Knapp. 1858. 157p.
P5-MA0539 — $31.00.

HISTORY OF NEWTON, Town &
City, from its Earliest Settlement to
the Present Time, 1630-1880. By S. F.
SMith. 1880. 851p.
P5-MA0023 — $89.50.

HISTORY OF THE EARLY
SETTLEMENT OF NEWTON
from 1639-1800, with a Gen. Register.
By F. Jackson. 1854. 555p.
P5-MA0076 — $58.00.

NEWTON, MASSACHUSETTS,
VITAL RECORDS TO THE YEAR
1850. 1905. 521p
P27320000 — $77.00.

HISTORY OF NORFOLK CO., with
Biogr. Sketches of Many of its
Pioneers & Prominent Men.
Comp. by D. H. Hurd. 1884. 1001p.
P5-MA0151 — $99.00.

INDEX TO THE PROBATE REC-
ORDS OF NORFOLK COUNTY,
MASSACHUSETTS, 1793 TO 1900,
in 2 vols. 1910. 1201p.
P26707500 — $188.00.

HISTORY OF NORTH BRIDGE-
WATER, Plymouth Co, from its First
Settlement to 1866, with Family
Register. By B. Kingman. 1866. 696p.
P5-MA0077 — $73.00.

For hardcover versions, see the order form on page v. To order, call 1-888-296-3447.

HISTORY OF NORTH BROOK-FIELD, with a Gen. Register. By J. Temple. 1887. 824p.
P5-MA0078 — $85.00.

SERVICE MEN FROM NORTH READING in the Revolution. 8p.
P5-MA0304 — $10.00.

EARLY NORTHAMPTON. 1914. 231p.
P5-MA0484 — $34.00.

HISTORY OF NORTHAMPTON, from its Settlement in 1654, 2-vol. set J. R. Trumbull. 1898. 2 vols., 628 + 699p.
P5-MA0417 — $125.00.

HISTORY OF NORTHAMPTON . . ., Vol. I. 1898. 628p.
P5-MA0417A — $65.00.

HISTORY OF NORTHAMPTON . . ., Vol. II. 1898. 699p.
P5-MA0417B — $65.00.

HISTORY OF NORTHAMPTON, NORTHAMPTON GENEALO-GIES Vol. 3. By James Russell Trumull. 1899. 576p.
P5-MA3000 — $59.50.

NORTHAMPTON of Today, Depicted by Pen and Camera . . . Northampton at the dawn of the 20th century . . . By Frederick Knab. 1902-1903. 96p.
P5-MA0483 — $17.50.

NORTHAMPTON, The Meadow City. Historical sketch of North-ampton, with over 250 photographics and illustrations. Comp. by F.N. Kneeland & L.P. Bryant. 1894. 108p.
P5-MA0482 — $19.50.
NORTHBOROUGH HISTORY. Dr Josiah M. Stanley. 1921. 529 + 62p.
P5-MA0485 — $61.00.

HISTORY OF THE TOWN OF NORTHFIELD FOR 150 YEARS, with Genealogies. By J. H. Temple & G. Sheldon. 1875. 636p.
P5-MA0079 — $64.00.

HISTORY OF THE TOWN OF NORTON, Bristol Co., from 1669 to 1859. By George F. Clark. 1859. 550p.
P5-MA0350A — $59.50.

NORTON, MASSACHUSETTS, VITAL RECORDS TO THE YEAR 1850. 1906. 405p
P27335000 — $66.00.

VITAL RECORDS OF NORTON, MASSACHUSETTS. 1906. 405p.
P5-MA3013 — $41.00.

SETTLEMENT & STORY OF OAKHAM. With 10 fold-out maps [Vol. I]. By H.B. Wright & E.D. Harvey. 1947. 361p. + maps.
P5-MA0357A — $46.50.

SETTLEMENT & STORY OF OAKHAM, Vol. II. 848p.
P5-MA0561 — $85.00.

SOLDIERS OF OAKHAM, in the Revolutionary War, the War of 1812, & the Civil War. By Henry Parks Wright. 1914. 325p.
P5-MA0457 — $39.50.

HISTORY OF THE TOWN OF OXFORD, with genealogies. By G. Daniels 1892. 856p.
P5-MA0081 — $87.00.

HUGUENOTS IN THE NIPMUCK COUNTRY, or Oxford Prior to 1713. By George F. Daniels. 1880. 168p.
P5-MA0351B — $22.50.

INDEX TO "RECORDS OF OXFORD" by Mary DeWitt Freeland. Comp. by Avis F. Clarke. 1942. 178p.
P5-MA0352b — $21.00.

RECORDS OF OXFORD, incl. Chapters of Nipmuck, Huguenot & English History from the Earliest Date, 1630 . . . Mary DeWitt Freeland. 1894. 429p.
P5-MA0165 — $45.00.

HISTORY OF PALMER, Early Known as the Elbow Tract, Incl. Records of the Plantation, District and Town, 1716-1889. By J. H. Temple. 1889. 602p.
P5-MA0082 — $67.00.

HISTORY OF PAXTON. By Ledyard Bill. 1889. 121p.
P5-MA0293 — $19.50.

HISTORY OF PELHAM, from 1738-1898, incl. the Early History of Prescott. C. O. Parmenter. 1898. 531p.
P5-MA0270 — $58.00.

PEMBROKE, MASSACHUSETTS, VITAL RECORDS TO THE YEAR 1850. 1911. 465p
P27350000 — $77.00.

HISTORY OF PITTSFIELD, Berkshire Co., from the Year 1734 to the year 1800. J.E.A. Smith. 1869. 518p.
P5-MA0322 — $54.00.

HISTORY OF PITTSFIELD, Berkshire Co., from the Year 1800 to the Year 1876. J.E.A. Smith. 1876. 725p.
P5-MA0166 — $73.00.

HISTORY OF PITTSFIELD, from the Year 1876 to 1916, By Edw. Boltwood. 1916. 387p.
P5-MA0462 — $44.00.

HISTORY OF THE TOWN OF PLAINFIELD, Hampshire Co., from it Settlement to 1891, including a Genealogical History of Twenty-Three of the Original Settlers & their Descendants. By Charles N. Dyer. 1891. 187p.
P5-MA0353B — $31.00.

ANCIENT LANDMARKS OF PLYMOUTH. Part 1, Hist. Sketch & Titles of Estates; Part 2, Gen. Reg. of Plymouth fams. By W. T. Davis. 1887. 662p.
P5-MA0191 — $69.00.

BURIAL HILL [PLYMOUTH, MA]: Its Monuments and Gravestones Numbered and Briefly Described. By Benjamin Drew 1894. xxii + 310p
P27870500 — $58.00.

ENGLISH ANCESTRY & HOMES OF THE PILGRIM FATHERS, who Came to Plymouth on the "Mayflower" in 1620, the "Fortune" in 1621, & the "Anne" & "Little James" in 1623. 1929. 187p.
P5-GR0016 — $19.50.

GENEALOGICAL REGISTER OF PLYMOUTH FAMILIES. A list of thousands of people with Mayflower and sister ship antecedents. By W.T. Davis. 1899. 363p.
P5-MA0281 — $27.50.

HISTORY OF THE TOWN OF PLYMOUTH from its Earliest Settlement in 1620 to the Present Time; with a Precise History of the Aborigines of New England & their Wars with the English. By James Thacher. 1835. 401p.
P5-MA0324 — $40.00.

Massachusetts, cont.

PLYMOUTH SCRAP BOOK, The Oldest Original Documents Extant in Plymouth Archives. 1918. 149p.
P5-MA0354B — $21.00.

RECORDS OF PLYMOUTH COLONY: Births, Marriages, Deaths, Burials & Other Records from 1633-1689. With Plymouth Colony Vital Records, a Supp. From Mayflower Desc. by G. E. Bowman. Ed. by N.B. Shurtleff. 1857, 1911, 1913. 293p.
P5-MA0344 — $27.50.

RECORDS OF THE TOWN OF PLYMOUTH, 3-vol. set. 1889-1903. 3 vols., 348 + 365 + 481p.
P5-MA0541 — $119.50/set.

RECORDS OF THE TOWN OF PLYMOUTH, Vol. I. 1889-1903. 348p.
P5-MA0541A — $45.00.

RECORDS OF THE TOWN OF PLYMOUTH, Vol. II. 1889-1903. 365p.
P5-MA0541B — $45.00.

RECORDS OF THE TOWN OF PLYMOUTH, Vol. III. 1889-1903. 481p.
P5-MA0541C — $47.50.

HISTORY OF PLYMOUTH COUNTY, with Biographical Sketches of Many of its Pioneers & Prominent Men. Comp. under supervision of D. H. Hurd. 1884. 1198p.
P5-MA0337 — $98.00.

PLYMOUTH COUNTY MARRIAGES, 1692-1746. Transcribed from Records of the Court of Common Pleas & Court of General Session. Contains records not found in Bailey's Early Mass. Marriages. 1900. 54p.
P5-MA0167 — $10.00.

PLYMPTON, MASSACHUSETTS, VITAL REOCRDS TO THE YEAR 1850. 1923. 540p
P27380000 — $75.00.

HISTORY OF PRESCOTT, one of four townships in the Swift River Valley which was "born, lived & died" to make way for Metro. Water Basin [Quabbin Reservoir]. With genealogies and biographies. By Lillie P. Coolidge. n.d. 288p.
P5-MA0461 — $39.50.

PRESCOTT FUR-EVER. By Raymond W. Whitaker. 2000. 97p.
P5-MA0570 — $17.50.

PRESCOTT YEARS, By Raymond W. Whitaker. 1997. 128p.
P5-MA0571 — $19.50.

HISTORY OF THE TOWN OF PRINCETON, in the County of Worcester & the Commonwealth of Massachusetts, 2-Vol. Set: Vol. I, History; Vol. II, Genealogies. By F.W. Blake. 1915. 2 vols., 428 + 336p.
P5-MA0556 — $78.00/set.

HISTORY OF THE TOWN OF PRINCETON . . ., Vol. I: History. 1915. 428p.
P5-MA0556A — $47.00.

HISTORY OF THE TOWN OF PRINCETON . . ., Vol. II: Genealogies.1915. 336p.
P5-MA0556B — $37.00.

SOLDIERS OF THE REVOLUTION, PRINCETON (Listed alphabetically with biog. information). 1897?. 8p.
P5-MA0355B — $10.00.

PROVINCETOWN, or Odds & Ends from the Tip End: A Brief Historical Description of Provincetown . . . with Thirty-Three Engravings. By Herman A. Jennings. 1890. 212p.
P5-MA0288 — $29.00.

QUABBIN: THE LOST VALLEY. [Contains biographical & historical information on the lost towns of Enfield, Smith's Village, Greenwich & Greenwich Village, Prescott, Dana & N. Dana, & Millington.] Comp. by Donald W. Howe, ed. by Roger Nye Lincoln. 1951. 631p.
P5-MA0168 — $65.00.

THREE HUNDRED YEARS OF QUINCY, 1625-1925: Historical Retrospect of Mt Wollaston, Braintree & Quincy, with a Chronicle of the the Tercentenary Celebration. By David M. Wilson & Timothy J. Collins. 1926. 455p.
P5-MA0358A — $49.00.

GENEALOGICAL HISTORY OF THE TOWN OF READING, incl. the Present Towns of Wakefield, Reading & No Reading, with Chronological & Historical Sketches, from 1639-1874. By L. Eaton. 1874. 815p.
P5-MA0196 — $82.00.

READING, MASSACHUSETTS, VITAL RECORDS TO THE YEAR 1850. 1912. 586p
P27400000 — $85.00.

HISTORY OF REHOBOTH: Its History for 275 Years, 1643-1918. By George H. Tilton. 1918. 417p.
P5-MA0260 — $45.50.

BIOGRAPHICAL SKETCHES OF REHOBOTH. Extr. from above. 88p.
P5-MA0262 — $18.00.

EARLY REHOBOTH: Documented Historical Studies of Families & Events in this Plymouth Colony Township. Vols. I-IV. By Richard L. Bowen. 1945. 4 vols., 164 + 177 + 186 + 189p.
P5-MA0359A — $84.00/set.

EARLY REHOBOTH . . ., Vol. I. 1945. 164p.
P5-MA0359A1 — $25.00.

EARLY REHOBOTH . . ., Vol. II. 1945. 177p.
P5-MA0359A2 — $25.00.

EARLY REHOBOTH . . ., Vol. III. 1945. 186p.
P5-MA0359A3 — $25.00.

EARLY REHOBOTH . . ., Vol. IV. 1945. 189p.
P5-MA0359A4 — $25.00.

REHOBOTH, MASSACHUSETTS, VITAL RECORDS TO THE YEAR 1850. 1897. 925p
P27410000 — $150.00.

HISTORY OF THE TOWN OF REVERE. By Benjamin Shurtleff. 1937. 618p.
P5-MA0513 — $65.00.

ROCHESTER, MASSACHUSETTS, VITAL RECORDS TO THE YEAR 1850. 1914. 318 + 450p
P27430000 — $120.00.

HISTORY OF THE TOWN OF ROCKPORT. L. Gott et al. 1888. 295p.
P5-MA0085 — $35.00.

NIPPERS, NIGHTCAPS and
NEEDLES: A Story of the Circle at
Pigeon Cove [Rockport]. **By Eleanor
C. Parsons. 1995. 118p.**
P5-MA0280 — $19.95.

ROCKPORT, MASSACHUSETTS,
VITAL RECORDS TO THE YEAR
1850. 1924. 120p
P27433300 — $27.00.

HISTORY OF ROWE. **By Percy
Whiting Brown. 1935. 114p.**
P5-MA10026 — $17.50.

EARLY SETTLERS OF ROWLEY.
By George B. Blodgette & Amos E.
Jewett. 1933. 472p.
P5-MA0469 — $47.50.

HISTORY OF ROWLEY, Anciently
incl. Bradford, Boxford & George-
town, from 1639-1840. **By T. Gage.
1840. 483p.**
P5-MA0090 — $48.50.

ROWLEY OLD CEMETERY
INSCRIPTIONS. 72p.
P5-MA0089 — $11.00.

ROWLEY TOWN RECORDS, 1639-
1672. Vol I. 254p.
P5-MA0087 — $32.00.
ROWLEY, MASSACHUSETTS,
VITAL RECORDS TO THE YEAR
1850. 1928. 537p
P27432500 — $75.00.

ROWLEY, RECORDS OF THE
FIRST CHURCH. 1898. 220p.
P5-MA0088 — $31.00.

HISTORY OF ROXBURY TOWN.
By Charles M. Ellis 1847. 146p
P5-MA3007 — $30.00.

ROXBURY, MASSACHUSETTS,
VITAL RECORDS TO THE YEAR
1850. 3-vol. set. 1925.
P27435000 — $171.00/set.

TOWN OF ROXBURY: Its
Memorable Persons & Places, Its
History & Antiquities, with numer-
ous Illustrations of Old Landmarks &
Noted Personages. **By F. S. Drake.
1905. 475p.**
P5-MA0017 — $48.00.

HISTORY OF THE TOWN OF
ROYALSTON, 1762-1917, including
Royalston's Soldier Record (by F.W.
Cross.) Lilley B. Caswell. 1917. 566 + 21p.
P5-MA0357B — $64.00.

REFLECTIONS ON ROYALSTON,
Worcester Co. By Hubert Carlton
Bartlett. 1927. 332p.
P5-MA1027 — $37.50.

BIOGRAPHIES OF THE FIRST
SETTLERS OF RUTLAND. From
History of Rutland. 1836. 76p.
P5-MA0091 — $11.00.

HISTORY OF RUTLAND, Worcester
County, from its Earliest Settlement,
with a Biography of its First Settlers. By
Jonas Reed. 1836. 168p.
P5-MA0169 — $27.00.

RUTLAND, MASSACHUSETTS,
VITAL RECORDS TO THE YEAR
1850. 1905. 255p
P27435500 — $49.00.

ANNALS OF SALEM, 2-vol. set. By
J.B. Felt. 2nd ed. 1845, 1849. 2 vols., 535
+ 563p.
P5-MA0189 — $110.00/set.

ANNALS OF SALEM, Vol. I. 1845.
535p.
P5-MA0189A — $60.00.

ANNALS OF SALEM, Vol. II. 1849.
563p.
P5-MA0189B — $60.00.

CHARTER STREET CEMETERY
BURIAL RECORDS: Genealogical
& Historical. With index and map of
cemetery. Comp. by William Carlson.
1996. 65p.
P5-MA0359B — $15.00.

ESSEX INSTITUTE HISTORICAL
COLLECTIONS, VOL. I: TOWN
RECORDS OF SALEM, MASSA-
CHUSETTS, 1634-1659. 1868. 243p
P2744300 — $44.00.

HISTORICAL SKETCH OF
SALEM, 1626-1879. By Chas. S.
Osgood & H.M Batchelder. 1879. 288p.
P5-MA0544 — $37.00.

HISTORY OF SALEM,
MASSACHUSETTS, Vol. I: 1626-
1637. Sidney Perley. 1924. viii + 539p
P27881000 — $82.00.

HISTORY OF SALEM,
MASSACHUSETTS, Vol. II: 1638-
1670. Sidney Perley. 1924. viii + 526p
P27881100 — $81.00.

HISTORY OF SALEM,
MASSACHUSETTS, Vol. III: 1671-
1716. Sidney Perley. 1924. vii + 508p
P27881200 — $77.00.

OLD SHIPMASTERS OF SALEM,
with Mention of Eminent Merchants.
By Chas. E. Trow. G.P. Putnams' Sons;
1905. 337p.
P5-MA0546 — $44.50.

RECORDS OF SALEM WITCH-
CRAFT Copied from the Original
Documents. By W. Eliot Woodward
1864. 2 vols. in 1, 279 + 281p.
P5-MA0543 — $61.50.

SALEM INSCRIPTIONS FROM
THE CHARTER STREET
CEMETERY. Comp. by P. Derby.
22p.
P5-MA0096 — $10.00 .

SALEM WITCHCRAFT, with An
Account of Salem Village & an
Opinion on Witchcraft & Kindred
Subjects, 2-vol. set. By Chas. W.
Upham. 1867. 2 vols., 469+553p.
P5-MA0542 — $99.50/set.

SALEM WITCHCRAFT . . ., Vol. I.
1867. 469p.
P5-MA0542A — $52.00.

SALEM WITCHCRAFT . . ., Vol. II.
1867. 553p.
P5-MA0542B — $52.00.

SALEM, MASSACHUSETTS, VITAL
RECORDS TO THE YEAR 1850,
Vol. I: Births, A-L. 1916. 536p
P27442000 — $82.00.

SALEM, MASSACHUSETTS, VITAL
RECORDS TO THE YEAR 1850,
Vol. II: Births, M-Z. 1918. 454p
P27442100 — $74.00.

SALEM, MASSACHUSETTS, VITAL
RECORDS TO THE YEAR 1850,
Vol. III: Marriages, A-L. 1924. 625p
P27442300 — $98.00.

SALEM, MASSACHUSETTS, VITAL
RECORDS TO THE YEAR 1850,
Vol. IV: Marriages, M-Z. 1924. 529p
P27442400 — $84.00.

SALEM, MASSACHUSETTS, VITAL
RECORDS TO THE YEAR 1850,
Vol. V: Deaths, A-L. 1925. 422p
P27442500 — $69.00.

SALEM, MASSACHUSETTS, VITAL
RECORDS TO THE YEAR 1850,
Vol. VI: Deaths, M-Z. 1925. 365p.
P27442600 — $61.00.

Massachusetts, cont.

SHIPS AND SAILORS OF OLD SALEM. Ralph D. Paine. 1912. 515 + 115p.
P5-MA3044 — $63.00.

THE WITCHCRAFT DELUSION. By S. Perley. Extr. from History of Salem. 1928. 42p.
P5-MA0097B — $10.00.

VITAL RECORDS OF SALEM, to the End of the Year 1849. 1916.
P5-MA0515 — 225.00.

WHEN I LIVED IN SALEM. By Caroline Howard King. 1937. 222p.
P5-MA0545 — $34.00.

WITCH HILL: A History of Salem Witchcraft. Rev. Z.A. Mudge. 1870. 322p.
P5-MA3037 — $22.00.

OLD FAMILIES OF SALISBURY & AMESBURY, incl. Towns of Ipswich, Newbury, Haverhill, Hampton & Coastal New Hampshire & Coastal York County, Me. 1897-1919. Traces nearly 300 families, most back to immigration. By D. W. Hoyt. 1897. 1097p.
P5-MA0266B — $115.00.

SALISBURY SECOND CHURCH RECORDS. Extr. from Old Families of Salisbury. 59pp.
P5-MA0097A — $11.00.

SKETCHES OF SAUGUS. By Benjamin Franklin Newhall. 1997. 262p.
P5-MA0547 — $41.50.

EARLY PLANTERS OF SCITUATE. A history of the town of Scituate, from its establishment to the end of the Rev. War. H. H. Pratt. 1929. 386p.
P5-MA0267 — $44.00.

HISTORY OF SCITUATE from First Settlement to 1831. About half of the book consists of genealogies. By S. Deane. 1831. 408p.
P5-MA0325 — $40.00.

SCITUATE, MASSACHUSETTS, VITAL RECORDS TO THE YEAR 1850. 1909. 436 + 473p
P27460000 — $138.00.

PUBLICATIONS OF SHARON HIST SOC, SHARON, MA, 1-5. 1904-1908. 234p.
P5-MA3034 — $32.00.

HISTORY OF THE TOWN OF SHIRLEY, from its Early Settlement to 1882. S. Chandler. 1883. 744p.
P5-MA0099 — $76.50.

SHIRLEY UPLANDS & INTER-VALES: Annals of a Border Town of Old Middlesex, with Some Genealogical Sketches. By Ethel Stanley Bolton. 1914. 394p.
P5-MA0171 — $41.00.

FAMILY REGISTER OF THE INHABITANTS OF SHREWSBURY, from its Settlement in 1717 to 1829. Rare early genealogy of Shrewsbury. By Andrew H. Ward. 1847. 294p.
P5-MA0305 — $35.00.

SHREWSBURY, MASSACHUSETTS, VITAL RECORDS TO THE YEAR 1850. 1904. 281pp.
P27477000 — $49.00.

HISTORY OF THE TOWN OF SOMERSET, Shawomet Purchase, 1677, Incorporated 1790. By Wm. A. Hart. 1940. 247p.
P5-MA0453 — $37.00.

HISTORY OF SOUTH BOSTON, formerly Dorchester Neck, now Ward XII of Boston. By Thomas C. Simonds. 1857. 331p.
P5-MA0247 — $37.00.

HISTORY OF SOUTH BOSTON. By John J. Toomey & Edward P.B. Rankin. 1901. 570 + 44p.
P5-MA3016 — $62.00.

IN OLD SOUTH HADLEY. By Sophie E. Eastman. 1912. 221p.
P5-MA0495 — $33.50.

NARRATIVE HISTORY OF SOUTH SCITUATE/NORWELL. By J. F. Merritt. 1938. 203p.
P5-MA0100 — $24.00.

HISTORICAL SKETCHES RELATING TO SPENCER. A variety of biographical and historical sketches. Vol. IV. By H.M. Tower. 1909. 234p.
P5-MA3043 — $29.50.

HISTORICAL SKETCHES RELATING TO SPENCER. Vol. I. By Henry M. Tower. 1901. 184p.
P5-MA3040 — $26.00.

HISTORICAL SKETCHES RELATING TO SPENCER. Vol. II. By H.M. Tower. 1902. 228p.
P5-MA3041 — $31.50.

HISTORICAL SKETCHES RELATING TO SPENCER. Vol. III. By H.M. Tower. 1903. 257p.
P5-MA3042 — $34.00.

HISTORY OF SPENCER, from its Early Settlement to the Year 1860, Incl. a Sketch of Leicester to 1753. By J. Draper. 2nd Ed. 1860. 276p.
P5-MA0101 — $34.00.

SPENCER, MASSACHUSETTS, VITAL RECORDS TO THE YEAR 1850. 1909. 276p.
P27500000 — $47.00.

FIRST CENTURY OF THE HISTORY OF SPRINGFIELD: The Official Records from 1636 to 1736, with an Historical Review & Biographical Mention of the Founders, 2-vol. set. By Henry M. Burt. 1899. 2 vols., 473 + 712p.
P5-MA0486 — $119.00/set.

FIRST CENTURY OF THE HISTORY OF SPRINGFIELD . . ., Vol. I. 1899. 473p.
P5-MA0486A — $48.50.

FIRST CENTURY OF THE HISTORY OF SPRINGFIELD . . ., Vol. II. 1899. 712p.
P5-MA0486B — $82.00.

SPRINGFIELD FAMILIES. By Warren B. White 1934-1935. 1007p.
P27891000 — $171.00.

SPRINGFIELD, 1636-1886, History of Town amd City, Including an Account of the Quarter-Millenial Celebration. By Mason A. Green. 1888. 645p.
P5-MA0340 — $69.00.

THE FIRST CENTURY OF THE HISTORY OF SPRINGFIELD: The Official Records from 1636 to 1736, with an Historical Review & Biographical Mention of the Founders, Vol. II. By Henry M. Burt. 1899. 712p.
P5-MA0486B — $74.50.

STOCKBRIDGE, 1739-1939: A Chronicle. By Sarah C. Sedgwick & Christina S. Marquand. 1939. 306p.
P5-MA0279 — $39.50.

STOCKBRIDGE, PAST & PRESENT, or Records of an Old Mission Station. By Miss Electa F. Jones. 1854. 275p.
P5-MA0277 — $37.00.

HISTORY OF STONEHAM. With biographical sketches of many of its pioneers & prominent men. By William B. Stevens. 1891. 352p.
P5-MA0173 — $37.50.

STOW, 1683-1933, Compiled in Honor of the 250th Anniversary of the Town. By Rev. & Mrs Preston R. Crowell. 1933. 131p.
P5-MA0360 — $17.50.

STOW, MASSACHUSETTS, VITAL RECORDS TO THE YEAR 1850. 1911. 270p
P27510000 — $46.00.

HISTORICAL SKETCH OF STURBRIDGE & SOUTHBRIDGE. By George Davis. 1856. 233p.
P5-MA0496 — $31.50.

STURBRIDGE, MASSACHUSETTS, VITAL RECORDS TO THE YEAR 1850. 1906. 393p
P27520000 — $61.00.

ANNALS OF SUDBURY, WAYLAND & MAYNARD, Middlesex Co., By Alfred Sereno Hudson. 1891. 219 + 40p.
P5-MA0420 — $35.00.

HISTORY OF SUDBURY, 1638-1889. By Alfred S. Hudson. 1889. 660p.
P5-MA0174 — $66.00.

SUDBURY, MASSACHUSETTS, VITAL RECORDS TO THE YEAR 1850. 1903. 332p.
P27530000 — $51.00.

DOCUMENTARY HISTORY OF SUFFIELD, MASSACHUSETTS, 1660-1749 By Hezekiah Spencer Sheldon 1879. 343p.
P27900000 — $55.00.

HISTORY OF THE TOWN OF SUNDERLAND, which originally embraced . . . Montague & Leverett. With Genealogies. By J. M. Smith. 1899. 696p.
P5-MA0022 — $71.50.

HISTORY OF THE TOWN OF SUTTON, 1704-1876, incl. Grafton until 1735; Millbury until 1813; and Parts of Northbridge, Upton & Auburn. By W. A. Benedict & H. A. Tracy. 1878. 837p.
P5-MA0296 — $83.00.

HISTORY OF THE TOWN OF SUTTON, Vol. II, 1876-1950. Comp. by the Town Hist. Comm., John C. Dudley, Chair. 1952. 634p.
P5-MA0472 — $65.00.

SUTTON, MASSCHUSETTS, VITAL RECORDS TO THE YEAR 1850. 1907. 478p
P27540000 — $72.00.

SWAMPSCOTT: Historical Sketches of the Town. By Waldo Thompson. 1885. 241p.
P5-MA0497 — $34.50.

HISTORY OF SWANSEA, 1667-1917. By Otis O. Wright. 1917. 248p.
P5-MA0265 — $31.00.

SWANSEA FAMILY RECORDS. Extr. from above. 55p.
P5-MA0266A — $11.00.

RECORDS OF SWANSEA, MASSACHUSETTS, BOOK A: 1662-1705. 1900. 82p
P27920000 — $42.00.

HISTORY OF TAUNTON. By S. H. Emery. 1893. 768 + 110p.
P5-MA0112 — $91.50.

TAUNTON, MASSACHUSETTS, VITAL RECORDS TO THE YEAR 1850, Vol. I: Births. 1929. 476p
P27930200 — $77.00.

TAUNTON, MASSACHUSETTS, VITAL RECORDS TO THE YEAR 1850, Vol. II: Marriages. 1928. 550p
P27930250 — $87.00.

TAUNTON, MASSACHUSETTS, VITAL RECORDS TO THE YEAR 1850, Vol. III: Deaths. 1929. 237p
P27930230 — $43.00.

STORY OF TEMPLETON. Comp. by Elizabeth W. Lord. 1946. 283p.
P5-MA0498 — $37.00.
ASK NOW OF THE DAYS THAT ARE PAST: A History of the Town of Tewksbury, 1734-1964. Comp. by Harold I. Patten. 1964. 312p.
P5-MA0499 — $39.50.

TEWKSBURY, MASSACHUSETTS, VITAL RECORDS TO THE YEAR 1850. 1912. 246p
P27550000 — $44.00.

RECORDS OF THE TOWN OF TISBURY, Beginning June 29, 1669, and Ending May 16, 1864. 1903. 841p.
P5-MA0500 — $87.00.

TISBURY, MASSACHUSETTS, VITAL RECORDS TO THE YEAR 1850. 1910. 244p
P27565000 — $47.00.

HISTORY OF TOPSFIELD. By G. F. Dow. 1940. 517p.
P5-MA0102 — $55.00.

TOPSFIELD, MASSACHUSETTS, VITAL RECORDS, Vol. I: To 1850. 1903. 258p
P27601000 — $46.00.

TOPSFIELD, MASSACHUSETTS, VITAL RECORDS, Vol. II: 1850-1899. 1916. 251p
P27602000 — $45.00.

HISTORY OF TOWNSEND from the Grant of Hathorn's Farm, 1676-1878. Ithamar B. Sawtelle. 1878. 455p.
P5-MA0326 — $45.00.

TRURO (Barnstable Co.) Births, 1850-1884. Comp. by W. Alden Burrell. 1949. 189p.
P5-MA0503 — $22.00.

TRURO (Barnstable Co.) Deaths, 1850-1885. Comp. by Mrs W. Alden Burrell. 1950. 124p.
P5-MA0501 — $16.50.

TRURO (Barnstable Co.) Marriage Records, 1850-1899. Comp. by Mrs W. Alden Burrell. 1950. 125p.
P5-MA0502 — $17.00.

TRURO, Cape Cod: Landmarks & Seamarks. By S. Rich. 1883. 580p.
P5-MA0203 — $63.00.

VITAL RECORDS OF THE TOWN OF TRURO, MASSACHUSETTS to the end of the year 1849. 1933. 480 + xiii p.
P5-MA3003 — $49.50.

UPTON, Massachusetts: 1735-1935. 1935. 194p.
P5-MA10029 — $29.50.

Massachusetts, cont.

UXBRIDGE, MASSACHUSETTS, VITAL RECORDS TO THE YEAR 1850. 1916. 420p
P27590000 — $69.00.

WABAN: EARLY DAY, 1681-1918. By Isabel L. Strong. 1944. 294p.
P5-MA0487 — $41.00.

WACHUSETT: Wajuset Gatherings from Then and When. By Warren M. Sinclair. 1995, 2000. 193p.
P5-MA0566 — $25.00.

HISTORY OF WAKEFIELD (Middlesex Co.) Wm. E. Eaton, with the History Committee. 1944. 263p.
P5-MA0361 — $37.00.

HISTORY OF WALPOLE, from its earliest times. I. N. Lewis. 1905. 217p.
P5-MA0103 — $32.00.

STORY OF WALPOLE, 1724-1924: A Narrative History. By Willard de Lue. 1925. vii + 374p.
P5-MA0473 — $44.00.

WALPOLE, MASSACHUSETTS, VITAL RECORDS TO THE YEAR 1850. 1902. 216p
P27599000 — $40.00.

WALTHAM AS A PRECINCT OF WATERTOWN & as a Town, 1630-1884. By Edmund L. Sanderson. 1936. 168p.
P5-MA0506 — $21.50.

WALTHAM PAST & PRESENT, & its Industries, with an Historical Sketch of Watertown from its Settlement in 1630 to the Incorporation of Waltham, 1738. By Charles A. Nelson. 1879. 152p.
P5-MA0505 — $22.50.

WALTHAM, MASSACHUSETTS, VITAL RECORDS TO THE YEAR 1850. 1904. 298p
P27600000 — $52.00.

EARLY GRANTS & INCORPOR-ATION OF THE TOWN OF WARE. Edw. H. Gilbert. 1891. 58p.
P5-MA0558 — $12.00.

HISTORY OF WARE. By Arthur Chase. 1911. 293p.
P5-MA0507 — $39.50.

HISTORY OF THE TOWN OF WARWICK, from its First Settlement to 1854. Brought down to (1873) by others. With appendix. By Jonathan Blake. 1873. 240p.
P5-MA0474 — $29.50.

WARWICK, Biography of a Town, 1763-1963. Charles A. Morse. 1963. 288p.
P5-MA0488 — $39.00.

GENEALOGIES OF THE FAM-ILIES & DESCENDANTS OF THE EARLY SETTLERS OF WATERTOWN, Incl. Waltham & Weston; to which is Appended the Early History of the Town. By Henry Bond. 2nd ed. 1860. 1094p, 2 vols. in 1.
P5-MA0330 — $98.00.

GREAT LITTLE WATERTOWN, 1630-1930, a Tercentary History. By G. Frederick Robinson & Ruth Robinson Wheeler. 1930. 150p. + 52 illus.
P5-MA0508 — $32.00.

WATERTOWN RECORDS: The First Book and Supplement of Births, Deaths, and Marriages 1894. 460p
P27935000 — $73.00.

WATERTOWN RECORDS comprising the third book of town proceedings and the second book of births, marriages, and deaths to the end of 1737. 1900. 517p.
P27592000 — $74.00.

WATERTOWN RECORDS comprising the fourth book of town proceedings and the second book of births, marriages, and deaths from 1738 to 1882. 273p.
P27592100 — $48.00.

NOW AND THEN: A WEBSTER SCRAP-BOOK, 1832-1932. 1932. 141p.
P5-MA9999 — $26.00.

HISTORY OF THE TOWN OF WELLESLEY. By Joseph E. Fiske. 1917. 92p.
P5-MA0509 — $17.50.

HISTORY OF WENHAM, Civil & Ecclesiastical, from its Settlement in 1639 to 1860. M. O. Allen. 1860. 220p.
P5-MA0216 — $26.00.

NOTES ON WENHAM HISTORY, 1643-1943. Comp. by Adeline P. Cole. 1943. 157p.
P5-MA0475 — $25.00.

HISTORY OF WESTBOROUGH: Part I, Early History; Part II, Later History. By Heman P. DeForest & Edw. C. Bates. 1891. 504p.
P5-MA0460 — $54.50.

THE HUNDREDTH TOWN: GLIMPSES OF LIFE IN WESTBOROUGH, 1717-1817. By Harriette M. Forbes. 1889. 209p.
P5-MA0476 — $27.50.

WESTBOROUGH, MASSA-CHUSETTS, VITAL RECORDS TO THE YEAR 1850. 258p.
P27612000 — $46.00.

WESTFIELD and its Historical Influences, 1669-1919: the Life of an Early Town, with a Survey of Events in New England & Bordering Regions to which it was Related in Colonial & Revolutionary Times, 2-vol. set. By Rev. John H. Lockwood. 1922. 2 vols., 621+506p.
P5-MA0510 — $105.00/set.

WESTFIELD and its Historical Influences . . ., Vol. I. 1922. 621p.
P5-MA0510A — $59.50.

WESTFIELD and its Historical Influences . . ., Vol. II. 1922. 506p.
P5-MA0510B — $59.50.

HISTORY OF THE TOWN OF WESTFORD IN THE COUNTY OF MIDDLESEX, 1659-1883. By E. A. Hodgman. 1883. 494p.
P5-MA0104 — $52.00.
HISTORY OF WESTMINSTER, from 1728-1893, with a Biog. and Gen. Reg. Of its Principal Families. By W. S. Heywood. 1893. 963p.
P5-MA0105 — $98.00.

HISTORY OF THE TOWN OF WESTON, 1630-1890. By Col. Daneil S. Lamson. 1913. 214p.
P5-MA0511 — $34.50.

TOWN OF WESTON Births, Deaths, & Marriages, 1707-1850; Gravestones, 1703-1900; Church Records, 1709-1825. Ed. by Mary F. Peirce. 1901. 649p.
P5-MA0244 — $65.00.

WESTON, MASSACHUSETTS, VITAL RECORDS TO THE YEAR 1850. 1901. 649pp.
P27610000 — $93.00.

HISTORY OF WEYMOUTH, VOLS I & II: HISTORICAL. 1923. 996p., 2 vols in 1.
P5-MA0106 — $97.50.

HISTORY OF WEYMOUTH, VOLS III & IV: GENEALOGY . . . hundreds of families of the 17th & 18th centuries, down to the 5th or 6th generations. G. W. Chamberlain. 1923. 849p.
P5-MA0421 — $85.00.

WEYMOUTH, MASSACHUSETTS, VITAL RECORDS TO THE YEAR 1850. 1910. 359 + 376p
P27620000 — $133.00.

HISTORY OF THE TOWN OF WHATELY, Incl. Events from the 1st Planting of Hatfield, 1661-1899. By J. M. Crafts. 1899. 636p.
P5-MA0107 — $66.00.

HISTORY OF THE TOWN OF WHATELY, including a Narrative of Leading Events from the First Planting of Hayfield, 1660-1871. With family genealogies. By J.H. Temple. 1872. 331p.
P5-MA0489 — $44.00.

HISTORICAL ADDRESS, Delivered at the Centennial Celebration of the Incorporation of the Town of Wilbraham. Rufus P. Stebbins. 1864. 317p.
P5-MA0458 — $42.50.

HISTORY OF WILBRAHAM. By Chauncey E. Peck. 1913. 469p.
P5-MA0468 — $49.50.

ORIGINS OF WILLIAMSTOWN. By Arthur L. Perry. Repr. of 2nd ed. 1896. 650p.
P5-MA0418 — $65.00.

WILLIAMSTOWN & WILLIAMS COLLEGE. By Arthur Latham Perry. 1899. 847p.
P5-MA0490 — $87.00.

WILLIAMSTOWN, MASSACHUSETTS, VITAL RECORDS TO THE YEAR 1850. 1907. 173p
P27630000 — $34.00.

WILLIAMSTOWN: The First Two Hundred Years, 1753-1953. 1953. 458p.
P5-MA0343 — $48.00.

WILMINGTON, MASSACHUSETTS, VITAL RECORDS TO THE YEAR 1850. 1898. 255p
P27950000 — $44.00.

HISTORY OF THE TOWN OF WINCHENDON, Worcester Co., from the Grant of Ipswich Canada in 1735. Rev. A.P. Marvin. 1868. 528p.
P5-MA0424 — $55.00.

WINCHENDON, MASSACHUSETTS, VITAL RECORDS TO THE YEAR 1850. 1919. 223p
P27635000 — $41.00.

HISTORY OF WINTHROP, 1630-1952. By W.H. Clark. 1952. 313p.
P5-MA0029B — $36.00.

HISTORY OF WOBURN, Middlesex Co., from the Grant of its Territory to Charlestown in 1640 to the Year 1860. Samuel Sewall. 1868. 677p.
P5-MA0327 — $65.00.

LEGENDS OF WOBURN, 1642-1892. Now First Written and Preserved in Collected Form . . . [with] Chrono-Indexical History of Woburn. By Parker L. Converse. 1892. 174p.
P5-MA0479 — $29.50.

LEGENDS OF WOBURN, 1642-1892. Second Series. By Parker L. Converse. 1896. 252p.
P5-MA0478 — $37.00.
WOBURN MARRIAGES, from 1640 to 1873; Pt. III of Woburn Records of Births, Deaths and Marriages. By Edw. F. Johnson. 1891. 338p.
P5-MA0492 — $41.00.

WOBURN RECORDS from 1640-1873, Parts 1 & 2, Births and Deaths & Epitaphs. By Edward F. Johnson. 1890. 297 + 218 + 160p.
P5-MA3006 — $67.00.

WOBURN, MASSACHUSETTS, VITAL RECORDS TO THE YEAR 1850: Births, Deaths, and Marriages from 1640 to 1873, and a transcript of epitaphs in Woburn First and Second Burial Grounds. 1890. 297 + 218 + 338 + 160p
P27970000 — $149.00.

STORY OF WORCESTER, MASSACHUSETTS. By Thomas F. O'Flynn 1877. 392p
P27985000 — $64.00.

WORCESTER, MASSACHUSETTS, VITAL RECORDS TO THE YEAR 1850. 1894. 527p
P27650000 — $78.00.

HISTORY OF WORCESTER COUNTY, Embracing a Comprehensive History of the County from its First Settlement to the Present Time with a History of Cities and Towns. 1879. 662 + 710p.
P5-MA0334 — $139.00.

HISTORY OF WORCESTER COUNTY, 3-vol. set. 1924. 3 vols., 1371p.
P5-MA0516 — $135.00/set.

HISTORY OF WORCESTER COUNTY, Vol. I. 1924.
P5-MA0516A — $50.00.

HISTORY OF WORCESTER COUNTY, Vol. II. 1924.
P5-MA0516B — $50.00.

HISTORY OF WORCESTER COUNTY, Vol. III. 1924.
P5-MA0516C — $50.00.

HISTORY OF WORCESTER COUNTY, with Biographical Sketches of Many of its Pioneers & Prominent Men, 2-vol. set. 1889. 2 vols., 1762p.
P5-MA0517 — $175.00/set.

HISTORY OF WORCESTER COUNTY . . ., Vol. I. 1889.
P5-MA0517A — $91.50.

HISTORY OF WORCESTER COUNTY . . ., Vol. II. 1889.
P5-MA0517B — $91.50.

HISTORY OF WORCESTER, from its Earliest Settlement to September, 1836, with Various Notices Relating to the History of Worcester County. By Wm. Lincoln. 1837. 383p.
P5-MA0493 — $46.00.

INDEX TO THE PROBATE RECORDS OF WORCESTER, MASSACHUSETTS, July 1731 to July 1, 1881. 1999. 1567p
P26720000 — $239.00.

INDEX TO THE PROBATE RECORDS OF WORCESTER, MASSACHUSETTS: July 1, 1881 to July 1, 1897, with supplement to January 1, 1898. By George H. Harlow 1898. 599 + 35p
P26730000 — $117.00.

HISTORY OF THE TOWN OF WORTHINGTON, from its first settlement to 1874. J. C. Rice. . 123p.
P5-MA0213 — $20.00.

Massachusetts, cont.

WRENTHAM, MASSACHUSETTS, VITAL RECORDS TO THE YEAR 1850. 1910. 518p
P27655000 — $77.00.

GRAVESTONE RECORDS IN THE ANCIENT CEMETERY & THE WOODSIDE CEMETERY IN YARMOUTH. Comp. by G. E. Brown. 1906. 46p.
P5-MA0307 — $10.00.

HISTORY OF OLD YARMOUTH, Comprising the Present Towns of Yarmouth & Dennis. By C. F. Swift. 1884. 281p.
P5-MA0328 — $35.00.

Michigan

CYCLOPEDIA OF MICHIGAN, Historical & Biographical, Comprising a Synopsis of General History of the State & Biographical Sketches . . . 1890. 346p.
P5-MI0067 — $45.00.

GAZETTEER OF THE STATE OF MICHIGAN, in Three Parts. By John T. Blois. 1840. 418p.
P5-MI0004 — $44.00.

HISTORY OF MICHIGAN, 4-vol. set Charles Moore. 1915. 4 vols., 2297p.
P5-MI0070 — $199.00/set.

HISTORY OF MICHIGAN, Vol. I. By Charles Moore. 1915.
P5-MI0070A — $57.50.

HISTORY OF MICHIGAN, Vol. II. By Charles Moore. 1915.
P5-MI0070B — $57.50.

HISTORY OF MICHIGAN, Vol. III. By Charles Moore. 1915.
P5-MI0070C — $57.50.

HISTORY OF MICHIGAN, Vol. IV. By Charles Moore. 1915.
P5-MI0070D — $57.50.

HISTORY OF THE NORTHERN PENINSULA OF MICHIGAN & ITS PEOPLE: Its Mining, Lumber & Agricultural Industries, 3-vol. set. Alvah L. Sawyer. 1911. 3 vols., 1552p.
P5-MI0066 — $149.00/set.

HISTORY OF THE NORTHERN PENINSULA OF MICHIGAN & ITS PEOPLE . . ., Vol. I By Alvah L. Sawyer. 1911.
P5-MI0066A — $59.00.

HISTORY OF THE NORTHERN PENINSULA OF MICHIGAN & ITS PEOPLE . . ., Vol. II. 1911.
P5-MI0066B — $59.00.

HISTORY OF THE NORTHERN PENINSULA OF MICHIGAN & ITS PEOPLE . . ., Vol. III. 1911.
P5-MI0066C — $59.00.

MEMORIAL [BIOGRAPHICAL] RECORDS OF THE NORTHERN PENINSULA OF MICHIGAN. 1895. 642p.
P5-MI0068 — $67.00.

PICTORIAL HISTORY OF BARNS AND OTHER FARM STRUCTURES IN MICHIGAN. By Mark Pickvet. 2004. 341p.
P5-MI0074 — $45.00.

HISTORY OF ALLEGAN & BARRY COUNTIES. 1880. 512p.
P5-MI0011A — $54.50.

PORTRAIT & BIOGRAPHICAL ALBUM OF BARRY & EATON COUNTIES, Containing Full Page Portraits & Biographical Sketches of Prominent & Representative Citizens of the County. 1891. 832p.
P5-MI0017 — $87.00.

OAK HILL CEMETERY RECORDS, Battle Creek, Calhoun. 1946. 638p., typescript.
P5-MI0018 — $65.00.

CITIES OF THE BAY, ILLUSTRATED [BAY CO.]. 1888. 64p.
P5-MI0071 — $19.00.

HISTORY OF BAY COUNTY & Representative Citizens. 1905. 726p.
P5-MI0072 — $79.00.

HISTORY OF BAY COUNTY, with Illustrations & Biographical Sketches of Some of its Prominent Men & Pioneers. 1883. 281p.
P5-MI0019 — $37.00.

HISTORY OF BERRIEN & VAN BUREN COUNTIES, with Illustrations & Biographical Sketches of its Prominent Men & Pioneers. 1880. 548p.
P5-MI0005 — $56.50.

TWENTIETH CENTURY HISTORY OF BERRIEN COUNTY. By Orville W. Coolidge. 1906. 1007p.
P5-MI0020 — $99.50.

HISTORY OF BRANCH COUNTY, with Illustrations & Biographical Sketches of Prominent Men & Pioneers. With every-name index. 1879. 347p.+ illus. + 180p. index.
P5-MI0061 — $59.00.

PORTRAIT & BIOGRAPHICAL ALBUM OF BRANCH COUNTY, Containing Full Page Portraits & Biographical Sketches of Prominent & Representative Citizens of the County. 1888. 653p.
P5-MI0022 — $68.00.

TWENTIETH CENTURY HISTORY & BIOGRAPHICAL RECORD OF BRANCH COUNTY. By Rev. Henry P. Collin. 1906. 879p.
P5-MI0021 — $91.50.

PORTRAIT & BIOGRAPHICAL ALBUM OF CLINTON & SHIAWASSEE COS., Containing Full Page Portraits & Biographical Sketches of Prominent & Representative Citizens of the County. 1891. 1001p.
P5-MI0023 — $99.00.

HISTORY OF DETROIT & MICHIGAN, or, the Metropolis Illustrated: Chronological Cyclopedia of the Past & Present, Including a Full Record of Territorial Days in Michigan & the Annals of Wayne Co. By Silas Farmer. 1884. 1024p.
P5-MI0024 — $99.50.

PIONEER HISTORY OF EATON COUNTY, 1833-1866. By David Strange. 1923. 192p.
P5-MI0063 — $31.50.

STORY OF FRANKFORT. By John H. Howard. 1930. 176p.
P5-MI0025 — $21.50.

GENESEE COUNTY CEMETERY RECORDS. 1946. 232p., typescript.
P5-MI0027 — $25.00.

PORTRAIT & BIOGRAPHICAL ALBUM OF GENESEE, LAPEER & TUSCOLA COUNTIES, Containing Biographical Sketches of Prominent & Representative Citizens of the Counties. 1892. 1062p.
P5-MI0026 — $101.50.

**HISTORIC GRAND HAVEN &
OTTAWA COUNTY.** By Leo C. Lillie.
1931. 414p.
P5-MI0064 — $49.00.

GRAND RAPIDS & KENT COUNTY:
Historical Account of their Progress
from First Settlement to the Present
Time [1918], 2-vol. set. 1918. 2 vols.,
1105p.
P5-MI0010 — $109.00/set.

**GRAND RAPIDS & KENT COUNTY
. . ., Vol. I.** 1918.
P5-MI0010A — $59.00.

**GRAND RAPIDS & KENT COUNTY
. . ., Vol. II.** 1918.
P5-MI0010B — $59.00.

**HISTORY OF THE CITY OF
GRAND RAPIDS.** By Albert Baxter.
1891. 845p.
P5-MI0006 — $87.00.

**MEMORIALS OF THE GRAND
RIVER VALLEY. With biographical
sketches. [GRAND RAPIDS]** By
Franklin Everett. 1878. 545 + 127p.
P5-MI0011B — $67.00.

**HISTORY OF HILLSDALE
COUNTY, with Illustrations & Bio-
graphical Sketches of Some of its
Prominent Men & Pioneers.** 1879. 334p.
P5-MI0029 — $43.50.

**HISTORY OF INGHAM & EATON
COUNTIES, with Illustrations &
Biographical Sketches of their Promi-
nent Men & Pioneers.** By Sam'l W.
Durant. 1880. 586p.
P5-MI0031 — $61.50.

**PIONEER HISTORY OF
INGHAM COUNTY. Vol. I.** Comp.
by Mrs. F.L. Adams. 1923. 856p.
P5-MI0030 — $89.50.

**PORTRAIT & BIOGRAPHICAL
ALBUM OF ISABELLA COUNTY,
Containing Portraits & Sketches of
Prominent & Representative Citizens
of the County.** 1884. 590p.
P5-MI0032 — $61.50.

**HISTORY OF JACKSON
COUNTY, Together with Sketches
of its Cities, Villages & Townships . .
. Civil, Military & Political History; &
Biographies of Representative
Citizens.** 1881. 1156p.
P5-MI0033 — $109.50.

**PORTRAIT & BIOGRAPHICAL
ALBUM OF JACKSON COUNTY,
Containing Full Page Portraits &
Biographical Sketches of Prominent
& Representative Citizens of the
County.** 1888. 885p.
P5-MI0034 — $91.00.

**HISTORY OF KALAMAZOO
COUNTY, with Illustrations &
Biographical Sketches.** 1880. 552p.
P5-MI0007 — $56.50.

**PORTRAIT & BIOGRAPHICAL
RECORD OF KALAMAZOO,
ALLEGAN & VAN BUREN
COUNTIES Containing Sketches of
Prominent & Representative Citizens.**
1892. 950p.
P5-MI0035 — $97.00.

**MEMORIES OF MANITOU
ISLAND, LAKE SUPERIOR,
KEWEENAW CO., MICHIGAN.** By
L.T. Fadner. 2003. 144 + x p.
P5-MI0075 — $25.00.

**HISTORY OF LAPEER COUNTY,
with Illustrations & Biographical
Sketches of some of its Prominent
Men & Pioneers.** 1894. 211p.
P5-MI0073 — $32.00.

**HISTORY & BIOGRAPHICAL
RECORD OF LENAWEE CO.,
Containing a History of the Organi-
zation & Early Settlement of the
County, together with a Biographical
Record of Many of the Oldest &
Most Prominent Settlers & Present
[1879] Residents. 2-vol set.** W.A.
Whitney & R.I. Bonner. 1879. 2 vols.,
536 + 491p.
P5-MI0037 — $99.00/set.

**HISTORY & BIOGRAPHICAL
RECORD OF LENAWEE CO . . .,
Vol. I.** 1879. 536p.
P5-MI0037A — $54.50.

**HISTORY & BIOGRAPHICAL
RECORD OF LENAWEE CO . . .,
Vol. II.** 1879. 491p.
P5-MI0037B — $54.50.

**PORTRAIT & BIOGRAPHICAL
ALBUM OF LENAWEE COUNTY,
Containing Full Page Portraits &
Biographical Sketches of Prominent
& Representative Citizens of the
County.** 1888. 1280p.
P5-MI0036 — $119.00.

**HISTORY OF THE EARLY LIFE
& BUSINESS INTERESTES OF
THE VILLAGE & TOWNSHIP OF
LESLIE, INGHAM CO.** Comp. & arr.
by Mina A Vliet et al. 1914. 120p.
P5-MI0038 — $17.50.

**HISTORY OF LIVINGSTON
COUNTY, with Illustrations &
Biographical Sketches of its Promi-
nent Men & Pioneers.** 1880. 462p.
P5-MI0039 — $51.00.

ANNALS OF FORT MACKINAC.
Revised edition. By Dwight H. Kelton.
1883. 129p., paper.
P5-MI0040 — $17.50.

**HISTORIC MACKINAC: Historical,
Picturesque & Legendary Features of
the Mackinac Country, 2-vol. set.** Edwin
O. Wood. 1918. 2 vols., 697 + 775p.
P5-MI0041 — $145.00/set.

HISTORIC MACKINAC . . ., Vol. I.
1918. 697p.
P5-MI0041A — $77.00.

HISTORIC MACKINAC . . ., Vol. II.
1918. 775p.
P5-MI0041B — $77.00.

**HISTORY OF MACOMB
COUNTY, Containing an Account of
its Settlement, Growth, Development;
an Extensive & Minute Sketch of its
cities, Towns & Villages; Biographical Sketches, Portraits of Prominent
Men & Early Settlers; etc.** 1882. 923p.
P5-MI0042 — $94.50.

**HISTORY OF MANISTEE (&
MASON) COUNTY, with Illustrations & Biographical Sketches of
some of its Prominent Men & Pioneers.** 1882. 154p.
P5-MI0008 — $25.00.

**HISTORY OF MANISTEE CO.,
with Illustrations & Biographical
Sketches of some of its Prominent
Men & Pioneers.** 1882. 88p.
P5-MI0069 — $23.00.

**HISTORY OF MONROE
COUNTY. With biographical
sketches.** 1890. 653p.
P5-MI0043 — $69.50.

**HISTORY OF MONTCALM
COUNTY: Its People, Industries &
Institutions, 2-vol. set** By John W.
Dasef. 1916. 2 vols., 517 + 668p.
P5-MI0044 — $119.00/set.

Michigan, cont.

**HISTORY OF MONTCALM
COUNTY . . ., Vol. I.** 1916. 517p.
P5-MI0044A — $64.50.

**HISTORY OF MONTCALM
COUNTY . . ., Vol. II.** 1916. 668p.
P5-MI0044B — $69.50.

**PORTRAIT & BIOGRAPHICAL
RECORD OF MUSKEGON &
OTTAWA COUNTIES, Containing
Biographical Sketches of Prominent
& Representative Citizens & the
Presidents of the U.S.** 1893. 577p.
P5-MI0065 — $61.50.

**HISTORY OF MUSKEGON
COUNTY, with Illustrations & Bio-
graphical Sketches of Some if its
Prominent Men & Pioneers.** 1882. 151p.
P5-MI0045 — $31.00.

**NEWAYGO WHITE PINE HERI-
TAGE: A Pictorial History of the
Lumbering Era along the Muskegon
River in Newaygo Co., 1837-1899.** By
Robert I. Thompson. 1976. 91p.
P5-MI0012 — $18.00.

**PORTRAIT & BIOGRAPHICAL
ALBUM OF NEWAYGO COUNTY,
Containing Portraits and Biographical Sketches of Prominent and
Representative Citizens. (Reprinted
without the first 174 pages which
contained biographies of Presidents
of the U.S. and governors of Mich.)**
1884. 478p.
P5-MI0013 — $53.00.

**BIOGRAPHICAL SKETCHES OF
OF LEADING CITIZENS OF
OAKLAND COUNTY.** 1903. 681p.
P5-MI0048 — $71.50.

**HISTORY OF OAKLAND COUNTY,
with Illustrations Descriptive of its
Scenery.** 1877. 334 + xviii p.
P5-MI0047 — $44.00.

**PORTRAIT & BIOGRAPHICAL
ALBUM OF OAKLAND COUNTY,
Containing Full-Page Portraits &
Biographical Sketches of Prominent
& Representative Citizens of the
County.** 1891. 964p.
P5-MI0046 — $98.50.

**OCEANA COUNTY PIONEERS &
BUSINESS MEN of Today [1890]:
History, Biography, Statistics &
Humorous Incidents.** By L.M.
Hartwick & W.H. Tuller. 1890. 432p.
P5-MI0049 — $48.00.

**HISTORY OF OTTAWA COUNTY,
with Illustrations & Biographical
Sketches of Some if its Prominent
Men & Pioneers.** 1882. 133p.
P5-MI0050 — $27.00.

**HISTORY OF SAGINAW COUNTY,
Together with Sketches of its Cities,
Villages & Toawnships . . . Civil,
Military & Political History; Portraits
of Prominent Persons; Biographies of
Representative Citizens.** 1881. 960p.
P5-MI0052 — $98.00.

**HISTORY OF SAGINAW
COUNTY: Historical, Commercial,
Biographical, Profusely Illustrated.**
By James Cooke Mills. 1918. 801p.
P5-MI0051 — $84.50.

**EARLY MEMORIES OF SAUGA-
TUCK, 1830-1930.** By May Francis
Heath. 1930. 225p.
P5-MI0056 — $31.50.

**HISTORY OF SHIAWASSEE &
CLINTON COUNTIES, with Illustrations & Biographical Sketches of
their Prominent Men & Pioneers.**
1880. 541p.
P5-MI0057 — $61.00.

**BIOGRAPHICAL MEMOIRS OF
ST CLAIR COUNTY.** 1903. 695p.
P5-MI0003 — $69.50.

**HISTORY OF ST CLAIR
COUNTY, Containing an Account of
its Settlement, Growth &
Development . . . its Cities, Towns &
Villages . . . Biographical Sketches,
Portraits of Prominent Men & Early
Settlers . . .** 1883. 790p.
P5-MI0053 — $84.50.

**ST CLAIR COUNTY, Its History &
its People: Narrative Account of its
Historical Progress & its Principal
Interests. Vol. I only, History.** By
Wm. Lee Jenks. 1912. 2 vols, 904p.
P5-MI0062 — $95.00/set.

**HISTORY OF ST JOSEPH COUNTY,
with Illustrations Descriptive of its
Scenery.** 1877. 232p.
P5-MI0055 — $34.00.

**PORTRAIT & BIOGRAPHICAL
ALBUM OF SAINT JOSEPH
COUNTY, Containing Full Page
Portraits & Biographical Sketches of
Prominent & Representative Citizens
of the County.** 1889. 609p.
P5-MI0054 — $65.00.

**HISTORY OF VAN BUREN
COUNTY: A Narrative Account of
its Historical Progress, its People, &
its Principal Interest, 2-vol. set.** By
Oran W. Rowland. 1912. 2 vols., 1158p.
P5-MI0009 — $115.00/set.

**HISTORY OF VAN BUREN
COUNTY . . ., Vol. I.** 1912.
P5-MI0009A — $59.50.

**HISTORY OF VAN BUREN
COUNTY . . ., Vol. II.** 1912.
P5-MI0009B — $59.50.

**HISTORY OF WASHTENAW
COUNTY, Together with Sketches
of its Cities, Villages & Townships
. . . Civil, Military & Political History;
Portraits of Prominent Persons; &
Biographies of Representative Citi-
zens.** 1881. 1452p.
P5-MI0058 — $139.00.

**LANDMARKS OF WAYNE
COUNTY & DETROIT. With
biographical & personal sketches,
2-vol. set.** By Robert B. Ross & Geo. B,
Catlin. 1898. 872 + 320p.
P5-MI0059 — $116.50/set.

**LANDMARKS OF WAYNE
COUNTY & DETROIT . . ., Vol. I.**
1898. 872p.
P5-MI0059A — $90.00.

**LANDMARKS OF WAYNE
COUNTY & DETROIT . . ., Vol. II.**
1898. 320p.
P5-MI0059B — $34.50.

**LANDMARKS OF WAYNE
COUNTY & DETROIT. With
biographical & personal sketches,
Vol. I** By Robert B. Ross & Geo. B,
Catlin. 1898. 872p.
P5-MI0059A — $90.00.

**WAYNE COUNTY HISTORICAL
& PIONEER SOCIETY CHRONO-
GRAPHY of Notable Events in the
History of the Northwest Territory &
Wayne County, 1651-1890 . . . with
Biographical Sketches of the Early
Explorers & Pioneers.** By Frederick
Carlisle. 1890. 484p.
P5-MI0060 — $54.50.

STORY OF YPSILANTI. By Harvey C. Colburn. 1923. 327p. **P5-MI0016 — $41.00.**

Minnesota

COMPENDIUM OF HISTORY & BIOGRAPHY OF CENTRAL & NORTHERN MINNESOTA, Containing a History of the State of Minnesota . . . and a Compendium of Biography. 1904. 828p. **P5-MN0040 — $86.50.**

COMPENDIUM OF HISTORY & BIOGRAPHY OF NORTHERN MINNESOTA: containing a History of the State of Minnesota. 1902. 1039p. **P5-MN0008 — $99.50.**

ENCYCLOPEDIA OF BIOGRAPHY OF MINNESOTA [AND] HISTORY OF MINNESOTA, Vol. I. By Judge Charles E. Flandrau. 1900. 497p. **P5-MN0064A — $55.50.**

HISTORY OF THE FOURTH REGIMENT of Minnesota Infantry Volunteers during the Great Rebellion, 1861-65. By Alonzo L. Brown. 1892. 592p. **P5-MNCW02 — $63.50.**

HISTORY OF THE MINNESOTA VALLEY, including the Explorers & Pioneers of Minnesota & History of the Sioux Massacre. Rev. Edward D. Neill & Charles S. Bryant. 1882. 1016p. **P5-MN0007 — $99.50.**

HISTORY OF THE SWEDISH-AMERICANS OF MINNESOTA, 3-vol. set. A.E. Strand. 1910. 3 vols., 1147p. **P5-MN0011 — $115.00/set.**

HISTORY OF THE SWEDISH-AMERICANS OF MINNESOTA, Vol. I. 1910. **P5-MN0011A — $45.00.**

HISTORY OF THE SWEDISH-AMERICANS OF MINNESOTA, Vol. II. 1910. **P5-MN0011B — $45.00.**

HISTORY OF THE SWEDISH-AMERICANS OF MINNESOTA, Vol. III. 1910. **P5-MN0011C — $45.00.**

HISTORY OF THE UPPER MISSISSIPPI VALLEY, including Explorers & Pioneers of Minnesota, Outlines of the History of Minnesota, Exploration & Development Above the Falls of St Anthony. By Rev. Edward D. Neill. 1881. 717p. **P5-MN0012 — $74.50.**

HISTORY OF THE WELSH IN MINNESOTA, Foreston & Lime Springs, Iowa, Gathered by the Old Settlers. 1895. 306p. **P5-MN0045 — $39.50.**

MEMORIAL RECORD OF SOUTH-WESTERN MINNESOTA. [Biographical sketches of prominent residents]. 1897. 560p. **P5-MN0010 — $59.50.**

MINNESOTA & DAKOTAH in Letters Descriptive of a Tour through the North-West in the Autumn of 1856. By C.C. Andrews. 1857. 216p. **P5-MN0043 — $31.00.**

MINNESOTA IN THE CIVIL & INDIAN WARS, 1861-1865, Vol. I: Narratives & Rosters of Minn. State Regiments, Companies and Batteries. 1890. 843p. **P5-MN0050B — $85.00.**

MINNESOTA IN THE CIVIL & INDIAN WARS, 1861-1865, Vol. II: Official Reports & Correspondence on Battles, Campaigns, Expeditions, Skirmishes, etc. 1899, Second ed. 634p. **P5-MN0034B — $65.00.**

MINNESOTANS IN THE CIVIL & INDIAN WARS, An Index to the Rosters in "Minnesota in the Civil & Indian Wars, 1861-1865." Includes more than 25,000 Minnesotans who participated in both wars. Comp. under the direction of Irene B. Warming 1936. **P5-MN0035B — $49.00.**

HISTORY OF ANOKA COUNTY & the Towns of Champlin & Dayton in Hennepin Co. By Albert M. Goodrich. 1905. 320p. **P5-MN0013 — $38.50.**

PIONEER HISTORY OF BECKER COUNTY, including a Brief Account of its Natural History. By Alvin H. Wilcox. 1907. 757p. **P5-MN0014 — $77.00.**

DAKOTA COUNTY, Its Past & Present, Geographical, Statistical & Historical, together with a General View of the State. With 1998 index by Dakota County Historical Society. By W.H. Mitchell. 1868. 174 + 52p. **P5-MN0046 — $23.50.**

HISTORY OF DAKOTA COUNTY & the City of Hastings, including the Explorers & Pioneers of Minnesota. By Rev. Edward D. Neill. 1881. 551p. **P5-MN0004 — $58.00.**

HISTORY OF DAKOTA COUNTY. Vol. I of "History of Dakota & Goodhue Counties," complete for Dakota Co. 1910. 662p. **P5-MN0034A — $68.00.**

HISTORY OF DOUGLAS & GRANT COUNTIES, Their People, Industries & Institutions, 2-vol. set. Constant Larson. 1916. 2 vols., 509 + 693p. **P5-MN0035A — $115.00/set.**

HISTORY OF DOUGLAS & GRANT COUNTIES . . ., Vol. I. 509p. **P5-MN0035A1 — $53.00.**

HISTORY OF DOUGLAS & GRANT COUNTIES . . ., Vol. II. 1916. 693p. **P5-MN0035A2 — $69.50.**

MEMORIAL HISTORY OF THE COUNTIES OF FARIBAULT, MARTIN, WATONWAN & JACKSON. 1895. 766p. **P5-MN0047 — $79.00.**

HISTORY OF FILLMORE COUNTY, Including Explorers & Pioneers of Minnesota & the Sioux Massacre of 1862. By Rev. Edward D. Neill & Charles Bryan. 1882. 626p. **P5-MN0016 — $65.00.**

HISTORY OF FREEBORN COUNTY. 1911. 883p. **P5-MN0017 — $89.00.**

GILLFORD. Biographical Sketch of People buried in the Gillford Cemetery, Lincoln, Gillford Twp., Wabasha Co. 22p. **P5-MN0002 — $10.00.**

GOODHUE COUNTY, Past & Present. By J.W. Hancock 1893. 349p. **P5-MN0048 — $41.50.**

Minnesota, cont.

HISTORY OF GOODHUE COUNTY, Including a Sketch of the Territory & State of Minnesota . . . with Biographical Sketches of Early & Prominent Settlers & Representative Men. 1878. 664p.
P5-MN0049 — **$71.50.**

HISTORY OF GOODHUE COUNTY. 1909. 1074p.
P5-MN0018 — **$105.00.**

HISTORY OF GOODHUE COUNTY. C.A. Rasmussen. 1935. 336p.
P5-MN0050A — **$42.00.**

HISTORY OF HENNEPIN COUNTY & the City of Minneapolis, including the Explorers & Pioneers of Minnesota. By Rev. Edw. D. Neill. 1881. 713p.
P5-MN0005 — **$74.00.**

EARLY HISTORY OF LINCOLN COUNTY, from the Early Writings of Old Pioneers, Historians & Later Writers. By A.E. Taker. 1936. 352p.
P5-MN0019 — **$39.50.**

ILLUSTRATED HISTORY OF LYON COUNTY. By Arthur P. Rose. 1912. 616p.
P5-MN0051A — **$66.50.**

MANKATO: Its First Fifty Years . . . [with] Brief Biographies of Early Settlers & Active Upbuilders of the City, 1852-1902. 1902. 347p.
P5-MN0052A — **$41.50.**

HISTORY OF McLEOD COUNTY. 1917. 862p.
P5-MN0053 — **$89.50.**

CONDENSED HISTORY OF MEEKER CO., 1855-1939. By Frank B. Lamson. 1939. 240 + vii p.
P5-MN0156 — **$33.00.**

RANDOM HISTORICAL SKETCH OF MEEKER COUNTY, from its First Settlement to July 4th, 1876. By A.C. Smith. 1877. 160p.
P5-MN0054 — **$19.50.**

COMPENDIUM OF HISTORY & BIOGRAPHY OF MINNEAPOLIS & HENNEPIN COUNTY. Maj. R.I. Holcombe & W.H. Bingham. 1914. 584p.
P5-MN0022 — **$59.50.**

HALF-CENTURY OF MINNE-APOLIS. Horace B. Hudson. 1908. 569p.
P5-MN0020 — **$59.00.**

HISTORY OF MINNEAPOLIS, Gateway to the Northwest, 3-vol. set. 1923. 3 vols., 711 + 831 + 826p.
P5-MN0055 — **The set: $215.00.**

HISTORY OF MINNEAPOLIS . . ., Vol. I. 1923. 711p.
P5-MN0055A — **$75.50.**

HISTORY OF MINNEAPOLIS . . ., Vol. II. 1923. 831p.
P5-MN0055B — **$75.50.**

HISTORY OF MINNEAPOLIS . . ., Vol. III. 1923. 826p.
P5-MN0055C — **$75.50.**

HISTORY OF MINNESOTA from the Earliest French Explorations to the Present Time [1883]. 5th ed., rev. & enlarged. By Rev. Edw. D. Neill. 1883. 929 + 18p.
P5-MN0042 — **$96.50.**

HISTORY OF THE CITY OF MINNEAPOLIS, 2-vol. set. By Isaac Atwater. 1893. 2 vols., 544 + 466p.
P5-MN0021 — **$97.50/set.**

HISTORY OF THE CITY OF MINNEAPOLIS, Vol. I. 1893. 544p.
P5-MN0021A — **$55.00.**

HISTORY OF THE CITY OF MINNEAPOLIS, Vol. II. 1893. 466p.
P5-MN0021B — **$55.00.**

History of Mower Co., MN. 1884. 610p.
P5-MN0154 — **$62.00.**

HISTORY OF MOWER COUNTY. Ed. by Franklyn Curtiss-Wedge. 1911. 1006p.
P5-MN0006 — **$99.50.**

BIOGRAPHICAL & STATISTICAL HISTORY OF THE COUNTY OF OLMSTED, together with a General View of the State of Minnesota from its Earliest Settlement to [1866]. By W.H. Mitchell. 1866. 132p.
P5-MN0056 — **$26.50.**

HISTORY OF OLMSTED COUNTY, with Sketches of Many of its Pioneers, Citizens, Families & Institutions. Joseph A. Leonard. 1910. 674p.
P5-MN0023 — **$69.50.**

COMPENDIUM OF HISTORY & BIOGRAPHY OF POLK COUNTY. 1916. 486p.
P5-MN0057 — **$54.00.**

HISTORY OF RAMSEY COUNTY & THE CITY OF ST PAUL, Including the Explorers & Pioneers of Minnesota. By Rev. Edw. D. Neill & J.F. Williams. 1881. 650p.
P5-MN0024 — **$67.00.**

ILLUSTRATED ALBUM OF BIOGRAPHY OF THE FAMOUS VALLEY OF THE RED RIVER of the North & the Park Regions, including the Most Fertile & Widely-Known Portions of Minn. & No. Dakota. 1889. 845p.
P5-MN0009 — **$87.00.**

ILLUSTRATED ALBUM OF BIOGRAPHY of the Famous Valley of the Red River of the North and the Park Regions..Containing Biogr. Sketches of Hundreds of Prominent Old Settlers and Representative Citizens . . . 1889. 844p.
P5-MN0051B — **$87.00.**

HISTORY OF RED WING. By Christian A. Rasmussen. 1933. 296p.
P5-MN0065 — **$39.50.**

HISTORY OF REDWOOD COUNTY, 2-vol. set. Comp. by Franklyn Curtiss-Wedge. 1916. 2 vols., 1016p.
P5-MN0068 — **$115.00.**

HISTORY OF REDWOOD COUNTY, Vol. I. 1916.
P5-MN0068A — **$62.50.**

HISTORY OF REDWOOD COUNTY, Vol. II. 1916.
P5-MN0068B — **$62.50.**

HISTORY OF RENVILLE COUNTY, Two-vol. set 1916. 2 vols., 675 + 701p.
P5-MN0025 — **$132.50/set.**

HISTORY OF RENVILLE COUNTY, Vol. I. 1916. 675p.
P5-MN0025A — **$69.50.**

HISTORY OF RENVILLE COUNTY, Vol. II. 1916. 701p.
P5-MN0025B — **$69.50.**

HISTORY OF RICE & STEELE COUNTIES, 2-vol. set. Comp. by Franklyn Curtiss-Wedge, et al. 1910. 2 vols., 1560p.
P5-MN0058 — **$155.00/set.**

HISTORY OF RICE & STEELE COUNTIES, Vol. I. 1910.
P5-MN0058A — **$84.50.**

HISTORY OF RICE & STEELE COUNTIES, Vol. II. 1910.
P5-MN0058B — $84.50.

HISTORY OF RICE COUNTY, including Explorers & Pioneers of Minnesota & Outline History of the State of Minnesota. By Rev. Edw. D. Neill & C.S. Bryant. 1882. 603p.
P5-MN0026 — $63.00.

ILLUSTRATED HISTORY OF THE COUNTIES OF ROCK & PIPESTONE. By Arthur P. Rose. 1911. 802p.
P5-MN0059 — $86.00.

MEET SHIELDSVILLE, the Story of St Patrick's Parish, Shieldsville. By Mary L. Hagerty. 1940. 174p.
P5-MN0061 — $27.00.

HISTORY OF THE ST CROIX VALLEY, 2-vol. set. 1909. 2 vols., 1289p.
P5-MN0052B — $125.00/set.

HISTORY OF THE ST CROIX VALLEY, Vol. I. 1909.
P5-MN0052B1 — $69.50.

HISTORY OF THE ST CROIX VALLEY, Vol. II. 1909.
P5-MN0052B2 — $69.50.

HISTORY OF ST PAUL, with Illustrations & Biographical Sketches of Some of its Prominent Men & Pioneers. 1890. 603 + 224p.
P5-MN0060 — $87.00.

HISTORY OF THE CITY OF ST PAUL & of the County of Ramsey. By J. Fletcher Williams. 1876. 475p.
P5-MN0027 — $49.50.

PAST & PRESENT OF ST PAUL. By W.B. Hennesey. 1906. 814p.
P5-MN0028 — $85.00.

PEN PICTURES OF ST PAUL & Biographical Sketches of Old Settlers, from the Earliest Settlement . . . to the Year 1857. By T.M. Newson. 1886. 746p.
P5-MN0029 — $77.00.

GEOGRAPHICAL & STATISTICAL HISTORY OF STEELE COUNTY, from its Earliest Settlement to [1868]. By W.H. Mitchell. 1868. 110p.
P5-MN0062 — $23.00.

HISTORY OF WABASHA COUNTY, together with Biographical Matter, etc.; also a History of Winona County. 1884. 1314p.
P5-MN0066 — $129.00.

HISTORY OF WABASHA COUNTY. 1920. 781p.
P5-MN0030 — $79.00.

HISTORY OF WASECA COUNTY, from its First Settlement in 1854 to the Close of Year 1904: A Record of Fifty Years, the Story of the Pioneers. By James E. Child. 1905. 848p.
P5-MN0063 — $89.50.

HISTORY OF WASHINGTON COUNTY & the St Croix Valley, including the Explorers & Pioneers of Minnesota. By Rev. Edw. D. Neill & J.F. Williams. 1881. 636p.
P5-MN0031 — $65.00.

WINONA & ITS ENVIRONS ON THE MISSISSIPPI in Ancient & Modern Days. By Lafayette H. Bunnell. 1897. 694p.
P5-MN0064B — $74.00.

HISTORY OF WINONA & OLMSTED COUNTIES. 1883. 1148p.
P5-MN0155 — $115.00.

HISTORY OF WINONA COUNTY, together with Biographical Matter, Statistics, etc. 1883. 951p.
P5-MN0032 — $95.00.

CONDENSED HISTORY OF WRIGHT COUNTY, 1851-1935. 1935. 228p.
P5-MN0003 — $29.50.

HISTORY OF WRIGHT COUNTY, 2-vol. set. 1915. 2 vols., 544 + 567p.
P5-MN0033 — $105.00.

HISTORY OF WRIGHT COUNTY, Vol. I. 1915. 544p.
P5-MN0033A — $55.00.

HISTORY OF WRIGHT COUNTY, Vol. II. 1915. 567p.
P5-MN0033B — $55.00.

ILLUSTRATED HISTORY OF YELLOW MEDICINE COUNTY, MINNESOTA. By Arthur P. Rose. 1914. 562 + 50 p.
P5-MN0153 — $74.00.

Mississippi

OFFICIAL & STATISTICAL REGISTER OF THE STATE OF MISSISSIPPI, Military History only. By Dunbar Rowland. 1908. 565p.
P5-MS0003A — $61.00.

BIOGRAPHICAL & HISTORICAL MEMOIRS OF MISSISSIPPI . . . an Authentic & Comprehensive Account of the Chief Events in the History of the State & a Record of . . . Illustrious Families & Individuals, 2-vol. set. 1891. 2 vols, 1260 + 1124p.
P5-MS0005 — $199.00/set.

BIOGRAPHICAL & HISTORICAL MEMOIRS OF MISSISSIPPI . . ., Vol. I. 1891. 1260p.
P5-MS0005A — $115.00.

BIOGRAPHICAL & HISTORICAL MEMOIRS OF MISSISSIPPI . . ., Vol. II. 1891. 1124p.
P5-MS0005B — $115.00.

HISTORY OF MISSISSIPPI, the Heart of the South, 2-vol. set. By Dunbar Rowland. 1925. 2 vols., 933 + 904p.
P5-MS0002 — $185.00/set.

HISTORY OF MISSISSIPPI . . ., Vol. I. 1925. 933p.
P5-MS0002A — $99.50.

HISTORY OF MISSISSIPPI . . ., Vol. II. 1925. 904p.
P5-MS0002B — $99.50.

INDIAN TRIBES OF THE LOWER MISSISSIPPI VALLY & Adjacent Coast of the Gulf of Mexico. By John R. Swanton. 1911. 386p.
P5-MS0006 — $44.00.

MISSISSIPPI VALLEY BEGIN-NINGS: An Outline of the Early History of the Earlier West. By Henry E. Chambers. 1922. 389p.
P5-MS0007 — $44.50.

OFFICIAL & STATISTICAL REGISTER of the State of Mississippi. Dunbar Rowland. 1908. 1317p.
P5-MS0003B — $129.00.

PRIVATE CEMETERIES IN ADAMS COUNTY. 1946. 101p., typescript.
P5-MS0008A — $16.50.

Mississippi, cont.

HISTORY OF HARRISON COUNTY. John H. Lang. 1936. 303p.
P5-MS0008B — $39.50.

HISTORY OF NEWTON COUNTY, from 1834 to 1894. A.J. Brown. 1894. 473p.
P5-MS0001 — $49.50.

Missouri

HISTORY OF NORTHEAST MISSOURI, Vol. I. 1913.
P5-MO0018A — $73.00.

HISTORY OF NORTHEAST MISSOURI, Vol. II. 1913.
P5-MO0018B — $73.00.

HISTORY OF NORTHEAST MISSOURI, Vol. III. 1913.
P5-MO0018C — $73.00.

HISTORY OF SOUTHEAST MISSOURI. 1888. 1215 + 67p.
P5-MO0075 — $128.00.

HISTORY OF THE PIONEER FAMILIES OF MISSOURI, with Numerous Sketches, Anecdotes, Adventures, etc., Relating to Early Days in Missouri. By W.S. Bryan & R. Rose. 1876, 1935. 569p.
P5-MO0001 — $42.50.

MARVELS OF THE NEW WEST. A Vivid Portrayal of the Stupendous Marvels in the Vast Wonderland West of the Missouri River. By William L. Thomas. 1891. 716 + xxxvi p.
P5-MISC0005 — $75.00.

REVOLUTIONARY SOLDIERS & THEIR DESCENDANTS: Genealogical Records, Missouri Records. n.d. 112p.
P5-MO0019 — $19.50.

HISTORY OF ADAIR COUNTY, Together with Reminiscences & Biographical Sketches. By E.M. Violette. 1911. 1188p.
P5-MO0020 — $116.00.

HISTORY OF AUDRAIN COUNTY . . . Including a History of its Townships, Towns and Villages . . . and Biographical Sketches. 1884. 973p.
P5-MO0016 — $97.50.

HISTORY OF BATES COUNTY, includes history of Missouri and biographical sketches. [Part II of the History of Cass and Bates Counties.] 1883. 728p.
P5-MO0014 — $74.50.

HISTORY OF BOONE COUNTY, including a History of the Townships, Towns & Villages . . . with Biographical Sketches. 1882. 1144p.
P5-MO0002 — $109.00.

Daily News' **HISTORY OF BUCHANAN COUNTY & ST JOSEPH, from the Time of the Platte Purchase to the End of 1898. With** biographical sketches. 1898. 569p.
P5-MO0007 — $59.00.

HISTORY OF BUCHANAN COUNTY & ST JOSEPH from the Time of the Platte Purchase to the End of the Year 1915 . . . Supplemented by Biographical Sketches of Noted Citizens, Living & Dead. 1915. 572p.
P5-MO0021 — $61.50.

HISTORY OF BUCHANAN COUNTY. 1881. 1073p.
P5-MO0008 — $105.00.

HISTORY OF CALDWELL & LIVINGSTON COUNTIES, Including a History of their Townships, Towns & Villages, Together with . . . their Pioneer Record; Biographical Sketches of Prominent Citizens, etc. 1886. 1274p.
P5-MO0022 — $121.50.

HISTORY OF CALLAWAY COUNTY. 1884. 954p.
P5-MO0009 — $95.00.

HISTORY OF CARROLL COUNTY, including a History of the Townships, Towns & Villages . . . with Biographical Sketches. [Reprinted without History of Missouri, which comprised first 200 pages of original ed.] 1881. 490p.
P5-MO0003 — $55.00.

HISTORY OF CASS COUNTY, includes biographical sketches and history of Missouri. [Part I of the History of Cass and Bates Counties.] 1883. 757p.
P5-MO0015 — $79.00.

HISTORICAL, PICTORIAL & BIOGRAPHICAL RECORD OF CHARITON COUNTY. By James G. Gallemore. 1896. 252p.
P5-MO0023 — $34.00.

HISTORY OF CHARITON & HOWARD COUNTIES. By T. Berry Smith & Pearl Sims Gehrig. 1923. 856p.
P5-MO0010 — $87.00.

HISTORY OF CLAY & PLATTE COUNTIES, Including a History of their Townships, Towns & Villages Together with . . . their Pioneer Record, Resources, Biographical Sketches of Prominent Citizens, Incidents & Reminiscences. 1885. 1121p.
P5-MO0025 — $109.00.

Hist of Clinton & Caldwell Cos, MO. By C.P. Johnston & W.H.S. McGlumphy. 1923. 900p.
P5-MO0076 — $90.00.

HISTORY OF COLE, MONITEAU, MORGAN, BENTON, MILLER, MARIES & OSAGE COUNTIES, from the Earliest Time to the Present [1889]. 1889. 1172p.
P5-MO0063 — $115.00.

HISTORY OF COOPER COUNTY. By W.F. Johnson. 1919. 1167p.
P5-MO0064 — $109.00.

HISTORY OF COOPER COUNTY: An Account from Early Times to the Present. By E.J. Melton. 1937. 584p.
P5-MO0059 — $61.00.

EARLY DAYS IN DALLAS COUNTY. By Elva M. Hemphill. 1954. 115p.
P5-MO0056 — $17.00.

HISTORY OF DAVIESS & GENTRY COUNTIES. Daviess Co. by J.C. & B. Leopard; Gentry Co. by R. McCammon & M. Hillman 1922. 1035p.
P5-MO0026 — $99.50.

HISTORY OF DAVIESS COUNTY: Encyclopedia of Useful Information & Actual Facts . . . its Pioneer Record, War History, Resources, Biographical Sketches & Portraits of Prominent Citizens, Incidents, etc. 1882. 868p.
P5-MO0027 — $89.50.

EARLY SETTLERS OF DOUGLAS COUNTY. Bessie J. Selleck. 1952. 307p.
P5-MO0060 — $41.00.

HISTORY OF DUNKLIN CO.,
1845-1895, Embracing an Historical
Acct. of the Towns & Post-Villages . .
. incl. a Dept. Devoted to the
Description of the Early Appearance,
Settlement, Development, Resources
. . . with an Album of its People and
Homes. Mary F. Smyth-Davis. 1896. 290p.
P5-MO0028 — $37.00.

HISTORY OF FRANKLIN,
JEFFERSON, WASHINGTON,
CRAWFORD & GASCONADE
COUNTIES, from the Earliest Time
to the Present, Including a Depart-
ment Devoted to the Preservation of
Sundry Personal, Business & Pro-
fessional Sketches, & Family
Records, etc. 1888. 1131p.
P5-MO0029 — $109.00.

HISTORY OF GENTRY &
WORTH COUNTIES. 1882. 839p.
P5-MO0004 — $84.00.

HISTORY OF GREENE COUNTY
. . . Including a History of its Town-
ships, Towns & Villages . . . its
Pioneer Record; War History;
Biographical Sketches & Portraits of
Prominent Citizens . . . 1883. 919p.
P5-MO0031 — $94.50.

PAST & PRESENT OF GREENE
COUNTY: Early & Recent History
& Genealogical Records of Many of
the Representative Citizens. With
index. 2-vol. set. By Jonathan
Fairbanks & Clyde E. Tuck. 1915. 2
vols., 1933p.
P5-MO0017 — $179.00/set.

PAST & PRESENT OF GREENE
COUNTY . . ., Vol. I. 1915.
P5-MO0017A — $94.50.

PAST & PRESENT OF GREENE
COUNTY . . ., Vol. II. 1915.
P5-MO0017B — $94.50.

PICTORIAL & GENEALOGICAL
RECORD OF GREENE COUNTY.
With 1932 index by J.R. Moll.
1893. 392 + 42p.
P5-MO0030 — $45.00.

CENTENNIAL HISTORY OF
GRUNDY COUNTY, 1839-1939. By
William Ray Denslow. 1939. 402p.
P5-MO0057 — $47.00.

HISTORY OF GRUNDY COUNTY,
. . . Containing its Pioneer Record,
War History, Resources, Biograph-
ical Sketches, Portraits of Prominent
Citizens, etc. 1881. 739p.
P5-MO0032 — $78.00.

HISTORY OF GRUNDY COUNTY
. . . its Transformation from the
Heart of the Wilderness of Yesterday
to the Heart of the Mighty Nation of
Today: A Tribute to the Pioneer &
Something of the Men who are Making the Grundy Co. of Tomorrow.
1908. 875p.
P5-MO0033 — $91.50.

HISTORY OF HENRY & SAINT
CLAIR COUNTIES, Containing a
History of their Cities, Towns, etc.,
Biographical Sketches of their
Citizens, etc. 1883. 1224p.
P5-MO0034 — $119.00.

HISTORY OF HOLT COUNTY,
From the Time of the Platte
Purchase to the End of the Year 1916,
Supplemented by Biographical
Sketches of Prominent Citizens. By
the History Publ. Comm. 1917. 481p.
P5-MO0035 — $51.00.

HISTORY OF HOWARD & COOPER
COUNTIES, Including a History of
its Townships, Towns & Villages . . .
its Pioneer Record; Biographical
Sketches of Prominent Citizens; Incidents & Reminiscences. 1883. 1167p.
P5-MO0061 — $117.00.

ABSTRACT OF THE CENSUS OF
1840, Jackson County. Comp. by Mrs
H.E. Poppino. n.d. 62p., typescript.
P5-MO0062 — $12.00.

BIOGRAPHICAL RECORD OF
JASPER COUNTY. By Malcolm G.
McGregor. 1901. 526p.
P5-MO0005 — $55.00.

HISTORY OF JASPER COUNTY,
Including a Condensed History of
the State, a Complete History of
Carthage & Joplin, together with
Numerous Portraits of Prominent
Men . . . Biographical Sketches . . .
Pioneers; Political History, etc. 1883.
1065p.
P5-MO0037 — $105.00.

HISTORY OF JEFFERSON CITY,
Missouri's State Capital, & of Cole
Co. By James E. Ford. 1938. 600p.
P5-MO0013 — $62.50.

HISTORY OF JOHNSON
COUNTY. 1881. 989p.
P5-MO0011 — $97.50.

HISTORY OF KANSAS CITY . . .
the True Account of the Founding,
Rise & Present Position Occupied by
Kansas City in Municipal America.
By Wm. Griffith. 1900. 132p.
P5-MO0038 — $19.50.

KANSAS CITY: Its History & its
People, 1808-1908, 3-vol. set. By Carrie
Westlake Whitney. 1908. 3 vols.,
706+688+684p.
P5-MO0039 — $199.00/set.

KANSAS CITY . . ., Vol. I. 1908. 706p.
P5-MO0039A — $74.00.

KANSAS CITY . . ., Vol. II. 1908.
688p.
P5-MO0039B — $74.00.

KANSAS CITY . . ., Vol. III. 1908.
684p.
P5-MO0039C — $74.00.

HISTORY OF LaCLEDE, CAMDEN,
DALLAS, WEBSTER, WRIGHT,
TEXAS, PULASKI, PHELPS &
DENT COUNTIES. With modern
typsecript index. 1889. 1219 + 97p.
P5-MO0040 — $119.00.

PORTRAIT & BIOGRAPHICAL
RECORD OF LAFAYETE &
SALINE COUNTIES, Containing
Biographical Sketches of Prominent
& Representative Citizens. 1893. 642p.
P5-MO0041 — $69.50.

OZARK REGION: Its History & Its
People. Including every-name index
courtesy of the Lawrence Co. Historical Society, 3-vol. set. 1917. 3 vols.,
371 + 414 +396p.
P5-MO0042 — $119.00/set.

OZARK REGION . . ., Vol. I. 1917.
371p.
P5-MO0042A — $43.50.

OZARK REGION . . .,Vol. II. 1917.
414p.
P5-MO0042B — $43.50.

OZARK REGION . . ., Vol. III. 1917.
396p.
P5-MO0042C — $43.50.

Missouri, cont.

HISTORY OF LEWIS, CLARK, KNOX & SCOTLAND COUNTIES, from the Earliest Times to [1887], together with Sundry Personal, Business & Professional Sketches & Numerous Family Records; etc., etc. 1887. 1229p.
P5-MO0043 — $119.50.

HISTORY OF MARION COUNTY, Including a History of its Townships, Towns & Villages Together with . . . their Pioneer Record, Resources, Biographical Sketches & Portraits of Prominent Citizens, Incidents & Reminiscences. 1884. 1003p.
P5-MO0044 — $99.50.

PORTRAIT & BIOGRAPHICAL RECORD OF MARION, RALLS & PIKE COUNTIES, Containing Biographical Sketches of Prominent & Representative Citizens of the Counties. 1895. 803p.
P5-MO0045 — $84.50.

HISTORY OF MILLER COUNTY, with Miller County Biography. By Gerard Schultz. 1933. 176p.
P5-MO0058 — $27.00.

HISTORY OF MONROE & SHELBY COUNTIES . . . Including a History of their Townships, Towns & Villages, Together with.. their Pioneer Record, Resources, Biographical Sketches of Prominent Citizens; Incidents & Reminiscences. 1884. 1176p.
P5-MO0047 — $116.50.

ORIGINAL LAND ENTRIES IN MONTGOMERY COUNTY. By Harris B. Dickey. 1937. 45p.
P5-MO0048 — $9.00.

HISTORY OF NEWTON, LAWRENCE, BARRY & McDONALD COUNTIES, from the Earliest Time to the Present, Including a Department Devoted to the Preservation of Sundry Personal, Business, Professional & Private Records, etc. With index. 1888. 1092 + 92p.
P5-MO0049 — $111.00.

ANNALS OF PLATTE COUNTY, From its Exploration Down to June 1, 1897, with Genealogies of its Noted Families & Sketches of its Pioneers & Distinguished People. W.M. Paxton. 1897. 1182p.
P5-MO0050 — $117.00.

HISTORY OF RANDOLPH & MACON COUNTIES . . . including a History of its Townships, Cities, Towns & Villages . . . with Biographical Sketches. 1884. 1123p.
P5-MO0006 — $109.50.

HISTORY OF RANDOLPH COUNTY. By Alexander H. Waller. 1920. 852p.
P5-MO0051 — $89.50.

HISTORY OF SALINE COUNTY. 1881. 960p.
P5-MO0012 — $97.50.

GENERAL HISTORY OF SHELBY COUNTY, MISSOURI. With new index. 1911. 671 + 13p.
P5-MO0067 — $69.50.

HISTORY & DIRECTORY OF SPRINGFIELD & NORTH SPRINGFIELD, Containing a Historical Sketch of the Early Settlement, etc. By Geo. S. Escott. 1878. 273p.
P5-MO0054 — $36.00.

OLD & NEW ST. LOUIS: Concise History of the Metropolis of the West & Southwest, with a Review of its Present Greatness & Immediate Prospects, with a 444-page Biographical Appendix. History by James Cox. 1894. 575p.
P5-MO0066 — $65.00.

PORT. & BIO. RECORD OF ST. CHARLES, LINCOLN, AND WARREN COS., MO. 1895. 573p.
P5-MO0073 — $60.00.

ANNALS OF SAINT LOUIS IN ITS EARLY DAYS, Under the French & Spanish Dominations. By Frederoc L. Billon. 1886. 499p.
P5-MO0053 — $54.00.

EARLY HISTORY OF ST LOUIS & MISSOURI, from its First Exploration by White Men in 1675 to 1843. By Elihu H. Shepard. 1870. 170p.
P5-MO0052 — $28.50.

ENCYCLOPEDIA OF THE HISTORY OF ST. LOUIS, 4-vol. set. 1899. 4 vols; 824 + 809 + 821 + 773p.
P5-MO0074 — $275.00/set.

ENCYCLOPEDIA OF THE HISTORY OF ST. LOUIS, Vol. I. 1899. 824p.
P5-MO0074A — $75.00.

ENCYCLOPEDIA OF THE HISTORY OF ST. LOUIS, Vol. II. 1899. 809p.
P5-MO0074B — $75.00.

ENCYCLOPEDIA OF THE HISTORY OF ST. LOUIS, Vol. III. 1899. 821p.
P5-MO0074C — $75.00.

ENCYCLOPEDIA OF THE HISTORY OF ST. LOUIS, Vol. IV. 1899. 773p.
P5-MO0074D — $75.00.

HISTORY OF SAINT LOUIS CITY & COUNTY, FROM THE Earliest Periods to the Present Day, including Biographical Sketches of Representative Men, 2-vol. set. By J. Thomas Scharf. 1883. 2 vols., 1643p.
P5-MO0065 — $155.00/set.

HISTORY OF SAINT LOUIS CITY & COUNTY . . . , Vol. I. 1883.
P5-MO0065A — $82.50.

HISTORY OF SAINT LOUIS CITY & COUNTY . . . , Vol. II. 1883.
P5-MO0065B — $82.50.

ST. LOUIS: HISTORY OF THE FOURTH CITY, 1763-1909. Vol. I, Historical. By Walter B. Stevens. 1909. 1132p.
P5-MO0070 — $110.00.

ST. LOUIS: HISTORY OF THE FOURTH CITY, 1763-1909. Vol. II, Biographical. By Walter B. Stevens. 1909. 1082 + vi p.
P5-MO0069 — $105.00.

ST. LOUIS THE FOURTH CITY, 1764-1909. Vol. III, Biography. By Walter B. Stevens. 1909. 1063 + vii p.
P5-MO0068 — $104.00.
HISTORY OF ST. LOUIS COUNTY, MISSOURI. Vol. I: Historical. By William L. Thomas. 1911. 416 + 88p.
P5-MO0071 — $55.00.

HISTORY OF ST. LOUIS COUNTY, MISSOURI. Vol. II: Biographical. By William L. Thomas. 1911. 558p.
P5-MO0072 — $59.00.

HISTORY OF VERNON COUNTY, Past & Present, Including an Account of the Cities, Towns & Villages of the County, 2-vol. set. 1911. 2 vols., 1086p.
P5-MO0055 — $105.00/set.

HISTORY OF VERNON COUNTY . . ., Vol. I. 1911.
P5-MO0055A — $59.50.

HISTORY OF VERNON COUNTY . . ., Vol. II. 1911.
P5-MO0055B — $59.50.

Montana

ILLUSTRATED HISTORY OF THE STATE OF MONTANA . . . From the Earliest Period of its Discovery to the Present Time . . . [and] Biographical Mention of Many of its Pioneers & Prominent Citizens. By Joaquin Miller. 1894. 822p.
P5-MT0001 — $88.00.

MONTANA, its Story & Biography: History of Aboriginal & Territorial Montana, & Three Decades of Statehood, 3-vol. set. 1921. 3 vols., 2343p.
P5-MT0002 — $215.00/set.

MONTANA . . ., Vol. I. 1921.
P5-MT0002A — $75.00.

MONTANA . . ., Vol. II. 1921.
P5-MT0002B — $75.00.

MONTANA . . ., Vol. III. 1921.
P5-MT0002C — $75.00.

Nebraska

COMPENDIUM OF HISTORY, REMINISCENCE & BIOGRAPHY OF WESTERN NEBRASKA, Containing a History of the State of Nebraska, Embracing an Account of Early Explorations, Early Settlement, Indian Occupancy . . . a Concise History of the Growth & Development of the State. 1909. 1135p.
P5-NE0009 — $109.00.

HISTORY OF THE STATE OF NEBRASKA. 1882. 1460p.
P5-NE0022 — $140.00.

HISTORY OF ANTELOPE COUNTY, From its First Settlement in 1868 to the Close of the Year 1883. By A.J. Leach. 1909. 262p.
P5-NE0010 — $37.00.

"LA BELLE VUE": Studies in the history of Bellevue. 1976. 378p.
P5-NE0021 — $45.00.

BIOGRAPHICAL SOUVENIR OF THE COUNTIES OF BUFFALO, KEARNEY & PHELPS, Containing Portraits . . . of Many of the Prominent & Representative Citizens & Sketches of Many of the Early Settled Families of these Counties. 1890. 716p.
P5-NE0011 — $76.00.

MEMORIAL & BIOGRAPHICAL RECORDS & Illustrated Compendium of Biography, Containing a Compendium of Local Biography, including Biographical Sketches of Hundreds of Prominent Old Settlers & Representative Citizens [BUTLER, POLK, SEWARD, YORK & FILLMORE COS.] 1899. 1119p.
P5-NE0001 — $89.50.

HISTORY OF CUSTER COUNTY: a Narrative of the Past, with Special Emphasis upon the Pioneer Period, its Social . . . and Civic Development from the Early Days to the Present Time [1919]. By W.L. Gaston & A.R. Humphrey. 1919. 1175p.
P5-NE0002 — $109.00.

HISTORY OF THE ELKHORN VALLEY: An Album of History & Biography Containing a Descriptive, Political.. Biographical History & Reminiscences. 1892. 779p.
P5-NE0012 — $83.50.

HISTORY OF GAGE COUNTY: Narrative of the Past, with Special Emphasis upon the Pioneer Period of the County's History, its Social. & Civic Development from the Early Days to the Present Time. By Hugh J. Dobbs. 1918. 1100p.
P5-NE0014 — $107.00.

PORTRAITS & BIOGRAPHICAL ALBUM OF GAGE COUNTY, Containing Full Page Portraits & Biographical Sketches of Prominent & Representative Citizens of the County. 1888. 784p.
P5-NE0013 — $83.00.

HISTORY OF HALL COUNTY: Narrative of the Past with Special Emphasis upon the Pioneer Period, & Chronological Presentation of its Social.. & Civic Develpment from the Early Days to [1920]. . . 1920. 965p.
P5-NE0015 — $99.00.

PORTRAIT & BIOGRAPHICAL ALBUM OF JOHNSON & PAWNEE COUNTIES, Containing Full Page Portraits & Biographical Sketches of Prominent & Representative Citizens of the Cos. 1885. 626p.
P5-NE0006 — $65.00.

PORTRAITS & BIOGRAPHICAL ALBUM OF LANCASTER COUNTY, Containing Full Page Portraits & Biographical Sketches of Prominent & Representative Citizens of the County. 1888. 800p.
P5-NE0016 — $84.50.

HISTORY OF THE CITY OF LINCOLN. By A.B. Hayes & Sam D. Cox. 1889. 379p.
P5-NE0004 — $42.50.

HISTORY OF OMAHA, from the Pioneer Days to the Present Time [1889]. By Alfred Sorenson. 1889, 2nd ed. 342p.
P5-NE0005 — $39.00.

HISTORY OF THE CITY OF OMAHA and SOUTH OMAHA. By James W. Savage & John T. Bell. 1894. 699p.
P5-NE0018 — $77.00.

OMAHA, THE GATE CITY, & DOUGLAS COUNTY: Record of Settlement, Organization, Progress & Achievement, 2-vol. set. 1917. 2 vols., 997p.
P5-NE0017 — $99.50/set.

OMAHA, THE GATE CITY, & COUGLAS COUNTY: Record of Settlement, Organization, Progress & Achievement, Vol. I. 1917.
P5-NE0017A — $57.00.

Nebraska, cont.

OMAHA, THE GATE CITY, & COUGLAS COUNTY: Record of Settlement, Organization, Progress & Achievement, Vol. II. 1917.
P5-NE0017B — $57.00.

HISTORY OF RICHARDSON COUNTY, Its People, Industries and Institutions. With biographical sketches of representative citizens and genealogical records of many of the old families. By Lewis C. Edwards. 1917. 1417p.
P5-NE0007 — $139.00.

HISTORY OF SEWARD COUNTY, together with a Chapter of Reminiscences of the Early Settlement of Lancaster County. W.W. Cox. 1888. 290p.
P5-NE0003 — $36.00.

MEN & WOMEN OF NEBRASKA: A Book of Portraits, Washington Co. Edition, Containing an Historical Review of Washington Co., Compiled from Public & Private Records. Ed. by Daniel M. Carr. 1903. 198p.
P5-NE0008 — $31.50.

OLD SETTLERS' HISTORY OF YORK COUNTY & INDIVIDUAL BIOGRAPHIES. Comp. by John Lett, Geo. B. France, et al. 1913. 175p.
P5-NE0020 — $27.00.

YORK COUNTY & Its People, Together with a Condensed History of the State: a Record of Settlement, Organization, Progress & Achievement, 2-vol. set. 1921. 2 vols., 1264p.
P5-NE0019 — $119.00/set.

YORK COUNTY & Its People . . ., Vol. I. 1921.
P5-NE0019A — $65.00.

YORK COUNTY & Its People . . ., Vol. II. 1921.
P5-NE0019B — $65.00.

Nevada

HISTORY OF NEVADA, with Illustrations & Biographical Sketches of its Prominent Men & Pioneers. 1881. 680p.
P5-NV0001 — $69.50.

New Hampshire

CAPTAIN JOHN MASON, Founder of New Hampshire. 1887. 491p.
P5-NH0112 — $49.50.

GENEALOGICAL & FAMILY HISTORY OF THE STATE OF NEW HAMPSHIRE: Record of the achievements of her people in the making of a commonwealth & the founding of a nation, 4-vol. set. 1908. 4 vols., 2067p.
P5-NH0249 — $199.00/set.

GENEALOGICAL & FAMILY HISTORY OF THE STATE OF NEW HAMPSHIRE . . ., Vol. I. 1908.
P5-NH0249A — $57.00.

GENEALOGICAL & FAMILY HISTORY OF THE STATE OF NEW HAMPSHIRE. . ., Vol. II. 1908.
P5-NH0249B — $57.00.

GENEALOGICAL & FAMILY HISTORY OF THE STATE OF NEW HAMPSHIRE. . ., Vol. III. 1908.
P5-NH0249C — $57.00.

GENEALOGICAL & FAMILY HISTORY OF THE STATE OF NEW HAMPSHIRE. . ., Vol. IV. 1908.
P5-NH0249D — $57.00.

GENEALOGICAL DICTIONARY OF MAINE & NEW HAMPSHIRE. By Noyes, Libby & Davis. 1928-39. 795p.
P5-ME0049 — $49.00.

HISTORY OF THE FIRST NEW HAMPSHIRE REGIMENT in the War of the Revolution with New Hampshire at the Battle of Bunker Hill. By Frederic Kidder. 1868 & 1903. 184 + 23p.
P5-NH0250 — $39.00.

MILITARY HISTORY OF THE STATE OF NEW HAMPSHIRE, Parts 1 & 2. By C.E. Potter. 1866, 1869. 2 vols., 394 + 401p.
P5-NH0272 — $79.00/set.

MILITARY HISTORY OF THE STATE OF NEW HAMPSHIRE, Part 1. 1866. 394p.
P5-NH0272A — $45.00.

MILITARY HISTORY OF THE STATE OF NEW HAMPSHIRE, Part 2. 1869. 401p.
P5-NH0272B — $45.00.

NEW HAMPSHIRE GRANTS: CHARTERS OF TOWNSHIPS By Albert Stillman Batchellor 1895. xii + 792p.
P28023000 — $123.00.

NORTHERN N.H. GRAVEYARDS & CEMETERIES. Comp. by Nancy L. Dodge. 1985. 443p.
P5-NH0001 — $45.00.

NORTHERN NEW HAMPSHIRE and its leading business men; embracing Littleton, Lancaster, Lisbon, Woodsville, Whitefield, Groveton, Berlin Falls, and Wells River, VT. By George F. Bacon 1890. 88p.
P5-NH0266 — $27.00.

PIONEERS OF MAINE & NEW HAMPSHIRE, 1623 to 1660: Descriptive List Drawn from Records of the Colonies, Towns, Churches, Courts & Other Contemporary Sources. By Charles Henry Pope. 1908. 252p.
P5-ME0054 — $24.50.

SKETCHES OF SUCCESSFUL NEW HAMPSHIRE MEN. With genealogical information & portraits. 1882. 315p.
P5-NH0224 — $41.00.

ACWORTH: Inscriptions from the Ancient Gravestones & Cemetery Records; Epitaphs. 1908, 1956. 23 + 71p.
P5-NH0223 — $17.50.

HISTORY OF ACWORTH, with the Proceedings of the Centennial Anniversary, Gen. Records & Register of Farms. By J.L. Merrill. 1869. 306p.
P5-NH0037 — $39.00.

COLONIAL AMHERST, The Early History, Customs & Homes. By Emma P. Boylston Locke. 1916. 122p.
P5-NH0144 — $16.00.

HISTORY OF THE TOWN OF AMHERST, Hillsborough Co., from 1728 to 1882, with Genealogies. By D.F. Secomb. 1883. 978p.
P5-NH0002 — $97.00.

HISTORY OF THE TOWN OF ANDOVER, 1751-1906, including Genealogies. J.R. Eastman. 1910. 450p.
P5-NH0003 — $48.00.

HISTORY OF ANTRIM, from its Earliest Settlement in 1727 to 1872. By W.R. Cochrane. 1880. 791p.
P5-NH0004 — $79.00.

TOWN REGISTER OF ASHLAND, PLYMOUTH, SANDWICH, CAMPTON, HOLDERNESS, CENTER HARBOR, MOULTONBORO, 1908. [Town histories & censuses]. 1908. 109 + 157p.
P5-NH0146 — $37.00.

HISTORY OF BARNSTEAD, from its First Settlement in 1727 to 1872. By J.P. Jewett & R.B. Caverly. 1871. 271p.
P5-NH0075 — $34.00.

HISTORY OF BARNSTEAD, NEW HAMPSHIRE By Jeremiah P. Jewett 1872. 264p
P28047500 — $50.00.

VITAL RECORDS OF BARRINGTON, 1720-1851. By Priscilla Hammond. 1934. 110p.
P5-NH0145 — $15.00.

ADDRESS DELIVERED TO THE INHABITANTS OF BATH on. . . January 23, 1854 . . . with an Historical Appendix. Address by Rev. David Sutherland; Historical Appendix by Rev. T. Boutel. 1855. 135p.
P5-NH0147 — $28.50.

HISTORICAL NOTES OF BATH, 1765-1965. By Edwin Chamberlin, Louise Bailey, Natalie Burton, et al. 1965. 144p.
P5-NH0235 — $21.00.

HISTORY OF BEDFORD, Being Statistics Compiled on the Occasion of the 100th Anniversary of the Town, May 19th, 1850. With genealogies. 1851. 364p.
P5-NH0119 — $39.50.

HISTORY OF BEDFORD, FROM 1737. 1903. 1132p.
P5-NH0148 — $109.50.

BERLIN, NEW HAMPSHIRE CENTENNIAL, 1829-1929. 1929. 89 + 55p.
P5-NH0265 — $30.00.

CITY OF BERLIN AND GORHAM: Their Past and Present Progress and Property Souvenir. n.d. 44p.
P5-NH0264 — $21.00.

ILLUSTRATED INDUSTRIAL EDITION: Berlin, New Hampshire. 1913. 76p.
P5-NH0263 — $27.00.

EARLY HISTORY OF THE TOWN OF BETHLEHEM. Simeon Bolles. 1883. 108p.
P5-NH0149 — $15.00.

150TH ANNIVERSARY OF THE SETTLEMENT OF BOSCAWEN & WEBSTER, Merrimack Co.; also Births Recorded on the Town Records from 1733 to 1850 & Biographical Sketches. 1884. 211p.
P5-NH0241 — $24.50.

BOSCAWEN GRAVESTONE INSCRIPTIONS. Comp. by Priscilla Hammond. 1932. 89p.
P5-NH0150 — $16.00.

HISTORY OF BOSCAWEN — WEBSTER, Fifty Years, 1883-1933. Comp. by Willis G. Buxton. 1933. 502p.
P5-NH0151 — $55.00.

HISTORY OF BOSCAWEN & WEBSTER, from 1733 to 1878, By Chas. C. Coffin. 1878. 666p.
P5-NH0259 — $67.00.

GRAVESTONE INSCRIPTIONS FROM BRADFORD. Comp. by Francis L. Childs. 1938. 59p.
P5-NH0219 — $12.00.

BRENTWOOD'S 225 YEARS, 1742-1967. Comp. by Brentwood Hist. Society. 1967?. 120p.
P5-NH0071 — $19.50.

GRAVESTONE INSCRIPTIONS FROM BRADFORD. Comp. by Francis L. Childs. 1938. 59p.
P5-NH0219 — $12.00.

HISTORY OF THE TOWN OF BRISTOL, Grafton Co., 2-vol. set. By Richard W. Musgrove. 1904. 2 vols., 570 + 526p.
P5-NH0260 — $105.00/set.

HISTORY OF THE TOWN OF BRISTOL, Grafton Co., Vol. I. 1904. 570p.
P5-NH0260A — $57.00.

HISTORY OF THE TOWN OF BRISTOL, Grafton Co., Vol. II. 1904. 526p.
P5-NH0260B — $57.00.

HISTORY OF BROOKLINE, formerly Raby, Hillsborough Co., with Tables of Family Records & Genealogies. E.E. Parker. 1913?. 664p.
P5-NH0051B — $71.50.

HISTORY OF CANAAN. By W.A. Wallace. 1910. 757p.
P5-NH0061 — $79.00.

HISTORY OF CANDIA, Once Known as Charmingfare; with Notices of Some of the Early Families. By F.B. Eaton. 1852. 151p.
P5-NH0057 — $25.00.

HISTORY OF THE TOWN OF CANDIA, Rockingham Co., from its First Settlement to the Present Time [1893]. By J.B. Moore. 1893. 528p.
P5-NH0110 — $55.00.

REMINISCENCES OF CANDIA. By Wilson Palmer. 1905. 345p.
P5-NH0152 — $41.50.

HISTORY OF THE TOWN OF CANTERBURY, 1727-1912, 2-vol. set. J.O. Lyford. 1912. 2 vols., 513 + 455p.
P5-NH0073 — $95.00/set.

HISTORY OF THE TOWN OF CANTERBURY. . ., Vol. I. 1912. 513p.
P5-NH0073A — $49.50.

HISTORY OF THE TOWN OF CANTERBURY. . . , Vol. II. 1912. 455p.
P5-NH0073B — $49.50.

TOWN REGISTER OF CANTERBURY, NORTHWOOD, EPSOM, LOUDON, CHICHESTER & DEERFIELD, 1909 [Town histories & censuses]. 1909. 120 + 119p.
P5-NH0153 — $31.00.

HISTORY OF CARROLL COUNTY. 1889. 984p.
P5-NH0036A — $97.50.

GAZETTEER OF CHESHIRE COUNTY, 1736-1885. With town histories & directories, biographical sketches, 2-vol. set. Comp. by Hamilton Child. 1885. 2 vols., 560 + 272p.
P5-NH0154 — $87.00/set.

GAZETTEER OF CHESHIRE COUNTY . . . , Vol. I. 1885. 560p.
P5-NH0154A — $58.00.

For hardcover versions, see the order form on page v. To order, call 1-888-296-3447.

New Hampshire, cont.

GAZETTEER OF CHESHIRE COUNTY. . . , Vol. II. 1885. 272p.
P5-NH0154B — $33.00.

HISTORY OF CHESHIRE & SULLIVAN COUNTIES, 2-vol. set. 1886. 2 vols., 516 + 409p.
P5-NH0030 — $97.00/set.

HISTORY OF CHESHIRE & SULLIVAN COUNTIES, Vol. I. 1886. 516p.
P5-NH0030A — $65.00.

HISTORY OF CHESHIRE & SULLIVAN COUNTIES, Vol. II. 1886. 409p.
P5-NH0030B — $42.50.

HISTORY OF CHESTER, includ–ing Auburn. Supplement to "History of Old Chester" (1869). By J.C. Chase. 1926. 535p.
P5-NH0006B — $59.00.

HISTORY OF CHESTERFIELD, Cheshire County, 1736 6o 1881, with Family Sketches. By O.E. Randall. 1882. 525p.
P5-NH0008 — $57.00.

HISTORY OF THE TOWN OF CLAREMONT, for a Period of 130 Years, from 1764 to 1894. By Otis F.R. Waite. 1895. 539p.
P5-NH0137 — $59.00.

ANNALS OF THE TOWN OF CONCORD, in the County of Merrimack, from its First Settlement in the Year 1726 to the Year 1823, with Several Biographical Sketches. By Jacob B. Moore. 1824. 112p.
P5-NH0138 — $21.00.

HISTORY OF CONCORD, from 1725 to 1853. By N. Bouton. 1856. 786p.
P5-NH0009 — $82.00.

HISTORY OF CONCORD, from the Original Grant in 1725 to the Open-ing of the 20th Century, 2-vol. set. 1903. 2 vols., 1477p.
P5-NH0117A — $135.00/set.

HISTORY OF CONCORD . . . , Vol. I. 1903.
P5-NH0117A1 — $75.00.

HISTORY OF CONCORD. . . , Vol. II. 1903.
P5-NH0117A2 — $75.00.

UTAH EXPEDITION, 1857-1858: Letters of Capt. Jesse A. Gove, of Concord, to Mrs Gove, & Special Correspondence of the N.Y. Herald. [Concord, N.H.] 1928. 442p.
P5-NH0141 — $49.50.

HIST SKETCHES OF THE DIS-COVERY & SETTLEMENT OF COOS COUNTY & VICINITY. By G. Powers. 1880. 240p.
P5-NH0271 — $34.00.

HISTORY OF COOS COUNTY. 1888. 956p.
P5-NH0120 — $89.50.

HISTORY OF THE TOWN OF CORNISH, with Genealogical Record, 1763-1910, 2-vol. set. By Wm. H. Child. 1911?. 2 vols., 392 + 463p.
P5-NH0156 — $89.50/set.

HISTORY OF THE TOWN OF CORNISH . . . , Vol. I. 1911?. 392p.
P5-NH0156A — $50.00.

HISTORY OF THE TOWN OF CORNISH . . . , Vol. II. 1911?. 463p.
P5-NH0156B — $50.00.

HISTORY OF THE TOWN OF CORNISH, with Genealogical Record, 1910-1960. Vol. III, Supple-mental narrative & genealogy. By Barbara E. Rawson. 1963. 207p.
P5-NH0240 — $31.50.

SOME THINGS ABOUT COVENTRY-BENTON. By William F. Whitcher. 1905. 313p.
P5-NH0206 — $38.50.

CROYDEN, 1866: Proceedings at the Centennial Celebration; a Brief Account of the Leading Men of the First Century; together with Histori-cal & Statistical Sketches of the Town. Edmund Wheeler. 1867. 173p.
P5-NH0158 — $29.00.

HISTORICAL & STATISTICAL SKETCH OF CROYDEN, from its incorporation to the year 1852, con-taining much local information . . . John Cooper. 1852. 52p.
P5-NH0157 — $11.00.

HOUSES OF DERRY VILLAGE: An Informal Story. By Harriett Chase Newell. 1951. 171p.
P5-NH0262 — $25.00.

DOVER MARRIAGES, 1623-1823. Comp. by John R. Ham. 1904. 245p.
P5-NH0159 — $34.00.

HISTORY OF DOVER, Containing Historical, Genealogical & Industrial Data of its Early Settlers: Their Struggles & Triumphs. Vol. I. By Johns Scales. 1923. 516p.
P5-NH0160 — $55.00.

HISTORY OF DUBLIN, Containing the Address by Charles Mason & the Proceedings at the Centennial Cele-bration, with a Register of Families. 1855. 433p.
P5-NH0161 — $49.50.

HISTORY OF DUBLIN, with a Reg-ister of Families. 1920, rev. ed. 1018p.
P5-NH0106 — $99.00.

HISTORY OF THE TOWN OF DUNBARTON, Merrimack Co., from 1751 to 1860. C. Stark. 1860. 272p.
P5-NH0010 — $37.00.

HISTORY OF THE TOWN OF DURHAM (Oyster River Plantation) with Genealogical Notes, 2-vol. set: Vol. I, Historical; Vol. II, Gene-alogical. E.S. Stackpole & L. Thompson. 1913. 2 vols., 436 + 502p.
P5-NH0066 — $93.50/set.

HISTORY OF THE TOWN OF DURHAM . . . , Vol. I: Historical. 1913. 436p.
P5-NH0066A — $45.00.

HISTORY OF THE TOWN OF DURHAM . . . , Vol. II: Genealog-ical. 1913. 502p.
P5-NH0066B — $52.00.

CHURCH RECORDS OF EPSOM, 1761-1774. Priscilla Hammond. 1933. 29p.
P5-NH0162 — $10.00.

HISTORY OF THE TOWN OF EXETER. With a family register. By Charles H. Bell. 1888. 559p.
P5-NH0052 — $58.00.

MEN AND THINGS OF EXETER: Sketches from the History of an Old New Hampshire Town. By Charles H. Bell. 1871?. 73p.
P5-NH0255 — $15.00.

MY GREAT-GRANDFATHER'S HOUSE IN EXETER, New Hamp-shire. James Emery Brooks. 1932. 64p.
P5-NH0163 — $13.00.

HISTORY OF FITZWILLIAM, from 1752 to 1887, with a Genealogical Record of many Fitzwilliam Families. By John F. Norton & Joel Wittemore. 1888. 829p.
P5-NH0133 — $87.00.

HISTORY OF FRANCESTOWN, from its Earliest Settlement, 1758-1891. By W.R. Cochrane & G.K. Wood. 1895. 1031p.
P5-NH0011 — $97.00.

HISTORY OF GILMANTON, Embracing its Civil, Ecclesiastical, Literary & Biographical History to 1875, & including the History of Belmont. William Badger. 1976. 116p.
P5-NH0226 — $19.00.

HISTORY OF GILMANTON, Embracing the . . . Civil, Biographical, Genealogical & Misc. History from the First Settlement to the Present Time [1845], including what is now Gilford. By Daniel Lancaster. 1845. 304p.
P5-NH0084 — $37.50.

HISTORY OF GILSUM, from 1752 to 1879. By S. Hayward. 1881. 468p.
P5-NH0034 — $53.00.

HISTORY OF THE TOWN OF GOFFSTOWN, 1733-1920, 2-vol. set. By George Plummer Hadley. 1923. 2 vols., 601 + 586p.
P5-NH0074 — $159.00/set.

HISTORY OF THE TOWN OF GOFFSTOWN, 1733-1920, Vol. I. 1923. 601p.
P5-NH0074A — $62.50.

HISTORY OF THE TOWN OF GOFFSTOWN, 1733-1920, Vol. II. 1923. 586p.
P5-NH0074B — $62.50.

HISTORY OF GOSHEN. With two chapters of genealogy. By W.R. Nelson. 1957. 471p.
P5-NH0100 — $49.00.

GAZETEER OF GRAFTON COUNTY, 1709-1886, 2-vol. set. Comp. by H. Child. 1886. 2 vols., 644 + 380p.
P5-NH0064 — $107.50/ set.

GAZETEER OF GRAFTON COUNTY, 1709-1886, Vol. I. 1886. 644p.
P5-NH0064A — $74.50.

GAZETEER OF GRAFTON COUNTY, 1709-1886, Vol. II. 1886. 380p.
P5-NH0064B — $44.50.

VITAL RECORDS OF GREENLAND, 1710-1851. By Priscilla Hammond. 1938. 172p.
P5-NH0164 — $22.50.

MEMORIAL OF THE TOWN OF HAMPSTEAD, Historic & Genealogical Sketches, etc. By H.E. Noyes. 1899. xi + 468p.
P5-NH0068 — $52.00.

MEMORIAL OF THE TOWN OF HAMPSTEAD, ADDITIONS & CORRECTIONS. From "Hist. of the Congregational Church of Hampstead," by H.E. Noyes. 1903. 50p.
P5-NH0078 — $10.00.

VITAL RECORDS OF HAMPSTEAD, 1731-1870. With supplement, Abstracts from the Church Records, 1752-1866. By Priscilla Hammond. 1936. 351+116p.
P5-NH0165 — $49.00.

GRANTEES & SETTLEMENT OF HAMPTON. By Victor C. Sanborn. 1917. 24p.
P5-NH0217 — $10.00.

HISTORY OF THE TOWN OF HAMPTON, from its Settlement in 1638 to the Autumn of 1892. With a genealogical regoster. By Joseph Dow. 1894. 2 vols. in 1, 1104p.
P5-NH0022 — $105.00.

HISTORY OF THE TOWN OF HAMPTON FALLS, from the Time of the First Settlement within its Borders, 1640 to 1900. By Warren Brown. 1900. 637p.
P5-NH0024 — $75.00.

HISTORY OF HANCOCK, 1764-1889. With genealogical register. By W.W. Hayward. 1889. 1070p.
P5-NH0012 — $97.50.

HISTORY OF THE TOWN OF HANOVER. John King Lord. 1928. 339p.
P5-NH0111 — $42.50.

HISTORY OF HAVERHILL. By J.Q. Bittinger. 1888. 443p.
P5-NH0050 — $49.00.

HISTORY OF THE TOWN OF HAVERHILL. By W.F. Whitcher. 1919. 781p.
P5-NH0006A — $79.50.

HISTORY OF HEBRON. By the Hebron Bicentennial Comm. 1976. 55p.
P5-NH0227 — $11.00.

HISTORY OF THE TOWN OF HENNIKER, Merrimac Co., from the Date of the Canada Grant by the Province of Mass. in 1735 to 1880, with a Gen. Register. By L.W. Cogswell. 1880. 807p.
P5-NH0038 — $85.00.

TOWN REGISTER OF HENNIKER, BRADFORD, WARNER & HOPKINTON, 1908 [Town histories & censuses]. 1908. 212p.
P5-NH0216 — $29.00.

STORY OF HILL, NEW HAMPSHIRE. By Dan Stiles. 1942. 72p.
P5-NH0268 — $25.00.

HISTORY OF HILLSBOROUGH COUNTY. 1885. 748p.
P5-NH0062 — $79.00.

HISTORY OF HILLSBOROUGH, 1735-1921, 2-vol. set. By George Waldo Browne. 1921-1922. 2 vols., 567 + 695p.
P5-NH0167 — $125.00/set.

HISTORY OF HILLSBOROUGH, 1735-1921, Vol. I. 1921-1922. 567p.
P5-NH0167A — $62.50.

HISTORY OF HILLSBOROUGH, 1735-1921, Vol. II. 1921-1922. 695p.
P5-NH0167B — $75.00.

HISTORY OF HILLSBOROUGH, 1921-1963. By Harrison C. Baldwin. 1963. 201p.
P5-NH0047 — $29.50.

HOLDERNESS: An Account of the Beginnings of a New Hampshire Town. By George Hodges. 1907. 102p.
P5-NH0168 — $15.00.

HISTORY OF THE TOWN OF HOLLIS, from its First Settlement to 1879. By S.T. Worcester. 1879. 394p.
P5-NH0013 — $43.50.

LIFE & TIMES IN HOPKINTON, in Three Parts: Descriptive & Historical; Personal & Biographical; Statistical & Documentary. By C.C. Lord. 1890. 583p.
P5-NH0118 — $59.00.

ISLE OF SHOALS: an Historical Sketch. By John Scribner Jenness. 3rd ed., 1884. 214p.
P5-NH0200 — $29.50.

New Hampshire, cont.

HISTORY OF JAFFREY (Middle Monadnock): An Average Country Town in the Heart of New England, 2-vol. set. Albert Annett & Alice E.E. Lehtinen. 1934-1937. 2 vols., 847 + 902p.
P5-NH0245 — $175.00/set.

HISTORY OF JAFFREY . . . Vol. I. 1934-1937. 847p.
P5-NH0245A — $91.50.

HISTORY OF JAFFREY . . . Vol. II. 1934-1937. 902p.
P5-NH0245B — $91.50.

HISTORY OF THE TOWN OF JAFFREY, from the Date of the Masonian Charter to the Present Time, 1749-1880, with a Genealogical Register of the Jaffrey Families. By Daniel B. Cutter. 1881. 648p.
P5-NH0169 — $69.50.

HISTORY OF THE TOWN OF JEFFERSON, 1773-1927. By George C. Evans. 1927. 320p.
P5-NH0207 — $41.00.

ANNALS OF THE TOWN OF KEENE, from its First Settlement in 1734 to the Year 1790, with Corrections, Additions & a Continuation from 1790 to 1815. Salma Hale. 1851. 120p.
P5-NH0171 — $16.50.

HISTORICAL NOTES, WITH KEYED MAP, OF KEENE & ROXBURY, Cheshire County. By Samuel Wadsworth. 1932. 84p. + map
P5-NH0170 — $18.00.

HISTORY OF THE TOWN OF KEENE, from 1732 to 1874. By F.H. Whitcomb. 1904. 792p.
P5-NH0015 — $84.00.

VITAL STATISTICS OF THE TOWN OF KEENE, Compiled from the Town Records, First Church & Family Records, the Original Fisher Record & the Newspapers. By Frank H. Whitcomb. 1905. 268p.
P5-NH0172 — $34.00.

HISTORY OF KENSINGTON, 1663 to 1945, with a Family & Homestead Register of the Pioneer Families, Early Settlers & Permanent Citizens of the Town. Roland D. Sawyer. 1946. 404p.
P5-NH0173 — $47.00.

HISTORY OF KINGSTON, 1694-1969. 1969. 134p.
P5-NH0236 — $19.50.

THE ILLUSTRATED LACONIAN: History & Industries of Laconia. By Charles W. Vaughan. 1899. 248p.
P5-NH0135 — $34.50.

LAKEPORT'S ANCIENT HOMES: Recollections of Major John Aldrich . . . & of the Homes of Lakeport in 1844 with Notes of their Occupants Then & Later. Maj. John Aldrich. 1917. 86p.
P5-NH0174 — $15.00.

HISTORY OF LANCASTER. By A.N. Somers. 1899. 652p.
P5-NH0016 — $68.00.

HISTORY OF LANDAFF. Stanley P. Currier & Edgar T. Clement. 1966. 165p.
P5-NH0222 — $21.50.

HISTORY & GENEALOGICAL RECORD OF THE TOWN OF LANGDON, Sullivan County, from the Date of its Severance from Walpole & Charlestown, from 1787 to 1930. By Frank B. Kingsbury. 1932. 777p.
P5-NH0175 — $81.00.

HISTORY OF LEBANON, 1761-1887. By C.A. Downs. 1908. xiiii + 459p.
P5-NH0070 — $49.50.

BURIAL PLACES IN THE TOWN OF LEE, including old Parish Cemetery on Mast Rd. & Town Cemetery on Lee Hill, N.H. comp. by L.E. Walker, M.B. Walker & M.F. Burpee. 1938. 159p., typescript, paperback.
P5-NH0258 — $25.00.

HISTORY OF LITTLETON, 3-vol. set. 1905. 3 vols., 771 + 733 + 771p.
P5-NH0107 — $189.00/set.

HISTORY OF LITTLETON, Vol. I. 1905. 771p.
P5-NH0107A — $75.00.

HISTORY OF LITTLETON, Vol. II. 1905. 733p.
P5-NH0107B — $75.00.

HISTORY OF LITTLETON, Vol. III. 1905. 771p.
P5-NH0107C — $75.00.

EARLY RECORDS OF LONDON-DERRY, WINDHAM, AND DERRY, NEW HAMPSHIRE 1719-1962, Vol. I. By George Waldo Browne. 1908. 416p
P28071300 — $67.00.

HISTORY OF LONDONDERRY, Comprising the Towns of Derry & Londonderry. E.L. Parker. 1851. 418p.
P5-NH0054 — $45.00.

VITAL RECORDS OF LONDON-DERRY: Full & Accurate Transcript of Births, Marriages & Deaths . . . from the Earliest Date to 1910. Comp. by Daniel G. Annis. 1914. 330p.
P5-NH0234 — $39.50.

WILLEY'S BOOK OF NUTFIELD: History of the Part of New Hampshire Comprised within the Limits of the Old Township of Londonderry, from its Settlement in 1719 to the Present Time: Biographical, Genealogical, Political, Anecdotal. By Geo. F. Willey. 1895. 414p.
P5-NH0176 — $47.00.

HISTORICAL SKETCHES OF LYMAN. By E.B. Hoskins. 1903. 148p.
P5-NH0177 — $27.00.

HISTORY OF LYNDEBOROUGH, 1735-1905. By D. Donovan & Jacob A. Woodward. 1906. 932p.
P5-NH0178 — $94.50.

HISTORY OF THE TOWN OF LYNDEBOROUGH, 1905-1955. With genealogies. 1958. 229p.
P5-NH0179 — $29.50.

MADBURY, Its People & Places. By Eloi A. Adams. 1968. 152p.
P5-NH0233 — $22.50.

AMOSKEAG MANUFACTURING CO. OF MANCHESTER: A History. By George Waldo Browne. 1915. 288p.
P5-NH0208 — $39.50.

HISTORY OF MANCHESTER, Formerly Derryfield, in New Hampshire, including that of Ancient Amoskeag, or the Middle Merrimack Valley. By C.E. Potter. 1856. 764p.
P5-NH0136 — $79.00.

MANCHESTER MEN, Soldiers & Sailors in the Civil War, 1861-66. By George C. Gilmore. 1898. 167p.
P5-NH0180 — $21.00.

MANCHESTER OF YESTERDAY: A Human Interest Story of its Past, with One Hundred Illustrations, Including Rate Wood Engravings of Old Pioneers and Places. By L. Ashton Thorp. 1939. 561p.
P5-NH0209 — $61.00.

MANCHESTER: BRIEF RECORD OF ITS PAST, also a Picture of its Present, Including an Account of its Settlement & of its Growth . . . and Sketches of its Representative Citizens. By John B. Clarke. 1875. 463p.
P5-NH0181 — $51.50.

RECORD OF THE MARRIAGES OF SAINT ANTOINE (1900-50) [MANCHESTER]. 1951. 77p., typescript. In French
P5-NH0244 — $15.00.

RECORD OF THE MARRIAGES OF SAINT JEAN-BAPTISTE (1914-51) [Manchester, NH]. 1951. 114p., typescript.
P5-NH0243 — $18.00.

WILLEY'S SEMI-CENTENNIAL BOOK OF MANCHESTER. By George Franklin Willey. 1896. 371p.
P5-NH0267 — $40.00.

TOWN REGISTER OF MARLBORO, TROY, JAFFREY & SWANZEY, 1908 [Town histories & censuses]. 1908. 96 + 120p.
P5-NH0182 — $29.50.

HISTORY OF THE TOWN OF MARLBOROUGH, Cheshire Co. With genealogical register. By C.A. Bemis. 1881. 726p.
P5-NH0101 — $69.50.

HISTORY OF THE TOWN OF MASON, from its First Grant in 1749 to 1858 (incl. Greenville). By John B. Hill. 1858. 324p.
P5-NH0113 — $38.00.

MEREDITH Annals & Genealogies. By Mary E.N. Hanaford. 1932. 760p.
P5-NH0184 — $79.50.

TOWN REGISTER OF MEREDITH, TILTON, GILMANTON, GILFORD, BELMONT, NEW HAMPTON, 1908. 1908. 87 + 165p.
P5-NH0183 — $34.00.

HISTORY OF MERRIMAC & BELKNAP COUNTIES. 1885. 915p.
P5-NH0029 — $91.00.

BIOGRAPHICAL REVIEW, MERRIMACK AND SULLIVAN COUNTIES, NEW HAMPSHIRE. 1897. 596p
P28035000 — $93.00.

HISTORICAL NOTES & PICTURES OF MILAN, N.H., 1771-1971. By the Bicentennial History Comm. 1971. 352p.
P5-NH0228 — $44.00.

HISTORY OF MILFORD, with Family Registers. By G.A. Ramsdell & W.P. Colburn. 1901. xii + 1210p.
P5-NH0069 — $125.00.

HISTORY OF MONROE, 1761-1954. With genealogical records. By Frances Ann Johnson. 1955. 642p.
P5-NH0130 — $67.00.

HISTORY OF THE TOWN OF MONT VERNON. By C.J. Smith. 1907. 443p.
P5-NH0049 — $47.00.

SKETCH OF THE EARLY HISTORY OF THE TOWN OF NELSON. By S.G. Griffith. 1903. 54p.
P5-NH0185 — $11.00.

GRAVESTONE INSCRIPTIONS FROM NEW BOSTON. Comp. by M. & W. Holman. 1931. 87p.
P5-NH0220 — $16.00.

HISTORY OF NEW BOSTON. By Elliott C. Cogswell. 1864. 470p.
P5-NH0201 — $49.00.

NEW CASTLE, Historic & Picturesque. With the Bi-Centennial Souvenir, 1693-1893 (compiled by chester B. Curtis). By John Albee. 1884. 154 + 51p.
P5-NH0239 — $31.00.

BAPTISMS, MARRIAGES & FUNERALS from the Notebooks of Rev. David Leighton Edgerly, 1818-1891 [NEW DURHAM]. Comp. by Edwin L. Edgerly. n.d. 39p.
P5-NH0221 — $10.00.

REMINISCENCES OF NEW HAMPTON; also a Genealogical Sketch of the Kelley & Simpson Families. Frank H. Kelley. 1929. 147p.
P5-NH0186 — $19.50.

HISTORY OF NEW IPSWICH, 1735-1914, with Genealogical Records of the Principal Families. By C.H. Chandler & S.F. Lee. 1914. 782p.
P5-NH0032 — $78.00.

HISTORY OF NEW IPSWICH, from its First Grant in 1736, with Genealogical Notices of the Principal Families & the Proceedings of the Centennial Celebrations. By A.A. Gould. 1852. 492p.
P5-NH0035A — $49.50.

HISTORY OF THE TOWN OF NEW LONDON, Merrimac Co., 1779-1899. 1899. 774p.
P5-NH0102 — $77.00.

HISTORY OF NEWFIELDS, 1638-1911. By J.H. Fitts. 1912. viii + 785p.
P5-NH0076 — $79.50.

VITAL RECORDS OF NEWINGTON, 1703-1853. By Priscilla Hammond. 1934. 29p.
P5-NH0187 — $10.00.

OLD NEWMARKET: Historical Sketches. By Nellie Palmer George. 1932. 133p.
P5-NH0210 — $30.00.

HISTORY OF NEWPORT, from 1766 to 1878, with Genealogical Register. By Edmund Wheeler. 1879. 600p.
P5-NH0116 — $59.50.

HISTORY OF NORTHFIELD, 1780-1905, in Two Parts with Many Biographical Sketches & Portraits, Part I: History. L.H.R. Cross. 1905. 293p.
P5-NH0055A — $38.50.

HISTORY OF NORTHFIELD, 1780-1905, in Two Parts with Many Biographical Sketches & Portraits, Part II: Genealogy. L.H.R. Cross. 1905. 410p.
P5-NH0055B — $49.50.

GRAVESTONES OF GUILDHALL, Vt. & Northumberland, NH. By Nancy L. Dodge. 1987. 185p.
P5-VT0006 — $39.00.

HISTORY OF NOTTINGHAM, DEERFIELD, NORTHWOOD, Nottingham and Rockingham Counties, with Genealogical Sketches. By E.C. Cogswell. 1878. 790p.
P5-NH0017 — $79.00.

HISTORY OF OLD CHESTER, NEW HAMPSHIRE, 1719-1869. By Benjamin Chase. 1869. xvi + 702p
P28073000 — $91.00.

HISTORY OF PEMBROKE, 1730-1895, in 2 vols. By N.F. Carter, with T.L. Fowler. 1895. 2 vols., 428 + 469p.
P5-NH0252 — $95.00/set.

HISTORY OF PEMBROKE, 1730-1895, Vol. I. 1895. 428p.
P5-NH0252A — $49.00.

New Hampshire, cont.

HISTORY OF PEMBROKE, 1730-1895, Vol. II. 1895. 469p.
P5-NH0252B — $49.00.

HISTORY OF PENACOOK from its First Settlement in 1734 up to 1900. Comp. by David Arthur Brown. 1902. 570p.
P5-NH0188 — $61.00.

HISTORY OF THE TOWN OF PETERBOROUGH, Hillsborough Co. By Albert Smith. 1876. 735p.
P5-NH0117 — $76.00.

PETERBOROUGH in the American Revolution. Jonathan Smith. 1913. 423p.
P5-NH0189 — $47.00.

PIERMONT, New Hampshire, 1764-1947. With genealogies. L.S. Horton, E.H. Underhill & E.D. Deal. 1947. 236p.
P5-NH0067 — $32.50.

PISCATAQUA PIONEERS, 1623-1775: Register of Members & Ancestors. By John Scales. 1919. 212p.
P5-NH0190 — $24.50.

HISTORY OF PITTSFIELD in the Great Rebellion. By H.L. Robinson. 1893. 217p.
P5-NH0191 — $31.00.

HISTORY OF PITTSFIELD, New Hampshire. E. Harold Young. 1953. 575p.
P5-NH0211 — $64.00.

GRAVESTONES OF PLAINFIELD, 1767-1946. Vernon A. Hood. 1946. 163p.
P5-NH0192 — $19.50.

HISTORY OF PLYMOUTH, Vol. I, Narrative [history]. By Ezra S. Stearns. 1906. 632p.
P5-NH0193 — $67.00.

ANNALS OF PORTSMOUTH. By Nathaniel Adams. 1825; Index, 1940. 400p.
P5-NH0103 — $39.00.

PORTSMOUTH & NEWCASTLE CEMETERY INSCRIPTIONS, Abstracted from some 2,000 Oldest Tombstones. Arthur Locke. 1907. 44p.
P5-NH0104 — $10.00.

PORTSMOUTH BOOK [Essays on history & architecture of Portsmouth]. 1899. 52 + xiv p.
P5-NH0254 — $13.50.

RANDOLPH, OLD & NEW: Its Ways & its By-ways. By George N. Cross. 1924. 260p.
P5-NH0242 — $34.50.

HISTORY OF RAYMOND. By Joseph Fullonton. 1875. 406p.
P5-NH0065 — $44.50.

HISTORY OF THE TOWN OF RICHMOND, Cheshire Co., from its First Settlement to 1882. By Wm. Bassett. 1884. 578p.
P5-NH0140 — $64.00.

HISTORY OF THE TOWN OF RINDGE, from the Date of the Rowley, Canada or Mass. Charter to the Present Time, 1736-1874, with Genealogical Register. By E.S. Stearns. 1875. 788p.
P5-NH0072 — $81.00.

HISTORY OF ROCHESTER, from 1722 to 1890. By F. McDuffee, 1892. 2 vols. in 1, 705p.
P5-NH0051A — $69.50.

HISTORY OF ROCKINGHAM & STRAFFORD COUNTY, with Biographical Sketches of Many of its Prominent Men & Pioneers. 1882. 889p.
P5-NH0031 — $92.00.

HISTORY OF ROCKINGHAM COUNTY & Representative Citizens. By Charles A. Hazlett. 1915. 1306p.
P5-NH0014 — $125.00.

RUMNEY, Then & Now. By Jesse A. Barney. 1967. 244p.
P5-NH0229 — $33.50.

HISTORY OF THE TOWN OF RYE, 1623-1903. By L.B. Parsons. 1905. 675p.
P5-NH0018 — $69.50.

RYE ON THE ROCKS: the Tale of a Town; a Yankee Saga told by a Yankee. By W.M. Varrell. 1962. 149p.
P5-NH0063 — $18.50.

HISTORY OF SALEM. By E. Gilbert. 1907. 444 + 160p.
P5-NH0019 — $79.50.

HISTORY OF SALISBURY, from Date of Settlement to 1890. By Dearborn, Adams & Rolfe. 1890. 892p.
P5-NH0020 — $89.50.

HISTORY OF SANBORNTON, 2-vol. set.. By M.T. Runnels. 1881-1882. 2 vols., 570 + 1022p.
P5-NH0021 — $150.00/set.

HISTORY OF SANBORNTON, Vol. I. 1881. 570p.
P5-NH0021A — $57.00.

HISTORY OF SANBORNTON, Vol. II. 1882. 1022p
P5-NH0021B — $96.00.

SANDWICH CEMETERIES. By Harriett Vittum Lighton. 1930. 161p.
P5-NH0194 — $19.50.

HISTORY OF SHELBURNE. By Mrs R.P. Peabody. 1882. 127p.
P5-NH0195 — $24.50.

FIRST ANNUAL REPORT OF THE CITY OF SOMERSWORTH, Containing the City Charter . . . , Vital Statistics for 1894 . . . , Prefaced with an Historical Sketch. 1894. 161p.
P5-NH0196 — $19.50.

HISTORY OF STARK, 1774-1974. Stark Bi-Centennial Comm. 1974. 228p.
P5-NH0230 — $34.00.

VITAL STATISTICS OF STEWARTS-TOWN, From Dec. 1770 to Jan. 1, 1888. With names & dates of the original grant, incorporation, settlement, marriages, births & deaths. By C.E. Tewksbury. 1888. 51p.
P5-NH0197 — $11.00.

HISTORY OF STODDARD, Cheshire Co., from the Time of its Incorporation in 1774 to 1854, with some Sketches from its First Settlement in 1768. Isaiah Gould. 1897. 139p.
P5-NH0256 — $22.00.

BIO. REVIEW [Vol. XXI] Containing Life Sketches of Citizens of Strafford and Belknap Cos. 1897. 604p.
P5-NH0270 — $62.00.

HISTORY OF STRAFFORD COUNTY, & Representative Citizens. By John Scales. 1914. 953p.
P5-NH0198 — $97.00.

HISTORY OF THE TOWN OF STRATFORD, 1733-1925. By Jeannette R. Thompson. 1925. 525p.
P5-NH0248 — $57.00.

HISTORY OF STRATHAM, 1631-1900. By Charles B. Nelson. n.d. 308p.
P5-NH0232 — $39.50.

HISTORY OF THE TOWN OF SULLIVAN, 1777-1917, with Genealogies, 2-vol. set. By J.L. Seward. 1921. 2 vols., 816 + 820p.
P5-NH0023 — $159.00/set.

HISTORY OF THE TOWN OF SULLIVAN . . . , Vol. I. 1921. 816p.
P5-NH0023A — $85.50.

HISTORY OF THE TOWN OF SULLIVAN . . . , Vol. II. 1921. 820p.
P5-NH0023B — $85.50.

STORY OF SUNAPEE. By John Henry Bartlett. 1941. 196p.
P5-NH0261 — $27.00.

HISTORY OF THE TOWN OF SURRY, Cheshire Co., from the Date of Severance from Gilsum & Westmoreland, 1769-1922, with a Genealogical Reg. of the Town. By F.B. Kingsbury. 1925. 1062p.
P5-NH0035B — $98.00.

HISTORY OF SUTTON, Consisting of the Hist. Collections of Erastus Wadleigh & A.H. Worthen, 2-vol. set. 1890. 2 vols., 595 + 510p.
P5-NH0046 — $114.00/set.

HISTORY OF SUTTON . . . , Vol. I. 1890. 595p.
P5-NH0046A — $60.00.

HISTORY OF SUTTON . . . , Vol. II. 1890. 510p.
P5-NH0046B — $59.00.

HISTORY OF SWANZEY, from 1734 to 1890. Benjamin Read. 1892. 585p.
P5-NH0025 — $59.50.

TAMWORTH NARRATIVE. By Marjorie Gane Harkness. 1958. 336p.
P5-NH0139 — $43.50.

HISTORY OF TEMPLE. By Henry Ames Blood. 1860. 352p.
P5-NH0203 — $39.00.

HISTORICAL SKETCH OF THE TOWN OF TROY & her Inhabitants, from the First Settlement of the Territory now within the Limits of the Town, 1764-1897. By M.T. Stone. 1897. 587p.
P5-NH0059 — $62.00.

HISTORICAL SKETCH OF TROY & her Inhabitants, from the First Settlement in 1764 to 1855. By A.M. Caverly. 1859. 298p.
P5-NH0204 — $36.50.

TUFTONBORO: An Historical Sketch. Rev. John W. Hayley. 1923. 111p.
P5-NH0199 — $15.00.

HISTORY OF WALPOLE, NEW HAMPSHIRE. By Martha McDanolds Frizzell. 1963. 772 + 343p.
P5-NH0269 — $124.00.

WALPOLE AS IT WAS AND AS IT IS: Containing the Complete Civil History of the Town from 1749 to 1879, also..a History of the 150 Families that Settled in the Town Previous to 1820 . . . George Aldrich. 1880. 404p.
P5-NH0134 — $44.50.

HISTORY OF WARREN, A Mountain Hamlet Located among the White Hills of New Hampshire. By William Little. 1870. 594p.
P5-NH0132 — $61.50.

HISTORY OF WASHINGTON, from 1768 to 1886, with Genealogies. By a Comm. of the Town. 1886. 696p.
P5-NH0026 — $69.50.

HISTORY OF WEARE, 1735-1888. 1888. 1064p.
P5-NH0048 — $105.00.

TOWN HISTORY OF WEARE, from 1888. By Helen E. Dearborn. 1959. 305 + 44p.
P5-NH0205b — $37.50.

HISTORY OF THE TOWN OF WENTWORTH. By Geo. F. Plummer. 1930. xix + 401p.
P5-NH0212 — $47.00.

WEST DUNSTABLE, MONSON & HOLLIS: An Acct. of Some of the Early Settlers. By C.S. Spaulding. 1915. 251p.
P5-NH0027 — $35.00.

HEART OF THE WHITE MOUNTAINS: Their Legend and Scenery. By Samuel Adams Drake. 1882. 318p.
P5-NH0131 — $39.50.

HISTORY OF THE WHITE MOUNTAINS, from the First Settlement of Upper Coos & Pequaket. By Lucy Crawford. 1846. 205p.
P5-NH0143 — $31.00.

HISTORY OF THE WHITE MOUNTAINS, from the First Settlement of Upper Coos & Pequaket. By L. Crawford. 1883. 230p
P5-NH0105 — $30.00.

INCIDENTS IN WHITE MOUNTAIN HISTORY, Containing Facts Relating to the Discovery & Settlement of the Mountains, Indian History & Traditions . . . Together with Humorous Anecdotes Illustrating Life in the Back Woods. By Rev. Benj. G. Willey. 1856. 326p.
P5-NH0142 — $41.50.

EARLY HISTORY OF WILMOT. By Caspar L. LeVarn. 1957. 214p.
P5-NH0213 — $34.00.

HISTORY OF THE TOWN OF WILTON, Hillsborough Co., with Genealogical Register. By A.A. Livermore & S. Putnam. 1888. 575p.
P5-NH0036B — $62.00.

VITAL RECORDS OF WILTON, 1718-1853. Priscilla Hammond. 1936. 170p.
P5-NH0214 — $21.50.

HISTORY OF THE PROCEEDINGS OF THE CELEBRATIONS OF THE 150TH ANNIVERSARY . . . OF WINDHAM in New Hampshire. 1892. 124p.
P5-NH0238 — $19.00.

HISTORY OF WINDHAM, 1719-1883, with the History & Genealogy of its First Settlers & Descendants. By Leonard A. Morrison. 1883. 862p.
P5-NH0028 — $88.00.

TOWN REGISTER OF WOLFBORO, OSSIPEE, EFFINGHAM, TUFTONBORO, TAMWORTH, FREEDOM, 1908 [Town histories & censuses]. 1908. 117 + 139p.
P5-NH0215 — $34.00.

HISTORY OF WOLFEBOROUGH. By B.F. Parker. 1901. 557p.
P5-NH0060 — $61.50.

New Jersey

EARLY GERMANS OF N.J., Their History, Churches & Genealogy. By T.F. Chambers. 1895. 667p.
P5-NJ0011 — $42.50.

EARLY QUAKER MARRIAGES from Various Records in N.J. Comp. by G. Haines. 1902. 32p.
P5-NJ0001 — $10.00.

New Jersey, cont.

EAST JERSEY UNDER THE PROPIETARY GOVERNMENTS: Narrative of Events Connected with the Settlement & Progress of the Province, until the Surrender of the Government to the Crown in 1703. With appendix containing "Model of the Govt. on East New-Jersey," 1685. By Wm. A. Whitehead. 1875. 486p.
P5-NJ0087 — $51.00.

ENCYCLOPEDIA OF AMERICAN QUAKER GENEALOGY, Vol. II, New Jersey & Pennsylvania. By William Wade Hinshaw. 1938. 1126p.
P5-NJ0060 — $85.00.

GEOGRAPHIC DICTIONARY OF N.J. By Henry Gannett. 1894. 131p.
P5-NJ0037 — $15.00.

HISTORICAL & GENEALOGICAL MISCELLANY: Data Relating to the Settlement & Settlers of New Jersey, Vol. I only. By John E. Stillwell, M.D. 1903-1932. 483p.
P5-NJ0021A — $45.00.

HISTORICAL & GENEALOGICAL MISCELLANY . . . , Vol. II only. 1903-1932. 503p.
P5-NJ0021B — $45.00.

HISTORICAL & GENEALOGICAL MISCELLANY . . . Vol. III only. 1903-1932. 546p.
P5-NJ0021C — $45.00.

HISTORICAL & GENEALOGICAL MISCELLANY . . . Vol. IV only. 1903-1932. 440p.
P5-NJ0021D — $45.00.

HISTORICAL & GENEALOGICAL MISCELLANY . . . , Vol. V only. 1903-1932. 575p.
P5-NJ0021E — $45.00.

HISTORICAL COLLECTIONS OF THE STATE OF NEW JERSEY, Containing a General Collection of the Most Interesting Facts, Traditions, Biographical Sketches, Anecdotes, etc., Relating to its History & Antiquities. With a geographical description of every township. By J.W. Barber & Henry Howe. 1844. 518p.
P5-NJ0018 — $55.00.

MISCELLANEOUS BIBLE RECORDS, Principally New Jersey Families. Comp. by Agnes F. Risley. 1929. 151p.
P5-NJ0085 — $22.00.

NEW JERSEY MARRIAGE NOTICES, 1830-1871, as Published in "The Christian Intelligencer" of the Reformed Dutch Church. Comp. by Ray. C. Sawyer. 1932-1933. 2 vols. in 1, 138 + 195p.
P5-NJ0088 — $39.00.

NEW JERSEY MARRIAGE RECORDS, 1665-1800. Documents Relating to the Colonial History of N.J.: Marriage Records. 1900. 678p.
P5-NJ0017B — $57.00.

PATENTS & DEEDS OF COLONIAL N.J.: Documents relating to the Colonial History, 1664-1703. 1899. 770p.
P5-NJ0022 — $75.00.

RECORD OF OFFICERS & MEN OF NEW JERSEY in the Civil War, 1861-5, 2-vol. set. Comp. by Wm. Stryker, Adjutant General. 1876. 2 vols., 1758 + 176p. index.
P5-NJ0151 — $165.00/set.

RECORD OF OFFICERS & MEN OF NEW JERSEY in the Civil War, 1861-5, Vol. I. 1876. 1758p.
P5-NJ0151A — $148.50.

RECORD OF OFFICERS & MEN OF NEW JERSEY in the Civil War, 1861-5, Vol. II. 1876. 176p.
P5-NJ0151B — $28.00.

RECORDS OF OFFICERS AND MEN OF NEW JERSEY IN WARS: 1791-1815. 1909. 286 + 19p.
P5-NJ0151C — $32.50.

STATE OF NEW JERSEY INDEX OF WILL, INVENTORIES, Etc., in the Office of the Secretary of State Prior to 1901, 3-vol. set. Comp. by the Office of the Secretary of State. 1913. 3 vols., 1452p.
P5-NJ0147 — $145.00.

STATE OF NEW JERSEY INDEX OF WILL, INVENTORIES . . . , Vol. I. 1913.
P5-NJ0147A — $52.00.

STATE OF NEW JERSEY INDEX OF WILL, INVENTORIES . . . , Vol. II. 1913.
P5-NJ0147B — $52.00.

STATE OF NEW JERSEY INDEX OF WILL, INVENTORIES . . . , Vol. III. 1913.
P5-NJ0147C — $52.00.

STORY OF AN OLD FARM, or, Life in N. J. in the 18th Century. With genealogical appendix (Mellick Family). By Andrew D. Mellick, Jr. 1889. 742p.
P5-NJ0035 — $77.00.

"THE DAILY UNION" HISTORY OF ATLANTIC CITY & COUNTY, Containing Sketches of the Past & Present of Atlantic City & Co., with Maps & Illustrations. By John F. Hall. 1899-1900. 517p.
P5-NJ0090 — $56.00.

ABSEGAMI ANNALS: Eyren Haven & Atlantic City, 1609 to 1904, Being an Account of the Settlement of Eyren Haven or Egg Harbor, and Reminiscences of Atlantic City during the 17th, 18th & 19th Centuries; also Indian Traditions & Sketches, 2-vol. set. Alfred M. Heston. 1904. 2 vols., 337 + 446p.
P5-NJ0093 — $79.50/set.

ABSEGAMI ANNALS . . . , Vol. I. 1904. 337p.
P5-NJ0093A — $40.00.

ABSEGAMI ANNALS . . . , Vol. II. 1904. 446p.
P5-NJ0093B — $45.50.

ATLANTIC CITY & COUNTY [History & Biography]: the City by the Sea & her People. 1899. 200 + 173p.
P5-NJ0091 — $44.50.

HISTORY OF ATLANTIC CITY. By A.L. English. 1884. 226p.
P5-NJ0092 — $31.50.

ANNALS OF THE CLASSIS OF BERGEN, of the Reformed Dutch Church, Including the Civil History of the Ancient Township of Bergen. By Benjamin C. Taylor. 1857. 479p.
P5-NJ0095 — $53.50.

BERGEN COUNTY MARRIAGE RECORDS, Copied from the Entries as Originally Made. Comp. by Frances A. Westervelt. 1929. 117p.
P5-NJ0094 — $15.00.

For hardcover versions, see the order form on page v. To order, call 1-888-296-3447.

HISTORY OF BERGEN &
PASSAIC COUNTIES, with Biographical Sketches of Many of its
Pioneers & Prominent Men. With
1993 every-name index by Jerri
Burket. 1882. 570 + 90p.
P5-NJ0026 — $67.00.

HISTORY OF BERGEN COUNTY,
1630-1923, Historical-Biographical.
Includes modern every-name index
by Jerri Burket, 3 vols. in 2. 1923. 3
vols. in 2, 709 + 516p.
P5-NJ0150 — $99.50/set.

HISTORY OF BERGEN COUNTY
. . . , Book I: History. 1923. 709p.
P5-NJ0150A — $67.50.

HISTORY OF BERGEN COUNTY
. . . , Book II: Genealogy. 1923. 516p.
P5-NJ0150B — $52.00.

HISTORY OF BERGEN COUNTY.
With 1994 Index, by Jerri Burket. By
J.M. Van Valen. 1900. 691 + 71p.
P5-NJ0023 — $76.50.

BLOOMFIELD, New Jersey. 1932.
110p.
P5-NJ0096 — $17.00.

BOTTLE HILL & MADISON:
Glimpses & Reminiscenses from its
Earliest Settlement to the Civil War.
By Wm. Parkhurst Tuttle. 1916. 237p.
P5-NJ0114 — $34.00.

CITY OF BRIDGETON: its
Settlement & Growth, its Attractions,
its Industries, its Advantages as a
Manufacturing Site. With Illustrations. By J.T. Nichols. 1889. 79p.
P5-NJ0097 — $14.00.

FRIENDS [Quakers] IN
BURLINGTON. By Amerlia Mott
Gummere. 1884. 100p.
P5-NJ0098 — $15.00.

BURLINGTON COUNTY
MARRIAGES. Comp. by H. Stanley
Craig. n.d. 339p.
P5-NJ0099 — $39.50.

HISTORY OF BURLINGTON &
MERCER COUNTIES, with
Biographical Sketches of its Pioneers
& Prominent Men. E.M. Woodward &
J.F. Hageman. 1883. 888p.
P5-NJ0002 — $95.00.

HISTORY OF CAMDEN
COUNTY. 1886. 769p.
P5-NJ0025 — $79.00.

CAPE MAY COUNTY Mayflower
Pilgrim Descendants. By P.S. Howe.
1921. 464p.
P5-NJ0069 — $45.00.

HISTORY OF CAPE MAY
COUNTY, from Aboriginal Times to
the Present Day [1897]. By Lewis T.
Stevens. 1897. 479p.
P5-NJ0024 — $49.50.

CUMBERLAND COUNTY
GENEALOGICAL DATA: Records
Pertaining to Persons Residing in
Cumberland County Prior to 1800.
Comp. by H. Stanley Craig. n.d. 248p.
P5-NJ0070 — $27.00.

CUMBERLAND COUNTY
MARRIAGES. Comp. by H. Stanley
Craig. n.d. 333p.
P5-NJ0102 — $39.00.

GENEALOGICAL DATA FROM
CUMBERLAND CO. WILLS. By H.
Stanley Craig. n.d. 157p.
P5-NJ0101 — $21.00.

HISTORY OF THE EARLY
SETTLEMENT & PROGRESS OF
CUMBERLAND COUNTY. By
Lucius Q.C. Elmer. 1869. 142p.
P5-NJ0100 — $19.50.

HISTORY OF ELIZABETH,
including the Early History of Union
County. Edwin F. Hatfield. 1868. 701p.
P5-NJ0005 — $75.00.

INSCRIPTIONS ON TOMBSTONES
& MONUMENTS in the Burying
Grounds of the First Presbyterian
Church & St Johns Church at
Elizabeth, 1664-1892. Comp. by W.O.
Wheeler & E.D. Halsey. 1892. 355p.
P5-NJ0080 — $39.50.

NOTES, HISTORICAL & BIOGRAPHICAL, Concerning
Elizabeth-Town: its Eminent Men,
Churches & Ministers. By Nicholas
Murray. 1844. 174p.
P5-NJ0103 — $28.50.

HISTORY OF ESSEX & HUDSON
COUNTIES, 2-vol. set. Comp. by
William H. Shaw. 1884. 2 vols., 678 + 734p.
P5-NJ0027 — $135.00/set.

HISTORY OF ESSEX & HUDSON
COUNTIES, Vol. I. 1884. 678p.
P5-NJ0027A — $74.50.

HISTORY OF ESSEX & HUDSON
COUNTIES, Vol. II. 1884. 734p.
P5-NJ0027B — $78.50.

MUNICIPALITIES OF ESSEX
COUNTY, 1666-1924, 4-vol. set in 2
books. 1925. 4 vols. in 2, 888 + 409p.
P5-NJ0061 — $125.00/set.

MUNICIPALITIES OF ESSEX
COUNTY, 1666-1924, Vols. I & II:
History. 1925. 888p.
P5-NJ0061A — $89.00.

MUNICIPALITIES OF ESSEX
COUNTY, 1666-1924, Vols. III & IV:
Biography. 1925. 409p.
P5-NJ0061B — $45.00.

HISTORIC NOTES ON FAIRMOUNT, NEW JERSEY. By
Freeman Leigh. 1926. 75p.
P5-NJ0256 — $23.00.

HISTORY OF FRENCHTOWN,
with Interesting Sidelights on
Surrounding Communities. By
Clarence B. Fargo. 1933. 220p.
P5-NJ0105 — $31.50.

GLOUCESTER COUNTY RESIDENTS, 1850. G.& F. Gibson. n.d. 337p.
P5-NJ0029 — $34.50.

HISTORY OF THE COUNTIES
OF GLOUCESTER, SALEM &
CUMBERLAND, with Biographical
Sketches of their Prominent Citizens.
By Thomas Cushing & Chas. E.
Sheppard. 1883. 726p.
P5-NJ0253 — $73.50.

NEW YORK-MAPLE GROVE
CEMETERY; Hackensack, NJ. H.S.
Acerkman & A.J. Goff. 1945. 209 + 6p.
P5-NJ0261 — $30.00.

HARDYSTON MEMORIAL: A
History of the Township & the No.
Presbyterian Church, Hardyston,
Sussex Co. Alanson A. Haines. 1888. 181p.
P5-NJ0106 — $29.00.

HISTORY OF HILLSIDE &
VICINITY, Including Lyons Farms,
Salem, Saybrook & Early History of
Newark & Elizabethtown. 1934. 278p.
P5-NJ0107 — $36.50.

PIONEERS OF OLD HOPEWELL,
with Sketches of her Revolutionary
Heroes. By Ralph Ege. 1908. 290p.
P5-NJ0109 — $37.00.

For hardcover versions, see the order form on page v. To order, call 1-888-296-3447.

New Jersey, cont.

TOWN RECORDS OF HOPEWELL.
By Lida Cokefair Gedney. 1931. 197p.
P5-NJ0108 — $24.00.

HISTORY OF HUDSON COUNTY,
from the Earliest Settlement to the
Present Time. With 1993 index by
Jerri Burket. By C.H. Winfield. 1874.
568 + 40p.
P5-NJ0003 — $62.50.

**GENEALOGICAL HISTORY OF
HUDSON & BERGEN COUNTIES.**
Ed. by Cornelius B. Harvey. 1900. 617p.
P5-NJ0030 — $63.50.

**HISTORY OF THE LAND TITLES
IN HUDSON CO., 1609-1871.** By
Charles H. Winfield. 1872. 443p.
P5-NJ0110 — $47.00.

**HISTORY OF THE MUNICIPAL-
ITIES OF HUDSON COUNTY,**
1630-1923, 3-vol. set. 1924. 3 vols; 534
+ 414 + 390p.
P5-NJ0071 — $129.00/set.

**HISTORY OF THE MUNICIPAL-
ITIES OF HUDSON COUNTY,**
1630-1923, Vol. I. 1924. 534p.
P5-NJ0071A — $55.00.

**HISTORY OF THE MUNICIPAL-
ITIES OF HUDSON COUNTY,**
1630-1923, Vol. II. 1924. 441p.
P5-NJ0071B — $45.00.

**HISTORY OF THE MUNICIPAL-
ITIES OF HUDSON COUNTY, 1630-
1923, Vol. III.** 1924. 390p.
P5-NJ0071C — $40.00 .

**HISTORY OF HUNTERDON &
SOMERSET COUNTIES, with
Illustraitons & Biographical Sketches
of its Prominent Men & Pioneers.**
Comp. by James P. Snell. 1881. 864p.
P5-NJ0014 — $89.50.

**PORT. & BIO. RECORD OF
HUNTERDON & WARREN COS.,**
NJ. 1898. 578p.
P5-NJ0258 — $58.00.

**GENEALOGICAL RECORDS OF
THE REFORMED PROTESTANT
DUTCH CHURCH OF BERGEN**
[now Jersey City], 1666-1788. Ed. &
trans. by C. Versteeg & T.E. Vermilye,
Jr. 1913-1915. 3 vols. in 1, 273p.
P5-NJ0112 — $25.00.

HISTORY OF JERSEY CITY: A
Record of its Early Settlement &
Corporate Progress, Sketches of
Towns & Cities that were Absorbed
om the Growth of the Present
Municipality . . . with Some Notice of
the Men who Built the City. By
Alexander McLean. 1895. 462p.
P5-NJ0111 — $51.50.

Jersey City of Today. 1910. 156p.
P5-NJ0260 — $25.00.

**OLD BERGEN HISTORY &
REMINISCENCES, with Maps &
Illustrations** [Jersey City]. By Daniel
Van Winkle. 1902. 319p.
P5-NJ0063 — $37.00.

**HISTORY OF LITTLE EGG
HARBOR TOWNSHIP, Burlington
Co., from its First Settlement to the
Present Time.** By Leah Blackman.
1880?. 468p.
P5-NJ0068 — $49.50.

**LIVINGSTON, The Story of a Com-
munity.** Writers of the WPA. 1939. 166p.
P5-NJ0113 — $19.00.

**HISTORY OF MIDDLESEX
COUNTY, 1664-1920, Historical —
Biographical, 3 vols. in 2 books.**
1921. 3 vols. in 2, 506 + 535p.
P5-NJ0115 — $109.00/set.

**HISTORY OF MIDDLESEX
COUNTY . . . , Book I.** 1921. 506p.
P5-NJ0115A — $57.00.

**HISTORY OF MIDDLESEX
COUNTY . . . , Book II.** 1921. 535p.
P5-NJ0115B — $57.00.

**STORY OF MIDDLETOWN, the
Oldest Settlement in New Jersey.** By
Ernest W. Mandeville. 1927. 143p.
P5-NJ0116 — $21.00.

**EARLY DUTCH SETTLERS OF
MONMOUTH COUNTY.** By Geo.
C. Beekman. 1901. 162p.
P5-NJ0118 — $21.00.

**HISTORY OF MONMOUTH &
OCEAN COUNTIES. Includes a
genealogical register.** By Edwin Salter.
1890. 510p.
P5-NJ0006 — $53.00.

**HISTORY OF MONMOUTH
COUNTY.** Franklin Ellis. 1885. 902p.
P5-NJ0012 — $89.50.

**HISTORY OF MONMOUTH
COUNTY, 1664-1920, Historical —
Biographical, 3 vols. in 2 books.**
1922. 3 vols. in 2, 559 + 501p.
P5-NJ0119 — $99.50.

**HISTORY OF MONMOUTH
COUNTY . . . , Book I.** 1922. 559p.
P5-NJ0119A — $57.00.

**HISTORY OF MONMOUTH
COUNTY . . . , Book II.** 1922. 501p.
P5-NJ0119B — $57.00.

**OLD TIMES IN OLD MON-
MOUTH, Historical Reminiscences
of Old Monmouth Co.** By E. Salter &
E.C. Beekman. 1887. 474p.
P5-NJ0028 — $48.00.

**SHARKRIVER DISTRICT,
Monmouth Co., & Genealogies of
Chambers, Corlies, Drummond,
Morris, Potter, Shafto, Webley &
White.** Geo. Castor Martin. 1914. 99p.
P5-NJ0117 — $16.50.

**THIS OLD MONMOUTH OF
OURS: History, Tradition, Bio-
graphy, Genealogy, Anecdotes
related to Monmouth Co.** By W.S.
Hornor. 1932. 444p.
P5-NJ0007 — $39.00.

**MONTCLAIR: Evolution of a Sub-
urban Town.** By Edwin B. Goodell.
1934. 303p.
P5-NJ0121 — $39.50.

**STORY OF MONTCLAIR, its
People in Peace & War Times.** By the
Montclair Capt. NJSAR. 1930. 202p.
P5-NJ0120 — $31.00.

**BIOGRAPHICAL & GENE-
ALOGICAL HISTORY OF MORRIS
COUNTY, 2-vol. set.** 1899. 2 vols., 803p.
P5-NJ0123 — $87.00.

**BIOGRAPHICAL & GENE-
ALOGICAL HISTORY OF MORRIS
COUNTY, Vol. I.** 1899.
P5-NJ0123A — $50.00.

**BIOGRAPHICAL & GENE-
ALOGICAL HISTORY OF MORRIS
COUNTY, Vol. II.** 1899.
P5-NJ0123B — $50.00.

**HISTORY OF MORRIS COUNTY,
Embracing Upwards of Two Centuries, 1710-1913, 2-vol. set.** 1914. 2
vols., 506 + 509p.
P5-NJ0124 — $99.00/set.

HISTORY OF MORRIS COUNTY
. . . , Vol. I. 506p.
P5-NJ0124A — $55.00.

HISTORY OF MORRIS COUNTY
. . . , Vol. II. 509p.
P5-NJ0124B — $55.00.

HISTORY OF MORRIS COUNTY,
with Illustrations & Biographical
Sketches of Prominent Citizens &
Pioneers. 1882. 407p.
P5-NJ0031 — $45.00.

HISTORIC MORRISTOWN: The
Story of its First Century. By Andrew
M. Sherman. 1906. 444 + 57 illus.
P5-NJ0149 — $57.00.

CHRONICLES OF NEW BRUNS-
WICK, 1667-1931. By John P. Wall.
1931. 487p.
P5-NJ0125 — $51.50.

NEW BRUNSWICK IN HISTORY.
Includes genealogical sketches. By
Williams H. Benedict. 1925. 391p.
P5-NJ0032 — $44.00.

HISTORY OF NEWARK, being a
Narrative of its Rise & Progress from
the Settlement in May, 1666. With
1938 index compiled by the Public
Library of Newark. By Joseph
Atkinson. 1878. 334 + 171p.
P5-NJ0064 — $52.50.

HISTORY OF THE CITY OF
NEWARK, Embracing Practically
Two and a Half Centuries, 1666-1913,
3-vol. set. 1913. 3 vols.
P5-NJ0126 — $169.00/set.

HISTORY OF THE CITY OF
NEWARK . . ., Vol. I. 1913.
P5-NJ0126A — $59.50.

HISTORY OF THE CITY OF
NEWARK . . . , Vol. II. 1913.
P5-NJ0126B — $59.50.

HISTORY OF THE CITY OF
NEWARK . . . , Vol. III. 1913.
P5-NJ0126C — $59.50.

WOODSIDE, The North End of
Newark: its History, Legends &
Ghost Stories Gathered from the
Records and the Older Inhabitants
Now Living [1909]. By C.G. Hine.
1909. 308p.
P5-NJ0145 — $39.50.

SKETCHES OF THE FIRST
EMIGRANT SETTLERS ON
NEWTON TOWNSHIP, Old
Gloucester Co., West N.J. By John
Clement. 1877. 444p.
P5-NJ0127 — $51.50.

FOUNDERS & BUILDERS OF
THE ORANGES, Comprising a
History of the Outlying District of
Newark, Subsequently Known as
Orange . . . also a History of the Early
Settlers or Founders . . . and the
Builders. Henry Whittemore. 1896. 468p.
P5-NJ0128 — $51.00.

HISTORY OF THE ORANGES, in
Essex Co. By Stephen Wickes. 1892.
334p.
P5-NJ0015B — $39.00.

HISTORY OF AMESBURY,
including the First Seventeen Years
of Salisbury to Separation in 1654, &
Merrimac from Incorporation in 1876.
By J. Merrill. 1880. 431p.
P5-MA0002 — $47.00.

HISTORY OF THE ORANGES TO
1921, Reviewing the Rise, Develop-
ment & Progress of an Influential
Community. By David Lawrence
Pierson. 1922. 3 vols. in 1, 749p.
P5-NJ0129 — $79.50.

THE MOUNTAIN SOCIETY:
History of the First Presbyterian
Church, Orange, Organized about
the Year 1719 [including local
history]. By James Hoyt. 1860. 281p.
P5-NJ0254 — $37.00.

HISTORY OF PASSAIC & ITS
ENVIRONS, Historical- Biographical,
3 vols. in 2 books. By Wm. W. Scott.
1922. 3 vols. in 2, 915 + 717p.
P5-NJ0152 — $159.00/set.

HISTORY OF PASSAIC & ITS
ENVIRONS . . . , Book I. 1922. 915p.
P5-NJ0152A — $93.50.

HISTORY OF PASSAIC & ITS
ENVIRONS . . . , Book II. 1922. 717p.
P5-NJ0152B — $73.50.

PASSAIC VALLEY (and Vicinity)
Family Records, or Genealogies of
the First Settlers. J. Littell. 1852. 512p.
P5-NJ0034 — $35.00.

THE NEWS' HISTORY OF
PASSAIC, from the Earliest
Settlement to the Present Day,
Embracing a Descriptive History of
its Municipal, Religious, Social and
Commercial Institutions, with
Biographical Sketches. 1899. 320p.
P5-nj0072 — $41.00.

THE PASSAIC VALLEY in Three
Centuries, Past & Present, 2-vol. set.
John Whitehead. n.d. 2 vols., 469 + 528p.
P5-NJ0033 — $99.00.

THE PASSAIC VALLEY . . . , Vol. I.
469p.
P5-NJ0033A — $52.00.

THE PASSAIC VALLEY . . . , Vol.
II. 528p.
P5-NJ0033B — $56.00.

CENSUS OF PATERSON, 1827-32.
By the Rev. Sam'l Fisher. n.d. 148p.
P5-NJ0130 — $19.00.

HISTORY OF INDUSTRIAL
PATERSON . . . a Compendium of
the Establishment, Growth & Present
[1882] Status of the Silk, Cotton, Flax,
Locomotive, Iron & Miscellaneous
Industries, Together with Outlines of
. . . History & Biographical Sketches
By L.R. Trumbull. 1882. 342p.
P5-NJ0131 — $43.50.

HISTORY OF PATERSON & ITS
ENVIRONS (The Silk City):
Historical-Genealogical-Biographical,
3-vol. set. 1920. 3 vols.; 371 + 208 + 298 p.
P5-NJ0132 — $114.00/set.

HISTORY OF PATERSON & ITS
ENVIRONS . . . , Vol. I. 1920. 371p.
P5-NJ0132A — $45.00.

HISTORY OF PATERSON & ITS
ENVIRONS . . . , Vol. II. 1920. 208p.
P5-NJ0132B — $34.00.

HISTORY OF PATERSON & ITS
ENVIRONS . . . , Vol. III. 1920. 298p.
P5-NJ0132C — $38.50.

HISTORY OF THE CITY OF
PATERSON & the County of
Passaic. With 1994 index by Jerri
Burket. Wm. Nelson. 1901. 448 + 132p.
P5-NJ0065 — $59.50.

For hardcover versions, see the order form on page v. To order, call 1-888-296-3447.

New Jersey, cont.

PATERSON: Its Advantages for Manufacturing and Residence, its Industries, Prominent Men, Banks, Schools, Churches, etc. With many photographs. Charles A. Shriner. 1890. 326p.
P5-NJ0133 — $41.00.

HISTORY OF THE OLD PRESBYTERIAN CONGREGATION OF THE PEOPLE OF MAIDENHEAD & HOPEWELL, at Pennington NJ. G. Hale. 1876. 128p.
P5-NJ0062 — $23.00.

CONTRIBUTIONS TO THE EARLY HISTORY OF PERTH AMBOY & Adjoining Country, with Sketches of Men & Events in NJ during the Provincial Era. By W.A. Whitehead. 1856. 428p.
P5-NJ0010 — $47.00.

HISTORY OF PERTH AMBOY, 1651-1958. By William C. McGinnis. 1958. 3 vols. in 1, 153 + 145 + 189.
P5-NJ0084 — $49.50.

PLAINFIELD & NORTH PLAINFIELD, Embracing a Descriptive History of the Municipal, Religious, Social & Commercial Institutions, with Biographical Sketches, Profusely Illustrated. F.T. Smiley. 1901. 108p. + illus.
P5-NJ0134 — $27.00.

PREAKNESS & THE PREAKNESS REFORMED CHURCH, Passaic Co.: a History, 1695 - 1902, with Genealogical Notes, the Records of the Church & Tombstone Inscriptions. By George W. Labaw. 1902. 344p.
P5-NJ0135 — $41.50.

RECORDS OF THE SWEDISH LUTHERAN CHURCHES AT RACCOON & PENNS NECK, 1713-1786. Trans.& comp. by Fed. Writers Project, WPA. 1938. 398p.
P5-NJ0136 — $44.50.

BIRTH OF RAMSEY. C.A. Smeltzer. 1976. 96p.
P5-NJ0257 — $23.00.

HISTORY OF RUMSON, 1665-1944. 1944. 364p.
P5-NJ0137 — $43.50.

HISTORY & GENEALOGY OF FENWICK'S COLONY [Salem Co.]. By Thomas Shourds. 1876. 581p.
P5-NJ0017A — $49.00.

SALEM COUNTY WILLS Recorded in the Office of the Surrogate at Salem. 1804-1830. 1941?. 2 vols. In 1 book, 214 + 203p.
P5-NJ0083 — $39.50.

CENTENNIAL HISTORY OF SOMERSET COUNTY. By Abraham Messler. 1878. 198p.
P5-NJ0139 — $28.50.

FIRST THINGS IN OLD SOMERSET: Collection of Articles Relating to Somerset County, By Rev. A. Messler, revised ed. 1899. 172p.
P5-NJ0138 — $21.00.

NORTHWESTERN NEW JERSEY: A History of Somerset, Morris, Hunterdon, Warren & Sussex Cos. 1927. 5 vols. in 2.
P5-NJ0089 — $169.00/set.

SOMERSET COUNTY HISTORICAL QUARTERLY, 2-vol. set. 1912-1913. 2 vols., 337 + 331p.
P5-NJ0073 — $75.00.

SOMERSET COUNTY HISTORICAL QUARTERLY, Vol. I. 1912. 337p.
P5-NJ0073A — $39.50.

SOMERSET COUNTY HISTORICAL QUARTERLY, Vol. II. 1913. 331p.
P5-NJ0073B — $39.50.

SOMERSET HILLS, Being a Brief Record of Significant Facts in the Early History of the Hill Country of Somerset Co. Ludwig Schmacher. 1900. 133p.
P5-NJ0140 — $17.50.

SOUTH JERSEY MARRIAGES, Supplementing the Cape May, Cumberland, Gloucester & Salem Co. Marriage Records. H. Stanley Craig. n.d. 164p.
P5-NJ0146 — $21.00.

SOUTH JERSEY, a History, 1664-1924, 5-vol. set. 1924. 5 vols.
P5-NJ0148 — $199.50/set.

SOUTH JERSEY, a History, 1664-1924, Vol. I. 1924.
P5-NJ0148A — $45.00.

SOUTH JERSEY, a History, 1664-1924, Vol. II. 1924.
P5-NJ0148B — $45.00.

SOUTH JERSEY, a History, 1664-1924, Vol. III. 1924.
P5-NJ0148C — $45.00.

SOUTH JERSEY, a History, 1664-1924, Vol. IV. 1924.
P5-NJ0148D — $45.00.

SOUTH JERSEY, a History, 1664-1924, Vol. V. 1924.
P5-NJ0148E — $45.00.

HISTORY OF SUSSEX & WARREN COUNTIES, with Illustrations & Biographical Sketches of Prominent Men & Pioneers. Comp. By James P. Snell 1881. 748p.
P5-NJ0013 — $81.00.

MEMOIRS & REMINSCENCES, together with Sketches of the Early History of Sussex County, NJ, with Notes & Genealogical Record of the Schaeffe, Shaver or Shafer family. By Caspar Schaeffer & William M. Johnson. 1907. 187p.
P5-NJ0081 — $29.50.

HISTORY OF THE OLD TENNENT CHURCH. With historical records, genealogical notes, graveyard transcriptions and much other information about the history of the town, as well as the church. By Rev. Frank R. Symmes. 1904. 472p.
P5-NJ0066 — $49.50.

OLD DUTCH CHURCH AT TOTOWA. By W. Nelson. 1892. 170p.
P5-NJ0259 — $27.00.

GENEALOGY OF EARLY SETTLERS IN TRENTON & EWING, "Old Hunterdon Co.," N.J. By F. & W.S. Cooley. 1883. 336p.
P5-NJ0004 — $35.00.

HISTORY OF TRENTON, NJ. The Record of Its Early Settlement & Corporate Progress. Comp. by F. B. Lee. 1895. 526p.
P5-NJ0262 — $53.00.

HISTORY OF THE CITY OF TRENTON, Embracing a Period of Nearly Two Hundred Years. By John O. Raum. 1871. 448p.
P5-NJ0015A — $49.50.

TRENTON, Old & New. By Harry J. Podmore. 1927. 166p.
P5-NJ0141 — $21.00.

HISTORY OF UNION COUNTY. 1897. 656p.
P5-NJ0036 — $68.00.

HISTORY OF UNION & MIDDLESEX COUNTIES, with Biographical Sketches of Many of their Prominent Men & Pioneers. 1882. 885p.
P5-NJ0067 — $89.50.

HISTORY OF UNION COUNTY,
1664-1923, 3-vol. set. 1923. 3 vols; 431
+ 276 + 283p.
P5-NJ0142 — $99.50/set.

HISTORY OF UNION COUNTY,
1664-1923, Vol. I. 1923. 431p.
P5-NJ0142A — $48.50.

HISTORY OF UNION COUNTY,
1664-1923, Vol. II. 1923. 276p.
P5-NJ0142B — $33.00.

HISTORY OF UNION COUNTY,
1664-1923, Vol. III. 1923. 283p.
P5-NJ0142C — $33.00.

HISTORY OF WARREN
COUNTY. By George Wyckoff
Cummins. 1911. 431p.
P5-NJ0143 — $49.50.

WASHINGTON VALLEY: An
Informal History, Morris County,
New Jersey. By B. Hoskins, C. Foster,
D. Roberts and G. Foster 1960.
P5-NJ0255 — $43.00.

HISTORY OF WOODBURY, from
1681 to 1936. With biographical
sketches. By Benj. F. Carter & Jas. D.
Carpenter. 1937. 184p.
P5-NJ0144 — $24.00.

New Mexico

LEADING FACTS OF NEW MEX-
ICAN HISTORY, Vols. 1 & 2. By
Ralph Emerson Twitchell. 1911, 1912. 2
vols., 694 + 853p.
P5-NM0001 — $150.00/set.

LEADING FACTS OF NEW MEX-
ICAN HISTORY, Vol. 1. 1911. 694p.
P5-NM0001A — $78.00.

LEADING FACTS OF NEW MEX-
ICAN HISTORY, Vol. 2. 1912. 853p.
P5-NM0001B — $89.00.

LEADING FACTS OF NEW MEX-
ICAN HISTORY, Vol. 3. 1917. 571 +
148p.
P5-NM0002 — $72.00.

LEADING FACTS OF NEW MEX-
ICAN HISTORY, Vol. 4. 567 + 114p.
P5-NM0003 — $68.00.

LEADING FACTS OF NEW MEX-
ICAN HISTORY, Vol. 5. 1917. 505 +
114p.
P5-NM0004 — $62.00.

SPANISH ARCHIVES OF NEW
MEXICO, 2-vol. set. Ralph Emerson
Twitchell. 1914. 2 vols; 586 + 725p.
P5-NM0005 — $130.00/set.

SPANISH ARCHIVES OF NEW
MEXICO, Vol. I. 1914. 586p.
P5-NM0005A — $65.00.

SPANISH ARCHIVES OF NEW
MEXICO, Vol. II. 1914. 725p.
P5-NM0005B — $75.00.

New York

CALENDAR OF HISTORICAL
MANUSCRIPTS in the Office of the
Secretary of State of N.Y. Part I,
Dutch Mss., 1630-1664. 1865. 423p.
P5-NY0178 — $47.00.

CENTRAL NEW YORK, An Inland
Empire Comprising Oneida, Cayuga,
Madison, Tompkins, Onondaga,
Cortland, Chenango Cos., & their
People, 4-vol. set. W. Freeman Galpin.
1941. 4 vols., 319 + 347 + 460 + 551p.
P5-NY0465A —$169.50/set.

CENTRAL NEW YORK . . . , Vol. I.
1941. 319p.
P5-NY0465A1 — $35.00.

CENTRAL NEW YORK . . . , Vol.
II. 1941. 347p.
P5-NY0465A2 — $38.50.

CENTRAL NEW YORK . . . , Vol.
III. 1941. 460p.
P5-NY0465A3 — $48.50.

CENTRAL NEW YORK . . . , Vol.
IV. 1941. 551p.
P5-NY0465A4 — $55.50.

CONTRIBUTIONS TO THE HIS-
TORY OF ANCIENT FAMILIES
OF NEW AMSTERDAM AND
NEW YORK. By Edwin R. Purple.
1881. 138 + 12p.
P5-NY0486 — $32.50.

DUTCH NEW YORK. By Esther
Singleton. 1909. 360p.
P5-NY0201 — $42.50.

EARLY SETTLERS OF WESTERN
NEW YORK, Their Ancestors &
Descendants. By J.W. Foley. 1934-
1936. 600+ p.
P5-NY0204 — $62.50.

EMPIRE OIL: The Story of Oil in
New York State. By John P. Herrick.
1949. 474 + 44p.
P5-NY0489 — $52.00.

FRONTIERSMEN OF NEW
YORK, Showing Customs of the
Indians, Vicissitudes of Pioneer
White Settlers & Border Strife in Two
Wars, with a Great Variety of Romantic
& Thrilling Stories, 2-vol. set. Jeptha
R. Simms. 1883. 2 vols., 712 + 759p.
P5-NY0130 — $135.00/set.

FRONTIERSMEN OF NEW YORK
. . . , Vol. I. 1883. 712p.
P5-NY0130A — $72.50.

FRONTIERSMEN OF NEW YORK
. . . , Vol. II. 1883. 759p.
P5-NY0130B — $72.50.

GAZETTEER OF THE STATE OF
NEW YORK, Comprehending its
Colonial History; General Geo-
graphy, Geology, Internal Improve-
ments; its Political State; Minute
Description of its Several Counties,
Towns & Villages; Statistical Tables.
By T.F. Gordon. 1836. 800p.
P5-NY0030 — $79.50.

GAZETTEER OF THE STATE OF
NEW YORK, Embracing a Compre-
hensive Account of the History &
Statistics of the State, with Geolog-
ical & Topographical Descriptions of
each County, City, Town & Village.
By Franklin B. Hough. 1872. 745p.
P5-NY0222 — $75.00.

GENEALOGICAL & BIOGRAPH-
ICAL DIRECTORY TO PERSONS
IN NEW NETHERLAND, from
1613 to 1674. David M. Riker 1999. 4 vols.
P5-NY0461B — $52.00/vol. or
$195.00/set.

GENEALOGICAL & FAMILY
HISTORY OF NORTHERN NEW
YORK: A Record of the Achievements
of her People in the Making of the
Commonwealth & the Building of a
Nation, 3-vol. set. 1910. 3 vols., 1247p.
P5-NY0035 — $124.00/set.

New York, cont.

GENEALOGICAL & FAMILY HISTORY OF NORTHERN NEW YORK . . . , Vol. I. 1910.
P5-NY0035A — $44.50.

GENEALOGICAL & FAMILY HISTORY OF NORTHERN NEW YORK . . . , Vol. II. 1910.
P5-NY0035B — $44.50.

GENEALOGICAL & FAMILY HISTORY OF SOUTHERN NEW YORK & THE HUDSON RIVER VALLEY: A Record of the Achievements of her People in the Making of the Commonwealth & the Building of a Nation, 3-vol. set. 1913. 3 vols; 416 + 317 + 351p.
P5-NY0034 — $115.00/set.

GENEALOGICAL & FAMILY HISTORY OF SOUTHERN NEW YORK & THE HUDSON RIVER VALLEY . . . , Vol. I. 1913. 416p.
P5-NY0034A — $43.50.

GENEALOGICAL & FAMILY HISTORY OF SOUTHERN NEW YORK & THE HUDSON RIVER VALLEY . . . , Vol. II. 1913. 317p.
P5-NY0034B — $40.00.

GENEALOGICAL & FAMILY HISTORY OF SOUTHERN NEW YORK & THE HUDSON RIVER VALLEY. . . , Vol. III. 1913. 351p.
P5-NY0034C — $41.50.

GENEALOGICAL NOTES of NEW YORK & NEW ENGLAND FAMILIES. Comp. by S.V. Talcott. 1883. 747 + 39p.
P5-NY0240 — $81.50.

HISTORICAL SKETCHES OF NORTHERN NEW YORK & THE ADIRONDACK WILDERNESS, Including Traditions of the Indians, Early Explorers, Pioneer Settlers, etc. Nathaniel Bartlett Sylvester. 1877. 316p.
P5-NY0046 — $39.00.

HISTORY OF NEW NETHER-LAND, or, New York under the Dutch, 2-vol. set. By E.B. O'Callaghan. 1848. 2 vols., 493 + 608p.
P5-NY0043 — The set: $105.00.

HISTORY OF NEW NETHER-LAND . . . , Vol. I. 1848. 493p.
P5-NY0043A — $51.00.

HISTORY OF NEW NETHER-LAND . . . Vol. II. 1848. 608p.
P5-NY0043B — $66.50.

HISTORY OF NEW YORK SHIP YARDS. John H. Morrison. 1909. 165p.
P5-NY0048 — $28.00.

HISTORY OF NORTHWESTERN NEW YORK: Erie, Niagara, Wyoming, Genesee & Orleans Counties, 3-vol. set. John T. Horton, Edw. T. Williams & Harry S. Douglass. 1947. 3 vols., 604 + 598 + 504p.
P5-NY0047 — $155.00/set.

HISTORY OF NORTHWESTERN NEW YORK . . . , Vol. I. 1947. 604p.
P5-NY0047A — $59.50.

HISTORY OF NORTHWESTERN NEW YORK . . . , Vol. II. 1947. 598p.
P5-NY0047B — $59.50.

HISTORY OF NORTHWESTERN NEW YORK . . . , Vol. III. 1947. 504p.
P5-NY0047C — $59.50.

HISTORY OF THE PIONEER SETTLEMENT OF PHELP'S & GORHAM'S PURCHASE & Morris' Reserve, to which is Added a . . . Continuation of the Pioneer History of Ontario, Wayne, Livingston, Yates & Allegany. By O. Turner. 1852. 588p.
P5-NY0049 — $61.00.

HISTORY OF THE SCHENEC-TADY PATENT, in the Dutch & English Times, Being Contributions Toward a History of the Lower Mohawk Valley. By Jonathan Pearson, et al. 1883. 466p.
P5-NY0354 — $51.00.

HISTORY OF THE SEVENTH REGIMENT, National Guard, State of N.Y., during the War of the Rebellion. By Wm. Swinton. 1876. 501p.
P5-NY0292B — $55.00.

HUDSON-MOHAWK GENE-ALOGICAL & FAMLY MEMOIR: Record of Achievements of the People of Hudson & Mohawk Vals., incl. within the Present Cos. of Albany, Rensselaer, Washington, Saratoga, Montgomery, Fulton, Schenectady, Columbia & Greene, 4-vol. set. 1911. 4 vols., 2076p.
P5-NY0103 — $175.00/set.

HUDSON-MOHAWK GENEALOGICAL & FAMLY MEMOIR . . . , Vol. I. 1911.
P5-NY0103A — $49.00.

HUDSON-MOHAWK GENEALOGICAL & FAMLY MEMOIR . . . , Vol. II. 1911.
P5-NY0103B — $49.00.

HUDSON-MOHAWK GENEALOGICAL & FAMLY MEMOIR . . . , Vol. III. 1911.
P5-NY0103C — $49.00.

HUDSON-MOHAWK GENEALOGICAL & FAMLY MEMOIR . . . , Vol. IV. 1911.
P5-NY0103D — $49.00.

IROQUOIS FOLK LORE, Gathered from the Six Nations of New York. 1922. 251p.
P5-NY0036 — $36.00.

MAKERS OF NEW YORK: An Historical Work. 1895. 348p.
P5-NY0506 — $36.00.

MILITARY BOUNTY LANDS: THE BALLOTING BOOK & Other Documents Relating to Them in N.Y. 1825. 189p.
P5-NY0106 — $19.50.

MILITARY MINUTES OF THE COUNCIL OF APPOINTMENT of the State of N.Y., 1783-1821. 1901. In 3 vols. + index, 3038p.
P5-NY0179 — $249.50.

MUSTER ROLLS OF N.Y. PROVINCIAL TROOPS, 1755-1764. 1897. 620p.
P5-NY0105 — $52.00.

NAMES OF PERSONS FOR WHOM MARRIAGE LICENSES WERE ISSUED BY THE SECRETARY OF THE PROVINCE OF NEW YORK, Previous to 1784. 1860. 480p.
P5-NY0042 — $51.50.

NEW YORK CONSIDERED & IMPROVED. From the original mss. in the British Museum. By John Miller. 1903. 135p.
P5-NY0044 — $18.50.

NEW YORK IN THE REVOLUTION AS COLONY & STATE. A Compilation of documents & records from the Office of the State Comptroller, given NY rolls of soldiers & sailors in the Rev. War, 2-vol. set. 1904. 2 vols., 533 + 336p.
P5-NY0014B — $91.00/set.

NEW YORK IN THE
REVOLUTION AS COLONY &
STATE . . . , Vol. I. 1904. 533p.
P5-NY0014B1 — $56.50.

NEW YORK IN THE
REVOLUTION AS COLONY &
STATE . . . , Vol. II. 1904. 336p.
P5-NY0014B2 — $39.50.

NORTH COUNTRY: A History
Enbracing Jefferson, St Lawrence,
Oswego, Lewis & Franklin Counties,
3-vol. set. By Harry F. Landon. 1932. 3
vols., 1647p.
P5-NY0045 — $149.50/set.

NORTH COUNTRY . . . , Vol. I. 1932.
P5-NY0045A — $59.00.

NORTH COUNTRY . . . , Vol. II. 1932.
P5-NY0045B — $59.00.

NORTH COUNTRY . . . , Vol. III. 1932.
P5-NY0045C — $59.00.

PIONEER HISTORY OF THE
HOLLAND PURCHASE, Western
New York. O. Turner. 1849. 666 + 50p.
P5-NY0501 — $75.00.

SCANDINAVIAN IMMIGRANTS
IN NEW YORK, 1630-1674. With
appendices on Scandanavians in
Mexico, So. America, Cananda, N.Y.,
plus Germans in N.Y. By John O.
Evjen. 1916. 24 + 438p.
P5-NY0137 — $47.00.

THE "ULSTER GUARD" [20th
N.Y. State Militia], and the War of
the Rebellion. By Theodore B. Gates.
1879. 619p.
P5-NY0470B — $67.00.

THE BELGIANS: First Settlers in
New York & in the Middle States,
with a Review of the Events which
Led to their Immigration. By Henry
G. Bayer. 1925. 373p.
P5-NY0032 — $41.50.

THE HISTORIC MOHAWK. By
Mary Riggs Diefendorf. 1910. 331p.
P5-NY0230 — $38.50.

ALBANY CHRONICLES: History
of the City Arranged Chronologically,
from the Earliest Settlement to the
Present Time [1906]. By Cuyler
Reynolds. 1906. 808p.
P5-NY0052 — $86.00.

BI-CENTENNIAL HISTORY OF
THE COUNTY OF ALBANY. from
1609 to 1886, with Portraits,
Biographies & Illustrations.
1886. 3 vols. in 1, 997p.
P5-NY0053 — $99.00.

EARLY RECORDS OF THE CITY
& COUNTY OF ALBANY, &
Colony of Resselaerwyck, 1656-1675,
Translated from the Dutch, with
Notes. Jonathan Pearson. 1869. 523p.
P5-NY0054 — $57.00.

HEROES OF ALBANY: A Memorial
of the Patriot-Martyrs of the City &
County of Albany, 1861-1865. By Rufus
W. Clark 1867. 870 + 16p.
P5-NY0515 — $88.00.

HISTORY OF THE CITY OF
ALBANY, from the Discovery of the
Great River in 1524, by Verrazzano, to
the Present [1884]. A.J. Weise. 1884. 528p.
P5-NY0010 — $57.50.

MINUTES OF THE COURT OF
ALBANY, RENSSELAERSWYCK &
SCHENECTADY, 1668-80. 2-vol. set.
1926-1928. 2 vols., 356 + 530p.
P5-NY0050 — $85.00/set.

MINUTES OF THE COURT OF
ALBANY, RENSSELAERSWYCK &
SCHENECTADY, 1668-80, Vol. I.
1926-1928. 356p.
P5-NY0050A — $35.00.

MINUTES OF THE COURT OF
ALBANY, RENSSELAERSWYCK &
SCHENECTADY, 1668-80, Vol. II.
1926-1928. 530p.
P5-NY0050B — $55.00.

MINUTES OF THE COURT OF
FORT ORANGE & BEVERWYCK
[ALBANY], 1652-60, 2-vol. set. 1920-
1923. 2 vols., 326 + 336p.
P5-NY0051 — $79.00/set.

MINUTES OF THE COURT OF
FORT ORANGE & BEVERWYCK
. . . , Vol. I. 1920-1923. 326p.
P5-NY0051A — $42.00.

MINUTES OF THE COURT OF
FORT ORANGE & BEVERWYCK
. . . , Vol. II. 1920-1923. 336p.
P5-NY0051B — $42.00.

LANDMARKS OF ALBANY
COUNTY. Part I, Historical; Part II,
Biographical. 2-vol. set. 1897. 2 vols.,
557 + 418p.
P5-NY0471B — $101.00/set.

LANDMARKS OF ALBANY
COUNTY. Pt. I, Historical. 1897. 557p.
P5-NY0471B1 — $60.00.

LANDMARKS OF ALBANY
COUNTY. Pt. II, Biographical. 1897.
418p.
P5-NY0471B2 — $50.00.

ALLEGANY COUNTY & ITS
PEOPLE: A Centennial Memorial
History of Allegany County; also,
Histories of the Towns of the
County. 1896. 951p.
P5-NY0279 — $97.00.

OLD HELLEBERGH: Historical
Sketches of the West Manor of
Rensselaerswyck [Altamont]. By
Arthur B. Gregg. 1936. 192p.
P5-NY0055 — $29.50.

HISTORICAL RECORDS OF A
HUNDRED & TWENTY-FIVE
YEARS: AUBURN. By J.H. Monroe.
1913. 278p.
P5-NY0121 — $35.00.

CENTENNIAL HISTORY OF
THE VILLAGE OF BALLSTON
SPA, Including the Towns of
Ballston and Milton. By Edw. F.
Grose, with J.C. Booth. 1907. 258p.
P5-NY0278 — $36.50.

BEDFORD Inscriptions from
Gravestones, with Genealogical
Notes & Index. By Francis F. Spies.
1933. 229p.
P5-NY0452 — $25.00.

HISTORY OF THE TOWN OF
BEDFORD, to 1917. By James Wood.
1925. 48p.
P5-NY0203 — $10.00.

TIMES REMEMBERED & MORE
TIMES REMEMBERED [Bethlehem,
NY]. By Allison Bennett. 1984, 1987. 2
vols. in 1, 110 + 122p.
P5-NY0475 — $34.00.

BINGHAMTON & BROOME
COUNTY: A History. With biographical sketches. 1924. 3 vols. in 2,
742 + 404p.
P5-NY0057 — $118.00/set.

New York, cont.

BINGHAMTON: Settlement, Growth & Development & the Factors in its History, 1800-1900, together with a History of the Villages & Towns of the County. 1900. 1035p.
P5-NY0056 — $99.50.

MEMORIALS OF OLD BRIDGE-HAMPTON. By James Truslow Adams. 1916. 399p.
P5-NY0058 — $47.50.

HISTORY OF BRONX BOROUGH, City of New York. By Randall Comfort. 1906. 422p.
P5-NY0474A — $48.50.

BRONX COUNTY HISTORICAL SOCIETY "JOURNAL," Vols. I-XXXII. Reprinted in 8 vols. 1964-1995.
P5-NY0409 — $356.00/set.

BRONX COUNTY HISTORICAL SOCIETY "JOURNAL," Vols. I-XXXII, Book One. 1964-1995.
P5-NY0409A — $42.50.

BRONX COUNTY HISTORICAL SOCIETY "JOURNAL," Vols. I-XXXII, Book Two. 1964-1995.
P5-NY0409B — $42.50.

BRONX COUNTY HISTORICAL SOCIETY "JOURNAL," Vols. I-XXXII, Book Three. 1964-1995.
P5-NY0409C — $42.50.

BRONX COUNTY HISTORICAL SOCIETY "JOURNAL," Vols. I-XXXII, Book Four. 1964-1995.
P5-NY0409D — $42.50.

BRONX COUNTY HISTORICAL SOCIETY "JOURNAL," Vols. I-XXXII, Book Five. 1964-1995.
P5-NY0409E — $53.50.

BRONX COUNTY HISTORICAL SOCIETY "JOURNAL," Vols. I-XXXII, Book Six. 1964-1995.
P5-NY0409F — $53.50.

BRONX COUNTY HISTORICAL SOCIETY "JOURNAL," Vols. I-XXXII, Book Seven. 1964-1995.
P5-NY0409G — $53.50.

BRONX COUNTY HISTORICAL SOCIETY "JOURNAL," Vols. I-XXXII, Book Eight. 1964-1995.
P5-NY0409H — $53.50.

BOROUGHS OF BROOKLYN & QUEENS, Counties of Nassau & Suffolk, Long Island, 1609-1924, Vol. I-III, History. 3-vol. set. By Henry Isham Hazelton. 1924. 1724p.
P5-NY0061 — $174.50/set.

BOROUGHS OF BROOKLYN & QUEENS, Counties of Nassau & Suffolk . . . , Vol. I. 1924.
P5-NY0061A — $61.00.

BOROUGHS OF BROOKLYN & QUEENS, Counties of Nassau & Suffolk . . . , Vol. II. 1924.
P5-NY0061B — $61.00.

BOROUGHS OF BROOKLYN & QUEENS, Counties of Nassau & Suffolk, . . . , Vol. III. 1924.
P5-NY0061C — $61.00.

BOROUGHS OF BROOKLYN & QUEENS, Counties of Nassau & Suffolk, Long Island, 1609-1924, Vols. IV-V, Biographies. By Henry Isham Hazelton. 1924. 2 vols. in 1, 486 + 336p.
P5-NY0060 — $89.50.

HISTORY OF THE CITY OF BROOKLYN, including the Old Town & Village of Brooklyn, the Town of Bushwick & the Village & City of Williamsburgh, 3 vols. By H.R. Stiles. 1869. 3 vols., 464 + 500 + 485p.
P5-NY0001 — $135.00/set.

HISTORY OF THE CITY OF BROOKLYN . . . , Vol. I. 1869. 464p.
P5-NY0001A — $49.00.

HISTORY OF THE CITY OF BROOKLYN . . . , Vol. II. 1869. 500p.
P5-NY0001B — $49.00.

HISTORY OF THE CITY OF BROOKLYN . . . , Vol. III. 1869. 485p.
P5-NY0001C — $49.00.

KESKACHAUGE, or the First White Settlement on Long Island [Brooklyn]. By Frederick Van Wyck. 1924. 778p.
P5-NY0059 — $81.00.

NOTES GEOGRAPHICAL and HISTORICAL, Relating to the Town of Brooklyn in Kings County on Long Island. By Gabriel Furman. 1824. 116p.
P5-NY0292A — $21.00.

BIOGRAPHICAL REVIEW OF THE LEADING CITIZENS OF BROOME COUNTY. 1894. 831p.
P5-NY0062 — $87.00.

DEATH NOTICES PUBLISHED IN THE BROOME CO. "REPUBLICAN," A Weekly Newspaper of Binghamton, 1851-1870. Comp. by Ray C. Sawyer. 1942. 195p.
P5-NY0439 — $24.50.

HISTORY OF BROOME CO., with Illustrations & Biographical Sketches of some of its Prominent Men & Pioneers. 1885. 630p.
P5-NY0110 — $66.50.

MARRIAGE ANNOUNCEMENTS PUBLISHED IN THE "BROOME CO. REPUBLICAN," a Weekly Newspaper of Binghamton, 1831-1870. Comp. by Ray C. Sawyer. 1941. 2 v. in 1, 135 + 114p.
P5-NY0432 — $29.00.

AUTHENTIC & COMPREHENSIVE HISTORY OF BUFFALO, with Some Account of its Early Inhabitants both "Savage & Civilized," 2-vol. set. By William Ketchum. 1864. 2 vols., 432 + 443p.
P5-NY0206 — $92.00/set.

AUTHENTIC & COMPREHENSIVE HISTORY OF BUFFALO . . . , Vol. I. 1864. 432p.
P5-NY0206A — $49.00.

AUTHENTIC & COMPREHENSIVE HISTORY OF BUFFALO . . . , Vol. II. 1864. 443p.
P5-NY0206B — $49.00.

HISTORY OF BUFFALO & ERIE COUNTY, with Illustrations & Biographical Sketches of its Prominent Men & Pioneers, 2-vol. set. 1884. 2 vols., 776 + 684p.
P5-NY0205 — $147.00/set.

HISTORY OF BUFFALO & ERIE COUNTY . . . , Vol. I: History of Erie County. 1884. 776p.
P5-NY0205A — $80.00.

HISTORY OF BUFFALO & ERIE COUNTY . . . , Vol. II: History of Buffalo. 1884. 684p.
P5-NY0205B — $72.00.

HISTORY OF THE GERMANS IN BUFFALO & ERIE CO., with Biographies & Portraits of German-Americans who have Contributed to the Development of the City of Buffalo. 1898. 338 + 125p.
P5-NY0464A — $45.00.

HOME HISTORY: Recollections of Buffalo during the Decade from 1830 to 1840, or Fifty Years Since. By Samuel M. Welch. 1891. 423p.
P5-NY0207 — $47.50.

MUNICIPALITY OF BUFFALO: A History, 1720-1923, 4 vols. in 2 books. 1923. 4 vols. in 2, 947 + 493p.
P5-NY0063 — $142.00/set.

MUNICIPALITY OF BUFFALO: A History, 1720-1923, Vols. I & II. 1923. 947p.
P5-NY0063A — $95.00.

MUNICIPALITY OF BUFFALO: A History, 1720-1923, Vols. III & IV. 1923. 493p.
P5-NY0063B — $58.00.

PICTURE BOOK OF EARLIER BUFFALO. Comp. by the Buffalo Hist. Soc. 1912. 508p.
P5-NY0145 — $55.00.

PIONEER HISTORY OF CAMDEN, Oneida County. 1897. 559p.
P5-NY0123 — $58.00.

CAPE VINCENT & ITS HISTORY. Comp. by Nelie Horton Casler. 1906. 240p.
P5-NY0064A — $34.00.

HISTORY OF THE TOWN OF CATHERINE, Schuyler County. By Mary Louise C. Cleaver. 1945. 686p.
P5-NY0064B — $68.50.

CATTARAUGUS COUNTY CEMETERIES. Comp. by G.A. Barber. 1930. 148p.
P5-NY0455 — $19.00.

HISTORICAL GAZETEER & BIOGRAPHICAL MEMORIAL OF CATTARAUGUS CO., with Map and Illustrations. 1893. 1164p.
P5-NY0242 — $115.00.

ABSTRACTS OF WILLS OF CAYUGA COUNTY, 1799-1842, 4-vol. set. Copied by G.A. Barber. 1947. 4 vols. in 1 book, 54 + 54 + 52 + 43p.
P5-NY0421 — $26.00/set.

ABSTRACTS OF WILLS OF CAYUGA COUNTY, 1799-1842, Vol. I. 1947. 54p.
P5-NY0421A — $12.00.

ABSTRACTS OF WILLS OF CAYUGA COUNTY, 1799-1842, Vol. II. 1947. 54p.
P5-NY0421B — $12.00.

ABSTRACTS OF WILLS OF CAYUGA COUNTY, 1799-1842, Vol. III. 1947. 52p.
P5-NY0421C — $12.00.

ABSTRACTS OF WILLS OF CAYUGA COUNTY, 1799-1842, Vol. IV. 1947. 43p.
P5-NY0421D — $12.00.

EARLY HISTORY OF FRIENDS IN CAYUGA COUNTY. By Emily Howland. 1882. 44p.
P5-NY0065 — $10.00.

HISTORY OF CAYUGA COUNTY, with Illustrations & Biographical Sketches of Some of its Prominent Men & Pioneers. 1879. 556p.
P5-NY0111B — $65.00.

CENTENNIAL HISTORY OF CHAUTAUQUA COUNTY: Detailed & Entertaining Story of 100 Years of Development, 2-vol. set. 1904. 2 vols., 698 + 1173p.
P5-NY0146 — $169.50/set.

CENTENNIAL HISTORY OF CHAUTAUQUA COUNTY . . . , Vol. I. 1904. 698p.
P5-NY0146A — $75.00.

CENTENNIAL HISTORY OF CHAUTAUQUA COUNTY . . . , Vol. II. 1904. 1173p.
P5-NY0146B — $110.00.

CHAUTAUQUA COUNTY GRAVESTONE INSCRIPTIONS [from various cemeteries]. Comp. by Minnie Cohen. 1931. 2 vols. in 1, 58 + 79p.
P5-NY0418 — $19.00.

HISTORY OF CHAUTAQUA, from its First Settlement to the Present Time, with Numerous Biographical & Family Sketches. By Andrew W. Young. 1875. 667p.
P5-NY0294 — $71.50.

HISTORY OF CHAUTAUQUA COUNTY & ITS PEOPLE. 1921. 3 vols. in 2, 475 + 702p.
P5-NY0067 — $129.00/set.

SKETCHES OF THE HISTORY OF CHAUTAUQUA COUNTY. By Emory F. Warren. 1846. 159p.
P5-NY0066 — $27.00.

ABSTRACTS OF WILLS OF CHEMUNG COUNTY. Comp. by G.A. Barber. 1941. 46p.
P5-NY0470A — $9.00.

BIOGRAPHICAL RECORD OF CHEMUNG COUNTY, Illustrated. 1902. 512p.
P5-NY0069 — $57.00.

OUR COUNTY & ITS PEOPLE: A History of the Valley & County of Chemung from the Closing Years of the 18th Century. With biographies & personal references. By Ausburn Towner. 1892. 702 + 160p.
P5-NY0295 — $89.50.

BRIEF HISTORY OF CHEMUNG COUNTY. Ausburn Towner. 1907. 103p.
P5-NY0068 — $15.00.

BIOGRAPHICAL & GENE-ALOGICAL: Biographical Sketches of Leading Citizens of Chenango County. 1898. 635p.
P5-NY0070 — $71.00.

HISTORY OF CHENANGO & MADISON COUNTIES, with Illustrations & Biographical Sketches of Some of its Prominent Men & Pioneers. James H. Smith. 1880. 760 + 29p.
P5-NY0148 — $79.50.

INDEX OF WILLS OF CHENANGO COUNTY, 1797-1850. Comp. by G.A. Barber. 1935. 21p.
P5-NY0425 — $10.00.

INDEX OF WILLS OF CHENANGO COUNTY, 1851-1875. Comp. by G.A. Barber. 1951. 54p.
P5-NY0424 — $11.00.

HISTORY OF CHERRY VALLEY, from 1740 to 1898. By John Sawyer. 1898. 156p.
P5-NY0071 — $19.50.

HISTORY OF CLARENDON, from 1810 to 1888. David Sturges Copeland. 1889. 382p.
P5-NY0149 — $44.00.

HISTORICAL SKETCH OF THE TOWN OF CLERMONT. By T. Hunt. 1928. 149p.
P5-NY0296 — $19.50.

HISTORY OF CLINTON & FRANKLIN COUNTIES, with Illustration & Biographical Sketches of its Prominent Men & Pioneers. 1880. 508p.
P5-NY0298 — $55.00.

HISTORY OF COHOCTON, NEW YORK. By William A Field 1916. 70p.
P5-NY0491 — $26.00.

New York, cont.

HISTORY OF COHOES from its Earliest Settlement to the Pesent Time [1877]. By Arthur M. Masten. 1877. 327p.
P5-NY0248 — $38.00.

ABSTRACTS OF WILLS OF COLUMBIA COUNTY, 1786-1851, 8 vols. in 1 book. Comp. by G.A. Barber. 1935.
P5-NY0469A — $69.50/set (8 vols. in 1 book).

ABSTRACTS OF WILLS OF COLUMBIA COUNTY . . ., Vol. I.
P5-NY0469A1 — $17.50.

ABSTRACTS OF WILLS OF COLUMBIA COUNTY . . ., Vol. II.
P5-NY0469A2 - $17.50.

ABSTRACTS OF WILLS OF COLUMBIA COUNTY . . ., Vol. III.
P5-NY0469A3 - $17.50.

ABSTRACTS OF WILLS OF COLUMBIA COUNTY . . ., Vol. IV.
P5-NY0469A4 - $17.50.

ABSTRACTS OF WILLS OF COLUMBIA COUNTY . . ., Vol. V.
P5-NY0469A5 - $17.50.

ABSTRACTS OF WILLS OF COLUMBIA COUNTY . . ., Vol. VI.
P5-NY0469A6 - $17.50.

ABSTRACTS OF WILLS OF COLUMBIA COUNTY . . ., Vol. VII.
P5-NY0469A7 - $17.50.

ABSTRACTS OF WILLS OF COLUMBIA COUNTY . . ., Vol. VIII.
P5-NY0469A8 - $17.50.

BIOGRAPHICAL REVIEW OF THE LEADING CITIZENS OF COLUMBIA COUNTY. 1894. 603p.
P5-NY0073 — $65.00.

BIOGRAPHICAL SKETCHES OF DISTINGUISHED MEN OF COLUMBIA COUNTY, Including an Account of the Most Important Offices they have Filled. By William Raymond. 1851. 119p.
P5-NY0072 — $17.00.

COLUMBIA COUNTY EPITAPHS [copied from many county graveyards]. Copied by M. Cohen [vol. 1 copied by M. Thomas]. 1935-1939. 9 vols in 2, 1008p.
P5-NY0413 — $94.50.

HISTORY OF COLUMBIA COUNTY, with Illustrations & Biographical Sketches of Some Prominent Men & Pioneers. 1878. 447p.
P5-NY0021 — $47.00.

HISTORY OF THE ORIGINAL TOWN OF CONCORD, Being the Present Towns of Concord, Collins, N. Collins and Sardinia, Erie County. By Erasmus Briggs. 1883. 977p.
P5-NY0299 — $97.50.

HISTORY OF THE TOWN OF CONESUS, Livingston Co., from its First Settlement in 1793, to 1887, with a brief genealogical records of the Conesus families. By William P. Boyd. 1887. 207p.
P5-NY0276 — $32.50.

CONDENSED HISTORY OF COOPERSTOWN, with a Biographical Sketch of J. Fenimore Cooper. By S.T. Livermore. 1862. 276p.
P5-NY0076 — $37.00.

HISTORY OF COOPERSTOWN, Including "Chronicles of Cooperstown," by James Fenimore Cooper; "History of Cooperstown, 1839-1886," by Samuel M. Shaw; "History of Cooperstown, 1886-1929," by Walter R. Littell. 1929. 259p.
P5-NY0074 — $37.00.

PIONEER DAYS & LATER TIMES IN CORNING & VICINITY, 1789-1920. By Uri Mulford. 1920. 528p.
P5-NY0077 — $57.00.

"GRIP'S" HISTORICAL SOUVENIR OF CORTLAND. "Grip." 1899. 240p.
P5-NY0078 — $34.50.

HISTORY OF CORTLAND COUNTY, with Illustrations & Biographical Sketches of Some of its Prominent Men & Pioneers. 1885. 543p.
P5-NY0079 — $59.50.

PIONEER HISTORY OF CORTLAND COUNTY, & the Border Wars of N.Y., from the Earliest Period. By H.C. Goodwin. 1859. 456p.
P5-NY0125 — $48.00.

CUTCHOGUE, Southold's First Colony. By Wayland Jefferson. 166p.
P5-NY0368 — $27.00.

DANSVILLE, 1789-1902: Historical, Biographical, Descriptive. 1902. 270 + 267p.
P5-NY0150 — $55.00.

HISTORICAL & BIOGRAPHICAL OF THE TOWNSHIP OF DAYTON, Cattaraugus Co., Comprising the Villages of Cottage, Wesley, Markham, Dayton, So. Dayton & Fairplain. 1901. 302p.
P5-NY0080 — $39.00.

HISTORY OF DEER PARK IN ORANGE COUNTY. By Peter E. Gumaer. 1890. 205p.
P5-NY0081 — $31.00.

ABSTRACTS OF WILLS OF DELAWARE COUNTY, 1796 to 1875, Copied from the Original Wills at the Surrogate's Office, Delhi, 6-vol. set in 1 book. Comp. by G.A. Barber. 1940. 6 vols., 54+54+53+53+53+74p., paper
P5-NY0412 — $37.50/set.

ABSTRACTS OF WILLS OF DELAWARE COUNTY . . ., Vol. I. 1940. 54p.
P5-NY0412A - $12.00.

ABSTRACTS OF WILLS OF DELAWARE COUNTY . . ., Vol. II. 1940. 54p.
P5-NY0412B - $12.00.

ABSTRACTS OF WILLS OF DELAWARE COUNTY . . ., Vol. III. 1940. 53p.
P5-NY0412C - $12.00.

ABSTRACTS OF WILLS OF DELAWARE COUNTY . . ., Vol. IV. 1940. 53p.
P5-NY0412D - $12.00.

ABSTRACTS OF WILLS OF DELAWARE COUNTY . . ., Vol. V. 1940. 53p.
P5-NY0412E - $12.00.

ABSTRACTS OF WILLS OF DELAWARE COUNTY . . ., Vol. VI. 1940. 74p.
P5-NY0412F - $12.00.

CENSUS RECORDS, 1855, OF DELAWARE COUNTY. Comp. by G.A. Barber. 1946. 537p.
P5-NY0440 — $47.50.

CHAPTERS IN THE HISTORY OF DELAWARE COUNTY. By John D. Monroe. 1949. 132p.
P5-NY0082 — $17.50.

DELAWARE COUNTY CEM-
ETERY INSCRIPTIONS [from 10
private graveyards]. 1953. 48p.
P5-NY0415 — $10.00.

DELAWARE COUNTY DEATHS,
1819-79, from the Delhi Gazette. 1934.
3 v. in 1, 257p.
P5-NY0414 — $27.00.

DELAWARE COUNTY MAR-
RIAGES, 1819-79, from the Delaware
& Delhi Gazettes, Vol. I: 1819-1844
Comp. by G.A. Barber. 1934. 114p.
P5-NY0472B1 — $17.50.

DELAWARE COUNTY MAR-
RIAGES . . . , Vol. II: 1844-1868.
1934. 120p.
P5-NY0472B2 — $18.00.

DELAWARE COUNTY MAR-
RIAGES . . . , Vol. III: 1868-1879.
1934. 62p.
P5-NY0472B3 — $13.50.

DELAWARE COUNTY: History of
the Century, 1797-1897. 1898. 604p.
P5-NY0153B — $65.00.

HISTORY OF DELAWARE
COUNTY & Border Wars of New
York, Containing a Sketch of Early
Settlement. By Jay Gould. 1856. 426p.
P5-NY0151 — $47.00.

HISTORY OF DELAWARE
COUNTY, with Illustrations,
Biographical Sketches & Portraits of
some Pioneers & Prominent Resi-
dents. Ed.by W. Munsell 1880. 363p.
P5-NY0227 — $42.50.

INDEX OF WILLS OF DELAWARE
COUNTY, 1795-1885. Comp. by
Gertrude A. Barber. 1934. 82p.
P5-NY0416 — $16.00.

LETTERS OF ADMINISTRATION
OF DELAWARE COUNTY, 1797 to
1875, Copied from the Original
Records at the Court House, Delhi.
Comp. by G.A. Barber. 1939. 4 v. in 1,
54 + 53 + 54 + 15p.
P5-NY0411 — $22.50.

MARRIAGES & DEATHS Taken
from the "Delaware Gazette" at
Delhi, 1880-1895. Comp. by G.A.
Barber. 1945?. 125p.
P5-NY0460A — $16.00.

CENTENNIAL HISTORY OF
THE TOWN OF DRYDEN, 1797-
1897. 1898. 272p.
P5-NY0209 — $35.00.

COMMEMORATIVE BIOGRAPH-
ICAL RECORD OF DUTCHESS
COUNTY. 1897. 950p.
P5-NY0208 — $95.00.

GENERAL HISTORY OF DUCHESS
COUNTY, from 1609 to 1876. By
Philip H. Smith. 1877. 507p.
P5-NY0476 — $55.00.

HISTORY OF "LITTLE 9
PARTNERS" of the N.E. Precinct &
Pine Plains. By I. Hunting. 1897. 411p.
P5-NY0004 — $45.00.

HISTORY OF DUTCHESS
COUNTY, with Illustrations &
Biographical Sketches of some of its
Prominent Men & Pioneers. By James
H. Smith. 1882. 562 + 28p.
P5-NY0153A — $59.50.

HISTORY OF DUTCHESS
COUNTY. 1909. 791 + 31p.
P5-NY0083 — $87.00.

OLD GRAVESTONES OF
DUTCHESS COUNTY: 19,000
Inscriptions. Coll. & ed. by J.W.
Poucher & H.W. Reynolds. 1924, 1958.
401 + 25p.
P5-NY0460B — $47.00.

OLD MISCELLANEOUS REC-
ORDS [of the Supervisors and
Assessors, through 1742]. 1909. 195p.
P5-NY0300 — $22.00.

INSCRIPTIONS COPIED FROM
ST. PAUL'S CHURCH YARD
[EAST CHESTER], with Gene-
alogical Notes, Index & Some Data
from Church Records. By Francis F.
Spies. 1931. 200p.
P5-NY0450 — $22.00.

HISTORY OF THE TOWN OF
EAST-HAMPTON, Including..an
Appendix and Genealogical Notes.
By Herbert P. Hedges. 1897. 345p.
P5-NY0085 — $45.00.

REMINISCENCES OF OLD EAST
HAMPTON BY THE SEA, as Given
by One of her Native Townsmen. By
Thomas M. Edwards. 1928. 300p.,
typescript.
P5-NY0084 — $39.00.

PLEASANT VALLEY: A History of
Elizabethtown, Essex Co. By George
L. Brown. 1905. 480p.
P5-NY0301 — $53.00.

HISTORY OF THE TOWN OF
ELMA, Erie County, 1620-1901. By
Warren Jackman. 1902. 331p.
P5-NY0086 — $42.00.

HISTORY OF ELMIRA, HORSE-
HEADS and the Chemung Valley,
with Sketches of the Churches,
Schools, Societies, Railroads,
Manufacturing Companies, etc. By
A.B. Galatian. 1868. 280 + 38p.
P5-NY0485 — $48.00.

CENTENNIAL HISTORY OF
ERIE COUNTY, Being its Annals
from the Earliest Recorded Events to
the Hundreth Year of American Independence. Crisfield Johnson. 1876. 512p.
P5-NY0129 — $55.00.

OUR COUNTY & ITS PEOPLE: A
Descriptive Work on Erie County, 2-
vol. set. 1898. 2 vols., 906 + 617p.
P5-NY0127 — $152.50/set.

OUR COUNTY & ITS PEOPLE
. . ., Vol. I. 1898. 906p.
P5-NY0127A - $93.00.

OUR COUNTY & ITS PEOPLE
. . ., Vol. II. 1898. 617p.
P5-NY0127B - $66.00.

HISTORY OF ESSEX COUNTY,
with Illustrations and Biographical
Sketches of Some of its Prominent
Men and Pioneers. 1885. 754p.
P5-NY0087 — $79.00.

MILITARY & CIVIL HISTORY OF
THE COUNTY OF ESSEX. By
Winslow C. Watson. 1869. 504p.
P5-NY0144 — $52.50.

FISHERS ISLAND, N.Y., 1614-1925.
By Henry L. Ferguson. 1925. 103p.
P5-NY0027 — $19.50.

HISTORY OF THE TOWN OF
FLATBUSH, in Kings Co., Long
Island. Thomas M. Strong. 1842. 178p.
P5-NY0090 — $29.00.

REFORMED DUTCH CHURCH
AT FLATBUSH, Ulster County,
New York. Copied by Kenneth E.
Hasbrouck. n.d. 297p.
P5-NY0497 — $41.00.

New York, cont.

SOCIAL HISTORY OF FLATBUSH,
& Manners & Customs of the Dutch
Settlers in Kings County. By Gertrude
Leffferts Vanderbilt. 1909. 391p.
P5-NY0088 — $46.00.

THE REALM OF AIR & LIGHT":
Flatbush of To-Day. 1908. 168p.
P5-NY0089 — $28.00.

FLUSHING, Long Island, Friends'
Records. Comp. by Frank Haviland.
1905. 193p.
P5-NY0091 — $23.50.

FLUSHING, Past & Present: A
Historical Sketch. By G. Henry
Mandeville. 1860. 180p.
P5-NY0092 — $29.00.

EARLY HISTORY OF FLUVANNA,
Chautauqua Co., with Numerous
Biographical & Family Sketches,
including Genealogy of the Griffith
Family. History by Hetty Sherwin;
Genealogy by Mary Griffith. 1927?. 126p.
P5-NY0465B — $15.00.

FORT EDWARD BOOK, Contain-
ing Some Historical Sketches, with
Illustrations and Family Records. By
Robert O. Bascom. 1903. 274p.
P5-NY0094 — $37.00.

OLD FORT EDWARD, Before 1800:
An Account of the Historic Ground
Now Occupied by the Village of Ft.
Edward. William H. Hill. 1929. 383p.
P5-NY0093 — $45.00.

HISTORICAL SKETCHES OF
FRANKLIN COUNTY & Its Several
Towns, with Many Short Biographies.
Frederick J. Seaver. 1918. 819p.
P5-NY0246 — $85.00.

FRANKLINVILLE in Pictures &
Story. Roy W. VanHoesen. 1914. 183p.
P5-NY0095 — $28.00.

TALES OF EARLY FREDONIA. By
Ellen E. Adams. 1931. 155p.
P5-NY0096 — $26.00.

HISTORY OF THE TOWNSHIP
OF GARDINER, 1853-1953. By
Kenneth E. Hasbrouck. 1953. 68p.
P5-NY0482 — $15.00.

A CENTURY & A QUARTER OF
HISTORY: GENEVA From 1787 to
1912. By Joel H. Monroe. 1912. 234p.
P5-NY0098 — $34.00.

REMINISCENCES OF EARLY
DAYS [with genealogy of] Abijih
Gilbert, 1747-1811, Joseph T. Gilbert,
1783-1867 **[Gilbertsville].** By Helen G.
Ecob. 1927. 61p.
P5-NY0099 — $12.00.

HISTORY OF GLENS FALLS & its
settlement. Louis Fiske Hyde. 1936. 347p.
P5-NY0181 — $42.00.

EARLY RECORDS OF THE FIRST
PRESBYTERIAN CHURCH AT
GOSHEN, 1767-1885. By Charles C.
Coleman. 1934. 215p.
P5-NY0182 — $25.00.

CENTENNIAL SOUVENIR HIS-
TORY OF GOUVERNEUR. With
personal sketches. By Jay S. Corbin et
al. 1905. 384p.
P5-NY0183 — $47.00.

GOVERNORS ISLAND: Its Military
History under Three Flaggs, 1637-
1922. By Edw. Banks Smith. 1923. 242p.
P5-NY0184 — $34.00.

HISTORICAL SKETCH OF
GOWANDA, in Commemoration of
the 50th Anniversary of its Incor-
poration, August, 8, 1898. Comp. by
I.R. Leonard. 1898. 147p.
P5-NY0185 — $27.00.

ABSTRACTS OF WILLS OF
GREENE COUNTY, 1800-1900, 3-
vol. set. Comp. by Ray. C. Sawyer. 1933.
3 vols., 138 + 135 + 189p.
P5-NY0433 — $54.00/set.

ABSTRACTS OF WILLS OF
GREENE COUNTY . . ., Vol. I.
1933. 138p.
P5-NY0433A - $18.00.

ABSTRACTS OF WILLS OF
GREENE COUNTY . . ., Vol. II.
1933. 135p.
P5-NY0433B - $18.00.

ABSTRACTS OF WILLS OF
GREENE COUNTY . . ., Vol. III.
1933. 189p.
P5-NY0433C - $20.00.

GRAVESTONE INSCRIPTIONS
OF GREENE COUNTY. Comp. by
M. Cohen. 1933. 3 v. in 1, 100 + 108 + 56p.
P5-NY0438 — $27.50.

HISTORY OF GREENE COUNTY,
with Biographical Sketches of its
Prominent Men. 1884. 462p.
P5-NY0012 — $56.50.

OFFICIAL HISTORY OF
GREENE COUNTY. Vol. I (all
published). Comp. by Jesse V.V.
Vedder. 1927. 207p.
P5-NY0235 — $29.50.

CEMETERIES OF THE TOWN
OF HALF MOON, Saratoga Co.
1963. 74p.
P5-NY0022 — $14.00.

HANNIBAL'S HISTORICAL
HIGHLIGHTS. By Gordon W. Sturge.
1949. 280p.
P5-NY0468B — $34.50.

REVISED HISTORY OF HARLEM
(City of New York); its Origin &
Early Annals..alsom Sketches of
Numerous Families. By James Riker.
1904. xiv + 908p.
P5-NY0025 — $92.50.

STORY OF HARTFORD: A
History. By Isabella Brayton, with J.B.
Norton. 1929. 212p.
P5-NY0187 — $31.00.

HISTORY OF HAUPPAUGE, Long
Island, Together with Genealogies.
By Simeon Woods. 1920. 92p.
P5-NY0188 — $18.00.

COLONIAL HEMPSTEAD. By
Bernice Schultz. 1937. 392p.
P5-NY0189 — $45.00.

HISTORY OF HERKIMER
COUNTY, including the Upper
Mohawk Valley from the Earliest
Period to the Present Time [1856]. By
Nathaniel S. Benton. 1856. 497p.
P5-NY0154 — $53.50.

NEW YORK EPITAPHS, from
Herkimer, Oneida & Otsego Cos.
1928. 147p.
P5-NY0427 — $18.00.

HISTORY OF HILLSDALE,
Columbia Co. a Memorabilia of
Persons and Things of Interest,
Passed and Passing. By John Francis
Collin. 1883. 195p.
P5-MA0290 — $32.50.

EARLY HISTORY OF THE TOWN
OF HOPKINTON. By C.E. Sanford.
1903. 604p.
P5-NY0100 — $65.00.

DEATHS FROM THE RURAL REPOSITORY, HUDSON, 1824-1851, 4-vol. set. Copied by Harriett M. Wiles. 1951. 4 vols., 86 + 67 + 67 + 81p.
P5-NY0422 — $35.00/set.

DEATHS FROM THE RURAL REPOSITORY, HUDSON . . ., Vol. I. 1951. 86p.
P5-NY0422A — $16.00.

DEATHS FROM THE RURAL REPOSITORY, HUDSON . . .,Vol. II. 1951. 67p.
P5-NY0422B — $16.00.

DEATHS FROM THE RURAL REPOSITORY, HUDSON . . ., Vol. III. 1951. 67p.
P5-NY0422C — $16.00.

DEATHS FROM THE RURAL REPOSITORY, HUDSON . . .,Vol. IV. 1951. 81p.
P5-NY0422D — $16.00.

HISTORICAL SKETCHES OF HUDSON, Embracing the Settlement of the City, City Government, etc. By Stephen B. Miller. 1862. 120p.
P5-NY0469B — $19.00.

HISTORY OF THE CITY OF HUDSON, with Biographical Sketches of Henry Hudson & Robert Fulton. Anna R. Bradbury. 1908. 223p.
P5-NY0190 — $31.50.

MARRIAGES FROM THE RURAL REPOSITORY 1824-5, 1838-32, 1840-6. H.M. White. 1947-1949. 2 vols. in 1, 155p.
P5-NY0451 — $19.00.

HUNTINGTON — BABYLON TOWN HISTORY. 1937. 296p.
P5-NY0191 — $39.00.

HUNTINGTON TOWN RECORDS, including Babylon, Long Island, 1653-1688. By Charles R. Street. 1887. 578p.
P5-NY0464B — $59.00.

RECORDS OF THE TOWN OF JAMAICA, Long Island, New York, 1656-1751. 1914. 464 + 457 + 448 pages.
P5-NY0493 — $140.00.

GENEALOGICAL & FAMILY HISTORY OF THE COUNTY OF JEFFERSON: A Record of her People & the Phenomonal Growth of her Agricultural & Mechanical Industries, 2-vol. set. 1905. 2 vols., 1349p.
P5-NY0193 — $135.00/set.

GENEALOGICAL & FAMILY HISTORY OF THE COUNTY OF JEFFERSON . . .,Vol. I. 1905.
P5-NY0193A — $77.00.

GENEALOGICAL & FAMILY HISTORY OF THE COUNTY OF JEFFERSON . . ., Vol. II. 1905.
P5-NY0193B — $77.00.

GEOGRAPHICAL GAZETTEER & BUSINESS DIRECTORY OF JEFFERSON CO., 1684-1890, in Two Parts. 1890. 2 parts, 887 + 340p.
P5-NY0228 — $125.50/set.

GEOGRAPHICAL GAZETTEER & BUSINESS DIRECTORY OF JEFFERSON CO. . . ., Part I. 1890. 887p.
P5-NY0228A — $93.00.

GEOGRAPHICAL GAZETTEER & BUSINESS DIRECTORY OF JEFFERSON CO. . ., Part II. 1890. 340p.
P5-NY0228B — $39.50.

HISTORY OF JEFFERSON COUNTY from the Earliest Period to the Present Time [1854]. By F.B. Hough. 1854. 601p.
P5-NY0014A — $65.00.

HISTORY OF JEFFERSON COUNTY, with Illustrations & Biographical Sketches of Some of its Prominent Men & Pioneers. 1878. 593p.
P5-NY0113 — $65.00.

OUR COUNTY & ITS PEOPLE: A Descriptive Work on Jefferson County. 2 parts in 1 book. 1898. 936 + 318p.
P5-NY0192 — $119.50.

HISTORY OF JERUSALEM. By Miles A. Davis. 1912. 103p.
P5-NY0194 — $17.50.

KATONAH: History of a New York Village & its People. By Frank R. Duncombe et al. 1961. 515p.
P5-NY0195 — $57.00.

KATSBAAN AND SAUGERTIES REFORMED CHURCH, Ulster county, New York. By Jean D. Worden. 1982. 355 + iv p.
P5-NY0500 — $40.00.

HISTORY OF OLD KINDERHOOK, from Aboriginal Days to the Present Time. Edward A. Collier. 1914. 572p.
P5-NY0211 — $59.50.

ABSTRACTS OF WILLS OF KINGS CO., Recorded at Brooklyn, Libers 1-7. Arr.by DeWitt Van Buren. 1934. 255p.
P5-NY0441 — $27.00.

INDEX TO PROBATE OF WILLS, Kings Co., Jan. 1, 1850 to Dec. 31, 1890, 3-vol. set in 1 book. Comp. by G.A. Barber. 1949. 3 vols., 102 + 112 + 120p.
P5-NY0454 — $37.50/set.

INDEX TO PROBATE OF WILLS . . ., Vol. I. 1949. 102p.
P5-NY0454A — $15.00.

INDEX TO PROBATE OF WILLS . . ., Vol. II. 1949. 112p.
P5-NY0454B — $15.00.

INDEX TO PROBATE OF WILLS . . ., Vol. III. 1949. 120p.
P5-NY0454C — $15.00.

KING'S COUNTY. Civil, Political, Professional & Ecclesiastical History, & Commercial & Industrial Record of the County of King's & the City of Brooklyn, 1638-1884, 2-vol. set. H.R. Stiles, et al. 1884. 2 vols., 632 + 770p.
P5-NY0005 — $146.00/set.

KING'S COUNTY. Civil, Political . . ., Vol. I. 1884. 632p.
P5-NY0005A — $69.50.

KING'S COUNTY. Civil, Political . . ., Vol. II. 1884. 770p.
P5-NY0005B — $80.50.

REGISTER OF THE EARLY SETTLERS of King's County, Long Island, N.Y., from its First Settlement by Europeans to 1700. By Teunis G. Bergen. 1881. 452p.
P5-NY0156 — $48.50.

INSCRIPTIONS ON TOMBSTONES AND OTHER RECORDS. Kings County Genealogical Club. 1882-1894. 96p
P28157500 — $43.00.

BAPTISMAL & MARRIAGE REGISTERS OF THE OLD DUTCH CHURCH OF KINGSTON, Ulster Co, for 150 Years from their Commencement in 1660. Comp. by R.R. Hoes. 1891. 797p.
P5-NY0015 — $82.00.

HISTORY OF KINGSTON, from its Early Settlement to the Year 1820. By Marius Schoonmaker. 1888. 558p.
P5-NY0197 — $59.00.

New York, cont.

PEOPLE'S HISTORY OF KINGSTON, RONDOUT & VICINITY, the First Capitol of N.Y. State (1820-1943). By Wm. C.DeWitt. 1943. 445p.
P5-NY0196 — $49.50.

HISTORY OF THE TOWN OF KIRKLAND. By Rev. A.D. Gridley. 1874. xiv + 232p.
P5-NY0157 — $32.00.

HISTORY OF LEWIS COUNTY in the State of New York, from the Beginning of its Settlement to the Present Time. By Franklin B. Hough. 1860. 320p.
P5-NY0212 — $38.00.

HISTORY OF LEWIS COUNTY in the State of New York, from the Beginning of its Settlement to the Present Time, with Biographical Sketches. By Franklin B. Hough. 1883. 606 + 37p.
P5-NY0213 — $68.00.

BIOGRAPHICAL REVIEW OF THE LEADING CITIZENS OF LIVINGSTON & WYOMING COUNTIES. 1895. 684p.
P5-NY0199 — $71.50.

HISTORY OF LIVINGSTON COUNTY, from its Earliest Traditions to its Part in the War for our Union; with an Account of Seneca Nation of Indians. 1876. 685p.
P5-NY0101 — $69.50.

HISTORY OF LIVINGSTON COUNTY, from its Earliest Traditions to the Present, together with Early Town Sketches. 1905. 1016 + 84 + 142p.
P5-NY0198 — $119.50.

HISTORY OF LIVINGSTON COUNTY, with Illustrations and Biographical Sketches of Some of its Prominent Men and Pioneers. By James H. Smith, with Hume H. Cale. 1881. 490 + 24p.
P5-NY0254 — $57.00.

AMERICAN FAMILIES OF HISTORIC LINEAGE, LONG ISLAND EDITION, 2-vol. set. 1921?. 2 vols., 714p.
P5-NY0041 — $75.00/set.

AMERICAN FAMILIES OF HISTORIC LINEAGE, LONG ISLAND EDITION, Vol. I. 1921?.
P5-NY0041A — $39.50.

AMERICAN FAMILIES OF HISTORIC LINEAGE, LONG ISLAND EDITION, Vol. II. 1921?.
P5-NY0041B — $39.50.

EARLY LONG ISLAND: A Colonial Study. By Martha B. Flint. 1896. 549p.
P5-NY0040 — $57.00.

HEROES OF THE AMERICAN REVOLUTION & THEIR DESCENDANTS: Battle of Long Island. Henry Whittemore. 1897. xxvi + 211 + 203p.
P5-NY0039 — $49.50.

HISTORY OF LONG ISLAND from its First Settlement by Europeans to the Year 1845. By Nathaniel S. Prime. 1845. 420p.
P5-NY0255 — $49.00.

HISTORY OF LONG ISLAND, from its Discovery & Settlement to the Present Time. 3rd ed., 3-vol. set. By Benj. F. Thompson. 1918. 3 vols., 538 + 647 + 677p.
P5-NY0256 — $165.00/set.

HISTORY OF LONG ISLAND, from its Discovery & Settlement . . ., Vol. I. 1918. 538p.
P5-NY0256A — $60.00.

HISTORY OF LONG ISLAND, from its Discovery & Settlement . . ., Vol. II. 1918. 647p.
P5-NY0256B — $60.00.

HISTORY OF LONG ISLAND, from its Discovery & Settlement . . ., Vol. III. 1918. 677p.
P5-NY0256C — $60.00.

HISTORY OF LONG ISLAND, from its Earliest Settlement to the Present Time [1902], 2-vol. set. By Peter Ross. 1902. 2 vols., 1080 + 562p.
P5-NY0293 — $155.00/set.

HISTORY OF LONG ISLAND, from its Earliest Settlement . . ., Vol. I. 1902. 1080p.
P5-NY0293A — $99.50.

HISTORY OF LONG ISLAND, from its Earliest Settlement . . ., Vol. II. 1902. 562p.
P5-NY0293B — $67.50.

LONG ISLAND COLONIAL PATENTS. By Frederick Van Wyck. 1935. 16 + 175p.
P5-NY0038 — $21.00.

LONG ISLAND GENEALOGIES . . . Desc. of Thomas Powell of Bethpage, Long Island, 1688. With genealogical material on over 60 early families. By M. Bunker. 1895. 350p.
P5-NY0013 — $48.00.

SKETCH OF THE FIRST SETTLEMENT OF LONG ISLAND. By D. Wood. 1865. 226p.
P28162500 — $44.00.
RATE LISTS OF LONG ISLAND: 1675, 1676, 1683. n.d. 102p.
P5-NY0426 — $15.00.

HISTORY OF LONG ISLAND CITY: A Record of its Early Settlement & Corporate Progress, Sketches of the Villages that Were Absorbed . . . with Some Notice of the Men who Built the City. J.S. Kelsey. 1896. 202p.
P5-NY0257 — $31.00.

HISTORICAL REVIEW OF THE TOWN OF LYSANDER. By L. Pearl Palmer. 1950. 191p.
P5-NY0258 — $23.50.

PIONEERS OF MACEDON, & Other Papers of the Macedon Center Historical Society. By Mary Louise Eldredge. 1905. 190p.
P5-NY0259 — $29.50.

HISTORY OF MADISON COUNTY, State of New York. By Mrs L.M. Hammond Whitney. 1872. 774p.
P5-NY0243 — $81.50.

OUR COUNTY & ITS PEOPLE: A Descriptive & Biographical Record of Madison County. 1890. 649 + 239p.
P5-NY0260 — $89.50.

CENTENNIAL HISTORY OF THE TOWN OF MARCELLUS. By Israel Parsons. 1878. 108p.
P5-NY0262 — $15.00.

HISTORY OF THE TOWN OF MARLBOROUGH, Ulster Co., from its Earliest Discovery By C.M. Woolsey. 1908. 471p.
P5-NY0302 — $53.00.

HISTORY OF MATTITUCK, Long Island. Charles E. Craven. 1906. 400p.
P5-NY0263 — $44.00.

BAPTIST CHURCH AT MERIDIAN, New York, 1810-1988. A.M. Meacham. 2006. 297 + x p.
P5-NY0514 — $40.00.

MEXICO, Mother of Towns: Fragments of Local History. By Elizabeth M. Simpson. 1949. 551p.
P5-NY0264 — $61.50.

MIDDLETOWN: A Biography. By Franklin B. Williams. 1928. 201p.
P5-NY0265 — $34.50.

BOOK OF NAMES, Esp. Relating to the Early Palatines & First Settlers in the Mohawk Valley. By L. MacWethy. 1933. 209p.
P5-NY0362B — $22.50.

HISTORY OF THE MONT-GOMERY CLASSIS, to Which is Added Sketches of Mohawk Valley Men & Events of Early Days, etc. By W.N.P. Daily. 1915?. 198p.
P5-NY0120 — $24.50.

MOHAWK VALLEY: Its Legends & History. By W. Max Reid, with photographs by J. Arthur Maney. 1907. 455p.
P5-NY0229 — $49.50.

STORY OF OLD FORT PLAIN & the Middle Mohawk Valley. A Review of Mohawk Valley History from 1609 to 1912-4. Nelson Greene. 1915. 399p.
P5-NY0214 — $45.00.

CHRONICLES OF MONROE in the Olden Time, Town & Village, Orange County. By Daniel Niles Freeland. 1898. 279p.
P5-NY0268 — $34.00.

HISTORY OF MONROE COUNTY, 1783-1877, with Illustrations Descriptive of its Scenery, Palatial Residences, Public Buildings . . . W.H. McIntosh 1877. 320p.
P5-NY0267 — $43.00.

LANDMARKS OF MONROE COUNTY, Containing an Historical Sketch of Monroe Co. & the City of Rochester . . . Followed by Brief Historical Sketches of the Towns, with Biography & Family History. Wm. F. Peck, et al. 1895. 492 + 339p.
P5-NY0269 — $87.00.

BRICK REFORMED CHURCH: MONTGOMERY, ORANGE COUNTY, NEW YORK. By Mrs. Jean D. Worden. 1982. 229p.
P5-NY0494 — $35.00.

HISTORY OF MONTGOMERY COUNTY. With biographies and family sketches. 1892. 450 + 349p.
P5-NY0169 — $81.50.

MONTGOMERY CO. MARRIAGE RECORDS, Performed by Rev. Elijah Herrick 1795-1844; also Records of Rev. Calvin Herricl, 1834-1876; Rev. John Calvin Toll, 1803-1844. Comp. by Melvin W. Lethbridge. 1922. 38p.
P5-NY0479 — $10.00.

HISTORICAL SKETCHES OF THE TOWN OF MORAVIA, from 1791 to 1918. James A. Wright. 1918. 525p.
P5-NY0270 — $57.00.

HISTORICAL SKETCHES OF OLD NEW BERLIN. By John Hyde. 1876, 1907. 108p.
P5-NY0271 — $15.00.

RECORDS OF THE REFORMED DUTCH CHURCH OF NEW HACKENSACK, Dutchess Co. 1932. 333p.
P5-NY0273A — $41.00.

NEW HARLEM, Past & Present: The Story of an Amazing Civic Wrong, Now at Last Righted. By Carl Horton Pierce. 1903. 332p.
P5-NY0186 — $41.50.

DUTCH REFORMED CHURCH: NEW HURLEY, Ulster County, New York. Mrs. Jean D. Worden. 1980. 224p.
P5-NY0495 — $34.00.

REGISTER OF NEW NETHER-LAND, 1626-1674. E.B. O'Callaghan. 1865. 198p.
P5-NY0480 — $24.50.

SUPPLEMENT TO THE 1999 "DIRECTORY TO PERSONS IN NEW NETHERLAND from 1613 to 1674." By David M. Riker. 2004. 456p.
P5-NY0498 — $51.00.

HISTORY OF NEW PALTZ & its Old Families, from 1678 to 1829. By Ralph LeFevre. 1903. 592p.
P5-NY0132 — $62.00.

HISTORY OF THE TOWN OF NEW WINDSOR, Orange Co. By Edw. M. Ruttenber. 1911. 213p.
P5-NY0273B — $31.00.

NEW WOODSTOCK & Vicinity, Past & Present. By Anzolette D. Ellsworth & Mary E. Richmond. 1901. 141p.
P5-NY0274 — $19.00.

HISTORY OF THE CITY OF NEW YORK. By David T. Valentine. 1853. 404p. + 5 folding maps.
P5-NY0303 — $49.50.

HISTORY OF THE CITY OF NEW YORK, 1609-1909. By John William Leonard. 1910. 954p.
P5-NY0492 — $95.00.

MANHATTAN IN 1628, as Described in the . . . Autographed Letter of Jonas Michaelius . . . with a Review of the Letter & an Historical Sketch of New Netherland to 1628. By Dingman Versteeg. 1904. 203p.
P5-NY0261 — $35.00.

NEW YORK [CITY] DIRECTORY FROM 1786, Prefaced by a General Description of N.Y. by Noah Webster & an Appendix of the Annals of N.Y.C., 1786. xxii + 216p.
P5-NY0216 — $29.50.

PHILLIP'S ELITE DIRECTORY of Private Families, 1881-1882, Containing the Names of 25,000 Householders. 1881. 515p.
P5-NY0217 — $54.50.

RECORDS OF THE REFORMED DUTCH CHURCH IN NEW AMSTERDAM & New York — Baptisms. 1902. 634p.
P5-NY0509 — $64.00.

INDEX OF WILLS FOR NEW YORK CO. (New York City), from 1662 to 1850. Comp. by Ray C. Sawyer. 1930. 496p.
P5-NY0449 — $49.50.

HISTORY OF THE TOWN OF NEWBURGH. By E.M. Ruttenber 1859. 322 + xx p.
P5-NY0200 — $39.50.

NEWBURGH Her Institutions, Industries and Leading Citizens. Comp. by J.J. Nutt. 1891. 335p.
P5-NY0503 — $45.00.

ANNALS OF NEWTOWN, Queen's County, Containing its History from its Settlement..with Many Interesting Facts Concerning the Adjacent Towns. With genealogies. James Riker. 1852. 437p.
P5-NY0131 — $47.00.

BIOGRAPHICAL & PORTRAIT CYCLOPEDIA OF NIAGARA COUNTY. 1892. 640p.
P5-NY0405A — $71.00.

New York, cont.

HISTORY OF NIAGARA CO., NY.
1878. 397 + 262p.
P5-NY0508 — $54.00.

NIAGARA COUNTY, One of the Most Wonderful Regions in the World: A Concise Record of her Progress & People, 1821-1921, 2-vol. set in 1 book.
Edw. T. Williams. 1921. 2 vols., 850p.
P5-NY0275 — $89.00/set.

NIAGARA COUNTY . . ., Vol. I.
1921.
P5-NY0275A — $49.50.

NIAGARA COUNTY . . ., Vol. II.
1921.
P5-NY0275B — $49.50.

CENTENNIAL HISTORY OF THE TOWN OF NUNDA, 1808-1908, with a Preliminary Recital of the Winning of Western N.Y. 1908.
637p.
P5-NY0159 — $66.00.

HISTORY OF THE CITY OF OGDENSBURG. By Rev. P.S. Garand. 1927. 469p.
P5-NY0310 — $51.50.

HISTORY OF ONONDAGA COUNTY, with Illustrations & Biographical Sketches of Some of its Prominent Men & Pioneers. By W.W. Clayton. 1878. 430p. + many illus.
P5-NY0410 — $54.00.

ABSTRACTS OF WILLS OF ONEIDA COUNTY, Six-vol. set By G.A. Barber. 1945. 6 v., 56+53+53+53+53+27p.
P5-NY0473B — $66.00/set.

ABSTRACTS OF WILLS OF ONEIDA COUNTY,Vol. I. 1945. 56p.
P5-NY0473B1 — $12.50.

ABSTRACTS OF WILLS OF ONEIDA COUNTY, Vol. II. 1945. 53p.
P5-NY0473B2 — $12.50.

ABSTRACTS OF WILLS OF ONEIDA COUNTY, Vol. III. 1945. 53p.
P5-NY0473B3 — $12.50.

ABSTRACTS OF WILLS OF ONEIDA COUNTY, Vol. IV. 1945. 53p.
P5-NY0473B4 — $12.50.

ABSTRACTS OF WILLS OF ONEIDA COUNTY, Vol. V. 1945. 53p.
P5-NY0473B5 — $12.50.

ABSTRACTS OF WILLS OF ONEIDA COUNTY, Vol. VI. 1945. 27p.
P5-NY0473B6 — $10.00.

ANNALS & RECOLLECTIONS OF ONEIDA COUNTY. By Pomroy Jones. 1851. 893p.
P5-NY0160 — $88.00.
HISTORY OF ONEIDA COUNTY, from 1700 to the Present Time, 2-vol. set. By Henry J. Cookinham. 1912. 2 vols., 568 + 699p.
P5-NY0311 — $132.00/set.

HISTORY OF ONEIDA COUNTY . . ., Vol. I. 1912. 568p.
P5-NY0311A — $66.00.

HISTORY OF ONEIDA COUNTY . . ., Vol. II. 696p.
P5-NY0311B — $72.50.

HISTORY OF ONEIDA COUNTY, with Illustration & Biographical Sketches of Some of its Prominent Men & Pioneers. 1878. 678p.
P5-NY0161 — $69.50.

OUR COUNTY & ITS PEOPLE: A Descriptive Work on Oneida County, 3 Parts in 2 Vols. 1896. 2 vols., 851 + 411p.
P5-NY0102 — $125.00/set.

OUR COUNTY & ITS PEOPLE . . ., Parts I & II: History & Biography. 1896. 851p.
P5-NY0102A — $88.00.

OUR COUNTY & ITS PEOPLE . . .,Part III: Family Sketches. 1896. 411p.
P5-NY0102B — $44.00.

HISTORY OF ONEONTA, from its Earliest Settlement to the Present Time. Dudley M. Campbell. 1906. 190p.
P5-NY0312 — $29.50.

ONONDAGA, or Reminiscences of Earlier & Later Times, Being a Series of Historical Sketches Relative to Onondaga; with Notes on the Several Towns in the County, & Oswego. By Joshua V.H. Clark. 1849. 2 vols. in 1, 408 + 392p.
P5-NY0313 — $86.00.

ONONDAGA'S CENTENNIAL: Gleanings of a Century, 2-vol. set.
1896. 2 vols., 1111 + 546p.
P5-NY0315 — $149.00/set.

ONONDAGA"S CENTENNIAL . . ., Vol. I. 1896. 1111p.
P5-NY0315A — $111.00.

ONONDAGA"S CENTENNIAL . . .,Vol. II. 1896. 546p.
P5-NY0315B — $56.00.

PIONEER IRISH OF ONONDAGA (about 1776-18470). By Theresa Bannan, M.D. 1911. 333p.
P5-NY0314 — $43.50.

PIONEER TIMES IN THE ONONDAGA COUNTRY. By Carroll E. Smith. 1904. 415p.
P5-NY0252 — $47.00.

REVOLUTIONARY SOLDIERS Resident or Dying in Onondaga Co., with Supplementary List of Possible Veterans. 1912. 307p.
P5-NY0218 — $34.50.

HISTORY OF ONTARIO COUNTY & Its People. 2-vol. set. By Charles F. Milliken. 1911. 2 vols., 505 + 506p.
P5-NY0408 — $109.00/set.

HISTORY OF ONTARIO COUNTY & Its People, Vol. I. 1911. 505p
P5-NY0408A — $57.00.

HISTORY OF ONTARIO COUNTY & Its People, Vol. II. 1911. 506p
P5-NY0408B — $57.00.

HISTORY OF ONTARIO COUNTY, with Illustrations and Family Sketches of some of the Prominent Men & Families. Comp. by Lewis C. Aldrich. 1893. 519 + 396p.
P5-NY0304 — $94.00.

HISTORY OF ONTARIO COUNTY, with Illustrations. 1876. 276p.
P5-NY0316 — $39.00.

ABTRACTS OF WILLS OF ORANGE & ROCKLAND COUNTIES. Comp. by M. Cohen. 1937. 2 vols. in 1, 84 + 84p.
P5-NY0467A — $16.00.

ANCESTORS OF ORANGE COUNTY, NEW YORK. By D.G. Van Curen 2003 viii + 749p.
P5-NY1003 — $78.00.

HISTORY OF ORANGE COUNTY, with an Enumeration of the Names of its Towns, Villages . . . and other Known Localities..with Short Biographical Sketches of Early Settlers. By Samuel W. Eager. 1846-1847. 652p.
P5-NY0175 — $68.00.

HISTORY OF ORANGE COUNTY, with Illustrations & Biographical Sketches of Many of its Pioneers & Prominent. By E.M. Ruttenber & L.H. Clark. 1881. 820p.
P5-NY0133 — $79.00.

HISTORY OF ORANGE COUNTY. 1908. 997p.
P5-NY0219 — $98.00.

HISTORY OF THE MINISINK REGION, which Includes the Present Towns of Minisink, Deerpark, Mount Hope, Greenville & Wayayanda, in Orange County, from their Organization & First Settlement to the Present [1867]. By Charles E. Stickney. 1867. 211p.
P5-NY0266 — $33.50.

MARRIAGES & DEATHS FROM 1828-1831, from "Orange Co. Patriot," Published in Goshen. Comp. by G.A. Barber. 1933. 41p.
P5-NY0435 — $10.00.

ORANGE COUNTY WILLS, 1787-1831, with Added Genealogical Notes. Mrs J.A. Weller, Jr. 1946. 221p.
P5-NY0434 — $25.00.

ORANGE COUNTY: A Narrative History. Comp. by Almet S. Moffat. 1928. 87p.
P5-NY0317 — $16.00.

PORTRAIT & BIOGRAPHICAL RECORD OF ORANGE COUNTY, Containing Portraits & Biopgrahical Sketches of Prominent & Representative Citizens of the County. Parts 1 & 2. 1895. 1547p.
P5-NY0318 — $149.50.

HISTORICAL ALBUM OF ORLEANS CO., NY. 1879. 320 + 120p.
P5-NY0507 — $44.00.

HISTORY OF THE MISSISCO VALLEY [Orleans Co.]. By Samuel Sumner. With intro. notice of Orleans Co. by Rev. S.R. Hall. 1860. 75p.
P5-NY0232 — $17.50.

LANDMARKS OF ORLEANS COUNTY, Illustrated. With biographical & family sketches. 1894. 688 + 241p.
P5-NY0319 — $97.00.

PIONEER HISTORY OF ORLEANS COUNTY, Containing Some Account of the Civil Divisions of Western N.Y., with Brief Biogr. Notices of Early Settlers. By Arad Thomas. 1871. 463p.
P5-NY0023 — $49.00.

HISTORY OF THE TOWN OF ORWELL, 1806 to 1887. Comp. by Hugh F. Murray. 1887. 236p.
P5-NY0320 — $33.50.

HISTORY OF OSWEGO COUNTY, with Illustrations & Biographical Sketches of Prominent Men & Pioneers. 1877. 450p.
P5-NY0114 — $54.50.

LANDMARKS OF OSWEGO COUNTY. Part I, History; Part II, Biographical; Part III, Family Sketches. 1895. 843 + 72 + 348p.
P5-NY0250 — $119.50.

BIOGRAPHICAL SKETCHES OF THE LEADING CITIZENS OF OTSEGO COUNTY. 1893. 857p.
P5-NY0322 — $89.50.

HISTORY OF OTSEGO COUNTY, with Illustrations & Biographical Sketches of some of its Prominent Men & Pioneers. 1878. 378p.
P5-NY0115 — $47.50.

INDEX OF WILLS FOR OTSEGO COUNTY, 1792-1875. Comp. by G.A. Barber. 1934. 2 vols. in 1, 54 + 67p.
P5-NY0419 — $16.00.

OTSEGO COUNTY ABSTRACTS OF WILLS, 1794-1850, 5-vol. set in 1 book. Comp. by G.A. Barber. 1945. 5 v., 53+53+53+52+59p., paper.
P5-NY0420 — $35.00/set.

OTSEGO COUNTY ABSTRACTS OF WILLS . . ., Vol. I. 1945. 53p.
P5-NY0420A — $12.00.

OTSEGO COUNTY ABSTRACTS OF WILLS . . ., Vol. II. 1945. 53p.
P5-NY0420B — $12.00.

OTSEGO COUNTY ABSTRACTS OF WILLS . . ., Vol. III. 1945. 53p.
P5-NY0420C — $12.00.

OTSEGO COUNTY ABSTRACTS OF WILLS . . ., Vol. IV. 1945. 52p.
P5-NY0420D — $12.00.

OTSEGO COUNTY ABSTRACTS OF WILLS . . ., Vol. V. 1945. 59p.
P5-NY0420E — $12.00.

OTSEGO COUNTY MARRIAGES, From the "Otsego Herald & Western Advertiser" & "Freeman's Journal," 3-vol. set in 1 book. Comp. by G.A. Barber. 1932. 3 vols., 157 + 121 + 147p.
P5-NY0453 — $45.00/set.

OTSEGO COUNTY MARRIAGES . . ., Vol. I. 1932. 157p.
P5-NY0453A — $16.50.

OTSEGO COUNTY MARRIAGES . . ., Vol. II. 1932. 121p.
P5-NY0453B — $16.50.

OTSEGO COUNTY MARRIAGES . . ., Vol. III. 1932. 147p.
P5-NY0453C — $16.50.

REMINISCENCES: Personal & Other Incidents; Early Settlement of Otsego Co. etc. By Levi Beardsley. 1852. 575p.
P5-NY0321 — $63.50.

EARLY OWEGO: Some Account of the Early Settlement of the Village in Tioga County. Called Ah-wa-ga by the Indians. LeRoy Wilson Kingman. 1907. 673p.
P5-NY0323 — $73.00.

ANNALS OF OXFORD, with Illustrations & Biographical Sketches of some of its Prominent Men & Early Pioneers. Henry J. Galpin. 1906. 568p.
P5-NY0134 — $59.00.

DOCUMENTARY HISTORY OF THE DUTCH CONGREGATION OF OYSTER BAY, Queens Co., Island of Nassau (Long Island), 2-vol. set. By Henry A. Stoutenburgh. 1902. 2 vols., 966p.
P5-NY0170 — $99.50/set.

DOCUMENTARY HISTORY OF THE DUTCH CONGREGATION OF OYSTER BAY . . ., Vol. I. 1902.
P5-NY0134A — $55.00.

DOCUMENTARY HISTORY OF THE DUTCH CONGREGATION OF OYSTER BAY . . ., Vol. II. 1902.
P5-NY0134B — $55.00.

New York, cont.

OYSTER BAY TOWN RECORDS,
Vol. I: 1653-1690. John Cox, Jr. 1916. 754p.
P28245400 — $116.00.

OYSTER BAY TOWN RECORDS,
Vol. II: 1691-1704. By D. Underhill, J.
Merritt & W. Pierce 1924. 747p.
P28254200 — $115.00.

HISTORY OF THE TOWN OF
PARIS & the Valley of the Sauquoit:
Anecdotes & Reminiscences. By
Henry C. Rogers. 1881. 398p.
P5-NY0142 — $44.00.

ATTACK AT PEEKSKILL BY THE
BRITISH IN 1777, and the Role of
the Fort Hill Site During the War of
Independence. John J. Curran. 1998. 153p.
P5-NY0490 — $23.00.

PEEKSKILL IN THE AMERICAN
REVOLUTION. By Emma L.
Patterson. 1944. 184p.
P5-NY0324 — $28.50.

PIONEERS, PATRIOTS &
PEOPLE, PAST & PRESENT:
History of Peekskill. By Wm. T.
Horton. 1953. 355p.
P5-NY0325 — $44.00.

BRIEF, BUT MOST COMPLETE
& TRUE ACCOUNT OF THE
SETTLEMENT OF THE ANCIENT
TOWN OF PELHAM, Westchester
Co., Known One Time . . . as the
Lordshipp & Monnour of Pelham;
also the Story of the Three Modern
Villages called the Pelhams. By
Lockwood Barr. 1946. 190p.
P5-NY0326 — $29.00.

HISTORY OF THE TOWN OF
PERRY. By Frank D. Roberts, with
C.G. Clarke. 1915. 385p.
P5-NY0327 — $44.00.

HISTORY OF PORT HENRY. By
Dr Charles B. Warner & C. Eleanor
Hall. 1931. 182p.
P5-NY0328 — $29.00.

HISTORY OF THE TOWN OF
PORTLAND, Comprising also the
Pioneer History of Chautauqua
County, with Biographical Sketches
of Early Settlers. By H.C, Taylor. 1873.
446p.
P5-NY0329 — $48.00.

PURCHASE QUAKER BURYING
GROUND, & Minutes of Monthly
Meetings, etc. Transcr. by Francis F.
Spies. 1932. 244p.
P5-NY0457 — $25.00.

HISTORY OF PUTNAM COUNTY,
with an Enumeration of its Towns,
Villages . . . and Geological Features,
Local Traditions, & Short Biograph-
ical Sketches of Early Settlers. By
Wm. J. Blake. 1849. 368p.
P5-NY0462B — $42.50.

HISTORY OF PUTNAM COUNTY,
with Biographical Sketches of its
Prominent Men. By Wm. S. Pelletreau.
1886. 769p.
P5-NY0466B — $82.00.

HISTORY OF QUEENS COUNTY,
NEW YORK. 1882. 576p
P28220000 — $91.00.

DESCRIPTION OF PRIVATE &
FAMILY CEMETERIES IN THE
BOROUGH OF QUEENS. Comp. by
the Topographical Bureau. 1932. 81p.
P5-NY0423 — $16.50.

ABSTRACTS OF WILLS FOR
QUEENS COUNTY, 1787-1850, 4
vols. in 1 book. Comp. by Ray C. Sawyer.
1934-1937. 4 v., 134 + 134 + 134 + 95p.
P5-NY0446 — $50.00/set.

ABSTRACTS OF WILLS FOR
QUEENS COUNTY, 1787-1850, Vol.
I. 1934-1937. 134p.
P5-NY0446A — $16.00.

ABSTRACTS OF WILLS FOR
QUEENS COUNTY, 1787-1850, Vol.
II. 1934-1937. 134p.
P5-NY0446B — $16.00.

ABSTRACTS OF WILLS FOR
QUEENS COUNTY, 1787-1850, Vol.
III. 1934-1937. 134p.
P5-NY0446C — $16.00.

ABSTRACTS OF WILLS FOR
QUEENS COUNTY, 1787-1850, Vol.
IV. 1934-1937. 95p.
P5-NY0446D — $16.00.

DOCUMENTS & LETTERS
INTENDED TO ILLUSTRATE
REVOLUTIONARY INCIDENTS
OF QUEENS CO., with Connecting
Narratives, Explanatory Notes &
Additions. By Henry Onderdonk, Jr.
1884. 70p.
P5-NY0330 — $14.00.

DOCUMENTS & LETTERS
INTENDED TO ILLUSTRATE
THE REVOLUTIONARY INCI-
DENTS OF QUEENS CO., with
Connecting Narratives, Explanatory
Notes & Additions. 1846. 264p.
P5-NY0331 — $38.00.

HISTORY OF THE TOWN OF
QUEENSBURY, with Biographical
Sketches of Many of its Distinguished
Men. A.W. Holden. 1874. 517p.
P5-NY0220 — $55.00.

STORY OF OLD RENSSELAER-
VILLE. By Mary Fisher Torrance. 1939.
72p.+ 6 maps.
P5-NY0333 — $17.50.

ABSTRACTS OF ALL WILLS, 1791-
1850, of Rensselaer Co., 3 vols. in 1
book. By Ralph D. Phillips. 1921. 3
vols., 99 + 117 + 137p.
P5-NY0442 — $42.00/set.

ABSTRACTS OF ALL WILLS . . . of
Rensselaer Co., Vol. I. 1921. 99p.
P5-NY0442A — $15.00.

ABSTRACTS OF ALL WILLS . . . of
Rensselaer Co., Vol. II. 1921. 117p.
P5-NY0442B — $15.00.

ABSTRACTS OF ALL WILLS . . . of
Rensselaer Co., Vol. III. 1921. 137p.
P5-NY0442C — $15.00.

HISTORY OF RENSSELAER
COUNTY, with Illustrations &
Biographical Sketches of its
Prominent Men & Pioneers. By
Nathaniel Bartlett Sylvester. 1880. 564p.
P5-NY0135 — $59.50.

HISTORY OF THE SEVENTEEN
TOWNS OF RENSSELAER
COUNTY, from the Colonization of
the Manor of Rensselaerwyck to the
Present Timw [1880]. By A.J. Weise.
1880. 158p.
P5-NY0332 — $21.00.

LANDMARKS OF RENSSELAER
COUNTY. By George Baker Anderson.
1897. 570 + 460p.
P5-NY0162 — $98.50.

HISTORIC OLD RHINEBECK,
Echoes of Two Centuries: A Hudson
River & Post Road Colonial Town . . .
Historical, Genealogical, Biograph-
ical, Traditional. By Howard H. Morse.
1908. 448p.
P5-NY0334 — $49.00.

ANNALS OF RICHFIELD. By Henry A. Ward. 1898. 102p.
P5-NY0335 — $18.00.

RICHFIELD SPRINGS & Vicinity: Historical, Biographical & Descriptive. By W.T. Bailey. 1874. 227p.
P5-NY0336 — $33.00.

HISTORY OF RICHMOND COUNTY (STATEN ISLAND) From its Discovery to the Present Time [1887]. 1887. 741p.
P5-NY0337 — $78.00.

HISTORY OF ROCHESTER, & MONROE COUNTY, from Earliest Historic Times to the Beginning of 1907. William F. Peck. 1908. 2 vols., 1434p.
P5-NY0136 — $119.50.

ROCHESTER: A Story Historical. By Jenny Marsh Parker. 1884. 412p.
P5-NY0338 — $47.00.

GRAVEYARD INSCRIPTIONS OF ROCKLAND COUNTY. Comp. by G.A. Barber. 1931. 3 v. in 1, 49 + 51 + 52p.
P5-NY0431 — $21.00.

HISTORY OF ROCKLAND COUNTY, with Biographical Sketches of its Prominent Men. 1884. 420p.
P5-NY0028 — $49.50.

CENSUSES OF THE TOWNS OF ROXBURY & SIDNEY, From the 1855 Delaware Co. Census. Comp. by Gertrude A. Barber. 1949. 71p.
P5-NY0417 — $14.00.

HISTORY OF THE TOWN OF ROXBURY. By Caroline E. More & Irma Mae Griffin. 1953. 281p.
P5-NY0339 — $39.00.

RUSHFORD & RUSHFORD PEOPLE. Helen J.W. Gilbert. 1910. 572p.
P5-NY0340 — $63.00.

RYE, Westchester Co., Inscriptions from Graveyards. Transcr. by Francis F. Spies. 1932. 371p.
P5-NY0456 — $36.00.

RYE. Chronicle of a Border Town: History of Rye, Westchester Co., 1660-1870, Including Harrison & White Plains till 1788. By C.W. Baird. 1871. 570p.
P5-NY0007 — $59.50.

SAG HARBOR IN EARLIER DAYS: A Series of Historical Sketches of the Harbor & Hampton Port. Harry D. Sleight. 1930. 284 + 9p.
P5-NY0341 — $38.00.

HAND-BOOK OF SARATOGA & STRANGERS' GUIDE. By R.L. Allen. 1859. 131p.
P5-NY0345 — $17.50.

REMINISCENCES OF SARATOGA. Comp. by Cornelius E. Durkee. 1927-1928. 316p.
P5-NY0346 — $39.00.

REMINISCENCES OF SARATOGA & BALLSTON. Wm. L. Stone. 1875. 451p.
P5-NY0347 — $49.50.

STORY OF OLD SARATOGA & The Burgoyne Campaign. 2nd ed. By John Henry Brandow. 1919. 528p.
P5-NY0344 — $57.00.

GRANTORS IN THE REGISTRY OF DEEDS OF SARATOGA COUNTY, as Contained in Libers A-S, 1792-1831. Comp. by Edw. Doubleday Harris. 1901-3. 391p.
P5-NY0343 — $47.00.

HISTORY OF SARATOGA COUNTY, with Historical Notes on its Various Towns, together with Biographical Sketches of its Prominent Men & Leading citizens. History by Nathaniel Bartlett Sylvester. 1893. 635p.
P5-NY0348 — $68.00.

OUR COUNTY AND ITS PEOPLE: A descriptive & biographical record of Saratoga Co. By "The Saratogian" (George Baker Anderson). 1899. 584 + 203p.
P5-NY0247 — $81.50.

CENTENNIAL ADDRESS RELATING TO THE EARLY HISTORY OF SCHENECTADY & Its First Settlers. By John Sanders. 1879. 346p.
P5-NY0353 — $41.00.

CONTRIBUTIONS FOR THE GENEALOGY of the Descendants of the First Settlers of the Patent & City of SCHENECTADY from 1662 to 1800. By J. Pearson. 1873. 324p.
P5-NY0138 — $32.50.

HISTORY OF SCHENECTADY DURING THE REVOLUTION, To Which is Appended a Contribution to the Individual Records of the Inhabitants of the Schenectady District During that Period. By Willis T. Hanson. 1916. 304p.
P5-NY0352 — $39.50.

MARRIAGE RECORDS OF THE REFORMED PROTESTANT DUTCH CHURCH OF SCHENECTADY. Comp. by Charlotte T. Luckhurst. 1917. 204p.
P5-NY0430 — $26.00.

OLD SCHENECTADY. By George S. Roberts. 1904. 296p.
P5-NY0351 — $38.00.

SCHENECTADY, Ancient & Modern: a Complete & Connected History of Schenetady from the Granting of the First Patent in 1661 to 1914. Joel Henry Monroe. 1914. 285p.
P5-NY0350 — $37.00.

VALE CEMETERY RECORDS, Schenectady. Comp. by Charlotte T. Luckhurst. 1926. 5 vols. in 1, 597p.
P5-NY0471A — $59.00.

ABSTRACTS OF WILLS OF SCHENECTADY COUNTY, 1809-1835, From the Original Records at the Surrogate's Office, Schenectady. Comp. by G. Barber. 1941. 3 vols. in 1, 140p.
P5-NY0462A — $19.00.

HISTORY OF THE COUNTY SCHENECTADY from 1662 to 1886, with Portraits, Biographies & Illustrations. 1886. 218p.
P5-NY0356B — $25.00.

SCHENECTADY COUNTY: Its History to the Close of the Nineteenth Century. With biographical sketches. 1902. 463 + 258p.
P5-NY0355 — $74.50.

ABSTRACTS OF WILLS, LETTERS OF ADMINISTRATION & GUARDIANSHIP, from the Original Records at the Surrogate's Office, 1795-1863. Copied by G.A. Barber. 1938. 5 v. in 1, 328p.
P5-NY0447 — $32.00.

BURIALS IN THE OLD STONE FORT CEMETERY AT SCHOHARIE, Copied from the Gravestones. By Frank D. Andrews. 1917. 31p.
P5-NY0445 — $10.00.

PAPERS RELATNG TO THE MANOR OF LIVINGSTON, Including the First Settlement of Schoharie, 1680-1795. n.d. 213p.
P5-NY0466A — $21.00.

New York, cont.

DEATHS & BURIALS IN SCHOHARIE COUNTY. Comp. by Charlotte T. Luckhurst. 1921. 200p.
P5-NY0356A — $24.50.

GRAVESTONE INSCRIPTIONS OF SCHOHARIE CO. Comp. by M. Cohen. 1933. 700p.
P5-NY0448 — $72.00.

HISTORY OF SCHOHARIE COUNTY, with Illustrations and Biographical Sketches of Some of its Prominent Men and Pioneers. By William E. Roscoe. 1882. 470 + 28p.
P5-NY03586 — $54.00.

BIOGRAPHICAL RECORD OF SCHUYLER COUNTY, Illustrated. 1903. 546p.
P5-NY0359 — $59.50.

PORTRAIT & BIOGRAPHICAL RECORD OF SENECA & SCHUYLER COUNTIES. 1895. 508p.
P5-NY0360 — $55.00.

LEGENDS OF THE SHAWAN-GUNK & its Environs, Including Historical Sketches, Biographical Notices & Thrilling Border Incidents & Adventures Relating to those Portions of Orange, Ulster & Sullivan Counties Lying in the Shawangunk Region. By Philip H. Smith. 1887. 168p.
P5-NY0033 — $27.00.

REFORMED PROTESTANT DUTCH CHURCH OF SHAWANGUNK, Ulster County, New York. Jean D. Worden. n.d. 405p.
P5-NY0499 — $45.00.

HISTORY OF SHELTER ISLAND, from its Settlement in 1652 to the Present Time, 1932. By Ralph G. Duvall. 1932. 229p.
P5-NY0361 — $34.00.

REMINISCENCES, ANECDOTES & STATISTICS of the Early Settlers & the "Olden Time" in the Town of Sherburne, Chenango Co. By Joel Hatch, Jr. 1862. 104p.
P5-NY0478 — $17.50.

SHERBURNE ILLUSTRATED: History of the Village of Sherburne, its Scenery, Development & Business Enterprises. John P. Gomph. 1896. 110p.
P5-NY0362A — $15.00.

SOUVENIR OF THE SHERBURNE CENTENNIAL CELEBRATION; Also Sketches of Families & Other Historical Data. 1893. 111p.
P5-NY0481 — $19.00.

SKANEATELES: History of Its Earliest Settlement & Reminiscences of Later Times. Edmund Norman Leslie. 1902. 477p.
P5-NY0364 — $51.00.

RECORDS OF THE TOWN OF SMITHTOWN. Long Island, with Other Ancient Documents of Historic Value, with Notes & Introduction. Wm. S. Pelletreau. 1898. 503p.
P5-NY0366 — $54.50.

EARLY YEARS IN SMYRNA, & Our First Old Home Week. By George A. Munson. 1905. 209p.
P5-NY0367 — $31.50.

OLD CHURCHYARD INSCRIPTIONS, South Salem, Westchester Co. 1908. 52p.
P5-NY0428 — $11.00.

EARLY HISTORY OF SOUTH-AMPTON, Long Island, with Genealogies. 2nd ed. By George Rogers Howell. 1887. 473p.
P5-NY0163 — $49.50.

HISTORY OF THE TOWN OF SOUTHAMPTON (East of Canoe Place). James Truslow Adams. 1918. 424p.
P5-NY0221 — $45.00.

SOUTHOLD TOWN RECORDS [with Explanatory Notes], 1651-1787. With appendix & index, 2-vol. set. Comp. by J. Wickham Case. 1884. 2 vols., 490 + 565p.
P5-NY0477 — $99.00/set.

SOUTHOLD TOWN RECORDS . . ., Vol. I. 1884. 490p.
P5-NY0477A — $56.00.

SOUTHOLD TOWN RECORDS . . ., Vol. II. 1884. 565p.
P5-NY0477B — $56.00.

SPAFFORD, Onondaga County. By George Knapp Collins. 1917. 112 + 280p.
P5-NY0164 — $42.50.

HISTORY OF SPRINGFIELD. By Kate M. Gray. 1935. 251p.
P5-NY0369 — $36.00.

HISTORY OF SAINT LAWRENCE COUNTY, 1749-1878, with Illustrations & Biographical Sketches of Prominent Men & Pioneers. By Sam'l W. Durant & Henry B. Pierce. 1878. 521p.
P5-NY0244 — $56.00.

HISTORY OF ST LAWRENCE & FRANKLIN COUNTIES, from the Earliest Period to the Present Time. By Franklin B. Hough. 1853. 719p.
P5-NY0342 — $75.00.

OUR COUNTY & ITS PEOPLE: A Memorial Record of St Lawrence County, 2 vols. in 1. 1894. 720 + 420p.
P5-NY0253 — $115.00.

ANNALS OF STATEN ISLAND, from its Discovery to the Present Time. By J.J. Clute. 1877. 464p.
P5-NY0143 — $49.00.

MORRIS'S MEMORIAL HISTORY OF STATEN ISLAND, 2-vol. set. By Ira K. Morris. 1900. 2 vols., 415 + 539p.
P5-NY0147 — $95.00/set.

MORRIS'S MEMORIAL HISTORY OF STATEN ISLAND . . ., Vol. I. 1900. 415p.
P5-NY0147A — $49.50.

MORRIS'S MEMORIAL HISTORY OF STATEN ISLAND . . ., Vol. II. 1900. 539p.
P5-NY0147B — $49.50.

HISTORICAL GAZETTEER OF STEUBEN COUNTY, with Memoirs & Illustrations. Part I: Historical & Biographical. Comp. by Millard F. Roberts. 1891. 592p.
P5-NY0305A — $66.50.

HISTORICAL GAZETTEER OF STEUBEN COUNTY, with Memoirs & Illustrations. Part II: Directory of Individuals & Businesses. Comp. by Millard F. Roberts. 1891. 354p.
P5-NY0305B — $41.50.

HISTORY OF STEUBEN COUNTY & ITS PEOPLE, 2-vol. set. By Irvin W. Near. 1911. 2 vols., 977p.
P5-NY0371 — $98.50/set.

HISTORY OF STEUBEN COUNTY & ITS PEOPLE, Vol. I. 1911.
P5-NY0371A — $52.50.

HISTORY OF STEUBEN COUNTY & ITS PEOPLE, Vol. II. 1911.
P5-NY0371B — $52.50.

HISTORY OF STEUBEN COUNTY, NEW YORK. G. McMaster 1853. 207p. P28235000 — $42.00.

HISTORY OF STEUBEN COUNTY, with Illustrations and Biographical Sketches of Some of its Prominent Men and Pioneers. By Prof. W.W. Clayton. 1879. 460 + 311p. P5-NY0372 — $77.00.

LANDMARKS OF STEUBEN COUNTY. 1896. 379 + 530p. P5-NY0370 — $92.50 (2 parts in 1).

STONY POINT ILLUSTRATED: An Account of the Early Settlement on the Hudson, with Traditions & Relics of the Revolution and some Genealogical Record of the Present [1888] Inhabitants. 1888. 166p. P5-NY0373 — $19.50.

STORMING OF STONY POINT on the Hudson, Midnight, July 15, 1779. Henry P. Johnston. 1900. 274p. P5-NY0374 — $37.00.

ABSTRACTS OF INTESTATE RECORDS OF SUFFOLK COUNTY, Recorded at Riverhead, Liber A-G. Comp. by Elizabeth R. Van Buren. 1931. 127p. P5-NY0444 — $17.00.

ABSTRACTS OF WILLS Recorded at Riverhead, Suffolk Co. Comp. by E.R. Van Buren. 1934?. 277p. P5-NY0461A — $29.50.

EARLY LONG ISLAND WILLS OF SUFFOLK COUNTY, 1691-1703, with Genealogical and Historical Notes. Wm. S. Pelletreau. 1897. 289p. P5-NY0291 — $39.50.

HISTORICAL AND DESCRIPTIVE SKETCHES, SUFFOLK COUNTY, NEW YORK. By Richard Bayles 1874. xii + 424 + 38p P28240000 — $73.00.

PORTRAIT & BIOGRAPHICAL RECORD OF SUFFOLK COUNTY (Long Island), Containing Portraits & Biographical Sketches of Prominent & Representative Citizens of the County. 1896. 1038p. P5-NY0376 — $102.50.

REVOLUTIONARY INCIDENTS OF SUFFOLK & KINGS COUNTIES, with an Account of the Battle of Long Island & the British Prisons & Prisonships at New York. 1849. 268p. P5-NY0375 — $38.50.

SUFFOLK COUNTY INDEX OF WILLS TO DECEMBER 31, 1850, Copied from the Index in the Surrogate's Office at Riverhead. Comp. by Edwin W. Wheat. 1930. 20p. P5-NY0443 — $10.00.

SUFFOLK COUNTY MARRIAGES, Taken from Suffolk Co. Newspapers, 4 vols. in 1 book. Comp. by G. Barber. 1950. 4 v., 108 + 112 + 108 + 105p. P5-NY0463 — $42.50/set.

SUFFOLK COUNTY MARRIAGES . . ., Vol. I. 1950. 108p. P5-NY0463A — $17.50.

SUFFOLK COUNTY MARRIAGES . . ., Vol. II. 1950. 112p. P5-NY0463B — $17.50.

SUFFOLK COUNTY MARRIAGES . . ., Vol. III. 1950. 108p. P5-NY0463C — $17.50.

SUFFOLK COUNTY MARRIAGES . . ., Vol. IV. 1950. 105p. P5-NY0463D — $17.50.

HISTORY OF SULLIVAN COUNTY, Embracing an Account of its Geology, Settlement, Towns, with Biographical Sketches of Prominent Residents, etc. By J.E. Quinlan. 1873. 700p. P5-NY0031 — $72.00.

SULLIVAN COUNTY GRAVESTONE INSCRIPTIONS [taken from various cemeteries]. Comp. by G.A. Barber. 1929. 10 vols. in 1. 596p. P5-NY0377 — $61.50.

EARLY LANDMARKS OF SYRACUSE. By Gurney S. Strong. 1894. 393p. P5-NY0379 — $47.00.

EARLY RECORDS OF THE FIRST PRESBYTERIAN CHURCH OF SYRACUSE, from the Date of its Establishmen in 1826 to 1850 [with marriages & baptisms]. 1902. 53p. P5-NY0478 — $11.00.

MEMORIAL HISTORY OF SYRACUSE, from its Settlement to the Present Time. With biographical sketches. 1891. 718 + 131p. P5-NY0378 — $87.00.

SYRACUSE & ITS ENVIRONS: A History. By Franklin H. Chase. 1924. 3 vols. in 2, 874 + 511p. P5-NY0380 — $135.00/set.

CHRONICLES OF TARRYTOWN & SLEEPY HOLLOW. By Edgar Mayhew Bacon. 1907. 163p. P5-NY0381 — $26.50.

FIRST ENGLISH RECORD BOOK OF THE REFORMED DUTCH CHURCH IN SLEEPY HOLLOW, Formerly the Manor Church of Philipsburgh, Now the First Reformed Church of Tarrytown. 1931. 122p. P5-NY0365 — $15.50.

OLD DUTCH BURYING GROUND OF SLEEPY HOLLOW, in N. Tarrytown, A Record of the Early Gravestones & Inscriptions. 1953. 192p. P5-NY0104 — $19.00.

SOUVENIR OF THE THOUSAND ISLANDS & RIVER ST. LAWRENCE. n.d. 78p. P5-NY0505 — $27.00.

TOUR AMONG THE THOUSAND ISLANDS. By G.J. Walsh. n.d. 110p. P5-NY0502 — $23.00.

BLACK WATCH AT TICONDEROGA. By Frederick B. Richards. 1925. 98p. P5-NY0382 — $17.00.

HISTORICAL GAZETTEER OF TIOGA COUNTY, 1785-1888. 1888. 493 + 245p. P5-NY0383 — $76.50.

HISTORY OF TIOGA, CHEMUNG, TOMPKINS & SCHUYLER COUNTIES, with Illustrations & Biographical Sketches of some of their Prominent Men & Pioneers. 1879. 687p. P5-NY0116 — $78.50.

LANDMARKS OF TOMPKINS COUNTY, Including a History of Cornell University (by Prof. W.T. Hewitt), in Two Parts. 1894. 2 parts, 704 + 276p. P5-NY0384 — $99.00/set.

For hardcover versions, see the order form on page v. To order, call 1-888-296-3447.

302 *Local Histories*

New York, cont.

LANDMARKS OF TOMPKINS COUNTY . . ., Part I. 1894. 704p.
P5-NY0384A — $75.00.

LANDMARKS OF TOMPKINS COUNTY . . ., Part II. 1894. 276p.
P5-NY0384B — $35.00.

HISTORY OF THE CITY OF TROY, from the Expulsion of the Mohegan Indians to [1876]. By A.J. Weise. 1876. 400p.
P5-NY0387 — $44.50.

REMINISCENCES OF TROY from its Settlement in 1790 to 1807, with Remarks on its Commerce, Enterprise, Improvements . . . etc. 2nd ed. John Woodworth. J. Munsell; 1860. 110p.
P5-NY0386 — $16.00.

TROY & RENSSELAER COUNTY, A History. By Rutherford Hayner. 1925. 3 vols. in 2, 778 + 464p.
P5-NY0385 — $131.00/set.

TROY'S ONE HUNDRED YEARS, 1789-1889. Arthur James Weise. 1891. 453p.
P5-NY0210 — $48.50.

ANNALS OF TRYON COUNTY, or the Border Warfare of N.Y. During the Revolution. By William W. Campbell. 1831; 1924. xx + 257p.
P5-NY0165 — $34.50.

THE WORLD WITH A FENCE AROUND IT: Tuxedo Park - The Early Days. By George M. Rushmore. 1957. 238p.
P5-NY0488 — $32.00.
COMMEMORATIVE BIOGRAPHICAL RECORD OF ULSTER COUNTY, Containing Sketches of Prominent & Representative Citizens, & of Many of the Early Settled Families. 1896. 1322.
P5-NY0483 — $125.00.

EARLIEST ENGLISH DEEDS OF ULSTER COUNTY, 1685-1709 [from Liber AA]. Transcribed by Louise H. Zimm. 1936. 105 + 24p.
P5-NY0437 — $16.00.

EARLIEST ENGLISH DEEDS OF ULSTER COUNTY, 1689-1718 [Liber BB]. Transcribed by Louise H. Zimm. 1936. 89 + 21p.
P5-NY0436 — $15.00.

HISTORY OF ULSTER COUNTY, with Illustrations & Biographical Sketches of its Prominent Men & Pioneers. N.B. Sylvester. 1880. 310 + 340p.
P5-NY0011 — $76.50.

HISTORY OF ULSTER COUNTY. 1907. 707p.
P5-NY0140 — $75.00.

MARBLETOWN REFORMED DUTCH CHURCH: Ulster County, New York; Stone Ridge Methodist Church: Ulster County, New York. By Mrs. Jean D. Worden. n.d. 396p.
P5-NY0496 — $44.00.

OLD GRAVESTONES OF ULSTER COUNTY: 22,000 Inscriptions. With index. Collected & ed. by J. Wilson Poucher & Byron J. Terwilliger. 1931. 407 + 27p.
P5-NY0473A — $47.00.

ULSTER COUNTY PROBATE RECORDS: a Careful Abstract & Translation of Dutch & English Wills, Letters of Admin. & Inventories, with Gen. & Hist. Notes. By G. Anjou. 1906. Vol. II, 280p.
P5-NY0166 — $32.00.

PIONEERS OF UNADILLA VILLAGE, 1784-1840, with Reminiscences of Village Life, and of Panama & California from 1840 to 1850. By Francis W. Halsey, with G.L. Halsey. 1902. 323p.
P5-NY0307 — $41.00.

MEMORIAL HISTORY OF UTICA, from its Settlement to the Present Time. With biographical sketches. 1892. 632 + 104p.
P5-NY0388 — $77.00.

PIONEER SETTLERS OF UTICA, being Sketches of its Inhabitants & its Institutions, with the Civil History of the Place, from the Earliest Settlement to 1825. By M.M Baggs, M.D. 1877. 665p.
P5-NY0167 — $68.50.

HISTORY OF WALTON, DELAWARE CO., NY. n.d. 65p.
P5-NY0504 — $18.00.

HISTORY OF WARREN COUNTY, with Illustrations and Biographical Sketches of Some of its Prominent Men and Pioneers. 1885. 702p.
P5-NY0390 — $77.00.

HISTORY OF WARREN COUNTY. 1963. 302p.
P5-NY0389 — $39.50.

HISTORY OF THE TOWN OF WARSAW, from its First Settlement to the Present Time, with Numerous Family Sketches & Biographical Notes. Andrew W. Young. 1869. 400p.
P5-NY0407 — $46.50.

ABSTRACTS OF WILLS OF WASHINGTON COUNTY, 1788-1850: 4-vol. set. Comp. by G.A. Barber. 1937. 4 vols., 88 + 83 + 100 + 25p.
P5-NY0474B — $55.50/set.

ABSTRACTS OF WILLS OF WASHINGTON COUNTY . . ., Vol. I: 1788-1806. 1937. 88p.
P5-NY0474B1 — $17.00.

ABSTRACTS OF WILLS OF WASHINGTON COUNTY . . ., Vol. II: 1806-1814. 1937. 83p.
P5-NY0474B2 — $16.50.

ABSTRACTS OF WILLS OF WASHINGTON COUNTY . . ., Vol. III: 1814-1825. 1937. 100p.
P5-NY0474B3 — $19.00.

ABSTRACTS OF WILLS OF WASHINGTON COUNTY . . ., Vol. IV: 1825-1850. 1937. 25p.
P5-NY0474B4 — $10.00.

HISTORY & BIOGRAPHY OF WASHINGTON COUNTY & the Town of Queensbury, with Historical Notes on the Various Towns. 1894. 436p.
P5-NY0391 — $49.00.

WASHINGTON COUNTY: its History to the Close of the Nineteenth Century. With biographical sketches. 1901. 570 + 318p.
P5-NY0392 — $89.50.

HISTORY OF THE CITY OF WATERVLIET, 1630 to 1910. By James T. Myers. 1910. 124p.
P5-NY0225 — $18.50.

HISTORY OF WAVERLY & Vicinity. Capt. Charles L. Albertson. 1943. 319p.
P5-NY0006 — $37.00.

ABSTRACTS OF WILLS OF WAYNE COUNTY, 1823-1866. Comp. by Harriett M. Wiles. 1935. 5 vols. in 1, 278p.
P5-NY0468A — $35.00.

LANDMARKS OF WAYNE COUNTY. With biographical and family sketches. 1895. 437 + 41 + 343p.
P5-NY0394 — $95.00.

MARRIAGES & DEATHS Copied from the Wayne Sentinel (1823-60) Published in Palmyra, & the Newark Weekly Courier (1869-73) [Wayne Co.]. Comp. by Harriett M. Wiles. 1934, 1941. 53 + 74p.
P5-NY0393 — $16.00.

MILITARY HISTORY OF WAYNE COUNTY: The County in the Civil War. By Lewis H. Clark. 1863. 691 + 173 + 60p.
P5-NY0395 — $94.50.

CEMETERY INSCRIPTIONS FROM SHRUB OAK CEMETERY, Westchester Co. Comp. by Robert B. Miller, copied by J.C. Frost. 1915. 99p.
P5-NY0399 — $15.00.

CEMETERY INSCRIPTIONS FROM WESTCHESTER COUNTY [Incl. Mt. Kisco, Bedford, Elmsford, Groton Village, Poundridge, New Canaan, Hastings-on-Hudson]. Comp. by Robert B. Miller, copied by J.C. Frost. 1915. 214p.
P5-NY0401 — $25.00.

CEMETERY INSCRIPTIONS FROM WESTCHESTER COUNTY [Incl. towns of Unionville, Greenville, Hartsdale, Mamaroneck, Harrison, Ossining]. Comp. by Robert B. Miller, copied by J.C. Frost. 1915. 145p.
P5-NY0400 — $19.00.

EARLY WILLS OF WESTCHESTER COUNTY, FROM 1664 TO 1784, with genealogical and historical notes. William S. Pelletreau 1898. 488p.
P28250000 — $78.00.

HISTORY OF THE SEVERAL TOWNS, MANORS & PATENTS OF THE COUNTY OF WESTCHESTER from its First Settlement, with Numerous Genealogies of County Families, 2-vol. set. By Robert Bolton. 1905, 3rd ed. 2 vols., 782 + 826p.
P5-NY0177 — $162.50/set.

HISTORY OF THE SEVERAL TOWNS... OF THE COUNTY OF WESTCHESTER, Vol. I. 1905, 3rd ed. 782p.
P5-NY0177A — $86.50.

HISTORY OF THE SEVERAL TOWNS... OF THE COUNTY OF WESTCHESTER, Vol. II. 1905, 3rd ed. 826p.
P5-NY0177B — $86.50.

HISTORY OF WESTCHESTER COUNTY, 5-vol. set. 1925. 5 vols.
P5-NY0397 — $205.00/set.

HISTORY OF WESTCHESTER COUNTY, from its Earliest Settlement to the Year 1900. By Frederic Shonnard & W.W. Spooner. 1900. 638p.
P5-NY0251 — $67.00.

HISTORY OF WESTCHESTER COUNTY, including Morrisania, Kings Bridge and West Farms, which have been added to New York City, 2-vol. set. By J. Thomas Scharf. 1886. 2 vols., 893 + 771p.
P5-NY0250 — $159.50/set.

HISTORY OF WESTCHESTER COUNTY, including Morrisania, Kings Bridge and West Farms, which have been added to New York City, Vol. I. By J. Thomas Scharf. 1886. 893p.
P5-NY0250A — $88.75.

HISTORY OF WESTCHESTER COUNTY, including Morrisania, Kings Bridge and West Farms, which have been added to New York City, Vol. II. By J. Thomas Scharf. 1886. 771p.
P5-NY0250B — $80.75.

HISTORY OF WESTCHESTER COUNTY, Vol. I. 1925.
P5-NY0397A — $45.00.

HISTORY OF WESTCHESTER COUNTY, Vol. II. 1925.
P5-NY0397B — $45.00.

HISTORY OF WESTCHESTER COUNTY, Vol. III. 1925.
P5-NY0397C — $45.00.

HISTORY OF WESTCHESTER COUNTY, Vol. IV. 1925.
P5-NY0397D — $45.00.

HISTORY OF WESTCHESTER COUNTY, Vol. V. 1925.
P5-NY0397E — $45.00.

WESTCHESTER COUNTY During the American Revolution. By Henry B. Dawson. 1886. 281p.
P5-NY0398 — $37.00.

WESTCHESTER COUNTY during the Revolution, 1775-1783. By Otto Hufeland. 1926. 471p.
P5-NY0396 — $51.50.

"BESSBORO": History of Westport, Essex Co. Caroline H. Royce. 1902. 616p.
P5-NY0467B — $64.00.

BESSBORO: History of Westport, Essex County. By Caroline H. Royce. 1902. 616p.
P5-NY0402 — $66.00.

WHEATLAND, Monroe County: A Brief Sketch of its History. By George E. Slocum. 1908. 138p.
P5-NY0403 — $17.50.

HISTORIC WHITE PLAINS. By John Rosch. 1939. 395p.
P5-NY0128 — $42.50.

INSCRIPTIONS FROM GRAVEYARDS, with Genealogical Notes & Index. Transcr. by Francis F. Spies. 1933. 312p.
P5-NY0458 — $35.00.

PIONEER HISTORY OF THE CHAMPLAIN VALLEY, being an Account of the Settlement of the Town of Willsborough by William Gilliland. By Winslow C. Watson. 1863. 231p.
P5-NY0226 — $32.00.

HISTORY OF WYOMING COUNTY, with Illustrations, Biographical Sketches of some Pioneers & Prominent Residents. 1880. 310p.
P5-NY0231 — $37.50.

HISTORY & DIRECTORY OF YATES COUNTY, Containing a Sketch of its Original Settlement, with an Account of Individual Pioneers & their Families. Vol. I. By Stafford C. Cleveland. 1873. 766p.
P5-NY0168 — $79.00.

HISTORY OF YATES COUNTY, Vol. II. By Stafford C. Cleveland. 1873, 1950. 407p.
P5-NY0404 — $47.00.

HISTORY OF YATES COUNTY, with Illustrations & Biographical Sketches of the Prominent Men & Pioneers. 1892. 671p.
P5-NY0406 — $71.00.

New York, cont.

HISTORY OF YONKERS, from the Earliest Times to the Present [1896], including an Elaborate Description of its Aborigines; a Narrative of its Discovery & Early Settlement; A Record of Events with its Borders, etc. By Rev. Charles Elmer Allison. 1896. 454p.
P5-NY0468C — $49.00.

INSCRIPTIONS COPIED FROM GRAVEYARDS, with Genealogical Notes, 2-vol. set in 1 book. Transcr. by Francis F. Spies. 1927, 1934. 2 vols., 204 + 237p.
P5-NY0459 — $42.50/set.

INSCRIPTIONS COPIED FROM GRAVEYARDS, with Genealogical Notes, Vol. I. Transcr. by Francis F. Spies. 204p.
P5-NY0459A — $25.00.

INSCRIPTIONS COPIED FROM GRAVEYARDS, with Genealogical Notes, Vol. II. Transcr. by Francis F. Spies. 237p.
P5-NY0459B — $25.00.

YONKERS, ILLUSTRATED. Comp. by Yonkers Board of Trade. 1904? 192p.
P5-NY0241 — $34.00.

North Carolina

ABSTRACT OF N.C. WILLS from the 1760 to about 1800. Suppl. Grimes Abstr. of N.C. Wills 1663 to 1760. 1925. 330p.
P5-NC0011 — $29.00.

ABSTRACT OF N.C. WILLS, 1690-1760. Comp. from original & recorded wills in the Office of the Sec. of State. 1910. 669p.
P5-NC0005 — $59.00.

CHRONICLES OF THE CAPE FEAR RIVER, 1660-1916. By James Sprunt. 1916. 732p.
P5-NC0014 — $77.00.

JOURNAL OF A LADY OF QUALITY; Being the Narrative of a Journey from Scotland to the West Indies, No. Carolina & Portugal, 1774-1776. By Janet Schaw. 1921. 341p.
P5-NC0015 — $43.50.

N.C. WILLS & INVENTORIES. Copied from original & recorded wills & inventories in the Office of the Secretary of State. Comp. by J. Bryan Grimes. 1912. 587p.
P5-NC0004 — $55.00.

ONE DOZEN PRE-REVOLUTIONARY FAMILIES OF EASTERN NO. CAROLINA and Some of their Descendants. By P.W. Fisher. 1958. 629p.
P5-NC0012 — $69.50.

SKETCHES OF WESTERN NORTH CAROLINA, Historical & Biographical, Illustrating Principally the Rev. Period of Mecklenburg, Rowan, Lincoln & Adjoining Cos. By C.L. Hunter. 1877. 357p.
P5-NC0001 — $34.50.

1880 FEDERAL CENSUS OF ASHE COUNTY. 1992. 311 + 67p.
P5-NC0003 — $39.00.

ASHEVILLE & BUNCOMBE COUNTY; Genesis of Buncombe County. By F.A. Sondley & Theodore F. Davidson. 1922. 200p.
P5-NC0017 — $31.00.

HERE WILL I DWELL: the Story of Caldwell County. By Nancy Alexander. 1956. 230p.
P5-NC0007 — $32.50.

CENTENNIAL HISTORY OF DAVIDSON COUNTY. By Rev. Jacob Calvin Leonard. 1927. 523p.
P5-NC0013 — $57.00.

HISTORY OF EDGECOMBE COUNTY. By J. Kelly Turner & J.L. Bridges, Jr. 1920. 486p.
P5-NC0018 — $53.50.

FOUNDERS & BUILDERS OF GREENSBORO, 1808-1908: Fifty Sketches. Bettie D. Caldwell. 1925. 356p.
P5-NC0020 — $41.00.

GREENSBORO, 1808-1904: Facts, Figures, Traditions & Reminiscences. Jas. W. Albright. 1904. 134p.
P5-NC0019 — $18.00.

HISTORY OF HALIFAX COUNTY. By W.C. Allen. 1918. 235p.
P5-NC0021 — $31.00.

ANNALS OF HAYWOOD COUNTY, 1808-1935, Historical, Sociological, Biographical & Genealogical. By W.C. Allen. 1935. 632p.
P5-NC0022 — $66.50.

COLONIAL & STATE POLITICAL HISTORY OF HERTFORD COUNTY. Benj. B. Winborne. 1906. 350p.
P5-NC0023 — $42.00.

BIOGRAPHICAL SKETCHES OF THE EARLY SETTLERS OF THE HOPEWELL SECTION, & Reminiscences of the Pioneers & their Descendants by Families, with Some Historical Facts Incidents. By J.B. Alexander. 1897. 104p.
P5-NC0024 — $16.00.

KING'S MTN. & ITS HEROES: History of the Battle of King's Mtn., Oct. 7th, 1780. L.C. Draper. 1881. 612p.
P5-NC1500 — $55.00.

ANNALS OF LINCOLN COUNTY, Containing Interesting & Authrntic Facts of Lincoln County History through the Years 1749 to 1937. By William L. Sherrill. 1937. 536p.
P5-NC0033 — $57.50.

HISTORY OF MECKLENBURG COUNTY & THE CITY OF CHARLOTTE. By D.A. Tompkins. 1903. 2 vols. in 1, 202 + 216p.
P5-NC0025 — $44.50.

HISTORY OF MECKLENBURG COUNTY, from 1740 to 1900. Enlarged & rev. ed. By J.B. Alexander. 1902. 431p.
P5-NC0026 — $48.00.

SKETCHES OF MONROE & UNION COUNTY, Together with General & Individual Characteristics of their People & a Description of the Natural Resources & Business Enterprises. By Stack & Beasley. 1902. 115p.
P5-NC0027 — $16.50.

HISTORY OF NEW HANOVER COUNTY & THE LOWER CAPE FEAR REGION. Vol. I, 1723-1800 [no more published]. By Alfred Moore Waddell. 1909. 232p.
P5-NC0028 — $31.50.

SKETCHES OF PITT COUNTY: Brief History of the County, 1704-1910. By Henry T. King. 1911. 275p. P5-NC0029 — $37.00.

HISTORICAL RALEIGH, with Sketches of Wake County from 1771 & its Important Towns, Descriptive, Biographical, Educational, Industrial, Religious. Moses N. Amis. 1913. 289p. P5-NC0031 — $36.00.

RICHMOND COUNTY RECORDS: Journal of the Society of Richmond County Descendants, Vol. I-Vol. 28. By Joe M McLaurin. 1988-97. 665p. P5-NC0036 — $59.00.

THE STATE OF ROBESON. By R.C. Lawrence. 1939. 279p. P5-NC0006 — $35.00.

HISTORY OF ROWAN COUNTY. By J. Rumple. 1881. 434p. P5-NC0035 — $46.50.

HISTORY OF WAKE COUNTY, with Sketches of Those who have Most Influenced its Development. By Hope S. Chamberlain. 1922. 302p. P5-NC0030 — $37.00.

HISTORY OF WATAUGA CO., with Sketches of Prominent Families, By John Preston Arthur. 1915. 363p. P5-NC0034 — $44.50.

BIOGRAPHICAL SKETCHES OF WILMINGTON CITIZENS. By R.H. Fisher. 1929. 316p. P5-NC0032 — $41.00.

North Dakota

HISTORY OF DICKEY COUNTY. 1930. 333p. P5-ND0004 — $39.50.

GRAND FORKS COUNTY Heritage Book: A History of Rural Grand Forks County, Grand Forks County, North Enoch Thorsgard. 1976. 534p. P5-ND0011 — $66.00.

COMPENDIUM OF HISTORY & BIOGRAPHY of North Dakota. 1900. 1410p. P5-ND0002 — $145.00.

HISTORY OF NORTH DAKOTA, 3-vol. set. By Lewis F. Crawford. 1931. 3 vols., 640 + 617 + 653p. P5-ND0010 — $174.50/set.

HISTORY OF NORTH DAKOTA, Vol. I. 1931. 640p. P5-ND0010A — $65.00.

HISTORY OF NORTH DAKOTA, Vol. II. 1931. 617p. P5-ND0010B — $65.00.

HISTORY OF NORTH DAKOTA, Vol. III. 1931. 653p. P5-ND0010C — $65.00.

PIONEERS & Their Sons: One Hundred Sixty-Five Family Histories. By Mon. George P. Aberle. [Vol. I only, but contains all 165 families.] 471p. P5-ND0001 — $49.50.

EARLY HISTORY OF RANSOM COUNTY, Including References to Sargent County, 1835-1885. By H.V. Arnold. 1918. 74p. P5-ND0006 — $15.00.

HISTORY OF THE RED RIVER VALLEY, Past & Present, 2-vol. set. 1909. 2 vols., 1165p. P5-ND0003 — $115.00/set.

HISTORY OF THE RED RIVER VALLEY, Vol. I. 1909. P5-ND0003A — $65.00.

HISTORY OF THE RED RIVER VALLEY, Vol. II. 1909. P5-ND0003B — $65.00.

HISTORY OF WELLS COUNTY & ITS PIONEERS, with a Sketch of No. Dakota History & the Origin of the Place Names. By Walter E. Spokesfield. 1929. 804p. P5-ND0005 — $82.50.

Ohio

BIBLIOGRAPHY OF THE STATE OF OHIO, Being a Catalog of the Books & Pamphlets Relating to the History of the State, the West & Northwest. Complete subject index. Peter G. Thomson. 1880. 427 + 108p. P5-OH0009 — $55.00.

BIOGRAPHICAL CYCLOPEDIA & PORTRAIT GALLERY OF THE STATE OF OHIO, Vol. I. 1894. P5-OH0255A — $50.00.

BIOGRAPHICAL CYCLOPEDIA & PORTRAIT GALLERY OF THE STATE OF OHIO, Vol. II. 1894. P5-OH0255B — $50.00.

BIOGRAPHICAL ENCYCLO-PEDIA OF OHIO of the 19th Century. Many portraits. 1876. 672p. + illus. P5-OH0111 — $75.00.

BIOGRAPHICAL HISTORY OF NORTHEASTERN OHIO, Embracing the Counties of Ashtabula, Geauga & Lake, with Biographies.. of a Large Number of the Early Settlers & Representative Families. 1893. 1028p. P5-OH0126 — $99.50.

FIRST OWNERSHIP OF OHIO LANDS. By A.M. Dyer. 1911. 85p. P5-OH0024 — $10.00.

HISTORICAL COLLECTIONS OF OHIO, 2-vol. set. Comp. by Henry Howe. 1888-1908. 2 vols., 992 + 911p. P5-OH0059 — $179.00/set.

HISTORICAL COLLECTIONS OF OHIO, Vol. I. 1888-1908. 992p. P5-OH0059A — $95.00.

HISTORICAL COLLECTIONS OF OHIO, Vol. II. 1888-1908. 911p. P5-OH0059B — $95.00.

HISTORICAL COLLECTIONS OF OHIO. With 177 engravings. Comp. by Henry Howe. First ed.; 1848. 599p. P5-OH0058 — $59.50.

HISTORY OF THE GIRTYS, a concise acct. of the Girty Bros. — Thomas, Simon, James & George, & their half-brother John Turner — also of the part taken by them in Lord Dunsmore's War, Western Border War of the Rev.; and the Indian War, 1790-5 [Ohio]. By Consul Willshire Butterfield. 1905. 425p. P5-OH0104 — $42.50.

HISTORY OF THE UPPER OHIO VALLEY, with Family History & Biographical Sketches, 2-vol. set. 1891. 2 vols, 404 + 432p. P5-OH0205 — $89.50/set.

HISTORY OF THE UPPER OHIO VALLEY . . ., Vol. I. 1891. 404p. P5-OH0205A — $47.00.

HISTORY OF THE UPPER OHIO VALLEY . . ., Vol. II. 1891. 432p. P5-OH0205B — $47.00.

Ohio, cont.

MEMOIRS OF THE LOWER OHIO VALLEY, Personal & Genealogical, 2-vol. set. 1905. 2 vols., 412 + 410p.
P5-OH0122 — $85.00/set.

MEMOIRS OF THE LOWER OHIO VALLEY . . ., Vol. I. 1905. 412p.
P5-OH0122A — $45.00.

MEMOIRS OF THE LOWER OHIO VALLEY . . ., Vol. II. 1905. 410p.
P5-OH0122B — $45.00.

OHIO RIVER: A Course of Empire. By Archer Butler Hulbert. 1906. 378p.
P5-OH0213 — $45.00.

OHIO VALLEY GENEALOGIES, Relating Chiefly to Families in Harrison, Belmont & Jefferson Cos., Oh., & Washington, Westmoreland & Fayette Cos., Pa. By C.A. Hanna. 1900. 172p., paper.
P5-OH0001A — $19.00.

OHIO VALLEY IN COLONIAL DAYS. Berthold Frenow. 1890. 299p.
P5-OH0124 — $38.00.

PIONEER HISTORY, Being an Account of the First Examinations of the Ohio Valley & the Early Settlement of the Northwest Territory. By S.P. Hildreth. 1848. 525p.
P5-OH0123 — $57.00.

RECOLLECTIONS OF LIFE IN OHIO, from 1813 to 1840. By Wm. Cooper Howells. 1895. 207p.
P5-OH0121 — $29.50.

STATE CENTENNIAL HISTORY OF OHIO, Covering the Periods of Indian, French and British Dominion, the Territory Northwest, and the Hundred Years of Statehood. By Rowland H. Rerick. 1902. 425p.
P5-OH0087 — $47.00.

HISTORY OF ADAMS COUNTY, from its Earliest Settlement to the Present Time, including Character Sketches of the Prominent Persons Identified with the First Century of the County's Growth. By N.W. Evans & E.B. Stivers. 1900. 946p.
P5-OH0093 — $96.50.

AKRON & SUMMIT COUNTY. By Karl H. Grismer. 1952. 834p.
P5-OH0078 — $85.00.

CENTENNIAL HISTORY OF AKRON, 1825-1925. 1925. 666p.
P5-OH0208 — $71.00.

HISTORY OF ALLEN COUNTY & Representative Citizens. 1906. 872p.
P5-OH0006 — $89.50.

STANDARD HISTORY OF ALLEN COUNTY: Authentic Narrative of the Past, with Particular Attention to the Modern Era, 2-vol. Set. 1921. 2 vols.
P5-OH0125 — $92.50/set.

STANDARD HISTORY OF ALLEN COUNTY . . ., Vol. I. 1921.
P5-OH0125A — $50.00.

STANDARD HISTORY OF ALLEN COUNTY . . ., Vol. II. 1921.
P5-OH0125B — $50.00.

HISTORY OF ASHLAND COUNTY, with Illustrations & Biographical Sketches. By George Wm. Hill, M.D. 1880. 408p.
P5-OH0007 — $44.50.

PIONEER SKETCHES: Scenes & Incidents of Former Days. An entertaining and very useful account of the early days of Crawford Co., Pa., & Ashtabula, Oh., incl. biographical sketches of early sett. By M. P. Sargent. 1891. 512p.
P5-PA0075 — $54.00.

HISTORY OF ASHTABULA COUNTY, with Illustrations & Biographical Sketches of its Pioneers & Most Prominent Men. By Wm. W. Williams. 1878. 256p. + many illustrations.
P5-OH0063A — $37.50.

PIONEER SKETCHES [ASHTABULA CO.]: Scenes & Incidents of Former Days. By M.P. Sargent. 1891. 512p.
P5-OH0008 — $54.00.

HISTORY OF ATHENS COUNTY, & Incidentally of the Ohio Land Company, & the First Settlement of the State at Marietta, with Personal & Biographical Sketches of the Early Settlers, etc. Charles M. Walker. 1869. 600p.
P5-OH0127 — $65.00.

CENTENNIAL HISTORY OF BELMONT COUNTY, & Representative Citizens. 1903. 833p.
P5-OH0100A — $85.00.

HISTORY OF BELMONT & JEFFERSON COUNTIES, & Incidentally Historical Collections Pertaining to Border Warfare & Early Settlement of the Adjacent Portion of the Ohio Valley. With biographical sketches. J.A. Caldwell. 1880. 611 + 30p.
P5-OH0128 — $69.50.

HISTORY OF BELPRE, Washington Co. By C.E. Dickinson. 1920. 243p.
P5-OH0113 — $36.00.

HISTORY OF BROWN COUNTY, Containing a History of the County, its Townships, Towns . . . Portraits of Early Settlers & Prominent Men, etc. 1883. 1070p.
P5-OH0216 — $105.00.

HISTORY OF BROWN COUNTY, Containing a History of the County; its Townships, Towns, etc.; [Biographical] Portraits of Early Settlers & Prominent Men; etc. 1883. 703 + 308p.
P5-OH0129 — $99.50.

HISTORY & BIOGRAPHICAL CYCLOPEDIA OF BUTLER COUNTY, with Illustrations & Sketches of its Representative Men & Pioneers. 1882. 666p.
P5-OH0089 — $69.50.

PIONEER BIOGRAPHY: Sketches of the Lives of Some of the Early Settlers of Butler Co. By James McBride. 1869-1871. 2 vols. in 1, 640p.
P5-OH0130 — $67.00.

HISTORY OF CARROLL & HARRISON COUNTIES, 2-vol. Set. 1921. 2 vols., 1039p.
P5-OH0131 — $99.50/set.

HISTORY OF CARROLL & HARRISON COUNTIES, Vol. I. 1921.
P5-OH0131A — $54.50.

HISTORY OF CARROLL & HARRISON COUNTIES, Vol. II. 1921.
P5-OH0131B — $54.50.

HISTORY OF CHAMPAIGN & LOGAN COUNTIES, from Their First Settlement. By Joshua Antrim. 1872. 460p.
P5-OH0133 — $51.50.

HISTORY OF CHAMPAIGN COUNTY, Containing a History of the County, its Cities, Towns, etc.; General & Local Statistics; Portraits of early Settlers & Prominent Men, etc. 1881. 921p.
P5-OH0004 — $89.50.

HISTORY OF CINCINNATI, 1789-1881, with Illustrations & Biographical Sketches. By Henry A. Ford & Kate B. Ford. 1881. 534p.
P5-OH0134 — $58.50.

HISTORY OF CINCINNATI & HAMILTON COUNTY: Their Past & Present . . . including Biographies & Portraits of Pioneers & Representative Citizens. 1894. 1056p.
P5-OH0067 — $99.50.

BIOGRAPHICAL RECORD OF CLARK COUNTY. 1902. 824p.
P5-OH0136 — $87.00.

HISTORY OF CLARK COUNTY, Containing a History of its Cities, Towns, etc. 1881. 1085p.
P5-OH0011 — $99.50.

PIONEER HISTORY OF CLARKSFIELD. By Dr F.E. Weeks. 1908. 175p.
P5-OH0137 — $28.50.

HISTORY OF CLERMONT & BROWN COUNTIES, From the Earliest Historical Times Down to the Present, 2-vol. Set. By Byron Williams. 1913. 2 vols., 459 + 853p.
P5-OH0138 — $119.00/set.

HISTORY OF CLERMONT & BROWN COUNTIES . . ., Vol. I. 1913. 459p.
P5-OH0138A — $55.00.

HISTORY OF CLERMONT & BROWN COUNTIES . . ., Vol. II. 1913. 853p.
P5-OH0138B — $88.00.

HISTORY OF CLERMONT COUNTY, with Illustrations & Biographical Sketches of its Prominent Men & Pioneers. With Index comp. by the Clermont Co. Genealogical Society. 1880. 557 + 121p.
P5-OH0060C — $68.00.

EARLY HISTORY OF CLEVELAND, with Biographical Notices of the Pioneers & Surveyors. By Col. Chas. Whittlesey. 1867. 487p.
P5-OH0139 — $54.00.

HISTORY OF CLEVELAND, OHIO, 2-vol. Set. By Samuel P. Orth 1910. 2 vols., 1255 + 1136p.
P5-OH0222 — $212.00/set.

HISTORY OF CLEVELAND, OHIO, Vol. I. 1910. 1255p.
P5-OH0222A — $121.00.

HISTORY OF CLEVELAND, OHIO, Vol. II. 1910. 1136p.
P5-OH0222B — $116.00.

HISTORY OF CLEVELAND, OHIO. Vol. III Biographical. 1910. 1104p.
P5-OH0223 — $110.00.

PIONEER FAMILIES OF CLEVELAND, 1796-1840. By Gertrude Van Rensselaer Wickham. 1914. 2 vols. in 1, 694p.
P5-OH0012 — $69.50.

HISTORY OF CLINTON COUNTY, Containing a History of its Townships, Cities, etc. 1882. 1180p.
P5-OH0013 — $105.00.

HISTORY OF COLUMBIANA COUNTY, and Representative Citizens. With every-name index. 1905. 848 + 49p.
P5-OH0096 — $91.50.

HISTORY OF COLUMBIANA COUNTY, 2-vol. set. By Harold B. Barth. 1926. 2 vols., 1032p.
P5-OH0140 — $99.50/set.

HISTORY OF COLUMBIANA COUNTY, Vol. I. 1926.
P5-OH0140A — $57.00.

HISTORY OF COLUMBIANA COUNTY, Vol. II. 1926.
P5-OH0140B — $57.00.

HISTORY OF COLUMBIANA COUNTY, with Illustrations & Biographical Sketches of some of its Prominent Men & Pioneers. 1879. 334p.
P5-OH0061B — $39.50.

HISTORY OF THE UPPER OHIO VALLEY, with Historical Account of Columbiana Co. With family history & biography, 2-vol. Set. 1891. 2 vols., 487 + 442p.
P5-OH0141 — $97.00/set.

HISTORY OF THE UPPER OHIO VALLEY . . ., Vol. I. 1891. 487p.
P5-OH0141A — $51.00.

HISTORY OF THE UPPER OHIO VALLEY . . ., Vol. II. 1891. 442p.
P5-OH0141B — $51.00.

CENTENNIAL HISTORY OF COLUMBUS & Franklin County, 2-vol. Set. By William Alexander Taylor. 1909. 2 vols., 839 + 824p.
P5-OH0014 — $159.50/set.

CENTENNIAL HISTORY OF COLUMBUS & Franklin County . . ., Vol. I. 1909. 839p.
P5-OH0014A — $85.00.

CENTENNIAL HISTORY OF COLUMBUS & Franklin County . . ., Vol. II. 1909. 824p.
P5-OH0014B — $85.00.

COLUMBUS: its History, Resources & Progress, with Numerous Illustrations. By Jacob J. Studer. 1873. 585p.
P5-OH0062 — $61.00.

HISTORY OF THE CITY OF COLUMBUS from the Founding of Franklinton in 1797, through the World War Period to the Year 1920. With biographical sketches. By Osman Castle Hooper. n.d. 481p.
P5-OH0143 — $53.50.

HISTORY OF THE CITY OF COLUMBUS, 2-vol. set. By Alfred E. Lee. 1892. 2 vols., 921 + 878p.
P5-OH0142 — $169.50/set.

HISTORY OF THE CITY OF COLUMBUS, Vol. I. 1892. 921p.
P5-OH0142A — $89.50.

HISTORY OF THE CITY OF COLUMBUS, Vol. II. 1892. 878p.
P5-OH0142B — $89.50.

PEOPLE, PLACES AND PIONEERS OF COSHOCTON. By Curtiss N. Stuart. 2004. 425p.
P5-OH0221 — $47.00.

CEMETERY RECORDS OF COSHOCTON COUNTY. Comp. by Helen M. Meredith. 1956?. 6 v. in 1, 1059p., typescript.
P5-OH0204 — $95.00.

CENTENNIAL HISTORY OF COSHOCTON COUNTY, 2-vol. set. William J. Bahmer. 1909. 2 vols., 531 + 488p.
P5-OH0018 — $95.00/set.

Ohio, cont.

CENTENNIAL HISTORY OF COSHOCTON COUNTY, Vol. I. 1909. 531p.
P5-OH0018A — $52.50.

CENTENNIAL HISTORY OF COSHOCTON COUNTY, Vol. II. 1909. 488p.
P5-OH0018B — $52.50.

GEOLOGY OF COSHOCTON COUNTY. Raymond E. Lamborn. 1954. 245p.
P5-OH0214 — $37.00.

HISTORICAL COLLECTIONS OF COSHOCTON COUNTY. A Complete Panorama of the County, from the Time of the Earliest Known Occupants unto the Present Time, 1764 — 1876. By Wm. E. Hunt. 1876; index, 1964. 264 + 27p. index.
P5-OH0015 — $32.00.

HISTORY OF COSHOCTON COUN-TY, its Past & Present, 1740-1881. Comp. by N.N. Hill, Jr. 1881. 838p.
P5-OH0017 — $86.00.

REVOLUTIONARY WAR SOLDIERS WITH COSHOCTON COUNTY CONNECTION. By C.N. Stuart. 2006. 421p.
P5-OH2226 — $43.00.

HISTORY OF CRAWFORD COUNTY & OHIO, Containing . . . Biographical Sketches & Portraits of Some Early Settlers & Prominent Men. William H. Perrin, et al. 1881. 1047p.
P5-OH0019 — $99.50.

HISTORY OF CUYAHOGA COUNTY & THE CITY OF CLEVELAND, Historical & Biographical. By Wm. R. Coates. 1924. 3 vols. in 2, 555 + 641p.
P5-OH0144 — $119.00/set.

HISTORY OF CUYAHOGA COUNTY, with Portraits & Bio-graphical Sketches of some of its Prominent Men & Pioneers. 1879. 534p.
P5-OH0060A — $57.00.

INDEX TO THE ADMINISTRA-TION DOCKETS OF THE PRO-BATE COURTS OF CUYAHOGA CO., Showing Estates Administered . . . from March 5, 1811 to Dec. 31, 1896. Comp. by F.M. Chandler. 1897. 192p.
P5-OH0145 — $22.50.

HISTORY OF DARKE COUNTY, Containing a History of the County, its Cities, Towns, etc.; Portraits of Early Settlers & Prominent Men, etc. 1880. 772p.
P5-OH0063B — $79.50.

HISTORY OF DARKE COUNTY, from its Earliest Settlement to the Present Time; also Biographical Sketches of Many Representative Citizens of the County, 2-vol. set. By Frazer E. Wilson. 1914. 2 vols., 623 + 571p.
P5-OH0146 — $124.00/set.

HISTORY OF DARKE COUNTY . . ., Vol. I. 1914. 623p.
P5-OH0146A — $64.50.

HISTORY OF DARKE COUNTY . . ., Vol. II. 1914. 571p.
P5-OH0146B — $64.50.

DAYTON, OHIO: An Intimate History, with One Hundred Twenty-Six Illustrations. By Charlotte Conover. 1932. 311p.
P5-OH0209 — $41.50.

EARLY DAYTON, with Important Facts & Incidents from the Founding of the City of Dayton to the 100th Anniversary. By Robert W. Steele & Mary Davies Steele. 1896. 247p.
P5-OH0147 — $35.00.

HISTORY OF THE CITY OF DAYTON & Montgomery County, 2-vol. set. Rev. A.W. Drury. 1909. 2 vols., 941 + 1078p.
P5-OH0021 — $185.00/set.

HISTORY OF THE CITY OF DAYTON . . ., Vol. I. 1909. 941p.
P5-OH0021A — $95.00.

HISTORY OF THE CITY OF DAYTON . . ., Vol. II. 1909. 1078p.
P5-OH0021B — $95.00.

PIONEER LIFE IN DAYTON & VICINITY. John F. Edgar. 1896. 289p.
P5-OH0020 — $37.00.

HISTORY OF DEFIANCE COUNTY, Containing a History of the County; its Townships, Twons, etc.; Military Record; [biographical] Portraits of Early Settlers & Prominent Men; etc. 1883. 374p.
P5-OH0148 — $45.50.

HISTORY OF DELAWARE COUNTY & Ohio, with Biographical Sketches. 1880. 885p.
P5-OH0022 — $89.50.

MEMORIAL [BIOGRAPHICAL] RECORD OF THE COUNTIES OF DELAWARE, UNION & MORROW. 1895. 501p.
P5-OH0149 — $55.00.

EARLY HISTORY OF ELYRIA & Her People. A.R. Webber. 1930. 326p.
P5-OH0044 — $39.50.

HISTORY OF ERIE COUNTY, with Illustration & Biographical Sketches of some of its Prominent Men & Pioneers. 1889. 653p.
P5-OH0023 — $68.00.

ETNA & KIRKERSVILLE. By Morris Schaff. 1905. 157p.
P5-OH0150 — $19.50.

COMPLETE HISTORY OF FAIRFIELD COUNTY, 1795-1876. By Hervey Scott. 1877. 304p.
P5-OH0065 — $35.00.

HISTORY OF FAYETTE COUNTY, together with Historic Notes on the Northwest & the State of Ohio. By R.S. Dills. 1881. 1039p.
P5-OH0064 — $99.50.

FRANKLIN COUNTY AT THE BEGINNING OF THE 20th CENTURY: Historical Record of its Development, Resources, Industries, Institutions & Inhabitants, with Illustrations . . . , Including Bio-graphical Sketches. 1901. 401p.
P5-OH0151 — $47.00.

HISTORY OF FRANKLIN & PICKAWAY COUNTIES, 1796-1880, with Illustrations & Biographical Sketches of Some of the Prominent Men & Pioneers. 1880. 593p.
P5-OH0132 — $67.00.

HISTORY OF FRANKLIN COUNTY, 3-vol. set. By Opha Moore. 1930. 3 vols., 1424p.
P5-OH0066 — $139.00/set.

HISTORY OF FRANKLIN COUNTY, Vol. I. 1930.
P5-OH0066A — $50.00.

HISTORY OF FRANKLIN COUNTY, Vol. II. 1930.
P5-OH0066B — $50.00.

HISTORY OF FRANKLIN
COUNTY, Vol. III. 1930.
P5-OH0066C — $50.00.

HISTORY OF FRANKLIN
COUNTY: A Collection of Reminis-
cences of the Early County with
Biographical Sketches & a Complete
History of the County to [1858]. By
Wm. T. Martin. 1858. 449p.
P5-OH0025 — $49.00.

STANDARD HISTORY OF FULTON
COUNTY: Authentic Narrative of
the Past, with an Extended Survey of
Modern Developments in the
Progress of Town & County. With
modern every-name index comp. by
the Fulton County Chapter, Ohio
Genealogical Society, 2-vol. set. 1920,
1997. 2 vols. + index, 508 + 558 + 139p.
P5-OH0152 — $119.00/set.

STANDARD HISTORY OF
FULTON COUNTY . . ., Vol. I.
1920. 508p.
P5-OH0152A — $65.00.

STANDARD HISTORY OF
FULTON COUNTY . . ., Vol. II &
Index. 1920, 1997. 558 + 139p.
P5-OH0152B — $65.00.

HISTORICAL SKETCHES OF
THE VILLAGE OF GATES MILLS.
1943. 132p.
P5-OH0153 — $17.50.

PIONEER & GENERAL HISTORY
OF GEAUGA COUNTY, with Sketches
of Some of its Pioneers & Prominent
Men, 1798-1880. 1880. 822p.
P5-OH0026 — $85.00.

PIONEER & GENERAL HISTORY
OF GEAUGA COUNTY. 1953. 783p.
P5-OH0085 — $79.50.

HISTORY OF GRANVILLE,
Licking Co. By Rev. Henry Bushnell.
1889. 372p.
P5-OH0027 — $45.00.

GREENE COUNTY, 1803-1908.
1908. 190 + 38p.
P5-OH0028 — $29.50.

HISTORY OF GREENE COUNTY,
embracing the Organization of the
County, its Division into Townships
. . . also a Roster of Ten Thousand of
the Early Settlers . . . to 1840. By
George F. Robinson. 1902. 927p.
P5-OH0091 — $92.50.

HISTORY OF GREENE COUNTY,
together with Historic Notes on the
Northwest. By R.S. Dills. 1881. 1018p.
P5-OH0154B — $99.00.

PORTRAIT & BIOGRAPHICAL
ALBUM OF GREENE & CLARK
COUNTIES, Containing Full-Page
Portraits of Prominent & Represen-
tative Citizens. 1894. 924p.
P5-OH0135 — $95.00.

PORTRAIT & BIOGRAPHICAL
RECORD OF GUERNSEY
COUNTY, Containing Biographical
Sketches of Prominent and Represen-
tative Citizens of the County. 1895. 541p.
P5-OH0114 — $59.50.

STORIES OF GUERNSEY COUNTY.
Wm. G. Wolfe. 1943. 1093p.
P5-OH0206 — $103.00.

HAMILTON COUNTY BIO-
GRAPHICAL SKETCHES (Vol. III
of "Memoirs of the Miami Valley").
1919. 537p.
P5-OH0101 — $56.50.

HISTORY OF HAMILTON
COUNTY, with Illustrations &
Biographical Sketches. Comp. by
Henry A. Ford & Kate B. Ford. 1881. 432p.
P5-OH0029 — $48.00.

MEMOIRS OF THE MIAMI
VALLEY [Hamilton Co.], Vols. I &
II: History. 1919. 636 + 669p.
P5-OH0215 — $136.00/set.

MEMOIRS OF THE MIAMI
VALLEY, Vol. I: History. 1919. 636p.
P5-OH0215A — $72.00.

MEMOIRS OF THE MIAMI
VALLEY, Vol. II: History. 1919.
669p.
P5-OH0215B — $72.00.

PAST & PRESENT OF MILL
CREEK VALLEY, Being a
Collection of Historical & Descrip-
tive Sketches of that Part of Hamilton
County. Henry B. Teetor. 1882. 328p.
P5-OH0155 — $41.00.

CENTENNIAL BIOGRAPHICAL
HISTORY OF HANCOCK COUNTY,
Embellished with Portraits of Many
Well Known Poeple of Hancock
County, who Have Been or are
Prominent in its History & Devel-
opment. 1903. 595p.
P5-OH0156 — $64.00.

HISTORY OF HANCOCK
COUNTY, Containing a History of
the County, its Townships, Villages
. . . Biographies, etc. 1886. 880p.
P5-OH0031 — $89.50.

HISTORY OF HANCOCK
COUNTY, from its Earliest Settlement to the Present Time, together
with Reminiscences of Pioneer Life
. . . and Biographical Sketches. By
D.B. Beardsley. 1881. 472p.
P5-OH0030 — $49.50.

HISTORY OF HANOVER,
Columbiana Co., 1804-1913. 1913. 191p.
P5-OH0157 — $29.50.

CENTENNIAL HISTORY OF
HARDIN COUNTY, 1833-1933,
including Centennial Celebration
Program. Herbert T.O. Blue. 1933. 180p.
P5-OH0086 — $27.00.

HISTORY OF HARDIN COUNTY,
Containing a history of the County;
its Townships, Towns, Churches,
Schools, etc.. With biographical
sketches. 1883. 1064p.
P5-OH0115 — $99.50.

BRIEF HISTORY OF HARRISON
COUNTY. S.B. McGavran. 1894. 56p.
P5-OH0158 — $11.00.

COMMEMORATIVE & BIOGRAPH-
ICAL RECORDS OF THE
COUNTIES OF HARRISON &
CARROLL, Containing Biographical
Sketches of Prominent & Represen-
tative Citizens & many of the Early
Settled Families. 1891. 1150p.
P5-OH0095 — $111.50.

HISTORICAL COLLECTIONS OF
HARRISON CO., with Lists of First
Landowners, Early Marriage to 1841,
Will Records to 1861, Burial Records
& Numerous Genealogies. By C.A.
Hanna. 1900. 636p.
P5-OH0032 — $65.00.

STORY OF THE "DINING FORK"
[HARRISON CO.]. By Joseph T.
Harrison. 1927. 370p.
P5-OH0068 — $43.00.

HISTORY OF HENRY &
FULTON COUNTIES, with
Illustrations & Biographical Sketches
of Some of its Prominent Men &
Pioneers. 1888. 712p.
P5-OH0159 — $76.50.

Ohio, cont.

**HISTORY OF HOCKING VALLEY,
Together with Sketches of its Cities,
Villages & Townships . . . Portraits of
Prominent Persons; & Biographies of
Representative Citizens.** 1883. 1392p.
P5-OH0120 — $129.00.

**GRAVE RECORDS OF HURON
COUNTY.** Comp. by Marjorie Cherry.
1957-1958. 3 vols. in 1, 138 + 151 + 237p.
P5-OH0203 — $53.00.

**HISTORY OF HURON COUNTY;
Its Progress & Development, with
Biographical Sketches of Prominent
Citizens of the County, 2-vol. set.** A.J.
Baughman. 1909. 2 vols., 513 + 549p.
P5-OH0160 — $109.00/set.

**HISTORY OF HURON COUNTY
. . ., Vol. I.** 1909. 513p.
P5-OH0160A — $59.50.

**HISTORY OF HURON COUNTY
. . ., Vol. II.** 1909. 549p.
P5-OH0160B — $59.50.

EARLY JACKSON. By Romaine Aten
Jones. 1942. 70p.
P5-OH0162 — $14.00.

**HISTORY OF JACKSON COUNTY.
Vol. I.** By D.W. Williams. 1900. 188p.
P5-OH0163 — $22.50.

**PATHFINDERS OF JEFFERSON
COUNTY.** Comp. by W.H. Hunter.
1898. 463p.
P5-OH0069 — $37.50.

**HISTORY OF JEROME TOWN-
SHIP, Union County.** By W.L. Curry.
1913. 205p.
P5-OH0164 — $31.00.

**HISTORY OF KNOX COUNTY,
from 1779 to 1862, comprising Bio-
graphical Sketches, Anecdotes &
Incidents of Men Connected with the
County from its First Settlement.** By
A. Banning Norton. 1862. 424p.
P5-OH0036 — $46.00.

**HISTORY OF KNOX COUNTY: Its
Past & Present.** Comp. by N.N. Hill,
Jr. 1881. 854p.
P5-OH0035 — $88.00.

**PAST & PRESENT OF KNOX
COUNTY, 2-vol. set.** 1912. 2 vols., 907p.
P5-OH0165 — $89.00/set.

**PAST & PRESENT OF KNOX
COUNTY, Vol. I.** 1912.
P5-OH0165A — $48.50.

**PAST & PRESENT OF KNOX
COUNTY, Vol. II.** 1912.
P5-OH0165B — $48.50.

**RECORD OF THE REVOLU-
TIONARY SOLDIERS BURIED IN
LAKE COUNTY, with a Partial List
of Those in Geauga Co.** By New
Conn. Chapter D.A.R. 1902. 94p.
P5-OH0166 — $17.00.

**CENTENNIAL HISTORY OF
LANCASTER & Lancaster People,
1898: the 100th Anniversary of the
Settlement.** C.M.L. Wiseman. 1898. 407p.
P5-OH0167 — $46.50.

**LANCASTER & FAIRFIELD
COUNTY.** 1901. 221p.
P5-OH0168 — $31.50.

**CENTENNIAL HISTORY OF
LICKING COUNTY.** By Isaac
Smucker. 1876. 80p.
P5-OH0169 — $15.00.

**HISTORY OF LICKING COUNTY,
its Past & Present.** Comp. by N.N.
Hill, Jr. 1881. 822p.
P5-OH0037 — $85.00.

**MEMORIAL RECORD OF
LICKING COUNTY, Containing
Biographical Sketches of Represen-
tative Citizens of the County.** 1894. 526p.
P5-OH0170A — $57.00.

**HISTORY OF LOGAN COUNTY &
OHIO, Containing a History of the
State . . . and Biographical Sketches.**
1880. 840p.
P5-OH0061A — $87.00.

**HISTORY OF LORAIN COUNTY,
with Illustrations & Biographical
Sketches of Some of its Prominent
Men & Pioneers.** 1879. 373p.
P5-OH0170B — $46.00.

**STANDARD HISTORY OF
LORAIN COUNTY, 2-vol. set.** 1916.
2 vols., 1062p.
P5-OH0070 — $105.00/set.
**STANDARD HISTORY OF
LORAIN COUNTY, Vol. I.** 1916.
P5-OH0070A — $55.00.

**STANDARD HISTORY OF
LORAIN COUNTY, Vol. II.** 1916.
P5-OH0070B — $55.00.

**ABSTRACTS OF LUCAS COUNTY
WILLS, Vols. 1 to 6, to the Year 1874.**
Blaine, Hughes, Lorenz, et al. 1954.
125p.
P5-OH0171 — $17.50.

**MEMOIRS OF LUCAS COUNTY &
THE CITY OF TOLEDO, from the
Earliest Historical Times Down to
the Present, Including a
Genealogical & Biographical Record
of Representative Families, 2-vol. set.**
1910. 2 vols., 636 + 685p.
P5-OH0172 — $129.00/set.

**MEMOIRS OF LUCAS COUNTY
. . ., Vol. I.** 1910. 636p.
P5-OH0172A — $69.50.

**MEMOIRS OF LUCAS COUNTY
. . ., Vol. II.** 1910. 685p.
P5-OH0172B — $69.50.

**HISTORY OF MADISON TOWN-
SHIP, Including Groveport & Canal
Winchester, Franklin County.** By
George F. Bareis. 1902. 515p.
P5-OH0038 — $55.00.

**HISTORY OF MADISON COUNTY,
Containing a History of the County;
its Townships, Towns, etc.; [Bio-
graphical] Portraits of Early Settlers
& Prominent Men; etc.** 1883. 1165p.
P5-OH0173 — $109.50.

**TWENTIETH CENTURY HISTORY
OF YOUNGSTOWN & MAHONING
COUNTY & Representative Citizens.**
1907. 1030p.
P5-OH0071 — $99.50.

**MAINEVILLE, OHIO, HISTORY:
100 Years as an Incorporated Town,
1850-1950.** Robert Brenner. 1950. 216p.
P5-OH0210 — $29.50.

HISTORY OF MARIETTA. By
Thos. J. Summers. 1903. 328p.
P5-OH0174 — $41.50.

**BIOGRAPHIES OF MANY RESI-
DENTS OF MARION CO., &
Review of the History of Marion
County.** 1950. 370p.
P5-OH0039 — $42.00.

**HISTORY OF MARION COUNTY,
Containing a History of the County;
its Townships, Towns . . . etc.;
Portraits of Early Settlers and
Prominent Men; etc. With biogra-
phies.** 1883. 1031p.
P5-OH0116 — $105.00.

HISTORY OF THE MAUMEE RIVER BASIN, from the Earliest Account to its Organization into Counties. By Charles E. Slocum. 1905. 638 + xx p.
P5-OH0060B — $68.50.

HISTORY OF THE MAUMEE VALLEY, TOLEDO and THE SANDUSKY REGION, 4-vol. set. By Charles Sumner Van Tassel. 1929. 4 vols., 3450p.
P5-OH0105 — $299.50/set.

HISTORY OF THE MAUMEE VALLEY . . ., Vol. I: History. 1929.
P5-OH0105A — $97.50.

HISTORY OF THE MAUMEE VALLEY . . ., Vol. II: History. 1929.
P5-OH0105B — $97.50.

HISTORY OF THE MAUMEE VALLEY . . ., Vol. III: Biography. 1929. 670p.
P5-OH0105C — $69.50.

HISTORY OF THE MAUMEE VALLEY . . ., Vol. IV: Biography. 1929. 688p.
P5-OH0105D — $69.50.

HISTORY OF MEDINA COUNTY. Medina County Historical Soc. 1948. 419p.
P5-OH0040 — $47.00.

HISTORY OF MEDINA COUNTY. With biographical sketches & portraits of early settlers & prominent citizens. 1881. 922p.
P5-OH0176 — $94.50.

PIONEER HISTORY OF MEDINA COUNTY. By N.B. Northrop. 1861. 224p.
P5-OH0175 — $31.50.

PIONEER HISTORY OF MEIGS COUNTY. By Stillman Carter Larkin. 1908. 208p.
P5-OH0094 — $34.50.

GENEALOGICAL & BIOGRAPHICAL RECORD OF MIAMI COUNTY (Reprinted without "Compendium of National Biography.") 1900. 682p.
P5-OH0177 — $71.50.

HISTORY OF MIAMI COUNTY (1807-1953). 1953. xii + 403p.
P5-OH0042 — $45.00.

HISTORY OF MIAMI COUNTY. 1880. 880p.
P5-OH0041 — $89.50.

TOWN OF MILAN. By Jas. A. Ryan. 1928. 96p.
P5-OH0179 — $17.50.

HISTORY OF MONTGOMERY COUNTY: History of the County; its Townships, Cities, Towns, etc.; [Biographical] Portraits of Early Settlers & Prominent Men; etc. 1882. 760 + 460p.
P5-OH0180 — $119.50.

HISTORY OF MORGAN COUNTY, with Portraits & Biographical Sketches of some of the Pioneers & Prominent Men. With modern every-name index. By Charles Robertson. 1886. 538 + 57p.
P5-OH0117 — $59.50.

HISTORY OF MORROW COUNTY & OHIO. With biographical sketches. 1880. 838p.
P5-OH0181 — $87.00.

HISTORY OF MUSKINGUM COUNTY, 1794-1882, with Illustrations & Biographical Sketches of Prominent Men & Pioneers. With 1955 every-name index. By J.F. Everhart. 1882. 481 + 64p.
P5-OH0043 — $55.00.

ACCOUNT OF THE REMARKABLE OCCURENCES in the Life & Travels of Col. James Smith, During his Captivity with the Indians, in the Years 1755-1759 [Ohio]. By Wm. M. Darlington. 1870. 190p.
P5-OH0033 — $19.00.

HISTORICAL ACCOUNT OF BOUQUET'S EXPEDITION Against the Indians in 1764 [Ohio]. Preface by Francis Parkman, with a Biographical Sketch of General Bouquet. 1868. xxiii + 162p.
P5-OH0034 — $18.00.

HISTORICAL SKETCH of the OLD VILLAGE OF NEW LISBON, with Biographical Notes of its Citizens Prominent in the Affairs of the Village, State & Nation. By C.S. Speaker, C.C. Connell & Geo. T. Farrell. 1903. 203p.
P5-OH0118 — $34.00.

CONDENSED HISTORY OF NEW LYME, Ashtabula Co., Compiled from Early Records & Verbal Accounts of Old Residents. 1877. 60p.
P5-OH0183 — $12.00.

HISTORY OF NOBLE COUNTY, with Portraits & Biographical Sketches of Some of its Pioneers & Prominent Men, with modern every-name index. 1887. 597 + 65p.
P5-OH0184 — $69.50.

"JUST LIKE OLD TIMES" BOOK I, 1972-1974. From the Norwalk Reflector. By Henry Reinier Timman. 1982. 164p.
P5-OH0220 — $31.50.

"JUST LIKE OLD TIMES" BOOK II, 1975-1977. 1983. 173p.
P5-OH0219 — $33.00.

"JUST LIKE OLD TIMES" BOOK III, 1978-1980. 1984. 182p.
P5-OH0218 — $33.50.

"JUST LIKE OLD TIMES" BOOK IV, 1981-1983. 1985. 157 + 28p.
P5-OH0224 — $33.50.

FAIR OXFORD. By Ophia D. Smith. 1947. 223p.
P5-OH0211 — $31.50.

HISTORY OF PICKAWAY COUNTY & Representative Citizens. 1906. 882p.
P5-OH0045 — $88.00.

HISTORY OF PORTAGE COUNTY, Containing a History of the County; its Townships, Towns, Villages, etc.; Portraits of Early Settlers & Prominent Men; Biographies; etc. 1885. 927p.
P5-OH0185 — $94.50.

PORTAGE HERITAGE. HISTORY OF PORTAGE COUNTY: its Towns & Townships, & the Men & Women who have Developed Them; its Life, Institutions & Biographies, Facts & Lore. 1957. 824p.
P5-OH0046 — $85.00.

PORTRAITS & BIOGRAPHICAL RECORD OF PORTAGE & SUMMIT COUNTIES, Containing Biographical Sketches of Many Prominent & Representative Citizens. 1898. 988p.
P5-OH0073 — $95.00.

For hardcover versions, see the order form on page v. To order, call 1-888-296-3447.

Ohio, cont.

BIOGRAPHICAL HISTORY OF PREBLE COUNTY (reprinted without "Compendium of National Biography.") 1900. 351p.
P5-OH0187 — $44.00.

HISTORY OF PREBLE COUNTY, with Illustration & Biographical Sketches & History of Ohio. 1881. 340 + 106p.
P5-OH0217 — $49.00.

HISTORY OF PREBLE COUNTY, with Illustrations & Biographical Sketches (reprinted without the History of Ohio section). 1881. 337p.
P5-OH0186 — $41.00.

CENTENNIAL BIOGRAPHICAL HISTORY OF RICHLAND & ASHLAND COUNTIES. 1901. 831p.
P5-OH0048 — $86.00.

HISTORY OF RICHLAND COUNTY (including the Original Boundaries): its Past & Present, Containing . . . its Cities, Towns & Villages..& Biographies & Histories. Comp. by A.A. Graham. 1880. 941p.
P5-OH0047 — $95.00.

HISTORY OF RICHLAND COUNTY, from 1808 to 1908, with Biographical Sketches of Prominent Citizens of the County, 2-vol. set. 1908. 2 vols., 1175p.
P5-OH0189 — $119.50/set.

HISTORY OF RICHLAND COUNTY . . ., Vol. I. 1908.
P5-OH0189A — $64.50.

HISTORY OF RICHLAND COUNTY . . ., Vol. II. 1908.
P5-OH0189B — $64.50.

PIONEER DIRECTORY & SCRAP BOOK, Including the Names of 300+ Richland County Pioneers. By E.B. McLaughlin. 1887. 82p.
P5-OH0188 — $15.00.

COUNTY OF ROSS: A History of Ross County from the Earliest Days . . . with Biographical Sketches. 1902. 736p.
P5-OH0088 — $77.00.

HISTORY OF ROSS & HIGHLAND COUNTIES, with Illustrations & Biographical Sketches. With every-name index. 1880. 532 + 110p.
P5-OH0049 — $69.00.

PIONEER RECORD & REMINISCENCES OF THE EARLY SETTLERS & SETTLEMENT OF ROSS COUNTY. By Isaac J. Finley & Rufus Putnam. 1871. 148p.
P5-OH0190 — $19.00.

PORTRAIT & BIOGRAPHICAL RECORD OF THE SCIOTO VALLEY [ROSS CO.]. 1894. 429p.
P5-OH0074 — $47.00.

STANDARD HISTORY OF ROSS COUNTY: Authentic Narrative of the Past, with Particular Attention to the Modern Era, 2-vol. set. 1917. 2 vols., 934p.
P5-OH0191 — $97.00/set.

STANDARD HISTORY OF ROSS COUNTY . . ., Vol. I. 1917.
P5-OH0191A — $52.00.

STANDARD HISTORY OF ROSS COUNTY . . ., Vol. II. 1917.
P5-OH0191B — $52.00.

HISTORY OF SALEM & the Immediate Vicinity, Columbiana Co. By George D. Hunt. 1898. 241p.
P5-OH0050 — $32.00.

HISTORICAL ACCOUNT OF THE EXPEDITION AGAINST SANDUSKY Under Col. William Crawford in 1782, with Biographical Sketches, Personal Reminiscences & Descriptions of Interesting Localities. By C.W. Butterfield. 1873. 403p.
P5-OH0051 — $45.00.

HISTORY OF SANDUSKY COUNTY, with Portraits & Biographies of Prominent Citizens & Pioneers. 1882. 834p.
P5-OH0192A — $87.00.

TWENTIETH CENTURY HISTORY OF SANDUSKY COUNTY & Representative Citizens. 1909. 934p.
P5-OH0075 — $95.00.

HISTORY OF SCIOTO COUNTY, Together with a Pioneer Record of Southern Ohio. By Nelson W. Evans. 1903. 1322p.
P5-OH0192B — $127.00.

CENTENNIAL BIOGRAPHICAL HISTORY OF SENECA COUNTY. 1902. 757p.
P5-OH0102 — $79.50.

HISTORY OF SENECA COUNTY, Containing a Detailed Narrative of the Principal Events that Have Occured Since its First Settlement . . . with Biographical Sketches. By Consul W. Butterfield. 1848. 252p.
P5-OH0103 — $37.00.

HISTORY OF SENECA COUNTY, Containing a History of the County, its Townships, Towns, Villages, etc.; Portraits of Early Settlers & Prominent Men; Biographies, etc. 1886. 1070p.
P5-OH0193 — $105.00.

HISTORY OF SENECA COUNTY, from the Close of the Revolutionary War to 1880. By W. Lang. 1880. 691p.
P5-OH0076 — $71.00.

HISTORY OF SHELBY COUNTY, & Representative Citizens. By A.B.C. Hitchcock. 1913. 862p.
P5-OH0090 — $89.50.

STANDARD HISTORY OF SPRINGFIELD & CLARK COUNTY: Authentic Narrative of the Past, with Particular Attention to the Modern Era in the Commercial, Industrial, Educational, Civic & Social Development, 2-vol. set. 1922. 2 vols., 562 + 432p.
P5-OH0194 — $105.00/set.

STANDARD HISTORY OF SPRINGFIELD & CLARK COUNTY . . ., Vol. I. 1922. 562p.
P5-OH0194A — $60.00.

STANDARD HISTORY OF SPRINGFIELD & CLARK COUNTY . . ., Vol. II. 1922. 432p.
P5-OH0194B — $60.00.

HISTORY OF STARK COUNTY, with an Outline Sketch of Ohio. 1881. 1010p.
P5-OH0100B — $99.50.

STANDARD HISTORY OF STARK COUNTY: Authentic Narrative of the Past, with Particular Attention to the Modern Era; Chronicle of the People, with Family Lineage & Memoirs, 3-vol. set. 1916. 3 vols., 1114p.
P5-OH0195 — $119.00/set.

STANDARD HISTORY OF STARK COUNTY . . ., Vol. I. 1916. P5-OH0195A — $43.00.

STANDARD HISTORY OF STARK COUNTY . . ., Vol. II. 1916. P5-OH0195B — $43.00.

STANDARD HISTORY OF STARK COUNTY . . ., Vol. III. 1916. P5-OH0195C — $43.00.

20TH CENTURY HISTORY OF STEUBENVILLE & JEFFERSON COUNTY, & Representative Citizens. By Joseph B. Doyle. 1910. 1190p. P5-OH0196 — $116.50.

HISTORICAL REMINISCENCES OF SUMMIT COUNTY. By Gen. L.V. Bierce. 1854. 157p. P5-OH0197 — $27.00.

HISTORY OF SUMMIT COUNTY. 1881. 1056p. P5-OH0077 — $99.50.

HISTORY OF TOLEDO & LUCAS COUNTY, 1623-1923, 3-vol. set in 2 books. 1923. 3 vols. in 2, 762 + 1383p. P5-OH0052 — $200.00/set.

HISTORY OF TOLEDO & LUCAS COUNTY . . ., Vol. I. 1923. 762p. P5-OH0052A — $80.00.

HISTORY OF TOLEDO & LUCAS COUNTY . . ., Vols. II & III. 1923. 1383p. P5-OH0052B — $130.00.

TROY, PIQUA, & MIAMI COUNTY, & Representative Citizens. 1909. 857p. P5-OH0178 — $89.50.

HISTORY OF TRUMBULL & MAHONING COUNTIES, with Illustrations & Biographical Sketches, 2-vol. set. 1882. 2 vols., 504 + 566p. P5-OH0053 — $99.50.

HISTORY OF TRUMBULL & MAHONING COUNTIES, with Illustrations & Biographical Sketches, Vol. I. 1882. 504p. P5-OH0053A — $54.50.

HISTORY OF TRUMBULL & MAHONING COUNTIES, with Illustrations & Biographical Sketches, Vol. II. 1882. 566p. P5-OH0053B — $54.50.

TWENTIETH CENTURY HISTORY OF TRUMBULL COUNTY: A Narrative Account of its Historical Progress, its People & its Principal Interests, 2-vol. set. Harriet Taylor Upton. 1909. 2 vols., 643 + 436p. P5-OH0054 — $107.50/set.

TWENTIETH CENTURY HISTORY OF TRUMBULL COUNTY . . ., Vol. I: History. 1909. 643p. P5-OH0054A — $68.00.

TWENTIETH CENTURY HISTORY OF TRUMBULL COUNTY . . ., Vol. II: Biography. 1909. 436p. P5-OH0054B — $46.00.

HISTORY OF TUSCARAWAS COUNTY. 1884. 1007p. P5-OH0079 — $99.50.

TWINSBURG, 1817-1917. Part I, History; Part II, Genealogies. 1917. 533p. P5-OH0198 — $58.00.

HISTORY OF UNION COUNTY: History of the County; its Townships, Towns, etc.; . . . [Biographical] Portraits of Early Settlers & Prominent Men; etc. 1883. 562 + 688p. P5-OH0199 — $119.00.

HISTORY OF VAN WERT COUNTY & Representative Citizens. Ed. By Thaddeus S. Gilliland. 803pp. (Richmond & Arnold; 1906) 1999. 1906. 803p. P5-OH0212 — $84.00.

HISTORY OF VINTON COUNTY, Wonderland of Ohio. By Lew Ogan. 1954. 314p. P5-OH0080 — $39.50.

HISTORY OF WARREN COUNTY, Containing a History of the County; its Townships, Towns, etc. . . . With biographies. 1882. 1070p. P5-OH0119 — $105.00.

HISTORY OF WASHINGTON COUNTY, 1788-1881, with Illustrations & Biographical Sketches. 1881. 739p. P5-OH0200 — $77.00.

COMMEMORATIVE BIO-GRAPHICAL RECORD OF WAYNE COUNTY, Containing Biographical Sketches of Prominent & Representative Citizens & Many of the Early Families. 1889. 608p. P5-OH0081 — $64.00.

HISTORY OF WAYNE COUNTY, from the Days of the Pioneers & First Settlers. By Ben Douglass. 1878. 868p. P5-OH0056 — $87.50.

HISTORY OF THE WESTERN RESERVE, Vol. I By Harriet Tayor Upton. 1910. P5-OH0112A — $69.50.

HISTORY OF THE WESTERN RESERVE, Vol. II By Harriet Tayor Upton. 1910. P5-OH0112B — $69.50.

HISTORY OF THE WESTERN RESERVE. With biographies & every-name index included in Vol. III. By Harriet Taylor Upton. 1910; Index, 1988. 3 vols., 1874p. Index: 184p. P5-OH0112 — $189.50/set.

HISTORY OF THE WESTERN RESERVE. With biographies & every-name index included in Vol. III. By Harriet Tayor Upton. 1910; Index, 1988. P5-OH0112C — $69.50.

COUNTY OF WILLIAMS, Historical & Biographical, with an Outline Sketch of the N.W. Territory, the State & Miscellaneous Matters. 1882. 820p. P5-OH0057 — $85.00.

COUNTY OF WILLIAMS: History of Williams Co. from the Earliest Days with Special Chapters on . . . Each of the Different Townships; also a Biographical Department. By Wm. Henry Shinn. 1905. 611p. P5-OH0201 — $66.50.

COMMEMORATIVE HISTORI-CAL & BIOGRAPHICAL RECORD OF WOOD COUNTY; its Past & Present, Early Settlement & Development. 1897. 1386p. P5-OH0082 — $129.50.

For hardcover versions, see the order form on page v. To order, call 1-888-296-3447.

Ohio, cont.

PIONEER SCRAP-BOOK OF WOOD COUNTY: Many Incidents & Reminiscences of the Early History of Wood County, Together with Some of the Historic Events of the Maumee Valley. With 1993 index by the Wood Co. Chapter of the Ohio Gen. Soc. Collected by C.W. Evers. 1910. 264p.
P5-OH0202 — $37.00.

HISTORY OF WYANDOT COUNTY. With Biographical Sketches. 1884. 1056p.
P5-OH0084 — $99.00.

HISTORY OF YOUNGSTOWN & THE MAHONING VALLEY, 3-vol. set. By Jos. G. Butler, Jr. 1921. 3 vols. 844 + 398 + 410p.
P5-OH0001B — $159.00/set.

HISTORY OF YOUNGSTOWN & THE MAHONING VALLEY, Vol. I. 1921. 844p.
P5-OH0001B1 — $85.00.

HISTORY OF YOUNGSTOWN & THE MAHONING VALLEY, Vol. II. 1921. 398p.
P5-OH0001B2 — $42.00.

HISTORY OF YOUNGSTOWN & THE MAHONING VALLEY, Vol. III. 1921. 410p.
P5-OH0001B3 — $48.00.

Y BRIDGE CITY: The Story of Zanesville & Muskingum County. By Norris F. Schneider. 1950. 414p.
P5-OH0207 — $47.00.

Oklahoma

PORTRAIT & BIOGRAPHICAL RECORD OF OKLAHOMA, Commemorating the Achievements of Citizens who have Contributed to the Progress of Oklahoma & the Development of its Resources. 1901. 1298p.
P5-OK0001 — $119.00.

PIONEERS OF THE PRAIRIE [Early Settlement of Follett, Texas & Ivanhoe, Oklahoma]. 1967. 211p.
P5-TX0020 — $35.00.

INVENTORY OF RECORD IN MUSKOGEE COUNTY COURT HOUSE. By Hist. Records Survey. 1936. 136p.
P5-OK0003 — $19.00.

TULSA COUNTY IN THE WORLD WAR. By Wm. T. Lampe. 1919. 300p.
P5-OK0002 — $39.00.

Oregon

CENTENNIAL HISTORY OF OREGON, 1811-1912. With notice of antecedent explorations, 4-vol. set. By Joseph Gaston. 1912. 4 vols., 684 + 1060 + 1096 + 1100p.
P5-OR0002 — $255.00/set.

CENTENNIAL HISTORY OF OREGON . . ., Vol. I. 1912. 684p.
P5-OR0002A — $65.00.

CENTENNIAL HISTORY OF OREGON . . ., Vol. II. 1912. 1060p.
P5-OR0002B — $95.00.

CENTENNIAL HISTORY OF OREGON . . ., Vol. III. 1912. 1096p.
P5-OR0002C — $95.00.

CENTENNIAL HISTORY OF OREGON . . ., Vol. IV. 1912. 1100p.
P5-OR0002D — $95.00.

HISTORY OF THE WILLAMETTE VALLEY, being a Description of the Valley & its Resources, with an Account of its discovery & Settlement by White Men, & its Subsequent History, together with Personal Reminiscences of its Early Pioneers. 1885. 902p.
P5-OR0006 — $94.50.

PORTRAIT & BIOGRAPHICAL RECORD OF WESTERN OREGON, Containing Original Sketches of Many Well Known Citizens of the Past & Present. 1904. 1033p.
P5-OR0003 — $109.00.

PORTRAIT & BIOGRAPHICAL RECORD OF THE WILLAMETTE VALLEY, Containing Original Sketches of Many Well Known Citizens of the Past & Present. 1903. 1571p.
P5-OR0007 — $149.00.

HISTORY OF BENTON COUNTY, together with the Early History of the Pacific Coast . . .; a Full Political History . . .; Incidents of Pioneer Life & Biographical Sketches of Early & Prominent Citizens; also the History of Cities, Towns, etc. With index comp. by Elizabeth Ritchie (1951); ed. by Ed Stratton. 1885. 532 + 57p.
P5-OR0004 — $59.50.

ILLUSTRATED HISTORY OF LANE COUNTY. Comp. & pub. by Albert G. Walling. 1884. 508p.
P5-OR0001 — $53.00.

PORTLAND, The Rose City, Pictorial & Biographical. With Deluxe Supplement, 2-vol. set. 1911. 2 vols, 584 + 488p.
P5-OR0005 — $99.50.

PORTLAND, The Rose City, Pictorial & Biographical, Vol. I. 1911. 584p.
P5-OR0005A — $60.00.

PORTLAND, The Rose City, Pictorial & Biographical. With Deluxe Supplement, Vol. II. 1911. 488p.
P5-OR0005B — $50.00.

Pennsylvania

ENCYCLOPEDIA OF AMERICAN QUAKER GENEALOGY, Vol. II, New Jersey & Pennsylvania. By William Wade Hinshaw. 1938. 1126p.
P5-NJ0060 — $85.00.

FINAL REPORT ON THE BATTLE OF GETTYSBURG, 3-vol. set. 1900. 3 vols., 1462p.
P5-PA9999 — $145.00/set.

FINAL REPORT ON THE BATTLE OF GETTYSBURG, Vol. I. 1900.
P5-PA9999A — $52.00.

FINAL REPORT ON THE BATTLE OF GETTYSBURG, Vol. II. 1900.
P5-PA9999B — $52.00.

FINAL REPORT ON THE BATTLE OF GETTYSBURG, Vol. III. 1900.
P5-PA9999C — $52.00.

CENTRAL PENNSYLVANIA MARRIAGES. C.A. Fisher. 1946. 90p.
P5-PA0141A — $12.00.

CHRONICLES OF CENTRAL PENNSYLVANIA, 4-vol. set. By Frederic A. Godcharles. 1944. 4 vols., 425 + 488 + 472 + 679p.
P5-PA0262 — $224.00/set.

CHRONICLES OF CENTRAL PENNSYLVANIA, Vol. I. 1944. 425p.
P5-PA0262A — $52.00.

CHRONICLES OF CENTRAL PENNSYLVANIA, Vol. II. 1944. 488p.
P5-PA0262B — $52.00.

CHRONICLES OF CENTRAL PENNSYLVANIA, Vol. III. 1944. 472p.
P5-PA0262C — $52.00.

CHRONICLES OF CENTRAL PENNSYLVANIA, Vol. IV. 1944. 679p.
P5-PA0262D — $72.00.

COLLECTION OF UPWARDS OF 30,000 NAMES OF German, Swiss, Dutch, French & other Immigr. in Penn., from 1727-1776, with a statement of names of ships, whence they sailed & the date of their arrival at Philadelphia. I. D. Rupp. 1875. 581p.
P5-PA0059B — $49.00.

COMMEMORATIVE BIOGRAPHICAL RECORD OF NORTH-EASTERN PENNSYLVANIA, including the Counties of Susquehanna, Wayne, Pike & Monroe, containing Biographical Sketches of Prominent & Representative Citizens & Many of the Early Settled Families, 2-vol. set. 1900. 2 vols., 1852p.
P5-PA0170 — $179.00/set.

COMMEMORATIVE BIOGRAPHICAL RECORD OF NORTH-EASTERN PENNSYLVANIA. . ., Vol. I. 1900.
P5-PA0170A — $95.00.

COMMEMORATIVE BIOGRAPHICAL RECORD OF NORTH-EASTERN PENNSYLVANIA. . ., Vol. II. 1900.
P5-PA0170B — $95.00.

EARLY 18TH CENTURY PALATINE EMIGRATION. By Walter A. Knittle. 1937. 320p.
P5-PA0141B — $29.00.

EARLY PA. BIRTHS, 1675-1875. By C. A. Fisher. 1947. 107p.
P5-PA1835 — $16.50.

EVERYDAY LIFE IN COLONIAL PENNSYLVANIA. By George & Virginia Schaun. 1963. 90p.
P5-PA0100B — $18.00.

FOREIGNERS WHO TOOK THE OATH OF ALLEGIANCE to the Province & State of Penna., 1727-1775, with Foreign Arrivals, 1786-1808. 1898. 787p.
P5-PA0053 — $75.00.

GAZETTEER OF THE STATE OF PENNSYLVANIA. This earliest gazetteer of Pa., is filled with very useful info. for the genealogist, esp. population surveys & geographical information. 1832. 63 + 508p.
P5-PA0008 — $59.50.

GENEALOGICAL & PERSONAL HISTORY OF WESTERN PENNSYLVANIA, Vol. I. 1915.
P5-PA0175A — $61.00.

GENEALOGICAL & PERSONAL HISTORY OF WESTERN PENNSYLVANIA, Vol. II. 1915.
P5-PA0175B — $61.00.

GENEALOGICAL & PERSONAL HISTORY OF WESTERN PENNSYLVANIA, Vol. III. 1915.
P5-PA0175C — $61.00.

HEADS OF FAMILIES AT THE FIRST CENSUS of the U.S. taken in the Year 1790. 1908. 422p.
P5-PA0026 — $42.50.

HISTORICAL COLLECTIONS OF THE STATE OF PENNSYLVANIA, Containing a Copious Selection of the Most Interesting Facts . . . Relating to the History and Antiquities . . . with Topographical Descriptions of Every County. By Sherman Day. 1843. 705p.
P5-PA0140A — $76.00.

HISTORICAL JOURNAL: MONTHLY REC OF LOCAL HISTORY & BIOGRAPHY, Northwestern, PA. J.F. Meginness. 1888. 853p.
P5-PA1848 — $85.00.

HISTORY OF THE 18TH REGIMENT OF CAVALRY, Pennsylvania Vols. (163rd Regiment of the Line), 1862-1865. 1909. 299p.
P5-PA0166 — $42.00.

MEMORIALS OF THE HUGUENOTS IN AMERICA, with Special Reference to their Emigration to Penn. By Rev. A. Stapleton. 1901. 164p.
P5-PA0179B — $19.00.

NAMES OF PERSONS WHO TOOK THE OATH OF ALLEGIANCE to the State of Pennsylvania Between the Years 1777 & 1789, with a History of the "Test Laws" of Pa. By Thompson Westcott. 1865. 145p.
P5-PA0062 — $19.00.

OHIO RIVER: A Course of Empire. By Archer Butler Hulbert. 1906. 378p.
P5-PA0158 — $45.00.

OTZINACHSON, or A History of the West Branch Valley of the Susquehanna, Embracing a Full Account of its Settlement . . . With Biographical Sketches of Some of the Leading Settlers, Families, etc. By J.F. Meginness. 1859. 511p.
P5-PA0174 — $56.50.

PENNSYLVANIA GENEALOGIES; Scotch-Irish & Germans. By W.H. Egle. 1886. 720p.
P5-PA0001 — $75.00.

PENNSYLVANIA-GERMAN IN THE REVOLUTIONARY WAR, 1775-1783. By Henry M. Muhlenberg. 1908. 542p.
P5-PA0173 — $57.00.

PIONEER OUTLINE HISTORY OF NORTHWESTERN PENNSYLVANIA, Embracing Cos. of Tioga, Potter, McKean, Warren, Crawford, Venango, Forest, Clarion, Elk, Jefferson, Cameron, Butler, Lawrence & Mercer; Pioneer Sketch of Cities of Allegheny, Beaver, du Bois & Towanda. By W.J. McKnight. 1905. 747p.
P5-PA0172 — $78.00.

PROGRESSIVE MEN OF THE COMMONWEALTH OF PENNSYLVANIA, 2-vol. set. By Col. C. Blanchard. 1900. 2 vols.; 498 + 552p.
P5-PA1844 — $105.00/set.

PROGRESSIVE MEN OF THE COMMONWEALTH OF PENNSYLVANIA, Vol. I. 1900. 498p.
P5-PA1844A — $57.50.

For hardcover versions, see the order form on page v. To order, call 1-888-296-3447.

Pennsylvania, cont.

PROGRESSIVE MEN OF THE COMMONWEALTH OF PENNSYLVANIA, Vol. II. 1900. 552p.
P5-PA1844B — $57.50.

PROMINENT & PROGRESSIVE PENNSYLVANIANS OF THE NINETEENTH CENTURY, 3-vol. set. 1898. 3 vols. 2630p.
P5-PA1846 — $240.00/set.

PROMINENT & PROGRESSIVE PENNSYLVANIANS . . ., Vol. I. 1898.
P5-PA1846A — $90.00.

PROMINENT & PROGRESSIVE PENNSYLVANIANS . . ., Vol. II. 1898.
P5-PA1846B — $90.00.

PROMINENT & PROGRESSIVE PENNSYLVANIANS . . ., Vol. III. 1898.
P5-PA1846C — $90.00.

SCHWENKFELDERS IN PENNSYLVANIA: A Historical Sketch. By Howard W. Kriebel. 1904. 246p.
P5-PA0138 — $36.00.

SOUTHEASTERN PENNSYL-VANIA: History of Berks, Bucks, Chester, Delaware, Montgomery, Philadelphia & Schuylkill, 3-vol. set. 1943. 3 vols, 576 + 500 + 560p.
P5-PA0269 — $159.00/set.

SOUTHEASTERN PENNSYL-VANIA . . ., Vol. I. 1943. 576p.
P5-PA0269A — $59.50.

SOUTHEASTERN PENNSYL-VANIA . . ., Vol. II. 1943. 500p.
P5-PA0269B — $59.50.

SOUTHEASTERN PENNSYL-VANIA . . ., Vol. III. 1943. 560p.
P5-PA0269C — $59.50.

SWEDISH SETTLEMENTS ON THE DELAWARE, 1638-1664. By A. Johnson. 1911. 879p.
P5-PA0024A — $89.50.

SWISS & GERMAN PIONEER SETTLERS OF S.E. PENN. Emphasizes Lancaster Co. genealogy & the emigr. from Palatine, with lists of early settlers & biogr. sketches of the "Pennsylvania Germans." H.F. Eshleman. 1917. 386p.
P5-PA0151A — $42.50.

TWENTIETH CENTURY BENCH AND BAR OF PENNSYLVANIA, 2-vol. set. 1903. 2 vols., 1203 + 561p.
P5-PA1843 — $160.00/set.

TWENTIETH CENTURY BENCH AND BAR OF PENNSYLVANIA, Vol. I. 1903. 1203p.
P5-PA1843A — $120.00.

TWENTIETH CENTURY BENCH AND BAR OF PENNSYLVANIA, Vol. II. 1903. 516p.
P5-PA1843B — $51.00.

WELSH SETTLEMENT OF PENNSYLVANIA: Welsh Quaker Emigr. Index incl. over 2,000 settlers. By C. H. Browning. 1912. 631p.
P5-PA0015 — $66.50.

WILLIAM PENN & THE DUTCH QUAKER MIGRATION TO PENNSYLVANIA. By Wm. I. Hull. 1935. 445p.
P5-PA0258 — $45.00.

HISTORY OF ALBANY TOWNSHIP, 1800-1885, with Biographical Sketches of the Pioneers. Wtih index. By C.F. Heverly. 1885. 117 + 42p. Index.
P5-PA0284 — $22.50.

HISTORY OF ALLEGHENY COUNTY, with Illustrations. [The original book is oversized. It has been reduced approximately 25% to fit an 8.5 x 11 format; the print is small but quite legible.] 1876. 242p.
P5-PA0156A — $34.00.

HISTORY OF ALLEGHENY COUNTY. Including its Early Settlement & Progress; a Description of its Historical & Interesting Localities; its Cities, Towns, & Villages; Portraits of Some Prominent Men & Biogr. of Many Citizens, 2-vol. set. 1889. 2 vols., 762 + 786p.
P5-PA0055 — $149.00/set.

HISTORY OF ALLEGHENY COUNTY . . ., Vol. I. 1889. 762p.
P5-PA0055A — $79.00.

HISTORY OF ALLEGHENY COUNTY . . ., Vol. II. 1889. 786p.
P5-PA0055B — $79.00.

MEMOIRS OF ALLEGHENY COUNTY, Personal & Genealogical, 2-vol. set. 1904. 2 vols., 560 + 530p.
P5-PA0176 — $109.00/set.

MEMOIRS OF ALLEGHENY COUNTY, Personal & Genealogical, Vol. I. 1904. 560p.
P5-PA0176A — $58.50.

MEMOIRS OF ALLEGHENY COUNTY, Personal & Genealogical, Vol. II. 1904. 530p.
P5-PA0176B — $58.50.

GENEALOGICAL & PERSONAL HISTORY OF THE ALLEGHENY VALLEY, 3-vol. set. 1913. 3 vols., 1162p.
P5-PA0157 — $119.00/set.

GENEALOGICAL & PERSONAL HISTORY OF THE ALLEGHENY VALLEY, Vol. I. 1913.
P5-PA0157A — $44.50.

GENEALOGICAL & PERSONAL HISTORY OF THE ALLEGHENY VALLEY, Vol. II. 1913.
P5-PA0157B — $44.50.

GENEALOGICAL & PERSONAL HISTORY OF THE ALLEGHENY VALLEY, Vol. III. 1913.
P5-PA0157C — $44.50.

ARMSTRONG COUNTY, Her People, Past & Present, Embracing a History of the County & a Gene-alogical & Biographical Record of Representative Families, 2 vols in 1 book. 1914. 2 vols., 995p.
P5-PA0177 — $98.50/set.

ARMSTRONG COUNTY . . ., Vol. I. 1914.
P5-PA0177A — $57.00.

ARMSTRONG COUNTY, Her People, Past & Present, Embracing a History of the County & a Genealogical & Biographical Record of Representative Families, Vol. II. 1914.
P5-PA0177B — $57.00.

HISTORY OF OLD TIOGA POINT & EARLY ATHENS. By Louis Welles Murray. 1908. 656p.
P5-PA0129 — $69.00.

BOOK OF BIOGRAPHIES: Biographical Sketches of Leading Citizens of Beaver Co. 1899. 435p.
P5-PA0142 — $53.00.

GENEALOGICAL & PERSONAL HISTORY OF BEAVER COUNTY, 2-vol. set. 1914. 2 vols., 1124p.
P5-PA0178 — $112.00/set.

For hardcover versions, see the order form on page v. To order, call 1-888-296-3447.

GENEALOGICAL & PERSONAL
HISTORY OF BEAVER COUNTY,
Vol. I. 1914.
P5-PA0178A — $59.50.

GENEALOGICAL & PERSONAL
HISTORY OF BEAVER COUNTY,
Vol. II. 1914.
P5-PA0178B — $59.50.

HISTORY OF BEAVER CO., 2-vol.
set. J. H. Bausman. 1904. 2 vols., 612 +
703p.
P5-PA0005 — $139.00/set.

HISTORY OF BEAVER CO., Vol. I.
1904. 612p.
P5-PA0005A — $73.00.

HISTORY OF BEAVER CO., Vol. II.
1904. 703p.
P5-PA0005B — $73.00.

HISTORY OF BEAVER COUNTY,
Including its Early Settlement. 1888.
908 + 123p.
P5-PA0100A — $99.50.

HISTORY OF BEDFORD &
SOMERSET COUNTIES, with
Genealogical & Personal History, 3-
vol. set. E. Howard Blackburn & Wm.
H. Welfley. 1906. 3 vols., 554 + 695 + 553p.
P5-PA0179A — $169.00/set.

HISTORY OF BEDFORD &
SOMERSET COUNTIES . . ., Vol. I.
1906. 554p.
P5-PA0179A1 — $59.00.

HISTORY OF BEDFORD &
SOMERSET COUNTIES . . ., Vol.
II. 1906. 695p.
P5-PA0179A2 — $59.00.

HISTORY OF BEDFORD &
SOMERSET COUNTIES . . ., Vol.
III. 1906. 553p.
P5-PA0179A3 — $59.00.

HISTORY OF BEDFORD,
SOMERSET & FULTON
COUNTIES. 1884. 672p .+ illus.
P5-PA0050 — $79.50.

ANNALS OF THE OLEY VALLEY
IN BERKS COUNTY, PA. Over
Two Hundred years of Local History
of an American Canaan. By Rev. P.C.
Croll, D.D. 1926. 148p.
P5-PA1836 — $19.00.

EARLY NARRATIVES OF BERKS
COUNTY. J. Bennett Nolan. 1927. 189p.
P5-PA0277 — $28.00.

HISTORICAL & BIOGRAPHICAL
ANNALS OF BERKS CO.: A Concise History of the Co., & Genealogical & Biogr. Records of Representative Families, 2-vol. set. 1909. 2
vols., 1700p.
P5-PA0067 — $155.00/set.

HISTORICAL & BIOGRAPHICAL
ANNALS OF BERKS CO. . . ., Vol.
I. 1909.
P5-PA0067A — $82.00.

HISTORICAL & BIOGRAPHICAL
ANNALS OF BERKS CO. . . ., Vol.
II. 1909.
P5-PA0067B — $82.00.

HISTORY OF BERKS COUNTY in
the Revolution, from 1774 to 1783.
Book I, Revolution; Book II,
Biographical Sketches. By Morton L.
Montgomery. 1894. 295p.
P5-PA0180 — $39.50.

HISTORY OF BERKS COUNTY.
By M. L. Montgomery. 1886. 1204p.
P5-PA0006A — $129.50.

HISTORY OF THE COUNTIES
OF BERKS & LEBANON. By I.
Daniel Rupp. 1844. 512p.
P5-PA0071 — $55.00.

LUTHERANS IN BERKS
COUNTY: Two Centuries of
Continuous Organized Church Life,
1723-1923. By H.S. Kidd. 1923. 503p.
P5-PA0280 — $54.00.

HISTORICAL BOOK OF BERRYS-
BURG & MIFFLIN TWP., 1819-
1969. 1969. 363p.
P5-PA0143 — $42.50.

BETHLEHEM, Long Ago & To-
day. By Raymond Walters. 1922. 159p.
P5-PA0181 — $20.00.

GUIDE TO THE OLD MORAVIAN
CEMETERY OF BETHLEHEM,
1742-1897. Augustus Schultze. n.d. 200p.
P5-PA0182 — $24.50.

HISTORY OF BETHLEHEM, 1741-
1892, with Some Account of its
Founders & their Early Activity in
America. Joseph M. Levering. 1903. 809p.
P5-PA0183 — $81.50.

BLAIR COUNTY'S FIRST
HUNDRED YEARS, 1846-1946.
1945. 526p.
P5-PA0282 — $57.00.

HISTORY OF BLAIR COUNTY.
1931. 2 vols. in 1, 527p.
P5-PA0147 — $59.50.

MILITARY SERVICES & GENE-
ALOGICAL RECORDS OF
SOLDIERS OF BLAIR COUNTY
[from the Revolutionary War to WW
I]. By Floyd G. Hoenstine. 1940. 426p.
P5-PA0279 — $48.00.

ILLUSTRATED HISTORY OF
BRADFORD, McKean Co. By
Vernelle A. Hatch. 1901. 261p.
P5-PA0101 — $32.00.

HISTORY & GEOGRAPHY OF
BRADFORD COUNTY, 1615-1924.
By Clement F. Heverly. 1926. 594p.
P5-PA0274 — $64.50.

HISTORY OF BRADFORD
COUNTY, 1770 — 1878, with
Illustrations & Biographical Sketches
of Some of its Prominent Men &
Pioneers. 1878. 501p.
P5-PA0184 — $54.50.

HISTORY OF BRADFORD
COUNTY, with Biographical
Selections. H.C. Bradsby. 1891. 1320p.
P5-PA0072 — $125.00.

BRISTOL PIKE. By Rev. S.F.
Hotchkin 1893. 410 + 16p.
P5-PA1840 — $47.00.

HISTORY OF BRISTOL BOROUGH,
in the Co. of Bucks, State of Penna.,
Anciently Known as "Buckingham,"
Being the Third Oldest Town &
Second Chartered Borough in
Penna., from its Earliest Times to the
Present Year. By Doron Green. 1911.
370p.
P5-PA0140B — $47.00.

EARLY FRIENDS FAMILIES OF
UPPER BUCKS CO., with Some
Account of their Descendants: Hist.
& Genealogical Information about
the Early Settlers in Upper Bucks
Co., Pa. By C. V. Roberts. 1925. 680p.
P5-PA0027 — $71.00.

HISTORY OF BUCKS COUNTY
from the Discovery of the Delaware
to the Present Time. By W.W.H.
Davis. 1876. 875 + 54p.
P5-PA0096A — $95.00.

For hardcover versions, see the order form on page v. To order, call 1-888-296-3447.

Pennsylvania, cont.

HISTORY OF BUCKS COUNTY,
from the Discovery of the Delaware
to the Present Time [1905], 3-vol. set.
By Wm. W.H. Davis. 1905. 3 vols., 486
+ 480 + 748p.
P5-PA0185 — $159.00/set.

HISTORY OF BUCKS COUNTY
. . ., Vol. I. 1905. 486p.
P5-PA0185A — $55.00.

HISTORY OF BUCKS COUNTY
. . ., Vol. II. 1905. 480p.
P5-PA0185B — $55.00.

HISTORY OF BUCKS COUNTY
. . ., Vol. III. By Wm. W.H. Davis.
1905. 748p.
P5-PA0185C — $75.00.

HISTORY OF BUCKS COUNTY,
including . . . Biographies of Many of
its Representative Citizens. 1887. 1176p.
P5-PA0102 — $109.00.

PLACE NAMES IN BUCKS
COUNTY, Alphabetically Arranged
in an Historical Narrative. Comp. by
George MacReynolds. 1942. 474p.
P5-PA0164 — $45.00.

RECORDS OF THE COURTS OF
QUARTER SESSIONS & COMMON
PLEAS OF BUCKS COUNTY, 1684-
1700. With complete index of per-
sons. 1943. 446p.
P5-PA0256 — $45.00.

ANNALS OF BUFFALO VALLEY,
1755-1855. John Blair Linn. 1877. 621p.
P5-PA0186 — $67.00.

TWENTIETH CENTURY OF
BUTLER & BUTLER CO. By James
A. McKee. 1909. 1487p.
P5-PA0103 — $139.50.

HISTORY OF BUTLER COUNTY,
1796-1883, with Illustrations & Bio-
graphical Sketches of Some of its
Prominent Men & Pioneers. 1883. 454p.
P5-PA0187 — $56.50.

HISTORY OF BUTLER COUNTY,
Embracing . . . Early Settlement &
Subsequent Growth; . . . Sketches of
Boroughs, Townships & Villages;
. . . Biographies & Portraits of Pio-
neers & Representative Citizens, etc.
1895. 1360p.
P5-PA0148 — $129.50.

BIOGRAPHICAL & PORTRAIT
CYCLOPEDIA OF CAMBRIA
COUNTY, Comprising About Five
Hundred Sketches of the Prominent
& Representative Citizens of the
County. 1896. 518p.
P5-PA0189A — $56.50.

CAMBRIA COUNTY PIONEERS:
Collection of Brief Biographical &
other Sketches Relating to the Early
History of Cambria County. By James
M. Swank. 1910. 138p.
P5-PA0188 — $18.50.

HISTORY OF CAMBRIA
COUNTY. With genealogical
memoirs, 2-vol. set. By Henry Wilson
Storey. 1907. 2 vols., 590 + 575p.
P5-PA0104 — $159.00/set.

HISTORY OF CAMBRIA
COUNTY. With genealogical
memoirs, Vol. I: History. 1907. 590p.
P5-PA0104A — $62.00.

HISTORY OF CAMBRIA
COUNTY. With genealogical
memoirs, Vol. II: History with
genealogical memoirs. 1907. 575p.
P5-PA0104B — $62.00.

HISTORY OF CAMBRIA
COUNTY, Vol. III, Biography. By
Henry Wilson Storey 1907. 679p.
P5-PA0288 — $69.50.

HISTORY OF CARBON COUNTY.
With biographical sketches. By Fred
Brenckman. 1913. 626p.
P5-PA0105 — $65.00.

20TH CENTURY HISTORY OF
THE CITY OF WASHINGTON &
WASHINGTON CO., & Represen-
tative Citizens. A Comprehensive
history of the city & county, with over
800 pages of biography. 1889. 527p.
P5-PA1842B — $55.00.

CARLISLE OLD & NEW. By the
Civic Club of Carlisle. 1907. 173p.
P5-PA0190 — $28.50.

CENT. MEM. OF PRESBYTERY
OF CARLISLE, 2-vol. set. 1889. 2
vols., 486 + 527p.
P5-PA1842 — $102.00/set.

CENT. MEM. OF PRESBYTERY
OF CARLISLE, Vol. I. 1889. 486p.
P5-PA1842A — $55.00.

CENT. MEM. OF PRESBYTERY
OF CARLISLE, Vol. II. 1889. 527p.
P5-PA1842B — $67.00.

EARLY HISTORY & GROWTH OF
CARLISLE; EARLY FOOTPRINTS
OF DEVELOPMENTS &
IMPROVEMENTS IN NORTH-
WESTERN PENNSYLVANIA. By
Theodore B. Klein & Isaac B. Brown.
1905. 75p. + foldout maps.
P5-PA0171 — $19.00.

HISTORY OF CENTRE &
CLINTON COUNTIES. With bio-
graphies. John Blair Linn. 1883. 672p.
P5-PA0106 — $71.00.

CHESTER & ITS VICINITY,
Delaware Co., with Gen. Sketches of
Some Old Families. John Hill Martin.
1877. 530p.
P5-PA0025 — $57.00.

BIOGRAPHICAL & PORTRAIT
CYCLOPEDIA OF CHESTER
COUNTY. Samuel T. Wiley. 1893. 879p.
P5-PA0107 — $89.50.

CHESTER COUNTY AND ITS
PEOPLE. 1898. 982p.
P5-PA0073 — $95.00.

HISTORIC HOMES & INSTITU-
TIONS, & GENEALOGICAL &
PERSONAL MEMOIRS OF
CHESTER & DELAWARE
COUNTIES, 2-vol. set. 1904. 2 vols.,
600 + 598p.
P5-PA0108 — $119.00/set.

HISTORIC HOMES &
INSTITUTIONS . . . OF CHESTER
& DELAWARE COUNTIES, Vol. I.
1904. 600p.
P5-PA0108A — $62.50.

HISTORIC HOMES &
INSTITUTIONS . . . OF CHESTER
& DELAWARE COUNTIES, Vol.
II. 1904. 598p.
P5-PA0108B — $62.50.

HISTORY OF CHESTER CO., with
Genealogical & Biographical Sketches.
Includes more than 320 illustrations.
J. S. Futhey & G. Cope. 1881. 782 + xliv p.
P5-PA0020 — $93.50.

HISTORY OF CHESTER COUNTY.
By Chas. W. Heathcote. 1926. 130p.
P5-PA0270 — $19.50.

HISTORY OF CHESTER COUNTY.
With biographies. 1932. 478p.
P5-PA0136 — $52.00.

**RECORD OF THE COURTS OF
CHESTER COUNTY, 1681-1697.**
With complete index of persons.
1910. 430p.
P5-PA0259 — $45.00.

HISTORY OF CLARION COUNTY,
with Illustrations & Biographical
Sketches of Some of its Prominent
Men & Pioneers. With 1997 index by
Clarion Co. Historical Society. 1887.
664 + 72 + 33p.
P5-PA0192 — $81.50.

**HISTORY OF CLEARFIELD
COUNTY,** with Illustrations & Bio-
graphical Sketches of Some of its
Prominent Men & Pioneers. 1887. 731p.
P5-PA0193 — $77.00.

**HISTORICAL & BIOGRAPHICAL
ANNALS OF COLUMBIA &
MONTOUR COUNTIES,** Contain-
ing a Concise History of the Two
Counties & a Genealogical & Bio-
graphical Record of Representative
Families, 2-vol. set. 1915. 2 vols., 1260p.
P5-PA0194 — $127.50.

**HISTORICAL & BIOGRAPHICAL
ANNALS OF COLUMBIA &
MONTOUR COUNTIES . . ., Vol. I.**
1915.
P5-PA0194A — $67.00.

**HISTORICAL & BIOGRAPHICAL
ANNALS OF COLUMBIA &
MONTOUR COUNTIES . . ., Vol.
II.** 1915.
P5-PA0194B — $67.00.

**HISTORY OF COLUMBIA &
MONTOUR COUNTIES,** Contain-
ing a History of each County, their
Townships, Towns & Villages . . . &
Biographies. 1887. 132 + 542 + 220p.
P5-PA0074 — $88.00.

**HISTORY OF COLUMBIA
COUNTY,** from the Earliest Times.
By John G. Freeze. 1883. 566p.
P5-PA0159 — $61.00.

VALLEY OF THE CONEMAUGH.
By Thomas J. Chapman. 1865. 202p.
P5-PA0167 — $31.00.

**CENTENNIAL HISTORY OF
THE BOROUGH OF CONNELLS-
VILLE, 1806-1906.** J.C. McClenathan,
Wm. A. Edie, et al. 1906. 564p.
P5-PA0149 — $59.00.

HISTORY OF CRAWFORD CO,
Containing a Hist. of the Co.; its
Twps., Towns . . . etc., Portraits of
Early Settlers & Prominent Men,
Biogr., etc. 1885. 1186p.
P5-PA0017 — $119.50.

OUR COUNTY & ITS PEOPLE:
Historical & Memorial Record of
Crawford County. Samuel P. Bates. 1899.
P5-PA0257 — $99.00.

**PIONEER SKETCHES: Scenes &
Incidents of Former Days.** An
entertaining and very useful account
of the early days of Crawford Co.,
Pa., & Ashtabula, Oh., incl. bio-
graphical sketches of early sett. By M.
P. Sargent. 1891. 512p.
P5-PA0075 — $54.00.

**BIOGRAPHICAL ANNALS OF
CUMBERLAND COUNTY,** Con-
taining Biographical Sketches of
Prominent & Representative Citizens
& of Many of the Early Settled
Families. 1905. 850p.
P5-PA0196 — $87.00.

**CUMBERLAND COUNTY
MARRIAGES, 1761-1800.** 1927. 40p.
P5-PA0260 — $10.00.

**CUMBERLAND COUNTY,
PENNSYLVANIA in the Civil War,
1861-1865 With Historical Sketches.**
John D. Hemminger. 1926. 144 + 50p.
P5-PA1838 — $32.00.

**HISTORY OF CUMBERLAND &
ADAMS COUNTIES.** With biogra-
phies. 1886. 132 + 588 + 516p.
P5-PA0135 — $119.50.

**HISTORY OF THE CUMBERLAND
VALLEY.** Harriet W. Stewart. n.d. 146p.
P5-PA0168 — $18.50.

**COMMEMORATIVE BIOGRAPH-
ICAL ENCYCLOPEDIA OF
DAUPHIN COUNTY,** Containing
Sketches of Prominent & Represen-
tative Citizens, & Many of the Early
Scotch-Irish & German Settlers. 1896.
1196p.
P5-PA0197 — $112.00.

**HISTORY & TOPOGRAPHY OF
DAUPHIN, CUMBERLAND,
FRANKLIN, BEDFORD, ADAMS
& PERRY COUNTIES.** By I. Daniel
Rupp. 1846. 606p.
P5-PA0110 — $65.00.

HISTORY OF DAUPHIN CO., with
Genealogical Memoirs. 2-vol. set. By
Luther Reily Kelker. 1907. 3 vols. in 2,
1136 + 727p.
P5-PA0006B — $184.00/set.

HISTORY OF DAUPHIN CO., with
Genealogical Memoirs, Vols. I & II:
History. 1907. 1136p.
P5-PA0006B1 — $115.00.

HISTORY OF DAUPHIN CO., with
Genealogical Memoirs, Vol. III:
Genealogy. 1907. 727p.
P5-PA0006B2 — $80.00.

**HISTORY OF THE COUNTIES
OF DAUPHIN & LEBANON** in the
Commonwealth of Pennsylvania,
Biogr. & Genealogical. By W. H. Egle.
1883. 616 + 360p.
P5-PA0016 — $103.50.

HISTORY OF DELANO, 1861-1931.
With biographical sketches. By H.O.
Moser. 1931. 227p.
P5-PA0111 — $32.00.

**BIOGRAPHICAL & HISTORICAL
CYCLOPEDIA OF DELAWARE
COUNTY,** Comprising a Historical
Sketch of the County, together with
Nearly Four Hundred Biographical
Sketches of the Prominent Men &
Families of the County. History by
Samuel T. Wiley. 1894. 500p.
P5-PA0198 — $55.00.

**HISTORY OF DELAWARE
COUNTY and Its People, 2-vol. set.**
1914. 2 Vols. , 558 + 596p.
P5-PA0139 — $115.00/set.

**HISTORY OF DELAWARE
COUNTY and Its People, Vol. I.**
1914. 558p.
P5-PA0139A — $61.50.

**HISTORY OF DELAWARE
COUNTY and Its People, Vol. II.**
1914. 596p.
P5-PA0139B — $61.50.

For hardcover versions, see the order form on page v. To order, call 1-888-296-3447.

Pennsylvania, cont.

HISTORY OF DELAWARE COUNTY, from the Discovery of the Territory included within its Limits to the Present Time [1862]. By George Smith. 1862. 581p.
P5-PA0199 — $61.50.

HISTORY OF DELAWARE COUNTY. By Henry Graham Ashmead. 1884. 767p.
P5-PA0076 — $78.00.

HISTORY OF DELAWARE COUNTY. 2 vols. in 1 book. 1932. 2 vols., 352 + 100p.
P5-PA0150 — $56.50.

SOME OF THE FIRST SETTLERS OF "THE FORKS OF THE DELAWARE" & THEIR DESCENDANTS [EASTON]. 1902. 404p.
P5-PA0052 — $44.00.

HISTORY OF ERIE CO., Containing a Hist. of the Co.; its Twps., Towns, & Villages; Early Settlers & Biogr., etc. By Whitman, Russell, Weakley & Mansfield. 1884. 1006 + 239p.
P5-PA0056 — $119.00.

HISTORY OF ERIE CO., from its First Settlement. Enlarged ed. of 1861 pub. Laura G. Sanford. 1894. 460p.
P5-PA0057 — $48.00.

HISTORY OF ERIE COUNTY, 2-vol. set. By John Elmer Reed. 1925. 2 vols., 1288p.
P5-PA0112 — $119.00/set.

HISTORY OF ERIE COUNTY, Vol. I. 1925.
P5-PA0112A — $67.50.

HISTORY OF ERIE COUNTY, Vol. II. 1925.
P5-PA0112B — $67.50.

NELSON'S BIOGRAPHICAL DICTIONARY & HISTORICAL REFERENCE BOOK OF ERIE COUNTY, Being a Condensed History of . . . Erie County, & of the Several Cities, Boroughs & Townships in the County. With biographies. By Benj. Whitman. 1896. 922p.
P5-PA0201 — $94.50.

TWENTIETH CENTURY HISTORY OF ERIE CO.: A Narrative acct. of its Historical Progress, its People, & its Principal Interests, 2-vol. set. By John Miller. 1909. 2 vols., 897 + 712p.
P5-PA0018 — $165.50/set.

TWENTIETH CENTURY HISTORY OF ERIE CO. . . ., Vol. I. 1909. 897p.
P5-PA0018A — $98.00.

TWENTIETH CENTURY HISTORY OF ERIE CO. . . ., Vol. II. 1909. 712p.
P5-PA0018B — $78.00.

BIOGRAPHICAL & PORTRAIT CYCLOPEDIA OF FAYETTE CO. 1889. 602p.
P5-PA0151B — $65.00.

GENEALOGICAL & PERSONAL HISTORY OF FAYETTE COUNTY, 3-vol. set. By John W. Jordan & James Hadden. 1912. 3 vols., 922p.
P5-PA0115 — $99.00/set.

GENEALOGICAL & PERSONAL HISTORY OF FAYETTE COUNTY, Vol. I. 1912.
P5-PA0115A — $36.50.

GENEALOGICAL & PERSONAL HISTORY OF FAYETTE COUNTY, Vol. II. 1912.
P5-PA0115B — $36.50.

GENEALOGICAL & PERSONAL HISTORY OF FAYETTE COUNTY, Vol. III. 1912.
P5-PA0115C — $36.50.

HISTORY OF FAYETTE COUNTY, with Biographical Sketches of many of its Prominent Men. By Franklin Ellis. 1882. 841p.
P5-PA0113 — $89.00.

HISTORY OF FORKS TOWNSHIP & FORKSVILLE BOROUGH, Including the Early Settlement, together with Biographical Sketches. By George Streby. 1904. 84p.
P5-PA0202 — $15.00.

BIOGRAPHICAL ANNALS OF FRANKLIN COUNTY. 1905. 706p.
P5-PA0114 — $74.00.

HISTORICAL SKETCH OF FRANKLIN COUNTY. By I.H. M'Cauley. 1878. 294p.
P5-PA0115 — $32.50.

HISTORY OF FRANKLIN COUNTY, Containing a History of the County, its Townships, Towns, etc. . . . & Biographies. By J. F. Richard. 1887. 968p.
P5-PA0078 — $97.00.

ANCIENT & MODERN GERMANTOWN, MOUNT AIRY & CHESTNUT HILL. History & biopgrahical sketches. By S.F. Hotchkin. 1889. 548p.
P5-PA0206 — $59.00.

HISTORY OF OLD GERMAN-TOWN, with a Description of its Settlement & Some Account of its Important Persons, Buildings & Places Connected with its Development. By Dr Naaman H. Keyser, et al. 1907. 453 + 20p.
P5-PA0203 — $51.50.

SETTLEMENT OF GERMAN-TOWN & the Beginning of German Emigration to North America. By Sam'l W. Pennypacker. 1899. 310p.
P5-PA0205 — $41.00.

TENMILE COUNTRY & ITS PIONEER FAMILY [GREEN CO.]: Genealogical history of the Upper Monongahela Valley, Vols. I-VII. Howard L. Leckey. 1950?. 484p.
P5-PA0273 — $49.00.

HISTORY OF GREENE CO. By Samuel P. Bates. 1888. xv + 898p.
P5-PA0058 — $89.50.

HISTORY OF HANOVER TOWN-SHIP, Including Sugar Notch, Ashley & Nanticoke Boroughs: also a History of Wyoming Valley in Luzerne Co. Incl. Genealogical tables for 73 Hanover twp. fams. By H. B. Plumb. 1885. 498p.
P5-PA0023 — $55.00.

HISTORY OF HUNTINGDON & BLAIR COUNTIES. By J. Simpson Africa. 1883. 500+p.
P5-PA0080 — $79.50.

HISTORY OF HUNTINGDON CO., from Earliest Times to the Centennial Anniversary of Amer. Independence. M. S. Lytle. 1876. 360p.
P5-PA0009 — $44.00.

HISTORY OF INDIANA COUNTY, 1745-1880. [The print of this oversized original has been reduced to fit an 8.5 x 11 format, but is clear and legible.] 1880. 543p.
P5-PA0007 — $59.50.

(INDEX TO) HISTORY OF INDIANA CO., 1745-1880. Comp. by Indiana Co. Historical Society. 1993. 52p.
P5-PA0116 — $11.00.

INDIANA COUNTY, Her People, Past & Present, with a Genealogical & Biographical Record of Representative Families, 2-vol. set. By Prof. J.T. Stewart. 1913. 2 vols., 1597p.
P5-PA0207 — $149.50/set.

INDIANA COUNTY, Her People, Past & Present . . ., Vol. I. 1913.
P5-PA0207A — $84.00.

INDIANA COUNTY, Her People, Past & Present . . ., Vol. II. 1913.
P5-PA0207B — $84.00.

JEFFERSON CO., PENNSYL-VANIA: Her Pioneers & People, 1800-1915, 2-vol. set. With modern every-name index (in Vol. II). Wm. J. McKnight. 2 vols., 542 + 701 + 27p.
P5-PA0021 — $127.50/set.

JEFFERSON CO., PENNSYL-VANIA . . ., Vol. I.
P5-PA0021A — $70.00.

JEFFERSON CO., PENNSYL-VANIA . . ., Vol. II. Includes every-name index.
P5-PA0021B — $70.00.

PIONEER HISTORY OF JEFFERSON CO., 1755-1844. By W.J. McKnight. 1898. 670p.
P5-PA0010 — $71.50.

HISTORY OF THE EARLY SETTLEMENT OF THE JUNIATA VALLEY, Embracing an Account of the Early Pioneers. By U.C. Jones. 1855. 440p.
P5-PA0019 — $47.50.

KANE & the Upper Allegheny. By J.E. Henrietta. 1929. 357p.
P5-PA0272 — $44.00.

HISTORY OF THE CERTIFIED TOWNSHIP OF KINGSTON, 1769 to 1929. By Wm. Brewster. 1930. 580p.
P5-PA0276 — $61.50.

CENTENNIAL HISTORY OF KUTZTOWN. Comp. by Committee, W.W. Deatrick, Chairman. 1915. 247p.
P5-PA0208 — $36.50.

JUBILEE HISTORY OF LACKA-WANNA COUNTY: Industrial, Religious, Financial, Educations & Cultural Development of County & Subdivisions, 2-vol. set. By Thomas Murphy. 1928. 2 vols, 1267p.
P5-PA0281 — $119.50/set.

JUBILEE HISTORY OF LACKA-WANNA COUNTY: Industrial, Religious, Financial, Educations & Cultural Development of County & Subdivisions, Vol. I. 1928.
P5-PA0281A — $64.50.

JUBILEE HISTORY OF LACKA-WANNA COUNTY: Industrial, Religious, Financial, Educations & Cultural Development of County & Subdivisions, Vol. II. 1928.
P5-PA0281B — $64.50.

PORTRAIT & BIOGRAPHICAL RECORD OF LACKAWANNA COUNTY, Containing Portraits & Biographical Sketches of Prominent & Representative Citizens of the County. 1897. 1077p.
P5-PA0210 — $105.00.

HISTORY OF LACKAWANNA VALLEY. 5th ed. By H. Hollister. 1885. 549p.
P5-PA0209 — $59.50.

(INDEX TO) HISTORY OF LANCASTER COUNTY (Ellis & Franklin, 1883). 1993. 337 + 12p.
P5-PA0117 — $39.50.

AUTHENTIC HISTORY OF LANCASTER COUNTY in the State of Pennsylvania. By J.I. Mombert. 1869. 617 + 175p.
P5-PA0118 — $79.50.

BIOGRAPHICAL ANNALS OF LANCASTER COUNTY, Containing Biographical & Genealogical Sketches of Prominent & Representative Citizens & Many of the Early Settlers. 1903. 1524p.
P5-PA0212 — $149.00.

BRIEF HISTORY OF LANCASTER COUNTY. By Israel Smith Clare. 1892. 317p.
P5-PA0119 — $36.00.

HISTORY OF LANCASTER CO., To Which is Prefixed a Brief Sketch of the Early History of Pa. By I. Daniel Rupp. 1844. 524p.
P5-PA0059A — $55.00.

HISTORY OF LANCASTER COUNTY, with Biographical Sketches of Many of its Prominent Men & Pioneers. By Franklin Ellis & Samuel Evans. 1883. 1101p.
P5-PA0081 — $105.00.

LANCASTER CO.; Index to the Will Books & Intestate Records, 1729-1850. By E.J. Fulton & B.K. Mylin. 1936. 136p.
P5-PA0100C — $19.00.

LANCASTER COUNTY: A History, 4 vols. in 2 books. 1924. 4 vols. in 2, 1172 + 484p.
P5-PA0211 — $159.00/set.

LANCASTER COUNTY: A History, Book I. 1924. 1172p.
P5-PA0211A — $119.00.

LANCASTER COUNTY: A History, Book II. 1924. 484p.
P5-PA0211B — $60.00.

PORTRAIT & BIOGRAPHICAL RECORD OF LANCASTER COUNTY. 1894. 685p.
P5-PA0120 — $72.50.

BOOK OF BIOGRAPHIES: Biographical Sketches of Leading Citizens of Lawrence County. 1897. 668p.
P5-PA0213 — $71.00.

BIOGRAPHICAL ANNALS OF LEBANON COUNTY, Containing Biographical Sketches of Prominent & Representative Citizens, & of Many of the Early Settled Families. 1904. 772p.,
P5-PA0214 — $81.00.

ANCIENT & HISTORIC LAND-MARKS IN THE LEBANON VALLEY. Rev. P.C. Croll. 1895. 334p.
P5-PA0215 — $41.50.

HISTORY OF THE LEBANON VALLEY IN PENNSYLVANIA. By Dr Hiram H. Shenk. 1930. 373 + 255p.
P5-PA0169 — $68.50/set.

For hardcover versions, see the order form on page v. To order, call 1-888-296-3447.

Pennsylvania, cont.

RELATED FAMILIES FROM THE LEBANON VALLEY [Anspach-Brecht-Breininger-Hickernell-Laucks-Meyer (Moyer)-Schaeffer-Van Hoosen-Womelsdorf-Weiser-Zerbe families]. By Robert L. Laucks. 2002. 424p.
P5-PA1839 — $54.50.

HISTORY OF LEHIGH COUNTY, with a Genealogical & Biographical Record of its Families, 3-vol. set. By Roberts, Stoudt, Krick & Dietrich. 1914. 3 vols., 1101 + 780 + 690p.
P5-PA0122 — $225.00/set.

HISTORY OF LEHIGH COUNTY . . ., Vol. I: History. 1914. 1101p.
P5-PA0122A — $105.00.

HISTORY OF LEHIGH COUNTY . . ., Vol. II: Genealogy & Biography. 1914. 780p.
P5-PA0122B — $72.50.

HISTORY OF LEHIGH COUNTY . . ., Vol. III. 1914. 690p.
P5-PA0122C — $69.00.

HISTORY OF THE COUNTIES OF LEHIGH & CARBON. By Alfred Mathews & A. Hungerford. 1884. 802p.
P5-PA0082 — $82.50.

PORTRAIT & BIOGRAPHICAL RECORD OF LEHIGH, NORTH-AMPTON & CARBON COUNTIES, Containing Biographical Sketches of Prominent & Representative Citizens of the Counties. 1894. 999p.
P5-PA0216 — $99.50.

HISTORIC HOMES & INSTITU-TIONS, & GENEALOGICAL & PERSONAL MEMOIRS OF THE LEHIGH VALLEY, 2-vol. set. Jordan, Breen & Ettinger. 1905. 2 vols., 516 + 528p.
P5-PA0083 — $99.00/set.

HISTORIC HOMES & INSTITU-TIONS . . . OF THE LEHIGH VALLEY, Vol. I. 1905. 516p.
P5-PA0083A — $56.00.

HISTORIC HOMES & INSTITU-TIONS . . . OF THE LEHIGH VALLEY, Vol. II. 1905. 528p.
P5-PA0083B — $56.00.

HISTORIC LOWER MERION & BLOCKLEY. Dora H. Develin. 1922. 131p.
P5-PA0162 — $21.00.

ANNALS OF LUZERNE COUNTY: A Record of Interesting Events, Traditions & Anecdotes from the First Settlement in Wyoming Valley to 1866. By Stewart Pearce. 1866. 564p.
P5-PA0152 — $61.50.

HISTORY OF LUZERNE COUNTY, with Biographical Selections. 1893. 1509p.
P5-PA0060 — $145.00.

HISTORY OF LUZERNE, LACKAWANNA & WYOMING COUNTIES, with Illustrations & Biographical Sketches of some of their Prominent Men & Pioneers. 1880. 540p. + illus.
P5-PA0287 — $75.00.

GENEALOGICAL & PERSONAL HISTORY OF LYCOMING COUNTY, 2-vol. set. Ed. by Emerson Collins & John W. Jordan. 1906. 2 vols., 513 + 560p.
P5-PA0218 — $109.00/set.

GENEALOGICAL & PERSONAL HISTORY OF LYCOMING COUNTY, Vol. I. 1906. 513p.
P5-PA0218A — $57.00.

GENEALOGICAL & PERSONAL HISTORY OF LYCOMING COUNTY, Vol. II. 1906. 560p.
P5-PA0218B — $57.00.

HISTORY OF LYCOMING COUNTY, Including . . . Portraits & Biographies of Pioneers & Representative Citizens, etc. 1892. 1268p.
P5-PA0217 — $123.00.

HISTORY OF LYCOMING COUNTY. With biographical sketches, 2-vol. set. By Col. Thomas W. Lloyd. 1929. 2 vols., 600 + 618p.
P5-PA0123 — $125.00/set.

HISTORY OF LYCOMING COUNTY. With biographical sketches, Vol. I. 1929. 600p.
P5-PA0123A — $65.00.

HISTORY OF LYCOMING COUNTY. With biographical sketches, Vol. II. 1929. 618p.
P5-PA0123B — $65.00.

HISTORY OF THE COUNTIES OF McKEAN, ELK, CAMERON & POTTER, with Biographical Selections. 1890. 1261p.
P5-PA0011 — $126.50.

HISTORY OF MERCER CO., its Past & Present. 1888. 1210p.
P5-PA0012 — $119.00.

TWENTIETH CENTURY HISTORY OF MERCER COUNTY: A Narrative Account of its Historical Progress, its People, & its Principal Interests, 2-vol. set. 1909. 2 vols., 1111p.
P5-PA0219 — $105.00/set.

TWENTIETH CENTURY HISTORY OF MERCER COUNTY . . ., Vol. I. 1909.
P5-PA0219A — $59.00.

TWENTIETH CENTURY HISTORY OF MERCER COUNTY . . ., Vol. II. 1909.
P5-PA0219B — $59.00.

OLD MERCERSBURG [Historical & genealogical sketches]. Woman's Club of Mercersburg. 1912. 215p.
P5-PA0220 — $31.50.

MERION IN THE WELSH TRACT, with Sketches of the twps. of Haverford & Radnor: Hist & Gen. collections concerning the Welsh Barony in the Province of Penn. By Thomas Allen Glenn 1896. 394p.
P5-PA0061 — $43.50.

CHRONICLES OF MIDDLETOWN, Containing a Compilation of Facts, Biographical Sketches, Reminiscences, Anecdotes, etc., Connected with the History of One of the Oldest Towns in Pennsylvania. By C.H. Hutchinson. 1906. 266p.
P5-PA0222 — $36.50.

HISTORY OF MIFFLIN COUNTY, Vol. I [no more published]. By Joseph Cochran. 1879. 422p.
P5-PA0223 — $51.00.

HISTORICAL MAGAZINE OF MONONGAHELA'S OLD HOME COMING WEEK, 1908. Includes a history of the city, as well as reminiscences, illustrations & miscellany. 1908. 267p.
P5-PA0096B — $34.50.

OLD & NEW MONONGAHELA. Includes lengthy sketches of early fams. of the Monongahela Valley. By J. S. Van Voorhis. 1893. 486p.
P5-PA0030 — $37.50.

HISTORY OF MONROE TOWN-SHIP & BOROUGH, 1779-1885, with Biographical Sketches of the Pioneers. By C.F. Heverly. 1885. 209p.
P5-PA0225 — $31.00.

HISTORY OF MONROE TWP. & BOROUGH [by Clement F. Heverly]: Genealogical Index & Abstract. Comp. by R.D. Macafee. 1951?. 69p., typescript.
P5-PA0285 — $14.00.

HISTORY OF MONROE COUNTY. Robert B. Keller. 1927. 500p.
P5-PA0224 — $54.50.

1890 PENNSYLVANIA (MONT-GOMERY COUNTY) Veterans Census Index. By Michael S. Ramage. 2003. 182 + viii p.
P5-PA1837 — $30.00.

BIOGRAPHICAL & PORTRAIT CYCLOPEDIA OF MONT-GOMERY COUNTY. By Samuel T. Wiley. 1895. 652p.
P5-PA0125 — $69.50.

BIOGRAPHICAL ANNALS OF MONTGOMERY COUNTY, 2-vol. set. By Ellwood Roberts. 1904. 2 vols., 544 + 542p.
P5-PA0124 — $105.00/set.

BIOGRAPHICAL ANNALS OF MONTGOMERY COUNTY, Vol. I. 1904. 544p.
P5-PA0124A — $55.00.

BIOGRAPHICAL ANNALS OF MONTGOMERY COUNTY, Vol. II. 1904. 542p.
P5-PA0124B — $55.00.

HISTORY OF MONTGOMERY CO. By T. W. Bean. 1884. 1197 + 98p.
P5-PA0013 — $129.50.

MONTGOMERY COUNTY: A History, 3-vol. set. Clifton S. Hunsicker. 1923. 3 vols. 416 + 340 + 357p.
P5-PA0226 — $120.00/set.

MONTGOMERY COUNTY: A History, Vol. I. 1923. 416p.
P5-PA0226A — $48.00.

MONTGOMERY COUNTY: A History, Vol. II. 1923. 340p.
P5-PA0226B — $40.00.

MONTGOMERY COUNTY: A History, Vol. III. 1923. 357p.
P5-PA0226C — $41.00.

HISTORY OF MOUNT UNION, SHIRLEYSBURG & SHIRLEY TOWNSHIP. By Charles H. Welch. 1909-1910. 752p.
P5-PA0227 — $78.00.

TWENTIETH CENTURY HIS-TORY OF NEW CASTLE & LAWRENCE COUNTY, & Representative Citizens. 1908. 1015p.
P5-PA0063 — $99.00.

DIRECTORY OF THE BOROUGHS OF NORRISTOWN & BRIDGE-PORT, Montgomery Co., for the Years 1860-1, Containing a Concise History of the Boroughs from their First Settlement to [1860], the Names of All the Inhabitants, etc. 1860. 228 + 57p.
P5-PA0229 — $37.00.

GENEALOGICAL INDEX OF THE WILLS OF NORTHAMPTON COUNTY, 1752-1802. 3rd edition. Comp. by John Eyerman. 1925. 111p.
P5-PA0261 — $15.00.

HISTORY OF NORTHAMPTON COUNTY, 1752-1877, with Illustra-tions Descriptive of its Scenery. 1877. 293p.
P5-PA0153 — $39.00.

HISTORY OF NORTHAMPTON, LEHIGH, MONROE, CARBON & SCHUYKILL COUNTIES. By I.D. Rupp. 1845. 568p.
P5-PA0051 — $59.00.

OLD GRAVEYARDS OF NORTHAMPTON & Adjacent Counties. Vol. I, Parts I-VI; Vol. II, Parts I & III. By John Eyerman. 1899. 149 + 121 + 58p.
P5-PA0230 — $32.50.

GENEALOGICAL & BIOGRAPH-ICAL ANNALS OF NORTHUM-BERLAND COUNTY, Containing a Genealogical Record of Representa-tive Families, including Many of the Early Settlers, & Biographical Sketches of Prominent Citizens. 1911. 988p.
P5-PA0231 — $99.50.

HISTORY OF NORTHUMBER-LAND COUNTY. 1891. 1256p.
P5-PA0084 — $109.00.

HISTORY OF OVERTON TOWN-SHIP, 1810-1885, with Biographical Sketches of the Pioneers. With index. By C.F. Heverly. 1885. 82 + 29p. Index.
P5-PA0283 — $17.50.

HISTORY OF PERRY CO., includ-ing Descriptions of Indian & Pioneer Life, from the Time of Earliest Settlement, with Sketches of its Noted Men & Women, and Many Pro-fessional Men. H. H. Hain. 1922. 1088p.
P5-PA0064 — $98.00.

HISTORY OF PERRY COUNTY in Pennsylvania, from the earliest Settlement to the Present Time. By Silas Wright. 1873. 290p.
P5-PA0085 — $34.00.

ANNALS OF PHILADELPHIA & PENNSYLVANIA IN THE OLDEN TIME, Being a Collection of Mem-oirs, Anecdotes & Incidents of the City & its Inhabitants, & of the Ear-liest Settlements of the Inland Part of Pennsylvania, 3-vol. set. By John F. Watson. 1891. 3 vols., 609 + 640 + 524p.
P5-PA0265 — $172.00/set.

ANNALS OF PHILADELPHIA & PENNSYLVANIA IN THE OLDEN TIME . . ., Vol. I. 1891. 609p.
P5-PA0265A — $61.50.

ANNALS OF PHILADELPHIA & PENNSYLVANIA IN THE OLDEN TIME . . ., Vol. II. 1891. 640p.
P5-PA0265B — $61.50.

ANNALS OF PHILADELPHIA & PENNSYLVANIA IN THE OLDEN TIME . . ., Vol. III. 1891. 524p.
P5-PA0265C — $61.50.

BAPTISMS & BURIALS FROM THE RECORDS OF CHRIST CHURCH, Philadelphia, 1709-1760. By C.R. Hildeburn. 1877-1883, 1888-1893. 231p.
P5-PA0031 — $19.50.

HISTORIC MANSIONS & BUILDINGS OF PHILADELPHIA, with some Notices of their Owners & Occupants. Thompson Westcott. 1877. 528p.
P5-PA0263 — $56.50.

HISTORY OF PHILADELPHIA, 1609-1884, 3-vol. set. By A. Thomas Scharf & Thompson Westcott. 1884. 3 vols., 2399p.
P5-PA0266 — $249.00/set.

HISTORY OF PHILADELPHIA, 1609-1884, Vol. I. 1884.
P5-PA0266A — $89.00.

Pennsylvania, cont.

HISTORY OF PHILADELPHIA,
1609-1884, Vol. II. 1884.
P5-PA0266B — $89.00.

HISTORY OF PHILADELPHIA,
1609-1884, Vol. III. 1884.
P5-PA0266C — $89.00.

HISTORY OF THE TOWNSHIPS OF BYBERRY & MORELAND in Philadelphia, from their Earliest Settlements to the Present Time. By Joseph C. Martindale, n.d. 416p.
P5-PA0086 — $46.00.

MEMORIAL HISTORY OF PHILADELPHIA from its First Settlement to the Year 1895, 2-vol. set. 1895-1898. 2 vols.
P5-PA0264 — $109.00/set.

MEMORIAL HISTORY OF PHILADELPHIA from its First Settlement to the Year 1895, Vol. I. 1895-1898.
P5-PA0264A — $60.00.

MEMORIAL HISTORY OF PHILADELPHIA from its First Settlement to the Year 1895, Vol. II. 1895-1898.
P5-PA0264B — $60.00.

PHILADELPHIA & HER MER-CHANTS, as Constituted Fifty to Seventy Years Ago, as Illustrated by Diagrams of the River Front & Portraits of Some of its Prominent Occupants, together with Sketches of Character & Incidents & Anecdotes of the Day. Abraham Ritter. 1860. 223p.
P5-PA0268 — $34.50.

PHILADELPHIA & ITS MANU-FACTURES: A Handbook Exhibiting the Development, Variety & Statistics of the Manufacturing Industry of Philadelphia in 1857, By Edwin T. Freedley. 1859. 504p.
P5-PA0267 — $56.50.

A CENTURY & A HALF OF PITTSBURG & HER PEOPLE, 4-vol. set. 1908. 4 vols., 544 + 539 + 475 + 491p.
P5-PA0232 — $199.00/set.

A CENTURY & A HALF OF PITTSBURG & HER PEOPLE, Vol. I. 1908. 544p.
P5-PA0232A — $54.50.

A CENTURY & A HALF OF PITTSBURG & HER PEOPLE, Vol. II. 1908. 539p.
P5-PA0232B — $54.50.

A CENTURY & A HALF OF PITTSBURG & HER PEOPLE, Vol. III. 1908. 475p.
P5-PA0232C — $54.50.

A CENTURY & A HALF OF PITTSBURG & HER PEOPLE, Vol. IV. 1908. 491p.
P5-PA0232D — $54.50.

HISTORY OF PITTSBURG, PA. 1898. 1074p.
P5-PA1847 — $108.00.

HISTORY OF PITTSBURGH, with a Brief Notice of its Facilities of Communication & other Advantages. By Neville B. Craig. 1851. 312p.
P5-PA0233 — $41.00.

SOCIAL MIRROR: A Character Sketch of the Women of Pittsburg & Vicinity During the First Century. By A.M. Nevin. 1888. 199p.
P5-PA1845 — $32.00.

HIST. SKETCHES OF PLYMOUTH, LUZERNE CO., incl. gen. info. on the founding families. H. B. Wright. 1873. 419 + 46p.
P5-PA0004 — $52.00.

READING & BERKS COUNTY: A History. 1925. 3 vols. in 2, 580 + 455p.
P5-PA0234 — $109.00/set.

HISTORY OF REYNOLDSVILLE & VICINITY, including Winslow Township. Ward C. Elliott. 1922. 100p.
P5-PA0235 — $14.50.

OLD RICHLAND FAMILIES, including Descendants of Edward Roberts, Thomas Roberts, Thomas Lancaster, Peter Lester [et al.]: Historical & Genealogical Data being Derived from the Records of Friends & Other Original Sources. By Ellwood Roberts. 1898. 246p.
P5-PA0236 — $35.00.

BRIEF HISTORY OF SCHAEFFERSTOWN. By A.S. Brendle. 1901. 233p.
P5-PA0237 — $31.50.

BIOGRAPHICAL & PORTRAIT CYCLOPEDIA OF SCHUYLKILL COUNTY, Comprising a Historical Sketch of the County. Over 550 biographical sketches. By S.T. Wiley & H.W. Ruoff. 1893. 752p.
P5-PA0127 — $75.00.

HISTORY OF SCHUYLKILL COUNTY, with Illustrations & Biographical Sketches of some of its Prominent Men & Pioneers. 1881. 390 + 60p.
P5-PA0126 — $49.50.

HALF CENTURY IN SCRANTON [History & reminiscences]. By Benj. H. Throop. 1895. 355p.
P5-PA0239 — $41.50.

HISTORY OF SCRANTON & ITS PEOPLE, Vol. I. By Frederick L. Hitchcock. 1914. 532p.
P5-PA0240 — $57.50.

HISTORY OF SCRANTON & ITS PEOPLE, Vol. II: Biographical Sketches. By Col. Frederick L. Hitchcock. 1914. 695p.
P5-PA0238 — $76.50.

SELINSGROVE CHRONOLOGY: Vol. I, 1700-1850; Vol. II, 1851-1920. Comp. by Wm. M. Schnure. 1918. Two vols. in one book, 150 + 215p.
P5-PA0241 — $46.50.

LIGHTS & SHADOWS OF SEWICKLEY LIFE. By A.L. Ellis. 1893. 316 + ii p.
P5-PA1841 — $44.00.

VILLAGE OF SEWICKLEY. By Franklin Taylor Nevin. 1929. 227p.
P5-PA0271 — $31.00.

HISTORICAL COLLECTIONS OF SHEFFIELD TOWNSHIP, Warren County. Bruce A. Smith. 1943. 565p.
P5-PA0242 — $61.00.

HISTORY OF SHESHEQUIN, 1777-1902, Including . . . Sketches of all the Pioneer Families, Thrilling Incidents of Early Times . . ., her Soldiers, etc. With 1949 index. By C.F. Heverly. 1902. 380 + 56p.
P5-PA0243 — $45.00.

SILVER LAKE TWP. [Susquehanna Co.] Tax Rolls, 1878-1879. Comp. by D.P. Hawley. 1994. 64p.
P5-PA0137 — $13.00.

SOUVENIR HISTORY OF SLIPPERY ROCK. By Rev. George S. Bowden. 1925. 117p. P5-PA0128 — $19.50.

SNYDER COUNTY MARRIAGES, 1835-1899, with Index of Surnames. Comp. by Geo. W. Wagenseller. 1899. 266p. P5-PA0245 — $27.50.

TOMBSTONE INSCRIPTIONS OF SNYDER COUNTY: All Epitaphs taken from the Markers in Every Burying Ground of Snyder County, Complete Record from the Time of Settlement of this Territory by the Pioneers before the Revolutionary War Down to the Year 1904. George W. Wagenseller. 1904. 279p. P5-PA0244 — $37.00.

HISTORY OF SULLIVAN COUNTY, with Biographical Compendium. Thomas J. Ingham. 1899. 239p. P5-PA0246 — $34.50.

EARLY TIMES ON THE SUSQUEHANNA (Athens, Bradford Co.) By Mrs George A. Perkins. 1906. 285p. P5-PA0160 — $37.00.

CENTENNIAL HISTORY OF SUSQUEHANNA COUNTY. By Rhamanthus M. Stocker. 1887. 851p. P5-PA0088 — $87.50.

HISTORY OF SUSQUEHANNA CO., from a Period Preceding its Settlement to Recent Times. By Emily C. Blackman. 1873. 640p. P5-PA0069 — $69.50.

HISTORY OF THAT PART OF THE SUSQUEHANNA & JUNIATA VALLEYS, Embraced In the Counties of Mifflin, Juniata, Perry, Union & Snyder. 1886. 2 vols., 1601p. P5-PA0068 — $125.00.

HISTORY OF TIOGA COUNTY, with Illustrations, Portraits & Sketches of Prominent Families & Individuals. 1883. 366 + 35p. P5-PA0089 — $45.00.

HISTORY OF TIOGA COUNTY. 1897. 1186p. P5-PA0003 — $109.00.

OLD TIOGA & NINETY YEARS OF ITS EXISTENCE: A Descriptive, Statistical & Chronological History of Tioga County from its Earliest Settlement to [1877]. By Maro O. Rolfe. 1877. 116p. P5-PA0247 — $15.00.

HISTORY OF UNIONTOWN, the County Seat of Fayette County. 1913. 824p. P5-PA0065 — $85.00.

HISTORY OF VALLEY FORGE. By Henry Woodman. 1920. 156p. P5-PA0248 — $19.50.

HISTORY OF VENANGO COUNTY & Incidentally of Petroleum, together with Accounts of the Early Settlement & Progress of each Township, Borough & Villagea, with Personal & Biographical Sketches of the Early Settlers, Representative Men, Family Records, etc. 1879. 651p., oversized. P5-PA0290 — $89.00.

HISTORY OF VENANGO COUNTY: Its Past & Present, including its Aboriginal History . . . its Early Settlement & Subsequent Growth . . . its Historic & Interesting Localities . . . Family History, etc. 1890. 1164p. P5-PA0066 — $108.50.

VENANGO COUNTY, Her Pioneers & People, 2-vol. set. 1919. 2 vols., 560 + 572p. P5-PA0130 — $105.00/set.
VENANGO COUNTY, Her Pioneers & People, Vol. I. 1919. 560p. P5-PA0130A — $55.00.

VENANGO COUNTY, Her Pioneers & People, Vol. II. 1919. 527p. P5-PA0130B — $55.00.

BOOK OF BIOGRAPHIES: Biographical Sketches of Leading Citizens of the 37th Judicial District [Warren Co.]. 1899. 609p. P5-PA0249 — $67.00.

HISTORY OF WARREN CO., with Illustrations & Biogr. Sketches of Some of its Prominent Men & Pioneers. 1887. 807p. P5-PA0070 — $82.00.

20TH CENTURY HISTORY OF THE CITY OF WASHINGTON & WASHINGTON CO., & Representative Citizens. A Comprehensive history of the city & county, with over 800 pages of biography. By Joseph F. McFarland. 1910. 1369p. P5-PA0095 — $125.00.

COMMEMORATIVE BIOGRAPHICAL RECORD OF WASHINGTON COUNTY, Containing Biographical Sketches of Prominent & Representative Citizens & Many of the Early Settled Families. 1893. 1486p. P5-PA0094 — $137.50.

HISTORY OF WASHINGTON COUNTY From its First Settlement. By Alfred Creigh. 1870. 386 + 121p. P5-PA0022 — $53.50.

HISTORY OF WASHINGTON COUNTY, with Biographical Sketches of Many of its Pioneers & Prominent Men. 1882. 1002p. P5-PA0090 — $94.50.

SOME PIONEERS OF WASHINGTON COUNTY: A Family History. By F.S. Reader. 1902. 154p. P5-PA0250 — $19.00.

CENTENNIAL & ILLUSTRATED WAYNE COUNTY: Historical, Biographical, Industrial, Picturesque . . . 1900. xii + 152p. P5-PA0251 — $27.00.

HISTORY OF WAYNE, PIKE & MONROE COUNTIES. By Alfred Mathews. 1886. 1283p. P5-PA0131 — $119.50.

WAYNESBORO: History of s Settlement in the County Formerly Called Cumberland . . . in its Beginnings through its Growth. By Benj. M. Nead. 1900. 427p. P5-PA0252 — $47.00.

HISTORY OF THE COUNTY OF WESTMORELAND, with Biographical Sketches of its Many Pioneers & Prominent Men. 1882. 496p. P5-PA0154 — $55.00.

HISTORY OF WESTMORELAND COUNTY, Part One. P5-PA0189A — $32.50.

HISTORY OF WESTMORELAND COUNTY, Part Two: Local History of Boroughs & Towns. 230p. P5-PA0189B — $32.50.

Pennsylvania, cont.

HISTORY OF WESTMORELAND COUNTY, 3-vol. set (in 2 books). By John N. Boucher & John W. Jordan. 1906. 3 vols. in 2, 678 + 1308p.
P5-PA0132 — $189.50/set.

HISTORY OF WESTMORELAND COUNTY, Vol. I: History. 1906. 678p.
P5-PA0132A — $68.00.

HISTORY OF WESTMORELAND COUNTY, Vols. II & III: Genealogy. 1906. 1308p.
P5-PA0132B — $127.50.

OLD & NEW WESTMORELAND [County]. 4-vol. set. By John N. Boucher. 1918. 4 vols., 581 + 665 + 622 + 749p.
P5-PA0253 — $229.00/set.
OLD & NEW WESTMORELAND [County], Vol. I. 1918. 581p.
P5-PA0253A — $66.00.

OLD & NEW WESTMORELAND [County], Vol. II. 1918. 665p.
P5-PA0253B — $66.00.

OLD & NEW WESTMORELAND [County], Vol. III. 1918. 622p.
P5-PA0253C — $66.00.

OLD & NEW WESTMORELAND [County], Vol. IV. 1918. 749p.
P5-PA0253D — $66.00.

WILKES-BARRE (The "Diamond City"), Luzerne County: its History, its Natural Resources, its Industries, 1769-1906. 1906. 160p.
P5-PA0254 — $20.00.

ANNALS OF OLD WILKINSBURG & Vicinity, the Village, 1788-1888. With index. 1940. 549 + 6p.
P5-PA0155 — $59.50.

HISTORY OF THE FIRST 100 YEARS IN WOOLRICH, 1830-1930. By M.B. Rich. 1930. 233p.
P5-PA0275 — $32.50.

FAMILIES OF THE WYOMING VALLEY, with Biographical, Genealogical & Historical Sketches of the Bench & Bar of Luzerne County. By George B. Kulp. 1885. 3 vols., 1423p.
P5-PA0133 — $135.00.

GENEALOGICAL & FAMILY HISTORY of the Wyoming & Lackawanna Valleys, 2-vol. set. 1906. 2 vols., 582 + 627p.
P5-PA0156B — $119.50/set.

GENEALOGICAL & FAMILY HISTORY of the Wyoming & Lackawanna Valleys, Vol. I. 1906. 582p.
P5-PA0156B1 — $67.00.

GENEALOGICAL & FAMILY HISTORY of the Wyoming & Lackawanna Valleys, Vol. II. 1906. 627p.
P5-PA0156B2 — $67.00.

STORY OF A DYNAMIC COMMUNITY: York, Pennsylvania. By Betty Peckham. 1945?. 257p.
P5-PA0161 — $27.50.

HISTORY OF YORK COUNTY, from the Earliest Period to the Present Time . . . With a Biographical Department Appended. 1886. 772 + 207p.
P5-PA0091 — $98.00.

HISTORY OF YORK COUNTY. With modern subject index, 2-vol. set. By George R. Prowell. 1907. 2 vols., 1118 + 1058.
P5-PA0092 — $195/set.

HISTORY OF YORK COUNTY . . ., Vol. I. 1907. 1118p.
P5-PA0092A — $110.00.

HISTORY OF YORK COUNTY . . ., Vol. II. 1907. 1058p.
P5-PA0092B — $108.00.

Rhode Island

A NEW ENGLAND CHILDHOOD [Rhode Island]. By Dorothy Crandall Bliss. 1997. 64 + 30p.
P5-RI0062 — $17.50.

ANCESTRY OF 33 RHODE ISLANDERS, Born in the 18th century; also 27 Charts of Roger Williams' Desc. to the 5th Generation. By J. O. Austin. 1889. 139p.
P5-RI0014 — $17.00.

BIOGRAPHICAL CYCLOPEDIA OF REPRESENTATIVE MEN OF RHODE ISLAND. With many portraits. 1881. 589p. + portraits.
P5-RI0035 — $69.50.

CENSUS OF THE INHABITANTS OF THE COLONY OF RHODE ISLAND & PROVIDENCE PLANTATIONS, taken in the Year 1774. 1854, 1858. 238 + 120p.
P5-RI0013 — $39.00.

CIVIL & MILITARY LIST OF RHODE ISLAND, 1647-1800: A List of All Officers Elected by the General Assembly from the Organization of the Legislative Government of the Colony to 1800. Comp. by Joseph Jencks Smith. 1900. 659p.
P5-RI0036 — $68.00.

CIVIL & MILITARY LIST OF RHODE ISLAND, 1800-50: A List of All Officers Elected by the General Assembly from 1800 to 1850; also All Officers in Revolutionary War, Appointed by Continental Congress, and in the Regular Army & Navy to 1850. Comp. by Joseph Jencks Smith. 1901. 799p.
P5-RI0037 — $81.50.

EARLY RHODE ISLAND HOUSES: An Historical & Architectural Study. By Norman M. Isham & Albert F. Brown. 1895. 100 + 59p.
P5-RI0034A — $22.50.

GENEALOGICAL DICTIONARY OF RHODE ISLAND, Comprising Three Generations of Settlers who Came before 1690. With many families carried to the 4th gen. By J.O. Austin. 1887. 446p.
P5-RI0020 — $51.00.

INDEX TO THE CIVIL & MILITARY LISTS OF RHODE ISLAND: Two Vols. in One, Giving Christian & Families Names; also, Additional Indexes of Both Vols. 1907. 182p.
P5-RI0072 — $27.00.

NAMES OF OFFICERS, SOLDIERS & SEAMEN in Rhode Island Regiments Belonging to the State of Rhode Island & Serving in the Regiments of Other States & in the Regular Army & Navy of the U.S. who Lost Their Lives in . . . the Late Rebellion. 1869. 32p.
P5-RI0038 — $10.00.

NARRAGANSETT PLANTERS: A Study of Causes. Edward Channing. 1886. 23p.
P5-RI0040 — $10.00.

ONE-HUNDRED & SIXTY ALLIED FAMILIES. J. O. Austin. 1893. 309p.
P5-RI0006 — $29.50.

RECORDS OF THE COLONY OF RHODE ISLAND AND PROVI-DENCE PLANTATIONS IN NEW ENGLAND, Vol. I. By John Russell Bartlett 1856. x + 549p
P28301000 — $84.00.

RECORDS OF THE COLONY OF RHODE ISLAND AND PROVI-DENCE PLANTATIONS IN NEW ENGLAND, Vol. II. By John Russell Bartlett 1857. 609p.
P28030200 — $95.00.

RECORDS OF THE PROPRIE-TORS OF THE NARRAGANSETT, otherwise called the "Fones Record." These records are the very valuable Land Evidences of the founders & settlers of Rhode Island. 1894. 199p.
P5-RI0016 — $21.50.

REPRESENTATIVE MEN & OLD FAMILIES OF RHODE ISLAND: Genealogical Records & Historical Sketches of Prominent & Represen-tative Citizens & of Many of the Old Families, 3-vol. set. 1908. 3 vols., 2336p.
P5-RI0041 — $219.50/set.

REPRESENTATIVE MEN & OLD FAMILIES OF RHODE ISLAND . . ., Vol. I. 1908.
P5-RI0041A — $81.00.

REPRESENTATIVE MEN & OLD FAMILIES OF RHODE ISLAND . . ., Vol. II. 1908.
P5-RI0041B — $81.00.

REPRESENTATIVE MEN & OLD FAMILIES OF RHODE ISLAND . . ., Vol. III. 1908.
P5-RI0041C — $81.00.

RHODE ISLAND IN THE COLO-NIAL WARS: List of R.I. Soldiers & Sailors in King George's War, 1740-1748; and List of R.I. Soldiers & Sailors in the Old French & Indian War, 1755-1762. H.M. Chapin. 1918, 1920. 193p.
P5-RI0032B — $31.00.

RHODE ISLAND: ITS MAKING AND ITS MEANING. A Survey of the Annals of the Commonwealth from its Settlement to the Death of Roger Williams, By Irving Bernine Richman 1902. 564 + vx p.
P5-RI0078 — $68.00.

RHODE ISLAND: Three Centuries of Democracy. Vol. I History. Charles Carroll. 1932. 598 + 57p.
P5-RI0079 — $65.00.

RHODE ISLAND: Three Centuries of Democracy. Vol. II, History. Charles Carroll. 1932. 618 + 37p.
P5-RI0080 — $65.00.

RHODE ISLAND: Three Centuries of Democracy. Vol. III, Biographical. Charles Carroll. 1932. 272 + 62p.
P5-RI0081 — $40.00.

RHODE ISLAND: Three Centuries of Democracy. Vol. IV, Biographical. Charles Carrol. 1932. 319 + 80p.
P5-RI0082 — $45.00.

SPIRIT OF '76 IN RHODE ISLAND, or Sketches of the Efforts of the Gov-ernment and People in the War of the Revolution, together with the names of those who belonged to R.I. regiments in the army, with biogr. notices, etc. Benj. Cowell. 1850. 560p.
P5-RI0032A — $58.00.

STATE OF RHODE ISLAND & PROVIDENCE PLANTATIONS at the end of the [20th] century: A history, 3-vol. set. 1902. 3 vols., 674 + 696 + 708p.
P5-RI0077 — $165.00/set.

STATE OF RHODE ISLAND & PROVIDENCE PLANTATIONS . . ., Vol. I. 1902. 674p.
P5-RI0077A — $72.00.

STATE OF RHODE ISLAND & PROVIDENCE PLANTATIONS . . ., Vol. II. 1902. 696p.
P5-RI0077B — $72.00.

STATE OF RHODE ISLAND & PROVIDENCE PLANTATIONS . . ., Vol. III. 1902. 708p.
P5-RI0077C — $72.00.

TOWN GOVERNMENT IN RHODE ISLAND [Brief history of the development of town organi-zation in Rhode Island]. By Wm. E. Foster. 1886. 36p.
P5-RI0042 — $10.00.

VITAL RECORDS OF RHODE ISLAND, 1636-1850 (THE ARNOLD COLLECTION), Vols. I-XXI. By James N. Arnold 1891-1912. 11,936p+
P28322200 — $1,900.00/set.

VITAL RECORDS OF RHODE ISLAND, 1636-1850 (THE ARNOLD COLLECTION), Vol. I: Kent County. 1891-1912. xxxvii + 601p.
P28320100 — $99.00.

VITAL RECORDS OF RHODE ISLAND, 1636-1850 (THE ARNOLD COLLECTION), Vol. II: Providence County. 1891-1912. xlii + 397p.
P28320200 — $71.00.

VITAL RECORDS OF RHODE ISLAND, 1636-1850 (THE ARNOLD COLLECTION), Vol. III: Provi-dence County. 1891-1912. xxxix + 443p.
P28320300 — $77.00.

VITAL RECORDS OF RHODE ISLAND, 1636-1850 (THE ARNOLD COLLECTION), Vol. IV: Newport County. 1891-1912. xxxvi + 655p.
P28320400 — $107.00.

VITAL RECORDS OF RHODE ISLAND, 1636-1850 (THE ARNOLD COLLECTION), Vol. V: Wash-ington County. 1891-1912. xxx + 503p.
P28320500 — $85.00.

VITAL RECORDS OF RHODE ISLAND, 1636-1850 (THE ARNOLD COLLECTION), Vol. VI: Bristol County. 1891-1912. xviii + 309p.
P28320600 — $53.00.

VITAL RECORDS OF RHODE ISLAND, 1636-1850 (THE ARNOLD COLLECTION), Vol. VII: Friends and Ministers. 1891-1912. xlv + 634p.
P28320700 — $105.00.

VITAL RECORDS OF RHODE ISLAND, 1636-1850 (THE ARNOLD COLLECTION), Vol. VIII: Episcopal and Congregational. 1891-1912. xlvi + 631p.
P28320800 — $105.00.

VITAL RECORDS OF RHODE ISLAND, 1636-1850 (THE ARNOLD COLLECTION), Vol. IX: Seekonk (Including East Providence, Paw-tucket, and Newman Congregational Church). 1891-1912. xxxviii + 596p.
P28320900 — $99.00.

VITAL RECORDS OF RHODE ISLAND, 1636-1850 (THE ARNOLD COLLECTION), Vol. X: Town and Church. 1891-1912. xlix + 590p.
P28321000 — $95.00.

For hardcover versions, see the order form on page v. To order, call 1-888-296-3447.

Rhode Island, cont.

VITAL RECORDS OF RHODE ISLAND, 1636-1850 (THE ARNOLD COLLECTION), Vol. XI: Church Records. 1891-1912. xlviii + 590p.
P28321100 — $99.00.

VITAL RECORDS OF RHODE ISLAND, 1636-1850 (THE ARNOLD COLLECTION), Vol. XII: Revolutionary Rolls and News-papers. 1891-1912. cv + 616pp.
P28321200 — $111.00.

VITAL RECORDS OF RHODE ISLAND, 1636-1850 (THE ARNOLD COLLECTION), Vol. XIII: News-papers. 1891-1912. lxxxv + 542p.
P28321300 — $98.00.

VITAL RECORDS OF RHODE ISLAND, 1636-1850 (THE ARNOLD COLLECTION), Vol. XIV: News-papers. 1891-1912. ci + 616p.
P28321400 — $110.00.

VITAL RECORDS OF RHODE ISLAND, 1636-1850 (THE ARNOLD COLLECTION), Vol. XV: News-papers. 1891-1912. lxxv + 577p.
P28321500 — $101.00.

VITAL RECORDS OF RHODE ISLAND, 1636-1850 (THE ARNOLD COLLECTION), Vol. XVI: Newspapers. 1891-1912. lxiv + 601p.
P28321600 — $103.00.

VITAL RECORDS OF RHODE ISLAND, 1636-1850 (THE ARNOLD COLLECTION), Vol. XVII: Newspapers. 1891-1912. lxxii + 599p.
P28321700 — $104.00.

VITAL RECORDS OF RHODE ISLAND, 1636-1850 (THE ARNOLD COLLECTION), Vol. XVIII: News-papers. 1891-1912. ci + 608p.
P28321800 — $109.00.

VITAL RECORDS OF RHODE ISLAND, 1636-1850 (THE ARNOLD COLLECTION), Vol. XIX: News-papers. 1891-1912. xcv + 601p.
P28321900 — $107.00

VITAL RECORDS OF RHODE ISLAND, 1636-1850 (THE ARNOLD COLLECTION), Vol. XX: News-papers. 1891-1912. xcvii + 640p.
P28322000 — $113.00.

VITAL RECORDS OF RHODE ISLAND, 1636-1850 (THE ARNOLD COLLECTION), Vol. XXI: News-papers. 1891-1912. cvii + 607p
P28322100 — $110.00.

WILLIAM CODDINGTON IN R.I. COLONIAL AFFAIRS: an Historical Inquiry. (No. 4, R.I. Hist. Tracts). Dr Henry E. Turner. 1878. 66p.
P5-RI0074 — $14.00.

HISTORY OF BARRINGTON. By Thomas Williams Bicknell. 1898. 619p.
P5-RI0025 — $64.50.

SOWAMS: with Ancient Records of Sowams & Parts Adjacent [Barrington]. By Thos. W. Bicknell. 1908. 204p.
P5-RI0043 — $31.00.

BLOCK ISLAND: I, Map & Guide; II, History. By Rev. S.T. Livermore. 1893. 137p.
P5-RI0044 — $19.00.

OLD CEMETERY AT BLOCK ISLAND. Comp. by Helen W. Mansfield. 1950? 101p.
P5-RI0067 — $15.00.
COPIES OF INSCRIPTIONS TAKEN FROM GRAVESTONES IN BRISTOL. Comp. by Oscar Frank Stetson. 1934?. 81p.
P5-RI0068 — $14.50.

HISTORY OF BRISTOL: The Story of the Mount Hope Lands, from the Visit of the Northmen to the Present Time. By W. H. Munro. 1880. 396p.
P5-RI0005 — $47.00.

SKETCHES OF OLD BRISTOL. By Charles O.F. Thompson. 1942. 418 + 26p.
P5-RI0045 — $50.00.

BURRILLVILLE: As it Was, & As it Is. By Horace A. Keach. 1856. 170p.
P5-RI0047 — $27.00.

CHARLESTOWN IN THE Mid-19th Century, as Seen Through the Eyes of "Uncle Phineas" (Nelson Byron Vars). Comp. & ed. by Earl P. Crandall. 1992. 79p.
P5-RI0033 — $16.00.

FIVE FAMILIES OF CHARLES-TOWN (Bliven, Crandall, Macomber, Money, Taylor families), with Appen-dix. Earl P. Crandall. 1993. 165 + 120p.
P5-RI0026 — $41.00.

HISTORICAL SKETCH OF THE TOWN CHARLESTOWN, from 1636 to 1876. By Wm. Franklin Tucker. 1877. 88p.
P5-RI0048 — $17.00.

HISTORY OF EAST GREEN-WICH, 1677-1960, with Related Genealogy. By Martha R. McPartland. Illus. by S.J. Hoxie. 1960. 300p.
P5-RI0063A — $39.50.

HISTORY OF THE TOWN OF EAST GREENWICH & ADJA-CENT TERRITORY, 1677-1877, By D.H. Greene. 1877. 263p.
P5-RI0001 — $32.50.

HISTORICAL SKETCH OF THE TOWN OF HOPKINTON, 1757-1876. By S.S. Griswold. 1876. 93p.
P5-RI0027 — $18.00.

DR JOSEPH TORREY & HIS RECORD BOOK OF MARRIAGES [Kingstown; 1736-1783]. By Wm. Davis Miller. 1925. 24p.
P5-RI0065 — $10.00.

LAFAYETTE: A Few Phases of its History from the Ice Age to the Atomic. George W. Gardiner. 1949. 267p.
P5-RI0028 — $35.00.

(Thomas Hazard, Son of Rob, Called College Tom) STUDY OF LIFE IN NARRAGANSETT in the Eighteenth Century. By Caroline Hazard. 1893. 324 + 18p.
P5-RI0083 — $35.00.

NARRAGANSETT FRIENDS' MEETING in the XVIII Century, with a Chapter on Quaker Begin-nings in R.I. Caroline Hazard. 1899. 197p.
P5-RI0017 — $21.00.

EARLY RECOLLECTIONS OF NEWPORT, from 1793 to 1811. By G. G. Channing. 1868. 284p.
P5-RI0002 — $31.00.

NEWPORT, Illustrated: a Series of Pen & Pencil Sketches by the Editor of "The Newport Mercury." 1854. 110p.
P5-RI0049 — $16.00.

REMINISCENCES OF NEWPORT. A charming history of Newport as a "watering-place," from the earliest days as a vacation spot. By George C. Mason. 1884. 407p.
P5-RI0009 — $44.00.

HISTORY OF NEWPORT
COUNTY. 1888. 1060p.
P5-RI0010 — $99.00.

HISTORICAL SKETCH OF THE
TOWN OF PAWTUCKET. By
Massena Goodrich. 1876. 189p.
P5-RI0052 — $28.50.

ILLUSTRATED HISTORY OF
PAWTUCKET, CENTRAL FALLS
& VICINITY: Narrative of the
Growth & Evolution of the Com-
munity. By Robert Grieve. 1897. 509p.
P5-RI0051 — $57.00.

EARLY RECORDS OF THE
TOWN OF PORTSMOUTH. 1901.
462p.
P5-RI0015 — $49.50.

HISTORY OF PORTSMOUTH,
1638-1936. Edward H. West. 1936. 65p.
P5-RI0071 — $12.50.

[Indexes to] EARLY TOWN REC-
ORDS, from 4th & 5th Reports of the
Record Commissioners. 1895-7. 228 +
155p.
P5-RI0076 — $37.50.

ACCOUNT OF THE ENGLISH
HOMES OF THREE EARLY
"PROPRIETORS" OF PROVI-
DENCE, Wm. Arnold, Stukeley
Westcott & Wm. Carpenter. By Fred
A. Arnold. 1921. 43p.
P5-RI0055 — $9.00.

ALPHABETICAL INDEX TO
BIRTHS Recorded in Providence
from 1851-1870. Gives vol. & page of
city records where birth is recorded
for 29,768 births. By Edwin M. Snow.
1882. 615p.
P5-RI0022 — $59.50.

ALPHABETICAL INDEX TO
MARRIAGES Recorded in Providence from 1851-1870. Gives vol. &
page of city records where marriage
is recorded for 13,135 marriages. By
Edwin M. Snow. 1880. 547p.
P5-RI0021 — $58.00.

ANNALS OF CENTERDALE in the
Town of North Providence: its Past
& Present, 1636-1909. By Frank C.
Angell. 1909. 196p.
P5-RI0050 — $29.00.

ANNALS OF THE TOWN OF
PROVIDENCE from its First
Settlement to June, 1832. By William
R. Staples. 1843. 670p.
P5-RI0020 — $69.50.

CIVIC AND ARCHITECTURAL
DEVELOPMENT OF PROVI-
DENCE, 1636-1950. By John Hutchins
Cady. 1957. 320p.
P5-RI0073 — $46.00.

HOME LOTS OF THE EARLY
SETTLERS OF THE PROVI-
DENCE PLANTAIONS, with Notes
& Plats. By Charles Wyman Hopkins.
1886. 78p.
P5-RI0053 — $15.00.

INDEX TO THE PROBATE
RECORDS OF THE MUNICIPAL
COURT OF THE CITY OF Provi-
dence, Rhode Island, 1646-1899 By
Edward Field 1902. 355p.
P28361500 — $57.00.

NAMES OF THE OWNERS OR
OCCUPANTS OF BUILDINGS IN
THE TOWN OF PROVIDENCE,
1749-1771. 1870. 25p.
P5-RI0064 — $10.00.

OWNERS & OCCUPANTS of the
Lots, Houses & Shops in the Town
of Providence in 1798. With Maps of
Providence, 1650-1765-1770. By Henry
R. Chace. 1914. 47 + 19p.
P5-RI0054 — $12.00.

PROVIDENCE BIRTHS, 1871 TO
1880, Inclusive. (Vol. IX, Alphabetical
Index of the Births, Marriages &
Deaths) Charles V. Chapin, MD. 1903.
545p.
P5-RI0046 — $59.00.

PROVIDENCE DEATHS From 1851
to 1870, Inclusive. Vol. III, Alphabetical Index of the Births, marriages
and Deaths Recorded in Providence.
By Edwin M. Snow, MD. 1881. 627p.
P5-RI0034B — $67.00.

PROVIDENCE IN COLONIAL
TIMES. By Gertrude S. Kimball. 1912.
392p. + illus,
P5-RI0011 — $45.00.

VITAL RECORDS OF PROVI-
DENCE, RHODE ISLAND, Vols. I-
IV. By Edwin M. Snow 1879-1882. 599
+ 547 + 627 + 615p
P28360500 — $340.00/set.

VITAL RECORDS OF PROVI-
DENCE, RHODE ISLAND Vol. I:
Births, Marriages, Deaths, 1636-1850.
By Edwin M. Snow 1879-1882. 599p
P28360100 — $94.00.

VITAL RECORDS OF PROVI-
DENCE, RHODE ISLAND, Vol. II:
Marriage, 1851-1870. By Edwin M.
Snow 1879-1882. 547p.
P28360200 — $87.00.

VITAL RECORDS OF PROVI-
DENCE, RHODE ISLAND, Vol.
III: Deaths, 1851-1870. By Edwin M.
Snow 1879-1882. 627p.
P28360300 — $98.00.

VITAL RECORDS OF PROVI-
DENCE, RHODE ISLAND, Vol.
IV: Births, 1851-1870. By Edwin M.
Snow 1879-1882. 615p.
P28360400 — $96.00.

HISTORY OF PROVIDENCE
COUNTY, 2-vol. set. 1891. 2 vols.,
821 + 639p.
P5-RI0018 — $135.00/set.

HISTORY OF PROVIDENCE
COUNTY, Vol. I
1891. 821p.
P5-RI0018A — $84.00.

HISTORY OF PROVIDENCE
COUNTY, Vol. II
1891. 639p.
P5-RI0018B — $69.00.

OLD REHOBOTH CEMETERY
. . . at East Providence, New
Newman's Church. #IX. Comp. by
Marion Pearce Carter. 1932. 58p.
P5-RI0070 — $12.00.

HISTORICAL SKETCH OF THE
TOWN OF RICHMOND, from 1747
to 1876, Comprising a Period of One
Hundred and Twenty-Nine Years. By
James R. Irish. 1877. 96p.
P5-RI0226 — $18.00.

HISTORY OF THE TOWN OF
SMITHFIELD, from its Organi-
zation in 1730 to its Division in 1871.
By T. Steere. 1881. 230p.
P5-RI0003 — $29.00.

COMPLETE CEMETERY INSCRIP-
TIONS OF TIVERTON. Comp. by
Durfee, Wilbour & Sprague. 1953-1954.
128p
P5-RI0066 — $16.00.

For hardcover versions, see the order form on page v. To order, call 1-888-296-3447.

Rhode Island, cont.

HILLSIDE CEMETERY, TIVERTON [Inscriptions]. Comp. by Mrs Hengry Durfee. 1937. 32p.
P5-RI0069 — $10.00.

HISTORY OF WARREN in the War of the Revolution, 1776-1783. By Virginia Baker. 1901. 68p.
P5-RI0056 — $14.50.

EARLY RECORDS OF THE TOWN OF WARWICK. 1926. 361p.
P5-RI0029 — $42.00.

HISTORY OF WARWICK, Settlement in 1642 to the Present Time; including Accounts of the Early Settlement & Development of its Several Villages; Sketches of the Origin & Progress of the Different Churches, &c., &c. By Oliver Payson Fuller. 1875. 380p.
P5-RI0057 — $44.00.

SAMUELL GORTON: Forgotten Founder of our Liberties, First Settler of Warwick. Lewis G. Janes. 1896. 141p.
P5-RI0058 — $18.50.

HISTORY OF WASHINGTON & KENT COUNTIES. By J.R. Cole. 1889. 1324p.
P5-RI0030 — $129.50.

VITAL RECORD OF [WEST GREENWICH], 1636-1850: Births, Marriages & Deaths. By James N. Arnold. 1891. 109p.
P5-RI0059 — $15.00.

THE TOWN THAT SAVED A STATE: WESTERLY. By Mary Agnes Best. 1943. 283p.
P5-RI0063B — $36.50.

VITAL RECORDS OF [WESTERLY], 1636-1850: Births, Marriages & Deaths. By James N. Arnold. 1894. 152p.
P5-RI0060 — $21.00.

WESTERLY & ITS WITNESSES, for Two Hundred & Fifty Years, 1626-1876, Including Charlestown, Hopkinton & Richmond until their Separate Organization. With index by Sallie E. Coy. By Frederic Denison. 1878. 314 + 28p.
P5-RI0031 — $37.00.

DEBUTS DE LA COLONIE FRANCO-AMERICAINE de Woonsocket [French Settlers of Woonsocket]. IN FRENCH. By Marie Louise Bonier. 1920. 342p.
P5-RI0061 — $41.00.

HISTORY OF WOONSOCKET. By E. Richardson. 1876. 264p.
P5-RI0007 — $34.50.

South Carolina

HISTORY OF SOUTH CAROLINA, 4-vol. set. By David Duncan Wallace. 1934.
P5-SC0021 — $229.00/set.
HISTORY OF SOUTH CAROLINA, Vol. I. 1934.
P5-SC0021A — $61.00.

HISTORY OF SOUTH CAROLINA, Vol. II. 1934.
P5-SC0021B — $61.00.

HISTORY OF SOUTH CAROLINA, Vol. III. 1934.
P5-SC0021C — $61.00.

HISTORY OF SOUTH CAROLINA, Vol. IV. 1934.
P5-SC0021D — $61.00.

INDEX TO COUNTY WILLS OF SOUTH CAROLINA, Containing Index of each County Will Book, except Charleston County. Comp. by M.L. Houston. 1939. 261p.
P5-SC0009 — $29.00.

MARRIAGE NOTICES IN THE S.C. & AMERICAN GENERAL GAZETTE, from May, 1766, to February, 1781, & in its Successor, The Royal Gazette (1781-1782). Comp. by A.S. Salley, Jr. 1914. 52p.
P5-SC0007 — $10.00.

MARRIAGE NOTICES in the SOUTH-CAROLINA GAZETTE, & its Successors (1732-1801). 1902. 174p.
P5-SC0012 — $19.50.

ORIGINAL INDEX BOOK SHOWING REVOLUTIONARY CLAIMS FILED IN S.C between Aug. 20, 1783, & Aug.31, 1786. By J. Revill. 1941. 387p.
P5-SC0002 — $35.00.

SOUTH CAROLINA BAPTISTS, 1670-1805. Leah Townsend. 1935. 391p.
P5-SC0005 — $39.00.

WARRANTS FOR LANDS IN SOUTH CAROLINA, 1672-1711, 3-vol. set in 1 book. By A.S. Salley, Jr. 1910-1915. 3 vols, 222 + 226 + 264p.
P5-SC0019 — $65.00/set.

WARRANTS FOR LANDS IN SOUTH CAROLINA, 1672-1711, Vol. I. 1910-1915. 222p.
P5-SC0019A — $25.00.

WARRANTS FOR LANDS IN SOUTH CAROLINA, 1672-1711, Vol. II. 1910-1915. 226p.
P5-SC0019B — $25.00.

WARRANTS FOR LANDS IN SOUTH CAROLINA, 1672-1711, Vol. III. 1910-1915. 264p.
P5-SC0019C — $25.00.

NINETY YEARS IN AIKEN COUNTY: Memories of Aiken County & its People. By Gasper Loren Toole, II. 1959. 404p.
P5-SC0010 — $44.50.

TRADITIONS & HISTORY OF ANDERSON COUNTY. By Louise A. Vandiver. 1928. 318p.
P5-SC0020 — $38.00.

CAMDEN DEATHS & MAR-RIAGES, 1822-1871. Comp. by Janie Revill. 1933-1935. 149p., typescript
P5-SC0023 — $19.50.

HISTORIC CAMDEN: Part II, Nineteenth Century. By Thomas J. Kirkland & Robt. M. Kennedy. 1926. 485p.
P5-SC0013 — $54.50.

CENSUS OF THE CITY OF CHARLESTON, for the Year 1848, Exhibiting the Condition & Prospects of the City. By J.L. Dawson & H.W. SeSaussure. 1849. 262p.
P5-SC0016A — $34.00.

CHARLESTON, SOUTH CAROLINA, 1670-1883: The Centennial of Incorporation. 1883. 259p. + 9 foldout maps.
P5-SC0015 — $39.50.

MARRIAGE NOTICES IN THE CHARLESTON COURIER, 1803-1808. Comp. by A.S. Salley, Jr. 1919. 83p.
P5-SC0001 — $15.00.

REGISTER OF ST PHILIPS, Charles Town, 1720-1758. 1904. 355p. P5-SC0003 — $39.00.

SIEGE OF CHARLESTON by the British Fleet & Army under the Command of Admiral Arbuthnot & Sir Henry Clinton. 1867. 223p. P5-SC0017 — $31.50.

HISTORY OF EDGEFIELD COUNTY, from the Earliest Settlements to 1897, Biographical & Anecdotal. Incl. Saluda Co., which separated from Edgefield. By John A. Chapman. 1897. 521 + 6p. P5-SC0006 — $55.00.

HISTORY OF FAIRFIELD COUNTY, From "Before the White Man Came" to 1942. By Fitz Hugh McMaster. 1946. 220p. P5-SC0018 — $31.00.

Marion Churches & Churchmen, 1735-1935. By V.B. Stanley, Jr. 1938. 109 + 4p. P5-SC0024 — $22.00.

HISTORY OF MARION COUNTY, from its Earliest Times to the Present, 1901. With family sketches. By W.W. Sellers. 1902. 647p. P5-SC0004 — $68.00.

HISTORY OF MARLBORO COUNTY, with Traditions & Sketches of Numerous Families. By Rev. J.A.W. Thomas. 1897. 292p. P5-SC0011 — $35.00.

HISTORY OF ORANGEBURG COUNTY, from its First Settlement to the Close of the Rev. War. By A.S. Salley, Jr. 1898. 572p. P5-SC0016B — $55.00.

HISTORY OF OLD PENDLETON DISTRICT, with a Genealogy of the Leading Families of the District. By R.W. Simpson. 1913. 226p. P5-SC0008 — $29.50.

South Dakota

BLACK HILLS SOUVENIR, a Pictorial & Historic Description of the Black Hills. By Rev. J.I. Sanford. 1902. 223p. P5-SD0006 — $29.95.

BLACK HILLS, or, the Last Hunting Ground of the Dakotahs. Heavily illustrated. Annie D. Tallent. 1899. 713p. P5-SD0005 — $69.50.

HISTORY OF FAULK COUNTY, together with Biographical Sketches of Pioneers & Prominent Citizens. By Capt. C.H. Ellis. 1909. 508p. P5-SD0002 — $53.00.

HUGHES COUNTY HISTORY. Comp. & arranged by the Office of Co. Superintendent of Schools. 1937. 205 + 27p. P5-SD0007 — $32.00.

HISTORY OF JERAULD COUNTY, from its Earliest Settlement to Jan. 1st, 1909. Niles J. Dunham. 1910. 441p. P5-SD0003 — $48.50.

COMPREHENSIVE HISTORY OF MINNEHAHA COUNTY. Charles A. Smith. 1949. 504p. P5-SD0004 — $54.50.

HISTORY OF MINNEHAHA COUNTY, Containing an Account of its Settlements, Growth, Development & Resource . . . and Biographical Sketches. By Dana R. Bailey. 1899. 1099 + xii p. P5-SD0001 — $99.50.

SEVENTY-FIVE YEARS OF SULLY COUNTY HISTORY, 1883-1958. 1958. 393 + 52p. P5-SD0008 — $49.00.

Tennessee

ANNALS OF TENNESSEE to the End of the 18th Century, Comprising its Settlement as the Watauga Assoc. from 1769 to 1777 . . . to the State of Tennessee, 1796 to 1800. By J.G.M. Ramsey. 1853. 743p. P5-TN0009 — $79.50.

GENEALOGY OF SOME EAST TENNESSEE FAMILIES of the Early 19th Century. By Ruth Ritchie. 1945. 96p. P5-TN0020A — $18.00.

HISTORY OF MIDDLE TENNESSEE, or, Life & Times of Gen. James Robertson. By A.W. Putnam. 1859. 668p. P5-TN0012 — $71.50.

HISTORY OF TENNESSEE, from the Earliest Time . . . together with an Historical & Biographical Sketch of from Twenty-five to Thirty Cos. of East Tenn., etc. East Tennessee ed. 1887. 1317p. P5-TN0003 — $125.00.

HISTORY OF THE LOST STATE OF FRANKLIN. By Samuel Cole Williams. 1924. 371p. P5-TN0017 — $47.00.

NOTABLE MEN OF TENNESSEE, Personal and Genealogical, with Portraits, 2-vol. set. 1905. 2 vols., 332 + 335p. P5-TN0010 — $71.50/set.

NOTABLE MEN OF TENNESSEE . . ., Vol. I. 1905. 332p. P5-TN0010A — $38.00.

NOTABLE MEN OF TENNESSEE . . ., Vol. II. 1905. 335p. P5-TN0010B — $38.00.

REPORT OF THE SOCIETY OF THE ARMY OF THE TENNESSEE at the 1st Annual Meeting, Nov. 14th & 15th, 1866 [Civil War]. 1877. 534p. P5-TN0020B — $57.50.

HISTORY OF DAVIDSON COUNTY, with Illustrations & Biographical Sketches of its Prominent Men & Pioneers. By W. Woodford Clayton. 1880. 499p. P5-TN0001 — $52.50.

HISTORY OF DEKALB COUNTY. By Will T. Hale. 1915. xii + 254p. P5-TN0002 — $32.50.

HISTORY OF DICKSON COUNTY, from the Earliest Times to the Present. Robert E. Corlew. 1956. 243p. P5-TN0008 — $32.00.

HISTORY OF HICKMAN COUNTY. By W. Jerome Spence & David L. Spence. 1900. 509p. P5-TN0007 — $53.00.

HISTORY OF HUMPHREYS COUNTY, TENNESSEE. By Jill Knight Garrett. 1963. 407 + 55p. P5-TN0021 — $54.00.

REMINISCENCES OF THE EARLY SETTLEMENT & EARLY SETTLERS OF McNAIRY COUNTY. By Gen. Marcus J. Wright. 1882. 96p. P5-TN0013 — $16.00.

Tennessee, cont.

**EARLY HISTORY OF NASH-
VILLE.** Lizzie P. Elliott. 1911. 286p.
P5-TN0005 — $35.00.

HISTORY OF NASHVILLE. By
H.W. Crew. 1890. 656p.
P5-TN0004 — $68.00.

**HISTORY OF OBION COUNTY,
Towns & Communities, Churches,
Schools, Farming, Factories, Social
& Political.** 1941. 272p.
P5-TN0014 — $36.50.

**HISTORY OF PUTNAM COUNTY,
TENNESSEE.** By Walter S. McClain.
1925. 152p.
P5-TN0022 — $27.00.

**HISTORIC SUMNER COUNTY,
with Genealogies of the Bledsoe,
Cage & Douglass Families & Gene-
alogical Notes of other County
Families.** Jay Guy Cisco. 1909. 319p.
P5-TN0006 — $38.00.

HISTORY OF WHITE COUNTY.
By Rev. Monroe Seals. 1935. 152p.
P5-TN0019 — $27.00.

Texas

**EVOLUTION OF A STATE:
Recollections of Old Texas Days.** By
Noah Smithwick. 1900. 354p.
P5-TX0025 — $39.00.

KINGDOM OF ZAPATA. 1953. 254p.
P5-TX0014 — $37.50.

**DIRECTORY OF ATHENS CITY,
TEXAS, Co. Site of Henderson Co.**
1904. 188p.
P5-TX0012 — $20.00.

**100 YEARS IN BANDERA, 1853-
1953.** By J. Marvin Hunter. 1953. 95p.
P5-TX0021 — $37.00.

**PIONEER HISTORY OF BANDERA
COUNTY: Seventy-five Years of
Intrepid History,** By J. Marvin Hunter.
1922. 292p.
P5-TX0006 — $39.00.

**HISTORY OF BEE COUNTY, with
Some Brief Sketches about Men &
Events in Adjoining Counties.** Mrs I.C.
Madray. 1939. 133p.
P5-TX0019 — $21.00.

HISTORY OF BELL COUNTY. By
George W. Tyler. 1936. xxiii + 425p.
P5-TX0001 — $48.00.

**INTO THE SETTING SUN:
History of Coleman Co.** By Beatrice
G. Gay. 1936. 193p.
P5-TX0004 — $34.00.

**THROUGH THE YEARS: History
of Crosby Co.,** By Nellie W. Spikes &
Temple Ann Ellis. 1952. 493 + 46p.
P5-TX0005 — $59.00.

**DALLAS COUNTY, A Record of its
Pioneers & Progress, being a
Supplement to John Henry Brown's
History of Dallas County (1887)..
with Much Additional Information
about Early Settlers & their Families.**
John H. Cochran. 1928. 296p.
P5-TX0003 — $36.00.

**SIXTY YEARS IN TEXAS, 2nd
Edition. (Sketches of old pioneers of
Dallas Co., especially the Jackson
family).** By Geo. Jackson. 1908. 384p.
P5-TX0014A — $46.50.

**HISTORY & REMINISCENCES
OF DENTON COUNTY.** By Ed. F.
Bates. 1918. 412p.
P5-TX0016 — $46.50.

**PIONEERS OF THE PRAIRIE
[Early Settlement of Follett, Texas &
Ivanhoe, Oklahoma.** 1967. 211p.
P5-TX0020 — $35.00.

**PIONEERS IN GOD'S HILLS:
Stories & biographies of the Brave
Men & Courageous Women who
Sought Homes & Peace . . . Among
the Hills of Fredericksburg & Gillespie
County.** 1960. 304p.
P5-TX0007 — $41.00.

**COMPLETE GALVESTON
HORROR.** The Survivors. 1900. 386p.
P5-TX0022 — $40.00.

HISTORY OF HALE COUNTY. By
Mary L. Cox. 1937. 230p.
P5-TX0008 — $35.00.

**HISTORY OF HENDERSON
COUNTY, Recording Names of
Early Pioneers, their Struggles &
Handicaps, Condition & Appearance
of the Co., Advancement & Progress
to [1929].** By J.J. Faulk. 1929. 322p.
P5-TX0018 — $39.00.

**MEN OF AFFAIRS OF
HENDERSON CO.** 1927. 120p.
P5-TX0017 — $19.00.

**IT OCCURED IN KIMBLE, and
How: Story of a Texas County.** By
O.C. Fisher. 1937. 240p.
P5-TX0009 — $34.00.

**HISTORIC MATAGORDA
COUNTY, vol. III.** S.L. Brown, C.S.
Gibbs, & M.B. Ingram 1988. 275 + viii p.
P5-TX10032 — $36.00.

**EASY SEARCH FOR MILAM
ANCESTORS: Milam Co. Censuses
for 1850, 1860 and 1870.** Trans. &
indexed by Dorothy Brown Crawford.
1985. 322p.
P5-TX0002 — $32.50.

**HISTORY OF MONTAGUE
COUNTY.** Mrs W.R. Potter. 1957.
184p.
P5-TX0010 — $29.00.

**HISTORY OF PALO PINTO
COUNTY (Word of Mouth Family
History) Palo Pinto County, Texas.**
Palo Pinto County Hist. Assn. 1978. 304p.
P5-TX10033 — $37.00.

**HISTORY OF REFUGIO
MISSION.** By William H. Oberste.
1942. 411p.
P5-TX0023 — $42.00.

**BRIEF HISTORY OF THE
LOWER RIO GRANDE VALLEY.**
ByFrank C. Pierce. 1917. 200p.
P5-TX0026 — $24.00.

HISTORY OF RUSK COUNTY. By
Dorman H. Winfrey. 1961. 179p.
P5-TX0011A — $32.00.

REALM OF RUSK COUNTY. By
Garland R. Farmer. 1951. 221p.
P5-TX0011B — $35.00.

**PIONEER HISTORY OF WISE
COUNTY.** Cliff D. Wise. 1907. 471p.
P5-TX0013 — $49.50.

Utah

**CASTLE VALLEY: History of
Emery Co.,** By Stella McElprang. 1949.
343p.
P5-UT0004 — $39.50.

MILESTONES OF MILLARD: 100 YEARS OF HISTORY OF MILLARD COUNTY. Comp. by S.H. Day & S.C. Ekins. 1951. 808p. **P5-UT0005 — $84.00.**

HISTORY OF SALT LAKE CITY. Comp. by Edward W. Tullidge. 1886. 896p. **P5-UT0001 — $91.50.**

SAGA OF SAN JUAN. By Perkins, Nielson & Jones. 1957. 367p. **P5-UT0002 — $44.00.**

UTAH EXPEDITION, 1857-1858: Letters of Capt. Jesse A. Gove, of Concord, to Mrs Gove, & Special Correspondence of the N.Y. Herald. 1928. 442p. **P5-NH0141 — $49.50.**

Vermont

BIBLIOGRAPHY OF VERMONT; or, a List of Books & Pamphlets Relating in any Way to the State. With biographical & other notes. By M.D. Gilman. 1897. 349p. **P5-VT0016 — $45.00.**

EARLY HISTORY OF VERMONT, 4-vol. set. By LaFayette Wilbur. 1899-1903. 4 vols., 362 + 419 + 397 + 463p. **P5-VT0120 — $165.00/set.**

EARLY HISTORY OF VERMONT, Vol. I. 1899-1903. 362p. **P5-VT0121 — $45.00.**

EARLY HISTORY OF VERMONT, Vol. II. 1899-1903. 419p. **P5-VT0122 — $45.00.**

EARLY HISTORY OF VERMONT, Vol. III. 1899-1903. 397p. **P5-VT0123 — $45.00.**

EARLY HISTORY OF VERMONT, Vol. IV. 1899-1903. 463p. **P5-VT0125 — $45.00.**

LIST OF THE PRINCIPAL OFFI-CERS OF VERMONT, from 1777 to 1918. 1918. 411p. **P5-VT0096 — $47.00.**

OVER THE DEAD LINE, or Tracked by Bloodhounds, Giving the Author's personal experience during eleven month that he was confined . . . as a [Confederate] prisoner of war . . .; with numerous & varied incidents & anecdoes of his prison life. S.M. Dufour. 1902. 283p. **P5-VT0097 — $41.00.**

RECORDS OF THE COUNCIL OF SAFETY & GOVERNOR AND COUNCIL OF THE STATE OF VERMONT, 8-vol. set. 1873. 8 Vols.; 4365p. **P5-VT0124 — $350.00/set.**

RECORDS OF THE COUNCIL OF SAFETY . . . OF THE STATE OF VERMONT, Vol. I. 1873. **P5-VT0124A — $46.00.**

RECORDS OF THE COUNCIL OF SAFETY . . . OF THE STATE OF VERMONT, Vol. II. 1873. **P5-VT0124B — $46.00.**

RECORDS OF THE COUNCIL OF SAFETY . . . OF THE STATE OF VERMONT, Vol. III. 1873. **P5-VT0124C — $46.00.**

RECORDS OF THE COUNCIL OF SAFETY & . . . OF THE STATE OF VERMONT, Vol. IV. 1873. **P5-VT0124D — $46.00.**

RECORDS OF THE COUNCIL OF SAFETY . . . OF THE STATE OF VERMONT, Vol. V. 1873. **P5-VT0124E — $46.00.**

RECORDS OF THE COUNCIL OF SAFETY . . . OF THE STATE OF VERMONT, Vol. VI. 1873. **P5-VT0124F — $46.00.**

RECORDS OF THE COUNCIL OF SAFETY . . . OF THE STATE OF VERMONT, Vol. VII. 1873. **P5-VT0124G — $46.00.**

RECORDS OF THE COUNCIL OF SAFETY . . . OF THE STATE OF VERMONT, Vol. VIII. 1873. **P5-VT0124H — $46.00.**

REVISED ROSTER OF VERMONT VOLUNTEERS and Lists of Vermonters who Served in the Army and Navy of the United States during the War of the Rebellion, 1861-66. 1892. 862p. **P5-VT0087 — $87.50.**

ROLLS OF THE SOLDIERS IN THE REVOLUTIONARY WAR, 1775-1783. 1904. 927p. **P5-VT0027 — $85.00.**

SETTLEMENT & CEMETERIES IN VERMONT'S NORTHEAST KINGDOM. Nancy L. Dodge. 1986. 197p. **P5-VT0007 — $39.00.**

VERMONT BRIGADE IN THE SHENANDOAH VALLEY, 1864 [Civil War]. Aldace F. Walker. 1869. 191p. **P5-VT0098 — $31.50.**

VERMONT HISTORICAL GAZET-TEER, Vol. I. A Magazine Embrac-ing a History of Each Town, Civil, Ecclesiastical, Biogr. & Military: Addison, Bennington, Caledonia, Chittenden & Essex Cos. 1868. 1092p. **P5-VT0038 — $107.00.**

VERMONT HISTORICAL GAZET-TEER, VOL. II: Franklin, Grand Isle, LaMoille, Orange Counties. 1871. 1200p. **P5-VT0039 — $119.50.**

VERMONT HISTORICAL GAZET-TEER, VOL. III: ORLEANS & RUTLAND COS. 1877. 1245p. **P5-VT0040 — $119.50.**

VERMONT HISTORICAL GAZET-TEER, Vol. IV (Washington Co.), including a County Chapter & the Histories of the Towns . . . 1882. 932p. **P5-VT0041 — $94.50.**

VERMONT HISTORICAL GAZET-TEER, Vol. V. The Towns of Windham County. 1891. 1204p. **P5-VT0042 — $117.00.**

VERMONT IN THE CIVIL WAR. History of the Part Taken by the Vermont Soldiers & Sailors in the War for the Union, 1861-1865. 2-vol. set. G.G. Benedict. 1886-1888. 2 vols, 620+808p. **P5-VT0086 — $90.00/set.**

VERMONT IN THE CIVIL WAR . . ., Vol. I. 1886-1888. 620p. **P5-VT0086A — $60.00.**

VERMONT IN THE CIVIL WAR . . ., Vol. II. 1886-1888. 808p. **P5-VT0086B — $75.00.**

For hardcover versions, see the order form on page v. To order, call 1-888-296-3447.

Vermont, cont.

VERMONT IN THE GREAT REBELLION, Containing Historical & Biographical Sketches. By Maj. Otis F.R. Waite. 1869. 288p.
P5-VT0099 — $39.50.

HISTORY OF ADDISON COUNTY, with Illustrations & Biographical Sketches of its Prominent Men & Pioneers. Ed. by H.P. Smith. 1886. 774 + 62p.
P5-VT0019 — $85.00.

HISTORY OF ATHENS. From Vt. Hist. Gazetteer, Vol. V. 1891. 20p.
P5-VT0043 — $10.00.

HISTORY OF BARNARD, with Family Genealogies, 1761-1927, 2-vol. set. By Wm. Monroe Newton. 1927. 2 vols., 368 + 511p.
P5-VT0088 — $89.00/set.

HISTORY OF BARNARD . . ., Vol. I. 1927. 368p.
P5-VT0088A — $38.50.

HISTORY OF BARNARD . . ., Vol. II. 1927. 511p.
P5-VT0088B — $53.00.

HISTORY OF BARNET, from the Outbreak of the French & Indian Wars to the Present. With genealogical records of many families. By Frederic Palmer Wells. 1923. 691p.
P5-VT0028 — $71.50.

HISTORY OF BELLOWS FALLS. From Vt. Hist. Gazetteer, Vol. V. 1891. 7p.
P5-VT0044A — $10.00.

HISTORY OF BENNINGTON. From Vt. Hist. Gazetteer, Vol. V. 1891. 108p.
P5-VT0045 — $19.50.

MEMORIALS OF A CENTURY, Embracing a Record of Individuals & Events, Chiefly in the Early History of Bennington & its First Church. By Isaac Jennings. 1869. 408p.
P5-VT0100 — $46.50.

SKETCHES OF HISTORIC BENNINGTON. By John V.D.S. & Caroline E. Merrill. 1908. 99p.
P5-VT0101 — $18.50.

BENNINGTON COUNTY GENEALOGICAL GLEANINGS. Trans. & gathered by Elijah E. Brownell. 1941. 207p.
P5-VT0102 — $24.50.

GAZETTEER AND BUSINESS DIRECTORY OF BENNINGTON CO. for 1880-81. Comp. by Hamilton Child. 1880. 500p.
P5-VT0089 — $55.00.

HISTORY OF BENNINGTON COUNTY, with Illustrations & Biographical Sketches of some of its Prominent Men & Pioneers. 1889. 584p.
P5-VT0029 — $59.50.

HISTORY OF BERLIN. From Vermont Historical Gazetteer, Vol. IV. 1882. 21p.
P5-VT0046 — $10.00.

HISTORY OF BRADFORD, Containing some Account of the Place from its First Settlement in 1765 & the Principle Improvements & Events to 1874. With gen. records. S. McKeen. 1875. 459p.
P5-VT0001 — $46.00.

HISTORY OF BRAINTREE. Including a Memorial of Families that have Resided in Town. By H. Royce Bass. 1883. 208p.
P5-VT0103 — $31.50.

ANNALS OF BRATTLEBORO, 1681-1895, 2-vol. set. Comp. & ed. by Mary R. Cabot. 1921-1922. 2 vols, 1104p.
P5-VT0104 — $109.00/set.

ANNALS OF BRATTLEBORO, 1681-1895, Vol. I. Comp. & ed. by Mary R. Cabot. 1921-1922.
P5-VT0104A — $63.00.

ANNALS OF BRATTLEBORO, 1681-1895, Vol. II. Comp. & ed. by Mary R. Cabot. 1921-1922.
P5-VT0104B — $63.00.

HISTORY OF BRATTLEBORO. From Vermont Historical Gazette, Vol. V. By Henry Burnham. 1891. 191p.
P5-VT0047 — $29.50.

HISTORY OF BROOKLINE. From Vt. Hist. Gazetteer, Vol. V. 1891. 27p.
P5-VT0048 — $10.00.

PICTURESQUE BURLINGTON: A Handbook of Burlington & Lake Champlain, with One Hundred & Sixty-Four Illustrations. By Joseph Auld. 1894. 190p.
P5-VT0026 — $29.50.

HISTORY OF CABOT. From Vermont Historical Gazetteer, Vol. IV. 1882. 54p.
P5-VT0049 — $11.00.

HISTORY OF CALAIS. From Vermont Historical Gazetteer, Vol. IV. 1882. 55p.
P5-VT0050 — $11.00.

SUCCESSFUL VERMONTERS: Modern Gazetteer of Caledonia, Essex & Orleans Counties, Containing an Historical Review ofthe Several Towns & a Series of Biographical Sketches . . . By Wm. H. Jeffrey. 1904. 361 + 274p.
P5-VT0119 — $66.50.

HISTORY OF THE TOWN CHARLESTON (Named "Navy," 1803-1825). Esther B. Hamilton. 1955. 129p.
P5-VT0030 — $22.50.

CHELSEA: The Origin of Chelsea and a Record of its Institutions and Individuals. By John Moore Comstock. 1944. 62p.
P5-VT0090B — $12.00.

HISTORY OF THE TOWN OF CORNWALL. Rev. Lyman Matthews. 1862. xii + 356p.
P5-VT0023 — $39.50.

HISTORY & MAP OF DANBY. By J.C. Williams. 1869. 391p.
P5-VT0024 — $42.50.

HISTORY OF DERBY. By Cecile B. Hay & Mildred B. Hay. 1967. 240p.
P5-VT0117 — $34.50.

STORY OF DORSET. By Zephine Humphrey. 1924. 288p.
P5-VT0116 — $38.00.

HISTORY OF DOVER. From Vt. Hist. Gazetteer, Vol. V. 1891. 20p.
P5-VT0051 — $10.00.

HISTORY OF DUMMERSTON. From Vermont Historical Gazetteer, Vol. V. By D.L. Mansfield. 1891. 216p.
P5-VT0052 — $32.50.

HISTORY OF THE TOWN OF FAIR HAVEN. By Andrew N. Adams. 1870. 516p.
P5-VT0008 — $54.00.

HISTORY OF FAYSTON. From Vermont Historical Gazetteer, Vol. IV. 1882. 21p.
P5-VT0053 — $10.00.

HISTORY OF FRANKLIN & GRAND ISLE COUNTIES. Ed. by L.C. Aldrich. 1891. 821p.
P5-VT0012 — $82.50.

HISTORY OF GRAFTON. From Vt. Hist. Gazetteer, Vol. V. 1891. 8p.
P5-VT0054 — $10.00.

HISTORY OF THE TOWN OF GRAFTON. By Francis A. Palmer. 1954. 120p.
P5-VT0032 — $21.00.

GRAVESTONES OF GUILDHALL, Vt. & Northumberland, NH. By Nancy L. Dodge. 1987. 185p.
P5-VT0006 — $39.00.

HISTORY OF GUILDHALL, Containing some Account of the . . . First Settlement in 1764 . . . and Events to 1886. With genealogical records. By Everett Chamberlin Benton. 1886. 270p.
P5-VT0033 — $34.50.

HISTORY OF GUILFORD. From Vt. Hist. Gazetteer, Vol. V. 1891. 80p.
P5-VT0055 — $16.00.

HISTORY OF HALIFAX. From Vt. Hist. Gazetteer, Vol. V. 1891. 15p.
P5-VT0056 — $10.00.

HISTORY OF HARTFORD, July 4, 1761-April 4, 1889. By Wm. Howard Tucker. 1889. 488p.
P5-VT0025 — $52.50.

HISTORICAL NOTES, JAMAICA, Windham County. Comp. & ed. by Warren E. Booker. 1940. 244p.
P5-VT0105 — $33.50.

HISTORY OF JAMAICA. From Vt. Hist. Gazetteer, Vol. V. 1891. 17p.
P5-VT0057 — $10.00.

HISTORY OF JERICHO. With family histories. Ed. by Chauncey H. Hayden, et al. 1916. 665p.
P5-VT0013 — $67.00.

HISTORY OF THE TOWN OF JOHNSON, 1784-1907. 1908. 83p.
P5-VT0095 — $15.00.

HISTORY OF LAKE CHAMPLAIN, from its First Exploration by the French in 1609, to the Close of the Year 1814. Peter S. Palmer. 1866. 276p.
P5-VT0115 — $35.00.

HISTORY OF LUDLOW. By Joseph N. Harris. 1949. 239p.
P5-VT0106 — $33.00.

HISTORY OF MARLBORO. From Vt. Hist. Gazetteer, Vol. V. 1891. 22p.
P5-VT0059 — $10.00.

HISTORY OF MARSHFIELD. From Vermont Historical Gazetteer, Vol. IV. 1882. 25p.
P5-VT0060 — $10.00.

HISTORY OF MIDDLESEX. From Vermont Historical Gazetteer, Vol. IV. 1882. 26p.
P5-VT0061 — $10.00.

HISTORY OF MIDDLETOWN, in Three Discourse delivered by Hon. Barnes Frisbie. 1867. 130p.
P5-VT0034 — $23.00.

HISTORY OF MONTPELIER, from the Time it was Chartered in 1781 to 1860, with Biographical Sketches of its Most Noted Deceased Citizens. By D.P. Thompson. 1860. 312p.
P5-VT0036 — $36.00.

HISTORY OF MONTPELIER. From Vermont Historical Gazetteer, Vol. IV. Incl. East Montpelier. By Eliakim P. Walton. 1882. 352p.
P5-VT0062 — $41.50.

MARRIAGES OF MONTPELIER [through 1852], Burlington [through 1833], Berlin [through 1876]. Comp. by Research Pub. Co. 1903. 92p.
P5-VT0035 — $18.00.

HISTORY OF MORETOWN. From Vermont Historical Gazetteer, Vol. IV. Incl. East Montpelier. 1882. 19p.
P5-VT0063 — $10.00.

HISTORY OF MORRISTOWN. By Anna L. Mower. 1935. 324p.
P5-VT0107 — $39.50.

HISTORY OF NEWBURY, from the Discovery of Coos Co. to 1902. With genealogical records. By F. Wells. 1902. 779p.
P5-VT0002 — $79.00.

1774-1874: CENTENNIAL PROCEEDINGS AND OTHER HISTORICAL FACTS and Incidents, Relating to Newfane, the County Seat of Windham County. 1877. 256p.
P5-VT0090A — $37.00.

HISTORY OF NEWFANE. From Vt. Hist. Gazetteer, Vol. V. 1891. 36p.
P5-VT0064 — $10.00.

FIRE OF LIFE. Sketches from the author's life; born & raised in Newport and much of the book is about the town in the first half of the 20th century. Raymond T. Lahar. 1998. 313p.
P5-VT0118 — $35.00.

CENTENNIAL PROCEEDINGS & HISTORICAL INCIDENTS OF THE EARLY SETTLERS OF NORTHFIELD, with Biographical Sketches. By John Gregory. 1878. 320p.
P5-VT0037 — $38.00.

HISTORY OF NORTHFIELD. From Vermont Historical Gazetteer, Vol. IV. Incl. East Montpelier. 1882. 101p.
P5-VT0065 — $17.50.

HISTORY OF NORWICH, with Portraits & Illustrations. By M.E. Goddard & Henry V. Partridge. 1905. 276p.
P5-VT0066 — $37.00.

GAZETTEER OF ORANGE COUNTY, VERMONT By Hamilton Child 1888. 755p
P28390000 — $116.00.

PAWLET FOR ONE HUNDRED YEARS. By Hiel Hollister. 1867. 272p.
P5-VT0091A — $38.00.

HISTORY OF THE TOWN OF PITTSFORD, with Biographical Sketches and Family Records. By A.M. Caverly. 1872. 756p.
P5-VT0067 — $79.00.

HISTORY OF PLAINFIELD. From Vermont Historical Gazetteer, Vol. IV. Incl. East Montpelier. 1882. 21p.
P5-VT0068 — $10.00.

POMFRET, VERMONT, in 2 Vols. By Henry Hobart Vail.1930. 2 vols., 338 + 327p.
P5-VT0021 — $69.50/set.

For hardcover versions, see the order form on page v. To order, call 1-888-296-3447.

Vermont, cont.

POMFRET, VERMONT, Vol. I.
1930. 338p.
P5-VT0021A — $39.00.

POMFRET, VERMONT, Vol. II.
1930. 327p.
P5-VT0021B — $39.00.

HISTORY OF THE TOWN OF POULTNEY, from its Settlement to the Year 1875, with Family & Biographical Sketches & Incidents.
By Joslin, Frisbie & Ruggles. 1875. 369p.
P5-VT0020 — $41.00.

MARRIAGES IN POWNAL, VERMONT TO 1850
Arranged by Elmer I. Shepard 1941. 54p
P28412700 — $15.00.

HISTORY OF PUTNEY. From Vermont Historical Gazetteer, Vol. V.
By A. Foster. 1891. 53p.
P5-VT0069 — $11.00.

CENTENNIAL CELEBRATION, Together with an Historical Sketch of Reading, Windsor Co., and its Inhabitants from the First Settlement of the Town to 1874. By Gilbert A. Davis. 1874. 169p.
P5-VT0091B — $19.50.

HISTORY OF READING, Windsor Co. 2nd ed. G.A. Davis. 1903. 375 + 12p.
P5-VT0003 — $43.00.

HISTORY OF THE TOWN OF ROCHESTER. 1869. 92p.
P5-VT0109 — $17.00.

HISTORY OF ROCKINGHAM. From Vt. Hist. Gazetteer, Vol. V.
1891. 16p.
P5-VT0070 — $10.00.

HISTORY OF THE TOWN OF ROCKINGHAM, including the Villages of Bellows Falls, Saxtons River, Rockingham, Cambridgeport & Bartonsville, 1753-1907, with family genealogies. By Lyman S. Hayes. 1907. 850p.
P5-VT0092 — $89.00.

HISTORY OF ROXBURY. From Vermont Historical Gazetteer, Vol. IV. Incl. East Montpelier. 1882. 33p.
P5-VT0071 — $10.00.

HISTORY OF ROYALTON, with Family Genealogies, 1769-1911. By E.M.W. Lovejoy. 1911. 1146p.
P5-VT0014 — $105.00.

GRAVESTONE INSCRIPTIONS OF RUPERT, BENNINGTON COUNTY, VERMONT. By Levi Henry Elwell 1913.
P28415000 — $110.00.

HISTORY OF RUTLAND COUNTY, VERMONT: Civil, Ecclesiastical, Biographical, and Military. 1882. 1244p; 1 vol. in 2 books.
P28395000 — $194.00.

HISTORY OF RUTLAND COUNTY, with Illustrations & Biographical Sketches of Some of its Prominent Men & Pioneers. 1886. 959p.
P5-VT0110 — $97.00.

HISTORY OF RYEGATE, from its Settlement by Scotch-American Farmers to 1912. By E. Miller & F.P. Wells. 1913. 604p.
P5-VT0004 — $62.00.

HISTORY OF SALISBURY. By John M. Weeks. 1860. 362p.
P5-VT0072 — $44.50.

HISTORY OF THE TOWN OF SPRINGFIELD, with a Genealogical Record. By C.H. Hubbard & J. Dartt. 1895. 618p.
P5-VT0009 — $66.50.

HISTORY OF ST ALBANS, Civil, Religious, Biographical & Statistical. With History of Sheldon. From "Vermont Gazeteer." By L.L. Dutcher, with by H.R. Whitney. 1872. 107p.
P5-VT0017 — $16.00.

TOWN OF ST JOHNSBURY: A Review of 125 Years. By E.T. Fairbanks. 1914. 592p.
P5-VT0015 — $59.00.

HISTORY OF STRATTON. From Vt. Hist. Gazetteer, Vol. V. 1891. 9p.
P5-VT0073 — $10.00.

HISTORY OF STRATTON-WRIGHT-WIITHED. From Vt. Hist. Gazetteer, Vol. V. 1891. 6p.
P5-VT0074B — $10.00.

HISTORY OF SUTTON. From Vt. Hist. Gazetteer, Vol. V. 1891. 56p.
P5-VT0074A — $11.50.

HISTORY OF THE TOWN OF SWANTON [from Vermont Gazetteer, part 2]. By J.B. Perry & G. Barney. 1882. 224 + 48p.
P5-VT0121 — $37.00.

HISTORY OF TOWNSEND. From Vt. Hist. Gazetteer, Vol. V. 1891. 21p.
P5-VT0075 — $10.00.

HISTORY OF VERNON. From Vermont Historical Gazetteer, Vol. V. 1891. 54p.
P5-VT0076 — $11.00.

HISTORY OF THE TOWN OF WAITSFIELD, 1782-1908, with Family Genealogies. By M.B. Jones. 1909. 534p.
P5-VT0005 — $57.00.

HISTORY OF WAITSFIELD. From Vermont Historical Gazetteer, Vol. IV. Incl. East Montpelier. 1882. 31p.
P5-VT0077 — $10.00.

HISTORY OF WALLINGFORD. By Walter Thorpe. 1911. 222p.
P5-VT0094 — $34.50.

PEOPLE OF WALLINGFORD. By Birney C. Batcheller. 1937. 317p.
P5-VT0093 — $41.50.

HISTORY OF WARDSBORO. From Vt. Hist. Gazetteer, Vol. V. 1891. 15p.
P5-VT0078 — $10.00.

HISTORY OF WARREN. From Vermont Historical Gazetteer, Vol. IV. Incl. East Montpelier. 1882. 12p.
P5-VT0079 — $10.00.

HISTORY OF WATERBURY. 1763-1915. 1915. 286p.
P5-VT0111 — $39.50.

HISTORY OF WATERBURY. From Vermont Historical Gazetteer, Vol. IV. Incl. East Montpelier. 1882. 60p.
P5-VT0080 — $12.00.

HISTORY OF WESTMINSTER. From Vt. Hist. Gazetteer, Vol. V. 1891. 11p.
P5-VT0081 — $19.50.

HISTORY OF WESTMINSTER: Vermont Sesquicentennial Souvenir of Westminster, 1791-1941. By M. Elizabeth Minard. 1941. 174p.
P5-VT0112 — $21.50.

GREEN LEAVES FROM WHITINGHAM: A History of the Town. By Clark Jillson. 1894. 244p.
P5-VT0113 — $37.00.

HISTORY OF WHITINGHAM. From Vt. Hist. Gazetteer, Vol. V. 1891. 40p.
P5-VT0082 — $10.00.

HISTORY OF WILMINGTON. From Vt. Hist. Gazetteer, Vol. V. 1891. 16p.
P5-VT0083A — $10.00.

HISTORY OF WINDHAM. From Vt. Hist. Gazetteer, Vol. V. 1891. 26p.
P5-VT0083B — $10.00.

INDUSTRIAL HISTORY OF WINDSOR, VERMONT. By G. Hubbard. 1922. 272p.
P5-VT0123 — $38.00.

Gazetteer & Business Directory of Windsor Co., VT. By H. Child. 1884. 666 + 22p.
P5-VT0122 — $73.00.

HISTORY OF WINDSOR COUNTY, with Illustrations & Biographical Sketches of some of its Prominent Men & Pioneers. 1891. 1005p.
P5-VT0018 — $97.50.

HISTORY OF WOODBURY. From Vermont Historical Gazetteer, Volume IV. Incl. East Montpelier. 1882. 9p.
P5-VT0084 — $10.00.

HISTORY OF WOODSTOCK. By Henry Swan Dana. 1889. 641p.
P5-VT0114 — $69.50.

HISTORY OF WORCESTER. From Vermont Historical Gazetteer, Vol. IV. Incl. East Montpelier. 1882. 29p.
P5-VT0085 — $10.00.

Virginia

DOCUMENTS CHEIFLY UNPUBLISHED RELATING THE HUGUENOT EMIGRATION TO VIRGINIA & the settlement at Manakin-town, with appendix of genealogies presenting data of the Fontaine, Maury, Dupuy, Trabue, Marye, Chastain, Cooke & other families. By R.A. Brock. 1886. 247p.
P5-VA0088 — $37.00.

EARLY VA. IMMIGRANTS, 1623-1666. George Cabell Greer. 1912. 376p.
P5-VA0037A — $39.50.

GERMAN ELEMENT OF THE SHENANDOAH VALLEY. By John Walter Wayland. 1907. 272p.
P5-VA0060 — $37.00.

GERMAN NEW RIVER SETTLEMENT, Virginia. By U.S.A. Heavener. 1929. 94p.
P5-VA0025 — $18.00.

GLEANINGS OF VIRGINIA HISTORY: An Hist. & Gen. Collection, Largely from Original Sources. William F. Boogher. 1903. 443p.
P5-VA0002 — $39.00.

HEADS OF FAMILIES AT THE FIRST CENSUS OF THE U.S. taken in the Year 1790: Va. Records of the State's Enumerations, 1782-1785. 1908. 189p.
P5-VA0022 — $19.50.

INDEX TO PRINTED VA. GENEALOGIES. Comp. by R.A. Stewart. 1930. 265p.
P5-VA0012 — $27.50.

KEGLEY'S VIRGINIA FRONTIER: Beginning of the Southwest, the Roanoke o fColonial Days, 1740-1783. By F.B. Kegley. 1938. 786p.
P5-VA0086 — $81.00.

LETTERS AND TIMES OF THE TYLERS [Letter of John Tyler, Sr., Pres. John Tyler & others], 3-vol. set. By Lyon G. Tyler. 1884-1897. 3 vols., 633 + 736 + 234p.
P5-VA0200 — $155.00/set.

LETTERS AND TIMES OF THE TYLERS . . ., Vol. I. By Lyon G. Tyler. 1884-1897. 633p.
P5-VA0200A — $63.00.

LETTERS AND TIMES OF THE TYLERS . . ., Vol. II. By Lyon G. Tyler. 1884-1897. 736p.
P5-VA0200B — $73.00.

LETTERS AND TIMES OF THE TYLERS . . ., Vol. III. By Lyon G. Tyler. 1884-1897. 234p.
P5-VA0200C — $25.00.

LIST OF THE REVOLUTIONARY SOLDIERS OF VIRGINIA: Special Report of the Department of Archives &History for 1911. By H.J. Eckenrode, Archivist. 1912. 488p.
P5-VA0089 — $49.50.

OLD CHURCHES, MINISTERS & FAMILIES OF VIRGINIA, 2-vol. set. By Bishop Wm. Meade. 1857, 1910. 2 vols, 490 + 495p.
P5-VA0084 — $99.00/set.

OLD CHURCHES, MINISTERS & FAMILIES OF VIRGINIA, Vol. I. 1857, 1910. 490p.
P5-VA0084A — $53.00.

OLD CHURCHES, MINISTERS & FAMILIES OF VIRGINIA, Vol. II. 1857, 1910. 495p.
P5-VA0084B — $53.00.

SOME EMIGRANTS TO VIRGINIA. By W.G. Stanard. 94p.
P5-VA0024 — $15.00.

SOME PROMINENT VIRGINIA FAMILIES, 4-vol. set (in 2 books). By Louise P. du Bellet. 1907. 4 vols. in 2, 1096 + 616p.
P5-VA0017 — $148.00/set.

SOME PROMINENT VIRGINIA FAMILIES, Vols. I & II (in 1 book). 1907. 1096p.
P5-VA0017A — $110.00.

SOME PROMINENT VIRGINIA FAMILIES, Vols. III & IV (in 1 book). 1907. 616p.
P5-VA0017B — $110.00.

VIRGINIA COUNTIES: Those resulting from Va. Legislation. By M.P. Robinson. 1916. 283p.
P5-VA0035 — $32.50.

VIRGINIA GENEALOGIES: Gen. of the Glassell Fam. of Scotland & Va., also of the Fams. of Ball, Brown, Bryan, Conway, Daniel, Ewell, Holladay, Lewis, Littlepages, Moncure, Peyton, Robinson, Scott, Taylor, Wallace & others, of Va. & Md. By H.E. Hayden. 1891. 759p.
P5-VA0028 — $59.00.

Virginia, cont.

VIRGINIA WILLS & ADMINI-STRATIONS, 1632-1800. An index of wills recorded in local courts of Virginia, 1632-1800, and of admins. on estates shown by inventories of the estates of intestates records in will and other books of local courts, 1632-1800. 1930. 483p.
P5-VA0047B — $45.00.

YE KINGDOM OF ACCAWMACKE, or the New Eastern Shore of Va. in the 17th Cent. By J.C. Wise. 1911. 416p.
P5-VA0003 — $47.00.

THE ALBEMARLE OF OTHER DAYS. Mary Rawlings. 1925. 146 + 22p.
P5-VA0080 — $27.00.

ALBEMARLE COUNTY IN VA. With genealogical sketches. By Edgar Woods. 1901. 412p.
P5-VA0009 — $39.00.

HISTORY OF OLD ALEXANDRIA, from July 13, 1749 to May 24, 1861. By Mary G. Powell. 1928. 367p.
P5-VA0083 — $43.00.

CENTENNIAL HISTORY OF ALLEGHANY COUNTY. By Oren F. Morton. 1923. 232p.
P5-VA0047A — $31.50.

AMHERST COUNTY MARRIAGE BONDS, 1753-1853. 1937. 177p.
P5-VA0061 — $18.50.

MARRIAGE BONDS & Other Marriage Records of Amherst County, 1763-1800. By W.M. Sweeny. 1937. 102p.
P5-VA0010 — $16.00.

ABSTRACTS OF LAND GRANT SURVEYS OF AUGUSTA & ROCKINGHAM COS., 1761-1791. By P.C. Kaylor. 1930. 150p.
P5-VA0008 — $19.50.

ANNALS OF AUGUSTA CO., with Reminiscences Illustrative of..its Pioneer Settlers, Biographical Sketches of Citizens . . . a Diary of the War, 1861-5, & a Chapter on Reconstruction. By Jos. A. Waddell. 1886. 492p.
P5-VA0063 — $53.00.

CHRONICLES OF THE SCOTCH-IRISH SETTLEMENT OF VA., Extracted from the Original Court Records of Augusta Co., 1745-1800, 3-vol. set. By Lyman Chalkley. 1912. 3 vols., 623 + 652 + 712p.
P5-VA0045A — $180.00/set.

CHRONICLES OF THE SCOTCH-IRISH SETTLEMENT OF VA. . . ., Vol. I. 1912. 623p.
P5-VA0045A1 — $65.00.

CHRONICLES OF THE SCOTCH-IRISH SETTLEMENT OF VA. . . ., Vol. II. 1912. 652p.
P5-VA0045A2 — $65.00.

CHRONICLES OF THE SCOTCH-IRISH SETTLEMENT OF VA. . . ., III. 1912. 712p.
P5-VA0045A3 — $65.00.

HISTORY OF AUGUSTA COUNTY. By J. Lewis Peyton. 1882. 387p.
P5-VA0062 — $43.00.

ANNALS OF BATH COUNTY. By Oren F. Morton. n.d. 208p.
P5-VA0020 — $19.50.

BEDFORD COUNTY MARRIAGE BONDS, 1800-1853. 1937. 227p.
P5-VA0076 — $24.50.

OUR KIN: Genealogies of Some of the Early Families . . . of Bedford County. By M. D. Ackerly & L. E. J. Parker. 812pp. (1930) 1997. By M.D. Ackerly & L.E.J. Parker. 1930. 812p.
P5-VA0085 — $82.00.

HISTORY OF BRISTOL PARISH, with Genealogies of Families Connected Therewith, & Historical Illustrations. 2nd ed. By Rev. Philip Slaughter. 1879. 237p.
P5-VA0048A — $34.00.

CAMPBELL COUNTY MARRIAGE BONDS, 1781-1854. 1937. 185p.
P5-VA0067 — $22.50.

CAROLINE COUNTY MARRIAGE BONDS, 1787-1852. 1937. 182p.
P5-VA0065 — $22.00.

HISTORY OF CAROLINE COUNTY, from its Formation in 1727 to 1924. Includes genealogies. M. Wingfield. 1924. 528p.
P5-VA0007 — $45.00.

CHARLOTTE COUNTY MARRIAGE BONDS, 1765-1863. 1937. 182p.
P5-VA0071 — $22.00.

CHESTERFIELD COUNTY MARRIAGE BONDS, 1771-1852. 1937. 132 + 42p.
P5-VA0066 — $21.50.

CULPEPER COUNTY Gen. & Hist. Notes, Embracing a Rev. & Enlarged Ed. of Dr Philip Slaughter's History of St Mark's Parish. By R.T. Green. 1900. 120 + 160p.
P5-VA0023 — $35.00.

CUMBERLAND PARISH, Lunenburg Co., Va., 1746-1816, Vestry Book, 1746-1816. By Landon C. Bell. 1930. 633p.
P5-VA0090 — $66.50.

FARQUIER COUNTY MARRIAGE BONDS, 1759-1854. 1937. 312p.
P5-VA0075 — $29.50.

FAUQUIER DURING THE PROPRIETORSHIP: A Chronicle of the Colonization Organization of a Northern Neck Co. By Harry C. Groome. 1927. 255p.
P5-VA0030 — $25.00.

SHENANDOAH VALLEY PIONEERS & their Descendants: History of Frederick Co. from its Formation in 1738 to 1908. By T.K. Cartmell. 1908. 522p.
P5-VA0036A — $53.50.

HISTORIC FREDERICKSBURG: Story of an Old Town. By John T. Goolrick. 1922. 200p.
P5-VA0049A — $31.50.

EPITAPHS OF GLOUCESTER and MATHEWS COS., in Tidewater Va., Through 1865. 1959. 168p.
P5-VA0051B — $21.00.

DOUGLAS REGISTER [GOOCHLAND CO.]: Being a Detailed Record of Births, marr. & Deaths, with Other Interesting Notes as Kept by the Rev. Wm. Douglas, 1750-97; Index of Goochland Wills; Notes on the French Huguenot Refugees who Lived in Manakin-Town. 1928. 412p.
P5-VA0050A — $47.00.

GOOCHLAND COUNTY MARRIAGE BONDS, 1730-1854. 1937. 129p.
P5-VA0077 — $15.00.

GRAYSON CO. PIONEER SETTLERS. B.F. Nuckolls. 1914. 219p.
P5-VA0041A — $29.00.

HALIFAX COUNTY MARRIAGE BONDS, 1753-1854. 1937. 295p.
P5-VA0074 — $29.50.

HANOVER COUNTY, its History & Legends. By Rosewell Page. 1926. 153p.
P5-VA0082 — $19.50.

QUAKER FRIENDS OF YE OLDEN TIME, Being in Part a Transcript of the Minute Books of Cedar Creek Meeting, Hanover Co., & the South River Meeting, Campbell Co. By J.P. Bell. 1905. 287p.
P5-VA0051A — $38.00.

ANNALS & HIST. OF HENRICO PARISH, Diocese of Va., & St John's P.E. Church. J.S. Moore. 1904. 578p.
P5-VA0040A — $55.00.

BIRTHS FROM BRISTOL PARISH REGISTER OF HENRICO, PRINCE GEORGE & DINWIDDIE COS., 1720-1798. Trans. by C.G. Chamberlayne. 1898. 121p.
P5-VA0011 — $16.50.

HENRICO COUNTY MARRIAGE BONDS, 1780-1861. 1937. 291p.
P5-VA0073 — $29.00.

HISTORY OF HIGHLAND COUNTY. O.F. Morton. 1911. 532p.
P5-VA0037B — $45.00.

ISLE OF WIGHT COUNTY MARRIAGES, 1628-1800. Comp. by Blanche Adams Chapman. 1939. 137p. Typescript.
P5-VA0052 — $19.50.

POCAHONTAS, Alias Matoaka, & her Desc. through her Marriage at Jamestown in April, 1614, with John Rolfe, Gentleman. With biogr. sketches by W. Robertson & hist. notes by R.A. Brock. 1887. 84p.
P5-VA0032 — $10.00.

KING & QUEEN COUNTY. With genealogies. By Rev. Alfred Bagby. 1908. 402p.
P5-VA0012 — $42.50.

HISTORY & COMPREHENSIVE DESCRIPTION OF LOUDON CO. By James W. Head. 1908. 186p.
P5-VA0031 — $21.00.

LOUISA COUNTY MARRIAGE BONDS, 1769-1856. 1937. 149p.
P5-VA0072 — $17.50.

OLD FREE STATE: A Contribution to the History of Lunenburg Co. & Southside Va., 2-vol. set. By Landon C. Bell. 1927. 2 vols., 623 + 644p.
P5-VA0048B — $119.00/set.

OLD FREE STATE . . ., Vol. I. 1927. 623p.
P5-VA0048B1 — $68.50.

OLD FREE STATE . . ., Vol. II. 1927. 644p.
P5-VA0048B2 — $68.50.

SUNLIGHT ON THE SOUTHSIDE: List of Tithes, Lunenburg Co., 1748-83. 1931. 505p.
P5-VA0091 — $53.00.

LYNCHBURG & its People. By Wm. Asbury Christian. 1900. 463p.
P5-VA0049B — $51.00.

PARISH REGISTER OF CHRIST CHURCH, Middlesex Co., 1652 to 1812. 1897. 341p.
P5-VA0027 — $35.00.

MONTGOMERY & FINCASTLE CO., Brief of Wills & Marriages, 1733-1831. By A.L. Worrell. 1932. 56p.
P5-VA0040B — $10.00.

HISTORICAL & DESCRIPTIVE SKETCHES OF NORFOLK & VICINITY, including Portsmouth & the Adjacent Counties during a Period of Two Hundred Years; also, Sketches of Williamsburg . . . & other Places in . . . Eastern Virginia. By Wm. S. Forrest. 1853. 496p.
P5-VA0055A — $55.00.

BRIEF ABSTRACT OF LOWER NORFOLK CO. & NORFOLK CO. WILLS, 1637-1710. By Charles F. McIntosh. 1914. 223p.
P5-VA0041B — $25.00.

HISTORY OF NORFOLK COUNTY & Representative Citizens, 1637-1900. 1902. 1042p.
P5-VA0053 — $99.50.

RECORD OF EVENTS IN NORFOLK COUNTY, from April 19th, 1861, to May 10th, 1862, with a History of the Soldiers & Sailors of Norfolk Co., Norfolk City & Portsmouth who Served in the Confederate Army or Navy. By John W.H. Porter. 1892. 366p.
P5-VA0054 — $44.00.

HISTORY OF ORANGE COUNTY, from its Formation in 1734 to the End of Reconstruction in 1870. By W.W. Scott. 1907. 292p.
P5-VA0033 — $35.00.

HISTORY OF PATRICK and HENRY COUNTIES. By Virginia G. & Lewis G. Pedigo. 1933. 400p.
P5-VA0050B — $44.50.

PITTSYLVANIA COUNTY MARRIAGE BONDS, 1767-1864. 1937. 368p.
P5-VA0070 — $35.00.

PRINCESS ANNE COUNTY LOOSE PAPER, 1700-89 (Vol. I of "Virginia Anitquary"). 1954. 221p.
P5-VA0056 — $27.50.

MARRIAGE BONDS, 1797-1853: Richmond City. By A.W. Reedy & A.L. Riffe, IV. 1939. 158p.
P5-VA0039 — $19.00.

RICHMOND IN BY-GONE DAYS, Being Reminiscences of an Old Citizen. By Geo. M. West. 1856. 321p.
P5-VA0059 — $39.50.

RICHMOND MANUFACTURING & TRADING CENTRE, Giving a Full & Complete List of All Wholesale & Manufacturing Houses & Transportation Facilities. 1880. 92p.
P5-VA0057 — $17.00.

RICHMOND, Her Past & Present. By W. Asbury Christian. 1912. 618p.
P5-VA0058 — $66.00.

HISTORY OF ROCKBRIDGE COUNTY. Oren F. Morton. 1920. 574p.
P5-VA0042B — $59.50.

HISTORY OF ROCKINGHAM COUNTY. John F. Wayland. 1912. 466p.
P5-VA0043 — $49.00.

Virginia, cont.

OLD 10TH LEGION RECORDS.
Marriages in Rockingham Co., 1778-
1816, Taken from Marriage Bonds. By
H.M. Strickler. 1928. 128p.
P5-VA0005 — $17.00.

RUSSELL CO. ABSTR. OF DEEDS,
from Deed Book I, 1781-1795. By Lois
Nix. 1985. 34p.
P5-VA0001 — $10.00.

LIFE ALONG HOLMAN'S CREEK
(Shenandoah, Virginia). By Joseph
Floyd Wine. 1982. 254 + 9p.
P5-VA3201 — $38.00.

SHENANDOAH COUNTY
MARRIAGE BONDS, 1772-1853.
1937. 355p.
P5-VA0068 — $34.00.

SMYTH COUNTY History &
Traditions. By Goodbridge Wilson.
1937. 397p.
P5-VA0044 — $45.00.

SOUTHAMPTON COUNTY
MARRIAGE BONDS, 1751-1853.
1937. 185p.
P5-VA0069 — $22.50.

SPOTSYLVANIA COUNTY
RECORDS. Vol. I of Va. Co. Records
series. By W.A. Crozier. 1905. 576p.
P5-VA0055B — $59.00.

HISTORY OF TAZEWELL
COUNTY & SOUTHWEST
VIRGINIA, 1748-1920. By Wm. C.
Pendleton. 1920. 700p.
P5-VA0045B — $69.50.

HISTORY OF THE UNIVERSITY
OF VIRGINIA, 1819-1919. By Philip
A. Bruce. 1920-1922.
P5-VA0087 — $235.00/set.

HISTORY OF SOUTHWEST VA.,
1746-86; WASHINGTON CO, 1777-
1870. By Lewis P. Summers. 1903. 912p.
P5-VA0029 — $89.00.

WILLS OF WESTMORELAND
CO., 1654-1800. A.B. Fothergill. 1925.
229p.
P5-VA0016 — $24.00.

VA. COUNTY RECORDS, Vol. III:
Williamsburg Wills. By W.A. Crozier.
1906. 77p.
P5-VA0042A — $14.50.

STORY OF WINCHESTER IN
VIRGINIA: Oldest Town in the
Shenandoah Valley. By Frederick
Morton. 1925. 336p.
P5-VA0079 — $39.50.

WINCHESTER & ITS BEGIN-
NINGS, 1743-1814. 1926. 441p.
P5-VA0046 — $47.50.

ST JOHN'S EVANGELICAL
LUTHERAN CHURCH, Wythe Co.,
its Pastors & their Records, 1800-
1924. Includes marriages, baptisms,
member lists, deaths. F.B. Kegley &
Mary B. Kegley. 1961. 416 + 48p.,
typescript.
P5-VA0081 — $39.00.

Washington

SEATTLE & ENVIRONS, 1852-
1924, 3-vol. set. 1924. 3 vols., 679 + 640
+ 630p.
P5-WA0002 — $185.00/set.

SEATTLE & ENVIRONS, 1852-
1924, Vol. I. 1924. 679p.
P5-WA0002B — $69.50.

SEATTLE & ENVIRONS, 1852-
1924, Vol. II. 1924. 640p.
P5-WA0002B — $69.50.

SEATTLE & ENVIRONS, 1852-
1924, Vol. III. 1924. 630p.
P5-WA0002C — $69.50.

VOLUME OF MEMOIRS &
GENEALOGY OF REPRESEN-
TATIVE CITIZENS OF THE CITY
OF SEATTLE & THE COUNTY
OF KING, including Biographies.
1903. 773p.
P5-WA0005 — $84.50.

ILLUSTRATED HISTORY OF
SPOKANE COUNTY. By Rev.
Jonathan Edwards. 1900. 726p.
P5-WA0003 — $77.00.

LYMAN'S HISTORY OF OLD
WALLA WALLA COUNTY,
Embracing Walla Walla, Columbia,
Garfield & Asotin Counties, 2-vol.
set. W.D. Lyman. 1918. 2 vols, 731 + 846p.
P5-WA0004 — $149.50/set.

LYMAN'S HISTORY OF OLD
WALLA WALLA COUNTY . . ., Vol.
I. 1918. 731p.
P5-WA0004A — $75.00.

LYMAN'S HISTORY OF OLD
WALLA WALLA COUNTY . . ., Vol.
II. 1918. 846p.
P5-WA0004B — $85.50.

HISTORY OF CENTRAL WASH-
INGTON, Including the Famous
Wenatchee, Entiat, Chelan &
Columbia Valleys, with . . . Eighty
Scenic-Historical Illustrations. Part I,
The Story of Pioneer Settlements,
Part II, The Development Period.
Comp. by Lindley M. Hull. 1929. 624p.
P5-WA0001A — $67.00.

West Virginia

BORDER SETTLERS OF
NORTHWESTERN VA. [present-
day W.Va.], from 1768-1795, embrac-
ing the Life of Jesse Hughes & other
Noted Scouts of the Great Woods of
the Trans-Alleghany. L.V. McWhorter;
add. notes by W.E. Connelley. 1915. 509p.
P5-WV0001 — $54.50.

DYER'S INDEX TO LAND
GRANTS IN WEST VIRGINIA. By
M.H. Dyer. 1895. 948p.
P5-WV0004 — $89.00.

GAZETTEER OF WEST VIRGINIA.
By Henry Gannett. 1904. 164p.
P5-WV0012 — $19.50.

GENEALOGICAL & PERSONAL
HISTORY OF THE UPPER
MONONGAHELA VALLEY, 3-vol.
set. James M. Callahan. 1912. 3 vols.,
1399p.
P5-WV0017 — $135.00/set.

GENEALOGICAL & PERSONAL
HISTORY OF THE UPPER
MONONGAHELA VALLEY, Vol. I.
1912.
P5-WV0017A — $49.50.

GENEALOGICAL & PERSONAL
HISTORY OF THE UPPER
MONONGAHELA VALLEY, Vol.
II. 1912.
P5-WV0017B — $49.50.

GENEALOGICAL & PERSONAL
HISTORY OF THE UPPER
MONONGAHELA VALLEY, Vol.
III. 1912.
P5-WV0017C — $49.50.

HISTORY OF MIDDLE NEW RIVER SETTLEMENTS & Contiguous Territory. By David E. Johnson. 1906. 500 + xxxi p.
P5-WV0006 — $57.00.

MYERS' HISTORY OF WEST VIRGINIA, 2-vol. set. By Sylvester Myers. 1915. 2 vols., 560 + 480p.
P5-WV0011 — $99.50/set.

MYERS' HISTORY OF WEST VIRGINIA, Vol. I. 1915. 560p.
P5-WV0011A — $52.50.

MYERS' HISTORY OF WEST VIRGINIA, Vol. II. 1915. 480p.
P5-WV0011B — $52.50.

OBITUARIES FROM NEWS-PAPERS OF NOTHERN W.V., Principally from the Cos. Of Barbour, Braxton, Calhoun, Doddrige, Gilmer, etc., 2-vol. set. 1933. 2 vols., 602 + 600p.
P5-WV0062 — $117.00/set.

OBITUARIES FROM NEWS-PAPERS OF NOTHERN W.V. . . ., Principally from the Cos. Of Barbour, Braxton, Calhoun, Doddrige, Gilmer, etc., Vol. I. 1933. 602p.
P5-WV0062A — $62.50.

OBITUARIES FROM NEWS-PAPERS OF NOTHERN W.V. . . ., Principally from the Cos. Of Barbour, Braxton, Calhoun, Doddrige, Gilmer, etc., Vol. II. 1933. 600p.
P5-WV0062B — $62.50.

OHIO RIVER: A Course of Empire. By Archer Butler Hulbert. 1906. 378p.
P5-WV0022 — $45.00.

WEST VA. REVOLUTIONARY ANCESTORS. A.W. Reddy. 1930. 93p.
P5-WV0008 — $16.00.

WEST VIRGINIA & ITS PEOPLE, 3-vol. set. By Thomas C. Miller & Hu Maxwell. 1913. 3 vols., 1909p.
P5-WV0024 — $175.00/set.

WEST VIRGINIA & ITS PEOPLE, Vol. I. 1913.
P5-WV0024A — $65.00.

WEST VIRGINIA & ITS PEOPLE, Vol. II. 1913.
P5-WV0024B — $65.00.

WEST VIRGINIA & ITS PEOPLE, Vol. III. 1913.
P5-WV0024C — $65.00.

HISTORY OF BARBOUR COUNTY, from its Earliest Exploration & Settlement to the Present Time. Hu Maxwell. 1899. 518p.
P5-WV0014 — $54.50.

ALER'S HISTORY OF MARTINS-BURG & BERKELEY CO. By F. Vernon Aler. 1888. 452p.
P5-WV0015 — $48.50.

HISTORY OF BRAXTON COUNTY & Central West Virginia. By John Davison Sutton. 1919. 465p.
P5-WV0025 — $51.00.

CABELL COUNTY ANNALS & FAMILIES. By George Selden Wallace. 1935. 589p.
P5-WV0054 — $64.50.

CEMETERY READING IN GIDEON MAGISTERIAL DISTRICT [Cabell Co.]. Comp. by WV Historical Records Survey. 1940. 317p., typescript.
P5-WV0026 — $29.50.

MARRIAGE RECORDS OF CABELL COUNTY, 1809-1851. Comp. by Annie W.B. Bell. n.d. 90p., typescript.
P5-WV0027 — $17.50.

HISTORY OF CHARLESTON & KANAWHA COUNTY, & Representative Citizens. By W.S. Laidley. 1911. 1021p.
P5-WV0028 — $99.00.

CENSUS RETURNS OF DODD-RIDGE, RITCHIE & GILMER COS. (West) Wa. for 1850, & Calhoun Co. (West) Va. for 1860. 1933. 360p.
P5-WV0060 — $39.00.

HISTORY OF FAYETTE COUNTY. J.T. Peters and H.B. Carden. 1926. 772p.
P5-WV0056 — $79.50.

RECORD OF THE EARLY SETTLE-MENT OF LOWER LOUP CREEK, Fayette Co., 1798-1865. By L. Neil Darlington. 1933. 68p.
P5-WV0032 — $14.00.

HISTORY OF THE GREAT KANAWHA VALLEY, with Family History and Biographical Sketches. 1891. 308 + 307p.
P5-WV0021 — $62.50.

HISTORY OF GREENBRIER COUNTY. With biographical sketches. By J.R. Cole. 1917?. 347p.
P5-WV0029 — $41.50.

CEMETERIES OF HAMPSHIRE COUNTY. By Ralph L. Triplett, 1974-8. 437p.
P5-WV0057 — $49.00.

EARLY RECORDS, HAMPSHIRE CO., Virginia, Now W.V. (including at the start most of known Va., aside from Augusta District): . . . Wills . . . to 1860, Grantee, Grantor Deeds up to 1800, Marriage Records 1824-8, . . . State Census 1782 & 1784, Rev. Sol-diers' Pensions. By Clara McC. Sage & Laura S. Jones. 1939. 170p.
P5-WV0030 — $21.50.

HISTORY OF HAMPSHIRE COUNTY, from its Earliest Settle-ment to the Present [1897]. By Hu Maxwell & H.L. Swisher. 1897. 744p.
P5-WV0050 — $77.00.

HISTORY OF HARRISON COUNTY, from the Early Days of Northwestern Virginia to the Present. By Henry Haymond. 1910. 451p.
P5-WV0051 — $49.50.

HISTORY OF JEFFERSON COUNTY. By Millard Kessler Bushong. 1941. 438p.
P5-WV0055 — $48.00.

HISTORY OF KANAWHA COUNTY from its Organization in 1789 until the Present Time [1876], Embracing Accounts of Early Settlements & Thrilling Adventures with the Indians; also, Biographical Sketches of a Large Number of the Early Settlers of the Great Kanawh. By George W. Atkinson. 1876. 338p.
P5-WV0031 — $41.00.

CENSUS RETURNES OF LEWIS COUNTY for 1850. By W. Guy Tetrick. 1930. 287p.
P5-WV0053 — $37.50.

HISTORY OF LEWIS COUNTY. By Edward C. Smith. 1920. 427p.
P5-WV0010 — $47.00.

CEMETERY READING IN FAIRMONT & GRANT MAGIS-TERIAL DISTRICTS [Marion Co.]. Comp. by WV Historical Records Survey. 1941. 245p., typescript.
P5-WV0033 — $25.00.

For hardcover versions, see the order form on page v. To order, call 1-888-296-3447.

West Virginia, cont.

FORT PRICKETT FRONTIER & MARION COUNTY. By W.L. Balderson. 1976. 316p.
P5-WV0064 — $40.00.

HISTORY & PROGRESS OF THE COUNTY OF MARION, from its Earliest Settlement by the Whites, Together with Biographical Sketches of its Most Prominent Citizens. By George A. Dunnington. 1880. 162p.
P5-WV0034 — $27.00.

HISTORY OF MARSHALL COUNTY, from Forest to Field. A Story of Early Settlement & Development of Marshall Co., with Incidents of Early Life. By Scott Powell. 1925. 334p.
P5-WV0005 — $39.50.

HISTORY OF MONONGALIA COUNTY, from its First Settlement to the Present Time. with Numerous Biographical & Family Sketches. By Samuel T. Riley 1883. 776p.
P5-WV0035 — $81.50.

HISTORY OF MONROE COUNTY. By Oren F. Morton. 1916. 509p.
P5-WV0007 — $53.50.

HISTORY OF NICHOLAS COUNTY. By Wm. Griffee Brown. 1954. 425p.
P5-WV0020 — $47.00.

HISTORY OF PENDLETON COUNTY. With family sketches (15,000 individuals). By Oren F. Morton. 1910. 493p.
P5-WV0002 — $45.00.

HISTORICAL SKETCHES OF POCAHONTAS COUNTY, WEST VIRGINIA. By William T. Price. 1901. 628 + iv p.
P5-WV0063 — $64.00.

AURORA COMMUNITY, Preston Co. With genealogies. By M.L. Peter. 1950. 44p.
P5-WV0013 — $10.00.

GENEALOGY OF SOME EARLY FAMILIES IN Grant & Pleasant District, Preston Co. By E.T. King. 1933. 233p.
P5-WV0003 — $29.50.

HISTORY OF PRESTON COUNTY. By S.T. Wiley. 1882. 529p.
P5-WV0019 — $55.00.

HISTORY OF PRESTON COUNTY. Oren F. Morton (History) & J.R. Cole (Biography). 1914. 2 vols. in 1 book, 887p.
P5-WV0036 — $91.00.

HISTORY OF RANDOLPH CO., from its Earliest Exploration & Settlement to the Present Time. By Hu Maxwell. 1898. 531p.
P5-WV0018 — $55.00.

HISTORY OF RANDOLPH COUNTY, from its Earliest Exploration & Settlement to the Present Time [1916]. By A.S. Baosworth. 1916. 448p.
P5-WV0037 — $49.00.

HISTORY OF RITCHIE COUNTY, with Biographical Sketches of its Pioneers & their Ancestors, & Interesting Reminiscences of Revolutionary & Indian Times. By Minnie Kendall Lowther. 1911. 679p.
P5-WV0038 — $71.50.

HISTORY OF ROANE COUNTY, from the Time of its Exploration (1774) to 1927. With genealogies. By Wm. H. Bishop. 1927. 711p.
P5-WV0009 — $74.50.

HISTORIC SHEPHERDSTOWN. By Danske Dandridge. 1910. 389p.
P5-WV0039 — $46.00.

HISTORY OF SUMMERS COUNTY, from the Earliest Settlement to the Present Time. James H. Miller. 1908. 838p.
P5-WV0040 — $87.00.

WAYNE COUNTY, WEST VIRGINIA IN THE CIVIL WAR. Jack L. Dickinson. 2003. 193p.
P5-WV10034 — $32.00.

MOCCASIN TRACKS AND OTHER IMPRINTS (sketches relating to pioneer history of Webster Co. & pioneer families). By William C. Dodrill. 1915. 298p.
P5-WV0052 — $39.50.

HISTORY OF WETZEL COUNTY. By John S. McEldowney, Jr. 1901. 187p.
P5-WV0041 — $28.50.

HISTORY OF WHEELING CITY AND OHIO COUNTY, and Representative Citizens. 1902. 853p.
P5-WV0023 — $87.00.

SKETCHES OF WOOD COUNTY: its Early History as Embraced in & Connected with Other Counties of West Virginia; also Brief Accounts of First Settlers & their Descendants. By S.C. Shaw. 1878. 65p.
P5-WV0042 — $13.00.

Wisconsin

BIOGRAPHICAL HISTORY OF CLARK & JACKSON COUNTIES, Containing . . . Engravings of Prominent Citizens of the Counties, with Personal Histories of Many of the Early Settlers & Leading Families. 1891. 387p.
P5-WI0041 — $45.50.

BIOGRAPHICAL HISTORY OF LA CROSSE, TREMPELEAU & BUFFALO COUNTIES, Containing . . . Engravings of Prominent Citizens of the Counties, with Personal Histories of Many of the Early Settlers & Leading Families. 1892. 794p.
P5-WI0045 — $81.50.

BIOGRAPHICAL HISTORY OF LaCROSSE, MONROE & JUNEAU COUNTIES, Containing . . . Engravings of Prominent Citizens with Personal Histories of Many of the Early Settlers & Leading Families. 1892. 936p.
P5-WI0067 — $97.00.

BIOGRAPHICAL SKETCHES OF OLD SETTLERS & PROMINENT PEOPLE OF WISCONSIN, Vol. I (all published). 1899. 298p.
P5-WI0034 — $37.00.

COMMEMORATIVE BIOGRAPHICAL RECORD OF PROMINENT & REPRESENTATIVE MEN OF RACINE & KENOSHA COUNTIES, Containing Biographical Sketches of Business & Professional Men & Many of the Early Settled Families. 1906. 645p.
P5-WI0056 — $69.00.

COMMEMORATIVE BIOGRAPHICAL RECORD OF THE COUNTIES OF ROCK, GREEN, GRANT, IOWA & LAFAYETTE, Containing Biographical Sketches of Prominent & Representative Citizens & Many of the Early Settled Families. 1901. 990p.
P5-WI0059 — $99.00.

COMMEMORATIVE BIOGRAPH-ICAL RECORD OF THE UPPER LAKE REGION, Containing Biographical Sketches of Prominent & Representative Citizens & Many of the Early Settled Families. 1905. 554p.
P5-WI0039 — $59.50.

FIFTY YEARS IN THE NORTH-WEST, with an Introduction and Appendix containing Reminiscences, Incidents and Notes. By W.H.C. Folsom. 1888. 763p.
P5-WI0013B — $78.00.

HISTORY OF NORTHERN WIS-CONSIN, containing an Account of its Settlement, Growth, Development & Resources; an Extensive Sketch of its Counties, Cities, Towns & Villages; Biographical Sketches, Portraits of Prominent Men & Early Settlers, etc. 1881. 1218p.
P5-WI0021 — $119.00.

HISTORY OF THE TERRITORY OF WISCONSIN, from 1836 to 1848. Preceded by an Account of Some Events . . . Previous to 1836. By Moses M. Strong. 1870. 637p.
P5-WI0003 — $67.00.

HISTORY OF WISCONSIN, comprising Sketches of Counties, Towns, Events, Institutions & Persons, arranged in Cyclopedic Form. 1906. 417p.
P5-WI0001 — $44.50.

ILLUSTRATED HISTORY OF THE STATE OF WISCONSIN, Being a Complete Civil, Political & Military History of the State, from its First Exploration to 1875, incl. . . . Historical & Descriptive Sketches of Each Co. . . ., Embracing Interesting Narratives of Pioneer Life By Charles R. Tuttle. 1875. 800p.
P5-WI0038 — $81.50.

WEST CENTRAL WISCONSIN: A History, 4-vol. set. John G. Gregory & Thomas J. Cunningham. 1933. 4 vols., 2460p.
P5-WI0015B — $210.00/set.

WEST CENTRAL WISCONSIN: A History, Vol. I. 1933.
P5-WI0015B1 — $57.50.

WEST CENTRAL WISCONSIN: A History, Vol. II. 1933.
P5-WI0015B2 — $57.50.

WEST CENTRAL WISCONSIN: A History, Vol. III. 1933.
P5-WI0015B3 — $57.50.

WEST CENTRAL WISCONSIN: A History, Vol. IV. 1933.
P5-WI0015B4 — $57.50.

WISCONSIN IN THE WAR OF THE REBELLION: History of All Regiments & Batteries. By Wm. DeLoss Love. 1866. 1144p.
P5-WI0037 — $109.00.

HISTORY OF BUFFALO AND PEPIN COUNTIES, 2-vol. set. By Franklyn Curtiss-Wedge. 1919. 2 vols., 1047p.
P5-WI0064 — $109.00/set.

HISTORY OF BUFFALO AND PEPIN COUNTIES, Vol. I. 1919.
P5-WI0064A — $59.00.

HISTORY OF BUFFALO AND PEPIN COUNTIES, Vol. II. 1919.
P5-WI0064B — $59.00.

HISTORY OF BUFFALO COUNTY, WISCONSIN. By L. Kessinger 1888. xvi + 656p.
P5-WI10035 — $65.00.

HISTORICAL & BIOGRAPHICAL ALBUM OF THE CHIPPEWA VALLEY, Including a General Historical Sketch; Ancestral Records of Leading Families; Biographies of Representative Citizens, Past & Present; & Portraits of Prominent Men. 1891-1892. 950p.
P5-WI0035 — $97.00.

HISTORY OF THE CHIPPEWA VALLEY: Faithful Record of all Important Events, Incidents & Circumstances that have Transpired in the Valley of the Chippewa . . .; also of the Counties Embracing the Valley . . .; also a Brief Biogr. Sketch of the Prominent Persons . . . By Thos. E. Randall. 1875. 207p.
P5-WI0040 — $31.00.

HISTORY OF COLUMBIA COUNTY, Containing an Acct. of its Settlement, Growth & Resources . . . & Biographical Sketches. 1880. 1095p.
P5-WI0004 — $105.00.

HISTORY OF CRAWFORD & RICHLAND COUNTIES, Together with Sketches of their Towns & Villages . . . and Biographies of Representative Citizens, with a History of Wisconsin. With 1981 index to Richland Co. section. 1884. 1308 + 36p.
P5-WI0022 — $129.00.

HISTORY OF DANE COUNTY, Containing an Account its Settlement, Growth, Development, etc..& Biographical Sketches. 1880. 1289p.
P5-WI0005 — $119.50.

HISTORY OF DANE COUNTY, 2-vol. set. 1906. 2 vols., 423 + 974p.
P5-WI0002 — $132.00/set.

HISTORY OF DANE COUNTY, Vol. I. 1906. 423p.
P5-Wi0002A — $45.00.

HISTORY OF DANE COUNTY, Vol. II. 1906. 974p.
P5-Wi0002B — $99.50.

PRAIRIE FARMER'S HOME & COUNTY DIRECTORY OF DANE COUNTY: Directory of the Farm Homes of Dane Co., with Information about Each Family & Farm. 1928. 351p.
P5-WI10036 — $39.50.

DODGE COUNTY, WISCONSIN., Past & Present, 2-vol. set. By Homer B. Hubbell. 1913. 2 vols., 432 + 494p.
P5-WI0016 — $95.00/set.

DODGE COUNTY, WISCONSIN., Past & Present, Vol. I. 1913. 432p.
P5-WI0016A — $49.50.

DODGE COUNTY, WISCONSIN., Past & Present, Vol. II. 1913. 494p.
P5-Wi0016B — $49.50.

HISTORY OF DODGE COUNTY, Containing . . . its Early Settlement . . . Biographical Sketche, etc. 1880. 766p.
P5-WI0023 — $81.00.

HISTORY OF DUNN COUNTY. With biographical sketches. Comp. by F. Curtiss-Wedge, G.O. Jones, et al. 1925. 966p.
P5-WI0024 — $97.00.

FOND du LAC COUNTY: Past & Present, Vol. I. 1912. 399p
P5-WI0025A — $42.00.

For hardcover versions, see the order form on page v. To order, call 1-888-296-3447.

Wisconsin, cont.

FOND du LAC COUNTY: Past & Present, Vol. II. 1912. 715p
P5-WI0025B — $77.00.

HISTORY OF FOND DU LAC COUNTY, containing a History of . . . its Early Settlement . . . and Biographical Sketches . . . 1880. 1063p.
P5-WI0015A — $105.00.

HISTORY OF THE FOX RIVER VALLEY, Lake Winnebago and the Green Bay Region, 3 vols. in 2. 1930. 3 vols. in 2, 853 + 683p.
P5-WI0026 — $149.00/set.

HISTORY OF THE FOX RIVER VALLEY . . ., Vols. I & II. 1930. 853p.
P5-WI0026A — $85.00.

HISTORY OF THE FOX RIVER VALLEY . . ., Vol. III. 1930. 683p
P5-WI0026B — $78.00.

HISTORY OF GRANT COUNTY, Containing an Account of its Settlement, Growth, Development; its Cities, Towns & Villages; Biographical Sketches, Portraits of Prominent Men & Early Settlers. 1881. 1046p.
P5-WI0042 — $99.50.

HISTORY OF GREEN COUNTY, Together with Sketches of its Towns & Villages . . . and Biographies of Representative Citizens. 1884. 1158p.
P5-WI0027 — $109.00.

HISTORY OF GREEN COUNTY. By Helen M. Bingham. 1877. 310p.
P5-WI0043 — $39.50.

PORTRAIT & BIOGRAPHICAL ALBUM OF GREEN LAKE, MARQUETTE & WAUSHARA COUNTIES. 1890. 850p.
P5-WI0006 — $89.50.

HISTORY OF IOWA COUNTY, Containing an Account of its Settlement, Growth, Development; . . . its Cities, Town & Villages; . . . Biographical Sketches; Portraits of Prominent Men & Early Settlers; etc. 1881. 970p.
P5-WI0044 — $99.50.

PRAIRIE FARMER'S HOME & COUNTY DIRECTORY OF IOWA CO., WI. 1929. 183p.
P5-WI0074 — $29.00.

HISTORY OF JEFFERSON COUNTY, its Early Settlement, Growth . . . etc.; an Extensive & Minute Sketch of its Cities, Towns & Villages . . . ; Biographical Sketches, Portraits of Prominent Men & Early Settlers . . . 1879. 733p.
P5-WI0028 — $77.00.

PRAIRIE FARMER'S HOME & COUNTY DIRECTORY OF JEFFERSON CO., WI. 1927. 245p.
P5-WI0073 — $34.00.

PRAIRIE FARMERS DIRECTORY OF KENOSHA AND RACINE COUNTIES, WISCONSIN. 1919. 367p
P5-WI10037 — $37.00.

HISTORY OF LaCROSSE COUNTY, Containing . . . an Account of its Settlement, Growth, Development & Resources; . . . Biographical Sketches & Portraits of Prominent Men & Early Settlers. 1881. 862p.
P5-WI0066 — $89.50.

HISTORY OF LaFAYETTE COUNTY, Containing an Account of its Settlement, Growth, Development . . .; Sketch of its Cities, Towns & Villages; Biographical Sketches & Portraits of Prominent Men & Early Settlers. 1881. 799p.
P5-WI0046 — $84.00.

LaGRANGE PIONEERS. By James & Esther Ellis. 1935. 395p.
P5-WI0047 — $46.50.

HISTORY OF LINCOLN, ONEIDA & VILAS COUNTIES. By George O. Jones, et al. 1924. 787p.
P5-WI0007 — $79.50.

MADISON, DANE COUNTY, & Surrounding Towns, being a History & Guide. 1877. 664p.
P5-WI0008 — $68.50.

HISTORY OF MANITOWOC COUNTY, 2-vol. set. By Dr Louis Falge. 1911-1912. 2 vols., 463 + 675p.
P5-WI0009 — $109.50/set.

HISTORY OF MANITOWOC COUNTY, Vol. I. By Dr Louis Falge. 1911-1912. 463p.
P5-WI0009A — $69.50.

HISTORY OF MANITOWOC COUNTY, Vol. II. By Dr Louis Falge. 1911-1912. 675p.
P5-WI0009B — $69.50.

HISTORY OF MARATHON & Representative Citizens. By Louis Marchetti. 1913. 984p.
P5-WI0048 — $99.50.

HISTORY OF MILWAUKEE from Pre-Historic Times to [1881], Embracing a Summary Sketch of the Native Tribes & an Exhaustive Record of Men & Events for the Past Century . . . including Nearly Four Thousand Biographical Sketches of Pioneers & Citizens. 1881. 1661p.
P5-WI0050 — $159.00.

HISTORY OF MILWAUKEE, City & County, 3-vol. set. 1922. 3 vols., 804 + 831 + 893p.
P5-WI0051 — $229.00/set.

HISTORY OF MILWAUKEE, City & County, Vol. I. 1922. 804p
P5-WI0051A — $85.00.

HISTORY OF MILWAUKEE, City & County, Vol. II. 1922. 831p
P5-WI0051B — $85.00.

HISTORY OF MILWAUKEE, City & County, Vol. III. 1922. 893p
P5-WI0051C — $85.00.

HISTORY OF MILWAUKEE, from its First Settlement to the Year 1895, 2-vol. set. 1895. 2 vols, 510 + 500p.
P5-WI0049 — $105.00/set.

HISTORY OF MILWAUKEE, from its First Settlement to the Year 1895, Vol. I. 1895. 510p
P5-WI0049A — $54.50.

HISTORY OF MILWAUKEE, from its First Settlement to the Year 1895, Vol. II. 1895. 500p
P5-WI0049B — $54.50.

PIONEER HISTORY OF MIL-WAUKEE, 4-vol. set. By James S. Buck. 1881-1890. 4 vols., 355 + 383 + 506 + 465p.
P5-WI0069 — $159.00/set.

PIONEER HISTORY OF MIL-WAUKEE, Vol. I. 1881-1890. 355p.
P5-WI0069A — $45.00.

PIONEER HISTORY OF MIL-WAUKEE, Vol. II. 1881-1890. 383p
P5-WI0069B — $45.00.

PIONEER HISTORY OF MIL-WAUKEE, Vol. III. 1881-1890. 506p
P5-WI0069C — $45.00.

PIONEER HISTORY OF MILWAUKEE, Vol. IV. 1881-1890. 465p.
P5-WI0069D — $45.00.

HISTORY OF MONROE COUNTY: Past & Present, Including an Account of the Cities, Towns & Villages of the County. By Randolph A. Richards. 1912. 946p.
P5-WI0030 — $97.00.

HISTORY OF THE TOWN OF MOSCOW, from 1848 to 1919. By Bjorn Holland. 1919. 175p.
P5-WI0052 — $22.50.

EARLY & LATE MOSINEE. By Edgar E. Ladu. 1907. 228p.
P5-WI0053 — $34.00.

HISTORY OF NEENAH, Being a Complete Historical Sketch from the "Early Days" to [1878], with Interesting Incidents & Personal Reminiscences. By G.A. Cunningham. 1878. 254 + 53p.
P5-WI0031 — $41.00.

LAND OF THE FOX: A Saga of Outagamie County. 1949. 302p.
P5-WI0018 — $36.00.

PIONEERS OF OUTAGAMIE COUNTY, Containing the Records of the Outagamie County Pioneer Association; a Biographical & Historical Sketch of Some of the Earliest Settlers of the County & their Families, their Children & Grand-Children. By Elihu Spencer. 1895. 303p.
P5-WI0054 — $39.00.

OUR COUNTY, OUR STORY: Portage County. By Malcolm Rosholt. 1959. 600p.
P5-WI0065 — $64.50.
STORY OF PRIMROSE, 1831-1895. By Albert Barton. 1895. 112p.
P5-WI0055 — $17.50.

HISTORY OF RACINE & KENOSHA COUNTIES, Containing a History of Each County, its Early Settlement, Growth, etc . . . & Biographical Sketches. 1879. 738p.
P5-WI0010 — $75.00.

OFFICIAL RECORD OF THE OLD SETTLERS SOCIETY OF RACINE CO., with Historical Address. By Charles E. Dyer. 1871. 84p.
P5-WI0057 — $16.00.

RACINE COUNTY MILITANT: Illustrated Narrative of War Times, also a Soldiers' Roster, a Pioneer Publication [Civil War]. By Eugene W.Leach. 1915. 394p.
P5-WI0058 — $43.50.

HISTORY OF REEDSBURG AND THE UPPER BARABOO VALLEY. By Merton Edwin Krug. 1929. 509 p.
P5-WI0071B — $57.00.

HISTORY OF RICHLAND COUNTY. With 1986 index. 1906. 698 + 50p.
P5-WI0032 — $79.50.

HISTORY OF ROCK COUNTY, Containing a History of Each County, its Early Settlement, Growth, etc . . . & Biographical Sketches. 1879. 897p.
P5-WI0011 — $89.50.

PRAIRIE FARMER'S RELIABLE DIRECTORY OF FARMERS AND BREEDERS, ROCK COUNTY, WISCONSIN. 1919. 375p.
P5-WI0070 — $39.50.

HISTORY OF SAUK COUNTY, Containing a History of Each County, its Early Settlement, Growth, etc. . . . & Biographical Sketches. 1880. 825p.
P5-WI0012 — $85.00.

HISTORY OF TREMPELEAU COUNTY. Comp. by Franklyn Curtis-Wedge. 1917. 922p.
P5-WI0013A — $92.00.

HISTORY OF VERNON COUNTY, Together with Sketches of its Towns, Villages & Townships; . . . Civil, Military & Political History; Portraits of Prominent Persons & Biographies of Representative Citizens. 1884. 826p.
P5-WI0060 — $87.00.

HISTORY OF WALWORTH COUNTY, Containing an Account of its Settlement . . . its Cities, Towns and Villages . . . and Biographical Sketches. 1862. 967p.
P5-WI0019 — $98.00.

HISTORY OF WAUKESHA COUNTY, Containing an Account of its Settlement, Growth, Development . . . ; Sketch of its Cities, Towns & Villages; Biographical Sketches & Portraits of Prominent Men & Early Settlers. 1880. 1007p.
P5-WI0061 — $99.50.

HISTORY OF WAUPACA COUNTY. By J. Wakefield. 1890. 219p.
P5-WI0033 — $34.00.

SKETCHES OF WAUWATOSA. By Elizabeth V. Foley. 1932. 110p.
P5-WI0068 — $17.50.

EARLY ANNALS OF WHITE-WATER, 1837-1867. By Prosper Cravath & Spencer Steele. 1906. 283p.
P5-WI0017 — $39.50.

HISTORY OF WINNEBAGO COUNTY & the Early History of the Northwest. Richard J. Harney. 1880. 349p.
P5-WI0063 — $41.50.

HISTORY OF WINNEBAGO COUNTY, Its Cities, Towns, Resources, People, 2-vol. set. 1908. 2 vols., 1208p.
P5-WI0062 — $119.00/set.

HISTORY OF WINNEBAGO COUNTY . . ., Vol. I. 1908.
P5-WI0062A — $64.00.

HISTORY OF WINNEBAGO COUNTY . . ., Vol. II. 1908.
P5-WI0062B — $64.00.

Wyoming

HISTORY & BUSINESS DIRECTORY OF CHEYENNE & Guide to Mining Regions of the Rocky Mountains. Comp. by E.H. Saltiel & George Barnett. 1868. 114p.
P5-WY0001 — $22.50.

MISCELLANEOUS

REGIONAL GENEALOGIES

"SAVAGE'S DICTIONARY" GENEALOGICAL DICTIONARY OF THE FIRST SETTLERS OF NEW ENGLAND, Showing Three Generations of Those who Came Before May, 1692, on the Basis of Farmer's Register. With genealogical cross-index. 4-vol. set By J. Savage. 1860-1862. 4 vols., 2541 + 38p.
P5-NEG001 — $145.00/set.

"SAVAGE'S DICTIONARY" GENEALOGICAL DICTIONARY OF THE FIRST SETTLERS OF NEW ENGLAND . . ., Vol. I. 1860-2.
P5-NEG001A — $39.50.

"SAVAGE'S DICTIONARY" GENEALOGICAL DICTIONARY OF THE FIRST SETTLERS OF NEW ENGLAND . . ., Vol. II. 1860-2.
P5-NEG001B — $39.50.

"SAVAGE'S DICTIONARY" GENEALOGICAL DICTIONARY OF THE FIRST SETTLERS OF NEW ENGLAND . . ., Vol. III. 1860-2.
P5-NEG001C — $39.50.

GENEALOGIES OF THE FAMILIES OF THE PRESIDENTS. By R.B. Henry. 1935. 340p.
P5-GR0030 — $38.50.

INDEX TO GENEALOGIES & PEDIGREES in the New England Historic Genealogical Register, Vols. 1-50. 11p.
P5-GR0002 — $10.00.

INDEX TO PERSONS in the New England Historic Genealogical Register, Vols. 1-50, 4-vol. set. 1907.
P5-GR0010A — $159.00/set.

INDEX TO PERSONS in the New England Historic Genealogical Register, Vols. 1-50, Vol. I. 1907.
P5-GR0010AB — $45.00.

INDEX TO PERSONS in the New England Historic Genealogical Register, Vols. 1-50, Vol. II. 1907.
P5-GR0010AC — $45.00.

INDEX TO PERSONS in the New England Historic Genealogical Register, Vols. 1-50, Vol. III. 1907.
P5-GR0010AD — $45.00.

INDEX TO PERSONS in the New England Historic Genealogical Register, Vols. 1-50, Vol. IV. 1907.
P5-GR0010AE — $45.00.

GENEALOGICAL GLEANINGS IN ENGLAND: Abstracts of Wills Related to Early American Families with Genealogical Notes & Pedigrees Constructed from Wills & other Records. With New Series. 2-vol. set. By Henry F. Waters. 1901, 1907. 2 vols., 1760p.
P5-WA0001B — $125.00/set.

GENEALOGICAL GLEANINGS IN ENGLAND . . . , Vol. I. By Henry F. Waters. 1901.
P5-WA0001BA — $68.50.

GENEALOGICAL GLEANINGS IN ENGLAND . . ., Vol. II. By Henry F. Waters. 1907.
P5-WA0001BB — $68.50.

SCHLEGEL'S GERMAN-AMERICAN FAMILIES in the United States, Genealogical & Biographical [New York ed.], 2-vol. set. 1917. 2 vols., 393 + 403p.
P5-NY0405B — $89.00/set (Two-vols. in one book).

SCHLEGEL'S GERMAN-AMERICAN FAMILIES . . ., Vol. I. 1917. 393p.
P5-NY0405B1 — $47.00.

SCHLEGEL'S GERMAN-AMERICAN FAMILIES . . ., Vol. II. 1917. 403p.
P5-NY0405B2 — $47.00.

AMERICAN FAMILIES OF HISTORIC LINEAGE, LONG ISLAND EDITION, Vol. II. 1921?.
P5-NY0041B — $39.50.

CATALOGUE OF AMERICAN GENEALOGIES in the Library of the Long Island Historical Society. 1935. 660p.
P5-GR0003 — $67.50.

LONG ISLAND GENEALOGIES, Being Kindred Desc. of Thomas Powell of Bethpage, Long Island, 1688. With genealogical material on over 60 early families. By M. Bunker. 1895. 350p.
P5-NY0013 — $48.00.

OTISFIELD GENEALOGIES ONLY. 340p.
P5-ME0035 — $34.00.

GENEALOGICAL & FAMILY HISTORY OF THE STATE OF NEW HAMPSHIRE: Record of the Achievements of her People in the Making of a Commonwealth & the Founding of a Nation, Vol. I. 1908.
P5-NH0249A — $57.00.

GENEALOGICAL & FAMILY HISTORY OF THE STATE OF NEW HAMPSHIRE . . ., Vol. II. 1908.
P5-NH0249B — $57.00.

GENEALOGICAL & FAMILY HISTORY OF THE STATE OF NEW HAMPSHIRE . . ., Vol. III. 1908.
P5-NH0249C — $57.00.

GENEALOGICAL & FAMILY HISTORY OF THE STATE OF NEW HAMPSHIRE . . ., Vol. IV. 1908.
P5-NH0249D — $57.00.

GENEALOGICAL & FAMILY HISTORY OF NORTHERN NEW YORK: A Record of the Achievements of her People in the Making of the Commonwealth & the Building of a Nation, 3-vol. set. 1910. 3 vols., 1247p.
P5-NY0035 — $124.00/set.

GENEALOGICAL & FAMILY HISTORY OF NORTHERN NEW YORK . . ., Vol. I. 1910.
P5-NY0035A — $44.50.

GENEALOGICAL & FAMILY HISTORY OF NORTHERN NEW YORK . . ., Vol. II. 1910.
P5-NY0035B — $44.50.

GENEALOGICAL & FAMILY HISTORY OF NORTHERN NEW YORK . . ., Vol. III. 1910.
P5-NY0035C — $44.50.

GENEALOGICAL & FAMILY HISTORY OF SOUTHERN NEW YORK & THE HUDSON RIVER VALLEY: A Record of the Achievements of her People in the Making of the Commonwealth & the Building of a Nation, 3-vol. set. 1913. 3 vols; 416 + 317 + 351p.
P5-NY0034 — $115.00/set.

GENEALOGICAL & FAMILY HISTORY OF SOUTHERN NEW YORK & THE HUDSON RIVER VALLEY . . ., Vol. I. 1913. 416p.
P5-NY0034A — $43.50.

For hardcover versions, see the order form on page v. To order, call 1-888-296-3447.

GENEALOGICAL & FAMILY HISTORY OF SOUTHERN NEW YORK & THE HUDSON RIVER VALLEY . . ., Vol. II. 1913. 317p.
P5-NY0034B — $40.00.

GENEALOGICAL & FAMILY HISTORY OF SOUTHERN NEW YORK & THE HUDSON RIVER VALLEY . . ., Vol. III. 1913. 351p.
P5-NY0034C — $41.50.

GENEALOGICAL NOTES OF NEW YORK & NEW ENGLAND FAMILIES. Compiled by S.V. Talcott. 1883. 747 + 39p.
P5-NY0240 — $81.50.

HUDSON-MOHAWK GENEA-LOGICAL & FAMLY MEMOIR: Record of Achievements of the People of Hudson & Mohawk Vals., incl. within the Present Cos. of Albany, Rensselaer, Washington, Saratoga, Montgomery, Fulton, Schenectady, Columbia & Greene, 4-vol. set. 1911. 4 vols., 2076p.
P5-NY0103 — $175.00/set.

HUDSON-MOHAWK GENEA-LOGICAL & FAMLY MEMOIR . . ., Vol. I. 1911.
P5-NY0103A — $49.00.

HUDSON-MOHAWK GENEA-LOGICAL & FAMLY MEMOIR . . ., Vol. II. 1911.
P5-NY0103B — $49.00.

HUDSON-MOHAWK GENEA-LOGICAL & FAMLY MEMOIR . . ., Vol. III. 1911.
P5-NY0103C — $49.00.

HUDSON-MOHAWK GENEA-LOGICAL & FAMLY MEMOIR . . ., Vol. IV. 1911.
P5-NY0103D — $49.00.

GENEALOGICAL & PERSONAL HISTORY OF WESTERN PENN-SYLVANIA, 3-vol. set. 1915. 1789p.
P5-PA0175 — $169.00/set.

GENEALOGICAL & PERSONAL HISTORY OF WESTERN PENNSYLVANIA, Vol. I. 1915.
P5-PA0175A — $61.00.

GENEALOGICAL & PERSONAL HISTORY OF WESTERN PENNSYLVANIA, Vol. II. 1915.
P5-PA0175B — $61.00.

GENEALOGICAL & PERSONAL HISTORY OF WESTERN PENNSYLVANIA, Vol. III. 1915.
P5-PA0175C — $61.00.

ENCYCLOPEDIA OF AMERICAN QUAKER GENEALOGY, Vol. III: New York. 1940. 540p.
P5-NY0122 — $45.00.

GENEALOGICAL DICTIONARY OF RHODE ISLAND, Comprising Three Generations of Settlers who Came before 1690. With many families carried to the 4th gen. By J.O. Austin. 1887. 446p.
P5-RI0020 — $51.00.

EMIGRANTS

THE BELGIANS: First Settlers in New York & in the Middle States, with a Review of the Events which Led to their Immigration. By Henry G. Bayer. 1925. 373p.
P5-NY0032 — $41.50.

WILLIAM PENN & THE DUTCH QUAKER MIGRATION TO PENNSYLVANIA. By Wm. I. Hull. 1935. 445p.
P5-PA0258 — $45.00.

[HOTTEN'S] ORIGINAL LISTS OF PERSONS OF QUALITY: Emigrants, Religious Exiles, Political Rebels . . . & Others who Went from Great Britain to the American Plantations, 1690-1700. J.C. Hotten. 1874. 580p.
P5-HT0001 — $49.00.

PLANTERS OF THE COMMON-WEALTH: Study of the Emigrants & Emigration in Colonial Times, to which are Added Lists of Passengers to Boston & the Bay Colony, the Ships which Brought Them, Their English Homes & the Places of Their Settlement in Mass., 1620-1640. Charles Edw. Banks. 1930. 231p.
P5-GR0015 — $29.50.

TOPOGRAPHICAL DICTIONARY OF 2885 ENGLISH EMIGRANTS TO NEW ENGLAND, 1620-1650. By Charles E. Banks. 1937. 295p.
P5-GR0025 — $37.00.

GERMAN ELEMENT OF THE SHENANDOAH VALLEY. By John Walter Wayland. 1907. 272p.
P5-VA0060 — $37.00.

GERMAN EMIGRANTS TO THE US, Series B, vol. I. By Dr. Heinz Marxkors. 2004. 137p.
P5-IL0242 — $26.00.

GERMAN EMIGRANTS TO THE US, Series B, vol. II. By Dr. Heinz Marxkors. 2004. 161p.
P5-IL0246 — $28.00.

GERMAN EMIGRANTS TO THE US, Series B, vol. III. By Dr. Heinz Marxkors. 2004. 358p.
P5-IL0247 — $45.00.

GERMAN EMIGRANTS TO THE US, Series B, vol. IV. By Dr. Heinz Marxkors. 2005. 262p.
P5-IL0252 — $36.00.

GERMAN EMIGRANTS TO THE US, series B, vol. V. By Dr. Heinz Marxkors. 2005. 130p.
P5-IL0255 — $25.00.

GERMAN EMIGRANTS TO US, Series B, vol. VI. By Dr. Heinz Marxkors. 2005. 197p.
P5-IL0256 — $32.00.

GERMAN EMIGRANTS TO THE US, Series B, vol. VII. By Dr. Heinz Marxkors. 2005. 257p.
P5-IL0257 — $37.00.

GERMAN EMIGRANTS TO THE US, Series B, vol. VIII. By Dr. Heinz Marxkors. 2005. 109p.
P5-IL0260 — $28.00.

GERMAN EMIGRANTS TO THE US, Series B, vol. IX. By Dr. Heinz Marxkors. 2005. 88p.
P5-IL0262 — $27.00.

GERMAN EMIGRANTS TO THE US, IL. Series B, Vol. X. By Dr. Heinz Marxkors. 2005. 98p.
P5-IL0261 — $27.00.

GERMAN EMIGRANTS TO THE US, Series B, vol. XI. By Dr. Heinz Marxkors. 2005. 216p.
P5-IL0259 — $33.00.

SCHLEGEL'S GERMAN-AMERICAN FAMILIES in the United States, Genealogical & Biographical [New York ed.], 2 vols in 1 book. 1917. 2 vols., 393 + 403p.
P5-NY0405B — $89.00/set.

SCHLEGEL'S GERMAN-AMERICAN FAMILIES in the United States, Genealogical & Biographical [New York ed.], Vol. I. 1917. 393p.
P5-NY0405B1 — $47.00.

DOCUMENTS CHIEFLY UNPUBLISHED RELATING THE HUGUENOT EMIGRATION TO VIRGINIA & the settlement at Manakin-town, with appendix of genealogies presenting data of the Fontaine, Maury, Dupuy, Trabue, Marye, Chastain, Cooke & other families. By R.A. Brock. 1886. 247p.
P5-VA0088 — $37.00.

HISTORY OF HUGUENOT EMIGRATION TO AMERICA. Charles W. Baird. 1885. 2 vols. in 1, 353 + 448p.
P5-FR0021 — $79.00.

MEMORIALS OF THE HUGUENOTS IN AMERICA, with Special Reference to their Emigration to Penn. Rev. A. Stapleton. 1901. 164p.
P5-PA0179B — $19.00.

MEMOIRS OF A HUGUENOT FAMILY: Translated & Compiled from the Original Autobiography of the Rev. James Fontainee, & Other Family Manuscripts. By Ann Maury. 1872. 512p.
P5-FR0002 — $57.00.

EARLY 18TH CENTURY PALATINE EMIGRATION. By Walter A. Knittle. 1937. 320p.
P5-PA0141B — $29.00.

PENNSYLVANIA-GERMAN IN THE SETTLEMENT OF MARYLAND. Daniel W. Nead. 1914. 304p.
P5-MD0024 — $39.50.

SCANDINAVIAN IMMIGRANTS IN NEW YORK, 1630-1674. With appendices on Scandinavians in Mexico, So. America, Cananda, N.Y., plus Germans in N.Y. By John O. Evjen. 1916. 24 + 438p.
P5-NY0137 — $47.00.

HISTORY OF THE SWEDES IN ILLINOIS, 2-vol. set. 1908. 2 vols., 933 + 684p.
P5-SW0001 — $139.00/set.

HISTORY OF THE SWEDES IN ILLINOIS, Vol. I. 1908. 933p.
P5-SW0001A — $78.00.

HISTORY OF THE SWEDES IN ILLINOIS, Vol. II. 1908. 684p.
P5-SW0001B — $65.00.

HISTORY OF THE SWEDISH-AMERICANS OF MINNESOTA, Three-vol. set By A.E. Strand. 1910. 3 vols., 1147p.
P5-MN0011 — $115.00/set.

HISTORY OF THE SWEDISH-AMERICANS OF MINNESOTA, Vol. I. By A.E. Strand. 1910.
P5-MN0011A — $45.00.

HISTORY OF THE SWEDISH-AMERICANS OF MINNESOTA, Vol. II. By A.E. Strand. 1910.
P5-MN0011B — $45.00.

HISTORY OF THE SWEDISH-AMERICANS OF MINNESOTA, Vol. III. By A.E. Strand. 1910.
P5-MN0011C — $45.00.

SWEDISH SETTLEMENTS ON THE DELAWARE, 1638-1664. By A. Johnson. 1911. 879p.
P5-PA0024A — $89.50.

SWISS & GERMAN PIONEER SETTLERS OF S.E. PENN. Emphasizes Lancaster Co. genealogy & the emigr. from Palatine, with lists of early settlers & biogr. sketches of the "Pennsylvania Germans." H.F. Eshleman. 1917. 386p.
P5-PA0151A — $42.50.

WELSH SETTLEMENT OF PENNSYLVANIA: Welsh Quaker Emigr. Index incl. over 2,000 settlers. By C. H. Browning. 1912. 631p.
P5-PA0015 — $66.50.

MAGNA CARTA

MAGNA CARTA BARONS & THEIR AMERICAN DESCENDANTS, together with the Pedigrees of the Founders of the Order of Runnymede deduced from the Sureties for the Enforcement of the Statutes of the Magna Carta of King John. Charles H Browning. 1898. 463p.
P5-MC0001 — $49.00.

THE MAGNA CHARTA: History & Romance of the Great Charter., 6-vol. set By John S. Wurts. 1939-1954. 7 parts in 6 vols.
P5-GR0103 — $225.00/set

THE MAGNA CHARTA: History & Romance of the Great Charter, Vol. I. By John S. Wurts. 1939-1954.
P5-GR0103A — $40.00.

THE MAGNA CHARTA: History & Romance of the Great Charter, Vol. II. By John S. Wurts. 1939-1954.
P5-GR0103B — $40.00.

THE MAGNA CHARTA: History & Romance of the Great Charter, Vol. III. By John S. Wurts. 1939-1954.
P5-GR0103C — $40.00.

THE MAGNA CHARTA: History & Romance of the Great Charter, Vol. IV. By John S. Wurts. 1939-1954.
P5-GR0103D — $40.00.

THE MAGNA CHARTA: History & Romance of the Great Charter, Vol. V. By John S. Wurts. 1939-1954.
P5-GR0103E — $40.00.

THE MAGNA CHARTA: History & Romance of the Great Charter, Vol. VI By John S. Wurts. 1939-1954.
P5-GR0103F — $40.00.

MAYFLOWER

CAPE COD SERIES. History and Genealogy of the Mayflower Planters and First Comers to Ye Olde Colonies, 2-vol. set By L. C. Hills. 1936-1941. 2 vols., 177+284p.
P5-MA0240 — $49.00/set.

For hardcover versions, see the order form on page v. To order, call 1-888-296-3447.

CAPE COD SERIES. History and Genealogy of the Mayflower Planters . . ., Vol. I. L. C. Hills 1936-1941. 177p.
P5-MA0240A — $25.00.

CAPE COD SERIES. History and Genealogy of the Mayflower Planters . . ., Vol. II. L. C. Hills 1936-1941. 284p.
P5-MA0240B — $32.50.

ENGLISH ANCESTRY & HOMES OF THE PILGRIM FATHERS who Came to Plymouth in the "Mayflower" in 1620, the Fortune" in 1621, & the "Anne" & "Little James" in 1623. By Charles Edw. Banks. 1929. 187p.
P5-GR0016 — $21.50.

FAMILIES OF THE PILGRIMS. Comp. for the Mass. Soc. of Mayflower Desc. by H.K. Shaw. 1956. 178p.
P5-MA0083 — $19.00.

GENEALOGICAL REGISTER OF PLYMOUTH FAMILIES. A list of thousands of people with Mayflower and sister ship antecedents. By W.T. Davis. 1899. 363p.
P5-MA0281 — $27.50.

MAYFLOWER DESCENDANTS & THEIR MARRIAGES FOR TWO GENERATIONS AFTER THE LANDING. By J.T. Landis. 1922. 37p.
P5-GR0001 — $10.00.

RECORDS OF PLYMOUTH COLONY: Births, Marriages, Deaths, Burials & Other Records from 1633-1689. With Plymouth Col Vital Records, a Supp. from May-flower Desc. by G. E. Bowman. Ed. by N.B. Shurtleff. 1857, 1911, 1913. 293p.
P5-MA0344 — $27.50.

CAPE MAY COUNTY MAYFLOWER Pilgrim Descendants. By P.S. Howe. 1921. 464p.
P5-NJ0069 — $45.00.

NATIVE AMERICANS

TRUE INDIAN STORIES, with Glossary of Indiana Indian Names. By Jacob Piatt Dunn. 1908. 320p.
P5-IN0067 — $39.50.

IROQUOIS FOLK LORE, Gathered from the Six Nations of New York. 1922. 251p.
P5-NY0036 — $36.00.

INDIAN TRIBES OF THE LOWER MISSISSIPPI VALLEY & Adjacent Coast of the Gulf of Mexico. John R. Swanton. 1911. 386p.
P5-MS0006 — $44.00.

LETTERS FROM THE ALLEGHANY MOUNTAINS [CHEROKEE]. By Charles Lanman. 1849. 198p.
P5-CH0001 — $32.50.

INDIAN TRIBES OF THE LOWER MISSISSIPPI VALLEY & Adjacent Coast of the Gulf of Mexico. John R. Swanton. 1911. 386p.
P5-IND001 — $42.00.

NOTES ON THE IROQUOIS, or Contributions to American History, Antiquities, & General Ethnology. By Henry Schoolcraft. 1847. 498p.
P5-NA0001 — $55.00.

RELIGIONS

ANNUAL REGISTER OF THE BAPTIST DENOMINATION in North America, to the First of Nov., 1790. Comp. by J. Asplund. 1791. 60p.
P5-GR0034 — $12.00.

HISTORY OF THE BAPTISTS IN MAINE. Henry S. Burrage. 1904. 497p.
P5-ME0127 — $56.00.

SOUTH CAROLINA BAPTISTS, 1670-1805. Leah Townsend. 1935. 391p.
P5-SC0005 — $39.00.

JEWS OF DES MOINES: The First Century. Frank Rosenthal. 1957. 213p.
P5-IA0128 — $34.00.

JEWS OF IOWA: Complete History & Accurate Account of their Religious, Social, Economical & Educational Progress on this State; History of the Jews of Europe, North & South America in Modern Times; & a Brief History of Iowa. By Rabbi Simon Glazer. 1904. 359p.
P5-IA0129 — $44.50.

JEWS STRUGGLE FOR RELIGIOUS & CIVIL LIBERTY IN MARYLAND. By E. Milton Altfeld. 1924. 211p.
P5-MD0053 — $22.50.

PAGES FROM THE EARLY HISTORY OF THE WEST & NORTH-WEST, Embracing Reminiscences & Incidents of Settlement & Growth . . . of the States of Ohio, Indiana, Illinois & Missouri, with Especial Reference to the History of Methodism. By Rev. S.R. Beggs. 1868. 325p.
P5-MH0001 — $39.95.

EARLY QUAKER MARRIAGES from Various Records in N.J. Comp. by G. Haines. 1902. 32p.
P5-NJ0001 — $10.00.

ENCYCLOPEDIA OF AMERICAN QUAKER GENEALOGY, Vol. II, New Jersey & Pennsylvania. By William Wade Hinshaw. 1938. 1126p.
P5-NJ0060 — $85.00.

WARS & MILITARY

Civil War

CAMP FIRES OF THE CONFEDERACY: A Vol. of Humorous Anecdotes, Reminiscences, Deeds of Heroism, Thrilling Narratives, Terrible Hardships Endured, Imprisonments, Sea Fights, etc. 1898. 560p.
P5-CW0001 — $59.50.

OUR YOUNGEST BLUE & GRAY: Callow, Brave & True. By Jay S. Hoar. 2005. 289 + 19p.
P5-CW0022 — $45.00.

THE NORTH'S LAST BOYS IN BLUE: Last Living Chapter of the American Civil War. By Jay S. Hoar. 2006. 566 + 22p.
P5-CW0023 — $70.00.

LIST OF INTERMENTS Made by the Expedition to Andersonville, Georgia, During the Months of July & August, 1865. 1866. 225p.
P5-CW0020 — $22.50.

RECORDS OF CALIFORNIA MEN IN THE WAR OF THE REBELLION, 1861 to 1867. Comp. by Richard H. Orton. 1890. 887p.
P5-CA0035 — $89.00.

RECORD OF SERVICE OF CONNECTICUT MEN in the Army and Navy of the United States, during the War of the Rebellion. 1889. 1071p.
P5-CT0315 — $105.00.

INDIANA IN THE WAR OF THE REBELLION. Part I, History; Part II, Statistics & Documents. By W.H.H. Terrell, Adj. General 1869. 2 parts, 466 + 372p.
P5-IN0065 — $86.50.

INDIANA IN THE WAR OF THE REBELLION, Part I: History. 1869. 466p.
P5-IN0065A — $46.00.

INDIANA IN THE WAR OF THE REBELLION, Part II: Statistics & Documents. 1869. 372p.
P5-IN0065B — $46.00.

MAINE AT GETTYSBURG: Report of Maine Commissioners. Prepared by the Executive Comm. 1898. 602p.
P5-ME0129 — $67.00.

MINNESOTA IN THE CIVIL & INDIAN WARS, 1861-1865, Vol. I: Narratives & Rosters of Minn. State Regiments, Companies and Batteries. 1890. 843p.
P5-MN0050B — $85.00.

MINNESOTA IN THE CIVIL & INDIAN WARS, 1861-1865, Vol. II: Official Reports & Correspondence on Battles, Campaigns, Expeditions, Skirmishes, etc. 1899, 2nd ed. 634p.
P5-MN0034B — $65.00.

MINNESOTANS IN THE CIVIL & INDIAN WARS, An Index to the Rosters in "Minnesota in the Civil & Indian Wars, 1861-1865." Includes more than 25,000 Minnesotans who participated in both wars. Comp. under the direction of Irene B. Warming 1936.
P5-MN0035B — $49.00.

RECORD OF OFFICERS & MEN OF NEW JERSEY in the Civil War, 1861-5, 2-vol. set. Comp. by Wm. Stryker, Adjutant General. 1876. 2 vols., 1758 + 176p. index.
P5-NJ0151 — $165.00/set.

RECORD OF OFFICERS & MEN OF NEW JERSEY in the Civil War, 1861-5, Vol. I. 1876. 1758p.
P5-NJ0151A — $148.50.

RECORD OF OFFICERS & MEN OF NEW JERSEY in the Civil War, 1861-5, Vol. II. 1876. 176p.
P5-NJ0151B — $28.00.

NAMES OF OFFICERS, SOLDIERS & SEAMEN in Rhode Island Regiments Belonging to the State of Rhode Island & Serving in the Regiments of Other States & in the Regular Army & Navy of the U.S. who Lost Their Lives in . . . the Late Rebellion. 1869. 32p.
P5-RI0038 — $10.00.

REVISED ROSTER OF VERMONT VOLUNTEERS and Lists of Vermonters who Served in the Army and Navy of the United States during the War of the Rebellion, 1861-66. 1892. 862p.
P5-VT0087 — $87.50.

VERMONT IN THE CIVIL WAR. History of the Part Taken by the Vermont Soldiers & Sailors in the War for the Union, 1861-1865. 2-vol. set. By G.G. Benedict. 1886-1888. 2 vols, 620+808p.
P5-VT0086 — $90.00/set.

VERMONT IN THE CIVIL WAR . . ., Vol. I. 1886-1888. 620p.
P5-VT0086A — $60.00.

VERMONT IN THE CIVIL WAR . . ., Vol. II. 1886-1888. 808p.
P5-VT0086B — $75.00.

WISCONSIN IN THE WAR OF THE REBELLION: History of All Regiments & Batteries. By Wm. DeLoss Love. 1866. 1144p.
P5-WI0037 — $109.00.

Colonial Wars

RHODE ISLAND IN THE COLONIAL WARS: List of R.I. Soldiers & Sailors in King George's War, 1740-1748; and List of R.I. Soldiers & Sailors in the Old French & Indian War, 1755-1762. H.M. Chapin. 1918, 1920. 193p.
P5-RI0032B — $31.00.

French & Indian War

CONNECTICUT SOLDIERS IN THE FRENCH & INDIAN WAR: Bills, Receipts & Documents. By Frank D. Andrews. 1925. 41p.
P5-CT0329 — $10.00.

King Philip's War

OLD INDIAN CHRONICLE, Being a Collection of Exceeding Rare Tracts Written and Published in the Time of King Philip's War by Persons Residing in the Country. By Samuel G. Drake. 1867. 333p.
P5-MA0297 — $43.50.

SOLDIERS IN KING PHILIP'S WAR, Containing Lists of Soldiers of Mass. Colony, who Served in the Indian Wars from 1620-77. Incl. sketches of principal offices & copies of ancient documents & records relating to the war. George M. Bodge. Third ed., 1906. 502p.
P5-MA0413 — $45.00.

Mexican War

INDIANA IN THE MEXICAN WAR. By Oran Perry. 1908. 496p.
P5-IN0103 — $55.00.

Revolutionary War

RECORD OF CONNECTICUT MEN in the Military & Naval Service during the War of the Revolution, 1775-1783. 1889. 777p.
P5-CT0141 — 79.5.

HISTORIC REGISTER OF OFFICERS OF THE CONTINENTAL ARMY DURING THE WAR OF THE REVOLUTION, April 1775 to December 1783. By F.B. Heitman. 1914, 1932. 698p.
P5-GR0080 — $61.00.

PIERCE'S REGISTER: Register of the Certificates Issued by John Pierce, Esq., Paymaster General & Commissioner of Army Accounts for the U.S., to Officers & Soldiers of the Continental Army Under the Act of July 4, 1783. 1915. 566p.
P5-REV001A — $55.00.

RECORDS OF THE REVOLUTIONARY WAR. Comp. by W.T.R. Saffell. 1894. 555 + 43p.
P5-GR0101 — $45.00.

GERMAN ALLIED TROOPS IN THE NORTH AMERICAN WAR OF INDEPENDENCE, 1776-1783. Trans. by M. Von Eelking. 1893. 360p.
P5-GE0001 — $39.00.

REVOLUTIONARY SOLDIERS IN KY., Containing Roll of the Officers of Va. Line who Rec'd Land Bounties; a Roll of the Revolutionary Pensioners in Ky.; List of the Ill. Regiment who Served under George Rogers Clark in the N.W. Campaign & roster of Va. Navy. Comp. by Anderson C. Quisenberry. 1895. 223p.
P5-KY0010 — $25.00.

KING'S MOUNTAIN & ITS HEROES: History of the Battle of King's Mountain, Oct. 7, 1780, & the Events Which Led to It. By L.C. Draper. 1881. 612p.
P5-AC1500 — $57.50.

MILITARY OPERATIONS IN EASTERN MAINE & NOVA SCOTIA During the Revolution. By Frederic Kidder. 1867. 336p.
P5-ME0135 — $43.00.

REVOLUTIONARY RECORDS OF MARYLAND. By G.M. Brumbaugh & M.R. Hodges. 1924. 96p.
P5-MD0003 — $10.00.

REVOLUTION ON THE UPPER OHIO, 1775-1777. 1908. 276p.
P5-REV001B — $37.00.

REVOLUTIONARY SOLDIERS & THEIR DESCENDANTS: Genealogical Records, Missouri Records. n.d. 112p.
P5-MO0019 — $19.50.

NEW YORK IN THE REVOLU-TION AS COLONY & STATE. A compilation of documents & records from the Office of the State Comptroller, given NY rolls of soldiers & sailors in the Rev. War, 2-vol. set. 1904. 2 vols., 533 + 336p.
P5-NY0014B — $91.00/set.

NEW YORK IN THE REVOLU-TION AS COLONY & STATE . . ., Vol. I. 1904. 533p.
P5-NY0014B1 — $56.50.

NEW YORK IN THE REVOLU-TION AS COLONY & STATE . . ., Vol. II. 1904. 336p.
P5-NY0014B2 — $39.50.

PENNSYLVANIA-GERMAN IN THE REVOLUTIONARY WAR, 1775-1783. By Henry M. Muhlenberg. 1908. 542p.
P5-PA0173 — $57.00.

IRISH RHODE ISLANDERS IN THE AMERICAN REVOLUTION. Thomas Hamilton Murray, 1903. 90p.
P5-RI0039 — $17.00.

SPIRIT OF '76 IN RHODE ISLAND, or Sketches of the Efforts of the Government and People in the War of the Revolution, together with the names of those who belonged to R.I. regiments in the army . . . By Benj. Cowell. 1850. 560p.
P5-RI0032A — $58.00.

ROLLS OF THE SOLDIERS IN THE REVOLUTIONARY WAR, 1775-1783. 1904. 927p.
P5-VT0027 — $85.00.

LIST OF THE REVOLUTIONARY SOLDIERS OF VIRGINIA: Special Report of the Department of Archives &History for 1911. By H.J. Eckenrode, Archivist. 1912. 488p.
P5-VA0089 — $49.50.

War of 1812

RECORD OF CONNECTICUT MEN in the Regular Army & the Militia in the War of 1812 & Mexican War. 1889. 180p.
P5-CT0143 — 22.5.

BRITISH INVASION OF MARY-LAND, 1812-1815. By Wm. M. Marine. 1913. 519p.
P5-MD0019 — $52.00.

Military — General

MAP HISTORY OF MY ARMY-NAVY YEARS, 1944-1966. By Rundlette K. Palmer. 1996. 324p.
P5-MISC0007 — $44.00.

MISCELLANEOUS

CROZIER'S GENERAL ARMORY: Registry of American Families Entitled to Coat Armor. With dictionary of heraldic terms. 1904. 155p.
P5-HE0002 — $22.50.

LA SCIENCE DU BLASON, Accompagnee d'un armorial general des fam. nobles de l'Europe. Par le Vicomte de Magny. 1858. 488p.
P5-HE0001 — $49.00.

HOW TO CLIMB YOUR FAMILY TREE. Dr. Robert Medford. 2001. 96p.
P5-MISC0001 — $12.00.

BIRTH AND THE BABYHOOD OF THE TELEPHONE. By T. A. Watson. 1913. 45 + 4p.
P5-MISC0010 — $17.00.

FOUR OF GOD'S CHOSEN ONES. Lorraine B. Bourassa. 2001. 235p.
P5-MISC — $29.00.

HOLMES-PITEZEL CASE: A History of the Greatest Crime of the Century. Det. F.P. Geyer. 1896. 502p.
P5-MISC0011 — $49.95.

LIFE AT DAWN. By Talbot A. Love. 2004. 53 + iii p.
P5-MISC0004 — $23.00.

MEET ME IN HEAVEN. A Collection of Epitaphs from the Simple to the Sublime. By Tina Pabst. 2004. 189 + 12p.
P5-MISC0003 — $25.50.

THE MORNING STARS: Ships of the Gospel Navy. By T.W. Livingston. 1971. 289 + 32p.
P5-MISC0009 — $45.00.

TWO COLLECTIONS OF STRATHSPEY REELS, with a Bass for the Violoncello or Harpsichord. Niel Gow of Dunkeld 1784, 1788. 72p.
P5-MISC0002 — $12.00.

WHAT'S IN A NAME? Being a Popular Explanation of Ordinary Christian Names of Men & Women. By T.N. Nickols. 1859. 128p.
P5-GR0005B — $19.50.